Cases and Materials on Contracts

SIXTH EDITION

Stephen Waddams
Faculty of Law
University of Toronto

Jassmine Girgis
Faculty of Law
University of Calgary

Bruce MacDougall
Peter A. Allard School of Law
University of British Columbia

John McCamus
Osgoode Hall Law School
York University

Jason W. Neyers
Faculty of Law
University of Western Ontario

Toronto, Canada
2018

Emond Montgomery Publications Limited
60 Shaftesbury Avenue
Toronto ON M4T 1A3
http://www.emond.ca/lawschool

Printed in Canada.

We acknowledge the financial support of the Government of Canada. Canadä

Emond Montgomery Publications has no responsibility for the persistence or accuracy of URLs for external or third-party Internet websites referred to in this publication, and does not guarantee that any content on such websites is, or will remain, accurate or appropriate.

Vice president, publishing: Anthony Rezek
Publisher: Danann Hawes
Director, development and production: Kelly Dickson
Production editor: Natalie Berchem
Copy editor: Valerie Adams
Typesetter: Tara Agnerian
Permissions editor: Lisa Brant
Proofreader: Michelle Waitzman

Library and Archives Canada Cataloguing in Publication

Waddams, S. M., 1942-, author
    Cases and materials on contracts / Stephen M. Waddams, Jassmine Girgis, John D. McCamus, Jason W. Neyers, Bruce MacDougall. — Sixth edition.

ISBN 978-1-77255-330-7 (hardcover)

    1. Contracts—Canada—Cases.   2. Contracts—Commonwealth countries—Cases.
3. Contracts—United States—Cases.   I. Girgis, Jassmine, author   II. McCamus, John D., author   III. Neyers, Jason W., author   IV. MacDougall, Bruce, author   V. Title.

    K840.W33 2018   346.02   C2018-901817-8

PREFACE TO THE SIXTH EDITION

We have attempted here to offer students and teachers of Canadian contract law a collection of materials suitable for the basic course in the subject. We have included cases from Canadian, Commonwealth, and American jurisdictions and relevant statutory provisions, notes, problems, and extracts from academic writing.

There has been a lively interest during the past 30 years in the theory of contract law, and we have taken particular account of this in the first chapter, "Perspectives on Contract Law." The second chapter is on remedies, and the third on enforceability. We do not expect that all users of the book will proceed through it sequentially, and we have designed it to be suitable for dealing with the material in several different orders. Some users will wish to start with contract formation. Others will wish to start with remedies. Others again may prefer to start with the theoretical perspectives. We hope that all will find the book equally suitable for their purposes.

The growing importance of the law of restitution, or unjust enrichment, and the intellectual interest and practical importance of its relation to contracts have been reflected in the introduction of separate sections on restitution in most chapters.

We have drawn from many sources in compiling this book, and acknowledge debts to our own teachers and students and to our predecessors in the field of contracts casebooks, in particular to the late JB Milner, who taught at the University of Toronto for many years until his death in 1968. We are grateful to Professor Michael Trebilcock and to Professor Mary Anne Waldron for their contributions to previous editions, the influence of which is apparent in the present edition.

The Editors, 2018

ACKNOWLEDGMENTS

A book of this nature borrows heavily from other published material. We have attempted to request permission from, and to acknowledge in the text, all sources of such material. We wish to make specific references here to the authors, publishers, journals, and institutions that have generously given permission to reproduce in this text works already in print. If we have inadvertently overlooked an acknowledgment or failed to secure a permission, we offer our sincere apologies and undertake to rectify the omission in the next edition.

American Law Institute. Restatement, Second, Contracts, copyright © 1981 by the American Law Institute. Reprinted with permission. All rights reserved.

Cambridge University Press. Stephen Waddams, *The Dimensions of Private Law* (Cambridge: Cambridge University Press, 2003). Reprinted with the permission of Cambridge University Press.

Canadian Bar Association. Law Revision Committee, "Sixth Interim Report," Cmnd 5449 (Eng) (1937) 15 Can Bar Rev 585. Reprinted with permission.

Capital University Law Review. Margaret J Radin, "Reconsidering Boilerplate: Confronting Normative and Democratic Degradation" (2012) 40 Cap UL Rev 617. Reprinted with permission.

Columbia Law Review. Randy E Barnett, "A Consent Theory of Contract" (1986) 86 Colum LR 269. Reprinted with permission.

Columbia Law Review. Lon L Fuller, "Consideration and Form" (1941) 41 Colum LR 799. Reprinted with permission.

Federation Press. Anthony Duggan, "Silence as Misleading Conduct: An Economic Analysis" in M Richardson and P Williams, eds, The Law and the Market (Sydney: Federation Press, © The Federation Press. Reprinted with permission.

Harvard University Press. Charles Fried, *Contract as Promise: A Theory of Contractual Obligations* (Cambridge, MA: Harvard University Press, 1981). Copyright © 1981 by the President and Fellows of Harvard College. Reprinted with permission.

Harvard University Press. Michael J Trebilcock, *The Limits of Freedom of Contract* (Cambridge, MA: Harvard University Press, 1993). Copyright 1993 by the President and Fellows of Harvard College. Reprinted with permission.

LexisNexis. Arthur L Corbin, *Corbin on Contracts* (Dayton, OH: LexisNexis, 2004). Copyright 2004 Matthew Bender & Company, Inc., a member of the LexisNexis Group. All rights reserved. Reprinted with permission.

New York University Annual Survey of American Law. Jeffrey L Harrison, "The Influence of Law and Economics Scholarship on Contract Law: Impressions Twenty-Five Years Later" (2012) 68 NYU Ann Surv Am L 1. Reprinted with permission.

New Zealand Universities Law Review. Brian Coote, "The Instantaneous Transmission of Acceptance" (1971) 4 NZ Univ L Rev 331. Reprinted with permission.

Oxford University Press. *Exploitative Contracts* by Bigwood (2003). By permission of Oxford University Press. Reprinted with permission.

Oxford University Press. *Contract Theory* by Smith (2004). Reprinted with permission.

Thomson Reuters (Professional) Australia Limited. Peter Heffey, Jeannie Paterson & Andrew Robertson, *Principles of Contract Law* (Sydney: Lawbook Co, 2005). Reproduced with permission.

UCLA Law Review. Jay M Feinman, "Critical Approaches to Contract Law" (1983) 30 UCLA L Rev 829. Reprinted with permission.

University of Chicago Press. Richard A Posner & Andrew M Rosenfield, "Impossibility and Related Doctrines in Contract Law: An Economic Analysis" (1977) 6 J Legal Stud 83. Reprinted with permission.

University of Pennsylvania Law Review. Arthur A Leff, "Unconscionability and the Code: The Emperor's New Clause" (1967) 115 U Pa L Rev 485. Reprinted with permission.

University of Toronto Press. Alan Brudner, "Reconstructing Contracts" (1993) 43 UTLJ 1. Reprinted by permission of University of Toronto Press Inc. (<www.utpjournals.com>).

University of Toronto Press. George G Triantis, "Contractual Allocations of Unknown Risks: A Critique of the Doctrine of Commercial Impracticability" (1992) 42 UTLJ 4500. Reprinted by permission of University of Toronto Press Inc. (<www.utpjournals.com>).

Wisconsin Law Review. Stewart Macaulay, "An Empirical View of Contract" (1985) Wis L Rev 465. Reprinted with permission.

The Yale Law Journal Company Inc. Fuller & Perdue, "The Reliance Interest in Contract Damages" (1936) 46 Yale LJ 52. Reprinted by permission of The Yale Law Journal Company Inc.

SUMMARY TABLE OF CONTENTS

DETAILED TABLE OF CONTENTS

xvii

TABLE OF CASES

A page number in boldface type indicates that the text of the case or a portion thereof is reproduced. A page number in lightface type indicates that the case is quoted briefly or discussed.

FREQUENTLY CITED REFERENCES

Benson, P, ed, *The Theory of Contract Law* (Cambridge: Cambridge University Press, 2001) [Benson].

Burrows, A & E Peel, eds, *Contract Formation and Parties* (Oxford: Oxford University Press, 2010) [Burrows & Peel].

Fridman, GHL, *The Law of Contract in Canada*, 6th ed (Toronto: Carswell, 2011) [Fridman].

MacDougall, B, *Introduction to Contracts*, 3rd ed (Toronto: LexisNexis, 2016) [MacDougall].

Maddaugh, PD & JD McCamus,*The Law of Restitution*, 2nd ed (Aurora, Ont: Canada Law Book, 2004) [Maddaugh & McCamus].

McCamus, JD, *The Law of Contracts*, 2nd ed (Toronto: Irwin Law, 2012) [McCamus].

Smith, SA, *Contract Theory* (Oxford: Oxford University Press, 2004) [Smith].

Swan, A, & J Adamski, *Canadian Contract Law*, 3rd ed (Markham, Ont: LexisNexis, 2012) [Swan & Adamski].

Trebilcock, MJ, *The Limits of Freedom of Contract* (Cambridge, Mass: Harvard University Press, 1993) [Trebilcock].

Waddams, SM, *The Law of Contracts*, 6th ed (Aurora, Ont: Canada Law Book, 2010) [Waddams].

CHAPTER ONE

PERSPECTIVES ON CONTRACT LAW

CHARLES FRIED, *Contract as Promise*
(Cambridge, Mass: Harvard University Press, 1981) at 1-5, 14-17
(footnotes omitted)

The promise principle, which in this book I argue is the moral basis of contract law, is that principle by which persons may impose on themselves obligations where none existed before.

Security of the person, stability of property, and the obligation of contract were for David Hume the bases of a civilized society. Hume expressed the liberal, individualistic temper of his time and place in treating respect for person, property, and contract as the self-evident foundations of law and justice. Through the greater part of our history, our constitutional law and politics have proceeded on these same premises. In private law particularly these premises have taken root and ramified in the countless particulars necessary to give them substance. The law of property defines the boundaries of our rightful possessions, while the law of torts seeks to make us whole against violations of those boundaries, as well as against violations of the natural boundaries of our physical person. Contract law ratifies and enforces our joint ventures beyond those boundaries. Thus the law of torts and the law of property recognize our rights as individuals in our persons, in our labor, and in some definite portions of the external world, while the law of contracts facilitates our disposing of these rights on terms that seem best to us. The regime of contract law, which respects the dispositions individuals make of their rights, carries to its natural conclusion the liberal premise that individuals have rights. And the will theory of contract, which sees contractual obligations as essentially self-imposed, is a fair implication of liberal individualism.

This conception of contractual obligation as essentially self-imposed has been under increasing pressure over the last fifty years. One essentially historicist line of attack points out that until the eighteenth century communal controls, whether of families, guilds, local communities, or of the general government, hardly conceded enough discretion to individuals over their labor or property to give the liberal conception much to work on. And beginning in the last century and proceeding apace since, the state, unions, corporations, and other intermediate institutions have again withdrawn large areas of concern from individual control and thus from the scope of purely contractual arrangements. That there has been such an ebb and flow

1

of collective control seems fairly clear. But from the fact that contract emerged only in modern times as a principal form of social organization, it does not follow that therefore the concept of contract as promise (which is indeed a centerpiece of nineteenth-century economic liberalism) was itself the invention of the industrial revolution; whatever the accepted scope for contract, the principle of fidelity to one's word is an ancient one. Still less does it follow that the validity, the rightness of the promise principle, of self-imposed obligation, depended on its acceptance in that earlier period, or that now, as the acceptance is in doubt, the validity of the principle is under a cloud. The validity of a moral, like that of a mathematical truth, does not depend on fashion or favor.

A more insidious set of criticisms denies the coherence or the independent viability of the promise principle. Legal obligation can be imposed only by the community, and so in imposing it the community must be pursuing its goals and imposing its standards, rather than neutrally endorsing those of the contracting parties. These lines of attack—found recently in the writings of legal scholars such as Patrick Atiyah, Lawrence Friedman, Grant Gilmore, Morton Horwitz, Duncan Kennedy, Anthony Kronman, and Ian Macneil, as well as in philosophical writings—will provide the foil for much of my affirmative argument. Here I shall just set out their main thrust so that my readers may be clear what I am reacting against.

Not all promises are legally enforced, and of those which are, different categories receive differing degrees of legal recognition: some only if in writing, others between certain kinds of parties, still others only to the extent that they have been relied on and that reliance has caused measurable injury. And some arrangements that are not promissory at all—preliminary negotiations, words mistakenly understood as promises, schemes of cooperation—are assimilated to the contractual regime. Finally, even among legally binding arrangements that are initiated by agreement, certain ones are singled out and made subject to a set of rules that often have little to do with that agreement. Marriage is the most obvious example, but contracts of employment, insurance, or carriage exhibit these features as well. Thus the conception of the will binding itself—the conception at the heart of the promise principle—is neither necessary nor sufficient to contractual obligation. Indeed it is a point of some of these critics (for example, Friedman, Gilmore, Macneil) that the search for a central or unifying principle of contract is a will-o'-wisp, an illusion typical of the ill-defined but much excoriated vice of conceptualism. These critics hold that the law fashions contractual obligation as a way to do justice between, and impose social policy through, parties who have come into a variety of relations with each other. Only some of these relations start in an explicit agreement, and even if they do, the governing considerations of justice and policy are not bound by the terms or implications of that agreement.

Though the bases of contract law on this view are as many and shifting as the politics of the judicial and legislative process, two quite general considerations of justice have figured prominently in the attack on the conception of contract as promise: benefit and reliance. The benefit principle holds that where a person has received a benefit at another's expense and that other has acted reasonably and with no intention of making a gift, fairness requires that the benefit be returned or paid for. I discuss this idea in detail in subsequent chapters. Here I shall make my point by the more pervasive notion of reliance. Proceeding from a theme established in Lon Fuller and William Perdue's influential 1936 article, a number of writers have argued that often what is taken as enforcement of a promise is in reality the compensation of an injury sustained by the plaintiff because he relied on the defendant's promise. At first glance the distinction between promissory obligation and obligation based on reliance may seem too thin to notice, but indeed large theoretical and practical matters turn on that distinction. To enforce a promise as such is to make a defendant render a performance (or its money equivalent) just because he has promised that very thing. The reliance view, by contrast, focuses on an injury suffered by the plaintiff and asks if the defendant is somehow sufficiently responsible for that injury that he should be made to pay compensation.

The latter basis of liability, the compensation of injury suffered through reliance, is a special case of tort liability. For the law of torts is concerned with just the question of compensation for harm caused by another: physical harm caused by willful or negligent conduct, pecuniary harm caused by careless or deceitful representations, injury to reputation caused by untrue statements. Now tort law typically deals with involuntary transactions—if a punch in the nose, a traffic accident, or a malicious piece of gossip may be called a transaction—so that the role of the community in adjudicating the conflict is particularly prominent: What is a safe speed on a rainy evening, what may a former employer say in response to a request for a reference? In contrast, so long as we see contractual obligation as based on promise, on obligations that the parties have themselves assumed, the focus of the inquiry is on the will of the parties. If we assimilate contractual obligation to the law of torts, our focus shifts to the injury suffered by the plaintiff and to the fairness of saddling the defendant with some or all of it. So, for instance, if there has been no palpable injury because the promisee has not yet relied on the promise there seems to be nothing to compensate, while at other times a generalized standard of fair compensation may move us to go beyond anything that the parties have agreed. The promise and its sequel are seen as a kind of encounter, giving rise to losses to be apportioned by the community's sense of fairness. This assimilation of contract to tort is (and for writers like Gilmore, Horwitz, and Atiyah is intended to be) the subordination of a quintessentially individualist ground for obligation and form of social control, one that refers to the will of the parties, to a set of standards that are ineluctably collective in origin and thus readily turned to collective ends.

Another line of attack on contract as promise denies the coherence of the central idea of self-imposed obligation. Some writers argue that obligation must always be imposed from outside. Others work from within: For promissory obligations to be truly self-imposed, the promise must have been freely given. If this means no more than that the promisor acted intentionally, then even an undertaking in response to a gunman's threat is binding. If, as we must, we insist that there be a *fair* choice to promise or not, we have imported external standards of fairness into the very heart of the obligation after all. Having said, for instance, that a promise to pay an exorbitant price for a vital medicine is not freely undertaken, while a promise to pay a reasonable price is, why not dispense with the element of promise altogether and just hold that there is an obligation to supply the medicine at an externally fixed price to all who need it? This and more subtle, related suggestions have been put forward by writers who are particularly concerned about the connection between contract as promise and the market as a form of economic organization. Some like Robert Hale, Duncan Kennedy, and Anthony Kronman see in the concepts of duress and unconscionability the undoing of the arguments for the free market and for the autonomy of contract law. Others, most particularly Richard Posner, also denying any independent force to promissory obligation, derive such force as the law gives to contracts from social policies such as wealth maximization and efficiency, which are usually associated with the operation of the market. ...

Once I have invoked the institution of promising, why exactly is it wrong for me then to break my promise?

My argument so far does not answer that question. The institution of promising is a way for me to bind myself to another so that the other may expect a future performance, and binding myself in this way is something that I may want to be able to do. But this by itself does not show that I am morally obligated to perform my promise at a later time if to do so proves inconvenient or costly. That there should be a system of currency also increases my options and is useful to me, but this does not show why I should not use counterfeit money if I can get away with it. In just the same way the usefulness of promising in general does not show why I should not take advantage of it in a particular case and yet fail to keep my promise. That the convention would cease to function in the long run, would cease to provide benefits if everyone felt free to violate it, is hardly an answer to the question of why I should keep a particular promise on a particular occasion.

Considerations of self-interest cannot supply the moral basis of my obligation to keep a promise. By an analogous argument neither can considerations of utility. For however sincerely and impartially I may apply the utilitarian injunction to consider at each step how I might increase the sum of happiness or utility in the world, it will allow me to break my promise whenever the balance of advantage (including, of course, my own advantage) tips in that direction. The possible damage to the institution of promising is only one fact in the calculation. Other factors are the alternative good I might do by breaking my promise, whether and by how many people the breach might be discovered, what the actual effect on confidence of such a breach would be. There is no a priori reason for believing that an individual's calculations will come out in favor of keeping the promise always, sometimes, or most of the time.

Rule-utilitarianism seeks to offer a way out of this conundrum. The individual's moral obligation is determined not by what the best action at a particular moment would be, but by the rule it would be best for him to follow. It has, I believe, been demonstrated that this position is incoherent: Either rule-utilitarianism requires that rules be followed in a particular case even where the result would not be best all things considered, and so the utilitarian aspect of rule-utilitarianism is abandoned; or the obligation to follow the rules is so qualified as to collapse into act-utilitarianism after all. There is, however, a version of rule-utilitarianism that makes a great deal of sense. In this version the utilitarian does not instruct us what our individual moral obligations are but rather instructs legislators what the best rules are. If legislation is our focus, then the contradictions of rule-utilitarianism do not arise, since we are instructing those whose decisions can *only* take the form of issuing rules. From that perspective there is obvious utility to rules establishing and enforcing promissory obligations. Since I am concerned now with the question of individual obligation, that is, moral obligation, this legislative perspective on the argument is not available to me.

The obligation to keep a promise is grounded not in arguments of utility but in respect for individual autonomy and in trust. Autonomy and trust are grounds for the institution of promising as well, but the argument for *individual* obligation is not the same. Individual obligation is only a step away, but that step must be taken. An individual is morally bound to keep his promises because he has intentionally invoked a convention whose function it is to give grounds—moral grounds—for another to expect the promised performance. To renege is to abuse a confidence he was free to invite or not, and which he intentionally did invite. To abuse that confidence now is like (but only *like*) lying: the abuse of a shared social institution that is intended to invoke the bonds of trust. A liar and a promise-breaker each *use* another person. In both speech and promising there is an invitation to the other to trust, to make himself vulnerable; the liar and the promise-breaker then abuse the trust. ...

The obligation to keep a promise is thus similar to but more constraining than the obligation to tell the truth. To avoid lying you need only believe in the truth of what you say when you say it, but a promise binds into the future, well past the moment when the promise is made. There will, of course, be great social utility to a general regime of trust and confidence in promises and truthfulness. But this just shows that a regime of mutual respect allows men and women to accomplish what in a jungle of unrestrained self-interest could not be accomplished. If this advantage is to be firmly established, there must exist a ground for mutual confidence deeper than and independent of the social utility it permits.

The utilitarian counting the advantages affirms the general importance of enforcing *contracts*. The moralist of duty, however, sees *promising* as a device that free, moral individuals have fashioned on the premise of mutual trust, and which gathers its moral force from that premise. The moralist of duty thus posits a general obligation to keep promises, of which the obligation of contract will be only a special case—that special case in which certain promises have attained legal as well as moral force. But since a contract is first of all a promise, the contract must be kept because a promise must be kept.

To summarize: There exists a convention that defines the practice of promising and its entailments. This convention provides a way that a person may create expectations in others. By virtue of the basic Kantian principles of trust and respect, it is wrong to invoke that convention in order to make a promise, and then to break it.

NOTE

For commentary on Fried's work, see PS Atiyah, "The Liberal Theory of Contract" in *Essays on Contract* (Oxford: Oxford University Press, 1986, reprinted 2001).

STEPHEN A SMITH, *Contract Theory*
(Oxford: Oxford University Press, 2004) at 7, 36 (footnotes omitted)

[W]hat makes a particular interpretive theory of the law a good one? What are the criteria, in other words, for evaluating interpretive theories? This is the most difficult of the methodological questions faced by legal theorists. It is rarely addressed explicitly in contract theory scholarship, although no theorist can avoid taking a position, explicitly or not, on the answer.

In what follows, I will suggest that four criteria are of particular relevance in assessing contract theories: (1) fit, (2) coherence, (3) morality, and (4) transparency ... .

[The discussion of the four criteria has been omitted.]

The most general lesson to be taken from this chapter is that disagreements between contract theories are often disagreements, typically unarticulated, about the appropriate criteria for evaluating contract theories. ...

More substantively, I explained that this book is concerned with interpretive theories of contract law. An interpretive theory is a theory that helps us to better understand the law by illuminating the significance of, and connections between, its different parts. As such, interpretive theories are linked to, but different than, historical, prescriptive, and descriptive theories. Interpretive theories are assessed according to: (1) how well they fit the rules and decisions that make up contract law, (2) how coherent they are, and (3) how well they explain the way that legal actors themselves explain what they are doing. The third criterion can be subdivided into two parts: (1) how well does the theory explain law's claims to authority (the claim that law is a legitimate or morally justified authority), and (2) how well does the theory explain law's claim to transparency (the claim that legal reasoning is meaningful)?

A further distinction was drawn between weak, moderate, and strong versions of what is required to explain the above claims to authority and transparency. The weak versions hold that any explanation is sufficient, even if it shows legal actors to be insincere in their claims. The strong versions hold that a good explanation of the law will show that the law's claims to authority and transparency are actually true, that is, that the law is actually morally justified and that the reasons alleged to motivate decision-making actually do motivate decision-making. Finally, the moderate—and, I argued, most persuasive—versions state that a good explanation must show that the law's claim to authority and claim to transparency might be thought to be true (even if they are not in fact true). This can be done either by advancing a functionalist explanation or, more plausibly, by advancing an interpretation that shows legal actors to have been mistaken. To fit within the latter approach, an interpretation of the law must propose a normative justification for the law that is recognizably "moral" (in order to make sense of law's claim to authority) and must explain the law in terms that are recognizably "legal" (in order to make sense of law's claim to transparency).

RANDY E BARNETT, "A CONSENT THEORY OF CONTRACT"
(1986) 86 Colum L Rev 269 at 269-70, 304-5 (footnotes omitted)

The mere fact that one man promises something to another creates no legal duty and makes no legal remedy available in case of non-performance. To be enforceable, the promise must be accompanied by some other factor. ... The question now to be discussed is what is this other factor. What fact or facts must accompany a promise to make it enforceable at law?

We look to legal theory to tell us when the use of legal force against an individual is morally justified. We look to contract theory, in particular, to tell us which inter-personal commitments the law ought to enforce. Contract theory at present, however, does not provide a satisfactory answer to this question. The five best known theories or principles of contractual obligation—the will theory, the reliance theory, the fairness theory, the efficiency theory and the bargain theory—each have very basic shortcomings. A consent theory of contract avoids these difficulties while explaining coherent obligation in a plausible and coherent manner.

Theories are problem-solving devices. We assess the merits of a particular theory by its ability to solve the problems that gave rise to the need for a theory. We do not, however, assess a particular theory in a vacuum. No theory in any discipline, from physics to biology to philosophy, can be expected to solve every problem raised by the discipline. Rather, we *compare* contending theories to see which theory handles problems the best.

Our criteria for comparing theories include at least three factors: (a) the number of known problems the theory handles as well [as] or better than its rivals, (b) the centrality of the problems that the theory handles well, and (c) the promise that the theory offers for solving future problems. When we assess legal theories, the better a particular theory explains cases where we are confident of the right outcome, the more confident we will be with the answers it suggests for those cases at the margin where our intuitions are less secure.

[The discussion of the assessment of current theories of contractual obligation and most of the elements of consent theory has been omitted.]

What exact meaning must a court conclude was conveyed by a promisor to a promisee to find that a contractual commitment was incurred? If consent is properly thought of as "objective" or "manifested" assent, what is it that must be assented to for a contractual obligation to arise? It is not enough that one manifests a commitment or promises to perform or refrain from doing some act. Such a manifestation would be nothing more than a promise. Contract theory searches for the "extra" factor that, if present, justifies the legal enforcement of a commitment or promise.

An entitlements theory specifies that consent to a transfer of rights is this factor. The consent that is required is a *manifestation of an intention to alienate rights*. In a system of entitlements where manifested rights transfers are what justify the legal enforcement of agreements, any such manifestation necessarily implies that one intends to be "legally bound," to adhere to one's commitment. Therefore, the phrase "a manifestation of an intention to be legally bound" neatly captures what a court should seek to find before holding that a contractual obligation has been created.

Charles Fried maintains that a promisor incurs a moral obligation because she intentionally invokes a social convention whose purpose is to cause others to expect the promised performance. By contrast, a consent theory specifies that a promisor incurs a contractual obligation the legal enforcement of which is morally justifiable by manifesting assent to legal enforcement and thereby invoking the institution of contract. In the circumstances described by Fried, a promisor may have a moral obligation to do what she promised. Without more she would not have a legal obligation and a promisee would not have a legal right to performance. She incurs a contractual obligation to perform only when she manifests to a promisee her intention to be legally bound. The basis of contractual obligation is not promising per se. The basis of contract is consent.

MARGARET J RADIN, "RECONSIDERING BOILERPLATE: CONFRONTING NORMATIVE AND DEMOCRATIC DEGRADATION"
(2012) 40 Cap U L Rev 617 at 619-20, 621-27 (footnotes omitted)

The law considers boilerplate to be a method of contract formation. That is, the law usually holds that a contract is formed between the firm and the recipient, and the terms of the contract are the fine print in the boilerplate. Even when there is no signature, such as when we click "I agree" online, courts are likely to find that a contract has been formed unless there is some other reason for invalidating the terms. Boilerplate has really come into its own in the online environment. Firms use other online procedures that are even further removed from the kind of consent we normally suppose is required for a contract, such as, "By browsing our website, you have agreed to all of the terms we have placed in the link entitled Terms of Service, together with any changes that we make from time to time." Courts may be less likely to find that these procedures form an enforceable contract. Firms today, however, are hopeful that courts will rule in their favor if these procedures are challenged—hopeful enough to use these procedures very widely. ...

Our basic conventional understanding of freedom of contract is at odds with this reality. Most people still think that a contract is a voluntary transaction, a consensual exchange. Indeed, the basis of contract law is the idea of free exchanges between willing parties. "Freedom of contract" is a revered ideal. Let me call the traditional world of our conventional understanding, and of contract theory, World A. World A is the world in which the revered ideal resides, the world of Agreement, the world of voluntary exchanges. It is sometimes the world of actual pre-exchange negotiation, but at minimum the world of realistic choice on whether to transact.

World B is another world, the world of Boilerplate, of fine-print schemes. World B does not fit the theory or the rationale of contract law, which developed to justify the scenarios of contract enforcement of World A. Yet World B is the primary world in which consumers transact in the marketplace. This article and the corresponding book essentially ask: What (if anything) should be done about this disconnect between theory and practice and between justification and reality?

Our courts consider boilerplate schemes contractual, but should they? Perhaps they should not, or at least not always. Meanwhile, as long as boilerplate terms are considered contractual, as our legal system currently does, that means that boilerplate is regulated under contract law. Why is boilerplate "regulated"? It is regulated because not everything that is *called* a contract actually *is* one. A purported contract obtained by coercion or fraud is not an enforceable contract; nor is a contract for an illegal purpose, a contract that is too indefinite, or a contract that lacks consideration.

If boilerplate schemes should not be regulated by contract law, that does not mean that boilerplate should not be regulated at all, or that boilerplate should not exist. If boilerplate schemes were not regulated at all but could still be freely used by firms to divest people of legal rights, we would not be living under the rule of law. If, however, all uses of boilerplate schemes to create an alternative legal universe for a firm were suddenly declared unenforceable, that would impose a disruption of current commercial practice.

Because boilerplate is regulated by—or, in other words, evaluated under—contract law, those who defend boilerplate schemes must argue that boilerplate schemes somehow meet the requirements of contract law. Thus, they must argue that recipients somehow agree to, or consent to, its terms. Or they must argue that there can be such a thing as a contract without consent. This is contrary to the basic rationale of contract law. Some, however, would argue that a contract without consent can be rescued by hypothetical consent. These arguments may be succeeding with U.S. courts because judges apparently believe that a boilerplate form signifies that the recipient has exercised freedom of contract.

Businesses that use forms to construct their own legal universe, and others who argue in defense of this practice, usually say something like the following: "We need to constrict recipients' legal rights to contain costs. When we reduce costs, we pass on our savings to recipients, so recipients benefit with lower prices. Furthermore, recipients, if given a choice, would choose lower prices over legal rights. So we are not really interfering with people's freedom of choice." Thus, hypothetical consent is often premised on the idea that firms pass on to recipients the money they save by curtailing recipients' rights. Therefore, recipients, if economically rational, "would" choose these passed-on savings and "would" consider it appropriate "compensation" for their loss of rights.

There is a lot wrong with this argument. Whether savings to firms are passed on and whether they would be equal to just the right amount of compensation is a difficult empirical question; it is not one that is properly answered by convenient assumption. Moreover, the argument does not take into account that some rights cannot be sold, even for just compensation. Furthermore, even if it were true that firms pass on savings that amount to just compensation, and that the rights are saleable, there is still the question of "private eminent domain": our legal system normally does not allow private parties (such as firms) to divest other private parties (such as consumers) of entitlements if compensation is paid.

We should not ignore the argument that adhesion contracts are justified as enforceable contracts because firms pass on to recipients the savings they realize from boilerplate schemes that delete legal rights. The argument should be reconsidered, however, in light of four factors: (1) the varying market circumstances that can make its premises true or untrue; (2) the nature of the various legal rights that firms are negating by using boilerplate schemes (for example whether the rights can be traded off); (3) the dubious normative premises that opportunity to read incomprehensible terms amounts to choice; and (4) that hypothetical choice is as good as real choice. ...

A. DECAY OF THE IDEA OF VOLUNTARY CHOICE

Given that firms are using boilerplate schemes to transport us into an alternative legal universe, why don't we read these things? Here are seven possible answers. First, we would not understand these things if we did read them, so it is not worth our time. Second, we may need the product or service and have no access to a supplier that does not impose onerous clauses, so reading the terms would not make a difference. Industry-wide standardization is common, so alternative terms are often not available.

Third, sometimes we do not even know that we are being made subject to these terms, so we do not know that there is anything to read. Fourth, we trust that the company did not include anything harmful. Fifth, we think that anything harmful would be unenforceable. Although this thought is common, it is wrong; many harmful clauses are often enforced. Sixth, we think that the company has power over us, and we are stuck with what it imposes on us. Finally, an important reason we do not read boilerplate is that we do not believe we will ever be in need of exercising our background legal rights. We do not expect to have misfortune befall us. As psychological research has shown, we are not able to make an accurate assessment of the risks.

Given the seven reasons why we do not read boilerplate schemes, they are problematic on the issue of consent. Because boilerplate schemes do not demonstrate the kind of consent that is presupposed by the notion of freedom of contract, they can be understood as a "normative degradation" of our legal system. Legal theorists and market apologists have attempted to cope with this degradation in various ways that amount to a devolution or decay of the idea of voluntary choice. This is a serious decay because the idea of voluntary choice is at the root of the underlying commitment to freedom of contract.

The boilerplate schemes in World B use the word "agreement" because that is the traditional word used for a contract. They are, however, using it in an Orwellian manner. The usual software End User License Agreement (EULA) is not what normal speakers would consider an agreement on the part of the user.

Procedures construed as acceptance have also been transmogrified. It has always been possible in traditional contract law to signify voluntary acceptance by a specified procedure, such as, signifying agreement to purchase by retaining or modifying a product sent on approval. Consider, however, the following (paraphrased) statement: "By looking at this website, you have agreed to a lot of internal boilerplate you do not know is there, as well as whatever changes the website owner might make from time to time." That pushes the traditional possibility of specified agreement procedure to an absurd length. One cannot make something into an agreement just by using that word.

The gerrymandering of the word agreement, along with the various other attempts to fit World B into the World A paradigm of voluntary transfer by agreement can be viewed as a sort of devolution or decay of the concept of voluntariness. Agreement gets assimilated to consent, and then to assent. Assent then becomes blanket assent to unknown terms, provided they are what a consumer might have expected. ...

Llewellyn excluded "unreasonable" or "indecent" terms from enforceability under blanket assent. Whatever Llewellyn may have meant by "indecency" in this context, his notion of blanket assent has played out in subsequent attempts to provide for exceptions to enforceability for unknown terms not within the recipient's "reasonable expectations," or for unknown terms not "radically unexpected." Assent devolves to fictional or constructive assent, then to fictional or constructive opportunity to assent, then to notice that the terms exist, and then to fictional or constructive notice of terms. Fictional or constructive notice further devolves to as-if or hypothetical consent, and from there to the elimination of consent entirely; that is, to mere (allegedly) efficient rearrangement of entitlements.

MICHAEL J TREBILCOCK, *The Limits of Freedom of Contract*
(Cambridge, Mass: Harvard University Press, 1993) at 15-17 (footnotes omitted)

THE ECONOMIC FUNCTIONS OF CONTRACT LAW

[N]eo-classical economists have a predilection for resource allocation through voluntary exchanges as opposed to collective decisions because they believe that one can have a higher degree of confidence in the welfare implications of private exchanges, where both parties stand to benefit, than in collective decisions, where typically there are both winners and losers and it is difficult to net out gains against losses. However, this predilection for the private exchange or market process in the allocation of resources does not speak to the economic role of contract *law*. From an economic perspective, we can identify several major functions of contract law.

CONTAINING OPPORTUNISM IN NON-SIMULTANEOUS EXCHANGES

Let us return to the earlier example of Tribe A's producing corn and Tribe B's producing beef. Even if a stable regime of property rights is established so that members of Tribe A and members of Tribe B agree to respect each other's property rights, this in itself does not ensure that mutual gains from trade will be realized. In other words, we have ruled out theft, but we have not yet facilitated exchange. Suppose that Tribe A's corn is ripe now and must be eaten within a few days and that Tribe A is prepared to trade a quantity of this corn for a calf from Tribe B, but that the calf will not be ready for delivery for another six weeks. If Tribe A delivers the corn today against the promise of delivery of the calf in six weeks' time, there is a serious risk of defection by Tribe B when it comes time to meet its delivery obligations. Tribe A, perceiving this risk, may be disinclined to deliver the corn. In this event, the potential for a Pareto superior exchange would not be realized. This is a variant of the Prisoner's Dilemma. Whereas in traditional societies conventions may develop that mitigate the problem, in contemporary societies the law of contracts—by providing remedies in the event of breach of contractual promises—provides an essential check on opportunism in non-simultaneous exchanges by ensuring that the first mover, in terms of performance, does not run the risk of defection, rather than cooperation, by the second mover.

REDUCING TRANSACTION COSTS

A second economic function of the law of contracts is to supply parties to given categories of exchanges with standard sets of implied terms, which in most cases save the parties the transaction costs entailed in fully specifying a complete contingent claims contract, but typically leave them free to contract out of these rules if they find them inappropriate to their particular transaction. In addition to various aspects of the common law of contracts, many statutes dealing with sales law and partnership law, and perhaps certain aspects of corporation statutes, can be thought of in these terms.

FILLING GAPS IN INCOMPLETE CONTRACTS

A related function of the law of contracts is to provide a set of default or background rules where the explicit terms of a contract are incomplete, not because the parties consciously adverted to the default or background rules and accepted them as appropriate to their transaction, but typically because particular contingencies were not consciously adverted to by one or the other party (or both) at all. Here, an economic framework of analysis would tend to ask, what rule would maximize the parties' joint welfare, on the assumption that this rule would generally be the rule that rational parties would have agreed to *ex ante*?

DISTINGUISHING WELFARE-ENHANCING AND WELFARE-REDUCING EXCHANGES

A central economic role of contract law is to formulate a set of excuses for contract performance that permits the enforcement of efficient exchanges but discourages the enforcement of inefficient exchanges. Individual exchanges might be evaluated from a Paretian perspective, where one would ask whether it is reasonable to infer that such exchanges are welfare-enhancing in the sense of making somebody better off and nobody worse off. Lack of voluntariness, imperfect information, and externalities are likely to provide the principal economic bases for declining to draw such an inference, whatever the legal forms that excuses reflecting these factors might take. Alternatively, one could employ a Kaldor-Hicks criterion of efficiency, asking whether society on net would be better off by permitting the class of transaction of which the instant transaction is representative or if, in contrast, society would be better off on net by imposing certain legal rules or constraints on the class of transaction in question. As we shall see in later chapters, economists are not always precise about which of these two concepts of efficiency should be employed and when.

Thus, neo-classical economists' predilection for private ordering turns centrally on legal regimes of well-defined and exclusive private property rights and a regime of contract law that facilitates the voluntary exchange of those rights. Liberal political theories of individual autonomy generally reflect a similar predilection, though not necessarily for the same reasons or with the same normative entailments.

NOTE

For an extensive and insightful critique of autonomy and welfare-based theories of contract law, see Peter Benson, "The Idea of a Public Basis of Justification for Contract" (1995) 33 Osgoode Hall LJ 273.

PÉTER CSERNE, "PATERNALISM AND CONTRACT LAW"
The Routledge Handbook of the Philosophy of Paternalism, ed by Kalle Grill
& Jason Hanna (Abingdon: Routledge, 2018) at 293-310

Contract regulation is a domain where the conflict between freedom of choice and paternalistic intervention is especially easy to notice. In most countries people are not allowed to sell or buy (although in some cases they can donate and receive) each other's body parts; certain substances deemed dangerous or harmful are not available for sale for the general public; individuals cannot legally commit themselves to servitude or slavery; consumers can access certain unhealthy goods or risky financial products only under strictly regulated terms and after having been confronted with graphic or heavily worded warnings about the risks involved.

In this chapter, contract law is understood as a body of legal rules that pertains to the enforcement and regulation of voluntary private agreements. Contract law provides a normative framework for the social practice of contracting. By enabling, regulating and selectively enforcing contracts, the state, both through legislation and adjudication, operates as a powerful governance mechanism for private transactions. The law can take various stances towards the social practice of contracting: expressive, constitutive and regulative. It expresses generally held ideas or aspirations about agency, autonomy, trust, fairness, cooperation or dependency. Although promises and agreements can operate without law, contract law constitutes categories, conventional forms (e.g. the formalities of offer and acceptance or consideration) in which these cooperative activities can be recognized and carried out. (I shall return to this constitutive element below.) Most conspicuously, the law also regulates the practice of contracting by prohibiting, limiting, or setting terms for various transactions. While paternalism is most visible in the regulatory aspect of contract law, it is traceable in the expressive and constitutive aspects as well.

For the purposes of this chapter, the term "paternalism" will refer to "[t]he interference of a state or an individual with another person, against their will, and defended or motivated by a claim that the person interfered with will be better off or protected from harm" (Dworkin 2017). Given that other chapters of this Handbook focus on the meaning, kinds and normative status of paternalism, this chapter focuses on how the normative problems of paternalism play out in the domain of contract law.

In the following, we shall call a certain rule or doctrine of contract law or a judicial decision paternalistic, when it limits the freedom of contract in order to protect from harm or grant benefits to at least one of the contracting parties. The interference of "contract law" typically happens through general rules enacted by legislators or introduced by decisions of state authorities, be they judges or other officials. Paternalism in contract law is easiest to grasp if we look at what legal rules do to contracts ex ante, i.e. at the formation of contracts. If we look at legal rules ex post, i.e. in case of a dispute, one of the parties willingly invokes a rule, presumably because it is in their interest to do so. So by looking at judicial actions in an individual contract case one would hardly find any intervention paternalistic in the sense of interfering against the current will of the party. The paternalistic character of the interference is clear, however, if we focus on the rule or principle that the court applies to override (some terms of) a binding contract, thus going against the party's will at the time of contracting.

The nature of the interference can vary from refraining from enforcing the contract or some of its terms, imposing mandatory terms through legislation or various judicial techniques, introducing default rules which, for various psychological or practical reasons, will be "sticky," i.e. while technically non-mandatory, still difficult to opt-out from (see below). Some rules are directly paternalistic, e.g. when they imply mandatory terms favorable to one party. Some rules are indirectly paternalistic, e.g. prohibiting the sale (but not the purchase) and punishing sellers (but not the buyers) of certain goods or services in order to protect potential purchasers from supposedly harmful goods and services.

Even the harshest sanctions of contract law do not amount to coercion ..., so paternalistic interference by contract law is generally seen as less intrusive to auton- omy, and in this respect, less morally troubling than coercive paternalistic interven- tions, e.g. by criminal law.

In sum, contract law is seen as an intelligible and in part systematizable normative practice which can be illuminated by moral and political principles. The main subject of this chapter is to explore the role of paternalism among these principles in the context of a body of legal rules and doctrines which relate, roughly speaking, to judicially enforceable agreements between private parties.

JEFFREY L HARRISON, "THE INFLUENCE OF LAW AND ECONOMICS SCHOLARSHIP ON CONTRACT LAW: IMPRESSIONS TWENTY-FIVE YEARS LATER"
(2012) 68 NYU Ann Surv Am L 1 at 22, 24-26 (footnotes omitted)

Although the numbers suggest varying conclusions with respect to the influence of law and economics [on contract law], an examination of actual decisions indicates that an economic way of thinking about issues has penetrated judicial reasoning. Here the focus is not on the number of citations. Instead, the inquiry centers on the development of an economically influenced manner of reasoning and discussion and on the diverse courts which employ this reasoning. For example, although the theory of efficient breach hardly explains the evolution of the expectancy measure of damages, courts have an appreciation of how the theory supports expectations. Thus as Justice Mosk of the Supreme Court of California observed in a 1995 opinion, "[t]he efficient breach occurs when the gain of the breaching party exceeds the loss to the party suffering the breach, allowing movement of resources to their more optimal use. Contract law must be careful 'not to exceed compensatory damages if it doesn't want to deter efficient breaches.'" In gauging the impact of law and eco- nomics on the vocabulary of courts, most telling is the trend in the use of the term ... [in this case, "efficient breach"].

More broadly, in *Bidlack v. Wheelabrator Corporation*, the court noted the potential application of the backbone of law and economics—the Coase Theorem—when it discussed the possibility that parties can contract around court-determined rules: "We should recognize initially that, when those affected by a chosen default rule can easily bargain around it to agree to a mutually beneficial course, the rule choice will generally make little difference to the parties' actual agreement." Indeed courts have recognized the relevance of the Coase Theorem forty-seven times. This may not be an impressive number for an article as well known to economists and lawyers as Coase's classic, but for the first twenty years of its existence—from 1960 to 1980—it was cited but six times.

Also pertinent as a measure of the penetration of economic analysis into judicial opinion is the use of the term "transaction costs." Transaction costs are the costs incurred in reaching an agreement. High transaction costs deter contract formation and low ones make contract formation more likely. The most well-known application of transaction costs is found in Coase's *The Problem of Social Cost.* ... By 1987, the date of the initial study, the term had appeared ninety-three times. In the twenty-five years since 1987, the usage of the term tripled over the number of times used since 1987. Clearly transaction costs have become part of the day-to-day vocabulary of courts.

These examples are far from exhaustive. The breadth of the topics addressed, as well as the jurisdictions represented, suggest that economic reasoning, or an effort to apply it, has become common in opinions dealing with contract matters. This is the sort of subterranean effect that may not be fully appreciated by focusing only on citations.

JAY M FEINMAN, "CRITICAL APPROACHES TO CONTRACT LAW"
(1983) 30 UCLA L Rev 829 at 849-54 (footnotes omitted)

The first critical approach to the social function of contract law shares the view of mainstream theory that law is useful to business people and that it is instrumental— that is, it is consciously used for economic ends. The differences lie in the effects on different groups in society and the precise source of the attempt. The essence of this view is that contract is a device by which a dominant class imposes and perpetuates a hierarchical capitalist economy on society. Contract law is continually refashioned to meet the changing needs of the dominant class.

In the early nineteenth century, traditional contract law hindered the enforcement of executory, speculative transactions. These transactions came into prominence with the rise of national markets and large-scale enterprises. Therefore, courts proceeded to undermine traditional notions of value and provided a system of free contract more advantageous to the new entrepreneurs. When the development of a mass economy made standardized transactions desirable, the courts created the objective theory of contract to facilitate them; the theoretical loss in individual autonomy was a necessary cost. But the defect of free contract was that from its premises, rules of law developed that were ill-suited to actual commercial practice. Examples include the technical development of the doctrine of consideration, such as the unenforceability of requirements contracts. In the twentieth century, these inconsistencies were simply swept away and a new law, more flexible and better suited to an interdependent capitalist system, was established.

Critical functional theories vary with respect to the level at which it is appropriate to speak of contract as an aid to capitalist domination. One approach suggests that all that is required for domination is the basic conception of free contract, the per-missibility and protection of formally free exchange. Particular doctrines within that general conception are the products of peculiar historical circumstances which may not reflect fundamental social relations. Thus, not every doctrinal development necessarily reflects class conflict. Another approach argues that it is possible to identify the source and effect of many individual doctrines in economic advantage or necessity. For example, there was the nineteenth century class-biased treatment of "entire contracts," in which builders, but not workers, who failed to complete their contracts could recover in quantum meruit.

A basic element of all versions of critical functionalism is that it rejects pluralism, the political theory which supports the mainstream theory. Pluralism assumes the existence of many groups in political society, none of which has a consistent advan-tage over any other. In the critical approach, the political situation is defined by the economic order. Capitalist society, by definition, is composed of two classes, capitalists and workers, who are distinguished from each other by ownership of the means of production. Contract law supports and legitimates the economic arrangement to the benefit of the capitalists. ...

Examining the strengths and the defects of the instrumental theories leads to no clear conclusion about the functional utility of contract law. Surely the claims of contract's central importance are exaggerated. Yet it is hard to dismiss entirely the ways in which contract law apparently facilitates commercial exchange. Further, the limited functional utility of contract law doctrine does not mean that the system of adjudication which uses the doctrine is irrelevant. The particular content of the doctrine may not have much effect, prospectively or retrospectively, on the activities of private parties, but its application in litigation may facilitate the economy. In a variation of the mainstream account, for example, contract litigation serves as a forum for dividing up the remains of a dead economic relation, a sort of salvage operation. It also serves as a low cost administrative device for routine debt collection. From a critical perspective, contract litigation is a device by which economically powerful parties discipline weaker parties. By and large, however, these functions are conveniences rather than necessities and are little affected by the form or content of contract law doctrine.

Critical theory's particular contribution to the study of the role of contract law in society is the recognition of a different function of the law: law as a legitimating ideology and as an expression of legal consciousness. The initial step is to consider the instrumental use of contract law as an ideology. In the instrumental view, contract doctrine is created and perpetuated as a belief system to conceal the reality of economic injustice in society. Society is composed of illegitimate hierarchies in which dominant economic groups systematically exploit their subordinates. The dominant class's hegemony is maintained by inducing acceptance of values and institutions that appear to support the status quo, as well as by using force. For example, the classical image's conceptualization of the economic world as composed of independent actors transacting on a voluntary basis suggests that whatever inequality exists in society is a product of individuals' unwise acts, not the system. On the other hand, the modern notion of commercial convenience suggests that the world is a well-ordered place in which people and firms carry on their affairs according to socially acceptable modes of behavior. To the extent that people accept these suggested ways of looking at the world, they will be more likely to accept their place in it.

Ideology is powerful, and contract law could well serve an instrumental function. But critical theory has moved beyond the instrumental approach for several reasons. The critical theory of ideology states that contract legitimates an illegitimate status quo. To legitimate an unjust social order, contract law decisions and the reasoning employed in reaching them must appear to derive from a coherent application of accepted principles of fairness. Because contract law relies on contradictory principles, however, it lacks coherence. The principles of contract law could be used to reach entirely different doctrinal results, just as the results could be generated by entirely different doctrines. Thus, there is no clear correspondence between a particular image of contract law and a particular social order. It is impossible to say that an image of contract law legitimates particular social relations without tautologically assigning the legitimating function to contract law throughout history.

There is also the problem of penetration. People must be aware of ideology if it is to serve as an effective legitimation device. The penetration of contract law doctrines into society is not great; first-year law students' common ignorance of its principles is annual evidence of this. On the other hand, people's general understanding of the nature of the economy may allow some basic contract law principles to penetrate deeply in society. Further, contract law as ideology may be most important to members of the legal elite, not to the common person. Lawyers and judges have the skill and the opportunity to see contract law as an instrument of inequality and domination. If the contract ideology prevents that perception, if it justifies the law and attorneys' and judges' role in its application to the elite, it thereby assists in the continued functioning of the system.

Finally, some instrumental conceptions of ideology are too unsophisticated to accord completely with reality. In its simpler form, instrumentalism requires the development and exploitation of the ideology by a dominant group. Actually, contract is not often the product of such conscious manipulation. Instead, its ideological form is generated in a different manner, one that both removes the conspiratorial aspect and opens the possibility of a more basic explanation of contract's source and its legitimating function.

A powerful function of contract law is to present a system of belief which affirms the legitimacy of the existing social order while denying its true nature. The law does so not through any conscious manipulation by judges, but by judges restating the basic facts of concrete social experience in abstract terms when they decide cases. These facts include the mode of production and "a concomitant organic culture, an interrelated, possibly internally contradictory, but characteristic complex of institutions, feelings, habits, beliefs, interpretations, morals, and doctrines." Judges sympathize with the goals, purposes, and "logic" of the social order because of their education, their favored economic position, their association with others similarly favored, and their peculiar training and role in a formalistic precedent- and stability-oriented legal system. In deciding cases, they fit the dispute at issue within this advantageous view of the organic whole. That mode of resolution tends to legitimate the basic social relations, however unjust they actually are. In the process of deciding many cases, judges construct legal concepts that embody the social relations. The result is a system of contract law which appears to shape economic affairs according to normative principles, but which actually is only a recast, idealized form of the underlying illegitimate socio-economic order.

GILLIAN K HADFIELD, "AN EXPRESSIVE THEORY OF CONTRACT: FROM FEMINIST DILEMMAS TO A RECONCEPTUALIZATION OF RATIONAL CHOICE IN CONTRACT LAW"
(1998) 146 U Pa L Rev 1235 at 1236-38, 1257-58, 1263-65
(footnotes omitted)

The idea of deliberate, rational choice is ... of importance in almost every field of law. In contract law, however, the idea takes on constitutive importance: The very obligations that an individual is under in contract are a product of that individual's choice. Indeed, this principle is what distinguishes contract from tort. In contract, one is obligated only if one chooses to be obligated. In tort, one is obligated regardless of one's desire to be obligated; the only choice is whether or not to run afoul of the obligation.

Or, at least, so goes the conventional doctrine. The idea of choice as the source of obligation in contract has come under scrutiny from a variety of scholars, most notably relational contract scholars and critical theorists such as feminists. Grant Gilmore, for example, announced in 1974 the "death of contract" as a distinctive mode of obligation—if obligations in "contract" arise from considerations of reliance or unjust enrichment, from fairness or justice, rather than from the will of the contracting parties, as Gilmore observed they do, then contract is not contract; it is tort. For relational contract scholars, modern contract law poses this puzzle: Is it possible to accept the idea that obligations arise from the norms of a contractual relationship without conceding the death of contract, of "choice"? For feminist contract scholars, the question is this: Is it possible to protect women from the oppressive consequences of harmful, constrained choices—in surrogacy or marital separation agreements, for example—without divesting women of agency? In all these instances, the idea of what it is to choose comes to the fore.

In this Article, I examine how our underlying conceptions of what it is to choose animate legal reasoning in contract. In particular, I contrast the economist's conception of rational choice—which I consider to be a sharply delineated representation of dominant legal conceptions of rational choice—with Elizabeth Anderson's conception of rational choice. Building on the ideas that values are plural, incommensurable, and socially mediated, and that choice is rational when it is adequately expressive of values, Anderson constructs a vision of what it is to choose that is a substantial challenge to the dominant conceptions that undergird conventional contract logic. In doing so, I argue, she provides the basis for reconceptualizing choice in contract law in a way that should alter radically our understanding of the source of contractual obligation.

In particular, I defend in this Article the following claim. Conventional contract logic rests on the idea that when someone makes the choice to enter into a contract, she does so primarily to select a preferred future state of affairs; enforcement of the contract is then seen as a neutral act on the part of the law, which merely gives to the chooser what she chose. If we adopt Anderson's view of what it means to make a choice, however, this logic no longer applies. For in that vision we admit the possibility that the chooser assessed her options in light of what the choice would express rather than what future states it would secure. That is, the conventional logic is flawed when it asserts that the chooser has, necessarily, by deciding today to contract, indicated her choice among future states of affairs. Rather she has indicated her choice among current states of affairs; the choice among current states has consequences for the future only if the law attaches them. Analytically, Anderson's challenge to conventional rational choice theory raises a question that conventional contract logic thinks it has answered, namely, why does a person's choice at one point in time determine her legal obligations at another point in time? Why does a choice in contract have legal significance? It cannot be, after Anderson, simply because the law is a neutral arm of the state, handing out to contractors what they have asked for. Instead, the very problem of contract enforcement is that one of the contractors does not want what the state is giving.

Anderson's theory ... tells us that we need to identify reasons, beyond the bare fact that a choice to enter a contract has been made, for attaching legal significance to this particular exercise of choice. I suggest in this Article what some such reasons might be, and in particular, explore two: the protection of reliance interests and the protection of an instrumentally valuable convention. The principal point I defend, however, is that reasons for enforcement are needed, and I observe that turning to reasons such as reliance or convention would create a contract law that exhibits more differentiation among types of contract. Faced with the need in a given type of contract to identify a reliance interest or the instrumental value of a particular convention of contracting, we may be led to conclude that not all contracts are enforceable and, moreover, not all are enforceable in the same way or with the same remedy. ...

ANDERSON'S CONCEPTION OF RATIONAL CHOICE AS EXPRESSIVE CHOICE

... The feminist dilemma lies in how to reject the implications of the economist's model of rational choice without adopting the position that women are not rational; that is, in Fried's view, infantile and ruled by emotion. This is the dilemma of choice, the apparently headlong confrontation between being an agent whose autonomous choices are respected and being an agent who seeks to avoid the legal enforcement of her choices.

Elizabeth Anderson's conception of rational choice offers, I believe, a way out of this dilemma by providing a foothold to a contract logic that does not see the decision to refrain from implementing a person's earlier choice as a failure to respect her autonomy. Anderson's conception of rational choice captures a greater share of the human experience without relinquishing rationality. Indeed, she defines rationality as requiring the integration of emotion, relation, and the possibility of growth into the process of valuing and choosing among alternatives. Moreover, she recaptures for rationality attributes of community and public meaning, releasing rationality from its narrow confines within our separate skulls. ...

IMPLICATIONS FOR CONTRACTS: SURROGACY BEGUN

If we adopt the economist's theory of rational choice, the decision to enter into a surrogacy contract is like any other choice. A potential birth mother assesses her personal preferences for the available options. She weighs the expected benefits of the income or satisfaction against the expected physical, emotional, and social costs. The woman who changes her mind about carrying through with the contract does so, on this theory of rational choice, for one of three reasons: (1) she is opportunistic and seeking to extort the father; (2) she erred in her calculation of the expected costs and benefits; or (3) she did not choose rationally to begin with, because of either diminished capacity or coercion.

According to the conventional logic, the first reason is not grounds for letting the woman out of the contract. Neither is the second reason, unless we find an extraordinary mistake. Both Fried's notion of autonomy and the fact that uncertainty is attendant on almost any choice lead us to the position that, unless there is something exceptional here, mere regret is no basis for release from the contract.

The third reason necessarily must be limited if we start with the economic model of rational choice. The economic model assumes that action is premised on rational choice and that coercion and irrationality are the exception and not the rule. Hence, law motivated by this vision of human behavior will look for extreme forms of coercion (rather than the ordinary coercion of gender or class) or irrationality. To do otherwise would be to unravel the core premises on which such law is built. ...

[Now] ... we turn to Anderson's theory of rational choice .... A birth mother's decision to enter into a surrogacy contract may have been expressive of her values, and it may have been fundamentally directed towards expressing, at that point in time, how she saw herself in relation to the world: how she valued herself, pregnancy, money, her family, and the intending parents. Suppose her act is not best understood as a calculation of expected costs and benefits, but rather as a means of expressing the values of compassion and generosity towards those unable to bear children or an act expressing her valuation of her body as a source of life. Or perhaps it is an expression of self-hatred, of her devaluation of herself as a responsible mother. Or it may be an expression of her valuation of money as evidence of her degraded value to her family. Perhaps at the moment she decided to enter into that contract, she was struggling to express to herself, her family, and the world that she was valuable and worthy of respect.

Anderson's understanding of what it is to choose requires that we attend to the framing of choice by, and hence the meaning of choice to, the chooser.

STEWART MACAULAY, "AN EMPIRICAL VIEW OF CONTRACT"
(1985) Wis L Rev 465 at 465-69 (footnotes omitted)

When Grant Gilmore called his lectures "The Death of Contract," he gave a name to a body of work that includes some of mine. He called me the "Lord High Executioner" of the "Contract is Dead" movement. However, Gilmore was not very interested in my empirical description of contract. He said this kind of work lacked theoretical relevance. I must credit him with an attention catching title. Nevertheless, he failed to see that the very limited practical role of what professors call contract law poses significant theoretical problems that we are only beginning to confront.

In a way, Gilmore's title is misleading. Contract as a living institution is very much with us. In the day-to-day flow of dealings, vast numbers of significant transactions take place to the reasonable satisfaction of all concerned. People and organizations bargain, they write documents, and they avoid, suppress, and resolve disputes little influenced by academic contract law. Some cases are taken to court and the formal process begun, although lawyers settle most of them before courts reach final decisions. There are even opinions by judges relying on traditional contract law, but they are relatively rare.

Furthermore, contract within the academy is still very much alive. Every morning in law schools all over the United States beginning law students struggle with offer, acceptance, and consideration. I never argued that contract law died. Rather, academic contract law is not now and never was a descriptively accurate reflection of the institution in operation. Moreover, this inaccuracy matters in many ways.

At the end of September in 1984, there was a conference in Madison marking the 21st birthday of the publication in the *American Sociological Review* of my article on non-contractual relations in business. I am pleased that the article has had a long shelf-life and people still find something in it. After listening to others at the conference consider long-term continuing relationships, it is a good time for me to reflect on developments over the past two decades. ...

The 1963 article challenges a model of contract law's functions, explicit or implicit in the work of contracts scholars and social theorists. This model makes contract law far more central than its actual role in society. One version of the model suggests that in a state of nature we are all selfish. Law supports needed interdependence by coercing us to honor obligations to others. The historical story is that we begin with trading within real communities. Capitalism breaks this up, and we become alienated strangers. Then the legal system supplies a kind of synthetic community based on rights and duties enforced by courts. A variant of the story is that market capitalism changes all personal relations into autonomous market trades—capitalism replaces a spirit of interdependence by "what's in it for me?" Contract law supplies the needed glue to hold individualists to their bargains.

More particularly, writers assume a number of things about the institution of contract. First there is careful planning of relationships in light of legal requirements and the possibilities of non-performance. We must spell out everything because parties will perform only to the letter of a contract, if they go that far. Second, contract law is a body of clear rules so that it can facilitate planning. It provides formal channels so that we know the right way to proceed to produce desired legal consequences. Finally, contract litigation is a primary means of deterring breach and directly and indirectly resolving disputes. Without contract law and the state's monopoly of the legitimate use of force, performance of contracts would be highly uncertain.

However, all of these assumptions about history and about human relationships are just wrong or so greatly overstated as to be seriously misleading. Contract planning and contract law, at best, stand at the margin of important long-term continuing business relations. Business people often do not plan, exhibit great care in drafting contracts, pay much attention to those that lawyers carefully draft, or honor a legal approach to business relationships. There are business cultures defining the risks assumed in bargains, and what should be done when things go wrong. People perform disadvantageous contracts today because often this gains credit that they can draw on in the future. People often renegotiate deals that have turned out badly for one or both sides. They recognize a range of excuses much broader than those accepted in most legal systems.

There are relatively few contracts litigated, and those that are have special characteristics. Few of those cases litigated produce anything like adequate compensation for the injuries caused. Frequently, limitations on liability in written contracts block remedies based on the reasonable expectations of the party who did not draft the instrument. At best, formal legal procedures usually are but a step in a larger process of negotiation. Filing a complaint and pre-trial procedure can be tactics in settlement bargaining; appeals often prompt reversals and remands, leaving the parties to settle or face continuing what seems to be an endless process. When final judgments are won, often they cannot be executed because of insolvency.

How do we explain this gap between the academic model and an empirical description of the system of contract law in action? Academic writers often make individualistic assumptions. Their theories rest on worlds of discrete transactions where people respond to calculations of short-term advantage. However, people engaged in business often find that they do not need contract planning and contract law because of relational sanctions. There are effective private governments and social fields, affected but seldom controlled by the formal legal system. Even discrete transactions take place within a setting of continuing relationships and interdependence. The value of these relationships means that all involved must work to satisfy each other. Potential disputes are suppressed, ignored, or compromised in the service of keeping the relationship alive.

While we often read that increasing bureaucratic organization has made the world impersonal, this is not always the case. Social fields cutting across formal lines exist within bureaucracies, creating rich sanction systems. Individuals occupying formal roles ignore organizational boundaries as they seek to overcome formal rationality to achieve goals, gain rewards, and avoid sanctions. Social networks serve as communications systems. People gossip and this creates reputational sanctions.

Power, exploitation, and dependence also are significant. Continuing relationships are not necessarily nice. The value of arrangements locks some people into dependent positions. They can only take orders. The actual lines of a bureaucratic structure may be much more extensive than formal ones. Seemingly independent actors may have little real freedom and discretion in light of the costs of offending dominant parties. Once they face sunk costs and comfortable patterns, the possibility of command rather than negotiation increases. In some situations parties may see relational sanctions as inadequate in view of the risks involved. However, instead of contract law, they usually turn to other techniques to provide security, ranging from collateral to vertical integration.

STEPHEN WADDAMS, *Dimensions of Private Law*
(Cambridge, UK: Cambridge University Press, 2003) 1-2, 4-12 (footnotes omitted)

Many attempts have been made to explain the relation to each other of categories (organizing divisions) and concepts (recurring ideas) in private law, leading, since Blackstone's time, to a great variety of suggested maps, schemes, and diagrams; none of these has commanded general assent or has fully explained the actual decisions of the courts. In this study a number of legal issues will be examined in which the interrelation of fundamental concepts has been crucial. It will appear that the concepts have, when looked at from the standpoint of these legal issues, operated not in isolation from each other, but cumulatively and in combination, and that their relation to each other is fully captured neither by the image of a map nor by that of a diagram. Often a legal obligation has been derived not from a single concept, but from the interaction of two or more concepts in such a way as to preclude the allocation of the legal issue to a single category.

A desire for precision and order naturally leads to a search for clear categories and good maps, but such a search, if pressed too far, may be self-defeating, for material that is inherently complex is not better understood by concealing its complexity. Schemes that have failed to account for the inherent complexity of the law have not been conducive to good intellectual order, and have engendered both academic scepticism and judicial resistance ... .

... Blackstone ... [divided] rights into "rights of persons" and "rights of things," and wrongs into "private wrongs" and "public wrongs," supplying titles for each of his four volumes. Despite the enormous success of the *Commentaries*, this scheme gained little following. It depended too much on doubtful verbal parallels and antitheses, and it omitted divisions that later came to be thought to be of fundamental importance, notably the distinctions between public and private law, and within private law between property and obligations, and within obligations between contractual and other kinds of obligation. ...

Though Blackstone's primary purpose was not to subject English law to critical analysis, his work paved the way for others to do so. Blackstone's scheme had found no explicit place for contract law. In the *Commentaries*, aspects of contracts formed part of rights of persons (employment) and of rights of things (transfers of property), general contract law being assigned to a chapter of the book on private wrongs entitled "Of Injuries to Personal Property," and very briefly treated. In 1790 the first English treatise on contract law gave conceptual unity to the topic, and in 1806 a treatise on *Obligations* by Blackstone's French contemporary Robert Joseph Pothier was published in English translation. So unfamiliar to English readers was the idea of a law of obligations that the translator found it necessary to add to the title, calling it *A Treatise on the Law of Obligations or Contracts*. The modern reader might naturally suppose that the purpose must have been to enlarge the meaning of "contracts," but the translator explained that his purpose was in fact to enlarge the meaning of "obligations" beyond the restricted meaning (i.e., penal bond) that it had in contemporary English legal usage ... .

Pothier did indeed devote the vast bulk of the treatise ... to contractual obligation, but he was notably concerned that his account should be conceptually complete.

He divided obligations into "contracts" and "other causes of obligations," and though he devoted only five pages to these "other causes" he took care to divide them in their turn into "quasi contracts" (one and a half pages), "injuries and neglects" (two and a half pages) and a residual class called "of the law" (one page), consisting of obligations derived directly from natural or positive law. ...

The demarcation of contract law from other bases of obligation had far-reaching implications, including a division between property and obligation, and divisions among different classes of obligation. It also implied that the contract law of a particular legal system was a manifestation of a universal order, with which, therefore, it might be critically contrasted and compared. This attitude is well illustrated by Charles Addison's preface to his *Treatise on Contracts* (1847), where he said that English contract law was not "a mere collection of positive rules" or "founded upon any positive or arbitrary regulations, but upon the broad and general principles of universal law." ...

This approach gave to contract law a high conceptual significance that had been absent from Blackstone. But attempts to subordinate English contract law to a single classifying concept, such as consent, have not succeeded. Actual consent to be bound has been neither sufficient nor necessary in Anglo-American contract law: not sufficient, because it is ineffective in the absence of a bargain or a formality; not necessary, because contractual words and conduct are given effect according to the meaning reasonably ascribed to them by the promisee, not that actually intended by the promisor. Thus, an offer may be effectively accepted even though the offeror has intended to withdraw it. On this last question the authority of Pothier was expressly rejected by an English court in 1880, relying on American law ... .

English contract law, as Blackstone's scheme reminds us, had developed by treating breach of contract as a species of wrong, associated with injury to property. The nineteenth century produced a large number of treatises on English contract law, and though the delictual and proprietary associations of the subject were neglected they were not altogether buried: the primary right of the promisee remained a right to compensation for loss caused by wrongdoing, overlaid on the earlier concepts of covenant and debt, and supplemented by the power of the court of equity, where it thought it appropriate, to decree specific performance, to issue injunctions, and to declare and enforce trusts. These delictual and proprietary associations have been an obstacle to schematic classification because they preclude a sharp demarcation between contractual and other sources of obligation. Such a demarcation would have required the abandonment, as a central concept, of breach of contract as a wrong, the abolition of covenant and debt, the abolition of equity as a source of contractual obligation, the dissociation of contract from property, and the substitution of a primary legal obligation of fulfilment of contracts, as in some other legal systems. Simultaneous changes of this magnitude could scarcely have been achieved without codifying legislation.

Most of the nineteenth-century treatises did not struggle with the precise relation of contracts to other kinds of obligation, but Anson (1879), like Pothier, did. Anson's attempt to reconcile conceptual completeness with the actual structure of English contract law led him to allocate to entirely separate categories the initial obligation to perform a contract and the obligation to pay compensation for loss caused by breach. Anson recognized also that the obligation to pay a judgment could not readily be accommodated under other headings; neither could matrimonial obligations, nor obligations arising from trusts. He thus found it necessary to postulate six categories of obligation: contract, delict, breach of contract, judgment, quasi-contract, and miscellaneous.

Anson's scheme, despite the very high repute of his book, and though carried through seventeen editions over fifty years, attracted no following. Nor was any similar scheme adopted. Halsbury's *Laws of England* (1907-17) organized the law alphabetically under 164 titles, with no title for "public law," "private law," "property," "obligation," "quasi-contract," or "unjust enrichment." The highly influential *Smith's Leading Cases* (12th edition, 1915) succeeded in arranging much of English private law in the form of annotations on sixty judicial decisions. The general tendency of English lawyers at this time was to think in terms of two general categories only of personal obligation, namely contract and tort, and this tendency was assisted by comparisons with Roman law, by curricula of legal education, by a statutory provision on costs in county courts, and by the prevailing desire for clarity, predictability, and certainty in the law. Though this was the general tendency, it did not receive the approval of the two most prominent contemporary English academic writers. F.W. Maitland, in a study published posthumously in 1909, after referring to the divisions of Roman law, said that "[t]he attempt to distribute our personal forms under the two heads of contract and tort was never very successful or very important." Frederick Pollock, writing at about the same date, pointed out that "[s]ince about the middle of the 19th century there has been a current assumption that all civil causes of action must be founded on either contract or tort," but added flatly, "there is no historical foundation for this doctrine."

Nevertheless the tendency to think in terms of only two categories went so far as to lead the House of Lords in 1914 to subordinate the category of quasi-contract (obligations imposed by law for the avoidance of unjust enrichment) to that of contract. ...

The revival of unjust enrichment has been one of the most important developments of the twentieth century in Anglo-American private law. The American Law Institute's *Restatement of Restitution* (1937) was welcomed in England by Lord Wright, who took the opportunity of expanding his views in the *Fibrosa* case (1942) ... .

... In one sense, this development may be viewed as a victory for the law of unjust enrichment and for the influence of academic writing. But Lord Wright's language, rejecting the notion of two categories only, and advocating "a third category," had the effect of entrenching a particular view of categories. The notion of three categories may be superior, from a historical perspective, to that of two, but it directs attention away from the question of whether it is necessary or desirable to think in terms of exhaustive and mutually exclusive divisions.

Some modern writers have accepted the threefold division, but there are still many kinds of obligation that cannot be comfortably fitted within it. For this reason, some have proposed "trust" or "fiduciary relationship" as a separate category. Others, following Pothier and Anson, have admitted a residual or "miscellaneous" class, but the need for it points to the limitations of this kind of diagrammatic classification. First, the contents of the residual class are potentially very large—"a huge and various assortment of rights." When the number of specimens that has to be classified as "sui generis" is indeterminate and far larger than the number of primary "genera," doubt is cast on the primacy and distinctiveness of the named classes. Secondly, most of the kinds of obligation called "sui generis" have not been *distinct* from the three primary classes, but have contained elements of two or more of them, often combined with elements of property and public policy. Thirdly, the admission of a residual class deprives the scheme of all excluding power: to establish, in response to a claim, that there is no obligation derived from contract, tort, or unjust enrichment is inconclusive, because it leaves open the possibility that there is another unnamed and hitherto unidentified kind of obligation that may lead to similar or analogous legal consequences. It is equally difficult to reconcile a miscellaneous category with the image of a map: the notion of a limitless and permanently unknowable residual territory demonstrates the limits of the mapping metaphor in its application to law.

CHAPTER TWO

REMEDIES FOR BREACH
OF PROMISE

I. THE INTERESTS PROTECTED

FULLER & PERDUE, "THE RELIANCE INTEREST
IN CONTRACT DAMAGES"
(1936) 46 Yale LJ 52 at 53-54, 56-57, 61-63

It is convenient to distinguish three principal purposes which may be pursued in awarding contract damages. These purposes, and the situations in which they become appropriate, may be stated briefly as follows:

First, the plaintiff has in reliance on the promise of the defendant conferred some value on the defendant. The defendant fails to perform his promise. The court may force the defendant to disgorge the value he received from the plaintiff. The object here may be termed the prevention of gain by the defaulting promisor at the expense of the promisee; more briefly, the prevention of unjust enrichment. The interest protected may be called the *restitution interest*. For our present purposes it is quite immaterial how the suit in such a case be classified, whether as contractual or quasi-contractual, whether as a suit to enforce the contract or as a suit based upon a rescission of the contract. These questions relate to the superstructure of the law, not to the basic policies with which we are concerned.

Secondly, the plaintiff has in reliance on the promise of the defendant changed his position. For example, the buyer under a contract for the sale of land has incurred expense in the investigation of the seller's title, or has neglected the opportunity to enter other contracts. We may award damages to the plaintiff for the purpose of undoing the harm which his reliance on the defendant's promise has caused him. Our object is to put him in as good a position as he was in before the promise was made. The interest protected in this case may be called the *reliance interest*.

Thirdly, without insisting on reliance by the promisee or enrichment of the promisor, we may seek to give the promisee the value of the expectancy which the promise created. We may in a suit for specific performance actually compel the defendant to render the promised performance to the plaintiff or, in a suit for damages, we may make the defendant pay the money value of this performance. Here our object is to put the plaintiff in as good a position as he would have occupied had the defendant performed his promise. The interest protected in this case we may call the *expectation interest*. ...

It is obvious that the three "interests" we have distinguished do not present equal claims to judicial intervention. It may be assumed that ordinary standards of justice would regard the need for judicial intervention as decreasing in the order in which we have listed the three interests. The "restitution interest," involving a combination of unjust impoverishment with unjust gain, presents the strongest case for relief. If, following Aristotle, we regard the purpose of justice as the maintenance of an equilibrium of goods among members of society, the restitution interest presents twice as strong a claim to judicial intervention as the reliance interest, since if A not only causes B to lose one unit but appropriates that unit to himself, the resulting discrepancy between A and B is not one unit but two.

On the other hand, the promisee who has actually relied on the promise, even though he may not thereby have enriched the promisor, certainly presents a more pressing case for relief than the promisee who merely demands satisfaction for his disappointment in not getting what was promised him. In passing from compensation for change of position to compensation for loss of expectancy we pass, to use Aristotle's terms again, from the realm of corrective justice to that of distributive justice. [The reference is to Aristotle, *Nicomachean Ethics*, 1132a-1132b.] The law no longer seeks merely to heal a disturbed status quo, but to bring into being a new situation. It ceases to act defensively or restoratively, and assumes a more active role. With the transition, the justification for legal relief loses its self-evident quality. It is as a matter of fact no easy thing to explain why the normal rule of contract recovery should be that which measures damages by the value of the promised performance. Since this "normal rule" throws its shadow across our whole subject it will be necessary to examine the possible reasons for its existence. It may be said parenthetically that the discussion which follows, though directed primarily to the normal measure of recovery where damages are sought, also has relevance to the more general question, why should a promise which has not been relied on ever be enforced at all, whether by a decree of specific performance or by an award of damages? ...

The rule measuring damages by the expectancy may also be regarded as a prophylaxis against the losses resulting from detrimental reliance. Whatever tends to discourage breach of contract tends to prevent the losses occasioned through reliance. Since the expectation interest furnishes a more easily administered measure of recovery than the reliance interest, it will in practice offer a more effective sanction against contract breach. It is therefore possible to view the rule measuring damages by the expectancy in a quasi-criminal aspect, its purpose being not so much to compensate the promisee as to penalize breach of promise by the promisor. The rule enforcing the unrelied-on promise finds the same justification, on this theory, as an ordinance which fines a man for driving through a stop-light when no other vehicle is in sight.

In seeking justification for the rule granting the value of the expectancy there is no need, however, to restrict ourselves by the assumption, hitherto made, that the rule can only be intended to cure or prevent the losses caused by reliance. A justification can be developed from a less negative point of view. It may be said that there is not only a policy in favor of preventing and undoing the harms resulting from reliance, but also a policy in favor of promoting and facilitating reliance on business agreements. As in the case of the stop-light ordinance we are interested not only in preventing collisions but in speeding traffic. Agreements can accomplish little, either for their makers or for society, unless they are made the basis for action. When business agreements are not only made but are also acted on, the division of labor is facilitated, goods find their way to the places where they are most needed, and economic activity is generally stimulated. These advantages would be threatened by any rule which limited legal protection to the reliance interest. Such a rule would in practice tend to discourage reliance. The difficulties in proving reliance and subjecting it to pecuniary measurement are such that the business man knowing, or sensing, that these obstacles stood in the way of judicial relief would hesitate to rely on a promise in any case where the legal sanction was of significance to him. To encourage reliance we must therefore dispense with its proof. For this reason it has been found wise to make recovery on a promise independent of reliance, both in the sense that in some cases the promise is enforced though not relied on (as in the bilateral business agreement) and in the sense that recovery is not limited to the detriment incurred in reliance. ...

The inference is therefore justified that the ends of the law of contracts and those of our economic system show an essential correspondence. One may explain this either on the ground that the law (mere superstructure and ideology) reflects inertly the conditions of economic life, or on the ground that economic activity has fitted itself into the rational framework of the law. Neither explanation would be true. In fact we are dealing with a situation in which law and society have interacted. The law measures damages by the expectancy *in part* because the law (for reasons more or less consciously articulated) gives protection to the expectancy.

WERTHEIM V CHICOUTIMI PULP COMPANY
[1911] AC 301 at 307 (PC)

LORD ATKINSON: ... And it is the general intention of the law that, in giving damages for breach of contract, the party complaining should, so far as it can be done by money, be placed in the same position as he would have been in if the contract had been performed. ... That is a ruling principle. It is a just principle.

BOLLENBACK V CONTINENTAL CASUALTY COMPANY
414 P 2d 802 (Oregon SC 1965)

HOLMAN J: Plaintiff was the holder of a policy issued by defendant under a group health and accident plan. The effective date of the policy was August 10, 1954. Premiums were due every six months and were paid by plaintiff. On September 28, 1963, while the policy was in full force and effect, plaintiff was hospitalized for six days with a back injury.

On November 12 he filed a claim with defendant for $107.33. He received no answer. On December 12 he wrote to the defendant calling to its attention that he had filed the claim and had received no acknowledgement. He still received no answer. On January 6, 1964, he wrote to the defendant a third time calling to its attention the filing of his claim and his previous correspondence. On January 20 both plaintiff and defendant wrote to each other. Plaintiff wrote to the assistant to the president of defendant, calling his attention to the plaintiff's payment of premiums, protesting the manner in which he was being ignored, enclosing copies of his previous letters, and asking for action. Defendant's correspondence was an answer to plaintiff's letter of January 6, informing plaintiff that his policy had lapsed in 1959 for non-payment of premiums. On January 30, defendant wrote again to plaintiff. This letter specified that it was an answer to plaintiff's letter of January 20 to the assistant to the president of defendant. This letter contained the same information previously given plaintiff about the lapse of his policy and called to his attention their previous notification to this effect.

On January 25, plaintiff wrote two more letters to the defendant, one to the accounting department requesting information from its records concerning the premiums it had received from him and the other to the claims department requesting information about the reason for the policy's lapse. Plaintiff had received no answer to these letters when, on February 4, he filed the present case stating that he had elected to rescind the contract because of its repudiation by defendant and requesting judgment against defendant for all premiums previously paid under the policy in the sum of $2,166.50.

To plaintiff's complaint defendant filed an answer denying its repudiation of the contract, pleading the affirmative defense of mistake and tendering the amount of plaintiff's claim into court. A trial without a jury ensued which resulted in findings and conclusions by the judge to the effect that defendant had repudiated the contract by non-payment of plaintiff's claim, that it had done so because of mistake and that plaintiff was entitled to recover as prayed for in his complaint.

Defendant assigns as error the court's denial of judgment in its favor at the close of testimony, its denial of a conclusion of law that plaintiff was not entitled to rescission, and the entering of the conclusion of law that plaintiff was entitled to recover. ...

(5) Defendant contends plaintiff has adequate redress in an action for damages and that rescission is an extraordinary remedy available only in exceptional cases. The right to rescission and restitution is an alternative remedy where there has been repudiation or a material breach of the contract. 5 Williston, *Contracts* §1455, at 4064 (Rev. ed. 1937) states as follows:

> The right of rescission and restitution generally exists as an alternative remedy to an action for damages where there has been repudiation or a material breach of contract. ...

In *Mohr v. Lear*, 239 Or. 41 at page 48, 395 P.2d 117 at page 120 (1964), Justice Rossman stated for this court as follows:

... When one party repudiates a contract or commits a total breach thereof the injured party has an election to pursue one of three remedies: he may treat the contract as at an end and sue for restitution, he may sue for damages, or he may sue for specific performance in certain cases. *Armsby v. Grays Harbor Commercial Co.*, 62 Or. 173, 123 P. 32; *Massey v. Becker*, 90 Or. 461, 176 P. 425; *Cornely v. Campbell*, 95 Or. 345, 186 P. 563, 187 P. 1103; *Paine v. Meier & Frank Co.*, 146 Or. 40, 27 P.2d 315, 29 P.2d 531; *Macomber v. Waxbom*, 213 Or. 412, 325 P.2d 253.

(6) Before a party to a contract is justified in rescinding it because of its breach by the other party, the breach must be substantial. Rescission is not warranted when the breach is not substantial and does not defeat the objects of the parties. *Walton v. Denhart*, 226 Or. 254, 262, 359 P.2d 890 (1961); *Mohr v. Lear*, supra, 239 Or. at 48, 395 P.2d 117. Have the ends the contract was designed to subserve been effectively frustrated? *Mohr v. Lear*, supra at 50, 395 P.2d 117.

The purpose of the contract, in so far as plaintiff was concerned, was to obtain protection in the form of defendant's promise to pay claims in case of his disability. It would hardly seem arguable but that defendant's refusal to pay claims, based upon its position that the policy has lapsed, effectively frustrated this purpose and was a substantial breach. ...

The defendant next contends the return of all the premiums is not the proper measure of relief. The law relative to relief that can be secured by the insured when the insurer wrongfully repudiates the contract is in much confusion. One reason is the failure to distinguish an action for restitution upon rescission of the contract from an action for damages for its breach. The first is based on an annulment of the contract, the latter upon an assertion of the contract. As an illustration of the confusion the Annotation, 48 A.L.R. 107 (1927), uses the following language at page 110:

As concerns the *measure of damages* for the wrongful cancellation, repudiation, or termination of the contract of insurance by the insurer, there seems to be an irreconcilable conflict between two principal lines of authority, as well as variations from these two rules. The first of these rules is to the effect that the insured may *recover as damages* the amount of premiums paid or premiums, with interest, where there has been a wrongful repudiation of the contract by the insurer, *and the assured has elected to rescind the contract rather than have it enforced*. The other of these two rules is to the effect that, if the assured is still in such a state of health that he can secure other insurance of like nature and kind, his measure of damages would be the difference between the cost of carrying the insurance which he has for the term stipulated for, and the cost of new insurance at the rate he would then be required to pay for a like term. ...

(Emphasis added.) See also Annotation 107 A.L.R. 1233, at 1235 (1937).

The fact is that recovery in each case is based upon a different theory. The purpose of rescission and restitution is to return the parties as near as possible to their respective positions prior to the formation of the contract so that each of the parties will be free to obtain his desired performance elsewhere. The purpose of an action for damages is to put the injured party as near as possible to the position where he would have been had the contract actually been performed. See 5 Corbin, Contracts §996 (1964) ... . A more consistent adherence by the courts to this distinction would enable a more accurate analysis and classification of cases.

Whether relief for wrongful repudiation of an insurance contract is granted by way of restitution upon rescission or upon an action for damages for breach of contract, there is a split in authority whether or not a proper measure of recovery is the return of *all* premiums. Probably the majority opinion in the United States is that all premiums may be recovered. At least, it is referred to as the majority rule. See Annotation 48 A.L.R. 107, at 111. Oregon is among the jurisdictions having recognized this rule. In *Hinkson v. Kansas City Life Ins. Co.*, 93 Or. 473, 183 P. 24 (1919) the defendant issued several policies of life insurance to plaintiff and subsequently wrongfully canceled them, claiming the premiums had not been paid when in fact they had. Plaintiff brought an action for restitution of premiums paid under the policies and received a jury verdict. Upon appeal this court affirmed, stating at 93 Or. at page 500, 183 P. at page 33 as follows:

> The verdict was for the full amount of each alleged payment, with accrued interest. Upon the theory that the policies were in force until such time as they were canceled and that the plaintiff had the benefit of insurance, the defendant claims that it was entitled to a reduction or an offset. 2 *Bacon on Benefit Societies and Life Insurance* (3 ed. [1904]) §376, lays down this rule:
>
> > If a company wrongfully declares the policy forfeited and refuses to accept the premium when duly tendered, and to give the insured the customary renewal receipt, evidencing the continued life of the policy, the assured has his choice of three courses: He may tender the premium and wait until the policy becomes payable by its terms and then try the question of forfeiture; or he may sue in equity to have the policy continued in force; or he may elect to consider the policy at an end and bring an action to recover the just value of the policy, in which case the measure of damages is the amount of the premiums paid with interest on each from the time it was made.

It is apparent that this court at times has also failed to distinguish between an action for restitution upon rescission and one for damages.

One of the cases which makes the best argument for the position that the insured is entitled to the recovery of all premiums is *American Life Ins. Co. v. McAden*, 109 Pa. 399, 1 A. 256 (1885), which states at pages 404-405, 1 A. at 258, as follows:

> In the case at bar, the rights of the parties under the contract of insurance had attached, but the plaintiffs had never received any actual benefit from it. They may, in some sense perhaps, be said to have enjoyed the protection which the policy afforded in the event of the husband's death; but as that event did not occur, the policy had as yet been of no appreciable actual advantage to the plaintiff, and no real disadvantage to the defendant. The parties for anything that appears, upon the plaintiffs' recovery are placed precisely in the same situation they were in before the contract was made; for, although the company carried the risk, and the plaintiff May F. McAden, at all times during the continuance of the contract upon the happening of the event provided against was entitled to the indemnity it secured, yet the company has paid nothing and the plaintiffs have received nothing. As in the case of any other contract, the parties were each entitled during its continuance according to its terms.
>
> The policy when made was admittedly valid; the premiums which were paid were voluntarily paid upon that policy; the risk had been running for 10 years; the obligations of the contract were long since in force on both sides; and it is clear that the plaintiffs could not on their own mere motion rescind it, so as to recover back the premiums paid; but if after receiving these several premiums, the company, without right, refuse to receive further premiums as they mature, deny their obligation, and declare the contract at an end, the plaintiff, we think, may take the defendants at their word, treat the contract as rescinded, and recover back the premiums paid as so much money had and received for their use. Rescission or avoidance, properly so called, annihilates the contract and puts the parties in the same position as if it had never existed. ...

There are also cases which hold that upon rescission there should be offset against the recovered premiums the value of the coverage actually received by the insured. The case which best illustrates the argument for this position is *Watson v. Massachusetts Mut. Life Ins. Co.*, 78 U.S. App. D.C. 248, 140 F.2d 673 (1943), cert. den. 322 U.S. 746, 64 S.Ct. 1156, 88 L.Ed. 1578 (1944). It states, at page 677, as follows:

> ... Therefore, when the defendant disclaimed liability it committed an immediate, not an anticipatory, breach of its contract to furnish insurance protection. Had the plaintiff chosen to do so he could have sued for damages, which ordinarily would have been the difference in cost between the repudiated policy and other insurance taken out at the advanced age of the subject of the policy.
>
> ·However, instead of seeking damages plaintiff has elected to rescind. We must, therefore, consider the second question—whether his right to rescission entitles him to return of the premiums. Some cases permit the recovery of premiums when an insurance company repudiates its liability, without reduction for the benefit of the insurance afforded while the policy was in force. This is in conflict with the well-established rule that if a party seeks restitution after rescinding on account of a breach of an executory contract he must deduct the benefits, if any, which he has received under such contract.
>
> Only a total failure of consideration should entitle the plaintiff to recover all his premiums. In this case the plaintiff was actually receiving full insurance protection prior to defendant's repudiation. It would require the application of the principle of punitive damages to permit him to recover the premiums which represented what it cost the defendant to carry the insurance for his benefit. A rule allowing the recovery of all premiums upon repudiation of an insurance contract can logically apply only to a case of intentional misrepresentation where it is shown that the defendant was at no time during the life of the policy willing to meet its obligation. There are no facts alleged which show such an intentional misrepresentation. So far as we can determine from the complaint, plaintiff received full value for all premiums paid prior to the disclaimer. *His right to rescind the contract does not carry with it the right to recover such premiums to the extent that they represent the cost of carrying insurance protection actually furnished the plaintiff.* No payments in excess of such costs are alleged.

(Emphasis added.)

(9) The theory of relief on an action for restitution is placing both parties in statu quo ante. Because insurance protection cannot be returned to defendant, the theory of recovery necessarily means the return to plaintiff of all premiums less the value of any benefits the plaintiff has actually received under the contract. ... Defendant contends plaintiff received the value of the protection for the ten-year period which, upon loss, could have been asserted by plaintiff at any time despite defendant's subsequent disavowal of the contract. Defendant's assertion upon repudiating the contract was that the policy had lapsed in 1959. There is no reason to believe that after that date defendant would have been any more willing to honor claims by plaintiff than it was in 1964 when it refused payment. By its own assertion that the policy lapsed in 1959 defendant demonstrated its unwillingness to meet contractual obligations since that time. Plaintiff therefore could not have been receiving the protection for which his premiums were being paid.

(10) It is our opinion that *Watson v. Massachusetts Mutual Life Ins. Co.*, supra, and similar cases correctly state the amount recoverable in restitution by an action for money had and received upon rescission of the insurance contract because of repudiation by the other party. To the extent that *Hinkson v. Kansas City Life Ins. Co.*, supra, is in conflict, it is hereby expressly overruled. There must be deducted from

the amount of premiums which are returned to him the value of the protection plaintiff has received.

Plaintiff has not claimed that the amount of premiums paid were in excess of the cost to defendant of carrying the risk of his policy. As was stated in *Watson v. Massachusetts Mut. Life Ins. Co.*, supra 78 U.S. App. D.C. 248, 140 F.2d at 677, "No payments in excess of such costs are alleged." Defendant, on the other hand, has not stated, nor did it prove when in 1959 it terminated plaintiff's policy. Not having shown this, it should be considered as terminated on January 1, 1959, or the time most unfavorable to defendant.

(11) As a result, plaintiff is not entitled to recover for those premiums paid prior to the year 1959 because it appears from the record that he received the protection these payments afforded. It would be inequitable for him to recover them. Defendant having wrongfully terminated plaintiff's policy in 1959, plaintiff is entitled to recover all premiums paid subsequent to January 1, 1959.

[See also McCamus at 1034-41; Waddams at paras 719-27.]

PROBLEMS

1. A agreed to buy goods from B for $14,000, and paid $5,000 in advance. B failed to deliver the goods, the value of which is $11,000. Advise A. See *Bush v Canfield*, 2 Conn 485 (1818).

2. A agreed with B to construct a dam for a price of $200,000, payable in installments according to the progress of the work. When nine-tenths of the work had been done, and A had been paid $180,000, a dispute arose between the parties, and B wrongfully ordered A off the construction site. A can prove that the market value of the services rendered is $400,000. Advise A. See *Boomer v Muir*, 24 P 2d 570 (Cal CA 1933).

ANGLIA TELEVISION LTD V REED
[1972] 1 QB 60 (CA)

LORD DENNING MR: Anglia Television Ltd., the plaintiffs, were minded in 1968 to make a film of a play for television entitled "The Man in the Wood." It portrayed an American man married to an English woman. The American has an adventure in an English wood. The film was to last for 90 minutes. Anglia Television made many arrangements in advance. They arranged for a place where the play was to be filmed. They employed a director, a designer and a stage manager, and so forth. They involved themselves in much expense. All this was done before they got the leading man. They required a strong actor capable of holding the play together. He was to be on the scene the whole time. Anglia Television eventually found the man. He was Mr. Robert Reed, the defendant, an American who has a very high reputation as an actor. He was very suitable for this part. By telephone conversation on August 30, 1968, it was agreed by Mr. Reed through his agent that he would come to England and be available between September 9 and October 11, 1968, to rehearse and play in this film. He was to get a performance fee of £1,050, living expenses of £100 a week, his first class fares to and from the United States, and so forth. It was all subject to the permit of the Ministry of Labour for him to come here. That was duly given on September 2, 1968. So the contract was concluded. But unfortunately there was some muddle with the bookings. It appears that Mr. Reed's agents had already booked him in America for some other play. So on September 3, 1968, the agent said that Mr. Reed would not come to England to perform in this play. He repudiated his contract.

Anglia Television tried hard to find a substitute but could not do so. So on September 11 they accepted his repudiation. They abandoned the proposed film. They gave notice to the people whom they had engaged and so forth.

Anglia Television then sued Mr. Reed for damages. He did not dispute his liability, but a question arose as to the damages. Anglia Television do not claim their profit. They cannot say what their profit would have been on this contract if Mr. Reed had come here and performed it. So, instead of claiming for loss of profits, they claim for the wasted expenditure. They had incurred the director's fees, the designer's fees, the stage manager's and assistant manager's fees, and so on. It comes in all to £2,750. Anglia Television say that all that money was wasted because Mr. Reed did not perform his contract.

Mr. Reed's advisers take a point of law. They submit that Anglia Television cannot recover for expenditure incurred *before* the contract was concluded with Mr. Reed. They can only recover the expenditure *after* the contract was concluded. They say that the expenditure *after* the contract was only £854.65, and that is all that Anglia Television can recover.

The master rejected that contention: he held that Anglia Television could recover the whole £2,750; and now Mr. Reed appeals to this court.

Mr. Butler, for Mr. Reed, has referred us to the recent case of *Perestrello & Companhia Limitada v. United Paint Co. Ltd.*, The Times, April 16, 1969, in which Thesiger J. quoted the words of Tindal C.J. in *Hodges v. Earl of Litchfield* (1835) 1 Bing. N.C. 492, 498: "The expenses preliminary to the contract ought not to be allowed. The party enters into them for his own benefit at a time when it is uncertain whether there will be any contract or not." Thesiger J. applied those words, saying: "In my judgment pre-contract expenditure, though thrown away, is not recoverable."

I cannot accept the proposition as stated. It seems to me that a plaintiff in such a case as this has an election: he can either claim for loss of profits; or for his wasted expenditure. But he must elect between them. He cannot claim both. If he has not suffered any loss of profits—or if he cannot prove what his profits would have been—he can claim in the alternative the expenditure which has been thrown away, that is, wasted, by reason of the breach. That is shown by *Cullinane v. British "Rema" Manufacturing Co. Ltd.* [1954] 1 Q.B. 292, 303, 308.

If the plaintiff claims the wasted expenditure, he is not limited to the expenditure incurred *after* the contract was concluded. He can claim also the expenditure incurred *before* the contract, provided that it was such as would reasonably be in the contemplation of the parties as likely to be wasted if the contract was broken. Applying that principle here, it is plain that, when Mr. Reed entered into this contract, he must have known perfectly well that much expenditure had already been incurred on director's fees and the like. He must have contemplated—or, at any rate, it is reasonably to be imputed to him—that if he broke his contract, all that expenditure would be wasted, whether or not it was incurred before or after the contract. He must pay damages for all the expenditure so wasted and thrown away. This view is supported by the recent decision of Brightman J. in *Lloyd v. Stanbury* [1971] 1 W.L.R. 535. There was a contract for the sale of land. In anticipation of the contract—and before it was concluded—the purchaser went to much expense in moving a caravan to the site and in getting his furniture there. The seller afterwards entered into a contract to sell the land to the purchaser, but afterwards broke his contract. The land had not increased in value, so the purchaser could not claim for any loss of profit. But Brightman J. held, at p. 547, that he could recover the cost of moving the caravan and furniture because it was "within the contemplation of the parties when the contract was signed." That decision is in accord with the correct principle, namely, that wasted expenditure can be recovered when it is wasted by reason of the defendant's breach of contract. It is true that, if the defendant had never entered into the contract, he would not be liable, and the expenditure would have been incurred by the plaintiff without redress; but, the defendant having made his contract and broken it, it does not lie in his mouth to say he is not liable, when it was because of his breach that the expenditure has been wasted.

I think the master was quite right and this appeal should be dismissed.

AI OGUS, NOTE, "DAMAGES FOR PRE-CONTRACT EXPENDITURE"
(1972) 35 Mod L Rev 423

[Two] questions arise for consideration.

(1) *Should the plaintiff have the right to elect between his reliance interest and his expectation interest?* The principle of election is stated broadly without qualification and yet concealed behind the question is a policy issue of fundamental importance. If the plaintiff is allowed recovery on the basis of his reliance interest the award will seek to put him in the position he would have been in if the contract had not been made. He may as a result be put in a better position than if the defendant had performed his contract. He may, in short, be able to protect himself against the consequences of having made a bad bargain. It may be sought to defend this result on the ground that it does not lie in the mouth of a person who has broken his contract to complain if the plaintiff is put in the position he would have been in if he had not entered into a contract with the defendant. But this view involves, by implication a punitive consideration. The opposing view, that a plaintiff should never be put in a better position than if the contract had been performed, seems to be more consistent with the doctrine of compensation. If this latter view were to be preferred then the principle of election enunciated by Lord Denning M.R. would be subject to the qualification that recovery of reliance interest damages should not exceed the value of the expectation.

(2) *Should pre-contract expenditure form part of the reliance interest award?* Having allowed the plaintiff to elect between the reliance and expectation interests, Lord Denning M.R. decided that an award of reliance interest damages might include pre-contract expenditure. This is, with respect, a doubtful proposition. The measure of damages so envisaged would not put the plaintiffs in the position they would have been in if the contract had not been made, for the expenses would still have been incurred. The expenses were incurred not in reliance on the defendant's promise to perform—they were incurred merely in the hope that agreement with the defendant would be secured. There was indeed no causal connection between the loss (the wasted expenses) and either the making of the contract or its breach. In the United States of America these theoretical objections have proved decisive: all attempts to recover pre-contract expenditure (where there was no special agreement binding the defaulting party to pay) have failed.

[See also McCamus at 890-95; MacDougall at 338-47; Waddams at paras 712-15.]

NOTES AND QUESTIONS

1. In *Bowlay Logging Ltd v Domtar Ltd* (1978), 135 DLR (3d) 179 (BCCA), a logging contract was terminated by the timber owner's breach. The contract price for full performance was $150,000. The logger's claim for expenses was held to be limited by proof that losses would have been incurred even if the contract had not been terminated. Seaton JA said: "On the evidence it seems clear that the appellant was losing heavily; not because of the respondent's breach, but because of an improvident contract and grossly inefficient work practices. The appellant's claim that it expended $232,905 partially completing a project that was to yield $150,000 demonstrates the extent to which it was losing money. The result of the breach was to release the appellant from further losses. In short, no damage was sustained by the appellant as a consequence of the respondent's breach."

2. The owners of a ship enter into a charterparty—that is, a contract to rent the carrying capacity of a ship—for five years and incur expenses to install special equipment for the particular needs of the charterer. Then the charterer repudiates the contract. Market rates for ship charters are now much higher than the contract rate, so that the owners recharter the ship at a higher rate and suffer no net loss, even taking account of the expenses of the special equipment, which is now useless. Are the owners entitled to recover damages? See *Omak Maritime Ltd v Mamola Challenger Shipping Co*, [2010] EWHC 2026 (Comm).

PITCHER V SHOEBOTTOM
[1971] 1 OR 106 (HC)

[Prior to August 1958, the plaintiff made an oral agreement with the defendant, S, to buy certain land. This agreement was reduced to writing in the summer of 1959, and the plaintiff made some payments to S under the agreement. In 1960, S, in breach of the agreement, sold the land to a third person.

The plaintiff brought an action against S for specific performance of the agreement for the sale of land, for a declaration that the subsequent purchasers had no interest in the land, or, alternatively, for damages against all the defendants. The claims for specific performance and for damages against the other purchasers were dismissed, but the claim for damages against S was allowed.]

LIEFF J: ... I find Shoebottom liable to the plaintiff for breach of contract but I also find that there is not sufficient evidence before me to ascertain the damages which the plaintiff suffered as a result of the breach. The only evidence led in this regard was contained in Kingshott's testimony where he stated that the value of the Pitcher lands is now more than $8,000 and in 1958 the value was $2,000. I therefore think it is necessary to direct a reference to the local Master at Parry Sound to ascertain the quantum of damage suffered by the plaintiff. ...

Therefore in the present case the Master must ascertain the value of the Pitcher lands at the date when the Pitcher agreement was to close, and the difference between that value and the contract price represents the loss of bargain damage to which I find the plaintiff to be entitled. The plaintiff is also entitled to the return of the moneys which he paid on account of the purchase price but he is not entitled to any expenditures relating to investigating title or any other expenditures which had been necessary if the transaction had been closed as planned. On the other hand, the cost of the survey which the plaintiff would have acquired must be deducted if in fact he did not need to have that survey made as a result of the vendor's breach. These items all flow from the principle that damages are being awarded to put the plaintiff in the same position he would have been in at the time when the contract was breached by the vendor. Thus any items of expenditure which would have been necessary in order to close the deal must be taken into consideration.

The last problem relates to the problem that the agreement of purchase and sale did not specify a closing date. In such a circumstance, a reasonable time is implied (*Shackleton v. Hayes*, [1954] 4 D.L.R. 81 at p. 89, *per* Cartwright J.). Hence, a reasonable time for closing the transaction would have been early 1960. It is a fact that a survey could not have been carried out prior to the spring of 1959 due to weather conditions. Therefore, early 1960 is the date which the Master should use in ascertaining the market value of the land at the date of the breach.

NOTES AND QUESTIONS

1. Assuming that the land had increased in value between 1960 and 1970, why was the plaintiff not entitled to recover that increase? This aspect is discussed in Section VIII, below.

2. In April, A agreed to sell 2,000 bushels of wheat to B at $1.03 a bushel, to be delivered July 25. On July 13, A sold the wheat to C at $1.16 a bushel. By July 25, the market price of wheat had dropped to 97¢ a bushel. B claims damages for breach of contract. Will B succeed? See *Acme Mills & Elevator Co v Johnson* (1911), 141 Ky 718, 133 SW 784.

HAWKINS V MCGEE
84 NH 114, 146 A 641 (1929)

Assumpsit against a surgeon for breach of an alleged warranty of the success of an operation. Trial by jury. Verdict for the plaintiff. The writ also contained a count in negligence upon which a nonsuit was ordered, without exception.

The defendant ... moved to set aside the verdict upon the grounds that it was contrary to the evidence; ... and because the damages awarded by the jury were excessive. The trial court ... found that the damages were excessive, and made an order that the verdict be set aside, unless the plaintiff elected to remit all in excess of $500. The plaintiff having refused to remit, the verdict was set aside "as excessive and against the weight of the evidence," and the plaintiff excepted.

[The case was transferred to the Supreme Court.]

BRANCH J: The operation in question consisted in the removal of a considerable quantity of scar tissue from the palm of the plaintiff's right hand and the grafting of skin taken from the plaintiff's chest in place thereof. The scar tissue was the result of a severe burn caused by contact with an electric wire, which the plaintiff received about nine years before the time of the transactions here involved. There was evidence to the effect that before the operation was performed the plaintiff and his father went to the defendant's office, and that the defendant, in answer to the question, "How long will the boy be in the hospital?" replied, "Three or four days, not over four; then the boy can go home and it will be just a few days when he will go back to work with a good hand." Clearly this and other testimony to the same effect would not justify a finding that the doctor contracted to complete the hospital treatment in three or four days or that the plaintiff would be able to go back to work within a few days thereafter. The above statements could only be construed as expressions of opinion or predictions as to the probable duration of the treatment and plaintiff's resulting disability, and the fact that these estimates were exceeded would impose no contractual liability upon the defendant. The only substantial basis for the plaintiff's claim is the testimony that the defendant also said before the operation was decided upon, "I will guarantee to make the hand a hundred per cent perfect hand or a hundred per cent good hand." The plaintiff was present when these words were alleged to have been spoken, and, if they are to be taken at their face value, it seems obvious that proof of their utterance would establish the giving of a warranty in accordance with his contention.

The defendant argues, however, that, even if these words were uttered by him, no reasonable man would understand that they were used with the intention of entering "into any contractual relation whatever," and that they could reasonably be understood only "as his expression in strong language that he believed and expected that as a result of the operation he would give the plaintiff a very good hand." It may be conceded, as the defendant contends that, before the question of the making of a contract should be submitted to a jury, there is a preliminary question of law for the trial court to pass upon, i.e. "whether the words could possibly have the meaning imputed to them by the party who founds his case upon a certain interpretation"; but it cannot be held that the trial court decided this question erroneously in the present case. It is unnecessary to determine at this time whether the argument of the defendant, based upon "common knowledge of the uncertainty which attends all surgical operations," and the improbability that a surgeon would ever contract to make a damaged part of the human body "one hundred per cent perfect," would, in the absence of countervailing considerations, be regarded as conclusive, for there were other factors in the present case which tended to support the contention of the plaintiff. There was evidence that the defendant repeatedly solicited from the plaintiff's father the opportunity to perform this operation, and the theory was advanced by plaintiff's counsel in cross-examination of defendant that he sought an opportunity to "experiment on skin grafting," in which he had had little previous experience. If the jury accepted this part of plaintiff's contention, there would be a reasonable basis for the further conclusion that, if defendant spoke the words attributed to him, he did so with the intention that they should be accepted at their face value, as an inducement for the granting of consent to the operation by the plaintiff and his father, and there was ample evidence that they were so accepted by them. The question of the making of the alleged contract was properly submitted to the jury.

The substance of the charge to the jury on the question of damages appears in the following quotation: "If you find the plaintiff entitled to anything, he is entitled to recover for what pain and suffering he has been made to endure and for what injury he has sustained over and above what injury he had before." To this instruction the defendant seasonably excepted. By it, the jury was permitted to consider two elements of damage: (1) Pain and suffering due to the operation; and (2) positive ill effects of the operation upon the plaintiff's hand. Authority for any specific rule of damages in cases of this kind seems to be lacking, but, when tested by general principle and by analogy, it appears that the foregoing instruction was erroneous. ...

The present case is closely analogous to one in which a machine is built for a certain purpose and warranted to do certain work. In such cases, the usual rule of damages for breach of warranty in the sale of chattels is applied, and it is held that the measure of damages is the difference between the value of the machine, if it had corresponded with the warranty and its actual value, together with such incidental losses as the parties knew, or ought to have known, would probably result from a failure to comply with its terms. ...

We therefore conclude that the true measure of the plaintiff's damage in the present case is the difference between the value to him of a perfect hand or a good hand, such as the jury found the defendant promised him, and the value of his hand in its present condition, including any incidental consequences fairly within the contemplation of the parties when they made their contract ... .

The extent of the plaintiff's suffering does not measure this difference in value. The pain necessarily incident to a serious surgical operation was a part of the contribution which the plaintiff was willing to make to his joint undertaking with the defendant to produce a good hand. It was a legal detriment suffered by him which constituted a part of the consideration given by him for the contract. It represented a part of the price which he was willing to pay for a good hand, but it furnished no test of the value of a good hand or the difference between the value of the hand which the defendant promised and the one which resulted from the operation. ...

It was also erroneous and misleading to submit to the jury as a separate element of damage any change for the worse in the condition of the plaintiff's hand resulting from the operation, although this error was probably more prejudicial to the plaintiff than to the defendant. Any such ill effect of the operation would be included under the true rule of damages set forth above, but damages might properly be assessed for the defendant's failure to improve the condition of the hand, even if there were no evidence that its condition was made worse as a result of the operation.

It must be assumed that the trial court, in setting aside the verdict, undertook to apply the same rule of damages which he had previously given to the jury, and, since this rule was erroneous, it is unnecessary for us to consider whether there was any evidence to justify his finding that all damages awarded by the jury above $500 were excessive. ...

New trial ordered.

II. PROBLEMS IN MEASURING DAMAGES

A. COST OF SUBSTITUTE PERFORMANCE, OR ECONOMIC VALUE?

CARSON V WILLITTS
(1930), 65 OLR 456 (CA)

[A contract was entered into to bore three oil wells. The defendant bored one well and then refused to carry on.]

MASTEN JA: Then what is the basis on which this court should now direct the damages to be assessed? In my opinion, what the plaintiff lost by the refusal of the defendant to bore two more wells was a sporting or gambling chance that valuable oil or gas would be found when the two further wells were bored. If the wells had been bored and no oil or gas of value had been found, the effect would be that the plaintiff has lost nothing by the refusal of the defendant to go on boring. On the other hand, if valuable oil or gas had been discovered, by the boring of these two wells, he had lost substantially. It may not be easy to compute what that chance was worth to the plaintiff, but the difficulty in estimating the quantum is no reason for refusing to award any damages.

In *Mayne on Damages*, 10th ed., p. 6, it is said:

A distinction must be drawn between cases where absence of evidence makes it impossible to assess damages, and cases where the assessment is difficult because of the nature of the damages proved. In the former case only nominal damages can be recovered. In the latter case, however, the difficulty of assessment is no ground for refusing substantial damages.

GROVES V JOHN WUNDER CO
286 NW 235 (Minn SC 1939)

STONE J (for the court): Action for breach of contract. Plaintiff got judgment for a little over $15,000. Sorely disappointed by that sum, he appeals.

In August 1927, S.J. Groves and Sons Company, a corporation (hereinafter mentioned simply as Groves), owned a tract of 24 acres of Minneapolis suburban real estate. It was served or easily could be reached by railroad trackage. It is zoned as heavy industrial property. But for lack of development of the neighborhood its principal value thus far may have been in the deposit of sand and gravel which it carried. The Groves company had a plant on the premises for excavating and screening the gravel. Near by defendant owned and was operating a similar plant.

In August 1927, Groves and defendant made the involved contract. For the most part it was a lease from Groves, as lessor, to defendant as lessee; its term seven years. Defendant agreed to remove the sand and gravel and to leave the property "at a uniform grade, substantially the same as the grade now existing at the roadway ... on said premises, and that in stripping the overburden ... it will use said overburden for the purpose of maintaining and establishing said grade."

Under the contract defendant got the Groves screening plant. The transfer thereof and the right to remove the sand and gravel made the consideration moving from Groves to defendant, except that defendant incidentally got rid of Groves as a competitor. On defendant's part it paid Groves $105,000. So that from the outset, on Groves' part the contract was executed except for defendant's right to continue using the property for the stated term. (Defendant had a right to renewal which it did not exercise.)

Defendant breached the contract deliberately. It removed from the premises only "the richest and best of the gravel" and wholly failed, according to the findings, "to perform and comply with the terms, conditions, and provisions of said lease ... with respect to the condition in which the surface of the demised premises was required to be left." Defendant surrendered the premises, not substantially at the grade required by the contract "nor at any uniform grade." Instead, the ground was "broken, rugged, and uneven." Plaintiff sues as assignee and successor in right of Groves.

As the contract was construed below, the finding is that to complete its performance 288,495 cubic yards of overburden would need to be excavated, taken from the premises and deposited elsewhere. The reasonable cost of doing that was found to be upwards of $60,000. But, if defendant had left the premises at the uniform grade required by the lease, the reasonable value of the property on the determinative date would have been only $12,160. The judgment was for that sum, including interest, thereby nullifying plaintiff's claim that cost of completing the contract rather than difference in value of the land was the measure of damages. The gauge of damage adopted by the decision was the difference between the market value of plaintiff's land in the condition it was when the contract was made [broken?] and what it would have been if defendant had performed. The one question for us arises upon plaintiff's assertion that he was entitled, not to that difference in value, but to the reasonable cost to him of doing the work called for by the contract which defendant left undone.

1. Defendant's breach of contract was wilful. There was nothing of good faith about it. Hence, that the decision below handsomely rewards bad faith and deliberate breach of contract is obvious. That is not allowable. Here the rule is well settled, ... that where the contractor wilfully and fraudulently varies from the terms of a construction contract he cannot sue thereon and have the benefit of the equitable doctrine of substantial performance. That is the rule generally. ...

2. In reckoning damages for breach of a building or construction contract, the law aims to give the disappointed promisee, so far as money will do it, what he was promised. ...

Never before, so far as our decisions show, has it even been suggested that lack of value in the land furnished to the contractor who had bound himself to improve it any escape from the ordinary consequences of a breach of the contract. ...

Even in case of substantial performance in good faith, the resulting defects being remediable, it is error to instruct that the measure of damage is "the difference in value between the house as it was and as it would have been if constructed according to contract." The "correct doctrine" is that the cost of remedying the defect is the "proper" measure of damages. ...

Value of the land (as distinguished from the value of the intended product of the contract, which ordinarily will be equivalent to its reasonable cost) is no proper part of any measure of damages for wilful breach of a building contract. The reason is plain.

The summit from which to reckon damages from trespass to real estate is its actual value at the moment. The owner's only right is to be compensated for the deterioration in value caused by the tort. That is all he has lost. But not so if a contract to improve the same land has been breached by the contractor who refuses to do the work, especially where, as here, he has been paid in advance. The summit from which to reckon damages for that wrong is the hypothetical peak of accomplishment (not value) which would have been reached had the work been done as demanded by the contract.

The owner's right to improve his property is not trammeled by its small value. It is his right to erect thereon structures which will reduce its value. If that be the result, it can be of no aid to any contractor who declines performance. As said long ago in *Chamberlain v. Parker*, 45 N.Y. 569, 572:

> A man may do what he will with his own, ... and if he chooses to erect a monument to his caprice or folly on his premises, and employs and pays another to do it, it does not lie with the defendant who has been so employed and paid for building it, to say that his own performance would not be beneficial to the plaintiff.

To the same effect is *Restatement, Contracts*, s. 346, p. 576, Illustrations of Subsection (1), par. 4. [See dissenting judgment, below.]

Suppose a contractor were suing the owner for breach of a grading contract such as this. Would any element of value, or lack of it, in the land have any relevance in reckoning damages? Of course not. The contractor would be compensated for what he had lost, i.e., his profit. Conversely, in such a case as this, the owner is entitled to compensation for what he has lost, that is, the work or structure which he has been promised, for which he has paid, and of which he has been deprived by the contractor's breach.

To diminish damages recoverable against him in proportion as there is presently small value in the land would favor the faithless contractor. It would also ignore and so defeat plaintiff's right to contract and build for the future. To justify such a course would require more of the prophetic vision than judges possess. This factor is important when the subject matter is trackage property in the margin of such an area of population and industry as that of the Twin Cities. ...

[Under] a construction contract, the thing lost by a breach such as we have there is a physical structure or accomplishment, a promised and paid for alteration in land. That is the "injury" for which the law gives him compensation. Its only appropriate measure is the cost of performance.

It is suggested that because of little or no value in his land the owner may be unconscionably enriched by such a reckoning. The answer is that there can be no unconscionable enrichment, no advantage upon which the law will frown, when the result is but to give one party to a contract only what the other has promised; particularly where, as here, the delinquent has had full payment for the promised performance.

3. It is said by the *Restatement, Contracts*, s. 346, Comment b:

> Sometimes defects in a completed structure cannot be physically remedied without tearing down and rebuilding, at a cost that would be imprudent and unreasonable. The law does not require damages to be measured by a method requiring such economic waste. If no such waste is involved, the cost of remedying the defect is the amount awarded as compensation for failure to render the promised performance.

The "economic waste" declaimed against by the decisions applying that rule has nothing to do with the value in money of the real estate, or even with the product of the contract. The waste avoided is only that which would come from wrecking a physical structure completed, or nearly so, under the contract. ... Absent such waste, as it is in this case, the rule of the *Restatement, Contracts*, s. 346, is that "the cost of remedying the defect is the amount awarded as compensation for failure to render the promised performance." That means that defendants here are liable to plaintiff for the reasonable cost of doing what defendants promised to do and have wilfully declined to do. ...

The judgment must be reversed with a new trial to follow.

JULIUS J. OLSON J (dissenting) (Holt J concurring): ... Since there is no issue of fact, we should limit our inquiry to the single legal problem presented: What amount in money will adequately compensate plaintiff for his loss caused by defendant's failure to render performance? ...

As the rule of damages to be applied in any given case has for its purpose compensation, not punishment, we must be ever mindful that, "if the application of a particular rule for measuring damages to given facts results in more than compensation, it is at once apparent that the wrong rule has been adopted." *Crowley v. Burns Boiler Co.*, 110 N.W. 969, 973.

We have here then a situation where, concededly, if the contract had been performed, plaintiff would have had property worth, in round numbers, no more than $12,000. If he is to be awarded damages in an amount exceeding $60,000 he will be receiving at least 500 per cent more than his property, properly leveled to grade by actual performance, was intrinsically worth when the breach occurred. To so conclude is to give him something far beyond what the parties had in mind or contracted for. There is no showing made, nor any finding suggested, that this property was unique, specially desirable for a particular or personal use, or of special value as to location or future use different from that of other property surrounding it. Under the circumstances here appearing, it seems clear that what the parties contracted for was to put the property in shape for general sale. And the lease contemplates just that, for by the terms thereof defendant agreed "from time to time, as the sand and gravel are removed from the various lots ... leased, it will surrender said lots to the lessor" if of no further use to defendant "in connection with the purposes for which this lease is made."

The theory upon which plaintiff relies for application of the cost of performance rule must have for its basis cases where the property or the improvement to be made is unique or personal instead of being of the kind ordinarily governed by market values. His action is one at law for damages, not for specific performance. As there was no affirmative showing of any peculiar fitness of this property to a unique or personal use, the rule to be applied is, I think, the one applied by the court. The cases bearing directly upon this phase so hold. Briefly, the rule here applicable is this: Damages recoverable for breach of a contract to construct is the difference between the market value of the property in the condition it was when delivered to and received by plaintiff and what its market value would have been if defendant had fully complied with its terms. ...

No one doubts that a party may contract for the doing of anything he may choose to have done (assuming what is to be done is not unlawful) "although the thing to be produced had no marketable value." In *Restatement, Contracts*, s. 346, pp. 576, 577, Illustrations of Subsection (1), par. 4, the same thought is thus stated:

> A contracts to construct a monumental fountain in B's yard for $5,000, but abandons the work after the foundation has been laid and $2,800 has been paid by B. The contemplated fountain is so ugly that it would decrease the number of possible buyers of the place. The cost of completing the fountain would be $4,000. B can get judgment for $1,800, the cost of completion less the part of price unpaid.

But that is not what plaintiff's predecessor in interest contracted for. Such a provision might well have been made, but the parties did not. They could undoubtedly have provided for liquidated damages for nonperformance ... or they might have determined in money what the value of performance was considered to be and thereby have contractually provided a measure for failure of performance.

The opinion also suggests that this property lies in an area where the owner might rightly look for future development, being in a so-called industrial zone, and that as such he should be privileged to so hold it. This he may of course do, but let us assume that on May 1, 1934, condemnation to acquire this area had so far progressed as to leave only the question of price (market value) undetermined; that the area had been graded in strict conformity with the contract but that the actual market value of the premises was only $12,160, as found by the court and acquiesced in by plaintiff what would the measure of his damages be? Obviously, the limit of his recovery could be no more than the then market value of his property. In that sum he has been paid with interest and costs; and he still has the fee title to the premises, something he would not possess if there had been condemnation. In what manner has plaintiff been hurt beyond the damages awarded? As to him "economic waste" is not apparent. Assume the defendant abandoned the entire project without taking a single yard of gravel therefrom but left the premises as they were when the lease was made, could plaintiff recover damages upon the basis here established? The trouble with the prevailing opinion is that here plaintiff's loss is not made the basis for the amount of his recovery but rather what it would cost the defendant. No case has been decided upon that basis until now. Plaintiff asserts that he knows of no rule "giving a different measure of damages for public contracts and for private contracts in case of nonperformance." It seems to me there is a clear distinction to be drawn with respect to the application of the rule for recoverable damages in case of breach of a public works contract from that applicable to contracts between private parties. The construction of a public building, a sewer, drainage ditch, highway, or other public work, permits of no application of the market value doctrine. There simply is and can be no "market value" as to such. And for this cogent reason there can be but one rule of damages to apply, that of cost of completion of the thing contracted to be done. I think the judgment should be affirmed.

NOTES AND PROBLEMS

1. If the "reasonable value of the property on the determinative date would have been only $12,160," why did the plaintiff originally obtain judgment for $15,000 representing the $12,160 plus interest? The defendant surrendered the land to the plaintiff; must it not have some value? Should this value not be deducted from the $12,160? Professors Dawson and Harvey in their casebook *Contracts and Contract Remedies* (Brooklyn, NY: Foundation Press, 1959) report (at 28) that the case was compromised and the defendant paid $55,000 in cash settlement. In 1953, three-fifths of the land was sold for $45,000 after $6,000 had been spent on levelling that portion. It was left at a higher level than planned, but was still suitable for a railroad siding.

2. See also *Peevyhouse v Garland Coal & Mining Co*, 382 P 2d 109 (SC Okla 1962), in which the Supreme Court of Oklahoma refused to follow *Groves v John Wunder Co* in a case where the plaintiff sought damages for breach of a promise to restore a strip-mining site and where the cost of restoration was about 100 times the estimated increase in land value.

3. See also McCamus at 898-905; MacDougall at 358-60; Waddams at paras 766-67.

4. J owned a 1980 Ford car to which he was sentimentally attached and which he referred to affectionately as "Esmerelda." As the result of an accident, Esmerelda's fender was in need of repair, and K agreed to repair it for $500. K now finds that the cost of repair will actually be $2,000 and, in breach of contract, she refuses to do the repairs. J has the repairs done elsewhere for $2,000, and sues K for $1,500. It is proved that the market value of the car now (as repaired) is $1,000; in its damaged condition it was $800, but J was so attached to Esmerelda that he would not consider buying another car. Advise K. See *O'Grady v Westminster Scaffolding Ltd*, [1962] 2 Lloyd's Rep 238 (QB); *Darbishire v Warran*, [1963] 3 All ER 310 (CA); *Nu-West Homes Ltd v Thunderbird Petroleums, Ltd* (1975), 59 DLR (3d) 292 at 307-8 (Alta CA).

5. A, a carpenter, agreed with B, acting on behalf of a church organization, to build pews for a church. When the work was completed it was discovered that the pews did not meet specifications; they were too narrow and made of weak material. To replace the pews with the proper ones would cost $200. The difference in cost between the material used and that specified is about $50. B sues for damages. Advise A. See *Wood v Stringer* (1890), 20 OR 148 (ChD).

6. A agrees with B to construct a swimming pool, to be 7 feet 6 inches in depth. When the pool is complete it is discovered that the depth is only 6 feet. The evidence is that this does not diminish the suitability of the pool for diving and that it does not affect the value of B's land. Nevertheless, B, who particularly wanted the specified depth, is distressed, and demands $100,000, the cost of reconstructing the pool to the contractual specifications. See *Ruxley Electronics and Construction, Ltd v Forsyth*, [1996] 1 AC 344 (HL).

7. The lease of an office building provides that the lessee will not alter the premises without written permission from the lessor. In breach of this provision, the lessee replaced the floor in the foyer, destroying the previous floor that had been made of rare stone. The evidence is that the alteration reduced the value of the building by $35,000. The cost of restoring the floor to its original condition would be $580,000 and involve the loss of $800,000 in rent while the restoration was carried out. What is the proper measure of damages? Does it make any difference whether the breach is deliberate or accidental? See *Tabcorp Holdings Ltd v Bowen Investments Pty Ltd*, [2009] HCA 8.

8. D agrees with C to build an office building and garage. On completion of the work, the garage is found to be smaller than required under the contract. The evidence is that it would cost $54,000 to enlarge the garage, but that such work would add nothing to the value of the property. What is the measure of damages? See *Diotte v Consolidated Development Co.* 2014 NBCA 55, 376 DLR (4th) 235.

B. LOST VOLUME

SALE OF GOODS ACT
RSO 1990, c S.1

48(1) Where the buyer wrongfully neglects or refuses to accept and pay for the goods, the seller may maintain an action against the buyer for damages for non-acceptance.

(2) The measure of damages is the estimated loss directly and naturally resulting in the ordinary course of events from the buyer's breach of contract.

(3) Where there is an available market for the goods in question the measure of damages is in the absence of evidence to the contrary to be ascertained by the difference between the contract price and the market or current price at the time or times when the goods ought to have been accepted, or, if no time was fixed for acceptance, then at the time of the refusal to accept.

49(1) Where the seller wrongfully neglects or refuses to deliver the goods to the buyer, the buyer may maintain an action against the seller for damages for non-delivery.

(2) The measure of damages is the estimated loss directly and naturally resulting in the ordinary course of events from the seller's breach of contract.

(3) Where there is an available market for the goods in question, the measure of damages is in the absence of evidence to the contrary to be ascertained by the difference between the contract price and the market or current price of the goods at the time or times when they ought to have been delivered, or, if no time was fixed, then at the time of the refusal to deliver.

THOMPSON (WL) LTD V ROBINSON (GUNMAKERS) LTD
[1955] Ch 177

[The defendants had contracted to buy a standard model car from the plaintiffs, who were dealers in cars. The defendants, in breach of contract, refused to accept delivery of the car, and the plaintiffs returned it to their suppliers, who took it back. The plaintiffs claimed that they had lost the profit that they would have made if the defendants had bought the car; the defendants relied on s 48 of the *Sale of Goods Act* (s 50 of the English Act).]

UPJOHN J: This action raises a question of some importance to the motor trade as to the true measure of damages where the buyer of a motor-car, in this case a Standard "Vanguard," refuses to complete his bargain and take delivery.

[His Lordship stated the facts and continued:] The law is not really in doubt; it is set out in section 50 of the Sale of Goods Act, 1893. That section was declaratory of the existing law, and the general principle which has been observed in all cases [is this:] "Subject to these observations I think that there are certain broad principles which are quite well settled. The first is that, as far as possible, he who has proved a breach of a bargain to supply what he contracted to get is to be placed, as far as money can do it, in as good a situation as if the contract had been performed." That is the general rule.

Apart altogether from authority and statute it would seem to me on the facts which I have to consider to be quite plain that the plaintiffs' loss in this case is the loss of their bargain. They have sold one "Vanguard" less than they otherwise would. The plaintiffs, as the defendants must have known, are in business as dealers in motor-cars and make their profit in buying and selling motor-cars, and what they have lost is their profit on the sale of this "Vanguard." ...

The main case, however, put by the defendants is this: they submit that subsection (3) of section 50 applies, because they say that there is an available market for the goods in question, and in that available market we know that the price of the "Vanguard" is fixed. It is fixed by the manufacturers. Therefore, they say, the measure of damages must necessarily be little more than nominal. Had the plaintiffs kept the car and sold it to another at a later stage, no doubt they would have been entitled to the costs of storage in the meantime, possibly interest on their money laid out, and so on, but as they had in fact, mitigated their damages by getting out of the contract, damages are nil. ...

Had the matter been res integra I think that I should have found that an "available market" merely means that the situation in the particular trade in the particular area was such that the particular goods could freely be sold, and that there was a demand sufficient to absorb readily all the goods that were thrust on it, so that if a purchaser defaulted, the goods in question could readily be disposed of. Indeed, such was the situation in the motor trade until very recently. It was, of course, notorious that dealers all over the country had long waiting lists for new motor-cars. People put their names down and had to wait five or six years, and whenever a car was spared by the manufacturer from export it was snatched at, and if any purchaser fell out there were many waiting to take his place, and it was conceded that if those circumstances were still applicable to the "Vanguard" motor-car the claim for damages must necessarily have been purely nominal. But on the assumed facts circumstances had changed in relation to "Vanguard" motor-cars, and in March of this year there was not a demand in the East Riding which could readily absorb all the "Vanguard" motor-cars available for sale. If a purchaser defaults, that sale is lost, and there is no means of readily disposing of the "Vanguard" contracted to be sold so that there is not even on the extended definition an available market. But there is this further consideration: even if I accepted Mr. Platts-Mills's broad argument that one must now look at the market as being the whole conspectus of trade, organization and marketing, I have to remember that subsection (3) provides only a *prima facie* rule, and if on investigation of the facts one finds that it is unjust to apply that rule, in the light of the general principles mentioned above, then it is not to be applied. In this case, as I said in the earlier part of my judgment, it seems to me plain almost beyond argument that in fact the loss to the plaintiffs is the sum of £61. Accordingly, however one interprets subsection (3), it seems to me on the facts that I have to consider one reaches the same result.

Judgment for the plaintiffs.

CHARTER V SULLIVAN
[1957] 2 QB 117 (CA)

[The defendant refused to accept delivery of a standard model car that he had contracted to buy from the plaintiff car dealer. There was evidence that the plaintiff could sell all the cars of this sort that he could get, and he did in fact resell the particular car in question.]

JENKINS LJ: I turn now to consider what, on the undisputed facts of the case, is in the eye of the law the true measure of the damages, if any, over and above merely nominal damages, which the plaintiff has suffered through the defendant's failure to take and pay for the car he agreed to buy.

Consideration of this question must inevitably begin with a reference to section 50 of the Sale of Goods Act, 1893.

[His Lordship read s 50 and continued:]

Mr. Collard, for the defendant, argued that in the present case there was an available market for "Hillman Minx" de luxe saloon cars within the meaning of section 50(3) of the Act, and accordingly that the measure of damages ought, in accordance with the prima facie rule laid down by that subsection, to be ascertained by the difference between the contract price and the market or current price at the time of the defendant's refusal to perform his contract.

The result of this argument, if accepted, would be that the plaintiff could claim no more than nominal damages, because the market or current price could only be the fixed retail price, which was necessarily likewise the price at which he sold to the defendant and resold to Wigley.

But the plaintiff is a motor-car dealer whose trade for the present purpose can be described as consisting in the purchase of recurrent supplies of cars of the relevant description from the manufacturers, and selling the cars so obtained, or as many of them as he can, at the fixed retail price. He thus receives, on each sale he is able to effect, the predetermined profit allowed by the fixed retail price, and it is obviously in his interest to sell as many cars as he can obtain from the manufacturers. The number of sales he can effect, and consequently the amount of profit he makes, will be governed, according to the state of trade, either by the number of cars he is able to obtain from the manufacturers, or by the number of purchasers he is able to find. In the former case demand exceeds supply, so that the default of one purchaser involves him in no loss, for he sells the same number of cars as he would have sold if that purchaser had not defaulted. In the latter case supply exceeds demand, so that the default of one purchaser may be said to have lost him one sale. ...

In *Thompson (W.L.) Ltd. v. Robinson (Gunmakers) Ltd.* Upjohn J. had before him a claim for damages in a case resembling the present case to the extent that the damages were claimed in respect of the defendants' refusal to perform a contract with the plaintiffs for the purchase from the plaintiffs of a car (in that instance a "Standard Vanguard" car) which, like the car in the present case, could only be sold by the plaintiffs at a fixed retail price. It is, however, important to note that the case to which I am now referring proceeded on certain admissions, including an admission to the effect that in the relevant district at the date of the contract (which was also the date of the breach) "there was no shortage of 'Vanguard' models to meet all immediate demands in the locality," which I take to mean, in effect, that the supply of such cars exceeded the demand. In these circumstances the plaintiffs by agreement with their suppliers rescinded their contract with them, and returned the car. In the ensuing action the plaintiffs claimed from the defendants damages amounting to the profit the plaintiffs would have made on the sale of the car to the defendants if the defendants had duly completed their purchase of it, and the judge held them entitled to those damages. The defendants raised the same argument as had been raised by the defendant in the present case, namely that there was an available market for a car of the kind in question, within the meaning of section 50(3), that there was a market or current price in the shape of the fixed retail price, and that as the fixed retail price was the same as the contract price the plaintiffs had suffered no damage. ...

It remains, therefore, to ascertain the loss (if any) "naturally resulting in the ordinary course of events" from the defendant's breach of contract, and the measure of that loss must, in my opinion, be the amount, if any, of the profit the plaintiff has lost by reason of the defendant's failure to take and pay for the car he agreed to buy. This accords with the view taken by Upjohn J. in *Thompson (W.L.) Ltd. v. Robinson (Gunmakers) Ltd.*, and also with the principle stated in *In re Vic Mill Ltd.* which Upjohn J. applied.

I should next refer to evidence of which I have deferred consideration earlier in this judgment. ...

Notwithstanding Mr. Aldous's submission to the contrary on the plaintiff's behalf, I think we should assume that the judge accepted as accurate the plaintiff's sales manager's own description of the state of the plaintiff's business in "Hillman Minx" cars. Moreover, I think we should take that description as signifying, according to the ordinary meaning of the language used, that the plaintiff could always find purchasers for all the "Hillman Minx" cars he was able to get. ...

The matter therefore stands thus. If the defendant had duly performed his bargain, the plaintiff would have made on that transaction a profit of £97 15s. The calculation accordingly starts with a loss of profit, through the defendant's default, of £97 15s. That loss was not cancelled or reduced by the sale of the same car to Wigley, for if the defendant had duly taken and paid for the car he agreed to buy, the plaintiff could have sold another car to Wigley, in which case there would have been two sales and two profits: see *In re Vic Mill Ltd.*, and particularly *per* Hamilton L.J. and Buckley L.J. But the matter does not rest there. The plaintiff must further show that the sum representing the profit he would have made if the defendant had performed his contract has in fact been lost. Here I think he fails, in view of Winter's evidence to the effect that the plaintiff could sell all the "Hillman Minx" cars he could get.

I have already expressed my opinion as to the meaning of this statement. It comes, I think, to this, that according to the plaintiff's own sales manager the state of trade was such that the plaintiff could always find a purchaser for every "Hillman Minx" car he could get from the manufacturers; and if that is right it inevitably follows that he sold the same number of cars and made the same number of fixed profits as he would have sold and made if the defendant had duly carried out his bargain.

Upjohn J.'s decision in favour of the plaintiff dealers in *Thompson's* case was essentially based on the admitted fact that the supply of the cars in question exceeded the demand, and his judgment leaves no room for doubt that if the demand had exceeded the supply his decision would have been the other way.

Appeal allowed. Damages reduced to nominal sum.

NOTE

The problem in *Thompson v Robinson* and *Charter v Sullivan*, sometimes called the "lost volume" problem, is not confined to contracts for the sale of goods. See e.g. *Inter-office Telephones, Ltd v Robert Freeman Co, Ltd*, [1958] 1 QB 190 (CA), which concerned a contract for the hire of goods.

C. NOTE ON LOSS OF CHANCE

In *Chaplin v Hicks*, [1911] 2 KB 786, the plaintiff, one of 50 persons shortlisted for 12 positions, was deprived by breach of contract of an opportunity to be interviewed. The English Court of Appeal held that she was entitled to proportionate damages for loss of the chance. The case has been frequently followed in Canada. In *Multi-Malls Inc v Tex-Mall Properties Ltd* (1980), 108 DLR (3d) 399 (Ont H Ct J), aff'd (1981), 128 DLR (3d) 192 (CA), the defendant's breach of contract resulted in the loss of a 20 percent chance of rezoning the plaintiff's property for a valuable use; proportionate damages were awarded. In *Folland v Reardon* (2005), 136 ACWS (3d) (Ont CA), Doherty JA said:

> The imposition of liability grounded in the loss of a chance of avoiding a harm or gaining a benefit is controversial in tort law, particularly where the harm alleged is not purely economic: see *Laferrière v. Lawson*, [1991] 1 S.C.R. 541, at 600-606 ... . Whatever the scope of the lost chance analysis in fixing liability for tort claims based on personal injuries, lost chance is well recognized as a basis for assessing damages in contract. In contract, proof of damage is not part of the liability inquiry. If a defendant breaches his contract with the plaintiff and as a result a plaintiff loses the opportunity to gain a benefit or avoid harm, that lost opportunity may be compensable. As I read the contract cases, a plaintiff can recover damages for a lost chance if four criteria are met. First, the plaintiff must establish on the balance of probabilities that but for the defendant's wrongful conduct, the plaintiff had a chance to obtain a benefit or avoid a loss. Second, the plaintiff must show that the chance lost was sufficiently real and significant to rise above mere speculation. Third, the plaintiff must demonstrate that the outcome, that is, whether the plaintiff would have avoided the loss or made the gain, depended on someone or something other than the plaintiff himself or herself. Fourth, the plaintiff must show that the lost chance had some practical value: *Chaplin v. Hicks*, [1911] 2 K.B. 786; *Spring v. Guardian Assurance Plc.*, [1995] 2 A.C. 296 per Lord Lowry at 327 (H.L.); *Eastwalsh Homes Ltd. v. Anatal Developments Ltd.* (1993), 12 O.R. (3d) 675 at 689-90 (C.A.) ... ; *Multi-Malls Inc. v. Tex-Mall Properties Ltd.*

III. REMOTENESS

BRITISH COLUMBIA AND VANCOUVER'S ISLAND SPAR, LUMBER AND SAW MILL CO LTD V NETTLESHIP
(1868), LR 3 CP 499 at 508

WILLES J: Cases of this kind [involving remoteness of damages] have always been found to be very difficult to deal with, beginning with a case said to have been decided about two centuries and a half ago, where a man going to be married to an heiress, his horse having cast a shoe on the journey, employed a blacksmith to replace it, who did the work so unskilfully that the horse was lamed, and, the rider not arriving in time, the lady married another; and the blacksmith was held liable for the loss of the marriage. The question is a very serious one; and we should inevitably fall into a similar absurdity unless we applied the rules of common sense to restrict the extent of liability for the breach of a contract of this sort. ...

[On this example FE Smith commented as follows: "It is hardly necessary to observe that the man of the anvil, even with notice of his customer's errand, could hardly have apprehended in the bride an *animus nubendi* so imperious and undiscriminating" ((1900) 16 Law Q Rev 279).]

HADLEY V BAXENDALE
(1854), 9 Exch 341, 156 ER 145

[The plaintiff owned a steam-powered mill at Gloucester. The shaft having broken, the plaintiff had to send it to Greenwich, near London, to serve as a pattern for the manufacture of a new one. The defendant was in the business of carrying goods. The plaintiff sent the shaft for an agreed price, but its delivery at Greenwich was delayed beyond what was found to be a reasonable delivery time. The final delivery of the new shaft to the plaintiff was consequently delayed, and the plaintiff brought an action against the defendant for the profits lost due to the mill standing idle during that period of delay. At the trial, the jury awarded a sum of money (beyond a sum for which the defendant had formally admitted liability) in respect of the lost profits. The defendant sought an order for a new trial.]

ALDERSON B: We think that there ought to be a new trial in this case; but, in so doing, we deem it to be expedient and necessary to state, explicitly the rule which the Judge, at the next trial, ought, in our opinion, to direct the jury to be governed by when they estimate the damages.

It is indeed, of the last importance that we should do this; for, if the jury are left without any definite rule to guide them, it will, in such cases as these, manifestly lead to the greatest injustice. ...

Now we think the proper rule in such a case as the present is this: Where two parties have made a contract which one of them has broken, the damages which the other party ought to receive in respect of such breach of contract should be such as may fairly and reasonably be considered either arising naturally, i.e., according to the usual course of things, from such breach of contract itself, or such as may reasonably be supposed to have been in the contemplation of both parties, at the time they made the contract, as the probable result of the breach of it. Now, if the special circumstances under which the contract was actually made were communicated by the plaintiffs to the defendants, and thus known to both parties, the damages resulting from the breach of such a contract, which they would reasonably contemplate, would be the amount of injury which would ordinarily follow from a breach of contract under these special circumstances so known and communicated. But, on the other hand, if these special circumstances were wholly unknown to the party breaking the contract, he, at the most, could only be supposed to have had in his contemplation the amount of injury which would arise generally, and in the great multitude of cases not affected by any special circumstances, from such a breach of contract. For, had the special circumstances been known, the parties might have specially provided for the breach of contract by special terms as to damages in that case; and of this advantage it would be very unjust to deprive them. Now the above principles are those by which we think the jury ought to be guided in estimating the damages arising out of any breach of contract. ...

Now, in the present case, if we are to apply the principles above laid down, we find that the only circumstances here communicated by the plaintiffs to the defendants at the time the contract was made, were, that the article to be carried was the broken shaft of a mill, and that the plaintiffs were the millers of that mill. But how do these circumstances shew reasonably that the profits of the mill must be stopped by an unreasonable delay in the delivery of the broken shaft by the carrier to the third person? Suppose the plaintiffs had another shaft in their possession put up or putting up at the time, and that they only wished to send back the broken shaft to the engineer who made it; it is clear that this would be quite consistent with the above circumstances, and yet the unreasonable delay in the delivery would have no effect upon the intermediate profits of the mill. Or again, suppose that, at the time of the delivery to the carrier, the machinery of the mill had been in other respects defective, then, also, the same results would follow. Here it is true that the shaft was actually sent back to serve as a model for a new one, and that the want of a new one was the only cause of the stoppage of the mill, and that the loss of profits really arose from not sending down the new shaft in proper time, and that this arose from the delay in delivering the broken one to serve as a model. But it is obvious that, in the great multitude of cases of millers sending off broken shafts to third persons by a carrier under ordinary circumstances, such consequences would not, in all probability, have occurred; and these special circumstances were here never communicated by the plaintiffs to the defendants. It follows, therefore, that the loss of profits here, cannot reasonably be considered such a consequence of the breach of contract as could have been fairly and reasonably contemplated by both parties when they made this con-tract. For such loss would neither have followed naturally from the breach of this contract in the great multitude of such cases occurring under ordinary circumstances, nor were the special circumstances, which, perhaps, would have made it a reasonable and natural consequence of such breach of contract, communicated to or known by the defendants. The Judge ought, therefore, to have told the jury that, upon the facts then before them, they ought not to take the loss of profits into consideration at all in estimating the damages. There must therefore be a new trial in this case.

NOTE

In *Jackson v Royal Bank of Scotland*, [2005] UKHL 3, Lord Walker of Gestinghope said:

In my opinion the familiar passage from the judgment of Baron Alderson ... cannot be con-strued and applied as if it were a statutory text, nor are its two limbs mutually exclusive. The first limb ... tends to beg the question, since it makes the damages recoverable under the first limb depend on how the breach of contract is characterised. If for instance (by reference to the facts of *Hadley v. Baxendale* itself) the breach is described simply as a carrier's failure to convey goods from Gloucester and deliver them to Greenwich within two days as promised, it is a matter of speculation what damages would arise naturally and in the ordinary course. If on the other hand the breach is described as a delay in delivering to the manufacturer at Greenwich a broken crankshaft to serve as a model for a new crankshaft urgently required for the only steam engine at a busy flour mill at Gloucester (which was standing idle until the new crankshaft arrived) then loss of business profits is seen to be an entirely natural conse-quence. The appropriate characterisation of the breach depends on the terms of the con-tract, its business context, and the reasonable contemplation of the parties.

JH JACKSON, *Contract Law in Modern Society*
(St Paul, Minn: West, 1973) at 10-11

The role of the jury has always had considerable effect on the law of contract. Before the eighteenth century, writes one noted scholar, "... [T]he jury by and large, had a free discretion when money damages were claimed, to determine the amount of the award." In theory the amount of damages was a "question of fact" and in England the itinerant trial justice sent out from London was little disposed to challenge the "yeoman of the neighborhood" who had knowledge of the affair. Because of outra-geous or excessive verdicts, however, judges began to exercise control over the jury by rulings on evidence, by granting new trials, and by instructing the jury about the amount which was proper. Thus legal doctrine began to grow. The famous 1854 case of *Hadley v. Baxendale* ... demonstrates this tendency and it is commonly said that the modern law of contract damages dates only from the middle of the nineteenth century.

NOTES AND QUESTIONS

1. Suppose that the plaintiffs had taken their shaft in at 10 o'clock in the morning, and that at 11 o'clock the plaintiffs' servant came in again and said: "The mill is stopped; we can't make any flour until we get that shaft back. Please hurry it." Then suppose that at 12 noon Samuel Stranger came in and the defendants agreed to take a chest in the only available conveyance to Penzance in time for Stranger's daughter's wedding the next day. Suppose that Stranger offered to pay £5, twice the usual rate. If the defendants accepted this proposal and returned the plaintiffs their £2 4s., should this deliberate breach of the promise after the work stoppage was known affect the calculation of damages? *Corbin on Contracts* (vol 5, s 1008) suggests that we distinguish between wilful and non-wilful breach, and in the former case make the material time for notice of unusual loss the time the defendant chose to commit the wilful breach. The distinction has not been adopted in Canadian or English cases. *Principles, Definitions and Model Rules of European Private Law: Draft Common Frame of Reference* (2009) provides, in book III, ch 3, s 703: "The debtor in an obligation which arises from a contract ... is liable only for loss which the debtor foresaw or could reasonably be expected to have foreseen at the time when the obligation was incurred as a likely result of the non-performance, unless the non-performance was intentional, reckless or grossly negligent."

2. Who, of Hadley and Baxendale, could more easily insure against the loss that occurred? Should such a question be relevant to the court's conclusion?

3. Able, a farmer, ordered tractor headlights from Baker's Department Store Ltd., at their usual price. He told the clerk in the store that he needed the lights to operate his tractor to harvest his crop at night, and that if the lights were not supplied he would lose part of his crop. The clerk promised that the lights would be supplied in time. The lights were not supplied, and Able lost half the crop, being unable to procure substitute lights in time. Is Baker's Department Store liable for the loss? See *Lamkins v International Harvester Co*, 182 SW 2d 203 (Ark SC 1944).

FULLER & PERDUE, "THE RELIANCE INTEREST IN CONTRACT DAMAGES"
(1936) 46 Yale LJ 52 at 84-88

[Reprinted by permission of The Yale Law Journal Company and Fred B. Rothman & Company from *The Yale Law Journal*.]

Before we discuss the relation between the reliance interest and *Hadley v. Baxendale* it will be necessary to state briefly what seems to us to be involved in that famous case, considering it not so much as an event in legal history but as the accepted symbol for a set of problems. The case may be said to stand for two propositions: (1) that it is not always wise to make the defaulting promisor pay for all the damage which follows as a consequence of his breach, and (2) that specifically the proper test for determining whether particular items of damage should be compensable is to inquire whether they should have been foreseen by the promisor at the time of the contract. The first aspect of the case is much more important than the second. In its first aspect the case bears an integral relation to the very bases of contract liability. It declares in effect that just as it is wise to refuse enforcement altogether to some promises (considerationless, unaccepted, "social" promises, etc.) so it is wise not to go too far in enforcing those promises which are deemed worthy of legal sanction. The answer to the question of *Hadley v. Baxendale* (where shall we stop?) must inevitably be as complex as the answer to the question (where shall we begin?) which is implicit in the law of mutual assent, consideration and the rules governing the formation of contracts generally.

In its second aspect *Hadley v. Baxendale* may be regarded as giving a grossly simplified answer to the question which its first aspect presents. To the question, how far shall we go in charging to the defaulting promisor the consequences of his breach, it answers with what purports to be a single test, that of foreseeability. The simplicity and comprehensiveness of this test are largely a matter of illusion. In the first place, it is openly branded as inappropriate in certain situations where the line is drawn much more closely in favor of the defaulting promisor than the test of foreseeability as normally understood would draw it. There are, therefore, exceptions to the test, to say nothing of authorities which reject it altogether as too burdensome to the defaulter. In the second place, it is clear that the test of foreseeability is less a definite test itself than a cover for a developing set of tests. As in the case of all "reasonable man" standards there is an element of circularity about the test of foreseeability. "For what items of damage should the court hold the defaulting promisor? Those which he should as a reasonable man have foreseen? but what should he have foreseen as a reasonable man? Those items of damage for which the court feels he ought to pay." The test of foreseeability is therefore subject to manipulation by the simple device of defining the characteristics of the hypothetical man who is doing the foreseeing. By a gradual process of judicial inclusion and exclusion this "man" acquires a complex personality; we begin to know just what "he" can "foresee" in this and that situation, and we end, with not one test but with a whole set of tests. This has obviously happened in the law of negligence, and is happening, although less obviously, to the reasonable man postulated by *Hadley v. Baxendale*.

Even if the reasonable man who does the foreseeing is a juristic construct, endowed precisely with those qualities which the court feels he ought to have for the purpose at hand, it does not seem that there is a complete *petitio principii* in the test of foreseeability. When we import into a question of liability the "reasonable man" standard we do at least two things. In the first place we increase the chance that the case will ultimately be determined by the jury. Though the court may define the reasonable man, it cannot be sure that its definition will be regarded by the jury, and any test which speaks of the reasonable man decreases the court's chance of removing the case from the jury. In the second place, whether the case is ultimately decided by the judge or the jury, stating the problem in terms of the reasonable man creates a bias in favor of exempting *normal* or *average* conduct from legal penalties. The reasonable man is not necessarily the average man, but he tends to be, and the notion of what is normal and average puts a bridle on the judicial power of defining reasonableness. But the restraint is far from complete. It becomes illusory in those situations where the concepts "normal" and "average" are without definite content: where the "average man" is as much a juristic construct as the "reasonable man." The restraint is often thrown off even in those fields where, because rather definite lay ways of thought and action are discoverable in them, the notion of the "normal" and "average" has some objective reality. The courts have not hesitated to invest the reasonable man with capacities either greater or less than those of the average man. For an example of this judicial autonomy within the reign of fact one need look no further than the case which originated the test of foreseeability, *Hadley v. Baxendale* itself. ("Thus, in *Hadley v. Baxendale* itself, the carrier was told of the use to which the broken shaft was to be put and that the mill was shut down, but it was held that this was not enough, since it was not told that another shaft was not available!" McCormick, *Damages* (1935) §140.)

HORNE V THE MIDLAND RAILWAY COMPANY
(1873), LR 8 CP 131 (Exch Ch)

[The plaintiffs, shoe manufacturers in Kettering, were under contract to supply a quantity of shoes to a firm in London for the use of the French army, at the unusually high price of 4s. per pair. By the terms of the contract with the London firm, the plaintiff was bound to deliver the shoes by February 3, 1871, and to meet this provision he sent the shoes to the defendant's station at Kettering in time to be delivered in the usual course in the evening of that day, when they would have been accepted and paid for by the consignees. Notice was given to the station master (which notice was, for the purpose of the case, deemed to be notice to the company) at the time the shoes were delivered to him that the plaintiffs were under contract to deliver the shoes by February 3 and that unless they were so delivered they would be thrown on their hands. The shoes were not delivered in London until the morning of February 4, when the consignee refused them, and the plaintiffs were obliged to sell them at the best price obtainable—namely, 2s. 9d. per pair.

In an action against the defendants for the delay in delivering the shoes, they paid into court a sum of £20, which would be sufficient to cover any ordinary loss such as expenses incidental to the resale, but the plaintiffs further claimed the sum of £267 as the difference between the price at which they had contracted to sell the shoes and the price which they ultimately received.

On a stated case to the Court of Common Pleas, the defendant received a judgment (LR 7 CP 583), which was affirmed in this appeal.]

BLACKBURN J: ... Then if there was no special contract, what was the effect of the notice? In the case of *Hadley v. Baxendale* it was intimated that, apart from all question of a special contract with regard to the amount of damages, if there were a special note of the circumstances the plaintiff might recover the exceptional damages. This doctrine has been adverted to in several subsequent decisions with more or less assent, but they appear to have all been cases in which it was held that the doctrine did not apply because there was no special notice. It does not appear that there has been any case in which it has been affirmatively held that in consequence of such a notice the plaintiff could recover exceptional damages. The counsel for the plaintiff could not refer to any such case, and I know of none. If it were necessary to decide the point, I should be much disposed to agree with what my Brother Martin has suggested, viz., that in order that the notice may have any effect, it must be given under such circumstances, as that an actual contract arises on the part of the defendant to bear the exceptional loss. Before, however, deciding the point, I should have wished to take time to consider.

Hydraulic Engineering Co Ltd v McHaffie. (1878), 4 QBD 670 (England). BRAMWELL LJ: It has occurred to me that the true explanation is that a person contemplates the performance and not the breach of his contract; he does not enter into a kind of second contract to pay damages, but he is liable to make good those injuries which he is aware that his default may occasion to the contractee. COTTON LJ: It cannot be said that damages are granted because it is part of the contract that they shall be paid: it is the law which imposes or implies the term that upon breach of a contract damages must be paid.

Rivers v George White & Sons Co. [1919] 2 WWR 189 (Sask CA). HAULTAIN CJS: It may be observed that this theory "of a kind of second contract to pay damages" has been mainly developed in actions against carriers on the ground that a common carrier has no discretion to decline a contract.

Kinghorne v The Montreal Telegraph Co. (1859), 18 UCQB 60 (Ont). In an action for failure to deliver a telegram that cost 60¢ and might have led to a contract that might have been carried out, the jury awarded £57 13s. 7d. as damages. On a motion for a non-suit, held, for the defendant, McLEAN J: It is, in my opinion, extremely doubtful whether in any such case a party who avails himself of the facilities afforded in communicating by telegraph can expect that a telegraph company shall be responsible for all damages, no matter what amount, which may arise in the hurry of transmitting a message from any verbal inaccuracy of an operator, or from an omission in forwarding or delivering it when received. It ought not to be expected that so great facilities are to be afforded for so small a remuneration, and at a risk which might bring ruin upon any company if obliged to indemnify for every possible loss.

VICTORIA LAUNDRY LTD V NEWMAN INDUSTRIES LTD
[1949] 2 KB 528 (CA)

ASQUITH LJ (for the court): This is an appeal by the plaintiffs against a judgment of Streatfeild J., in so far as that judgment limited the damages to £110 in respect of an alleged breach of contract by the defendants which is now uncontested. The breach of contract consisted in the delivery of a boiler sold by the defendants to the plaintiffs some twenty odd weeks after the time fixed by the contract for delivery. The short point is whether, in addition to the £110 awarded, the plaintiffs were entitled to claim in respect of loss of profits which they say they would have made if the boiler had been delivered punctually.

The defendants are and were at all material times a limited company which described itself on its invoices as "Electrical and Mechanical Engineers and Manufacturers." They did not manufacture the boiler in question. They just happened to own it. The plaintiffs were at all material times a limited company carrying on the business of laundrymen and dyers in the neighbourhood of Windsor. In January, 1946, the plaintiffs were minded to expand their business, and to that end required a boiler of much greater capacity than the boiler they then possessed. ... Seeing an advertisement by the defendants on Jan. 17, 1946, of two boilers, which appeared suitable ... they negotiated for the purchase of one of them, and by Apr. 26, 1946, had concluded a contract for its purchase at a price of £2,150, loaded free on transport at Harpenden.

Seeing that the issue is as to the measure of recoverable damages and the application of the rules in *Hadley v. Baxendale* it is important to inquire what information the defendants possessed at the time when the contract was made as to such matters as the time at which, and the purpose for which, the plaintiffs required the boiler. The defendants knew before and at the time of the contract that the plaintiffs were laundry-men and dyers and required the boiler for purposes of their business as such. They also knew that the plaintiffs wanted the boiler for immediate use. On the latter point the correspondence is important. The contract was concluded by, and is contained in, a series of letters ... and finally, on Apr. 26, in the concluding letter of the series by which the contract was made: "We are most anxious that this" (that is, the boiler) "should be put into use"—we call attention to this expression—"in the shortest possible space of time." Hence, up to and at the very moment when a concluded contract emerged, the plaintiffs were pressing on the defendants the need for expedition, and the last letter was a plain intimation that the boiler was wanted for immediate use. This is none the less so because when, later, the plaintiffs encountered delays in getting the necessary permits and licences, the exhortations to speed come from the other side, who wanted their money, which, in fact, they were paid in advance of delivery. The defendants knew the plaintiffs needed the boiler as soon as the delays should be overcome, and they knew by the beginning of June that such delays had by then, in fact, been overcome. The defendants did not know at the material time the precise role for which the boiler was cast in the plaintiffs' economy, *e.g.*, whether (as the fact was) it was to function in substitution for an existing boiler of inferior capacity, or in replacement of an existing boiler of equal capacity, or as an extra unit to be operated side by side with and in addition to any existing boiler. It has, indeed, been argued strenuously that, for all they knew, it might have been wanted as a "spare" or "standby," provided in advance to replace an existing boiler, when, perhaps some time hence the latter should wear out, but such an intention to reserve it for future use seems quite inconsistent with the intention expressed in the letter of Apr. 26 to "put it into use in the shortest possible space of time." In this connection, certain admissions made in the course of the hearing are of vital importance. The defendants formally admitted what in their defence they had originally traversed, namely, the facts alleged in para. 2 of the statement of claim. That paragraph reads as follows:

> At the date of the contract hereinafter mentioned the defendants well knew as the fact was that the plaintiffs were launderers and dyers carrying on business at Windsor and required the said boiler for use in their said business and the said contract was made upon the basis that the said boiler was required for the said purpose.

On June 5, the plaintiffs, having heard that the boiler was ready, sent a lorry to Harpenden to take delivery. Mr. Lennard, a director of the plaintiff company, pre-ceded the lorry in a car. He discovered on arrival that four days earlier the contractors employed by the defendants to dismantle the boiler had allowed it to fall on its side, receiving damage. Mr. Lennard declined to take delivery of the damaged boiler in its existing condition and insisted that the damage must be made good. He was, we think, justified in this attitude, since no similar article could be bought on the market. After a long wrangle, the defendants agreed to perform the necessary repairs, and, after further delay through the difficulty of finding a contractor who was free and able to perform them, completed the repairs by Oct. 28. Delivery was taken by the plaintiffs on Nov. 8 and the boiler was erected and working by early December. The plaintiffs claim, as part—the disputed part—of the damages, loss of the profits they would have earned if the machine had been delivered in early June instead of November.

Evidence was led for the plaintiffs with the object of establishing that, if the boiler had been punctually delivered, then, during the twenty odd weeks between then and the time of actual delivery (1) they could have taken on a very large number of new customers in the course of their laundry business, the demand for laundry services at that time being insatiable—they did, in fact, take on extra staff in the expectation of its delivery—and (2) that they could and would have accepted a number of highly lucrative dyeing contracts for the Ministry of Supply. In the statement of claim, para. 10, the loss of profits under the first of these heads was quantified at £16 a week and under the second at £262 a week. The evidence, however, which promised to be voluminous, had not gone very far when counsel for the defendants submitted that in law no loss of profits was recoverable at all, and that to continue to hear evidence as to its *quantum*, was mere waste of time. He suggested that the question of remoteness of damage under this head should be decided on the existing materials, including the admissions to which we have referred. The learned judge accepted counsel's submission, and on that basis awarded £110 damages under certain minor heads, but nothing in respect of loss of profits, which he held to be too remote. It is from that decision that the plaintiffs now appeal. It was a necessary consequence of the course which the case took that no evidence was given on behalf of the defendants, and only part of the evidence available to the plaintiffs. It should be observed parenthetically that the defendants had added as third party the contractors who, by dropping the boiler, so causing the injuries to it, prevented its delivery in early June and caused the defendants to break their contract. Those third party proceedings have been adjourned pending the hearing of the present appeal as between the plaintiffs and the defendants. The third party, nevertheless, was served with notice of appeal by the defendants and argument was heard for him at the hearing of the appeal.

The ground of the learned judge's decision ... may be summarised as follows. He took the view that the loss of profit claimed was due to special circumstances, and, therefore, recoverable, if at all, only under the second rule in *Hadley v. Baxendale*, and not recoverable in the present case because such special circumstances were not at the time of the contract communicated to the defendants. He also attached much significance to the fact that the object supplied was not a self-sufficient profit-making article, but part of a larger profit-making whole. ...

What propositions applicable to the present case emerge from the authorities as a whole, including those analysed above? We think they include the following: (1) It is well settled that the governing purpose of damages is to put the party whose rights have been violated in the same position, so far as money can do so, as if his rights had been observed. This purpose, if relentlessly pursued, would provide him with a complete indemnity for all loss *de facto* resulting from a particular breach, however improbable, however unpredictable. This, in contract at least, is recognised as too harsh a rule. Hence: (2) In cases of breach of contract the aggrieved party is only entitled to recover such part of the loss actually resulting as was at the time of the contract reasonably foreseeable as liable to result from the breach. (3) What was at that time reasonably foreseeable depends on the knowledge then possessed by the parties, or at all events, by the party who later commits the breach. (4) For this purpose, knowledge "possessed" is of two kinds—one imputed, the other actual. Everyone, as a reasonable person, is taken to know the "ordinary course of things" and consequently what loss is liable to result from a breach of that ordinary course. This is the subject-matter of the "first rule" in *Hadley v. Baxendale*, but to this knowledge, which a contract-breaker is assumed to possess whether he actually possesses it or not, there may have to be added in a particular case knowledge which he actually possesses of special circumstances outside the "ordinary course of things" of such a kind that a breach in those special circumstances would be liable to cause more loss. Such a case attracts the operation of the "second rule" so as to make additional loss also recoverable. (5) In order to make the contract-breaker liable under either rule it is not necessary that he should actually have asked himself what loss is liable to result from a breach. As has often been pointed out, parties at the time of contracting contemplate, not the breach of the contract, but its performance. It suffices that, if he had considered the question, he would as a reasonable man have concluded that the loss in question was liable to result. ... (6) Nor, finally, to make a particular loss recoverable, need it be proved that on a given state of knowledge the defendant could, as a reasonable man, foresee that a breach must necessarily result in that loss. It is enough if he could foresee it was likely so to result. It is enough ... if the loss (or some factor without which it would not have occurred) is a "serious possibility" or a "real danger." For short, we have used the word "liable" to result. Possibly the colloquialism "on the cards" indicates the shade of meaning with some approach to accuracy.

If these, indeed, are the principles applicable, what is the effect of their application to the facts of the present case? We have, at the beginning of this judgment, summarised the main relevant facts. The defendants were an engineering company supplying a boiler to a laundry. We reject the submission for the defendants that an engineering company knows no more than the plain man about boilers or the purposes to which they are commonly put by different classes of purchasers, including laundries. The defendant company were not, it is true, manufacturers of this boiler or dealers in boilers, but they gave a highly technical and comprehensive description of this boiler to the plaintiffs by letter of Jan. 19, 1946, and offered both to dismantle the boiler at Harpenden and to re-erect it on the plaintiffs' premises. Of the uses or purposes to which boilers are put, they would clearly know more than the uninstructed layman. Again, they knew they were supplying the boiler to a company carrying on the business of laundrymen and dyers, for use in that business. The obvious use of a boiler, in such a business, is surely to boil water for the purpose of washing or dyeing. A laundry might conceivably buy a boiler for some other purpose, for instance, to work radiators or warm bath water for the comfort of its employees or directors, or to use for research, or to exhibit in a museum. All these purposes are possible, but the first is the obvious purpose which, in the case of a laundry, leaps to the average eye. If the purpose then be to wash or dye, why does the company want to wash or dye, unless for purposes of business advantage? ...

We agree that in order that the plaintiffs should recover specifically and as such the profits expected on [the lucrative dyeing contracts], the defendants would have had to know, at the time of their agreement with the plaintiffs, of the prospect and terms of such contracts. We also agree that they did not, in fact, know these things. It does not, however, follow that the plaintiffs are precluded from recovering some general (and perhaps conjectural) sum for loss of business in respect of dyeing contracts to be reasonably expected any more than in respect of laundering contracts to be reasonably expected.

We are, therefore, of opinion that the appeal should be allowed and the issue referred to an official referee as to what damage, if any, is recoverable in addition to the £110 awarded by the learned trial judge. The official referee would assess those damages in consonance with the findings in this judgment as to what the defendants knew or must be taken to have known at the material time, either party to be at liberty to call evidence as to the *quantum* of the damage in dispute.

Appeal allowed.

QUESTIONS

Asquith LJ cited the *British Columbia Saw Mill* case, but he did not quote Bovill CJ, who said: "It is to be observed that the defendant is a carrier, and not a manufacturer of goods supplied for a particular purpose." Stuart J drew attention to this distinction in *Canada Foundry Co Ltd v Edmonton Portland Cement Co Ltd*, [1913] 1 WWR 382 (Alberta), and he also said: "There are indeed numbers of cases in which loss of profits has been awarded for breach of contract. ... In actions against carriers the Courts have perhaps hesitated more than they have in actions against manufacturers and builders." Is the distinction valid? Should a distinction be made between a carrier, a seller, and a manufacturer?

MUNROE EQUIPMENT SALES LTD V CANADIAN
FOREST PRODUCTS LTD
(1961), 29 DLR (2d) 730 (Man CA)

[The plaintiff agreed early in December 1956 to rent a second-hand Allis Chalmers HD 15 tractor to the defendant at the rate of $1,500 a month. The defendant wanted the tractor to be used along with his other equipment (including other tractors) in road-clearing operations that winter, so that his pulpwood could be brought to market. When the contract was made the defendant stressed that the tractor was needed to open roads, that time was short, and that frost had set in. Nevertheless, the contract was made on December 13 when the defendant's superintendent "accidentally bumped into" a salesman of the plaintiff. The tractor broke down within two days and thereafter its performance was sporadic and it was not much used until January 20, 1957. During this time the defendant made no effort to get a replacement, largely because the plaintiff's salesman thought the tractor could be repaired sooner than it could be replaced. Two subcontractors got additional equipment "when they became tired of waiting for the HD 15." The final breakdown occurred on February 20, and from then until the end of the season the tractor was abandoned. By agreement, no rent was charged for the month ending January 17, but in this action the plaintiff claimed $6,667.99. The trial judge allowed him $2,075, made up of $1,500 for one month's rent and freight charges. But he also allowed a counterclaim of $6,958.37 (the defendant asked for $14,298.12), most of which was based on lost profits because the defendant was prevented from removing 3,500 cords of pulpwood. He relied on *Hadley v Baxendale* and found the defendant's loss "was a natural and probable consequence that ought to have been in plaintiff's contemplation." On appeal the court divided three to two in modifying the verdict by reducing the plaintiff's award to $1,826.43 and dismissing the counterclaim altogether.]

MILLER CJM (Guy JA concurring): With respect, I do not think *Victoria Laundry (Windsor) Ltd. v. Newman Industries Ltd.*, [1949] 1 All E.R. 997, 2 K.B. 528, quoted by the learned trial Judge, is of much help to defendant. In any event, that decision is not binding on this Court. I prefer the reasoning of the trial Judge to that of the Judges of appeal so far as the application of the law to the facts is concerned. ... [*Anson on Contract*, 21st ed at 460-63, quoted and adopted.]

It seems to me that in the case at bar the defendant cannot succeed on its counterclaim unless it establishes that the special circumstances in connection with the use of the tractor were communicated and made known to the plaintiff company. There was nothing discussed in the negotiations for the tractor which would indicate whether the defendant company intended to remove 100 cords or 100,000 cords of wood; nor, so far as the knowledge of, or the knowledge imparted to, the plaintiff company was concerned, how much wood was cut and ready to be moved. Nor was it in any way indicated to the plaintiff that all the wood which the defendant company had cut by itself or its subcontractors had to be moved that year. The fact that the defendant had labour trouble in the fall of 1956, as deposed by Knelman the general manager of defendant, was not disclosed to plaintiff, or that, as a result thereof, the defendant was going to attempt to remove all wood that season. As stated above, it is not uncommon in the business in question to leave a substantial portion of 1 year's cut in the bush for removal in another year. Neither was it made known to the plaintiff company that the defendant company had a sale for any specific quantity of wood. The rental contract covering the HD 15 was of indeterminate duration and presumably could have been determined by either party at virtually any time.

It seems to me that the defendant company was seeking—and urgently seeking—a tractor, and was glad to obtain this rebuilt tractor. The defendant (not the plaintiff) was the originator of the contract in issue.

It appears to me that if it were a matter of such urgency to the defendant company that this tractor should bear the brunt of the roadwork, the defendant company would not have left the securing of same until as late as December 1956 when hauling operations were ready to begin. It also seems logical to me that if the defendant company were going to hold the plaintiff company responsible in such large damages for any failure to a second-hand rebuilt unit, the defendant company should have made clear to the plaintiff the extent of the work to be done. I do not believe the plaintiff acted in any improper way and I do believe that any representations the salesman of the plaintiff company may have made were made innocently, in good faith, and were not intended as a guarantee: but, as above pointed out, the learned trial Judge found that the salesman had guaranteed the tractor to be in good mechanical condition—whatever that may have meant with respect to a second-hand unit. There is no warranty or guarantee in the written rental agreement ex. 3.

In my opinion it is unreasonable to expect that such a burden of responsibility for damages as now claimed by the defendant should be assumed from the rental of a second-hand unit. Surely no reasonable person could contemplate, under the circumstances of the renting of this machine, that the lessor of one second-hand tractor was underwriting and virtually insuring the removal of all this pulpwood from the bush. ...

Had the plaintiff contemplated possible liability for such damage as claimed by the counterclaim, it is scarcely conceivable that it would have risked letting a second-hand tractor bear such responsibility; nor would any reasonable person do so. Such damages do not ordinarily flow from the fact that a second-hand tractor does not "stand-up," and therefore in order to fix the plaintiff with responsibility for such damages the defendant, at the time of making the contract, should have made clear its version of the extraordinary responsibility the defendant might seek to impose upon the plaintiff. At least it should have warned the plaintiff of its (defendant's) intention to remove all wood that season, the quantity involved, the sale contracts for wood that defendant had made, and such like. If this had been done it is probable the defendant would not have secured the tractor or the plaintiff would have insisted upon contracting itself out of any liability.

SCYRUP V ECONOMY TRACTOR PARTS LTD
(1963), 40 DLR (2d) 1026 (Man CA)

MILLER CJM (dissenting) (Guy JA concurring): This is an appeal from the judgment of Maybank J., who allowed plaintiff judgment for $2,001.14 damages. The damages were agreed upon as being out-of-pocket expenses amounting to $541.14 (against which there was a credit of $190, leaving a balance of $351.14) plus loss of profits of $1,650.

The action arose out of a purchase by plaintiff from defendant of a second-hand La Plante Hydraulic attachment for a D8 caterpillar tractor.

Plaintiff had, or expected to secure, a contract from Supercrete Limited to do certain work with this equipment in a gravel pit. His equipment was needed to replace that owned and operated by Supercrete during a period when Supercrete's equipment was being repaired. Plaintiff testified that he had entered into the contract before he ever attempted to purchase the equipment from defendant, although some doubt was raised on this point by the evidence of an employee of Supercrete Ltd., who indicated the deal between plaintiff and Supercrete was made just a few days before July 10, 1961, whereas the equipment was ordered by plaintiff in May or early in June, 1961.

With a view to obtaining the desired equipment the plaintiff approached defendant company in Winnipeg, but as suitable equipment was not available from defendant in Winnipeg, plaintiff was referred to defendant's parent company in Fargo, North Dakota, called Surplus Tractor Parts Inc., from which it was finally secured.

After delivery was made to plaintiff, he settled with defendant for the equipment at around $1,000, plus import duty. Plaintiff duly assembled the attachment and placed it on his tractor but when he commenced to work with it in July it did not operate properly and it now appears that various parts, including hoses and pumps, were either missing or were practically useless. When plaintiff communicated with defendant regarding these deficiencies, the defendant or its parent company co-operated and supplied the missing parts. The pumps were immediately replaced (actually during the course of the trouble the pumps were replaced more than once). The defendant company, under instructions from the parent company in Fargo, made an adjustment of $40 for hoses and a further $150 was later paid plaintiff in compensation for the repairs made, including repairs to defective pumps. Finally Supercrete became impatient because plaintiff's equipment was not in proper condition and hired someone else to do the job, with the result that plaintiff lost the contract.

Plaintiff testified that he had told defendant and also Surplus Tractor Parts Inc. that he had this contract and needed the equipment for the purpose of the contract. The following appears on pp. 13 and 14 of the evidence:

> Q. What did you tell the Defendant? A. I told him I needed the hydraulic dozer as soon as possible. I had picked out one down in Fargo.
>
> Q. Before we get to there, what did you tell the Defendant while you were in Winnipeg? A. I told him I had a job to go to with a hydraulic dozer. He told me fine, we have dozers like that in Fargo, North Dakota. ...
>
> Q. I believe this was a conversation with Mr. Swartz you are still referring to? A. Yes, I am.
>
> Q. Did you tell him who your job was with? A. Yes I did.

And at p. 19 of the evidence:

> Q. What happened then? A. I explained to Mr. Goodman that I had to have this piece of equipment in quite a hurry and it had to be in good working order. He showed

me this one that I have purchased and it was not all ... there was pieces missing here and there which he said. ...

A. Yes, but he said he had those parts to go with it and that it would be all checked over before delivery in good working order.

And at p. 22 of the evidence:

Q. What did he say? Tell us what he said, not just what you understood but what was actually said. A. I explained to him that I did not want it unless it was going to be in good working order and he agreed with me that it would be all checked over and in good working order. There wasn't a pump at the time on the machine that the hydraulic system was on but he said if they did not have one they would make up a good pump for it. And I explained the necessity of having all parts because I would be quite a ways from the city putting this machine together when it did arrive.

This does not indicate too clearly that much information was given defendant as to the scope of the contract, including whether it was a small or large contract, what type of work was involved, where or when it was to be performed, or its duration. In other words, the paucity of essential information communicated to defendant by plaintiff seems to me to be fatal to plaintiff's claim for profits.

The representative of the Surplus Tractor Parts in Fargo gave evidence that plaintiff only intimated to him that he possibly had a contract; but the learned trial Judge believed plaintiff and it must therefore be assumed by this Court that the communication, to the extent set out in the quoted evidence at least, was made by plaintiff to defendant.

The learned trial Judge found as follows:

I have no doubt that judgment herein should be for the plaintiff. I accept the evidence of him and his witnesses wherever it is in conflict with other evidence. The defendant sold to the plaintiff the equipment detailed in the statement of claim and warranted it fully. The machinery was quite defective. It would not work. The defendant was apprised at the time of the purchase that the plaintiff wanted the apparatus for use on a contract of work he had just obtained. When the apparatus was found to be inoperative this contract was lost to the plaintiff. Such loss was clearly foreseeable at the time the plaintiff dealt with the defendant for the purchase of the said machinery.

These are strong findings, conclusions, and inferences in favour of plaintiff. I am of the opinion that the "foreseeability" inferred by the learned trial Judge is not supported by the evidence, and that indeed on the evidence it is not supportable in law.

With respect, I feel it is very doubtful that this second-hand machinery should be saddled with a claim for damages for loss of profits unless it was clearly indicated to defendant at the time the equipment was purchased exactly what kind of contract was being entered into by plaintiff, the type of work that was to be done and the magnitude of the operation. All the evidence in this case discloses is that plaintiff wanted the equipment because he had a contract. It might have been a contract of a very minor nature so far as the evidence is concerned; it might have been a contract involving $100 or one involving $100,000; or a contract that would take a week or a month, or two years. In other words, it is doubtful whether the evidence discloses that sufficient information was given defendant to indicate the responsibilities to be assumed by this second-hand equipment.

This Court recently dealt with a somewhat similar problem in *Munroe Equipment Sales Ltd. v. Canadian Forest Products Ltd.* (1961), 29 D.L.R. (2d) 730. (This was not cited to the learned trial Judge nor incorporated in either factum, but was referred to us in defendant's oral submission.) In that case the various decisions dealing with the principle involved in such claims, particularly *Hadley v. Baxendale* (1854), 9 Exch. 341, 156 E.R. 145, were examined. *Hadley v. Baxendale* first established the rule or rules governing liability for damages in circumstances such as existed in the instant case.

The following quotations from the *Munroe Equipment* case seem pertinent to the appeal now before us, page 731 (headnote):

> *Held*, on appeal by a majority, defendant hirer failed to establish the damages which would ordinarily flow from the failure of the tractor to come up to expectations, and the large damages awarded were not reasonably foreseeable as flowing from the failure of the tractor. No reasonable person could contemplate in the circumstances that the owner of the second-hand tractor was virtually insuring the removal of the timber from the bush.
>
> Nor was it established that the special circumstances in connection with the use of the tractor were communicated and made known to the owner, either as to the amount of wood cut, or the amount to be removed. Since the tractor broke down almost immediately, defendant hirer was under a duty to mitigate damages and it was its duty in the circumstances to seek another tractor from plaintiff or elsewhere rather than pin its faith on a broken down article for a short winter season when so much was at stake.

Page 739:

> It seems to me that in the case at bar the defendant cannot succeed on its counterclaim unless it establishes that the special circumstances in connection with the use of the tractor were communicated and made known to the plaintiff company. There was nothing discussed in the negotiations for the tractor which would indicate whether the defendant company intended to remove 100 cords or 100,000 cords of wood; nor, so far as the knowledge of, or the knowledge imparted to, the plaintiff company was concerned, how much wood was cut and ready to be moved. Nor was it in any way indicated to the plaintiff that all the wood which the defendant company had cut by itself or its subcontractors had to be moved that year.

Pages 741-2:

> I cannot see how any person or company dealing in second-hand machinery would contemplate for a moment that if the rebuilt machine broke down the vendor or lessor thereof would be liable for the type of damages claimed and allowed in this action.
>
> Had the plaintiff contemplated possible liability for such damage as claimed by the counterclaim, it is scarcely conceivable that it would have risked letting a second-hand tractor bear such responsibility; nor would any reasonable person do so. Such damages do not ordinarily flow from the fact that a second-hand tractor does not "stand-up," and therefore in order to fix the plaintiff with responsibility for such damages the defendant, at the time of making the contract, should have made clear its version of the extraordinary responsibility the defendant might seek to impose upon the plaintiff. At least it should have warned the plaintiff of its (defendant's) intention to remove all wood that season, the quantity involved, the sale contracts for wood that defendant had made, and such like. If this had been done it is probable the defendant would not have secured the tractor or the plaintiff would have insisted upon contracting itself out of any liability.

The rule referred to in the *Baxendale* case is discussed in *Hammond & Co. v. Bussey* (1887), 20 Q.B.D. 79, and a quotation from the latter appears in the *Munroe Equipment Sales* case, supra. *Burrard Dry Dock Co. v. Canadian Union Line Ltd.*, [1954] 3 D.L.R. 561, [1954] S.C.R. 307; *Victoria Laundry (Windsor) Ltd. v. Newman Industries, Ltd.*, [1949] 1 All E.R. 997, [1949] 2 K.B. 528; *Anson on Contract*, 21st ed., pp. 460-3 and *Overseas Tankship (U.K.), Ltd. v. Morts Dock & Engineering Co.*, [1961] 1 All E.R. 404, were all reviewed in *Munroe Equipment Sales*, supra, and clearly established the tests to be applied on such a claim for damages as the one with which we now have to deal.

Counsel for plaintiff argued before us that these damages for loss of profit naturally flow from breach of contract by defendant and therefore come under the first rule in the *Baxendale* case; that these would be in the same category as damages for the repair costs of the defective parts. I am unable to accept this argument. I do not think that damages for loss of profit naturally flow from the defective character of the equipment or that they could have been reasonably foreseen or anticipated by defendant, because, as I have said above, defendant was not given sufficient information regarding the actual contract in which plaintiff was interested to permit it to determine the scope of its liability if the machine did not work satisfactorily. Defendant was not given an opportunity, by full disclosure or communication, to be put in the position where it could reasonably have anticipated damages for loss of profit by plaintiff on this particular contract and had no opportunity to contract itself out of liability if unwilling to be subjected to damages of unascertained magnitude. That being so, I would not allow the judgment against defendant for loss of profits of $1,650 to stand. The damages, $351.14, allowed to plaintiff for the balance of the repair costs is proper because they flow naturally from the breach of contract disclosed in the evidence.

I would therefore allow the appeal and vary the judgment by reducing the amount awarded from $2,001.14 to $351.14. Defendant should have its costs of appeal in this Court.

FREEDMAN JA (Schultz and Monnin JJA concurring): This is an appeal by the defendant from a judgment of Maybank J., holding the defendant liable to the plaintiff for damages for breach of contract arising from the sale of a hydraulic dozer attachment for the plaintiff's D8 caterpillar tractor.

There was contradiction in the testimony concerning the facts. The learned trial Judge resolved this in favour of the plaintiff, saying "I accept the evidence of him and his witnesses wherever it is in conflict with other evidence." The brief recital of facts which follows takes due account of that finding.

Prior to the matters in question in this case the plaintiff had entered into a contract, requiring the use of his tractor, with a company known as Supercrete Ltd. It was to make the tractor fit and suitable for the Supercrete job that the plaintiff needed the hydraulic dozer attachment. It is common ground that he purchased this attachment from the defendant. The plaintiff's evidence establishes that he made known to the defendant the fact that the attachment was for a tractor which was to be used by him on a job with Supercrete Ltd. He also made it plain that he needed this equipment in a hurry and that it had to be in good working order.

The attachment was duly sold and delivered by the defendant to the plaintiff. But the learned trial Judge found, on substantial evidence, that the equipment did not measure up to the terms of the contract. The plaintiff first discovered that certain parts were missing. Then, after these were replaced, it was found that the hydraulic attachment would not function. Tests showed that the hydraulic pump did not generate sufficient pressure to operate the unit. The plaintiff later received in turn, three replacing pumps, not one of which proved adequate. Finally the plaintiff had to rebuild one of the pumps in order to make the attachment operable.

In consequence of the attachment equipment being defective the caterpillar could not function. For Supercrete Ltd., it was imperative to have a tractor effectively working at its gravel pit. Since the plaintiff's tractor, in the condition it then was, could not do the job, Supercrete cancelled the contract with the plaintiff and hired another tractor from a third party to do the work. The plaintiff's loss of profit, which he would have earned on the Supercrete contract, represents the main item of the damages which he now claims from the defendant.

Both plaintiff and defendant referred to *Hadley v. Baxendale*, 9 Exch. 341, 156 E.R. 145, and to several of the cases which later considered that earlier decision, including *Victoria Laundry (Windsor), Ltd. v. Newman Industries Ltd.*, [1949] 1 All E.R. 997, [1949] 2 K.B. 528. I do not think it necessary in the present case to make any lengthy examination of the jurisprudence on this subject. The guiding principles are clear. It is usual to think of *Hadley v. Baxendale* as enunciating two rules, or, at all events, one rule with two branches. Under the first rule (or branch) damages for breach of contract should be such as arise naturally—that is, according to the usual course of things—from the breach of contract itself, or such as may reasonably be supposed to have been in the contemplation of the parties, at the time they made the contract, as the probable result of its breach. Under the second rule, if there are special circumstances relating to the contract—and these are actually communicated by the plaintiff to the defendant—damages reasonably contemplated would be the amount of injury which would ordinarily follow from a breach of contract under these special circumstances so known and communicated.

The *Victoria Laundry v. Newman* case, in considering the *Hadley v. Baxendale* rules, made it clear that damages for breach of contract should be measured by what was reasonably foreseeable as liable to result from the breach. That in turn would depend on the knowledge possessed by the parties or, at all events, by the party who later commits the breach. Knowledge could be either imputed or actual. Imputed knowledge is sufficient to bring into play the first rule; actual knowledge is required for the second.

Reasonable foreseeability is the test under both rules. Indeed it is not always easy to make a rigid division between the two rules, and one writer comments that "the modern restatement of the rule as a totality is a salutary trend": *vide Mayne & McGregor on Damages*, 12th ed., p. 127.

It seems to me that whether we say there is one rule or two, or one rule with two branches, the test of reasonable foreseeability in either case operates here in favour of the plaintiff. For if imputed knowledge under the first rule is sufficient, it is not unrealistic to ascribe to the defendant an awareness that his breach of contract in selling this defective equipment to the plaintiff would in the ordinary course of events result in damages in the form of loss of profits as here sustained. If, on the other hand, actual knowledge of special circumstances attaching to the contract is required, the evidence on the record shows that the defendant had such knowledge.

I would accordingly agree with the learned trial Judge that the defendant is liable as claimed. The amount of the damages had been agreed to, subject to liability being established.

I would therefore dismiss the appeal and affirm the judgment of the Court below, with costs.

Appeal dismissed.

KOUFOS V C CZARNIKOW, LTD (THE HERON II)
[1969] 1 AC 350 (HL)

LORD REID: My Lords, by charterparty of October 15, 1960, the respondents chartered the appellant's vessel, *Heron II*, to proceed to Constanza, there to load a cargo of 3,000 tons of sugar; and to carry it to Basrah, or, in the charterer's option, to Jeddah. The vessel left Constanza on November 1, 1960. The umpire has found that "a reasonably accurate prediction of the length of the voyage was twenty days." But the vessel had in breach of contract made deviations which caused a delay of nine days.

It was the intention of the respondents to sell the sugar "promptly after arrival at Basrah and after inspection by merchants." The appellant did not know this, but he was aware of the fact that there was a market for sugar at Basrah. The sugar was in fact sold at Basrah in lots between December 12 and 22, 1960, but shortly before that time the market price had fallen, partly by reason of the arrival of another cargo of sugar. It was found by the umpire that if there had not been this delay of nine days the sugar would have fetched £32 10s. 0d. per ton. The actual price realised was only £31 2s. 9d. per ton. The respondents claim that they are entitled to recover the difference as damage for breach of contract. The appellant admits that he is liable to pay interest for nine days on the value of the sugar and certain minor expenses but denies that fall in market value can be taken into account in assessing damages in this case.

McNair J., following the decision in *The Parana* (1877), 2 P.D. 118, decided this question in favour of the appellant. He said: "In those circumstances, it seems to me almost impossible to say that the shipowner must have known that the delay in prosecuting the voyage would probably result, or be likely to result, in this kind of loss."

The Court of Appeal by a majority (Diplock and Salmon L.JJ., Sellers L.J. dissenting) reversed the decision of the trial judge. The majority held that *The Parana* laid down no general rule, and, applying the rule (or rules) in *Hadley v. Baxendale* as explained in *Victoria Laundry (Windsor) Ltd. v. Newman Industries Ltd.* they held that the loss due to fall in market price was not too remote to be recoverable as damages.

It may be well first to set out the knowledge and intention of the parties at the time of making the contract so far as relevant or argued to be relevant. The charterers intended to sell the sugar in the market at Basrah on arrival of the vessel. They could have changed their mind and exercised their option to have the sugar delivered at Jeddah but they did not do so. There is no finding that they had in mind any particular date as the likely date of arrival at Basrah or that they had any knowledge or expectation that in late November or December there would be a rising or a falling market. The shipowner was given no information about these matters by the charterers. He did not know what the charterers intended to do with the sugar. But he knew there was a market in sugar at Basrah, and it appears to me that, if he had thought about the matter, he must have realised that at least it was not unlikely that the sugar would be sold in the market at market price on arrival. And he must be held to have known that in any ordinary market prices are apt to fluctuate from day to day; but he had no reason to suppose it more probable that during the relevant period such fluctuation would be downwards rather than upwards—it was an even chance that the fluctuation would be downwards.

So the question for decision is whether a plaintiff can recover as damages for breach of contract a loss of a kind which the defendant, when he made the contract, ought to have realised was not unlikely to result from a breach of contract causing delay in delivery. I use the words "not unlikely" as denoting a degree of probability considerably less than an even chance but nevertheless not very unusual and easily foreseeable. ...

In cases like *Hadley v. Baxendale* or the present case it is not enough that in fact the plaintiff's loss was directly caused by the defendant's breach of contract. It clearly was so caused in both. The crucial question is whether, on the information available to the defendant when the contract was made, he should, or the reasonable man in his position would, have realised that such loss was sufficiently likely to result from the breach of contract to make it proper to hold that the loss flowed naturally from the breach or that loss of that kind should have been within his contemplation.

The modern rule of tort is quite different and it imposes a much wider liability. The defendant will be liable for any type of damage which is reasonably foreseeable as liable to happen even in the most unusual case, unless the risk is so small that a reasonable man would in the whole circumstances feel justified in neglecting it. And there is good reason for the difference. In contract, if one party wishes to protect himself against a risk which to the other party would appear unusual, he can direct the other party's attention to it before the contract is made, and I need not stop to consider in what circumstances the other party will then be held to have accepted responsibility in that event. But in tort there is no opportunity for the injured party to protect himself in that way, and the tortfeasor cannot reasonably complain if he has to pay for some very unusual but nevertheless foreseeable damage which results from his wrongdoing. I have no doubt that today a tortfeasor would be held liable for a type of damage as unlikely as was the stoppage of Hadley's mill for lack of a crankshaft: to anyone with the knowledge the carrier had that may have seemed unlikely but the chance of it happening would have been seen to be far from negligible. But it does not at all follow that *Hadley v. Baxendale* would today be differently decided. ...

[Lord Reid and the other law lords held that the shipowner was liable for the loss claimed.]

Appeal dismissed.

NOTE

The effect of *The Heron II* was summed up in *Aruna Mills Ltd v Dhanrajmal Gobindram*, [1968] 1 QB 655 at 668:

DONALDSON J: In the course of the speeches in the *Czarnikow* case their Lordships expressed varying degrees of enthusiasm for the *Victoria Laundry* case; but, subject to two possible qualifications, it seems to me to remain unimpaired as the classic authority on the topic. These two qualifications are as follows. First, reference in the judgment in the *Victoria Laundry* case to a loss being "reasonably foreseeable" should perhaps be taken as referring to the loss having been within "actual or assumed contemplation" (see the speech of Lord Reid). Second, the phrase "liable to result" is not correctly paraphrased by the use of the expression "on the cards," but conveys the relevant shade of likelihood by its own wording (Lord Hodson) or when defined (as it was in proposition (6) in the *Victoria Laundry* case) as indicating that a loss is a "serious possibility" or "real danger" (see Lord Pearce and Lord Upjohn), words that, among others, had the approval of Lord Morris of Borth-y-Gest.

TRANSFIELD SHIPPING INC V MERCATOR SHIPPING INC (THE ACHILLEAS)
[2009] 1 AC 61 (HL)

LORD HOFFMANN:

[1] The *Achilleas* is a single-decker bulk carrier of some 69,000 dwt built in 1994. By a time charter dated 22 January 2003 the owners let her to the charterers for about five to seven months at a daily hire rate of US$13,500. By an addendum dated

12 September 2003 the parties fixed the vessel for a further five to seven months at a daily rate of US$16,750. The latest date for redelivery was 2 May 2004.

[2] By April 2004, market rates had more than doubled compared with the previous September. On 20 April 2004 the charterers gave notice of redelivery between 30 April and 2 May 2004. On the following day, the owners fixed the vessel for a new four to six month hire to another charterer, following on from the current charter, at a daily rate of US$39,500. The latest date for delivery to the new charterers, after which they were entitled to cancel, was 8 May 2004.

[3] With less than a fortnight of the charter to run, the charterers fixed the vessel under a subcharter to carry coals from Quingdao in China across the Yellow Sea to discharge at two Japanese ports, Tobata and Oita. If this voyage could not reasonably have been expected to allow redelivery by 2 May 2004, the owners could probably have refused to perform it: see *Torvald Klaveness A/S v. Arni Maritime Corpn (The Gregos)* [1995] 1 Lloyd's Rep 1. But they made no objection. The vessel completed loading at Quingdao on 24 April. It discharged at Tobata, went on to Oita, but was unfortunately delayed there and not redelivered to the owners until 11 May.

[4] By 5 May it had become clear to everyone that the vessel would not be available to the new charterers before the cancelling date of 8 May. By that time, rates had fallen again. In return for an extension of the cancellation date to 11 May, the owners agreed to reduce the rate of hire for the new fixture to $31,500 a day.

[5] The owners claimed damages for the loss of the difference between the original rate and the reduced rate over the period of the fixture. At US$8,000 a day, that came to US$1,364,584.37. The charterers said that the owners were not entitled to damages calculated by reference to their dealings with the new charterers and that they were entitled only to the difference between the market rate and the charter rate for the nine days during which they were deprived of the use of the ship. That came to $158,301.17.

[6] The arbitrators, by a majority, found for the owners. They said that the loss on the new fixture fell within the first rule in *Hadley v. Baxendale* (1854) 9 Exch. 341, 354 as arising "naturally, ie according to the usual course of things, from such breach of contract itself." It fell within that rule because it was damage "of a kind which the [charterer], when he made the contract, ought to have realised was not unlikely to result from a breach of contract [by delay in redelivery]": see Lord Reid in *C. Czarnikow Ltd. v. Koufos (The Heron II)* [1969] 1 A.C. 350, 382-383. The dissenting arbitrator did not deny that a charterer would have known that the owners would very likely enter into a following fixture during the course of the charter and that late delivery might cause them to lose it. But he said that a reasonable man in the position of the charterers would not have understood that he was assuming liability for the risk of the type of loss in question. The general understanding in the shipping market was that liability was restricted to the difference between the market rate and the charter rate for the overrun period and "any departure from this rule [is] likely to give rise to a real risk of serious commercial uncertainty which the industry as a whole would regard as undesirable."

[7] The majority arbitrators, in their turn, did not deny that the general understanding in the industry was that liability was so limited. They said (at para. 17):

> The charterers submitted that if they had asked their lawyers or their Club what damages they would be liable for if the vessel was redelivered late, the answer would have been that they would be liable for the difference between the market rate and the charter rate for the period of the late delivery. We agree that lawyers would have given such an answer.

[8] But the majority said that this was irrelevant. A broker "in a commercial situation" would have said that the "not unlikely" results arising from late delivery would include missing dates for a subsequent fixture, a dry docking or the sale of the vessel. Therefore, as a matter of law, damages for loss of these types was recoverable. The understanding of shipping lawyers was wrong.

[9] On appeal from the arbitrators, Christopher Clarke J. [2007] 1 Lloyd's Rep. 19 and the Court of Appeal (Ward, Tuckey and Rix L.JJ.) [2007] 2 Lloyd's Rep. 555 upheld the majority decision. The case therefore raises a fundamental point of principle in the law of contractual damages: is the rule that a party may recover losses which were foreseeable ("not unlikely") an external rule of law, imposed upon the parties to every contract in default of express provision to the contrary, or is it a prima facie assumption about what the parties may be taken to have intended, no doubt applicable in the great majority of cases but capable of rebuttal in cases in which the context, surrounding circumstances or general understanding in the relevant market shows that a party would not reasonably have been regarded as assuming responsibility for such losses?

[10] Before I come to this point of principle, I should say something about the authorities upon which the understanding of shipping lawyers was based. There is no case in which the question now in issue has been raised. But that in itself may be significant. This cannot have been the first time that freight rates have been volatile. There must have been previous cases in which late redelivery caused the loss of a profitable following fixture. But there is no reported case in which such a claim has been made. Instead, there has been a uniform series of dicta over many years in which judges have said or assumed that the damages for late delivery are the difference between the charter rate and the market rate. ... Nowhere is there a suggestion of even a theoretical possibility of damages for the loss of a following fixture.

[11] The question of principle has been extensively discussed in the literature. Recent articles by Adam Kramer ("An Agreement-Centred Approach to Remoteness and Contract Damages") in Cohen and McKendrick (ed), *Comparative Remedies for Breach of Contract* (2004) pp. 249-286, Andrew Tettenborn ("Hadley v. Baxendale Foreseeability: A Principle Beyond its Sell-by Date") in (2007) 23 *Journal of Contract Law* 120-147, and Andrew Robertson ("The basis of the remoteness rule in contract") (2008) 28 *Legal Studies* 172-196 are particularly illuminating. They show that there is a good deal of support in the authorities and academic writings for the proposition that the extent of a party's liability for damages is founded upon the interpretation of the particular contract; not upon the interpretation of any particular language in the contract, but (as in the case of an implied term) upon the interpretation of the contract as a whole, construed in its commercial setting. Professor Robertson considers this approach somewhat artificial, since there is seldom any helpful evidence about the extent of the risks the particular parties would have thought they were accepting. I agree that cases of departure from the ordinary foreseeability rule based on individual circumstances will be unusual, but limitations on the extent of liability in particular types of contract arising out of general expectations in certain markets, such as banking and shipping, are likely to be more common. There is, I think, an analogy with the distinction which Lord Cross of Chelsea drew in *Liverpool City Council v. Irwin* [1977] A.C. 239, 257-258 between terms implied into all contracts of a certain type and the implication of a term into a particular contract.

[12] It seems to me logical to found liability for damages upon the intention of the parties (objectively ascertained) because all contractual liability is voluntarily undertaken. It must be in principle wrong to hold someone liable for risks for which

the people entering into such a contract in their particular market, would not reasonably be considered to have undertaken.

[13] The view which the parties take of the responsibilities and risks they are undertaking will determine the other terms of the contract and in particular the price [that] is paid. Anyone asked to assume a large and unpredictable risk will require some premium in exchange. A rule of law which imposes liability upon a party for a risk which he reasonably thought was excluded gives the other party something for nothing. And as Willes J. said in *British Columbia Saw Mill Co. Ltd. v Nettleship* (1868) L.R. 3 C.P. 499, 508:

> I am disposed to take the narrow view, that one of two contracting parties ought not to be allowed to obtain an advantage which he has not paid for.

[14] In their submissions to the House, the owners said that the "starting point" was that damages were designed to put the innocent party, so far as it is possible, in the position as if the contract had been performed: see *Robinson v. Harman* (1848) 1 Exch 850, 855. However, in *Banque Bruxelles Lambert S.A. v. Eagle Star Insurance Co. Ltd.* (*sub. nom South Australia Asset Management Corpn v. York Montague Ltd.*) [1997] A.C. 191, 211, I said (with the concurrence of the other members of the House):

> I think that this was the wrong place to begin. Before one can consider the principle on which one should calculate the damages to which a plaintiff is entitled as compensation for loss, it is necessary to decide for what kind of loss he is entitled to compensation. A correct description of the loss for which the valuer is liable must precede any consideration of the measure of damages.

[15] In other words, one must first decide whether the loss for which compensation is sought is of a "kind" or "type" for which the contract-breaker ought fairly to be taken to have accepted responsibility. In the *South Australia* case the question was whether a valuer, who had (in breach of an implied term to exercise reasonable care and skill) negligently advised his client bank that property which it proposed to take as security for a loan was worth a good deal more than its actual market value, should be liable not only for losses attributable to the deficient security but also for further losses attributable to a fall in the property market. The House decided that he should not be liable for this kind of loss:

> In the case of an implied contractual duty, the nature and extent of the liability is defined by the term which the law implies. As in the case of any implied term, the process is one of construction of the agreement as a whole in its commercial setting. The contractual duty to provide a valuation and the known purpose of that valuation compel the conclusion that the contract includes a duty of care. The scope of the duty, in the sense of the consequences for which the valuer is responsible, is that which the law regards as best giving effect to the express obligations assumed by the valuer: neither cutting them down so that the lender obtains less than he was reasonably entitled to expect, nor extending them so as to impose on the valuer a liability greater than he could reasonably have thought he was undertaking. (p. 212)

[16] What is true of an implied contractual duty (to take reasonable care in the valuation) is equally true of an express contractual duty (to redeliver the ship on the appointed day). In both cases, the consequences for which the contracting party will be liable are those which "the law regards as best giving effect to the express obligations assumed" and "[not] extending them so as to impose on the [contracting party] a liability greater than he could reasonably have thought he was undertaking."

[17] The effect of the *South Australia* case was to exclude from liability the damages attributable to a fall in the property market notwithstanding that those losses were foreseeable in the sense of being "not unlikely" (property values go down as well as up) and had been caused by the negligent valuation in the sense that, but for the valuation, the bank would not have lent at all and there was no evidence to show that it would have lost its money in some other way. It was excluded on the ground that it was outside the scope of the liability which the parties would reasonably have considered that the valuer was undertaking.

[18] That seems to me in accordance with the careful way in which Robert Goff J. stated the principle in *Satef-Huttenes Albertus Sp.A. v. Paloma Tercera Shipping Co. S.A. (The Pegase)* [1981] Lloyd's Rep. 175, 183, where the emphasis is upon what a reasonable person would have considered to be the extent of his responsibility:

> The test appears to be: have the facts in question come to the defendant's knowledge in such circumstances that a reasonable person in the shoes of the defendant would, if he had considered the matter at the time of making the contract, have contemplated that, in the event of a breach by him, such facts were to be taken into account when considering his responsibility for loss suffered by the plaintiff as a result of such breach.

[19] A similar approach was taken by the Court of Appeal in *Mulvenna v. Royal Bank of Scotland plc.* [2003] E.W.C.A. Civ 1112, mentioned by Professor Robertson in the article to which I have referred. This was an application to strike out a claim for damages for the loss of profits which the claimant said he would have made if the bank had complied with its agreement to provide him with funds for a property development. The Court of Appeal held that even on the assumption that the bank knew of the purpose for which the funds were required and that it was foreseeable that he would suffer loss of profit if he did not receive them, the damages were not recoverable. Sir Anthony Evans said:

> The authorities to which we were referred ... demonstrate that the concept of reasonable foreseeability is not a complete guide to the circumstances in which damages are recoverable as a matter of law. Even if the loss was reasonably foreseeable as a consequence of the breach of duty in question (or of contract, for the same principles apply), it may nevertheless be regarded as "too remote a consequence" or as not a consequence at all, and the damages claim is disallowed. In effect, the chain of consequences is cut off as a matter of law, either because it is regarded as unreasonable to impose liability for that consequence of the breach (*The Pegase* [1981] 1 Lloyd's Rep. 175 Robert Goff J.), or because the scope of the duty is limited so as to exclude it (*Banque Bruxelles S.A. v. Eagle Star* [1997] A.C. 191), or because as a matter of commonsense the breach cannot be said to have caused the loss, although it may have provided the opportunity for it to occur. ...

[20] By way of explanation for why in such a case liability for lost profits is excluded, Professor Robertson (at p. 183) offers what seem to me to be some plausible reasons:

> It may be considered unjust that the bank should be held liable for the loss of profits simply because the bank knew of the proposed development at the time the refinancing agreement was made. The imposition of such a burden on the bank may be considered unjust because it is inconsistent with commercial practice for a bank to accept such a risk in a transaction of this type, or because the quantum of the liability is disproportionate to the scale of the transaction or the benefit the bank stood to receive.

[21] It is generally accepted that a contracting party will be liable for damages for losses which are unforeseeably large, if loss of that type or kind fell within one or other of the rules in *Hadley v. Baxendale*: see, for example, Staughton J. in *Transworld Oil Ltd. v. North Bay Shipping Corpn (The Rio Claro)* [1987] Lloyd's Rep 173, 175 and *Jackson v. Royal Bank of Scotland plc.* [2005] 1 W.L.R. 377. That is generally an inclusive principle: if losses of that type are foreseeable, damages will include compensation for those losses, however large. But the *South Australia* and *Mulvenna* cases shows that it may also be an exclusive principle and that a party may not be liable for foreseeable losses because they are not of the type or kind for which he can be treated as having assumed responsibility.

[22] What is the basis for deciding whether loss is of the same type or a different type? It is not a question of Platonist metaphysics. The distinction must rest upon some principle of the law of contract. In my opinion, the only rational basis for the distinction is that it reflects what would have reasonably have been regarded by the contracting party as significant for the purposes of the risk he was undertaking. In *Victoria Laundry (Windsor) Ltd. v. Newman Industries Ltd.* [1949] 2 K.B. 528, where the plaintiffs claimed for loss of the profits from their laundry business because of late delivery of a boiler, the Court of Appeal did not regard "loss of profits from the laundry business" as a single type of loss. They distinguished (at p. 543) losses from "particularly lucrative dyeing contracts" as a different type of loss which would only be recoverable if the defendant had sufficient knowledge of them to make it reasonable to attribute to him acceptance of liability for such losses. The vendor of the boilers would have regarded the profits on these contracts as a different and higher form of risk than the general risk of loss of profits by the laundry.

[23] If, therefore, one considers what these parties, contracting against the background of market expectations found by the arbitrators, would reasonably have considered the extent of the liability they were undertaking, I think it is clear that they would have considered losses arising from the loss of the following fixture a type or kind of loss for which the charterer was not assuming responsibility. Such a risk would be completely unquantifiable, because although the parties would regard it as likely that the owners would at some time during the currency of the charter enter into a forward fixture, they would have no idea when that would be done or what its length or other terms would be. If it was clear to the owners that the last voyage was bound to overrun and put the following fixture at risk, it was open to them to refuse to undertake it. What this shows is that the purpose of the provision for timely redelivery in the charterparty is to enable the ship to be at the full disposal of the owner from the redelivery date. If the charterer's orders will defeat this right, the owner may reject them. If the orders are accepted and the last voyage overruns, the owner is entitled to be paid for the overrun at the market rate. All this will be known to both parties. It does not require any knowledge of the owner's arrangements for the next charter. That is regarded by the market as being, as the saying goes, *res inter alios acta*.

[24] The findings of the majority arbitrators shows that they considered their decision to be contrary to what would have been the expectations of the parties, but dictated by the rules in *Hadley v. Baxendale* as explained in *The Heron II* [1969] 1 A.C. 350. But in my opinion these rules are not so inflexible; they are intended to give effect to the presumed intentions of the parties and not to contradict them.

[25] The owners submit that the question of whether the damage is too remote is a question of fact on which the arbitrators have found in their favour. It is true that the question of whether the damage was foreseeable is a question of fact: see *Monarch Steamship Co Ltd. v. Karlshamns Oljefabriker (A/B)* [1949] A.C. 196. But the question of

whether a given type of loss is one for which a party assumed contractual responsibility involves the interpretation of the contract as a whole against its commercial background, and this, like all questions of interpretation, is a question of law.

[26] The owners say that the parties are entirely at liberty to insert an express term excluding consequential loss if they want to do so. Some standard forms of charter do. I suppose it can be said of many disputes over interpretation, especially over implied terms, that the parties could have used express words or at any rate expressed themselves more clearly than they have done. But, as I have indicated, the implication of a term as a matter of construction of the contract as a whole in its commercial context and the implication of the limits of damages liability seem to me to involve the application of essentially the same techniques of interpretation. In both cases, the court is engaged in construing the agreement to reflect the liabilities which the parties may reasonably be expected to have assumed and paid for. It cannot decline this task on the ground that the parties could have spared it the trouble by using clearer language. In my opinion, the findings of the arbitrators and the commercial background to the agreement are sufficient to make it clear that the charterer cannot reasonably be regarded as having assumed the risk of the owner's loss of profit on the following charter. I would therefore allow the appeal.

• • •

LORD RODGER OF EARLSFERRY:

[60] Returning to the present case, I am satisfied that, when they entered into the addendum in September 2003, neither party would reasonably have contemplated that an overrun of nine days would "in the ordinary course of things" cause the owners the kind of loss for which they claim damages. That loss was not the "ordinary consequence" of a breach of that kind. It occurred in this case only because of the extremely volatile market conditions which produced both the owners' initial (particularly lucrative) transaction, with a third party, and the subsequent pressure on the owners to accept a lower rate for that fixture. Back in September 2003, this loss could not have been reasonably foreseen as being likely to arise out of the delay in question. It was, accordingly, too remote to give rise to a claim for damages for breach of contract.

• • •

BARONESS HALE OF RICHMOND:

[89] My Lords, this could be an examination question. Although the context is a specialised one, the answer has mainly to be found in the general principles to be derived from the well-known authorities to which your Lordships have all referred, principally *Hadley v. Baxendale* (1854) 9 Exch. 341, *Victoria Laundry (Windsor) Ltd. v. Newman Industries Ltd.* [1949] 2 K.B. 528 and, above all, *C. Czarnikow Ltd v. Koufos (The Heron II)* [1969] 1 A.C. 350. There is no obviously right answer: two very experienced commercial judges have reached one answer, your lordships have reached another. There is no obviously just answer: the charterer's default undoubtedly caused the owner's loss, but a loss for which no-one has ever had to pay before. The examiners would surely have given first class marks to all the judges who have answered the question so far.

• • •

[92] Another answer to the question, given as I understand it by my noble and learned friends, Lord Hoffmann and Lord Hope, is that one must ask, not only whether the parties must be taken to have had this *type of loss* within their contemplation when the contract was made, but also whether they must be taken to have had *liability for this type of loss* within their contemplation then. In other words, is

the charterer to be taken to have undertaken legal responsibility for this type of loss? What should the unspoken terms of their contract be taken to be? If that is the question, then it becomes relevant to ask what has been the normal expectation of parties to such contracts in this particular market. If charterers would not normally expect to pay more than the market rate for the days they were late, and ship-owners would not normally expect to get more than that, then one would expect something extra before liability for an unusual loss such as this would arise. That is essentially the reasoning adopted by the minority arbitrator.

[93] My Lords, I hope that I have understood this correctly, for it seems to me that it adds an interesting but novel dimension to the way in which the question of remoteness of damage in contract is to be answered, a dimension which does not clearly emerge from the classic authorities. There is scarcely a hint of it in *The Heron II*, apart perhaps from Lord Reid's reference, at p. 385, to the loss being "sufficiently likely to result from the breach of contract *to make it proper* to hold that the loss flowed naturally from the breach or that loss of that kind should have been within his contemplation" (emphasis supplied). In general, *The Heron II* points the other way, as it emphasises that there are no special rules applying to charterparties and that the law of remoteness in contract is not the same as the law of remoteness in tort. There is more than a hint of it in the judgment of Waller L.J. in *Mulvenna v. Royal Bank of Scotland plc.* [2003] E.W.C.A. Civ. 1112, but in the context of the "second limb" of *Hadley v. Baxendale* where knowledge of an unusual risk is posited. To incorporate it generally would be to introduce into ordinary contractual liability the principle adopted in the context of liability for professional negligence in *South Australia Asset Management Corpn v. York Montague Ltd.* [1997] A.C. 191, 211. In an examination, this might well make the difference between a congratulatory and an ordinary first class answer to the question. But despite the excellence of counsels' arguments it was not explored before us, although it is explored in academic textbooks and other writings, including those cited by Lord Hoffmann in paragraph 11 of his opinion. I note, however, that the most recent of these, Professor Robertson's article on "The basis of the remoteness rule in contract" (2008) 28 *Legal Studies* 172 argues strongly to the contrary. I am not immediately attracted to the idea of introducing into the law of contract the concept of the scope of duty which has perforce had to be developed in the law of negligence. The rule in *Hadley v. Baxendale* asks what the parties must be taken to have had in their contemplation, rather than what they actually had in their contemplation, but the criterion by which this is judged is a factual one. Questions of assumption of risk depend upon a wider range of factors and value judgments. This type of reasoning is, as Lord Steyn put it in *Aneco Reinsurance Underwriting Ltd v. Johnson & Higgins Ltd.* [2002] 1 Lloyd's Rep. 157, para 186, a "deus ex machina." Although its result in this case may be to bring about certainty and clarity in this particular market, such an imposed limit on liability could easily be at the expense of justice in some future case. It could also introduce much room for argument in other contractual contexts. Therefore, if this appeal is to be allowed, as to which I continue to have doubts, I would prefer it to be allowed on the narrower ground identified by Lord Rodger, leaving the wider ground to be fully explored in another case and another context.

Appeal allowed.

[Lord Hope agreed in substance with Lord Hoffmann. Lord Walker agreed with all three of Lords Hoffmann, Hope, and Rodger.]

CORNWALL GRAVEL CO LTD V PUROLATOR COURIER LTD
(1978), 83 DLR (3d) 266 (Ont HC), aff'd (1979), 115 DLR (3d) 511 (CA) and [1980] 2 SCR 118, 120 DLR (3d) 575

R.E. HOLLAND J: This is an action for damages for breach of contract and negligence brought by Cornwall Gravel Company Limited (Cornwall Gravel) against Purolator Courier Ltd. (Purolator) and Bernard Levert and Rheal Boisvenue who, at the material time, were employees of Purolator, arising out of the late delivery of a tender prepared by the plaintiff for submission to the Ontario Ministry of the Environment.

It is admitted that had the tender been delivered in time Cornwall Gravel would have been awarded a contract for $698,246.79 and would have made a profit on the contract of $70,000.

The information for tenderers which governed the submission of the tender provided that tenders were to be delivered on or before 3 p.m. Toronto time on October 2, 1973, at the office of the contracts officer of the Ministry in Toronto and further that under no circumstances would any tender be considered which was received after that time. The tender in question was delivered by Purolator at 3:17 p.m. on October 2, 1973, and was therefore rejected.

The tender was ready for delivery at Cornwall shortly after 6 p.m. on October 1, 1973. Cornwall Gravel had used the services of Purolator to deliver tenders on prior occasions. Ronald Paymemp, who was at the time the controller of Cornwall Gravel, telephoned the office of Purolator around noon on October 1st to advise that there was a pick-up for Toronto that evening. ...

When the tender was picked up by Boisvenue, there was a conversation between Paymemp, John Fleming, who was an engineer employed by Cornwall Gravel and who had worked on the tender, and Boisvenue. Paymemp and Fleming wished to make sure that the tender would be delivered on time. If there was any question about late delivery one or the other of them would have driven with the tender to Toronto. They were assured by Boisvenue that there would be no problem with delivery. Paymemp had inserted the time as 12 noon rather than 3 p.m. to make the time consistent with other tenders that had previously been delivered to Toronto for other departments where the time for delivery was 12 noon. There was no conversation with Boisvenue or anyone from Purolator as to the amount of the tender.

Boisvenue was not called as a witness at the trial and I was advised by counsel that he was no longer in the employ of Purolator and his whereabouts were unknown. He was examined for discovery and part of his examination was read in by counsel for the plaintiff. He admitted that he was told that the document was very important, that he had read the bill of lading and had noticed the incorrect date which he changed. He was then asked these questions and made these answers:

Q. I see, at that time you left the office of Cornwall Gravel with this parcel, did you know it was a tender?
A. I think so because I had read it, yes.
Q. Did you at that time know what a tender was?
A. As a rule I do, yes.
Q. What did you understand?
A. Well, I know that it has—it—
Q. Generally, when someone says, "here is a tender."
A. Yes?
Q. Did you believe you understood what a tender was?
A. Yes.
Q. What did you understand it to be?
A. That it is fairly important and it has to be there a certain time to my own personal knowledge. ...

[Holland J then discussed a clause in the contract, and regulations under a statute, and concluded that neither was effective to limit the defendant's liability.]

There remains the question whether or not this loss was in the contemplation of the parties and this takes us back to *Hadley et al. v. Baxendale et al.* (1854), 9 Ex. 341, 156 E.R. 145. At pp. 354-5, Alderson, B., said this:

> Where two parties have made a contract which one of them has broken, the damages which the other party ought to receive in respect of such breach of contract should be such as may fairly and reasonably be considered arising naturally, i.e., according to the usual course of things, from such breach of contract itself, or such as may reasonably be supposed to have been in the contemplation of both parties, at the time they made the contract, as the probable result of the breach of it. Now, if the special circumstances under which the contract was actually made were communicated by the plaintiffs to the defendants, and thus known to both parties, the damages resulting from the breach of such a contract, which they would reasonably contemplate, would be the amount of injury which would ordinarily follow from a breach of contract under those special circumstances, so known and communicated. But, on the other hand, if those special circumstances were wholly unknown to the party breaking the contract, he, at the most, could only be supposed to have had in his contemplation the amount of injury which would arise generally, and in the great multitude of cases not affected by any special circumstances, from such a breach of contract. For, had the special circumstances been known, the parties might have specially provided for the breach of contract by special terms as to the damages in that case; and of this advantage it would be very unjust to deprive them.

In the present case Purolator, through its employee, Boisvenue, knew that the item to be transported was a tender and that it was required to be delivered by 12 noon on October 2, 1973. Boisvenue was told of the importance of the document and must have realized that if delivered late the tender would be worthless and a contract could well be lost. In these particular circumstances it is my opinion that "the special circumstances under which the contract was actually made were communicated by the plaintiff to the defendant" and the damage which in fact flowed from the breach of such contract was damage "which they would reasonably contemplate ... which would ordinarily follow from a breach of contract under those special circumstances, so known and communicated."

It is not necessary, in view of my findings, to deal with the allegation that there is liability for the misrepresentation of Boisvenue that the tender would be delivered by 12 noon the next day.

For the above reasons there will be judgment for the plaintiff for $70,000, with interest in accordance with s. 38 of the *Judicature Act*, R.S.O. 1970, c. 228, as amended, from the date of the coming into force of s. 3 of the *Judicature Amendment Act, 1977 (No. 2)*, 1977, c. 51, to the date of judgment, together with costs against the defendant Purolator. The action as against the individual defendants will be dismissed without costs.

Judgment for plaintiff.

[Appeal to the Court of Appeal and Supreme Court of Canada dismissed without written reasons.]

[See also McCamus at 912-25; MacDougall at 348-53; Waddams at paras 734-42.]

NOTES AND PROBLEMS

1. A bought a ticket on the midnight train to Sudbury. The train did not go on to Sudbury as it was supposed to do, but stopped several miles outside the city, where A was forced to disembark. Because no transport or accommodation was available, A walked the 5 miles to her home through freezing rain. As a result, she caught a severe cold and was off work for several days. A sues for pain and suffering and loss of wages. Will she succeed? See *Hobbs v London & SW Rlwy* (1875), LR 10 QB 111.

2. C visits horse shows in order to display and promote the sale of his products. At the London fair, he met the agent of D, a railway company, who was at the fair for the purpose of delivering and receiving goods. C delivered his samples to the agent for delivery at the Toronto fair, and marked the consignment note "must be at Toronto by Monday certain." The samples were not delivered in time for the fair. C sues for loss of profits. Will he succeed? See *Simpson v London & NW Rlwy* (1876), 1 QBD 274.

3. X contracted to employ Y for five years at a salary of $10,000 a year plus any bonuses X might give, as X saw fit. After two years, X wrongfully dismissed Y. The next year, X discontinued the bonus system, and instead increased employees' salaries by $1,000 a year. Y claims that her damages should include the extra $2,000 she would have received. Advise her. See *Lavarack v Woods of Colchester, Ltd*, [1967] 1 QB 278.

4. In *BDC Ltd v Hofstrand Farms Ltd*, [1986] 1 SCR 228, the plaintiff sued a courier for failing to deliver a document that the plaintiff desired to register by a certain date in a land registry office. There was no contract between the plaintiff and the courier, and the action was in tort for negligence. The plaintiff's loss was held to be too remote. The court distinguished the *Cornwall Gravel* case: "There the courier had been told that the package contained a tender and that delivery had to be made before a certain time. In the ordinary course of events it would be obvious that unless the tender arrived before the deadline, a contract could be lost. Therefore, the defendant had actual knowledge of 'special circumstances,' and this fact justified holding it liable for the plaintiff's lost profit."

IV. INTANGIBLE INJURIES

ADDIS V GRAMOPHONE COMPANY LIMITED
[1909] AC 488 (HL)

[The plaintiff was employed by the defendants as manager of their business in Calcutta at £15 per week as salary and a commission on the trade done. He could be dismissed by six months' notice.

In October 1905, the defendants gave him six months' notice, but at the same time they appointed Mr. Gilpin to act as his successor, and took steps to prevent the plaintiff from acting any longer as manager. In December 1905, the plaintiff came back to England.

The plaintiff brought this action in 1906, claiming an account and damages for breach of contract. That there was a breach of contract is quite clear. If what happened in October 1905 did not amount to a wrongful dismissal, it was, at all events, a breach of the plaintiff's right to act as manager during the six months and to earn the best commission he could make.

When the action came to trial it was agreed to refer the matters of account to arbitration. The causes of action for breach of contract were tried by Darling J and a jury. The jury found for the plaintiff in respect of wrongful dismissal £600, and £340 in respect of excess commission over and above what was earned by the plaintiff's successor between October 1905 and April 1906.

The Court of Appeal by a majority held that on their views of the facts there was (apart from the account which must be taken) no cause of action, and they entered judgment for the defendants.]

LORD ATKINSON: My Lords, I entirely concur with the judgment of my noble and learned friend on the woolsack. Much of the difficulty which has arisen in this case is due to the unscientific form in which the pleadings, as amended, have been framed, and the loose manner in which the proceedings at the trial were conducted.

The rights of the plaintiff, disembarrassed of the confusing methods by which they were sought to be enforced, are, in my opinion, clear. He had been illegally dismissed from his employment. He could have been legally dismissed by the six months' notice, which he, in fact, received, but the defendants did not wait for the expiry of that period. The damages plaintiff sustained by this illegal dismissal were (1) the wages for the period of six months during which his formal notice would have been current; (2) the profits or commission which would, in all reasonable probability, have been earned by him during the six months had he continued in the employment; and possibly (3) damages in respect of the time which might reasonably elapse before he could obtain other employment. He has been awarded a sum possibly of some hundreds of pounds, not in respect of any of these heads of damage, but in respect of the harsh and humiliating way in which he was dismissed, including, presumably, the pain he experienced by reason, it is alleged, of the imputation upon him conveyed by the manner of his dismissal. This is the only circumstance which makes the case of general importance, and this is the only point I think it necessary to deal with.

I have been unable to find any case decided in this country in which any countenance is given to the notion that a dismissed employee can recover in the shape of exemplary damages for illegal dismissal, in effect damages for defamation, for it amounts to that, except the case of *Maw v. Jones* (1890), 25 Q.B.D. 107.

In that case Matthew J., as he then was, during the argument, while counsel was urging ... that the measure of damages for the improper dismissal of an ordinary domestic servant was a month's wages and nothing more, no doubt interjected in the shape of a question the remark, "Have you ever heard the principle applied to a case where a false charge of misconduct has been made?" But the decision was that the direction of the judge at the trial was right.

Now, what was the character of that direction? The defendant had power to dismiss his apprentice, the plaintiff, on a week's notice, and had also power to dismiss him summarily if he should show a want of interest in his work. He dismissed the apprentice summarily without notice, assigning as a reason that he had been guilty of frequent acts of insubordination and that he had gone out at night without leave.

The judge at the trial told the jury that they were not bound to limit the damages to the week's notice he had lost, but that they might take into consideration the time the plaintiff would require to get new employment—the difficulty he would have as a discharged apprentice in getting employment elsewhere—and it was on this precise ground the direction was upheld. I do not think that this case is any authority what ever for the general proposition that exemplary damages may be recovered for wrongful dismissal, still less, of course, for breach of contract generally; but, such as it is, it is the only authority in the shape of a decided case which can be found upon the first-mentioned point.

I have always understood that damages for breach of contract were in the nature of compensation, not punishment. ...

For instance, in actions of tort, motive, if it may be taken into account to aggravate damages, as it undoubtedly may be, may also be taken into account to mitigate them, as may also the conduct of the plaintiff himself who seeks redress. Is this rule to be applied to actions of breach of contract? There are few breaches of contract more common than those which arise where men omit or refuse to repay what they have borrowed, or to pay for what they have bought. Is the creditor or vendor who sues for one of such breaches, to have the sum he recovers lessened if he should be shown to be harsh, grasping, or pitiless, or even insulting, in enforcing his demand, or lessened because the debtor has struggled to pay, has failed because of misfortune, and has been suave, gracious, and apologetic in his refusal? On the other hand, is that sum to be increased if it should be shewn that the debtor could have paid readily without any embarrassment, but refused with expression of contempt and contumely, from a malicious desire to injure his creditor?

Few parties to contracts have more often to complain of ingratitude and baseness than sureties. Are they, because of this, to be entitled to recover from the principal, often a trusted friend, who has deceived and betrayed them, more than they paid on that principal's behalf? If circumstances of aggravation are rightly to be taken into account in actions of contract at all, why should they not be taken into account in the case of the surety, and the rules and principles applicable to cases of tort applied to the full extent?

In many other cases of breach of contract there may be circumstances of malice, fraud, defamation, or violence, which would sustain an action of tort as an alternative remedy to an action for breach of contract. If one should select the former mode of redress, he may, no doubt, recover exemplary damages, or what is sometimes styled vindicative damages; but if he should choose to seek redress in the form of an action for breach of contract, he lets in all the consequences of that form of action. One of these consequences is, I think, this: that he is to be paid adequate compensation in money for the loss of that which he would have received had his contract been kept, and no more.

I can conceive nothing more objectionable and embarrassing in litigation than trying in effect an action of libel or slander as a matter of aggravation in an action for illegal dismissal, the defendant being permitted, as he must in justice be permitted, to traverse the defamatory sense, rely on privilege, or raise every point which he could raise in an independent action brought for the alleged libel or slander itself.

In my opinion, exemplary damages ought not to be, and are not according to any true principle of law, recoverable in such an action as the present, and the sums awarded to the plaintiff should therefore be decreased by the amount at which they have been estimated, and credit for that item should not be allowed in his account.

NOTE

In *Mahmud v Bank of Credit and Commerce Int SA*, [1998] AC 20 (HL), it was held that, in a contractual action, bank employees could claim compensation for damage to their reputation caused by improper activities of the bank. The holdings in *Addis* on intangible loss and exemplary damages have also been substantially modified, as seen in the following material.

KOLAN V SOLICITOR
(1969), 7 DLR (3d) 481 (Ont H Ct J)

[The plaintiff brought an action for damages against her solicitor. The solicitor failed to discover that premises purchased by the plaintiff were subject to a city demolition order. The plaintiff proved that consequent anxiety had caused injury to her health.]

LACOURCIÈRE J (on the question of damages): In the present case the plaintiff relies on *Cook v. S.* [1967] 1 All E.R. 299, a decision of the Court of Appeal dealing with the measure of damages against a solicitor as a result of his negligence. It had been pleaded that the plaintiff suffered an anxiety state and could not work, and that the defendant knew that she was peculiarly liable to nervous shock. The plaintiff was awarded damages but nothing with respect to her claim for mental distress. It was held as summarized in the headnote:

> [T]he plaintiff's breakdown in health owing to anxiety was not a reasonably foreseeable consequence of the defendant's negligence, and, although damages for reasonably foreseeable injury in health due to nervous shock or anxiety could be recovered for breach of duty to use care and skill where, as in the present case, the cause of action lay in contract, yet in this case the ruling of the trial judge that the damage was too remote should stand. ...

The following dictum appears in the judgment of Lord Denning, M.R., at p. 303:

> In these circumstances I think that, just as in the law of tort, so also in the law of contract, damages can be recovered for nervous shock or anxiety state if it is a reasonably foreseeable consequence.
>
> So the question became this: when a client goes to a solicitor, is it a reasonably foreseeable consequence that, if anything goes wrong with the litigation owing to the solicitor's negligence, there will be a breakdown in health? It can be foreseen that there will be injured feelings; mental distress; anger, and annoyance. But for none of these can damages be recovered. It was so held in *Groom v. Crocker* on the same lines as *Addis v. Gramophone Co. Ltd.* ([1908-10] All E.R. Rep. 1, [1909] A.C. 488). Is it reasonably foreseeable that there may be an actual breakdown in health? I do not think so. It was suggested in this case that there were special circumstances in that the plaintiff was peculiarly liable to nervous shock. I am afraid that she was. The history of her life shows one nervous breakdown after another. If this special circumstance was brought home to the defendant, it might enlarge the area of foreseeability so as to make him liable; but it was not pleaded. Moreover when counsel for the plaintiff put questions to the defendant, he did not succeed in showing that special circumstances were brought home to him. All the defendant knew was that she was a woman obviously highly strung and worried as any woman would be in the circumstances. That does not mean, however, that he should foresee that, if he was negligent, she would suffer injury to health. In all these cases of nervous shock and breakdown in mental health, it is very difficult to draw the line. In *King v. Phillips* ([1953] 1 All E.R. 617, at p. 624) I asked: "Where is the line to be drawn?" I found the answer given by Lord Wright: "Only where 'in the particular case the good sense of the ... judge, decides.'" In this present case the judge thought that the damages for the breakdown in health were too remote. I am not prepared to disturb his ruling. On this point the appeal fails.

In the case at bar, it is undisputed that the plaintiff did suffer physical illness, and the question is therefore whether such illness was reasonably foreseeable to the defendant at the time of the contract. Mr. Starr argued that such consequence was foreseeable in that Mrs. Kolan was a widow of modest means who was using her limited cash reserve to complete the purchase of an old potentially substandard house, and that a demolition order of the Housing Standards Board would therefore place her in a critical position where a woman of her age and in her position would suffer illness. I am not prepared to find that the health breakdown of the plaintiff was a reasonably foreseeable consequence of the defendant's negligence, and I am not prepared to award the plaintiff any damages under that heading or refer any for assessment.

JARVIS V SWANS TOURS LTD
[1973] QB 233 (CA)

LORD DENNING MR (Edmund Davies and Stephenson LJJ concurring): Mr. Jarvis is a solicitor, employed by a local authority at Barking. In 1969 he was minded to go for Christmas to Switzerland. He was looking forward to a skiing holiday. It is his one fortnight's holiday in the year. He prefers it in the winter rather than in the summer.

Mr. Jarvis read a brochure issued by Swans Tours Ltd. He was much attracted by the description of Mörlialp, Giswil, Central Switzerland. I will not read the whole of it, but just pick out some of the principal attractions:

> House Party Centre with special resident host. ... Mörlialp is a most wonderful little resort on a sunny plateau ... Up there you will find yourself in the midst of beautiful alpine scenery, which in winter becomes a wonderland of sun, snow and ice, with a wide variety of fine ski-runs, a skating rink and exhilarating toboggan run ... Why did we choose the Hotel Krone ... mainly and most of all because of the "Gemütlichkeit" and friendly welcome you will receive from Herr and Frau Weibel. ... The Hotel Krone has its own Alphütte Bar which will be open several evenings a week. ... No doubt you will be in for a great time, when you book this house-party holiday ... Mr. Weibel, the charming owner, speaks English.

On the same page, in a special yellow box, it was said:

> Swans House Party in Mörlialp. All these House Party arrangements are included in the price of your holiday. Welcome party on arrival. Afternoon tea and cake for 7 days. Swiss dinner by candlelight. Fondue party. Yodler evening. Chali farewell party in the "Alphütte Bar." Service of representative.

Alongside on the same page there was a special note about ski-packs. "Hire of Skis, Sticks and Boots ... Ski Tuition ... 12 days £11.10."

In August 1969, on the faith of that brochure, Mr. Jarvis booked a 15-day holiday, with ski-pack. The total charge was £63.45, including Christmas supplement. He was to fly from Gatwick to Zurich on December 20, 1969, and return on January 3, 1970.

The plaintiff went on the holiday, but he was very disappointed. He was a man of about 35 and he expected to be one of a house party of some 30 or so people. Instead, he found there were only 13 during the first week. In the second week there was no house party at all. He was the only person there. Mr. Weibel could not speak English. So there was Mr. Jarvis, in the second week, in this hotel with no house party at all, and no one could speak English, except himself. He was very disappointed, too, with the skiing. It was some distance away at Giswil. There were no ordinary length skis. There were only mini-skis about 3 ft. long. So he did not get his skiing as he wanted to. In the second week he did get some longer skis for a couple of days, but then, because of the boots, his feet got rubbed and he could not continue even with the long skis. So his skiing holiday, from his point of view, was pretty well ruined.

There were many other matters, too. They appear trivial when they are set down in writing, but I have no doubt they loomed large in Mr. Jarvis's mind, when coupled with the other disappointments. He did not have the nice Swiss cakes which he was hoping for. The only cakes for tea were potato crisps and little dry nut cakes. The yodler evening consisted of one man from the locality who came in his working clothes for a little while, and sang four or five songs very quickly. The "Alphütte Bar" was an unoccupied annex which was only open one evening. There was a representative, Mrs. Storr, there during the first week, but she was not there during the second week.

The matter was summed up by the judge: "During the first week he got a holiday in Switzerland which was to some extent inferior ... and, as to the second week, he got a holiday which was very largely inferior" to what he was led to expect.

What is the legal position? I think that the statements in the brochure were representations or warranties. The breaches of them give Mr. Jarvis a right to damages. It is not necessary to decide whether they were representations or warranties: because since the *Misrepresentation Act 1967*, there is a remedy in damages for misrepresentation as well as for breach of warranty.

The one question in the case is: What is the amount of damages? The judge seems to have taken the difference in value between what he paid for and what he got. He said that he intended to give "the difference between the two values and no other damages" under any other head. He thought that Mr. Jarvis had got half of what he paid for. So the judge gave him half the amount which he had paid, namely, £31.72. Mr. Jarvis appeals to this court. He says that the damages ought to have been much more. ...

What is the right way of assessing damages? It has often been said that on a breach of contract damages cannot be given for mental distress. Thus in *Hamlin v. Great Northern Railway Co.* (1856) 1 H. & N. 408, 411 Pollock C.B. said that damages cannot be given "for the disappointment of mind occasioned by the breach of contract." And in *Hobbs v. London & South Western Railway Co.* (1875) L.R. 10 Q.B. 111, 122, Mellor J. said that "for the mere inconvenience, such as annoyance and loss of temper, or vexation, or for being disappointed in a particular thing which you have set your mind upon, without real physical inconvenience resulting, you cannot recover damages."

The courts in those days only allowed the plaintiff to recover damages if he suffered physical inconvenience, such as having to walk five miles home, as in *Hobbs*'s case; or to live in an over-crowded house, *Bailey v. Bullock* [1950] 2 All E.R. 1167.

I think that those limitations are out of date. In a proper case damages for mental distress can be recovered in contract, just as damages for shock can be recovered in tort. One such case is a contract for a holiday, or any other contract to provide entertainment and enjoyment. If the contracting party breaks his contract, damages can be given for the disappointment, the distress, the upset and frustration caused by the breach. I know that it is difficult to assess in terms of money, but it is no more difficult than the assessment which the courts have to make every day in personal injury cases for loss of amenities. Take the present case. Mr. Jarvis has only a fortnight's holiday in the year. He books it far ahead, and looks forward to it all that time. He ought to be compensated for the loss of it.

A good illustration was given by Edmund Davies L.J. in the course of the argument. He put the case of a man who has taken a ticket for Glyndbourne. It is the only night on which he can get there. He hires a car to take him. The car does not turn up. His damages are not limited to the mere cost of the ticket. He is entitled to general damages for the disappointment he has suffered and the loss of the entertainment which he should have had. Here, Mr. Jarvis's fortnight's winter holiday has been a grave disappointment. It is true that he was conveyed to Switzerland and back and had meals and bed in the hotel. But that is not what he went for. He went to enjoy himself with all the facilities which the defendants said he would have. He is entitled to damages for the lack of those facilities, and for his loss of enjoyment.

A similar case occurred in 1951. It was *Stedman v. Swan's Tours* (1951) 95 S.J. 727. A holiday-maker was awarded damages because he did not get the bedroom and the accommodation which he was promised. The county court judge awarded him £13.15. This court increased it to £50.

I think the judge was in error in taking the sum paid for the holiday £63.45 and halving it. The right measure of damages is to compensate him for the loss of entertainment and enjoyment which he was promised, and which he did not get.

Looking at the matter quite broadly, I think the damages in this case should be the sum of £125. I would allow the appeal, accordingly.

[See also *Jackson v Horizon Holidays Ltd*, Chapter 4.]

HEYWOOD V WELLERS
[1976] QB 446 (CA)

[H, a woman, instructed a firm of solicitors to seek an injunction to restrain a man, M, from molesting her. The solicitors failed to institute the proper proceedings, and M continued to molest H. H sued the solicitors for the return of the fees she had paid and for damages for negligence. The trial judge ordered repayment of the fees, but refused to award further damages. H appealed (conducting the appeal in person).]

LORD DENNING MR (James and Bridge LJJ concurring): So the solicitors were entitled to nothing for costs; and Mrs. Heywood could recover the £175 as money paid on a consideration which had wholly failed. She was, therefore, entitled to recover it as of right. And she is entitled to recover as well damages for negligence. Take this instance. If you engage a driver to take you to the station to catch a train for a day trip to the sea, you pay him £2—and then the car breaks down owing to his negligence. So that you miss your holiday. In that case you can recover not only your £2 back but also damages for the disappointment, upset and mental distress which you suffered: see *Jarvis v. Swan's Tours Ltd.* [1973] Q.B. 233 and *Jackson v. Horizon Holidays Ltd.* [1975] 1 W.L.R. 1468.

So here Mrs. Heywood employed the solicitors to take proceedings at law to protect her from molestation by Mr. Marrion. They were under a duty by contract to use reasonable care. Owing to their want of care she was molested by this man on three or four occasions. This molestation caused her much mental distress and upset. It must have been in their contemplation that if they failed in their duty she might be further molested and suffer much upset and distress. This damage she suffered was within their contemplation within the rule in *Hadley v. Baxendale* (1854) 9 Exch. 341. That was the test applied by Lawson J. in the recent case of *Cox v. Philips Industries Ltd.* (October 15, 1975) reported only in *The Times*, October 21, 1975. Mr. Keith Simpson urged that damages for mental distress were not recoverable. He relied on *Groom v. Crocker* [1939] 1 K.B. 194 and *Cook v. Swinfen* [1967] 1 W.L.R. 457, 461. But those cases may have to be reconsidered. In any case they were different from this. Here the solicitors were employed to protect her from molestation causing mental distress— and should be responsible in damages for their failure.

It was suggested that even if the solicitors had done their duty and taken the man to court he might still have molested her. But I do not think they can excuse themselves on that ground. After all, it was not put to the test: and it was their fault that it was not put to the test. If they had taken him to court as she wished—and as they ought to have done—it might well have been effective to stop him from molesting her any more. We should assume that it would have been effective to protect her, unless they prove that it would not: see *Coldman v. Hill* [1919] 1 K.B. 443, 457 by Scrutton L.J. and *Scottish Co-operative Wholesale Society Ltd. v. Meyer* [1959] A.C. 324, 367.

So the remaining question is: What damages should be awarded to Mrs. Heywood for the molestation she suffered on three or four occasions and the mental distress and upset she suffered? The judge, unfortunately, did not quantify the damages. In her claim as amended she put them at £150. I would allow her that sum.

NOTES

1. In *Hayes v James & Charles Dodd*, [1990] 2 All ER 815 (CA), the plaintiffs were a married couple in business together. The defendants, the plaintiffs' solicitors, wrongly advised them that there was a right of way attached to a property they proposed to buy for their business. They bought the property, and suffered loss when access to it was restricted. The plaintiffs' claim for damages for mental distress was rejected. Staughton LJ said: "I am not convinced that it is enough to ask whether mental distress was reasonably foreseeable as a consequence, or even whether it should have been contemplated as not unlikely to result from a breach of contract. It seems to me that damages for mental distress in contract are, as a matter of policy, limited to certain classes of case. I would broadly follow the classification ... 'where the contract which has been broken was itself a contract to provide peace of mind or freedom from distress.' It may be that the class is somewhat wider than that. But it should not, in my judgment, include any case where the object of the contract was not comfort or pleasure, or the relief of discomfort, but simply carrying on a commercial activity with a view to profit. So I would disallow the item of damages for anguish and vexation."

2. In *Turczinski v Dupont Heating & Air Conditioning Ltd* (2004), 246 DLR (4th) 95, the Ontario Court of Appeal said that "generally before damages for mental distress can be awarded for breach of contract, the contract must be one where peace of mind is what is being contracted for, such as a contract for a holiday ... or for insurance," adding that "there are persuasive reasons to confine within narrow limits the circumstances when damages will be awarded for exacerbation of mental illness for breach of a consumer contract." On the other hand, in *Farley v Skinner*, [2002] 2 AC 732 (HL), it was held that it was not necessary for the contract as a whole to be one for peace of mind so long as one important object of it was peace of mind.

VORVIS V INSURANCE CORPORATION OF BRITISH COLUMBIA
[1989] 1 SCR 1085

McINTYRE J: This appeal raises questions concerning the amount and nature of damages which may be payable in an action for wrongful dismissal from employment. The appellant is a fifty-four year old solicitor who commenced employment as a junior solicitor in the respondent's legal department in September of 1973. His employment terminated on January 20, 1981. The respondent initially purported to dismiss for cause, that is, incompetence, but, as the trial judge determined, it had no cause for dismissal. The trial judge therefore found that the plaintiff was wrongfully dismissed and that he was entitled to damages. Upon his dismissal the appellant received salary until February 15, 1981, a period of about one month, and he was able to obtain new employment, but not as a lawyer, on September 15, 1981, some seven months since his last payment. At trial, it was agreed by counsel that damages should be assessed on the basis of a seven-month notice requirement, because the plaintiff was able to mitigate his loss by finding other employment at a similar salary by September 15, 1981. ...

In this Court, the appellant ... argued that the court was in error in denying his claim for punitive damages. Damages for mental distress, properly characterized as aggravated damages, were not claimed in this Court as a separate head but it was argued that they were included in the general concept of punitive damages. ...

Before dealing with the question of punitive damages, it will be well to make clear the distinction between punitive and aggravated damages, for in the argument before us and in some of the materials filed there appeared some confusion as to the distinction. Punitive damages, as the name would indicate, are designed to punish. In this, they constitute an exception to the general common law rule that damages are designed to compensate the injured, not to punish the wrongdoer. Aggravated damages will frequently cover conduct which could also be the subject of punitive damages, but the role of aggravated damages remains compensatory. The distinction is clearly set out in Waddams, *The Law of Damages* (2nd ed. 1983), at p. 562, para. 979. ... Aggravated damages are awarded to compensate for aggravated damage. As explained by Waddams, they take account of intangible injuries and by definition will generally augment damages assessed under the general rules relating to the assessment of damages. Aggravated damages are compensatory in nature and may only be awarded for that purpose. Punitive damages, on the other hand, are punitive in nature and may only be employed in circumstances where the conduct giving the cause for complaint is of such nature that it merits punishment. The issue which is faced by this Court is whether punitive damages may be awarded by the Court in an action for breach of contract, based on wrongful dismissal of an employee, and, if so, whether the circumstances of this case would merit such an award. Also, before the Court is a similar question with respect to aggravated damages. ...

From the foregoing authorities, I would conclude that while aggravated damages may be awarded in actions for breach of contract in appropriate cases, this is not a case where they should be given. The rule long established in the *Addis* and *Peso Silver Mines* cases has generally been applied to deny such damages, and the employer/employee relationship (in the absence of collective agreements which involve consideration of the modern labour law regime) has always been one where either party could terminate the contract of employment by due notice, and therefore the only damage which could arise would result from a failure to give such notice.

I would not wish to be taken as saying that aggravated damages could never be awarded in a case of wrongful dismissal, particularly where the acts complained of were also independently actionable, a factor not present here. ...

[Weatherstone JA said, in *Brown v Waterloo Regional Board of Commissioners of Police* (1983), 43 OR (2d) 113, 150 DLR (3d) 729 (CA): "Damages, to be recoverable, must flow from an actionable wrong. It is not sufficient that a course of conduct not in itself actionable be somehow related to an actionable course of conduct."]

Furthermore, while the conduct complained of, that of Reid, was offensive and unjustified, any injury it may have caused the appellant cannot be said to have arisen out of the dismissal itself. The conduct complained of preceded the wrongful dismissal and therefore cannot be said to have aggravated the damage incurred as a result of the dismissal. Accordingly, I would refuse any claim for aggravated damages in respect of the wrongful dismissal.

[See also McCamus at 875-79; MacDougall at 355-57; Waddams at paras 743-54.]

FIDLER V SUN LIFE ASSURANCE CO OF CANADA
[2006] 2 SCR 3

McLACHLIN CJC and ABELLA J (for the court):

[1] For more than five years, Sun Life Assurance Company of Canada denied Connie Fidler the long-term disability benefits to which she was entitled. The trial judge found that, while there was no bad faith on the part of the insurer justifying an award of punitive damages, the denial caused Ms. Fidler significant mental distress. Sun Life was found liable to pay Ms. Fidler $20,000 in damages for mental distress resulting from Sun Life's breach of a group disability insurance contract. In the Court of Appeal for British Columbia, that award was upheld. In addition, a majority of the Court of Appeal found that, in reaching the conclusion that there was no bad faith, the trial judge had made a palpable and overriding error and awarded $100,000 in punitive damages to Ms. Fidler.

[2] Since mental distress of the kind experienced by Ms. Fidler was reasonably within the contemplation of the parties when they entered into the contract of disability insurance, we see no reason to deny her compensation for the damages for mental distress directly flowing from the breach. However, the trial judge's finding that Sun Life did not act in bad faith should not be interfered with and precludes an award of punitive damages. Accordingly, we reverse the Court of Appeal's order as to punitive damages and restore the award made by the trial judge.

• • •

DAMAGES FOR MENTAL DISTRESS FOR BREACH OF CONTRACT

[27] Damages for breach of contract should, as far as money can do it, place the plaintiff in the same position as if the contract had been performed. However, at least since the 1854 decision of the Court of Exchequer Chamber in *Hadley v. Baxendale* ..., it has been the law that these damages must be "such as may fairly and reasonably be considered either arising naturally ... from such breach of contract itself, or such as may reasonably be supposed to have been in the contemplation of both parties."

[28] Until now, damages for mental distress have not been welcome in the family of remedies spawned by this principle. The issue in this appeal is whether that remedial ostracization continues to be warranted.

[29] In *Hadley v. Baxendale*, the court explained the principle of reasonable expectation as follows:

> Where two parties have made a contract which one of them has broken, the damages which the other party ought to receive in respect of such breach of contract should be such as may fairly and reasonably be considered either arising naturally, i.e., according to the usual course of things, *from such breach of contract itself, or such as may reasonably be supposed to have been in the contemplation of both parties, at the time they made the contract, as the probable result of the breach of it.* [Emphasis added.] ...

[30] *Hadley v. Baxendale* makes no distinction between the types of loss that are recoverable for breach of contract. The principle of reasonable expectation is stated as a general principle. Nevertheless, subsequent cases purported to rule out damages for mental distress for breach of contract except in certain defined situations.

[31] While courts have always accepted that some non-pecuniary losses arising from breach of contract are compensable, including physical inconvenience and discomfort, they have traditionally shied away from awarding damages for mental suffering caused by the contract breach.

[32] This tradition of refusing to award damages for mental distress was launched in *Hobbs v. London and South Western Rail. Co.* (1875), L.R. 10 Q.B. 111, and *Hamlin v. Great Northern Railway Co.* (1856), 1 H. & N. 408, 156 E.R. 1261 (Ex.). In 1909, in the case of *Addis v. Gramophone Co.* ... the House of Lords "cast a long shadow over the common law" when it rejected a claim for mental distress because the conduct said to cause the distress was not actionable ... .

[33] To this day, *Addis* is cited for the proposition that mental distress damages are not generally recoverable for breach of contract.

[34] In short, the foundational concepts of reasonable expectations had a ceiling: mental distress. ...

[35] A number of policy considerations have been cited in support of this restriction. One is the perceived minimal nature of mental suffering:

> [A]s a matter of ordinary experience, it is evident that, while the innocent party to a contract will generally be disappointed if the defendant does not perform the contract, the innocent party's disappointment and distress are seldom so significant as to attract an award of damages on that score.

(*Baltic Shipping Co. v. Dillon* (1993), 176 C.L.R. 344 (Austl. H.C.) at p. 365, *per* Mason C.J.)

[36] Others have suggested that a "stiff upper lip" expectation in commercial life is the source of the prohibition. In *McGregor on Damages* (17th ed. 2003), the author explains:

> The reason for the general rule is that contracts normally concern commercial matters and that mental suffering on breach is not in the contemplation of the parties as part of the business risk of the transaction. [p. 63]

This resonated in *Johnson v. Gore Wood & Co.*, [2001] 2 W.L.R. 72 (H.L.) at p. 108, where Lord Cooke observed: "Contract-breaking is treated as an incident of commercial life which players in the game are expected to meet with mental fortitude."

[37] This Court's jurisprudence has followed the restrictive interpretation of *Addis*, generally requiring that a claim for compensation for mental distress be grounded in independently actionable conduct. The general rule that damages for mental distress should not be awarded for breach of contract was thus preserved: *Peso Silver Mines Ltd. (N.P.L.) v. Cropper*, [1966] S.C.R. 673. ...

[38] Without resiling from the general rule that damages for mental suffering could not be awarded at contract, the courts in the 1970s acknowledged that the reasons of principle and policy for the rule did not always apply, and began to award such damages where the contract was one for pleasure, relaxation or peace of mind. The charge was led, as so many were, by Lord Denning. In *Jarvis v. Swans Tours Ltd.*, [1973] 1 All E.R. 71 (C.A.), the plaintiff had contracted with the defendant to arrange a holiday. The defendant breached the contract by providing a terrible vacation. Acknowledging but declining to follow what he referred to as the "out of date" decisions in *Hamlin* and *Hobbs*, which had sired *Addis*, Lord Denning held that mental distress damages could be recovered for certain kinds of contracts:

> In a proper case damages for mental distress can be recovered in contract, just as damages for shock can be recovered in tort. One such case is a contract for a holiday, or any other contract to provide entertainment and enjoyment. If the contracting party breaks his contract, damages can be given for the disappointment, the distress, the upset and frustration caused by the breach. [p. 74]

[39] This holding in *Jarvis* emerged from the common law chrysalis as the "peace of mind exception" to the general rule against recovery for mental distress in contract

breaches. This exception was confined to contracts which had as their object the peace of mind of a contracting party. Bingham L.J. in *Watts v. Morrow* stated: "Where the very object of [the] contract is to provide pleasure, relaxation, peace of mind or freedom from molestation, damages will be awarded" (para. 1445).

[40] More recently, the House of Lords in *Farley v. Skinner*, [2001] 4 All E.R. 801, [2001] UKHL 49, loosened the peace of mind exception so as to permit recovery of mental distress not only when pleasure, relaxation, or peace of mind is "the very object of the contract," but also when it is a "major or important object of the contract" (para. 24).

[41] The right to obtain damages for mental distress for breach of contracts that promise pleasure, relaxation or peace of mind has found wide acceptance in Canada. ...

[43] The view taken by this Court in *Vorvis* that damages for mental distress in "peace of mind" contracts should be seen as an expression of the general principle of compensatory damages of *Hadley v. Baxendale*, rather than as an exception to that principle, is shared by others. ... Professor J.D. McCamus in *The Law of Contracts* (2005) argues at p. 877 that once peace of mind is understood as a reflection of, or "proxy" for the reasonable contemplation of the contracting parties, "there is no compelling reason not to simply apply the foreseeability test itself." At this point, the apparent inconsistency between the general rule in *Hadley v. Baxendale* and the exception vanishes. ...

[44] We conclude that damages for mental distress for breach of contract may, in appropriate cases, be awarded as an application of the principle in *Hadley v. Baxendale*: see *Vorvis*. The court should ask "what did the contract promise?" and provide compensation for those promises. The aim of compensatory damages is to restore the wronged party to the position he or she would have been in had the contract not been broken. As the Privy Council stated in *Wertheim v. Chicoutimi Pulp Co.*, [1911] A.C. 301 at p. 307: "the party complaining should, so far as it can be done by money, be placed in the same position as he would have been in if the contract had been performed." The measure of these damages is, of course, subject to remoteness principles. There is no reason why this should not include damages for mental distress, where such damages were in the reasonable contemplation of the parties at the time the contract was made. This conclusion follows from the basic principle of compensatory contractual damages: that the parties are to be restored to the position they contracted for, whether tangible or intangible. The law's task is simply to provide the benefits contracted for, whatever their nature, if they were in the reasonable contemplation of the parties.

[45] It does not follow, however, that all mental distress associated with a breach of contract is compensable. In normal commercial contracts, the likelihood of a breach of contract causing mental distress is not ordinarily within the reasonable contemplation of the parties. It is not unusual that a breach of contract will leave the wronged party feeling frustrated or angry. The law does not award damages for such incidental frustration. The matter is otherwise, however, when the parties enter into a contract, an object of which is to secure a particular psychological benefit. In such a case, damages arising from such mental distress should in principle be recoverable where they are established on the evidence and shown to have been within the reasonable contemplation of the parties at the time the contract was made. The basic principles of contract damages do not cease to operate merely because what is promised is an intangible, like mental security.

[46] This conclusion is supported by the policy considerations that have led the law to eschew damages for mental suffering in commercial contracts. As discussed

above, this reluctance rests on two policy considerations—the minimal nature of the mental suffering and the fact that in commercial matters, mental suffering on breach is "not in the contemplation of the parties as part of the business risk of the transaction" ... . Neither applies to contracts where promised mental security or satisfaction is part of the risk for which the parties contracted.

[47] This does not obviate the requirement that a plaintiff prove his or her loss. The court must be satisfied: (1) that an object of the contract was to secure a psychological benefit that brings mental distress upon breach within the reasonable contemplation of the parties; and (2) that the degree of mental suffering caused by the breach was of a degree sufficient to warrant compensation. These questions require sensitivity to the particular facts of each case.

[48] While the mental distress as a consequence of breach must reasonably be contemplated by the parties to attract damages, we see no basis for requiring it to be the dominant aspect or the "very essence" of the bargain. ... Principle suggests that as long as the promise in relation to state of mind is a part of the bargain in the reasonable contemplation of the contracting parties, mental distress damages arising from its breach are recoverable. This is to state neither more nor less than the rule in *Hadley v. Baxendale*.

[49] We conclude that the "peace of mind" class of cases should not be viewed as an exception to the general rule of the non-availability of damages for mental distress in contract law, but rather as an application of the reasonable contemplation or foreseeability principle that applies generally to determine the availability of damages for breach of contract. ...

[54] It follows that there is only one rule by which compensatory damages *for breach of contract* should be assessed: the rule in *Hadley v. Baxendale*. The *Hadley* test unites all forms of contractual damages under a single principle. It explains why damages may be awarded where an object of the contract is to secure a psychological benefit, just as they may be awarded where an object of the contract is to secure a material one. ... In all cases, these results are based on what was in the reasonable contemplation of the parties at the time of contract formation. They are not true aggravated damages awards.

[55] The recognition that *Hadley* is the single and controlling test for compensatory damages in cases of breach of contract therefore refutes any argument that an "independent actionable wrong" is a prerequisite for the recovery of mental distress damages. Where losses arise from the breach of contract itself, damages will be determined according to what was in the reasonable contemplation of the parties at the time of contract formation. An independent cause of action will only need to be proved where damages are of a different sort entirely: where they are being sought on the basis of aggravating circumstances that extend beyond what the parties expected when they concluded the contract. ...

[58] People enter into disability insurance contracts to protect themselves from this very financial and emotional stress and insecurity. An unwarranted delay in receiving this protection can be extremely stressful. Ms. Fidler's damages for mental distress flowed from Sun Life's breach of contract. To accept Sun Life's argument that an independent actionable wrong is a precondition would be to sanction the "conceptual incongruity of asking a plaintiff to show *more* than just that mental distress damages were a reasonably foreseeable consequence of breach." ...

[59] The second question is whether the mental distress here at issue was of a degree sufficient to warrant compensation. Again, we conclude that the answer is yes. The trial judge found that Sun Life's breach caused Ms. Fidler a substantial loss which she suffered over a five-year period. He found as a fact that Ms. Fidler "genuinely

suffered significant additional distress and discomfort *arising out of the loss of the disability coverage*" (para. 30 (emphasis added)). This finding was amply supported in the evidence, which included extensive medical evidence documenting the stress and anxiety that Ms. Fidler experienced. He concluded that merely paying the arrears and interest did not compensate for the years Ms. Fidler was without her benefits. His award of $20,000 seeks to compensate her for the psychological consequences of Sun Life's breach, consequences which are reasonably in the contemplation of parties to a contract for personal services and benefits such as this one. We agree with the Court of Appeal's decision not to disturb it.

[An award of punitive damages of $100,000 given by the BC Court of Appeal was set aside.]

NOTES

1. In *Mustapha v Culligan of Canada*, 2008 SCC 27, [2008] 2 SCR 114, the court set aside a substantial award of damages granted at trial to the buyer of a bottle of drinking water who saw a dead fly in the unopened bottle. The court's reasons dealt mainly with the action in tort. On the contractual action, the court said (para 19), "I have concluded that personal injury to Mr. Mustapha was not reasonably foreseeable by the defendant at the time of the alleged tort. The same evidence suggests that Mr. Mustapha's damage could not be reasonably supposed to have been within the contemplation of the parties when they entered into their agreement."

2. In *Honda Canada Inc v Keays*, 2008 SCC 39, [2008] 2 SCR 362, awards of damages for mental distress and punitive damages were set aside in a wrongful dismissal case, the Supreme Court finding that there was no bad faith or very improper conduct on the employer's part. The court, referring to para 48 of the *Fidler* case, said (at para 58) that "as long as the promise in relation to state of mind is a part of the bargain in the reasonable contemplation of the contracting parties, mental distress damages arising from its breach are recoverable."

V. PUNITIVE DAMAGES

WHITEN V PILOT INSURANCE CO
2002 SCC 18, [2002] 1 SCR 595

[1] BINNIE J (McLachlin CJC, L'Heureux-Dubé, Gonthier, Major, and Arbour JJ concurring): This case raises once again the spectre of uncontrolled and uncontrollable awards of punitive damages in civil actions. The jury was clearly outraged by the high-handed tactics employed by the respondent, Pilot Insurance Company, following its unjustified refusal to pay the appellant's claim under a fire insurance policy (ultimately quantified at approximately $345,000). Pilot forced an eight-week trial on an allegation of arson that the jury obviously considered trumped up. It forced the appellant to put at risk her only remaining asset (the insurance claim) plus approximately $320,000 in legal costs that she did not have. The denial of the claim was designed to force her to make an unfair settlement for less than she was entitled to. The conduct was planned and deliberate and continued for over two years, while the financial situation of the appellant grew increasingly desperate. Evidently concluding that the arson defence from the outset was unsustainable and made in bad faith, the jury added an award of punitive damages of $1 million, in effect providing

the appellant with a "windfall" that added something less than treble damages to her actual out-of-pocket loss. The respondent argues that the award of punitive damages is itself outrageous.

[2] The appellant, Daphne Whiten, bought her home in Haliburton County, Ontario, in 1985. Just after midnight on January 18, 1994, when she and her husband Keith were getting ready to go to bed, they discovered a fire in the addition to their house. They and their daughter, who had been upstairs, fled the house wearing only their nightclothes. It was minus 18 degrees Celsius. Mr. Whiten gave his slippers to his daughter to go for help and suffered serious frostbite to his feet for which he was hospitalized. He was thereafter confined to a wheelchair for a period of time. The fire totally destroyed the Whitens' home and its contents, including their few valuable antiques and many items of sentimental value and their three cats.

[3] The appellant was able to rent a small winterized cottage nearby for $650 per month. Pilot made a single $5,000 payment for living expenses and covered the rent for a couple of months or so, then cut off the rent without telling the family, and thereafter pursued a hostile and confrontational policy which the jury must have concluded was calculated to force the appellant (whose family was in very poor financial shape) to settle her claim at substantially less than its fair value. The allegation that the family had torched its own home was contradicted by the local fire chief, the respondent's own expert investigator, and its initial expert, all of whom said there was no evidence whatsoever of arson. The respondent's position, based on wishful thinking, was wholly discredited at trial. Pilot's appellate counsel conceded here and in the Ontario Court of Appeal that there was no air of reality to the allegation of arson.

[4] A majority of the Ontario Court of Appeal allowed the appeal in part and reduced the punitive damage award to $100,000. In my view, on the exceptional facts of this case, there was no basis on which to interfere with the jury award. The award, though very high, was rational in the specific circumstances disclosed in the evidence and within the limits that a jury is allowed to operate. The appellant was faced with harsh and unreasoning opposition from an insurer whose policy she had purchased for peace of mind and protection in just such an emergency. The jury obviously concluded that people who sell peace of mind should not try to exploit a family in crisis. Pilot, as stated, required the appellant to spend $320,000 in legal costs to collect the $345,000 that was owed to her. The combined total of $665,000 at risk puts the punitive damage awards in perspective. An award of $1 million in punitive damages is certainly at the upper end of a sustainable award on these facts but not beyond it. I would allow the appeal and restore the jury award of $1 million punitive damages. ...

[5] The facts surrounding the fire itself have already been briefly mentioned. The origin of the fire was never discovered but everyone who investigated the fire in the six months after it occurred concluded that it was accidental. The first persons to investigate the fire were the fire chief and firefighters called to the scene. The fire chief thought, and he was eventually shown to be correct, that the fire was caused at a single point of origin by a malfunctioning kerosene heater in the porch of the addition. This was where the fire was first observed and also the area which had sustained the most fire damage. The firefighters saw no evidence of arson and therefore they did not request the Fire Marshal's office to investigate.

[6] Pilot retained an experienced independent insurance adjuster, Derek Francis, to investigate the loss. Francis inspected the site and interviewed the Whitens, who freely acknowledged that they had both been unemployed and had financial difficulties. Francis also interviewed the firefighters about the speed at which the fire

spread, a key indicator of arson. Both the physical evidence and the Whitens' conduct satisfied Francis that the fire was accidental and on February 3, 1994 he reported to Pilot that "there is no suspicion of arson on behalf of the insureds or any members of their family."

• • •

[25] The Whitens lived in a small community. People were aware that their home was not being rebuilt because the insurer was alleging arson. The stigma persisted. Pilot continued to allege arson throughout the trial. Pilot now concedes that the evidence as a whole unequivocally demonstrates that the fire was accidental.

• • •

[36] Punitive damages are awarded against a defendant in exceptional cases for "malicious, oppressive and high-handed" misconduct that "offends the court's sense of decency": *Hill v. Church of Scientology of Toronto*, [1995] 2 S.C.R. 1130; 126 D.L.R. (4th) 129, at para. 196. The test thus limits the award to misconduct that represents a marked departure from ordinary standards of decent behaviour. Because their objective is to punish the defendant rather than compensate a plaintiff (whose just compensation will already have been assessed), punitive damages straddle the frontier between civil law (compensation) and criminal law (punishment).

[37] Punishment is a legitimate objective not only of the criminal law but of the civil law as well. Punitive damages serve a need that is not met either by the pure civil law or the pure criminal law. In the present case, for example, no one other than the appellant could rationally be expected to invest legal costs of $320,000 in lengthy proceedings to establish that on this particular file the insurer had behaved abominably. Overcompensation of a plaintiff is given in exchange for this socially useful service.

[38] Nevertheless, the hybrid nature of punitive damages offends some jurists who insist that legal remedies should belong to one jurisprudential field or the other. That is one major aspect of the controversy, often framed in the words of Lord Wilberforce's comments, dissenting, in *Broome v. Cassell & Co.*, [1972] A.C. 1027 (H.L.), at p. 1114:

> It cannot lightly be taken for granted, even as a matter of theory, that the purpose of the law of tort is compensation, still less that it ought to be, an issue of large social import, or that there is something inappropriate or illogical or anomalous (a question-begging word) in including a punitive element in civil damages, or, conversely, that the criminal law, rather than the civil law, is in these cases the better instrument for conveying social disapproval, or for redressing a wrong to the social fabric, or that damages in any case can be broken down into the two separate elements. As a matter of practice English law has not committed itself to any of these theories: it may have been wiser than it knew.

[39] A second major aspect of the controversy surrounding punitive damages is related to the quantum. Substantial awards are occasionally assessed at figures seemingly plucked out of the air. The usual procedural protections for an individual faced with potential punishment in a criminal case are not available. Plaintiffs, it is said, recover punitive awards out of all proportion to just compensation. They are subjected, it is said, to "palm tree justice": *Cassell*, supra, at p. 1078. They are handed a financial windfall serendipitously just because, coincidentally with their claim, the court desires to punish the defendant and deter others from similar outrageous conduct. Defendants on the other hand say they suffer out of all proportion to the actual wrongs they have committed. Because the punishment is tailored to fit not

only the "crime" but the financial circumstances of the defendant (i.e., to ensure that it is big enough to "sting"), defendants complain that they are being punished for who they are rather than for what they have done. The critics of punitive awards refer *in terrorem* to the United States experience where, for example, an Alabama jury awarded $4 million in punitive damages against a BMW dealership for failure to disclose a minor paint job to fix a cosmetic blemish on a new vehicle in *BMW of North America, Inc. v. Gore*, 517 U.S. 559 (1996). In 1994, a jury in New Mexico awarded 81-year-old Stella Liebeck $160,000 in compensatory damages and $2.7 million in punitive damages against McDonald's Restaurants for burns resulting from a spilled cup of coffee, notwithstanding that she tried to open the cup while balancing it on her lap in the passenger seat of a car (*Liebeck v. McDonald's Restaurants, P.T.S. Inc.*, 1995 WL 360309 (N.M. Dist.)). Critics of punitive damages warn against an "Americanization" of our law that, if adopted, would bring the administration of justice in this country into disrepute.

[40] These are serious concerns, but in fact, the punitive damage controversies have little if anything to do with Americanization of our law. Jury awards of punitive damages in civil actions have a long and important history in Anglo-Canadian jurisprudence. They defy modern attempts at neat classification of remedies. The jury is invited to treat a plaintiff as a public interest enforcer as well as a private interest claimant. Almost 240 years ago, government agents broke into the premises of a Whig member of Parliament and pamphleteer, John Wilkes, to seize copies of a publication entitled *The North Briton*, No. 45, which the Secretary of State regarded as libellous. Lord Chief Justice Pratt (later Lord Camden L.C.) on that occasion swept aside the government's defence. "If such a [search] power is truly invested in a Secretary of State," he held, "and he can delegate this power, it certainly may affect the person and property of every man in this kingdom, and is totally subversive of the liberty of the subject." As to punitive damages, he affirmed that:

> [A] jury have it in their power to give damages for more than the injury received. Damages are designed not only as a satisfaction to the injured person, but likewise as a punishment to the guilty, to deter from any such proceeding for the future, and as a proof of the detestation of the jury to the action itself.

(*Wilkes v. Wood* (1763), Lofft. 1, 98 E.R. 489 (K.B.), at pp. 498-99.)

[41] Long before the days of Lord Pratt C.J., the related idea of condemning a defendant to a multiple of what is required for compensation (in the present appeal, as stated, the punitive damages were roughly triple the award of compensatory damages) reached back to the Code of Hammurabi, Babylonian law, Hittite law (1400 B.C.), the Hindu Code of Manu (200 B.C.), ancient Greek codes, the Ptolemaic law in Egypt and the Hebrew Covenant Code of Mosaic law (see Exodus 22:1: "If a man shall steal an ox, or a sheep, and kill it, or sell it; he shall restore five oxen for an ox, and four sheep for a sheep."). Roman law also included provisions for multiple damages. Admittedly, in these early systems, criminal law and civil law were not always clearly differentiated. The United States Supreme Court in *BMW, supra*, referred at p. 581 to "65 different enactments [in English statutes] during the period between 1275 and 1753 [that] provided for double, treble, or quadruple damages."

[42] Even in terms of quantum, the use of punitive damages in the eighteenth century was aggressive. In *Huckle v. Money* (1763), 2 Wils. K.B. 205, 95 E.R. 768 (K.B.), the journeyman Huckle (who had actually printed the pamphlet *The North Briton*, No. 45 at issue in *Wilkes, supra*) won a cause of action for trespass, assault and false imprisonment and received 300 pounds in damages from the jury despite the comfortable and short six-hour duration of his confinement. The government's motion

for a new trial on the basis that the award was "outrageous" was denied, even though actual damages totalled only 20 pounds (i.e., a multiplier of 15) (p. 768 E.R.). The Lord Chief Justice, in introducing the expression "exemplary damages," thought there was no precedent for judges "intermeddling" with damages awarded by juries.

[43] The three objectives identified by Lord Chief Justice Pratt, in *Wilkes, supra*—punishment, deterrence and denunciation ("proof of the detestation")—are with us still, even though some scholarly critics have argued that these rationales "have very particular and divergent implications" that occasionally wind up undermining each other: B. Chapman and M. Trebilcock, "Punitive Damages: Divergence in Search of a Rationale" (1989), 40 *Ala. L. Rev.* 741, at p. 744. No doubt, as a matter of language, the word "punishment" includes both retribution and denunciation, and the three object-ives should perhaps better be referred to as retribution, deterrence and denunciation.

[44] The notion of private enforcers (or "private Attorneys General"), particularly where they act for personal gain, is worrisome unless strictly controlled. Thus, while the availability of punitive damages in Canada was affirmed early on by this Court in *Collette v. Lasnier* (1886), 13 S.C.R. 563, a patent case, they were not widely awarded until the 1970s. Since then the awards have multiplied in number and escalated in amount. A report on punitive damages by the Ontario Law Reform Commission, issued in 1991, which examined research begun in 1989, predicted limited and principled development in the law of punitive damages in Canada: Ontario Law Reform Commission, *Report on Exemplary Damages*, June 1, 1991, at pp. 93 and 98. By 1998, the report's research director, Dean Bruce Feldthusen, conceded that the law was "certainly developing quite differently in Canada than one would have predicted only a short time ago" and that "many of the doctrinal pillars on which the Report's predictions of limited and principled development in the law governing punitive damages were based have since cracked or collapsed": B. Feldthusen, "Puni-tive Damages: Hard Choices and High Stakes," [1998] *N.Z.L. Rev.* 741, at p. 742. Con-trary to expectations, the awards were much larger, more frequent, appeared to rely more often on the defendant's wealth in support, and included more high profile jury awards. The kinds of causes of action had expanded; punitive damages were the "norm" and had "proliferated" in actions in sexual battery, were now "clearly available" for breach of fiduciary duty, and "persisted" in contract actions. Prior crim-inal convictions, he concluded, no longer automatically barred punitive awards. He added: "Perhaps most significantly, the courts seem to have accepted general deter-rence, not retributive punishment, as the dominant purpose behind punitive damage awards in a number of important decisions" (p. 742).

[45] This Court more recently affirmed a punitive damage award of $800,000 in *Hill, supra*. On that occasion some guidelines were set out to keep this remedy within reasonable limits. The Court on this occasion has an opportunity to clarify further the rules governing whether an award of punitive damages ought to be made and, if so, the assessment of a quantum that is fair to all parties.

· · ·

[66] For present purposes, I draw the following assistance from the experience in other common law jurisdictions which I believe is consistent with Canadian practice and precedent.

[67] First, the attempt to limit punitive damages by "categories" does not work and was rightly rejected in Canada in *Vorvis, supra*, at pp. 1104-6. The control mechanism lies not in restricting the category of case but in rationally determining circum-stances that warrant the addition of punishment to compensation in a civil action. It is in the nature of the remedy that punitive damages will largely be restricted to intentional torts, as in *Hill, supra*, or breach of fiduciary duty as in *M.(K.) v. M.(H.)*, [1992]

3 S.C.R. 6, 96 D.L.R. (4th) 289, but *Vorvis* itself affirmed the availability of punitive damages in the exceptional case in contract. In *Denison v. Fawcett*, [1958] O.R. 312, 12 D.L.R. (2d) 537, the Ontario Court of Appeal asserted in obiter that on proper facts punitive damages would be available in negligence and nuisance as well. In *Robitaille v. Vancouver Hockey Club Ltd.* (1981), 124 D.L.R. (3d) 228, the British Columbia Court of Appeal awarded punitive damages in a negligence case on the principle that they ought to be available whenever "the conduct of the defendant [was] such as to merit condemnation by the [c]ourt" (p. 250). This broader approach seems to be in line with most common law jurisdictions apart from England.

[68] Second, there is a substantial consensus that coincides with Lord Pratt C.J.'s view in 1763 that the general objectives of punitive damages are punishment (in the sense of retribution), deterrence of the wrongdoer and others, and denunciation (or, as Cory J. put it in *Hill, supra*, at para. 196, they are "the means by which the jury or judge expresses its outrage at the egregious conduct").

[69] Third, there is recognition that the primary vehicle of punishment is the criminal law (and regulatory offences) and that punitive damages should be resorted to only in exceptional cases and with restraint. Where punishment has actually been imposed by a criminal court for an offence arising out of substantially the same facts, some jurisdictions, such as Australia and New Zealand, bar punitive damages in certain contexts ... but the dominant approach ... is to treat it as another factor, albeit a factor of potentially great importance. ... The Ontario Law Reform Commission ... recommended that the "court should be entitled to consider the fact and adequacy of any prior penalty imposed in any criminal or other similar proceeding brought against the defendant." ...

[70] Fourth, the incantation of the time-honoured pejoratives ("high-handed," "oppressive," "vindictive," etc.) provides insufficient guidance (or discipline) to the judge or jury setting the amount. Lord Diplock in *Cassell, supra*, at p. 1129, called these the "whole gamut of dyslogistic judicial epithets." A more principled and less exhortatory approach is desirable.

[71] Fifth, all jurisdictions seek to promote rationality. In directing itself to the punitive damages, the court should relate the facts of the particular case to the underlying purposes of punitive damages and ask itself how, in particular, an award would further one or other of the objectives of the law, and what is the lowest award that would serve the purpose, i.e., because any higher award would be irrational.

[72] Sixth, it is rational to use punitive damages to relieve a wrongdoer of its profit where compensatory damages would amount to nothing more than a licence fee to earn greater profits through outrageous disregard of the legal or equitable rights of others.

[73] Seventh, none of the common law jurisdictions has adopted (except by statute) a formulaic approach, as advocated by the intervener the Insurance Council of Canada in this appeal, such as a fixed cap or fixed ratio between compensatory and punitive damages. The proper focus is not on the plaintiff's loss but on the defendant's misconduct. A mechanical or formulaic approach does not allow sufficiently for the many variables that ought to be taken into account in arriving at a just award.

[74] Eighth, the governing rule for quantum is proportionality. The overall award, that is to say compensatory damages plus punitive damages plus any other punishment related to the same misconduct, should be rationally related to the objectives for which the punitive damages are awarded (retribution, deterrence and denunciation). Thus there is broad support for the "if, but only if" test formulated, as mentioned, in *Rookes*, ... , and affirmed here in *Hill, supra*.

[75] Ninth, it has become evident that juries can and should receive more guidance and help from the judges in terms of their mandate. They should be told in some detail about the function of punitive damages and the factors that govern both the award and the assessment of a proper amount. Juries should not be thrown into their assignment without any help, then afterwards be criticized for the result.

[76] Tenth, and finally, there is substantial consensus (even the United States is moving in this direction) that punitive damages are not at large (as pointed out by Cory J. in *Hill, supra* ...) and that an appellate court is entitled to intervene if the award exceeds the outer boundaries of a rational and measured response to the facts of the case.

[77] With the benefit of these general principles, I now turn to the specific issues raised by this appeal.

(1) PUNITIVE DAMAGES FOR BREACH OF CONTRACT

[78] This, as noted, is a breach of contract case. In *Vorvis, supra*, this Court held that punitive damages are recoverable in such cases provided the defendant's conduct said to give rise to the claim is itself "an actionable wrong" (p. 1106). The scope to be given this expression is the threshold question in this case, i.e., is a breach of an insurer's duty to act in good faith an actionable wrong independent of the loss claim under the fire insurance policy? *Vorvis* itself was a case about the employer's breach of an employment contract. This is how McIntyre J. framed the rule at pp. 1105-6:

> When then can punitive damages be awarded? It must never be forgotten that when awarded by a judge or a jury, a punishment is imposed upon a person by a Court by the operation of the judicial process. What is it that is punished? It surely cannot be merely conduct of which the Court disapproves, however strongly the judge may feel. Punishment may not be imposed in a civilized community without a justification in law. *The only basis for the imposition of such punishment must be a finding of the commission of an actionable wrong which caused the injury complained of by the plaintiff.* [Emphasis added.]

This view, McIntyre J. said (at p. 1106), "has found approval in the *Restatement on the Law of Contracts* 2d in the United States," which reads as follows:

> Punitive damages are not recoverable for a breach of contract unless the conduct constituting the breach is also a *tort* for which punitive damages are recoverable. [Emphasis added.]

Applying these principles in *Vorvis*, McIntyre J. stated, at p. 1109:

> Each party had the right to terminate the contract without the consent of the other, and where the employment contract was terminated by the employer, the appellant was entitled to reasonable notice of such termination or payment of salary and benefits for the period of reasonable notice. The termination of the contract on this basis by the employer is not *a wrong in law* and, where the reasonable notice is given or payment in lieu thereof is made, the plaintiff—subject to a consideration of aggravated damages which have been allowed in some cases but which were denied in this case—is entitled to no further remedy. ... [Emphasis added.]

Wilson J., with whom L'Heureux-Dubé J. concurred, dissented. She did not agree "that punitive damages can only be awarded when the misconduct is in itself an 'actionable wrong.'" She stated, at p. 1130:

In my view, the correct approach is to assess the conduct in the context of all the circumstances and determine whether it is deserving of punishment because of its shock-
ingly harsh, vindictive, reprehensible or malicious nature. Undoubtedly some conduct
found to be deserving of punishment will constitute an actionable wrong but other
conduct might not.

[79] In the case at bar, Pilot acknowledges that an insurer is under a duty of good
faith and fair dealing. Pilot says that this is a contractual duty. *Vorvis*, it says, requires
a tort. However, in my view, a breach of the contractual duty of good faith is
independent of and in addition to the breach of contractual duty to pay the loss. It
constitutes an "actionable wrong" within the *Vorvis* rule, which does not require an
independent tort. I say this for several reasons.

[80] First, McIntyre J. chose to use the expression "actionable wrong" instead of
"tort" even though he had just reproduced an extract from the *Restatement* which
does use the word tort. It cannot be an accident that McIntyre J. chose to employ a
much broader expression when formulating the Canadian test.

[81] Second, in *Royal Bank of Canada v. W. Got & Associates Electric Ltd.*, [1999] 3
S.C.R. 408, 178 D.L.R. (4th) 385, at para. 26, this Court, referring to McIntyre J.'s holding in *Vorvis*, said "the circumstances that would justify punitive damages for breach
of contract *in the absence* of actions also constituting *a tort* are rare" (emphasis
added). Rare they may be, but the clear message is that such cases do exist. The Court
has thus confirmed that punitive damages can be awarded in the absence of an
accompanying tort.

[82] Third, the requirement of an independent tort would unnecessarily compli-
cate the pleadings, without in most cases adding anything of substance. *Central Trust
Co. v. Rafuse*, [1986] 2 S.C.R. 147, 31 D.L.R. (4th) 481, held that a common law duty of
care sufficient to found an action in tort can arise within a contractual relationship,
and in that case proceeded with the analysis in tort instead of contract to deprive an
allegedly negligent solicitor of the benefit of a limitation defence. To require a plaintiff to formulate a tort in a case such as the present is pure formalism. An independent
actionable wrong is required, but it can be found in breach of a distinct and separate
contractual provision or other duty such as a fiduciary obligation.

[83] I should add that insurance companies have also asserted claims for punitive
damages against their insured for breach of the mutual "good faith" obligation in
insurance contracts.

• • •

[91] The appellant also pleaded that Pilot's manner of dealing with her claim had
created "hardship" of which "the Defendants, through their agents and employees
always had direct and ongoing knowledge" (para. 8). In para. 14 she pleaded that "as
a result of the actions of the Defendants, the Plaintiff has suffered and continues to
suffer great emotional stress" (although there was no claim for aggravated damages).
The respondent specifically denied acting in bad faith (Statement of Defence and
Counterclaim of the Defendant, at para. 6). The statement of claim was somewhat
deficient in failing to relate the plea for punitive damages to the precise facts said to
give rise to the outrage, but Pilot was content to go to trial on this pleading and I do
not think it should be heard to complain about it at this late date.

[92] As to the respondent's objection that the pleading does not allege separate and
distinct damages flowing from the independent actionable wrong, the respondent's
argument overlooks the fact that punitive damages are directed to the quality of the
defendant's conduct, not the quantity (if any) of the plaintiff's loss. As Cory J. observed
in *Hill, supra*, at para. 196: "Punitive damages bear no relation to what the plaintiff should
receive by way of compensation. Their aim is not to compensate the plaintiff, but

rather to punish the defendant. It is the means by which the jury or judge expresses its outrage at the egregious conduct of the defendant." In any event, there is a good deal of evidence of emotional stress and financial cost over and above the loss that would have been incurred had the claim been settled in good faith within a reasonable time. ...

(3) WAS THE JURY CHARGE ADEQUATE?

[93] The respondent argues that the trial judge did not give the jury adequate guidance on how to assess punitive damages. There is considerable merit in this submission. The judge's charge on this point was skeletal. It is my view, for the reasons already discussed, that the charge on punitive damages should not be given almost as an afterthought but should be understood as an important source of control and discipline. The jurors should not be left to guess what their role and function is.

[94] To this end, not only should the pleadings of punitive damages be more rigorous in the future than in the past ... but it would be helpful if the trial judge's charge to the jury included words to convey an understanding of the following points, even at the risk of some repetition for emphasis. (1) Punitive damages are very much the exception rather than the rule, (2) imposed only if there has been high-handed, malicious, arbitrary or highly reprehensible misconduct that departs to a marked degree from ordinary standards of decent behaviour. (3) Where they are awarded, punitive damages should be assessed in an amount reasonably proportionate to such factors as the harm caused, the degree of the misconduct, the relative vulnerability of the plaintiff and any advantage or profit gained by the defendant, (4) having regard to any other fines or penalties suffered by the defendant for the misconduct in question. (5) Punitive damages are generally given only where the misconduct would otherwise be unpunished or where other penalties are or are likely to be inadequate to achieve the objectives of retribution, deterrence and denunciation. (6) Their purpose is not to compensate the plaintiff, but (7) to give a defendant his or her just desert (retribution), to deter the defendant and others from similar misconduct in the future (deterrence), and to mark the community's collective condemnation (denunciation) of what has happened. (8) Punitive damages are awarded only where compensatory damages, which to some extent are punitive, are insufficient to accomplish these objectives, and (9) they are given in an amount that is no greater than necessary to rationally accomplish their purpose. (10) While normally the state would be the recipient of any fine or penalty for misconduct, the plaintiff will keep punitive damages as a "windfall" in addition to compensatory damages. (11) Judges and juries in our system have usually found that moderate awards of punitive damages, which inevitably carry a stigma in the broader community, are generally sufficient.

[95] These particular expressions are not, of course, obligatory. What is essential in a particular case will be a function of its particular circumstances, the need to emphasize the nature, scope and exceptional nature of the remedy, and fairness to both sides.

[96] The trial judge should keep in mind that the standard of appellate review applicable to punitive damages ultimately awarded, is that a reasonable jury, properly instructed, could have concluded that an award in that amount, and no less, was rationally required to punish the defendant's misconduct, as discussed below.

[97] If counsel can agree on a "bracket" or "range" of an appropriate award, the trial judge should convey these figures to the jury, but at the present time specific figures should not be mentioned in the absence of such agreement (Hill, supra, per Cory J., at paras. 162-63. This prohibition may have to be re-examined in future,

based on further experience). Counsel should also consider the desirability of asking the trial judge to advise the jury of awards of punitive damages made in comparable circumstances that have been sustained on appeal.

[98] The foregoing suggestions are put forward in an effort to be helpful rather than dogmatic. They grow out of the observation in *Hill* that punitive damages are not "at large" (para. 197). Unless punitive damages can be approached rationally they ought not to be awarded at all. To the extent these suggestions are considered useful, they will obviously have to be both modified and elaborated to assist the jury on the facts of a particular case. The point, simply, is that jurors should not be left in any doubt about what they are to do and how they are to go about it.

[99] It is evident that I am suggesting a more ample charge on the issue of punitive damages than was given in this case. Finlayson J.A. said that he was "not entirely happy with the trial judge's charge to the jury on the issue of punitive damages" (p. 661), and Laskin J.A. agreed that "[t]he trial judge might have given the jury more help than he did" (p. 656). However, both Finlayson and Laskin JJ.A. agreed that the jury charge covered the essentials, however lightly. This conclusion is reinforced by the fact that no objection was made by either counsel. With some hesitation, I agree with the Court of Appeal, unanimous on this point, that in the circumstances this ground of appeal should be rejected. ...

(4) REVIEWING THE JURY AWARD

(A) WHETHER THE AWARD OF PUNITIVE DAMAGES IN THIS CASE WAS A RATIONAL RESPONSE TO THE RESPONDENT'S MISCONDUCT

[100] The applicable standard of review for "rationality" was articulated by Cory J. in *Hill, supra,* at para. 197:

Unlike compensatory damages, punitive damages are not at large. Consequently, courts have a much greater scope and discretion on appeal. The appellate review should be based upon the court's estimation as to whether the punitive damages serve a rational purpose. In other words, was the misconduct of the defendant so outrageous that punitive damages were rationally required to act as deterrence?

[101] The "rationality" test applies both to the question of whether an award of punitive damages should be made at all, as well as to the question of its quantum.

[102] The respondent claims that an insurer is entirely within its rights to thoroughly investigate a claim and exercise caution in evaluating the circumstances. It is not required to accept the initial views of its investigators. It is perfectly entitled to pursue further inquiries. I agree with these points. The problem here is that Pilot embarked on a "train of thought" as early as February 25, 1994 ... that led to the arson trial, with nothing to go on except the fact that its policyholder had money problems.

[103] The "train of thought" mentioned in the letter to Pilot from Derek Francis kept going long after the requirements of due diligence or prudent practice had been exhausted. There is a difference between due diligence and wilful tunnel vision. The jury obviously considered this case to be an outrageous example of the latter. In my view, an award of punitive damages (leaving aside the issue of quantum for the moment) was a rational response on the jury's part to the evidence. It was not an inevitable or unavoidable response, but it was a rational response to what the jury had seen and heard. The jury was obviously incensed at the idea that the respondent would get away with paying no more than it ought to have paid after its initial investigation in 1994 (plus costs). It obviously felt that something more was required to demonstrate to Pilot that its bad faith dealing with this loss claim was not a wise or

profitable course of action. The award answered a perceived need for retribution, denunciation and deterrence.

[104] The intervener, the Insurance Council of Canada, argues that the award of punitive damages will over-deter insurers from reviewing claims with due diligence, thus lead to the payment of unmeritorious claims, and in the end drive up insurance premiums. This would only be true if the respondent's treatment of the appellant is not an isolated case but is widespread in the industry. If, as I prefer to believe, insurers generally take seriously their duty to act in good faith, it will only be rogue insurers or rogue files that will incur such a financial penalty, and the extra economic cost inflicted by punitive damages will either cause the delinquents to mend their ways or, ultimately, move them on to lines of work that do not call for a good faith standard of behaviour.

[105] The Ontario Court of Appeal was unanimous that punitive damages in some amount were justified and I agree with that conclusion. This was an exceptional case that justified an exceptional remedy. The respondent's cross-appeal will therefore be dismissed.

• • •

(ii) Proportionate to the Degree of Vulnerability of the Plaintiff

[115] I add two cautionary notes on the issue of vulnerability [of the plaintiff]. First, this factor militates *against* the award of punitive damages in most commercial situations, particularly where the cause of action is contractual and the problem for the Court is to sort out the bargain the parties have made. Most participants enter the marketplace knowing it is fuelled by the aggressive pursuit of self-interest. Here, on the other hand, we are dealing with a homeowner's "peace of mind" contract.

[116] Second, it must be kept in mind that punitive damages are not compensatory. Thus the appellant's pleading of emotional distress in this case is only relevant insofar as it helps to assess the oppressive character of the respondent's conduct. Aggravated damages are the proper vehicle to take into account the additional harm caused to the plaintiff's feelings by reprehensible or outrageous conduct on the part of the defendant. Otherwise there is a danger of "double recovery" for the plaintiff's emotional stress, once under the heading of compensation and secondly under the heading of punishment.

• • •

(6) CONCLUSION ON "RATIONALITY"

[128] I would not have awarded $1 million in punitive damages in this case but in my judgment the award is within the rational limits within which a jury must be allowed to operate. The award was not so disproportionate as to exceed the bounds of rationality. It did not overshoot its purpose. I have already outlined the reasons why I believe this to be the case.

[129] The jury followed the "if but only if" model, i.e., punitive damages should be awarded "if but only if" the compensatory award is insufficient. The form and order of the questions put to the jury required them first of all to deal with compensation for the loss of the plaintiff's house (replacement or cash value), its contents, and any increase in her living and moving expenses. Only after those matters had been dealt with was the jury instructed to turn their minds to a final question on punitive damages. They were clearly aware that compensatory damages might well be sufficient punishment to avoid a repetition of the offence and a deterrent to others. In this case, the jury obviously concluded that the compensatory damages ($345,000) were

not sufficient for those purposes. It was no more than the respondent had contractually obligated itself to pay under the insurance policy. In this case, the power imbalance was highly relevant. Pilot holds itself out to the public as a sure guide to a "safe harbour." In its advertising material it refers to itself as "Your Pilot" and makes such statements as:

> At Pilot Insurance Company, guiding people like you into safe harbours has been our mission for nearly 75 years.

Insurance contracts, as Pilot's self-description shows, are sold by the insurance industry and purchased by members of the public for peace of mind. The more devastating the loss, the more the insured may be at the financial mercy of the insurer, and the more difficult it may be to challenge a wrongful refusal to pay the claim. Deterrence is required. The obligation of good faith dealing means that the appellant's peace of mind should have been Pilot's objective, and her vulnerability ought not to have been aggravated as a negotiating tactic. It is this relationship of reliance and vulnerability that was outrageously exploited by Pilot in this case. The jury, it appears, decided a powerful message of retribution, deterrence and denunciation had to be sent to the respondent and they sent it.

[130] The respondent points out that there is no evidence this case represents a deliberate corporate strategy as opposed to an isolated, mishandled file that ran amok. This is true, but it is also true that Pilot declined to call evidence to explain why this file ran amok, and what steps, if any, have been taken to prevent a recurrence.

[131] The respondent also argues that at the end of the day, it did not profit financially from its misbehaviour. This may also be true, but if so, that result was not for want of trying. The respondent clearly hoped to starve the appellant into a cheap settlement. Crabbe's letter of June 9, 1994, quoted earlier, suggests as much. That it failed to do so is due in no small part to appellant's counsel who took a hotly contested claim into an eight-week jury trial on behalf of a client who was effectively without resources of her own; and who obviously could have been starved into submission but for his firm's intervention on her behalf.

[132] While, as stated, I do not consider the "ratio" test to be an appropriate indicator of rationality, the ratio of punitive damages to compensatory damages in the present case would be either a multiple of three (if only the insurance claim of $345,000 is considered) or a multiple of less than two (if the claim plus the award of solicitor–client costs is thought to be the total compensation). Either way, the ratio is well within what has been considered "rational" in decided cases.

[133] The majority opinion of the Ontario Court of Appeal recognized that punitive damages are not "at large" and appellate courts have "much greater scope and discretion on appeal" than they do in the case of general damages (*Hill, supra*, at para. 197). If the court considers the award or its quantum to be irrational, it is its duty to interfere.

[134] This was the view taken by the majority judgment of Finlayson J.A. The appellant complains that Finlayson J.A. applied a standard of "simply too high" (p. 661). It is true that he thought the award was too high, but that observation must be understood in light of other comments made in the course of his reasons. Finlayson J.A. concluded there was "no justification for such a radical departure from precedent" (pp. 661-62), which revealed awards in the range of $7,500 to $15,000. ... Finlayson J.A. looked at "the degree of reprehensibility of the defendant's conduct" (p. 666) and concluded that "[t]his case does not demonstrate that there was such insidious, pernicious and persistent malice as would justify an award of this magnitude" (p. 666).

[135] With respect to precedent, it must be remembered that the respondent's trial counsel objected to any range or "bracket" of appropriate figures being given to the jury. Had the jury been given the information, it may have influenced their views. The respondent itself appears to have been unimpressed by the size of prior awards of punitive damages. In its factum, commenting on Crabbe's letter of June 9, 1994, counsel states, "However, it should also be noted that Mr. Crabbe was clearly attempting to allay Pilot's concern about the Whiten's bad faith claim at a time when punitive damage awards against insurers were in the range of $7,500-$15,000." Pilot's concern may have been easy to allay when the expected exposure to punitive damages was only $15,000.

[136] The respondent objects that, prior to this judgment, the highest previous award in an insurer bad faith case was $50,000. However, prior to the $800,000 award of punitive damages upheld in *Hill, supra*, the highest award in punitive damages in a libel case in Canada was $50,000 ... . One of the strengths of the jury system is that it keeps the law in touch with evolving realities, including financial realities. ...

[140] Having accepted with some hesitation the adequacy of the trial judge's instructions to the jury, and there being no convincing demonstration that the jury's subsequent imposition and assessment of punitive damages were irrational, I would affirm the award of punitive damages. ...

[141] I would allow the appeal and restore the jury award of $1 million in punitive damages, with costs in this Court and in the Court of Appeal on a party-and-party basis.

[142] The respondent's cross-appeal against the award of any punitive damages is dismissed with costs to the appellant, also on a party-and-party basis.

• • •

LeBEL J (dissenting):

[147] The purpose of this part of our legal system remains to make good the loss suffered, no less, no more ... .

[148] The award of punitive damages in discussion here leads us far away from that principle. It tends to turn tort law upside down. It transmogrifies what should have remained an incident of a contracts case into the central issue of the dispute. The main purpose of the action becomes the search for punishment, not compensation ... .

[See also McCamus at 944-63; MacDougall at 378-79; Waddams at paras 740-41.]

NOTES

1. In *Performance Industries Ltd v Sylvan Lake Golf & Tennis Club Ltd*, [2002] 1 SCR 678, decided concurrently with *Whiten*, the court unanimously upheld the setting aside of an award of $200,000 punitive damages for fraud, on the ground that the award would serve no rational purpose. Binnie J said (at para 87) that "fraud is generally reprehensible, but only in exceptional cases does it attract punitive damages."

2. The economic concept of "efficient breach" asserts that it is not always desirable to deter breach of contract, because breach may in some cases enhance the joint welfare of the contracting parties: the plaintiff (on receipt of full compensatory damages) is no worse off than she would have been on performance, and the defendant, if he finds a more valuable use of his resources, is better off. In *Bank of America Canada v Mutual Trust Co*, [2002] 2 SCR 601, decided two months after *Whiten*, the court said that "[e]fficient breach should not be discouraged by the courts. This lack of disapproval emphasizes that a court will usually award money damages for breach of contract equal to the value of the bargain to the plaintiff."

3. Punitive damages were refused by the Supreme Court of Canada in both *Fidler* and *Keays*, above.

VI. MITIGATION OF LOSS

PAYZU LIMITED V SAUNDERS
[1919] 2 KB 581 (CA)

[By a contract in writing, dated November 9, 1917, the defendant, who was a dealer in silk, agreed to sell the plaintiffs 200 pieces of crepe de Chine at 4s. 6d. a yard and 200 pieces at 5s. 11d. a yard, "delivery as required January to September, 1918; conditions 2½ percent 1 month," which meant that payment for goods delivered up to the 20th day of the month should be made on the 20th day of the following month, subject to a 2½ percent discount. At the request of the plaintiffs, the defendant delivered, in November 1917, a certain quantity of the goods under the contract, the price of which amounted to £76 less the 2½ percent discount. On December 21 the plaintiffs drew a cheque in favour of the defendant in payment of these goods, but the cheque was never received by the defendant. Early in January 1918, the defendant telephoned to the plaintiffs asking why she had not received a cheque. The plaintiffs then drew another cheque, but owing to a delay in obtaining the signature of one of the plaintiffs' directors, this cheque was not sent to the defendant until January 16. On that day the plaintiffs gave an order by telephone for further deliveries under the contract. The defendant, in the belief, which was in fact erroneous, that the plaintiffs' financial position was such that they could not have met the cheque that they alleged had been drawn in December, wrote to the plaintiffs on January 16, refusing to make any further deliveries under the contract, unless the plaintiffs paid cash with each order. The plaintiffs refused to do this, and after some further correspondence brought this action claiming damages for breach of contract. The damages claimed were the difference between the market price in the middle of February 1918 and the contract price of the two classes of goods; the difference alleged being respectively 1s. 3d. and 1s. 4d. a yard.]

McCARDIE J: ... [I]n my opinion, the defendant's letter of January 16 did in fact and in law amount to an unjustifiable refusal by her to carry out her contractual obligations, for she announced in clear terms that she would thenceforth deliver no further goods to the plaintiffs under the contract unless the plaintiffs paid cash to cover each invoice. The market price of these goods was rising from the beginning of January and continued to rise up to the middle of February. The plaintiffs claim to be entitled to damages based on the market price at that date. I find as a fact that the market prices in February were respectively 6d. and 7d. per yard in excess of the contract prices. The plaintiffs did not in fact purchase goods as against their contract with the defendant. They asserted that the market was so bare of goods as to render purchases impracticable.

Now a serious question of law arises on the question of damages. I find as a fact that the defendant was ready and willing to supply the goods to the plaintiffs at the times and places specified in the contract, provided the plaintiffs paid cash on delivery. Mr. Matthews [of counsel for the plaintiffs] argued with characteristic vigour and ability that the plaintiffs were entitled to ignore that offer on the ground that a person who has repudiated a contract cannot place the other party to the contract under an obligation to diminish his loss by accepting a new offer made by the party in default.

The question is one of juristic importance. What is the rule of law as to the duty to mitigate damages? I will first refer to the judgment of Cockburn C.J., in *Frost v. Knight* (1872), L.R. 7 Ex. 111, 115, where he said: "In assessing the damages for breach of the performance, a jury will of course take into account whatever the plaintiff has done, or has had the means of doing and, as a prudent man, ought in reason to have done, whereby his loss has been or would have been, diminished." ...

The question, therefore, is what a prudent person ought reasonably to do in order to mitigate his loss arising from a breach of contract. I feel no inclination to allow in a mercantile dispute an unhappy indulgence in farfetched resentment or an undue sensitiveness to slights or unfortunately worded letters. Business often gives rise to certain asperities. But I agree that the plaintiffs in deciding whether to accept the defendant's offer were fully entitled to consider the terms in which the offer was made, its bona fides or otherwise, its relation to their own business methods and financial position, and all the circumstances of the case; and it must be remembered that an acceptance of the offer would not preclude an action for damages for the actual loss sustained. Many illustrations might be given of the extraordinary results which would follow if the plaintiffs were entitled to reject the defendant's offer and incur a substantial measure of loss which would have been avoided by their accept-ance of the offer. The plaintiffs were in fact in a position to pay cash for the goods but instead of accepting the defendant's offer, which was made perfectly bona fide, the plaintiffs permitted themselves to sustain a large measure of loss which as pru-dent and reasonable people, they ought to have avoided. But the fact that the plain-tiffs have claimed damages on an erroneous principle does not preclude me from awarding to them such damages as they have in fact suffered, calculated upon the correct bases. ... They have suffered serious and substantial business inconvenience, and I conceive that I am entitled to award them damages for that. ... Moreover, even if the plaintiffs had accepted the defendant's offer, they would nevertheless have lost a very useful period of credit which the contract gave them. Taking into considera-tion all the circumstances of the case I have come to the conclusion that the right sum to award as damages is £50. I give judgment for the plaintiffs for that amount, and in view of the important points involved, I give costs on the High Court Scale.

[The plaintiffs appealed to the Court of Appeal on the question of damages.]

BANKS LJ: At the trial of this case the defendant, the present respondent, raised two points: first, that she had committed no breach of the contract of sale, and secondly that, if there was a breach, yet she had offered and was always ready and willing to supply the pieces of silk, the subject of the contract, at the contract price for cash; that it was unreasonable on the part of the appellants not to accept that offer, and that therefore they cannot claim damages beyond what they would have lost by paying cash with each order instead of having a month's credit and a discount of 2½ per cent. We must take it that this was the offer made by the respondent. The case was fought and the learned judge has given judgment on that footing. It is true that the correspondence suggests that the respondent was at one time claiming an increased price. But in this court it must be taken that the offer was to supply the contract goods at the contract price except that payment was to be by cash instead of being on credit.

In these circumstances the only question is whether the appellants can establish that as a matter of law they were not bound to consider any offer made by the respondent because of the attitude she had taken up. ...

It is plain that the question what is reasonable for a person to do in mitigation of his damages cannot be a question of law but must be one of fact in the circumstances of each particular case. There may be cases where as matter of fact it would be unreasonable to expect a plaintiff to consider any offer made in view of the treatment he had received from the defendant. If he had been rendering personal services and had been dismissed after being accused in presence of others of being a thief, and if after that his employer had offered to take him back into his service, most persons would think he was justified in refusing the offer and that it would be unreasonable to ask him in this way to mitigate the damages in an action of wrongful dismissal. But that is not to state a principle of law, but a conclusion of fact to be arrived at on a consideration of all the circumstances of the case. Mr. Matthews complained that the respondents had treated his clients so badly that it would be unreasonable to expect them to listen to any proposition she might make. I do not agree. In my view each party was ready to accuse the other of conduct unworthy of a high commercial reputation and there was nothing to justify the appellants in refusing to consider the respondent's offer. I think the learned judge came to a proper conclusion on the facts, and that the appeal must be dismissed.

SCRUTTON LJ: I am of the same opinion. Whether it be more correct to say that a plaintiff must minimize his damages, or to say that he can recover no more than he would have suffered if he had acted reasonably, because any further damages do not reasonably follow from the defendant's breach, the result is the same. ... In certain cases of personal service it may be unreasonable to expect a plaintiff to consider an offer from the other party who has grossly injured him; but in commercial contracts it is generally reasonable to accept an offer from the party in default. However, it is always a question of fact. About the law there is no difficulty.

Appeal dismissed.

[Parts of the opinions reproduced, as well as Eve J's opinion, are omitted.]

ROTH & CO V TAYSEN, TOWNSEND & CO
(1896), 1 Comm Cas 306 (CA)

[This was an action for damages for the non-acceptance by the defendants, Grant and Grahame, of a cargo of maize. The alleged contract was contained in telegrams that passed between the parties on May 23, 1895, and the trial judge and the Court of Appeal found it to be a contract to ship the cargo by a named ship, the ship to be ready to load on July 15, and the buyers to have the power of cancelling on August 15 if the ship was not ready to load by that day. On May 29 the defendants repudiated. The plaintiff did not sue until July 24 and did not resell the cargo until September 5, the last day in which a delivery might have been made under the contract. The resale on September 5 was at a loss of £3807 3s. 8d. The trial court (Matthew J) fixed the damages at £1,557, which would have been the amount of the loss if the cargo had been sold on July 24, when the plaintiffs issued the writ.

Against this judgment the defendants, Grant and Grahame, appealed on the ground that there was no binding contract between the parties, and that the damages were excessive. The damages, they contended, if payable, were £688 only, the amount of the loss if the cargo had been sold on May 29, when they repudiated the contract. The plaintiffs entered a cross-appeal, claiming by way of damages £3,807 3s. 8d., the amount of the loss sustained by the sale of the cargo on September 5.]

LORD ESHER MR: ... Then comes the question of damages. When there is a repudiation which the other party chooses to treat as a breach, the primary rule is that the damages are the difference between the contract price and the market price of the goods at the date of the breach. If the repudiation takes place before the day of delivery, the other party has the right to bring an action immediately, and it follows that he has the right to have his damages assessed at the time he brings his action. In such a case the damages are not the difference between the contract and market price on the day the action is brought. It is the duty of the jury to assess them, having regard to, and making allowance for, the fact that the party plaintiff is receiving damages before the date of delivery has arrived. There is this further rule. The party who has treated a repudiation as a breach is bound to do what is reasonable to prevent the damages from being inflamed or increased. Now, did the plaintiffs do what was unreasonable in declining to sell till September 5? ...

The evidence before the judge was that the market was falling steadily from day to day and from week to week, and was still falling when the writ was issued. Any one acquainted with the market must have seen the strong probability that the market would continue to fall. The plaintiffs had no right to suppose that the market would begin to rise, and no ordinary business man who was not a speculator would have thought that it was likely to do so. Buyers were refusing to come forward, being of opinion that they would have to sell at a still lower price. The judge had the right to come to the conclusion, as a jury, that ordinary business men (such as the plaintiffs), who were desirous of diminishing the loss, would have sold the maize at an earlier date, and I cannot undertake to say that his finding was wrong. The appeal and the cross-appeal therefore fail.

LOPES LJ: ... What are the plaintiff's rights? Ever since the case of *Hochster v. De La Tour* (1852), 118 E.R. 922, it has been the rule that if a payor repudiates a contract and the payee accepts his repudiation, the payee may bring an action. If no time has been fixed for the fulfilment of the contract, the plaintiff is entitled to such damage as he has sustained calculated at the date of the breach; if a time has been fixed for fulfilment, the damages are the loss of the plaintiff calculated as at the date of fulfilment. Here the breach was on July 24. The plaintiffs were bound to take reasonable steps to mitigate the damages; and, if they could have sold the cargo at any time previous to the date of fulfilment of the contract, or about the time of the breach, they ought to have done so. The learned judge held that they might have sold, and that they ought to have done so, about July 24. It is said for the plaintiffs that, though there is that rule of law, there was no evidence upon which a judge or jury could hold that it would have been prudent for the plaintiffs to sell. Of course, it is true that if the plaintiffs had sold and the market had then risen, they might have been told that they were wrong to sell; but I think that they were indiscreet in holding on when the market was falling, and that they would have been well advised if they had sold at an earlier date. The learned judge has held that they did not act reasonably, and I am not prepared to say that he was wrong. I think the amount of damages which he awarded was right.

RIGBY LJ: ... The only question, then, is as to the measure of damages. Now, taking in its full effect in favour of the plaintiffs the rule laid down in *Roper v. Johnson* (1873), L.R. 8 C.P. 167, it may be that prima facie, this being the breach of a contract to deliver goods, the damages are to be assessed as at the agreed date of delivery. But here the plaintiffs put an end to the contract at an earlier date. Judges have always held that a person availing himself of his right to accept repudiation of a contract must take measures to mitigate the damages which he has sustained by the breach. It is true that by so doing he may take some risk upon himself, but the tribunal will take that fact into consideration. In the present case there seems to be sufficient evidence though it is not conclusive, to justify the learned judge in holding that the plaintiffs ought to have sold the cargo when they put an end to the contract by accepting the defendants' repudiation. I gather that there was evidence that the market was falling, and that the state of things did not render a recovery of prices probable within a reasonable time. I cannot accept the argument of Mr. Bigham [of counsel for the plaintiffs] that it is sufficient to show that the plaintiffs acted to the best of their judgment. The standard which one must use in these cases is the conduct of an ordinary prudent man under similar circumstances. The result is that both appeals must be dismissed.

Appeal and cross-appeal dismissed.

[Only that part of the case dealing with the question of damages is reproduced.]

PROBLEMS

1. C bought a house with the assistance of her solicitor, D. A year later, a defect in the title of the house came to light, and C sued D for negligence. D admitted the negligence, but on the question of damages, claimed that C should have mitigated her loss by suing the vendor, E. Advise C. See *Pilkington v Wood*, [1953] Ch 770.

2. P was employed as general manager of Q Company. He had an employment contract for five years at $5,000 a year. After three years, Q Company went bankrupt and P was dismissed. At this point, P bought certain goods from Q Company, and sold them to make $11,000 profit. P now sues for damages for wrongful dismissal. Advise Q Company. See *Cockburn v Trusts & Guarantee Co* (1917), 55 SCR 264, 37 DLR 159.

3. Pharmacist B supplied tranquilizers instead of birth control pills to C, a married woman with seven children. As a result, an unwelcome eighth child was born. B claims that C has suffered no damages, or, alternatively, that she should have mitigated her loss either by abortion or by giving the child up for adoption. Advise C. See *Troppi v Scarf*, 187 NW 2d 511 (Mich CA 1971).

4. F, who operated a ski resort, bought a ski lift from P. The lift proved defective, F lost all his customers, and his business was ruined. He could not mitigate those losses because he had no money to purchase another ski lift. Is P liable for the loss of the business? See *Freedhoff v Pomalift Industries Ltd*, [1971] 2 OR 773 (CA); *All-Up Consulting Enterprises Inc v Dalrymple*, 2013 NSSC 46 at para 215.

5. A, in breach of contract, delivers defective goods to B, who has agreed to supply them to C, an old customer. The contract between B and C contains a clause in fine print exempting B from liability to C, and obliging C to pay for the goods even if defective. B buys sound goods from another seller and delivers them to C. In B's action against A, A argues that B should have mitigated his loss by foisting the defective goods on C in accordance with B's strict rights. B replies that he could not so treat an old and valued customer. Advise A. See *James Finlay & Co v NV Kwik Hoo Tong HM*, [1929] 1 KB 400.

6. B enters into an employment contract providing that if B's employment is terminated without cause, B will receive six months' notice or pay in lieu thereof. B's employment is terminated without cause, and B immediately finds alternative employment at the same salary. Is B entitled to six months' pay? See *Bowes v Goss Power Products Ltd*, 2012 ONCA 425.

WHITE & CARTER (COUNCILS), LTD V MCGREGOR
[1962] AC 413 (HL (Scot))

LORD REID: My Lords, the pursuers supply to local authorities litter bins which are placed in the streets. They are allowed to attach to these receptacles plates carrying advertisement and they make their profit from payments made to them by the advertisers. The defender carried on a garage in Clydebank and in 1954 he made an agreement with the pursuers under which they displayed advertisements of his business on a number of these bins. In June 1957, his sales manager made a further contract with the pursuers for the display of these advertisements for a further period of three years. The sales manager had been given no specific authority to make this contract and when the defender heard of it later on the same day he at once wrote to the pursuers to cancel the contract. The pursuers refused to accept this cancellation.

[The contract itself stated that it could not be cancelled by the advertiser.]

They prepared the necessary plates for attachment to the bins and exhibited them on the bins from Nov. 2, 1957, onwards.

[It was found by the Court of Session and the Sheriff Court that the appellants made no effort to minimize their loss by procuring another advertiser to take up the advertising space included in the contract.]

The defender refused to pay any sums due under the contract and the pursuers raised the present action in the Sheriff Court craving payment of £196 4s., the full sum due under the contract for the period of three years. After sundry procedure the sheriff-substitute on Mar. 15, 1960 dismissed the action. He held that the sales manager's action in renewing the contract was within his apparent or ostensible authority and that is not now disputed. The ground on which he dismissed the action was that in the circumstances an action for implement of the contract was inappropriate. He relied on the decision in *Langford & Co., Ltd. v. Dutch*, [1952] S.C. 15, and cannot be criticised for having done so.

The pursuers appealed to the Court of Session and on Nov. 29, 1960, the Second Division refused the appeal. The present appeal is taken against their interlocutor of that date. That interlocutor sets out detailed findings of fact and, as this case began in the Sheriff Court, we cannot look beyond those findings. The pursuers must show that on those findings they are entitled to the remedy which they seek.

The case for the defender (now the respondent) is that, as he repudiated the contract before anything had been done under it, the appellants were not entitled to go on and carry out the contract and sue for the contract price: he maintains that in the circumstances the appellants' only remedy was damages, and that, as they do not sue for damages, this action was rightly dismissed.

The contract was for the display of advertisements for a period of 156 weeks from the date when the display began. This date was not specified but admittedly the display began on Nov. 2, 1957, which seems to have been the date when the former contract came to an end. The payment stipulated was 2s. per week per plate together with 5s. per annum per plate both payable annually in advance, the first payment being due seven days after the first display. The reason why the appellants sued for the whole sum due for the three years is to be found in cl. 8 of the conditions:

> 8. In the event of an instalment or part thereof being due for payment, and remaining unpaid for a period of four weeks or in the event of the advertiser being in any way in breach of this contract then the whole amount due for the 156 weeks or such part of the said 156 weeks as the advertiser shall not yet have paid shall immediately become due and payable.

A question was debated whether this clause provides a penalty or liquidated damages but on the view which I take of the case it need not be pursued. The clause merely provides for acceleration of payment of the stipulated price if the advertiser fails to pay an instalment timeously. As the respondent maintained that he was not bound by the contract he did not pay the first instalment within the time allowed.

Accordingly, if the appellants were entitled to carry out their part of the contract notwithstanding the respondent's repudiation, it was hardly disputed that this clause entitled them to sue immediately for the whole price and not merely for the first instalment.

The general rule cannot be in doubt. It was settled in Scotland at least as early as 1848 and it has been authoritatively stated time and again in both Scotland and England. If one party to a contract repudiates it in the sense of making it clear to the other party that he refuses or will refuse to carry out his part of the contract, the other party, the innocent party, has an option. He may accept that repudiation and sue for damages for breach of contract whether or not the time for performance has come; or he may if he chooses disregard or refuse to accept it and then the contract remains in full effect. ...

I need not refer to the numerous authorities. They are not disputed by the respondent but he points out that in all of them the party who refused to accept the repudiation had no active duties under the contract. The innocent party's opinion is generally said to be to wait until the date of performance and then to claim damages estimated as at that date. There is no case in which it is said that he may, in face of the repudiation, go on and incur useless expense in performing the contract and then claim the contract price. The option, it is argued, is merely as to the date as at which damages are to be assessed. Developing this argument, the respondent points out that in most cases the innocent party cannot complete the contract himself without the other party doing, allowing or accepting something and that it is purely fortuitous that the appellants can do so in this case. In most cases by refusing co-operation the party in breach can compel the innocent party to restrict his claim to damages. Then it was said that even where the innocent party can complete the contract without such co-operation it is against the public interest that he should be allowed to do so. An example was developed in argument. A company might engage an expert to go abroad and prepare an elaborate report and then repudiate the contract before anything was done. To allow such an expert then to waste thousands of pounds in preparing the report cannot be right if a much smaller sum of damages would give him full compensation for his loss. It would merely enable the expert to extort a settlement giving him far more than reasonable compensation.

The respondent founds on the decision of the First Division in *Langford & Co., Ltd. v. Dutch*. There an advertising contractor agreed to exhibit a film for a year. Four days after this agreement was made the advertiser repudiated it but, as in the present case, the contractor refused to accept the repudiation and proceeded to exhibit the film and sue for the contract price. The sheriff-substitute dismissed the action as irrelevant and his decision was affirmed on appeal. In the course of a short opinion the Lord President (Lord Cooper) said:

> It appears to me that, apart from wholly exceptional circumstances of which there is no trace in the averments on this record, the law of Scotland does not afford to a person in the position of the pursuers the remedy which is here sought. The pursuers could not force the defender to accept a year's advertisement which she did not want, though they could of course claim damages for her breach of contract. On the averments the only reasonable and proper course, which the pursuers should have adopted, would have been to treat the defender as having repudiated the contract and as being on that account liable in damages, the measure of which we are, of course, not in a position to discuss.

The Lord President cited no authority and I am in doubt what principle he had in mind. In the earlier part of the passage which I have quoted he speaks of forcing the defender to accept the advertisement. Of course, if it had been necessary for the defender to do or accept anything before the contract could be completed by the pursuers, the pursuers could not and the court would not have compelled the defender to act, the contract would not have been completed, and the pursuers' only remedy would have been damages. But the peculiarity in that case, as in the present case, was that the pursuers could completely fulfil the contract without any co-operation of the defender. The Lord President cannot have meant that because of non-acceptance the contract had not been completely carried out, because that in itself would have been a complete answer to an action for the contract price. He went on to say that the only reasonable and proper course which the pursuers should have adopted would have been to treat the defender as having repudiated the contract, which must, I think, mean to have accepted the repudiation. It is this reference to "the only reasonable and proper course" which I find difficult to explain. It might be, but it never has been the law that a person is only entitled to enforce his contractual rights in a reasonable way and that a court will not support an attempt to enforce them in an unreasonable way. One reason why that is not the law is no doubt because it was thought that it would create too much uncertainty to require the court to decide whether it is reasonable or equitable to allow a party to enforce his full rights under a contract. The Lord President cannot have meant that. ...

Langford & Co. Ltd. v. Dutch is indistinguishable from the present case. Quite properly the Second Division followed it in this case as a binding authority and did not develop Lord Cooper's reasoning: they were not asked to send this case to a larger court. We must now decide whether that case was rightly decided. In my judgment it was not. It could only be supported on one or other of two grounds. It might be said that, because in most cases the circumstances are such that an innocent party is unable to complete the contract and earn the contract price without the assent or co-operation of the other party, therefore in cases where he can do so he should not be allowed to do so. I can see no justification for that.

The other ground would be that there is some general equitable principle or element of public policy which requires this limitation of the contractual rights of the innocent party. It may well be that, if it can be shown that a person has no legitimate interest, financial or otherwise, in performing the contract rather than claiming damages, he ought not to be allowed to saddle the other party with an additional burden with no benefit to himself. If a party has no interest to enforce a stipulation he cannot in general enforce it: so it might be said that if a party has no interest to insist on a particular remedy he ought not to be allowed to insist on it. And, just as a party is not allowed to enforce a penalty, so he ought not to be allowed to penalise the other party by taking one course when another is equally advantageous to him. If I may revert to the example which I gave of a company engaging an expert to prepare an elaborate report and then repudiating before anything was done, it might be that the company could show that the expert had no substantial or legitimate interest in carrying out the work rather than accepting damages. I would think that the de minimis principle would apply in determining whether his interest was substantial and that he might have a legitimate interest other than an immediate financial interest. But if the expert had no such interest then that might be regarded as a proper case for the exercise of the general equitable jurisdiction of the court. But that is not this case. Here the respondent did not set out to prove that the appellants had no legitimate interest in completing the contract and claiming the contract price rather than claiming damages, there is nothing in the findings of fact to support such a case, and it seems improbable that any such case could have been proved. It is, in my judgment, impossible to say that the appellants should be deprived of their right to claim the contract price merely because the benefit to them as against claim-ing damages and reletting their advertising space might be small in comparison with the loss to the respondent: that is the most that could be said in favour of the respondent. Parliament has on many occasions relieved parties from certain kinds of improvident or oppressive contracts, but the common law can only do that in very limited circumstances. Accordingly, I am unable to avoid the conclusion that this appeal must be allowed and the case remitted so that decree can be pronounced as craved in the initial writ.

LORD MORTON OF HENRYTON (dissenting): My Lords, the facts of this case have already been fully stated. It is plain that the respondent (defender in the action) repudiated the contract of June 26, 1957, immediately after his sales manager had entered into it and some months before the time for performance of it by the appellants, and per-sisted in his repudiation throughout. Notwithstanding this, the appellants proceeded with the preparation of plates advertising the respondent's garage business and, as the sheriff-substitute held, they "made no effort to procure another advertiser to take up the advertising space included in said contract and thus minimise their loss."

The plates were first exhibited on the litter bins on Nov. 2, 1957, and they remained on display during the whole of the contract period of 156 weeks. The respondent throughout made it clear that he did not want the advertisements and refused to pay for them. The present action is brought to recover £196 4s., the full sum payable under the contract. Alternatively, the appellants claim the same sum as liquidated damages. The respondent contends that in the circumstances of the present case the only remedy of the appellants was damages, to be assessed according to ordinary principles.

My Lords, I think that this is a case of great importance, although the claim is for a comparatively small sum. If the appellants are right, strange consequences follow in any case in which, under a repudiated contract, services are to be performed by the party who has not repudiated it, so long as he is able to perform these services without the co-operation of the repudiating party. Many examples of such contracts could be given. One, given in the course of the argument and already mentioned by my noble and learned friend, Lord Reid, is the engagement of an expert to go abroad and write a report on some subject for a substantial fee plus his expenses. If the appellants succeed in the present case, it must follow that the expert is entitled to incur the expense of going abroad, to write his unwanted report, and then to recover the fee and expenses, even if the other party has plainly repudiated the contract before any expense has been incurred.

It is well established that repudiation by one party does not put an end to a con-tract. The other party can say "I hold you to your contract, which still remains in force." What, then, is his remedy if the repudiating party persists in his repudiation and refuses to carry out his part of the contract? The contract has been broken. The innocent party is entitled to be compensated by damages for any loss which he has suffered by reason of the breach, and in a limited class of cases the court will decree specific implement. The law of Scotland provides no other remedy for a breach of contract, and there is no reported case which decides that the innocent party may act as the appellants have acted. The present case is one in which specific implement could not be decreed, since the only obligation of the respondent under the contract was to pay a sum of money for services to be rendered by the appellants. Yet the appellants are claiming a kind of inverted specific implement of the contract. They first insist on performing their part of the contract, against the will of the other party, and then claim that he must perform his part and pay the contract price for unwanted services. In my opinion, my Lords, the appellants' only remedy was damages and they were bound to take steps to minimise their loss, according to a well-established rule of law. Far from doing this, having incurred no expense at the date of the repudiation, they made no attempt to procure another advertiser, but deliberately went on to incur expense and perform unwanted services with the intention of creating a money debt which did not exist at the date of the repudiation.

The only cases cited in which a claim of the kind now put forward has been considered are *Langford & Co. Ltd. v. Dutch* when it was rejected by the Court of Session, and *White & Carter (Councils) Ltd.* [that is, the present appellants] *v. A.R. Harding* (May 21, 1958; unreported). The latter case is, I think, distinguishable from the present case; but, if it cannot be distinguished, it was, in my opinion, wrongly decided by the Court of Appeal. The former case is directly in point and was, in my opinion, rightly decided, and rightly followed by the Court of Session in the present case.

The facts in Langford's case have been stated by my noble and learned friend, Lord Reid. The Court of Session held that the law of Scotland did not "afford to a person in the position of the pursuers the remedy which is here sought." These words are quoted from the short opinion of the Lord President (Lord Cooper), and he continued:

> [T]he pursuers could not force the defender to accept a year's advertisement which she did not want, though they could of course claim damages for her breach of contract.

These two sentences embodied, I think the basis of the learned Lord President's opinion, but he added:

> On the averments the only reasonable and proper course, which the pursuers should have adopted, would have been to treat the defender as having repudiated the contract and as being on that account liable in damages the measure of which we are, of course, not in a position to discuss.

My Lords, I think that this last sentence was merely a comment on the behaviour of the pursuers, which applies with equal force to the appellants in the present case. The course of action followed by the appellants seems to me unreasonable and oppressive, but it is not on that ground that I would reject their claim. I would reject it for the reasons which I have already given. ...

I would dismiss the appeal.

LORD KEITH OF AVONHOLM (dissenting): ... The contract was to come into operation on Nov. 2, 1957, when the previous contract expired. But it involved, in the absence of other advertising matter supplied by the defender, the display by the appellants of at least the name, business and address of the advertiser. I should hesitate to say that any contractor was entitled to display these particulars of the defender against his wish, even if the withholding of his assent be in breach of contract.

Some play was made by counsel for the appellants with an expression used by Asquith L.J., in *Howard v. Pickford Tool Co., Ltd.,* [1951] 1 K.B. 417 at p. 421 that "[a]n unaccepted repudiation is a thing writ in water ... ." A graphic phrase or expression has its uses even in a law report and can give force to a legal principle, but it must be related to the circumstances in which it is used. Howard was a managing director with a six years contract of service. He thought that the company with which he was serving had shown by the conduct of its chairman that it no longer intended to be bound by its agreement. He brought an action which, as amended, sought a declaration that the company by so acting had repudiated the contract and excused the plaintiff from further performance and his obligations under it. Evershed M.R., said at p. 420:

It is quite plain ... that if the conduct of one party to a contract amounts to a repudiation, and the other party does not accept it as such but goes on performing his part of the contract and affirms the contract, the alleged act of repudiation is wholly nugatory and ineffective in law.

Asquith L.J. said:

An unaccepted repudiation is a thing writ in water and of no value to anybody: it confers no legal rights of any sort or kind.

The declaration was held to be academic and the claim struck out. These observations must be read in the light of the facts which they relate. They were directed to an alleged repudiation unaccepted by the man who said there was a repudiation before any cause of action had arisen. At best the case was no more than one of an intended repudiation, for performance was going on. The servant was still serving and the employer was continuing to employ him. What the court was saying was that the plaintiff had at that time no cause of action. But in the case of repudiation of a contract when performance is tendered, or due to be given by the other party, the repudiation cannot be said to be writ in water. It gives rise immediately to a cause of action. This does not involve acceptance of the repudiation. There has been a breach of contract which the complaining party denies the other had any right to commit. I know of no authority for saying that the offended party can go quietly on as if the contract still continued to be fully operative between both parties. He is put to his remedy at the date of the breach. It has been said that when an anticipatory repudiation is not treated as a cause of action the contract remains alive. It does until the contract would become operative, when the repudiation, if still maintained, then becomes a cause of action and all pleas and defences then existing are available to the respective parties.

The party complaining of the breach also has a duty to minimize the damage he has suffered, which is a further reason for saying that after the date of breach he cannot continue to carry on his part of an executory contract. A breach of a contract of employment will serve to illustrate the nature of this duty. A person is engaged to serve for a certain period, say three months, to commence at a future date. When that date arrives the prospective employer wrongfully refuses to honour the engagement. The servant is not entitled to see out the three months and then sue the recalcitrant employer for three months' wages. He must take steps by seeking other employment to minimize his loss. It is true, of course, that a servant cannot invoke a contract to force himself on an unwilling master, any more than a master can enforce the service of an unwilling servant. But if the appellants' contention is sound, it is difficult to see why, by parity of reasoning, it should not apply to a person who keeps himself free to perform the duties of his contract of service during the whole period of the contract and is prevented from doing so by the refusal of the other contracting party. Yet in *Hochster v. De La Tour*, from which the whole law about anticipatory repudiation stems, Lord Campbell C.J., plainly indicated that if the courier in that case, instead of accepting as he did the repudiation of his engagement as a cause of action, before it was due to commence, had waited till the lapse of the three months of the engagement he could not have sued as for a debt. The jury, he said, would be entitled to look at all that might "increase or mitigate the loss of the plaintiff down to the day of trial." There is no difference in this matter between the law of England and the law of Scotland. ...

This brings me to *Langford & Co. Ltd. v. Dutch*. I took part in the judgment in this case, though the only opinion delivered in the case was given by the Lord President (Lord Cooper), with whom I and the other judges of the division concurred. The judgment was not a reserved judgment and the case was not, I think, so fully argued as the case now before your Lordships. It is, if rightly decided, determinative of the present appeal and is, so far as I am aware, the only other case in which the question raised on this appeal has ever been considered. ... I have reconsidered the decision in *Langford & Co. Ltd. v. Dutch* in the light of the further argument on this appeal. I have come to the conclusion that it was rightly decided and that the Second Division in the present case was bound to follow it. ...

[Lord Tucker agreed with Lord Hodson, whose decision is omitted, in allowing the appeal. The opinion of Lord Keith is considerably cut.]

NOTE

White & Carter v McGregor was criticized by Goodhart in (1962) 78 LQR 263. Goodhart gives the example of an order placed for the building of an expensive machine, and then immediately cancelled. If the law is that the seller can disregard the cancellation, build the machine (now useless to the buyer) and claim the full price, it follows that the seller would be in the position to demand a very large sum from the buyer as payment for the surrender of the right to build the machine. Professor Goodhart points out that American authority almost unanimously holds that the innocent party to an anticipatory breach of contract must take reasonable steps to mitigate his loss, and that the American Law Institute's *Restatement of Contracts* is to this effect (s 388). Goodhart concludes: "In the present case there can be no question that if the pursuers had sued the defender on the day when he gave notice of repudiation they could have recovered as damages only the reasonable profits they would have made; it seems odd that by deliberately doing something that was of no value to the defender they could increase the damages he had to pay."

FINELLI V DEE
(1968), 67 DLR (2d) 393 (Ont CA)

LASKIN JA (orally): This case arises out of a written contract between the plaintiffs and the male defendant, for the paving of the driveway at the defendants' home. The contract was made on June 18, 1966, and while a price was fixed and other terms included, it did not fix any particular time for the commencement or completion of the work. It appears from the evidence that the parties agreed that the work would not begin immediately because the defendant was then in no position to pay for it, but that it would be performed sometime in October or about that time, in 1966.

There is evidence, which was accepted by the trial judge, that the defendant telephoned the office of the plaintiffs, after the contract was made and before any performance was contemplated, cancelling the contract, and that the plaintiff's sales manager at the office who received the telephone call, agreed that it would be cancelled. On or about November 1, 1966, when the defendants were away from home, the plaintiffs carried out the contract and the defendants were confronted with the completed work on their return to their premises in the evening. The plaintiffs sued for the price of the work done under the contract but their claim was rejected by the trial judge.

On appeal, a question was raised whether the cancellation of the contract amounted to rescission or simply represented a repudiation by the defendant. Of course, if there was rescission (and I should say that, notwithstanding the contrary argument of the plaintiffs' counsel, rescission could be effected by oral agreement even though the contract in question was in writing), then there would be no basis on which an action to enforce the provision as to price could be founded. If, on the other hand, the cancellation amounted to repudiation, a question arises as to the applicability of the principles canvassed by the House of Lords in *White & Carter (Councils), Ltd. v. McGregor*, [1961] 3 All E.R. 1178. It was the view of the majority of that Court that a repudiation by one party to a contract does not preclude the innocent party from carrying out the contract and suing for the price, at least where this can be done without the assent or cooperation of the party in breach. I am not, of course, bound by this judgment, but, respecting as I do the considered opinion of the majority, I must say that I am attracted by the reasons of the two dissenting members of the Court. Repudiation is not something that calls for acceptance when there is no question of rescission, but merely excuses the innocent party from performance and leaves him free to sue for damages. But, even accepting the majority view in the *McGregor* case, I should point out that it was a case in which the innocent party could carry out the contract notwithstanding the repudiation, without the assent or cooperation of the party in breach. This is not the situation here.

In the first place, it was necessary for the plaintiffs to enter upon the defendants' land in order to perform; and without wishing to embark on any issue as to trespass, the plaintiffs, in my view, were obliged to give previous intimation to the defendant that they were prepared to do the work called for by the contract and proposed to do it on a certain day. This, of course, was not done.

It follows that whether the cancellation amounts to rescission or merely to repudiation by the defendant, the plaintiffs are not entitled to recover the contract price. Accordingly, I would dismiss the appeal with costs and with a counsel fee of $25 to the defendants.

Appeal dismissed.

NOTES AND QUESTIONS

1. In *Hounslow London Borough Council v Twickenham Garden Developments Ltd*, [1971] 1 Ch 233, the defendant, a building contractor, refused to leave the plaintiff's building site and continued to work, despite the council's demand that he depart. The plaintiff's repudiation was found to be in breach of contract, but the plaintiff sought an interim injunction to keep the defendant off the site. The court, although holding that *White & Carter v McGregor* did not apply, refused to grant the injunction on the basis that equity would not assist a breach of contract.

2. C delivered some pictures to M to be cleaned. After M had begun work on the pictures, C changed his mind and asked M to stop. M refused, completed cleaning the pictures, and now sues C for the full price agreed. Advise C. Would it make any difference if C's repudiation was based on expert advice that cleaning the pictures would reduce their value on the art market? Would M be liable in tort for that reduction in value? See *Clark v Marsiglia*, 43 Am Dec 670 (NYSC 1843).

3. In *Asamera Oil Corp Ltd v Sea Oil & General Corp*, [1979] 1 SCR 633, the defendant had wrongfully failed to return shares in 1960. Their value then was 29¢. They subsequently rose to a value of $46.50, falling back by the time of the trial to $22.00. The Supreme Court of Canada held that damages were to be assessed at the date when, acting reasonably, the plaintiff could have purchased substitute shares. In the circumstances, this led to damages based on a share value of $6.50. Estey J referred to *White & Carter v McGregor* as follows:

It is, of course, an eminently reasonable position to take if, as Lord Reid suggests in *White & Carter (Councils) Ltd. v. McGregor*, [1962] A.C. 413, in the case of anticipatory breach, there is a substantial and legitimate interest in looking to performance of a contractual obligation. So a plaintiff who has agreed to purchase a particular piece of real estate, or a block of shares which represent control of a company, or has entered into performance of his own obligations, and where to discontinue performance might aggravate his losses, might well have sustained the position that the issuance of a writ for specific performance would hold in abeyance the obligation to avoid or reduce losses by acquisition of replacement property. Yet, even in these cases, the action for performance must be instituted and carried on with due diligence. This is but another application of the ordinary rule of mitigation which insists that the injured party act reasonably in all of the circumstances. Where those circumstances reveal a substantial and legitimate interest in seeking performance as opposed to damages, then a plaintiff will be able to justify his inaction and on failing in his plea for specific performance might then recover losses which in other circumstances might be classified as avoidable and thus unrecoverable; but such is not the case here.

See also McCamus at 926-31; MacDougall at 361-67; Waddams at paras 769-70.

VII. SPECIFIC PERFORMANCE

In the preceding sections, the remedy awarded by the courts usually resulted in the payment of money damages. It was not an "order" to pay a particular sum promised in a contract, although in some cases, of course, the award may have been calculated by direct reference to such a sum. The successful litigant "recovered" damages. If the defendant failed to pay the damages the state's long arm could reach out and seize his property (if any) to be sold to raise the amount. Generally speaking, this was the extent of the remedy and its sanction in the common law courts.

However, along with the development of the "law" in the common law courts, there also developed a supplementary system commonly called "equity." If an aggrieved party wanted to have her expectation interest more specifically satisfied, if she wanted to have the promise actually performed, she could turn to equity. Equity was administered by the Court of Chancery. Generally speaking, its remedies were available when it considered the remedies of the common law inadequate. The Chancery Court commonly ordered specific performance of contracts for the sale of land on the theory that any land is unique and no amount of damages could compensate for its loss, but in *Semelhago v Paramadevan*, [1996] 2 SCR 415, it was held that specific performance was only available where land was unique, and where damages were inadequate.

Equitable orders can be enforced by imprisonment for contempt of court. Today in most jurisdictions the two systems have been merged by merging the courts and providing that where the rules of law and equity conflict, the rules of equity prevail.

Stewart v Kennedy. (1890), 15 App Cas 75 (HL (Scot)). LORD WATSON: I do not think that upon this matter any assistance can be derived from English decisions; because the laws of the two countries regard the right to specific performance from different standpoints. In England the only legal right arising from a breach of contract is a claim of damages; specific performance is not a matter of legal right, but a purely equitable remedy, which the Court can withhold when there are sufficient reasons of conscience or expediency against it. But in Scotland the breach of a contract for the sale of a specific subject such as landed estate, gives the party aggrieved the legal right to sue for implement, and, although he may elect to do so, he cannot be compelled to resort to the alternative of an action of damages unless implement is shewn to be impossible, in which case, *loco facti imprestabilis subit damnum et interesse*. Even where implement is possible, I do not doubt that the Court of Session has inherent power to refuse the legal remedy upon equitable grounds, although I know of no instance in which it has done so. It is quite conceivable that circumstances might occur, which would make it inconvenient and injust to enforce specific performance of a contract of sale; but I do not think that any such case is presented in this appeal. The fact that the construction of a term in the contract is attended with doubt and difficulty, evidenced it may be by the different meanings attributed to it by Courts or individual judges, ought not, in my opinion, to prevent its receiving its full legal effect, according to the interpretation finally put upon it by a competent tribunal. The argument that, in this case, a decree for specific performance would necessarily impose upon the appellant the duty of performing a long series of personal acts under the supervision of the court does not appear to me to have a solid basis in fact. The acts which such a decree enjoins would be entirely within his power, and practically might be performed *uno flatu, viz.*, by his signing a conveyance in favour of the respondent, and at the same time giving instructions to his agents to take the necessary steps for obtaining its approval by the Court.

CIVIL CODE OF QUÉBEC
LRQ, c C-1991

1601. A creditor may, in cases which admit of it, demand that the debtor be forced to make specific performance of the obligation.

FALCKE V GRAY
(1859), 29 LJ Ch 28

[In a suit for specific performance of a contract giving Mr. Falcke the option of purchasing two valuable china jars, it appeared that Mr. Falcke had rented a house from Mrs. Gray and had accepted an option to buy some furniture including what Mr. Falcke's counsel described as "a couple of large Oriental jars, with great ugly Chinese pictures upon them." The jars were valued by agreement at £40. Later, Mrs. Gray was offered £200 by Messrs. Watson, to whom she promptly sold them. Mrs. Gray stated the jars were left her by a lady who had been offered £100 for them by King George IV. Mr. Falcke was a dealer in the same trade as Messrs. Watson and should have known the actual value of the jars.]

KINDERSLEY VC: The defendants insist, in the first place, that this bill cannot be maintained on the ground that the plaintiff can have no right to the specific performance of a contract relating solely to chattels. On this question, my opinion is entirely in favour of the plaintiff, that the Court will not refuse such relief. In the eye of this Court, there is no difference between real and personal estate in the performance of a contract; and a contract for one stands in no position different from a contract for the other. The principle upon which this Court decrees specific performance, as enunciated by Lord Redesdale, in *Harnett v. Yielding*, 2 Sch. & Lef. 549, is, that a Court of laws deals with the contract, and gives such a decree as it is competent to give in consequence of non-performance—that is, by giving compensation in the shape of damages for the non-performance. But a Court of equity says that it is not enough; and in many cases the mere remuneration and compensation in damages is not sufficient satisfaction. Apply that principle to chattels—and why is it less applicable to them than to real estate? In ordinary contracts, as for the purchase of ordinary articles of use and consumption, such as coals, corn or consols, this Court will not decree specific performance. And why? Because you have only to go into the market and buy another equally good article, and so you can get your compensation. It is not because it is a chattel, but because you can get adequate compensation for it. Now, here these articles are of unusual distinction and curiosity, if not unique; and it is altogether doubtful what price they will fetch. I am of opinion, therefore, that this is a contract which this Court can enforce; and if the case stood alone upon that ground I would decree specific performance. ...

[The bill was dismissed on another ground, and part of the judgment of the vice-chancellor is omitted.]

Carter v Long & Bisby. (1896), 26 SCR 430. STRONG CJ: Although not ordinarily interfering in the case of chattels, courts of equity would always take jurisdiction in two cases viz., where the chattel was of particular value so that damages would be no adequate compensation. ... The other ground was where a fiduciary relationship existed between the parties; there, irrespective altogether of the nature and value of the property, the jurisdiction of equity could always be invoked for the protection of the *cestui que trust*.

COHEN V ROCHE
[1927] 1 KB 169

[At an auction sale, Hepplewhite chairs (lot 145), which belonged to the auctioneer himself, the defendant, were knocked down to the plaintiff. After the sale the auctioneer refused to hand over the chairs to the plaintiff. Thereupon the plaintiff brought an action against the defendant in which he claimed for the delivery up of the chairs and alternatively damages for alleged breach of contract.]

McCARDIE J: ... I now take the final point in the case. The plaintiff sued in detinue only. The writ and statement of claim contain no alternative demand for damages for breach of contract. They ask (a) for delivery up of the chairs or payment of their value, and (b) damages for detention. I have however allowed an amendment whereby the statement of claim asks damages for breach of contract. The plaintiff vigorously contends that he is entitled as of right, once a binding contract is established, to an order for the actual delivery of the chairs, and that he is not limited to damages for breach of bargain. This point raises a question of principle and practice. Here I may again state one or two of the facts. The Hepplewhite chairs in lot 145 possessed no special feature at all. They were ordinary Hepplewhite furniture. The plaintiff bought them in the ordinary way of his trade for the purpose of ordinary resale at a profit. He had no special customer in view. The lot was to become a part of his usual trade stock.

The form of order in detinue cases for the delivery of goods is, in substance, this: "It is this day adjudged that the plaintiff do have a return of the chattels in the statement of claim mentioned and described (here set out description) or recover against the defendant their value (here set out value) ... and damages for their detention." ... By order XLVIII., r. 1, however, the Court has power to direct that execution shall issue for the delivery of the goods without giving to the defendant the option to retain the property upon payment of the assessed value. Now in the case before me, the plaintiff desires to secure a warrant for the compulsory and specific delivery of the chairs to him. ...

But at this point there arise other considerations. In *Chinery v. Viall* (1860), 5 H. & N. 288, it was laid down that as between buyer and seller the buyer cannot recover larger damages by suing in tort instead of contract. ... Bearing *Chinery v. Viall* in mind, it is necessary to mention next s. 52 of the *Sale of Goods Act*, 1893, which provides that in any action for breach of contract to deliver specific or ascertained goods the Court may, if it thinks fit, on the application of the plaintiff, direct by its judgment that the contract shall be performed specifically without giving the defendant the option of retaining the goods on payment of damages. It has been held that s. 52 applies to all cases where the goods are ascertained, whether the property therein has passed to the buyer or not: see Parker J. in *Jones v. Earl of Tankerville*, [1909] 2 Ch. 440, 445. It seems clear that the discretionary provisions of s. 52 cannot be consistent with an absolute right of a plaintiff to an order for compulsory delivery under a detinue judgment in such a case as the present. How, then, does the law stand as to detinue? In my view the power of the Court in an action of detinue rests upon a footing which fully accords with s. 52 of the *Sale of Goods Act*, 1893. In *Whitely, Ltd. v. Hilt*, [1919] 2 K.B. 808, 819 (an action of detinue), Swinfen Eady, M.R. said: "The power vested in the Court to order the delivery up of a particular chattel is discretionary, and ought not to be exercised when the chattel is an ordinary article of commerce and of no special value or interest, and not alleged to be of any special value to the plaintiff, and where damages would fully compensate." In equity, where a plaintiff alleged and proved the money value of the chattel, it was not the practice of the Court to order its specific delivery: see *Dowling v. Betjemann* (1862), 2 J. & H. 544. The law is thus, I am glad to find, consistent in its several parts. In the present case the goods in question were ordinary articles of commerce and of no special value or interest and no grounds exist for any special order for delivery. The judgment should be limited to damages for breach of contract. The plaintiff in his evidence said that the chairs were worth from £70 to £80. With this I agree. I assess the damages at the sum of £15.

For the reasons given I therefore enter judgment for the plaintiff for £15 damages for breach of contract. ...

[The statement of facts is abridged, and part of the judgment of McCardie J dealing with the *Statute of Frauds* is omitted. Section 50 of the *Sale of Goods Act*, RSO 1990, c S.1 is substantially the same as s 52 of the English Act, which has been adopted in all the common law provinces of Canada.]

QUESTION

Suppose the plaintiff buyer in *Cohen v Roche* had agreed to sell the chairs to someone else at a specially lucrative price, which, naturally enough, she had not mentioned to the defendant seller. Should specific performance be granted to enable the plaintiff to take advantage of the contract at no extra expense to the defendant where the advantage might not be accounted for in calculating damages?

SKY PETROLEUM LTD V VIP PETROLEUM LTD
[1974] 1 WLR 576 (Ch)

[The plaintiffs had entered into a contract with the defendants to purchase from the defendants, at fixed prices, their entire requirements of motor gasoline and diesel fuel for the plaintiffs' filling stations, with a minimum annual quantity being stipulated. At a time when the supply of petroleum was restricted and the plaintiffs had no prospect of finding an alternative source of supply, the defendants purported to terminate the contract on the ground that the plaintiffs had exceeded the credit provisions in the contract.]

GOULDING J: This is a motion for an injunction brought by the plaintiff company, Sky Petroleum Ltd., as buyer under a contract dated March 11, 1970, made between the defendant company, V.I.P. Petroleum Ltd., as seller of the one part and the plaintiffs of the other part. That contract was to operate for a period of ten years, subject to certain qualifications, and thereafter on an annual basis unless terminated by either party giving to the other not less than three months' written notice to that effect. It was a contract at fixed prices, subject to certain provisions which I need not now mention. Further, the contract obliged the plaintiffs—and this is an important point—to take their entire requirement of motor gasoline and diesel fuel under the contract, with certain stipulated minimum yearly quantities. After the making of the agreement, it is common knowledge that the terms of trade in the market for petroleum and its different products changed very considerably, and I have little doubt that the contract is now disadvantageous to the defendants. After a long correspondence, the defendants, by telegrams dated November 15 and 16, 1973, have purported to terminate the contract under a clause therein providing for termination by the defendants if the plaintiffs fail to conform with any of the terms of the bargain. What is alleged is that the plaintiffs have exceeded the credit provisions of the contract and have persistently been, and now are, indebted to the defendants in larger amounts than were provided for. So far as that dispute relates, as for the purposes of this motion it must, to the date of the purported termination of the contract, it is impossible for me to decide it on the affidavit evidence. It involves not only a question of construction of the contract, but also certain disputes on subsequent arrangements between the parties and on figures in account. I cannot decide it on motion, and the less I say about it the better.

What I have to decide is whether any injunction should be granted to protect the plaintiffs in the meantime. There is trade evidence that the plaintiffs have no great prospect of finding any alternative source of supply for the filling stations which constitute their business. The defendants have indicated their willingness to continue to supply the plaintiffs, but only at prices which, according to the plaintiffs' evidence, would not be serious prices from a commercial point of view. There is, in my judgment, so far as I can make out on the evidence before me, a serious danger that unless the court interferes at this stage the plaintiffs will be forced out of business. In those circumstances, unless there is some specific reason which debars me from doing so, I should be disposed to grant an injunction to restore the former position under the contract until the rights and wrongs of the parties can be fully tried out.

It is submitted for the defendants that I ought not to do so for a number of reasons. It is said that, on the facts, the defendants were entitled to terminate and the plaintiffs were in the wrong. That, of course, is the very question in the action, and I have already expressed my inability to resolve it even provisionally on the evidence now before me. Then it is said that there are questions between the parties as to arrangements subsequent to the making of the contract, in particular regarding the price to be paid, and that they give rise to uncertainties which would make it difficult to enforce any order made by way of interlocutory relief. I do not think I ought to be deterred by that consideration, though I can see it has some force. In fact, during September and October, to go no further back, the defendants have gone on supplying and the plaintiffs have gone on paying. There has been nothing apparently impracticable in the contract, although the defendants say, of course, that the plaintiffs have not been paying large enough sums quickly enough.

Now I come to the most serious hurdle in the way of the plaintiffs which is the well known doctrine that the court refuses specific performance of a contract to sell and purchase chattels not specific or ascertained. That is a well-established and salutary rule, and I am entirely unconvinced by Mr. Christie, for the plaintiffs, when he tells me that an injunction in the form sought by him would not be specific enforcement at all. The matter is one of substance and not of form, and it is, in my judgment, quite plain that I am, for the time being, specifically enforcing the contract if I grant an injunction. However, the ratio behind the rule is, as I believe, that under the ordinary contract for the sale of non-specific goods, damages are a sufficient remedy. That, to my mind, is lacking in the circumstances of the present case. The evidence suggests, and indeed it is common knowledge that the petroleum market is in an unusual state in which a would-be buyer cannot go out into the market and contract with another seller, possibly at some sacrifice as to price. Here, the defendants appear for practical purposes to be the plaintiffs' sole means of keeping their business going, and I am prepared so far to depart from the general rule as to try to preserve the position under the contract until a later date. I therefore propose to grant an injunction.

Dealing first with its duration, it will restrain the defendants (in terms I will come to in a moment) until judgment in the action or further order, but not in any event beyond June 30, 1974, without further order of the court. I say that because of a provision in the contract which requires further steps to be taken in relation to the price of supply after that date. The terms which I suggest must, with certain qualifications, follow the notice of motion. If counsel are able to arrive at something more convenient and easier to enforce, they may mention the matter to me at an early date and the wording can be reconsidered, but for the moment I will order that the defendants by themselves, or their servants or agents, in the usual form be restrained from withholding supplies of "motor gasoline and DERV" from the plaintiffs in accordance with the terms of the contract dated March 11, 1970, and such other arrangements, if any, as were agreed between the parties before the issue of the writ in this action. There will be a proviso that the plaintiffs are not to require delivery of more than a specified number of gallons in any one month, and that number is to be ascertained by taking the arithmetical mean of the three months of supply, August, September, and October. That will, I hope, prevent any abuse of the injunction by the plaintiffs.

I would be sympathetic to any application by the defendants for the provision of security in some particular sum and form. I do not know whether the plaintiffs can make any specific offer in that respect, or whether the best thing is that all the details should be considered by counsel.

Order accordingly.

Behnke v Bede Shipping Co, Ltd. [1927] 1 KB 649. An action for specific performance of a contract for the sale of a ship. WRIGHT J: In the present case there is evidence that the *City* was of peculiar and practically unique value to the plaintiff. She was a cheap vessel, being sold, having been built in 1892, but her engines and boilers were practically new and such as to satisfy the German regulations, and hence the plaintiff could, as a German shipowner, have her at once put on the German register. A very experienced ship valuer has said that he knew of only one other comparable ship, but that may now have been sold. The plaintiff wants the ship for immediate use, and I do not think damages would be an adequate compensation. I think he is entitled to the ship and a decree of specific performance in order that justice may be done. [It had been contended that the plaintiff had the option of inspecting the vessel and of requiring the sellers to repair any damages found and because the court would not order performance of a contract to do work the option constituted a bar to specific relief. Wright J rejected the contention. The sellers were not dry dock owners nor ship-repairers and anyway the plaintiff might not require the inspection.]

GILBERT V BARRON
(1958), 13 DLR (2d) 262 (Ont HC)

WILSON J: ... The company, Amerwood (Eastern) Canada Ltd., is incorporated as a public company under the Ontario *Companies Act* by letters patent of this Province dated October 26, 1948. Under agreement with an American company it manufactures and sells a plywood product known as Amerwood, and since 1954 it also manufactures and distributes another product known as Cellotex. The dispute in this action arises out of a struggle for control of the ownership of the shares of the Ontario company, hereinafter called Amerwood.

The plaintiff MacDonald, a successful salesman who resides in the City of Toronto, is responsible for the organization of Amerwood. He sold much treasury stock at Owen Sound, where the company, when organized, carried on its manufacturing operations. As was natural, he became one of the principal shareholders. The other two principal shareholders were one Parkes and the plaintiff Gilbert, an investment broker of many years' standing, who resides in Toronto. Gilbert became a shareholder in 1948, and at the annual meeting in February 1950 he was elected a director. In June 1954 he was elected president, an office he held until he was succeeded by Barron in 1956 in the circumstances hereinafter related. Shortly after his election as a director in 1948, he and Parkes, who was the general manager of the company from its inception until his resignation and retirement on account of ill-health on January 1, 1954, and MacDonald, who was a director and vice-president from the organization of the company until the annual meeting in 1957, entered into an agreement with the object of holding and preserving among the three of them stock control of the company. The terms of this agreement were that if any one of the three should purchase shares in the company, he would offer one-third to each of the other two at cost price. The agreement did not necessarily require the two shareholders to take up the offer but at least they had this right to purchase. This agreement was acted upon when Parkes' son sold his shares to his father. Gilbert and Macdonald agreed that they should be sold to Parkes Sr. because the quantity of shares made no real difference as to the balance of control.

Early in 1953 Parkes became ill, and subsequent to his resignation in January 1954, he died. In January 1954, before his resignation, he sold most of his shares to the defendant Barron, with the approval of Gilbert and MacDonald, after Barron agreed to the same arrangement with respect to the acquisition of future shares as had existed among Parkes, Gilbert and MacDonald. This agreement was made before Barron acquired his shares. The exact date of the agreement is not of great importance.

I am satisfied it was made before Barron acquired Parkes' shares. Moreover, as appears later, the agreement was acted upon, and, later again, acknowledged on a Sunday in February 1955 at a meeting, at which Barron, MacDonald and Gilbert were present in Barron's office at Port Credit. I find that Barron acted upon the agreement when he purchased in December 1954 the shares which were known as the 500 Russell shares. This number did not lend itself to an even division, and after negotiation among the three they were divided 150 shares to each of Gilbert, MacDonald and Barron and 50 shares to a member of the staff, Miss Dorothy Gilbank.

By February 1956, without the knowledge of his two fellow shareholders Gilbert and MacDonald, Barron had decided to secure control of the company. He purchased options to buy enough shares to give him voting control of the company and at the annual meeting he had enough proxies and shares in his name to give him voting control of it. After the meeting he took up the options thus acquiring stock control.

Gilbert and MacDonald learned of this control just before the annual meeting and in due course made demands upon Barron for their shares in accordance with the agreement among them. These demands were not replied to, and on February 8, 1957, this action was commenced. In the interval between this annual meeting and the commencement of the action the plaintiffs were acting upon legal advice. ...

[After considering and rejecting three defences, (1) a denial of the agreement, (2) no consideration, and (3) the *Statute of Frauds*, Wilson J continued:]

The plaintiffs are entitled to specific performance of the agreement in respect of all shares claimed by them. He must tender one-third—that is to say, 816 common and 816 preferred—to each of the plaintiffs who will, upon such tender, pay for them in accordance with the agreement. ...

The plaintiffs also ask an injunction restraining the defendants from voting the shares to which they are entitled, and from selling, pledging or transferring them. They will have judgment for this relief (directly and indirectly) in respect of Barron. He has apparently placed the shares in the name of Port Credit Lumber Co., of which he has voting share control. However, it is quite apparent that Barron was only using this company as well as his co-defendants as his agent to break the agreement with the plaintiffs. In any event, Barron has not pleaded that it is impossible for him to comply with the contract.

The plaintiffs also ask damages. To this they are entitled as against Barron. No evidence was adduced to prove the amount of damages suffered. I should think there would be some at least loss of salary as directors, but I am unable to conclude there was more. I think the sum of $200 to each of the plaintiffs as nominal damages would suffice. These are the directors' fees they appear to have lost. In other circumstances, even though the task seems an impossible one from the practical point of view, the damages could be assessed at a much higher figure.

In addition to the costs already dealt with, the plaintiffs will have their costs of the action against the defendant Barron, which includes the costs they have incurred against the other defendants.

[See also Waddams at para 681.]

TANENBAUM V WJ BELL PAPER CO LTD
(1956), 4 DLR (2d) 177 (Ont H Ct J)

[W.J. Bell Paper Co. Ltd., in October 1951, purchased a parcel of land, marked parcel "A" on the sketch, from one Tanenbaum, as a site for its new head office and plant. Tanenbaum retained the parcel "C" on the sketch, and the contract of sale contained a promise by Bell Paper that it would construct "a roadway not less than twenty-eight feet in width, similar to that at present constructed on Wicksteed Avenue" along the western boundary of parcel "A," and that Tanenbaum should have a right of way over it. Bell Paper also agreed to install sewer and water pipes of unspecified size along the new road to provide service for parcel "C," which was to be used for "industrial operations." Wicksteed Avenue, a street built by the Town of Leaside, is 28 feet wide, without sidewalks. It had an 8-inch Portland cement base with 2½ inches of asphalt "hot-mix" top. The surface was 26 feet wide and on each side were 12-inch brick gutters and concrete curbs. After some delay Bell Paper actually constructed a road with an 8-inch crushed stone base and with 1½ to 3 inches of asphalt, hot or cold mix, on top, with no gutters or curbing. The road was finished in May 1953, at a cost of about $25,000. Bell Paper also installed a 2-inch water main from its own plant to the northern limits of parcel "C." The road proved troublesome and in this action for specific performance and damages the court interpreted the contract as calling for a road like Wicksteed Avenue, with a concrete base and gutters and curbs, and a water main at least 6 inches in diameter.]

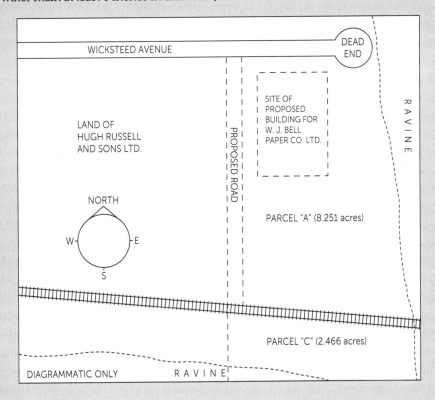

GALE J: ... The defendant must, therefore, be held accountable for the breach of contract. The plaintiff asks for specific performance of the covenants but the defendant urges that such relief would be inappropriate and too drastic in the circumstances of this case.

Generally the Court will not order a contract to build or to repair to be specifically performed. But an exception to that rule is now recognized and it is my understanding of the authorities that specific performance ought to be decreed where a person undertakes accommodation works on lands possessed by him in consideration for obtaining those lands or in consideration of the purchase-price of other lands sold by him, if the particulars of the work are sufficiently clear and defined and the Court comes to the conclusion that damages will not provide an adequate remedy for the breach of the contract. ...

That the Court will enforce building contracts in certain circumstances was firmly established in *Wolverhampton Corp. v. Emmons*, [1901] 1 K.B. 515. That was a decision of the English Court of Appeal and may well be regarded as the leading modern authority on the subject. In pursuance of a scheme of improvement the plaintiffs, an urban sanitary authority, conveyed to the defendant some lands abutting on a street. The defendant covenanted that he would erect buildings thereon within a certain time. Subsequently the nature and particulars of the houses to be erected were agreed upon, but the defendant failed to fulfil his covenant to build. The plaintiffs thereupon brought the action and were held entitled to a decree of specific performance. That was not a case involving a railway company. Romer L.J. at pp. 524-5 describes the exception to which I have alluded as follows:

> There is no doubt that as a general rule the Court will not enforce specific performance of a building contract, but an exception from the rule has been recognised. It has, I think, for some time been held that, in order to bring himself within that exception, a plaintiff must establish three things. The first is that the building work, of which he seeks to enforce the performance, is defined by the contract; that is to say, that the particulars of the work are so far definitely ascertained that the Court can sufficiently see what is the exact nature of the work of which it is asked to order the performance. The second is that the plaintiff has a substantial interest in having the contract performed, which is of such a nature that he cannot adequately be compensated for breach of the contract by damages. The third is that the defendant has by the contract obtained possession of land on which the work is contracted to be done.

The exception so defined by Romer L.J. was considered and expanded somewhat by Farwell J., as he then was, in *Carpenters Estates Ltd. v. Davies*, [1940] Ch. 160. In that case the defendant sold certain land to the plaintiffs for building development and agreed to install roads, mains, sewers and drains on other lands retained by her. The covenant having been broken, the plaintiffs succeeded in an action for specific performance. After setting out, *inter alia*, the passage in the *Emmons* case which I have quoted above, Farwell J. seemed to express himself as being of the view that if the conditions as to clarity and inadequacy of damages were present, the plaintiff would be entitled to succeed on his quest for a decree by showing merely that the defendant was in possession of the lands upon which the work was to have been done, and the exception may now perhaps be regarded as being as broad as that. I do not have to settle that question here.

It may be that the learned Judge did not intend to carry the extension of the exception so far because later in his judgment he said at p. 165: "The defendant has contracted to do the work on her own land in consideration of the purchase price of other land belonging to her, and if the other two conditions are fulfilled, I am unable to see why the Court should be debarred from granting relief by way of specific performance." He was not, however, prepared to accept as being completely exhaustive the statement of Romer L.J. and for the moment, therefore, I prefer to express the exception to the general rule as I have done.

Perhaps it is scarcely necessary to add that the exception which I have outlined has been worked into the fabric of the law of Canada. It was acknowledged and applied by two of the three Judges in *Colton v. Rookledge* (1872), 19 Gr. 121, and was reasserted by Idington J. in one of the judgments of the Supreme Court of Canada in *Gross v. Wright*, [1923] 2 D.L.R. 171, S.C.R. 214. In the latter case the litigants entered into a party-wall agreement under which the defendant was to build a wall 2 ft. or more in thickness with its middle line to coincide with the boundary-line. The wall erected by the defendant complied with the agreement to the level of the second storey but was narrowed from there up on the defendant's side, while remaining perpendicular on the plaintiff's side. The latter discovered this situation some years after the wall formed part of the defendant's building and sued for a mandatory injunction to compel the latter to pull down that which had been erected and for specific performance of the agreement. The majority of the Court granted a mandatory injunction on the theory that having obtained a licence to enter on the land for a particular purpose and having breached that licence, the defendant was committing a trespass. However, Idington J. expressly awarded the decree which was sought on the ground that the court had jurisdiction to grant specific performance of the agreement itself. Indeed at p. 176 D.L.R., p. 219 S.C.R., he stated that in his opinion specific performance was the only appropriate remedy in the circumstances and certainly the other members of the court did not take the position that the relief being ordered could not have been based on the claim for specific performance of the contract between the parties.

Here the defendant argues that specific performance is not available to the plaintiff, firstly because the terms of the agreement, ex. 1, as to the road and watermain are not sufficiently explicit; secondly, because the plaintiff can be appropriately compensated in damages if those works do not comply with the provisions of the agreement; and lastly, because the plaintiff has had some performance from the defendant.

As already indicated, I am of the opinion that the road and watermain which were to have been installed by the defendant were sufficiently described by the contract and that the defendant failed to fulfil its obligations in that respect. It is very difficult, if not impossible, to set down a general formula as to what degree of certainty is required in a contract before the Court will enforce its performance, so much depends upon the facts of each case. But I think it may be said with confidence that the certainty which is essential must be a reasonable one, having regard to the nature and subject-matter of the undertaking and the attendant conditions under which and with regard to which it was entered into. The authorities on this point substantiate such a conclusion. ...

All the defendant had to do here was to have copied the essential elements of a named street and to have installed a main which, in view of what must have been in the minds of the parties, would be at least 6 ins. in diameter. There was no room for doubt as to what was to be done and accordingly I hold that the plaintiff is not to be denied his decree by reason of any suggestion of uncertainty or ambiguity as to the nature of the work.

Probably the most serious objection to the granting of specific performance comes from the submission that if the road and watermain do not meet the terms of the agreement, the plaintiff can be properly and sufficiently compensated in damages. Let me say at once, however, that it is my view that such relief, even if capable of being calculated, would be quite inadequate to atone for the inadequacy of the watermain. As long as that pipe remains its sole source of water, parcel "C" cannot be put to its full use and certainly its potential sale value cannot be realized. I suspect that counsel for the defendant was aware of the hopelessness of his arguments that a pecuniary award could counterbalance the lack of a suitable main, because, while stoutly resisting all efforts to have the road replaced, he conceded that the installation of a new watermain would not be a very serious matter.

The question whether damages ought to be substituted for performance with respect to the road has not been easy to decide but here again I do not subscribe to the idea that an award of damages would give the proper relief. It would be futile to attempt to lay down a general rule as to when damages will be ordered in lieu of enforcing performance. ...

The best statement on the subject that I have been able to find appears in *Williston on Contracts*, rev. ed., vol. 5, s. 1423, pp. 3976-7, where this appears:

> In contracts other than those ordinarily designated as contracts of service, it is generally true so far as affirmative relief is concerned, that "Equity will not award specific performance where the duty to be enforced is continuous and reaches over a long period of time, requiring constant supervision by the court." Therefore, "There is no doubt that as a general rule the Court will not enforce specific performance of a building contract." The basis of equity's disinclination to enforce building contracts specifically is the difficulty of enforcing a decree without an expenditure of effort disproportionate to the value of the result. But where the inadequacy of damages is great, and the difficulties not extreme, specific performance will be granted and the tendency in modern times has been increasingly towards granting relief, where under the particular circumstances of the case damages are not an adequate remedy.

In this instance certainly the difficulties which would follow a decree of specific performance would not be extreme. The present roadway would have to be taken up and replaced with what should have been installed there in the first place and that would, of course, be an expensive undertaking. Indeed, the defendant protests strenuously that the cost of having to supplant the present road would not only be substantial but would also be out of all proportion to the advantages to be achieved by doing so. However, in many judgments upon the subject it has frequently been declared that mere hardship on the party in default should not be allowed to overcome the exercise of the Court's discretion in favour of ordering performance. Needless to say, if damages could be easily ascertained and were relatively insignificant in amount, I would pause long before making an order which might seriously prejudice the defendant's existence. Obviously that is not the situation here. As I shall point out in a moment, any attempt to assess damages is likely to prove abortive and the cost of building a proper road, while heavy by some standards, will by no means cripple the defendant company. And it must never be forgotten that if the decree were withheld the Court would, in one sense, be permitting the defendant to take advantage of its own wrong. ...

If for no other reason ... the conduct of the defendant and its contractor would probably induce me to grant that relief, for, as I have already mentioned, the reckless and almost wilful manner in which the plaintiff's rights were put aside would cause any Court to deal with the defendant quite dispassionately.

However, perhaps the most formidable obstacle to the granting of damages comes from the fact that to try to calculate those damages would be an almost insuperable task. They arise in several ways. The plaintiff should have an amount equivalent to the difference between the estimated cost of repairing the private roadway and that of repairing one like Wicksteed Ave. during the life span of the latter. Counsel for the defendant urged that a monetary allowance for that difference would represent the full loss sustained by its adversary, but I do not agree, for clearly the enjoyment of parcel "C" and its disposal-value will continue to be adversely affected so long as the present road is there. I propose to examine those two sources of damages to determine whether either can be properly ascertained.

In the first place, it is questionable who will be making any future repairs. Certainly the defendant has the right to rebuild or repair the road but it is not obliged to do so since the agreement contains no covenant to that effect. Conversely, the plaintiff has no right to alter or rebuild that which is there. But can he repair the road? On behalf of the defendant it was said that Mr. Tanenbaum could enter upon it to make minor repairs at his own expense and counsel for the plaintiff concurred in that suggestion. It is extremely difficult to say, however, to what extent that privilege can be exercised. For example, the plaintiff could not close off the road at any time for that purpose without obtaining permission, for the defendant has already granted further rights of way over it to the Russell company and perhaps to others. It occurs to me, therefore, that it would not be easy to define in advance the scope of the repairs which the plaintiff might make; assuredly he could not make material alterations to that which is there.

Even assuming that the plaintiff is at liberty to mend the surface of the road as it deteriorates, how could the present value of the cost of doing so be reckoned? The evidence proved beyond doubt that Wicksteed Ave. would not require as much in the way of maintenance as the private road but that on occasions when repairs will have to be made the cost of doing so will exceed that which will have to be expended for individual repairs to the private road. That being so, anyone fastened with the unenviable duty of assessing damages would be required to determine the life-expectancy of a cement-based road and then try to estimate what the repairs to this road over that period of time would amount to. I am completely convinced that it would be quite impossible to do that with any degree of accuracy because the extent of future repairs and their frequency will depend on the volume and weight of the traffic the road will be called upon to carry and the speeds at which the vehicles will pass over it. Even if the magnitude and volume of repairs could be predicted, how could anyone come to a conclusion as to what those repairs would cost, bearing in mind that no one can know when they will be needed? Prices ten years hence may bear no relation to to-day's prices. And if all of these data could in some miraculous way be calculated, they would still have to be compared with similar data concerning an imaginary cement-based road.

If the damages relating to the comparative cost of repairs could be determined the struggle would not be over, for there would still have to be a decision as to the amount of damages accruing to the plaintiff because the present road causes and will continue to cause some reduction in the disposal-value of parcel "C." ...

The defendant finally contended that specific performance ought not to be granted because the plaintiff has been provided with a hard-surfaced road which can be used. In other words, counsel suggested that since the plaintiff has had some measure of performance, he is precluded from obtaining anything but damages. Once again I do not agree and I am substantiated by the authorities. In *Lane v. Newdigate* (1804), 10 Ves. 192, 21 E.R. 818, the decree was made and again in *Gross v. Wright*, [1923] 2 D.L.R. 171, S.C.R. 214, the Court, and particularly Idington J., did not hesitate to order the demolition of a substantial part of an existing building and the reconstruction of a wall which had been built but did not comply with the agreement between the parties. If it were otherwise, it would mean that a person who has determined upon non-observance of a contract could arbitrate on what was to be done. I concede, of course that specific performance would probably be refused if the disparity of execution were slight, but that is not the situation here. The differences between the two roads are notable and the fact that the plaintiff will always be out of possession of the lands on which the road is laid and that he has no certain or clear right to effect even minor repairs to it is one which should never be overlooked.

For those reasons I order the defendant to cause to be installed along the westerly boundary of its lands a roadway similar to Wicksteed Ave. and by that I have in mind that there should be laid a road at least 28 ft. wide, having an 8-in. Portland cement base, a 2½-in. asphaltic standard highway hot-mix top, two brick gutters 12 ins. in width and consisting of 3 courses of brick and cement curbs. That roadway should extend, of course, from the southerly limit of Wicksteed Ave. to the north rail of the present railway siding. In addition, the defendant must also cause to be installed a 6-in. watermain leading from or close to the defendant's hydrant which is approximately 363 ft. south of the Town main to parcel "C." If the plaintiff desires to have an 8-in. main he will have to pay the difference between the installation of one of that dimension and the 6-in. main I have ordered. I see no reason why both of these works cannot be completed within 4 months from the date of this judgment. ...

[A large part of the judgment dealing with damages arising from the delay in performance and the resulting inaccessibility of steel stored on Tanenbaum's land is omitted.]

[See also McCamus at 998-1003; Waddams at para 680.]

NOTE

In *Posner v Scott-Lewis*, [1987] Ch 25, the court, departing from an 1893 case, decreed specific performance of a landlord's obligation to employ a resident porter to provide certain services to tenants. Mervyn Davies J: "Damages here could hardly be regarded as an adequate remedy."

CO-OPERATIVE INSURANCE SOCIETY LTD V
ARGYLL STORES (HOLDINGS) LTD
[1998] AC 1 (HL)

[The defendant operated a supermarket in the plaintiff's shopping centre, and undertook, by a lease entered into in 1979, to keep it in operation for a term of 35 years. In 1995, the defendant announced that the store would close, and proceeded to close it over the plaintiff's protest. The plaintiff sought a decree of specific performance, which was refused at first instance, but granted by the Court of Appeal. On further appeal the House of Lords restored the order of the judge of first instance.]

LORD HOFFMANN: Specific performance is traditionally regarded in English law as an exceptional remedy, as opposed to the common law damages to which a successful plaintiff is entitled as of right. There may have been some element of later rationalisation of an untidier history, but by the 19th century it was orthodox doctrine that the power to decree specific performance was part of the discretionary jurisdiction of the Court of Chancery to do justice in cases in which the remedies available at common law were inadequate. This is the basis of the general principle that specific performance will not be ordered when damages are an adequate remedy. ...

The most frequent reason given in the cases for declining to order someone to carry on a business is that it would require constant supervision ... . It is the possibility of the court having to give an indefinite series of ... rulings in order to ensure the execution of the order which has been regarded as undesirable. Why should this be so? A principal reason is that ... the only means available to the court to enforce its order is the quasi-criminal procedure of punishment for contempt. This is a powerful weapon; so powerful, in fact, as often to be unsuitable as an instrument for adjudicating upon the disputes which may often arise over whether a business is being run in accordance with the terms of the court's order. The heavy-handed nature of the enforcement mechanism is a consideration which may go to the exercise of the court's discretion in other cases as well, but its use to compel the running of a business is perhaps the paradigm case of its disadvantages ... . First, the defendant, who ex hypothesi did not think that it was in his economic interest to run the business at all, now has to make decisions under a sword of Damocles which may descend if the way the business is run does not conform to the terms of the order ... . Secondly, the seriousness of a finding of contempt for the defendant means that any application to enforce the order is likely to be a heavy and expensive piece of litigation ... in terms of cost to the parties and the resources of the judicial system. ...

There is a further objection to an order requiring the defendant to carry on a business ... . This is that it may cause injustice by allowing the plaintiff to enrich himself at the defendant's expense. The loss which the defendant may suffer through having to comply with the order (for example by running the business at a loss for an indefinite period) may be far greater than the plaintiff would suffer from the contract being broken. As Professor Sharpe explains in "Specific Relief for Contract Breach," ch. 5 of *Studies in Contract Law* (1980), edited by Reiter and Swan, p. 129:

> In such circumstances, a specific decree in favour of the plaintiff will put him in a bargaining position vis-à-vis the defendant whereby the measure of what he will receive will be the value to the defendant of being released from performance. If the plaintiff bargains effectively, the amount he will set will exceed the value to him of performance and will approach the cost to the defendant to complete.

... It is true that the defendant has, by his own breach of contract, put himself in such an unfortunate position. But the purpose of the law of contract is not to punish wrongdoing but to satisfy the expectations of the party entitled to performance. A remedy which enables him to secure, in money terms, more than the performance due to him is unjust. From a wider perspective, it cannot be in the public interest for the courts to require someone to carry on business at a loss if there is any plausible alternative by which the other party can be given compensation. It is not only a waste of resources but yokes the parties together in a continuing hostile relationship. The order for specific performance prolongs the battle. If the defendant is ordered to run a business, its conduct becomes the subject of a flow of complaints, solicitors' letters and affidavits. This is wasteful for both the parties and the legal system. An award of damages, on the other hand, brings the litigation to an end. The defendant pays damages, the forensic link between them is severed, they go their separate ways and the wounds of conflict can heal.

The cumulative effect of these various reasons, none of which would necessarily be sufficient on its own, seems to me to show that the settled practice is based upon sound sense.

WARNER BROS PICTURES INCORPORATED V NELSON
[1937] 1 KB 209

BRANSON J: The facts of this case are few and simple. The plaintiffs are a firm of film producers in the United States of America. In 1931 the defendant then not well known as a film actress [Bette Davis], entered into a contract with the plaintiffs. Before the expiration of that contract the present contract was entered into between the parties. Under it the defendant received a considerably enhanced salary, the other conditions being substantially the same. This contract was for fifty-two weeks and contains options to the plaintiffs to extend it for further periods of fifty-two weeks at ever-increasing amounts of salary to the defendant. No question of construction arises upon the contract, and it is not necessary to refer to it in any great detail; but in view of some of the contentions raised it is desirable to call attention quite generally to some of the provisions contained in it. It is a stringent contract, under which the defendant agrees "to render her exclusive services as a motion picture and/or legitimate stage actress" to the plaintiffs, and agrees to perform solely and exclusively for them. She also agrees, by way of negative stipulation, that "she will not, during such time"—that is to say, during the term of the contract—"render any services for or in any other photographic, stage or motion picture production or productions or business of any other person ... or engage in any other occupation without the written consent of the producer being first had and obtained."

With regard to the term of the contract there is further clause, clause 23, under which, if the defendant fails, refuses or neglects to perform her services under the contract, the plaintiffs "have the right to extend the term of this agreement and all of its provisions for a period equivalent to the period during which such failure, refusal or neglect shall be continued."

In June of this year the defendant, for no discoverable reason except that she wanted more money, declined to be further bound by the agreement, left the United States and, in September, entered into an agreement in this country with a third person. This was a breach of contract on her part, and the plaintiffs on September 9 commenced this action claiming a declaration that the contract was valid and binding, an injunction to restrain the defendant from acting in breach of it, and damages. The defence alleged that the plaintiffs had committed breaches of the contract which entitled the defendant to treat it as at an end; but at the trial this contention was abandoned and the defendant admitted that the plaintiffs had not broken the contract and that she had; but it was contended on her behalf that no injunction could as a matter of law be granted in the circumstances of the case.

At the outset of the considerations of law which arise stands the question, not raised by the pleadings but urged for the defendant in argument, that this contract is unlawful as being in restraint of trade. The ground for this contention was that the contract compelled the defendant to serve the plaintiffs exclusively and might in certain circumstances endure for the whole of her natural life. No authority was cited to me in support of the proposition that such a contract is illegal, and I see no reason for so holding. Where, as in the present contract, the covenants are all concerned with what is to happen whilst the defendant is employed by the plaintiffs and not thereafter, there is no room for the application of the doctrine of restraint of trade. ...

I turn then to the consideration of the law applicable to this case on the basis that the contract is a valid and enforceable one. It is conceded that our Courts will not enforce a positive covenant of personal service; and specific performance of the positive covenants by the defendant to serve the plaintiffs is not asked in the present case. The practice of the Court of Chancery in relation to the enforcement of negative covenants is stated on the highest authority by Lord Cairns in the House of Lords in *Doherty v. Allman* (3 App. Cas. 709). His Lordship says:

> My Lords, if there had been a negative covenant, I apprehend, according to well-settled practice, a Court of equity would have had no discretion to exercise. If parties, for valuable consideration, with their eyes open, contract that a particular thing shall not be done, all that a Court of Equity has to do is to say, by way of injunction, that which the parties have already said by way of covenant, that the thing shall not be done; and in such case the injunction does nothing more than give the sanction of the process of the Court to that which already is the contract between the parties. It is not then a question of the balance of convenience or inconvenience, or of the amount of damage or of injury—it is the specific performance, by the Court, of that negative bargain which the parties have made, with their eyes open, between themselves.

That was not a case of a contract of personal service; but the same principle had already been applied to such a contract by Lord St. Leonards in *Lumley v. Wagner* (1852), 1 De G.M. & G. 604; 42 E.R. 687. The Lord Chancellor used the following language:

> Wherever this Court has not proper jurisdiction to enforce specific performance, it operates to bind men's consciences, as far as they can be bound, to a true and literal performance of their agreements; and it will not suffer them to depart from their contract at their pleasure, leaving the party with whom they have contracted to the mere chance of any damages which a jury may give. The exercise of this jurisdiction has, I believe, had a wholesome tendency towards the maintenance of that good faith which exists in this country to a much greater degree perhaps than in any other; and although the jurisdiction is not to be extended, yet a judge would desert his duty who did not act up to what his predecessors have handed down as the rule for his guidance in the administration of such an equity. ...

The defendant, having broken her positive undertakings in the contract without any cause or excuse which she was prepared to support in the witness-box, contends that she cannot be enjoined from breaking the negative covenants also. The mere fact that a covenant which the Court would not enforce, if expressed in positive form, is expressed in the negative instead, will not induce the Court to enforce it. ... The Court will attend to the substance, and not to the form of the covenant. Nor will the Court, true to the principle that specific performance of a contract of personal service will never be ordered, grant an injunction in the case of such a contract to enforce negative covenants if the effect of so doing would be to drive the defendant either to starvation or to specific performance of the positive covenants. ...

[In] *Rely-a-Bell Burglar and Fire Alarm Co., Ltd. v. Eisler*, [1926] Ch. 609 which was strongly relied upon by the defendant, ... Russell, J., as he then was, said,

> It was said that the covenants ... were so framed that the servant, if the covenants were enforced, could make his living neither by serving nor by carrying on business independently; whereas in the present case the covenant only prohibited serving. Therefore, it was said, he was still free to start in business on his own account, and it could not be said, if an injunction were granted in the terms of the covenant, that he would be forced to remain idle and starve. That distinction seems to me somewhat of a mockery. It would be idle to tell this defendant, a servant employed at a wage, that he must not serve anybody else in that capacity, but that the world was still open to him to start business as an independent man. It seems to me that if I were to restrain this man according to the terms of the covenant, he would be forced to remain idle and starve.

Had it not been for that view of the facts, I think that the learned Judge would have granted an injunction in that case.

The conclusion to be drawn from the authorities is that, where a contract of personal service contains negative covenants the enforcement of which will not amount either to a decree of specific performance of the positive covenants of the contract or to the giving of a decree under which the defendant must either remain idle or perform those positive covenants, the Court will enforce those negative covenants; but this is subject to a further consideration. An injunction is a discretionary remedy and the Court in granting it may limit it to what the Court considers reasonable in all the circumstances of the case.

This appears from the judgment of the Court of Appeal in *William Robinson & Co., Ltd. v. Heuer,* [1898] 2 Ch. 451. The particular covenant in that case is set out at p. 452 and provides that "Heuer shall not during this engagement, without the previous consent in writing of the said W. Robinson & Co., Ltd.," and so forth, "carry on or be engaged either directly or indirectly, as principal agent, servant, or otherwise, in any trade, business or calling, either relating to goods of any description sold or manufactured by the said W. Robinson & Co., Ltd. ... or in any other business whatsoever." ...

Before parting with that case, I should say that the Court there proceeded to sever the covenants and to grant an injunction, not to restrain the defendant from carrying on any other business whatsoever, but framed so as to give what was felt to be a reasonable protection to the plaintiffs and no more. The plaintiffs waived an option which they possessed to extend the period of service for an extra five years, and the injunction then was granted for the remaining period of unextended time. ...

The case before me is, therefore, one in which it would be proper to grant an injunction unless to do so would in the circumstances be tantamount to ordering the defendant to perform her contract or remain idle or unless damages would be the more appropriate remedy.

With regard to the first of these considerations, it would, of course, be impossible to grant an injunction covering all the negative covenants in the contract. That would, indeed, force the defendant to perform her contract or remain idle; but this objection is removed by the restricted form in which the injunction is sought. It is confined to forbidding the defendant, without the consent of the plaintiffs, to render any services for or in any motion picture or stage production for anyone other than the plaintiffs.

It was also urged that the difference between what the defendant can earn as a film artiste and what she might expect to earn by any other form of activity is so great that she will in effect be driven to perform her contract. That is not the criterion adopted in any of the decided cases. The defendant is stated to be a person of intelligence, capacity and means, and no evidence was adduced to show that, if enjoined from doing the specified acts otherwise than for the plaintiffs, she will not be able to employ herself both usefully and remuneratively in other spheres of activity, though not as remuneratively as in her special line. She will not be driven, although she may be tempted to perform the contract, and the fact that she may be so tempted is no objection to the grant of an injunction. This appears from the judgment of Lord St. Leonards in *Lumley v. Wagner* where he used the following language:

> It was objected that the operation of the injunction in the present case is mischievous, excluding the defendant J. Wagner from performing at any other theatre while this Court had no power to compel her to perform at Her Majesty's Theatre. It is true, that I have not the means of compelling her to sing, but she has no cause of complaint, if I compel her to abstain from the commission of an act which she has bound herself not to do, and thus possibly cause her to fulfil her engagement. The jurisdiction which I now exercise is wholly within the power of the Court and being of the opinion that it is a proper case for interfering, I shall leave nothing unsatisfied by the judgment I pronounce. The effect,

too, of the injunction, in restraining J. Wagner from singing elsewhere may, in the event of an action being brought against her by the plaintiff, prevent any such amount of vindictive damages being given against her as a jury might probably be inclined to give if she had carried her talents and exercised them at the rival theatre: the injunction may also, as I have said, tend to the fulfilment of her engagement; though, in continuing the injunction, I disclaim doing indirectly what I cannot do directly.

With regard to the question whether damages is not the more appropriate remedy, I have the uncontradicted evidence of the plaintiffs as to the difficulty of estimating the damages which they may suffer from the breach by the defendant of her contract. I think it is not inappropriate to refer to the fact that, in the contract between the parties, in clause 22, there is a formal admission by the defendant that her services, being "of a special, unique, extraordinary and intellectual character" gives them a particular value "the loss of which cannot be reasonably or adequately compensated in damages" and that the breach may "cost the producer great and irreparable injury and damage," and the artist expressly agrees that the producer shall be entitled to the remedy of injunction. Of course, parties cannot contract themselves out of the law; but it assists, at all events, on the question of evidence as to the applicability of an injunction in the present case, to find the parties formally recognizing that in cases of this kind injunction is a more appropriate remedy than damages.

Furthermore, in the case of *Grimston v. Cunningham*, [1894] 1 Q.B. 125, which was also a case in which a theatrical manager was attempting to enforce against an actor a negative stipulation against going elsewhere, Wills, J., granted an injunction and used the following language:

> This is an engagement of a kind which is pre-eminently subject to the interference of the Court by injunction, for in cases of this nature it very often happens that the injury suffered in consequence of the breach of the agreement would be out of all proportion to any pecuniary damages which could be proved or assessed by a jury. This circumstance affords a strong reason in favour of exercising the discretion of the court by granting an injunction.

I think that that applies to the present case also, and that an injunction should be granted in regard to the specified services.

Then comes the question as to the period for which the injunction should operate. The period of the contract, now that the plaintiffs have undertaken not as from October 16, 1936, to exercise the rights of suspension conferred upon them by clause 23 thereof, will, if they exercise their options to prolong it, extend to about May, 1942. As I read the judgment of the Court of Appeal in *Robinson v. Heuer* the Court should make the period such as to give reasonable protection and no more to the plaintiffs against the ill effects to them of the defendant's breach of contract. The evidence as to that was perhaps necessarily somewhat vague. The main difficulty that the plaintiffs apprehend is that the defendant might appear in other films whilst the films already made by them and not yet shown are in the market for sale or hire and thus depreciate their value. I think that if the injunction is in force during the continuance of the contract or for three years from now, whichever period is the shorter, that will substantially meet the case.

The other matter is as to the area within which the injunction is to operate. The contract is not an English contract and the parties are not British subjects. In my opinion all that properly concerns this Court is to prevent the defendant from committing the prohibited acts within the jurisdiction of this Court, and the injunction will be limited accordingly.

Bette Davis, *The Lonely Life* **(1962).** Chapter 11 and the first part of chapter 12 of this autobiography tell in some detail the story of *Warner Bros v Nelson* from Mrs. Nelson's point of view. When she left the United States she had already won an Academy Award, and felt confined by her contract and convinced that Warner Brothers had no serious intention of letting her choose her own parts or find parts she would approve. A few other actors and actresses were also battling the restrictive terms of the standard form of actor's contract. Mrs. Nelson mentions familiar names, James Cagney, Margaret Sullivan, Carole Lombard, and Eddie Cantor. In a comparatively new industry, the "stars" were beginning to realize their contribution and were rebelling against the "slavery" of the contract designed to serve the convenience of a more experienced business management. Apparently Mrs. Nelson thought she could not be stopped from working abroad. The litigation cost her over $30,000.

NOTES

1. In *Detroit Football Co v Dublinski* (1956), 4 DLR (2d) 688, McRuer CJHC held that an injunction in favour of the Detroit Football Club restraining Dublinski from playing for the Toronto Argonauts was not appropriate because the clubs were in separate leagues, and Dublinski's playing for Toronto "did the plaintiff no more harm than if he had remained idle." The Court of Appeal awarded damages but did not deal with the question of the injunction: (1957), 7 DLR (2d) 9.

2. In *Yashin v National Hockey League* (2000), 192 DLR (4th) 747, a hockey player agreed to play exclusively for a period of time for the Ottawa Senators Hockey Club. An arbitrator's decision that the player did not become a free agent under NHL rules until he had fulfilled his contract was upheld by the Ontario Superior Court. According to reports, Yashin tried to sign with a Swiss team, but the International Ice Hockey Federation prevented him from playing internationally until the NHL dispute was resolved.

PAGE ONE RECORDS LTD V BRITTON
[1968] 1 WLR 157 (Ch)

[On February 1, 1966, Charles Christopher Britton, Ronald James Bullis, Reginald Maurice Ball, and Peter Lawrence Staples, a group of "pop" musicians known as "The Troggs," appointed Page One Records Ltd. (the first plaintiff) to be their managers, and on April 22 and 25 they made two further agreements, one an agency and the other a recording agreement, with the plaintiff. On January 3, 1967, they made a publishing agreement with the second plaintiff, Dick James Music Ltd. In March 1967, the first plaintiff appointed Harvey Block Associates Ltd. as booking agents for the Troggs for ballrooms, but subsequently the Troggs considered inviting that company to become their manager and agent in place of the first plaintiff. On June 19, 1967, by two letters written one to the first plaintiff and the other to the second plaintiff, the Troggs purported to determine the four agreements they had made with the plaintiffs.

The first plaintiff sought an injunction to restrain the Troggs until trial from engaging anyone else as their manager or agent or from publishing any music performed by them otherwise than through the medium of the plaintiffs. The plaintiffs also sought an injunction against the second defendant restraining it from inducing any breaches of the agreements between the plaintiffs and the Troggs.

The defendants alleged that, even if the plaintiffs had acted impeccably toward the group at all times, which they denied, no injunction amounting to specific performance of a contract for personal services could be granted. Nor should any employer be prevented by injunction from dismissing an agent who occupied a fiduciary position. They also claimed that because the group could not have brought an action against their manager for specific performance of its agreement, no injunction could be granted against them.

The facts are stated more fully in the judgment.]

STAMP J: The defendants have not, in my judgment, established a prima facie case for the view that there were such breaches by the first plaintiff of its duty to the Troggs as to justify the Troggs in repudiating the agreements they made with it. If all I had to do was to determine whether the plaintiffs had made out a prima facie case of breach of contract entitling them to damages, I would hold that they had, entitling the plaintiffs to make a heavy claim for damages against the defendants.

But it does not follow that because the plaintiffs have made out a prima facie case for succeeding in recovering damages in the action, that they have made out a prima facie case, or any case, for an interlocutory, or any, injunction.

The plaintiffs, replying on *Lumley v. Wagner* and the cases which followed it, claim, as regards the first plaintiff, an order that the first four defendants and each of them be restrained until trial from engaging as their managers or agents, or personal representatives in the branches of the entertainment industry referred to in clause 1 of the agreement of February 1, 1966, or from engaging as their managers conducting all their affairs relating to their professional careers in any medium of professional entertainment, any person, firm or corporation other than the first named plaintiff, and further, an injunction restraining each of the four Troggs acting as a group, from publishing or causing to be published any music performed by them, otherwise than through the medium of the first or second named plaintiffs. Then for an order that the second named defendant be restrained until the trial from inducing or procuring any breach or further breach by the Troggs as a group or otherwise of agreements between the plaintiffs and the Troggs for the management of the Troggs by the first plaintiff or the publication by either plaintiff of the music of the first-named defendants in accordance with the terms of the four written agreements, to which I have referred.

Sir Andrew Clark submits that even if the plaintiffs had throughout acted impeccably towards the Troggs, no such injunction as is asked for ought to be granted. He advances three propositions on behalf of the Troggs. (1) Specific performance is never granted to enforce a contract for personal services. (2) An injunction is never granted which would have the effect of preventing an employer discharging an agent who is in a fiduciary position vis-à-vis the employer. He emphasises that here the first plaintiff, as manager and agent of the Troggs, is in the position of an employee. (3) An injunction is never granted at the suit of the party against whom the party to be restrained could not obtain specific performance.

It is urged—and, in my judgment, correctly—that the Troggs could have no action for specific performance of the management or agency agreements against the first plaintiff.

The present case is clearly distinguished, in principle, from such cases as *Lumley v. Wagner*, for there the only obligation on the part of the plaintiffs seeking to enforce the negative stipulation was an obligation to pay remuneration and an obligation which could clearly be enforced by the defendants. But here the obligations of the first plaintiff, involving personal services, were obligations of trust and confidence and were obligations which, plainly, could not be enforced at the suit of the Troggs. Here, indeed, so it seems to me, the totality of the obligations between the parties are more a joint venture, almost approaching the relationship of partners than anything else, involving mutual confidence and reciprocal obligations on all sides. ...

So it was said in this case that if an injunction is granted the Troggs could, without employing any other manager or agent, continue as a group on their own or seek other employment of a different nature. So far as the former suggestion is concerned, in the first place I doubt whether consistently with the terms of the agreements which I have read, the Troggs could act as their own managers; and, in the second place, I think I can, and should, take judicial notice of the fact that these groups, if they are to have any great success, must have managers. Indeed, it is the plaintiffs' own case that the Troggs are simple persons, of no business experience, and could not survive without the services of a manager. As a practical matter on the evidence before me, I entertain no doubt that they would be compelled, if the injunction was granted, on the terms that the plaintiffs seek, to continue to employ the first plaintiff as their manager and agent and it is, I think, on this point that this case diverges from *Lumley v. Wagner* and the cases which have followed it, including the *Warner Brothers* case: for it would be a bad thing to put pressure upon these four young men to continue to employ as a manager and agent in a fiduciary capacity one who, unlike the plaintiff in those cases (who had merely to pay the defendant money) has duties of a personal and fiduciary nature to perform and in whom the Troggs, for reasons good, bad or indifferent, have lost confidence and who may, for all I know, fail in its duty to them.

On the facts before me on this interlocutory motion, I should, if I granted the injunction, be enforcing a contract for personal services in which personal services are to be performed by the first plaintiff. In *Lumley v. Wagner*, Lord St. Leonards, in his judgment, disclaimed doing indirectly what he could not do directly; and in the present case, by granting an injunction I would, in my judgment, be doing precisely that. I must, therefore, refuse the injunction which the first plaintiff seeks. The claim of the second plaintiff seems to me to be inextricably mixed up with the claim by the first plaintiff and no separate argument has really been addressed to me on the basis that the second plaintiff might succeed although the first plaintiff failed to obtain an injunction at the trial.

Motion dismissed.

NOTE

This case was approved in *Warren v Mendy*, [1989] 1 WLR 853 (CA), where, in similar circumstances, the court refused to grant an injunction restraining a prospective new manager from committing the tort of inducing breach of contract (a tort first recognized in *Lumley v Gye* (1853), 2 El & Bl 216). See also McCamus at 1016-26; MacDougall at chapter 24; Waddams at paras 682-83.

VIII. TIME OF MEASURING DAMAGES

WROTH V TYLER
[1974] Ch 30

[The plaintiffs, a young married couple, made an agreement to purchase the defendant's house. The day after the agreement was made, the defendant's wife registered a charge against the title under the *Matrimonial Homes Act, 1967*, an English statute designed to protect the wife from eviction from the matrimonial home. The registration of such a charge was binding on a subsequent purchaser. The plaintiffs consequently demanded removal of the charge. The defendant's wife refused to remove the charge and the plaintiffs sued for specific performance with compensation, or damages. The portion of the judgment reproduced here concerns the proper time for measurement of damages, an important question because the value of the house rose dramatically between the date agreed for conveyance and the date of the trial. The contract price was £6,000; the value at the date agreed for conveyance, £7,500; and the value at the date of trial, £11,500. The plaintiff's action for specific performance was dismissed on the ground that a decree of specific performance would split the family (the wife, only, being entitled by statute to stay in the house).]

MEGARRY J: It was common ground that the normal rule is that the general damages to which a purchaser is entitled for breach of a contract for the sale of land are basically measured by the difference between the contract price and the market price of the land at the date of the breach, normally the date fixed for completion. On the facts of this case, the damages under this rule would be of the order of £1,500. The real issue was whether that rule applies to this case, or whether some other rule applies.

Now the principle that has long been accepted is that stated by Parke B. in *Robinson v. Harman* (1848) 1 Exch. 850, in which, incidentally, the rule in *Flureau v. Thornhill*, 2 Wm. Bl. 1078, was considered. Parke B. said, at p. 855: "The rule of the common law is, that where a party sustains a loss by reason of a breach of contract, he is, so far as money can do it, to be placed in the same situation, with respect to damages, as if the contract had been performed."

In the present case, if the contract had been performed, the plaintiffs would at the date fixed for completion have had the house, then worth £7,500 in return for the contractual price of £6,000. If in lieu of the house they had been paid £1,500 damages at that date, they could, with the addition of the £6,000 that they commanded, have forthwith bought an equivalent house. I am satisfied on the evidence that the plaintiffs had no financial resources of any substance beyond the £6,000 that they could have put together for the purchase of the defendant's bungalow, and that the defendant knew this when the contract was made. The plaintiffs were therefore, to the defendant's knowledge, unable at the time of the breach to raise a further £1,500 in order to purchase an equivalent house forthwith, and so, as events have turned out, mitigate their loss. Today, to purchase an equivalent house they need £5,500 in addition to their £6,000. How, then, it may be asked, would the award today of £1,500 damages place them in the same situation as if the contract had been performed? The result that would have been produced by paying £1,500 damages at the date of the breach can today be produced only by paying £5,500 damages, with in each case the return of the deposit. On facts such as these, the general rule of assessing damages as at the date of the breach seems to defeat the general principle, rather than carry it out. In the ordinary case of a buyer of goods which the seller fails to deliver, the buyer can at once spend his money in purchasing equivalent goods from another, as was pointed out in *Gainsford v. Carroll* (1824) 2 B. & C. 624, and so the rule works well enough; but that is a very different case. It therefore seems to me that on the facts of this case there are strong reasons for applying the principle rather than the rule. The question is whether it is proper to do so.

I do not think that I need inquire whether such an award could be made at common law. It may be that it could. The rule requiring damages to be ascertained as at the date of the breach does not seem to be inflexible, and in any case the rule may be one which, though normally carrying out the principle, does on occasion fail to do so; and on those occasions the rule may have to be modified so as to accord with the principle. However, as I have said, I do not think I need explore that; for it seems to me that this case, in which there is a proper claim for specific performance, falls within the Chancery Amendment Act 1858 (better known as Lord Cairns' Act), and that damages assessed under that Act are to be ascertained in accordance with that Act on a basis which is not identical with that of the common law. That Act provides, by section 2:

> In all cases in which the Court of Chancery has jurisdiction to entertain an application for an injunction against a breach of any covenant, contract, or agreement, or against the commission or continuance of any wrongful act, or for the specific performance of any covenant, contract, or agreement, it shall be lawful for the same court, if it shall think fit, to award damages to the party injured, either in addition to or in substitution for such injunction or specific performance, and such damages may be assessed in such manner as the court shall direct. [Section 112 of the Ontario Courts of Justice Act is in similar terms]. ...

On the wording of the section, the power "to award damages to the party injured, ... in substitution for such ... specific performance," at least envisages that the damages awarded will in fact constitute a true substitute for specific performance. Furthermore, the section is speaking of the time when the court is making its decision to award damages in substitution for specific performance, so that it is at that moment that the damages must be a substitute. The fact that a different amount of damages would have been a substitute if the order had been made at the time of the breach must surely be irrelevant. In the case before me, I cannot see how £1,500 damages would constitute any true substitute for a decree of specific performance of the contract to convey land which at the time of the decree is worth £5,500 more than the contract price. A choice between the inadequate and the equivalent seems to me to be no real choice at all. It may seem strange that nearly 115 years should have elapsed before this aspect of Lord Cairns' Act should have emerged; but the economic conditions which reveal its significance have not been with us long.

There are dicta in *Leeds Industrial Co-operative Society Ltd. v. Slack* [1924] A.C. 851 which support this view, or are at least consistent with it. In a speech with which the Earl of Birkenhead expressed his agreement, Viscount Finlay said, at p. 859: "... the power to give damages in lieu of an injunction must in all reason import the power to give an equivalent for what is lost by the refusal of the injunction; for this purpose compensation only for what has passed would be futile."

He added:

> It has been urged that the word "damages" must be used as denoting compensation for what has already happened. It is, of course, true that a court of common law gives damages as compensation for past wrongs, but the word "damages" is perfectly apt to denote compensation for the damage which will be sustained if a building is allowed to proceed so as to obstruct ancient lights. If an injunction is granted the obstruction

will never take place. If damages are given instead of the injunction, they must be in respect of an injury which is still in the future.

Lord Dunedin expressly concurred in Lord Finlay's speech; but he also said, at p. 865, that the words referring to damages in substitution for an injunction "clearly point to a pecuniary payment equalling the loss to be occasioned by the act against which, but for the provision in question, an injunction would have been obtained. ..."

I must, of course, have care in applying dicta uttered in a case where the problem before me was obviously not in view, even though section 2 of the Act lays down the same rule for injunctions and specific performance alike. Yet on principle I would say simply that damages "in substitution" for specific performance must be a substitute, giving as nearly as may be what specific performance would have given. There are, moreover, certain other authorities which provide assistance. In *Fritz v. Hobson* (1880) 14 Ch.D. 542 it was held that damages awarded under the Act in substitution for an injunction were not confined to damages down to the issue of the writ, as at law, but included damages down to the hearing. Fry J. said, at p. 556: "Now it is manifest that damages cannot be an adequate substitute for an injunction unless they cover the whole area which would have been covered by the injunction ... ."

In *Chapman, Morsons & Co. v. Guardians of Auckland Union* (1889) 23 Q.B.D. 294, the Court of Appeal approved the view taken by Fry J. in *Fritz v. Hobson*, 14 Ch.D. 542, 556. In *Dreyfus v. Peruvian Guano Co.* (1889) 43 Ch.D. 316, 342, Fry L.J. said of Lord Cairns' Act: "I am clear that the statute often enables the court, where a wrong has been done, to give damages upon a different scale from what was done by the Courts of Common Law, because it may give them in substitution for an injunction ... ."

Cotton L.J., who had previously delivered the leading judgment, then said that he agreed with what Fry L.J. had said about Lord Cairns' Act.

I should say at once that these additional authorities were not discussed before me, but as they support the view which I took without their aid, it seems proper for me to cite them without incurring the costs and delay of restoring the case for further argument. There seems to me to be adequate authority for the view that damages under Lord Cairns' Act may be awarded in cases in which there is no claim at all at law, and also that the quantum of damages is not limited by the rules at law. No doubt in exercising the jurisdiction conferred by the Act a court with equitable jurisdiction will remember that equity follows the law, and will in general apply the common law rules for the assessment of damages; but this is subject to the overriding statutory requirement that damages shall be "in substitution for" the injunction or specific performance. In the words of Cardozo C.J., "Equity follows the law, but not slavishly nor always": *Graf v. Hope Building Corporation* (1930) 254 N.Y. 1, 9. Obedience to statute, whether in its precise words or in its spirit, is an excellent and compelling reason for not following the law.

In my judgment, therefore, if under Lord Cairns' Act damages are awarded in substitution for specific performance, the court has jurisdiction to award such damages as will put the plaintiffs into as good a position as if the contract had been performed, even if to do so means awarding damages assessed by reference to a period subsequent to the date of the breach. This seems to me to be consonant with the nature of specific performance, which is a continuing remedy, designed to secure (inter alia) that the purchaser receives in fact what is his in equity as soon as the contract is made, subject to the vendor's right to the money, and so on. On the other hand, a decree may be sought before any breach of contract has occurred, and so before any action lies for common law damages; and on the other hand the right to a decree may continue long after the breach has occurred. On the facts of this case, the damages that may be awarded are not limited to the £1,500 that is appropriate to the date of the breach, but extend to the £5,500 that is appropriate at the present day, when they are being awarded in substitution for specific performance. I should add that no contention has been advanced (in my judgment, quite rightly) that the case does not fall within Lord Cairns' Act. The sale of a house is a case par excellence in which the court "has jurisdiction to entertain an application ... for the specific performance" of a contract, and the plaintiffs have done nothing to disentitle themselves to a decree. The undesirability of granting the decree if any suitable alternative exists springs from the position of the defendant and his wife.

That brings me to a subsidiary point which Mr. Lyndon-Stanford urged upon me. He contended that an award of damages of the order of £5,500 was precluded by the operation of what is often called the "second rule" in *Hadley v. Baxendale* (1854) 9 Exch. 341, relating to what was in the contemplation of the parties. I was very properly referred to that case in the light of the discussion in later cases set out in *McGregor on Damages*, 13th ed. (1972) principally at pp. 124-132. It was beyond question that a rise in the price of houses was in the contemplation of the parties when the contract was made in this case. But Mr. Lyndon-Stanford took it further. He contended that what a plaintiff must establish is not merely a contemplation of a particular head of damage, but also of the quantum under that head. Here, the parties contemplated a rise in house prices, but not a rise of an amount approaching that which in fact took place. A rise which nearly doubled the market price of the property was, as the evidence showed, outside the contemplation of the parties, and so it could not be recovered. Thus ran the argument.

I do not think that this can be right. On principle, it seems to me to be quite wrong to limit damages flowing from a contemplated state of affairs to the amount that the parties can be shown to have had in contemplation, for to do this would require evidence of the calculation in advance of what is often incalculable until after the event. The function of the so-called "second rule" in *Hadley v. Baxendale*, 9 Exch. 341, seems to me to be not so much to add to the damages recoverable as to exclude from them any liability for any type or kind of loss which could not have been foreseen when the contract was made. No authority was put before me which appeared to me to provide any support for the alleged requirement that the quantum should have been in contemplation. So far as it went, the language used in the authorities that were cited seems to me to have been directed to the heads of damage rather than to quantum. Thus one finds phrases such as "special circumstances" and the "type" or "kind" of damage. I would therefore on principle reject the defendant's contention, and hold that a plaintiff invoking the so-called "second rule" in *Hadley v. Baxendale*, 9 Exch. 341, need show only a contemplation of circumstances which embrace the head or type of damage in question, and need not demonstrate a contemplation of the quantum of damages under that head or type. Accordingly, in my judgment, this subsidiary contention of the defendant's fails, even if it is one that would apply, either directly or by analogy, to damages under Lord Cairns' Act.

During the argument it seemed to me surprising that the point should not be covered by authority; yet the only authority put before me that seemed to bear on the point was *Vacwell Engineering Co. Ltd. v. B.D.H. Chemicals Ltd.* [1971] 1 Q.B. 88. Mr. Lyndon-Stanford referred me to this case in performance of his duty of assisting the court, although it was against him. The point does not seem to have been argued there in terms, but it was held that where the parties to a contract could reasonably have foreseen that there might be a small or minor explosion, with some damage to property, if a proper warning was not given as to the precautions to be taken in handling the chemical sold, but could not reasonably have foreseen the major explosion which in fact occurred, killing a scientist and doing extensive damage to property, the vendors were nevertheless liable for the whole of the damage done. As Rees J. said, at p. 110: "... the explosion and the type of damage being foreseeable, it matters not in the law that the magnitude of the former and the extent of the latter were not." An appeal was settled: see [1971] 1 Q.B. 111, 112 (note).

That case, however, does not stand alone. In *Great Lakes Steamship Co. v. Maple Leaf Milling Co. Ltd.* (1924) 41 T.L.R. 21, the respondents, in breach of contract, had failed "to lighter immediately" the appellants' vessel on its arrival at the respondents' wharf on Lake Erie. Three days later, before any lightering had taken place, the vessel settled on the bottom as a result of a fall in the level of the water in the lake that was within the contemplation of the parties. Unknown to either party, a large anchor was resting on the bottom at that point, projecting two feet above the rock floor which there formed the bottom. This anchor caused serious injuries to the hull, for which the appellants claimed over $40,000 damages. In delivering the advice of the Judicial Committee, Lord Carson said, at p. 23:

> There can be no doubt that it was from breach of the contract immediately to lighter that the vessel grounded by reason of the lowering of the water, the very thing which it was anticipated might occur and which rendered the immediate lightering so important, and it must, in their Lordship's opinion, be held that it was the breach of contract in not lightering the vessel which was the immediate cause of the damage, and the fact that such damage might not have occurred if the anchor had not been sunk can make no difference. If grounding takes place in breach of contract, the precise nature of the damage incurred by grounding is immaterial.

That case seems to me to provide strong support for the view that I take. In the present case, the argument is directed purely to quantum. The precise head of damage, a general rise in the price of houses, was admittedly in contemplation: all that could be said to be outside the contemplation was the full amount, or the higher stages of the rise from £6,000 to £11,500. In *Great Lakes Steamship Co. v. Maple Leaf Milling Co. Ltd.*, 41 T.L.R. 21, what was in contemplation was the fact that delay in lightering might cause the vessel to rest on the bottom by the wharf, a bottom consisting of rock; nobody contemplated the anchor, yet the damages recoverable included those stemming from the anchor. On the authority of that case, the case before me seems a fortiori. I therefore find confirmation in that case of the view that at the hearing I took without its aid.

The conclusion that I have reached, therefore, is that as matters stand I ought to award damages to the plaintiffs of the order of £5,500, in substitution for decreeing specific performance, with all the doubts and difficulties and probably undesirable consequences that a decree in either form would produce. An award of damages on this scale, I accept, will bear hardly on the defendant. Though able in one way or another to raise £1,500 without selling his bungalow, £5,500 is another matter; in all probability he could not raise that sum without selling the bungalow with vacant possession, and he has no power to do this. If, however, he becomes bankrupt, then his trustee in bankruptcy can sell the bungalow free from the wife's rights, even though they are registered: see section 2(5) of the Act of 1967. With the money so raised, the trustee in bankruptcy will then be able to pay the plaintiffs their damages, one hopes in full; or it may be possible for the plaintiffs to take the bungalow in satisfaction of their claim. This is a dismal prospect for the defendant, but if the plaintiffs obtain neither a decree of specific performance nor £5,500 by way of damages, theirs also is a dismal prospect. Having made a binding contract to purchase for £6,000 a bungalow now worth £11,500, they would recover neither the bungalow nor damages that would enable them to purchase anything like its equivalent. It is the plaintiffs who are wholly blameless. Nothing whatever can be said against them, or has been, save as to the contention that delay barred them from a decree of specific performance; and that I have rejected. Nor do I think that there was any delay on their part that could affect the measure of damages.

The ultimate truth as between the defendant and his wife I do not know. As the evidence stands, his wife did nothing whatever to warn the plaintiffs that she was not willing to leave the bungalow, but conducted herself so as to lead them to believe that she concurred in the sale. So far as the defendant was concerned, his wife was very cool about the move, and it may well be that the move was one which a strong-willed husband was in effect imposing on a reluctant yet secretive wife. Nevertheless, the consequences of disputes between husband and wife, whether open or concealed, ought not to be visited upon innocent purchasers.

In these circumstances, I think that what I ought to do is to make no order today, but, subject to what counsel may have to say, to adjourn the case until the first day of next term. In ordinary circumstances, I would adjourn the case for only a week, but unfortunately the impending vacation makes this impossible. During the adjournment I hope that the defendant and his wife will take advice, separately or together. When I resume the hearing, it may be that the defendant's wife will not have changed her mind about her charge. In that case, I shall award the plaintiffs damages against the defendant of the order of £5,500, even though the probable consequence will be the bankruptcy of the defendant and the sale of the bungalow with vacant possession by his trustee in bankruptcy, free from the wife's rights. On the other hand, the defendant's wife may by then have changed her mind, and rather than force her husband into bankruptcy without avoiding having to vacate the bungalow, she may have taken effective steps to enable the defendant to convey the bungalow to the plaintiffs free from her rights. In that case I shall decree specific performance of the contract. In this way the plaintiffs will obtain either the bungalow that they bought or else an amount of damages which will enable them to purchase its equivalent. I may add that of course I give each side liberty to apply in the meantime; and I should say that I shall be available until 4 p.m. today. As I have indicated, I feel much sympathy for the defendant as well as for the plaintiffs at being embroiled in this way. Yet as between the two sides both the law and the merits seem to me to point to the plaintiffs as being the parties who should be as little hurt as possible; and they have already suffered considerably, not least in relation to their temporary accommodation pending these proceedings. Counsel will no doubt assist me with any submissions that they may have on this proposed adjournment, which was not mooted during the argument.

January 11, 1973. The defendant's wife refused to remove the notice. Damages of £5,500 assessed as at January 11, 1973, were awarded in lieu of specific performance, with costs.

Order accordingly.

QUESTION

What if the land is an apartment building, and the purchaser has ample funds on hand to purchase another as soon as the vendor defaults? See *AVG Management Science Ltd v Barwell Developments Ltd* (1976), 69 DLR (3d) 741 (BCSC), aff'd on this point, [1979] 2 SCR 43.

RG LAWSON, "DAMAGES: AN APPRAISAL OF WROTH V TYLER"
(1975) 125 New LJ 300

Damages for breach of contract, Parke B. once suggested, should place the innocent party in the position he would have occupied had the contract been performed (*Robinson v. Harrian* (1848) 1 Ex. 850, 855). Generally speaking, this is done by awarding a measure of compensation based on the difference in sale price and market price at the date of breach. A buyer fortified with such damages, the theory goes, is able to purchase equivalent goods in the market, and so occupy the position originally promised him by the seller.

Of course, if the market price at the date of judgment exceeds the market price at the date of breach, compensation based on the earlier date may be unsatisfactory. The objection that the buyer should mitigate his loss by making a substitute purchase before the date of judgment is valid only if he has sufficient cash in hand. This may not be so; particularly if he paid the defaulting seller in advance.

The situation canvassed above had rarely engaged authoritative attention. In *Gainsford v. Carroll* (1824) 2 B. & C. 624, the buyer was denied the rate prevailing at judgment: he had not prepaid, and could have made a replacement purchase at the date of breach. Although this indicates that the latter date would have been apposite where advance payment had been made, a later court ruled otherwise where precisely this had happened: *Startup v. Cortazzi* (1835) 2 C.M. & R. 165.

When the matter later arose, the facts, as Megarry J. put it, were "as simple as the law is complex" (*Wroth v. Tyler* [1973] 1 All E.R. 897, 901). Put briefly, the plaintiff sought specific performance of a contract for the sale of land. This was refused. Megarry J. then proceeded to award damages: but the date chosen was not the £7,500 at the date of breach, but the £11,500 which the land was worth at the date of judgment.

In *Wroth v. Tyler*, the damages were assessed under the Chancery Amendment Act, 1858 ("Lord Cairns' Act"). They were not awarded as common law damages, but were awarded under this statute in lieu of specific performance. Section 2 speaks of damages being awarded "in substitution" for specific performance which "at least envisages that the damages awarded will in fact constitute a true substitute for specific performance. Furthermore, the section is speaking of the time when the court is making its decision to award damages in substitution, so that it is at that moment that the damage must be a substitute" (*ibid.* at 920).

Perhaps an even clearer statement had come from Sholl J. in *Bosaid v. Andrey* [1963] V.L.R. 465. Damages would be given by a Chancery Court in lieu of specific performance, he believed, "on the hypothesis that the contract came to an end by the act of the Court itself in withholding specific performance—that is to say, at the time (usually of the decree) when the Court substituted an order for damages, even if it did not at once assess them."

If it follows inexorably from this reasoning that damages under Lord Cairns' Act are based as at the date of judgment, it is not self-evident that the same approach would obtain at law. Megarry J. was content to say only that it might; but he did add that the "rule requiring damages to be ascertained as at the date of breach does not seem to be inflexible," and that the normal principle of common law damages "may have to be modified so as to accord with the principle."

In *Horsler v. Zorro* [1973] 2 W.L.R. 183, Megarry J. was content once more to leave open the question whether damages at law could be awarded as at the date of judgment. Goff J., too, in *Grant v. Dawkins* [1973] 3 All E.R. 897, 900, has gone no further than to say that "there may be exceptions" to the normal date of assessment for damages at law. But in *Souster v. Epsom Plumbing Contractors Ltd.* [1974] 2 N.Z.L.R. 515

McMullin J. put the view, *obiter dicta*, that the same measure of damages would be allowable at common law since Lord Cairns' Act was merely a procedural section designed to permit the employment of common law remedies in Courts of Equity.

This is doubtless so; but it is no support for the further argument that damages at law may also be assessed as at the date of judgment. The special factor in Lord Cairns' Act, and this was recognised by McMullin J. as well as Megarry and Sholl JJ., is that the contract is terminated only when the Court judges that specific performance is inappropriate. Such considerations are absent when damages are sought at law.

There is, furthermore, the flatly contradictory decision in *Chitholie v. Nash & Co.* (1974) 229 E.G. 786. This was an action where the defendants conceded that they had no authority to act for the vendor in the sale of a dwelling-house. Talbot J. refused to award damages on the higher rate prevailing at the date of judgment. He was bound, so the report runs, "to follow the normal common law rule as to the measure of damages for breach of a contract for sale of land ... to depart from that normal rule would be to place upon the shoulders of the defendants the burden of a higher award of damages due not to their breach, but to events which had occurred after the breach and over which they had no control."

[See also McCamus at 1011-16; MacDougall at 360-61; Waddams at paras 700-5.]

IX. RESTITUTION

In previous sections of this chapter, we have examined the traditional remedies available to the victim of a breach of contract—damages, specific performance, and the injunction. These remedies are considered to be contractual remedies in the sense that they form a part of that branch of the law commonly referred to as the law of contracts. As we have seen, some of these remedial principles were developed by courts of common law. Others were developed by the courts of equity. In this section we turn to consider remedies that might be available to the victim of a breach of contract under what is now treated as a third branch of the law of obligations, in addition to contract and tort, the law of restitution.

The professional convention or practice of treating the doctrines of common law and equity relating to the enforcement of promises as a subject or branch of the law known as "contracts" emerged in the early 19th century as the first treatises on this subject were written and absorbed into the professional understanding of these materials. Treatises drawing together the great variety of doctrines relating to compensation for harms resulting from wrongful conduct and labelling them "torts" appeared only in the last decades of the century. Emergence of restitution or, as it is sometimes called, "unjust enrichment" as a third branch of the private law of obligations occurred only in the 20th century.

Recognition of the subject came first in the United States with the publication of the American Law Institute's *Restatement of Restitution* in 1937. It was the thesis of the *Restatement* that common law and equity doctrines concerning the recovery of benefits obtained by the defendant in various circumstances could be usefully restated as a new branch of the law. The restated jurisprudence concerned such matters as the recovery of benefits conferred by the plaintiff (1) by mistake; (2) under duress or other forms of coercion; (3) under ineffective transactions; (4) to preserve the life, health, or property of another; or (5) to discharge a duty owed by another and, additionally, a broad range of rules that have as their object the recovery of benefits obtained by the defendant as a result of some form of wrongdoing recognized either at common law or in equity. The theoretical premise of the *Restatement of Restitution* was that this rather large and seemingly disparate body of material could be seen to have the unity of a branch of law because the various doctrines in question could be said to be grounded on a general principle in favour of preventing unjust enrichment. Thus, the first article of the *Restatement* set out the general underlying principle of the *Restatement* in the following terms:

A person who has been unjustly enriched at the expense of another is required to make restitution to the other.

It was the view of the authors of the *Restatement* that the common law material dealing with these matters suffered from an unfortunate and misleading connection with the law of contracts. For reasons that need not be explored here, the nature of common law restitutionary doctrine or, as it was often called, quasi-contract, rested on the court's ability to imply a contractual obligation to restore the benefit received by the defendant to the plaintiff. In other words, the liability imposed in a restitutionary claim was, on this view, essentially contractual in nature. In its extreme version, this theory would lead to the conclusion that if for some reason an actual contract could not be factually inferred from the circumstances or, if inferred, would prove to be unenforceable as a matter of contract law for some reason, restitution must be denied. A leading illustration of the phenomenon is *Sinclair v Brougham*, [1914] AC 398, a decision of the House of Lords arising from the insolvency of a building society (a financial institution similar to the Canadian credit union or caisse populaire) that had been carrying on an unlawful banking business. The banking business was *ultra vires*—that is, beyond the lawful powers or capacity of the society. It was held that moneys advanced to a building society under *ultra vires* and therefore unenforceable deposit agreements could not be recovered by the depositors in a restitutionary claim. If a contract to return the funds were inferred, in the sense that an actual contract was implied to exist, such a contract would also be *ultra vires* the building society. On this view, then, the depositors who had been encouraged by the building society to deposit their money in accounts that proved to be beyond the capacity of the building society would have no restitutionary claim for the value of their deposits. On the basis of the unjust enrichment theory, by way of contrast, it would be possible to conclude that although the contract of deposit is unenforceable in such a case, it is a separate question whether the building society should be allowed to retain the deposits or, on the principle that otherwise the building society would be unjustly enriched, should be subject to an obligation to restore the deposits to the depositors.

The *Restatement* offers a similar explanation for conceptual difficulties manifest in the traditional law concerning equitable restitutionary claims that involved the awarding of constructive trust relief. At the risk of oversimplification, it may be said that, under the traditional English view, the constructive trust was considered to be a type of actual trust and therefore available only where the relationship between plaintiff and defendant bore some of the hallmarks of or was reasonably analogous to the relationship recognized in equity between a trustee and a beneficiary of a trust. Thus, under English law, constructive trust relief was essentially restricted to cases where the plaintiff and defendant had a so-called fiduciary relationship. Under the approach taken by the *Restatement*, the constructive trust was considered to be merely a remedy imposed to prevent unjust enrichment and, accordingly, could be considered to be more broadly available in restitution cases.

In a remarkable series of cases, beginning with *Deglman v Guaranty Trust Co and Constantineau*, below, in 1954, the Supreme Court of Canada essentially adopted the basic theory of the *Restatement* and accepted the view that basic to both quasi-contract and constructive trust is the principle against unjust enrichment. For a detailed account of this line of jurisprudence, see Maddaugh & McCamus, ch 3.

In *Deglman*, the restitutionary claim concerned the value of benefits conferred in the form of services rendered by a nephew to his aunt under an agreement that was unenforceable by reason of the *Statute of Frauds*. The English *Statute of Frauds*, enacted in 1677 and copied in most common law jurisdictions, although later varied and repealed in some, provided that no action could be brought on a number of kinds of agreements unless evidenced by a note or memorandum in writing signed by the party to be charged. The classes of agreement to which the original statute applied were contracts for the sale of land, guarantees, contracts for the sale of goods over a certain price, agreements not to be performed within a year, contracts in consideration of marriage, and promises by executors or administrators to assume personal liability. Judicial interpretation of the statute has given rise to many complexities. See generally Waddams, ch 6.

DEGLMAN V GUARANTY TRUST CO OF CANADA AND CONSTANTINEAU
[1954] SCR 725, 3 DLR 785

RAND J (Rinfret CJC and Taschereau J concurring): In this appeal the narrow question is raised as to the nature of part performance which will enable the Court to order specific performance of a contract relating to lands unenforceable at law by reason of s. 4 of the *Statute of Frauds*, R.S.O. 1950, c. 371. The respondent Constantineau claims the benefit of such a contract and the appellant represents the next-of-kin other than the respondent of the deceased, Laura Brunet, who resist it.

The respondent was the nephew of the deceased. Both lived in Ottawa. When he was about 20 years of age, and while attending a technical school, for 6 months of the school year 1934-35 he lived with his aunt at No. 550 Besserer St. Both that and the house on the adjoining lot, No. 548, were owned by the aunt and it was during this time that she is claimed to have agreed that if the nephew would be good to her and do such services for her as she might from time to time request during her lifetime she would make adequate provision for him in her will, and in particular that she would leave to him the premises at No. 548. While staying with her the nephew did the chores around both houses which, except for an apartment used by his aunt, were occupied by tenants. When the term ended he returned to the home of his mother on another street. In the autumn of that year he worked on the national highway in the northern part of Ontario. In the spring of 1936 he took a job on a railway at a point outside of Ottawa and at the end of that year, returning to Ottawa, he obtained a position with the city police force. In 1941 he married. At no time did he live at the house No. 548 or, apart from the 6 months, at the house No. 550.

The performance consisted of taking his aunt about in her own or his automobile on trips to Montreal and elsewhere, and on pleasure drives, of doing odd jobs about the two houses, and of various accommodations such as errands and minor services for her personal needs. ...

[Rand J considered the argument that the agreement was enforceable on the basis of the doctrine of part performance, which he rejected, reversing the courts below and holding the contract unenforceable under the *Statute of Frauds*, and continued:]

There remains the question of recovery for the services rendered on the basis of a *quantum meruit*. On the findings of both Courts below the services were not given gratuitously but on the footing of a contractual relation: they were to be paid for. The statute in such a case does not touch the principle of restitution against what would otherwise be an unjust enrichment of the defendant at the expense of the plaintiff. This is exemplified in the simple case of part or full payment in money as the price under an oral contract; it would be inequitable to allow the promisor to keep both the land and the money and the other party to the bargain is entitled to recover what he has paid. Similarly is it in the case of services given.

This matter is elaborated exhaustively in the *Restatement of the Law of Contract* issued by the American Law Institute and Professor Williston's monumental work on *Contracts*, 1936, vol. 2, s. 536 deals with the same topic. On the principles there laid down the respondent is entitled to recover for his services and outlays what the deceased would have had to pay for them on a purely business basis to any other person in the position of the respondent. The evidence covers generally and perhaps in the only way possible the particulars, but enough is shown to enable the Court to make a fair determination of the amount called for; and since it would be to the benefit of the other beneficiaries to bring an end to this litigation, I think we should not hesitate to do that by fixing the amount to be allowed. This I place at the sum of $3,000.

The appeal will therefore be allowed and the judgment modified by declaring the respondent entitled to recover against the respondent administrator the sum of $3,000; all costs will be paid out of the estate, those of the administrator as between solicitor and client.

CARTWRIGHT J (Estey, Locke, and Fauteux JJ concurring): ... I agree with the conclusion of my brother Rand that the respondent is entitled to recover the value of these services from the respondent administrator. This right appears to me to be based, not on the contract, but on an obligation imposed by law.

In *Fibrosa Spolka Akcyjna v. Fairbairn Lawson Combe Barbour Ltd.*, [1943] A.C. 32, at p. 61, Lord Wright said:

> It is clear that any civilized system of law is bound to provide remedies for cases of what has been called unjust enrichment or unjust benefit, that is to prevent a man from retaining the money of or some benefit derived from another which it is against conscience that he should keep. Such remedies in English law are generically different from remedies in contract or in tort, and are now recognized to fall within a third category of the common law which has been called quasi-contract or restitution.

And at p. 62:

> Lord Mansfield does not say that the law implies a promise. The law implies a debt or obligation which is a different thing. In fact, he denies that there is a contract; the obligation is as efficacious as if it were upon a contract. The obligation is a creation of the law, just as much as an obligation in tort. The obligation belongs to a third class, distinct from either contract or tort, though it resembles contract rather than tort.

Lord Wright's judgment appears to me to be in agreement with the view stated in Williston on Contracts referred to by my brother Rand. ...

In the case at bar all the acts for which the respondent asks to be paid under his alternative claim were clearly done in performance of the existing but unenforceable contract with the deceased that she would devise 548 Besserer St. to him, and to infer from them a fresh contract to pay the value of the services in money would be ... to draw an inference contrary to the fact.

In my opinion when the *Statute of Frauds* was pleaded the express contract was thereby rendered unenforceable, but the deceased having received the benefits of the full performance of the contract by the respondent, the law imposed upon her, and so on her estate, the obligation to pay the fair value of the services rendered to her.

If this is, as I think, the right view of the nature of the obligation upon which the respondent's claim rests it follows that the *Limitations Act* can have no application. ... In my opinion the obligation which the law imposes upon the respondent administrator did not arise until the deceased died intestate. It may well be that throughout her life it was her intention to make a will in fulfillment of the existing although unenforceable contract and until her death the respondent had no reason to doubt that she would do so. The statutory period of limitation does not commence to run until the plaintiff's cause of action has accrued; and on the facts of the case at bar the cause of action upon which the respondent is entitled to succeed did not accrue until the death of the deceased intestate.

For the above reasons I would dispose of the appeal as proposed by my brother Rand.

NOTES AND QUESTIONS

1. As illustrated by the well-known passage from the reasons of Lord Wright in the *Fibrosa* case, quoted by Cartwright J in *Deglman*, some English observers welcomed the American Law Institute's initiative. Such views remained heterodox in England, however, until the last decade or so of the 20th century when the American unjust enrichment analysis was finally absorbed into English restitutionary doctrine.

2. How does the measure of relief made available in *Deglman* differ from the measure of relief available for damages for breach of contract—that is, expectancy damages?

3. What should have been the result if the value of the nephew's services had exceeded the value of the house?

Boone v Coe. 154 SW 900 (Ky CA 1913). The plaintiffs, Boone and J.T. Coe, were farmers in Kentucky. The defendant, J.F. Coe, a farmer in Texas, orally promised them a lease of his farm for a year, to commence on their arrival at the farm in Texas. He also promised to build them a dwelling ready for occupancy on their arrival, to provide materials for a stock and grain barn, and to share with them a portion of the crop that the plaintiffs were to sow and cultivate. The plaintiffs did move to Texas, with their families, wagons, horses, and camping outfit, taking about 55 days, at an expense of $1,387.80, including $8 a day for the 55 days and 22 days while they remained in Texas; cash outlay en route $361.80; $100 for loss of time on the return trip, which took 4 days; and $150 for losses suffered in abandoning their homes and businesses in Kentucky. They returned because the defendant J.F. Coe failed to carry out any of his promises. In an action for damages the court held the contract was unenforceable under the *Statute of Frauds*, which required a promise for a lease for more than a year to be in writing and refused relief. CLAY C said:

> In the case under consideration the plaintiffs merely sustained a loss. Defendant received no benefit. Had he received a benefit, the law would imply an obligation to pay therefor. Having received no benefit, no obligation to pay is implied. The statute says that the contract of defendant made with plaintiffs is unenforceable. Defendant therefore had the legal right to decline to carry it out. To require him to pay plaintiffs for losses and expenses incurred on the faith of the contract, without any benefit accruing to him, would, in effect, uphold a contract upon which the statute expressly declares no action shall be brought. The statute was enacted for the purpose of preventing frauds and perjuries. That it is a valuable statute is shown by the fact that similar statutes are in force in practically all, if not all, of the states of the Union. Being a valuable statute, the purpose of the lawmakers in its enactment should not be defeated by permitting recoveries in cases to which its provisions were intended to apply.

NOTES AND QUESTIONS

1. Why is the *Statute of Frauds* not intended to apply when the plaintiff confers a benefit, but is intended to apply when the plaintiff confers no benefit? What does *Boone v Coe* tell us about the nature of restitutionary relief?

2. If *Deglman v Guaranty Trust* represents the triumph, for the purposes of Canadian law, of the unjust enrichment theory over the implied contract theory of restitutionary relief, it is of interest to note that, in an earlier era, some English judges adopted a similar view of the nature of restitutionary relief.

Moses v Macferlan. (1760), 2 Burr 1005, 97 ER 676. LORD MANSFIELD: If the defendant be under an obligation, from the ties of natural justice to refund; the law implies a debt, and gives this action, founded in the equity of the plaintiff's case, as it were upon a contract (*quasi ex contractu*, as the Roman law expresses it). ... This kind of equitable action, to recover back money, which ought not in justice to be kept, is very beneficial, and therefore much encouraged. It lies only for money which, *ex aequo et bono*, the defendant ought to refund ... it lies for money paid by mistake; or upon a consideration which happens to fail; or for money got through imposition (express or implied); or extortion; or oppression; or an undue advantage taken of the plaintiff's situation, contrary to laws made for the protection of persons under those circumstances.

In one word, the gist of this kind of action is that the defendant, upon the circumstances of the case, is obliged by the ties of natural justice and equity to refund the money.

The adoption of the unjust enrichment theory as an explanation for restitutionary recovery may thus be considered, in part at least, to achieve a restoration of the view of Lord Mansfield that common law relief in so-called quasi-contractual cases did not require the factual inference of a contractual obligation to restore the value received to the plaintiff.

The critical modern Canadian case adopting the unjust enrichment theory as an explanation for equity jurisprudence involving the imposition of a "remedial constructive trust" is *Pettkus v Becker*, [1980] 2 SCR 834, a case making constructive trust relief available to a female partner in a cohabiting relationship so as to require the male partner to share the assets acquired by the couple through their joint effort but with respect to which title had been taken exclusively by the male partner.

In subsequent chapters, we will examine the restitutionary remedies available in the context of ineffective transactions of various kinds where transactions have been rendered unenforceable by principles of either common law or equity. In the present chapter, however, it is pertinent to consider the restitutionary remedies that might be available to the victim of a breach of contract.

As a preliminary point, we might consider why a victim of a breach of contract might prefer to pursue restitutionary relief rather than damages for breach of contract. Keeping in mind that the measure of relief in a restitution claim is benefit-based rather than expectancy-based, one can imagine circumstances in which restitutionary relief might be preferable to the victim. Assume, for example, that a plaintiff entered into an unprofitable contract for the purchase of an asset at a rather disadvantageous price, paying a substantial deposit to the seller. In the event of the seller's default, the plaintiff might prefer to sue for restitutionary recovery of the deposit rather than be subject, in a contract damages claim, to the negative effects of the expectancy principle. See e.g. *Bowlay Logging Ltd v Domtar Ltd* (1982), 135 DLR (3d) 179 (BCCA). Alternatively, it may be that the complexity of proving expectancy damages may be such that the plaintiff would prefer the convenience of proof of the value of benefits conferred on the defendant in a restitutionary claim.

A further element of complexity is introduced, however, when it is revealed that the restitutionary doctrines drawn together in the *Restatement of Restitution* involve two different types of benefit-based liability. Many claims, such as that illustrated by *Deglman*, involve the recovery of benefits acquired by the defendant directly from or at the expense of the plaintiff. Other cases, however, both at common law and in equity, award recovery of benefits obtained by the defendant as a result of wrongful conduct constituting the breach of a duty owed to the plaintiff. Such relief is often referred to by contemporary scholars as disgorgement relief and involves the defendant disgorging to the plaintiff benefits acquired in this fashion. To illustrate, it is well established that in the context of some kinds of tortious wrongdoing and in the contexts of breach of fiduciary obligation and breach of confidence, the plaintiff is entitled to recover the value of benefits secured by the defendant through the wrongful conduct.

It is a distinguishing feature of disgorgement relief that its availability is not dependent on a demonstration by the plaintiff that, were it not for the defendant's breach of duty, the plaintiff would have acquired a similar benefit. Thus, where, for example, the defendant has, in breach of a fiduciary obligation owed to the plaintiff, secured benefits or profits that could not, in any event, have been enjoyed by the plaintiff, the defendant may nonetheless be required to disgorge such benefits to the plaintiff. See e.g. *Can Aero v O'Malley*, [1974] SCR 592. A question much debated in the law reviews in recent decades is whether, in the context of a breach of contract, the victim of the breach of contract may bring a restitutionary claim in the disgorgement measure to recover profits secured through the breach even though the plaintiff would not have secured such profits if the contract had been performed. For an analysis of the arguments for and against such relief, see L Smith, "Disgorgement of the Profits of Breach of Contract: Property, Contract and 'Efficient Breach'" (1994) 24 Can Bus LJ 121. Recovery in both measures of relief—recovery of the value of benefits conferred on the defendant by the plaintiff and the disgorgement of benefits secured through breach—are considered in the cases set out below.

HUNT V SILK
(1804), 5 East 449

The defendant landlord agreed to rent a house to the plaintiff, to repair it and to execute the lease within ten days in return for the plaintiff's initial payment of £10. The plaintiff paid the £10 and took immediate possession of the premises. The defendant, however, refused to make the repairs or to execute the lease, notwithstanding several requests from the plaintiff after expiry of the ten-day period. The plaintiff quit the premises and sought recovery of the £10.

LORD ELLENBOROUGH CJ: ... [I]nstead of making his stand, as he might have done, on the defendant's non-performance of what he had undertaken to do, [the plaintiff] waived his right, and voluntarily paid the money, giving the defendant credit for his future performance of the contract, and afterwards he continued in possession notwithstanding the defendant's default. Where a contract is to be rescinded at all, it must be rescinded in toto, and the parties put in *statu quo*. But here was an intermediate occupation, a part execution of the agreement, which was incapable of being rescinded. If the plaintiff might occupy the premises two days beyond the time when the repairs were to have been done and the lease executed, and yet rescind the contract, why might he not rescind it after a twelvemonth on the same account? This objection cannot be got rid of: the parties cannot be put in statu quo.

NOTES

1. The unwillingness of the court in *Hunt v Silk* to apportion and then deduct the benefit received by the tenant appears archaic in the light of the complex kinds of valuations that we have seen the courts making in some of the damages cases examined in this chapter. Nonetheless, the "total failure of consideration" requirement has remained a part of the English law of restitution for recovery of money payments in cases like *Hunt v Silk* until quite recently. To be sure, the requirement has sometimes been applied in a somewhat manipulative fashion. Thus, it has been held in a line of English cases that a buyer of goods may recover deposits paid to a seller, notwithstanding the fact that the buyer has enjoyed interim use of the goods, in cases where the seller has been unable to make title. Failure to make title is said to be a "total failure of consideration" because the transferring of title is the main object of the agreement. See e.g. *Rowland v Divall*, [1923] 2 KB 500 (CA).

2. The capacity of the rule to work an injustice is neatly illustrated by the decision of the Australian High Court in *Baltic Shipping Company v Dillon* (1993), 176 CLR 344. The plaintiff had paid a deposit on a 14-day cruise. On the 8th day of the cruise the ship struck a rock and sank. The plaintiff sued to recover, *inter alia*, the deposit paid, but this aspect of her claim failed on the basis that, inasmuch as she had received the first half of the cruise, there existed no total failure of consideration. The plaintiff was allowed, however, a claim for damages for breach of contract.

3. More recently, it has been suggested by the House of Lords that, at least in cases where the benefit received by the plaintiff is money, as in the case of an annuity, the total failure of consideration requirement does not constitute a bar for relief. See *Westdeutsche Landesbank Girozentrale v Islington LBC*, [1996] AC 669 (HL). More important, in *Goss v Chilcott*, [1996] AC 788, the Privy Council held that a restitutionary claim for moneys paid to the defendant could succeed, notwithstanding the fact that the plaintiff had received some benefit in return, "at least in cases in which an apportionment can be carried out without difficulty" (at 798).

4. It is unlikely that a contemporary Canadian court would apply the total failure of consideration requirement so as to defeat a restitutionary claim for moneys paid under a contract discharged by the defendant's breach. Certainly, the requirement has been ignored in the context of contracts for the sale of goods, where the buyer has enjoyed interim use of the goods but has nonetheless successfully sued to recover moneys paid, subject to an appropriate deduction for the value of the interim enjoyment. See e.g. *Gibbons v Trapp Motors Ltd* (1970), 9 DLR (3d) 742 (BCSC). Moreover, for historical reasons, the requirement was applied only in the context of money claims and is not applied, for example, where the plaintiff has supplied goods and services to a defendant who has breached the contract. See e.g. *Alkok v Grymek*, [1968] SCR 452. Could it be argued that this anomalous distinction should no longer be applied once the underlying unjust enrichment basis of these claims is recognized? Further, the requirement seems to be routinely ignored in money claims in contexts other than claims for moneys paid under agreements discharged by the defendant's breach of contract. For a more detailed account, see generally Maddaugh & McCamus, ss 4:200.10 and 19:200.

ATTORNEY GENERAL V BLAKE
[2000] UKHL 45, [2000] 4 All ER 385

LORD NICHOLLS OF BIRKENHEAD: George Blake is a notorious, self-confessed traitor. He was employed as a member of the security and intelligence services for 17 years, from 1944 to 1961. In 1951 he became an agent for the Soviet Union. From then until 1960 he disclosed valuable secret information and documents gained through his employment. On 3 May 1961 he pleaded guilty to five charges of unlawfully communicating information contrary to section 1(1)(c) of the *Official Secrets Act 1911*. He was sentenced to 42 years' imprisonment. This sentence reflected the extreme gravity of the harm brought about by his betrayal of secret information.

In 1966 Blake escaped from Wormwood Scrubs prison and fled to Berlin and then to Moscow. He is still there, a fugitive from justice. In 1989 he wrote his autobiography. Certain parts of the book related to his activities as a secret intelligence officer. By 1989 the information in the book was no longer confidential, nor was its disclosure damaging to the public interest. On 4 May 1989 Blake entered into a publishing contract with Jonathan Cape Ltd. He granted Jonathan Cape an exclusive right to publish the book in this country in return for royalties. Jonathan Cape agreed to pay him advances against royalties: £50,000 on signing the contract, a further £50,000 on delivery of the manuscript, and another £50,000 on publication. Plainly, had Blake not been an infamous spy who had also dramatically escaped from prison, his autobiography would not have commanded payments of this order.

The book, entitled *No Other Choice*, was published on 17 September 1990. Neither the security and intelligence services nor any other branch of the Government were aware of the book until its publication was announced. Blake had not sought any prior authorisation from the Crown to disclose any of the information in the book relating to the Secret Intelligence Service. Jonathan Cape has, apparently, already paid Blake about £60,000 under the publishing agreement. In practice that money is irrecoverable. A further substantial amount, in the region of £90,000, remains payable. These proceedings concern this unpaid money. ...

Blake's disclosure of the information in his autobiography to his publishers was a breach of section 1(1) of the *Official Secrets Act 1989*:

> A person who is or has been ... a member of the security and intelligence services ... is guilty of an offence if without lawful authority he discloses any information ... relating to security or intelligence which is or has been in his possession by virtue of his position as a member of any of those services. ...

... On 16 August 1944 Blake signed an *Official Secrets Act* declaration. This declaration included an undertaking:

> ... I undertake not to divulge any official information gained by me as a result of my employment, either in the press or in book form. I also understand that these provisions apply not only during the period of service but also after employment has ceased.

This undertaking was contractually binding. Had Blake not signed it he would not have been employed. By submitting his manuscript for publication without first obtaining clearance Blake committed a breach of this undertaking. The Court of Appeal suggested that the Crown might have a private law claim to "restitutionary damages for breach of contract," and invited submissions on this issue. The Attorney General decided that the Crown did not wish to advance argument on this point in the Court of Appeal. The Attorney General, however, wished to keep the point open for a higher court. The Court of Appeal expressed the view, necessarily tentative in the circumstances, that the law of contract would be seriously defective if the court were unable to award restitutionary damages for breach of contract. The law is now sufficiently mature to recognise a restitutionary claim for profits made from a breach of contract in appropriate situations. These include cases of "skimped" performance, and cases where the defendant obtained his profit by doing "the very thing" he contracted not to do. The present case fell into the latter category: Blake earned his profit by doing the very thing he had promised not to do.

This matter was pursued in your Lordship's House ... . This is a subject on which there is a surprising dearth of judicial decision. By way of contrast, over the last 20 years there has been no lack of academic writing ... . Most writers have favoured the view that in some circumstances the innocent party to a breach of contract should be able to compel the defendant to disgorge the profits he obtained from his breach of contract. However, there is a noticeable absence of any consensus on what are the circumstances in which this remedy should be available ... . The broad proposition that a wrongdoer should not be allowed to profit from his wrong has an obvious attraction. The corollary is that the person wronged may recover the amount of this profit when he has suffered no financially measurable loss. ... [T]he corollary is not so obviously persuasive. ...

INTERFERENCE WITH RIGHTS OF PROPERTY

So I turn to established, basic principles. I shall first set the scene by noting how the court approaches the question of financial recompense for interference with rights of property. As with breaches of contract, so with tort, the general principle regarding assessment of damages is that they are compensatory for loss or injury. The general rule is that, in the oft quoted words of Lord Blackburn, the measure of damages is to be, as far as possible, that amount of money which will put the injured party in the same position he would have been in had he not sustained the wrong: *Livingstone v. Rawyards Coal Co.* (1880) 5 App. Cas. 25, 39. Damages are measured by the plaintiff's loss, not the defendant's gain. But the common law, pragmatic as ever, has long recognised that there are many commonplace situations where a strict application of this principle would not do justice between the parties. Then compensation for the wrong done to the plaintiff is measured by a different yardstick. A trespasser who enters another's land may cause the landowner no financial loss. In such a case damages are measured by the benefit received by the trespasser, namely, by his use of the land. The same principle is applied where the wrong consists of use of another's land for depositing waste, or by using a path across the land or using passages in an underground mine. In this type of case the damages recoverable will be, in short, the price a reasonable person would pay for the right of user: see *Whitwam v. Westminster Brymbo Coal Co.* [1892] 2 Ch. 538, and the "wayleave" cases such as *Martin v. Porter* (1839) 5 M. and W. 351 and *Jegon v. Vivian* (1871) L.R. 6 Ch. 742. A more recent example was the non-removal of a floating dock, in *Penarth Dock Engineering Co. Ltd. v. Pounds* [1963] 1 Lloyd's Rep. 359.

The same principle is applied to the wrongful detention of goods. An instance is the much cited decision of the Court of Appeal in *Strand Electric and Engineering Co. Ltd. v. Brisford Entertainments Ltd.* [1952] 2 Q.B. 246, concerning portable switchboards. But the principle has a distinguished ancestry. Earl of Halsbury L.C. famously asked in *The Mediana* [1900] A.C. 113, 117, that if a person took away a chair from his room and kept it for 12 months, could anybody say you had a right to diminish the damages by showing that I did not usually sit in that chair, or that there were plenty of other chairs in the room? To the same effect was Lord Shaw's telling example in *Watson, Laidlaw & Co. Ltd. v. Pott, Cassels, and Williamson* (1914) 31 R.P.C. 104, 119. It bears repetition:

If A, being a liveryman, keeps his horse standing idle in the stable, and B, against his wish or without his knowledge, rides or drives it out, it is no answer to A for B to say: "Against what loss do you want to be restored? I restore the horse. There is no loss. The horse is none the worse; it is the better for the exercise."

Lord Shaw prefaced this observation with a statement of general principle:

[W]herever an abstraction or invasion of property has occurred, then, unless such abstraction or invasion were to be sanctioned by law, the law ought to yield a recompense under the category or principle ... either of price or of hire.

That was a patent infringement case. The House of Lords held that damages should be assessed on the footing of a royalty for every infringing article.

This principle is established and not controversial. More difficult is the alignment of this measure of damages within the basic compensatory measure. Recently there has been a move towards applying the label of restitution to awards of this character: see, for instance, *Ministry of Defence v. Ashman* [1993] 2 E.G.L.R. 102, 105, and *Ministry of Defence v. Thompson* [1993] 2 E.G.L.R. 107. However that may be, these awards cannot be regarded as conforming to the strictly compensatory measure of damage for the injured person's loss unless loss is given a strained and artificial meaning. The reality is that the injured person's rights were invaded but, in financial terms, he suffered no loss. Nevertheless the common law has found a means to award him a sensibly calculated amount of money. Such awards are probably best regarded as an exception to the general rule.

Courts of equity went further than the common law courts. In some cases equity required the wrongdoer to yield up all his gains. In respect of certain wrongs which originally or ordinarily were the subject of proceedings in the Court of Chancery, the standard remedies were injunction and, incidental thereto, an account of profits. These wrongs included passing off, infringement of trade marks, copyrights and patents, and breach of confidence. Some of these subjects are now embodied in statutory codes. An injunction restrained the continuance of the wrong, and the wrongdoer was required to account for the profits or benefits he had obtained from breaches or infringements which had already occurred. The court always had a discretion regarding the grant of the remedy of an account of profits, and this remains the position. Further, the circumstances in which an account of profits is available under the statutes vary. For instance, an account of profits may not be ordered against a defendant in a patent infringement action who proves that at the date of the infringement he was not aware, and had no reasonable grounds for supposing, that the patent existed: *Patents Act 1977*, section 62(1).

In these cases the courts of equity appear to have regarded an injunction and account of profits as more appropriate remedies than damages because of the difficulty of assessing the extent of the loss. Thus, in 1803 Lord Eldon L.C. stated, in *Hogg v. Kirby* 8 Ves. Jun. 215, 223, a passing off case:

> [W]hat is the consequence in Law and in Equity? ... [A] Court of Equity in these cases is not content with an action for damages; for it is nearly impossible to know the extent of the damage; and therefore the remedy here, though not compensating the pecuniary damage except by an account of profits, is the best: the remedy by an injunction and account.

Whether this justification for ordering an account of profits holds good factually in every case must be doubtful. Be that as it may, in these types of case equity considered that the appropriate response to the violation of the plaintiff's right was that the defendant should surrender all his gains, and that he should do so irrespective of whether the violation had caused the plaintiff any financially measurable loss. Gains were to be disgorged even though they could not be shown to correspond with any disadvantage suffered by the other party. This lack of correspondence was openly acknowledged. In *Lever v. Goodwin* (1887) 36 Ch. D. 1, 7, Cotton L.J. stated it was "well known" that in trade mark and patent cases the plaintiff was entitled, if he succeeded in getting an injunction, to take either of two forms of relief: he might claim from the defendant either the damage he had sustained from the defendant's wrongful act or the profit made by the defendant from the defendant's wrongful act.

Considered as a matter of principle, it is difficult to see why equity required the wrongdoer to account for all his profits in these cases, whereas the common law's response was to require a wrongdoer merely to pay a reasonable fee for use of another's land or goods. In all these cases rights of property were infringed. This difference in remedial response appears to have arisen simply as an accident of history.

In some instances the common law itself afforded a wronged party a choice of remedies. A notable example is the wrong of conversion. A person whose goods were wrongfully converted by another had a choice of two remedies against the wrongdoer. He could recover damages, in respect of the loss he had sustained by the conversion. Or he could recover the proceeds of the conversion obtained by the defendant: see *United Australia Ltd. v. Barclays Bank Ltd.* [1941] A.C. 1, 34, *per* Lord Romer. Historically, the latter alternative was achieved by recourse to an element of legal fiction, whereby the innocent party "waived the tort." The innocent party could suppose that the wrongful sale had been made with his consent and bring an action for money "had and received to his use": see *Lamine v. Dorrell* (1701) 2 Ld. Raym. 1216, 1217. Holt C.J. observed that these actions had "crept in by degrees."

BREACH OF TRUST AND FIDUCIARY DUTY

I should refer briefly to breach of trust and breach of fiduciary duty. Equity reinforces the duty of fidelity owed by a trustee or fiduciary by requiring him to account for any profits he derives from his office or position. This ensures that trustees and fiduciaries are financially disinterested in carrying out their duties. They may not put themselves in a position where their duty and interest conflict. To this end they must not make any unauthorised profit. If they do, they are accountable. Whether the beneficiaries or persons to whom the fiduciary duty is owed suffered any loss by the impugned transaction is altogether irrelevant. The accountability of the army sergeant in *Reading v. Attorney General* [1951] A.C. 507 is a familiar application of this principle to a servant of the Crown.

DAMAGES UNDER LORD CAIRNS' ACT

I must also mention the jurisdiction to award damages under section 2 of the *Chancery Amendment Act 1858*, commonly known as *Lord Cairns' Act*. This Act has been repealed but the jurisdiction remains. Section 2 empowered the Court of Chancery at its discretion, in all cases where it had jurisdiction to entertain an application for an injunction or specific performance, to award damages in addition to or in substitution for an injunction or specific performance. Thus section 2 enabled the Court of Chancery, sitting at Lincoln's Inn, to award damages when declining to grant equitable relief rather than, as had been the practice since Lord Eldon's decision in *Todd v. Gee* (1810) 17 Ves. 273, sending suitors across London to the common law courts at Westminster Hall.

Lord Cairns' Act had a further effect. The common law courts' jurisdiction to award damages was confined to loss or injury flowing from a cause of action which had accrued before the writ was issued. Thus in the case of a continuing wrong, such as maintaining overhanging eaves and gutters, damages were limited to the loss suffered up to the commencement of the action: see *Battishill v. Reed* (1856) 18 C.B. 696. *Lord Cairns' Act* liberated the courts from this fetter. In future, if the court declined to grant an injunction, which had the effect in practice of sanctioning the indefinite continuance of a wrong, the court could assess damages to include losses likely to follow from the anticipated future continuance of the wrong as well as losses already suffered. The power to give damages in lieu of an injunction imported the power to give an equivalent for what was lost by the refusal of an injunction: see *Leeds Industrial Co-operative Society Ltd. v. Slack* [1924] A.C. 851, 859, *per* Viscount Finlay L.C. It is important to note, however, that although the Act had the effect of enabling the court in this regard to award damages in respect of the future as well as the past, the Act did not alter the measure to be employed in assessing damages: see *Johnson v. Agnew* [1980] A.C. 367, 400, *per* Lord Wilberforce. Thus, in the same way as damages at common law for violations of a property right may be measured by reference to the benefits wrongfully obtained by a defendant, so under *Lord Cairns' Act* damages may include damages measured by reference to the benefits likely to be obtained in future by the defendant. This approach has been adopted on many occasions. Recent examples are *Bracewell v. Appleby* [1975] Ch. 408 and *Jaggard v. Sawyer* [1995] 1 W.L.R. 269, both cases concerned with access to a newly-built house over another's land.

The measure of damages awarded in this type of case is often analysed as damages for loss of a bargaining opportunity or, which comes to the same, the price payable for the compulsory acquisition of a right. This analysis is correct. The court's refusal to grant an injunction means that in practice the defendant is thereby permitted to perpetuate the wrongful state of affairs he has brought about. But this analysis takes the matter now under discussion no further forward. A property right has value to the extent only that the court will enforce it or award damages for its infringement. The question under discussion is whether the court will award substantial damages for an infringement when no financial loss flows from the infringement and, moreover, in a suitable case will assess the damages by reference to the defendant's profit obtained from the infringement. The cases mentioned above show that the courts habitually do that very thing.

BREACH OF CONTRACT

Against this background I turn to consider the remedies available for breaches of contract. The basic remedy is an award of damages. In the much quoted words of Baron Parke, the rule of the common law is that where a party sustains a loss by reason of a breach of contract, he is, so far as money can do it, to be placed in the same position as if the contract had been performed: *Robinson v. Harman* (1848) 1 Ex. 850, 855. Leaving aside the anomalous exception of punitive damages, damages are compensatory. That is axiomatic. It is equally well established that an award of damages, assessed by reference to financial loss, is not always "adequate" as a remedy for a breach of contract. The law recognises that a party to a contract may have an interest in performance which is not readily measurable in terms of money. On breach the innocent party suffers a loss. He fails to obtain the benefit promised by the other party to the contract. To him the loss may be as important as financially measurable loss, or more so. An award of damages, assessed by reference to financial loss, will not recompense him properly. For him a financially assessed measure of damages is inadequate.

The classic example of this type of case, as every law student knows, is a contract for the sale of land. The buyer of a house may be attracted by features which have little or no impact on the value of the house. An award of damages, based on strictly financial criteria, would fail to recompense a disappointed buyer for this head of loss. The primary response of the law to this type of case is to ensure, if possible, that the contract is performed in accordance with its terms. The court may make orders compelling the party who has committed a breach of contract, or is threatening to do so, to carry out his contractual obligations. To this end the court has wide powers to grant injunctive relief. The court will, for instance, readily make orders for the specific performance of contracts for the sale of land, and sometimes it will do so in respect of contracts for the sale of goods. In *Beswick v. Beswick* [1968] A.C. 58 the court made an order for the specific performance of a contract to make payments of money to a third party. The law recognised that the innocent party to the breach of contract had a legitimate interest in having the contract performed even though he himself would suffer no financial loss from its breach. Likewise, the court will compel the observance of negative obligations by granting injunctions. This may include a mandatory order to undo an existing breach, as where the court orders the defendant to pull down building works carried out in breach of covenant.

All this is trite law. In practice, these specific remedies go a long way towards providing suitable protection for innocent parties who will suffer loss from breaches of contract which are not adequately remediable by an award of damages. But these remedies are not always available. For instance, confidential information may be published in breach of a non-disclosure agreement before the innocent party has time to apply to the court for urgent relief. Then the breach is irreversible. Further, these specific remedies are discretionary. Contractual obligations vary infinitely. So do the circumstances in which breaches occur, and the circumstances in which remedies are sought. The court may, for instance, decline to grant specific relief on the ground that this would be oppressive.

An instance of this nature occurred in *Wrotham Park Estate Co. Ltd. v. Parkside Homes Ltd.* [1974] 1 W.L.R. 798. For social and economic reasons the court refused to make a mandatory order for the demolition of houses built on land burdened with a restrictive covenant. Instead, Brightman J. made an award of damages under the jurisdiction which originated with *Lord Cairns' Act.* The existence of the new houses did not diminish the value of the benefited land by one farthing. The judge considered that if the plaintiffs were given a nominal sum, or no sum, justice would manifestly not have been done. He assessed the damages at five per cent of the developer's anticipated profit, this being the amount of money which could reasonably have been demanded for a relaxation of the covenant.

In reaching his conclusion the judge applied by analogy the cases mentioned above concerning the assessment of damages when a defendant has invaded another's property rights but without diminishing the value of the property. I consider he was right to do so. Property rights are superior to contractual rights in that, unlike contractual rights, property rights may survive against an indefinite class of persons. However, it is not easy to see why, as between the parties to a contract, a violation of a party's contractual rights should attract a lesser degree of remedy than a violation of his property rights. As Lionel Smith has pointed out in his article "Disgorgement of the Profits of Contract: Property, Contract, and 'Efficient Breach'" (1994), 24 *Can. B.L.J.* 121, it is not clear why it should be any more permissible to expropriate personal rights than it is permissible to expropriate property rights. ...

[Lord Nicholls then considered and rejected as unsatisfactory a decision of the Court of Appeal that was inconsistent with the decision in *Wrotham Park.*]

The *Wrotham Park* case, therefore, still shines, rather as a solitary beacon, showing that in contract as well as tort damages are not always narrowly confined to recoupment of financial loss. In a suitable case damages for breach of contract may be measured by the benefit gained by the wrongdoer from the breach. The defendant must make a reasonable payment in respect of the benefit he has gained. In the present case the Crown seeks to go further. The claim is for all the profits of Blake's book which the publisher has not yet paid him. This raises the question whether an account of profits can ever be given as a remedy for breach of contract. The researches of counsel have been unable to discover any case where the court has made such an order on a claim for breach of contract. ...

There is a light sprinkling of cases where courts have made orders having the same effect as an order for an account of profits, but the courts seem always to have attached a different label. A person who, in breach of contract, sells land twice over must surrender his profits on the second sale to the original buyer. Since courts regularly make orders for the specific performance of contracts for the sale of land, a seller of land is, to an extent, regarded as holding the land on trust for the buyer: *Lake v. Bayliss* [1974] 1 W.L.R. 1073. In *Reid-Newfoundland Co. v. Anglo-American Telegraph Co., Ltd.* [1912] A.C. 555 a railway company agreed not to transmit any commercial messages over a particular telegraph wire except for the benefit and account of the telegraph company. The Privy Council held that the railway company was liable to account as a trustee for the profits it wrongfully made from its use of the wire for commercial purposes. In *British Motor Trade Association v. Gilbert* [1951] 2 All E.R. 641 the plaintiff suffered no financial loss but the award of damages for breach of contract effectively stripped the wrongdoer of the profit he had made from his wrongful venture into the black market for new cars.

These cases illustrate that circumstances do arise when the just response to a breach of contract is that the wrongdoer should not be permitted to retain any profit from the breach. In these cases the courts have reached the desired result by straining existing concepts. Professor Peter Birks has deplored the "failure of jurisprudence when the law is forced into this kind of abusive instrumentalism": see (1993) 109 *L.Q.R.* 518, 520. Some years ago Professor Dawson suggested there is no inherent reason why the technique of equity courts in land contracts should not be more widely employed, not by granting remedies as the by-product of a phantom "trust" created by the contract, but as an alternative form of money judgment remedy. That well known ailment of lawyers, a hardening of the categories, ought not to be an obstacle: see "Restitution or Damages" (1959) 20 *Ohio L.J.* 175.

My conclusion is that there seems to be no reason, in principle, why the court must in all circumstances rule out an account of profits as a remedy for breach of contract. I prefer to avoid the unhappy expression "restitutionary damages." Remedies are the law's response to a wrong (or, more precisely, to a cause of action). When, exceptionally, a just response to a breach of contract so requires, the court should be able to grant the discretionary remedy of requiring a defendant to account to the plaintiff for the benefits he has received from his breach of contract. In the same way as a plaintiff's interest in performance of a contract may render it just and equitable for the court to make an order for specific performance or grant an injunction, so the plaintiff's interest in performance may make it just and equitable that the defendant should retain no benefit from his breach of contract.

The state of the authorities encourages me to reach this conclusion, rather than the reverse. The law recognises that damages are not always a sufficient remedy for breach of contract. This is the foundation of the court's jurisdiction to grant the remedies of specific performance and injunction. Even when awarding damages, the law does not adhere slavishly to the concept of compensation for financially measurable loss. When the circumstances require, damages are measured by reference to the benefit obtained by the wrongdoer. This applies to interference with property rights. Recently, the like approach has been adopted to breach of contract. Further, in certain circumstances an account of profits is ordered in preference to an award of damages. Sometimes the injured party is given the choice: either compensatory damages or an account of the wrongdoer's profits. Breach of confidence is an instance of this. If confidential information is wrongfully divulged in breach of a non-disclosure agreement, it would be nothing short of sophistry to say that an account of profits may be ordered in respect of the equitable wrong but not in respect of the breach of contract which governs the relationship between the parties. With the established authorities going thus far, I consider it would be only a modest step for the law to recognise openly that, exceptionally, an account of profits may be the most appropriate remedy for breach of contract. It is not as though this step would contradict some recognised principle applied consistently throughout the law to the grant or withholding of the remedy of an account of profits. No such principle is discernible.

The main argument against the availability of an account of profits as a remedy for breach of contract is that the circumstances where this remedy may be granted will be uncertain. This will have an unsettling effect on commercial contracts where certainty is important. I do not think these fears are well founded. I see no reason why, in practice, the availability of the remedy of an account of profits need disturb settled expectations in the commercial or consumer world. An account of profits will be appropriate only in exceptional circumstances. Normally the remedies of damages, specific performance and injunction, coupled with the characterisation of some contractual obligations as fiduciary, will provide an adequate response to a breach of contract. It will be only in exceptional cases, where those remedies are inadequate, that any question of accounting for profits will arise. No fixed rules can be prescribed. The court will have regard to all the circumstances, including the subject matter of the contract, the purpose of the contractual provision which has been breached, the circumstances in which the breach occurred, the consequences of the breach and the circumstances in which relief is being sought. A useful general guide, although not exhaustive, is whether the plaintiff had a legitimate interest in preventing the defendant's profit-making activity and, hence, in depriving him of his profit.

It would be difficult, and unwise, to attempt to be more specific. In the Court of Appeal Lord Woolf, M.R. suggested there are at least two situations in which justice requires the award of restitutionary damages where compensatory damages would be inadequate: see [1998] Ch. 439, 458. Lord Woolf was not there addressing the question of when an account of profits, in the conventional sense, should be available. But I should add that, so far as an account of profits is concerned, the suggested categorisation would not assist. The first suggested category was the case of "skimped" performance, where the defendant fails to provide the full extent of services he has contracted to provide. He should be liable to pay back the amount of expenditure he saved by the breach. This is a much discussed problem. But a part refund of the price agreed for services would not fall within the scope of an account of profits as ordinarily understood. Nor does an account of profits seem to be needed in this context. The resolution of the problem of cases of skimped performance, where the plaintiff does not get what was agreed, may best be found elsewhere. If a shopkeeper supplies inferior and cheaper goods than those ordered and paid for, he has to refund the difference in price. That would be the outcome of a claim for damages for breach of contract. That would be so, irrespective of whether the goods in fact served the intended purpose. There must be scope for a similar approach, without any straining of principle, in cases where the defendant provided inferior and cheaper services than those contracted for.

The second suggested category was where the defendant has obtained his profit by doing the very thing he contracted not to do. This category is defined too widely to assist. The category is apt to embrace all express negative obligations. But something more is required than mere breach of such an obligation before an account of profits will be the appropriate remedy.

Lord Woolf, at [1998] Ch. 439, 457, 458, also suggested three facts which should not be a sufficient ground for departing from the normal basis on which damages are awarded: the fact that the breach was cynical and deliberate; the fact that the breach enabled the defendant to enter into a more profitable contract elsewhere; and the fact that by entering into a new and more profitable contract the defendant put it out of his power to perform his contract with the plaintiff. I agree that none of these facts would be, by itself, a good reason for ordering an account of profits.

THE PRESENT CASE

The present case is exceptional. The context is employment as a member of the security and intelligence services. Secret information is the lifeblood of these services. In the 1950s Blake deliberately committed repeated breaches of his undertaking not to divulge official information gained as a result of his employment. He caused untold and immeasurable damage to the public interest he had committed himself to serve. In 1990 he published his autobiography, a further breach of his express undertaking. By this time the information disclosed was no longer confidential. In the ordinary course of commercial dealings the disclosure of non-confidential information might be regarded as venial. In the present case disclosure was also a criminal offence under the *Official Secrets Acts*, even though the information was no longer confidential. Section 1 of the *Official Secrets Act 1989* draws a distinction in this regard between members of the security and intelligence services and other Crown servants. Under section 1(3) a person who is or has been a Crown servant is guilty of an offence if without lawful authority he makes "a damaging disclosure" of information relating to security or intelligence. The offence is drawn more widely in the case of a present or past member of the security and intelligence services. Such a person is guilty of an offence if without lawful authority he discloses "any information" relating to security or intelligence which is or has been in his possession by virtue of his position as a member of those services. This distinction was approved in Parliament after debate when the legislation was being enacted. ...

When he joined the Secret Intelligence Service Blake expressly agreed in writing that he would not disclose official information, during or after his service, in book form or otherwise. He was employed on that basis. That was the basis on which he acquired official information. The Crown had and has a legitimate interest in preventing Blake [from] profiting from the disclosure of official information, whether classified or not, while a member of the service and thereafter. Neither he, nor any other member of the service, should have a financial incentive to break his undertaking. It is of paramount importance that members of the service should have complete confidence in all their dealings with each other, and that those recruited as informers should have the like confidence. Undermining the willingness of prospective informers to co-operate with the services, or undermining the morale and trust between members of the services when engaged on secret and dangerous operations, would jeopardise the effectiveness of the service. An absolute rule against disclosure, visible to all, makes good sense.

In considering what would be a just response to a breach of Blake's undertaking the court has to take these considerations into account. The undertaking, if not a fiduciary obligation, was closely akin to a fiduciary obligation, where an account of profits is a standard remedy in the event of breach. Had the information which Blake has now disclosed still been confidential, an account of profits would have been ordered, almost as a matter of course. In the special circumstances of the intelligence services, the same conclusion should follow even though the information is no longer confidential. That would be a just response to the breach. I am reinforced in this view by noting that most of the profits from the book derive indirectly from the extremely serious and damaging breaches of the same undertaking committed by

Blake in the 1950s. As already mentioned, but for his notoriety as an infamous spy his autobiography would not have commanded royalties of the magnitude Jonathan Cape agreed to pay.

LORD HOBHOUSE (dissenting): ... I must also sound a further note of warning that if some more extensive principle of awarding non-compensatory damages for breach of contract is to be introduced into our commercial law, the consequences will be very far-reaching and disruptive. I do not believe that such is the intention of your Lordships but if others are tempted to try to extend the decision of the present exceptional case to commercial situations so as to introduce restitutionary rights beyond those presently recognized by the law of restitution, such a step will require very careful consideration before it is acceded to ... . The policy which is being enforced is that which requires Blake to be punished by depriving him of any benefit from anything connected with his past deplorable conduct. Your Lordships consider that this policy can be given effect to without a departure from principle. I must venture to disagree.

[The court granted an order declaring that the attorney general was entitled to be paid a sum equal to whatever amount was due and owing to Blake from Jonathan Cape under the publishing agreement. Lord Hobhouse dissented on the ground that no principle was available to support the result favoured by the majority.]

NOTES AND QUESTIONS

1. What is the nature of the test identified by Lord Nicholls for determining whether a case is an appropriate one for the awarding of the disgorgement remedy? Would it apply to the following fact situation? Esso adopted a "Pricewatch" program to deal with the intermittent type of price war that breaks out among service stations. Service stations participating in Esso's program received an extra discount on gas supplied by Esso to them in return for an undertaking to participate in the program, which required the provision of information concerning prices charged by competitors and an agreement to charge prices required, from time to time, by Esso under the program. The defendant agreed to participate but then failed to charge the prices required by Esso with resulting profit. Should Esso be entitled to recover such profit under the test set out in *Attorney General v Blake*? See *Esso Petroleum Co Ltd v Niad*, [2001] All ER (D) 324 (Ch) (applying *Blake* and allowing such relief).

2. Did the attorney general or the Crown suffer a financially compensable loss? If not, on the basis of what policy considerations can the recovery of profits made by Blake be justified?

3. In *Bank of America Canada v Mutual Trust Co*, 2002 SCC 43, [2002] 2 SCR 601, the Supreme Court of Canada acknowledged, without discussion of the innovative nature of the point, the existence of a discretion to award disgorgement relief in the context of a breach of contract case. Major J (for the court) observed:

Contract damages are determined in one of two ways. Expectation damages, the usual measure of contract damages, focus on the value which the plaintiff would have received if the contract had been performed. Restitution damages, which are infrequently applied, focus on the advantage gained by the defendant as a result of his or her breach of contract.

With respect to the latter, Major J observed:

The other side of the coin is to examine the effect of the breach on the defendant. In contract, restitution damages can be invoked when a defendant has, as a result of his or her own breach, profited in excess of his or her expected profit had the contract been performed but the plaintiff's loss is less than the defendant's gain. So the plaintiff can be fully paid in damages with a surplus left in the hands of the defendant. This occurs with what has been described as an efficient breach of contract. In some but not all cases, the defendant may be required to pay such profits to the plaintiff as restitution damages. ...

Courts generally avoid this measure of damages so as not to discourage efficient breach (i.e., where the plaintiff is fully compensated and the defendant is better off than if he or she had performed the contract) ... . Efficient breach is what economists describe as a Pareto optimal outcome where one party may be better off but no one is worse off, or expressed differently, nobody loses. Efficient breach should not be discouraged by the courts. This lack of disapproval emphasizes that a court will usually award money damages for breach of contract equal to the value of the bargain to the plaintiff.

4. Canadian courts, both before and after *Blake*, have occasionally awarded disgorgement relief for breach of contract. See e.g. *Arbutus Park Estates Ltd v Fuller* (1976), 74 DLR (3d) 257 (BCSC); *Jostens Canada Ltd v Gibsons Studio Ltd*, [1998] 5 WWR 403 (BCCA); *Amertek Inc v Canadian Commercial Corp* (2003), 229 DLR (4th) 419 (Ont Sup Ct J).

5. For discussion of the concept of efficient breach, see R Posner, *Economic Analysis of Law*, 5th ed (New York: Aspen Law & Business, 1998) at 130-40; D Friedmann, "The Efficient Breach Fallacy" (1989) 18 J Legal Stud 1; R O'Dair, "Restitutionary Damages for Breach of Contract and Efficient Breach: Some Reflections" (1993) 46 CLP 113; L Smith, above.

6. For discussion of the *Blake* decision, see M McInnes, "Gain-Based Relief for Breach of Contract: Attorney General v Blake" (2001) 35 CBLJ 72; J McCamus, "Disgorgement for Breach of Contract: A Comparative Perspective" (2003) 36 Loy LA L Rev 943; J Edelman, *Gain-Based Damages* (Oxford: Oxford University Press, 2002) ch 5; Maddaugh & McCamus, ch 25.

7. In *Smith v Landstar Properties Inc*, 2011 BCCA 44, 320 DLR (4th) 664, the plaintiff had advanced moneys to the defendant on a loan that was agreed to be secured by a registered charge on the defendant's property. The defendant never intended to perform his contractual obligation to provide security and did not do so. The loan was, however, fully repaid with interest. The plaintiff successfully claimed the difference between the interest actually paid and the interest that would have been paid on an unsecured loan. Is this a disgorgement claim? Is it relevant that the plaintiff would not have loaned the money to the defendant on an unsecured loan?

CHAPTER THREE

THE KINDS OF PROMISES LEGALLY ENFORCED

The materials in this chapter are divided into bargains and non-bargain promises. A bargain is an agreed-on exchange, and the existence of a bargain has been the chief criterion for the enforceability of promises in the common law. The constituent parts of a bargain are intention, mutual assent to sufficiently certain terms (commonly called offer and acceptance), and an exchange of value (commonly called consideration). In the 19th century, the view developed that all contracts were bargains—that is, that the existence of a bargain was the *only* reason for the enforcement of promises. The materials in Section III, below, however, suggest that the bargain theory may not be a full account of contract law and that there may be other reasons for the enforcement of promises.

I. BARGAINS

A. OFFERS AND PRELIMINARY NEGOTIATIONS

CORBIN ON CONTRACTS, § 11
(St Paul, Minn: West, 1952)

OFFER DEFINED

An offer is an expression by one party of his assent to certain definitive terms, provided that the other party involved in the bargaining transaction will likewise express his assent to the identically same terms. An offer looks forward to an agreement—to mutual expression of assent. ...

[W]hat change in legal relations is brought about by the making of an offer? It is believed that the best short description of this change is that the offer creates a power of acceptance in the offeree. It will not be disputed by any one that, after an offer is made, a voluntary expression of assent by the offeree is all that is necessary to create what we call contract. This is what is meant, and it is all that is meant, by saying that an offer creates a power of acceptance in the offeree. ...

What kind of act creates a power of acceptance and is therefore an offer? It must be an expression of will or intention. It must be an act that leads the offeree reasonably to believe that a power to create a contract is conferred upon him. ... It is on this ground that we must exclude invitations to deal or acts of mere preliminary negotiations, and acts evidently done in jest ... .

An expression of willingness to make a contract is not operative as an offer unless it is made in such a manner as justifies another person in thinking that it is directed to him for his acceptance. ...

In order to be legally operative and to create a power of acceptance, it is necessary that the offer shall contain all the terms of the contract to be made. It is not enough for one party to say what he himself will promise to do; he must also say what he will do it for, that is, what the other party must do in exchange. If A says to B: "I will sell and convey Blackacre to you," and B replies: "I will pay you $5,000," no contract has been made yet.

NOTES

1. What you have just read is one academic's attempt to synthesize, in a formal manner, some of the basic rules relating to offers. As you examine the cases and materials excerpted below, ask yourself whether Corbin's postulates are an accurate reflection of the law.

2. Issues relating to offers and unilateral contracts are dealt with in Section IV, below.

DENTON V GREAT NORTHERN RAILWAY COMPANY
(1856), 5 E & B 860, 119 ER 701 (QB)

The plaintiff being in London in March, 1855, and having business at Peterborough on the 25th March, 1855, and at Hull on the 26th March, 1855, consulted the printed time tables issued in the usual way by the defendants for that month. In these time tables a train was advertised to leave London at 5 p.m. and reach Peterborough about 7 p.m. and thence to proceed, amongst other towns, to Hull, to arrive there about midnight. At the bottom of the time tables was the following notice:

> The Companies make every exertion that the trains shall be punctual, but their arrival or departure at the times stated will not be guaranteed, nor will the companies hold themselves responsible for delay or any consequences arising therefrom.

The time tables advertising this train were, till after 26th March, exhibited by the defendants at their stations, where the plaintiff had seen them, and were printed and circulated; and on the 25th March the plaintiff had one in his possession.

The plaintiff, having made his arrangements on the faith of these time tables, went down to Peterborough by an early train of the defendants, transacted his business at Peterborough, and went to the defendants' station at Peterborough in due time to take a ticket to Hull by the evening train so advertised: but there was no such train to Hull; nor had there been one during any part of the month of March. The explanation of this was that the whole line of railway from Peterborough to Hull was not the property of the defendants, their line ending at Askerne on the route from Peterborough to Hull. They had running power over the line of the Lancashire and Yorkshire Railway Company from Askerne to Milford Junction, where the line of the North Eastern Railway Company joins that of The Lancashire and Yorkshire Railway Company. There had been, in February, an arrangement between the three companies by which passengers booked at the stations on the line of The Great Northern Railway Company were carried in the carriages of that company to Milford Junction, and thence were conveyed by The North Eastern Railway Company to Hull by a train departing a few minutes after the arrival of the train leaving Peterborough about 7 p.m. Toward the end of February, prior to the publication by the defendants of their time tables, but after they had been prepared and printed, The North Eastern Railway Company gave notice to the defendants that, after the 1st day of March, the train from Milford Junction to Hull would be discontinued. The defendants nevertheless made no alteration in their time tables, which were published and issued for March. The plaintiff consulted them and was misled as above stated. In consequence of the absence of this train the plaintiff could not get to Hull in time for an appointment which he had made for the morning of the 26th March, and sustained damage to the amount of £5 10s. It did not appear in or by the time tables whether the train from Peterborough to Hull was or was not entirely under the control of the defendants. ...

LORD CAMPBELL CJ: This is a case of some importance, both as regards the public and the railway companies. It seems to me that the representations made by railway companies in their time tables cannot be treated as mere waste paper; and in the present case I think the plaintiff is entitled to recover, on the ground that there was a contract with him, and also on the ground that there was a false representation by the Company.

It seems to me that, if the Company promised to give tickets for a train, running at a particular hour to a particular place, to any one who would come to the station and tender the price of the ticket, it is a good contract with any one who so comes. I take it to be clear that the issuing of the time tables in this way amounts in fact to such a promise; any one who read them would so understand them. Then, is it a good contract in law? The consideration is one which is a prejudice to the person who makes his arrangements with a view to the fulfilment of the contract, and comes to the station on the faith of it. Is it not then within the principle of those cases in which it has been held that an action lies on a contract to pay a reward? There the promise is to the public at large, exactly as it is here; it is in effect the same as if made to each individual conditionally; and, on an individual fulfilling the condition, it is an absolute contract with him, and he may sue. That being so, there is, I think, a contract and there is no excuse shown for breaking it. It is immaterial that the defendants are not owners of the line the whole way to Hull. It is admitted to have been often rightly held that, where there is a ticket taken out to go to a station, the contract binds the company issuing the ticket, though it is not specified how much of the line over which the journey is to be belongs to that company. Then reliance is placed on the class of cases which decide that an absolute contract must be fulfilled whatever happens, which, it is said, shows that there cannot be a contract here. But from the nature of the contract I think that there might be implied exceptions. A carrier by sea excepts the perils of the sea. It may be from the nature of this contract that the perils of the railroad are excepted. I see no inconvenience likely to arise from holding this a contract. It is put, as an example of inconvenience, that a shipowner who has advertised that his ship is bound for Calcutta as a general ship, and that he will take on board goods brought to her, would be liable to an action if when goods were brought on the faith of the advertisement he said he had got a better freight, and was now bound for Jamaica; but I see no reason why he should not be liable. It seems to me, therefore, that this is a contract, and that the plaintiff who has acted on it has his remedy on that ground. But on the other ground there is no doubt. The statement in the time tables was untrue, and was made so as to be what the law calls a fraudulent representation. It was not the original printing that was blamable; but, after notice that the train was withdrawn, the defendants continue, down to the 25th March, to issue these tables. Was not that a representation that there was such a train? And, as they knew it had been discontinued for some time, was it not a false representation? It is all one as if a person, duly authorized by the company, had, knowing it was not true, said to the plaintiff: "There is a train from Milford Junction to Hull at that hour." The plaintiff believes this, acts upon it, and sustains loss. It is well established law that, where a person makes an untrue statement, knowing it to be untrue, to another who is induced to act upon it, an action lies. The facts bring the present case within that rule.·

WIGHTMAN J: It seems to me that the publication of these time tables amounted to a promise to any one of the public who would come to the station and pay for a ticket, that he shall have one by the train at seven. It is said that this will make the Company liable though there be inevitable accidents. But the provision at the foot of the time tables protects the Company in cases of delay by accident, though the proviso does not apply to the present case where the train is altogether taken off.

But, whether there be a contract or not, the defendants are liable as having induced the plaintiff by a continued knowingly false representation to believe that there was a train at seven to Hull, which he, believing, acted upon to his prejudice. All the essentials for an action for a false representation are here. The representation is untrue; it is known by the persons making it to be untrue; it is calculated to induce the plaintiff to act; and he, believing it, is induced to act accordingly.

CROMPTON J: I think also that the plaintiff is entitled to judgment.

I entirely agree in what has been said by my Lord and my brother Wightman, that an action in the nature of an action for deceit lies here. The Company make a fresh statement at every moment whilst they continue to hold out these time tables as theirs. I am besides much inclined to think that they are liable also on the ground that they have committed a breach of their duty as public carriers. A public carrier of goods must carry according to his public profession; I think, however, that there has been no decision that carriers of passengers are under the same obligation: though in *Story on Bailments*, s. 591, it is said they are. I cannot doubt that the defendants publicly professed to be carriers of passengers by this train; and therefore I am inclined to think an action would lie on that ground.

But I am not prepared to say that there is a contract. As I agree that the defendants are liable, there is no occasion to decide this; and it is true that the cases as to the recovery of rewards have an analogy to this case. But there is a difference; where a reward is offered, it is generally offered to procure a service which is entirely performed by the party claiming the reward. I never was able to see any good reason why in such cases he might not sue for work and labour done at the request of the defendant. But in the present case, or in that which might be put of a shopkeeper advertising that he had cheap goods in his shop, I doubt if the labour of coming to the station, or of crossing the threshold of the shop, really is part of the consideration at all. If it be, it is a very small one. I agree, however, that any consideration, however small, will support a promise; and perhaps the difference between me and my Lord and my brother Wightman is rather as to the fact than the law. I doubt whether the promise here in fact was in consideration of coming to the station. If it was, I see difficulty in saying that the shopkeeper does not promise to have his wares for those who will take the trouble to leave the street and come into his shop. But it is quite unnecessary for the decision of this case to come to a determination on that. I am clearly of opinion that the action lies as for a false representation. I think, though less decidedly, that it lies on the ground of their duty as public carriers of passengers to act up to their public profession. But I doubt whether they are answerable on a contract to do all that may be found in the time tables, if there be anything there beyond what would be implied as part of their duty as carriers.

Judgment for the plaintiff.

QUESTIONS

1. Are the decisions of Lord Campbell CJ and Wightman J consistent with the case law that follows?

2. What offer was made by the railway company?

JOHNSTON BROTHERS V ROGERS BROTHERS
(1899), 30 OR 150 (Div Ct)

An appeal by the defendants from the judgment of William Elliott, senior Judge of the County Court of Middlesex, in favour of the plaintiffs in an action in that Court, the facts of which are fully set out in the following [portion of the] opinion delivered by that Judge:

The plaintiffs are bakers, and seek to recover damages from the defendants for breach of a contract for the sale and delivery of a quantity of flour.

The following letter is the basis of the plaintiff's claim:

Toronto, April 26, 1898.

Dear Sir,—We wish to secure your patronage, and, as we have found the only proper way to get a customer is to save him money, we therefore are going to endeavour to save you money.

It is hardly prudent for us to push the sale of flour just now, as prices are sure to advance at least 50 cents per barrel within a very few days, and to give you the advantage of a cut from 20 to 25 cents per barrel seems a very foolish thing, but nevertheless we are going to do it, just to save you money and secure your patronage.

> We quote you (R.O.B. or F.O.B.) your station, Hungarian $5.40, and strong Bakers $5.00, car lots only, and subject to sight draft with bill of lading.
>
> We would suggest your using the wire to order, as prices are so rapidly advancing that they might be beyond reach before a letter would reach us.
>
> Yours respectfully,
> Rogers Bros.

This communication was received by the plaintiffs on the 27th April. The plaintiffs telegraphed the defendants the same morning as follows:

> London, April 27, 1898.
> To Rogers Bros., Confederation Life Building, Toronto.
> We will take two cars Hungarian at your offer of yesterday.
>
> Johnston Bros.

On the same day, namely, the 27th April, the plaintiffs received the following communication by telegraph:

> Toronto, Ont., April 27, 1898.
> Flour advanced sixty. Will accept advance of thirty on yesterday's quotations. Further advance certain.
>
> Rogers Bros.

Then followed a letter, dated the 28th April, from Messrs. Hellmuth & Ivey, solicitors for the plaintiffs, calling upon the defendants to fulfil the order "according to the offer contained in your letter of the 26th and duly accepted by them by wire on April 27th; and upon your refusal damages will be demanded."

FALCONBRIDGE J (for the court): ... The real crux of the case is whether there is a contract.

Leaving out the matters of inducement (in both the legal and the ordinary sense) in the letter of the 26th, the contract, if there is one, is contained in the following words:

> Letter, Defendants to Plaintiffs
> 27th April, 1898.
> We quote you, F.O.B. your station, Hungarian $5.40, and strong Bakers $5.00, car lots only, and subject to sight drafts with bills of lading.

> Telegram, Plaintiffs to Defendants
> 27th April, 1898.
> We will take 2 cars Hungarian at your offer of yesterday.

I should expect to find American authority as to the phrase "we quote you" which must be in very common use among brokers, manufacturers, and dealers in the United States; but we were referred to no decided case, and I have found none where that phrase was used.

In the *American and English Encyclopedia of Law*, 2nd ed., vol. 7, p. 138, the law is stated to be: "A quotation of prices is not an offer to sell, in the sense that a complete contract will arise out of the mere acceptance of the rate offered or the giving of an order for merchandise in accordance with the proposed terms. It requires the acceptance by the one naming the price, of the order so made, to complete the transaction. Until thus completed there is no mutuality of obligation."

Of the cases cited in support of this proposition, *Mouton v. Kershaw* (1884), 59 Wis. 316, 48 Am. Rep. 516, is the nearest to the present one, but in none is the word "Quote" used.

The meaning of "quote" is given in modern dictionaries as follows:

Standard (Com.)—To give the current market price of, as bonds, stocks, commodities, etc.

Imperial, ed. 1884—In com., to name as the price of an article; to name the current price of; as, what can you quote sugar at?

Century (Com.)—To name as the price of stocks, produce, etc.; name the current price of.

Webster (Com.)—To name the current price of.

Worcester—To state the price as the price of merchandise.

See also Black's *Law Dictionary, sub tit.* "Quotation."

There is little or no difference between any of these definitions. Now if we write the equivalent phrase into the letter—"We give you the current or market price, F.O.B. your station, of Hungarian Patent $5.40"—can it be for a moment contended that it is an offer which needs only an acceptance in terms to constitute a contract?

The case of *Harty v. Gooderham* (1871), 31 U.C.R. 18, is principally relied on by the plaintiffs. But that case presents more than one point of distinction. There the first inquiry was from the plaintiff, which, I think, is an element in the case. He writes the defendants to let him "know your lowest prices for 50 O.P. spirits," etc. To which defendants answered, mentioning prices and particulars: "Shall be happy to have an order from you, to which we will give prompt attention," which the court held to be equivalent to saying "We will sell it at those prices. Will you purchase from us and let us know how much?" And so the contract was held to be complete on the plaintiff's acceptance.

But there is no such offer to sell in the present defendant's letter. *Harvey v. Facey*, [1893] A.C. 552, is strong authority against the plaintiffs.

I have not overlooked the concluding paragraph of the letter, viz., "We would suggest your using the wire to order, as prices are so rapidly advancing that they might be beyond reach before a letter would reach us." The learned Judge considers this to be one of the matters foreign to a mere quotation of prices. I venture, on the contrary, to think that this suggestion is more consistent with a mere quotation of prices, which might vary from day to day or from hour to hour. There could be no question of the prices becoming "beyond reach" in a simple offer to sell at a certain price.

In my opinion, the plaintiffs have failed to establish a contract, and this appeal must be allowed with costs, and the action dismissed with costs.

QUESTIONS

1. Suppose the plaintiff in *Harty v Gooderham* had ordered more "spirits," etc. than the defendant could reasonably have possessed or acquired. Is *Harvey v Facey* such a strong authority against the plaintiffs? What is *Harvey v Facey* authority for? See (1923) 1 Can Bar Rev at 398ff and 694, 713.

2. What problems do you foresee if this quote of flour prices was an offer? Could you think of any way to overcome the problem?

HARVEY V FACEY
[1893] AC 552 (PC)

LORD MORRIS: The appellants are solicitors carrying on business in partnership at Kingston, [Jamaica], and it appears that in the beginning of October, 1891, negotiations took place between the respondent L.M. Facey and the Mayor and council of Kingston for the sale of the property in question; that Facey had offered to sell it to them for the sum of £900; that the offer was discussed by the Council at their meeting on the 6th of October, 1891, and the consideration of its acceptance deferred; that on the 7th of October, 1891, L.M. Facey was travelling in the train from Kingston to Porus, and that the appellants caused a telegram to be sent after him from Kingston addressed to him "on the train for Porus," in the following words: "Will you sell us Bumper Hall Pen? Telegraph lowest cash price—answer paid"; that on the same day L.M. Facey replied by telegram to the appellants in the following words: "Lowest price for Bumper Hall Pen £900"; that on the same day the appellants replied to the last-mentioned telegram by a telegram addressed to L.M. Facey "on train at Porus" in the words following: "We agree to buy Bumper Hall Pen for the sum of nine hundred pounds asked by you. Please send us your title deed in order that we may get early possession." The above telegrams were duly received by the appellant and by L.M. Facey. ... Their Lordships concur in the judgment of Mr. Justice Curran that there was no concluded contract between the appellants and L.M. Facey to be collected from the aforesaid telegrams. The first telegram asks two questions. The first question is as to the willingness of L.M. Facey to sell to the appellants; the second question asks the lowest price, and the word "Telegraph" is in its collocation addressed to that second question only. L.M. Facey replied to the second question only, and gives his lowest price. The third telegram from the appellants treats the answer of L.M. Facey stating his lowest price as an unconditional offer to sell to them at the price named. Their Lordships cannot treat the telegram from L.M. Facey as binding him in any respect, except to the extent it does by its terms, viz., the lowest price. Everything else is left open, and the reply telegram from the appellants cannot be treated as an acceptance of an offer to sell to them; it is an offer that required to be accepted by L.M. Facey. The contract could only be completed if L.M. Facey had accepted the appellants' last telegram. It has been contended for the appellants that L.M. Facey's telegram should be read as saying "yes" to the first question put in the appellants' telegram, but there is nothing to support that contention. L.M. Facey's telegram gives a precise answer to a precise question, viz., the price. The contract must appear by the telegrams, whereas the appellants are obliged to contend that an acceptance of the first question is to be implied. Their Lordships are of the opinion that the mere statement of the lowest price at which the vendor would sell contains no implied contract to sell at that price to the persons making the inquiry.

QUESTIONS

1. What if Facey's telegram had said, "I am prepared to offer you Bumper Hall Pen for £900"? See *Clifton v Palumbo*, [1944] 2 All ER 497 (CA).

2. In another case, the vendor's letter said, "For a quick sale, I would accept £26,000." Was that an offer? See *Bigg v Boyd Gibbons Ltd*, [1971] 1 WLR 913 (CA).

Grainger & Son v Gough. [1896] AC 325 (HL). LORD HERSCHELL: The transmission of such a price list does not amount to an offer to supply an unlimited quantity of the wine described at the price named, so that so soon as an order is given there is a binding contract to supply that quantity. If it were so, the merchant might find himself involved in any number of contractual obligations to supply wine of a particular description which he would be quite unable to carry out, his stock of that wine being necessarily limited.

Boyer and Co v D & R Duke. [1905] 2 IR 617 (KBD). MADDEN J: It is a matter of common knowledge that quotations of prices are scattered broadcast among possible customers. Business could not be carried on if each such recipient of a priced catalogue offering a desirable article—say a rare book—at an attractive price, were in a position to create a contract of sale by writing that he would buy at the price mentioned. The catalogue had probably reached many collectors. The order of one only can be honoured. Has each of the others who write for the book the right of action? Wholesale dealers have not in stock an unlimited supply of the articles the price of which they quote to the public at large. This stock usually bears some proportion to the orders which they may reasonably expect to receive. Transactions of the kind under consideration are intelligible and business-like, if we bear in mind the distinction between a quotation, submitted as a basis of a possible order, and an offer to sell which, if accepted, creates a contract for the breach of which damages may be recovered.

These observations seem to apply with special force to a quotation furnished by a manufacturer, in the position of the defendants, stating the terms on which he is prepared to work, as to price and time for completion. He may receive and comply with many applications for quotations on the same day. If his reply in each case can be turned into a contract by acceptance, his looms might be burdened with an amount of work which would render it impossible for him to meet his engagements. In my opinion, a merchant, dealer, or manufacturer, by furnishing a quotation invites an offer which will be honoured or not according to the exigencies of the business. A quotation based on current prices usually holds good for a limited time. But it remains a quotation on the basis of which an offer will not be entertained after a certain date.

LEFKOWITZ V GREAT MINNEAPOLIS SURPLUS STORE
86 NW 2d 689 (Minn SC 1957)

MURPHY J: This is an appeal from an order of the Municipal Court of Minneapolis denying the motion of the defendant for amended findings of fact, or, in the alternative, for a new trial. The order for judgment awarded the plaintiff the sum of $138.50 as damages for breach of contract.

This case grows out of the alleged refusal of the defendant to sell to the plaintiff a certain fur piece which it had offered for sale in a newspaper advertisement. It appears from the record that on April 6, 1956, the defendant published the following advertisement in a Minneapolis newspaper:

Saturday 9 A.M. Sharp

3 Brand New

Fur Coats

Worth to $100.00

First Come

First Served

$1

Each

On April 13, the defendant again published an advertisement in the same newspaper as follows:

> Saturday 9 A.M.
> 2 Brand New Pastel
> Mink 3-Skin Scarfs
> Selling for $89.50
> Out they go
> Saturday. Each ... $1.00
> 1 Black Lapin Stole
> Beautiful,
> worth $139.50 ... $1.00
> First Come
> First Served.

The record supports the findings of the court that on each of the Saturdays following the publication of the above-described ads, the plaintiff was the first to present himself at the appropriate counter in the defendant's store and on each occasion demanded the coat and the stole so advertised and indicated his readiness to pay the sale price of $1. On both occasions, the defendant refused to sell the merchandise to the plaintiff, stating on the first occasion that by a "house rule" the offer was intended for women only and sales would not be made to men, and on the second visit that the plaintiff knew defendant's house rules.

[After agreeing with the trial judge that the plaintiff could not recover damages for the coats because their value "Worth to $100.00" was too vague, the court also found that the value of the Lapin stole was sufficiently certain to form the basis of a damage award. The court continued as follows:]

The defendant contends that a newspaper advertisement offering items of merchandise for sale at a named price is a "unilateral offer" which may be withdrawn without notice. He relies upon authorities which hold that, where an advertiser publishes in a newspaper that he has a certain quantity or quality of goods which he wants to dispose of at certain prices and on certain terms, such advertisements are not offers which become contracts as soon as any person to whose notice they may come signifies his acceptance by notifying the other that he will take a certain quantity of them. Such advertisements have been construed as an invitation for an offer of sale on the terms stated, which offer, when received, may be accepted or rejected and which therefore does not become a contract of sale until accepted by the seller; and until a contract has been so made, the seller may modify or revoke such prices or terms.

[Authorities cited omitted.]

The test of whether a binding obligation may originate in advertisements addressed to the general public is "whether the facts show that some performance was promised in positive terms in return for something requested." 1 Williston, Contracts (Rev. ed.) s. 27. ...

Whether in any individual instance a newspaper advertisement is an offer rather than an invitation to make an offer depends on the legal intention of the parties and the surrounding circumstances ... . We are of the view on the facts before us that the offer by the defendant of the sale of the Lapin fur was clear, definite, and explicit, and left nothing open for negotiation. The plaintiff having successfully managed to be the first one to appear at the seller's place of business to be served, as requested by the advertisement, and having offered the stated purchase price of the article, he was entitled to performance on the part of the defendant. We think the trial court was correct in holding that there was in the conduct of the parties a sufficient mutuality of obligation to constitute a contract of sale.

The defendant contends that the offer was modified by a "house rule" to the effect that only women were qualified to receive the bargains advertised. The advertisement contained no such restriction. This objection may be disposed of briefly by stating that, while an advertiser has the right at any time before acceptance to modify his offer, he does not have the right, after acceptance, to impose new or arbitrary conditions not contained in the published offer.

Affirmed.

QUESTION

The argument that the contract was formed, in the case of the first visit by Mr. Lefkowitz to the store, before the inclusion of the "house rule" as a term still leaves open the question of why the words of the defendant were not effective to modify the second offer when, by that time, Mr. Lefkowitz knew of the rule. On what basis could the court decide that the "house rule" was also not part of the second contract?

PHARMACEUTICAL SOCIETY OF GREAT BRITAIN V BOOTS CASH CHEMISTS (SOUTHERN) LTD
[1953] 1 QB 401 (CA)

[The Pharmaceutical Society is charged with the enforcement of the *Pharmacy and Poisons Act*, 1933, s 18 of which provides in part that no person shall "sell any poison included in Part I of the Poisons List, unless ... the sale is effected by, or under the supervision of, a registered pharmacist." "Boots," well-known chain store druggists (chemist's shops) in England, operated a shop in Edgware where substances included in Part I of the Poisons List were displayed in a self-service area. A customer taking one of these substances could only escape from the area by passing a cashier's desk that was near and under the supervision of the pharmacist. The cashier and the pharmacist were instructed to prevent any customers from removing any drug from the shop if the pharmacist thought fit. The Pharmaceutical Society brought this action on an agreed statement of facts to determine whether, as the Society contended, the sale took place when the customer helped himself from the shelf, or as Boots maintained, the sale took place when the cashier decided whether she would accept the payment. The Society supposed that if the sale had already taken place it had not taken place under the supervision of a registered pharmacist and that Boots could not, therefore, refuse to accept payment or stop the customer from leaving with the prescribed drugs. Lord Goddard CJ decided that the sale took place when the cashier accepted payment and under proper supervision. The Society appealed.]

SOMERVELL LJ: It is not disputed that in a chemist's shop where this self-service system does not prevail a customer may go in and ask a young woman assistant, who will not herself be a registered pharmacist, for one of these articles on the list, and the transaction may be completed and the article paid for, although the registered pharmacist, who will no doubt be on the premises, will not know anything himself of the transaction, unless the assistant serving the customer, or the customer, requires to put a question to him. It is right that I should emphasize, as did the Lord Chief Justice, that these are not dangerous drugs. They are substances which contain very small portions of poison, and I imagine that many of them are the type of drug which has a warning as to what doses are to be taken. They are drugs which can be obtained, under the law, without a doctor's prescription.

The point taken by the plaintiff is this: it is said that the purchase is complete if and when a customer going round the shelves takes an article and puts it in the receptacle which he or she is carrying, and that therefore, if that is right, when the customer comes to the pay desk, having completed the tour of the premises, the registered pharmacist, if so minded, has no power to say: "This drug ought not to be sold to this customer." Whether and in what circumstances he would have that power we need not inquire, but one can, of course, see that there is a difference if super-vision can only be exercised at a time when the contract is completed.

I agree with the Lord Chief Justice in everything that he said, but I will put the matter shortly in my own words. Whether the view contended for by the plaintiffs is a right view depends on what are legal implications of this layout—the invitation to the customer. Is a contract to be regarded as being completed when the article is put into the receptacle, or is this to be regarded as a more organized way of doing what is done already in many types of shops—and a bookseller is perhaps the best example—namely, enabling customers to have free access to what is in the shop, to look at the different articles, and then, ultimately, having got the ones which they wish to buy, to come up to the assistant saying "I want this"? The assistant in 999 times out of 1,000 says "That is all right," and the money passes and the transaction is completed. I agree with what the Lord Chief Justice has said, and with the reasons which he has given for his conclusion, that in the case of an ordinary shop, although goods are displayed and it is intended that customers should go and choose what they want, the contract is not completed until, the customer having indicated the articles which he needs, the shop-keeper, or someone on his behalf, accepts that offer. Then the contract is completed. I can see no reason at all, that being clearly the normal position, for drawing any different implication as a result of this layout.

The Lord Chief Justice, I think, expressed one of the most formidable difficulties in the way of the plaintiffs' contention when he pointed out that, if the plaintiffs are right, once an article has been placed in the receptacle the customer himself is bound and would have no right, without paying for the first article, to substitute an article which he saw later of a similar kind and which he perhaps preferred. I can see no reason for implying from this self-service arrangement any implication other than that which the Lord Chief Justice found in it, namely, that it is a convenient method of enabling customers to see what there is and choose, and possibly put back and substitute, articles which they wish to have, and then go up to the cashier and offer to buy what they have so far chosen. On that conclusion the case fails, because it is admitted that there was supervision in the sense required by the Act and at the appropriate moment of time. For these reasons, in my opinion, the appeal should be dismissed.

[The judgments of Birkett and Romer LJJ, who agreed, are omitted.]

Fisher v Bell. [1960] 3 All ER 731 (QB). [A 1959 statute made it an offence for anyone to "manufacture, sell or hire or offer for sale or hire, or lend or give to any other per-son" a spring blade knife, commonly known as a "flick knife." The respondent had such a knife displayed in his shop window, with a price tag "Ejector knife—4s." attached. A police constable gave the respondent his opinion that it was a flick knife, to which the respondent asked: "Why do the manufacturers still bring them round for us to sell?" The constable told the respondent he would be reported for offering for sale a flick knife, to which he said: "Fair enough." On a prosecution, held, for the respondent. The display of the knife was a mere invitation to treat, not an "offer for sale."]

LORD PARKER CJ: I think that most lay people would be inclined to the view (as, indeed, I was myself when I first read these papers), that if a knife were displayed in a window like that with a price attached to it, it was nonsense to say that that was not offering it for sale. The knife is there inviting people to buy it, and in ordinary language it is for sale; but any statute must be looked at in the light of the general law of the country, for Parliament must be taken to know the general law. It is clear that, according to the ordinary law of contract, the display of an article with a price on it in a shop window is merely an invitation to treat. ... [In] many statutes and orders which prohibit selling and offering for sale of goods, it is very common, when it is so desired, to insert the words, "offering or exposing for sale," "exposing for sale" being clearly words which would cover the display of goods in a shop window. ... I, for my part, though I confess reluctantly, am driven to the conclusion that no offence was here committed.

SWISS FEDERAL CODE OF OBLIGATIONS

7. ... The display of merchandise with a price tag is considered as a rule as an offer.

QUESTIONS

1. If the decision in *Boots* had gone the other way, would it follow that once a customer had handled a product she would have to pay for it?

2. Is there any reason why the decision in these quasi-criminal cases should depend on the contractual concept of "offer"? Are not the courts here dealing with entirely different problems? If you were legislative counsel, what would you do? For a discussion, see Waddams at para 57; McCamus at 38-41; MacDougall at 24-25.

3. Given that many civil law systems have a rule similar to that of the *Swiss Federal Code of Obligations*, could it be said that the common law's "invitation to treat" presumption regarding advertisements and the display of merchandise is arbitrary? For just such an argument, see Smith at 188; JM Feinman & SR Brill, "Is an Advertisement an Offer? Why It Is, and Why It Matters" (2006) 58 Hastings LJ 61. Would the judges who decided *Grainger & Son v Gough* and *Boyer and Co v D & R Duke*, above, have agreed that the common law is arbitrary?

STORER V MANCHESTER CITY COUNCIL
[1974] 3 All ER 825 (CA)

LORD DENNING MR: In May, 1971 there was a change in the control of the defendants, Manchester Corporation. Previously the Conservatives had been in control. Afterwards it was Labour. The change had legal repercussions. During the Conservative administration the policy of the corporation was to sell their council houses to tenants on favourable terms. They were willing to sell to any sitting tenant who had been in occupation more than a year. The sale price was to be the market value of the house if sold with vacant possession, but with a reduction for the tenant according to the length of time he had been in the premises as a tenant. He might get a reduction of from 10 to 20 per cent on the price. Furthermore, the corporation were ready to give him a 100 per cent mortgage.

When the Labour administration took over in May, 1971 that policy was reversed. The Labour-controlled administration decided that they would not sell council houses to tenants. But they realised that they could not go back on existing contracts. So they gave instructions to their officers that they were to fulfil existing contracts but not to make any fresh contracts. Now in many cases tenants had filled in various forms applying to buy their houses, but the contracts of sale had not been exchanged. The tenants claim that firm contracts had been made even though the contracts had not been exchanged. But the town clerk thought that the contracts were only binding when contracts of sale had been exchanged. So he wrote this letter to the tenants: "At their meeting on the 7th July, 1971 the Council decided to discontinue the Scheme for the sale of Council houses, and to proceed only with those cases where Contracts have been exchanged. As Contracts have not been formally exchanged in this case, I am unable to proceed with the proposed sale." Now the plaintiff, Mr. Storer, one of the tenants, has brought this action to test that ruling.

The facts are these. Mr. Storer was a tenant of a council house, 167 Moorcroft Road, Wythenshawe. On 15th November 1970 he filled in a request for information asking for the price and details of any mortgage. On 14th January 1971 the corporation wrote saying that they "may be prepared to sell the house to you at the purchase price of £2,750," less a discount of 17 per cent (as he had had a council house for several years), making a net sum of £2,282. If he were granted a mortgage, it would be for £2,279 repayable over 25 years. They said in their letter: "This letter should not be regarded as a firm offer of a mortgage." Later on, however, they did make a firm offer, as I will show.

On 11th February 1971 Mr. Storer filled in an application form to buy a council house. He said: "I ... now wish to purchase my Council house." In it he asked for a loan on mortgage. On 9th March 1971 the city treasurer wrote to him: "The Corporation will lend £2,279 repayable over 25 years with interest at 8½% ... the total monthly instalment payable will be £14.98." On the same day, 9th March 1971, the town clerk himself wrote a letter which is of crucial importance in the case:

Dear Sir,

Sale of Council Houses

I understand you wish to purchase your Council house and enclose the Agreement for sale. If you will sign the Agreement and return it to me I will send you the Agreement signed on behalf of the Corporation in exchange. From the enclosed list of Solicitors, who are prepared to act for you and advise you on the purchase, please let me know the name of the firm that you select, as soon as possible.

Enclosed with that letter there was a form headed: "City of Manchester. Agreement for Sale of a Council House." The corporation had filled in various details, such as the name of the purchaser, the address of the property, the price, the mortgage, amount, and the monthly repayments. There was this item left blank: "7. Date when your tenancy ceases and mortgage repayments will commence," followed by these clauses:

8. *Freehold* to be conveyed or transferred by the Corporation.
9. There will be no abstract or investigation of title. ...
10. *Deeds* of Conveyance or Transfer and Mortgage to be in the Corporation's standard forms including conditions against use except as a private dwelling-house and against advertising and a restriction not to sell or lease the property for five years.

11. *Warning.* As from the date mentioned in 7 above the property is at your risk. If you are taking a mortgage from the Corporation it will be insured for you but the cost recharged to you. *If you are not taking a Mortgage insure it at once.* Your responsibility for repairs and for payment of rates also start from that day. My solicitors are ...

Mr. Storer filled in that form. He filled in the name of solicitors, Messrs. Hargreaves & Co. He signed the form himself and returned it on 20th March 1971. So he had done everything which he had to do to bind himself to the purchase of the property. The only thing left blank was the date when the tenancy was to cease.

The sale would have gone through, no doubt, within a short time but for the corporation and the town clerk's office being so pressed. The housing manager passed a note to the town clerk suggesting that the sale be completed with effect from Monday 22nd March or Monday 12th April. But nothing more was done before the election which brought a change of control in the corporation. The town clerk's staff were, apparently, overworked and did not deal with the matter in time. Then in May, 1971 there was the election. In July, 1971 the corporation, under the new control, resolved that there were to be no more sales to council tenants; but the corporation recognised that they had to go on with the cases where the corporation were legally bound.

Thereupon the town clerk wrote to Mr. Storer and other tenants in like situation a letter saying: "As Contracts have not been formally exchanged in this case, I am unable to proceed with the proposed sale." Mr. Storer took the advice of Messrs. Hargreaves & Co. Some 120 other tenants also took advice. They were advised that there was a binding contract, even though formal contracts had not been exchanged. So this case of Mr. Storer has come as a test case for Manchester Corporation. It is to decide whether or not "exchange" is necessary in order to form a concluded contract.

When parties arrange for a sale "subject to contract," that means, as a rule, that there is no binding contract until the contracts of sale have been formally exchanged. That is clear from *Eccles v. Bryant.* But where there is no arrangement "subject to contract," the only question is whether a contract has been concluded: see *Bigg v. Boyd Gibbins Ltd.* One example is where one solicitor is acting for both sides, such as in *Smith v. Mansi.* It is "artificial nonsense," Danckwerts L.J. said, to have an exchange of contracts where there is only one solicitor acting. The present case is, I think, another example. The corporation put forward to the tenant a simple form of agreement. The very object was to dispense with legal formalities. One of the formalities—exchange of contracts—was quite unnecessary. The contract was concluded by offer and acceptance. The offer was contained in the letter of 9th March in which the town clerk said: "I ... enclose the Agreement for Sale. If you will sign the Agreement and return it to me I will send the Agreement signed on behalf of the Corporation in exchange." The acceptance was made when the tenant did sign it, as he did, and return it, as he did on 20th March. It was then that a contract was concluded. The town clerk was then bound to send back the agreement signed on behalf of the corporation. The agreement was concluded on Mr. Storer's acceptance. It was not dependent on the subsequent exchange.

I appreciate that there was one space in the form which was left blank. It was cl. 7 for "Date when your tenancy ceases." That blank did not mean there was no concluded contract. It was left blank simply for administrative convenience. A similar point arose in *Smith v. Mansi* where Russell L.J. said:

There was nothing left for the parties themselves to do but agree the date. Its insertion in the already signed document—in the hands of the common solicitor—could surely be nothing but an administrative tidying up to be done, if at all, at the solicitor's convenience.

So here the filling in of the date was just a matter of administrative tidying up, to be filled in by the town clerk with a suitable date for the change-over—the date on which the man ceased to be a tenant and become a purchaser.

A further point was taken. It was said that the town clerk had not actually signed the form of agreement. No matter. He had signed a letter of 9th March 1971 and that was sufficient. It was a note or memorandum sufficient to satisfy the Law of Property Act 1925, s. 40.

The final point was this. Counsel for the corporation said that the town clerk did not intend to be bound by the letter of 9th March 1971. He intended that the corporation should not be bound except on exchange. There is nothing in this point. In contracts you do not look into the actual intent in a man's mind. You look at what he said and did. A contract is formed when there is, to all outward appearances, a contract. A man cannot get out of a contract by saying: "I did not intend to contract," if by his words he has done so. His intention is to be found only in the outward expression which his letters convey. If they show a concluded contract that is enough.

It seems to me that the judge was quite right in holding that there was a binding contract in this case, even though there was no exchange. It is a proper case for specific performance; and I would dismiss the appeal.

NOTE

In a subsequent case, *Gibson v Manchester City Council*, [1979] 1 WLR 294 (HL), negotiations had not proceeded as far as in *Storer*'s case. The Council had written to Gibson saying, "[T]he Corporation may be prepared to sell the house to you at ... £2,180." The House of Lords held that this was not an offer. See also Waddams at para 25; McCamus at 37-38; MacDougall at 24-26.

B. THE POWER OF ACCEPTANCE

It is frequently said that the rules of "offer" and "acceptance" in contract are technical and arbitrary. The following cases, however, illustrate the difficulties in determining whether an assent has been given to a proposed bargain. Apart from determining whether a bargain has been made, when an acceptance has been given can have other implications as well. In some cases, acceptance has been used to determine where a contract has been made and therefore which courts can claim jurisdiction over disputes arising out of the contract. In others, the timing of acceptance has been used to help determine actual terms of the contract bargained between the parties. Consider these issues as you examine the materials that follow.

NOTE

Issues of acceptance in relation to unilateral contracts are dealt with in Section IV, below.

SHATFORD V BC WINE GROWERS LTD
[1927] 2 DLR 759 (BCSC)

MURPHY J: Plaintiff's case, on his pleadings, is that the letter of April 21, 1926 (ex. 3) with enclosure is an offer from the defendants to plaintiff for the purchase of loganberries ... . I think plaintiff's action must fail because he did not accept this offer within a reasonable time. The causes of this delay are immaterial. The facts are that ex. 3 was mailed on April 22, and was received probably on the 23rd, or, at latest, on the 24th. Plaintiff did not sign the contract enclosed with ex. 3 until April 30—a delay of at least some six days. He mailed the signed document to defendant on the evening of April 30. Ordinarily a proposal sent by mail calls for an acceptance, if not by return of post, at least during business hours of the day on which such offer is received (*Dunlop v. Higgins* (1848), 1 H.L. Cas. 381, 9 E.R. 805). In all cases the offer must be accepted within a reasonable time. Here, having regard to the commodity being bargained for, the time of year of the offer, and the necessity, under the circumstances, as shown by the evidence of prompt decision, as to whether an offer would be accepted or not, I hold the plaintiff did not accept defendants' offer within a reasonable time. Action dismissed with costs.

MANCHESTER DIOCESAN COUNCIL FOR EDUCATION V COMMERCIAL & GENERAL INVESTMENTS LTD
[1969] 3 All ER 1593 (ChD)

BUCKLEY J: ... It has long been recognised as being the law that, where an offer is made in terms which fix no time limit for acceptance, the offer must be accepted within a reasonable time to make a contract (*Chitty on Contracts* (22nd edn.), vol. 1, p. 47, para. 89; *Williams on Vendor and Purchaser* (4th edn.), vol. 1, p. 16; 8 *Halsbury's Laws of England* (3rd edn.), p. 71, para. 124). There seems, however, to be no reported case in which the reason for this is explained.

There appear to me to be two possible views on methods of approaching the problem. First, it may be said that by implication the offer is made on terms that, if it is not accepted within a reasonable time, it must be treated as withdrawn. Alternatively, it may be said that, if the offeree does not accept the offer within a reasonable time, he must be treated as having refused it. On either view the offer would cease to be a live one on the expiration of what in the circumstances of the particular case should be regarded as a reasonable time for acceptance. The first of these alternatives involves implying a term that if the offer is not accepted within a reasonable time, it shall be treated as withdrawn or lapsing at the end of that period if it has not then been accepted; the second is based on an inference to be drawn from the conduct of the offeree, that is, that having failed to accept the offer within a reasonable time he has manifested an intention to refuse it. If, in the first alternative, the time which the offeror is to be treated as having set for acceptance is to be such a time as is reasonable at the date of the offer, what is reasonable must depend on circumstances then existing and reasonably likely to arise during the continuance of the offer; but it would be not unlikely that the offeror and offeree would make different assessments of what would be reasonable even if, as might quite possibly not be the case, they based those judgments on identical known and anticipated circumstances. No doubt a court could resolve any dispute about this, but this approach clearly involves a certain degree of uncertainty about the precise terms of the offer. If on the other hand the time which the offeror is to be treated as having set for acceptance is to be such a time as turns out to be reasonable in the light of circumstances then existing and of circumstances arising thereafter during the continuance of the offer, whether foreseeable or not, an additional element of uncertainty is introduced. The second alternative on the other hand involves simply an objective assessment of facts and the determination of the question whether on the facts the offeree should in fairness to both parties be regarded as having refused the offer.

It does not seem to me that either party is in greater need of protection by the law in this respect than the other. Until his offer has been accepted it is open to the offeror at any time to withdraw it or to put a limit on the time for acceptance. On the other hand, the offeree can at any time refuse the offer or, unless he has been guilty of unreasonable delay, accept it. Neither party is at a disadvantage. Unless authority constrains me to do otherwise, I am strongly disposed to prefer the second alternative to the first.

QUESTIONS

1. If Buckley J is correct that the second alternative is to be preferred, does this mean that the same offer made to different people might lapse at different times? For a discussion, see MacDougall at 34-35.

2. On November 15, B wrote to C, offering to sell C his farm for $150,000. The letter said that the deal could be closed immediately and that the title would be transferred on January 1, and ended, "Trusting to hear from you as soon as possible." C was away when the letter arrived, and did not accept the offer until December 10; meanwhile, B sold the farm to H. Both C and H claim the farm. How would you advise C? See *Barrick v Clark*, [1951] SCR 177, [1950] 4 DLR 529.

3. A sends an offer to B to sell goods, asking for a reply within a week. Eight days after receiving the offer, B replies accepting it. Two days later B changes his mind and withdraws his acceptance. How would you advise A, who has incurred expense in preparing the goods for shipment?

4. D sues N to enforce N's guarantee of the indebtedness of a related company. The Court of Appeal finds that N owes D approximately $315,000. N applies for leave to appeal to the Supreme Court. After N has filed the leave application and D has responded to it, N makes D an offer to settle the case for $250,000. A few hours after the settlement offer has been made (and sooner than either party had expected), the Supreme Court advises the parties that leave to appeal has been granted. D purports to accept N's offer to settle. Is D able to accept the offer or has it lapsed because of a fundamental change in circumstances? For a discussion, see *Nielsen v Dysart Timbers Ltd*, [2009] NZSC 43, noted (2011) 27 J of Contract L 222.

LARKIN V GARDINER
(1895), 27 OR 125 (Div Ct)

This was an action for the specific performance of a contract for the sale of land, brought by Jane Larkin, alleging herself to be the vendor, against the defendant, who had, as she alleged, entered into a contract with her.

The defendant denied the making of any contract, and alleged a want of title in the vendor and a cancellation of the contract if any existed.

The property had been placed in the hands of one Nesbitt, a land agent, by the plaintiff for sale on her behalf. The defendant went to Nesbitt and offered $1,900 for the property. Nesbitt stated, as the fact was, that he was not authorized to sell at that price, but that if the defendant would sign an agreement to purchase at that price, he would submit the matter to the plaintiff. Thereupon Nesbitt prepared a form of agreement, beginning "I, Jane Larkin of Toronto, married woman, agree to sell, through John A. Nesbitt as my agent, and I, David Gardiner of the city of Toronto, baker, agree to buy, all that certain parcel," etc.

This was signed by the defendant at about seven p.m. on the 22nd April, 1895, and left by him with Nesbitt. Early next morning Nesbitt went to the plaintiff's house and she signed the agreement. At about one o'clock on the same day, the defendant gave written notice to Nesbitt withdrawing from the offer he had made. At the time he received his notice, Nesbitt had taken no step to communicate to the defendant the fact that the plaintiff had accepted his offer or had signed the agreement. The agreement with the two signatures attached to it, had simply remained in his possession as agent for the plaintiff without communication to any one of the fact that the plaintiff had completed it by her signature. Subsequently the defendant, while always repudiating the existence of any agreement on his part to purchase, and expressly without prejudice to that position, upon being served with an abstract of title, made objections to it, and upon these not being satisfactorily answered, refused to do anything further, whereupon the present action was brought.

STREET J: The instrument signed by the defendant, although drawn in the form of an agreement, must, in my opinion, be treated as a mere offer to purchase which might be withdrawn before it had been accepted by the plaintiff; and the only question to be determined is, whether the mere signature of the plaintiff without anything more was a sufficient acceptance.

In *Brogden v. Metropolitan R. W. Co.* (1877), 2 App. Cas. 666, Lord Blackburn, at p. 691, says: "I have always believed the law to be this, that whenever an offer is made to another party, and in that offer there is a request express or implied that he must signify his acceptance by doing some particular thing, then as soon as he does that thing, he is bound." And he goes on to say, at p. 692, "But when you come to the general proposition which Mr. Justice Brett seems to have laid down, that a simple acceptance in your mind, without any intimation to the other party and expressed by a mere private act, such as putting a letter into a drawer, completes a contract, I must say I differ from that."

Now, I think it would be unreasonable to hold in the present case that the defendant having made his offer to purchase, did not impliedly stipulate that in some form or other he should be made aware of the plaintiff's decision with regard to it—either by a letter informing him of the fact, or by the delivery to him of the contract signed by the plaintiff. I do not think it would be consistent with what we must assume the intention of the parties to have been that the mere signature of the plaintiff not communicated to him, should convert his offer into a binding contract. If I am right in so viewing the matter, then it follows that until the plaintiff had done something irrevocable towards communicating to him her acceptance of his offer, he was at liberty to withdraw it. The posting of a letter to him, or the verbal communication to him, of the fact that she had signed the contract, would have been sufficient. But the delivery to her own agent of the contract with her signature to it, was a revocable act until it had been communicated to the defendant, and was of no more force than if she had kept the instrument in her own drawer after signing it. If it had been possible to hold that Nesbitt was agent for the defendant to receive notice of the completion of the contract, his knowledge that the plaintiff had signed, would of course have bound the defendant, but there is not the slightest ground for any such finding.

In my opinion, therefore, the defendant was within his rights when he withdrew the offer he had made, and no contract binding upon either party ever existed.

[The judgment of Armour CJ is omitted. Falconbridge J concurred.]

Dominion Building Corporation, Ltd v The King. [1933] 3 DLR 577 (Canada PC). One, Forgie, on July 27, 1925 offered in writing to purchase from His Majesty property at the corner of King and Yonge Streets in Toronto. The offer concluded with these words: "This offer of purchase, if accepted by Order of His Excellency the Governor General in Council, shall constitute a binding contract of purchase and sale, subject to all the terms and provisions thereof and which contract shall enure to the benefit of the undersigned [Forgie], his heirs, etc. and to the benefit of His Majesty, etc." An Order in Council was duly passed and a certified copy sent to Forgie, who could not remember when he received it or whether he had received a covering letter with it. The Exchequer Court held there was a binding contract, which decision the Supreme Court unanimously reversed on the ground that there was no written acceptance. The Privy Council then reversed the decision of the Supreme Court.

LORD TOMLIN: Their Lordships think that if any notification of acceptance of the offer was necessary, the only possible inference upon the evidence is that there was a notification of acceptance by the sending to the appellant Forgie of a certified copy of the Order in Council.

But in fact, in their Lordships' opinion, there was not upon the true construction of the contract any need for a notification of acceptance. The language of the offer is ... not the language of precision, but the meaning which can most naturally be and ought, in their Lordships' opinion, to be attributed to it, is that the offer shall be deemed to have been accepted when the necessary Order in Council has been made.

DICKINSON V DODDS
(1876), 2 ChD 463 (CA)

On Wednesday, the 10th of June, 1874, the defendant John Dodds signed and delivered to the plaintiff, George Dickinson, a memorandum, of which the material part was as follows:

> I hereby agree to sell to Mr. George Dickinson the whole of the dwelling houses, garden ground, stabling, and outbuildings thereto belonging, situated at Croft, belonging to me, for the sum of £800. As witness my hand this tenth day of June, 1874. John Dodds.
>
> P.S.—This offer to be left over until Friday, 9 o'clock, a.m. J.D. (the twelfth), 12th June, 1874. (signed) J. Dodds.

The bill alleged that Dodds understood and intended that the plaintiff should have until Friday, 9 a.m., within which to determine whether he would or would not purchase, and that he should absolutely have, until that time, the refusal of the property at the price of £800, and that the plaintiff in fact determined to accept the offer on the morning of Thursday, the 11th of June, but did not at once signify his acceptance to Dodds, believing that he had the power to accept it until 9 a.m. on the Friday.

In the afternoon of Thursday the plaintiff was informed by a Mr. Berry that Dodds had been offering or agreeing to sell the property to Thomas Allan the other defendant. Thereupon the plaintiff, at about half-past seven in the evening, went to the house of Mrs. Burgess, the mother-in-law of Dodds, where he was then staying, and left with her a formal acceptance, in writing, of the offer to sell the property. According to the evidence of Mrs. Burgess, this document never in fact reached Dodds, she having forgotten to give it to him.

On the following (Friday) morning, at about seven o'clock, Berry, who was acting as agent for Dickinson, found Dodds at the Darlington railway station, and handed to him a duplicate of the acceptance by Dickinson, and explained to Dodds its purport. He replied that it was too late, as he had sold the property. A few minutes later

Dickinson himself found Dodds entering a railway carriage, and handed him another duplicate of the notice of acceptance, but Dodds declined to receive it, saying, "You are too late. I have sold the property."

It appeared that on the day before, Thursday, the 11th of June, Dodds had signed a formal contract for the sale of the property to the defendant Allan for £800, and had received from him a deposit of £40.

Bacon V.C. decreed specific performance in favor of the plaintiff, on the ground that by the original offer or agreement with the plaintiff, and by relation back of the acceptance to the date of the offer, Dodds had lost the power to make a sale to Allan. From this decision the defendants appealed.

JAMES LJ: ... That shows it was only an offer. There was no consideration given for the undertaking or promise, to whatever extent it may be considered binding, to keep the property unsold until 9 o'clock on Friday morning; but apparently Dickinson was of opinion, and probably Dodds was of the same opinion, that he (Dodds) was bound by that promise, and could not in any way withdraw from it, or retract it, until 9 o'clock on Friday morning, and this probably explains a good deal of what afterwards took place. But it is clear settled law, on one of the clearest principles of law, that this promise, being a mere *nudum pactum*, was not binding, and that at any moment before a complete acceptance by Dickinson of the offer, Dodds was as free as Dickinson himself. Well, that being the state of things, it is said that the only mode in which Dodds could assert that freedom was by actually and distinctly saying to Dickinson, "Now I withdraw my offer." It appears to me that there is neither principle nor authority for the proposition that there must be an express and actual withdrawal of the offer, or what is called a retraction. It must, to constitute a contract, appear that the two minds were at one at the same moment of time; that is, that there was an offer continuing up to the time of the acceptance. If there was not such a continuing offer, then the acceptance comes to nothing. Of course it may well be that the one man is bound in some way to let the other know that his mind with regard to the offer has been changed; but in this case, beyond all question, the plaintiff knew that Dodds was no longer minded to sell the property to him as plainly and clearly as if Dodds had told him in so many words, "I withdraw the offer." This is evident from the plaintiff's own statements in the bill.

The plaintiff says, in effect that, having heard and knowing that Dodds was no longer minded to sell to him, and that he was selling or had sold to someone else, thinking that he could not, in point of law, withdraw his offer, meaning to fix him to it, and endeavoring to bind him, "I went to the house where he was lodging, and saw his mother-in-law, and left with her an acceptance of the offer, knowing all the while that he had entirely changed his mind. I got an agent to watch for him at 7 o'clock the next morning, and I went to the train just before 9 o'clock, in order that I might catch him and give him my notice of acceptance just before 9 o'clock, and when that occurred he told my agent, and he told me, you are too late, and he then threw back the paper." It is to my mind quite clear that, before there was any attempt at acceptance by the plaintiff, he was perfectly well aware that Dodds had changed his mind, and that he had in fact agreed to sell the property to Allan. It is impossible, therefore, to say there was ever that existence of the same mind between the two parties which is essential in point of law to the making of an agreement. I am of opinion, therefore, that the plaintiff has failed to prove that there was any binding contract between Dodds and himself.

[The decision of Mellish LJ is omitted. Baggallay JA concurred.]

GERMAN CIVIL CODE

Section 145. An offer to contract is binding upon the offeror unless he has provided for the contrary.

UNIFORM COMMERCIAL CODE
American Law Institute, 1978

SECTION 2-205. FIRM OFFERS

An offer by a merchant to buy or sell goods in a signed writing which by its terms gives assurance that it will be held open is not revocable for lack of consideration during the time stated or if no time is stated for a reasonable time, but in no event may such period of irrevocability exceed three months; but any such term of assurance on a form supplied by the offeree must be separately signed by the offeror.

NOTES AND QUESTIONS

1. What are the actual facts of *Dickinson v Dodds*? Mellish LJ remarked that "Berry does not tell us from whom he heard it, but he says that he did hear it, that he knew it, and that he informed Dickinson of it." Later he referred to the offeree receiving notice "in some way" that the property has been sold. What "way" would be effective? If Dickinson had heard of the revocation from a friend of his who had heard from a friend of the defendant that the deal was off, would that be an effective revocation?

2. It was held in *Dickinson v Dodds* to be "clear settled law" that a promise to hold an offer open for a certain time is unenforceable unless there is consideration for the promise or unless it is under seal. James LJ thought that both parties assumed the contrary, and it has often been suggested that business practice is not in accord with the law in this matter. Should common law jurisdictions adopt the rules proposed by the *German Civil Code* or *Uniform Commercial Code*? Would your opinion change if you were informed that German businesses customarily "provide for the contrary" (which is said to be the case)?

3. If a promise to hold an offer open is made under seal, it is enforceable even though there is no consideration for it. But the offeree may still not be in quite as good a position as he would have been in had he accepted the offer before revocation because equity will not generally grant specific performance in the absence of consideration. Thus the seal makes the promise enforceable at law, but is not recognized by equity as a substitute for consideration: see *Savereux v Tourangeau* (1908), 16 OLR 600 (Div Ct).

4. For a discussion of the firm offer problem, see Waddams at paras 114, 127-29; McCamus at 86-90; MacDougall at 30-32.

FELTHOUSE V BINDLEY
(1862), 11 CB (NS) 869, 142 ER 1037 (Ex Ch)

Action for the conversion of a horse. A verdict was found for the plaintiff, damages £33, leave being reserved to the defendant to move to enter a nonsuit. A rule nisi was obtained.

WILLES J: I am of opinion that the rule to enter a nonsuit should be made absolute. The horse in question had belonged to the plaintiff's nephew, John Felthouse. In December, 1860, a conversation took place between the plaintiff and his nephew relative to the purchase of the horse by the former. The uncle seems to have thought that he had on that occasion bought the horse for £30, the nephew that he had sold it for 30 guineas: but there was clearly no complete bargain at that time. On the 1st of January, 1861, the nephew writes, "I saw my father on Saturday. He told me that you considered you had bought the horse for £30. If so, you are labouring under a mistake, for, 30 guineas was the price I put upon him, and you never heard me say less. When you said you would have him, I considered you were aware of the price." To this the uncle replies on the following day, "Your price, I admit, was 30 guineas. I offered £30; never offered more: and you said the horse was mine. However, as there may be a mistake about him, I will split the difference. If I hear no more about him, I consider the horse mine at £30 15s." It is clear that there was no right to complete the bargain on the 2nd of January; and it is also clear that the uncle had no right to impose upon the nephew a sale of his horse for £30 15s. unless he chose to comply with the condition of writing to repudiate the offer. The nephew might, no doubt, also have retracted his offer at any time before acceptance. It stood an open offer: and so things remained until the 25th of February, when the nephew was about to sell his farming stock by auction. The horse in question being catalogued with the rest of the stock, the auctioneer (the defendant) was told that it was already sold. It is clear, therefore, that the nephew in his own mind intended his uncle to have the horse at the price which he (the uncle) had named, £30 15s.: but he had not communicated such his intention to his uncle, or done anything to bind himself. Nothing, therefore, had been done to vest the property in the horse in the plaintiff down to the 25th of February, when the horse was sold by the defendant. It appears to me, that, independently of the subsequent letters, there had been no bargain to pass the property in the horse to the plaintiff, and therefore that he had no right to complain of the sale. Then, what is the effect of the subsequent correspondence? The letter of the auctioneer amounts to nothing. The more important letter is that of the nephew, of the 27th of February, which is relied on as shewing that he intended to accept and did accept the terms offered by his uncle's letter of the 2nd of January. The letter, however, may be treated either as an acceptance then for the first time by him, or as a memorandum of a bargain complete before the 25th of February, sufficient within the statute of frauds. It seems to me that the former is the more likely construction: and if so, it is clear that the plaintiff cannot recover. But, assuming that there had been a complete parole bargain before the 25th of February, and that the letter of the 27th was a mere expression of the terms of that prior bargain, and not a bargain then for the first time concluded, it would be directly contrary to the decision of the Contract of Exchequer in *Stockdale v. Dunlop* (1840), 6 M. & W. 224; 151 E.R. 391, to hold that that acceptance had relation back to the previous offer so as to bind third persons in respect of a dealing with the property by them in the interim. ...

[Byles J agreed, as did Keating J, who said, "Had the question arisen as between uncle and nephew, there would probably have been some difficulty." The record shows that Bindley simply forgot that the horse had been sold. The decision was affirmed by the Court of Exchequer Chamber in (1863), 7 LT 835.]

Lucy v Mouflet. (1860), 5 H & N 229, 157 ER 1168 (Ex Ch). POLLOCK CB: Now though is it true that if a stranger were to write and say to a person, "If I do not hear I will send goods," the omission to reply would be no evidence of a contract, yet it is different where two persons are actually engaged in dealing or under contract with each other. Then, if a proposal is made to which assent might be reasonably expected amongst men of business, and no answer is sent to it, acquiescence may be presumed.

WHEELER V KLAHOLT
178 Mass 141, 59 NE 756 (Sup Jud Ct 1901)

HOLMES CJ: This is an action for the price of one hundred and seventy four pairs of shoes, and the question raised by the defendants' exception is whether there was any evidence, at the trial, of a purchase by the defendants. ...

The evidence of the sale was this. The shoes had been sent to the defendants on the understanding that a bargain had been made. It turned out that the parties disagreed, and if any contract had been made it was repudiated by them both. Then, on September 11, 1899, the plaintiffs wrote to the defendants that they had written to their agent, Young, to inform the defendants that the latter might keep the goods "at the price you offer if you send us net spot cash at once. If you cannot send us cash draft by mail please return the goods to us immediately via Wabash & Fitchburg Railroad, otherwise they will go through New York City and it would take three or four weeks to get them." On September 15, the defendants enclosed a draft for the price less four per cent, which they said was the proposition made by Young. On September 18 the plaintiffs replied, returning the draft, saying that there was no deduction of four per cent, and adding, "if not satisfactory please return the goods at once by freight via Wabash & Fitchburg Railroad." This letter was received by the defendants on or before September 20, but the plaintiffs heard nothing more until October 25, when they were notified by the railroad company that the goods were in Boston.

It should be added that when the goods were sent to the defendants they were in good condition, new, fresh, and well packed, and that when the plaintiffs opened the returned cases their contents were more or less defaced and some pairs of shoes were gone. It fairly might be inferred that the cases had been opened and the contents tumbled about by the defendants, although whether before or after the plaintiff's final offer perhaps would be little more than a guess.

Both parties invoke *Hobbs v. Massasoit Whip Co.* (1893), 33 N.E. 495, the defendants for the suggestion on page 495, that a stranger by sending goods to another cannot impose a duty of notification upon him at the risk of finding himself a purchaser against his own will. We are of opinion that this proposition gives the defendants no help. The parties were not strangers to each other. The goods had not been foisted upon the defendants, but were in their custody presumably by their previous assent, at all events by their assent implied by their later conduct. The relations between the parties were so similar to those in the case cited, that if the plaintiffs' offer had been simply to let the defendants have the shoes at the price named, with an alternative request to send them back at once, as in their letters, the decision would have applied, and a silent retention of the shoes for an unreasonable time would have been an acceptance of the plaintiffs' terms, or, at least would have warranted a finding that it was. ...

The defendants seek to escape the effect of the foregoing principle, if held applicable, on the ground of the terms offered by the plaintiffs. They say that those terms made it impossible to accept the plaintiffs' offer, or to give the plaintiffs any reasonable ground for understanding that their offer was accepted, otherwise than by promptly forwarding the cash. They say that whatever other liabilities they may have incurred they could not have purported to accept an offer to sell for cash on the spot by simply keeping the goods. But this argument appears to us to take one half of the plaintiffs' proposition with excessive nicety, and to ignore the alternative. Probably the offer could have been accepted and the bargain have been made complete before sending the cash. At all events we must not forget the alternative, which was the immediate return of the goods.

The evidence warranted a finding that the defendants did not return the goods immediately or within a reasonable time, although subject to a duty in regard to them. The case does not stand as simple offer to sell for cash received in silence, but as an alternative offer and demand to and upon one who was subject to a duty to return the goods, allowing him either to buy for cash or to return the shoes at once, followed by a failure on his part to do anything. Under such circumstances a jury would be warranted in finding that a neglect of the duty to return imported an acceptance of the alternative offer to sell, although coupled with a failure to show that promptness on which the plaintiffs had a right to insist if they saw fit, but which they also were at liberty to waive.

Exceptions overruled.

RESTATEMENT OF THE LAW OF CONTRACTS (SECOND)
American Law Institute, 1981

69(1) Where an offeree fails to reply to an offer, his silence and inaction operate as an acceptance in the following cases only:

(a) Where an offeree takes the benefit of offered services with reasonable opportunity to reject them and reason to know that they were offered with the expectation of compensation.

(b) Where the offeror has stated or given the offeree reason to understand that assent may be manifested by silence or inaction, and the offeree in remaining silent and inactive intends to accept the offer.

(c) Where because of previous dealings or otherwise it is reasonable that the offeree should notify the offeror if he does not intend to accept.

(2) An offeree who does any act inconsistent with the offeror's ownership of offered property is bound in accordance with the offered terms unless they are manifestly unreasonable. But if the act is wrongful against the offeror it is an acceptance only if ratified by him.

NOTES AND QUESTIONS

1. Modern consumer protection statutes indicate that, in general, a consumer has no legal obligation in respect of the use or disposal of unsolicited goods or services and that if the consumer has paid for such goods or services, he or she may demand a refund. See *Consumer Protection Act, 2002*, SO 2002, c 30, s 13; *Business Practices and Consumer Protection Act*, SBC 2004, c 2, ss 11-14.

2. A writes to B: "I hereby offer to sell you volume 1 of the *Acme Encyclopaedia* for the bargain price of $39.99. If I do not hear from you by Monday I shall assume that you wish to buy it." B, who wishes to buy the volume, does nothing, but A refuses to supply it. How would you advise B?

3. T made a contract with I, whereby T was to supply standby tugboat services at a specified pay rate. After the contract expired, T continued to supply the tugs and send invoices. I continued to use the service, but did not pay the bills. How would you advise T? See *Saint John Tugboat Co Ltd v Irving Refinery Ltd*, [1964] SCR 6143, 49 MPR 284. See also Waddams at paras 92-96; Fridman at 52-57.

ELIASON V HENSHAW
4 Wheaton 225 (USSC 1819)

WASHINGTON J (for the Court): It is an undeniable principle of the law of contracts that an offer of a bargain by one person to another imposes no obligation upon the former, until it is accepted by the latter according to the terms in which the offer was made. Any qualification of or departure from those terms invalidates the offer, unless the same be agreed to by the person who made it. Until the terms of the agreement have received the assent of both parties, the negotiation is open, and imposes no obligation upon either.

In this case, the plaintiffs in error offered to purchase from the defendant two or three hundred barrels of flour, to be delivered at Georgetown by the first water, and to pay for the same $9.50 per barrel. To the letter containing this offer they required an answer by the return of the wagon by which the letter was despatched. This wagon was at that time in the service of the defendant, and employed by him in hauling flour from his mill to Harper's Ferry, near to which place the plaintiffs then were. The meaning of the writers was obvious. They could easily calculate, by the usual length of time which was employed by this wagon in travelling from Harper's Ferry to Mill Creek, and back again with a load of flour, about what time they should receive the desired answer; and, therefore, it was entirely unimportant whether it was sent by that or another wagon, or in any other manner, provided it was sent to Harper's Ferry, and was not delayed beyond the time which was ordinarily employed by wagons engaged in hauling flour from the defendant's mill to Harper's Ferry. Whatever uncertainty there might have been as to the time when the answer would be received, there was none as to the place to which it was to be sent; this was distinctly indicated by the mode pointed out for the conveyance of the answer. The place, therefore, to which the answer was to be sent constituted an essential part of the plaintiff's offer.

It appears, however, from the bill of exceptions, that no answer to this letter was at any time sent to the plaintiffs at Harper's Ferry. Their offer, it is true, was accepted by the terms of a letter addressed Georgetown, and received by the plaintiffs at that place; but an acceptance communicated at a place different from that pointed out by the plaintiffs, and forming a part of their proposal, imposed no obligation binding upon them, unless they had acquiesced in it, which they declined doing.

It is no argument that an answer was received at Georgetown; the plaintiffs in error had a right to dictate the terms upon which they would purchase the flour; and, unless they were complied with, they were not bound by them. All their arrangements may have been made with a view to the circumstances of place, and they were the only judges of its importance. There was, therefore, no contract concluded between these parties; and the Court ought, therefore, to have given the instruction to the jury which was asked for.

Judgment reversed.

MANCHESTER DIOCESAN COUNCIL FOR EDUCATION V COMMERCIAL & GENERAL INVESTMENTS LTD
[1969] 3 All ER 1593 (ChD)

BUCKLEY J: It may be that an offeror, who by the terms of his offer insists on acceptance in a particular manner, is entitled to insist that he is not bound unless acceptance is effected or communicated in that precise way, although it seems probable that, even so, if the other party communicates his acceptance in some other way, the offeror may by conduct or otherwise waive his right to insist on the prescribed method of acceptance. Where, however, the offeror has prescribed a particular method of acceptance, but not in terms insisting that only acceptance in that mode shall be binding, I am of opinion that acceptance communicated to the offeror by any other mode which is no less advantageous to him will conclude the contract. Thus in *Tinn v. Hoffman & Co.*, where acceptance was requested by return of post, Honeyman J. said: "That does not mean exclusively a reply by letter by return of post, but you may reply by telegram or by verbal message, or by any means not later than a letter written and sent by return of post ... " If an offeror intends that he shall be bound only if his offer is accepted in some particular manner, it must be for him to make this clear.

HYDE V WRENCH
(1840), 3 Beav 334, 49 ER 132 (Rolls Ct)

LORD LANGDALE MR: Under the circumstances stated in this bill, I think there exists no valid binding contract between the parties for the purchase of the property. The defendant offered to sell it for £1,000, and if that had been at once unconditionally accepted, there would undoubtedly have been a perfect binding contract; instead of that, the plaintiff made an offer of his own to purchase the property for £950, and he thereby rejected the offer previously made by the defendant. I think that it was not afterwards competent for him to revive the proposal of the defendant, by tendering an acceptance of it; and that therefore there exists no obligation of any sort between the parties; the demurrer must be allowed.

Re Cowan and Boyd. (1921), 49 OLR 335 (AD). A's lease being about to expire, he wrote his landlord B on March 17 about a renewal. B replied on March 24, offering a renewal at an advanced rent of $75. A replied on March 31, saying that he was paying as high a rent as he felt he should pay, "[S]o if you do not see your way clear to renew at the present rental we would appreciate an early reply." On April 5, B wrote that he would call and see A at the end of the month. On April 19, A wrote B, saying, "I have decided to accept your terms of $75 per month." Held, the letter of April 5 left the offer open.

NOTES AND QUESTIONS

1. Must a counteroffer of necessity reject a previous offer? Compare the following suggestion by H Oliphant, "The Duration and Termination of an Offer" (1920) 18 Mich L Rev 201: "Suppose, in reply to an offer by A, B writes, 'I shall want to consider your offer for more than the time which you have allowed me for that purpose because I am so situated now that I cannot return an immediate answer. However, the situation is such that if you want to settle the matter at once, I will close with you now at 5 percent less than the price you name.'" See

189

also the following suggestion in the same article: "Suppose the offeror says when making the offer, 'I expect you to reject this offer upon first consideration, but I want you to consider it further because I think you will accept when you have thought about it a while.' The offeree immediately sends a rejection, which the offeror ignores. On further thought, the offeree sends an acceptance." Is the offeror bound?

2. D offered to sell an airplane to N for £27,000, £5,000 payable in advance. No delivery time was specified. N replied accepting the offer, stipulating delivery within 30 days, and sent £5,000 to D's bank to be payable on delivery. D thought there was a contract but later repudiated. How would you advise N? See *Northland Airlines Ltd v Dennis Ferranti Meters, Ltd* (1970), 114 SJ 845 (QL) (CA).

3. E offered to sell his land to L for $1,800. L replied by telegram, saying, "Send lowest cash price. Will give $1,600 cash." E answered by telegram, "Cannot reduce price," upon which L wrote accepting the original offer. E refused to sell. How would you advise L? See *Livingstone v Evans*, [1925] 4 DLR 269 (Alta SC).

4. Sometimes it may not be easy to tell whether, in fact, a counteroffer has been made. In *Anglo-Newfoundland Fish Co v Smith & Co Ltd* (1902), 35 NSR 267 (SC en banc), the plaintiffs agreed to buy cod cleaned "free from black skin." The defendants objected, but, upon receiving a justification from the plaintiffs, replied that they would do their best to remove the black skin. The plaintiffs ordered "according to previous arrangement as to quality and price." The defendants failed to deliver and contended there was no contract. The court divided, two judges holding that there was no material difference between the plaintiffs and defendants; two holding that the defendants' reply was a counteroffer. In the result, the appeal failed and the decision of the lower court that had held for the plaintiffs stood. However, contrast *McIntosh v Brill* (1870), 20 UCCP 426, in which the response to an offer to sell butter was "I will take your butter, if good." No agreement was found by the court. For a discussion, see Waddams at para 60; Fridman at 58-59.

BUTLER MACHINE TOOL CO LTD V EX-CELL-O CORPORATION (ENGLAND) LTD
[1979] 1 WLR 401, 1 All ER 965 (CA)

[On May 23, 1969, Butler Machine Tool Co. Ltd. ("the seller") offered to sell a machine to Ex-Cell-O Corporation (England) Ltd. ("the buyer") for £75,535. The offer was stated to be subject to terms and conditions that "shall prevail over any terms and conditions in the Buyer's order." These conditions included a price variation clause that provided for an increase in the price if there was an increase in production costs. On May 27, the buyer placed an order for the machine. The order was stated to be subject to terms and conditions that were materially different from those put forward by the seller and which contained no price variation clause. On the bottom of the buyer's order there was a tear-off acknowledgment slip that stated: "We accept your order on the Terms and Conditions stated thereon." On June 5, the seller completed and signed the acknowledgment slip and returned it to the buyer. An accompanying letter stated that the buyer's order was being "entered in accordance with our revised quotation of 23rd May for delivery in 10/11 months." When the seller delivered the machine, it claimed that the price had increased by £2,892 and that it was entitled to this amount due to the price variation clause. The buyer refused to pay the increase because it claimed that the contract had been formed on the basis of its terms and conditions. The seller sued and was awarded judgment. The buyer then appealed.]

LORD DENNING MR: No doubt a contract was ... concluded. But on what terms? ...

If those documents are analysed in our traditional method, the result would seem to me to be this: the quotation of 23rd May 1969 was an offer by the sellers to the buyers containing the terms and conditions on the back. The order of 27th May 1969 purported to be an acceptance of that offer in that it was for the same machine at the same price, but it contained such additions as to cost of installation, date of delivery and so forth, that it was in law a rejection of the offer and constituted a counter-offer. That is clear from *Hyde v. Wrench* (1840) 3 Beav. 334. As Megaw J. said in *Trollope & Colls Ltd. v. Atomic Power Constructions Ltd.* [1962] 3 All E.R. 1035 at 1038, [1963] 1 W.L.R. 333 at 337: "... the counter-offer kills the original offer." The letter of the sellers of 5th June 1969 was an acceptance of that counter-offer, as is shown by the acknowledgment which the sellers signed and returned to the buyers. The reference to the quotation of 23rd May 1969 referred only to the price and identity of the machine.

... The judge held that the sellers were entitled to the sum of £2,892 under the price variation clause. He did not apply the traditional method of analysis by way of offer and counter-offer. He said that in the quotation of 23rd May 1969 "one finds the price variation clause appearing under a most emphatic heading stating that it is a term or condition that is to prevail." So he held that it did prevail.

I have much sympathy with the judge's approach to this case. In many of these cases our traditional analysis of offer, counter-offer, rejection, acceptance and so forth is out-of-date. ... The better way is to look at all the documents passing between the parties and glean from them, or from the conduct of the parties, whether they have reached agreement on all material points, even though there may be differences between the forms and conditions printed on the back of them. ...

Applying this guide, it will be found that in most cases when there is a "battle of forms" there is a contract as soon as the last of the forms is sent and received without objection being taken to it. ... The difficulty is to decide which form, or which part of which form, is a term or condition of the contract. In some cases the battle is won by the man who fires the last shot. He is the man who puts forward the latest term and conditions: and, if they are not objected to by the other party, he may be taken to have agreed to them. ... In some cases, however, the battle is won by the man who gets the blow in first. If he offers to sell at a named price on the terms and conditions stated on the back and the buyer orders the goods purporting to accept the offer on an order form with his own different terms and conditions on the back, then, if the difference is so material that it would affect the price, the buyer ought not to be allowed to take advantage of the difference unless he draws it specifically to the attention of the seller. There are yet other cases where the battle depends on the shots fired on both sides. There is a concluded contract but the forms vary. The terms and conditions of both parties are to be construed together. If they can be reconciled so as to give a harmonious result, all well and good. If differences are irreconcilable, so that they are mutually contradictory, then the conflicting terms may have to be scrapped and replaced by a reasonable implication.

In the present case the judge thought that the sellers in their original quotation got their blow in first; especially by the provision that "These terms and conditions shall prevail over any terms and conditions in the Buyer's order." It was so emphatic that the price variation clause continued through all the subsequent dealings and that the buyer must be taken to have agreed to it. I can understand that point of view. But I think that the documents have to be considered as a whole. And, as a matter of construction, I think the acknowledgment of 5th June 1969 is the decisive document. It makes it clear that the contract was on the buyers' terms and not on the sellers' terms: and the buyers' terms did not include a price variation clause.

I would therefore allow the appeal and enter judgment for the buyers.

LAWTON LJ: The modern commercial practice of making quotations and placing orders with conditions attached, usually in small print, is indeed likely, as in this case, to produce a battle of forms. The problem is how should that battle be conducted? The view taken by the judge was that the battle should extend over a wide area and the court should do its best to look into the minds of the parties and make certain assumptions. In my judgment, the battle has to be conducted in accordance with set rules. It is a battle more on classical 18th century lines when convention decided who had the right to open fire first rather than in accordance with the modern concept of attrition.

The rules relating to a battle of this kind have been known for the past 130-odd years ... [I]f anyone should have thought they were obsolescent, Megaw J. in *Trollope & Colls Ltd. v. Atomic Power Constructions Ltd.* [1962] 3 All E.R. 1035, [1963] 1 W.L.R. 333 called attention to the facts that those rules are still in force.

When those rules are applied to this case, in my judgment, the answer is obvious. ...

[BRIDGE LJ gave a concurring judgment which stated that the case was "plainly governed by ... the classical doctrine that a counter-offer amounts to a rejection of an offer and puts an end to the effect of the offer."]

NOTES AND QUESTIONS

1. Do you agree with Lord Denning that the current rules of offer and acceptance are outmoded? For a philosophical defence of these rules, see Benson at 139-49.

2. Would the result of the case have been different if the seller had not signed and returned the tear-off acknowledgment slip? See *Tywood Industries Ltd v St Anne-Nackawic Pulp & Paper Co Ltd* (1979), 100 DLR (3d) 374 (Ont H Ct J) and the discussions in Waddams at para 76; McCamus at 62-64; MacDougall at 21-23; Fridman at 60-61.

3. What remedies would a seller have if the court concluded that no contract had been formed? See E McKendrick, "The Battle of the Forms and the Law of Restitution" (1988) 8 Oxford J Legal Stud 197; M Spence, *Protecting Reliance* (Oxford: Hart, 1999) at 114-17.

4. In *Tekdata Interconnections Ltd v Amphenol Ltd*, [2010] 2 All ER (Comm) 302 (CA) (noted (2011) Can Bus LJ 307), the court concluded that there could be circumstances in which the traditional "battle of the forms" analysis would be displaced if it could be shown that the parties had intended that the standard form terms printed on the "counter offer" were to be ignored (such that there was an acceptance on the terms of the original offer). The court noted that the most plausible way for the litigants to prove this intention would be to reference the conduct of the parties over a long-term relationship. The court insisted, however, that it would be difficult to displace the usual analysis and that a finding that the contract was on the terms of the original offer would be rare.

5. For a discussion of other solutions to "battle of the forms" problems in both consumer and commercial contexts, see DB King, "New Perspective on Standard Form Contracts: A Subject Revisited" (1993) Comm Law Ann 87. See also Waddams at paras 80-89, and McCamus at 64-68, where it is suggested that more flexibility can be achieved by using traditional principles of contract formation.

Tinn v Hoffmann and Co. (1873), 29 LTR 271 (Ex Ch). BRETT J: If I write to a person and say, "If you give me 6000 [pounds] for my house, I will sell it to you," and on the same day, and before the letter reaches him, he writes to me saying, "If you sell me your house for 6000 [pounds] I will buy it," that would be two offers crossing each other, and cross offers are not an acceptance of each other, therefore there will be no offer of either party accepted by the other. That is the case where the contract is to be made by the letters, and by the letters only. I think it would be different if there were already a contract in fact made in words, and then the parties were to write letters to each other, which crossed in the post, those might make a very good memorandum of the contract already made, unless the *Statute of Frauds* intervened. But where the contract is to be made by the letters themselves, you cannot make it by cross offers, and say that the contract was made by one party accepting the offer which was made to him. It seems to me, therefore, in both views, that the judgment of the court below was right.

HONYMAN J (dissenting): What, then is the effect of when the letters are written on the same day and crossed each other in the post? Does it make any difference? ... I cannot see why the fact of the letters crossing each other should prevent their making a good contract. If I say I am willing to buy a man's house on certain terms, and he at the same moment says that he is willing to sell it, and these two letters are posted so that they are irrevocable with respect to the writers, why should that not constitute a good contract. The parties are *ad idem* at one and the same moment. On these grounds it appears to me that the judgment of the court below was wrong, and ought to be reversed, I speak with some hesitation in this case when I find that the opinion of the majority of my brothers is against me.

NOTES AND QUESTIONS

1. Whose reasoning do you find more persuasive? For an argument that the majority position is to be preferred, see Benson at 139-49.

2. For an argument that it might be possible to form a contract without acceptance following offer, see *Corbin on Contracts*, §12.

BRISTOL, CARDIFF, AND SWANSEA AËRATED BREAD COMPANY V MAGGS
(1890), 44 ChD 616

This was an action by the Plaintiffs, the Bristol, Cardiff, and Swansea Aërated Bread Company (Limited), against the Defendant, a baker and confectioner carrying on business at 15, Duke Street, Cardiff, for the specific performance of a contract alleged to be constituted by two letters. The first was written by the Defendant to Colonel Guthrie, a director of the Plaintiff company, and was as follows:

> Cardiff, 29th of May, 1889
>
> Dear Sir,—I beg to submit to you the following conditions for disposal of my business carried on at 15, Duke Street, Cardiff. Lease and goodwill, £450 (lease from the 29th of September, 1888, for fourteen years). All fixtures, fittings, utensils, & c., stock-in-trade connected with the premises to be taken at valuation.
>
> Yours truly,
> R. Maggs.
>
> This offer to hold good for ten days.

The letter did not on the face of it shew to whom it was written. Colonel Guthrie, writing with the authority of the board of directors of the company, replied as follows:

Cardiff, 1st of June, 1889.

Dear Sir,—On behalf of the Bristol, Cardiff, and Swansea Aërated Bread Company (Limited), I accept your offer for shop and lease, & c., 15, Duke Street, Cardiff.

Yours truly,

John Guthrie,

For B., C., and S. Aërated Bread Company.

Mr. R. Maggs,

15, Duke Street, Cardiff.

On the 2nd of June, 1889, the Defendant's solicitor sent Colonel Guthrie a formal memorandum of agreement for approval, with an accompanying letter. This memorandum was altered by the Plaintiff's solicitors, mainly by the insertion of a clause preventing the vendor for five years from carrying on a like business within the borough of Cardiff or within a distance of five miles from the Townhall. The memorandum so altered was returned on the 4th of June, with a letter of the Plaintiff's solicitors. On the 5th of June the Defendant's solicitor wrote sending the draft again to the Plaintiffs' solicitors, with a modification of the proposed additional clause. On the 6th of June the Plaintiffs' solicitors wrote that they could not themselves agree to the proposed modification, but that they had asked Colonel Guthrie to call about it.

On the 7th the Defendant's solicitor wrote that he regretted the Plaintiffs' solicitors had not agreed to the terms of the draft contract, and continued: "Colonel Guthrie has not been near me, and by my client's instructions I beg to inform you that he declines to proceed further in the matter."

On the 8th Colonel Guthrie saw the Defendant's solicitor and said he had come to settle the agreement, which had been returned to him. The answer was that he was too late; the Defendant had made other arrangements. Colonel Guthrie replied he was prepared to sign the agreement leaving out the disputed clause. The solicitor declined; and Colonel Guthrie went immediately to the Defendant, who told him that he wished to have the agreement cancelled, because his son was very much against his parting with the shop. The Defendant, it appeared, did not suggest that there was no agreement, but asked Colonel Guthrie to use his influence with his co-directors to get the sale cancelled. The memorandum of agreement contained several terms not expressed in the letters; for example, it provided for the book debts and books of account being reserved to the vendor and for the payment of a deposit of £45; it fixed the 24th of June as the day for completion of the purchase and delivery of possession; it provided for delivery of abstract of title and the date from which it was to commence, and for other matters, all of which were more or less of a formal nature.

KAY J (after stating the facts, continued): The contested stipulation in the memorandum of agreement as to restricting the vendor from carrying on a like business to that which he had sold was not by any means a matter of form. After some conflict of opinion, it has been decided by the Court of Appeal, in *Pearson v. Pearson* (1884), 27 Ch.D. 145, that a man who sells the goodwill of a business may not only set up a similar business next door and say that he is the person who carried on the old business, but that he may also solicit the customers of the old business to continue to deal with him, although by these proceedings he might not only destroy all benefit to the purchaser of the thing which he had bought, but might recover to himself the actual possession of it. Such a fraudulent proceeding, according to the decision, cannot be prevented by any Court of Law or Equity. It follows that the stipulation which the company's solicitors introduced into the draft was one which they were not entitled to insert if the two letters which I have read were a complete contract.

In other words, they were trying to obtain an additional and most important concession from the vendor. Now ... suppose this to pass in conversation: A. offers to B. his business, lease, and goodwill for £450. B. says, "I accept." A day or two afterwards B. asks A. to engage not to carry on a similar business within a distance of five miles. A. answers, "I cannot agree to that, but I will if you say three miles." B. takes time to consider, saying he will send an agent next day to settle the terms. The agent does not go next day, and A. accordingly says to B., "I put an end to the matter." No one could doubt that would be a continuous negotiation, and that B. could not say, "I will disregard all that followed the acceptance of the first offer, and insist on there being a complete contract by that acceptance." Well, then, still leaving out of sight the statute and authorities suppose all this to take place by letters between A. and B. instead of conversation; it is obvious the result must be the same. Some of the letters being by the principals and some by the solicitors could not make any difference.

It was suggested that the ten days during which the offer was to remain open had not expired when it was withdrawn. But this can make no difference. The offer was not a contract, and the term that it should remain open for ten days was therefore not binding. It has often been held that such an offer may, notwithstanding, be withdrawn within the time limited. ...

I decide this case against the Plaintiffs upon the ground, that although the two letters relied on would, if nothing else had taken place, have been sufficient evidence of a complete agreement, yet the Plaintiffs have themselves shewn that the agreement was not complete by stipulating afterwards for an important additional term, which kept the whole matter of purchase and sale in a state of negotiation only, and that the Defendant was therefore at liberty to put an end to the negotiations, as he did, by withdrawing his offer. ...

[Part of the opinion dealing with the *Statute of Frauds* has been omitted.]

Bellamy v Debenham. (1890), 45 ChD 481. NORTH J: Some of the phrases used by Mr. Justice Kay, in *Bristol, Cardiff, and Swansea Aërated Bread Co. v. Maggs* seem to me to go further than that. By way of illustration he put a case of a definite offer to sell a business, lease, and goodwill, and a definite acceptance, and after that negotiations between the parties as to whether a new term, limiting the area within which the vendor of the business was to carry on a similar business, should be introduced, and said that in such a case he thought that the purchaser could not disregard all that followed the acceptance of the prior offer, and insist on there being a complete contract by that acceptance. ...

In my opinion, subsequent negotiations, first commenced on new points after a contract complete in itself has been signed, cannot be regarded as constituting a part of the negotiations going on at the time when it was signed, because, *ex hypothesi*, the Court has arrived at the conclusion that they were not going on then—that they were not thought of at that time, but related to matters first thought of subsequently.

I do not in any way dissent from the view which Mr. Justice Kay took of the case then before him; but those remarks of his, if they meant as much as they might possibly mean, seem to me to go too far, and I should not be prepared to follow them.

Harvey v Perry. [1953] 1 SCR 233, [1953] 2 DLR 465. Negotiations were spread over several months leading to an alleged contract for the sale of eight oil leases in Alberta. Correspondence starting in January 1950 included a letter from Perry dated May 2, rejecting terms so high that "we cannot handle it at all" and continuing, "However, you might consider the following and if you feel that you could accept these terms, I am sure we could put a deal over for you." On May 8, Harvey wrote, "I will accept your proposition." On May 15, Perry wrote, "We will proceed immediately to try and consummate a deal for you at the earliest possible moment. There will, in all probability, be a counter proposal or two from our clients, and if such is the case, we will submit them to you at once." On August 24, Perry's solicitor wrote that "Mr. A.C. Perry ... advises that he is in a position to take these leases under the terms and conditions contained in his letter to you of the 2nd May and your letter to his firm dated May 8th, 1950. Mr. Perry has asked us to prepare the Assignment ... it will be necessary that we have access to the above leases now in your possession." In due course Harvey forwarded the leases. On August 26, the solicitor again wrote, "[S]ome discussion between you will be necessary before adequate instructions can be given to draw such an Agreement." On the same day Perry himself wrote that "Mr. Howatt of Howatt and Howatt, my solicitor, is sending through a copy of the proposed agreement. However you and I will get together and complete the terms." The "get together" took place on September 1, when, Perry contended, "[W]e had made a deal ... and we shook hands on that deal right there and then in front of the Hotel." On September 2, Perry's solicitor sent a letter and draft agreement with some variations from the oral agreement, which Harvey's solicitors objected to on September 7, and to the correction of which Perry's solicitor agreed, on September 9, saying, "[T]he terms are acceptable." On September 13, Perry forwarded a second agreement in identical terms with the first, and containing another variation from the oral agreement of September 1. Neither Harvey nor his solicitors made any further communication and Perry's letters remained unanswered. About September 15, Harvey announced that he would drill his own wells, which concluded the negotiations. The trial judge found a contract in the letters of May 2, 8, 15, and August 24, and in Harvey's sending the leases. The Alberta Court of Appeal agreed. The Supreme Court of Canada, following the *Maggs* case, reversed, ESTEY J saying, "The letter of September 2nd, the proposed agreement enclosed therewith and respondent's solicitors' letter of September 9th, might support a conclusion that the parties had agreed, but, when read, as they must be, with respondent's solicitors' letter of September 13th and the proposed agreement enclosed therewith, it is clear that the respondent had not agreed. ... There was no consensus ad idem because the respondent was still negotiating for better terms."

NOTES AND QUESTIONS

As the cases above illustrate, the problem of when a contract has actually been formed is a difficult one that can have far-reaching consequences. Consider the following set of facts. X and Y have entered into a contract for the sale of X's house to Y. As is normal practice when property is bought and sold, numerous formal documents must be prepared by the parties' solicitors to effect the actual legal transfer of the property. To one of these documents, Y's lawyer adds the term: "And the vendor warrants that the house has not been insulated with Urea Formaldehyde Foam." Is there a contract? On which terms? For a discussion of the subsequent negotiation problem, see Waddams at para 29; McCamus at 53-56.

C. THE TENDERING PROCESS

The process of contract formation has also been crucial to the development of the tender system for construction contracts. A contractor or owner sends out a call for tenders under which it asks interested parties to submit a bid for a particular job. The party calling for the tenders usually provides extensive terms and conditions for the tender, including detailed specifications for the work to be done. Once the bid process has closed, the tenders are considered and one is selected, again according to the criteria set out in the original call for tenders. The contract is awarded to the successful bid. To make this process work, the parties submitting the tender must be unable to amend or revoke their tenders during the consideration period. Further, they must be willing to accept the job if awarded. How can this be accomplished using the paradigm of offer and acceptance? Consider the following case.

MJB ENTERPRISES LTD V DEFENCE CONSTRUCTION (1951)
[1999] 1 SCR 619, 170 DLR (4th) 577

[The defendant (the respondent) invited tenders for construction and received four tenders, including one from the plaintiff (the appellant). The contract was awarded to Sorochan Enterprises Ltd. The specifications in the tender documents contemplated a lump-sum price, notwithstanding the fact that a significant cost to the project would be the cost of material to backfill pipeline trenches. A choice among several possible materials would be made later by the site engineer and the result of that choice would considerably alter the cost of performance of the construction contract. This imposed a significant cost risk on the tendering company. The successful bid addressed this risk by accompanying its tender with a handwritten note that stated: "Unit Prices per metre are based on native backfill (Type 3). If Type 2 material is required ... add $60.00 per metre." The tenderers argued that this note invalidated the tender, but the respondent accepted the bid and relied on a "privilege" clause in the tender documents that stated: "The lowest or any tender shall not necessarily be accepted." M.J.B. Enterprises sued for breach of contract.]

IACOBUCCI J:

I. INTRODUCTION

The central issue in this appeal is whether the inclusion of a "privilege clause" in the tender documents allows the person calling for tenders (the "owner") to disregard the lowest bid in favour of any other tender, including a non-compliant one. The leading Canadian case on the law of tenders is *R. in Right of Ontario v. Ron Engineering & Construction (Eastern) Ltd.*, [1981] 1 S.C.R. 111, 119 D.L.R. (3d) 267, which concerned the obligations of a contractor who submitted a bid in response to a call for tenders. This Court held that, upon the submission of this tender, a contract arose between the contractor and the owner in that case and imposed certain obligations upon the contractor. The contract, referred to as "Contract A," was distinguished from the construction contract, "Contract B," to be entered into if the tender was accepted. Contract A imposed certain obligations upon the contractor. The present appeal instead asks whether contract A arose in this case and what obligations, if any, it imposes on the owner. It is the contention of M.J.B. Enterprises Ltd. (the "appellant") that in the circumstances of this case Defence Construction (1951) Limited (the "respondent") was obligated to accept the lowest valid tender. The respondent argues that the privilege clause precludes the finding of such an obligation.

• • •

V. ANALYSIS

A. GENERAL PRINCIPLES

As I have already indicated, any discussion of contractual obligations and the law of tendering must begin with this Court's decision in *Ron Engineering, supra*. That case concerned whether the owner had to return the contractor's tender deposit, a sum of $150,000. The terms and conditions attaching to the call for tenders had included the statement (at pp. 113-14) that:

> Except as otherwise herein provided the tenderer guarantees that if his tender is withdrawn before the commission shall have considered the tenders or before or after he has been notified that his tender has been recommended to the Commission for acceptance or that if the Commission does not for any reason receive within the period of seven days as stipulated and as required herein, the Agreement executed by the tenderer, the Performance Bond and the Payment Bond executed by the tenderer and the surety company and the other documents required herein, the Commission may retain the tender deposit for the use of the Commission and may accept any tender, advertise for new tenders, negotiate a contract or not accept any tender as the Commission may deem advisable.

Other terms and conditions included the ability to withdraw a tender, under seal, until the official closing (at p. 120). In rushing to compile its tender, the contractor omitted to add its own labour costs to its bid, but only discovered its error after the close of the tender call. It was the lowest out of eight bids. The contractor did not seek to withdraw its tender, but instead maintained that because it gave notice of this error to the owner prior to the acceptance of its tender by the owner ... the owner could not, in law, accept its tender, and therefore had to return the contractor's $150,000 deposit.

Estey J., for the Court, held that a contract arose upon the contractor's submission of the tender. This contract, which Estey J. termed "Contract A," was to be distinguished from the construction contract to be entered into upon the acceptance of one of the tenders, which Estey J. termed "Contract B." The terms of Contract A were governed by the terms and conditions of the tender call, which included that the contractor submit a deposit that could only be recovered under certain conditions. ...

This Court therefore held that it is possible for a contract to arise upon the submission of a tender and that the terms of such a contract are specified in the tender documents. The submissions of the parties in the present appeal appear to suggest that *Ron Engineering* stands for the proposition that Contract A is always formed upon the submission of a tender and that a term of this contract is the irrevocability of the tender; indeed, most lower courts have interpreted *Ron Engineering* in this manner. There are certainly many statements in *Ron Engineering* that support this view. However, other passages suggest that Estey J. did not hold that a bid is irrevocable in all tendering contexts and that his analysis was in fact rooted in the terms and conditions of the tender call at issue in that case. ...

Therefore it is always possible that Contract A does not arise upon the submission of a tender, or that Contract A arises but the irrevocability of the tender is not one of its terms, all of this depending upon the terms and conditions of the tender call. To the extent that *Ron Engineering* suggests otherwise, I decline to follow it. ...

What is important, therefore, is that the submission of a tender in response to an invitation to tender may give rise to contractual obligations, quite apart from the obligations associated with the construction contract to be entered into upon the acceptance of a tender, depending upon whether the parties intend to initiate contractual relations by the submission of a bid. If such a contract arises, its terms are governed by the terms and conditions of the tender call. ...

So this brings us to ask whether Contract A arose in this case and, if so, what were its terms?

B. CONTRACT A

Both parties in the present appeal agree with the Contract A/Contract B analysis outlined in *Ron Engineering* and that the terms of Contract A, if any, are to be determined through an examination of the terms and conditions of the tender call. In particular, they agree that Contract A arose, but disagree as to its terms. However, this agreement is influenced by an interpretation of *Ron Engineering* that I have rejected. Because of this, it is important to discuss whether contract A arose in this case.

As I have already mentioned, whether or not Contract A arose depends upon whether the parties intended to initiate contractual relations by the submission of a bid in response to the invitation to tender. In the present case I am persuaded that this was the intention of the parties. At a minimum, the respondent offered, in inviting tenders through a formal tendering process involving complex documentation and terms, to consider bids for Contract B. In submitting its tender, the appellant accepted this offer. The submission of the tender is good consideration for the respondent's promise, as the tender was a benefit to the respondent, prepared at a not insignificant cost to the appellant, and accompanied by the Bid Security. The question to be answered next is the precise nature of the respondent's contractual obligations.

The main contention of the appellant is that the respondent was under an obligation to award Contract B to the lowest compliant tender. As the Sorochan bid was invalid, Contract B should have been awarded to the appellant. In this regard, the appellant makes two arguments: first, that it was an explicit term of Contract A that the construction contract be awarded to the lowest compliant bid and second, that even if such a term was not expressly incorporated into the tender package it was an implied term of Contract A. ...

[The court concluded that Contract A contained no such explicit term, nor was it possible to imply such a term. The court proceeded to consider the effect of the "privilege" clause.]

(b) Effect of the Privilege Clause

Although the respondent has not disputed the trial judge's finding that the Sorochan tender was non-compliant, the respondent argues that the privilege clause gave it the discretion to award the contract to anyone, including a non-compliant bid, or to not award the contract at all, subject only to a duty to treat all tenderers fairly. It argues that because it accepted the Sorochan tender with the good faith belief that it was a compliant bid, it did not breach its duty of fairness.

The words of the privilege clause are clear and unambiguous. As this Court stated in *Cartwright & Crickmore, Ltd. v. MacInnes*, [1931] S.C.R. 425 at p. 431, [1931] 3 D.L.R. 693, "there can be no recognized custom in opposition to an actual contract, and the special agreement of the parties must prevail." However, the privilege clause is only one term of Contract A and must be read in harmony with the rest of the Tender Documents. To do otherwise would undermine the rest of the agreement between the parties.

I do not find that the privilege clause overrode the obligation to accept only compliant bids, because on the contrary, there is a compatibility between the privilege clause and this obligation. ...

Therefore even where, as in this case, almost nothing separates the tenderers except the different prices they submit, the rejection of the lowest bid would not imply that a tender could be accepted on the basis of some undisclosed criterion. The discretion to accept not necessarily the lowest bid, retained by the owner through the privilege clause, is a discretion to take a more nuanced view of "cost" than the prices quoted in the tenders. ...

The additional discretion not to award a contract is presumably important to cover unforeseen circumstances, which is not at issue in this appeal. ...

Therefore I conclude that the privilege clause is compatible with the obligation to accept only a compliant bid. As should be clear from this discussion, however, the privilege clause is incompatible with an obligation to accept only the lowest compliant bid. With respect to this latter proposition, the privilege clause must prevail. ...

C. BREACH OF CONTRACT A

Applying the foregoing analysis to the case at bar, I find that the respondent was under no contractual obligation to award the contract to the appellant, who the parties agree was the lowest compliant bid. However, this does not mean that Contract A was not breached.

Sorochan was only the lowest bidder because it failed to accept, and incorporate into its bid, the risk of knowing how much of Type 2, Type 3, and Type 4 fill would be required. As the Court of Appeal outlined, this risk was assigned to the contractor. Therefore Sorochan's bid was based upon different specifications. Indeed, it is conceded that the Sorochan bid was non-compliant. Therefore, in awarding the contract to Sorochan, the respondent breached its obligation to the appellant, and the other tenderers, that it would accept only a compliant tender.

The respondent's argument of good faith in considering the Sorochan bid to be compliant is no defence to a claim for breach of contract: it amounts to an argument that because it thought it had interpreted the contract properly it cannot be in breach. Acting in good faith or thinking that one has interpreted the contract correctly are not valid defences to an action for breach of contract. ...

[The court determined that the damages for breach of the contract should protect the expectation interest of the plaintiff. The court was convinced on a balance of probabilities that had the defective tender been ignored, the bid of M.J.B. would have been the successful bid, thus making the expectancy loss the profit it would have realized on Contract B. The court further held that this loss was not too remote.]

Double N Earthmovers Ltd v Edmonton (City). [2007] 1 SCR 116. CHARRON J (dissenting): The parties agree that these two implied terms formed part of Contract A: the City was obliged to accept only a compliant bid ... and the City was also obliged to treat all bidders fairly and equally. ... The test for compliance in the tendering process is "substantial" rather than strict. Estey J.'s remark in *Ron Engineering* that it would be "anomalous indeed if the march forward to a construction contract could be halted by a simple omission" is often cited in support of the substantial compliance test ... . Although Estey J. made this remark in reference to the Contract B stage of the tendering process, there is no reason to doubt that these same considerations apply to the Contract A stage as well. It would make tendering unworkable if an owner and bidder were prevented from entering into Contract B based on an unchecked box. Substantial compliance requires that all material conditions of a tender, determined on an objective standard, be complied with ... . A bid is substantially compliant if any departures from the tender call concern mere irregularities.

Maystar General Contractors Inc v Newmarket (Town). 2009 ONCA 675. FELD-MAN JA: The law governing the tender process for public construction contracts has been discussed and explained by the Supreme Court of Canada in a number of cases ... . Some basic principles for interpreting and applying the terms of tender documents have emerged from these cases. *Ron Engineering* established the two layers of contractual relations that arise in the tender process. When a contractor submits a tender that complies with the requirements set out by the owner in the tender documents, a contract arises, known as Contract A. The owner then enters into the construction contract, known as Contract B, with the Contract A contractor whose bid is the best bid in terms of price and other factors that the owner is entitled to take into account under the terms of the tender. The terms of Contract A are found in the express provisions of the tender requirements or can also be implied where the criteria for the implication of terms in a contract are met. In *M.J.B. Enterprises*, the Supreme Court found from the presumed intentions of the parties based on the express terms of the contract, that there was an implied term that the owner is obliged to accept only compliant bids. At para. 41, the court reasoned that it would not make sense for contractors to engage in the tendering process, which is expensive and time-consuming, if the owner could then "circumscribe this process and accept a non-compliant bid." In *Double N Earthmovers* ... the court clarified that the compliance required is "substantial compliance" with the tender documents and that substantial compliance requires compliance with all material conditions of a tender. In [*Martel Building Ltd v Canada*, [2000] 2 SCR 860] ... the court found that in order to give business efficacy to the tendering process, it was necessary to imply a term that the owner must treat all bids fairly and equally.

NOTES AND QUESTIONS

1. What are the terms of the offers that are being made by the parties in these cases? For a discussion, see Waddams at paras 36-41; McCamus at 150-59; Fridman at 36-40; MacDougall at 28-30.

2. As *Maystar* notes, the Contract A/Contract B theory of tendering has been the subject of much recent litigation and refinement in the Supreme Court of Canada. Does this indicate that the analysis might be flawed in some respect? Is the court's reasoning backward?

3. Industry guidebooks often advise users not to enforce the legal rights created under Contract A. Does this mean that the current tendering rules are inconsistent with common sense and the reasonable expectations of business people? For just such an argument, see P Sandori, "Construction Bidding and Tendering" (2015) 44 Construction L Report (4th) 62.

4. In *Naylor Group Inc v Ellis-Don Construction Ltd*, [2001] 2 SCR 943, the Supreme Court decided that the Contract A/Contract B analysis can also apply to the relationship between a main contractor (who assembles a bid) and the subcontractors (who supply sub-bids) when both parties implicitly or explicitly intended that such an analysis should apply. For a discussion of the case, see N Rafferty, "Developments in Contract and Tort Law: The 2001-2002 Term" (2002) 18 SCLR (2d) 154.

5. Could a subcontractor who suffered economically as a result of an owner's breach of Contract A with the head contractor sue in tort to recoup these losses? For judicial rejection of this possibility, see *Design Services Ltd v Canada*, [2008] 1 SCR 737. Could the subcontractor make a claim under the principled exception of privity of contract outlined in *Fraser River Pile*

and Dredge Ltd v Can-Dive Services Ltd, excerpted in Chapter 4? For just such an argument, see Swan & Adamski at 216.

6. Although Charron J was in the dissent in *Double N Earthmovers Ltd*, there was no dispute as between the majority and dissent as to the test for a compliant bid. The dispute instead focused on whether the failure to provide serial numbers and licence registration numbers for the vehicles to be supplied under Contract B in the tender documents prevented substantial compliance on the facts of the case. See WD Goodfellow, "*Double N Earthmovers Ltd*: A New Direction for the Supreme Court of Canada?" (2007) 61 Colum L Rev (3d) 163.

7. For a situation where a tender call or request for proposals (RFP) was not held to constitute Contract A, see *Budget Rent-A-Car of BC Ltd v Vancouver International Airport Authority* (2009), 89 BCLR (4th) 249 (CA). In that case the RFP stated: "This RFP does not constitute an offer. No agreement shall result upon submission of Proposals. [The owner] shall not be under obligation to enter into any agreement with anyone in connection with this RFP and responses received. [The owner] will not have any obligation to anyone in connection with this RFP unless [the owner] executes and delivers an agreement in writing approved by [the owner's] senior management."

8. Would the following exclusion clause included in an RFP be effective to negate liability for breach of Contract A? "Except as expressly and specifically permitted in these Instructions to Proponents, no Proponent shall have any claim for any compensation of any kind whatsoever, as a result of participating in this RFP, and by submitting a proposal each proponent shall be deemed to have agreed that it has no claim." For a negative answer, see *Tercon Contractors Ltd v British Columbia (Transportation and Highways)*, 2010 SCC 4, [2010] 1 SCR 69, excerpted in Chapter 6, Section IV.

9. Can a clause contained in an RFP giving the owner the sole discretion to accept any bid, including a materially non-compliant one, allow the creation of Contract A between the owner and the non-compliant bidder? Would the creation of Contract A in such a situation be consistent with the rules of offer and acceptance as generally understood? For a negative answer to both these questions, see *Graham Industrial Services Ltd v Greater Vancouver Water District* (2004), 25 BCLR (4th) 214 (CA).

10.   What should a tender-calling authority do if the lowest bid is over its budget for the project? Should it matter legally if the bid is slightly over budget (requiring a 15 percent or less reduction) or significantly over budget? For a discussion of the legal rules, the practice of industry, and the suggestion of industry guidebooks, see WD Goodfellow, "Advanced Tendering" (2016) JCCCL 105.

11. Should a distinction be made between situations involving private entities and those involving public entities? Has the Supreme Court's failure to make such a differentiation distorted the private law of contract? Would a legislative regime governing public procurement be preferable to the Contract A/Contract B analysis? For a discussion, see S Waddams, "Canadian Contract Law, 1970-2010" (2010) 50 Can Bus LJ 409; BA De Rubeis, "Public Procurement in Canada: A Comparative View of Remedies and the Tendering Contract" (2011) JCCCL 307.

12. For more on the tendering process, see *R (Ont) v Ron Engineering*, excerpted in Chapter 9, Section V, and the discussion of the Supreme Court in *Martel Building Ltd v Canada*, [2000] 2 SCR 860.

D. FORMALIZATION AND CERTAINTY

The cases below illustrate a tension between the way business is carried out and the legal requirements of an enforceable agreement. For example, business people often negotiate only the main terms of the deal, assuming that their solicitors will "work out the details later." Likewise, business people often want a degree of flexibility in their contracts to deal with future contingencies, such as fluctuating prices. It is, however, a fundamental principle of contract law that offer and acceptance must state the significant terms of the proposed contract with sufficient certainty and definitiveness; otherwise, there will be no contract. After reading the cases below, ask yourself whether the courts have properly dealt with this tension.

Brogden v Metropolitan Railway Company. (1876-77) LR 2 App Cas 666. LORD CAIRNS: My Lords, there are no cases upon which difference of opinion may more readily be entertained, or which are always more embarrassing to dispose of, than cases where the Court has to decide whether or not, having regard to letters and documents which have not assumed the complete and formal shape of executed and solemn agreements, a contract has really been constituted between the parties. But, on the other hand, there is no principle of law better established than this, that even although parties may intend to have their agreement expressed in the most solemn and complete form that conveyancers and solicitors are able to prepare, still there may be a *consensus* between the parties far short of a complete mode of expressing it, and that *consensus* may be discovered from letters or from other documents of an imperfect and incomplete description; I mean imperfect and incomplete as regards form.

BRITISH AMERICAN TIMBER CO V ELK RIVER TIMBER CO
[1933] 4 DLR 286 (BCCA)

MACDONALD CJBC: The parties entered into what is contended to be a binding and enforceable contract, as far as it went, to purchase timber limits, dated June 15, 1931. The said contract has been partially performed. Shortly it provides for a survey and cruise of the limits as preliminary, it is contended, to a formal agreement of sale to be drawn up in fulfilment of cl. 10 of the agreement. That clause reads as follows:

> 10. So soon as the cruise and survey as hereinbefore provided for shall have been completed, a formal contract shall be executed between the parties hereto according to the usual form adopted in such cases in the Province of British Columbia and containing inter alia, such of the provisions of this agreement as shall be applicable.

The formal agreement was not drawn up and the plaintiff sues for specific performance of the executed agreement of June 15, 1931. The appellant submits that the execution of the formal agreement was a condition precedent to the respondent's right to sue. It is necessary to consider the said agreement and particularly the said cl. 10. It will be noted that the clause provides that so soon as the cruise and survey have been completed, and this was on September 5, 1931, a "formal contract shall be executed between the parties according to the usual form adopted in such cases in the Province of British Columbia and containing inter alia, such of the provisions of this agreement as shall be applicable." I do not think that there is any such thing as a "usual form" of agreement in cases of this kind in British Columbia. The parties have agreed to the terms of such a form whether it exists or not and have not left any of the terms of the formal agreement for further negotiation. That usual form of agreement may be merely an imaginary one, but whatever it is its terms have been agreed upon by both parties. But in addition to that usual form it is to include "such of the provisions of this agreement (that of June 15) as shall be applicable."

The provisions of "this agreement" show an agreement of sale and purchase describing the timber to be sold; the parties to the agreement; the purchase-price; and the time of payment of the purchase-price. Leaving cl. 10 out of consideration for the moment, I think that agreement would be a complete and enforceable agreement of sale. Clause 10 does not permit of anything being introduced into the formal agreement except what they have assented to, namely, terms usual in formal agreements of that character to which with the added terms of June 15, the parties are in actual accord. There is to be embodied in that agreement the terms of the agreement of June 15, 1931, which are applicable to the transaction and nothing more. It was contended, however, on the argument by appellant's counsel that the agreement of June 15 did not specify a time fixed for payment of the purchase-money. This submission, I think, is not sustainable.

By cl. 2 of said agreement the purchase-money is "to be payable as to $25,000.00 in cash so soon" as the survey and cruise have been completed which was on September 5, 1931; and the balance in annual instalments the times of payment whereof were already agreed upon. I think, therefore the times of payment are clearly established. Those provisions of cl. 2 are clearly applicable to the formal agreement. There being no formal agreement what is left is the agreement of June 15 and nothing additional which must be supposed to be included in it. The purchase-money is to be paid in cash upon the execution of the formal agreement and the formal agreement is to be executed so soon as a cruise and survey have been made. This, I think sufficiently fixes the time for payment of the purchase-money. All the other provisions, except those already performed are, I think, applicable to the formal agreement and are to be deemed to be incorporated in it.

Therefore, I think, it is clear that the parties have agreed to all the terms of the sale. Nothing has been left for further negotiation and in these circumstances the Courts have had regard to the fact that the parties were *ad idem* with regard to the essentials of their contract. The agreement of June 15 is the whole agreement and includes all they agreed upon or intended to agree upon. When an agreement is complete in itself the fact that a formal contract is to be drawn up embodying its terms does not render it unenforceable.

We have been referred to a very large number of authorities which I do not think it necessary to consider in detail, but I shall refer to one or two as reflecting substantially the others. One of very high authority indeed is that of the House of Lords—*Love & Stewart Ltd. v. Instone & Co. Ltd.* (1917), 33 T.L.R. 475, at p. 476. In that case the agreement had been come to by correspondence except in one particular. Lord Loreburn, in his opinion said that he had come to the conclusion

> that the parties agreed on price and quantity and period of delivery and time of payment, and he thought also on the port of shipment. It seemed also that they intended to make a firm bargain and not to make it conditional upon the completion of the formal document. But had come to the conclusion that they also bound themselves to have a strike clause in the formal contract.
>
> The inclusion of such a term would make no difficulty if it could be said that by usage or by previous dealing or by law these parties, in binding themselves to a strike clause, bound themselves to something certain, because *id certum est quod certum reddi potest*. But no one said, and no proof was given, that it was so. There might be various kinds of strike clauses. No doubt both parties would have agreed as to the strike clause to be inserted in the formal document had the business … [eventuated], but they had not agreed upon such a clause at the time when the business came to be broken off. If, therefore, their Lordships were to say these parties had made a binding contract not subject to the completion of the formal document they must hold that a contract could be binding when the parties were not *ad idem* with regard to one of the intended terms of it,

and he held that the contract was not complete in the absence of a formal agreement including a strike clause. The same view was taken by the other members of the House.

In *Chinnock v. Marchioness of Ely*, 4 De G.J. & S. 638, at pp. 645-6, 46 E.R. 1066, the Lord Chancellor said:

> I entirely accept the doctrine contended for by the Plaintiff's counsel, and for which they cited the cause of *Fowle v. Freeman* (9 Ves. 351 [32 ER 638]), *Kennedy v. Lee* (3 Mer. 441 [36 ER 170]), and *Thomas v. Dering* (1 Keen, 729 [48 ER 488]), which establish that if there had been a final agreement, and the terms of it are evidenced in a manner to satisfy the Statute of Frauds, the agreement shall be binding, although the parties may have declared that the writing is to serve only as instructions for a formal agreement, or although it may be an express term that a formal agreement shall be prepared and signed by the parties. As soon as the fact is established of the final mutual assent of the parties to certain terms, and those terms are evidenced by any writing signed by the party to be charged or his agent lawfully authorized, there exist all the materials, which this Court requires, to make a legally binding contract.

It was held in that case that the agent who had made the contract had no authority to make it and that therefore it could not be enforced, but that the mutual assent to terms of an informal agreement may be sufficient where a formal agreement is contemplated notwithstanding the failure to execute it.

In this case there is a contract to which all the parties assented and intended to be bound by. It was intended to be put in legal form which was not done but no term in the contract was left as a matter for negotiation and further their informal agreement was complete. The rule of law is also referred to in *Chitty on Contracts*, 18th ed., at p. 13, in these words:

> If the terms in which the proposal is accepted show that the parties intended that a formal instrument should be prepared and agreed upon between them, and that, until that be done, no contract should arise: they will not be bound, until such formal instrument has been agreed upon. But where certain terms have been mutually assented to, the mere fact that the parties have expressly stipulated that a formal instrument shall be prepared, embodying those terms, does not, by itself, show that they have not come to a final agreement, nor does the fact that the acceptance contains a statement that the acceptor has instructed his solicitor to prepare the necessary documents.

In support of that is cited inter alia *Rossiter v. Miller* (1878), 3 App. Cas. 1124, and *Chinnock v. Marchioness of Ely, supra*. There are cases in our own Courts which show that a contract which has been duly assented to by the parties but in which they stipulate for a formal agreement has been itself enforceable. In *Horsnail v. Shute* (1919), 27 B.C.R. 474, at p. 478, this is quoted with approval from *Rossiter v. Miller* (p. 1149):

> But when an agreement embracing all the particulars essential for finality and completeness, even though it may be desired to reduce it to shape by a solicitor, is such that those particulars must remain unchanged, it is not, in my mind, less coercive because of the technical formality which remains to be made.

To the same effect are quotations made by McPhillips, J.A., from *Love & Stewart Ltd. v. Instone & Co., supra*. It was argued that where an informal agreement is made *subject* to a formal contract being drawn up it cannot be enforced unless the condition is performed. I am not sure that that is strictly correct. It is not correct when all the terms have been assented to according to law. But it does not matter in this case since the drawing up of the formal contract was provided for by agreement and not put in the form of a condition.

I therefore think that the appeal must be dismissed since the parties, I am convinced, came to a concluded contract and the respondent's attempt to now recede from it cannot be countenanced.

[Macdonald JA agreed. He made this comment on the appellant's motives:]

Appellant, rueing its bargain, doubtless because of depressed economic conditions, refused to execute the formal contract and claims that, without it, and a consensus as to its terms, the agreement cannot be enforced. In reality it submits that it may capriciously refuse to agree to terms and resist performance. That is the true deduction notwithstanding any contrary pretentions. I do not overlook the fact that appellant professed willingness to discuss a formal contract on the basis that it was not already bound and that its terms should be mutually agreed to. If it ever had in mind the arrival at a consensus in this regard (and I doubt it) it would be, not by carrying out the terms of the main contract but by materially altering it. That could not be considered by respondent. I make no further comment; we are concerned with the legal aspect of the case.

Green v Ainsmore Consolidated Mines Ltd. [1951] 3 DLR 632 (BCSC). A letter outlining in some detail clauses for an agreement was approved by the plaintiff and signed by the appropriate officers of the defendant company. It requested that the plaintiff "submit to us a draft form of agreement" and concluded with the words: "This memorandum shall be subject to a formal agreement of sale and undertaking being prepared, satisfactory in form to the solicitors of both parties." WILSON J found that the agreement submitted by the plaintiff, prepared by overzealous attorneys, did not conform to the meaning of the letter but that this difficulty might have been overcome by further honest discussion, and that the refusal of the defendant company to execute a written agreement was entirely due to advice given it by its solicitor that the chief disadvantage to the company arose out of resulting income tax liability. He held that the letter was not an enforceable contract, following *Chillingworth v Esche*, [1924] 1 Ch 97. "It is [not] open to me to review the reasonableness or *bona fides* of the refusal to execute a formal contract."

NOTES AND QUESTIONS

1. A signed an agreement to purchase B's farm. The document ended: "This is a provisional agreement until a fully legalized agreement, drawn up by a solicitor, and embodying all the conditions herewith stated, is signed." No "legalized" agreement was ever signed. Do A and B have a contract? See *Branca v Cobarro*, [1947] KB 854 (CA).

2. The defendant company was in the business of selling franchise rights to retail stores. It provided the plaintiff company with an information package, including a draft franchise agreement in standard form. The agreement was 50 pages long and the plaintiff was advised to get professional advice. At a meeting, the companies' agents agreed on some changes to the standard agreement and the meeting closed with the defendant's representative stating that they "had a deal." The final document that was submitted to the plaintiff company did not comply fully with the oral terms. The plaintiff refused to sign and the defendant withdrew from the transaction. At trial, the plaintiff's representative testified that he had no idea what was in the 50-page draft except for the specifically agreed-on terms. Was there a binding contract? See *Bawitko Investments Ltd v Kernels Popcorn Ltd* (1991), 79 DLR (4th) 97 (Ont CA).

3. For another case dealing with the issue of formalization, this time in relation to the purchase and sale of shares, see *UBS Securities Canada, Inc v Sands Brothers Canada, Ltd* (2009), 95 OR (3d) 93 (CA). In that case, the court held that, because it is customary in the securities industry to make binding contracts orally, a written document was not necessary in order for the parties to be bound because they had agreed to all the material terms (that is, the

price, quantity, and closing date) via telephone. See also *Hoban Construction Ltd v Alexander*, 2012 BCCA 75.

4. What effect does the subsequent conduct of the parties have on the courts' willingness to enforce agreements reached before the preparation of formal documents? See *Wallace v Allen* (2009), 93 OR (3d) 723 (CA), where the court held that a letter of intent was binding and enforceable because the parties' conduct (such as announcing the plaintiff as the new owner) demonstrated that they considered themselves bound before execution of the formal purchase agreement. See also *Erie Sand and Gravel Limited v Tri-B Acres Inc*, 2009 ONCA 709 and the discussion in *Foley v Classique Coaches, Limited*, below.

MAY AND BUTCHER, LIMITED V THE KING
(1929), [1934] 2 KB 17n (HL)

[The suppliants, May & Butcher, Ltd., who were general contractors, alleged in a petition of right that it was mutually agreed between them and the controller of the Disposals Board for the purchase by the suppliants of the whole of the tentage that might become available in the United Kingdom for disposal up to March 31, 1923. The material letters for the purposes of the case were dated June 29, 1921 and January 7, 1922. By the earlier of these letters written by the controller to the suppliants it was stated that "in consideration of your agreeing to deposit with the [Disposals & Liquidation] Commission the sum of £1000 as security for the carrying out of this extended contract, the Commission hereby confirm the sale to you of the whole of the old tentage which may become available ... up to and including December 31, 1921, upon the following terms":

(1) The Commission agrees to sell and [the suppliants] agree to purchase the total stock of old tentage. ...

(3) The price or prices to be paid, and the date or dates on which payment is to be made by the purchasers to the Commission for such old tentage shall be agreed upon from time to time between the Commission and the purchasers as the quantities of the said old tentage become available for disposal, and are offered to the purchasers by the Commission.

(4) Delivery ... shall be taken by the purchasers in such period or periods as may be agreed upon between the commission and the purchasers when such quantities of old tentage are offered to the purchasers by the Commission. ...

(10) It is understood that all disputes with reference to or arising out of this agreement will be submitted to arbitration in accordance with the provisions of the Arbitration Act, 1889.

By the second letter dated January 7, 1922, the disposals controller, referring to verbal negotiations that had taken place for an extension of the agreement between the Commission and the suppliants, confirmed the sale to the latter of the tentage that might become available for disposal up to March 31, 1923. This letter, which varied in certain respects the earlier terms, stated that "the prices to be agreed upon between the Commission and the purchasers in accordance with the terms of clause 3 of the said earlier contract shall include delivery free on rail ... nearest to the depots at which the said tentage may be lying. ..."

Some time later the proposals made by the suppliants for purchase were not acceptable to the controller, and in August 1922, the Disposals Board said it considered itself no longer bound by the agreement, whereupon the suppliants filed their petition of right claiming an injunction restraining the Commission from disposing elsewhere than to the suppliants of the remainder of the tentage; an account of the tentage that had become available; and compensation for the damage done to them.

By the demurrer, answer, and plea the attorney general said that the petition of right disclosed no sufficient and binding contract for the sale to the suppliants of any tentage, and further that it was a term of the contract (if any) that the suppliants should pay a reasonable price for the tentage and that the suppliants were not at the material time ready and willing to pay a reasonable price.

Rowlatt J held that the letters of June 29, 1921 and January 7 and 18, 1922 constituted no contract but contained merely a series of clauses for adoption if and when contracts were made, because the price, date of payment, and period of delivery had still to be agreed; and that the arbitration clause did not apply to differences of opinion upon these questions. The Court of Appeal (Scrutton LJ dissenting) affirmed Rowlatt J's decision. The suppliants appealed.]

LORD BUCKMASTER: ... In my opinion there never was a concluded contract between the parties. It has long been a well recognized principle of contract law that an agreement between two parties to enter into an agreement in which some critical part of the contract matter is left undetermined is no contract at all. It is of course perfectly possible for two people to contract that they will sign a document which contains all the relevant terms, but it is not open to them to agree that they will in the future agree upon a matter which is vital to the arrangement between them and has not yet been determined. It has been argued that as the fixing of the price has broken down, a reasonable price must be assumed. That depends in part upon the terms of the Sale of Goods Act, which no doubt reproduces, and is known to have reproduced, the old law upon the matter. That provides in s. 8 that

> the price in a contract of sale may be fixed by the contract, or may be left to be fixed in manner thereby agreed, or may be determined by the course of dealing between the parties. Where the price is not determined in accordance with the foregoing provisions the buyer must pay a reasonable price

while, if the agreement is to sell goods on the terms that the price is to be fixed by the valuation of a third party, and such third party cannot or does not make such valuation, s. 9 says that the agreement is avoided. I find myself quite unable to understand the distinction between an agreement to permit the price to be fixed by a third party and an agreement to permit the price to be fixed in the future by the two parties to the contract themselves. In principle it appears to me that they are one and the same thing. ...

The next question is about the arbitration clause, and there I entirely agree with the majority of the Court of Appeal and also with Rowlatt J. The clause refers "disputes with reference to or arising out of this agreement" to arbitration, but until the price has been fixed, the agreement is not there. The arbitration clause relates to the settlement of whatever may happen when the agreement has been completed and the parties are regularly bound. There is nothing in the arbitration clause to enable a contract to be made which in fact the original bargain has left quite open. ...

VISCOUNT DUNEDIN: ... In the system of law in which I was brought up, that was expressed by one of those brocards of which perhaps we have been too fond, but which often express very neatly what is wanted: "Certum est quod certum reddi potest." [That is certain that can be made certain.] Therefore, you may very well agree that a certain part of the contract of sale, such as price, may be settled by some one else. As a matter of the general law of contracts all the essentials have to be settled. What are the essentials may vary according to the particular contract under consideration. We are here dealing with sale, and undoubtedly price is one of the essentials of sale, and if it is left still to be agreed between the parties, then there is no contract. It may be left to the determination of a certain person, and if it was so left and that person either would not or could not act, there would be no contract because the price was to be settled in a certain way and it has become impossible to settle it in that way, and therefore there is no settlement. No doubt as to goods, the Sale of Goods Act, 1893, says that if the price is not mentioned and settled in the contract it is to be a reasonable price. The simple answer in this case is that the Sale of Goods Act provides for silence on the point and here there is no silence, because there is a provision that the two parties are to agree. As long as you have something certain it does not matter. For instance, with regard to price it is a perfectly good contract to say that the price is to be settled by the buyer. I have not had time, or perhaps I have not been industrious enough, to look through all the books in England to see if there is such a case; but there was such a case in Scotland in 1760, where it was decided that a sale of a landed estate was perfectly good, the price being left to be settled by the buyer himself.

[Lord Warrington of Clyffe also delivered reasons for dismissing the appeal.]

UNIFORM COMMERCIAL CODE
American Law Institute, 1978

SECTION 2-204. FORMATION IN GENERAL

• • •

(3) Even though one or more terms are left open, a contract for sale does not fail for indefiniteness if the parties have intended to make a contract and there is a reasonably certain basis for giving an appropriate remedy.

Ko v Hillview Homes Ltd. 2012 ABCA 245. CÔTÉ JA: Many writers imply that uncertainty of contractual terms is a technical defence, virtually unethical. ... Certainty of terms is not a separate self-contained defence, like failure to register a mortgage in a registry, or failure to have an Alberta guarantor appear before a notary public. Quite the contrary; certainty is an integral part of the very heart of contract. ... In contracts, as in many areas of the law, all the rules interlock. The rules of certainty of terms and the rules of offer and acceptance overlap ... . Why are there various "topics" in contracts law which overlap? That is because one cannot teach all aspects of contracts at once, especially to first-year law students. (See Justinian's *Institutes*, Book I, Title 1.) So law teachers have worked out a convenient instructional design, explaining different concepts separately and in an order easy to understand. ... Requiring that a contract be certain is thus far from a freestanding concept; it is the diametric opposite of a technical requirement divorced from principle, policy, or logic.

WN Hillas and Co, Limited v Arcos, Limited. (1932), 38 Com Cas 23 (HL). LORD WRIGHT: Business men often record the most important agreements in crude and summary fashion; modes of expression sufficient and clear to them in the course of their business may appear to those unfamiliar with the business far from complete or precise. It is accordingly the duty of the Court to construe such documents fairly and broadly, without being too astute or subtle in finding defects; but, on the contrary, the Court should seek to apply the old maxim of English law, *Verba ita sunt* *intelligenda ut res magis valeat quam pereat* [words are to be so understood that the subject matter may be preserved rather than destroyed]. That maxim, however, does not mean that the Court is to make a contract for the parties, or to go outside the words they have used, except in so far as there are appropriate implications of law, as for instance, the implication of what is just and reasonable to be ascertained by the Court as matter of machinery where the contractual intention is clear but the contract is silent on some detail. Thus in contracts for future performances over a period, the parties may neither be able to nor desire to specify many matters of detail, but leave them to be adjusted in the working out of the contract. Save for the legal implication I have mentioned, such contracts might well be incomplete or uncertain: with that implication in reserve they are neither incomplete nor uncertain. As obvious illustrations I may refer to such matters as prices or times of delivery in contracts for the sale of goods, or times for loading or discharging in a contract of sea carriage. Furthermore, even if the construction of the words used may be difficult, that is not a reason for holding them too ambiguous or uncertain to be enforced if the fair meaning of the parties can be extracted. ...

... Some confusion has been imported, as I think, into the question by dwelling on the exact words—"The option of entering into contract," and it is said that this is merely a contract to enter into a contract. The phrase is epigrammatic, but may be either meaningless or misleading. A contract *de praesenti* to enter into what, in law, is an enforceable contract, is simply that enforceable contract, and no more or no less; and if what may not very accurately be called the second contract is not to take effect till some future date but is otherwise an enforceable contract, the position is as in the preceding illustration, save that the operation of the contract is postponed. But in each case there is *eo instanti* a complete obligation. If, however, what is meant is that the parties agree to negotiate in the hope of effecting a valid contract, the position is different. There is then no bargain except to negotiate, and negotiations may be fruitless and end without any contract ensuing yet even then, in strict theory, there is a contract (if there is good consideration) to negotiate, though in the event of repudiation by one party the damages may be nominal, unless a jury think that the opportunity to negotiate was of some appreciable value to the injured party.

QUESTION

M, a dealer in mustard seed, agreed with G, a mustard farmer, to buy his entire 1961 crop. In the contract, the only price specified was for "Grade #1 seed *only*." G found that his seed was not Grade #1, and, believing that the contract was therefore not enforceable, he sold his crop on the open market at an increased price. Does M have a claim for breach of contract? See *Montana Mustard Seed Co v Gates* (1963), 42 WWR 303 (Sask QB).

FOLEY V CLASSIQUE COACHES, LIMITED
[1934] 2 KB 1 (CA)

SCRUTTON LJ: In this appeal I think that the Lord Chief Justice's decision was right, and I am glad to come to that conclusion, because I do not regard the appellant's contention as an honest one.

The nature of the case is this: the respondent, the plaintiff in the action, had some land, part of which was occupied by petrol pumps. Adjoining that land was some vacant land belonging to him which the appellants wanted to use as the headquarters for their charabancs, and they approached the respondent, who was willing to sell on the terms that the appellants obtained all their petrol from him. It is quite clear that unless the appellants had agreed to this they would never have got the land. There was a discussion whether this term about the petrol and the agreement to purchase the land should be put in one document or in two, but ultimately it was decided to put them in two documents of even date. One relates specifically to the sale and purchase of the land, and that was to go through on condition that the appellants undertook to enter into the petrol agreement, the terms of which had been already agreed. On the same day the second agreement was signed reciting that it was supplemental to the agreement of even date, that is the agreement for the sale of the land. The petrol agreement included a clause that if any dispute or difference should arise on the subject-matter or construction "the same shall be submitted to arbitration in the usual way."

[The petrol agreement also included a clause that stated: "The vendor shall sell to the company and the company shall purchase from the vendor all petrol which shall be required by the company for the running of their said business at a price to be agreed by the parties in writing and from time to time."]

It is quite clear that the parties intended to make an agreement, and for the space of three years no doubt entered the mind of the appellants that they had a business agreement, for they acted on it during that time. The petrol supplied by the respondent was non-combine petrol, but he had also combine petrol pumps. The non-combine petrol was supplied to the appellants at a price lower than that paid by the public, and an account was rendered periodically in writing and paid. In the third year some one acting for the appellants thought he could get better petrol elsewhere, and on September 29, 1933, their solicitor, thinking he saw a way out of the agreement, wrote on behalf of the appellants the letter of September 29, 1933, repudiating the agreement. Possibly the solicitor had heard something about the decision of the House of Lords in *May and Butcher, Limited v. The King* but probably had not heard of *Braithwaite v. Foreign Hardwood Co.* [1905] 2 K.B. 543, in which the Court of Appeal decided that the wrongful repudiation of a contract by one party relieves the other party from the performance of any conditions precedent. If the solicitor had known of that decision he would not have written the letter in the terms he did. Thereafter the respondent brought his action claiming damages for breach of the agreement, a declaration that the agreement is binding, and an injunction to restrain the appellants from purchasing petrol from any other person. The Lord Chief Justice decided that the respondent was entitled to judgment, as there was a binding agreement by which the appellants got the land on condition, that they should buy their petrol from the respondent. I observe that the appellants' solicitor in his letter made no suggestion that the land would be returned, and I suppose the appellants would have been extremely annoyed if they had been asked to return it when they repudiated the condition.

A good deal of the case turns upon the effect of the two decisions of the House of Lords which are not easy to fit in with each other. The first of these cases is *May and Butcher, Limited v. The King*, which related to a claim in respect of a purchase of surplus stores from a Government department. In the Court of Appeal two members of the Court took the view that inasmuch as there was a provision that the price of the stores which were to be offered from time to time was to be agreed there was no binding contract because an agreement to make an agreement does not constitute a contract, and that the language of clause 10 that any dispute as to the construction of the agreement was to be submitted to arbitration was irrelevant, because there was not an agreement, although the parties thought there was. In the second case, *Hillas & Co. v. Arcos*, there was an agreement between Hillas & Co. and the Russian authorities under which Hillas & Co. were to take in one year 22,000 standards of Russian timber, and in the same agreement they had an option to take in the next year 100,000 standards, with no particulars as to the kind of timber or as to the terms of shipment or any of the other matters one expects to find dealt with on a sale of a large quantity of Russian timber over a period. The Court of Appeal, which included Greer L.J. and myself, both having a very large experience in these timber cases, came to the conclusion that as the House of Lords in *May and Butcher, Limited v. The King* considered that where a detail had to be agreed upon there was no agreement until that detail was agreed, we were bound to follow the decision in *May and Butcher, Limited v. The King* and hold that there was no effective agreement in respect of the option, because the terms had not been agreed. It was, however, held by the House of Lords in *Hillas & Co. v. Arcos* that we were wrong in so deciding and that we had misunderstood the decision in *May and Butcher, Limited v. The King*. The House took this line: it is quite true that there seems to be considerable vagueness about the agreement but the parties contrived to get through it on the contract for 22,000 standards, and so the House thought there was an agreement as to the option which the parties would be able to get through also despite the absence of details. It is true that in the first year the parties got through quite satisfactorily; that was because during that year the great bulk of English buyers were boycotting the Russian sellers. In the second year the position was different. The English buyers had changed their view and were buying large quantities of Russian timber, so that different conditions were then prevailing. In *Hillas & Co. v. Arcos* the House of Lords said that they had not laid down universal principles of construction in *May and Butcher, Limited v. The King*, and that each case must be decided on the construction of the particular document, while in *Hillas & Co. v. Arcos* they found that the parties believed they had a contract. In the present case the parties obviously believed they had a contract and they acted for three years as if they had; they had an arbitration clause which relates to the subject-matter of the agreement as to the supply of petrol, and it seems to me that this arbitration clause applies to any failure to agree as to the price. By analogy to the case of a tied house there is to be implied in this contract a term that the petrol shall be supplied at a reasonable price and shall be of reasonable quality. For these reasons I think the Lord Chief Justice was right in holding that there was an effective and enforceable contract, although as to the future no definite price had been agreed with regard to the petrol. ...

The appeal therefore fails, and no alteration is required in the form of the injunction that has been granted.

[The judgments of Greer and Maugham LJJ have been omitted.]

SCAMMELL (G) AND NEPHEW, LIMITED V OUSTON
[1941] AC 251 (HL)

[On December 8, 1937, Ouston agreed to purchase a Commer van from Scammell and Nephew, Limited for £268 in exchange for a 1935 Bedford van and "the balance of purchase price ... on hire-purchase terms over a period of two years." Later Scammell wrote to Ouston: "[W]e have now received advice from the United Dominion Trust Co. Ltd. of their acceptance of the hire-purchase in connection with the vehicle we are supplying, and we will, in due course, forward the documents to you." A few days later on February 10, 1938 Scammell reported that the van would be ready for collection in a few days "subject to mutual acceptance of the hire-purchase agreement." He added, "We make it a condition of the supply of vehicles on hire-purchase terms that we approve terms of agreement before supply." Before the hire-purchase agreement was entered into, Scammell refused to go ahead on the ground that the Bedford van was a 1934 model and not in satisfactory condition. This ground was abandoned at the subsequent trial. Tucker J awarded damages, the Court of Appeal dismissed the appeal, and Scammell accordingly appealed to the House of Lords.]

LORD WRIGHT: ... There are in my opinion two grounds on which the court ought to hold that there was never a contract. The first is that the language used was so obscure and so incapable of any definite or precise meaning that the court is unable to attribute to the parties any particular contractual intention. The object of the court is to do justice between the parties, and the court will do its best, if satisfied that there was an ascertainable and determinate intention to contract, to give effect to that intention, looking at the substance and not mere form. It will not be deterred by mere difficulties of interpretation. Difficulty is not synonymous with ambiguity so long as any definite meaning can be extracted. But the test of intention is to be found in the words used. If these words, considered however broadly and untechnically and with due regard to all just implications, fail to evince any definite meaning on which the court can safely act, the court has no choice but to say that there is no contract. Such a position is not often found. But I think that it is found in this case. My reason for so thinking is not only based on the actual vagueness and unintelligibility of the words used, but is confirmed by the startling diversity of explanations, tendered by those who think there was a bargain, of what the bargain was. I do not think it would be right to hold the appellants to any particular version. It was all left too vague. There are many cases in the books of what are called illusory contracts, that is, where the parties may have thought they were making a contract but failed to arrive at a definite bargain. It is a necessary requirement that an agreement in order to be binding must be sufficiently definite to enable the court to give it a practical meaning. Its terms must be so definite, or capable of being made definite without further agreement of the parties, that the promises and performances to be rendered by each party are reasonably certain. In my opinion that requirement was not satisfied in this case.

But I think the other reason, which is that the parties never in intention nor even in appearance reached an agreement, is a still sounder reason against enforcing the claim. In truth, in my opinion, their agreement was inchoate and never got beyond negotiations. They did, indeed, accept the position that there should be some form of hire-purchase agreement, but they never went on to complete their agreement by settling between them what the terms of the hire-purchase agreement were to be. The furthest point they reached was an understanding or agreement to agree upon hire-purchase terms. ... It is here necessary to remember what a hire-purchase agreement is. It is not a contract of sale, but of bailment. ... Terms must accordingly be arranged in respect of the period of the bailment as to user, repairs, insurance, rights of retaking possession on the hirer's default and various other matters. A hire-purchase agreement is therefore in practice a complex arrangement. ...

[After discussing the three possible ways that a hire-purchase agreement could be structured his Lordship continued:]

... [T]he court has in proper circumstances found itself able to determine what is a reasonable price when the price is not specified in the contract as was done in *Foley's* case, rightly, as I think, distinguishing *May & Butcher's* case, or to determine what is a reasonable time, or what are reasonable instalments. Many other examples of this principle might be given. And in addition the court may import terms on the proof of custom or by implication. But it is in my opinion a very different matter to make an entire contract for the parties ... . The law has not defined and cannot of itself define what are the normal and reasonable terms of a hire-purchase agreement. Though the general character of such an agreement is familiar, it is necessary for the parties in each case to agree upon the particular terms. It may, perhaps, be that this might be done in particular circumstances by general words of reference. For instance if it were stipulated that there should be "a usual" hire-purchase agreement, the court might be able if supplied with appropriate evidence to define what are the terms of such an agreement. But there was nothing of the sort in this case.

I think this appeal should be allowed.

[The judgments of Viscount Simon LC, Viscount Maugham, and Lord Russell of Killowen, who concurred in allowing the appeal, are omitted.]

NOTES AND QUESTIONS

1. An agreement to finance the purchase of real property by a future agreement containing the "usual terms" was held to be too uncertain to constitute an enforceable agreement. See *Buyers v Begg*, [1952] 1 DLR 313 (BCCA). The current *Land Title Act* (RSBC 1996, c 250) of that province now contains a set of required mortgage terms. Would an agreement to provide a mortgage in the "usual form" be enforceable? On what factors might your answer depend? See *Thomson Groceries Ltd v Scott*, [1943] 3 DLR 25 (Ont CA).

2. When will the court consider that the boundary line between filling a contractual gap by reference to some implied term and making a new contract for the parties has been crossed?

3. Have factors such as detrimental reliance and bad faith been taken into account by the courts when deciding issues of certainty? Are these factors that should have been taken into account?

4. The question of illusory promises is dealt with in more detail in Section I.G, Mutual Promises, below.

Calvan Consolidated Oil & Gas Co v Manning. [1959] SCR 253, 17 DLR (2d) 1. An agreement provided for the exchange of part interests in petroleum and natural gas permits. Calvan was to have power to deal with a permit in which Manning had a 20 percent interest. The possibility was envisaged that Calvan might itself want to develop the land instead of selling or farming it out. In such a case it was provided that an operating agreement would be drawn up, and if the terms of such an operating agreement could not be agreed on, they were to be settled by arbitration. The agreement concluded: "It is also agreed that a formal agreement will be drawn up as soon as possible." A few days later a clause was added: "It is agreed that the terms of the formal agreement are to be subject to our mutual agreement, and if we are unable to agree, the terms of such agreement are to be settled for us by arbitration by a single arbitrator, pursuant to [t]he *Arbitration Act* of the Province of Alberta." It was argued that the agreement was unenforceable, first because the terms of the envisaged operating agreement had not been settled, and, second, because the reference to a later formal contract indicated that the present agreement was not meant to be binding. On the first point, JUDSON J for the Supreme Court, said, "The learned trial Judge was of the opinion that the provision for arbitration in relation to a possible operating agreement was meaningless and unenforceable. If this were so, the consequence would be that contracting parties in the position of Calvan and Manning who do not know what their ultimate intentions may be if they retain the property must provide in detail for a contingency that may never arise unless they wish to run the risk of having the rest of their contractual efforts invalidated and declared unenforceable. I agree with the opinion of the Court of Appeal that such a situation may be dealt with by an agreement to arbitrate and I can see no legal or practical difficulty in the way. No more could the learned author of Russell on Arbitration, 16th ed., p. 10, when he said: 'Since an arbitrator can be given such powers as the parties wish, he can be authorised to make a new contract between the parties. The parties to a commercial contract often provide that in certain events their contract shall be added to or modified to fit the circumstances then existing, intending thereby to create a binding obligation although they are unwilling or unable to determine just what the terms of the new or modified agreement shall be. To a court such a provision is ineffective as being at most a mere "agreement to agree"; but a provision that the new or modified terms shall be settled by an arbitrator can without difficulty be made enforceable.'"

On the second point, JUDSON J said: "Only two questions remain to be considered and these arise from the provision in the amending agreement for arbitration on the terms of the formal agreement. The questions are, first, whether this indicates an intention not to be bound until the formal agreement is executed, and, second, what terms may be incorporated in the formal agreement by the arbitrator. My opinion is that the parties were bound immediately on the execution of the informal agreement, that the acceptance was unconditional and that all that was necessary to be done by the parties or possibly by the arbitrator was to embody the precise terms, and no more, of the informal agreement in a formal agreement. This is not a case of acceptance qualified by such expressed conditions as 'subject to the preparation and approval of a formal contract,' 'subject to contract' or 'subject to the preparation of a formal contract, its execution by the parties and approval by their solicitors.' Here we have an unqualified acceptance with a formal contract to follow. Whether the parties intend to hold themselves bound until the execution of a formal agreement is a question of construction and I have no doubt in this case."

QUESTIONS

1. Would an agreement to sign a loan agreement containing certain agreed-on terms and "such other terms as the lender's solicitor reasonably may require" be enforceable? See *First City Investments Ltd v Fraser Arms Hotel Ltd*, [1979] 6 WWR 125 (BCCA).

2. It is generally the case that most contractual rights can be "sold" (*assigned*) by the party owning them. Would an agreement between "ABC Property Ltd. and X or nominee" be enforceable? What if the agreement read "Between ABC Property Ltd. and one of X, Y, or Z"? See *Santelli v Bifano Enterprises* (1981), 33 BCLR 266 (SC) and *Finlay Investments Ltd v Abraham* (1983), 26 RPR 188 (BCSC).

3. Can some of the problems with flexibility be solved by making an "agreement to negotiate in good faith"?

EMPRESS TOWERS LTD V BANK OF NOVA SCOTIA
(1990), 50 BCLR (2d) 126 (CA)

LAMBERT JA: The landlord, Empress Towers Ltd., brought a petition under s. 18 of the Commercial Tenancy Act against the tenant, the Bank of Nova Scotia, seeking to obtain a writ of possession under s. 21 of the Act.

The first lease between the parties was made in 1972. It expired in 1984. A new lease was made. It contained this clause:

> The landlord hereby grants to the Tenant right of renewal of this Lease for two succes-sive periods of five (5) years each, such rights to be exercisable by three (3) months' written notice from the Tenant, subject to all the terms and conditions herein contained excepting any right of renewal beyond the second five (5) year period and excepting the rental for any renewal period, which shall be the market rental prevailing at the commencement of that renewal term as mutually agreed between the Landlord and the Tenant. If the Landlord and the Tenant do not agree upon the renewal rental within two (2) months following the exercise of a renewal option, then this agreement may be terminated at the option of either party.

The 1984 lease was due to expire on 31st August 1989. On 25th May 1989 the bank exercised its option to renew the lease for a further term of five years from 1st Sep-tember 1989. On 23rd June 1989 the bank proposed a rental rate of $5,400 a month up from $3,097.92 under the lease that was about to expire. No written reply was received from Empress Towers. There may have been a telephone response. On 26th July 1989 the bank wrote again to Empress Towers. It said that its proposal of $5,400 a month was a rate which independent appraisers had advised the bank was appro-priate. It said it was willing to negotiate. Also on 26th July the solicitor for Empress Towers wrote to the bank saying that his client was still reviewing the offer. On 23rd August the bank asked whether Empress Towers was making progress in its delibera-tions and it said that it remained ready to discuss the matter at Empress Towers' convenience. On 31st August, on the day when the first five year term was due to expire, Empress towers made its response. It said it would allow the bank to remain on a month-to-month basis if $15,000 was paid before 15th September 1989 and a rent of $5,400 a month was paid thereafter. The tenancy that Empress Towers wished to create in that way was to be terminable on 90 days written notice. (There was evidence that an employee of Empress Towers had been robbed of $30,000 in a branch of the bank and that Empress Towers' insurance had paid only $15,000, leav-ing a loss to Empress Towers of $15,000.) ...

The principal question in the appeal is whether the renewal clause was void either for uncertainty or, what is fundamentally the same, as an agreement to agree. The obverse of that question is: If the renewal clause is not void, what does it mean? ...

The law is generally to the same effect in England. It is discussed by Mr. Justice Megarry in *Brown v. Gould*, [1972] 1 Ch. 53, where three categories of options are analyzed. The first category is where the rent is simply "to be agreed." Usually such a clause cannot be enforced. The second category is where the rent is to be established by a stated formula but no machinery is provided for applying the formula to produce the rental rate. Often the courts will supply the machinery. The third category is where the formula is set out but is defective and the machinery is provided for apply-ing the formula to produce the rental rate. In those cases the machinery may be used to cure the defect in the formula. What is evident from a consideration of all three categories is that the courts will try, wherever possible, to give the proper legal effect to any clause that the parties understood and intended was to have legal effect.

In this case, if the parties had intended simply to say that if the tenant wished to renew it could only do so at a rent set by or acceptable to the landlord, then they could have said so. Instead, they said that if the tenant wished to renew it could do so at the market rental prevailing at the commencement of the renewal term. If nothing more had been said, then the market rental could have been determined on the basis of valuations and, if necessary, a court could have made the determination.

It would have been an objective matter. But the clause goes on to say that not only must the renewal rental be the prevailing market rental but also it must be the prevailing market rental as mutually agreed between the landlord and the tenant. It could be argued that the additional provision for mutual agreement meant only that the first step was to try to agree, but if that step failed, then other steps should be adopted to set the market rental. However, the final sentence of cl. 23, which contemplates a failure to agree giving rise to a right of termination, precludes the acceptance of that argument. In my opinion, the effect of the requirement for mutual agreement must be that the landlord cannot be compelled to enter into a renewal tenancy at a rent which it has not accepted as the market rental. But, in my opinion, that is not the only effect of the requirement of mutual agreement. It also carries with it, first, an implied term that the landlord will negotiate in good faith with the tenant with the objective of reaching an agreement on the market rental rate and, second, that agreement on a market rental will not be unreasonably withheld. ... Those terms are to be implied under the officious bystander and business efficacy principle in order to prevent the renewal clause, which was clearly intended to have legal effect, from being struck down as uncertain. The key to implying the terms that I have set out is that the parties agreed that there should be a right of renewal at the prevailing market rental. (I do not have to decide in this case whether a bare right of renewal at a rental to be agreed carries with it an obligation to negotiate in good faith or not to withhold agreement unreasonably.)

[Lambert JA accepted the finding of the trial judge that Empress Towers had not negotiated in good faith. He therefore dismissed the claim for the writ of possession under the *Commercial Tenancy Act*. Taggart JA concurred. The dissenting judgment of Wallace JA is omitted. Leave to appeal to the SCC refused 79 DLR (4th) vii; 133 NR 238n.]

Walford v Miles. [1992] 2 AC 128 (HL). LORD ACKNER: The reason why an agreement to negotiate, like an agreement to agree, is unenforceable is simply because it lacks the necessary certainty. The same does not apply to an agreement to use best endeavours. This uncertainty is demonstrated in the instant case by the provision which it is said has to be implied in the agreement for the determination of the negotiations. How can a court be expected to decide whether, subjectively, a proper reason existed for the termination of negotiations? The answer suggested depends upon whether the negotiations have been determined "in good faith." However, the concept of a duty to carry on negotiations in good faith is inherently repugnant to the adversarial position of the parties when involved in negotiations. Each party to the negotiations is entitled to pursue his (or her) own interest, so long as he avoids making misrepresentations. To advance that interest he must be entitled, if he thinks it appropriate, to threaten to withdraw from further negotiations or to withdraw in fact in the hope that the opposite party may seek to reopen the negotiations by offering him improved terms. ... A duty to negotiate in good faith is as unworkable in practice as it is inherently inconsistent with the position of a negotiating party. It is here that the uncertainty lies.

Jet2.com Ltd v Blackpool Airport Ltd. [2012] EWCA Civ 417. MOORE-BICK LJ: In general an obligation to use best endeavours, or all reasonable endeavours, is not in itself regarded as too uncertain to be enforceable, provided that the object of the endeavours can be ascertained with sufficient certainty ... . In my view the obligation to use best endeavours to promote [a] business is no more uncertain than the obligation to use best endeavours to develop a railway's traffic (*Sheffield District Railway Co. v Great Central Railway Co.*), or to promote the sales of fountain pens and ink bottles (*Terrell v Mabie Todd and Co. Ltd*). There may be argument about what constitutes best endeavours in any particular circumstances (see, for example, *Terrell v Mabie Todd and Co. Ltd.*), but that is a different matter.

Greenberg v Meffert (1985), 50 OR (2d) 755 (CA). ROBINS JA, interpreting a contract whereby the payment of a commission to a terminated real estate agent was "at the sole discretion" of the company, held as follows: In my opinion, the company's discretion in this matter is not unbridled, firstly, because the nature of this contract and the subject-matter of the discretion are such that the company's decision should be construed as being controlled by standards and secondly, because the exercise of the discretion, whether measured by subjective or objective standards, is subject to a requirement of honesty and good faith. Provisions in agreements making payment or performance subject to "the discretion," "the opinion" or "the satisfaction" of a party to the agreement or a third party, broadly speaking, fall into two general categories. In contracts in which the matter to be decided or approved is not readily susceptible of objective measurement—matters involving taste, sensibility, personal compatibility or judgment of the party for whose benefit the authority was given— such provisions are more likely construed as imposing only a subjective standard. On the other hand, in contracts relating to such matters as operative fitness, structural completion, mechanical utility or marketability, these provisions are generally construed as imposing an objective standard of reasonableness ... . In any given transaction, the category into which such a provision falls will depend upon the intention of the parties as disclosed by their contract. In the absence of explicit language or a clear indication from the tenor of the contract or the nature of the subject-matter, the tendency of the cases is to require the discretion or the dissatisfaction to be reasonable ... . This construction imposes the least hardship in that it produces a result that cannot be said to be unfair or unjust to either of the parties. Other things being equal, I think it preferable that provisions of this kind be construed as implying the less arbitrary standards of the objective test.

NOTES AND QUESTIONS

1. Lambert JA appears to believe that the parties intended that the landlord could not be required to accept a rent that it did not accept as market. What is the effect of implying a clause that the landlord would not unreasonably withhold its agreement? Who would decide whether the landlord had acted unreasonably? Is there any difference in the effect of the clause, with the implied terms, and a clause by which the parties agreed that the rent would be market value?

2. Good faith was recognized as an organizing principle of Canadian contract law in *Bhasin v Hrynew* 2014 SCC 71 (which is excerpted and discussed in Chapter 8). Does this recognition mean that Lord Ackner's statement of principle in *Walford* is no longer cogent in Canada? For a general discussion of good faith, see McCamus, ch 5; Swan & Adamski at 312-30; MacDougall at 67-70; Waddams at paras 500-14.

3. Are the rules relating to certainty too rigidly enforced? Consider this question as you read the following excerpt dealing with issues of pre-contractual liability.

STEPHEN A SMITH, *Contract Theory*
(Oxford: Oxford University Press, 2004) at 194-95 (footnotes omitted)

NON-CONTRACTUAL PROTECTION

In considering [the rigidity question] ..., the possibility that disappointed parties may have recourse to non-contractual protection must also be kept in mind. If the full range of such protection is not recognized by courts, a neutral application of the offer and acceptance rules may indeed lead to harsh results. Equally, a failure by critics to appreciate such protection may lead to unfair criticism of the offer and acceptance rules. Three sources of non-contractual protection are particularly important.

The first is unjust enrichment law, which supports claims to recover the value of benefits conveyed in anticipation of a contract that did not materialize. A claim for what is sometimes called *quantum valebat* (for goods) and *quantum meruit* (for services) is reasonably well-established in common law, although the late recognition that such claims are part of a general duty to reverse unjust enrichments has meant this source of liability has not always been foremost in the minds of contract scholars.

A second source of non-contractual protection is a duty to pay for requested services. A party that has provided services requested in anticipation of a contract may be able to recover on this basis if he has not been paid. There is a debate amongst scholars as to whether such an action is part of unjust enrichment law or part of a distinct species of obligation, but for our purposes it is sufficient to acknowledge that plaintiffs normally can recover the value of services provided in anticipation of a contract.

Finally, a disappointed plaintiff may try to recover on the basis not that he conveyed a benefit to the defendant, but that he incurred expenses in justifiable reliance on the defendant's representations that he would be paid. In other words, the plaintiff may seek protection on the basis of a claim in estoppel. This is potentially the widest basis for relief, since the plaintiff has the possibility of claiming for all reliance-induced losses, regardless of whether those losses transmit to a benefit for the defendant. The main hurdle to making such a claim, at least in England, is the rule that estoppel may not be used to found a cause of action. In a contractual setting, estoppel is generally available only to prevent plaintiffs from insisting on their already-existing contractual rights. Some common law jurisdictions have abandoned this controversial limitation, and even in England there are exceptions to the rule.

NOTES

1. For an example of estoppel mitigating the rigours of offer and acceptance, see *Lim Teng Huan v Ang Swee Chuan*, [1992] 1 WLR 113 (Brunei PC). In that case, the Privy Council decided that a plaintiff might rely on proprietary estoppel to enforce a promise to exchange interests in land even though the promise was contained in a contract that was too uncertain to be enforceable. The contract was said to be void because one of the interests was in an unspecified piece of land expected to be allotted by the government at some uncertain future date. Proprietary estoppel is discussed in Section III.C.2, below. See also M Spence, *Protecting Reliance* (Oxford: Hart, 1999) at 99-106.

2. For a more detailed discussion of pre-contractual liability from an unjust enrichment perspective, see, *inter alia*, P Birks, *Unjust Enrichment*, 2nd ed (Oxford: Oxford University Press, 2005), 143ff; Maddaugh & McCamus, chs 17 and 21; J Edelman, "Liability in Unjust Enrichment Where a Contract Fails to Materialize" in Burrows & Peel 159; M McInnes, *The Canadian Law of Unjust Enrichment and Restitution* (Toronto: LexisNexis Canada, 2014) ch 13.

3. For a more detailed discussion of how the law of tort informs pre-contractual liability, see P Giliker, "A Role for Tort in Pre-Contractual Negotiations? An Examination of English, French, and Canadian Law" (2003) 52 ICLQ 969.

E. CONTRACTS NEGOTIATED BY CORRESPONDENCE

When negotiations for a contract are carried on through the medium of the mail, telephone, email, or fax, certain technical difficulties may cause problems. Mail may be misdelivered; telephones may fail; fax machines may run out of paper. Are special rules needed to deal with these situations? Consider the following excerpts.

HOUSEHOLD INSURANCE CO V GRANT
(1879), 4 Ex D 216 (CA)

THESIGER LJ: In this case the defendant made an application for shares in the plaintiffs' company under circumstances from which we must imply that he authorized the company, in the event of their allotting to him the shares applied for, to send the notice of allotment by post. The company did allot him the shares, and duly addressed to him and posted a letter containing the notice of allotment, but upon the finding of the jury it must be taken that the letter never reached its destination. In this state of circumstances Lopes J. has decided that the defendant is liable as a shareholder. ...

The leading case upon the subject is *Dunlop v. Higgins* (1848), 9 E.R. 805. ... [In that case] the Lord Justice General directed the jury in point of law that, if the pursuers posted their acceptance of the offer in due time according to the usage of trade they were not responsible for any casualties in the post office establishment. This direction was wide enough in its terms to include the case of the acceptance never being delivered at all; and Lord Cottenham, in expressing his opinion that it was not open to objection, did so after putting the case of a letter containing a notice of dishonour posted by the holder of a bill of exchange in proper time, in which case he said, "Whether that letter be delivered or not is a matter quite immaterial, because for accidents happening at the post office he is not responsible." In short, Lord Cottenham appears to me to have held that, as a rule, a contract formed by correspondence through the post is complete as soon as the letter accepting an offer is put into the post, and is not put an end to in the event of the letter never being delivered. My view of the effect of *Dunlop v. Higgins* is that taken by James L.J., in *Harris' Case* (1872), 7 Ch. App. 587, where he speaks of the former case as "a case which is binding upon us, and in which every principle argued before us was discussed at length by the Lord Chancellor in giving judgment." He adds, the Lord Chancellor "arrived at the conclusion that the posting of the letter of acceptance is the completion of the contract; that is to say, the moment one man has made an offer, and the other has done something binding himself to that offer, then the contract is complete and neither party can afterwards escape from it." ... Now, whatever in abstract discussion may be said as to the legal notion of its being necessary, in order to the effecting of a valid and binding contract, that the minds of the parties should be brought together at one and the same moment, that notion is practically the foundation of English law upon the subject of the formation of contract. Unless therefore a contract constituted by correspondence is absolutely concluded at the moment that the continuing offer is accepted by the person to whom the offer is addressed, it is difficult to see how the two minds are ever to be brought together at one and the same moment. This was pointed out by Lord Ellenborough in the case of *Adams v. Lindsell* (1818), 106 E.R. 250 which is a recognized authority upon this branch of the law. But on the other hand it is a principle of law, as well established as the legal notion to which I have referred, that the minds of the two parties must be brought together by mutual communication. An acceptance, which only remains in the breast of the acceptor without being actually and by legal implication communicated to the offeror, is no binding acceptance. ... How then are these elements of law to be harmonized in the case of contracts formed by correspondence through the post? I see no better mode than that of treating the post office as the agent of both parties. ... But if the post office be such common agent, then it seems to me to follow that, as soon as the letter of acceptance is delivered to the post office, the contract is made as complete and as final and absolutely binding as if the acceptor had put his letter into the hands of a messenger sent by the offeror himself as his agent to deliver the offer and receive the acceptance. What other principle can be adopted short of holding that the contract is not complete by acceptance until and except from the time that the letter containing the acceptance is delivered to the offeror, a principle which has been distinctly negatived. ... The acceptor, in posting the letter, has, to use the language of Lord Blackburn, in *Brogden v. Directors of Metropolitan Ry. Co.* (1877), 2 App. Cas. 666, 691, "put it out of his control and done an extraneous act which clenches the matter, and shows beyond all doubt that each side is bound." How then can a casualty in the post, whether resulting in delay, which in commercial transactions is often as bad as no delivery, or in non-delivery, unbind the parties or unmake the contract? To me it appears that in practice a contract complete upon the acceptance of an offer being posted, but liable to be put an end to by an accident in the post, would be more mischievous than a contract only binding upon the parties to it upon the acceptance actually reaching the offeror, and I can see no principle of law from which such an anomalous contract can be deduced.

There is no doubt that the implication of a complete, final, and absolutely binding contract being formed, as soon as the acceptance of an offer is posted, may in some cases lead to inconvenience and hardship. But such there must be at times in every view of the law. It is impossible in transactions which pass between parties at a distance, and have to be carried on through the medium of correspondence, to adjust conflicting rights between innocent parties, so as to make the consequences of mistake on the part of a mutual agent fall equally upon the shoulders of both. At the same time I am not prepared to admit that the implication in question will lead to any great or general inconvenience or hardship. An offeror, if he chooses, may always make the formation of the contract which he proposes dependent upon the actual communication to himself of the acceptance. If he trusts to the post he trusts to a means of communication which, as a rule, does not fail, and if no answer to his offer is received by him, and the matter is of importance to him he can make inquiries of the person to whom his offer was addressed. On the other hand, if the contract is not finally concluded, except in the event of acceptance actually reaching the offeror, the door would be opened to the perpetration of much fraud, and, putting aside this consideration, considerable delay in commercial transactions, in which despatch is, as a rule, of the greatest consequence, would be occasioned; for the acceptor would never be entirely safe in acting upon his acceptance until he had received notice that his letter of acceptance had reached its destination.

Upon balance of conveniences and inconveniences it seems to me, applying with slight alterations the language of the Supreme Court of the United States in *Tayloe v. Merchants Fire Insurance Co.* (1850), 9 Howard S. Ct. Rep. 390, more consistent with the acts and declarations of the parties in this case to consider the contract complete and absolutely binding on the transmission of the notice of allotment through the post, as the medium of communication that the parties themselves contemplated, instead of postponing its completion until the notice had been received by the defendant. Upon principle, therefore, as well as authority, I think that the judgment of Lopes J. was right and should be affirmed, and that this appeal should therefore be dismissed.

BRAMWELL LJ (dissenting): The question in this case is not whether the post office was a proper medium of communication from the plaintiffs to the defendant. There is no doubt that it is so in all cases where personal service is not required. It is an ordinary mode of communication, and every person who gives anyone the right to communicate with him, gives the right to communicate in an ordinary manner and so in this way and to this extent, that if an offer were made by letter in the morning to a person at a place within half-an-hour's railway journey of the offeror, I should say that an acceptance by post, though it did not reach the offeror till the next morning, would be in time. Nor is the question whether, when the letter reaches an offeror, the latter is bound and the bargain made from the time the letter is posted or despatched, whether by post or otherwise. The question in this case is different. I will presently state what in my judgment it is. Meanwhile I wish to mention some elementary propositions which, if carefully borne in mind, will assist in the determination of this case.

First. Where a proposition to enter into a contract is made and accepted, it is necessary, as a rule, to constitute the contract that there should be a communication of that acceptance to the proposer, per Brian C.J., and Lord Blackburn: *Brogden v. Metropolitan Ry. Co.*, 2 App. Cas. at p. 692.

Secondly. That the present case is one of proposal and acceptance.

Thirdly. That as a consequence of or involved in the first proposition, if the acceptance is written or verbal, i.e., is by letter or message, as a rule, it must reach the proposer or there is no communication, and so no acceptance of the offer.

Fourthly. That if there is a difference where the acceptance is by a letter sent through the post which does not reach the offeror, it must be by virtue of some general rule or some particular agreement of the parties. As for instance, there might be an agreement that the acceptance of the proposal may be sending the article offered by the proposer to be bought, or hanging out a flag or sign to be seen by the offeror as he goes by, or leaving a letter at a certain place, or any other agreed mode, and in the same way there might be an agreement that dropping a letter in a post pillar box or other place of reception should suffice.

Fifthly. That as there is no such special agreement in this case, the defendant, if bound, must be bound by some general rule which makes a difference when the post office is employed as the means of communication.

Sixthly. That if there is any such general rule applicable to the communication of the acceptance of offers, it is equally applicable to all communications that may be made by post. Because, as I have said, the question is not whether this communication may be made by post. If, therefore, posting a letter which does not reach is a sufficient communication of acceptance of an offer, it is equally a communication of everything else which may be communicated by post, e.g., notice to quit. It is impossible to hold, if I offer my landlord to sell him some hay and he writes accepting my offer, and in the same letter gives me notice to quit, and posts his letter which, however, does not reach me, that he has communicated to me his acceptance of my offer, but not his notice to quit. Suppose a man has paid his tailor by cheque or banknote, and posts a letter containing a cheque or banknote to his tailor, which never reaches, is the tailor paid? If he is, would he be if he had never been paid before in that way? Suppose a man is in the habit of sending cheques and banknotes to his banker by post, and posts a letter containing cheques and banknotes, which never reaches. Is the banker liable? Would he be if this was the first instance of a remittance of the sort? In the cases I have supposed, the tailor and banker may have recognized this mode of remittance by sending back receipts and putting the money to the credit of the remitter. Are they liable with that? Are they liable without it? The question then is, is posting a letter which is never received a communication to the person addressed, or an equivalent, or something which dispenses with it? It is for those who say it is to make good their contention. I ask why is it? My answer beforehand to any argument that may be urged is, that it is not a communication, and that there is no agreement to take it as an equivalent for or to dispense with a communication. That those who affirm the contrary say the thing which is not. That if Brian C.J. had had to adjudicate on the case, he would deliver the same judgment as that reported. That because a man, who may send a communication by post or otherwise, sends it by post, he should bind the person addressed, though the communication never reaches him, while he would not so bind him if he had sent it by hand, it is impossible. There is no reason in it; it is simply arbitrary. I ask whether anyone who thinks so is prepared to follow that opinion to its consequence; suppose the offer is to sell a particular chattel, and the letter accepting it never arrives, is the property in the chattel transferred? Suppose it is to sell an estate or grant a lease, is the bargain completed? The lease might be such as not to require a deed, could a subsequent lessee be ejected by the would-be acceptor because he had posted a letter? Suppose an article is advertised at so much, and that it would be sent on receipt of a post office order. Is it enough to post the letter? If the word "receipt" is relied on, is it really meant that that makes a difference? If it should be said let the offeror wait, the answer is, maybe he may lose his market meanwhile. Besides, his offer may be advertisement to all mankind. Suppose a reward for information, information posted does not reach, someone else gives it and is paid, is the offeror liable to the first man?

It is said that a contrary rule would be hard on the would-be acceptor, who may have made his arrangements on the footing that the bargain was concluded. But to hold as contended would be equally hard on the offeror, who may have his arrangements on the footing that his offer was not accepted; his non-receipt of any communication may be attributable to the person to whom it was made being absent. What is he to do but to act on the negative, that no communication has been made to him? Further, the use of the post office is no more authorized by the offeror than the sending an answer by hand, and all these hardships would befall the person posting the letter if he sent it by hand. Doubtless in that case he would be the person to suffer if the letter did not reach its destination. Why should his sending it by post relieve him of the loss and cast it on the other party? It was said, if he sends it by hand it is revocable, but not if he sends it by post, which makes the difference. But it is revocable when sent by post, not that the letter can be got back, but its arrival might be anticipated by a letter by hand or telegram, and there is no case to shew that such anticipation would not prevent the letter from binding. It would be a most alarming thing to say that it would. That a letter honestly but mistakenly written and posted must bind the writer if hours before its arrival he informed the person addressed that it was coming, but was wrong and recalled; suppose a false but honest character given, and the mistake found out after the letter posted, and notice that it was wrong given to the person addressed.

Then, as was asked, is the principle to be applied to telegrams? Further, it seems admitted that if the proposer said, "unless I hear from you by return of post the offer is withdrawn," that the letter accepting it must reach him to bind him. There is indeed a case recently reported in the Times before the Master of the Rolls, where the offer was to be accepted within fourteen days, and it is said to have been held that it was enough to post the letter on the 14th, though it would and did not reach the offeror till the 15th. Of course there may have been something in that case not mentioned in the report. But as it stands it comes to this, that if an offer is to be accepted in June, and there is a month's post between the places, posting the letter on the 30th of June will suffice, though it does not reach till the 31st of July; but that case does not affect this. There the letter reached, here it has not. If it is not admitted that "unless I hear by return the offer is withdrawn" makes the receipt of the letter a condition, it is to say an express condition goes for nought. If it is admitted, is it not what every letter says? Are there to be fine distinctions, such as, if the words are "unless I hear from you by return post, & c.," it is necessary the letter should reach him, but "let me know by return of post," it is not; or if in that case it is, yet it is not where there is an offer without those words. Lord Blackburn says that Mellish L.J. accurately stated that where it is expressly or impliedly stated in the offer, "you may accept the offer by posting a letter," the moment you post this letter the offer is accepted. I agree; and the same thing is true of any other mode of acceptance offered with the offer and acted on—as firing a cannon, sending off a rocket, give your answer to my servant the bearer. Lord Blackburn was not dealing with the question before us; there was no doubt in the case before him that the letter had reached. ...

I am of opinion that this judgment should be reversed. I am of opinion that there was no bargain between these parties to allot and take shares, that to make such bargain there should have been an acceptance of the defendant's offer and a communication to him of that acceptance. That there was no such communication. That posting a letter does not differ from other attempts at communication in any of its consequences, save that it is irrevocable as between the poster and post office. The difficulty has arisen from a mistake as to what was decided in *Dunlop v. Higgins*, and from supposing that because there is a right to have recourse to the post as a means of communication, that right is attended by some peculiar consequences, and also from supposing that because if the letter reaches it binds from the time of posting, it also binds though it never reaches. Mischief may arise if my opinion prevails. It probably will not, as so much has been said on the matter that principle is lost sight of. I believe equal if not greater, will, if it does not prevail. I believe the latter will be obviated only by the rule being made nugatory by every prudent man saying, "[Y]our answer by post is only to bind if it reaches me." But the question is not to be decided on these considerations. What is the law? What is the principle? If Brian C.J. had had to decide this a public post being instituted in his time, he would have said the law is the same, now there is a post, as it was before, viz., a communication to affect a man must be a communication, i.e., must reach him.

[Judgment affirmed. The opinion of Baggallay LJ, who agreed with Thesiger LJ, is omitted.]

CIVIL CODE OF QUÉBEC
LRQ, c C-1991

Article 1387. A contract is formed when and where acceptance is received by the offeror, regardless of the method of communication used.

NOTE

The only "circumstances" from which Thesiger LJ thought he must imply that the defendant had authorized the plaintiff company to use the post would appear to be that the defendant *handed* to one Kendrick, the plaintiff company's local agent, a written application for shares, which Kendrick duly forwarded, presumably by post, to his principals in London.

Nunin Holdings Pty Ltd v Tullamarine Estates Pty Ltd. [1994] 1 VR 74 (SC). HEDIGAN J: Notwithstanding that we live in the electronic age of telephones, telexes, facsimile transmissions, courier services and document exchange facilities, the use of the post, perhaps less reliable and speedy for all its modern equipment, is still commonplace. The rule has not been expanded but it has not been abandoned either.

HENTHORN V FRASER
[1892] 2 Ch 27 (CA)

[After two futile attempts by Henthorn to purchase property in Birkenhead from Fraser, the secretary of the Huskisson Benefit Building Society in Liverpool (the two cities are across the mouth of the Mersey River from each other), Fraser, on July 7, orally offered to sell it for £750 and handed Henthorn a written note stating, "I hereby give you the refusal of the Flamank Street property at £750 for fourteen days." On July 8 Fraser agreed to sell the same property to someone else, subject to his being able to cancel if he could not cancel his offer to Henthorn. Fraser posted a letter to Henthorn about noon that day, but it was not delivered to Henthorn's address until five o'clock and Henthorn did not in fact have it until he returned home about eight o'clock. Meanwhile Henthorn's solicitor had posted a letter in Birkenhead at ten to four that afternoon accepting the offer. The letter of acceptance was delivered at eight thirty that evening and was received by Fraser the next morning. Fraser denied the contract and Henthorn sued for specific performance in the Court of the County Palatine. His action was dismissed and he appealed.]

LORD HERSCHELL: ... If the acceptance by the plaintiff of the defendant's offer is to be treated as complete at the time the letter containing it was posted, I can entertain no doubt that the society's attempted revocation of the offer was wholly ineffectual. I think that a person who has made an offer must be considered as continuously making it until he has brought to the knowledge of the person to whom it was made that it is withdrawn ... . The grounds upon which it has been held that the acceptance of an offer is complete when it is posted have, I think, no application to the revocation or modification of an offer. These can be no more effectual than the offer itself, unless brought to the mind of the person to whom the offer is made. But it is contended on behalf of the defendants that the acceptance was complete only when received by them, and not on the letter being posted. It cannot, of course, be denied, after the decision in *Dunlop v. Higgins* (1848), 9 E.R. 805, in the House of Lords, that where an offer has been made through the medium of the post, the contract is complete as soon as the acceptance of the offer is posted, but that decision is said to be inapplicable here, inasmuch as the letter containing the offer was not sent by post to Birkenhead, but handed to the plaintiff in the defendant's office at Liverpool. The question therefore arises in what circumstances the acceptance of an offer is to be regarded as complete as soon as it is posted. In the case of the *Household Insurance Company v. Grant* (1879), 4 Ex. D. 216, Lord Justice Baggallay said: "I think that the principle established in *Dunlop v. Higgins* is limited in its application to cases in which by reason of general usage, or of relations between the parties to any particular transactions, or of the terms in which the offer is made, the acceptance of such offer by a letter through the post is expressly or impliedly authorized." ... Applying the law [there] laid down by the Court of Appeal I think in the present case an authority to accept by post must be implied. Although the plaintiff received the offer at the defendant's office in Liverpool, he resided in another town, and it must have been in contemplation that he would take the offer, which by its terms was to remain open for some days with him to his place of residence, and those who made the offer must have known that it would be according to the ordinary usages of mankind that if he accepted it he should communicate his acceptance by means of the post. I am not sure that I should myself have regarded the doctrine that an acceptance is complete as soon as the letter containing it is posted as resting upon an implied authority by the person making the offer to the person receiving it to accept by those means. It strikes me as somewhat artificial to speak of the person to whom the offer is made as having the implied authority of the other party to send his acceptance by post. He needs no authority to transmit the acceptance through any particular channel; he may select what means he pleases, the post-office no less than any other. The only effect of the supposed authority is to make the acceptance complete as soon as it is posted, and authority will obviously be implied only when the tribunal considers that it is a case in which this result ought to be reached.

I should prefer to state the rule thus: Where the circumstances are such that it must have been within the contemplation of the parties that, according to the ordinary usages of mankind, the post might be used as a means of communicating the acceptance of an offer, the acceptance is complete as soon as it is posted. It matters not in which way the proposition be stated, the present case is in either view within it. The learned Vice-Chancellor appears to have based his decision to some extent on the fact that before the acceptance was posted the defendants had sold the property to another person. The case of *Dickinson v. Dodds* (1876), 2 Ch. D. 463, was relied upon in support of that defence. In that case, however, the plaintiff knew of the subsequent sale before he accepted the offer, which, in my judgment, distinguishes it entirely from the present case. For the reasons I have given I think the judgment must be reversed, and the usual decree for specific performance made. The respondents must pay the costs of the appeal and of the action.

[The judgments of Lindley and Kay LJJ to the same effect are omitted.]

BYRNE & CO V LEON VAN TIENHOVEN & CO
(1880), 5 CPD 344

LINDLEY J: This was an action for the recovery of damages for the non-delivery by the defendants to the plaintiffs of 1,000 boxes of tin plates, pursuant to an alleged contract, which I will refer to presently. The action was tried at Cardiff before myself without a jury; and it was agreed at the trial that in the event of the plaintiffs being entitled to damages they should be £375.

The defendants carried on business at Cardiff and the plaintiffs at New York, and it takes ten or eleven days for a letter posted at either place to reach the other. The alleged contract consists of a letter written by the defendants to the plaintiffs on the 1st of October, 1879, and received by them on the 11th, and accepted by telegram and letter, sent to the defendants on the 11th and 15th of October respectively. These letters and telegrams were as follows:

[On October 1, 1879, the defendants wrote the plaintiffs offering them 1,000 boxes of tin plates at 15s. 6d. per box. On October 11, 1879, the plaintiffs cabled the defendants accepting this offer and on October 15 wrote the defendants confirming their previous cable of acceptance. On October 8, however, the defendants wrote a letter to the plaintiffs informing them that because there had been a big run on the tinplate market in the last few days, causing prices to rise considerably, they withdrew their offer and considered it cancelled from this date.]

... There is no doubt that an offer can be withdrawn before it is accepted, and it is immaterial whether the offer is expressed to be open for acceptance for a given time or not. ... For the decision of the present case, however, it is necessary to consider two other questions, viz., 1. Whether a withdrawal of an offer has any effect until it is communicated to the person to whom the offer has been sent? 2. Whether posting a letter of withdrawal is a communication to the person to whom the letter is sent?

It is curious that neither of these questions appears to have been actually decided in this country. As regards the first question, I am aware that Pothier and some other writers of celebrity are of opinion that there can be no contract if an offer is withdrawn before it is accepted, although the withdrawal is not communicated to the person to whom the offer has been made. The reason for this opinion is that there is not in fact any such consent by both parties as is essential to constitute a contract between them. Against this view, however, it has been urged that a state of mind not notified cannot be regarded in dealings between man and man; and that an uncommunicated revocation is for all practical purposes and in point of law no revocation at all. This is the view taken in the United States: see *Tayloe v. Merchants Fire Insurance Co.* (1850), 9 How. Sup. Ct. Rep. 390, cited in *Benjamin on Sales*, pp. 56-58, and it was adopted by Mr. Benjamin. The same view is taken by Mr. Pollock in his excellent work on *Principles of Contract*, 2nd ed., p. 10, and by Mr. Leake in his *Digest of the Law of Contracts*, p. 43. This view, moreover, appears to me much more in accordance with the general principles of English law than the view maintained by Pothier.

I pass, therefore, to the next question, viz., whether posting the letter of revocation was a sufficient communication of it to the plaintiff. The offer was posted on the 1st of October, the withdrawal was posted on the 8th, and did not reach the plaintiff until after he had posted his letter of the 11th, accepting the offer. It may be taken as now settled that where an offer is made and accepted by letters sent through the post, the contract is completed the moment the letter accepting the offer is posted: *Harris' Case* (1872), 7 Ch. App. 587; *Dunlop v. Higgins* (1848), 1 H.L.C. 381; 9 E.R. 805, even although it never reaches its destination. When, however, these authorities are looked at, it will be seen that they are based upon the principle that the writer of the offer has expressly or impliedly assented to treat an answer to him by a letter duly posted as a sufficient acceptance and notification to himself, or, in other words, he has made the post office his agent to receive the acceptance and notification of it. But this principle appears to me to be inapplicable to the case of the withdrawal of an offer. In this particular case I can find no evidence of any authority in fact given by the plaintiffs to the defendants to notify a withdrawal of their offer by merely posting a letter; and there is no legal principle or decision which compels me to hold, contrary to the fact, that the letter of the 8th of October is to be treated as communicated to the plaintiff on that day or any day before the 20th, when the letter reached them. But before that letter had reached the plaintiffs they had accepted the offer, both by telegram and by post; and they had themselves resold the tinplates at a profit. In my opinion the withdrawal of the defendants on the 8th of October of their offer of the 1st was inoperative and a complete contract binding on both parties was entered into on the 11th of October, when the plaintiff accepted the offer of the 1st, which they had no reason to suppose had been withdrawn. Before leaving this part of the case it may be as well to point out the extreme injustice and inconvenience which any other conclusion would produce. If the defendants' contention were to prevail no person who had received an offer by post and had accepted it would know his position until he had waited such a time as to be quite sure that a letter withdrawing the offer had not been posted before his acceptance of it. It appears to me that both legal principles, and practical convenience require that a person who has accepted an offer not known to him to have been revoked, shall be in a position safely to act upon the footing that the offer and acceptance constitute a contract binding on both parties.

[The facts have been considerably abbreviated, and only that part of the case is given that deals with revocation of the offer.]

F Pollock, *Principles of Contract at Law and in Equity.* (London: Stevens, 1876) at 9-10. A proposal is revoked only when the intention to revoke it is communicated to the other party. Therefore a revocation communicated after acceptance, though determined upon before the acceptance, is too late ... . The civilians differ on the point. Pothier lays down a directly contrary rule in a well-known passage (Contrat de Vente, s. 32) ... . He does not fail to see the manifestly unjust consequences of letting a revocation take effect, though the other party has received, accepted, and acted upon the proposal without knowing anything of the proposer's intention to revoke it; but he escapes them by imposing an obligation on the proposer upon grounds of natural equity independent of contract, to indemnify the party so accepting against any damage resulting to him from the transaction. [Pollock describes this solution as "cumbrous and inelegant" and continues:] The declaration of an *animus contrahendi* [intention of contracting] (whether by way of proposal or of acceptance) when once made must be regarded as continuing so long as no revocation of it is communicated to the other party. A revocation not communicated is in point of law no revocation at all. In this respect the revocation of a proposal or acceptance must be governed by the same rules as the proposal or acceptance itself. These principles, it seems to us, are entirely right if tested by common sense and convenience, and are in accordance with the authorities of the common law when rightly understood.

RESTATEMENT OF THE LAW OF CONTRACTS (SECOND)
American Law Institute, 1981

40. Rejection or counter-offer by mail or telegram does not terminate the power of acceptance until received by the offeror, but limits the power so that a letter or telegram of acceptance started after the sending of an otherwise effective rejection or counter-offer is only a counter-offer unless the acceptance is received by the offeror before he receives the rejection or counter-offer.

HOLWELL SECURITIES LTD V HUGHES
[1974] 1 All ER 161 (CA)

[By clause 1 of an agreement dated October 19, 1971 made between the defendant of the one part and the plaintiffs of the other, the plaintiffs were granted an option to purchase certain freehold property from the defendant. Clause 2 of the agreement provided: "The said option shall be exercisable by notice in writing to the [defendant] at any time within six months from the date hereof." On April 14, 1972, the plaintiffs' solicitors wrote a letter to the defendant giving notice of the exercise of the option. The letter was posted, properly addressed, and prepaid, on April 14, but it was never in fact delivered to the defendant or to his address. No other written communication of the exercise of the option was given or sent to the defendant before the expiry of the time limit on April 19.]

RUSSELL LJ: It is not disputed that the plaintiffs' solicitors letter dated 14th April 1972 addressed to the defendant at his residence and place of work, the house which was the subject of the option to purchase, was posted by ordinary post in a proper way, enclosing a copy of the letter of the same date delivered by hand to the defendant's solicitors. It is not disputed that the letter and enclosure somehow went astray and never reached the house nor the defendant. It is not disputed that the language of the letter and enclosure would have constituted notice of exercise of the option had they reached the defendant. It is not contended that the handing of the letter to the solicitor constituted an exercise of the option.

The plaintiffs' main contention below and before this court has been that the option was exercised and the contract for sale and purchase was constituted at the moment that the letter addressed to the defendant with its enclosure was committed by the plaintiffs' solicitors to the proper representative of the postal service, so that its failure to reach its destination is irrelevant.

It is the law in the first place that prima facie acceptance of an offer must be communicated to the offeror. On this principle the law has engrafted a doctrine that, if in any given case the true view is that the parties contemplated that the postal service might be used for the purpose of forwarding an acceptance of the offer, committal of the acceptance in a regular manner to the postal service will be acceptance of the offer so as to constitute a contract, even if the letter goes astray and is lost. Nor, as was once suggested, are such cases limited to cases in which the offer has been made by post. It suffices I think at this stage to refer to *Henthorn v. Fraser*. In the present case, as I read a passage in the judgment below, Templeman J. concluded that the parties here contemplated that the postal service might be used to communicate acceptance of the offer (by exercise of the option); and I agree with that.

But that is not and cannot be the end of the matter. In any case, before one can find that the basic principle of the need for communication of acceptance to the offeror is displaced by this artificial concept of communication by the act of posting, it is necessary that the offer is in its terms consistent with such displacement and not one which by its terms points rather in the direction of actual communication. We were referred to *Henthorn v. Fraser* and to the obiter dicta of Farwell J. in *Bruner v. Moore*, which latter was a case of an option to purchase patent rights. But in neither of those cases was there apparently any language in the offer directed to the manner of acceptance of the offer or exercise of the option.

The relevant language here is, "The said option shall be exercisable by notice in writing to the Intending Vendor ...," a very common phrase in an option agreement. There is, of course, nothing in that phrase to suggest that the notification to the defendant could not be made by post. But the requirement of "notice ... to," in my judgment, is language which should be taken expressly to assert the ordinary situation in law that acceptance requires to be communicated or notified to the offeror, and is inconsistent with the theory that acceptance can be constituted by the act of posting, referred to by Anson as "acceptance *without notification*."

It is of course true that the instrument could have been differently worded. An option to purchase within a period given for value has the characteristic of an offer that cannot be withdrawn. The instrument might have said "The offer constituted by this option may be accepted in writing within six months": in which case no doubt the posting would have sufficed to form the contract. But that language was not used, and, as indicated, in my judgment the language used prevents that legal outcome. Under this head of the case hypothetical problems were canvassed to suggest difficulties in the way of that conclusion. What if the letter had been delivered through the letterbox of the house in due time, but the defendant had either deliberately or fortuitously not been there to receive it before the option period expired? This does not persuade me that the artificial posting rule is here applicable. The answer might well be that in the circumstances the defendant had impliedly invited communication by use of an orifice in his front door designed to receive communications.

LAWTON LJ: Counsel for the plaintiffs submitted that the option was exercised when the letter was posted, as the rule relating to the acceptance of offers by post did apply. The foundation of his argument was that the parties to this agreement must have contemplated that the option might be, and probably would be, exercised by means of a letter sent through the post. I agree. This, submitted counsel, was enough to bring the rule into operation. I do not agree. In *Henthorn v. Fraser* Lord Herschell stated the rule as follows: "Where the circumstances are such that it must have been within the contemplation of the parties that, according to the ordinary usages of mankind, the post might be used as a means of communicating the acceptance of an offer, the acceptance is complete as soon as it is posted." It was applied by Farwell J. in *Bruner v. Moore* to an option to purchase patent rights. The option agreement, which was in writing, was silent as to the manner in which it was to be exercised. The grantee purported to do so by a letter and a telegram.

Does the rule apply in *all* cases where one party makes an offer which both he and the person with whom he was dealing must have expected the post to be used as a means of accepting it? In my judgment, it does not. First, it does not apply when the express terms of the offer specify that the acceptance must reach the offeror. The public nowadays are familiar with this exception to the general rule through their handling of football pool coupons. Secondly, it probably does not operate if its application would produce manifest inconvenience and absurdity. This is the opinion set out in Cheshire and Fifoot's *Law of Contract*. It was the opinion of Bramwell B. as is seen by his judgment in *British & American Telegraph Co. v. Colson*, and his opinion is worthy of consideration even though the decision in that case was overruled by this court in *Household Fire and Carriage Accident Insurance Co. Ltd. v. Grant*. The illustrations of inconvenience and absurdity which Bramwell B. gave are as apt today as they were then. Is a stockbroker who is holding shares to the orders of his client liable in damages because he did not sell in a falling market in accordance with the instructions in a letter which was posted but never received? Before the passing of the Law Reform (Miscellaneous Provisions) Act 1970 (which abolished actions for breach of promise of marriage), would a young soldier ordered overseas have been bound in contract to marry a girl to whom he had proposed by letter, asking her to let him have an answer before he left and she had replied affirmatively in good time but the letter had never reached him? In my judgment, the factors of inconvenience and absurdity are but illustrations of a wider principle, namely, that the rule does not apply if, having regard to all the circumstances, including the nature of the subject-matter under consideration, the negotiating parties cannot have intended that there should be a binding agreement until the party accepting an offer or exercising an option had in fact communicated the acceptance or exercise to the other. In my judgment, when this principle is applied to the facts of this case it becomes clear that the parties cannot have intended that the posting of a letter should constitute the exercise of the option.

QUESTIONS

1. The rule that acceptance is effective when posted has sometimes been justified on the basis that the post office was the "agent" of the offeror. The *Canada Post Corporation Act*, RSC 1985, c C-10, s 2(2), which provides that mail is the property of the addressee when deposited in a post office, has also been argued to support the rule. The first justification seems little more than a restatement of the rule that acceptance is effective when posted; the second does not have much rational connection with the question of when it is reasonable to find that a contract has been completed. What other justifications for the rule can you find in the case law? For an argument that the postal acceptance rule is arbitrary, because all possible rationales for the rule are unpersuasive, see Smith at 188-92.

2. Given that the postal acceptance rule imposes a degree of risk on the offeror, what would justify the imposition of such risk?

3. Does the existence of the postal acceptance rule mean that the common law is not concerned with consensus *ad idem*? For a discussion, see Waddams at para 145; MacDougall at 50-51.

4. What would happen if A mailed an acceptance of an offer, but subsequently changed her mind and posted a rejection? Assume that due to the vagaries of the mail the rejection arrived first. Given that the postal acceptance rule protects the offeree, should the offeree now be permitted to reject it? Why or why not? See also Waddams at paras 99-107; MacDougall at 41-45.

Entores, Ltd v Miles Far East Corporation. [1955] 2 All ER 493 (CA). DENNING LJ: [T]ake a case where two people make a contract by telephone. Suppose, for instance, that I make an offer to a man by telephone and, in the middle of his reply, the line goes "dead" so that I do not hear his words of acceptance. There is no contract at that moment. The other man may not know the precise moment when the line failed. But he will know that the telephone conversation was abruptly broken off, because people usually say something to signify the end of the conversation. If he wishes to make a contract, he must therefore get through again so as to make sure that I heard. Suppose next that the line does not go dead, but it is nevertheless so indistinct that I do not catch what he says and I ask him to repeat it. He then repeats and I hear his acceptance. The contract is made, not on the first time when I do not hear, but only the second time when I do hear. If he does not repeat it, there is no contract. The contract is only complete when I have his answer accepting the offer. ...

But suppose that [the offeree] does not know that his message did not get home. He thinks it has. This may happen if the listener on the telephone does not catch the words of acceptance, but nevertheless does not trouble to ask for them to be repeated: or if the ink on the teleprinter fails at the receiving end, but the clerk does not ask for the message to be repeated: so that the man who sends an acceptance reasonably believes that his message has been received. The offeror in such circumstances is clearly bound, because he will be estopped from saying that he did not receive the message of acceptance. It is his own fault that he did not get it. But if there should be a case where the offeror without any fault on his part does not receive the message of acceptance—yet the sender of it reasonably believes it has got home when it has not—then I think there is no contract.

EASTERN POWER LIMITED V AZIENDA COMUNALE ENERGIA AND AMBIENTE
(1999), 178 DLR (4th) 409 (Ont CA)

[Eastern Power Ltd. (EP) negotiated with Azienda Comunale Energia & Ambiente (ACEA) with a view to concluding a joint venture agreement to construct and operate an electricity generation plant in Italy. ACEA, which was located in Italy, signed a letter of intent and faxed it to EP, which was located in Ontario. EP signed the letter of intent and faxed it back to ACEA. The parties were unable to conclude the joint venture agreement and EP brought an action in the Ontario courts for breach of contract. ACEA moved to stay the action on *forum non conveniens* grounds. The motions judge granted the motion and EP appealed.]

MacPHERSON JA (for the court):

INTRODUCTION

[1] This is an appeal from the judgment of Juriansz J. dated November 26, 1998 in which he set aside service in Italy of a statement of claim by an Ontario company and stayed the company's action in Ontario on forum non conveniens grounds. In addition to the standard forum non conveniens factors that need to be addressed, the appeal poses the interesting question of where a contract is formed when the acceptance of an offer is communicated by facsimile transmission. Is the contract formed, in accordance with the general rule of contract law, in the place where the acceptance is received? Or should the postal exception to the general rule, which says that a contract is formed when and where an acceptance is placed in the mail, apply to acceptances communicated by facsimile transmission? ...

[After discussing the factors to be taken into account when staying actions on the basis of *forum non conveniens*, MacPherson JA continued:]

(A) LOCATION WHERE THE CONTRACT WAS SIGNED

[21] The contract which forms the basis of EP's action in contract and tort against ACEA is the Co-operation Agreement: see Statement of Claim, paragraphs 5, 26, 30 and 31. The motions judge found that the Co-operation Agreement was made in Italy because "acceptance was communicated to Italy." Since EP's acceptance was communicated by facsimile transmission, this raises the interesting question of the legal relationship between a faxed acceptance of an offer and the place where a contract is formed.

[22] The general rule of contract law is that a contract is made in the location where the offeror receives notification of the offeree's acceptance: see Fridman, *The Law of Contract in Canada*, 3rd ed., (1994), at p. 65; and *Re Viscount Supply Co.*, [1963] 1 O.R. 640, 40 D.L.R. (2nd) 501 (S.C.). However, there is an exception to this general rule. It is the postal acceptance rule. As expressed by Ritchie J. in *Imperial Life Assurance Co. of Canada v. Colmenares*, [1967] S.C.R. 443 at 447, 62 D.L.R. (2d) 138:

It has long been recognized that when contracts are to be concluded by post the place of mailing the acceptance is to be treated as the place where the contract was made.

See also: Fridman, *The Law of Contract in Canada*, supra, at pp. 67-68.

[23] EP contends that the rule with respect to facsimile transmissions should follow the postal acceptance exception. With respect, I disagree. EP has cited no authority in support of its position. There is, however, case authority for the proposition that acceptance by facsimile transmission should follow the general rule, which would mean that a contract is formed when and where acceptance is received by the offeror.

[24] In *Brinkibon Ltd. v. Stahag Stahl G.m.b.H.*, [1983] 2 A.C. 34 (H.L.), a contract was concluded when the buyer in London transmitted its acceptance to the seller in Vienna. The mode of acceptance was a message sent by telex, a form of instantaneous communication like the telephone. The law lords were unanimous in concluding that the contract was formed in Vienna where the acceptance was received by the offeror. Lord Brandon of Oakbrook analyzed the issue in this fashion, at p. 48:

> Mr. Thompson's second and alternative case, that the contract was concluded by the buyers transmitting to the sellers their telex of May 4, 1979, seems to me to be the correct analysis of the transaction. On this analysis, however, the buyers are up against the difficulty that it was decided by the Court of Appeal in *Entores Ltd. v. Miles Far East Corporation* [1955] 2 Q.B. 327 that, when an offer is accepted by telex, the contract thereby made is to be regarded as having been so made at the place where such telex was received (in this case Vienna) and not in the place from which such telex was sent (in this case London).
>
> Mr. Thompson invited your Lordships to hold that the *Entores* case was wrongly decided and should therefore be overruled. In this connection he said that it was well-established law that, when acceptance of an offer was notified to an offeror by post or telegram, the concluding of the contract took place when and where the letter of acceptance was posted or the telegram of acceptance was despatched. He then argued that the same rule should apply to cases where the acceptance of an offer was communicated by telex, with the consequence that the contract so made should be regarded as having been made at the place from which the telex was sent and not the place where it was received.
>
> My Lords, I am not persuaded that the *Entores* case [1955] 2 Q.B. 327 was wrongly decided and should therefore be overruled. On the contrary, I think that it was rightly decided and should be approved. The general principle of law applicable to the formation of a contract by offer and acceptance is that the acceptance of the offer by the offeree must be notified to the offeror before a contract can be regarded as concluded, *Carlill v. Carbolic Smoke Ball Co.* [1893] 1 Q.B. 256, 262, per Lindley L.J. The cases on acceptance by letter and telegram constitute an exception to the general principle of the law of contract stated above. The reason for the exception is commercial expediency: see, for example, *Imperial Land Co. of Marseilles, In re (Harris' Case)* (1872) L.R. 7 Ch. App. 587, 692 per Mellish L.J. That reason of commercial expediency applies to cases where there is bound to be a substantial interval between the time when the acceptance is sent and the time when it is received. In such cases the exception to the general rule is more convenient, and makes on the whole for greater fairness, than the general rule itself would do. In my opinion, however, that reason of commercial expediency does not have any application when the means of communication employed between the offeror and the offeree is instantaneous in nature, as is the case when either the telephone or telex is used. In such cases the general principle relating to the formation of contracts remains applicable, with the result that the contract is made where and when the telex of acceptance is received by the offeror.

[25] In my view, this analysis is equally applicable to facsimile transmissions, another form of instantaneous communication. Indeed, there is at least one Canadian authority that has reached this conclusion. In *Joan Balcom Sales Inc. v. Poirier* (1991), 49 C.P.C. (2d) 180 (N.S. Co. Ct.), an acceptance of a real estate listing offer was communicated by two vendors in Ottawa to a real estate company in Berwick, Nova Scotia. The mode of communication was a facsimile transmission. The vendors' position was that the contract was formed in Ottawa; they argued that the "mailbox doctrine" should be applied to communication by facsimile transmission.

[26] Haliburton Co. Ct. J. did not accept the vendors' argument. He reviewed the English academic writing about the postal acceptance exception to the general rule of contract formation. He then concluded, at p. 187:

> The writers then discuss the practical need of special rules to be applied to contracts entered into by post in the age when post was the primary method of commercial communication. The considerations which made it highly practical, if not imperative, in the interests of commerce, for the offeree to have knowledge in a timely fashion that he had a firm contract do not apply to facsimile transmissions. The communication is instantaneous. The offeree could easily have confirmed within minutes that they had a binding contract.
>
> I, therefore, find that the *contract was executed at Berwick*. [Emphasis in original.]

[27] I agree with this analysis, and with the analysis of the law lords in *Brinkibon*. I would hold that in contract law an acceptance by facsimile transmission should follow the general rule of contract formation, not the postal acceptance exception.

[28] I do not say that this rule should be an absolute one; like Lord Wilberforce in his separate speech in *Brinkibon*, "I think it a sound rule, but not necessarily a universal rule." (p. 42). Lord Wilberforce discussed some of the factors that might suggest caution about applying the general rule to telex communications in all cases, including the many variants in such communications and whether the message was sent and received by the principals to the contemplated contract. However, he concluded, at p. 42:

> The present case is ... the simple case of instantaneous communication between principals, and, in accordance with the general rule, involves that the contract (if any) was made when and where the acceptance was received.

[29] In my view, the present appeal is also "the simple case." The acceptance was faxed by the principals of EP in Ontario to the principals of ACEA in Italy. There is nothing to suggest that the communication between these principals was not instantaneous. Hence, applying the general rule, the contract was formed in Italy.

[The judgment has been significantly shortened to remove further discussion of *forum non conveniens* issues.]

NOTES AND QUESTIONS

1. As *Eastern Power* indicates, forms of instantaneous communication, such as the telephone, are usually treated differently than mail, despite possible technical failures. The justification appears to be that the offeree will realize that her acceptance has not been received. Of course, this will not always be true: see *Joan Balcom Sales Inc v Poirier* (1991), 106 NSR (2d) 377 (Co Ct).

2. In his judgment in *Brinkibon* (which is partially quoted in *Eastern Power*), Lord Wilberforce added: "No universal rule can cover all such cases; they must be resolved by reference

to the intentions of the parties, by sound business practice, and in some cases by a judgment where the risks should lie." Do you agree with this statement?

3. The problem before the court in *Eastern Power* was whether it should take jurisdiction over the dispute. For the purpose of solving that problem, is it relevant to consider whether an offeror is bound by an acceptance that fails to arrive? Is not the latter an entirely different problem? Compare the differing answers given to these questions by the Ontario Court of Appeal and Supreme Court of Canada in *Lapointe Rosenstein Marchand Melançon LLP v Cassels Brock & Blackwell LLP*, 2014 ONCA 497 (sub nom *Trillium Motor World Ltd v General Motors of Canada Limited*), affirmed [2016] 1 SCR 851.

4. In *Inukshuk Wireless Partnership v NextWave Holdco LLC*, 2013 ONSC 5631, Newbould J held that, in relation to the postal acceptance rule, "an e-mail is no different than a fax. Both are instantaneous communications" (para 25). Do you agree? Should the reliability of email be a factor? For a discussion, see D Capps, "Electronic Mail and the Postal Rule" (2004) 15 Intl Co & Com L Rev 207; V Watnick, "The Electronic Formation of Contracts and the Common Law 'Mailbox Rule'" (2004) 56 Baylor L Rev 175; E Mik, "The Effectiveness of Acceptances Communicated by Electronic Means, Or: Does the Postal Acceptance Rule Apply to Email?" (2009) J of Contract L 68; DP Nolan, "Offer and Acceptance in the Electronic Age" in Burrows & Peel 61.

5. A sent B by fax an offer to purchase B's property. B accepted by the same method. It was the procedure in A's office to clear the fax machine and distribute the transmissions only twice a day: once in the morning and once after lunch. B's fax arrived at 3:00 p.m. That evening, B received a better offer for her property, which she accepted. She immediately telephoned A to reject A's offer. The telephone message was left on A's answering machine and A received it at 10:00 p.m. that night. The fax accepting A's offer was handed to A as he came into the office at 8:45 a.m. the next morning. Do A and B have a contract? In answering this question consider the excerpts below.

BRIAN COOTE, "THE INSTANTANEOUS TRANSMISSION OF ACCEPTANCES"
(1971) 4 NZULR 331 at 338-40 (footnotes omitted)

[I]t is submitted that there is no universal rule that an acceptance must in fact be received by the offeror before a contract can be formed, to which rule communications by post and telegraph form the only exceptions. There are gaps in the law, but there are also available well established elements from which a general system of rules could be constructed and the gaps filled. ...

From these elements the following rules can be posited:

(1) Where offeror and offeree are face to face in instantaneous communication with each other, an acceptance must either actually be received by the offeror or reasonably appear to the offeree to have been so received.

(2) Where the offeror and offeree are apart and not in instantaneous communication with each other then, unless the offeror has stipulated for actual receipt, the contract will be formed once the offeree, using a mode of transmission contemplated by the parties for the purpose, has done all he can to ensure communication to the offeror. ...

Applying these rules, an acceptance by post or telegraph, if correctly addressed, would take effect as hitherto when posted or lodged, because this would be as far as the offeree could control its transmission. Should the parties be at each end of a telephone link, acceptance would take effect, again as hitherto, once the offeror had appeared to hear and understand it.

In the case of a telex link, the contract would be formed at that point in time when the party transmitting the acceptance (or his operator) could reasonably assume that the message had been received (if there were an operator at the other end) or recorded (if there were no such operator). It would follow in such a case that the acceptance could be binding even though not in fact received by the operator or recorded and this, too, would be consistent with the dicta of Denning L.J. in the *Entores* case. The *rationale* would, however, be different. The acceptance would take effect even though not received or recorded, not, as Denning L.J. suggested, as a consequence of the offeror's fault or neglect, but because the offeree would have given the degree of notice required by law and the risks would accordingly have passed to the offeror. Similarly, the acceptance could take effect when received by the operator, or recorded, even though it did not subsequently come to the mind of the offeror himself. The same would apply in the case of acceptances dictated into a telephone recording device at the offeror's address provided the offeree could not reasonably have been aware of any defect in the recording apparatus, if any should exist.

Under these same rules, an acceptance delivered by hand at the offeror's ordinary address for service would take effect from delivery to his door if the post were a contemplated mode of transmission. If it were not, the result would depend on the mode of transmission contemplated in the particular case. Delivery to a receptionist at the offeree's address would, for example, ordinarily be sufficient, unless the parties had in the particular circumstances contemplated delivery into the hands of the offeror.

RESTATEMENT OF THE LAW OF CONTRACTS (SECOND)
American Law Institute, 1981

63. Unless the offer provides otherwise,

(a) an acceptance made in a manner and by a medium invited by an offer is operative and completes the manifestation of mutual assent as soon as put out of the offeree's possession, without regard to whether it ever reaches the offeror; but

(b) an acceptance under an option contract is not operative until received by the offeror.

64. Acceptance by telephone or other medium of substantially instantaneous two-way communication is governed by the principles applicable to acceptances where the parties are in the presence of each other.

65. Unless circumstances known to the offeree indicate otherwise, a medium of acceptance is reasonable if it is the one used by the offeror or one customary in similar transactions at the time and place the offer is received.

NOTES AND QUESTIONS

1. According to Coote, the important question is not whether the parties are using a form of instantaneous communication but whether the parties are in instantaneous communication *with each other*. Thus, for him the key is not the technology used but rather how it is used. Would such a distinction be helpful in justifying why the court in *Eastern Power* stated that the rule relating to facsimiles was not absolute?

2. How would Coote answer the hypothetical posed by Russell LJ in *Holwell Securities*, above, concerning placing acceptances through a letterbox in the door of a house?

3. How does the Restatement's formulation differ from that of Coote? Which formulation do the Commonwealth cases support? Why, for example, does the Restatement have a separate rule for option contracts?

ELECTRONIC COMMERCE ACT, 2000
SO 2000, c 17

DEFINITIONS

1(1) In this Act,

"electronic" includes created, recorded, transmitted or stored in digital form or in other intangible form by electronic, magnetic or optical means or by any other means that has capabilities for creation, recording, transmission or storage similar to those means and "electronically" has a corresponding meaning;

"electronic agent" means a computer program or any other electronic means used to initiate an act or to respond to electronic documents or acts, in whole or in part, without review by an individual at the time of the response or act; ...

ELECTRONIC TRANSACTIONS AND ELECTRONIC AGENTS

FORMATION AND OPERATION OF ELECTRONIC CONTRACTS

19(1) An offer, the acceptance of an offer or any other matter that is material to the formation or operation of a contract may be expressed,
   (a) by means of electronic information or an electronic document; or
   (b) by an act that is intended to result in electronic communication, such as,
      (i) touching or clicking on an appropriate icon or other place on a computer screen, or
      (ii) speaking.

CONTRACTING OUT

(2) Subsection (1) applies unless the parties agree otherwise.

LEGAL RECOGNITION OF ELECTRONIC CONTRACTS

(3) A contract is not invalid or unenforceable by reason only of being in electronic form.

INVOLVEMENT OF ELECTRONIC AGENTS

20. A contract may be formed by the interaction of an electronic agent and an individual or by the interaction of electronic agents.

ERRORS, TRANSACTIONS WITH ELECTRONIC AGENTS

21. An electronic transaction between an individual and another person's electronic agent is not enforceable by the other person if,
   (a) the individual makes a material error in electronic information or an electronic document used in the transaction;
   (b) the electronic agent does not give the individual an opportunity to prevent or correct the error;

(c) on becoming aware of the error, the individual promptly notifies the other person; and

(d) in a case where consideration is received as a result of the error, the individual,

(i) returns or destroys the consideration in accordance with the other person's instructions or, if there are no instructions, deals with the consideration in a reasonable manner, and

(ii) does not benefit materially by receiving the consideration.

TIME OF SENDING OF ELECTRONIC INFORMATION OR DOCUMENT

22(1) Electronic information or an electronic document is sent when it enters an information system outside the sender's control or, if the sender and the addressee use the same information system, when it becomes capable of being retrieved and processed by the addressee.

CONTRACTING OUT

(2) Subsection (1) applies unless the parties agree otherwise.

PRESUMPTION, TIME OF RECEIPT

(3) Electronic information or an electronic document is presumed to be received by the addressee,

(a) if the addressee has designated or uses an information system for the purpose of receiving information or documents of the type sent, when it enters that information system and becomes capable of being retrieved and processed by the addressee; or

(b) if the addressee has not designated or does not use an information system for the purpose of receiving information or documents of the type sent, when the addressee becomes aware of the information or document in the addressee's information system and it becomes capable of being retrieved and processed by the addressee.

PLACES OF SENDING AND RECEIPT

(4) Electronic information or an electronic document is deemed to be sent from the sender's place of business and received at the addressee's place of business.

CONTRACTING OUT

(5) Subsection (4) applies unless the parties agree otherwise.

PLACE OF BUSINESS

(6) If the sender or the addressee has more than one place of business, the place of business for the purposes of subsection (4) is the one with the closest relationship to the underlying transaction to which the electronic information or document relates or, if there is no underlying transaction, the person's principal place of business.

HABITUAL RESIDENCE

(7) If the sender or the addressee does not have a place of business, the person's place of habitual residence is deemed to be the place of business for the purposes of subsection (4).

NOTES AND QUESTIONS

1. All common law provinces have legislation in force to deal with issues surrounding e-commerce. Moreover, the legislation is substantially similar because each act is based on the *Uniform Electronic Commerce Act* (UECA) developed by the Uniform Law Conference of Canada. (The UECA itself was based on a model act promulgated by the United Nations Commission on International Trade Law.) For a discussion of the UECA and the various legislation, see BJ Freeman, "Electronic Contracts Under Canadian Law—A Practical Guide" (2000) 28 Man LJ 1; JD Gregory, "Canadian Electronic Commerce Legislation" (2002) 17 BFLR 277; McCamus at 76-82.

2. Does the *Electronic Commerce Act* (ECA) apply to faxes or email?

3. Can you think of ways in which to rebut the presumption of receipt created by s 22(3) of the ECA? Can you think of a reason why the legislator used the word "presumed" rather than "deemed"?

4. Was the ECA necessary or should the common law have been left to deal with these issues? For examples of the common law in action, see *Rudder v Microsoft Corp* (1999), 47 CCLT (2d) 168 (Ont Sup Ct J); *Century 21 Canada Limited Partnership v Rogers Communications Inc*, 2011 BCSC 1196, 338 DLR (4th) 32. For a discussion of these cases, see MacDougall at 38-41.

F. CONSIDERATION: THE BARGAIN THEORY

Golding's Case. (1586), 2 Leon 72, 74 ER 367. EGERTON SG: In every action on the case [on an *assumpsit*], there are three things considerable: consideration, promise and breach of promise.

Currie v Misa. (1875), LR 10 Ex 153, 162, aff'd 1 App Cas 554. LUSH J: A valuable consideration, in the sense of the law, may consist either in some right, interest, profit, or benefit accruing to the one party, or some forbearance, detriment, loss or responsibility, given, suffered, or undertaken by the other.

Dunlop Pneumatic Tyre Co Ltd v Selfridge & Co. [1915] AC 847, 855. LORD DUNEDIN: My Lords, I am content to adopt from a work of Sir Frederick Pollock, to which I have often been under obligation, the following words as to consideration: "An act or forbearance of one party, or the promise thereof, is the price for which the promise of the other is bought, and the promise thus given for value is enforceable" (*Pollock on Contracts*, 8th ed., p. 175).

Westlake v Adams. (1858), 5 CB (NS) 248, 141 ER 99, 106. BYLES J: It is an elementary principle, that the law will not enter into an enquiry as to the adequacy of the consideration.

Hobbes, *Leviathan*. (1651). The value of all things contracted for is measured by the appetite of the contractors, and therefore the just value is that which they be contented to give.

Chappell & Co Ltd v Nestlé Co Ltd. [1960] AC 87 (HL). LORD SOMERVELL: A contracting party can stipulate for what consideration he chooses. A peppercorn does not cease to be good consideration if it is established that the promisee does not like pepper and will throw away the corn.

Vernon v Bethell. (1762), 2 Eden 110, 28 ER 839 (Ch). NORTHINGTON LC: [N]ecessitous men are not, truly speaking, free men, but, to answer a present exigency, will submit to any terms that the crafty may impose upon them. [This attitude is representative of a court of equity, in this case deciding that a mortgagee had made "an undue use of the influence of a mortgage."]

PS Atiyah, *Consideration in Contracts*. (Canberra: Australian National University Press, 1971). To talk of abolition of the doctrine of consideration is nonsensical. Consideration means a reason for the enforcement of a promise. Nobody can seriously propose that all promises should become enforceable; to abolish the doctrine of consideration, therefore, is simply to require the courts to begin all over again the task of deciding what promises are to be enforceable.

PS Atiyah, *Essays on Contract*. (Oxford: Oxford University Press, 1986). I would today wish to qualify the suggestion that consideration "means" a reason for the enforcement of a promise. It now seems to me to be more accurate to suggest that consideration really was and is a reason for the recognition of an obligation, rather than a reason for the enforcement of a promise. Given that ... reliance and benefit are often themselves good reasons for recognition of obligations in the law ... and given that many cases in contract law are based on implied promises which seem more or less fictitious, the wider formulation of the function of consideration seems more accurate.

NOTES AND QUESTIONS

1. It is obvious that numerous difficulties will arise in the application of these definitions: What is an exchange? Must it be equal in value to the promise? If so, who is to decide the relative values? Must it be contemporaneous with the promise? And so on. These difficulties are raised by the cases in this section. On thinking about them, it is important to remember that many people feel (as a matter of intuition) that a person who makes a serious promise ought to keep it, whether he exacted anything in exchange or not. The result is that courts are usually under some pressure to enforce a "barren" promise by "implying" a requested exchange, or "interpreting" the facts to show that there was one in circumstances where it is quite easy to reach the opposite conclusion.

2. When reading the cases below one should also keep in mind that the requirement of consideration is one that is not shared by the civil law tradition; see e.g. *Civil Code of Québec*, art 1371ff. Does this fact render the doctrine of consideration suspect?

3. For general theoretical discussions of the theory of consideration, see Trebilcock, ch 8; Benson at 153-85; Smith at 215-32; MacDougall, ch 8; M Chen-Wishart, "In Defence of Consideration" (2013) 13 OUCLJ 209.

WHITE (EXECUTOR) V WILLIAM BLUETT
(1853), 23 LJ Ex (NS) 36 (Eng Ex Ct)

This is an action upon a promissory note made payable to John Bluett; the testator: Plea that Bluett was the father of the defendant, and that in his lifetime, the defendant William Bluett complained to his father that he had not received at his hands so much money or so many advantages as the other children and controversies arose between them. Bluett afterward admitted the defendant's complaints were well founded, and it was agreed that the defendant should forever cease to make such complaints, and that in consideration thereof, and in order to do justice to the defendant, and also out of Bluett's natural love and affection toward the defendant, he, Bluett, would discharge the defendant of and from all liability in respect of the promissory note.

Demurrer and joinder.

[Parke B, during the argument, asked: "Is an agreement by a father in consideration that his son will not bore him, a binding contract?"]

POLLOCK CB: The plea is clearly bad. By the argument a principle is pressed to an absurdity, as a bubble blown until it bursts. Looking at the words merely, there is some foundation for the argument, and, following the words only, the conclusion may be arrived at. It is said the son had a right to an equal distribution of his father's property, and did complain to his father because he had not an equal share, and said to him, "I will cease to complain if you will not sue upon this note." Whereupon the father said, "If you will promise me not to complain I will give up the note." If such a plea as this could be supported, the following would be a binding promise: A man might complain that another person used the public highway more than he ought to do, and that the other might say, "Do not complain, and I will give you £5." It is ridiculous to suppose that such promises could be binding. So, if the holder of a bill of exchange were suing the acceptor, and the acceptor were to complain that the holder had treated him hardly, or that the bill ought never to have been circulated, and the holder were to say, "Now if you will not make any more complaints I will not sue you." Such a promise would be like that now set up. In reality, there was no consideration whatever. The son had no right to complain, for the father might make what distribution of his property he liked; and the son's abstaining from doing what he had no right to do can be no consideration.

Judgment for the plaintiff.

QUESTIONS

1. In the sentence beginning "The son had no right to complain," what does the word "right" mean? Is Pollock CB saying that the son could not succeed in an action against his father, or his father's estate, for a share of that estate; or is he saying that the son was not entitled to annoy his father with his complaints? If the word "right" involves this ambiguity, would it not be better to find two words instead of one? Try "claim" for the first and "privilege" for the second. Could giving up a privilege at the request of the promisor constitute consideration?

2. Would a promise by the son to be happy be a valid consideration? If not, could *White* be explained on this basis? For a discussion, see Benson at 155-56.

3. Can a promise to accept a gift be consideration for a promise to give a gift? Consider this question in the light of *Thorp v Thorp*, below.

4. Could *White* be explained on the basis that the promise was made under duress or that the parties lacked the intent to enter legal relations? See Smith at 226-27; MacDougall at 106-7.

HAMER V SIDWAY
27 NR 256 (NYCA (2d) 1891)

[At a family celebration, Storey Sr. promised his nephew, Storey Jr., that if the young man would refrain from drinking, using tobacco, swearing, and playing cards until age 21, the uncle would give his nephew $5,000. The promise was made in front of the invited guests. Upon attaining 21, the nephew wrote to his uncle to inform him that the conditions had been fulfilled. The uncle replied by letter that the money had been set aside for the nephew, that he would certainly have it, but that the uncle would hold the money until he considered the young man capable of taking care of it. In a postscript, the uncle wrote that his nephew could consider the money "on interest." The uncle died without having paid the nephew. This claim was brought against the executor of the estate of Storey Sr. by a woman who had acquired the debt from a third party after the nephew had sold his claim to another.]

PARKER J: The defendant contends that the contract was without consideration to support it, and therefore invalid. He asserts that the promisee, by refraining from the use of liquor and tobacco, was not harmed, but benefited; that which he did was best for him to do, independently of his uncle's promise—and insists that it follows that, unless the promisor was benefited, the contract was without consideration—a contention which, if well founded, would seem to leave open for controversy in many cases whether that which the promisee did or omitted to do was in fact of such benefit to him as to leave no consideration to support the enforcement of the promisor's agreement. Such a rule could not be tolerated and is without foundation in the law. The exchequer chamber in 1875 defined "consideration" as follows: "A valuable consideration, in the sense of the law, may consist either in some right, interest, profit, or benefit accruing to the one party, or some forbearance, detriment, loss or responsibility given, suffered, or undertaken by the other." Courts "will not ask whether the thing which forms the consideration does in fact benefit the promisee or a third party, or is of any substantial value to any one. It is enough that something is promised, done, forborne, or suffered by the party to whom the promise is made as consideration for the promise made to him." ...

Now, applying this rule to the facts before us, the promisee used tobacco, occasionally drank liquor, and he had a legal right to do so. That right he abandoned for a period of years upon the strength of the promise of the testator that for such forbearance he would give him $5,000. ... It is sufficient that he restricted his lawful freedom of action within certain prescribed limits upon the faith of his uncle's agreement, and now, having fully performed the conditions imposed, it is of no moment whether such performance actually proved a benefit to the promisor, and the court will not inquire into it; but, were it a proper subject of inquiry, we see nothing in this record that would permit a determination that the uncle was not benefited in a legal sense.

Allegheny College v National Chautauqua County Bank of Jamestown. 246 NY 369 (CA 1927). CARDOZO JA: A classic form of statement identifies consideration with detriment to the promisee sustained by virtue of the promise (*Hamer v. Sidway* ... [above]). So compendious a formula is little more than a half truth. There is need of many a supplementary gloss before the outline can be so filled in as to depict the classic doctrine. "The promise and the consideration must purport to be the motive each for the other, in whole or at least in part. It is not enough that the promise induces the detriment or that the detriment induces the promise if the other half is wanting" (*Wisc. & Mich. Ry. Co. v. Powers*, 191 U.S. 379 ...). If A promises B to make him a gift, consideration may be lacking, though B has renounced other opportunities for betterment in the faith that the promise will be kept. ... As far back as 1881, Judge Holmes in his lectures on the Common Law (page 292), separated the detriment, which is merely a consequence of the promise from the detriment, which is in truth the motive or inducement.

QUESTIONS

1. Compare and contrast *White v Bluett* and *Hamer v Sidway*. In both cases, the person making the promise had died. In which case would you be more certain a promise had actually been made as alleged? Why?

2. Suppose in each case that the deceased's estate had numerous creditors who would not be paid in full. In which of the two cases would it seem fairer to include the claim of the plaintiff with the other creditors? Why?

3. Is the motive inquiry one that is subjective or objective? The issue of motive is also discussed in Section IV, below.

ELEANOR THOMAS V BENJAMIN THOMAS
(1842), 2 QB 851, 114 ER 330

[The defendant was executor with Samuel Thomas (since deceased) of the will of John Thomas, who had intended that his widow, the plaintiff, should have some further protection and orally expressed a wish that she should have the house he lived in, with all its contents, or £100 instead. Shortly after his death his executors attempted to put his wish into effect. A written agreement was executed by the parties reciting this desire and the desire of the executors to fulfill it, and the executors promised "in consideration of such desire and of the premises" to convey the house to the widow for life or as long as she continued unmarried, "provided nevertheless, and it is hereby further agreed and declared, that the said Eleanor Thomas ... shall ... at all times during which she shall have possession of the said dwelling house ... pay to the ... executors ... the sum of £1 yearly towards the ground rent ... and shall ... keep the said ... house ... in good ... repair." The plaintiff was left in possession for some time, but the defendant, after the death of the co-executor, refused to execute a conveyance and ejected the plaintiff. The plaintiff sued on the agreement. Verdict for plaintiff. A rule nisi was obtained to enter a non suit.]

LORD DENMAN CJ: There is nothing in this case but a great deal of ingenuity, and a little wilful blindness to the actual terms of the instrument itself. There was nothing whatever to show that the ground-rent was payable to a superior landlord; and the stipulation for the payment of it is not a mere proviso, but an express agreement. (His Lordship here read the proviso.) This is in terms an express agreement, and shows a sufficient legal consideration quite independent of the moral feeling which disposed the executors to enter into such a contract. Mr. Williams' definition of consideration is too large: the word *causa* in the passage referred to means one which confers what the law considers a benefit to the party. Then the obligation to repair is one which might impose charges heavier than the value of the life estate.

PATTESON J: It would be giving to *causa* too large a construction if we were to adopt the view urged for the [plaintiff]; it would be confounding consideration with motive. Motive is not the same thing with consideration. Consideration means something which is of some value in the eye of the law, moving from the plaintiff: it may be some detriment to the plaintiff, or some benefit to the defendant; but at all events it must be moving from the plaintiff. Now that which is suggested as the consideration here—a pious respect for the wishes of the testator—does not in any way move from the plaintiff: it moves from the testator; therefore, legally speaking, it forms no part of the consideration. Then it is said that, if that be so, there is no consideration at all, it is a mere voluntary gift: but when we look at the agreement we find that this is not a mere proviso that the donee shall take the gift with the burthens; but it is an express agreement to pay what seems to be a fresh apportionment of the ground-rent, and which is made payable not to a superior landlord but to the executors. So that this rent is clearly not something incident to the assignment of the house; for in that case, instead of being payable to the executors; it would be payable to the landlord. Then as to the repairs: these houses may very possibly be held under a lease containing covenants to repair, but we know nothing about it; for anything that appears, the liability to repair is created by this instrument. The proviso certainly struck me at first as Mr. Williams [one of counsel] put it, that the rent and repairs were merely attached to the gift of the donors; and, had the instrument been executed by the donors only; there might have been some ground for that construction; but the fact is not so. Then it is suggested that this would be held to be a mere voluntary conveyance as against a subsequent purchaser for value: possibly that might be so: but suppose it would: the plaintiff contracts to take it, and does take it, whatever it is, for better for worse: perhaps a bona fide purchase for a valuable consideration might override it, but that cannot be helped.

Rule discharged.

[The opinion of Coleridge J is omitted.]

NOTES AND QUESTIONS

1. "Nominal consideration" means some practically valueless item or trivial amount of money that bears no relation to the value of the promise for which it is exchanged—for example, a valuable option to purchase property given for $1. Should promises for which nominal consideration has been given be enforced? Why or why not? See Waddams at paras 178-81; McCamus at 226-30; MacDougall at 105-6; and Benson at 161.

2. Should it matter if Mr. Thomas had died owing large sums of money to creditors?

3. Has Eleanor Thomas expressly or impliedly promised to take possession or keep possession? Is there mutuality of obligation here? If Eleanor had no right to possession, did she, by remaining in possession, incur a detriment such that a court would find that she had provided good consideration?

4. Is a contract to "sell" $100 in return for 1¢ binding? See *Schnell v Nell*, 17 Ind 29 (US Sup Ct 1861).

G. MUTUAL PROMISES

Thorp v Thorp. (1702), 12 Mod 455, 88 ER 1448, 1450 (KB). HOLT CJ: [W]here the doing of a thing will be a good consideration, a promise to do that thing will be so too.

Harrison v Cage. (1698), 5 Mod 411, 87 ER 736 (KB). A case of mutual promises to marry, breach by the woman. Action on the case. HOLT CJ: Why should not a woman be bound by her promise as well as a man is bound by his? Either all is *nudum pactum*, or else the one promise is as good as the other. You agree a woman shall have an action; now what is the consideration of a man's promise? Why, it is the woman's. Then why should not his promise be a good consideration for her promise as much as her promise is a good consideration for his? There is the same parity of reason in the one case as there is in the other, and the consideration is mutual. TURTON J: This action is grounded on mutual promises.

Nichols v Raynbred. (1615), Hobart 88, 80 ER 88 (KB). [T]he promises must be at one instant, for else they will be both *nuda pacta*.

NOTES

1. The ease with which an 18th-century judge could hold the exchange of a promise as good consideration for a promise has not been characteristic of later centuries, notably the latter half of the 19th and the first half of the 20th. Pollock, for example, in his *Contracts* (13th ed at 144), inclines to the view that an exchange of promises cannot be logically explained in terms of benefit and detriment. This rule, "the most important for the business of life," has "no conclusive reason other than the convenience of so holding." Unless the promise given in exchange is binding, how has the promisee suffered a legal detriment, or changed his position at the request of the promisor? It seems rather unconvincing to argue that the promisee is privileged to utter words or not, as he pleases, and that he gives up this privilege, because there is no reason to think that the promisor requests such an utterance. He requests a binding promise—that is, a legal thing—not a mere physical noise. On the other hand, if the promise is considered binding because of the exchanged promise, and the exchanged promise is binding because it, in turn, is given in consideration of the first promise, the circular argument is objectionable. One simple escape from this dilemma is to accept the existence of a bargain as a sufficient reason for enforcement and to include within the concept of bargain an executory exchange.

2. For different answers to Pollock's conundrum and the conceptual difficulty posed by *Nichols*, see Benson at 160-61, 173-74; B Coote, "The Essence of Contract (Part II)" (1988-89) 1 JCL 183 at 191-93.

GREAT NORTHERN RAILWAY COMPANY V WITHAM
(1873), LR 9 CP 16

In October, 1871, the plaintiffs advertised for tenders for the supply of goods (amongst other things iron) to be delivered at their station at Doncaster, according to a certain specification. The Defendant sent in a tender as follows:

> I, the undersigned, hereby undertake to supply the Great Northern Railway Company, for twelve months from the 1st of November, 1871, to 31st of October, 1872, with such quantities of each or any of the several articles named in the attached specification as the company's storekeeper may order from time to time, at the price set opposite each article respectively, and agree to abide by the conditions stated on the other side.
>
> (Signed) Samuel Witham.

The tender was accepted and several orders for iron were given by the company, which were from time to time duly executed by the defendant: but ultimately the defendant refused to supply any more, whereupon this action was brought.

A verdict having been found for the plaintiffs, Digby Seymour, Q.C., moved to enter a nonsuit, on the ground that the contract was void for want of mutuality. He contended that, as the company did not bind themselves to take any iron whatever from the defendant, his promise to supply them with iron was a promise without consideration. ...

BRETT J: The company advertised for tenders for the supply of stores such as they might think fit to order, for one year. The defendant made a tender offering to supply them for that period at certain fixed prices; and the company accepted his tender. If there were no other objection, the contract between the parties would be found in the tender and the letter accepting it. This action is brought for the defendant's refusal to deliver goods ordered by the company; and the objection to the plaintiff's right to recover is, that the contract is unilateral. I do not, however, understand what objection that is to a contract. Many contracts are obnoxious to the same complaint. If I say to another, "If you will go to York, I will give you £100" that is in a certain sense a unilateral contract. He has not promised to go to York; but if he goes it cannot be doubted that he will be entitled to receive the £100. His going to York at my request is a sufficient consideration for my promise. So, if one says to another, "If you will give me an order for iron, or other goods, I will supply it at a given price": if the order is given, there is a complete contract which the seller is bound to perform. There is in such a case ample consideration for the promise. So, here, the company having given the defendant an order at his request, his acceptance of the order would bind them. If any authority could have been found to sustain Mr. Seymour's contention, I should have considered that a rule ought to be granted. But none has been cited. *Burton v. Great Northern Railway Company*, 9 Ex. 507, is not at all to the purpose. This is matter of every day's practice; and I think it would be wrong to countenance the notion that a man who tenders for the supply of goods in this way is not bound to deliver them when an order is given. I agree that this judgment does not decide the question whether the defendant might have absolved himself from the further performance of the contract by giving notice.

Rule refused.

[The concurring opinions of Keating and Grove JJ are omitted.]

NOTES AND QUESTIONS

1. With his expression "unilateral contract" does Brett J refer to the same situation that Digby Seymour, QC does with his expression "want of mutuality"? Did the court find a contract in this case? Was it unilateral or bilateral? What do these expressions mean? How do you "absolve yourself" from performance of a contract by giving notice if the contract itself does not provide for notice or notice cannot reasonably be implied? Under the contract found by

the court, does the railway have to buy any iron? Is it free to buy iron from anybody else if it chooses? Unilateral contracts are discussed in Section IV, below.

2. Speaking of this case, Professor Corbin, in "The Effect of Options on Consideration" (1925) 34 Yale LJ 571, said: "In cases like this it may be reasonably argued that there was no contract because of lack of acceptance in accordance with the offer rather than for lack of consideration; orders were asked of the offeree and not illusory promises. Often however, the offeror does not so understand his own offer and makes no such contention; lack of consideration is a good defense. If an order is given before the offer is withdrawn, a contract is made." Do you agree? What are the terms of the "contract" that is so made?

3. By "illusory promise" Professor Corbin means a "promise that is not a promise. ... [T]he chief feature of contract law is that by an expression of his will today the promisor limits his freedom of voluntary choice in the future. ... To fall within this field, therefore, a promise must in its terms express a willingness to effect this limitation on freedom of choice. ... [An] illusory promise is neither enforceable against the one making it, nor is it operative as a consideration for a return promise."

4. Should a promise to sell the *entire output* of the promisor's plant be regarded as equally illusory? What about a promise to buy all the promisor's *needs* in a certain line from the promisee? Will the analysis differ if there are promises not to sell the *output* to third persons, or to buy *needs* from third persons?

Percival v London Etc Committee. (1918), 87 LJKB 677. ATKIN J: One knows that these tenders are very often in a form under which the purchasing body is not bound to give the tenderer any order at all; in other words, the contractor offers to supply goods at a price, and if the purchasing body chooses to give him an order for goods during the stipulated time, then he is under an obligation to supply the goods in accordance with the order; but apart from that nobody is bound.

In Re The Gloucester Municipal Election Petition. [1901] 1 KB 693. A tender to supply goods that the council might want in a certain period, when accepted was held to result in a contract. DARLING J: There is a good obligation to order from the respondent such of the goods included in his tender as the council might require ... for I do not think that the council would have been justified in treating the respondent's tender as a mere price list, and ordering the goods which they required from any one whom they might choose. ... There was a contract, because there was an obligation on both sides.

Greenberg v Lake Simcoe Ice Supply Co. (1917), 39 OLR 32 (H Ct J). The Lake Simcoe Company, a dealer in coal, confirmed an arrangement with Greenberg, a retailer of coal, in these words: "We beg to confirm our quotation on coal taken by you at our Dupont or Florence street yards, namely, ... $6.75 per ton for all coal taken from September 1st to April 30, 1917." No quantity of coal was agreed to be supplied and there was no undertaking to purchase any coal. In fact, about 40 tons were supplied before the company sought to put aside the arrangement because of suspected dishonest dealings. Greenberg sued for damages. Held, no contract. LATCHFORD J: The plaintiff was not under the slightest obligation to purchase a single ton of coal from the defendants. There was no consideration from him to the defendants, and no acceptance ... except in so far as the plaintiff from time to time prior to the revelation of his fraud, applied for and was supplied with coal. Until each such transaction was completed, there was no mutuality of obligation.

TOBIAS V DICK AND T EATON CO
[1937] 4 DLR 546 (Man KB)

DYSART J: The plaintiff sues John Dick and the T. Eaton Co. Ltd.,—the one for a breach of an alleged contract, and the other for interfering with his rights under that contract. He also charges both defendants with conspiracy, and asks for an injunction and damages.

The "contract" in question was originally drawn up by the plaintiff Tobias himself, who, by trickery, induced the defendant to sign it in its present changed form; but this defendant has by conduct since confirmed it, and cannot repudiate it. It reads thus—

Morden, Manitoba, April th., 1935.

AGREEMENT

This is to confirm that A.M. Tobias of Morden, Manitoba has the exclusive selling agency, to sell and organize territory and appoint his own agents for the John Dick Crushers, from the above date, April th., 1935 to December 31st, 1937, for all Manitoba, Saskatchewan and Alberta.

John Dick reserves the right to sell in the district and tributary of Emerson, Manitoba, and for a radius of 30 miles East, West, North and South of the Town of Emerson, Manitoba.

The cost of the grain grinders to A.M. Tobias is $43.00 F.O.B. Emerson. ...

At no time must there be more than five machines unpaid for, and all machines must be paid for in cash, unless with the consent of John Dick.

Witness H. Dueck   A.M. Tobias
                                                          John E. Dick.

The parties to this litigation assumed to the very last day of the trial that this document constituted a contract binding on both parties thereto. In my opinion, it is not a contract at all. It has no mutuality—it is entirely a one-sided arrangement. By it, Tobias gets the exclusive right "to sell" Dick's machines within a stated territory for a stated time, but does not promise to sell any of the machines. The term "to sell" by implication gives Tobias the right first to *buy*, in order that he may then sell. In essence therefore, the document gives him the exclusive right to *buy* Dick's entire output of machines. This construction finds confirmation in the later provisions of the document fixing the price and terms upon which Tobias may buy the machines from Dick.

These provisions taken together clearly indicate that there is no control left in Dick over the machines, nor over Tobias' dealings in respect of the machines after Tobias has bought them; nor over the appointment of agents or the organization of a selling staff. Tobias' profits are not based on commission, but he is free to resell the machines at his own price and terms, and through his own appointed agents. Clearly, therefore, the agreement, notwithstanding an express declaration to that effect, does not create an agency.

The indirect promise by Dick "to sell" to Tobias is not supported by any consideration moving from Tobias, and so is not binding upon Dick. There is therefore no contract. The document evidences nothing more than an offer from Dick open for a given time. This offer of course remains open for acceptance until withdrawn, and has never been formally withdrawn. It is of such a nature, having regard to Dick's method of manufacturing, that it could be accepted in part, from time to time. And so far as it was accepted, it was accepted by instalments.

Tobias ordered a number of machines on two separate occasions, took delivery of them and paid for them. Some of these he is unable to sell, but he does not pretend that he can return them to Dick and have the price refunded, as he might do if he were an agent.

Apart from these two partial acceptances, Tobias has not requested any more machines, and there has therefore been no refusal by Dick to live up to his offer. Dick was only too anxious to sell more machines to Tobias, and repeatedly urged Tobias to take those that were already completed. Only after Dick had lost all hope of disposing of his machines to Tobias did he decide to ignore his "agreement" altogether and sell his machines elsewhere.

To sum up, there was no contract between these two parties, and therefore no breach. The plaintiff's action against Dick must be dismissed with costs. ...

The plaintiff's action against the T. Eaton Co. will also be dismissed with costs. ...

Action dismissed.

WOOD V LUCY, LADY DUFF-GORDON
118 NE 214 (NYCA 1917)

CARDOZO J: The defendant styles herself "a creator of fashions." Her favour helps a sale. Manufacturers of dresses, millinery, and like articles are glad to pay for a certificate of her approval. The things which she designs, fabrics, parasols, and what not, have a new value in the public mind when issued in her name. She employed the plaintiff to help her to turn this vogue into money. He was to have the exclusive right, subject always to her approval, to place her endorsements on the designs of others. He was also to have the exclusive right to place her own designs on sale, or to license others to market them. In return she was to have one-half of "all profits and revenues" derived from any contracts he might make. The exclusive right was to last at least one year from April 1, 1915, and thereafter from year to year unless terminated by notice of 90 days. The plaintiff says that he kept the contract on his part, and that the defendant broke it. She placed her endorsement on fabrics, dresses, and millinery without his knowledge, and withheld the profits. He sues her for the damages and the case comes here on demurrer.

The agreement of employment is signed by both parties. It has a wealth of recitals. The defendant insists, however, that it lacks the elements of a contract. She says that the plaintiff does not bind himself to anything. It is true that he does not promise in so many words that he will use reasonable efforts to place the defendant's designs. We think, however, that such a promise is fairly to be implied. The law has outgrown its primitive stage of formalism when the precise word was the sovereign talisman, and every slip was fatal. It takes a broader view to day. A promise may be lacking and yet the whole writing may be "instinct with an obligation," imperfectly expressed. ...

The implication is that the plaintiff's business organization will be used for the purpose for which it is adapted. But the terms of the defendant's compensation are even more significant. Her sole compensation for the grant of an exclusive agency is to be one-half of all the profits resulting from the plaintiff's efforts. Unless he gave his efforts, she could never get anything. Without an implied promise, the transaction cannot have such business "efficacy, as both parties must have intended that at all events it should have." Bowen, L.J. in the *Moorcock*, 14 P.D. 64, 68. But the contract does not stop there. The plaintiff goes on to promise that he will account monthly for all moneys received by him, and that he will take out all such patents and copy-rights and trade-marks as may in his judgment be necessary to protect the rights and articles affected by the agreement. It is true, of course, as the appellate Division has said, that if he was under no duty to try to market designs or to place certificates of endorsement, his promise to account for profits or take out copyrights would be valueless. But in determining the intention of the parties the promise has a value. It helps to enforce the conclusion that the plaintiff had some duties. His promise to pay the defendant one-half of the profits and revenues resulting from the exclusive agency and to render accounts monthly was a promise to use reasonable efforts to bring profits and revenues into existence.

QUESTIONS AND PROBLEMS

1. Why do business people enter into the kinds of agreements found in cases such as *Witham*, *Tobias*, and *Wood*?

2. What features of *Wood* persuaded the court that there was, at least, an implicit obliga-tion on Wood?

3. If Lady Duff-Gordon were suing Wood because he failed to bring any profits and rev-enues into existence, what standard of effort on Wood's part would she have to prove? How would the damages be measured? If Wood were also under the same "contract" with another equally prominent person, how would he have to divide his efforts? Is the business incentive on Wood's part enough to justify holding Lady Duff-Gordon to her promise? Could we say that Lady Duff-Gordon exchanged her promise for the chance, given her by Wood, that he would likely bring into existence profits and revenues?

4. A signs a document that gives B "sole and exclusive right to act as my agent in the sale of my home for 30 days from today's date." A promises to pay B a commission of 5 percent of the selling price upon B finding a purchaser. After 15 days, A is very dissatisfied with the service given her by B. She purports to cancel the agreement. Can she do so? See also Waddams at paras 124-25; McCamus at 224-26.

H. PRE-EXISTING DUTY

HARRIS V WATSON
(1791), Peake 102, 170 ER 94 (KB)

In this case the declaration stated that the plaintiff being a seaman on board the ship "Alexander" of which the defendant was master and commander, and which was bound on a voyage to Lisbon: whilst the ship was on her voyage, the defendant, in consideration that the plaintiff would perform some extra work, in navigating the ship, promised to pay him five guineas over and above his common wages. There were other counts for work and labour, & c.

The plaintiff proved that the ship being in danger, the defendant, to induce the seamen to exert themselves, made the promise stated in the first count.

LORD KENYON: If this action was to be supported, it would materially affect the navi-gation of this kingdom. It has been long since determined that when the freight is lost, the wages are also lost. This rule was founded on a principle of policy, for if sailors were in all events to have their wages, and in times of danger entitled to insist on an extra charge on such a promise as this, they would in many cases suffer a ship to sink, unless the captain would pay any extravagant demand they might think proper to make. The plaintiff was nonsuited.

STILK V MYRICK
(1809), 2 Camp 317, 170 ER 1168

This was an action for a seaman's wages, on a voyage from London to the Baltic and back.

By the ship's articles, executed before the commencement of the voyage, the plaintiff was to be paid at the rate of £5 a month; and the principal question in the cause was whether he was entitled to a higher rate of wages. In the course of the voyage two of the seamen deserted; and the captain having in vain attempted to supply their places at Cronstadt, there entered into an agreement with the rest of the crew, that they should have the wages of the two who had deserted equally divided among them, if he could not procure two other hands at Gottenburgh. This was found impossible; and the ship was worked back to London by the plaintiff and eight more of the original crew, with whom the agreement had been made at Cronstadt.

LORD ELLENBOROUGH: I think *Harris v. Watson* [the preceding case] was rightly decided; but I doubt whether the ground of public policy, upon which Lord Kenyon is stated to have proceeded, be the true principle on which the decision is to be supported. Here, I say the agreement is void for want of consideration. There was no consideration for the ulterior pay promised to the mariners who remained with the ship. Before they sailed from London they had undertaken to do all they could under all the emergencies of the voyage. They had sold all their services till the voyage should be completed. If they had been at liberty to quit the vessel at Cronstadt, the case would have been quite different; or if the captain had capriciously discharged the two men who were wanting, the others might not have been compellable to take the whole duty upon themselves, and their agreeing to do so might have been a sufficient consideration for the promise of an advance of wages. But the desertion of a part of the crew is to be considered an emergency of the voyage as much as their death; and these who remain are bound by the terms of their original contract to exert themselves to the utmost to bring the ship in safety to her destined port. Therefore, without looking to the policy of this agreement, I think it is void for want of consideration, and that the plaintiff can only recover at the rate of £5 a month.

Verdict accordingly.

Hartley v Ponsonby. (1857), 7 El & Bl 872, 119 ER 1471. The crew of a ship was so reduced in number that "for the ship to go to sea with so few hands was dangerous to life. If so, it was not incumbent on the plaintiff to perform the work; and he was in the condition of a free man." It was held there was consideration for the contract to pay him an additional sum to work the ship home.

New Zealand Shipping Co Ltd v AM Satterthwaite & Co Ltd (The Eurymedon). [1975] AC 154. LORD WILBERFORCE: An agreement to do an act which the promisor is under an existing obligation to a third party to do, may quite well amount to valid consideration ... the promisee obtains the benefit of a direct obligation ... . This proposition is illustrated and supported by *Scotson v. Pegg* (1861), 6 H. & N. 295 which their Lordships consider to be good law.

NOTES AND QUESTIONS

1. Suppose the captain in *Stilk v Myrick* had requested the seamen to give him a pepper-corn (if they had one with them). Suppose he had put his promise in writing and under seal. Would the result have been different?

2. A substantially different report of *Stilk v Myrick* is found at (1809), 6 Esp 129, 170 ER 851. In that report, Lord Ellenborough CJ was quoted as saying that "he recognised the principle of the case of *Harris v Watson* as founded on just and proper policy." The word "consideration" was not mentioned. The reporter of this second version was Espinasse, who was also counsel for the plaintiff. Espinasse, however, was not held in high esteem by the judiciary as an accurate reporter and hence the version excerpted above has traditionally been regarded as more reliable.

HOLMES, *The Common Law* (1881)

The only universal consequence of a legally binding promise is that the law makes the promisor pay damages if the promised event does not come to pass. In every case it leaves him free from interference until the time for fulfilment has gone by, and therefore free to break his contract if he chooses. ...

If, when a man promised to labour for another, the law made him do it, his relation to his promise might be called a servitude *ad hoc* with some truth. But that is what the law never does. It never interferes until a promise has been broken, and therefore cannot possibly be performed according to its tenor. It is true that in some instances equity does what is called compelling specific performance. But, in the first place, I am speaking of the common law, and in the next, this only means that equity compels the performance of certain elements of the total promise which are still capable of performance.

NOTES AND QUESTIONS

1. Holmes is suggesting that the duty of the promisor under a contract is *either* to perform his contract *or* to pay damages. It is then arguable that because the promisor has his choice—that is, this privilege of performing one duty or the other—by giving up this privilege and agreeing to perform the contract rather than pay damages he has given up a valuable legal right, called in technical terms a *privilege*. And that, of course, is a valid exchange constituting a legal detriment. On this basis *Stilk v Myrick* must be wrongly decided, but *Harris v Watson* may be right.

2. Is Holmes's view of the law consistent with the modern remedy of specific performance discussed in Chapter 2 or with the existence of the tort of inducing breach of contract? What good is a theory of contract damages that cannot account for these doctrinal facts?

3. Does Holmes's reasoning not lead to an absurdity? For example, if every promise allows the promisor a "perform or pay" privilege, why is the second promise to actually perform any different?

4. What difficulties might we have with the rule that giving up your "right" to break a contract is good consideration? Does one have a right to breach a contract? Consider the following.

Coulls v Bagot's Executor and Trustee Co Ltd (1967), 119 CLR 460. WINDEYER J: It is ... a faulty analysis of legal obligations to say that the law treats a promisor as having a right to elect either to perform his promise or to pay damages. Rather ... the promisee has "a legal right to the performance of the contract."

SMITH V DAWSON
(1923), 53 OLR 615 (CA)

The plaintiffs agreed with the defendant to build her a house for $6,464. When the house was nearly finished, a fire took place in it doing considerable damage.

The defendant effected insurance on the house as it was being built. The plaintiffs effected no insurance. After the fire the defendant asked the plaintiffs to go ahead and complete the house. The plaintiffs said they would if the defendant promised to pay them the insurance monies.

RIDDELL J (Logie J concurring): ... The situation then seems quite clear—the plaintiffs, learning that the defendant had received some insurance money on the house, objected to go on without some kind of assurance that they were to get the insurance money—the defendant demurred, as she had lost considerably by the destruction of her furniture, but finally said, "All right, go ahead and do the work." If this constituted a contract at all, it was that she would give them the insurance money which she had received, if they would go ahead and do the work they were already under a legal obligation to do.

In some of the United States a doctrine has been laid down that (at least in building contracts) the contractor has the option either to complete his contract or to abandon it and pay damages. These Courts have accordingly held that the abandonment by the contractor of his option to abandon is sufficient consideration for a promise to pay an extra amount.

The Courts of Illinois, Indiana, and Massachusetts seem to have adopted this rule. ... But such a course is to allow a contractor to take advantage of his own wrong, and other American Courts reprobate it: 9 *Corpus Juris*, 720; 13 *Corpus Juris*, 354, sec. 210, and cases cited in notes.

This is not and never was law in Ontario, as it is not and never was law in England. It has long been text-book law that "not the promise or the actual performance of something which the promisee is legally bound to perform" is a consideration for a promise.

Halsbury's *Laws of England*, 385, para. 798: "the performance of an existing contract by one of the parties is no consideration for a new promise by the other party": *Leake on Contracts*, 7th ed., p. 455, and cases cited.

I am of the opinion that the promise (if there was one) to pay for the work to be done was not binding for want of consideration, and would allow the appeal with costs here and below. If there be any difficulty in moulding the judgment, one of us may be spoken to.

[The judgments of Latchford and Middleton JJ are omitted.]

England v Davidson. (1840), 11 Ad & E 856, 113 ER 640. The defendant offered a reward of £50 to anyone giving information leading to the conviction of persons who broke into his house. The plaintiff, a police constable on duty in the area in which the defendant's house was located, did give such information and claimed the reward. The defendant paid him five guineas but failed to pay the balance. In an action to recover the balance it was objected that the plaintiff had given no consideration because as a police constable he was bound to give such information anyway. Judgment for the plaintiff. LORD DENMAN CJ: I think there may be services which the constable is not bound to render and which he may therefore make the ground of a contract. We should not hold a contract to be against the policy of the law, unless the grounds for so deciding were very clear.

Reif v Page. 55 Wisc 496 (1882). A husband offered a reward to anyone who would rescue his wife, dead or alive, from a burning building. A fireman who took out the dead body was held entitled to recover. The court said that a fireman was not legally bound to risk his life in effecting a rescue.

Pao On v Lau Yiu Long. [1980] AC 614 (PC). LORD SCARMAN: When one turns to consider cases where a pre-existing duty imposed by law is alleged to be valid consideration for a promise, one finds cases in which public policy has been held to invalidate the consideration. A promise to pay a sheriff in consideration of his performing his legal duty, a promise to pay for discharge from illegal arrest, are to be found in the books as promises which the law will not enforce .... Yet such cases are also explicable upon the ground that a person who promises to perform, or performs, a duty imposed by law provides no consideration. In cases where the discharge of a duty imposed by law has been treated as valid consideration, the courts have usually (but not invariably) found an act over and above, but consistent with, the duty imposed by law.

NOTES AND QUESTIONS

1. Counsel for the defendant in *Davidson* argued that the contract was against public policy. To what policy is it obnoxious? Do rewards operate to deflect a policeman's attention from his regular duties? Should this fact, if it is a fact, justify the promisor's failure to carry out his promise? Should a court concern itself with such a question, or should it be left to the legislator or chief of police? For a discussion, see MacDougall at 109-10.

2. Could a different conclusion in these cases have been reached on the basis of motive? See the reward cases in Section IV, below.

3. If the pre-existing duty rule is based on policy, is the policy at play in the public service cases the same as that involved when business people make adjustments to their contractual relationships? What would motivate business people to agree to pay a higher price for work already contracted for at a lower price? Consider the following cases.

RAGGOW V SCOUGALL AND CO
(1915), 31 TLR 564 (Div Ct)

This was an appeal by the defendants, Messrs. Scougall and Co., who were a firm of mantle-makers, from a decision of Judge Rentoul in the City of London Court, by which plaintiff, a mantle designer, recovered judgment for £58.

In August, 1913, the plaintiff by an agreement in writing agreed to become the defendants' designer for two years at a certain salary. It was provided that if the business should be discontinued during the period the agreement should cease to be of any effect. When the war broke out many customers cancelled orders which they had given to the firm, and the defendants had to consider whether they should close the business altogether. They called their employees together, and most of them agreed to a reduction of wages during the war if the defendants would continue the business. The plaintiff entered into a new agreement in writing, in which he, like other employees of the firm, agreed to accept a smaller salary for the duration of the war, provided that when the war was over the terms of the old agreement should be revived. He went on with his work and accepted the new salary until February last, when the defendants received a solicitor's letter claiming payment in full at the rate fixed in the old agreement; and as they refused to pay the excess this action was brought.

In the Court below judgment was given for the plaintiff on the ground that no consideration had been shown for the new agreement to accept a reduced payment. ...

MR. JUSTICE DARLING said that the appeal must be allowed. It was clear from the provision in the new agreement that the terms of the old one should be reviewed when the war came to an end and that until the war ended the old agreement was dead. The parties had in fact torn up the old agreement and made a new one by mutual consent. They could have done it by recitals setting out the existence and rescission of the old agreement, but they had adopted a shorter course. The new agreement was an agreement contemplating employment on certain terms while the war lasted, and on certain other terms, which could be ascertained by reference to the older document, after the war had ended. The point, therefore, as to want of consideration failed and the appeal succeeded. He was the more glad to be able to arrive at this conclusion on the law, for it was evident that the plaintiff was trying to do a very dishonest thing.

[Coleridge J agreed.]

QUESTION

Could the court have found consideration in this case? What might distinguish this case from *Smith v Dawson*, in which the plaintiff argued he had given up his "right" to break the contract?

GILBERT STEEL LTD V UNIVERSITY CONSTRUCTION LTD
(1976), 67 DLR (3d) 606 (Ont CA)

WILSON JA: This is an appeal from the order of Mr. Justice Pennell dismissing the plaintiff's action for damages for breach of an oral agreement for the supply of fabricated steel bars to be incorporated into apartment buildings being constructed by the defendant. The case raises some fundamental principles of contract law.

The circumstances giving rise to the action are as follows. On September 4, 1968, the plaintiff entered into a written contract to deliver to the defendant fabricated steel for apartment buildings to be erected at three separate sites referred to in the contract as the "Flavin, Tectate and University projects." The price fixed by that contract was $153 per ton for "Hard grade" and $159 per ton for "Grade 60,000." Deliveries for the Flavin and Tectate projects were completed in August, 1969, and October, 1969, respectively, and paid for at the agreed-upon prices.

Two apartment buildings calling for the supply of 3,000 tons of fabricated steel were to be erected at the University site. However, prior to the defendant's notifying the plaintiff of its intention to commence construction on the first of these two buildings, the owners of the steel mill announced an increase in the price of unfabricated steel. They also gave warning of a further increase to come. The plaintiff approached the defendant about a new contract for the University project and a written contract dated October 22, 1969, was entered into for the supply of fabricated steel for the first building. The new price was $156 per ton for "Hard grade" and $165 per ton for "Grade 60,000." In fact this increase in price did not reflect the full amount of the initial increase announced by the mill owners.

On March 1, 1970, while the building under construction was still far from completion, the mill owners announced the second increase in price and a further discussion took place between John Gilbert and his brother Harry representing the plaintiff and Mendel Tenenbaum and Hersz Tenenbaum representing the defendant with respect to the price to be paid for the steel required to complete the first building. It is this discussion which the plaintiff alleges resulted in a binding oral agreement that the defendant would pay $166 per ton for "Hard grade" and $178 per ton for "Grade 60,000." Although the plaintiff submitted to the defendant a written contract embodying these revised prices following their meeting, the contract was not executed. It contained, in addition to the increased prices, two new clauses which the trial Judge found had not been the subject of any discussion with the defendant but were unilaterally imported into the document by the plaintiff. The trial Judge also found, however, that the defendant agreed at the meeting to pay the increased price.

From March 12, 1970, until the completion of the first building the defendant accepted deliveries of the steel against invoices which reflected the revised prices but, in making payments on account, it remitted cheques in rounded amounts which at the date of the issuance of the writ resulted in a balance owing to the plaintiff in accordance with the invoices.

Having found on the evidence that the defendant had orally agreed to pay the increased prices, the legal issue confronting Mr. Justice Pennell was whether that agreement was legally binding upon the defendant or whether it failed for want of consideration and that the plaintiff was already obliged before the alleged oral agreement was entered into to deliver the steel at the original prices agreed to in the written contract of October 22, 1969. Where then was the *quid pro quo* for the defendant's promise to pay more?

Counsel for the plaintiff sought to supply this omission from the evidence of Hersz Tenenbaum who, during the course of discussions which took place in September, 1970, with a view to a contract for the supply of steel for the second building at the University site, asked whether the plaintiff would give him "a good price" on steel for this building. Plaintiff's counsel argued that the promise of a good price on the second building was the consideration the defendant received for agreeing to pay the increased price on the first. The trial Judge rejected this submission and found the oral agreement unenforceable for want of consideration. In the course of his reasons for judgment the trial Judge adverted briefly to an alternate submission made by the Plaintiff's counsel. He said:

> I should, in conclusion, mention a further point which was argued with ingenuity by Mr. Morphy. His contention was that the consideration for the oral agreement was the mutual abandonment of right under the prior agreement in writing. I must say, with respect, that this argument is not without its attraction for me.

On the appeal Mr. Morphy picked up and elaborated upon this submission which had intrigued the trial Judge. In launching his main attack on the trial Judge's finding that the oral agreement was unenforceable for want of consideration, he submitted that the facts of this case evidenced not a purported oral variation of a written contract which failed for want of consideration but an implied rescission of the written contract and the creation of a whole new contract, albeit oral, which was subsequently reneged on by the defendant. The consideration for this new oral agreement, submitted Mr. Morphy, was the mutual agreement to abandon the previous written contract and to assume the obligations under the new oral one. Mr. Morphy submitted to the Court for its consideration two lines of authority, the first line illustrated by the leading case of *Stilk v. Myrick* (1809), 2 Camp. 317, 170 E.R. 1168, in which the subsequent agreement was held to be merely a variation of the earlier agreement and accordingly failed for want of consideration, and the other line illustrated by *Morris v. Baron & Co.*, [1918] A.C. 1, in which the subsequent agreement was held to have rescinded the former one and was therefore supported by the mutual agreement to abandon the old obligations and substitute the new. Mr. Morphy invited us to find that the oral agreement to pay the increased price for steel fell into the second category. There was, he acknowledged, no express rescission of the written contract but price is such a fundamental term of a contract for the supply of goods that the substitution of a new price must connote a new contract and impliedly rescind the old.

It is impossible to accept Mr. Morphy's submission in face of the evidence adduced at the trial. It is clear that the sole reason for the discussions between the parties in March, 1970, concerning the supply of steel to complete the first building at the University site was the increase in the price of steel by the mill owners. No changes other than the change in price were discussed. The trial Judge found that the other two changes sought to be introduced into the written document submitted by the plaintiff to the defendant for signature following the discussions had not even been mentioned at the meeting. Moreover, although repeated references were made at trial by the Gilbert brothers to the fact that the parties had made a "new contract" in March, 1970, it seems fairly clear from the evidence when read as a whole that the "new contract" referred to was the agreement to pay the increased price for the steel, *i.e.*, the agreement which effected the variation of the written contract and not a new contract in the sense of a contract replacing *in toto* the original contract of October 22, 1969.

I am not persuaded that either of the parties intended by their discussions in March, 1970, to rescind their original contract and replace it with a new one. Indeed, it is significant that no such plea was made in the statement of claim which confined itself to an allegation that "it was orally agreed in March 1970 that the prices as set forth in the said contract [that is, of October 22, 1969] would be varied ... ." Accordingly, consideration for the oral agreement is not to be found in a mutual agreement to abandon the earlier written contract and assume the obligations under the new oral one.

Nor can I find consideration in the vague references in the evidence to the possibility that the plaintiff would give the defendant "a good price" on the steel for the second building if it went along with the increased prices on the first. The plaintiff, in my opinion, fell far short of making any commitment in this regard.

Counsel for the appellant put before us as an alternate source of consideration for the agreement to pay the increased price, the increased credit afforded by the plaintiff to the defendant as a result of the increased price. The argument went something like this. Whereas previously the defendant had credit outstanding for 60 days in the amount owed on the original prices, after the oral agreement was made he had credit outstanding for 60 days in the amount owed on the higher prices. Therefore, there was consideration flowing from the promisee and the law does not inquire into its sufficiency. Reliance was placed by counsel on the decision of Chief Justice Meredith in *Kilbuck Coal Co. v. Turner & Robinson* (1915), 7 O.W.N. 673. This case, however, is clearly distinguishable from the case at bar, as Mr. Justice Pennell pointed out in his reasons, on the basis of the *force majeure* clause which had relieved the plaintiff of its obligations under the original contract. In undertaking to supply coal despite the strike the plaintiff was unquestionably providing consideration of real substance in that case. I cannot accept counsel's contention, ingenious as it is, that the increased credit inherent in the increased price constituted consideration flowing from the promisee for the promisor's agreement to pay the increased price.

The final submission put forward by counsel for the appellant was that the defendant, by his conduct in not repudiating the invoices reflecting the increase in price when and as they were received, had in effect acquiesced in such increase and should not subsequently be permitted to repudiate it. There would appear to be two answers to this submission. The first is summed up in the maxim that estoppel can never be used as a sword but only as a shield. A plaintiff cannot found his claim in estoppel. Secondarily, however, it should perhaps be pointed out that in order to found an estoppel the plaintiff must show, not only that the conduct of the defendant was clearly referable to the defendant's having given up its right to insist on the original prices, but also that the plaintiff relied on the defendant's conduct to its detriment. I do not think the plaintiff can discharge either of these burdens on the facts of this case.

In summary, I concur in the findings of the trial Judge that the oral agreement made by the parties in March, 1970, was an agreement to vary the written contract of October 22, 1969, and that it must fail for want of consideration.

WILLIAMS V ROFFEY BROS LTD
[1991] 1 QB 1 (CA)

[The plaintiff was a carpenter employed by the defendant contractor to work on the refurbishing of some flats. The defendant made interim payments on the total contract price of £20,000. After six months, £16,200 had been paid. The plaintiff then experienced financial difficulty due, first, to the fact that the contract price had been too low and, second, to his failure to supervise his workers properly. The defendants were particularly concerned to avoid delays because the main contract contained a penalty clause. They agreed to pay the plaintiff a further £10,300 to be paid as flats were completed. The plaintiff continued working for approximately one and one half months after the agreement, but received only one further payment of £1,500. The plaintiff sued for the remaining contract price and the extra payments agreed to by the defendants. Among other arguments, the defendants argued that the variation of the contract had been made without consideration.]

GLIDEWELL LJ (after reviewing the facts and discussing another issue raised by the defendants): Was there consideration for the defendants' promise made on 9 April 1986 to pay an additional price at the rate of £575 per completed flat?

The judge made the following findings of fact which are relevant on this issue. (i) The subcontract price agreed was too low to enable the plaintiff to operate satisfactorily and at a profit. Mr. Cottrell, the defendants' surveyor, agree that this was so. (ii) Mr. Roffey (managing director of the defendants) was persuaded by Mr. Cottrell that the defendants should pay a bonus to the plaintiff. The figure agreed at the meeting on 9 April 1986 was £10,300.

The judge quoted and accepted the evidence of Mr. Cottrell to the effect that a main contractor who agrees too low a price with a subcontractor is acting contrary to his own interests. He will never get the job finished without paying more money. The judge therefore concluded:

> In my view where the original subcontract price is too low, and the parties subsequently agree that additional moneys shall be paid to the subcontractor, this agreement is in the interests of both parties. This is what happened in the present case, and in my opinion the agreement of 9 April 1986 does not fail for lack of consideration.

In his address to us, Mr. Evans outlined the benefits to his clients, the defendants, which arose from their agreement to pay the additional £10,300 as: (i) seeking to ensure that the plaintiff continued work and did not stop in breach of the subcontract; (ii) avoiding the penalty for delay; and (iii) avoiding the trouble and expense of engaging other people to complete the carpentry work.

However, Mr. Evans submits that, though his clients may have derived, or hoped to derive, practical benefits from their agreement to pay the "bonus," they derived no benefit in law since the plaintiff was promising to do no more than he was already bound to do by his sub-contract, i.e. continue with the carpentry work and complete it on time. Thus there was no consideration for the agreement.

Counsel for the defendants relies on the principle of law which, traditionally, is based on the decision in *Stilk v. Myrick*. That was a decision at first instance of Lord Ellenborough CJ. On a voyage to the Baltic, two seamen deserted. The captain agreed with the rest of the crew that if they worked the ship back to London without the two seamen being replaced, he would divide between them the pay which would have been due to the two deserters. On arrival at London this extra pay was refused and the plaintiff's action to recover his extra pay was dismissed. Counsel for the defendant argued that such an agreement was contrary to public policy, but Lord Ellenborough CJ's judgment (as reported in Campbell's Reports) was based on lack of consideration. ...

It was suggested to us in argument that, since the development of the doctrine of promissory estoppel, it may well be possible for a person to whom a promise has been made, on which he has relied, to make an additional payment for services which he is in any event bound to render under an existing contract or by operation of law, to show that the promisor is estopped from claiming that there was no consideration for his promise. However, the application of the doctrine of promissory estoppel to facts such as those of the present case has not yet been fully developed: see e.g. the judgment of Lloyd J. in *Syros Shipping Co. SA v. Elaghill Trading Co., The Proodos C*, [1981] 3 All E.R. 189 at 191. Moreover, this point was not argued in the court below, nor was it more than adumbrated before us. Interesting though it is, no reliance can in my view be placed on this concept in the present case.

There is, however, another legal concept of relatively recent development which is relevant, namely that of economic duress. Clearly, if a sub-contractor has agreed to undertake work at a fixed price, and before he has completed the work declines to continue with it unless the contractor agrees to pay an increased price, the sub-contractor may be held guilty of securing the contractor's promise by taking unfair advantage of the difficulties he will cause if he does not complete the work. In such a case an agreement to pay an increased price may well be voidable because it was entered into under duress. Thus this concept may provide another answer in law to the question of policy which has troubled the courts since before *Stilk v. Myrick* and no doubt led at the date of that decision to a rigid adherence to the doctrine of consideration.

[After discussion of authorities, Glidewell LJ continued.]

Accordingly ... the present state of the law on this subject can be expressed in the following proposition: (i) if A has entered into a contract with B to do work for, or to supply goods or services to, B in return for payment by B and (ii) at some stage before

A has completely performed his obligations under the contract B has reason to doubt whether A will, or will be able to, complete his side of the bargain and (iii) B thereupon promises A an additional payment in return for A's promise to perform his contractual obligations on time and (iv) as a result of giving his promise B obtains in practice a benefit, or obviates a disbenefit, and (v) B's promise is not given as a result of economic duress or fraud on the part of A, then (vi) the benefit to B is capable of being consideration for B's promise, so that the promise will be legally binding.

As I have said, counsel for the defendants accepts that in the present case by promising to pay an extra £10,300 the defendants secured benefits. There is no finding, and no suggestion, that in this case the promise was given as a result of fraud or duress.

If it be objected that the propositions above contravene the principle in *Stilk v. Myrick* I answer that in my view they do not: they refine and limit the application of that principle, but they leave the principle unscathed, e.g. where B secures no benefit by this promise. It is not in my view surprising that a principle enunciated in relation to the rigours of seafaring life during the Napoleonic wars should be subjected during the succeeding 180 years to a process of refinement and limitation in its application in the present day.

It is therefore my opinion that on his findings of fact in the present case, the judge was entitled to hold, as he did, that the defendants' promise to pay the extra £10,300 was supported by valuable consideration, and thus constituted an enforceable agreement.

[The concurring judgments of Russell and Purchas LJJ have been omitted.]

M. Chen-Wishart, "The Enforceability of Additional Contractual Promises: A Question of Consideration?" (1991) 14 NZULR 270 at 270: Via the concept of 'practical benefit' the court significantly widened the content of consideration with the effect that it is easier to satisfy the requirement that consideration move from the party seeking to enforce the additional promise. ... It is clear that any reluctance to enforce additional promises given after a contract has been agreed to, arises out of a concern that the promisor may have been unfairly pressured into making the additional promise. Since the problem in this context is inherently not about the existence of valuable exchange, the doctrine of consideration is an inappropriate test of enforceability. Tinkering with the definition of what constitutes valuable exchange, whether by the concept of practical benefit or some other concept, does not alter this inherent unsuitability for the task.

NAV CANADA V GREATER FREDERICTON
AIRPORT AUTHORITY INC
2008 NBCA 28, 290 DLR (4th) 405

ROBERTSON JA (for the court):

I. OVERVIEW

[1] Ultimately, this Court must rule on the enforceability of what amounts to a variation to an existing contract or, as it is commonly described, a post-contractual modification to an executory contract. It is a case of first impression that brings into

issue fundamental principles of contract law tied to the articulation and application of the doctrines of consideration and economic duress.

[2] By federal prerogative, the appellant, Nav Canada, has the exclusive right and responsibility to provide aviation services and equipment to the respondent, the Greater Fredericton Airport Authority Inc. Their contractual relationship is governed by the Aviation and Services Facilities Agreement ("ASF Agreement"). The litigation stems from the Airport Authority's decision to extend one of its two runways, at a cost of $6 million, and its request that Nav Canada relocate the instrument landing system situated on the other runway to the one being extended. Part of that system consisted of a navigational aid labeled a "NDB" (a non-directional beacon). Nav Canada concluded that it made better economic sense to replace that navigational aid with another labeled a "DME" (distance measuring equipment). However, a disagreement soon arose as to which of the parties should pay the acquisition cost of $223,000. In a letter to the Airport Authority, Nav Canada refused to make provision in its fiscal budget for the upcoming year for the purchase of the DME, unless the Airport Authority agreed to pay the $223,000. From the outset, the Airport Authority insisted that it was not contractually bound to pay, but capitulated in a letter written "under protest" in order to ensure that the extended runway became operational. On the basis of that letter, Nav Canada installed the necessary equipment. Subsequently, the Airport Authority refused to pay and the parties agreed to arbitrate the matter in accordance with the *Arbitration Act*, S.N.B. 1992, c. A-10.1.

[3] The arbitrator held that Nav Canada possessed the exclusive right under the ASF Agreement to decide whether to replace navigational aids but that there was nothing in that agreement that entitled Nav Canada to claim reimbursement for the cost of acquiring the DME. Hence, according to the arbitrator, the Airport Authority was not contractually obligated to pay for the navigational aid. However, the arbitrator went on to hold that the subsequent exchange of correspondence between the parties gave rise to a separate and binding contract, supported by consideration, and therefore Nav Canada was entitled to recover the acquisition cost on that basis. In reaching that conclusion, the arbitrator rejected the argument that the words "under protest" were sufficient to negate contractual liability.

• • •

IV. THE "CONSIDERATION" ISSUE

[16] The question of whether the arbitrator erred in law in finding that the parties had entered into an enforceable agreement by which the Airport Authority promised to pay for the DME raises the immediate question of whether that promise was supported by consideration. The arbitrator so held but without offering reasons for his conclusion. While I have characterized the Airport Authority's promise to pay for the navigational aid as a variation to an existing contract, Nav Canada disagrees, maintaining that it is an agreement which falls outside the ASF Agreement ... .

• • •

[18] Nav Canada's argument that it was the Airport Authority that elected to replace the old NDB with a new DME is in conflict with the arbitrator's findings of fact: Nav Canada was the party that insisted on installing the DME rather than relocating the old NDB, and Nav Canada had the contractual authority to make that election. Having done so, Nav Canada cannot turn around and argue that it was not obligated to install the navigational aid in accordance with the underlying contract, the ASF Agreement.

[19] I return to the question whether the Airport Authority's subsequent promise to pay for the cost of the navigational aid was supported by "fresh" consideration.

Accepting that the hallmark of every bilateral contract is a consensual bargain (a promise in exchange for a promise), it must be asked whether the party seeking to enforce the post-contractual modification (Nav Canada) had agreed to do more than originally promised (in the ASF agreement) in return for the agreement to modify the contract. It is a well-established feature of the traditional doctrine of consideration that consideration must move from the promisee (Nav Canada) or, in other words, the promisee must suffer a detriment in return for the promise of the promisor (the Airport Authority). That something more provides the consideration necessary to enforce what otherwise would be a gratuitous and unenforceable promise. But as we know, under the rule in *Stilk v. Myrick* (1809), 2 Camp. 317, 170 E.R. 1168, the performance of a pre-existing obligation does not qualify as fresh or valid consideration and, therefore, such an agreement to vary an existing contract remains unenforceable. In this case, Nav Canada's pre-existing contractual obligation was to pay for the DME once it exercised its contractual right to insist on purchasing new equipment rather than relocating the old. In short, Nav Canada promised nothing in return for the Airport Authority's promise to pay for a navigational aid that it was not contractually bound to pay for under the ASF Agreement.

[20] The parties quite properly point out that, in Canada, the lead decision on the unenforceability of gratuitous promises in the context of a post-contractual modification is *Gilbert Steel Ltd. v. University Construction Ltd.* ... [After summarizing *Gilbert Steel*, Robertson JA continued.]

[22] Nav Canada's argument, that the Airport Authority's promise to pay for the navigational aid is enforceable, runs afoul of other tenets of the consideration doctrine. In the years following *Stilk v. Myrick*, the law would impose other barriers to the enforcement of post-contractual modifications. The first came in the form of a rule declaring that the plaintiff's forbearance from breaching the existing contract does not qualify as fresh consideration. Thus, the plaintiff (e.g., Nav Canada) cannot argue that the consideration for the defendant's promise to pay more was the plaintiff's forbearance from exercising its legal right to breach the contract by refusing to deliver promised goods or by withholding promised services (e.g. refusing to acquire and install the DME). Another rule that prevents the enforcement of a variation to an executory contract was articulated in *Combe v. Combe* ... namely that a plea of detrimental reliance is not a valid basis for enforcing an otherwise gratuitous promise. The plaintiff who argues detrimental reliance is in fact pleading that the defendant should be estopped from asserting that the agreement is unenforceable because of a lack of fresh consideration for the promise. Regrettably, the fact that the plaintiff may have relied on the agreement to his or her detriment is of no consequence as promissory estoppel may be invoked only as a [shield] and not as a [sword]. Thus, Nav Canada's estoppel-based argument—that it relied to its own detriment on the Airport Authority's gratuitous promise—must be rejected also.

[23] To this point, I have merely outlined the classical contract law approach to the enforcement of variations to an existing contract. The question which remains is whether this case should be decided on the basis of a "failure of consideration." I say this because in truth the courts have developed a number of ways to avoid the application of the classical tenets of the consideration doctrine when the court is convinced that the contractual variation was not procured under economic duress. Indeed, courts have adopted a number of "legal fictions" to avoid the blind application of the classical rules, thereby turning a gratuitous promise into an enforceable one. The principal techniques courts use to avoid the rule in *Stilk v. Myrick* were identified by the Ontario Law Reform Commission in its *Report on Amendment of the Law of Contract* (Toronto: Ministry of the Attorney General, 1987) at page 14: (1) finding that

on the facts of the case the plaintiff promised to do more than originally obliged to do; (2) finding that the circumstances have changed after the original contract was formed so that the plaintiff's promise to do exactly what was agreed to is consideration for a promise of more from the defendant; (3) accepting the plea of detrimental reliance on the basis of justice and equity, despite the application of the orthodox rules; and (4) holding that the original contract was mutually rescinded and replaced by a new agreement which incorporated the variation to the original contract. ...

[24] Two relatively recent cases reveal the extent to which some courts are unwilling to take a rigid or classical approach when it comes to applying the doctrine of consideration and the rule in *Stilk v. Myrick*. The first is the decision of the Ontario Court of Appeal in *Techform Products Ltd. v. Wolda* (2001), 56 O.R. (3d) 1 (C.A.), [2001] O.J. No. 3822 (QL), leave to appeal refused, [2001] S.C.C.A. No. 603 (QL). The defendant was retained in 1989 as an independent contractor to undertake research on behalf of the plaintiff. The parties were governed by a yearly contract that either side could terminate by giving sixty days' notice. Eventually, the plaintiff became concerned that, in future, the defendant might assert a right to any patentable invention that resulted from research undertaken pursuant to their contract. To address this concern, the plaintiff produced a written agreement that mandated that the defendant assign all of his inventions to the plaintiff in consideration of his continued engagement. The defendant signed the agreement in 1993. In 1997, the defendant invented a patentable device and sought compensation from the plaintiff, who refused to pay. The contractual relationship was terminated and questions arose as to whom had the legal right to the invention and whether the 1993 agreement was enforceable. The trial judge held that the 1993 agreement failed for want of consideration and was unenforceable on the ground of economic duress. The Court of Appeal disagreed. It was able to find the necessary consideration by implying a term into the contract, namely that the plaintiff implicitly promised to forbear from dismissing the defendant for a reasonable period of time after the signing of the agreement. Citing *Maguire v. Northland Drug Co. Ltd.*, [1935] S.C.R. 412, [1935] S.C.J. No. 11 (QL), the Court of Appeal held that continued employment and implied forbearance from dismissal for a reasonable period of time is adequate consideration. The fact that the original contract stated that the contractual relationship could be terminated by either party on sixty days' notice did not impede the court's willingness to imply a term broader in scope. The subsequent agreement being enforceable under the doctrine of consideration, the court went on to hold that it was not procured under economic duress. ...

[25] While Canadian courts continue to struggle with the rule in *Stilk v. Myrick* and the concept of "fresh" consideration, in recent years the English Court of Appeal has effectively modified the consideration doctrine by asking whether the promisor obtained a benefit or advantage from the agreement to vary, irrespective of whether the promisee has agreed to do more. Under the classical concept of consideration, it is expected that the promisee suffer a detriment even if it be a promise to pay a "peppercorn," unless of course the gratuitous promise is reduced to writing under seal. In *Williams v. Roffey Bros. & Nicholls (Contractors) Ltd.*, [1990] 1 All E.R. 512 (C.A.), [1991] 1 Q.B. 1, the defendant contractor voluntarily promised to pay the plaintiff subcontractor more than was agreed to in their original contract. ...

[26] In *The Law of Contracts* (Toronto: Irwin Law Inc., 2005), Professor J.D. McCamus, at p. 249, explains the *ratio* of the Court of Appeal's decision in *Williams v. Roffey Bros. & Nicholls (Contractors) Ltd.* as follows: "For all three members of the court, then, it appears that the fact that the contractor would obtain a benefit, albeit one arising from the defendant's relationship with the owner of the flats, could serve as con-

sideration rendering the promise to pay more an enforceable one." In short, the English Court of Appeal was prepared to "relax" the tenets of the consideration doctrine in order to render enforceable a gratuitous promise to pay more. Under English law, then, it is no longer necessary to look for an exchange of promises or detriment on the part of the promisee to enforce a variation of a contract, so long as the promisor obtains some benefit or advantage.

[27] In my opinion, this is a proper case to consider whether this Court should build upon the English Court of Appeal's decision in *Williams v. Roffey Bros. & Nicholls (Contractors) Ltd.* in order to avoid the rigid application of the rule in *Stilk v. Myrick*. I am prepared to accept that there are valid policy reasons for refining the consideration doctrine to the extent that the law will recognize that a variation to an existing contract, unsupported by consideration, is enforceable if not procured under economic duress. ...

[28] I offer several reasons for this incremental change in the law. First, the rule in *Stilk v. Myrick* is an unsatisfactory way of dealing with the enforceability of post-contractual modifications. As Professor McCamus points out, the rule is both overinclusive and underinclusive. It is overinclusive because it captures renegotiations induced by coercion so long as there is consideration for the modification. It is underinclusive in cases where there is no consideration because it excludes voluntary agreements that do not offend the tenets of the economic duress doctrine (see pp. 381-382 of his text). The reality is that existing contracts are frequently varied and modified by tacit agreement in order to respond to contingencies not anticipated or identified at the time the initial contract was negotiated. As a matter of commercial efficacy, it becomes necessary at times to adjust the parties' respective contractual obligations and the law must then protect their legitimate expectations that the modifications or variations will be adhered to and regarded as enforceable.

[29] Second, the consideration doctrine and the doctrine of promissory estoppel work in tandem to impose an injustice on those promisees who have acted in good faith and to their detriment in relying on the enforceability of the contractual modification. The notion that detrimental reliance can only be invoked if the promisee is the defendant to the action (*i.e.*, as a shield and not a sword) is simply unfair and leads to an unjust result if the promisor was not acting under economic duress. In *The Law of Contracts*, 5th ed. (Toronto: Canada Law Book, 2005) at p. 83, Professor S.M. Waddams points out that some gratuitous promises have been enforced because of detrimental reliance on the part of the promisee. He notes that these cases should not be met by a fictional attempt to find consideration in the sense of a bargained exchange. Professor Waddams opines that courts should openly recognize that, while these promises are not bargains, there may be other sound reasons for enforcement. In my view, this reasoning is persuasive in the context of the enforcement of a post-contractual modification. I agree with Professor Waddams' exhortation that courts should avoid "fictional" attempts to find consideration. We should not be seduced into adhering to a hunt and peck theory in an effort to find consideration where none exists, nor should we manipulate the consideration doctrine in such a way that it is no longer recognizable. Frankly, law professors spend far too much time trying to explain to law students what qualifies as valid consideration and why the cases seem to be irreconcilable, except in result, while judges spend more time avoiding the rule in *Stilk v. Myrick* than they do in applying it. Parties to a contract and to litigation are entitled to expect that there is some certainty in the law and that it is not dependent on the length of the chancellor's foot. For courts to find consideration by holding, for example, that the parties implicitly agreed to a mutual rescission of the original contract or that they implicitly agreed to a new term is to weaken the law of contract, not strengthen it.

[30] My third reason for refining the tenets of the consideration doctrine is tied to the reality that it developed centuries before the recognition of the modern and evolving doctrine of economic duress. The doctrine of consideration and the concept of bargain and exchange should not be frozen in time so as to reflect only the commercial realities of another era. If the courts are willing to formulate and adopt new contractual doctrines, they are equally capable of modifying the old. To the extent that the old doctrines interfere with the policy objectives underscoring the new, change is warranted. In my view, this is precisely what the English Court of Appeal did in *Williams v. Roffey Bros. & Nicholls (Contractors) Ltd*.

[31] For the above reasons, I am prepared to accept that a post-contractual modification, unsupported by consideration, may be enforceable so long as it is established that the variation was not procured under economic duress. In reaching this conclusion, I am mindful that the Supreme Court has cautioned that it is not the role of the courts to undertake "major" reforms in the common law or those that may have "complex ramifications." That is the prerogative of the legislature. "Incremental" changes, however, are permissible ... .

[32] In my view, the modernization of the consideration doctrine as it is tied to the rule in *Stilk v. Myrick* qualifies as an incremental change. It relieves the courts of the embarrassing task of offering unconvincing reasons why a contractual variation should be enforced. Again having regard to the Supreme Court's admonition, I wish to emphasize that I am not advocating the abrogation of the rule in *Stilk v. Myrick*. Simply, the rule should not be regarded as determinative as to whether a gratuitous promise is enforceable. Nor am I suggesting that the doctrine of consideration is irrelevant when it comes to deciding whether a contractual variation was procured under economic duress. There will be cases where the post-contractual modification is in fact and law supported by valid or fresh consideration. In my view, that type of evidence is important when it comes to deciding whether the contractual variation was procured with the "consent" of the promisor. After all, why would anyone agree to pay or do more than is required under an existing contract in return for nothing? But if the contractual variation was supported by fresh consideration, the argument that the variation was procured under economic duress appears, on the face of it, less convincing and the circumstances more in line with what one expects to see in every commercial contract: a "consensual bargain." On the other hand, for example, a person who agrees to pay more than the original contract price either in writing under seal or in return for a "peppercorn" is entitled to argue that the agreement was procured under economic duress.

[Robertson JA's discussion of economic duress is excerpted in Chapter 6, Section VI.]

River Wind Ventures Ltd v British Columbia. 2009 BCSC 589, rev'd (on other grounds) 2011 BCCA 79. MEIKLEM J: I agree with the reasoning of the court in the *Greater Fredericton Airport Authority* case in deciding to modernize the requirement of consideration in the context of variations of existing contracts. With respect, however, it is not clear to me that the first sentence in para. 31 ... fully captures the modernized principle intended to be enunciated by the court. That sentence seems to state that the only prerequisite for the enforceability of a post-contractual modification is that the variation was not procured by duress, but I note that the second reason (set out in the quoted para. 29) for making what is characterized as an incremental change in the law was to avoid imposing an injustice: "... on those promisees who have acted in good faith and to their detriment in relying on the enforceability of the contractual modification. ..." While I find that the facts of this case represent a situation where it would be unjust to adhere to the entrenched principle that equitable estoppel can only be relied upon as a shield, and not as a sword, I would follow the reasoning in the *Greater Fredericton Airport Authority* case only so far as enforcing a post-contractual variation in the absence of consideration if the evidence established either detrimental reliance by the plaintiff or the gaining of a benefit or advantage by the defendant. I am not persuaded that equity calls for enforceability where neither of those elements are present.

RICHCRAFT HOMES LTD V URBANDALE CORP
2016 ONCA 622

[In 2001, Urbandale Corporation and Richcraft Homes Ltd. entered into a limited partnership agreement ("LPA"). Clause 3.4 of the LPA allowed Riverdale to purchase, from the partnership, "residential house lots to meet Richcraft's needs." A dispute arose between the parties as to the correct interpretation of the clause. In response, the principals of Urbandale and Richcraft signed a document related to the LPA (the "2005 document"), which provided the parties would divide the building lots equally. When Richcraft sought to enforce the 2005 agreement, Urbandale contended that the agreement was unenforceable for lack of consideration].

LAUWERS JA (for the court):

[43] While the developing case law outside Ontario suggests that the time might be ripe for this court to re-consider the role that consideration plays in the enforceability of contractual variations, in my view, *Gilbert Steel* was a fundamentally different case on the facts and its holding has no application to this case.

[44] The 2005 document lacks the formality of the LPA. As the application judge found, it was intended by ... [the principals] to clarify the terms of the LPA. The potential for a dispute between the parties was plain enough on the language of Article 3.4 LPA to cause ... anxiety. On the facts, Richcraft was in no position to exert any kind of pressure on its senior partner, and Urbandale was not in a vulnerable position. The 2005 agreement was not, in my view, entirely one-sided in Richcraft's favour.

• • •

[46] Certainty in a long-term, ongoing business relationship is of value to the contracting parties because it avoids disputes and allows the parties to plan both their own affairs and also the orderly and reasonable unfolding of their business relationship. In *Gilbert Steel*, the respective obligations of each of the contracting parties were already clear: Gilbert Steel was supplying fabricated steel; University Construction was purchasing it at an agreed-upon price. Therefore, it was also clear to see that when University Construction promised to pay a higher price than it had previously agreed, it received nothing in return over and above the steel to which it was already entitled under the contract.

[47] The appellant's assertion that the 2005 document represented a compromise of its entitlement to a greater than equal share of the lots, or in other words, a promise for which it received no consideration, assumes that it was in fact originally entitled to a greater than equal share. However, in my view, under the original terms of the LPA it was far from clear how many lots Urbandale Construction and Richcraft were each entitled to under Article 3.4. That article entitled Richcraft to "such residential house lots to meet Richcraft's needs," with no limitation. The 2005 document clarified

the issue of quantum: Richcraft was entitled to share equally in the available lots with Urbandale Construction. Clarifying an unclear term in a long-term contract, in order to create certainty and to avoid future costly disputes, enures to the parties' mutual benefit, and is something of value that flows from and to each contracting party. It thus serves as a functional form of consideration.

NOTES AND QUESTIONS

1. Why was the court in *Gilbert Steel* unwilling to use the implied rescission analysis of *Raggow v Scougall*?

2. In *Roffey Bros* it is suggested that the presence of economic duress would negative a finding that a particular "practical benefit" could constitute good consideration. What do concepts like economic duress (discussed in Chapter 6, Section VI) have to do with the question of whether something amounts to consideration? Consider and contrast the pairing of promissory estoppel and duress discussed by Lord Denning in *D & C Builders, Ltd v Rees*, below.

3. Is the reasoning in *Roffey Bros* consistent with the idea that the consideration must move from the promisee at the promisor's request? For arguments that it is not, see *South Caribbean Trading Co v Trafigura Beheer BV*, [2004] EWHC 2676 at para 108; J O'Sullivan, "Unconsidered Modifications" (2017) 133 Law Q Rev 191. Could the promisor sue the promisee if the practical benefits do not materialize? To the extent that this is not possible, does this cast doubt on the concept of practical benefit as consideration? For an analysis, see M Roberts, "The Practical Benefit Doctrine Marches On" (2017) 80 Mod L Rev 339 at 343-46.

4. Could the result in *Roffey Bros* or *NAV Canada* be explained using the principles of promissory estoppel discussed in Section III.C.2, below?

5. If the law on promissory estoppel is broken, unjust, and unfair (as is argued in *NAV Canada* and *River Wind Ventures*) is the most efficient solution to change the law on consideration or to fix the law on estoppel directly? For the evolution of the doctrine of promissory estoppel in Australia and the United States that addresses the sword and shield issue, see Section III.C.2, below.

6. Given the fact that duress cannot explain the contours of the pre-existing duty doctrine (a fact that Robertson JA notes at para 28), why does the court in *NAV Canada* assume that it is the justification of that doctrine? Is it the only possible explanation of what the common law is doing? Can the ideas of "transfer" or "rights to performance" shed any light on the doctrine? For example, can one give the same gift to the same person more than once?

7. Do you agree that Robertson JA is not advocating the abrogation of the rule from *Stilk v Myrick*? Do you agree that what he proposes is merely an incremental change? Is Robertson JA really building on and applying *Roffey Bros*?

8. Is the decision of the Ontario Court of Appeal in *Richcraft* consistent with the practical benefits analysis espoused in *Roffey Bros*? Was the court's attempt to distinguish *Gilbert Steel* convincing? Might the case be viewed as one of compromise (see Section I, below)?

9. Why should consideration be necessary to modify an existing contract—that is, one that already states a valid consideration? Is an attack on the pre-existing duty doctrine not an attack on the doctrine of consideration itself? For judicial examination of this issue, see *Antons Trawling Co Ltd v Smith*, [2003] 2 NZLR 23 (CA).

10. For more discussion of pre-existing duty, see Fridman at 96-106; MacDougall at 112-16; Swan & Adamski at 72-100; V Aivazan, M Trebilcock & M Penny, "The Law and Economics of Contract Modification: The Uncertain Quest for a Benchmark of Enforceability" (1984) 22 Osgoode Hall LJ 173; B Reiter, "Courts, Consideration and Common Sense" (1977) 27 UTLJ 439; M Chen-Wishart, "A Bird in the Hand: Consideration and Contract Modifications" in Burrows & Peel 89.

FOAKES V BEER
(1884), LR 9 App Cas 605 (HL)

[In 1875, Mrs. Beer recovered judgment against Dr. Foakes for £2,090 19s. including costs. In an agreement dated December 21, 1876, Dr. Foakes promised to pay "the whole sum," £500 down and the balance in fixed payments over some five years; and Mrs. Beer promised not to take any proceedings on the judgment. This in effect meant that Mrs. Beer would not claim any interest on the unpaid part of the judgment. In 1882 Mrs. Beer commenced this action on the judgment for the interest, the principal amount having been paid as agreed. Cave J held that Mrs. Beer was not entitled to judgment because of the agreement. The Queen's Bench Division discharged an order for a new trial on the ground of misdirection. The Court of Appeal reversed that decision and entered judgment for the respondent for the interest due, with costs. Dr. Foakes appealed to the House of Lords.]

HOLL QC (for the appellant): Apart from the doctrine of *Cumber v. Wane* (1721), 1 St. 425; 93 E.R. 613, there is no reason in sense or law why the agreement should not be valid, and the creditor prevented from enforcing his judgment if the agreement be performed. It may often be much more advantageous to the creditor to obtain immediate payment of part of his debt than to wait to enforce payment, or perhaps by pressing his debtor to force him into bankruptcy, with the result of only a small dividend. Moreover if a composition is accepted friends, who would not otherwise do so, may be willing to come forward to assist the debtor. And if the creditor thinks that the acceptance of part is for his benefit who is to say it is not? The doctrine of *Cumber v. Wane* has been continually assailed, as in *Couldery v. Bartrum* (1880), 19 Ch. D. 394, by Jessel M.R. In the note to *Cumber v. Wane* (1 Smith L.C. 4th ed. p. 253, 8th ed. p. 367) which was written by J.W. Smith and never disapproved by any of the editors, including Willes and Keating JJ., it is said "that its doctrine is founded upon vicious reasoning and false views of the office of a Court of law, which should rather strive to give effect to the engagements which persons have thought proper to enter into, than cast about for subtle reasons to defeat them upon the ground of being unreasonable. Carried to its full extent the doctrine of *Cumber v. Wane* embraces the exploded notion that in order to render valid a contract not under seal, the adequacy as well as the existence of the consideration must be established. Accordingly in modern times it has been, as appears by the preceding part of the note, subjected to modification in several instances," *Cumber v. Wane* was decided on a ground now admitted to be erroneous, viz. that the satisfaction must be found by the Court to be reasonable. The Court cannot inquire into the adequacy of the consideration. *Reynolds v. Pinhowe* (1595), Cro. Eliz. 429; 78 E.R. 669, which was not cited in *Cumber v. Wane* ... decided that the saving of trouble was a sufficient consideration; "for it is a benefit unto him to have his debt without suit or charge." ... *Pinnel's Case* (1602), 5 Coke's Rep. 117a; 77 E.R. 237, was decided on a point of pleading; the dictum that payment of a smaller sum was no satisfaction of a larger, was extra-judicial, and overlooked all considerations of mercantile convenience, such as mentioned in *Reynolds v. Pinhowe*; and it is also noticeable that it was a case of a bond debt sought to be set aside by a parol agreement. It is every day practice for tradesmen to take less in satisfaction of a larger sum, and give discount, where there is neither custom nor right to take credit. ... The result of the cases is that if *Cumber v. Wane* be right, payment of a less sum than the debt due, by a bill, promissory note or cheque is a good discharge; but payment of such less sum by sovereigns or Bank of England notes is not. Here the agreement is not to take less than the debt, but to give time for payment of the whole without interest. Mankind have never acted on the doctrine of *Cumber v. Wane*, but the contrary; nay few are aware of it. By overruling it the House will only declare the universal practice to be good law as well as good sense.

[EARL OF SELBORNE LC: Whatever may be the ultimate decision of this appeal the House is much indebted to Mr. Holl for his exceedingly able argument.]

EARL OF SELBORNE LC: ... The question, therefore, is nakedly raised by this appeal, whether your Lordships are now prepared, not only to overrule, as contrary to law, the doctrine stated by Sir Edward Coke to have been laid down by all the judges of the Common Pleas in *Pinnel's Case* in 1602, and repeated in his note to Littleton, sect. 344, but to treat a prospective agreement, not under seal, for satisfaction of a debt, by a series of payments on account to a total amount less than the whole debt, as binding in law, provided those payments are regularly made; the case not being one of a composition with a common debtor, agreed to, *inter se*, by several creditors. I prefer so to state the question instead of treating it (as it was put at the Bar) as depending on the authority of the case of *Cumber v. Wane*, decided in 1718. It may well be that distinctions, which in later cases have been held sufficient to exclude the application of that doctrine, existed and were improperly disregarded in *Cumber v. Wane*, and not really contradicted by any later authorities. And this appears to me to be the true state of the case. The doctrine itself, as laid down by Sir Edward Coke, may have been criticised, as questionable in principle, by some persons whose opinions are entitled to respect, but it has never been judicially overruled; on the contrary I think it has always since the sixteenth century, been accepted as law. If so, I cannot think that your Lordships would do right, if you were now to reverse, as erroneous, a judgment of the Court of Appeal, proceeding upon a doctrine which has been accepted as part of the law of England for 280 years.

The distinction between the effect of a deed under seal, and that of an agreement by parol, or by writing not under seal, may seem arbitrary but it is established in our law; nor is it really unreasonable or practically inconvenient that the law should require particular solemnities to give to a gratuitous contract the force of a binding obligation. If the question be (as, in the actual state of the law, I think it is), whether consideration is, or is not, given in a case of this kind, by the debtor who pays down part of the debt presently due from him, for a promise by the creditor to relinquish, after certain further payments on account, the residue of the debt, I cannot say that I think consideration is given, in the sense in which I have always understood that word as used in our law. It might be (and indeed I think it would be) an improvement in our law, if a release or acquittance of the whole debt, or payment of any sum which the creditor might be content to receive by way of accord and satisfaction (though less than the whole), were held to be, generally, binding, though not under seal; nor should I be unwilling to see equal force given to a prospective agreement, like the present, in writing though not under seal; but I think it impossible, without refinements which partially alter the sense of the word, to treat such a release or acquittance as supported by any new consideration proceeding from the debtor. ...

My conclusion is, that the order appealed from should be affirmed, and the appeal dismissed, with costs, and I so move your Lordships.

[The opinions of Lords Blackburn, Fitzgerald, and Watson are omitted.]

Couldery v Bartrum. (1880), 19 ChD 394. JESSEL MR: According to English Common Law a creditor might accept anything in satisfaction of his debt except a less amount of money. He might take a horse, or a canary, or a tomtit if he chose, and that was accord and satisfaction; but, by a most extraordinary peculiarity of the English Common Law, he could not take 19s. 6d. in the pound; that was *nudum pactum*. Therefore, although the creditor might take a canary, yet, if the debtor did not give him a canary together with his 19s. 6d., there was no accord and satisfaction; if he did, there was accord and satisfaction. That was one of the mysteries of English Common Law.

NOTES AND QUESTIONS

1. Do the arguments of Holl QC, namely that *Pinnel's Case* was decided on the basis of deficiencies in the pleadings and that there existed lines of authority that challenged *Cumber v Wane*, change your view as to the cogency of *Foakes v Beer*?

2. Payment of a debt, or part of a debt, by a third person has been held to operate as a discharge of the original debtor. "The effect of such an agreement between a creditor and a third party with regard to the debt is to render it impossible for the creditor afterwards to sue the debtor for it. The way in which this is worked out in law may be that it would be an abuse of the process of the court to allow the creditor under such circumstances to sue, or it may be, and I prefer that view, that there is an extinction of the debt; but whichever way it is put, it comes to the same thing, namely that, after acceptance by a creditor of a sum offered by a third party in settlement of the claim against the debtor, the creditor cannot maintain an action for the balance." Fletcher Moulton LJ, in *Hirachand v Temple*, [1911] 2 KB 330 (CA).

3. Where several creditors agree with the debtor to accept a proportion of their claim in satisfaction, such composition agreements are held good. See *Good v Cheesman* (1831), 2 B & Ad 328, 109 ER 1165. It is usually stated that the promise of each creditor is consideration for the promise of every other creditor. If the creditors promise not to sue the debtor, how can this avail the debtor? That it does operate in his favour is undoubted.

4. Could agreeing to become a several debtor of a portion of a joint debt be consideration for a promise by the creditor to accept this lesser amount? For a judicial rejection of this possibility, see *Collier v P & M J Wright (Holdings) Ltd*, [2008] 1 WLR 643 (CA). For criticism of this position, see Richard Austen-Baker, "A Strange Sort of Survival for *Pinnel's Case*" (2008) 71 Mod L Rev 611, where the author argues that this agreed-on change in status is consideration because it is a detriment to the debtor that moves to the creditor at the creditor's request.

5. Could application of the practical benefits test from *Roffey Bros* help deal with the problem raised by *Foakes v Beer*? For a judicial rejection of this possibility, see *Re Selectmove Ltd*, [1995] 2 All ER 531 (CA). For a different view, see *MWB Business Exchange Centres Ltd v Rock Advertising Ltd*, [2016] EWCA Civ 553, where the court held that practical benefits over and above accommodating the debtor (such as ensuring that a licensee continued to occupy property) could count as consideration.

6. Has promissory estoppel solved the problems raised by *Foakes v Beer*? See *D & C Builders, Ltd v Rees* and *Collier v P & M J Wright (Holdings) Ltd*, Section III.C.2, below.

7. Should judges change the common law when its principles are inconsistent with modern business practice?

LAW REVISION COMMITTEE, SIXTH INTERIM REPORT
(1937) Cmnd 5449 (Eng)

34. In *Foakes v. Beer* Lord Blackburn was evidently disposed to hold that it was still open to the House of Lords to reconsider the rule based on the dictum [in *Pinnel's Case*], but in deference to his colleagues who were of a different opinion he did not press his views. In a few words (at p. 622) he summed up what appears to us to be a powerful argument for the abolition of the rule. He said:

What principally weighs with me in thinking that Lord Coke made a mistake of fact is my conviction that all men of business, whether merchants or tradesmen, do every day recognize and act on the ground that prompt payment of a part of their demand may be more beneficial to them than it would be to insist on their rights and enforce payment of the whole. Even where the debtor is perfectly solvent, and sure to pay at last, this often is so. Where the credit of the debtor is doubtful it must be more so.

35. In our opinion this view is as valid as it was fifty years ago, and we have no hesitation in recommending that legislation should be passed to give effect to it. This legislation would have the additional value of removing the logical difficulty involved in finding a consideration for the creditor's promises in a composition with creditors when not under seal. It would be possible to enact only that actual payment of the lesser sum should discharge the obligation to pay the greater, but we consider that it is more logical and more convenient to recommend that the greater obligation can be discharged either by a promise to pay a lesser sum or by actual payment of it, but that if the new agreement is not performed then the original obligation shall revive.

MERCANTILE LAW AMENDMENT ACT
RSO 1990, c M.10

16. Part performance of an obligation, either before or after a breach thereof, when expressly accepted by the creditor in satisfaction, or rendered in pursuance of an agreement for that purpose, though without any new consideration, shall be held to extinguish the obligation.

NOTES AND QUESTIONS

1. This section was originally enacted in 1885 as s 6 of the *Administration of Justice Act*. Like any statute, it is better understood when applied to specific facts. Would it have produced a different result in *Foakes v Beer*? Suppose Mrs. Beer had commenced her action before Dr. Foakes had made the £500 down payment. Could the statute have been invoked? Suppose after Dr. Foakes had completed all but the last payment Mrs. Beer had made her claim. What would the result be applying the Act?

2. Does s 16 of the *Mercantile Law Amendment Act* apply where the agreement is founded on economic duress, undue influence, or unconscionability? See *Process Automation Inc v Norstream Intertec Inc*, 2010 ONSC 3987, noted (2011) 90 Can Bar Rev 199, where the court reasoned that because the section is not an exhaustive code it was not meant to oust these principles.

3. Many provinces and some US states have adopted similar legislation. For a discussion of these enactments, see Waddams at paras 139-40; Fridman at 118-20.

4. Was s 16 of the Act necessary or could the application of the common law concept of a collateral unilateral contract have reached a commercially reasonable result? For just such an argument, see *MWB Business Exchange Centres Ltd v Rock Advertising Ltd*, [2016] EWCA Civ 553 at paras 89-90. For criticism of the idea, see M Roberts, "The Practical Benefit Doctrine Marches On" (2017) 80 Mod L Rev 339 at 344-47.

I. COMPROMISES

COOK V WRIGHT
(1861), 1 B & S 559, 121 ER 822 (QB)

BLACKBURN J: In this case it appeared on the trial that the defendant was agent for a Mrs. Bennett, who was non-resident owner of houses in a district subject to a local act. Work had been done in the adjoining street by the commissioners for executing the act, the expenses of which, under the provisions of their act, they charged on the owners of the adjoining houses. Notice had been given to the defendant, as if he had himself been owner of them. He attended at a board meeting of the commissioners, and objected both to the amount and nature of the charges, and also stated that he was not the owner of the houses, and that Mrs. Bennett was. He was told that if he did not pay he would be treated as one Goble had been. It appeared that Goble had refused to pay a sum charged against him as owner of some houses, and the commissioners had taken legal proceedings against him, and he had then submitted and paid with costs. In the result it was agreed between the commissioners and the defendant that the amount charged upon him should be reduced, and that time should be given to pay it in three instalments; he gave three promissory notes for the three instalments; the first was duly honoured, the others were not, and were the subject of the present action. At the trial it appeared that the defendant was not in fact owner of the houses. As agent for the owner he was not personally liable under the act. In point of law, therefore, the commissioners were not entitled to claim the money from him; but no case of deceit was alleged against them. It must be taken that the commissioners honestly believed that the defendant was personally liable, and really intended to take legal proceedings against him, as they had done against Goble. The defendant, according to his own evidence, never believed that he was liable in law, but signed the notes in order to avoid being sued as Goble was. Under these circumstances the substantial question reserved (irrespective of the form of the plea) was whether there was any consideration for the notes. We are of opinion that there was.

There is no doubt that a bill or note given in consideration of what is supposed to be a debt is without consideration if it appears that there was a mistake in fact as to the existence of the debt, *Bell v. Gardiner* (1842), 4 M. & Gr. 11; 134 E.R. 5; and, according to the cases of *Southall v. Rigg* and *Forman v. Wright* (1851), 11 C.B. 481; 138 E.R. 560, the law is the same if the bill or note is given in consequence of a mistake of law as to the existence of the debt. But here there was no mistake on the part of the defendant either of law or fact. What he did was not merely the making an erroneous account stated, or promising to pay a debt for which he mistakenly believed himself liable. It appeared on the evidence that he believed himself not to be liable; but he knew that the plaintiffs thought him liable, and would sue him if he did not pay, and in order to avoid the expense and trouble of legal proceedings against himself he agreed to compromise; and the question is, whether a person who has given a note as a compromise of a claim honestly made on him, and which but for that compromise would have been at once brought to a legal decision, can resist the payment of the note on the ground that the original claim thus compromised might have been successfully resisted.

If the suit had been actually commenced, the point would have been concluded by authority. In *Longridge v. Dorville* (1821), 5 B. & A. 117; 106 E.R. 1136, it was held that the compromise of a suit instituted to try a doubtful question of law was a sufficient consideration for a promise. In *Atlee v. Blackhouse* (1838), 3 M. & W. 633; 150 E.R. 1298 where the plaintiff's goods had been seized by the excise, and he had afterwards entered into an agreement with the commissioners of excise that all proceedings should be terminated, the goods delivered up to the plaintiff, and a sum of money paid by him to the commissioners, Parke B., rests his judgment, p. 650, on the ground that this agreement of compromise honestly made was for consideration, and binding. In *Cooper v. Parker* (1885), 15 C.B. 822; 139 E.R. 650 the Court of Exchequer Chamber held that the withdrawal of an untrue defence of infancy in a suit, with payment of costs, was a sufficient consideration for a promise to accept a smaller sum in satisfaction of a larger.

In these cases, however, litigation had been actually commenced; and it was argued before us that this made a difference in point of law, and that though, where a plaintiff has actually issued a writ against a defendant, a compromise honestly made is binding, yet the same compromise, if made before the writ actually issues, though the litigation is impending, is void. *Edwards v. Baugh* (1843), 11 M. & W. 641; 152 E.R. 962, was relied upon as an authority for this proposition. But in that case Lord Abinger expressly bases his judgment (pp. 645, 646) on the assumption that the declaration did not, either expressly or impliedly, show that a reasonable doubt existed between the parties. It may be doubtful whether the declaration in that case ought not to have been construed as disclosing a compromise of a real bona fide claim, but it does not appear to have been so construed by the court. We agree that unless there was a reasonable claim on the one side, which it was bona fide intended to pursue, there would be no ground for a compromise; but we cannot agree that (except as a test of the reality of the claim in fact) the issuing of a writ is essential to the validity of the compromise. The position of the parties must necessarily be altered in every case of compromise, so that, if the question is afterward opened up they cannot be replaced as they were before the compromise. The plaintiff may be in a less favorable position for renewing his litigation, he must be at an additional trouble and expense in again getting up his case, and he may no longer be able to produce the evidence which would have proved it originally. Besides, though he may not in point of law be bound to refrain from enforcing his rights against third persons during the continuance of the compromise to which they are not parties, yet practically the effect of the compromise must be to prevent his doing so. For instance, in the present case, there can be no doubt that the practical effect of the compromise must have been to induce the commissioners to refrain from taking proceedings against Mrs. Bennett, the real owner of the houses, while the notes given by the defendant, her agent, were running; though the compromise might have afforded no ground of defence had such proceedings been resorted to. It is this detriment of the party consenting to a compromise arising from the necessary alteration in his position which, in our opinion forms the real consideration for the promise, and not the technical and almost illusory consideration arising from the extra cost of litigation. The real consideration therefore depends, not on the actual commencement of a suit, but on the reality of the claim made and the bona fides of the compromise.

In the present case we think that there was sufficient consideration for the notes in the compromise made as it was.

The rule to enter a verdict for the plaintiff must be made absolute.

Callisher v Bischoffsheim. (1870), LR 5 QB 449. COCKBURN CJ: If the defendant's contention were adopted, it would result that in no case of a doubtful claim could a compromise be enforced. Every day a compromise is effected on the ground that the party making it has a chance of succeeding in it; and if he bona fide believes he has a fair chance of success, he has a reasonable ground for suing, and his forbearance to sue will constitute a good consideration. When such a person forbears to sue he gives up what he believes to be a right of action, and the other party gets an advantage; and, instead of being annoyed with an action, he escapes from the vexation incident to it.

FAIRGRIEF V ELLIS
(1935), 49 BCR 413 (SC)

MACDONALD J: Defendant is a retired gentleman, 72 years of age, owning and residing upon a small parcel of land on Lulu Island, worth approximately $2,500. For some years his relations with his wife have been strained; she refused to live with him in British Columbia and maintained her residence in California.

Plaintiffs are sisters, cultured maiden ladies about 50 years of age, who until the year 1933 lived in Winnipeg where they had been employed in clerical work though in recent times they were for considerable periods out of employment. They had been close friends of the defendant over a period of some 25 years and their relations may be judged from the fact that they called him "Dad." In the spring of 1933 the plaintiff Cornelia Fairgrief came to British Columbia on an excursion and visited with the defendant for some three days. Following that occasion some letters passed between the defendant and the plaintiff Anne Fairgrief wherein the plaintiff Anne Fairgrief was invited to visit the defendant. This invitation she declined. In August of that year defendant's son, who had for some months been residing with him, departed for the United States whereupon defendant wrote the plaintiff Anne Fairgrief stating that he was alone and that he required a housekeeper and that he wished the plaintiffs to come and keep house for him, final arrangements to be made after their arrival. Plaintiffs thereupon came to the defendant's home and took up their residence with him upon a verbal agreement that if they would become his housekeepers and take charge of his home during his lifetime the home would become theirs upon his death.

Pursuant to the above agreement plaintiffs entered upon their duties, took full charge of the home, performed all the household duties and did a good deal of work outside including painting, cleaning up the ground and other works of a more or less permanent nature. In addition to being his housekeepers they were his congenial companions and the three lived comfortably and happily until August, 1934, when the defendant's wife (much to his surprise for he had expected nothing of the sort) suddenly arrived in Vancouver. Defendant requested the plaintiffs to remain and be kind to his wife while she should reside with them, he feeling quite assured that her stay would not be a lengthy one. At the end of about a month defendant told the plaintiffs that he was grieved to be obliged to tell them that his wife insisted that they should depart the premises as she intended to remain and take charge. Defendant, knowing of his obligation to the plaintiffs, promised them if they would give up their rights under the agreement already entered into and would depart from his home he would on or about the 1st of October, 1934, pay them $1,000. That offer was accepted and plaintiffs removed themselves from the premises. The plaintiffs now bring action to recover that sum of $1,000. I have no doubt at all that the defendant's repudiation of his agreement resulted from the interference of his wife. Having persistently refused to live with him and assist him in making a happy and comfortable home, she was determined that the plaintiffs should not be allowed to render that assistance which she herself declined to render. Incidentally it may be said that her further actions justify to some extent this assumption for she again left her husband on November 2nd, 1934, and has not returned to him. Although there is a conflict of evidence I find the facts to be as above stated.

On the above facts, can the plaintiffs succeed? It is contended in the first instance that the agreement first made cannot be enforced by reason of the 4th section of the Statute of Frauds, the agreement being one relating to an interest in land. With that contention I agree and I also agree that the plaintiffs cannot rely upon the fact that they have partly performed their contract for the reason that the acts which they performed are not necessarily referable to the contract alleged by them but might equally be referable to the contract set out by the defendant, *viz.*:

> That the agreement under which the plaintiffs came to reside with the defendant ... was that in return for their board and lodging the plaintiffs were to keep house for the defendant until the defendant's wife came up from California.

See *Haddock v. Norgan* (1923), 33 B.C. 237; (1924), 34 B.C. 74.

Notwithstanding the above, however, I cannot understand why the plaintiffs cannot succeed in their claim for $1,000. When the agreement was made in September to pay the plaintiffs $1,000 the defendant thought that he was under an obligation to the plaintiffs and in order to be released from that obligation and so that the plaintiffs might agree to peacefully vacate his premises, he made the second agreement. Even although he was not in law bound to perform the first agreement nevertheless I think there was good consideration to support the promise to pay $1,000. ...

There will be judgment for the plaintiffs for $1,000.

NOTES AND QUESTIONS

1. For an example of a compromise agreement that was found to be unenforceable on the basis that the party pursuing the action could have no bona fide belief in the merits of their claim, see *B(DC) v Arkin*, [1996] 8 WWR 100 (Man QB), aff'd [1996] 10 WWR 689 (Man CA).

2. Might the result in *Fairgrief* be supported as a compromise of an unjust enrichment claim? See *Deglman v Guaranty Trust Co*, excerpted in Chapter 2, Section IX.

3. Why must the party pursuing the action have a bona fide belief in its merits? For example, if the rules of civil procedure would allow someone to bring a claim without such a bona fide belief, why should surrender of this claim not count as consideration? See Waddams at paras 129-32; McCamus at 230-33; Fridman at 93-96; MacDougall at 106-7.

4. If the sailors in *Stilk v Myrick*, above, had had a bona fide belief that they did not have to continue the voyage, would the captain's promise to pay more have been enforceable as a compromise?

5. For the interplay between the law of mistake and contracts of compromise, see *Toronto-Dominion Bank v Fortin et al (No 2)*, noted in Chapter 9, Section V.

J. CHARITABLE SUBSCRIPTIONS

DALHOUSIE COLLEGE V BOUTILIER ESTATE
[1934] SCR 642

CROCKET J (for the court): This appeal concerns a claim which was filed in the Probate Court for the County of Halifax, Nova Scotia, in the year 1931, by the appellant College against the respondent Estate for $5,000, stated as having been "subscribed to Dalhousie Campaign Fund (1920)," and attested by an affidavit of the College Bursar, in which it was alleged that the stated amount was justly and truly owing to the College Corporation.

The subscription, upon which the claim was founded, was obtained from the deceased on June 4, 1920, in the course of a canvass which was being conducted by a committee, known as the Dalhousie College Campaign Committee, for the raising of a fund to increase the general resources and usefulness of the institution and was in the following terms:

> For the purpose of enabling Dalhousie College to maintain and improve the efficiency of its teaching, to construct new buildings and otherwise to keep pace with the growing need of its constituency and in consideration of the subscription of others, I promise to pay to the Treasurer of Dalhousie College the sum of Five Thousand Dollars, payment as follows:
>
> Terms of payment as per letter from Mr. Boutilier.
>
> A. 399.   Name Arthur Boutilier.
>
> Date June 4th, 1920.
>
> Make all cheques payable to the Treasurer of Dalhousie College.

So far as the record disclosed, the subscription was not accompanied or followed by any letter from the deceased as to the terms of payment. He died on October 29, 1928, without making any payment on account. It appears that some time after he signed the subscription form he met with severe financial reverses which prevented him from honouring his pledge. That he desired and hoped to be able to do so is evidenced by a brief letter addressed by him to the President of the University on April 12, 1926, in reply to a communication from the latter, calling his attention to the subscription and the fact that no payments had been made upon it. The deceased's letter, acknowledging receipt of the President's communication states:

> In reply I desire to advise you that I have kept my promise to you in mind. As you are probably aware, since making my promise I suffered some rather severe reverses, but I expect before too long to be able to redeem my pledge.

... There is, of course, no doubt that the deceased's subscription can be sustained as a binding promise only upon one basis, viz.: as a contract, supported by a good and sufficient consideration. The whole controversy between the parties is as to whether such a consideration is to be found, either in the subscription paper itself or in the circumstances as disclosed by the evidence.

So far as the signed subscription itself is concerned, it is contended in behalf of the appellant that it shews upon its face a good and sufficient consideration for the deceased's promise in its statement that it was given in consideration of the subscription of others. As to this, it is first to be observed that the statement of such a consideration in the subscription paper is insufficient to support the promise if, in point of law, the subscriptions of others could not provide a valid consideration therefor. I concur in the opinion of Chisholm C.J., that the fact that others had signed separate subscription papers for the same common object or were expected so to do does not of itself constitute a legal consideration. ...

As to finding the consideration for the subscription outside the subscription itself, the only evidence relied upon is that of Dr. MacKenzie that increased expenditures were made by the College for the purposes stated between the years 1920 and 1931 on the strength of the subscriptions obtained in the canvass of 1920. It is contended that this fact alone constituted a consideration for the subscription and made it binding. The decisions in *Sargent v. Nicholson; Y.M.C.A. v. Rankin*; and the judgment of Wright J., of the Supreme Court of Ontario, in *Re Loblaw*, adopting the two former decisions, are relied upon to sustain this proposition as well as some earlier Ontario cases and several American decisions.

There seems to be no doubt that the first three cases mentioned unqualifiedly support the proposition relied upon, as regards at least a subscription for a single distinct and definite object, such as the erection of a designated building, whether or not the expenditure would not have been made nor any liability incurred by the promisee *but for the promise* or not. The earlier Ontario cases relied upon, however, do not appear to me to go that far. They all shew that there was either a direct personal interest on the part of the subscriber in the particular project undertaken or some personal participation in the action of the promisee as a result of which the expenditure or liability was incurred.

Regarding the American decisions, upon which *Sargent v. Nicholson* appears to have entirely proceeded—more particularly perhaps on the dictum of Gray C.J., in *Cottage Street M.E. Church v. Kendall* than any other—it may be pointed out that there are other American cases which shew that there must be something more than the mere expenditure of money or the incurring of liability by the promisee on the faith of the promise. *Hull v. Pearson* (1899), 56 N.Y. Sup. 518, a decision of the Appellate Division of the Supreme Court of New York, in which many of the American cases are reviewed, should perhaps be mentioned in this regard. One W. subscribed a certain sum for the work of the German department of a theological seminary. There was no consideration expressed in the memorandum, and there was no evidence of a request in the part of W. that the work should be continued, or of any expenditures on the part of the theological seminary in reliance on such request. Such department had been continued, but there was no evidence that it would not have been continued as it had been for a series of years but for the subscription. It was held that the subscription was without consideration and could not be enforced. Woodward J., in the course of his reasons, in which the full court concurred, said:

> It is true that there is evidence that the German department has been continued, but this does not meet the requirement. There is no evidence that it would not have been continued as it had been for a series of years if the subscription of Mr. Wild had not been made.

And further:

> He undoubtedly made the subscription for the purpose of aiding in promoting the work of the German department; but, in the absence of some act or word which clearly indicated that he accompanied his subscription by a request to do something which the corporation would not have done except for his subscription, there is no such request as would justify a constructive consideration in support of this promise.

These latter dicta seem to accord more with the English decisions, which give no countenance to the principle applied in *Sargent v. Nicholson* and *Y.M.C.A. v. Rankin* and in the earlier American cases, as is so pointedly illustrated by the judgments of

Pearson J., in *In Re Hudson*, and Eve J., in *In Re Cory* (1912), 29 T.L.R. 18. The head note in *In Re Hudson* states:

> A. verbally promised to give £20,000 to the Jubilee Fund of the Congregational Union, and also filled up and signed a blank form of promise not addressed to anyone, but headed "Congregational Union of England and Wales Jubilee Fund," whereby he promised to give £20,000 in five equal annual instalments of £4,000 each, for the liquidation of chapel debts. A. paid three instalments of £4,000 to the fund within three years from the date of his promise, and then died, leaving the remaining two instalments unpaid and unprovided for.
>
> The Congregational Union claimed £8,000 from A.'s executors, on the ground that they had been led by A.'s promise to contribute larger sums to churches than they would otherwise have done; that money had been given and promised by other persons in consequence of A.'s promise; that grants from the Jubilee Fund had been promised to cases recommended by A.; and that churches to which promises had been made by the committee, and the committee themselves, had incurred liabilities in consequence of A.'s promise.

His Lordship held there was no consideration for the promise. "There really was," he said, "in this matter, nothing whatever in the shape of a consideration which could form a contract between the parties."

And he added:

> I am bound to say that this is an attempt to turn a charity into something very different from a charity. I think it ought to fail, and I think it does fail. I do not know to what extent a contrary decision might open a new form of posthumous charity. Posthumous charity is already bad enough, and it is quite sufficiently protected by law without establishing a new principle which would extend the doctrine in its favour far more than it has been extended or ought to be extended.

In the *Cory* case a gift of 1,000 guineas was promised to a Y.M.C.A. Association for the purpose of building a memorial hall. The sum required was £150,000, of which £85,000 had been promised or was available. The committee in charge decided not to commit themselves until they saw that their efforts to raise the whole fund were likely to prove successful. The testator, whose estate it was sought to charge, promised the 1,000 guineas and subsequently the committee felt justified in entering into a building contract, which they alleged they were largely induced to enter into by the testator's promise. Eve J., held there was no contractual obligation between the parties and therefore no legal debt due from the estate.

Chisholm C.J., in the case at bar, said that without any want of deference to eminent judges who have held otherwise he felt impelled to follow the decisions in the English cases. I am of opinion that he was fully justified in so doing, rather than apply the principle contended for by the appellant in reliance upon the decision in *Sargent v. Nicholson* based, as the latter case is, upon the decisions of United States courts, which are not only in conflict with the English cases, but with decisions of the Court of Appeals of the State of New York, as I have, I think, shewn, and which have been subjected to very strong criticism by American legal authors, notably by Prof. Williston, as the learned Chief Justice of Nova Scotia has shewn in his exhaustive and, to my mind, very convincing judgment.

To hold otherwise would be to hold that a naked, voluntary promise may be converted into a binding legal contract by the subsequent action of the promisee alone without the consent, express or implied, of the promisor. There is no evidence here which in any way involves the deceased in the carrying out of the work for which the promised subscription was made other than the signing of the subscription paper itself.

I may add that, had I come to the opposite conclusion upon the legal question involved, I should have felt impelled, as Chisholm C.J. did, to seriously question the accuracy of the statement relied upon by the appellant that "this work was done and the increased expenditures were made on the strength of the subscriptions promised," if that statement was meant to refer to all the increased expenditures listed in the comparative statements produced by Dr. MacKenzie. The statement relied on does not profess to set out verbatim the language of the witness. The record of the evidence is apparently but a brief summary taken down by the Registrar. That the summary is inaccurate was shewn by the admission made on the argument before us that it was not $220,000 which was subscribed in all in 1920, but $2,200,000. The statement produced of expenditures on buildings, grounds and equipment since 1920 shews a grand total for the more than ten years of but $1,491,687—over $700,000 less than the aggregate of the 1920 campaign subscriptions—and this grand total includes over $400,000 for Shirriff Hall, which it is well known was the object of a special donation contributed by a wealthy lady, now deceased, as a memorial to her father. In the light of this correction it becomes quite as difficult to believe that the College Corporation, in doing "this work" and making "the increased expenditures" did so in reliance upon the deceased's subscription, as if the aggregate of the subscriptions had been but $220,000, as the Registrar took the figures down, and the Nova Scotia Supreme Court supposed, and the total expenditures $1,491,687. This evidence would assuredly seem to shut out all possibility of establishing a claim against the deceased's estate on any such ground as estoppel.

The appeal, I think, should be dismissed with costs.

NOTES AND QUESTIONS

1. Two Canadian jurisdictions give statutory protection to subscriptions to public undertakings: *Public Subscriptions Act*, RSNS 1989, c 378 and *Statute of Frauds*, RSPEI 1988, c S-6, s 4.

2. The decision of Anglo-Canadian courts that promises to give to charity are not enforceable without consideration is a controversial one. What policies justify the rule formulated in *Dalhousie College*? Could concerns about protecting creditors or family members be driving the result? See Waddams at para 126; *Eastwood v Kenyon* (1840), 11 Ad & E 438, 113 ER 482 (per Lord Denman). Compare the result of *Dalhousie College* with that reached in *Hutchison v The Royal Institution for the Advancement of Learning*, [1932] SCR 57, which applied the Quebec civil law rules relating to promise enforcement.

3. What if the charitable institution suffers a detriment as a result of the promise? Would that detriment constitute consideration or ground an estoppel? See McCamus at 233-36.

II. INTENTION

It is sometimes said that a contract is not formed between parties unless they had an "intention" to contract. We should not, however, assume this intention has anything to do with a subjective decision to make a contract. Instead, a finding of "intention" to contract reflects a court's decision as to whether a reasonable person in the position of the promisee would consider that the promisor "intended" to make a promise that would affect the promisor's legal status.

Sometimes one is convinced that the promisor was making a statement only as a joke or as a social engagement and that no one would seriously consider a promise that might subject the maker to legal obligations. Other situations will not be so obvious. Consider the following instances of "family arrangements" in which the matter wound up before the courts. What made the court think there was or was not an "intention" to create a contract?

BALFOUR V BALFOUR
[1919] 2 KB 571 (CA)

Appeal from a decision of SARGENT J., sitting as an additional judge of the King's Bench Division.

The plaintiff sued the defendant (her husband) for money which she claimed to be due in respect of an agreed allowance of £30 a month. The alleged agreement was entered into under the following circumstances. The parties were married in August, 1900. The husband, a civil engineer, had a post under the Government of Ceylon as Director of Irrigation, and after the marriage he and his wife went to Ceylon, and lived there together until the year 1915, except that in 1906 they paid a short visit to this country, and in 1908 the wife came to England in order to undergo an operation, after which she returned to Ceylon. In November, 1915, she came to this country with her husband, who was on leave. They remained in England until August, 1916, when the husband's leave was up and he had to return. The wife however on the doctor's advice remained in England. On August 8, 1916, the husband being about to sail, the alleged parol agreement sued upon was made. The plaintiff, as appeared from the judge's note, gave the following evidence of what took place: "In August, 1916, defendant's leave was up. I was suffering from rheumatic arthritis. The doctor advised my staying in England for some months, not to go out till November 4. On August 8 my husband sailed. He gave me a cheque from 8th to 31st for £24, and promised to give me £30 per month till I returned." Later on she said: "My husband and I wrote the figures together on August 8; £34 shown. Afterwards he said £30." In cross-examination she said that they had not agreed to live apart until subsequent differences arose between them, and that the agreement of August, 1916, was one which might be made by a couple in amity. Her husband in consultation with her assessed her needs, and said he would send £30 per month for her maintenance. She further said that she then understood that the defendant would be returning to England in a few months, but that he afterwards wrote to her suggesting that they had better remain apart. In March, 1918, she commenced proceedings for restitution of conjugal rights, and on July 30 she obtained a decree nisi. On December 16, 1918, she obtained an order for alimony.

SARGENT J. held that the husband was under an obligation to support his wife, and the parties had contracted that the extent of that obligation should be defined in terms of so much a month. The consent of the wife to that agreement was a sufficient consideration to constitute a contract which could be sued upon. He accordingly gave judgment for the plaintiff. The husband appealed.

ATKIN LJ: The defence to this action on the alleged contract is that the defendant, the husband, entered into no contract with his wife, and for the determination of that it is necessary to remember that there are agreements between parties which do not result in contracts within the meaning of that term in our law. The ordinary example is where two parties agree to take a walk together, or where there is an offer and an acceptance of hospitality. Nobody would suggest in ordinary circumstances that those agreements result in what we know as a contract, and one of the most usual forms of agreement which does not constitute a contract appears to me to be the arrangements which are made between husband and wife. It is quite common, and it is the natural and inevitable result of the relationship of husband and wife, that the two spouses should make arrangements between themselves—agreements such as are in dispute in this action—agreements for allowances, by which the husband agrees that he will pay to his wife a certain sum of money, per week, or per month, or per year, to cover either her own expenses or the necessary expenses of the household and of the children of the marriage, and in which the wife promises either expressly or impliedly to apply the allowance for the purpose for which it is given. To my mind those agreements, or many of them, do not result in contracts at all, and they do not result in contracts even though there may be what as between other parties would constitute consideration for the agreement. ... Nevertheless they are not contracts, and they are not contracts because the parties did not intend that they should be attended by legal consequences. To my mind it would be of the worst possible example to hold that agreements such as this resulted in legal obligations and could be enforced in the Courts. It would mean this, that when the husband makes his wife a promise to give her an allowance of 30s. or £2 a week, whatever he can afford to give her, for the maintenance of the household and children, and she promises to apply it, not only could she sue him for his failure in any week to supply the allowance, but he could sue her for non-performance of the obligation, express or implied, which she had undertaken on her part. All I can say is that the small Courts of this country would have to be multiplied one-hundredfold if these arrange-ments were held to result in legal obligations. They are not sued upon, not because the parties are reluctant to enforce their legal rights when the agreement is broken, but because the parties, in the inception of the arrangements, never intended that they should be sued upon. Agreements such as these are outside the realm of con-tracts altogether. The common law does not regulate the form of agreements between spouses. Their promises are not sealed with seals and sealing wax. The consideration that really obtains for them is that natural love and affection which counts for so little in these cold Courts. The terms may be repudiated, varied or renewed as performance proceeds or as disagreements develop, and the principles of the common law as to exoneration and discharge and accord and satisfaction are such as find no place in the domestic code. The parties themselves are advocates, judges, Courts, sheriff's officer and reporter. In respect of these promises each house is a domain into which the King's writ does not seek to run, and to which his officers do not seek to be admitted. The only question in this case is whether or not this promise was of such a class or not. For the reasons given by my brethren it appears to me to be plainly established that the promise here was not intended by either party to be attended by legal consequences. I think the onus was upon the plaintiff, and the plaintiff has not established any contract. The parties were living together, the wife intending to return. The suggestion is that the husband bound himself to pay £30 a month under all circumstances, and she bound herself to be satisfied with that sum under all circumstances, and, although she was in ill-health and alone in this country, that out of that sum she undertook to defray the whole of her medical expenses that might fall upon her, whatever might be the development of her illness, and in whatever expenses it might involve her. To my mind neither party contem-plated such a result. I think that the parol evidence upon which the case turns does not establish a contract. I think that the letters do not evidence such a contract, or amplify the oral evidence which was given by the wife, which is not in dispute. For these reasons I think the judgment of the Court below was wrong and that this appeal should be allowed.

WARRINGTON LJ: ... These two people never intended to make a bargain which could be enforced in law. The husband expressed his intention to make this payment, and he promised to make it, and was bound in honour to continue it so long as he was in a position to do so. The wife on the other hand, so far as I can see, made no bargain at all. That is in my opinion sufficient to dispose of the case. ...

DUKE LJ: ... I am satisfied that there was no consideration moving from the wife to the husband or promise by the husband to the wife which was sufficient to sustain this action founded on the contract.

NOTES AND QUESTIONS

1. Is this case decided on the basis of "consideration" or "intent to contract"?

2. Does the rule propounded in *Balfour* work to the disadvantage of vulnerable family members? For an affirmative answer, see MacDougall at 57; P Saprai, "*Balfour v Balfour* and the separation of contract and promise" (2017) 37 LS 468 at 473-76.

3. For a justification of *Balfour* on the basis that it respects the value inherent in family relationships and the ability to be free *from* contract, see Smith at 214; D Kimel, *From Promise to Contract: Towards a Liberal Theory of Contract* (Oxford: Hart, 2003) at 136-42.

Simpkins v Pays. [1955] 3 All ER 10 (HC). The defendant, a lady of 83, had been living with her granddaughter and the plaintiff, who had been a boarder since 1950, in circumstances that had "some element of a family circle" about it, although the plaintiff was not related to the defendant. The three ladies competed regularly in a newspaper competition under a not very formal arrangement that if they won, they would "go shares." The defendant and her granddaughter would put their guesses on a slip of paper and the plaintiff would fill in the coupon, putting her own guess first, then the granddaughter's and the defendant's last. Whoever happened to have stamps handy seems to have supplied the trifling amount involved each week. When the weekly entry finally won £750 on the granddaughter's entry, the defendant claimed the whole amount. The plaintiff sued to recover £250. Held, for the plaintiff. SELLERS J: It may well be there are many family associations where some sort of rough and ready statement is made which would not, in a proper estimate of the circumstances, establish a contract which was contemplated to have legal consequences, but I do not so find here. I think that in the present case there was a mutuality in the arrangement between the parties. ... This was in the nature of a very informal syndicate so that they should all get the benefit of success.

MERRITT V MERRITT
[1970] 2 All ER 760 (CA)

The husband and wife were married in 1941 and had three children. In 1966, the husband became attached to another woman, and left the matrimonial home to live with her. At that time, the matrimonial home, a freehold house, was in the joint names of the husband and wife, and was subject to an outstanding mortgage of some £180. The wife pressed the husband to make arrangements for the future, and on 25th May 1966, they met and talked the matter over in the husband's car. The husband said that he would pay the wife £40 a month out of which she must make the outstanding mortgage payments on the house and he gave her the building society mortgage book. Before leaving the car the wife insisted that the husband should put down in writing a further agreement, and on a piece of paper he wrote: "In consideration of the fact that you will pay all charges in connection with the house ... until such time as the mortgage repayment has been completed, when the mortgage has been completed I will agree to transfer the property in to your sole ownership." The husband signed and dated that agreement, and the wife took the piece of paper away with her. In the following months she paid off the mortgage, partly out of the husband's monthly payment to her and partly out of her own earnings. When the mortgage was paid off the husband refused to transfer the house to the wife.

This was an appeal by the husband, John Bertram Merritt, against the judgment of Stamp J., given on 14th May 1969, whereby he held that the wife, Millicent Joan Merritt, was entitled to a declaration that she was now the sole beneficial owner of the matrimonial home, a freehold property known as 133 Clayton Road, Hook, Surrey, and ordered the husband to join with the wife in transferring the property to her. Stamp J. also dismissed the husband's counterclaim that the property was owned by the parties in equal shares.

LORD DENNING MR: ... The first point taken on his behalf by counsel for the husband was that the agreement was not intended to create legal relations. It was, he says, a family arrangement such as was considered by the court in *Balfour v. Balfour* and in *Jones v. Padavatton*. So the wife could not sue on it. I do not think that those cases have any application here. The parties there were living together in amity. In such cases their domestic arrangements are ordinarily not intended to create legal relations. It is altogether different when the parties are not living in amity but are separated, or about to separate. They then bargain keenly. They do not rely on honourable understandings. They want everything cut and dried. It may safely be presumed that they intend to create legal relations.

Counsel for the husband then relied on the recent case of *Gould v. Gould*, when the parties had separated, and the husband agreed to pay the wife £12 a week "so long as he could manage it." The majority of the court thought that those words introduced such an element of uncertainty that the agreement was not intended to create legal relations. But for that element of uncertainty, I am sure that the majority would have held the agreement to be binding. They did not differ from the general proposition which I stated: "When ... husband and wife, at arm's length, decide to separate and the husband promises to pay a sum as maintenance to the wife during the separation, the court does, as a rule, impute to them an intention to create legal relations."

In all these cases the court does not try to discover the intention by looking into the minds of the parties. It looks at the situation in which they were placed and asks itself: would reasonable people regard the agreement as intended to be binding?

Counsel for the husband sought to say that this agreement was uncertain because of the arrangement for £40 a month maintenance. That is obviously untenable. Next he said that there was no consideration for the agreement. That point is no good. The wife paid the outstanding amount to the building society. That was ample consideration. It is true that the husband paid her £40 a month which she may have used to pay the building society. But still her act in paying was good consideration. Counsel for the husband took a small point about rates. There was nothing in it. The rates were adjusted fairly between the parties afterwards. Finally, counsel for the husband said that, under s. 17 of the Married Women's Property Act 1882, this house would be owned by the husband and the wife jointly; and that, even if this house were transferred to the wife, she should hold it on trust for them both jointly. There is nothing in this point either. The paper which the husband signed dealt with the beneficial ownership of the house. It was intended to belong entirely to the wife.

I find myself in entire agreement with the judgment of Stamp J. This appeal should be dismissed.

FAMILY LAW ACT
RSO 1990, c F.3

55(1) A domestic contract [such as a marriage contract, separation agreement, or cohabitation agreement] and an agreement to amend or rescind a domestic contract are unenforceable unless made in writing, signed by the parties and witnessed.

NOTE

In Canadian law, support obligations between family members are generally regulated by legislation, although, as the excerpt from the *Family Law Act* indicates, certain matters may still be the subject of contract.

JONES V PADAVATTON
[1969] 2 All ER 616 (CA)

[A mother and daughter agreed that the mother would pay an allowance of $200 per month if the daughter would leave her employment as an embassy secretary to read for the Bar in England. On faith of the arrangement, the daughter gave up her job, moved to the United Kingdom, and commenced legal studies. Due to difficulties in finding suitable housing, their arrangement was subsequently altered, with the mother providing a house in which the daughter could reside. A dispute arose between them and the mother commenced an action to evict her daughter from the house.]

DANCKWERTS LJ: This is an action between the mother and the daughter, and one which is really deplorable. The points of difference between the two parties appear to be comparatively small, and it is distressing that they could not settle their differences amicably and avoid the bitterness and expense which is involved in this dispute carried as far as this court. ...

There is no doubt that this case is a most difficult one, but I have reached a conclusion that the present case is one of those family arrangements which depend on the good faith of the promises which are made and are not intended to be rigid, binding agreements. *Balfour v. Balfour* was a case of husband and wife, but there is no doubt that the same principles apply to dealings between other relations, such as father and son and daughter and mother. This, indeed, seems to me a compelling case. The mother and the daughter seem to have been on very good terms before 1967. The mother was arranging for a career for the daughter which she hoped would lead to success. This involved a visit to England in conditions which could not be wholly foreseen. What was required was an arrangement which was to be financed by the mother and was such as would be adaptable to circumstances, as it in fact was. The operation about the house was, in my view, not a completely fresh arrangement, but an adaptation of the mother's financial assistance to the daughter due to the situation which was found to exist in England. It was not a stiff contractual operation any more than the original arrangement.

In the result, of course, on this view, the daughter cannot resist the mother's rights as the owner of the house to the possession of which the mother is entitled. ... In my opinion, therefore, the appeal should be allowed.

SALMON LJ: I agree with the conclusion at which Danckwerts, L.J., has arrived, but I have reached it by a different route. The first point to be decided is whether or not there was ever a legally binding agreement between the mother and the daughter in relation to the daughter's reading for the Bar in England. The daughter alleges that there was such an agreement, and the mother denies it. She says that there was nothing but a loose family arrangement which had no legal effect. The onus is clearly on the daughter. There is no dispute that the parties entered into some sort of arrangement. It really depends on: (a) whether the parties intended it to be legally binding; and (b) if so, whether it was sufficiently certain to be enforceable.

Did the parties intend the arrangement to be legally binding? This question has to be solved by applying what is sometimes (although perhaps unfortunately) called an objective test. The court has to consider what the parties said and wrote in the light of all the surrounding circumstances, and then decide whether the true inference is that the ordinary man and woman, speaking or writing thus in such circumstances, would have intended to create a legally binding agreement.

Counsel for the mother has said, quite rightly that as a rule when arrangements are made between close relations, for example, between husband and wife, parent and child or uncle and nephew in relation to an allowance, there is a presumption against an intention of creating any legal relationship. This is not a presumption of law, but of fact. It derives from experience of life and human nature which shows that in such circumstances men and women usually do not intend to create legal rights and obligations, but intend to rely solely on family ties of mutual trust and affection. This has all been explained by Atkin L.J., in his celebrated judgment in *Balfour v. Balfour.* There may, however, be circumstances in which this presumption, like all other presumptions of fact, can be rebutted. ...

In the present case the learned county court judge, having had the advantage of seeing the mother and the daughter in the witness box, entirely accepted the daughter's version of the facts. He came to the conclusion that on these very special facts the true inference must be that the arrangement between the parties prior to the daughter's leaving Washington were intended by both to have contractual force. On the facts as found by the learned county court judge this was entirely different from the ordinary case of a mother promising her daughter an allowance whilst the daughter read for the Bar, or a father promising his son an allowance at university if the son passed the necessary examinations to gain admission. The daughter here was 34 years of age in 1962. She had left Trinidad and settled in Washington as long ago as 1949. In Washington she had a comfortable flat and was employed as an assistant accountant in the Indian embassy at a salary of $500 a month (over £2,000 a year). This employment carried a pension. She had a son of seven years of age who was an American citizen, and had, of course, already begun his education. There were obviously solid reasons for her staying where she was. For some years prior to 1962, however, the mother, who lived in Trinidad, had been trying hard to persuade her to throw up all that she had achieved in Washington and go to London to read for the Bar. The mother would have been very proud to have a barrister for a daughter. She also thought that her plan was in the interest of her grandson, to whom she was much attached. She envisaged that, after the daughter had been called to the Bar, she would practise in Trinidad and thereafter presumably she (the mother) would be able to see much more of the daughter than formerly. The daughter was naturally loath to leave Washington, and did not regard the mother's suggestion as feasible. The mother, however, eventually persuaded the daughter to do as she wished by promising her that, if she threw up her excellent position in Washington and came to study for the Bar in England, she would pay her daughter an allowance of $200 a month until she had completed her studies. The mother's attorney in Trinidad wrote to the daughter to confirm this. I cannot think that either intended that if, after the daughter had been in London, say, for six months, the mother dishonoured her promise and left her daughter destitute, the daughter would have no legal redress.

In the very special circumstances of this case, I consider that the true inference must be that neither the mother nor the daughter could have intended that the daughter should have no legal right to receive, and the mother no legal obligation to pay, the allowance of $200 a month. ...

[Salmon LJ went on to hold that the agreement was enforceable despite its uncertainties; the court could imply reasonable terms where the parties had left the details unsettled. However, he agreed in the result reached by Danckwerts LJ on the ground that in the circumstances a reasonable time for the duration of the daughter's legal studies had elapsed, and hence her right to stay in the house had expired. Fenton Atkinson LJ, the other member of the court, agreed with Danckwerts LJ that there was no intent to enter into a legally binding contract.]

ROSE AND FRANK COMPANY V JR CROMPTON & BROTHERS, LIMITED
[1923] 2 KB 261 (Eng CA)

J.R. Crompton and Brothers, Ltd., were English manufacturers of carbonizing tissue papers. Rose and Frank Co. were merchants in the United States handling the product of the former firm. A series of contracts had been entered into by both parties dating from 1905 which contracts having been performed, the two companies in 1913 entered into negotiations for an arrangement which was to govern future dealings.

A lengthy document was drawn up and signed by both parties in July and August, 1913. This document provided *inter alia* for the duration of the arrangement, the method of determining it, the territory covered, the fixation of prices. In the body of the document there was inscribed the following paragraph:

> This arrangement is not entered into, nor is this memorandum written, as a formal or legal agreement, and shall not be subjected to legal jurisdiction in the Law Courts either of the United States or England, but it is only a definite expression and record of the purpose and intention of the three parties concerned to which they each honourably pledge themselves with the fullest confidence, based on past business with each other, that it will be carried through by each of the ... parties with mutual loyalty and friendly co-operation.

J.R. Crompton and Bros. Ltd., becoming dissatisfied with the manner in which the plaintiffs were conducting the business in America, refused to continue the arrangement. The plaintiffs then brought this action. At the trial Bailhache J. found for the plaintiffs, adjudging the agreement of 1913 to be a legally binding contract. The defendants appealed.

SCRUTTON LJ: ... Now it is quite possible for parties to come to an agreement by accepting a proposal with the result that the agreement concluded does not give rise to legal relations. The reason of this is that the parties do not intend that their agreement shall give rise to legal relations. This intention may be implied from the subject-matter of the agreement, but it may also be expressed by the parties. In social and family relations such an intention is readily implied, while in business matters the opposite result would ordinarily follow. But I can see no reason why, even in business matters, the parties should not intend to rely on each other's good faith and honour and to exclude all idea of settling disputes by any outside intervention, with the accompanying necessity of expressing themselves so precisely that outsiders may have no difficulty in understanding what they mean. If they clearly express such an intention I can see no reason in public policy why effect should not be given to their intention.

Both legal decisions and the opinions of standard text writers support this view. ... In the early years of the war, when a member of a club brought an action against the committee to enforce his supposed rights in a golf club competition, I nonsuited him for the same reason, that from the nature of the domestic and social relations I drew the inference that the parties did not intend legal consequences to follow from them: *Lens v. Devonshire Club* (Unreported. See *The Times*, Dec. 4, 1914.) ... Judged by this test, I come to the same conclusion as the learned judge, that the particular clause in question shows a clear intention by the parties that the rest of their arrangement or agreement shall not affect their legal relations, or be enforceable in a Court of Law, but in the words of the clause, shall be "only a definite expression and record of the purpose and intention of the three parties concerned to which they each honourably pledge themselves," "and shall not be subject to legal jurisdiction." If the clause stood first in the document, the intention of the parties would be exceedingly plain.

The cases cited to us to the contrary were cases in which the form of the other part of the document, as a covenant in a deed, or a grant of a right in property in legal terms, clearly showed an intention to create a legal right, and where subsequent words, purporting not to define but to negative the creation of such a right, were rejected as repugnant. In *Ellison v. Bignold* (1821), 2 Jac. & W. 503; 37 E.R. 720, where the parties under seal "resolved and agreed and did by way of declaration and not of covenant spontaneously and fully consent and agree," Lord Eldon laid aside "the nonsense about agreeing and declaring without covenanting." An agreement under seal is quite inconsistent with no legal relations arising therefrom. And in the present case I think the parties, in expressing their vague and loosely worded agreement or arrangement, having expressly stated their intention that it shall not give rise to legal relations but shall depend only on mutual honourable trust. This destroys the decision of Bailhache J. so far as it is based on the view that the document of 1913 gives rise to legal rights which can be enforced.

[The opinions of Bankes and Atkin LJJ are omitted, and only the facts and the opinion as they relate to the validity of the written agreement as a contract are given. Insofar as the Court of Appeal declared the written agreement invalid as a contract their judgment was affirmed by the House of Lords in [1925] AC 445.]

Jones v Vernon's Pools, Ltd. [1938] 2 All ER 626 (KB). The plaintiff claimed that he had accurately completed a coupon which he entered in the defendant's weekly pool on football matches, a lottery which paid large sums to the successful applicants. The defendant denied that it had received the plaintiff's coupon, and relied on a statement printed on the back of all its coupons that "the sending in and acceptance of the coupon" should not "give rise to any legal relationship ... but [be] binding in honour only." Held, for the defendant. ATKINSON J: I am told that there are a million coupons received every weekend. Just imagine what it would mean if half the people in the country could come forward and suddenly claim that they had posted and sent in a coupon which they never had, bring actions against the pool alleging that, and calling evidence to prove that they had sent in a coupon containing the list of winning teams, and if Vernon's had to fight case after case to decide whether or not those coupons had been sent in and received. The business could not be carried on for a day on terms of that kind. ... There is to be no legal liability to pay. He has got to trust to them, and, if something goes wrong, as I say, it is his funeral, and not theirs.

Canadian Taxpayers Federation v Ontario (Minister of Finance). (2004), 73 OR (3d) 621 (Sup Ct J). ROULEAU J: In the course of election campaigns, politicians and their parties present their election platform to the electorate. In so doing they commonly make promises and pledge that they will or will not do various things if and when they are elected. It is hoped that, if elected, the politicians and their parties will keep their promises and will follow through with the pledges given. This said, however, few people would consider that all of the promises made and pledges given constitute legally-binding agreements between the candidate and the elector or electors to whom these promises or pledges were made. ... It is a well-settled principle that, when elected into government, commitments previously made by a Minister regarding future conduct cannot fetter that Minister's freedom to "propose, consider and, if they think fit, vote for laws, even laws which are inconsistent with the contractual obligations." ... [U]ndertakings given as to what the government will or will not legislate in the future are without value, do not amount to consideration and cannot form the basis of a contract. ... While it is no doubt desirable and important to the proper functioning of a democracy that candidates and parties do their best to follow through with the promises and pledges made, it is not the role of the courts ... to intervene to enforce such promises and pledges. Rather, the remedy is for the electorate to consider and weigh the record of each candidate and party at the time of voting.

QUESTIONS

1. Powell lived in the Pershore fire district and the Upton police district. When his barn caught fire, he telephoned the Upton police office to ask for "the fire brigade" and the police telephoned the Upton fire brigade, which responded to the call. The Upton brigade apparently believed the fire was in its district. Unknown to Powell, although the Upton brigade was allowed to attend fires outside its district, it charged for such service. Had the Pershore brigade come, it would have done so for free. Powell was held liable to pay the Upton brigade (*Upton-on-Severn Rural District Council v Powell*, [1942] 1 All ER 220 (CA), noted (1942) 20 Can Bar Rev 557). What "intention" did Powell have in this case? See Waddams at para 148; Fridman at 42-43. Was this really an unjust enrichment case? See J Edelman, "Liability in Unjust Enrichment Where a Contract Fails to Materialize" in Burrows & Peel 166.

2. Is there a presumption against an intention to form a legal relationship between (i) a holder of an ecclesiastical office and his church (see *Brewer v Incorporated Synod of the Diocese of Ottawa of the Anglican Church of Canada*, [1996] OJ No 634 (QL) (Gen Div); *Preston v President of the Methodist Conference*, [2013] UKSC 29) and (ii) two consumers engaging in the exchange of rapid-fire emails (see *Girouard v Druet*, 2012 NBCA 40, noted (2014) 65 UNBLJ 403)? Should there be?

3. Is the intention requirement one that is based in public policy or one that is discernible from principle (or perhaps some combination of the two)? For a discussion, see MacDougall at 53-54; Waddams at para 159-60; MG Pratt, "Disclaimers of Contractual Liability and Voluntary Obligations" (2014) 51 Osgoode Hall LJ 767; and the excerpts below.

4. Can the results of the cases excerpted above be accounted for on alternative grounds—for example, lack of consideration, lack of certainty, or presence of exclusion clauses? For such an argument, see J Swan, "Consideration and the Reasons for Enforcing Contracts" (1976) 15 UWO L Rev 83. If they were so accountable, would this bolster Williston's argument (set out below)?

Pollock on Contracts. 13th ed at 3, n 5: An appointment between two friends to go out for a walk or to read a book together is not an agreement in the legal sense: for it is not meant to produce, nor does it produce, any new legal duty or right or any change in existing ones. Nothing but the absence of intention seems to prevent a contract from arising in many cases of this kind. A asks B for dinner. Here is a proposal of something to be done by B at A's request, namely, coming to A's house at the appointed time. If B accepts, there is in form a contract by mutual promises. ... Why is A not legally bound to have meat and drink ready for B, so that if A had forgotten his invitation and gone elsewhere B should have a right for action? Only because no legal bond was intended by the parties.

Williston on Contracts. Students' ed rev, s 21: The further statement of Savigny, which has been popularized for English and American lawyers by Sir Frederick Pollock and others, that not only mental assent to a promise in fact, but an intent to form a legal relation is a requisite for the formation of contracts ... cannot be accepted. ... In a system of law ... which does not enforce promises unless some benefit to the promisor or detriment to the promisee has been asked and given, there is no propriety in such a limitation. The only proof of its existence will be the production of cases holding that, although consideration was asked and given for a promise, it is, nevertheless, not enforceable because a legal relation was not contemplated.

III. NON-BARGAIN PROMISES

A. THE SEAL

An early form of action, called covenant, permitted enforcement of promises, even without any element of exchange, if under seal. The seal, originally molten wax dropped onto the document and impressed with a die, later took the form of a gummed paper wafer. A sealed document (also known as a deed, a covenant, a formal contract, or a specialty) usually contains formal language and ends with the words "signed, sealed, and delivered." Through the passage of time, the requirements of signing, sealing, and delivering have become much attenuated.

Friedmann Equity Developments Inc v Final Note Ltd. 2000 SCC 34, [2001] 1 SCR 842. BASTARACHE J: Because a contract under seal derives its validity from its form alone, there are several incidents of such a contract which differ from those of a simple contract. The fundamental difference between contracts under seal and simple contracts is in relation to the doctrine of consideration. The law will enforce a contract under seal even without consideration. Therefore, a gratuitous promise which is expressed in an instrument under seal is enforceable. There are other incidents of a contract under seal, which may be summarized as follows:

1. Where a debtor covenants in a deed to pay a debt antecedently based in simple contract, the right to sue in debt merges in the right to sue on the covenant and is extinguished in law.
2. In an action on a deed, a statement in the deed may operate by way of estoppel against the maker of the statement.
3. At common law, only a person named in an instrument under seal as a party to it could sue on a covenant in the instrument expressed to be for his benefit.
4. The limitation period for an action for a breach of a contract under seal may be longer than for a simple contract in some provinces.

Linton v Royal Bank of Canada. [1967] 1 OR 315 (H Ct J). HARTT J: Here we have a document which ends with the words "signed, sealed and delivered" and which has the word "seal" in parentheses beside the space provided for a signature or signatures. The guarantor signed the document without altering either of those printed items, and had it delivered to the creditor. Is it reasonable to say that the addition of a paper seal beside the signature in these circumstances was a material alteration of the agreement between the parties? Would it not be more accurate to say that it was an alteration "which carried out the intention of the parties already apparent on the face of the document." When a party signs a document, which by its language purports to be a deed, he cannot afterwards deny that it is so. ... When the guarantee in question was signed by Mr. Linton with the intention of constituting the document a deed, it became such. The important evidence in this regard was the markings on the document itself, namely "signed, sealed and delivered" and the word "seal" beside the space provided for signature. The document being a deed from the outset, the addition of a paper wafer by the bank cannot be considered a material alteration affecting the "legal incidence" of the document.

Vincent v Premo Enterprises Ltd. [1969] 2 WLR 1256 (CA). LORD DENNING MR: The law as to "delivery" of a deed is of ancient date. But it is reasonably clear. A deed is very different from a contract. On a contract for the sale of land, the contract is not binding on the parties until they have exchanged their parts. But with a deed it is different. A deed is binding on the maker of it, even though the parts have not been exchanged, as long as it has been signed, sealed and delivered. "Delivery" in this connection does not mean "handed over" to the other side. It means delivered in the old legal sense, namely, an act done so as to evince an intention to be bound. Even though the deed remains in the possession of the maker, or of his solicitor, he is bound by it if he has done some act evincing an intention to be bound, as by saying: "I deliver this my act and deed." He may, however, make the "delivery" conditional: in which case the deed is called an "escrow" which becomes binding when the condition is fulfilled. WINN LJ: [I]t might be very helpful in modern life if there were some modification of the law, departing somewhat from the strictness of the old rule the effect of which my Lord has indicated, viz., that a man becomes bound when he executes a deed in the form usually adopted ... . I think it might be more realistic to depend upon physical movement or legal control of the document after the time when it is sealed.

NOTES AND QUESTIONS

1. Although Lord Denning correctly states the modern rule, his summary is not historically accurate because this understanding of "delivery" is of fairly recent origin. See *Xenos v Wickham* (1866), LR 2 HL 296. Ironically, the reform suggested by Winn LJ would not be novel because the traditional common law position was that there had to be an actual delivery or a change in legal control of the document; see DEC Yale, "The Delivery of a Deed" (1970) 28:1 Cambridge LJ 52.

2. For a view of sealing that is somewhat different to that taken in *Linton*, see *Royal Bank of Canada v Kiska* (1967), 2 OR 379 (CA) per Laskin JA (dissenting) and *872899 Ontario Inc v Iacovoni* (1998), 163 DLR (4th) 263 (Ont CA).

3. For general discussions of sealed contracts and their idiosyncratic application vis-à-vis other areas of the law, see Waddams at paras 171-77; McCamus at 263-76; MacDougall at 99-100; Swan & Adamski at 148-62; TG Youdan, "The Formal Requirements of a Deed" (1979) 5 Bus L Rev 71; GHL Fridman, "Some Words About Deed" (2002) 81 Can Bar Rev 69.

4. The requirements of signing, sealing, and delivering look to be further affected by legislation dealing with e-commerce. For example, the *Electronic Commerce Act, 2000*, SO 2000, c 17 (ECA) has "functional equivalency rules" that provide for electronic signatures and the electronic provision of written documents (see ss 4-11). Section 11(6) of the ECA also contemplates that rules for seal equivalency will be prescribed in the regulations. These regulations have yet to be promulgated. For more on the ECA, see the Notes and Questions section following its excerption in section I.E, above. For a general examination of the issues surrounding electronic documents and evidentiary issues, see GS Takach, *Computer Law*, 2nd ed (Toronto: Irwin Law, 2003) ch 6.

5. Why should a modern court enforce a promise simply because the promisor affixed a red sticker to his or her written promise? Consider the following excerpts.

FULLER, "CONSIDERATION AND FORM"
(1941) 41 Colum L Rev 799 at 800-1

The Evidentiary Function. The most obvious function of a legal formality is, to use Austin's words, that of providing "evidence of the existence and purport of the contract, in case of controversy." The need for evidentiary security may be satisfied in a variety of ways: by requiring a writing, or attestation, or the certification of a notary. It may even be satisfied, to some extent, by such a device as the Roman *stipulatio*, which compelled an oral spelling out of the promise in a manner sufficiently ceremonious to impress its terms on participants and possible bystanders.

The Cautionary Function. A formality may also perform a cautionary or deterrent function by acting as a check against inconsiderate action. The seal in its original form fulfilled this purpose remarkably well. The affixing and impressing of a wax wafer—symbol in the popular mind of legalism and weightiness—was an excellent device for inducing the circumspect frame of mind appropriate in one pledging his future. To a less extent any requirement of a writing, of course, serves the same purpose, as do requirements of attestation, notarization, etc.

The Channeling Function. Though most discussions of the purposes served by formalities go no further than the analysis just presented, this analysis stops short of recognizing one of the most important functions of form. That a legal formality may perform a function not yet described can be shown by the seal. The seal not only insures a satisfactory memorial of the promise and induces deliberation in the making of it. It serves also to mark or signalize the enforceable promise; it furnishes a simple and external test of enforceability. This function of form Ihering described as "the facilitation of judicial diagnosis" and he employed the analogy of coinage in explaining it.

> Form is for a legal transaction what the stamp is for a coin. Just as the stamp of the coin relieves us from the necessity of testing the metallic content and weight—in short, the value of the coin (a test which we could not avoid if uncoined metal were offered to us in payment), in the same way legal formalities relieve the judge of an inquiry *whether* a legal transaction was intended, and—in case different forms are fixed for different legal transactions—*which* was intended.

In this passage it is apparent that Ihering has placed an undue emphasis on the utility of form for the judge, to the neglect of its significance for those transacting business out of court. If we look at the matter purely from the standpoint of the convenience of the judge, there is nothing to establish the forms used in legal transactions from the "formal" element which to some degree permeates all thinking. Even in the field of criminal law "judicial diagnosis" is "facilitated" by formal definitions, presumptions, and artificial construction of fact. The thing which characterizes the law of contracts and conveyances is that in this field forms are deliberately used, and are intended to be so used, by the parties whose acts are to be judged by the law. To the business man who wishes to make his own or another's promise binding, the seal was at common law available as a device for the accomplishment of his objective. In this aspect form offers a legal framework into which the party may fit his actions, or, to change the figure, it offers channels for the legally effective expression of intention. It is with this aspect of form in mind that I have described the third function of legal formalities as "the channeling function."

ALAN BRUDNER, "RECONSTRUCTING CONTRACTS"
(1993) 43 UTLJ 1 at 34-35 (footnotes omitted)

The fact that promises under seal are binding without consideration has led many to surmise that consideration must be a functional substitute for a seal. If the purpose of the seal is to give evidence of an intention to beget legal consequences or to encourage careful deliberation, then the doctrine of consideration must have this purpose as well. And then it is a short step to the conclusion that many things (such as a signed writing) besides consideration may perform the evidentiary or cautionary function, so that the bargain requirement begins to look like a fetish if insisted upon without regard to the contextual features that might make it superfluous. Taken to its extreme, this reasoning issues in a proposal to redefine consideration to mean any good reason for enforcing a promise, of which the existence of a bargain is only one.

The flaw in this reasoning is the assumption that consideration and the seal are interchangeable means by which to test the legal seriousness of a promise. Those who start from this premise forget that the enforcement of promises in an action for debt long predates the writ of *assumpsit* from which the modern action for breach of contract derives; and they forget too that promises under seal are enforceable only upon delivery to the donee. These phenomena suggest that the enforcement of promises under seal rests on the theoretical foundations different from that of enforcement of promises *per se*. In fact, promises under seal are enforced not as executory promises but as executed gifts. A gift does not pass title to the donee until delivered, but the delivery of a sealed deed of gift counts as a symbolic delivery of the object. In the same way, a promise signed, sealed, and delivered passes possessory title to the donee, and the court enforces the title. Thus, the seal is not an alternative to consideration in triggering the enforcement of a promise; rather it is something that (along with delivery) transforms a promise into an executed transfer. By contrast, the element required for the enforceability of a promise *as promise* is consideration. This distinction will perhaps seem artificial to those who see only the identical act of promising in both cases. However, what matters for our understanding of deeds and contracts is not that the same raw acts of promising underlie both; what matters is the theory behind the legal enforcement of these acts. Before the law attained the sophistication of enforcing executory contracts, it enforced promises by interpreting them as symbolic transfers when accompanied by formalities signifying the crossing of a boundary between promise and "deed." But if the legal theory behind enforcement differs as between deeds and contracts, then the formalities attached to these instruments must also differ in significance, since the only meaning these formalities can have is the one that theory gives them. If promises under seal are enforced only as executed transfers of possessory title, while unsealed promises for consideration are enforced as promises, then the seal provides no hint to the meaning of consideration.

QUESTIONS

1. Which view of the law, that of Fuller or Brudner, is more compelling?
2. Which of the three functions indicated by Fuller (evidentiary, cautionary, or channelling) does the seal continue to further?

LAW REVISION COMMITTEE, SIXTH INTERIM REPORT
(1937) Cmnd 5449 (Eng), 15 Can Bar Rev 585

[29] Basing themselves on the views of Lord Mansfield stated in *Pillans v. Van Mierop* [(1765), 3 Burr 1663] ... many judges and writers of textbooks (see, in particular, Professor Holdsworth, *History of English Law*, Vol. VII, p. 48) have advocated that a promise in writing, though not under seal and not supported by consideration, should be enforceable. The only justification for the doctrine of consideration at the present day, it is said, is that it furnishes persuasive evidence of the intention of the parties concerned to create a binding obligation, but it does not follow from this that consideration should be accepted as the *sole* test of such intention. This intention ought to be provable by other and equally persuasive evidence such as, e.g., the fact that the promisor has put his promise in writing. We agree with this view, and we therefore recommend that consideration should not be required in those cases in which the promise is in writing.

We must make it clear when we speak of the promise being in writing we mean the promise which is being sued upon, and we do not mean that, in the case of a contract consisting of mutual promises both the promises must be in writing.

[30] On the other hand we are of the opinion that the entire promise should be in writing to bring it within the rule and that no other evidence of the promise, whether in writing or partly in writing and partly oral, should be considered sufficient. Nor do we recommend that the written promise must be signed: all that is necessary is that the Court should be satisfied that the writing (which includes typescript and print) is that of the promisor or his agent. This can be proved in the same way as any other question of fact is proved. Thus the requirement of writing which we are now recommending has nothing to do with the old "memorandum or note" of the Statute of Frauds. It differs both in purpose and in content.

This recommendation does not mean that a promise in writing will be binding in every case. It will still be necessary for the Court to find that the parties intended to create a binding obligation. Just as the presence of consideration today does not convert a social engagement into a legal contract, so the presence of writing will not convert a gratuitous promise into a legally binding one unless the Court determines that the parties intended it to be legally binding.

LAW REFORM COMMISSION OF BRITISH COLUMBIA,
Report on Deeds and Seals, 1988
(Vancouver: Commission, 1988)

[The Law Reform Commission recommended in this report that specialty obligations be retained, but that they operate in the same manner as simple contracts. The commission commented:]

This approach to reform raises the question: what advantage is there to retaining the concept of specialty obligations if they are to be indistinguishable from simple obligations? There is a very significant advantage.

For the most part, paralleling simple and specialty obligations should dramatically simplify the law. The parties may use either a contract or a deed to record their arrangements and be assured that the legal consequences are the same. There is, consequently, little advantage to using a deed, except in one respect.

As a general rule the law will not enforce a gratuitous obligation unless it is recorded by deed. The law of contract depends upon the concept of consideration. There are, however, circumstances where the parties will wish to enter into gratuitous obligations confident that they will be binding. That has been the chief utility of the deed in modern times and, in our view, it should be retained ...

The point may be raised that a similar result could be achieved simply by enacting legislation that provides that obligations intended by the parties to be binding shall be binding. Reform along these lines would remove the need to retain the concept of specialty obligations.

We fear, however, that it would also do grave injury to the modern law of contract. Would these obligations be contractual? If not, what kind of obligations would they be? In our view it is simpler by far to retain the concept of specialty obligations, altered as we have proposed, than to define a new kind of statutory obligation or to provide that there are contractual obligations enforceable by some theory totally inconsistent with that which underlies the enforcement of contractual obligations generally. (pp. 42-43)

NOTES AND QUESTIONS

1. Canadian legislatures have not hastened to "abolish the seal," whatever that expression may mean, but legislatures in the United States have been quite active. For example, several American jurisdictions have language like California's *Civil Code*, s 1629: "All distinctions between sealed and unsealed instruments are abolished." As a result of this section, are unsealed promises as enforceable as sealed ones used to be? Or are sealed instruments no longer enforceable unless consideration is proved? The California Code also provided, in s 1614: "A written instrument is presumptive evidence of consideration."

2. Compare California's *Civil Code* with the *Uniform Written Obligations Act* approved by the Commissioners on Uniform State Laws in 1925. It is in force only in Pennsylvania:

A written release or promise hereafter made and signed by the person releasing or promising shall not be invalid or unenforceable for lack of consideration, if the writing also contains an additional express statement, in any form of language, that the signer intends to be legally bound.

3. Williston, who advocated the model Act, says (*Williston on Contracts*, 3rd ed, s 219 at 794): "[E]fforts to fill the gap created by statutory abolition of the seal have proved largely unsuccessful." See *Corbin on Contracts*, § 257, for a short criticism. Critics have also suggested that the form of words can become as sterile as the seal through mass reproduction in fine print on ready-made forms of contracts, and the further suggestion has been made that the model Act be modified to require that the words be in the handwriting of the promisor after the principle of holograph wills. See also Steele, "The Uniform Written Obligations Act: A Criticism" (1920) 21 Ill L Rev 185.

B. PAST CONSIDERATION

LAMPLEIGH V BRATHWAIT
(1615), Hobart 105, 80 ER 255

Anthony Lampleigh brought an assumpsit against Thomas Brathwait, and declared that, whereas the defendant had feloniously slain one Patrick Mahume, the defendant, after said felony done, instantly required the plaintiff to labor and do his endeavor to obtain his pardon from the king; whereupon the plaintiff upon the same request did, by all the means he could and many days' labor, do his endeavor to obtain the king's pardon for the said felony; viz., in riding and journeying at his own charges from London to Reiston, when the king was there, and to London back, and so to and from Newmarket, to obtain pardon for the defendant for the said felony. Afterwards in consideration of the premises, the said defendant did promise the said plaintiff to give him £100 and that he had not, to his damage £120.

To this, the defendant pleaded *non assumpsit*, and found for the plaintiff, damage £100. It was said in arrest of judgment that the consideration was past.

It was agreed that a mere voluntary courtesy will not have a consideration to uphold an assumpsit. But if that courtesy were moved by a suit or request of the party that gives the assumpsit, it will bind; for the promise, though it follows, yet it is not naked, but couples itself with the suit before, and the merits of the party procured by that suit, which is the difference.

Kennedy v Broun. (1863), 13 CB (NS) 677, 143 ER 268, 292. ERLE CJ: In *Lampleigh v. Brathwait*, it was assumed that the journeys which the plaintiff performed at the request of the defendant, and the other services he rendered, would have been sufficient to make any promise binding if it had been connected therewith in one contract; the peculiarity of the decision lies in connecting a subsequent promise with a prior consideration after it had been executed. Probably at the present day, such service or such request would have raised a promise by implication to pay what it was worth; and the subsequent promise of a sum certain would have been evidence for the jury to fix the amount.

Pao On v Lau Yiu Long. [1980] AC 614 (PC). LORD SCARMAN: An act done before the giving of a promise to make a payment or to confer some other benefit can sometimes be consideration for the promise. The act must have been done at the promisors' request: the parties must have understood that the act was to be remunerated either by a payment or the conferment of some other benefit: and payment, or the conferment of a benefit, must have been legally enforceable had it been promised in advance. ... It matters not whether the [promise] thus given be regarded as the best evidence of the benefit intended to be conferred ... or as the positive bargain which fixes the benefit on the faith of which the promise was given—though where, as here, the subject is a written contract, the better analysis is probably that of the "positive bargain."

QUESTIONS

1. What if the later promise is unreasonably low in comparison to the market value of the requested act? Could the promisee sue for this higher amount? What if the later promise is unreasonably high? Could the promisor refuse to perform her promise in full?

2. X is taken ill at his club. Y, a doctor, attends him. On recovering, X orally promises to give Y Blackacre, worth $100,000, for his services. Can A claim Blackacre? Would the third requirement of enforceability from *Pao On* come into play?

3. Are these cases really bargains in disguise? Are past consideration cases better seen as instances of unjust enrichment? See McCamus at 237-43.

4. Should the court be prepared to imply a request when, for whatever reason, the promisor is unable to do so herself? For an example of where a request was implied, see *Webb v McGowin*, 3 Div 768 (Alabama CA 1935). The facts of the case are as follows: W and M both worked at the local mill. W was responsible for keeping the upper floor of the mill free of pine block remnants. The usual and ordinary way of clearing the floor was to drop the blocks from the upper level to the level below. As W started to turn one of the blocks loose, which in this case weighed 75 pounds, he noticed that M was standing directly where the block was to fall. Had W let go of the block it would have struck M with enough force to have seriously injured or killed him. In order to save M, W diverted the block by falling with it. Although M was saved, W was so severely injured that he was unable to work for the rest of his life. In consideration of this act of bravery, M promised that he would pay $15 every two weeks to W during the remainder of W's life. M made the payments for almost nine years but after M's death, his estate refused to make further payments. W then brought suit to recover the unpaid installments. The court found that M's promise was enforceable on the basis that M's material benefit of being saved meant that his "express promise to pay appellant for the services rendered was an affirmance or ratification of what appellant had done raising the presumption that the services had been rendered at [M's] request." Would the judges in the cases that follow be willing to imply requests?

ROSCORLA V THOMAS
(1842), 3 QB 234, 114 ER 496

The plaintiff bought a horse from the defendant for £30. There was apparently no promise made at the time about the horse's qualities. Later the defendant did promise the plaintiff that the horse was not over five years old and was sound and free from vice. It then appeared that the horse was "very vicious, restive, ungovernable, and ferocious." In an action based on the later promise (assumpsit) there was a verdict for the plaintiff but the defendant obtained a rule nisi to arrest the judgment on the ground that there was no consideration.

LORD DENMAN CJ (for the court): ... It may be taken as a general rule, subject to exception not applicable to this case, that the promise must be co-extensive with the consideration. In the present case, the only promise that would result from the consideration as stated, and be co-extensive with it, would be to deliver the horse upon request. The precedent sale without a warranty, though at the request of the defendant, imposes no other duty or obligation upon him. It is clear therefore that the consideration stated would not raise an implied promise by the defendant that the horse was sound or free from vice.

But the promise in the present case must be taken to be, as in fact it was, express and the question is, whether that fact will warrant the extension of the promise beyond that which would be implied by law; and whether the consideration, though insufficient to raise an implied promise, will nevertheless support an express one. And we think that it will not.

The cases in which it has been held that, under certain circumstances, a consideration insufficient to raise an implied promise, will nevertheless support an express one, will be found collected and reviewed in the note (a) to *Wennall v. Adney* (1802), 3 B. & P. 247; 127 E.R. 137 and in the case of *Eastwood v. Kenyon*. They are cases of voidable contracts subsequently ratified, of debts barred by operation of law subsequently revived, and of equitable and moral obligations which, but for some rule of law, would of themselves have been sufficient to raise an implied promise. All these cases are distinguishable from, and indeed inapplicable to the present, which appears to us to fall within the general rule, that a consideration past and executed will support no other promise than such as would be implied by law.

The rule for arresting the judgment upon the first count must therefore be made absolute.

Mills v Wyman. 3 Pick [20 Mass] 207 (SJC 1825). PARKER CJ: If moral obligation, in its fullest sense, is a good substratum for an express promise, it is not easy to perceive why it is not equally good to support an implied promise. What a man ought to do, generally he ought to be made to do, whether he promise or refuse. But the law of society has left most of such obligations to the interior forum, as the tribunal of conscience has been aptly called. Is there not a moral obligation upon every son who has become affluent by means of the education and advantages bestowed upon him by his father, to relieve that father from pecuniary embarrassment, to promote his comfort and happiness, and even to share with him his riches, if thereby he will be made happy? And yet such a son may, with impunity, leave such a father in any degree of penury above that which will expose the community in which he dwells to the danger of being obliged to preserve him from absolute want. ... Without doubt there are great interests of society which justify withholding the coercive arm of the law from these duties of imperfect obligation as they are called; imperfect, not because they are less binding upon the conscience than those which are called perfect, but because the wisdom of the social law does not impose sanctions upon them.

NOTES AND QUESTIONS

1. As indicated in the above cases, there was a school of thought in the 18th and early 19th centuries that maintained that the existence of a moral obligation should in itself be sufficient reason for enforcing a promise to fulfill that obligation. In *Lee v Muggeridge* (1813), 5 Taunt 36, Lord Mansfield said: "It has long been established that where a person is bound morally and conscientiously to pay a debt, though not legally bound, a subsequent promise to pay will give

a right of action." Since *Eastwood v Kenyon* (1840), 11 Ad & E 438, this view has been regarded as overruled, but there are several situations where relics of the earlier view may still be found. One principle is that promises to pay prior debts may sometimes be enforceable, even though the debt itself is for some reason unenforceable. For a discussion, see Waddams at paras 182-91.

2. Section 53 of the *Bills of Exchange Act* provides that antecedent debt or liability constitutes sufficient consideration for a bill of exchange. Why is this thought necessary? Consider: A borrows money from B agreeing to repay the sum with interest in one month. At the end of the month, A gives B a cheque. Without s 53, would there be good consideration for the giving of the cheque? What arguments could be made? See *Currie v Misa* (1875), LR 10 Exch 153.

3. A, seeing B's house on fire, hires men to assist him in putting out the fire at an expense of $2,000. B, who was absent at the time, hears of A's actions and promises to pay him $1,000. The house burns to the ground and is now practically worthless (that is, worth $200). Can A recover as a matter of common law? In which amount? Would A fare any better using the legal doctrines excerpted below?

RESTATEMENT OF THE LAW OF CONTRACTS (SECOND)
American Law Institute, 1981

86(1) A promise made in recognition of a benefit previously received by the promisor from the promisee is binding to the extent necessary to prevent injustice.

(2) A promise is not binding under Subsection (1)

(a) if the promisee conferred the benefit as a gift or for other reasons the promisor has not been unjustly enriched; or

(b) to the extent that its value is disproportionate to the benefit.

CIVIL CODE OF QUÉBEC
LRQ, c C-1991

1482. Management of the business of another exists where a person, the manager, spontaneously and under no obligation to act, voluntarily and opportunely undertakes to manage the business of another, the principal, without his knowledge .... .

1484. The manager is bound to continue the management undertaken until he can withdraw without risk of loss or until the principal ... is able to provide for it. ...

1486. When the conditions of management of the business of another are fulfilled, even if the desired result has not been attained, the principal shall reimburse the manager for all the necessary or useful expenses he has incurred and indemnify him for any injury he has suffered by reason of his management and not through his own fault. ...

1487. Expenses or obligations are assessed as to their necessity or usefulness at the time they were incurred or contracted by the manager. ...

1490. Management inopportunely undertaken by a manager is binding on the principal only to the extent of his enrichment.

C. SUBSEQUENT RELIANCE

KN LLEWELLYN, "WHAT PRICE CONTRACT? AN ESSAY IN PERSPECTIVE"
(1931) 40 Yale LJ 704 at 741-44

[Reprinted by permission of the Yale Law Journal Company and Fred B. Rothman & Company from the *Yale Law Journal*.]

Neither causes nor processes of the development of the consideration concept are at all clear in detail. We do not know how the Germanic system of awarding what one may speak of as the advantage of proof to the apparently sounder side came to degenerate into the debt-defendant's power as of right to swear himself out of judgment. We do not know whether the fear of stout swearers or the growth of commercial transactions was the more vital factor in developing assumpsit; we know little if anything of the details of the latter pressure on the courts from, say, 1570 to 1620. We do not know in any clarity the process by which the case-misfeasance-tort root and the *quid-pro-quo* root out of debt were built together. What is clear, is the emergence of a current definition in terms of benefit to the promisor or detriment to the promisee as the agreed equivalent and inducing cause of the promise; a definition which purports both to show what is adequate and what is necessary to a successful action in assumpsit or its heirs. The current formulation has the merit of covering most cases, even if it does not cover all. Indeed, it is obvious that as soon as the arbitrary but utterly necessary logical jump is made, of making mutual promises serve to support each other, the great bulk of business promises are comfortably cared for.

Four troublesome classes of cases remain. There are business promises such as "firm offers," understood to be good for a fixed time, but revoked before. They are frequent; they are and should be relied on. As to them our consideration doctrine is badly out of joint. Closely related in orthodox doctrine, less so in practice, is the second class; promises which call for acceptance by extended action (such as laying twenty miles of track), revoked while the work is in process. A third and hugely important class is that of either additional or modifying business promises made after an original deal has been agreed upon. Law and logic go astray whenever such dealings are regarded as truly comparable to new agreements. They are not. No business man regards them so. They are going-transaction adjustments, as different from agreement-formation as are corporate organization and corporate management; and the line of legal dealing with them which runs over waiver and estoppel is based on sound intuition. The fourth main trouble-making class has only a doctrinal connection with business; it lies chiefly in the field of family affairs; it includes the promise made and relied on, but which did not bargain for reliance, and in the case of promises to provide it laps over into the third party beneficiary problem. As to all of these classes but the first, a distinct but very uneven tendency is observable in the courts to strain by one dodge or another toward enforcement. That tendency is healthy. It may be expected to increase. It has already had some effects on orthodox doctrine, and may be expected to have more. Meanwhile the first class mentioned goes largely untouched.

1. Gratuitous Undertakings

Ames, "The History of Assumpsit." (1888) 2 Harv L Rev 1: The action against a bailee for negligent custody was looked upon ... as a tort, and not as a contract. The immediate cause of the injury in the case of the bailee was, it is true, a nonfeasance, and not, as in the case of the surgeon or carpenter, a misfeasance. ... The action against the bailee sounding in tort, consideration was no more an essential part of the count than it was in action against a surgeon ... . Oddly enough, the earliest attempts to charge bailees in assumpsit were made when the bailment was gratuitous. These attempts, just before and after 1600, were unsuccessful, because the plaintiff could not make out any consideration. The gratuitous bailment was of course not a benefit, but a burden to the defendant; and, on the other hand, it was not regarded as a detriment, but an advantage to the plaintiff. But in 1623 it was finally decided, not without a great straining, it must be conceded, of the doctrine of consideration, that a bailee might be charged in assumpsit on a gratuitous bailment.

Baxter v Jones. (1903), 6 OLR 360 (CA). The plaintiff asked the defendant, his fire insurance agent, through whom he was placing extra insurance on his mills and machinery, to notify the other companies who held his insurance. The defendant gratuitously agreed to do this but failed to carry out his promise. On a fire damage claim the other companies, not having been notified of the extra insurance, denied liability, but settled for $1,000 less than they would have had to pay under the increased policies. This action was to recover the $1,000. Held, for the plaintiff. MacLENNAN JA: Mr. Baxter says he went to [Mr. Jones] for this additional insurance just because his other risks were in his office, and, it is not contended that there was any consideration between the plaintiffs and the defendant in connection with the business. The only consideration in the matter was the premium which was paid to the company. As between the plaintiffs and defendant, therefore, the whole business was voluntary. It was contended that the procurement of the policy and the promise to notify the companies were one single transaction, and that having undertaken the business and performed it negligently, the defendant was responsible although there was no consideration for the contract: *Coggs v. Bernard* and *Elsee v. Gatward*.

De La Bere v Pearson, Limited. [1908] 1 KB 280 (Eng CA). The defendants published a newspaper in which "readers ... desiring financial advice in these columns" were invited to address their queries to the city editor. The plaintiff, a regular reader (it is not reported that he was a purchaser or subscriber), wrote asking how best he could invest £800, and specifically requesting the name of a "good stock broker." The city editor turned the letter over to an "outside stock broker" who persuaded the plaintiff to invest £1400 with him. No shares were bought, the money instead was appropriated to the stock broker's private affairs. He was an undischarged bankrupt. The city editor knew that the broker was not on the stock exchange, but did not know of his bankruptcy, although he could have found out. The publishers had done what they could to help several of their readers who had lost money to the broker. The plaintiff sued the defendant publishers for damages for breach of contract to exercise due care in giving financial advice to the plaintiff. The lord chief justice held that the plaintiff was entitled to recover the £1,400 sent by him to the broker for investment. The defendant appealed, but the appeal was dismissed. On the question of consideration, nothing appears in the report of the argument. VAUGHAN WILLIAMS LJ: In the first place, I think there was a contract as between the plaintiff and the defendants. The defendants advertised, offering to give advice with reference to investments. The plaintiff, accepting that offer, asked for advice, and asked for the name of a good stock broker. The questions and answers were, if the defendants chose, to be inserted in their paper as published; such publication might obviously have a tendency to increase the sale of the defendants' paper. I think that this offer, when accepted, resulted in a contract for good consideration.

Hedley Byrne & Co Ltd v Heller & Partners Ltd. [1964] AC 465 (HL). LORD DEVLIN: Many cases could be cited in which the same result has been achieved by setting up some nominal consideration and suing in contract instead of in tort. In *Coggs v. Bernard*, Holt C.J. put the obligation on both grounds. He said: "... [S]econdly, it is objected, and there is no consideration to ground this promise upon, and therefore the undertaking is but *nudum pactum*. But to this I answer, that the owners trusting him with the goods is a sufficient consideration to oblige him to a careful management. Indeed, if the agreement had been executory, to carry these brandies from the one place to the other on such a day, the defendant had not been bound to carry them. But this is a different case, for assumpsit does not only signify a future agreement, but in such a case as this, it signifies an actual entry upon the thing, and taking the trust upon himself. And if a man will do that, and miscarries in the performance of his trust, an action will lie against him for that, though nobody could have compelled him to do the thing."

De La Bere v. Pearson Ltd. is an example of a case of this sort decided on the ground that there was a sufficiency of consideration. ... The case being brought in contract, Vaughan Williams L.J. thought that there was sufficient consideration in the fact that the plaintiff consented to the publication of his question in the defendants' paper if the defendants so chose. For Barnes P. the consideration appears to have lain in the plaintiff addressing an inquiry as invited. In the same way when in *Everett v. Griffiths* the Court of Appeal was considering the liability of a doctor towards the person he was certifying, Scrutton L.J. said that the submission to treatment would be a good consideration.

My Lords, I have cited these instances so as to show that in one way or another the law has ensured that in this type of case a just result has been reached. But I think that today the result can and should be achieved by the application of the law of negligence and that it is unnecessary and undesirable to construct an artificial consideration.

NOTES AND QUESTIONS

1. Negligent misrepresentation in tort is dealt with in more detail in Chapter 9.

2. Why should an action on the supposedly gratuitous promise of the defendant in *Jones* be justified by the ancient law? For a discussion of the rationale behind the gratuitous undertakings cases, see WA Seavey, "Reliance on Gratuitous Promises" (1951) 64 Harv L Rev 913; CO Gregory, "Gratuitous Undertakings and the Duty of Care" (1951-52) 1 DePaul L Rev 30; MP Gergen, "Negligent Misrepresentation as Contract" (2013) 101 Cal L Rev 953.

3. Could *Jones* be explained on the basis that the plaintiff agreed to buy insurance through the defendant agent at his request so that he would earn a commission on the premium? Then could not the one act be consideration for two promises, to procure and to notify?

2. Estoppel

Skidmore v Bradford. (1869), LR 8 Eq 134. An uncle promised his nephew, Edward Bradford, that he would buy him a warehouse for £5,000. The uncle paid £1,000 and Edward Bradford entered into a contract to buy the warehouse. The uncle paid a further £500, but died before making any further payment. The estate was held liable to pay the balance. STUART VC: If Edward Bradford were a mere volunteer there is no principle on which he would be entitled to come to this Court to have the testator's intended act of bounty completed. ... But if on the faith of the testator's representation he has involved himself in any liability, or had incurred any obligation, he cannot be regarded as a volunteer, and if so, the testator's assets are liable to make good the representation on the faith of which the nephew had entered into this contract.

Re Hudson. (1885), 54 LJ Ch 811. COOKSON QC (in the argument): [T]he testator signed a document by which he represented that the committee of the Jubilee Fund had £20,000 coming from him at their disposal, and relying on that document they have collected and expended money and incurred liabilities, and have in fact come under an obligation to provide £3,500 more than has come to their hands. The consideration for a contract need not consist of money; if a person suffers any detriment or inconvenience, that is sufficient consideration moving from him to support a contract by which another person comes under an obligation to him.

DAVEY QC: The argument is that that which is a mere *nudum pactum* can be converted into a contract by something subsequently done by one of the parties. But that is not so. *Hammersly v. De Beil*, 12 Cl. & F. 45, [one of a group of cases relied on in *Skidmore v Bradford*, above] was for a time supposed to have established the rule that a man who changes his position in reliance on an expression of intention can insist upon effect being given to that expression of intention. But that idea is now exploded. If A represents to B that something is an existing fact, and B acts on the faith of that representation, A is bound, but that is not so where the representation is of an intention and not of a fact.

Maddison v Alderson. (1883), 8 App Cas 467, 473. LORD SELBORNE: I have always understood it to have been decided ... that the doctrine of estoppel by representation is applicable only to representation as to some state of facts alleged to be at the time actually in existence, and not to promises *de futuro*, which, if binding at all, must be binding as contracts.

HUGHES V METROPOLITAN RAILWAY CO
(1877), 2 App Cas 439

[By the terms of a lease, the landlord had the right to demand repairs on six months' notice to the tenant. In October the landlord gave the notice. In November and December the parties negotiated about the possibility of the landlord's buying the tenant's interest in the property. On December 31 the negotiations broke off, and in April the landlord asserted a right to forfeit the lease on the expiry of the six-month period from October. The House of Lords held that the landlord was not entitled to assert such a right.]

LORD CAIRNS LC: It is the first principle upon which all courts of equity proceed, that if parties who have entered into definite and distinct terms involving certain legal results—certain penalties or legal forfeiture—afterwards by their own act or with their own consent enter upon a course of negotiation which has the effect of leading one of the parties to suppose that the strict rights arising under the contract will not be enforced, or will be kept in suspense, or held in abeyance, the person who otherwise might have enforced those rights will not be allowed to enforce them where it would be inequitable having regard to the dealings which have then taken place between the parties.

CENTRAL LONDON PROPERTY TRUST LTD V HIGH TREES HOUSE LTD
[1947] KB 130

[The plaintiffs leased a block of flats to the defendants, a wholly owned subsidiary, for 99 years from September 29, 1937, at a rent of £2,500 a year. Only about one-third of the flats had been let by the outbreak of war in 1939 and, on January 3, 1940, the plaintiffs agreed with the defendants to accept a reduced rent of £1,250 a year "as from the commencement of the lease." In March of 1941 the affairs of the plaintiffs were handed over to a receiver, who after that managed the company. Only the reduced rent was paid until the receiver looked at the lease in September of 1945, when he claimed the whole amount for the quarter ending September 29, 1945, and arrears of £7,916. The defendants did not pay and these "friendly proceedings" were commenced to recover £625 rent for each of the quarters ending September 29, 1945, and December 25, 1945. By early 1945 the flats were fully let.]

DENNING J: ... If I were to consider this matter without regard to recent developments in the law, there is no doubt that had the plaintiffs claimed it, they would have been entitled to recover ground rent at the rate of £2,500 a year from the beginning of the term, since the lease under which it was payable was a lease under seal which, according to the old common law, could not be varied by an agreement by parol (whether in writing or not), but only by deed. Equity, however stepped in, and said that if there has been a variation of a deed by a simple contract (which in the case of a lease required to be in writing would have to be evidenced by writing), the courts may give effect to it as is shown in *Berry v. Berry*, [1929] 2 K.B. 316. That equitable doctrine, however, could hardly apply in the present case because the variation here might be said to have been made without consideration. With regard to estoppel, the representation made in relation to reducing the rent, was not a representation of an existing fact. It was a representation, in effect, as to the future, namely, that payment of the rent would not be enforced at the full rate but only at the reduced rate. Such a representation would not give rise to an estoppel, because, as was said in *Jorden v. Money* (1854), 5 H.L.C. 185; 10 E.R. 868, a representation as to the future must be embodied as a contract or be nothing.

But what is the position in view of developments in the law in recent years? The law has not been standing still since *Jorden v. Money*. There has been a series of decisions over the last fifty years which, although they are said to be cases of estoppel are not really such. They are cases in which a promise was made which was intended to create legal relations and which, to the knowledge of the person making the promise, was going to be acted on by the person to whom it was made, and which was in fact so acted on. In such cases the courts have said that the promise must be honoured. The cases to which I particularly desire to refer are: *Fenner v. Blake*, [1900] 1 Q.B. 426, *In re Wickham* (1917), 34 T.L.R. 158, *Re William Porter & Co., Ltd.*, [1937] 2 All E.R. 361 and *Buttery v. Pickard*, [1946] W.N. 25. As I have said they are not cases of estoppel in the strict sense. They are really promises—promises intended to be binding, intended to be acted on, and in fact acted in. *Jorden v. Money* can be distinguished, because there the promisor made it clear that she did not intend to be legally bound, whereas in the cases to which I refer the proper inference was that the promisor did intend to be bound. In each case the court held the promise to be binding on the party making it, even though under the old common law it might be difficult to find any consideration for it. The courts have not gone so far as to give a cause of action in damages for the breach of such a promise, but they have refused to allow the party making it to act inconsistently with it. It is in that sense, and that sense only, that such a promise gives rise to an estoppel. The decisions are a natural result of the fusion of law and equity: for the cases of *Hughes v. Metropolitan Ry. Co.* (1877), 2 App. Cas. 439, *Birmingham and District Land Co. v. London & North Western Ry. Co.* (1888), 40 Ch. D. 268 and *Salisbury (Marquess) v. Gilmore*, [1942] 2 K.B. 38, afford a sufficient basis for saying that a party would not be allowed in equity to go back on such a promise. In my opinion, the time has now come for the validity of such a promise to be recognized. The logical consequence, no doubt is that a promise to accept a smaller sum in discharge of a larger sum, if acted upon, is binding notwithstanding the absence of consideration: and if the fusion of law and equity leads to this result, so much the better. That aspect was not considered in *Foakes v. Beer* (1884), 9 App. Cas. 605. At this time of day however, when law and equity have been joined together for over seventy years, principles must be reconsidered in the light of their combined effect. It is to be noticed that in the Sixth Interim Report of the Law Revision Committee, paras. 35, 40, it is recommended that such a promise as that to which I have referred, should be enforceable in law even though no consideration for it has been given by the promisee. It seems to me that, to the extent I have mentioned, that result has now been achieved by the decisions of the courts.

I am satisfied that a promise such as that to which I have referred is binding and the only question remaining for my consideration is the scope of the promise in the present case. I am satisfied on all the evidence that the promise here was that the ground rent should be reduced to £1,250 a year as a temporary expedient while the block of flats was not fully, or substantially fully let, owing to the conditions prevailing. That means that the reduction in the rent applied throughout the years down to the end of 1944, but early in 1945 it is plain that the flats were fully let, and, indeed the rents received from them (many of them not being affected by the Rent Restrictions Acts), were increased beyond the figure at which it was originally contemplated that they would be let. At all events the rent from them must have been very considerable. I find that the conditions prevailing at the time when the reduction in rent was made, had completely passed away by the early months of 1945. I am satisfied that the promise was understood by all parties only to apply under the conditions prevailing at the time when it was made, namely, when the flats were only partially let, and that it did not extend any further than that. When the flats became fully let, early in 1945, the reduction ceased to apply.

In those circumstances, under the law as I hold it, it seems to me that rent is payable at the full rate for the quarters ending September 29 and December 25, 1945.

If the case had been one of estoppel, it might be said that in any event the estoppel would cease when the conditions to which the representation applied came to an end, or it also might be said that it would only come to an end on notice. In either case it is only a way of ascertaining what is the scope of the representation. I prefer to apply the principle that a promise intended to be binding, intended to be acted on and in fact acted on, is binding so far as its terms properly apply. Here it was binding as covering the period down to the early part of 1945, and as from that time full rent is payable.

I therefore give judgment for the plaintiff company for the amount claimed.

COMBE V COMBE
[1951] 1 All ER 767 (CA)

ASQUITH LJ: I will ask Denning, L.J., to deliver the first judgment.

DENNING LJ: In this case a wife who has divorced her husband claims maintenance from him—not in the Divorce Court, but in the King's Bench on an agreement which is said to be embodied in letters. The parties were married in 1915. They separated in 1939. On Feb. 1, 1943, on the wife's petition, a decree *nisi* of divorce was pronounced. Shortly afterwards letters passed between the solicitors with regard to maintenance. On Feb. 9, 1943 (eight days after the decree *nisi*), the solicitor for the wife wrote to the solicitor for the husband:

With regard to permanent maintenance, we understood that your client is prepared to make [the wife] an allowance of £100 per year free of income tax.

In answer, on Feb. 19, 1943, the husband's solicitors wrote:

The respondent has agreed to allow your client £100 per annum free of tax.

On Aug. 11, 1943, the decree was made absolute. On Aug. 26, 1943, the wife's solicitors wrote to the husband's solicitors, saying:

Referring to your letter of Feb. 19 last, our client would like the £100 per annum agreed to be paid to her by your client to be remitted to us on her behalf quarterly. We shall be glad if you will kindly let us have a cheque for £25 for the first quarterly instalment and make arrangements for a similar remittance to us on Nov. 11, Feb. 11, May 11, and Aug. 11 in the future.

A reply did not come for nearly two months because the husband was away, and then he himself, on Oct. 18, 1943, wrote a letter which was passed on to the wife's solicitors:

... [R]egarding the sum of £25 claimed on behalf of Mrs. Coombe ... I would point out that whilst this is paid quarterly as from Aug. 11, 1943, the sum is not due till Nov. 11, 1943, as I can hardly be expected to pay this allowance in advance.

He never paid anything. The wife pressed him for payment, but she did not follow it up by an application to the divorce court. It is to be observed that she herself has an income of her own of between £700 and £800 a year, whereas her husband has only £650 a year. Eventually, after nearly seven years had passed since the decree absolute, she brought this action in the King's Bench Division on July 28, 1950, claiming £675 being arrears for six years and three quarters at £100 a year. Byrne, J., held that the first three quarterly instalments of £25 were barred by the Limitation Act, 1939, but he gave judgment for £600 in respect of the instalments which accrued within the six years before the action was brought. He held, on the authority of *Gaisberg v. Storr*, [1949] 2 All E.R. 411, that there was no consideration for the husband's promise to pay his wife £100 but, nevertheless, he held that the promise was enforceable on the principle stated in *Central London Property Trust Ltd. v. Hightrees House, Ltd.* and *Robertson v. Minister of Pensions*, [1949] 2 All E.R. 767, because it was an unequivocal acceptance of liability, intended to be binding, intended to be acted on, and, in fact, acted on.

Much as I am inclined to favour the principle of the *Hightrees* case, it is important that it should not be stretched too far lest it should be endangered. It does not create new causes of action where none existed before. It only prevents a party from insisting on his strict legal rights when it would be unjust to allow him to do so, having regard to the dealings which have taken place between the parties. That is the way it was put in the case in the House of Lords which first stated the principle. ... It is also implicit in all the modern cases in which the principle has been developed. Sometimes it is a plaintiff who is not allowed to insist on his strict legal rights. Thus, a creditor is not allowed to enforce a debt which he has deliberately agreed to waive if the debtor has carried on business or in some other way changed his position in reliance on the waiver. A landlord who has told his tenant that he can live in his cottage rent free for the rest of his life is not allowed to go back on it if the tenant stays in the house on that footing. Sometimes it is a defendant who is not allowed to insist on his strict legal rights. His conduct may be such as to debar him from relying on some condition, denying some allegation, or taking some other point in answer to the claim. Thus, a government department, who had accepted a disease as due to war service, were not allowed afterwards to say it was not, when the soldier in reliance on the assurance, had abstained from getting further evidence about it: *Robertson v. Minister of Pensions*. A buyer who had waived the contract date for delivery was not allowed afterwards to set up the stipulated time as an answer to the seller. A tenant who had encroached on an adjoining building, asserting that it was comprised in the lease, was not allowed afterwards to say that it was not included in the lease. A tenant who had lived in a house rent free by permission of his landlord, thereby asserting that his original tenancy had ended, was not afterwards allowed to say that his original tenancy continued. In none of these cases was the defendant sued on the promise, assurance, or assertion as a cause of action in itself. He was sued for some other cause, for example, a pension or a breach of contract, or possession, and the promise, assurance, or assertion only played a supplementary role, though, no doubt, an important one. That is, I think, its true function. It may be part of a cause of action, but not a cause of action in itself. The principle, as I understand it, is that where one party intended to affect the legal relations between them and to be acted on accordingly, then, once the other party has taken him at his word and acted on it, the one who gave the promise or assurance cannot afterwards be allowed to revert to the previous legal relations as if no such promise or assurance had been made by him, but he must accept their legal relations subject to the qualification which he himself has so introduced, even though it is not supported in point of law by any consideration, but only by his word.

Seeing that the principle never stands alone as giving a cause of action in itself, it can never do away with the necessity of consideration when that is an essential part of the cause of action. The doctrine of consideration is too firmly fixed to be overthrown by a side-wind. Its ill effects have been largely mitigated of late, but it still remains a cardinal necessity of the formation of a contract, although not of its modification or discharge. I fear that it was my failure to make this clear in *Central London Property Trust Ltd. v. Hightrees House, Ltd.*, which misled Byrne, J., in the present case. He held that his wife could sue on the husband's promise as a separate and independent cause of action by itself, although, as he held, there was no consideration for it. That is not correct. The wife can only enforce the promise if there was consideration for it. That is, therefore, the real question in the case: Was there sufficient consideration to support the promise?

If it were suggested that, in return for the husband's promise, the wife expressly or impliedly promised to forbear from applying to the court for maintenance—that is, a promise, in return for a promise—there would clearly be no consideration because the wife's promise would not be binding on her and, therefore, would be worth nothing. Notwithstanding her promise, she could always apply to the divorce court for maintenance—perhaps, only with leave—but nevertheless she could apply. No agreement by her could take away that right. There was, however, clearly no promise by the wife, express or implied, to forbear from applying to the court. All that happened was that she did, in fact, forbear—that is, she did an act in return for a promise. Is that sufficient consideration? Unilateral promises of this kind have long been enforced so long as the act of forbearance is done on the faith of the promise and at the request of the promisor, express or implied. The act done is then in itself sufficient consideration for the promise, even though it arises, *ex post facto*, as Parker J., pointed out in *Wigan v. English and Scottish Law Life Assurance Assocn.*, [1909] 1 Ch. 291 at p. 298. If the findings of Byrne, J., are accepted, they are sufficient to bring this principle into play. His finding that the husband's promise was intended to be binding, intended to be acted upon, and was, in fact, acted on—although expressed to be a finding on the principle of the *Hightrees House* case—is equivalent to a finding that there was consideration within this long-settled rule, because it comes to the same thing expressed in different words: see *Oliver v. Davis.* My difficulty, however, is to accept the findings of Byrne, J., that the promise was "intended to be acted on." I cannot find any evidence of any intention by the husband that the wife should forbear from applying to the court for maintenance, or, in other words, any request by the husband, express or implied, that the wife should so forbear. He left her to apply, if she wished to do so. She did not do so, and I am not surprised, because it is very unlikely that the divorce court would have made any order in her favour, since she had a bigger income than her husband. Her forbearance was not intended by him, nor was it done at his request. It was, therefore, no consideration.

It may be that the wife has suffered some detriment because, after forbearing to apply to the court for seven years, she might not now get leave to apply. The court, however, is nowadays much more ready to give leave than it used to be; and I should have thought that, if the wife fell on hard times, she would still get leave. Assuming, however, that she has suffered some detriment by her forbearance, nevertheless, as the forbearance was not at the husband's request, it is no consideration.

The doctrine of consideration is sometimes said to work an injustice, but I see none in this case, nor was there any in ... *Gaisberg v. Storr.* I do not think it would be right for this wife, who is better off than her husband, to take no action for six or seven years and then demand from him the whole £600. The truth is that in these maintenance cases the real remedy of the wife is, not by action in the King's Bench Division, but by application in the Divorce Court. ... For these reasons I think the appeal should be allowed.

[The opinions of Asquith and Birkett LJJ are omitted.]

Waltons Stores (Interstate) Ltd v Maher. (1988), 164 CLR 387 (Aus HC). BRENNAN J: The object of the equity is not to compel the party bound to fulfil the assumption or expectation; it is to avoid the detriment which, if the assumption or expectation goes unfulfilled, will be suffered by the party who has been induced to act or to abstain from acting thereon. If this object is kept steadily in mind, the concern that a general application of the principle of equitable estoppel would make non-contractual promises enforceable as contractual promises can be allayed. ... [T]here are differences between a contract and an equity created by estoppel. A contractual obligation is created by the agreement of the parties; an equity created by estoppel may be imposed irrespective of any agreement by the party bound. A contractual obligation must be supported by consideration; an equity created by estoppel need not be supported by what is, strictly speaking, consideration. The measure of a contractual obligation depends on the terms of the contract and the circumstances to which it applies; the measure of an equity created by estoppel varies according to what is necessary to prevent detriment resulting from unconscionable conduct.

NOTES AND QUESTIONS

1. *Combe v Combe* is often cited for the proposition that promissory estoppel can be used only as a "shield" and not a "sword": see *Gilbert Steel*, above. Does that mean that a plaintiff cannot raise promissory estoppel? Consider the following comment:

> The rule that promissory estoppel creates no new cause of action is often confused with a rule that only defendants can invoke the doctrine. Perhaps the aphorism that states that promissory estoppel is a shield and not a sword is responsible for this confusion. Clearly the second rule does not follow from the first and accepted rule. A plaintiff can indeed invoke promissory estoppel if her action is founded on an independently existing right, contractual or otherwise. The case of *Charles Rickards Ltd. v. Oppenhaim* ([1950] 1 All E.R. 420 (C.A.)) provides an example. The plaintiff agreed to build a body on a Rolls-Royce chassis owned by the defendant. The completed car was to be delivered by a stipulated date. It became clear that delivery in conformity with the contract would be impossible. The defendant agreed to a number of extensions until, in frustration, he refused any further extensions. When the car was finally ready, he refused to accept delivery. While recovery was denied because the defendant had brought the estoppel to an end, the plaintiff clearly could have invoked promissory estoppel if the defendant had not revoked the promise. The plaintiff would sue on the basis of the contract. The defendant would then argue that delivery was late under the original contract. The plaintiff could use promissory estoppel to prevent the defendant from invoking his right to delivery on the date stipulated in the contract. Promissory estoppel can only be used as a defense, but both plaintiffs and defendants have need of defenses.

(JA Manwaring, "Promissory Estoppel in the Supreme Court of Canada" (1986-87) 10:3 Dal LJ 43 at 57.)

2. Manwaring suggests at 51-52 in the above article that courts have two choices in attempting to provide remedies in cases in which a party has relied on a representation and incurred loss. They may either "continually redefine the concept of consideration ... [or] use the tools that Equity places at the disposition of the court in order to mitigate the harshness of the requirement of consideration." Does *Williams v Roffey Bros*, above, illustrate this point?

3. If Brennan J is correct, would using estoppel as a cause of action eviscerate the doctrine of consideration?

4. Did the court correctly analyze the estoppel claim in *Gilbert Steel*, above?

5. Is *Combe v Combe* consistent with *Owen Sound*, excerpted below?

6. For an alternative justification of the result in *Combe v Combe*, one that is based on the policy of protecting the jurisdiction of the Divorce Court, see J Swan, "Consideration and the Reasons for Enforcing Contracts" (1976) 15 UWO L Rev 83.

JOHN BURROWS LIMITED V SUBSURFACE SURVEYS LIMITED
[1968] SCR 607, 68 DLR (2d) 354

[As per a negotiated purchase agreement, the plaintiff (John Burrows Ltd.) sold substantially all of its assets to the defendant (Subsurface Surveys Ltd.) for $150,000. The majority of the purchase price was paid in cash with the balance payable by way of a promissory note. As security for this arrangement, the defendant deposited a number of shares with the plaintiff. The terms of the promissory note dictated that interest accrued at 6 percent per annum and was payable monthly. A further provision stated that, upon any default by the defendant, the entire outstanding amount became immediately payable. Although the defendant always made the requisite interest payments, they were frequently late. Nonetheless, the principals of the two companies were friends and 11 payments were accepted more than 10 days after they were due without consequence. After a falling out between the principals, the plaintiff advised the defendant that because the current interest installment was over 36 days overdue it was triggering the accelerated payment clause in the promissory note. In response, the defendant tendered a sum amounting to the overdue interest. Such payment was rejected and the plaintiff subsequently commenced an action seeking full payment of the amount outstanding on the promissory note. The plaintiff won at trial but the defendant succeeded on appeal. The plaintiff then appealed to the Supreme Court of Canada.]

RITCHIE J: ... The two defences raised by the respondents which form the subject of the appeal are:

(a) That the document referred to in paragraph 2 of the Statement of Claim is not a promissory note because it is not due at a fixed or determinable future time and is not for a sum certain as required by Section 176(1) of the Bills of Exchange Act. ... (and)

(c) ...

   (i) the Plaintiff is estopped from saying that the Defendants defaulted in the payment of such interest because by its conduct ... it represented to the Defendants that late payment would be accepted without penalty of default which said representation was intended to affect the legal relations between the Plaintiff and the Defendants and which said representation was relied on and acted on by the Defendants. ...

I am ... of opinion that the instrument in question was a promissory note, and there can be no doubt that the respondents were in default in their interest payments for more than 10 days after the same became due.

It remains to be considered whether the circumstances disclosed by the evidence were such as to justify the majority of the Court of Appeal in concluding that this was a case to which the defence of equitable estoppel or estoppel by representation applied.

Since the decision of the present Lord Denning in the case of *Central London Property Trust Ltd. v. High Trees House Ltd.*, [1947] K.B. 130 there has been a great deal of discussion, both academic and judicial, on the question of whether that decision extended the doctrine of estoppel beyond the limits which had been therefore fixed, but in this Court in the case of *Conwest Exploration Co. Ltd. et al. v. Letain*, 41 D.L.R. (2d) 198 at pp. 206-7, [1964] S.C.R. 20, Judson J., speaking for the majority of the Court, expressed the view that Lord Denning's statement had not done anything more than restate the principle expressed by Lord Cairns in *Hughes v. Metropolitan R. Co.* (1877), 2 App. Cas. 439 at p. 448 ... .

[After discussing the *Hughes* case and *Combe v Combe*, RITCHIE J continued:]

It seems clear to me that this type of equitable defence cannot be invoked unless there is some evidence that one of the parties entered into a course of negotiation which had the effect of leading the other to suppose that the strict rights under the contract would not be enforced, and I think that this implies that there must be evidence from which it can be inferred that the first party intended that the legal relations created by the contract would be altered as a result of the negotiations.

It is not enough to show that one party has taken advantage of indulgences granted to him by the other for if this were so in relation to commercial transactions, such as promissory notes, it would mean that the holders of such notes would be required to insist on the very letter being enforced in all cases for fear that any indulgences granted and acted upon could be translated into a waiver of their rights to enforce the contract according to its terms.

As Viscount Simonds said in *Tool Metal Mfg. Co. v. Tungsten Electric Co., Ltd.* [1955] 2 All E.R. 657 at p. 660: "... [T]he gist of the equity lies in the fact that one party has by his conduct led the other to alter his position. I lay stress on this, because I would not have it supposed, particularly in commercial transactions, that mere acts of indulgence are apt to create rights. ..."

The learned trial judge dealt with the rule of estoppel by representation as applied to the circumstances of the present case in the following brief paragraphs:

> It is my opinion, however, that for such a rule to apply, the plaintiff must have known or should have known that his action or inaction was being acted upon by the defendant and that the defendant thereby changed his legal position. I do not believe that John Burrows ever gave any consideration to the fact that in accepting late payments of interest on the note, he was thereby leading Mr. Whitcomb—as an officer of the defendant corporation—into thinking that strict compliance would not be required at any time.
>
> It is a matter of regret that Mr. Burrows did not see fit to advise Mr. Whitcomb by letter or verbally of his intention to require strict adherence to the terms of the note; but be that as it may, it is my opinion that both defendants were always aware of the terms of P. 1 and knew that default in payment of interest exceeding 10 days could result in the plaintiff demanding full payment, as the plaintiff has now done.

Ritchie J.A., who did not agree with the learned trial judge's interpretation of the evidence, made the following observations in the course of his reasons for judgment [62 DLR (2d) at 720]:

> By its conduct in accepting payments of interest after they were more than 10 days in default and, over a period of 16 months, not proceeding to enforce payment of the principal amount owing under P-1, the plaintiff gave the defendants a promise, or assurance, which it intended would affect the legal relations between them. Thereby, the plaintiff lulled the defendants into a false sense of security and misled them into the belief its strict rights to enforce immediate payment of the principal amount of $42,000 would be held in obeyance or be suspended until they were informed otherwise. It was reasonable for the defendants so to interpret the plaintiff's conduct. As a result, the position of each defendant was prejudiced. In my respectful opinion, the evidence supports that conclusion.

With the greatest respect for the reasoning of the majority of the Court of Appeal, I prefer the interpretation placed on the evidence by the learned trial judge and by Bridges C.J.N.B., in his dissenting reasons for judgment where he said [at 705]:

For estoppel to apply, I think we must be satisfied that the conduct of Burrows amounted to a promise or assurance, intended to affect the legal relations of the parties to the extent that if an interest instalment became in default for 10 days the plaintiff would not claim the principal as due unless it had previously notified the defendants of its intention to do so or, if it had not so notified them, that notice would be given them the principal would be claimed if such instalment so in default were not paid. This is, I think, a great deal to infer.

I do not think that the evidence warrants the inference that the appellant entered into any negotiations with the respondents which had the effect of leading them to suppose that the appellant had agreed to disregard or hold in suspense or abeyance that part of the contract which provided that: "... on default being made by both Subsurface Surveys Ltd. and the Debtor in paying any principal or interest due at any time according to the terms of the said note the Company may forthwith cause the pledged shares to be transferred to the name of the Company on the share register of Subsurface Surveys Ltd. and the pledged shares shall thereupon become the absolute property of the Company." I am on the other hand of opinion that the behaviour of Mr. Burrows is much more consistent with his having granted friendly indulgences to an old associate while retaining his right to insist on the letter of the obligation, which he did when he and Whitcomb became estranged and when the respondents were in default in payment of an interest payment for a period of 36 days.

For all these reasons I would allow the appeal and restore the judgment of the learned trial Judge. The appellant is entitled to its costs both here and in the Appeal Division.

Appeal allowed; trial judgment restored.

OWEN SOUND PUBLIC LIBRARY BOARD
V MIAL DEVELOPMENTS LTD
(1979), 102 DLR (3d) 685 (Ont CA)

[The Owen Sound Public Library Board ("the appellant") and Mial Developments Ltd. entered into a construction contract for substantial renovations to the local public library building. The contract provided that the Library Board should make payment of any amounts due within five days of being presented with an architect's certificate. The contract further provided that if the Library Board should fail to pay within seven days, Mial might upon five days' written notice terminate the contract. On November 4, the architect certified that a sum was due on December 12. On November 16, the Library Board requested that Mial secure the corporate seal of the subcontractor on one of the documents supporting the certificate. This was done in order to ensure that the subcontractor had been paid by Mial. Mial undertook to secure the subcontractor's seal although such an action was unnecessary under the contract. The Library Board did not pay on December 12 because Mial had not secured the subcontractor's corporate seal. On December 20, Mial wrote giving five days' notice of termination . That letter was received by the Library Board on Friday, December 22. Due to the holidays, a cheque was not mailed until December 28. The cheque was received by Mial on January 2. On December 28, Mial purported to terminate the contract because it was in its financial interest to do so. The Library Board then sued for breach of contract.]

LACOURCIÈRE JA: This appeal, which turns on the applicability of the doctrine of promissory estoppel, is brought by the Owen Sound Public Library Board (the "Library Board") from the judgment of the Honourable Mr. Justice Henry dismissing with costs the Library Board's claim for damages for breach of contract and allowing with costs the counterclaim of the defendant, Mial Developments Limited ("Mial"), for payment for all work executed. ...

The fundamental issue at trial, *i.e.* the contractor's right to terminate the contract, was resolved in the contractor's favour. The circumstances disclosed by the evidence must be examined in the light of the appellant's main submission that the learned trial Judge erred in his understanding and application of the principles of promissory estoppel. The promissory estoppel doctrine was invoked on the basis of the allegation that the contractor had failed to honour its promise to obtain the affixing of a seal to a certain document, which promise was relied on by the appellant in delaying payment of the account. ...

[After outlining the facts, LACOURCIÈRE JA continued:]

The learned trial Judge found, on these facts, that the clear and unambiguous language of the articles quoted above entitled Mial legally to terminate the contract. He did not consider that the doctrine of promissory estoppel precluded Mial from relying on the strict terms of the contract. In his view, Brown's promise, on behalf of Mial, to obtain a document bearing the corporate seal of the subcontractor (although admittedly such action was meaningless and unnecessary) caused Mr. McReavy to "put the matter aside without processing the architect's certificate for payment in reliance on *his* understanding that he need not act until the document was received."

Notwithstanding that important inference, the learned trial Judge refused to exercise the Court's equitable jurisdiction on the basis that there was no intention on the part of Brown or Mial, in spite of the promise, to alter the Library Board's strict legal obligation under the contract. ...

It was submitted on behalf of the appellant that the learned trial Judge erred in law in requiring intention or knowledge on the part of the promisor as a prerequisite to the operation of the equitable doctrine of estoppel. Counsel for the appellant relied on *Hughes v. Metropolitan R. Co. et al.* (1877), 2 App. Cas. 439, for the proposition that it is sufficient if a party to a contract, by his words or conduct, induces the other party to believe that strict performance of the terms of the contract will not be insisted upon. ...

The appellant further submitted that, in the present case, the request for the corporate seal of the subcontractor was made by the Library Board and its architect for the purpose of advising Mial that its application for payment of the holdback could not otherwise be processed. In that Mial could have refused this request and insisted upon payment pursuant to the certificate, its promise to obtain the seal could only be interpreted as a withdrawal of the certificate until the requested documentation was secured. Thus, counsel asked this Court to conclude that the words and conduct of Brown, as Mial's representative, could only induce the Library Board's agent into the belief that the operation of the time-limit under art. 38 was suspended, and that the time would begin to run upon Mial's production of the requested seal.

The appellant stressed in argument that the promisor's words and conduct, not his intent, are material to the proper invocation of the promissory estoppel doctrine. After referring to *Hughes v. Metropolitan R. Co.*, *supra*, Bowen, L.J., in *Birmingham & District Land Co. v. London North Western R. Co.* (1888), 40 Ch.D. 268, put the principle to be applied as follows at p. 286:

It seems to me to amount to this, that if persons who have contracted rights against others induce by their conduct those against whom they have such rights to believe that such rights will either not be enforced or will be kept in suspense or abeyance for some particular time, those persons will not be allowed by a Court of Equity to enforce the rights until such time has elapsed, without at all events placing the parties in the same position as they were before.

The principle as stated by Lord Cairns in *Hughes v. Metropolitan R. Co.*, which I have already quoted above, was approved by the Supreme Court of Canada in *Conwest Exploration Co. Ltd. et al. v. Letain*, [1964] S.C.R. 20 ... .

The learned trial Judge, in refusing to apply the doctrine of promissory estoppel in favour of the Library Board, on the basis that the Board failed to satisfy him that Mial, as promisor, had the requisite intention or knowledge, did not refer specifically to the authorities which appear to support this prerequisite.

In *Snell's Principles of Equity*, 27th ed. (1973), at p. 563, the learned co-authors, the Honourable Sir Robert Megarry and P.V. Baker, state the rule in the following words:

Where by his words or conduct one party to a transaction makes to the other an unambiguous promise or assurance *which is intended to affect the legal relations between them* (whether contractual or otherwise), and the other party acts upon it, altering his position to his detriment, the party making the promise or assurance will not be permitted to act inconsistently with it. ...

I interpret these cases as authority for the proposition that a promise, whether express or inferred from a course of conduct, is intended to be legally binding if it reasonably leads the promisee to believe that a legal stipulation, such as strict time of performance, will not be insisted upon. In *Charles Rickards Ltd. v. Oppenheim*, *supra*, Lord Justice Denning, with whom Singleton and Bucknill, L.JJ., concurred, said at p. 623:

If the defendant, as he did, led the plaintiffs to believe that he would not insist on the stipulation as to time, and that, if they carried out the work, he would accept it, and they did it, he could not afterwards set up the stipulation as to the time against them. Whether it be called waiver or forbearance on his part, or an agreed variation or substituted performance, does not matter. It is a kind of estoppel. *By his conduct he evinced an intention to affect their legal relations.* He made, in effect, a promise not to insist on his strict legal rights. That promise was intended to be acted on, and was in fact acted on. He cannot afterwards go back on it.

(Emphasis added.) Reference also may be made to Spencer Bower and Turner, *The Law Relating to Estoppel by Representation*, 3rd ed. (1977), at p. 377.

The prerequisite of intention to alter legal relations was not mentioned or discussed in *Hughes v. Metropolitan R. Co.*, *supra*, or in the *Birmingham* case, *supra*. However, it was stressed by Ritchie, J., delivering the judgment of the Supreme Court of Canada in *John Burrows Ltd. v. Subsurface Surveys et al.*, [1968] S.C.R. 607, 68 D.L.R. (2d) 354, in discussing a defence of promissory estoppel raised by a debtor against a creditor who had accepted without complaint habitually late repayments but later had invoked an acceleration clause without notice. ...

[After quoting from *John Burrows*, LACOURCIÈRE JA continued:]

The respondent argued that Brown's assertion that he would get the corporate seal affixed to the statutory declaration was not made with any reference to payment of the valid certificate. Counsel stated that there is no evidence that the assertion was related to payment, and the learned trial Judge found expressly that "there was no discussion of the effect of this undertaking [to obtain the document] on payment of the holdback … ." He said: "The terms of payment were not raised or discussed." The evidence appears to support the conclusion that no one on behalf of Mial expressly agreed to the suspension of the time requirement for payment pending delivery of the seal, and no one on behalf of the Library Board made any request to that effect.

Nevertheless, the more difficult and relevant question is whether Brown's statement and conduct could logically or reasonably be interpreted by the Library Board as an agreement by Mial that it would postpone the Board's strict obligation to pay the certificate. If that were so, Mial would be seeking to take advantage of a default induced by its own conduct. There is no direct evidence to the effect that the Board delayed payment because of the promise, although two members of the Library Board testified at trial. However, the learned trial Judge made an inference to the effect that McReavy "put the matter aside without processing the architect's certificate for payment in reliance on *his* understanding that he need not act until the document was received." With all due respect, and notwithstanding the respondent's submissions to the contrary, this inference is fully supported by the evidence. Counsel for the respondent submitted that it was incumbent on the Board to lead evidence on this specific point, and that there is no sworn testimony to support it. He contended that the letter of December 22, 1972, referring to the request to obtain the seal, was an attempt following cancellation of the contract to provide *ex post facto* a reason for non-payment of the certificate, which reason the Board's witnesses did not support in the witness-box.

On the basis of the authorities mentioned, I agree with the learned trial Judge that intent and knowledge on the part of the promisor are necessary ingredients of promissory estoppel. However, the authorities make it clear that intent to create legal relations does not require a direct statement to that effect. Rather, such an intent can be based on an inference drawn from the evidence. Knowledge by the promisor that the promisee is likely to regard the promise as affecting their legal relations constitutes an appropriate basis from which the inference of the existence of a sufficient intent can be drawn.

In this case, as found by the learned trial Judge, the Library Board's agent did in fact understand Mial's position to be that the Board need not make payment under the certificate until the sealed document was received. He relied on that understanding, which arose out of a discussion between representatives of the parties. I am of the opinion that both the agent's understanding and his reliance were reasonable. It was not necessary for the Court below to find specific words spoken by the parties to the effect that Mial's agreement to provide further documentation suspended the Library Board's obligation. As a matter of common business sense, the respondent, an experienced contractor, would interpret a request for further documentation as a suspension of the effect of the architect's certificate, particularly when the request was made in the presence of the architect's representative and repeated on behalf of the architect. As stated by Riddell, J., in *Grimsby Steel Furniture Co. Ltd. v. Columbia Gramophone Co.* (1922), 23 O.W.N. 188 at p. 189, "Silence is sometimes as cogent as speech … ." The predictable and reasonable interpretation placed on Brown's promise to obtain the seal, in the circumstances, is sufficient to support a finding that the requisite intent and knowledge existed. This Court is free to draw such an inference from the proven facts. It would be neither equitable nor just to view Mial's statement and conduct as having any other effect than that of leading the Library Board's representative to suppose that the strict payment obligations within the time-limits would not be enforced. In my view, the only proper inference on the facts found by the learned trial Judge is that the Library Board failed to pay the Friesen holdback because of the promise made by Mial, which promise remained unfulfilled at the time of the cancellation. In this respect the case is quite different from the factual situation in *John Burrows Ltd., supra*. I find, therefore, that the contractor Mial was not entitled to cancel the contract and that the purported cancellation was unjustified and ineffective. The Board was consequently entitled to judgment for damages assessed on established principles. In view of this conclusion, it becomes unnecessary to discuss the other grounds of appeal raised.

I would accordingly, allow the appeal with costs and set aside the judgment below. In place thereof I would enter judgment for the plaintiff and direct a reference to the Master to ascertain the amount of damages suffered by the plaintiff. I would also dismiss with costs the counterclaim of Mial.

Appeal allowed.

Amalgamated Investment & Property Ltd v Texas Commerce International Bank Ltd. [1982] QB 84 (CA). BRANDON LJ: I turn to the second argument advanced on behalf of the plaintiffs, that the bank is here seeking to use estoppel as a sword rather than a shield, and that that is something which the law of estoppel does not permit. Another way in which the argument is put is that a party cannot found a cause of action on an estoppel. ... This illustrates what I would regard as the true proposition of law, that, while a party cannot in terms found a cause of action on an estoppel, he may, as a result of being able to rely on an estoppel, succeed on a cause of action on which, without being able to rely on that estoppel, he would necessarily have failed.

NOTES AND QUESTIONS

1. Consider the meaning of the terms "estoppel," "waiver," and "promissory estoppel." How do courts differentiate among them? See Waddams at paras 206-7; McCamus, ch 8; MacDougall, ch 9; Fridman at 548-55. See also B MacDougall, *Estoppel* (Toronto: LexisNexis, 2012), ch V.

2. It is sometimes suggested that the "shield" in the *Owen Sound* case had become very pointed. How? What did the court do here that was different from what it did in the earlier cases in this section?

3. Does it matter to the court that it will have to add or rewrite a term?

4. Is *Owen Sound* an application of *John Burrows* or a complete reinterpretation of it? Has *Owen Sound* moved the focus from intention to the issue of whether the reliance was reasonable?

5. Suppose X and Y have a contract that X will build a website for Y in return for $10,000. After the contract is totally complete, Y promises X an additional $3,000 because Y is very pleased with X's work. X detrimentally relies on Y's promise to the value of $3,000. Relying on the *Amalgamated Investment* case, can X sue Y for breach of contract and then attempt to estop Y from denying that the contract price was $13,000? For judicial doubting of this possibility, see *Canadian Superior Oil Ltd v Hambly*, [1970] SCR 932.

6. What makes reliance reasonable? When would it be unreasonable to rely on a promise? See A Robertson, "Reasonable Reliance in Estoppel by Conduct" (2000) 23 UNSWLJ 87; *A-G for Hong Kong v Humphries Estate*, [1987] AC 114 (PC); *Cobbe v Yeoman's Row Management Ltd*, [2008] UKHL 55; Waddams at para 164; E Bant & M Bryant, "Fact, Future and Fiction: Risk and Reasonable Reliance in Estoppel" (2015) 35 OJLS 427; *Cowper-Smith v Morgan*, 2017 SCC 61 (excerpted below).

D & C BUILDERS, LTD V REES
[1965] 3 All ER 837 (CA)

LORD DENNING MR: D. & C. Builders, Ltd. ("the plaintiffs") are a little company. "D" stands for Mr. Donaldson, a decorator; "C" for Mr. Casey, a plumber. They are jobbing builders. The defendant, Mr. Rees, has a shop where he sells builders' materials.

In the spring of 1964 the defendant employed the plaintiffs to do work at his premises, 218, Brick Lane. The plaintiffs did the work and rendered accounts in May and June, which came to £746 13s. 1d. altogether. The defendant paid £250 on account. In addition the plaintiffs made an allowance of £14 off the bill. So in July, 1964, there was owing to the plaintiffs the sum of £482 13s. 1d. At this stage there was no dispute as to the work done. But the defendant did not pay.

On Aug. 31, 1964, the plaintiffs wrote asking the defendant to pay the remainder of the bill. He did not reply. On Oct. 19, 1964, they wrote again, pointing out that the "outstanding account of £480 is well overdue." Still the defendant did not reply. He did not write or telephone for more than three weeks. Then on Friday, Nov. 13, 1964, the defendant was ill with influenza. His wife telephoned the plaintiffs. She spoke to Mr. Casey. She began to make complaints about the work; and then said: "My husband will offer you £300 in settlement. That is all you'll get. It is to be in satisfaction." Mr. Casey said he would have to discuss it with Mr. Donaldson. The two of them talked it over. Their company was in desperate financial straits. If they did not have the £300, they would be in a state of bankruptcy. So they decided to accept the £300 and see what they could do about the rest afterwards. Thereupon Mr. Donaldson telephoned to the defendant's wife. He said to her: "£300 will not even clear our commitments on the job. We will accept £300 and give you a year to find the balance." She said: "No, we will never have enough money to pay the balance. £300 is better than nothing." He said: "We have no choice but to accept." She said: "Would you like the money by cash or by cheque. If it is cash, you can have it on Monday. If by cheque, you can have it tomorrow (Saturday)." On Saturday, Nov. 14, 1964, Mr. Casey went to collect the money. He took with him a receipt prepared on the company's paper with the simple words: "Received the sum of £300 from Mr. Rees." She gave him a cheque for £300 and asked for a receipt. She insisted that the words "in completion of the account" be added. Mr. Casey did as she asked. He added the words to the receipt. So she had the clean receipt: "Received the sum of £300 from Mr. Rees in completion of the account. Paid, M. Casey." Mr. Casey gave in evidence his reason for giving it: "If I did not have the £300 the company would have gone bankrupt. The only reason we took it was to save the company. She knew the position we were in."

The plaintiffs were so worried about their position that they went to their solicitors. Within a few days, on Nov. 23, 1964, the solicitors wrote complaining that the defendant had "extracted a receipt of some sort or other" from them. They said that they were treating the £300 as a payment on account. On Nov. 28, 1964, the defendant replied alleging bad workmanship. He also set up the receipt which Mr. Casey gave to his wife, adding: "I assure you she had no gun on her." The plaintiffs brought this action for the balance. The defendant set up a defence of bad workmanship and also that there was a binding settlement. The question of settlement was tried as a preliminary issue. The judge made these findings:

> I concluded that by the middle of August the sum due to the plaintiffs was ascertained and not then in dispute. I also concluded that there was no consideration to support the agreement of Nov. 13 and 14. It was a case of agreeing to take a lesser sum, when a larger sum was already due to the plaintiffs. It was not a case of agreeing to take a

cheque for a smaller account instead of receiving cash for a larger account. The payment by cheque was an incidental arrangement.

The judge decided, therefore, the preliminary issue in favour of the plaintiffs. The defendant appeals to this court. He says that there was here an accord and satisfaction—an *accord* when the plaintiffs agreed, however reluctantly, to accept £300 in settlement of the account—and *satisfaction* when they accepted the cheque for £300 and it was duly honoured.

This case is of some consequence for it is a daily occurrence that a merchant or tradesman, who is owed a sum of money, is asked to take less. The debtor says he is in difficulties. He offers a lesser sum in settlement, cash down. He says he cannot pay more. The creditor is considerate. He accepts the proffered sum and forgives him the rest of the debt. The question arises: is the settlement binding on the creditor? The answer is that, in point of law, the creditor is not bound by the settlement. He can the next day sue the debtor for the balance, and get judgment. The law was so stated in 1602 by Lord Coke in *Pinnel's Case*—and accepted in 1884 by the House of Lords in *Foakes v. Beer.*

Now, suppose that the debtor, instead of paying the lesser sum in cash, pays it by cheque. He makes out a cheque for the amount. The creditor accepts the cheque and cashes it. Is the position any different? I think not. No sensible distinction can be taken between payment of a lesser sum by cash and payment of it by cheque. The cheque, when given, is conditional payment. When honoured, it is actual payment. It is then just the same as cash. If a creditor is not bound when he receives payment by cash, he should not be bound when he receives payment by cheque. ... In point of law payment of a lesser sum, whether by cash or by cheque, is no discharge of a greater sum.

This doctrine of the common law has come under heavy fire. It was ridiculed by Sir George Jessel M.R., in *Couldery v. Bartrum.* It was held to be mistaken by Lord Blackburn in *Foakes v. Beer.* It was condemned by the Law Revision Committee in their Sixth Interim Report (Cmnd. 5449), para. 20 and para. 22. But a remedy has been found. The harshness of the common law has been relieved. Equity has stretched out a merciful hand to help the debtor. The courts have invoked the broad principle stated by Lord Cairns L.C., in *Hughes v. Metropolitan Ry. Co.* (1877) 2 App. Cas. 439. ...

This principle has been applied to cases where a creditor agrees to accept a lesser sum in discharge of a greater. So much so that we can now say that, when a creditor and a debtor enter on a course of negotiation, which leads the debtor to suppose that, on payment of the lesser sum, the creditor will not enforce payment of the balance, and on the faith thereof the debtor pays the lesser sum and the creditor accepts it as satisfaction: then the creditor will not be allowed to enforce payment of the balance when it would be inequitable to do so. This was well illustrated during the last war. Tenants went away to escape the bombs and left their houses unoccupied. The landlords accepted a reduced rent for the time they were empty. It was held that the landlords could not afterwards turn round and sue for the balance: see *Central London Property Trust, Ltd. v. High Trees House, Ltd.* This caused at the time some eyebrows to be raised in high places. But they have been lowered since. The solution was so obviously just that no one could well gainsay it.

In applying this principle, however, we must note the qualification. The creditor is barred from his legal rights only when it would be *inequitable* for him to insist on them. Where there has been a *true accord* under which the creditor voluntarily agrees to accept a lesser sum in satisfaction, and the debtor *acts on* that accord by paying the lesser sum and the creditor accepts it, then it is inequitable for the creditor afterwards to insist on the balance. But he is not bound unless there has been truly an accord between them.

In the present case, on the facts as found by the judge, it seems to me that there was no true accord. The debtor's wife held the creditor to ransom. The creditor was in need of money to meet his own commitments, and she knew it. When the creditor asked for payment of the £480 due to him, she said to him in effect: "We cannot pay you the £480. But we will pay you £300 if you will accept it in settlement. If you do not accept it on those terms, you will get nothing. £300 is better than nothing." She had no right to say any such thing. She could properly have said: "We cannot pay you more than £300. Please accept it on account." But she had no right to insist on his taking it in settlement. When she said: "We will pay you nothing unless you accept £300 in settlement," she was putting undue pressure on the creditor. She was making a threat to break the contract (by paying nothing) and she was doing it so as to compel the creditor to do what he was unwilling to do (to accept £300 in settlement): and she succeeded. He complied with her demand. That was on recent authority a case of intimidation. ... In these circumstances there was no true accord so as to found a defence of accord and satisfaction. ... There is also no equity in the defendant to warranty any departure from the due course of law. No person can insist on a settlement procured by intimidation.

In my opinion there is no reason in law or equity why the creditor should not enforce the full amount of the debt due to him. I would, therefore, dismiss this appeal.

Collier v P & M J Wright (Holdings) Ltd. [2008] 1 WLR 643 (CA). ARDEN LJ: [I]f (1) a debtor offers to pay part only of the amount he owes, (2) the creditor voluntarily accepts that offer, and (3) in reliance on the creditor's acceptance the debtor pays that part of the amount he owes in full, the creditor will, by virtue of the doctrine of promissory estoppel, be bound to accept that sum in full and final satisfaction of the whole debt. For him to resile will of itself be inequitable. In addition, in these circumstances, the promissory estoppel has the effect of extinguishing the creditor's right to the balance of the debt. This part of our law originated in the brilliant *obiter dictum* of Denning J. in the *High Trees* case ... . To a significant degree it achieves in practical terms the recommendation of the Law Revision Committee chaired by Lord Wright MR in 1937.

MWB Business Exchange Centres Ltd v Rock Advertising Ltd. [2016] EWCA Civ 553. KITCHIN LJ: It may be the case that it would be inequitable to allow the promisor to go back upon his promise without giving reasonable notice ... or it may be that it would be inequitable to allow the promisor to go back on his promise at all with the result that the right is extinguished. All will depend upon the circumstances. It follows that I do not for my part think that it can be said, consistently with the authorities ... that in every case where a creditor agrees to accept payment of a debt by instalments, and the debtor acts upon that agreement by paying one of the instalments, and the creditor accepts that instalment, then it will necessarily be inequitable for the creditor later to go back upon the agreement and insist on payment of the balance. Again, all will depend upon the circumstances.

NOTES AND QUESTIONS

1. Would the pressure applied by Mrs. Rees have constituted duress? See Chapter 6, Section VI.

2. For criticism of Arden LJ's approach in *Collier*, see M Chen-Wishart, "A Bird in the Hand: Consideration and Contract Modifications" in Burrows & Peel at 102-5; MH Ogilvie, "Part Payment, Promissory Estoppel and Lord Denning's 'Brilliant Balance'" (2010) 49 Can Bus LJ 287; M Roberts, "The Practical Benefit Doctrine Marches On" (2017) 80 Mod L Rev 339 at 348-50.

3. Is promissory estoppel a unitary doctrine? For an argument against, see B McFarlane, "Promissory Estoppel and Debts" in Burrows & Peel at 115, where it is contended that cases commonly thought of as "promissory estoppel" are best explained as applications of three more specific doctrines, each with their own legal incidents, which concern the relinquishment, acquisition, and creation of rights.

4. What detriment was suffered by the defendant in *D & C Builders*? Is detrimental reliance a necessary element to ground a promissory estoppel? Consider the following excerpts.

Ajayi v RT Briscoe (Nigeria) Ltd. [1964] 1 WLR 1326 (PC). LORD HODSON: The principle which has been described as quasi estoppel and perhaps more aptly as promissory estoppel is that when one party to a contract in the absence of fresh consideration agrees not to enforce his rights an equity will be raised in favour of the other party. This equity is, however, subject to the qualification (a) that the other party has altered his position, (b) that the promisor can resile from his promise on giving reasonable notice, which need not be a formal notice, giving the promisee a reasonable opportunity of resuming his position, (c) the promise only becomes final and irrevocable if the promisee cannot resume his position.

The Post Chaser. [1981] 1 All ER 19 (QB). ROBERT GOFF J: The fundamental principle is ... that the representor will not be allowed to enforce his rights "where it would be inequitable ... ." To establish such inequity, it is not necessary to show detriment; indeed, the representee may have benefited from the representation, and yet it may be inequitable, at least without reasonable notice, for the representor to enforce his legal rights. Take the facts of ... [*High Trees*]. The representation was by a lessor to the effect that he would be content to accept a reduced rent. In such a case, although the lessee has benefited from the reduction in rent, it may well be inequitable for the lessor to insist upon his legal right to the unpaid rent, because the lessee has conducted his affairs on the basis that he would only have to pay rent at the lower rate; and a Court might well think it right to conclude that only after reasonable notice could the lessor return to charging rent at the higher rate specified in the lease. Furthermore it would be open to the Court, in any particular case, to infer from the circumstances of the case that the representee must have conducted his affairs in such a way that it would be inequitable for the representor to enforce his rights, or to do so without reasonable notice.

Bertkey Development Ltd v Incorporated Owners of Fine Mansion. [1999] 2 HKLRD 662 (CA). LIU JA: Lord Denning has tried, time and again, to dispense with the requirement of detriment altogether ... . His Herculean efforts were not well received. It is generally accepted today that some detriment in the sense expounded by the distinguished Australian jurist Dixon J. would be required to feed an estoppel.

Grundt v Great Boulder Proprietary Gold Mines Ltd. (1937), 59 CLR 641 (Aus HC). DIXON J: [T]he real detriment or harm from which the law seeks to give protection is that which would flow from the change of position if the assumption were deserted that led to it. So long as the assumption is adhered to, the party who altered his situation upon the faith of it cannot complain. His complaint is that when afterwards the other party makes a different state of affairs the basis of an assertion of right against him then, if it is allowed, his own original change of position will operate as a detriment.

Ryan v Moore. 2005 SCC 38, [2005] 2 SCR 53. BASTARACHE J: The jurisprudence and academic comments support the requirement of detrimental reliance as lying at the heart of true estoppel ... . Detrimental reliance encompasses two distinct, but interrelated, concepts: reliance and detriment. The former requires a finding that the party seeking to establish the estoppel changed his or her course of conduct by acting or abstaining from acting in reliance upon the assumption, thereby altering his or her legal position. If the first step is met, the second requires a finding that, should the other party be allowed to abandon the assumption, detriment will be suffered by the estoppel raiser because of the change from his or her assumed position.

The Commonwealth of Australia v Verwayen. (1990), 170 CLR 394 (Aus HC). McHUGH J: Once the detriment has ceased or been paid for, there is nothing unconscionable in a party insisting on reverting to his or her former relationship with the other party and enforcing his or her strict legal rights.

Woodhouse AC Israel Cocoa Ltd SA v Nigerian Produce Marketing Co Ltd. [1972] AC 741 (HL). LORD HAILSHAM OF MARYLEBONE LC: [T]he time may soon come when the whole sequence of cases based on promissory estoppel since the war, beginning with ... *High Trees* ..., may need to be reviewed and reduced to a coherent body of doctrine by the courts. I do not mean to say that they are to be regarded with suspicion. But as is common with an expanding doctrine they do raise problems of coherent exposition which have never been systematically explored.

NOTES AND QUESTIONS

1. Does *The Post Chaser*, properly understood, stand for the proposition that no detriment is needed for promissory estoppel? If it does stand for that proposition is it consistent with the Privy Council's advice in *Ajayi*?

2. Is it in good conscience for a wealthy person not to give money to the needy? Should such a promise be enforced because it would be inequitable not to do so? Is this the type of unconscionability that the courts do, or should, have in mind?

3. What is the theoretical basis of promissory estoppel—is it unconscionability, promise enforcement, or the elimination of detrimental reliance? Which view is best supported by the criteria of liability? Which view is best supported by the choice of the court's remedy? Which view is more consistent with justice? For various arguments, see Smith at 233-44; M Spence, *Protecting Reliance* (Oxford: Hart, 1999); Elizabeth Cooke, *The Modern Law of Estoppel* (Oxford: Oxford University Press, 2000); P Heffey, J Paterson & A Robertson, *Principles of Contract Law*, 2nd ed (Sydney: Lawbook Co, 2005) at 193-95; Benson at 174-79; A Robertson, "Situating Equitable Estoppel Within the Law of Obligations" (1997) 19 Sydney L Rev 32.

4. What are the current doctrinal rules in regard to promissory estoppel that can be distilled from the case? Fridman at 127-35 describes them as follows: (1) there must have been an existing legal relationship between the parties at the time the statement on which the estoppel is founded was made; (2) there must be a clear promise or representation made by the party against whom the estoppel is raised, establishing his intent to be bound by what she has said; (3) there must have been reliance, by the party raising the estoppel, on the statement or conduct of the party against whom the estoppel is raised; (4) the party to whom the representation was made must have acted on it to her detriment; (5) the promisee must have acted equitably. Which cases stand for which propositions?

5. What issues of coherence might Lord Hailsham LC have had in mind in *Woodhouse*? Consider this question as you examine the following cases dealing with proprietary estoppel.

Dillwyn v Llewelyn. (1862), 6 LT 878, 4 De G F & J 517, 31 LJ Ch 658. The owner of a piece of land, then worth £1,500, promised (in a signed writing) to give it to his son "for the purpose of furnishing himself with a dwelling-house." The son made extensive improvements to the land at a cost of £20,000. The owner died leaving the land by will to other persons. The Chancery court held that the son was entitled to be declared the owner of the land in equity. LORD WESTBURY LC: Now, about the rules of the court there can be no controversy. A voluntary agreement will not be completed or assisted by a court of equity; in cases of mere gift, if anything be wanting to complete the title of the donee, a court of equity will not assist him in obtaining it, for a mere donee can have no right to claim more than he has received. But the subsequent acts of the donor may give the donee that right or ground of claim which he did not acquire from the original gift .... So if A puts B in possession of a piece of land, and tells him, I give it to you, that you may build a house on it; and B, on the strength of that promise, with the knowledge of A, expends a large sum of money in building a house accordingly, I cannot doubt that the donee acquires a right from the subsequent transaction to call on the donor to perform that contract which arises from the contract, and to complete the imperfect donation which was made. [Note: Money figures are from the LT report; De G F & J's report omits "which arises from the contract" in the second-last line; LJ has "which arises therefrom."]

CRABB V ARUN DISTRICT COUNCIL
[1976] Ch 179 (CA)

LORD DENNING MR (Lawton and Scarman LJJ concurring): This case cannot be properly understood without a map: but I will try to explain it as best I can. Near Bognor Regis there is a village called Pagham. There is a road there called Hook Lane running east and west. On the south side of that road there is an area of land called Windmill Park. In 1946 a Mr. Alford bought 5½ acres of it. It formed a big square field with its north side next to the road. Now you must imagine that big field divided into two parts by a line running from north to south, with two acres on the eastern side of the line and 3½ acres on the western side, and the two acres divided by a line horizontally into two halves, the front portion (1 acre) being next to the road and the back portion (1 acre) with no access to the road. Mr. Alford developed the two acres and left the other 3½ acres undeveloped. On these two acres Mr. Alford put two industrial buildings. On the front portion he erected offices and showrooms. On the back portion he erected a building for the manufacture of caravans. And he made a road on these two acres connecting the back portion to the front.

In 1962 Mr. Alford died. His executors decided to develop the remaining 3½ acres on the western side of the field. They obtained planning permission to erect dwelling houses on it. Under this proposal there was to be a new estate road made to give access from Hook Lane to the new housing estate. It was to be made on the 3½ acres but was to run alongside the boundary line between the 3½ acres and the two acres. It was to be called Mill Park Road. This road was to be to the advantage also of the buildings on the two-acre portion, because they could have access on to the near road. The proposal at that time was, however, that there should be only one access from the two acres on to the new road. This was to be at a point marked "A" in the front portion, about halfway up from Hook Lane. It was thought at that time that one access would be sufficient because the whole of the two acres were in one occupation. The vehicles from the back portion (where caravans were made) could go along their own existing road to the front portion (where the offices and showrooms were), and then out at point A. This was to be the only access to the two acres. The previous access (from a side lane) was to be closed.

Planning permission was given for this development. But the executors of Mr. Alford did not carry it out themselves. They sold the two acres to the plaintiff; and they sold the 3½ acres to the defendants, the Chichester Rural District Council. The conveyances are of importance. By a conveyance dated September 1, 1965, the executors of Mr. Alford sold the whole of the two acres with the two industrial buildings to the plaintiff, and in the conveyance they agreed to erect a fence 5 ft. 6 in. high along the boundary line (save for the access gap at point A). They also granted him a right of access at point A to the proposed new road and a right of way along it to Hook Lane. By a conveyance dated December 8, 1966, the executors of Mr. Alford sold the 3½ acres of the defendants, but they expressly reserved the right (which they had already granted to the plaintiff) for the owner of the two acres to have access at point A to the proposed new road and a right of way along it to Hook Lane. In the same deed the defendants agreed to erect the fence 5 ft. 6 in. high along the boundary line (save for the access gap at point A).

So, on the conveyances the owners and occupiers of the two acres had a right of access at one point, namely, point A (halfway up the front portion). It was shown on the map as a gap about 20 feet wide; and from that point they had a right of way along the proposed new estate road, to get to Hook Lane. The defendants were to erect a close-boarded fence 5 ft. 6 in. high along the whole boundary between the two acres and the 3½ acres, except for the 20 feet gap at point A.

In 1967 the plaintiff had a new idea about his two acres. He thought it would be desirable to split up the two portions and sell them separately for separate use. The front portion (with the offices and showrooms) was clearly separated from the back portion (with the manufacturing). But, if they were split up, he would need another access. The access at point A would serve the front portion. But he would need another access at another point (to be called point B) so as to serve the back portion, together with a right of way along the new estate road from point B to Hook Lane.

Now, by this time the plaintiff had engaged as his architect, Mr. Alford, who was the son of the original owner of the land. On June 22, 1967, Mr. Alford, as architect for the plaintiff, wrote this letter to the engineer of the defendant council:

For the attention of Mr. Stonier:
    Dear Sir ... It would appear that Mr. Crabb may require two entrances off the new road, one to each of his two buildings. If you could let me know when you hope to get this fence line out I would be glad of the opportunity of meeting a representative of your department on the site so that these matters can be finally settled and the line of the fence agreed.

In pursuance of that letter there was a meeting on July 26, 1967, which was attended by the plaintiff and his architect, Mr. Alford, and by a representative of the defendants. There is no written note of what took place. Both the plaintiff and his architect, Mr. Alford, gave evidence about the meeting. But unfortunately the defendants gave no evidence about it. They undoubtedly had a representative there, but we do not know who it was. The engineer, Mr. Stonier, said that he himself was not present. The only other person who might have represented the defendants was a Mr. Queen. He was in Canada and not available to give evidence. But there is no doubt that they agreed the line of the fence which was to separate the plaintiff's land from the defendant's land. There is also no doubt that there was an agreement in principle that the plaintiff should have, not only the access at point A, but also an additional access at point B, so as to give access from the back portion of his land on to the new estate road. The plaintiff said that the defendant's representative made a firm commitment for a second access at B, but the judge said that the plaintiff was rather over sanguine. The judge preferred the evidence of Mr. Alford who was rather more cautious. Mr. Alford said: "I thought we had got final agreement in that there was to be access at point B, but I saw further processes beyond the meeting." He foresaw, no doubt, that there might have to be a document drawn up between the solicitors. Later on, in his evidence, Mr. Alford was asked whether there was to be any payment for this additional access. He said: "The normal anticipation at that time would be that some consideration would be demanded." But the defendants' representatives did not ask for any payment. Mr. Alford said: "My strong feeling is we would not be asked to pay that consideration when talking to the defendants in 1967."

Summing up the evidence, as accepted by the judge, the result of the meeting on July 22, 1967 was that there was an agreement in principle that the plaintiff should have an additional access at point B to the land, because it was envisaged that he would sell his two acres of land in two portions: the front portion with access at point A to the new road, and the back portion with access at point B to the new road. But the judge found there was no definite assurance to that effect, and, even if there had been, it would not have been binding in the absence of either writing or consideration. In order to be binding, there would have to be the legal processes foreseen by Mr. Alford.

As it happened, no legal processes were gone through. The defendants made no formal grant to the plaintiff of any access at point B or any easement over the new road. But, nevertheless, the parties acted in the belief that he had or would be granted such a right. During the winter of 1967 the defendants erected a fence along the line of the agreed boundary, but they left gaps at point A with access to the front portion of the plaintiff's land and at point B with access to the back portion. These two gaps were used by lorries which went in and out at points A and B as if they were exits and entrances. It was creating such a mess and disturbance of the plaintiff's land that there was a meeting on the site on January 31, 1968, at which the defendants agreed that they would undertake a tidying-up operation; and they did so.

On February 6, 1968, there was an important development. The defendants gave orders for gates to be constructed at points A and B, and they were in fact constructed. We have before us the contractors' account dated March 30, 1968. The contractors erected a fence 5 ft. 6 in. high all the way along the boundary, but they put gates in the fence at points A and B. At point A they erected a pair of oak close-boarded gates 18 ft. 0 ins. wide, 5 ft. 6 ins. high, complete with posts and fittings, at a cost of £117 5s. 6d. At point B they erected a similar pair 12 ft. 3 ins. wide and 5 ft. 6 ins. high, at a cost of £76 6s. 0d. The gateposts were set firmly in concrete at points A and B, and were clearly intended to be permanent.

Some months later, in the autumn of 1968, the plaintiff agreed to sell the front portion of his land to a purchaser and assigned to the purchaser the right of access at point A. But, here is the important matter. In the conveyance of the front portion of October 4, 1968, the plaintiff did not reserve any right for himself (as the owner of the back portion) to go over the front portion so as to get out at point A. The plaintiff thought that he already had a right of access at point B (where gates had already been erected) and so he did not need to reserve any right to get to point A. The judge found that "... Mr. Crabb believed that he had an assurance by the council that he would have access at point B from the council's land and was content to rely on that assurance. He did not reserve any right of access over [the front portion] ... . Mr. Crabb would not have been prepared to proceed with the sale of [the front portion] to [the purchaser] without reserving access over it ... if he had not believed ... that he would have access over the council's land."

But then, in January 1969, there was a new development. The plaintiff put a padlock on the inside of the gate at point B. The defendants were incensed by this. But they did not say a word to the plaintiff. They went on to his land. They took down the gates at point B. They pulled them out of the concrete. They took them away and filled the gap with extra posts and a close-boarded fence to match the existing fence. In short, they shut up the access at point B. The judge said: "The council gave no notice to Mr. Crabb of its intention to take this step; it seems to me that it was a discourteous and high-handed act. ..."

It is that action, depriving the plaintiff of his access, which has led to all the trouble. The plaintiff sought to settle the matter by agreement. The defendants did not object to his having access at point B and an easement to serve the back portion of the land, but they wanted £3,000 for it. This was more than the plaintiff was willing to pay. So no agreement was reached. In consequence this back portion of land has been rendered sterile. The plaintiff has been unable to sell it or make use of it because it has no outlet anywhere.

In June 1971 the plaintiff brought this action claiming a right of access at point B and a right of way along the estate road. He had no such right by any deed or conveyance or written agreement. So, in strict law, on the conveyance, the defendants were entitled to their land, subject only to an easement at point A, but none at point B. To overcome this strict law, the plaintiff claimed a right of access at B on the ground of equitable estoppel, promissory or proprietary. The judge held that he could not avail himself of any estoppel. He said: "In the absence of a definite assurance by the representative of the council, no question of estoppel can arise, and that really concludes the action." The plaintiff appeals to this court.

When Mr. Millett, for the plaintiff, said that he put his case on an estoppel, it shook me a little; because it is commonly supposed that estoppel is not itself a cause of action. But that is because there are estoppels and estoppels. Some do give rise to a cause of action. Some do not. In the species of estoppel called proprietary estoppel, it does give rise to a cause of action. We had occasion to consider it a month ago in *Moorgate Mercantile Co. Ltd. v. Twitchings* [1975] 3 W.L.R. 286 where I said, at p. 297, that the effect of estoppel on the true owner may be that "... his own title to the property, be it land or goods, has been held to be limited or extinguished, and new rights and interests have been created therein. And this operates by reason of his conduct — what he has led the other to believe — even though he never intended it." The new rights and interests, so created by estoppel, in or over land, will be protected by the courts and in this way give rise to a cause of action. This was pointed out in Spencer Bower and Turner, *Estoppel by Representation*, 2nd ed. (1966), pp. 279-282.

The basis of this proprietary estoppel—as indeed of promissory estoppel—is the interposition of equity. Equity comes in, true to form, to mitigate the rigours of strict law. The early cases did not speak of it as "estoppel." They spoke of it as "raising an equity." If I may expand what Lord Cairns L.C. said in *Hughes v. Metropolitan Railway Co.* (1877) 2 App. Cas. 439, 448: "[I]t is the first principle upon which all courts of equity proceed" that it will prevent a person from insisting on his strict legal rights—whether arising under a contract, or on his title deeds, or by statute—when it would be inequitable for him to do so having regard to the dealings which have taken place between the parties.

What then are the dealings which will preclude him from insisting on his strict legal rights? If he makes a binding contract that he will not insist on the strict legal position, a court of equity will hold him to his contract. Short of a binding contract, if he makes a promise that he will not insist upon his strict legal rights—then, even though that promise may be unenforceable in point of law for want of consideration or want of writing—then, if he makes the promise knowing or intending that the other will act upon it, and he does act upon it, then again a court of equity will not allow him to go back on that promise: see *Central London Property Trust Ltd. v. High Trees House Ltd.* [1947] K.B. 130 and *Charles Rickards Ltd. v. Oppenhaim* [1950] 1 K.B. 616, 623. Short of an actual promise, if he, by his words or conduct, so behaves as to lead another to believe that he will not insist on his strict legal rights—knowing or intending that the other will act on that belief—and he does so act, that again will raise an equity in favour of the other; and it is for a court of equity to say in what way the equity may be satisfied. The cases show that this equity does not depend on agreement but on words or conduct. In *Ramsden v. Dyson* (1866) L.R. 1 H.L. 129, 170 Lord Kingsdown spoke of a verbal agreement "or what amounts to the same thing, an expectation, created or encouraged." In *Birmingham and District Land Co. v. London and North Western Railway Co.* (1888) 40 Ch. D. 268, 277, Cotton L.J. said that "... what passed did not make a new agreement, but ... what took place ... raised an equity against him." And it was the Privy council in *Plimmer v. Wellington Corporation* (1884) 9 App. Cas. 699, 713-714 who said that "... the court must look at the circumstances in each case to decide in what way the equity can be satisfied" giving instances.

Recent cases afford illustrations of the principle. In *Inwards v. Baker* [1965] 2 Q.B. 29 it was held that, despite the legal title being in the plaintiffs, the son had an equity to remain in the bungalow "as long as he desired to use it as his home." Danckwerts L.J. said, at p. 38: "[E]quity protects him so that an injustice may not be perpetrated." In *E.R. Ives Investment Ltd. v. High* [1967] 2 Q.B. 379, it was held that Mr. High and his successors had an equity which could only be satisfied by allowing him to have a right of access over the yard, "so long as the block of flats has its foundations on his land." In *Siew Soon Wah v. Yong Tong Hong* [1973] 2 M.L.J. 3 the Privy Council held that, despite the fact that the defendant had no protection under the Rent Acts, he had an equity to remain "so long as he continued to practise his profession."

The question then is: were the circumstances here such as to raise an equity in favour of the plaintiff? True the defendants on the deeds had the title to their land, free of any access at point B. But they led the plaintiff to believe that he had or would be granted a right of access at point B. At the meeting of July 26, 1967, Mr. Alford and the plaintiff told the defendants' representative that the plaintiff intended to split the two acres into two portions and wanted to have an access at point B for the back portion; and the defendants' representative agreed that he should have this access. I do not think the defendants can avoid responsibility by saying that their represent-ative had no authority to agree this. They entrusted him with the task of setting out the line of the fence and the gates, and they must be answerable for his conduct in the course of it: see *Attorney-General to the Prince of Wales v. Collom* [1916] 2 K.B. 193, 207; and *Moorgate Mercantile Co. Ltd. v. Twitchings* [1975] 3 W.L.R. 286, 298.

The judge found that there was "no definite assurance" by the defendants' representative, and "no firm commitment," but only an "agreement in principle," meaning I suppose that, as Mr. Alford said, there were "some further processes" to be gone through before it would become binding. But if there were any such processes in the mind of the parties, the subsequent conduct of the defendants was such as to dispense with them. The defendants actually put up the gates at point B at considerable expense. That certainly led the plaintiff to believe that they agreed that he should have the right of access through point B without more ado.

The judge also said that, to establish this equity or estoppel, the defendants must have known that the plaintiff was selling the front portion without reserving a right of access for the back portion. I do not think this was necessary. The defendants knew that the plaintiff *intended* to sell the two portions separately and that he would need an access at point B as well as point A. Seeing that they knew of his intention—and they did nothing to disabuse him but rather confirmed it by erecting gates at point B—it was their conduct which led him to act as he did: and this raises an equity in his favour against them.

In the circumstances it seems to me inequitable that the council should insist on their strict title as they did, and to take the highhanded action of pulling down the gates without a word of warning, and to demand of the plaintiff £3,000 as the price for the easement. If he had moved at once for an injunction in aid of his equity—to prevent them removing the gates—I think he should have been granted it. But he did not do so. He tried to negotiate terms, but these failing, the action has come for trial. And we have the question: in what way now should the equity be satisfied?

Here equity is displayed at its most flexible, see *Snell's Principles of Equity*, 27th ed. (1973), p. 568, and the illustrations there given. If the matter had been finally settled in 1967, I should have thought that, although nothing was said at the meeting in July 1967, nevertheless it would be quite reasonable for the defendants to ask the plaintiff to pay something for the access at point B, perhaps—and I am guessing—some hundreds of pounds. But, as Mr. Millett pointed out in the course of the argument, because of the defendants' conduct, the back land has been landlocked. It has been sterile and rendered useless for five or six years, and the plaintiff has been unable to deal with it during that time. This loss to him can be taken into account. And at the present time, it seems to me that in order to satisfy the equity, the plaintiff should have the right of access at point B without paying anything for it.

I would, therefore, hold that the plaintiff, as the owner of the back portion, has a right of access at point B over the verge on to Mill Park and a right of way along that road to Hook Lane without paying compensation. I would allow the appeal and declare that he has an easement, accordingly.

Loranger v Haines. (1921), 50 OLR 268 (CA). Action by the purchaser for specific performance. The facts of the case were as follows: L was associated with H in promoting a patent. H purchased a large parcel of land intending to build a house on part and sell the rest. H suggested that he would give L a building site on which a house might be built next to his own. L accepted and drafted an agreement in which, for "consideration hereinafter mentioned," H promised to convey a parcel of land to him. The agreement called for L to build a residence on this parcel and to share in the cost of sewers, watermains, and a common roadway. L built, without any conveyance, a house costing $12,500, and spent $1,500 improving the land. After a falling out, H refused to convey the agreed-on parcel to L. Held, for the plaintiff. On appeal, affirmed. The things that Loranger undertook to do were a sufficient consideration. MEREDITH CJCP: And quite apart from any question of contract, the defendant should assuredly be estopped from claiming title to and taking possession of the land upon which, not only with his knowledge, but at his request, the plaintiff has expended so much money—with the defendant's knowledge and before his eyes—on the faith of his promise to convey it to the plaintiff.

COWPER-SMITH V MORGAN
2017 SCC 61

MCLACHLIN CJ (Abella, Moldaver, Karakatsanis, Wagner, Gascon and Rowe JJ concurring):

[1] Equity enforces promises that the law does not. This appeal concerns such a promise, part of an arrangement between siblings to provide care for their aging mother. The sister assured the brother that, if he moved back into the family home to do so, he would be able to acquire her share of that property after their mother's death. The question before us is whether equity—and specifically the doctrine of proprietary estoppel—now binds her to her word.

[2] The trial judge concluded that all the elements of proprietary estoppel were established: the sister promised the brother that he would be able to purchase her eventual interest in their mother's property; the brother reasonably relied on the expectation that he would be able to do so; and, because of the detriment the brother suffered as a result of his reliance, it would be unfair and unjust in the circumstances to permit the sister to resile from her promise. The evidence supports that conclusion.

[3] That the sister did not have an interest in the property at the time her brother relied on her promise does not negate her obligation to keep her promise; proprietary estoppel will attach to the sister's interest in the property as soon as she receives it from their mother's estate. I would allow the appeal.

• • •

III. ANALYSIS

[15] An equity arises when (1) a representation or assurance is made to the claimant, on the basis of which the claimant expects that he will enjoy some right or benefit over property; (2) the claimant relies on that expectation by doing or refraining from doing something, and his reliance is reasonable in all the circumstances; and (3) the claimant suffers a detriment as a result of his reasonable reliance, such that it would be unfair or unjust for the party responsible for the representation or assurance to go back on her word: see *Thorner v. Major*, [2009] UKHL 18 ... . The representation or assurance may be express or implied ... . An inchoate equity arises at the time of detrimental reliance on a representation or assurance. It is not necessary to determine, in this case, whether this equity is personal or proprietary in nature. When the party responsible for the representation or assurance possesses an interest in the property sufficient to fulfill the claimant's expectation, proprietary estoppel may give effect to the equity by making the representation or assurance binding.

[16] Proprietary estoppel protects the equity, which in turn protects the claimant's reasonable reliance ... . Like other estoppels, proprietary estoppel avoids the

unfairness or injustice that would result to one party if the other were permitted to break her word and insist on her strict legal rights ... .

[17]   Where protecting the equity of the case may demand the recognition of "new rights and interests ... in or over land" (*Crabb v. Arun District Council* ...), proprietary estoppel can do what other estoppels cannot—it can found a cause of action: see MacDougall [*Estoppel* (Toronto: LexisNexis, 2012)], at p. 424 ... . Where the ingredients for a proprietary estoppel are present, the court must determine whether it is appropriate to satisfy the equity by recognizing the modification or creation of property rights "in situations where there is want of consideration or of writing" ... .

[18]   Consensus as to the elements of proprietary estoppel has proved elusive ... .

• • •

[20]   Unfairness or injustice—sometimes referred to as "unconscionability," albeit not in the sense in which that term is used in contract law (see *Ryan*, [2005 SCC 38] at para. 74)—are not stand-alone criteria; they are what proprietary estoppel aims to avoid by keeping the owner to her word.

[21]   It has commonly been understood in Canada that proprietary estoppel is concerned with interests in land ... .

[22]   We need not decide, in this case, whether proprietary estoppel may attach to an interest in property other than land; Max's expectation was that he would enjoy a right over the family home, namely, the right to acquire Gloria's eventual interest in it. Nor need we determine whether equity more broadly enforces non-contractual promises on which claimants have detrimentally relied: see, e.g., *Waltons Stores (Interstate) Ltd. v. Maher* (1988), 76 A.L.R. 513 (H.C.) ... .

A. WAS MAX'S RELIANCE REASONABLE?

[23]   As we have seen, to establish proprietary estoppel one must first establish an equity of the kind that proprietary estoppel protects. This requires three things: a representation or assurance on the basis of which the claimant expects to enjoy a right or benefit over property, reasonable reliance on that expectation, and detriment as a result of the reliance. When the owner of an interest in the property over which the claimant expects to enjoy a right or benefit is responsible for the representation or assurance, then the equity established by the claimant's reasonable reliance may be given effect by proprietary estoppel.

[24]   There is no question that Gloria assured Max that, if he moved back to Victoria to care for their mother, he would be able to acquire her eventual interest in the house. Nor is it disputed that, as a result of his reliance on that assurance, Max has suffered a detriment. The trial judge determined, and all now agree, that "Max acted to his detriment in moving from England to Victoria, giving up employment income, the long-term lease of a cottage, his contacts with his children, and his social life to look after his aged dementing mother" and that "[h]e did so relying on Gloria's agreement to his conditions for the move": para. 118.

[25]   The question is whether Max's reliance was reasonable. If not, then no equity arose in his favour. Gloria argues—and the Court of Appeal majority accepted—that Max's reliance could not have been reasonable because Gloria did not own an interest in the property. As Willcock J.A. wondered, at para. 111 of his reasons, "[h]ow can there be reasonable reliance upon a promise to convey an interest in property made by one who does not have such an interest or whose interest is uncertain?"

[26]   Reasonableness is circumstantial. As Lord Walker put it in *Thorner*, "to establish a proprietary estoppel the relevant assurance must be clear enough," that is, "[t]he promise must be unambiguous and must appear to have been intended to be taken

seriously. Taken in its context, it must have been a promise which one might reasonably expect to be relied upon by the person to whom it was made" ... . What matters is what one party induced the other to expect; as Lord Hoffmann stated in *Thorner*, the question is whether "the meaning ... conveyed would reasonably have been understood as intended to be taken seriously as an assurance which could be relied upon" ... .

[27] In *Thorner*, one party had induced the other to expect that he would inherit farm property. Since the parties knew "that the extent of the farm was liable to fluctuate (as development opportunities arose, and tenancies came and went)," "[t]here is no reason to doubt that their common understanding was that [the] assurance related to whatever the farm consisted of at [the owner's] death": para. 62. This was not the sort of uncertainty which would make reliance on the assurance unreasonable because "it is unprofitable, in view of the retrospective nature of the assessment which the doctrine of proprietary estoppel requires, to speculate on what might have been": para. 65.

[28] This approach to assessing certainty—and thus the reasonableness of reliance—permits equity "to mitigate the rigours of strict law": *Crabb*, at p. 871; see also *Thorner*, at para. 98, per Lord Neuberger. Unlike a contract, which, "subject to the narrow doctrine of frustration, must be performed come what may," equity "looks backwards from the moment when the promise falls due to be performed and asks whether, in the circumstances which have actually happened, it would be unconscionable for the promise not to be kept": *Walton*, [EWCA, April 14, 1994 (unreported)] at paras. 20-21, quoted in *Thorner*, at para. 57.

[29] In a proprietary estoppel claim, where the equity is said to have arisen when the claimant relied on an expectation that he would enjoy some right or benefit over property, it may be that the party responsible for the expectation had such a speculative interest in the property that the claimant's reliance could not have been reasonable: see *Cobbe v. Yeoman's Row Management Ltd.*, [2008] UKHL 55 ... . But whether this is so will depend on context, not on *ex ante* doctrinal restrictions. The Court of Appeal majority's proposed bright line rule—namely, that reliance on a promise by a party with no present interest in property can *never* be reasonable—is out of step with equity's purpose, which is to temper the harsh effects of strict legal rules.

[30] Whether, in a particular case, a claimant's reliance was reasonable in the circumstances is a question of mixed fact and law. A trial judge's determination of this point is, absent palpable and overriding error, entitled to deference ... .

[31] Here, on the trial judge's findings, both Max and Gloria had clearly understood for well over a decade that their mother's estate, including the house in which she lived, would be divided equally among her three children upon her death. Nathan, Max, and Max's ex-wife each testified to a conversation with Elizabeth and Arthur, just prior to Arthur's death in 1992, in which both parents made clear that everything they owned would be divided equally among their three children once Elizabeth passed away. Max's evidence was that Elizabeth confirmed as much to him in 2002. Gloria conceded at trial that, in the years before her mother's death, she made statements evincing the same expectation. She departed from that position—and asserted that she was entitled to *all* of her mother's assets, the house included—only in April 2011.

[32] It was thus sufficiently certain that Gloria would inherit a one-third interest in the property for her assurance to be taken seriously as one on which Max could rely. Max and Gloria negotiated for an extended period before Max uprooted his life in England and returned to Victoria. Gloria promised unequivocally that he would be able to acquire her share of the property if he did so. She made that commitment,

among others, with the purpose of enticing him back to the family home. In this, she succeeded. I see no basis on which to overturn the trial judge's conclusion that, in these circumstances, Max's reliance was reasonable.

[33] Max reasonably relied on the expectation that he would be able to acquire Gloria's interest in the property once their mother's estate had been administrated in the usual course. Gloria was responsible for that expectation; she promised Max as much before he returned to Victoria from England. Max suffered a detriment as a result, such that it would be unfair or unjust to permit Gloria to break her word. An equity thus arose in Max's favour. It is this equity that proprietary estoppel will protect, if its elements are established.

B. DOES PROPRIETARY ESTOPPEL PROTECT THE EQUITY?

[34] The dispute as to whether the elements of proprietary estoppel are made out in this case turns on whether, at the time of the claimant's reliance, the party responsible for the claimant's expectation that he will enjoy a right or benefit over property must own an interest in the property sufficient to meet the claimant's expectation. The Court of Appeal majority concluded that, since Gloria did not own such an interest at the time of Max's reliance, his proprietary estoppel claim could not succeed. ...

[35] I cannot agree. With respect, the conclusion reached by the Court of Appeal majority conflates proprietary estoppel with the equity to which it gives effect. ...

[36] An equity arose in Max's favour when he reasonably relied to his detriment on the expectation that he would be able to acquire Gloria's one-third interest in their mother's house. That equity could not have been protected by proprietary estoppel at the time it arose, because Gloria did not then own an interest in the property. But that does not mean that proprietary estoppel cannot attach to Gloria's share of the house once she receives it. I conclude that it can.

• • •

C. WHAT IS THE APPROPRIATE REMEDY?

[46] Where a claimant has established proprietary estoppel, the court has considerable discretion in crafting a remedy that suits the circumstances ... . As with any exercise of discretion, an appellate court should not interfere unless the trial judge's decision evinces an error in principle or is plainly wrong ... .

[47] Still, "the court must take a principled approach, and cannot exercise a completely unfettered discretion according to the individual judge's notion of what is fair in any particular case": *Jennings v. Rice*, [2002] EWCA Civ. 159 ... . A claimant who establishes the need for proprietary estoppel is entitled only to the minimum relief necessary to satisfy the equity in his favour ... . Since the equity aims to address the unfair or unjust detriment the claimant would suffer if the owner were permitted to resile from her inducement, encouragement, or acquiescence, "there must be a proportionality between the remedy and the detriment which is its purpose to avoid" ... .

[48] This approach recognizes that, while proprietary estoppel arises where the claimant's expectations are frustrated, the reasonableness of the claimant's expectations must be assessed in light of, among other things, the detriment the claimant has actually suffered ... . Courts of equity must therefore strike a balance between vindicating the claimant's subjective expectations—which, in their full context, may or may not reflect a reasonable valuation of the claimant's detriment—and correcting that detriment, which may be difficult or even impossible to measure ... . In no case, however, may the claimant obtain more than he expected ... .

[49] Here, Max's detriment lay in his returning to Victoria to live with and care for his aging mother. He expected, among other things, that he would be able to acquire Gloria's share of their mother's house after their mother's death and once her estate had been administered. Having kept up his end of the bargain, he sought an order requiring Gloria to keep up hers by selling him her one-third interest in the property. The trial judge concluded that this was the minimum required to satisfy the equity.

[50] Requiring Gloria to sell her interest in the house to Max is the minimum necessary to satisfy the equity in Max's favour. The question is, at what price?

[51] Max submits that he should be entitled to purchase Gloria's share for $223,333.33, which reflects the property's 2011 appraised value of $670,000.00. Gloria argues that, if she is ordered to sell her interest to Max, it should be at its current fair market value, which the parties agree is higher than it was in 2011.

[52] I agree with Max. As soon as Gloria receives an interest in the property from their mother's estate, all of the elements of proprietary estoppel will be satisfied. But the relevant equity will have arisen long before—namely, at the time of Max's reliance. The equity in Max's favour exists to avoid the unfairness and injustice that would result if Gloria were permitted to break her word and not sell her interest to Max, notwithstanding the detriment Max suffered in returning to Victoria from England. Max valued that detriment as being worth the concessions he obtained from Gloria. One of those concessions was that Max would be able to acquire Gloria's interest in the property in exchange for an amount equal to one third of its total fair market value once the estate had been administered.

· · ·

[56] To hold otherwise would disregard the difference between the equity and the estoppel. That no estoppel was available at the time the equity arose is of no moment. Max's expectations must be considered broadly. ...

[57] Still, as the trial judge recognized, satisfying the equity does not require Gloria to sustain a loss. Had events unfolded as Max reasonably expected them to, Gloria would have given up her interest in the property in early 2011 in exchange for its fair market value. She would have had the benefit of those funds during the intervening years. And her mother's estate would have been relieved of the cost of maintaining the property, increasing the residue in which Gloria and her siblings are to share equally.

[58] Max will therefore be entitled to purchase Gloria's interest in the property for $223,333.33, plus an amount equal to the post-judgment interest that would be payable on a judgment in that amount issued on February 2, 2011, once Gloria has received that interest from Elizabeth's estate. Upon his acquisition of Gloria's interest in the property, Max is to account to the estate for the amount of any expenses incurred by the estate in maintaining the property since February 2, 2011.

· · ·

[60] I would allow the appeal ... .

[The partially concurring judgments of BROWN J and CÔTÉ J are omitted.]

NOTES AND QUESTIONS

1. Are cases like *Dillwyn, Crabb, Cowper-Smith,* and *Loranger* really contract cases? If not, how should the rule applied in these cases be classified? In SM Waddams, *Dimensions of Private Law: Categories and Concepts in Anglo-American Legal Reasoning* (Cambridge: Cambridge University Press, 2003), the author suggests that this issue (reliance on gratuitous promises) has, like many other issues in private law, not been allocated to a single category,

but has been influenced concurrently by several concepts, including contract, wrongdoing, unjust enrichment, property, and public policy. Do you agree with this analysis?

2. A promises to give to B a vacant lot next to the family cottage in Muskoka. The lot is worth $1 million, and B builds a cabin there at a cost of $50,000. A dies leaving all her property by will to C. How would you advise B?

3. A is the owner of land and enters into negotiations with B for the sale of that land to B. They reach an oral "agreement in principle" on the core terms of the sale but no written contract is produced. There remain some non-trivial terms still to be agreed on. The structure of the agreement in principle is that B, at his own expense, will apply for planning permission and, if that permission is obtained, A will sell the land to B at a stipulated price. Both A and B know that the agreement in principle is not legally binding but both lead the other person to believe that they feel themselves honour bound to enter into the formal contract once planning permission is obtained. The application for planning permission is successful and A then seeks to renegotiate the core financial terms of the sale. B is unwilling to agree to the new financial terms. Can B sue A in proprietary estoppel to enforce their agreement in principle? Has B's reliance on the agreement in principle been reasonable? For a negative answer to both these questions, see *Cobbe v Yeoman's Row Management Ltd*, [2008] UKHL 55.

4. Why might a court allow estoppel to be used as a cause of action in relation to promises to convey interests in land? For a multifaceted historical explanation based on the prevalence of formalities required to transfer interests in land, the sympathetic nature of the persons relying, and the lack of respect for consideration in the equity tradition, see E Cooke, *The Modern Law of Estoppel* (Oxford: Oxford University Press, 2000) at 127-28. See also, the discussions in B MacDougall, *Estoppel* (Toronto: LexisNexis, 2012); B McFarlane, *The Law of Proprietary Estoppel* (Oxford: Oxford University Press, 2014); and J McGhee, *Snell's Equity*, 33rd ed (London: Sweet & Maxwell, 2015); all of which were relied on by the Supreme Court in *Cowper-Smith*.

5. As the Supreme Court noted in *Cowper-Smith*, courts deciding cases of proprietary estoppel have shown a willingness, in certain circumstances, to limit a claimant's remedy to one that undoes detrimental reliance rather than one that meets the claimant's expectation. Courts deciding cases of promissory estoppel have not shown this same willingness. Is there any compelling reason for this difference?

6. Is the current law of estoppel coherent when both the rules of proprietary and promissory estoppel are viewed together? For arguments that it is not, see JW Neyers, "A Coherent Law of Estoppel?" (2003) J of Obligations & Remedies 25; B McFarlane & P Sales, "Promises, Detriment, and Liability" (2015) 131 Law Q Rev 610. Sensing these incoherences, Australian courts have moved to merge the rules of promissory and proprietary estoppel. The excerpts that follow describe this process and its effect on Canadian courts.

PETER HEFFEY, JEANNIE PATERSON & ANDREW ROBERTSON, *Principles of Contract Law*, 2ND ED
(Sydney: Lawbook Co, 2005) at 162–63 (footnotes omitted)

Both the principles of proprietary estoppel and promissory estoppel came to be applied in the Australian courts. In *Waltons Stores (Interstate) Ltd v. Maher* [(1988), 164 CLR 387], the High Court recognised a unity of principle between promissory and proprietary estoppel, and recognised that they are manifestations of a broader principle of equitable estoppel, which is of general application. It was said that the common thread that links promissory and proprietary estoppel together is the principle that equity will come to the relief of a plaintiff who has acted to his or her detriment on the basis of an assumption induced by the defendant's conduct.

Waltons Stores negotiated to lease land from Mr. and Mrs. Maher, on terms that required the Mahers to demolish a building on their land and construct a new building to Waltons' specifications. Time was short, and the terms of the lease needed to be finalised quickly so that the Mahers could complete the construction work by the date stipulated by Waltons. The Mahers were concerned to ensure that there were no problems with the lease before they demolished a new brick part of the old building. When negotiations were essentially complete, Waltons' solicitors sent to the Mahers' solicitors a copy of the lease which incorporated some final amendments requested by the Mahers. Waltons' solicitors told the Mahers' solicitors that they would let them know the next day if Waltons disagreed with any of the amendments. The Mahers heard no more from Waltons' solicitors on this issue. The lease was signed by the Mahers and returned to Waltons on November 11 "by way of exchange." Waltons then instructed its solicitors to "go slow" on the transaction, pending a review of its retailing strategy. Waltons became aware in December that the Mahers had begun to demolish the existing building, but still delayed signing. On 19 January, when the construction of the new building was 40 per cent complete, Waltons' solicitors informed the Mahers' solicitors that Waltons did not intend to proceed with the lease.

No contract existed between the parties because Waltons had not executed the lease. Deane and Gaudron JJ. found that the Mahers had acted on the assumption that exchange *had* taken place and a binding agreement for lease had been made. This was an assumption of existing fact which, when relied upon, established an estoppel in pais or common law estoppel. The effect of that estoppel was to prevent Waltons from denying that they had signed the lease. The rights of the parties were therefore determined on the basis that Waltons had signed the lease. Mason C.J., Wilson and Brennan JJ. preferred the conclusion that the Mahers had acted on the assumption that Waltons *would* complete the transaction. This was an assumption as to Waltons' future conduct, which could only give rise to a promissory or equitable estoppel.

Mason C.J. and Wilson J. accepted that a promissory estoppel could arise between parties involved in pre-contractual negotiations, and could be used to support a cause of action in contract. Here, they said, Waltons' inaction encouraged the Mahers to continue to act on the assumption that the completion of the transaction was merely a formality. It was unconscionable for Waltons to act as it did, and Waltons was estopped from retreating from its implied promise to complete the contract. Brennan J. recognised that promissory estoppel could operate as an independent source of rights. If the proper inference from the facts was that the Mahers had been led to believe that a contract would come into existence, then Waltons' unconscionable conduct raised an equity in favour of the Mahers, which the Court had to satisfy by granting appropriate relief. The appropriate relief was to treat Waltons as though it had signed and exchanged the lease.

The decision in *Waltons Stores v. Maher* was a significant development in Australian contract law because it involved a departure from the classical idea that a promise creates a legal obligation only when consideration has been given in return for the promise and a contract has been formed. The decision greatly expanded the range of situations in which liability could result from reliance on non-contractual promises.

NM V ATA
2003 BCCA 297, 13 BCLR (4th) 73

HUDDART JA (for the court):

[1] This appeal arises out of a failed relationship. It is from an order dismissing Ms. A.'s claim to enforce a promise by Mr. M. to pay the balance outstanding on the mortgage on her home in England (GBP 73,048.53) if she would come to live with him in Canada with a view to marriage.

[2] In reliance on that promise, Ms. A. resigned her permanent job with the Bank of America and moved to Vancouver in July 1993. The relationship was stormy, in part, because Mr. M. did not pay off her mortgage. He did, however, loan her $100,000 on a promissory note dated 6 April 1994. Ms. A. applied those funds to her mortgage. About a week later, Mr. M. evicted Ms. A. from his home. She has not been able to find permanent employment since, in England or Vancouver.

[3] The only issue on this appeal is whether the trial judge erred in refusing to enforce the promise on which Ms. A. relied to her detriment. ...

[4] The essence of the appeal is that the trial judge took too narrow a view of the equitable doctrine of promissory estoppel ... . Ms. A.'s counsel frankly acknowledged he was asking this Court ... to extend the application of promissory estoppel to right a wrong that is otherwise being done to Ms. A., she having suffered from her reliance on Mr. M.'s promise, albeit in a romantic relationship. He asks us to follow the path already well trod by the courts of New Zealand, Australia, and the United States, and being opened in England to an equitable remedy for injurious reliance on a promise intended to bind its maker and to be acted upon by the promisee, and acted upon by the promisee to the knowledge of the promisor.

[5] This is the approach to promissory estoppel about which Professor Waddams wrote in *The Law of Contracts* (4th ed.) Canada Law Book, 1999, at p. 141 ...

> ... It may therefore be suggested that Commonwealth law is moving, though rather slowly, in the direction of the Second Restatement, section 90, that is, towards the protection of promises by reason of and to the extent of subsequent reliance.

[6] The relevant part of *Restatement of the Law Second, Contracts 2d*, The American Law Institute, American Law Institute Publishers (1981) states:

> ### 90. Promise Reasonably Inducing Action or Forbearance
> (1) A promise which the promisor should reasonably expect to induce action or forbearance on the part of the promisee or a third person and which does induce such action or forbearance is binding if injustice can be avoided only by enforcement of the promise. The remedy granted for breach may be limited as justice requires.

[7] The appellant finds further support for this extension of promissory estoppel beyond its reach as accepted currently in Canadian authorities in *Waltons Stores (Interstate) Limited v. Maher and Another* (1988), 164 C.L.R. 387 (H.C.A.). At para. 26, Brennan J. summarized the Australian position:

> A non-contractual promise can give rise to an equitable estoppel only when the promisor induces the promisee to assume or expect that the promise is intended to affect their legal relations and he knows or intends that the promisee will act or abstain from acting in reliance on the promise, and when the promisee does so act or abstain ... and the promisee would suffer detriment by his action or inaction if the promisor were not to fulfill the promise.

• • •

[9] [O]n the basis of this view of promissory estoppel, Ms. A. considers the minimum equity to do her justice is that she not be required to pay back the loan of $100,000.00. ...

[10] The respondent says this Court should not make such a revolutionary change to the law in circumstances where the unfulfilled promise was made at the outset of a romantic relationship that by its nature involves risk-taking, and, he might have said, many promises. This is particularly so, he submits, because Parliament and the Legislature have provided statutory remedies for losses suffered on the breakdown of romantic or marriage-like relationships, among which they have not chosen to include the enforcement of an unfulfilled promise. Finally, he asks, what better test is there for the enforcement of a promise than that the common law (as understood in British Columbia) provides: did the parties intend to affect their legal relations? Here, he points out, there is no evidence either party thought a legal relationship had been created by the promise, that their legal relations had been affected, or that the promise was legally binding.

[11] The appellant replies that, if this is the correct test for the enforcement of a promise, Mr. Justice Cohen's order dismissing her claim must be set aside and the matter remitted to the trial court for consideration as to whether the parties thought the promise of Mr. M. to be legally binding.

[12] I find merit in the respondent's submission given the current status of the law of promissory estoppel in Canada, but need consider only the appellant's submission to resolve this appeal. If equitable estoppel is seen as a flexible doctrine requiring a broad approach to preclude unconscionable conduct or injustice, I am not persuaded by the findings of the trial judge or the evidence in this case that Mr. M.'s failure to keep his promise to Ms. A. is unconscionable as the law understands that concept, and, thus, unjust. This is because, even on the analyses in *Waltons*, *supra*, a necessary element of promissory estoppel is the promisee's assumption or expectation of a legal relationship.

• • •

[17] None of the Australian High Court justices would have extended the reach of the doctrine of promissory estoppel to provide the equivalent of the American injurious reliance remedy. By no reading of any of their opinions, would the doctrine reach to the facts of this case. ...

[18] While it may be, as Professor Waddams suggests, that the law is moving slowly toward a more generous approach to promissory estoppel than that said ... to be well settled, I can see little evidence of that movement in Canadian authorities, or for that matter, in English authorities.

• • •

[20] The absence of any evidence as to what interest, if any, Mr. M. might acquire in her home, significant references in their correspondence to a future equal partnership and to joint plans for the English house to produce income for them jointly, and the lack of any reference to when the promise was to or could be fulfilled, suggest the promise was made in the context of a relationship both of them thought would be permanent, and result in marriage, at which point they would be life partners, not that it would be fulfilled to compensate Ms. A. for the detriment she would suffer from leaving her job and home. There was also a lack of mutuality, in that Ms. A. could be under no enforceable obligation to stay with Mr. M. if he fulfilled the promise.

[21] In these circumstances, I can see no reason to remit the matter to the trial court for further consideration, even if the trial judge can be said to have erred in

requiring proof of an existing legal relationship as a necessary element of promissory estoppel. Whether he did err in that regard I prefer to leave for another case where the question requires to be answered.

[22] It follows I would dismiss the appeal.

NOTES AND QUESTIONS

1. Although not made clear in the excerpt above, Ms. A's claim in promissory estoppel was a counterclaim to Mr. M's attempt to recover $100,000 under a promissory note signed by her. While his claim succeeded in full (see *McLeod v Amiras*, (2001), 94 BCLR (3d) 359 (SC)), her counterclaim was unsuccessful. Does it seem just that she has to repay the loan, but that he has no obligation to pay for her substantial detriment? Is it not realistic to assume that, before the breakup, the parties would have understood the repayment of the loan to be conditional on Mr. M fulfilling his side of the bargain?

2. Is the court's discussion of intention consistent with that given in *Owen Sound*, above? Is its discussion of certainty consistent with that given in *Crabb*, above?

3. American law has been much more willing to enforce non-proprietary gratuitous promises that have been relied on (in contrast to Canadian cases such as *NM v ATA* and *Calgary Fire Fighters Association (International Association of Fire Fighters, Local 255) v Calgary (City)*, 2011 ABCA 121). What is the conceptual basis underpinning s 90 of the *Restatement of Contracts*, 2d? Consider the following excerpt.

WARREN A SEAVEY, "RELIANCE UPON GRATUITOUS PROMISES OR OTHER CONDUCT"
(1950-51) 64 Harv L Rev 913 at 925-27 (footnotes omitted)

This brings us ... to the ... situation, where there has been a failure to perform a gratuitous promise which, it is assumed, was made in good faith. ... The ... way of dealing with the situation is to use tort principles. This will avoid the indefiniteness of the application of Section 90 and will also clarify the matter of damages. The colloquial explanation for the rule of the section is that it creates "promissory estoppel." Estoppel is basically a tort doctrine and the rationale of the section is that justice requires the defendant to pay for harm caused by foreseeable reliance upon performance of his promise. The wrong is not primarily in depriving the plaintiff of the promised reward but in causing the plaintiff to change position to his detriment. It would follow that the damages should not exceed the loss caused by the change of position, which would never be more in amount, but might be less, than the promised reward. ...

The limitations [of the tort analysis] ..., which do not appear in Section 90 of the *Restatement of Contracts*, are that the defendant is not liable if the plaintiff had no other means of securing the result or if the defendant had notified the plaintiff of an intent not to perform while the other still had available means to secure performance. Both limitations seem necessary for tort liability and it may be that this is merely spelling out what is implicit ... in Section 90. Thus, ... if a person gives the promise to insure a vessel at a time when the plaintiff could not have secured any other person to do the work for him, there would be no liability. Likewise, if the defendant, having decided not to perform his promise, notified the plaintiff in time for other insurance to be secured, no harm would have resulted from his failure to perform the undertaking. If there is reliance, it would seem unjust not to allow recovery where the defendant has reason to know of the reliance and where, without excuse, the defendant fails to perform. If the promisor attempted good faith performance and, in the exercise of due care, failed to carry our his promise, there should be no liability since it was not a bargaining transaction.

NOTES AND QUESTIONS

1. For a view of s 90 that is very different than that offered by Seavey, see T Yorio & S Thel, "The Promissory Basis of Section 90" (1991) 101 Yale LJ 111. In that article the authors argue that the purpose of s 90 is to enforce serious promises. Thus, detrimental reliance is important only insofar as it helps to identify serious promises and distinguish them from promises not warranting enforcement. Which view of s 90 would Fuller or Brudner support (recall their excerpts in Section III.A, above)? For a discussion of s 90, see Waddams at paras 192-94; McCamus at 298-301.

2. Surveys of American case law have found that judges routinely award expectation damages and specific performance for breach of s 90 (see e.g. the discussion of Yorio & Thel, above; DA Farber & JH Matheson, "Beyond Promissory Estoppel: Contract Law and the Invisible Handshake" (1985) 52 U Chicago L Rev 903; Smith at 239-40). Does this undermine Seavey's justification? Why might a court award expectation damages when it was concerned about detrimental reliance? For various explanations, see A Robertson, "Satisfying the Minimum Equity: Equitable Estoppel Remedies after *Verwayen*" (1996) 20 Melbourne UL Rev 805; A Robertson, "The Reliance Basis of Proprietary Estoppel Remedies" [2008] The Conveyancer 295; B McFarlane & P Sales, "Promises, Detriment, and Liability" (2015) 131 Law Q Rev 610; and Fuller & Perdue, "The Reliance Interest in Contract Damages," which is excerpted in Chapter 2, Section I.

3. A promises B $50,000 as a gift. B buys a car for $25,000. A revokes his promise. B's car is worth $20,000. What should be B's measure of recovery? Would it make any difference if A, instead of revoking the promise, had died leaving unpaid creditors and needy dependants?

IV. UNILATERAL CONTRACTS

A "unilateral contract" is made by accepting an offer; not by making a counterpromise (which would create a "bilateral contract" of mutual promises) but by performing a requested overt act. The contract is said to be unilateral because there is only one relationship of right and duty created between the parties—the promisor is under a duty to perform her promise and the promisee has a right to the promised performance (provided in each case that the requested act is performed).

Unilateral contract situations present a number of problems, many arising in what are sometimes called the "reward cases." To whom is a reward offered? Must the offeree, whoever she may be, notify the offeror? If so, when? Another interesting problem arises when the offeror wants to revoke her offer after the offeree has substantially performed the requested act. When should the courts protect the interests of the parties? What interests ought to be protected?

Looking back through the materials presented thus far, where before have you seen unilateral contracts? How was the concept used by the courts?

WILLIAMS V CARWARDINE
(1833), 4 B & Ad 621, 110 ER 590

At the trial before Park J., at the last Spring Assizes for the county of Hereford, the following appeared to be the facts of the case: One Walter Carwardine, the brother of the defendant, was seen on the evening of the 24th of March, 1831, at a public house at Hereford, and was not heard of again till his body was found on the 12th of April in the river Wye, about two miles from the city. An inquest was held on the body on the 13th of April and the following days till the 19th; and it appearing that the plaintiff was at a house with the deceased on the night he was supposed to have been murdered, she was examined before the magistrates but did not give them any information which led to the apprehension of the real offender. On the 25th of April the defendant caused a handbill to be published, stating that whoever would give such information as would lead to a discovery of the murderer of Walter Carwardine, should, on conviction receive a reward of £20; and any person concerned therein, or privy thereto (except the party who actually committed the offence), should be entitled to such reward, and every exertion used to procure a pardon; and it then added, that information was to be given, and application for the above reward was to be made, to William Carwardine, Holmer, near Hereford. Two persons were tried for the murder at the Summer Assizes, 1831, but acquitted. Soon after this the plaintiff was severely beaten and bruised by one William Williams; and on the 23rd of August, 1831, believing she had not long to live, and to ease her conscience, she made a voluntary statement, containing information which led to the subsequent conviction of Williams. Upon this evidence it was contended, that as the plaintiff was not induced by the reward promised by the defendant to give evidence, the law would not imply a contract by the defendant to pay her the £20. The learned Judge was of opinion that the plaintiff, having given the information which led to the conviction of the murderer, had performed the condition on which the £20 was to become payable, and was therefore entitled to recover it; and he directed the jury to find a verdict for the plaintiff, but desired them to find specially whether she was induced to give the information by the offer of the promised reward. The jury found that she was not induced by the offer of the reward, but by other motives.

Curwood [counsel for the defendant] now moved for a new trial. There was no promise to pay the plaintiff the sum of £20. That promise could only be enforced in favor of persons who should have been induced to make disclosures by the promise of the reward. Here the jury found that the plaintiff was induced by other motives to give the information. They have, therefore, negatived any contract on the part of the defendant with the plaintiff.

DENMAN CJ: The plaintiff, by having given information which led to the conviction of the murderer of Walter Carwardine, has brought herself within the terms of the advertisement, and therefore is entitled to recover.

LITTLEDALE J: The advertisement amounts to a general promise to give a sum of money to any person who shall give information which might lead to the discovery of the offender. The plaintiff gave that information.

PARKE J: There was a contract with any person who performed the condition mentioned in the advertisement.

PATTESON J: I am of the same opinion. We cannot go into the plaintiff's motives.

[Rule refused. From the report of the trial in 5 C & P 566 at 574, it might appear from an admission of the defendant's counsel that the plaintiff knew of the offer at the time she gave the information. If she did not, could she be treated as a party to a contract? Could she have given the information in fulfillment of its condition?]

THE CROWN V CLARKE
(1927), 40 CLR 227 (Aus HC)

ISAACS ACJ: This is an appeal from the judgment of the Full Court of Western Australia. Evan Clarke proceeded, by petition of right under the *Crown Suits Act* 1898, to sue the Crown for £1,000 promised by proclamation for such information as should lead to the arrest and conviction of the person or persons who committed the murders of two police officers, Walsh and Pitman. ... At the trial the Chief Justice gave judgment for the Crown. In the Full Court, by a majority, the judgment of McMillan C.J., the trial Judge, was reversed. In the result, two learned Judges thought the Crown should succeed while two others thought Clarke should succeed. ...

The facts of this case, including inferences, are not, as I understand, in dispute. They amount to this: The information for which Clarke claims the reward was given by him when he was under arrest with Treffene on a charge of murder, and was given by him in circumstances which show that in giving the information he was not acting on or in pursuance of or in reliance upon or in return for the consideration contained in the proclamation, but exclusively in order to clear himself from a false charge of murder. In other words, he was acting with reference to a specific criminal charge against himself, and not with reference to a general request by the community for information against other persons. It is true that without his information and evidence no conviction was probable, but it is also abundantly clear that he was not acting for the sake of justice or from any impulse of conscience or because he was asked to do so, but simply and solely on his own initiative, to secure his own safety from the hand of the law and altogether irrespective of the proclamation. He has, in my opinion, neither a legal nor a moral claim to the reward. The learned Chief Justice held that Clarke never accepted or intended to accept the offer in the proclamation, and unless the mere giving of the information without such intention amounted in law to an acceptance of the offer or to performance of the condition, there was neither "acceptance" nor "performance," and therefore there was no contract. I do not understand either of the learned Judges who formed the majority to controvert this. But they held that *Williams v. Carwardine* (1833), 110 E.R. 590, has stood so long that it should be regarded as accurate, and that, so regarded, it entitled the respondent to judgment. ...

The controlling principle, then, is that to establish the *consensus* without which no true contract can exist, acceptance is as essential as offer, even in a case of the present class where the same act is at once sufficient for both acceptance and performance. But acceptance and performance of condition, as shown by the judicial reasoning quoted, involve that the person accepting and performing must act on the offer. ...

Instances easily suggest themselves where precisely the same act done with reference to an offer would be performance of the condition, but done with reference to a totally distinct object would not be such a performance. An offer of £100 to any person who should swim a hundred yards in the harbour on the first day of the year, would be met by voluntarily performing the feat with reference to the offer, but would not in my opinion be satisfied by a person who was accidentally or maliciously thrown overboard on that date and swam the distance simply to save his life, without any thought of the offer. The offeror might or might not feel morally impelled to give the sum in such a case, but would be under no contractual obligation to do so. ...

The appeal ... should, in my opinion, for the reasons stated, be allowed, and the judgment of McMillan C.J. restored.

[The opinion is considerably abbreviated. The opinions of Higgins and Starke JJ are omitted.]

CIVIL CODE OF QUÉBEC
LRQ, c C-1991

Article 1395. The offer of a reward made to anyone who performs a particular act is deemed to be accepted and is binding on the offeror when the act is performed, even if the person who performs the act does not know of the offer, unless, in cases which admit of it, the offer was previously revoked expressly and adequately by the offeror.

NOTES AND QUESTIONS

1. For a discussion of the reward cases and issues of motive and reliance, see P Mitchell & J Phillips, "The Contractual Nexus: Is Reliance Essential?" (2002) 22 Oxford J Leg Stud 115.
2. Should the common law adopt the rule espoused in the *Civil Code of Québec*?
3. Does the issue of motive help explain why two simultaneous and identical offers are not treated as offer and acceptance but rather as cross-offers? Recall *Tinn v Hoffmann*, above.
4. Would a promise by X to give Y "a million dollars for being female" be contractually binding (assuming Y is and has always been female)? Do the reward cases help formulate an answer?

CARLILL V CARBOLIC SMOKE BALL COMPANY
[1893] 1 QB 256 (CA)

The defendants, who were the proprietors and vendors of a medical preparation called "The Carbolic Smoke Ball," inserted in the *Pall Mall Gazette* of November 13th, 1891, and in other newspapers, the following advertisement:

> £100 reward will be paid by the Carbolic Smoke Ball Company to any person who contracts the increasing epidemic of influenza, colds, or any disease caused by taking cold, after having used the ball three times daily for two weeks according to the printed directions supplied with each ball. £1000 is deposited with the Alliance Bank, Regent Street, shewing our sincerity in the matter.
>
> During the last epidemic of influenza many thousand carbolic smoke balls were sold as preventives against this disease, and in no ascertained case was the disease contracted by those using carbolic smoke ball.
>
> One carbolic smoke ball will last a family several months, making it the cheapest remedy in the world at the price, 10s., post free. The ball can be refilled at a cost of 5s. Address, Carbolic Smoke Ball Company, 27 Princes Street, Hanover Square London.

The plaintiff, a lady, on the faith of this advertisement, bought one of the balls at a chemist's, and used it as directed three times a day, from November 20, 1891, to

January 17, 1892, when she was attacked by influenza. Hawkins J. held that she was entitled to recover the £100. The defendants appealed.

LINDLEY LJ: I will begin by referring to two points which were raised in the court below. I refer to them simply for the purpose of dismissing them. First, it is said no action will lie upon this contract because it is a policy. You have only to look at the advertisement to dismiss that suggestion. Then it is said that it is a bet. Hawkins J. came to the conclusion that nobody ever dreamt of a bet, and that the transaction had nothing whatever in common with a bet. I so entirely agree with him that I pass over this contention also as not worth serious attention.

Then, what is left? The first observation I will make is that we are not dealing with any inference of fact. We are dealing with an express promise to pay £100 in certain events. Read the advertisement how you will, and twist it about as you will, here is a distinct promise expressed in language which is perfectly unmistakable—"£100 reward will be paid by the Carbolic Smoke Ball Company to any person who contracts the influenza after having used the ball three times daily for two weeks according to the printed directions supplied with each ball."

We must first consider whether this was intended to be a promise at all, or whether it was a mere puff which meant nothing. Was it a mere puff? My answer to that question is No, and I base my answer upon this passage: "£1000 is deposited with the Alliance Bank, shewing our sincerity in the matter." Now, for what was that money deposited or that statement made except to negative the suggestion that this was a mere puff and meant nothing at all? The deposit is called in aid by the advertiser as proof of his sincerity in the matter—that is, the sincerity of his promise to pay this £100 in the event which he has specified. I say this for the purpose of giving point to the observation that we are not inferring a promise; there is the promise, as plain as words can make it.

Then it is contended that it is not binding. In the first place, it is said that it is not made with anybody in particular. Now that point is common to the words of this advertisement and to the words of all other advertisements offering rewards. They are offers to anybody who performs the conditions named in the advertisement, and anybody who does perform the conditions accepts the offer. In point of law this advertisement is an offer to pay £100 to anybody who will perform these conditions, and the performance of the conditions is the acceptance of the offer. That rests upon a string of authorities, the earliest of which is *Williams v. Carwardine* (1833), 110 E.R. 590, which has been followed by many other decisions upon advertisements offering rewards.

But then it is said, "Supposing that the performance of the condition is an acceptance of the offer, that acceptance ought to have been notified." Unquestionably, as a general proposition, when an offer is made, it is necessary in order to make a binding contract, not only that it should be accepted, but that the acceptance should be notified. But is that so in cases of this kind? I apprehend that they are an exception to that rule, or, if not an exception, they are open to the observation that the notification of the acceptance need not precede the performance. This offer is a continuing offer. It was never revoked, and if notice of acceptance is required—which I doubt very much, for I rather think the true view is that which was expressed and explained by Lord Blackburn in the case of *Brogden v. Metropolitan Ry. Co.* (1877), 2 App. Cas. 666, 691—if notice of acceptance is required, the person who makes the offer gets the notice of acceptance contemporaneously with his notice of the performance of the condition. If he gets notice of the acceptance before his offer is revoked, that in principle is all you want. I, however, think that the true view, in a case of this kind, is that the person who makes the offer shews by his language and from the nature of the transaction that he does not expect and does not require notice of the accept-ance apart from notice of the performance. ...

It appears to me, therefore, that the defendants must perform their promise, and, if they have been so unwary as to expose themselves to a great many actions, so much the worse for them.

BOWEN LJ: I am of the same opinion. ...

It was said that there was no notification of the acceptance of the contract. One cannot doubt that, as an ordinary rule of law, an acceptance of an offer made ought to be notified to the person who makes the offer, in order that the two minds may come together. Unless this is done the two minds may be apart, and there is not that consensus which is necessary according to the English law—I say nothing about the laws of other countries—to make a contract. But there is this clear gloss to be made upon that doctrine, that as notification of acceptance is required for the benefit of the person who makes the offer, the person who makes the offer may dispense with notice to himself if he thinks it desirable to do so, and I suppose there can be no doubt that where a person in an offer made by him to another person, expressly or impliedly intimates a particular mode of acceptance as sufficient to make the bargain binding, it is only necessary for the other person to whom such offer is made to follow the indicated method of acceptance; and if the person making the offer, expressly or impliedly intimates in his offer that it will be sufficient to act on the proposal without communicating acceptance of it to himself, performance of the condition is a sufficient acceptance without notification.

That seems to me to be the principle which lies at the bottom of the acceptance cases, of which two instances are the well-known judgment of Mellish L.J. in *Harris' Case* (1872), 7 Ch. App. 587, and the very instructive judgment of Lord Blackburn in *Brogden v. Metropolitan Ry. Co.*, in which he appears to me to take exactly the line I have indicated.

Now, if that is the law how are we to find out whether the person who makes the offer does intimate that notification of acceptance will not be necessary in order to constitute a binding bargain? In many cases you look to the offer itself. In many cases you extract from the character of the transaction that notification is not required, and in the advertisement cases it seems to me to follow as an inference to be drawn from the transaction itself that a person is not to notify his acceptance of the offer before he performs the condition, but that if he performs the condition noti-fication is dispensed with. It seems to me that from the point of view of common sense no other idea could be entertained. If I advertise to the world that my dog is lost, and that anybody who brings the dog to a particular place will be paid some money, are all the police or other persons whose business it is to find lost dogs to be expected to sit down and write me a note saying they have accepted my proposal? Why, of course, they at once look after the dog, and as soon as they have found the dog they have performed the condition. The essence of the transaction is that the dog should be found, and it is not necessary under such circumstances, as it seems to me, that in order to make the contract binding there should be any notification of acceptance. It follows from the nature of the thing that the performance of the condition is suf-ficient acceptance without notification of it, and a person who makes an offer in an advertisement of that kind makes an offer which must be read by the light of that common sense reflection. He does, therefore, in his offer impliedly indicate that he does not require notification of the acceptance of the offer.

[Appeal dismissed. Only part of the opinions is given and the concurring opinion of AL Smith LJ is omitted.]

NOTES

1. In 1893, an advertisement appeared in *The Illustrated London News*. The Carbolic Smoke Ball Company stated in this new ad that thousands of smoke balls had been sold due to the first ad and that only three people had claimed the reward. The company went on to offer a larger reward of £200. It neglected to mention that Mrs. Carlill, at least, had only recovered after legal action.

2. In *Kolodziej v Mason*, 774 F 3d 736, 741 (11th Cir 2014), the plaintiff, a law student, filed a breach of contract claim against a criminal defence lawyer who had stated on national television that he would "pay a million dollars" to anyone who could prove that his client could get from the Atlanta airport to a specific hotel in only 28 minutes as the prosecution had alleged. Without contacting the defendant lawyer, the plaintiff made the journey in under 28 minutes and demanded payment. After citing *Carlill* and other similar American authorities, the court affirmed the judgment below dismissing the plaintiff's action. The court stated that "We do not find that [the defendant's] ... statements were such that a reasonable, objective person would have understood them to be an invitation to contract." The court added: "We simply are driven to ask ... : 'Why did you not just call?' Perhaps a jurist's interpretation of an old aphorism provides the answer: If, as Alexander Pope wrote, 'a little learning is a dangerous thing' then a little learning in law is particularly perilous."

Goldthorpe v Logan. [1943] 2 DLR 519 (Ont CA). LAIDLAW JA: The female appellant had some hairs on her face and wanted to have them removed. She saw advertisements published in a newspaper by the defendant Anne Graham Logan. She went to the place of business stated in the advertisement and consulted the defendant Kathleen Fitzpatrick, a registered nurse, who was an employee of the defendant Logan. She was told that her face could be definitely "cleared," that the hair could be removed permanently, and the result was guaranteed. She then submitted to a number of "treatments" by electrolysis for the purpose of removing the hairs but the result was not satisfactory. Hairs continued to grow on her face in the same way as before, and in spite of the efforts of the defendants to remedy the condition. ... [T]he alternative allegation to the effect that the defendant Logan is responsible in law by reason of a breach of contract made by or on her behalf with the female plaintiff requires careful consideration. The elements of a valid contract are well known, and it is only necessary to analyze the evidence to determine whether or not they exist in this case. I at once examined the advertisement ... : "Hairs ... removed safely and permanently by Electrolysis. ... No marks, No Scars, Results Guaranteed ... ." What is the true nature and construction of this advertisement? ... [T]he sensible interpretation of her words is this: "If you will submit yourself to my treatment and pay me (certain charges) I undertake to remove hairs safely and permanently by electrolysis and I promise to obtain a satisfactory result." The effect in law of such a statement is to create an offer from the person by whom it is made to every person who is willing to accept the terms and conditions of it. ... If the vendor's self-confidence had persuaded her into an excessive, extravagant promise, she cannot now escape a complaint from a credulous and distressed person to whom she gave assurance of future excellence and relief from her burden.

NOTES AND QUESTIONS

1. The use of contractual analysis to impose strict liability in the interests of consumer protection is not uncommon but has become less necessary in light of the rise of universal health care, expansions in the law of negligence, and the passage of consumer protection legislation in various provinces.

2. Was it necessary for the court to find that the advertisement created a unilateral contract given that the plaintiff was given further assurances by the defendant?

3. If a person with an incurable facial hair condition had presented herself at the defendant's office and been told that there was nothing that the defendant could do, would that person have been able to sue for breach of contract on the court's reasoning?

DALE V MANITOBA
(1997), 147 DLR (4th) 605 (Man CA)

SCOTT CJM (for the court):

The principal issue on this appeal is whether, as found by the trial judge, a legally enforceable contract was entered into between the plaintiffs and the defendant.

In 1992, each of the plaintiffs (and others) were accepted into the affirmative action program known as the ACCESS program (the program) created by the defendant [the government of Manitoba]. ACCESS was the generic name adopted to describe a number of programs funded by the provincial Department of Education, and administered by various education institutions and organizations, in this instance the University of Manitoba (the University), to provide post-secondary educational opportunities to disadvantaged persons. ...

At the outset, it is essential to address the findings of fact made by the trial judge, which were vigorously assailed by appellant's counsel. In my opinion, Schulman J. was undoubtedly correct when he concluded not only that the plaintiffs believed that they had a contractual arrangement with the government not to alter the terms and conditions of the funding arrangements that existed at the time of their entry into the program in 1992, but that in fact such an understanding had been communicated to them by the designated ACCESS staff at the University. There was ample evidence to support these findings.

This being so, the central question becomes whether the communication of this information to the students committed the government or the University of Manitoba, or both.

Before moving on to this question, the answer to which depends on whether the University ACCESS staff had the ostensible or apparent authority to commit the government, I turn briefly to consideration of one of the most venerable authorities concerning the law of contract, namely *Carlill v. Carbolic Smoke Ball Company,* [1893] 1 Q.B. 256 (C.A.), where the principle was established that an enforceable offer could be made to a "stranger" or an unknown member of the general public. Of particular relevance for this case is the statement of principle found in *Carlill* that, where an offer—such as that found to be made here—is continuing in nature, then notification need not precede performance. In other words, notification of acceptance need not be made so long as the offer continues to remain unrevoked. For an interesting review of the modern application of what has now come to be called unilateral contracts, see Professor G.H.L. Fridman, Q.C., *The Law of Contract in Canada* 3rd ed. (Toronto: Carswell, 1994). In C. 2(3)(h) at p. 75, Professor Fridman points out that the applicability of this principle in any given situation depends on whether the "offer" was intended to be taken seriously, or was merely promotion or "puffing." His conclusion is that "practical considerations have ousted logical analysis." Applying a "robust and pragmatic view" to the facts of this case, it is plain to me that by virtue of the role assigned by government to the University that a binding offer was made to the student applicants, open for acceptance without specific and direct communication to government.

As noted earlier, the determining question is on whose behalf was the offer communicated. For the purposes of this decision, I accept (without necessarily so finding) that the University ACCESS personnel did not have the actual or real authority to commit the Government of Manitoba with respect to the level and continuation of funding. ... It is clear, however, that the staff who dealt with the ACCESS students, and were their sole source of information concerning all particulars and requirements of the program, sincerely and honestly believed—and communicated to the students—the contrary: that is that the commitment made to the students at the time of their entry into the program in 1992 would continue up to the time they obtained their undergraduate degree. ...

[After discussing the leading cases on ostensible authority, the justice continued:]

I have no difficulty in concluding that the program administrators had the apparent or ostensible authority to speak on behalf of the "owner" of the program, namely, the government of Manitoba. Here the government, after defining all of the terms and parameters of the program, left it entirely to the University program staff to deal with the student applicants throughout the course of the four-year program. To the "outside world" they were the only ones, up until the changes that are the subject-matter of this action, with whom the students made their arrangements, a fact well known to the government. How can it be said in these circumstances that the University staff did not have the apparent authority to make a commitment on behalf of the government which had delegated all the administrative responsibilities to them while nonetheless maintaining, as the trial judge found, a "hands-on involvement" in the operation of the program? Given this role, it was incumbent on government, if it was concerned that this authority might be abused, to give clear instructions about the full implications of changes to the program regime. This was not done.

The trial judge concluded that the offers of funding by University ACCESS staff were made on behalf of the joint operators of the program, or alternatively as the agent of the government. He was entirely correct in the latter part of his conclusion. Indeed, given the evidence accepted by him concerning the role that the government expected the ACCESS staff to play, and that they did play throughout the program (and specifically with respect to the four applicants before the court), it is difficult to see how he could have come to any other conclusion.

In my opinion, this is sufficient to decide this appeal. There was a legally enforceable offer made to the students on behalf of the government, which these applicants accepted. The terms of the contract were as found by the trial judge. While Schulman J. felt obliged to deal with a multitude of other legal issues put before him by counsel (about which I intentionally make no comment), the legal effect of his judgment, now affirmed by this decision, is correctly set forth in the precise terms of the formal judgment roll taken out after trial:

> THIS COURT DECLARES that the Defendant Government of Manitoba is a party to a contract with the Plaintiffs, whereby the said Defendant is required to continue to provide, subject to assessed needs, the same base level of grants and other supports for living allowances, rental subsidies, transportation, day care, medical and dental and

optical care, special support costs, and tuition and books, as was provided to the said Plaintiffs during their year of initial registration.

The appeal is accordingly dismissed with costs.

Appeal dismissed.

GRANT V PROVINCE OF NEW BRUNSWICK
(1973), 35 DLR (3d) 141 (NB App Div)

HUGHES CJNB: This is an appeal by the Province of New Brunswick (herein referred to as "the Province") from a judgment in the Queen's Bench Division directed against it in favour of the plaintiff for $4,800, being the value of 4,000 barrels of potatoes which the plaintiff alleged he sold to the Province in 1967 under a potato price sta-bilization programme, with costs to be taxed.

On this appeal as well as at trial, the Province contended that the evidence does not establish a contract between the parties and that consequently, the action should be dismissed. In the spring of 1967, there was in Canada a considerable surplus of potatoes produced in 1966 which could not be marketed. To stabilize the price of potatoes the Governor-General in Council passed Order in Council P.C. 1967-892 dated May 4, 1967, pursuant to the *Agricultural Stabilization Act*, 1957-58 (Can.), c. 22 [now RSC 1970, c A-9], designating potatoes as an agricultural commodity for the purpose of the Act and authorizing the Agricultural Stabilization Board to make payments to producers for potatoes grown in 1966, limited to deliveries of 1,000 barrels per producer, for use for starch manufacture and for other non-food uses approved by the Board. Pro-grammes carried out under this Order in Council are referred to Program respectively. By a subsequent Order in Council the limitation of 1,000 barrels per producer was raised to 5,000 barrels.

These programmes were found inadequate to absorb the surplus potatoes in New Brunswick and an arrangement was entered into by the Minister of Agriculture for the Province with the Government of Canada to implement a potato price stabiliz-ation programme under which the Province undertook to purchase potatoes direct from growers resident in New Brunswick at the support price of $1.20 per barrel and to make payment for such potatoes direct to the producers. Under the programme purchases were limited to 5,000 barrels per producer including all potatoes sold under the Potato Starch Diversion Program and the Livestock Feed Diversion Pro-gram. The Agricultural Stabilization Board undertook as a term of the arrangement to pay the Province ½¢ per lb. for all potatoes purchased by the Province under the programme.

In entering into the agreement with the Government of Canada neither the Minister of Agriculture nor the Government of the Province had statutory authority to do so and the cost of the programme was financed by special warrants. To imple-ment the programme the Province appointed an administrator and established a committee consisting of potato farmers, officials of the Department of Agriculture and one representing the Agricultural Stabilization Board.

The committee's function was to process applications made by potato growers to ensure that the applicants were eligible and the potatoes offered for purchase qualified under the programme. In all, the Province received about 735 applications of which an estimated 700 were approved without question. Of the remaining 35, 25 were approved after the applicants satisfied the committee as to their eligibility.

The remaining 10, of which the plaintiff was one, were refused the benefits of the programme.

The Province publicized the programme and prepared a form of application which was made available to growers who wished to dispose of their surplus potatoes by selling them to the Province. In the form, the grower was required to state his potato acreage, his 1966 production, the capacity of storage used by him, the number of acres which he rented in 1966, and the estimated quantity of potatoes which he offered for purchase, and the applicant was required to make a statutory declaration as to the truth of his statements. On the reverse side of the application there was printed certain general information relating to the programme ... .

At the foot of the application there is a form to be completed by a federal Government inspector certifying the grade of potatoes offered for purchase and a certificate to be completed by a provincial inspector as to the grade and volume of the potatoes referred to in the application and stating there was evidence of excessive breakdown of the potatoes and that they had been disposed of in a manner satisfactory to the inspector. The certificate on the plaintiff's application was duly completed and signed by a federal Government inspector and by a provincial inspector.

After these certificates were completed and the potatoes disposed of, the plaintiff's application was placed by the administrator before the committee for its approval. Owing to certain information which came to its attention, the committee refused the plaintiff's application and the administrator wrote the plaintiff under date of October 5, 1967, stating, *inter alia*:

> The administration of this program is the responsibility of the Board appointed by the Minister of Agriculture and is subject to the guide lines and regulations established at the outset, through negotiation between the Federal Stabilization Board and the Province. One such regulation states that the potatoes offered must be the property of the applicant. Information received by the Board indicates that you do not qualify under this regulation.
>
> I have been instructed by the Board to inform you that for this reason your application has not been approved. We cannot, therefore, pay any assistance on the potatoes offered in your application.

The plaintiff replied protesting he was in fact the owner of the potatoes offered. Later he appeared before the committee but was unable to satisfy its members that he owned the potatoes which he had offered. Later, he brought the present action claiming the price of 4,000 barrels of potatoes at $1.20 per barrel. At the trial he testified he owned the potatoes and his evidence was accepted by the learned trial Judge who directed that judgment be entered against the Province for the price claimed. On this appeal the Province did not challenge the trial Judge's finding that the plaintiff was the owner of the potatoes which he offered for purchase, but contended that payments made to applicants under the potato price stabilization programme constituted subsidies, the payment of which the applicant had no legal right to enforce.

Counsel for the plaintiff admitted that to succeed in the action the plaintiff must prove there was an offer to purchase or to sell made by one of the parties to the other and that the party to whom it was made accepted it. It is elementary that until an offer open for acceptance by a person to whom it is made has been accepted by him, no contract results.

If the plaintiff's application is to be construed as an offer by him to the Province of potatoes for purchase, I am unable to find anything in the evidence to establish that the Province accepted his offer since the administrator who must be taken to be the agent of the Province refused to approve the application by letter dated October 5, 1967, and nothing which occurred thereafter can be regarded as constituting an acceptance.

In his opening remarks at trial, counsel for the plaintiff stated that the plaintiff based his case on the acceptance by him of terms offered by the Province. I interpret this submission to mean that the plaintiff claims the Province made a general offer to all eligible potato producers resident in New Brunswick to purchase any potatoes grown by them in 1966, subject to the limitations and conditions specified in the general information on the reverse side of the application form which it had prepared and that the plaintiff, by offering his potatoes, having them measured and inspected, and by disposing of them in a manner satisfactory to the inspector appointed by the Province, had accepted the Province's offer. This is essentially the view taken by the trial Judge who interpreted the general information as an offer and not merely as a statement by the Province of its intention to purchase potatoes.

It may well be that the Province in publicizing the general information concerning its potato price stabilization intended merely to inform eligible potato growers resident in New Brunswick of a policy without any intention of making a binding offer which would obligate it to purchase all eligible potatoes offered by all eligible growers. In interpreting an offer the objective test should, I think, be applied. *Williston on Contracts*, 3rd ed., (1957), vol. 1, s. 94, contains the following statement at p. 339:

> It follows that the test of the true interpretation of an offer or acceptance is not what the party making it thought it meant or intended it to mean, but what a reasonable person in the position of the parties would have thought it meant.

It is to be observed that para. 3 of the general information does not expressly state that the Province will purchase all potatoes offered nor does para. 7 promise to approve applications and authorize payment when an inspector appointed by the Minister has certified the quantity of the potatoes is correctly stated and that the potatoes have broken down and been disposed of in a manner satisfactory to the inspector. It only states that the application will not be approved nor will payment be authorized until these things are done. There is, nevertheless, an implication in the general information that if and when these things have been done, payment will be authorized. Had the Province intended to reserve the right to select from whom it chose to purchase potatoes, it could have indicated there was a limit to the quantity or the value of the potatoes which it was prepared to purchase or it could have stated that the decision of the committee appointed to administer the programme was final or made it clear that the committee's approval was a condition to the right to payment.

I am not satisfied that the trial Judge erred in finding that the Province offered to purchase potatoes at the support price from all eligible growers resident in New Brunswick who offered their potatoes for purchase within the guide-lines set out in the information. Indeed, I accept the view that a reasonable person in the position of the plaintiff would be entitled to assume that if he complied with the conditions set out in the general information and disposed of his potatoes to the satisfaction of the inspector appointed by the Province, he was entitled to sell his potatoes to the Province and that the Province was legally bound to purchase and pay for them. I would accordingly affirm the decision of the trial Judge and dismiss the appeal with costs.

Appeal dismissed.

NOTES AND QUESTIONS

1. In *Dale*, what was the act that was requested by the government to make its promise of funding binding?

2. Compare the result in *Grant* with that in *Australian Woollen Mills Ltd v Commonwealth of Australia*, [1956] 1 WLR 11 (PC), where their Lordships held that information about a government subsidy program was merely a statement of policy rather than a contractual offer that could have been accepted by the plaintiff. See also *Canada v South Yukon Forest Corp*, 2012 FCA 165, where the court refused to find a unilateral contract (a guaranteed supply of timber in exchange for building of a timber mill) because a statutory process for allocating timber (which required a grant by order in council) meant that departmental officials could not bind the Crown.

ERRINGTON V ERRINGTON
[1952] 1 All ER 149 (CA)

DENNING LJ: The facts are reasonably clear. In 1936 the father bought the house for his son and daughter-in-law to live in. The father put down £250 in cash and borrowed £500 from a building society on the security of the house, repayable with interest by instalments of 15s. a week. He took the house in his own name and made himself responsible for the instalments. The father told the daughter-in-law that the £250 was a present for them, but he left them to pay the building society instalments of 15s. a week themselves. He handed the building society book to the daughter-in-law and said to her: "Don't part with this book. The house will be your property when the mortgage is paid." He said that when he retired he would transfer it into their names. She has, in fact, paid the building society instalments regularly from that day to this with the result that much of the mortgage has been repaid, but there is a good deal yet to be paid. The rates on the house came to 10s. a week. The couple found that they could not pay those as well as the building society instalments so the father said he would pay them and he did so.

It is to be noted that the couple never bound themselves to pay the instalments to the building society, and I can see no reason why any such obligation should be implied. It is clear law that the court is not to imply a term unless it is necessary, and I do not see that it is necessary here. Ample content is given to the whole agreement by holding that the father promised that the house should belong to the couple as soon as they had paid off the mortgage. The parties did not discuss what was to happen if the couple failed to pay the instalments to the building society, but I should have thought it clear that, if they did fail to pay the instalments, the father would not be bound to transfer the house to them. The father's promise was a unilateral contract—a promise of the house in return for their act of paying the instalments. It could not be revoked by him once the couple entered on performance of the act, but it would cease to bind him if they left it incomplete and unperformed, which they have not done. If that was the position during the father's lifetime, so it must be after his death. If the daughter-in-law continues to pay all the building society instalments, the couple will be entitled to have the property transferred to them as soon as the mortgage is paid off, but if she does not do so, then the building society will claim the instalments from the father's estate and the estate will have to pay them. I cannot think that in those circumstances the estate would be bound to transfer the house to them, any more than the father himself would have been. ...

In the present case it is clear that the father expressly promised the couple that the property should belong to them as soon as the mortgage was paid, and impliedly promised that, so long as they paid the instalments to the building society, they should be allowed to remain in possession. They were not purchasers because they never bound themselves to pay the instalments but nevertheless they were in a position analogous to purchasers. They have acted on the promise and neither the father nor his widow, his successor in title, can eject them in disregard of it. The result is that, in my opinion, the appeal should be dismissed and no order for possession should be made. I come to this conclusion on a different ground from that reached by the learned judge, but it is always open to a respondent to support the judgment on any ground. If there is a dispute between the son and the daughter-in-law as to their respective rights in the house, that must be decided under s. 17 of the Married Women's Property Act, 1882. If the father's widow should cease to pay the rates, the actual occupier must pay them, because the father did not bind himself to pay them. He only did so out of paternal affection.

[The concurring opinions of Somervell and Hodson LJJ are omitted.]

DAWSON V HELICOPTER EXPLORATION
[1955] SCR 868, 5 DLR 404

[Dawson, a US citizen, had been negotiating by mail with Kidd and Springer, in Vancouver, an arrangement to get at some mineral deposits at the head of the Leduc River in British Columbia, in very rough country, which Dawson had discovered 20 years earlier. On January 13, 1951, Dawson wrote: "A large mining company in Salt Lake is showing a definite interest. To protect my interest, it will be necessary for me to arrive at some definite arrangement soon." Springer replied on January 17: "I would be interested in making some arrangement next summer to finance you in staking claims for which we would give you an interest. I would suggest that we should pay for your time and expenses and carry you for a ten per cent non-assessable interest in the claims." Dawson replied on January 22: "Your proposition ... appeals to me as being a fair one."

Thereafter Dawson was recalled to active duty in the United States Naval Reserve Engineering Corps, and sent to the Marshall Islands. Correspondence continued under rather difficult conditions, and on February 28 Dawson wrote: "As I informed you in a previous letter, your offer of a 10% non-assessable interest for relocating and finding these properties is acceptable to me, provided there is a definite arrangement to this effect in the near future." On March 5, Springer wrote, "I hereby agree that, if you take us in to the showings and we think they warrant staking, that we will stake the claims and give you a 10% non-assessable interest. The claims would be recorded in our name and we will have full discretion in dealing with them—you to get 10% of the vendor interest." Dawson replied on April 12: "If you will inform me, if and when you obtain a pilot for your copter, I will immediately take steps for a temporary release in order to be on hand." Dawson wrote again, on May 27: "Would like to know if your plans for further exploration work in the Unuk River area have become definite. ... For me to get away from my present duties on a furlough it may be necessary for me to have several weeks notice."

On June 7, Springer wrote:

Up to a little over a week ago it did not look as though we would be able to secure a pilot for our helicopter. However, we have a man now who we hope will be satisfactory.

I was talking to Tom McQuillan, who is prospecting for us this year; he said he had been over your showings at the head of the Leduc River, and in his opinion it would be practically impossible to operate there, as the showings were in behind ice fields, which along with the extreme snow falls made it very doubtful if an economic operation could be carried on.

We have also been delayed in getting away this year, due to pilot trouble, and have so much work lined up that I am doubtful whether we will have time to visit your showings, also I do not think we would be warranted in making the effort to get in there due to the unfavorable conditions. I must advise you therefore, not to depend on our making this trip, and suggest if you are still determined to go in, to make other arrangements.

Dawson did not reply. In 1952 he discovered that the helicopter company had made investigations and in 1953 arrangements were made for development by the company to which Springer had sold the claims in exchange for paid-up stock. Dawson commenced this action in November 1953, and his claim was dismissed by the trial judge, who was affirmed by the BC Court of Appeal.]

RAND J (Fauteux J concurring): ... The substantial contention of the respondent is that any offer contained in the correspondence and in particular the letter of March 5th called for an acceptance not by promise but by performance of an act, the location of the claims by Dawson for the respondent. It is based upon the well-known conception which in its simplest form is illustrated by the case of a reward offered for some act to be done. To put it in other words, no intention was conveyed by Springer when he said "I hereby agree" that Dawson, if agreeable, should have replied, "I hereby accept" or words to that effect: the offer called for and awaited only the act to be done and would remain revocable at any time until every element of that act had been completed.

The error in this reasoning is that such an offer contemplates acts to be performed by the person only to whom it is made and in respect of which the offeror remains passive, and that is not so here. What Dawson was to do was to proceed to the area with Springer or persons acting for him by means of the respondent's helicopter and to locate the showings. It was necessarily implied by Springer that he would participate in his own proposal. This involved his promise that he would do so, and that the answer to the proposal would be either a refusal or a promise on the part of Dawson to a like participation. The offer was unconditional but contemplated a performance subject to the condition that a pilot could be obtained by the respondent.

Dawson's answer of April 12th was, as I construe it, similarly an unqualified promissory acceptance, subject as to performance to his being able to obtain the necessary leave. It was the clear implication that Springer, controlling the means of making the trip, should fix the time and should notify Dawson accordingly. As the earlier letters show, Dawson was anxious to conclude some arrangement and if he could not make it with Springer he would seek it in other quarters.

Although in the circumstances, because the terms proposed involve such complementary action on the part of both parties as to put the implication beyond doubt, the precept is not required, this interpretation of the correspondence follows the tendency of Courts to treat offers as calling for bilateral rather than unilateral action when the language can be fairly so construed, in order that the transaction shall have such "business efficacy as both parties must have intended that at all events it should have": Bowen L.J. in The "Moorcock" (1889), 14 P.D. 64 at p. 68. In theory and as conceded by Mr. Guild, an offer in the unilateral sense can be revoked up to the last moment before complete performance. At such a consequence many Courts have balked; and it is in part that fact that has led to a promissory construction where that can be reasonably given. What is effectual is the real intention of both parties to close a business bargain on the strength of which they may, thereafter, plan their courses. ...

ESTEY J (Cartwright J concurring): ... It is contended that the appellant's silence, after his receipt of the letter of June 7, 1951, until his interview in December, 1952, constitutes an abandonment of the contract. ...

The letter of repudiation is dated June 7, 1951, and during the next month Kvale and McQuillan were taken into the area by helicopter. They were again taken into the area where, on August 2nd of that year, they staked a number of claims which were duly recorded. The record does not indicate when respondent changed its mind as indicated by Springer's remark to appellant at its office in December, 1952, but it is apparent that many of the difficulties emphasized in the letter of June 7th had either disappeared or been overcome by the following month. Upon this record it rather appears that the respondent concluded it could continue without assistance from the appellant and, therefore, wrote the letter of repudiation.

The respondent, in this letter of repudiation, set forth its reasons therefore which it would be difficult for the appellant, stationed as he was in the Marshall Islands, to effectively appraise. I do not think that under such circumstances a conclusion adverse to the appellant can be drawn from his failure to further press the respondent at that time. Immediately upon his return in December, 1950, he "wrote to the Mining Recorder at Prince Rupert" and apparently continued his examination to ascertain what had, in fact, taken place. He visited the premises in June and July, 1950, and relocated the three claims which he had found in 1931. When he had ascertained, at least in part, what had taken place, he made his position known to the respondent in December of 1952. Moreover, while silence may be evidence of repudiation, its weight must depend upon the circumstances and here I do not think his silence, coupled with the steps he took immediately upon his return from the Marshall Islands, sufficiently supports a conclusion that he, at any time, intended to abandon his rights under the contract.

Upon receipt of the letter of repudiation dated June 7, 1951, the appellant might have accepted it and forthwith claimed damages. Since, however, he did not accept it, the contract remained in force and binding upon both parties. It, therefore, remained the duty of the respondent, having obtained a pilot, to take the appellant into the area in August or September. Not only did the respondent not do so, but, notwithstanding the terms of its letter of repudiation, it, in fact, took Kvale and McQuillan into the area where they staked claims on behalf of the respondent. This conduct constituted a breach of its contract.

The appeal should be allowed with costs throughout and the matter referred back to the Supreme Court of British Columbia to determine the damages.

[Kerwin CJ dissented.]

QUESTIONS

1. Is the result in *Errington v Errington* consistent with the rules of contract formation? Would a double unilateral contract explanation be one that would be plausible on the facts? For a discussion, see McCamus at 86-90; MacDougall at 32-33.

2. Would some sort of reliance-based liability, such as that based on s 90 of the *Restatement* or equitable estoppel, be a simpler solution to the problem of the revocation of unilateral offers after substantial performance? See *Mobil Oil Australia Ltd v Wellcome International Pty Ltd* (1998), 81 FCR 475. Might it even be possible to explain all of "unilateral contract" on the basis of the promise-detriment principle? For just such an argument, see B McFarlane & P Sales, "Promises, Detriment, and Liability" (2015) 131 Law Q Rev 610 at 620, 626-27.

3. Do you think that the Supreme Court would have found a bilateral contract if the company had sued Dawson for non-performance?

4. What was the wrong that the defendant in *Dawson* committed: failing to take the plaintiff to the site or developing the site without the participation of the plaintiff? Would an action for breach of confidence, similar to that pursued in *Lac Minerals Ltd v International Corona Resources Ltd*, [1989] 2 SCR 574, have been a better solution to the problem posed by the facts of *Dawson*?

RESTATEMENT OF THE LAW OF CONTRACTS (SECOND)
American Law Institute, 1981

25. Option Contracts.
An option contract is a promise which meets the requirements for the formation of a contract and limits the promisor's power to revoke an offer. ...

32. Invitation of Promise or Performance.
In case of doubt an offer is interpreted as inviting the offeree to accept either by promising to perform what the offer requests or by rendering the performance, as the offeree chooses.

• • •

45. Option Contract created by Part Performance or Tender.
(1) Where an offer invites an offeree to accept by rendering a performance and does not invite a promissory acceptance, an option contract is created when the offeree tenders or begins the invited performance or tenders a beginning of it.
(2) The offeror's duty of performance under any option contract so created is conditional on completion or tender of the invited performance in accordance with the terms of the offer.

• • •

62. Effect of Performance by Offeree where Offer invites either Performance or Promise.
(1) Where an offer invites an offeree to choose between acceptance by promise and acceptance by performance, the beginning of the invited performance or a tender of a beginning of it is an acceptance by performance.
(2) Such an acceptance operates as a promise to render complete performance.

UNIFORM COMMERCIAL CODE
American Law Institute, 1978

Section 2-206. Offer and Acceptance in Formation of Contract
(1) Unless otherwise unambiguously indicated by the language or circumstances
(a) an offer to make a contract shall be construed as inviting acceptance in any manner and by any medium reasonable in the circumstances;
(b) an order or other offer to buy goods for prompt or current shipment shall be construed as inviting acceptance either by a prompt promise to ship or by the prompt or current shipment of conforming or non-conforming goods, but such a shipment of non-conforming goods does not constitute an acceptance if the seller seasonably notifies the buyer that the shipment is offered only as an accommodation to the buyer.

(2) Where the beginning of a requested performance is a reasonable mode of acceptance an offeror who is not notified of acceptance within a reasonable time may treat the offer as having lapsed before acceptance.

NOTES

1. There are problems in fitting together these sections of the *Restatement* and the *Uniform Commercial Code*. See JE Murray, "Contracts: A New Design for the Agreement Process" (1968) 53 Cornell L Rev 785.

2. Unilateral contracts should also be considered in the light of *R (Ont) v Ron Engineering*, considered in Chapter 9, Section V. See also Waddams, ch 4; MacDougall at 32-33, 46-48; Fridman at 70-77; Swan at 246-48.

CHAPTER FOUR

CONTRACTS AND THIRD PARTIES

I. THIRD-PARTY BENEFICIARIES

TWEDDLE V ATKINSON
(1861), 1 B & S 393, 121 ER 762

The declaration stated that the plaintiff was the son of John Tweddle, deceased and before the making of the agreement hereafter mentioned, married the daughter of William Guy, deceased; and before the marriage the parents of the parties to the marriage orally promised to give the plaintiff a marriage portion; and after the marriage in order to give effect to their promises the parents entered into the following written agreement for the plaintiff's benefit:

> High Coniscliffe, July 11, 1855.
> Memorandum of agreement made this day between William Guy, of, & c., of the one part, and John Tweddle, of, & C., of the other part. Whereas it is mutually agreed that the said William Guy shall and will pay the sum of £200 to William Tweddle, his son-in-law; and the said John Tweddle, father to the aforesaid William Tweddle, shall and will pay the sum of £100 to the said William Tweddle, each and severally the said sums on or before the 21st day of August, 1855. And it is hereby further agreed by the aforesaid William Guy and the said John Tweddle that the said William Tweddle has full power to sue the said parties in any court of law or equity for the aforesaid sum, hereby promised and specified.

The declaration further alleged that afterwards and before this suit, the plaintiff and his said wife, who is still living, ratified and assented to the said agreement, yet neither the said William Guy nor his executor has paid the promised sum of £200. Demurrer and joinder therein.

CROMPTON J: It is admitted that the plaintiff cannot succeed unless this case is an exception to the modern and well-established doctrine of the action of assumpsit. At the time when the cases which have been cited were decided the action of assumpsit was treated as an action of trespass upon the case, and therefore in the nature of a tort; and the law was not settled, as it now is, that natural love and affection is not a sufficient consideration for a promise upon which an action may be maintained; nor was it settled that the promisee cannot bring an action unless the consideration for the promise moved from him. The modern cases have, in effect, overruled the old decisions; they show that the consideration must move from the party entitled to sue upon the contract. It would be a monstrous proposition to say that a person was a party to the contract for the purpose of suing upon it for his own advantage and not a party to it for the purpose of being sued. It is said that the father in the present case was agent for the son in making the contract, but that argument ought also to make the son liable upon it. I am prepared to overrule the old decisions, and to hold that, by reason of the principles which now govern the action of assumpsit, the present action is not maintainable.

[Judgment was given for the defendant. The concurring opinions of Wightman and Blackburn JJ are omitted.]

DRIVE YOURSELF HIRE CO LTD V STRUTT
[1954] 1 QB 250 at 273-74

DENNING L: In 1861 ... came the unfortunate case of *Tweddle v. Atkinson* in which the Court of Queen's Bench departed from the law as it had been understood for the previous 200 years and held, quite generally, that no stranger could take advantage of a contract though made for his benefit: and that was assumed, without argument, to be the law by the House of Lords in *Dunlop Pneumatic Tyre Co. Ltd. v. Selfridge & Co. Ltd.* I do not pause to consider whether this new rule was legitimately introduced into the law. Incidentally, the courts of the United States have not adopted this new rule. They have followed the original common law, which is much more in accord with the needs of a civilised society. So is the Scots law.

BESWICK V BESWICK
[1966] 1 Ch 549 (CA), [1968] AC 70 (HL)

LORD DENNING MR: Old Peter Beswick was a coal merchant in Eccles, Lancashire. He had no business premises. All he had was a lorry, scales and weights. He used to take the lorry to the yard of the National Coal Board, where he bagged coal and took it round to his customers in the neighbourhood. His nephew, John Joseph Beswick, helped him in the business.

In March, 1962, old Peter Beswick and his wife were both over 70. He had had his leg amputated and was not in good health. The nephew was anxious to get hold of the business before the old man died. So they went to a solicitor, Mr. Ashcroft, who drew up an agreement for them. The business was to be transferred to the nephew: old Peter Beswick was to be employed in it as a consultant for the rest of his life at £6 10s. a week. After his death the nephew was to pay to his widow an annuity of £5 per week, which was to come out of the business. The agreement was quite short and I will read it in full:

1. Peter Beswick to assign to John Joseph Beswick the goodwill, motor lorry, scales, weights and other trade utensils of the business of a coal merchant hitherto carried on by him in consideration of the transferee employing the transferor as consultant to the said business for the remainder of the transferor's life at a weekly salary of £6 10s.

2. For the like consideration the transferee, in the event of the death of the transferor, to pay to the transferor's widow an annuity to be charged on the said business at the rate of £5 per week.

3. The transferee not to sell the said business in any way freed from his liability to the transferor, which liability shall cease only on the death of the survivor of them the transferor and his said widow.

4. The agreement between the parties to be deemed for all purposes to have commenced to operate as from March 1, 1962.

5. The transferor to be free to devote only such time to the conduct of the said business as he shall find convenient or shall at his own absolute discretion decide.

6. For the consideration aforesaid the transferee to take over the transferor's liability to the following creditors of the transferor: George and Lydia Turner in the sum of £187, Joseph Beswick in the sum of £250 or such lesser sums as shall be agreed with the said creditors whether by compounding or otherwise.

After the agreement was signed, the nephew took over the business and ran it. The old man seems to have found it difficult at first to adjust to the new situation, but he settled down. The nephew paid him £6 10s. a week. But, as expected, he did not live long. He died on November 3, 1963, leaving his widow, who was 74 years of age and in failing health. The nephew paid her the first £5. But he then stopped paying her and has refused to pay her any more.

On June 30, 1964, the widow took out letters of administration to her husband's estate. On July 15, 1964, she brought an action against the nephew for the promised £5 a week. She sued in the capacity of administratrix of the estate of Peter Beswick, deceased, and in her personal capacity she claimed £175 in arrears and a declaration. By amendment she claimed specific performance and the appointment of a receiver. The action came for hearing before the Vice-Chancellor of the County Palatine of Lancaster, who held that she had no right to enforce the agreement. He dismissed the action.

If the decision of the Vice-Chancellor truly represents the law of England, it would be deplorable. It would mean that the nephew could keep the business to himself, and at the same time repudiate his promise to pay the widow. Nothing could be more unjust. I am sure the Vice-Chancellor would have decided in favour of the widow if he had not felt himself bound by the decision of Wynn-Parry J. in *In re Miller's Agreement*, [1947] Ch. 615. That case is cited in the textbooks as if it were the last word on the subject: see Anson on Contracts, 22nd ed. (1964) p. 381; Cheshire and Fifoot on Contracts, 5th ed. (1960), p. 377. It is very like this case. So we must examine it with some care. In *In re Miller's Agreement* there were three partners. One of them had retired and transferred his interest to the other two. By a deed of covenant made by the three partners, the two continuing partners agreed to pay the retiring partner £5,000 a year during his life, and after his death to pay £1,000 a year to his three daughters during their lives. The two continuing partners also charged their interest in the firm with payment of those sums. The Revenue authorities claimed that estate duty was payable on the annuities payable to the daughters. That depended on whether the daughters had such an interest in property as would be protected in a court of law of equity. Wynn-Parry J. held that they had no such interest. "At common law," he said, "so far as the plaintiffs" (the daughters) "are concerned, the deed is res inter alios acta, and they have no right thereunder." As to section 56 of the Law of Property Act, 1925, "the section," he said, "has not the effect of creating rights, but only of assisting the protection of rights shown to exist." As to the charge: "The central function of a charge is to secure the performance of an obligation, and the charge is essentially ancillary." He concluded: "I cannot find ... that the deed confers upon any of the daughters any right to sue ... . [T]he payments, if and when made, will be no more than voluntary payments. ..." He held, accordingly, that estate duty was not payable on the daughters' annuities.

I can understand the desire of the judge in that case to save the daughters from death duties, but I cannot subscribe to the way he did it. He was wrong in saying that the daughters had no enforceable interest. We have here the standard pattern of a contract for the benefit of a third person. A man has a business or other assets. He transfers them to another and, instead of taking cash, takes a promise by that other that he will pay an annuity or other sum to his widow or children. Can the transferee take the assets and reject the promise? I think not. In my opinion a contract such as this, for the benefit of widow and children, is binding. The party who makes the promise must honour it, unless he has some good reason why he should not do so. He may, for instance, be able to say that the contract should be rescinded as being induced by fraud or misrepresentation, or that it was varied or rescinded by agreement between the parties, before the widow or children knew about it and adopted it. But unless he has some good reason, he is bound. The executor of the dead man can sue to enforce it on behalf of the widow and children. The widow and children can join with the executor as plaintiffs in the action. If he refuses to sue they may sue in their own names joining him as a defendant. In this way they have a right which can be enforced. I will prove this by reference to the common law, reinforced by equity, and now by statute.

1. THE COMMON LAW

The common law on this subject was much considered in *Dutton v. Poole*, (1678) T. Raym. 302, in 1678. It was regarded at the time as a case of great consequence and is reported by no less than five of the old reporters. It was similar in principle to our present case. The facts were these: Sir Edward Poole owned timber trees in a wood in Oaksey Park, Wiltshire. He had several children, including his son and heir, Nevil, and a daughter Grizel. Sir Edward proposed to cut down the trees and sell them so as to raise portions for the younger children. The eldest son did not want him to do this, because he was the heir and would inherit the trees if they were left standing. There was a meeting between the father and mother and the eldest son. The son asked the father not to cut down the trees, and promised him that, if he did not cut them down, he would pay £1,000 to the daughter Grizel. In reliance on the promise, the father did not cut down any of the trees, and died. The eldest son inherited and had the benefit of them. The daughter Grizel (who had married Sir Ralph Dutton) claimed £1,000 from the eldest son. He refused to pay it to her.

The mother was the executrix of the father's estate. She could as executrix have sued to enforce the agreement. But she was the only person present when it was made, and if she brought the action, she would not be a competent witness. So the daughter and her husband themselves sued the eldest son for the £1,000. In that action the mother was a competent witness. She proved the agreement, and the plaintiffs obtained judgment for £1,000. The eldest son appealed to the Court of King's Bench sitting in banc. The case was argued twice. John Holt appeared for the eldest son. He said that the action ought to be brought by the father's executor for the benefit of the daughter; and not by the daughter herself, as she was "not privy to the promise nor consideration." Pollexsen appeared for the daughter. He said that the action was maintainable either by the party to whom the promise was made, or by the daughter. When the case was first argued, two of the four judges were disposed to accept Holt's argument and hold that the daughter could not sue. But at the second argument Scroggs C.J. with his three brethren all held that the daughter could sue, "for the son hath the benefit by having of the wood, and the daughter hath lost her portion by this means." The eldest son appealed to the Court of Exchequer Chamber, but the appeal was dismissed.

Two things appear from that case: First, it was accepted on all hands that the father's executrix could have sued for the benefit of the daughter. Second, that in the special circumstances of that case (when a party could not give evidence), the daughter herself could sue on the contract although she was not a party to it. It was a decision of the Court of Exchequer Chamber and has never been overruled. It was approved by Lord Mansfield himself in 1776 who thought it so plain that "it is matter of surprise how a doubt could have arisen in that case." I know that in the 19th century some judges said that it was wrongly decided, but the criticism is not merited. It would have been shocking if the daughter had been refused a remedy.

The case of *Tweddle v. Atkinson* is readily distinguishable. John Tweddle married Miss Guy. After the marriage the two fathers of the young couple made an agreement between themselves, the two fathers, to pay these sums: The husband's father promised to pay his son £100: the wife's father promised to pay his son-in-law £200: such payments to be made on or before August 21, 1855. Clearly the payments were to be mutual for the benefit of the young couple. Neither of the fathers made the promised payments: and afterwards both fathers died. Then the young husband sued the executor of his wife's father for the £200. The action failed for the very good reason that the husband's father had not done his part. He had not paid his promised £100. The son could not himself be sued for his father's failure to pay the £100: for he was no party to the contract. So he could not be allowed to sue his wife's father for the £200. Crompton J. said: "It would be a monstrous proposition to say that a person was a party to the contract for the purpose of suing upon it for his own advantage, and not a party to it for the purpose of being sued." But if the husband's father had paid his £100 and thus wholly performed his part, then the husband's father in his lifetime, or his executor after his death, could have sued the wife's father or his executor for the £200. As Wightman J. observed: "If the father of the plaintiff had paid the £100 which he promised, might not he have sued the father of the plaintiff's wife on his express promise?" To which the answer would undoubtedly be: "Yes, he could sue and recover the £200," but he would recover it not for his own benefit, or for the benefit of the estate, but for the benefit of the son.

Those two cases give the key at common law to the whole problem of contracts for the benefit of a third person. Although the third person cannot as a rule sue alone in his own name, nevertheless there is no difficulty whatever in the one contracting party suing the other party for breach of the promise. The third person should, therefore, bring the action in the name of the contracting party, just as an assignee used to do. Face to face with the contracting party, the defaulter has no defence. He is sued by one who has provided consideration and to whom he has given his promise to pay the third person. He has broken his promise and must pay damages. The defaulter sometimes seeks to say that the contracting party can only recover nominal damages because it is not he but the third person who has suffered the damage. The common law has never allowed the defaulter to escape by such a shifty means. It holds that the contracting party can recover the money which should have been paid to the third person. He can get judgment for the sum and issue a writ of fi. fa. or other machinery to enforce payment: but when he recovers it, he holds the proceeds for the benefit of the third person. He cannot retain the money himself because it belongs to the third person and not to him: see *In re Schebsman, Ex parte the Official Solicitor, the Trustee, Cargo Superintendents (London) Ltd. v. Schebsman* [1944] Ch. 83. It is money had and received to the use of the third person. In *Robertson v. Wait*, (1853) 8 Exch. 299, Martin B. said: "If a person makes a contract whereby another obtains a benefit, why may not the former sue for it?" And in *Lloyd's v. Harper* (1880), 16 Ch. D. 290, Lush L.J. said: "I consider it to be an established rule of law that where a contract is made with A for the benefit of B, A can sue on the contract for the benefit of B and recover all that B could have recovered if the contract had been made with B himself."

Such was the position at common law if the action was brought in the name of the contracting party by himself alone. But nowadays when joinder of parties is freely permissible, it is far better for the contracting party and the third person to join as co-plaintiffs. Judgment will be given for the plaintiffs for the amount: and on payment, it will go at once to the third person who is entitled to it.

2. EQUITY

Sometimes one of the contracting parties makes the contract on trust for the third person, in this sense, that from the very beginning the right to sue is vested in him as trustee for the third person as beneficiary. Such a contract is different from those we are considering. It cannot be rescinded or varied except with the consent of the third person beneficiary: see *In re Empress Engineering Co.* (1880), 16 Ch. D. 125. In such a case it is clearly established that the third person himself can sue in equity to enforce the contract: ... but even so, he ought as a rule to join the trustee as a party. Here we have a case where there is admittedly no trust of the contractual right. Peter Beswick and his nephew might by agreement before his death have rescinded or varied the agreement, if they so wished. Nevertheless, although there is no trust, I do not think equity is powerless. It has in its hands the potent remedy of ordering a party specifically to perform his contract. If a party makes a promise to pay money to a third person, I see no reason why a court of equity should not order him to perform his promise. The action must be brought, of course, in the name of the other contracting party; but, that being done, there is no bar to a decree for specific performance being made. True it is for the payment of money, but a court of equity often decrees specific performance of a promise to pay money. It can enforce it by the appointment of a receiver, or other appropriate machinery. We have been referred to three cases where this has been done, although there was no trust. The first is *Keenan v. Handley* (1864), 13 W.R. 930. Ellen Keenan was the mistress of Captain Handley. They lived as Mr. and Mrs. Coverdale and had a baby daughter called Lucy Coverdale. Captain Handley wrote this letter to Miss Keenan: "I will allow you £150 a year, to be continued to you while you live and to your child after your death, should she survive you." She and her daughter sued for specific performance. Kindersley V.-C. granted it. He ordered deeds to be executed for payment of the annuities, including the amounts to the daughter, although she was not a party to the agreement. The next case is *Peel v. Peel*, (1869) 17 W.R. 586. William Peel was in financial difficulty. His brother Edmund Peel agreed with his cousin, Sir Robert Peel, that Edmund would pay off William's debts and that Sir Robert would during his life pay William an annuity of £164 a year. Edmund paid off the debts but Sir Robert Peel did not pay the amounts. Edmund Peel and William Peel sued for specific performance. James V.-C. granted it. He ordered Sir Robert to pay William Peel £164 a year, although William was not a party to the agreement. The third case is *Hohler v. Aston*, [1920] 2 Ch. 420, where Mrs. Aston agreed with her nephew, Mr. Hohler, to make provision for her niece and her husband, Mr. and Mrs. Rollo. Mrs. Aston died before doing so. Mr. Hohler and Mr. and Mrs. Rollo sued the executors for specific performance. Sargant J. granted it. He said: "Mr. E.T. Hohler was entitled, and is now entitled, to enforce for the benefit of the third parties, Mr. and Mrs. Rollo, a contract made with Mrs. Aston for those third parties. The third parties, of course, cannot themselves enforce a contract made for their benefit, but the person with whom the contract is made is entitled to enforce the contract."

These cases in equity fit in exactly with the common law. The contracting party is entitled by himself alone, or jointly with the third person, to have the contract performed according to its terms, and the court will decree specific performance of it. ...

[Lord Denning then examined s 56(1) of the *Law of Property Act*, 1925 (UK).]

• • •

4. CONCLUSION

The general rule undoubtedly is that "no third person can sue, or be sued, on a contract to which he is not a party": but at bottom that is only a rule of procedure. It goes to the form of remedy, not to the underlying right. Where a contract is made for the benefit of a third person who has a legitimate interest to enforce it, it can be enforced by the third person in the name of the contracting party or jointly with him or, if he refuses to join, by adding him as a defendant. In that sense, and it is a very real sense, the third person has a right arising by way of contract. He has an interest which will be protected by law. The observations to the contrary in *In re Miller's Agreement* and *Green v. Russell*, [1959] 2 Q.B. 226 are in my opinion erroneous. It is different when a third person has no legitimate interest, as when he is seeking to enforce the maintenance of prices to the public disadvantage, as in *Dunlop Pneumatic Tyre Co. Ltd. v. Selfridge & Co. Ltd.*, [1915] A.C. 847: or when he is seeking to rely, not on any right given to him by the contract, but on an exemption clause seeking to exempt himself from his just liability. He cannot set up an exemption clause in a contract to which he was not a party: see *Midland Silicones Ltd. v. Scruttons Ltd.*, [1962] A.C. 446.

The widow here sues in her capacity as executrix of her husband's estate (and therefore as contracting party), and also in her personal capacity (and therefore as a third person). This joint claim is clearly good. She is entitled to an order for specific performance of the agreement, by ordering the defendant to pay the arrears of £175, and the instalments of £5 a week as they fall due. The order for paying the arrears of £175 is equivalent to a judgment for that sum and can be enforced by fi. fa. or other appropriate machinery: see R.S.C. Ord. 42, r. 3. When the money is recovered, it will go to the widow for her own benefit, and not to her husband's estate. I would allow the appeal accordingly.

[The nephew appealed to the House of Lords.]

LORD REID: My Lords, before 1962 the respondent's deceased husband carried on business as a coal merchant. By agreement of March 14, 1962, he assigned to his nephew, the appellant, the assets of the business and the appellant undertook first to pay him £6 10s. per week for the remainder of his life and then to pay the respondent an annuity of £5 per week in the event of her husband's death. The husband died in November, 1963. Thereupon, the appellant made one payment of £5 to the respondent but he refused to make any further payment to her. The respondent now sues for £175 arrears of the annuity and for an order for specific performance of the continuing obligation to pay the annuity. The Vice-Chancellor of the County Palatine of Lancaster decided against the respondent but the Court of Appeal reversed this decision and, besides ordering payment of the arrears, ordered the appellant to pay to the respondent for the remainder of her life an annuity of £5 per week in accordance with the agreement.

It so happens that the respondent is administratrix of the estate of her deceased husband and she sues both in that capacity and in her personal capacity. So it is necessary to consider her rights in each capacity.

For clarity I think it best to begin by considering a simple case where, in consideration of a sale by A to B, B agrees to pay the price of £1,000 to a third party X. Then the first question appears to me to be whether the parties intended that X should receive the money simply as A's nominee so that he would hold the money for behoof of A and be accountable to him for it, or whether the parties intended that X should receive the money for his own behoof and be entitled to keep it. That appears to me to be a question of construction of the agreement read in light of all the circumstances which were known to the parties. There have been several decisions involving this question. I am not sure that any conflicts with the view which I have expressed: but if any does, ... I would not agree with it. I think that *In re Schebsman* was rightly decided and that the reasoning of Uthwatt J. and the Court of Appeal supports what I have just said. In the present case I think it clear that the parties to the agreement intended that the respondent should receive the weekly sums of £5 in her own behoof and should not be accountable to her deceased husband's estate for them. Indeed the contrary was not argued.

Reverting to my simple example the next question appears to me to be: Where the intention was that X should keep the £1,000 as his own, what is the nature of B's obligation and who is entitled to enforce it? It was not argued that the law of England regards B's obligation as a nullity, and I have not observed in any of the authorities any suggestion that it would be a nullity. There may have been a time when the existence of a right depended on whether there was any means of enforcing it, but today the law would be sadly deficient if one found that, although there is a right, the law provides no means for enforcing it. So this obligation of B must be enforceable either by X or by A. I shall leave aside for the moment the question whether section 56(1) of the Law of Property Act, 1925, has any application to such a case, and consider the position at common law.

Lord Denning's view, expressed in this case not for the first time, is that X could enforce this obligation. But the view more commonly held in recent times has been that such a contract confers no right on X and that X could not sue for the £1,000. Leading counsel for the respondent based his case on other grounds, and as I agree that the respondent succeeds on other grounds, this would not be an appropriate case in which to solve this question. It is true that a strong Law Revision Committee recommended so long ago as 1937 (Cmd. 5449): "That where a contract by its express terms purports to confer a benefit directly on a third party it should be enforceable by the third party in his own name. ..." (p. 31). And, if one had to contemplate a further long period of Parliamentary procrastination, this House might find it necessary to deal with this matter. But if legislation is probable at any early date I would not deal with it in a case where that is not essential. So for the purposes of this case I shall proceed on the footing that the commonly accepted view is right.

What then is A's position? I assume that A has not made himself a trustee for X, because it was not argued in this appeal that any trust has been created. So, if X has no right, A can at any time grant a discharge to B or make some new contract with B. If there were a trust the position would be different. X would have an equitable right and A would be entitled and, indeed, bound to recover the money and account for it to X. And A would have no right to grant a discharge to B. If there is no trust and A wishes to enforce the obligation, how does he set about it? He cannot sue B for the £1,000 because under the contract the money is not payable to him, and, if the contract were performed according to its terms, he would never have any right to get the money. So he must seek to make B pay X.

The argument for the appellant is that A's only remedy is to sue B for damages for B's breach of contract in failing to pay the £1,000 to X. Then the appellant says that A can only recover nominal damages of 40s. because the fact that X has not received the money will generally cause no loss to A: he admits that there may be cases where A would suffer damage if X did not receive the money but says that the present is not such a case.

Applying what I have said to the circumstances of the present case, the respondent in her personal capacity has no right to sue, but she has a right as administratrix of her husband's estate to require the appellant to perform his obligation under the agreement. He has refused to do so and he maintains that the respondent's only right is to sue him for damages for breach of his contract. If that were so, I shall assume that he is right in maintaining that the administratrix could then only recover nominal damages because his breach of contract has caused no loss to the estate of her deceased husband.

If that were the only remedy available the result would be grossly unjust. It would mean that the appellant keeps the business which he bought and for which he has only paid a small part of the price which he agreed to pay. He would avoid paying the rest of the price, the annuity to the respondent, by paying a mere 40s. damages.

The respondent's first answer is that the common law has been radically altered by section 56(1) of the Law of Property Act, 1925, and that that section entitles her to sue in her personal capacity and recover the benefit provided for her in the agreement although she was not a party to it.

[After an examination of the history of the section, Lord Reid held that it did not have the wide meaning contended for by the widow and accepted by Lord Denning and the majority of the Court of Appeal.]

The respondent's second argument is that she is entitled in her capacity of administratrix of her deceased husband's estate to enforce the provision of the agreement for the benefit of herself in her personal capacity, and that a proper way of enforcing that provision is to order specific performance. That would produce a just result, and, unless there is some technical objection, I am of opinion that specific performance ought to be ordered. For the reasons given by your Lordships I would reject the arguments submitted for the appellant that specific performance is not a possible remedy in this case. I am therefore of opinion that the Court of Appeal reached a correct decision and that this appeal should be dismissed.

[The other Lords agreed, in substance, with Lord Reid.]

QUESTION

Was Lord Reid (with whom the majority agreed on this point) correct in assuming that no loss was suffered by the promisee? If so, in what sense would nominal damages be "inadequate"? If damages were awarded to the promisee would they belong entirely to the promisee? (In *Beswick*, would they form part of the estate?) When can a claim by a third-party beneficiary be framed in non-contractual terms (consider property, wrongdoing, unjust enrichment, and estoppel)? See *Glanzer v Shepherd*, 223 NY 236 (1922); *White v Jones*, [1995] 2 AC 207 (HL); *Trident General Ins Co v McNiece Bros Pty Ltd* (1988), 165 CLR 107 (Aus HC).

DUNLOP PNEUMATIC TYRE CO LTD V SELFRIDGE & CO LTD
[1915] AC 847 (HL)

The facts of this case are shortly stated by Lord Sumner. There are two instances of sale and delivery complained of by Dunlop in this case. The steps in the Jameson transaction are as follows. Those in the other, the Strauss transaction, are similar, and need not be analysed. On October 12, 1911, Messrs. Dew & Co., motor accessory factors, contracted with the appellants, the Dunlop Company, in terms of the latter's price maintenance agreement then current. By this contract Dew became bound, inter alia, to buy from the Dunlop Company motor tyres, covers, tubes, and sundries to the net value of £2000 before the expiration of September, 1912, and the appellants became bound, if the contract continued to subsist, as it did, to sell and deliver such goods up to that value, whenever reasonably required to do so.

On December 21, 1911, a Captain Jameson thought fit to ask the respondents, Selfridge's, who are described as wholesale and retail merchants, for their lowest price for a Dunlop motor tyre, grooved and non-skid, 815 by 105. Their answer was that, on receipt of his order, such a tyre would be procured and the price would be £5 18s. 2d., which was the appellants' list price, less $7\frac{1}{2}$ per cent.

On January 1, 1912, Captain Jameson sent to the respondents an order for the tyre, and also the money for it, and on the same day the order was accepted, and delivery of the tyre was promised for the following day. In fact, on January 2 the respondents ordered this tyre from Dew by telephone. Dew, in turn, ordered it by telephone from the appellants; it was delivered by them to Dew, and they sent it to the respondents. These were the events of January 2. On the next day the respondents delivered it to Captain Jameson. Of course, the respondents did not mention Captain Jameson to Dew, nor did Dew mention the respondents to the appellants.

So far the respondents had signed no price maintenance agreement. They had been pressed to do so, and no doubt knew that the reason why they were being pressed by Dew was because the appellants, in turn, strictly required them to obtain these agreements from those of their customers to whom they sold. Within two or three days of January 3 they did sign such an agreement, dating it January 2, and delivering it to Dew, to whom it was addressed, a week or so afterwards. It is for breach of this agreement that the appellants sued.

The parties have been desirous of knowing their reciprocal rights and duties, if any, arising out of this agreement, and have accordingly raised two broad questions: (1) Is there any agreement between these parties at all? (2) If so, is there any consideration moving from the appellants to support it and make it bind the respondents to them? But for this there would have been a good deal to be said for the proposition that a bargain and sale, clearly complete before this agreement was signed or dated, could be no breach of it, and that the performance of that bargain by delivery of the goods after the price maintenance agreement was made could hardly be a ground for the grant of an injunction.

Phillimore J. gave judgment for the appellants for £10, the liquidated damages in respect of the two breaches, and granted an injunction restraining the respondents from selling Dunlop motor tyres, etc., below the appellants' current list prices.

The Court of Appeal reversed this decision and gave judgment for the respondents. They held that the contract of January 2 was not a contract between the appellants and the respondents at all, but was a contract between Dew and the respondents only, and that Dew were not legally competent at one and the same time to make a contract with the respondents by themselves as principals and as agents of the appellants. They therefore held that the action was not sustainable.

VISCOUNT HALDANE LC: My Lords, in my opinion this appeal ought to fail. ...

My Lords, in the law of England certain principles are fundamental. One is that only a person who is a party to a contract can sue on it. Our law knows nothing of a *jus quaesitum tertio* arising by way of contract. Such a right may be conferred by way of property, as, for example, under a trust, but it cannot be conferred on a stranger to a contract as a right to enforce the contract in personam. A second principle is that if a person with whom a contract not under seal has been made is to be able to enforce it consideration must have been given by him to the promisor or to some other person at the promisor's request. These two principles are not recognized in the same fashion by the jurisprudence of certain continental countries or of Scotland, but here they are well established. A third proposition is that a principal not named in the contract may sue upon it if the promisee really contracted as his agent. But again, in order to entitle him so to sue, he must have given consideration either personally or through the promisee, acting as his agent in giving it.

My Lords, in the case before us, I am of opinion that the consideration, the allowance of what was in reality part of the discount of which Messrs. Dew, the promisees, were entitled as between themselves and the appellants, was to be given by Messrs. Dew on their own account, and was not in substance, any more than in form, an allowance made by the appellants. The case for the appellants is that they permitted and enabled Messrs. Dew, with the knowledge and by the desire of the respondents, to sell to the latter on the terms of the contract of January 2, 1912, but it appears to me that even if this is so the answer is conclusive. Messrs. Dew sold to the respondents goods which they had a title to obtain from the appellants independently of this contract. The consideration by way of discount under the contract of January 2 was to come wholly out of Messrs. Dew's pocket, and neither directly nor indirectly out of that of the appellants. If the appellants enabled them to sell to the respondents on the terms they did, this was not done as any part of the terms of the contract sued on.

No doubt it was provided as part of these terms that the appellants should acquire certain rights, but these rights appear on the face of the contract as *jura quaesita tertio* which the appellants could not enforce. Moreover, even if this difficulty can be got over by regarding the appellants as the principals of Messrs. Dew in stipulating for the rights in question, the only consideration disclosed by the contract is one given by Messrs. Dew, not as their agents, but as principals acting on their own account.

The conclusion to which I have come on the point as to consideration renders it unnecessary to decide the further question as to whether the appellants can claim that a bargain was made in this contract by Messrs. Dew as their agents; a bargain which, apart from the point as to consideration, they could therefore enforce. If it were necessary to express an opinion on this further question, a difficulty as to the position of Messrs. Dew would have to be considered. Two contracts—one by a man on his own account as principal, and another by the same man as agent—may be validly comprised in the same piece of paper. But they must be two contracts, and not one as here. I do not think that a man can treat one and the same contract as made by him in two capacities. He cannot be regarded as contracting for himself and for another *uno flatu*.

My Lords, the form of the contract which we have to interpret leaves the appellants in this dilemma, that, if they say that Messrs. Dew contracted on their behalf, they gave no consideration, and if they say they gave consideration in the shape of a permission to the respondents to buy, they must set up further stipulations, which are neither to be found in the contract sued upon nor are germane to it, but are really inconsistent with its structure. That contract has been reduced to writing, and it is in the writing that we must look for the whole of the terms made between the parties.

These terms cannot, in my opinion, consistently with the settled principles of English law, be construed as giving to the appellants any enforceable rights as against the respondents.

I think that the judgment of the Court of Appeal was right, and I move that the appeal be dismissed with costs.

LORD DUNEDIN: My Lords, I confess that this case is to my mind apt to nip any budding affection which one might have had for the doctrine of consideration. For the effect of that doctrine in the present case is to make it possible for a person to snap his fingers at a bargain deliberately made, a bargain not in itself unfair, and which the person seeking to enforce it has a legitimate interest to enforce. Notwithstanding these considerations I cannot say that I have ever had any doubt that the judgment of the Court of Appeal was right. ...

That there are methods of framing a contract which will cause persons in the position of Selfridge to become bound, I do not doubt. But that has not been done in this instance; and as Dunlop's advisers must have known of the law of consideration, it is their affair that they have not so drawn the contract.

[Opinions to the like effect were given by Lords Atkinson, Parker of Waddington, Sumner, and Parmoor.]

THE SATANITA
[1895] P 248 (CA)

On July 5, 1894, the Valkyrie and the Satanita were manoeuvring to get into position for starting for the fifty mile race at the Mudhook Yacht Club Regatta, when the Satanita ran into and sank the Valkyrie.

The entry for the Satanita for the regatta was signed by the defendant, and contained the following clause: "I undertake that, while sailing under this entry, I will obey and be bound by the sailing rules of the Yacht Racing Association and the by-laws of the club."

The rules of the Yacht Racing Association, adopted by the club, provided among other things as follows:

> Rule 24: "... If a yacht, in consequence of her neglect of any of these rules, shall foul another yacht ... she shall forfeit all claim to the prize, and shall pay all damages."

The plaintiffs, in an action in personam in the Admiralty Division ... alleged that by the terms of the entry and in consideration that the owner of the Valkyrie would race with the defendant under these rules, the defendant agreed that if the Satanita fouled the Valkyrie in consequence of her neglect of any of the rules, the Satanita would pay all damages. ... The defendant denied that he had entered into such agreement as alleged. ...

LORD ESHER MR: This is an action by the owner of a yacht against the owner of another yacht, and although brought in the Admiralty Division, the contention really is that the yacht which is sued has broken the rules which by her consent governed her sailing in a regatta in which she was contesting for a price.

The first question raised is whether, supposing her to have broken a rule, she can be sued for that breach of the rules by the owner of the competing yacht which has been damaged; in other words, was there any contract between the owners of those two yachts? Or it may be put thus: Did the owner of the yacht which is sued enter into obligation to the owner of the other yacht, that if his yacht broke the rules, and thereby injured the other yacht, he would pay damages? It seems to me clear that he did; and the way that he has undertaken that obligation is this. A certain number of gentlemen formed themselves into a committee and proposed to give prizes for matches sailed between yachts at a certain place on a certain day, and they promulgated certain rules, and said: "If you want to sail in any of our matches for our prizes, you cannot do so unless you submit yourselves to the conditions which we have thus laid down. And one of the conditions is, that if you do sail for one of such prizes you must enter into an obligation with the owners of the yachts who are competing, which they at the same time enter into similarly with you, that if by a breach of any of our rules you do damage or injury to the owner of a competing yacht, you shall be liable to make good the damage which you have so done." If that is so, then when they do sail, and not till then, that relation is immediately formed between the yacht owners. There are other conditions with regard to these matches which constitute a relation between each of the yacht owners who enters his yacht and sails it and the committee; but that does not in the least do away with what the yacht owner has undertaken, namely, to enter into a relation with the other yacht owners, that relation containing an obligation.

Here the defendant, the owner of the Satanita, entered into a relation with the plaintiff Lord Dunraven, when he sailed his yacht against Lord Dunraven's yacht, and that relation contained an obligation that if, by any breach of any of these rules, he did damage to the yacht of Lord Dunraven, he would have to pay the damages.

[Only that part of the opinion is given that deals with the formation of the contract. Rigby and Lopes LJJ gave judgments to the same effect. Rigby LJ said: "To whom is the owner of that yacht to pay those damages? He cannot pay them to the club, nor do I think the club could recover them. The true and sensible construction is that he must pay the owner of the yacht fouled." The judgments were affirmed in the House of Lords *sub nom Clarke v Dunraven*, [1897] AC 59.]

MULHOLLAND V MERRIAM
(1872), 19 Grant 288 (Ont Ch)

STRONG VC: About the 6th of November, 1868, John Mulholland being possessed of a considerable amount in money and securities, the proceeds of the sale of his farm and also of some other property, executed an instrument in a very peculiar form. This document, which was prepared by Philip Green, a schoolmaster, residing in the neighbourhood of the defendant, may be thus described. The first part of it purports to be a bond by the defendant to John Mulholland in the penal sum of $400. What is declared to be the condition is as follows: John Mulholland purports thereby to assign to the defendant "all his estate real and personal, with notes and accounts, to the said William Merriam on condition that he pay his heirs in the manner following, namely," and then follows a direction to pay to each of the living children of John Mulholland except the defendant's wife $400, and the like sum to the children of two deceased daughters. It then contains the following clause: "The said William Merriam hereby becomes bound to pay the above mentioned sums to the parties herein named at the time of the decease of the said John Mulholland or as soon after as can conveniently be done." A covenant on the part of Merriam to provide a maintenance for John Mulholland during the remainder of his life, completes the document.

This bond or agreement was executed by sealing by both John Mulholland and his son-in-law, the defendant, William Merriam.

The bill is filed by George B. Mulholland one of the sons of John Mulholland, to enforce payment of the $400, which by the instrument set forth was to be paid to him on his father's death, which took place in April, 1870. The defendant by his answer to the original bill alleges in paragraph 7 that he has "in all things fully performed the trusts and covenants in the said bond and agreement on his part to be performed."

At the hearing it was contended for the defendant, in the first place, that there was no jurisdiction; that no trust was created by the agreement, and that there was an absence of any privity, either at law or in equity, between the plaintiff and the defendant, the proper remedy of the instrument being an action at law, to be brought by the personal representative of John Mulholland. ...

As to the first point raised by the defendant. I have had much doubt and difficulty, for it seemed to me at first that the bond could be considered in legal effect as nothing more than a personal covenant by Merriam the defendant with John Mulholland, and that consequently the only remedy on it could have been action at law by the personal representative of the latter. More mature consideration has led me to think I was wrong in my first impression both as to the proper construction of the instrument, and also as to the consequence which I thought would have attached, if that construction had been correct. ...

[Strong VC then concluded that on the true construction of the document, Merriam was a trustee of the property conveyed to him, and so was bound to account to George, the beneficiary of that trust. The learned judge then went on to consider whether Merriam's promise could be enforced even if there were no trust of the property.]

I think there could be no doubt but that a personal representative of the testator recovering this money in an action at law would be considered as a trustee for the plaintiff, and, if so, it would, I think, follow that the plaintiff can maintain this suit. I quite agree that, in the naked case, where there is a covenant by one person with another to pay a sum of money to a stranger, or do any act for the benefit of a stranger who is not a party to the instrument or agreement, the person to whom the money is to be paid, or who is to be benefited, cannot sue either at law or in equity, inasmuch as there is no privity of contract. ... There appears, it is true, to be an exception to this general rule recognized in some of the older cases where it is laid down that the person to receive the benefit of the contract, though a stranger to it, may maintain an action upon it if he stand in such a relationship to the contracting party that it may be considered that the contract was made for his benefit, and in the very case of a contract made with a father to pay money to his son or daughter, it has been held upon this principle that the son or daughter might sue on the contract. ... *Dutton v. Poole* (1678), 83 E.R. 523. ...

This doctrine is not, however, now approved as regards courts of law, as appears from the late case of *Tweddle v. Atkinson* (1861), 121 E.R. 762. This, however, in my opinion, only goes to shew the applicability to a case like the present of a remedy in this Court proceeding on a doctrine which I will endeavour to point out. There can be no doubt, as I have already said, that this $400, if recovered in an action at law by a personal representative of John Mulholland, would not be assets in his hands to be distributed by him according to the *Statute of Distributions*, but would be impressed with a trust in equity in favor of the plaintiff. This *must* be so, for the only other alternative is, that it was in the power of the defendant entirely to defeat any or all of the gifts which the settlor made to his children, by compelling the personal representative to bring an action, the fruits of which would be free from any trust and liable to be distributed amongst the next of kin; which would of course, be absurd.

Then if the money, when recovered by the administrator, would be affected by a trust, it must also be, that the right of action which the personal representative has is also bound by a like trust; and, if this is so, there is the highest authority for saying that, even though the obligation of Merriam rests (as I have already determined it does not) merely on contract, and he should not be bound by any trust, yet, as the personal representative would be a trustee for the plaintiff, he and the plaintiff conjointly might maintain this bill. The authority which I refer to is the case of *Gregory v. Williams* (1817), 36 E.R. 224, decided by a very great Judge (Sir William Grant, M.R.), and it is approved by Mr. Spence, who, in his treatise, 2 *Equitable Jurisdiction*, 286, thus states both the case and the principle which it establishes: he says:

> There are instances where a third person has been expressly allowed to treat the party exacting the stipulation as his trustee, though such third person was a mere stranger to the parties. In the case of *Gregory v. Williams*, one Parker, who was in the possession of a farm belonging to the defendant Williams, was considerably indebted to Williams; he also owed a large debt to one Gregory. Parker, as Williams knew, was under apprehension that Gregory would arrest him; Williams, the landlord, and Parker, the tenant, entered into an agreement in writing, to which Gregory, the creditor, was neither party nor privy, to the following effect, namely: that, if Parker would make over to Williams all his stock and effects of every kind, he would pay the debt due to Gregory, Gregory subsequently was informed of this arrangement, and he and Parker filed their bill against Williams to enforce it. The stock and effects assigned to Williams by Parker had been sold at a loss; it was insisted by Williams that, if Gregory had any remedy, it was at law. Sir W. Grant considered it was at least doubtful whether Gregory could recover at law, for the engagement of Williams was not made directly to Gregory, but to Parker only, and the consideration was furnished by Parker only, for he alone did the act which constituted the consideration; Gregory was not a party to the contract; however, that learned Judge supported Gregory's right to sue in equity, saying "Parker acts as his trustee, and Gregory may derive an equitable right through the medium of Parker's agreement, though it was at least questionable whether he could have maintained an action at law; it was like the case where a man promised the widow that, if she would allow his name to be joined with hers in the administration, he would make up the deficiency of the assets for the payment of the testator's debts; which promise was held to be binding in favour of the creditors, though they could not sue at law, as the promise was not made to them; so here, Gregory had a right to insist upon the benefit of the promise made to Parker to the extent of £900, which Parker represented to be the amount of the debt."

This case which never appears to have been overruled or even doubted, lays down a reasonable and convenient doctrine applying directly to the present case, and shewing that the plaintiff has an equitable right to enforce the contract (if it is nothing more than a contract) which the defendant entered into with John Mulholland. It is true that in the case of *Gregory v. Williams* the quasi trustee, Parker, was a co-plaintiff, and it may be said that a personal representative of the settlor John Mulholland ought to be a party here. But there is no such representative in existence, and if one was constituted it would only be for the express purpose of this suit since all the property of the intestate was made over by this assignment to the defendant, and there are now no assets to administer or debts to pay; and such an administrator would be a mere formal party as a trustee having not the slightest interest. I am therefore perfectly justified in directing as I do under the Consolidated Order 56, that the suit may proceed in the absence of any person representing the estate of John Mulholland.

> Therefore in my judgment the suit is maintainable, *first* because the defendant is a trustee under the instrument of the 6th November, 1868, and the plaintiff is one of the *cestuis que trust; second*, even though the defendant be not a trustee, and is liable on contract only, the plaintiff has nevertheless an equitable right of suit on the authority of the case referred to.

Les Affréteurs Réunis Société Anonyme v Leopold Walford (London) Limited. [1919] AC 801 (Eng HL). LORD WRENBURY: We have here to do with a contract between two parties reserving a benefit to a third. The two parties are the shipowners and the charterers, the third party is the broker of one of them, who is to be remunerated in respect of a contract which is being made for the hire of a ship. The particular form of contract in question is of course prepared by, or is under the eyes of the broker who is negotiating the matter. It is sent to the principals for signature, and they sign it, and there is contained in it a clause which reserves a benefit to the broker. Under those circumstances an action is brought by the broker against the shipowner for the commission which is expressed to be payable to him under the contract between the shipowner and the charterer—a contract to which he himself, I agree, was not a party. By agreement between the parties the record is to be treated as if the charterer were joined as a plaintiff in the action. The case is one in which an action can be brought on behalf of a person to whom a benefit is reserved although he is not a party to it. That is the subject of the decision in *Robertson v. Wait*. Under those circumstances the shipowners, the defendants in the action, defend the action and in effect are here saying: "It is perfectly true that we attached our signature to this document; it is perfectly true that it contains in Article 29 this stipulation in favour of a third party; but that means nothing at all—that is not the bargain at all to which we were parties. The matter is governed by a certain custom."

My Lords, I feel myself in great difficulty in understanding a contention of that sort. It is said that in this particular business there exists a custom (and I will take it for the moment that the custom is proved) that in time charterparties broker's commission is payable out of hire earned and is not payable unless hire is earned. In this contract, however, there is a stipulation that the commission shall be on the estimated gross amount of hire on signing the charter ship lost or not lost. I find myself quite unable to understand how it can be set up that into a contract expressed in those terms there can be introduced a custom to an exactly contrary effect. Directly it is conceded that the broker, although not a party to the contract, can sue on the contract, inasmuch as he can sue by the charterer as trustee for him, it appears to me that the case really is over. I have only to read Article 29 and I find there an express stipulation—a stipulation which is accepted by the signature of the defendants, that this payment shall be made, and for that payment it appears to me that the defendants are liable.

NOTE ON THE TRUST CONCEPT

The concept of trust involves a separation between legal and beneficial ownership: legal title to property is vested in one person (the trustee) and the beneficial interest in another (the *cestui que trust*, or beneficiary). The interest of the beneficiary is enforceable against the trustee and anyone else except a good-faith purchaser of the legal estate for value without notice. The subject of a trust may be intangible as well as tangible property and may include a promise. Trusts were developed by the courts of equity.

The notion of a trust of a promise, which found favour in *Mulholland v Merriam* and in *Walford*, is clearly capable of making great inroads on the rule denying an action to a third-party beneficiary. For if the making of the promise in favour of the third party is in itself sufficient to create a trust, it is always open to a court to hold that the promise is enforceable at the suit of the third party. Even without the promisee's cooperation, the third party could succeed, for once a trust is found a court will never allow the rights of a beneficiary to be defeated because of the recalcitrance of the trustee. Indeed, it was argued by Corbin in "Contracts for the Benefit of Third Persons" (1930) 46 Law Q Rev 12 that the way was open, by means of the concept of trust of a promise, effectively to abolish the rule against third-party beneficiaries. This suggestion was, however, rejected in *Re Schebsman*, [1944] Ch 83 (CA) and in *Green v Russell*, [1959] 2 QB 226 (CA), where proof of a "real" intention to create a trust was required.

JACKSON V HORIZON HOLIDAYS LTD
[1975] 3 All ER 92 (CA)

LORD DENNING MR: Mr. Jackson is a young man, in his mid-twenties. He has been very successful in his business. He is married with three small children. In November 1970 there were twin boys of three years of age; and his wife had just had her third child. He had been working very hard. They determined to have a holiday in the sun. He decided on Ceylon. He enquired of Horizon Holidays Ltd. He made arrangements with their agent, a Mrs. Bremner, for a holiday at a hotel, the Pegasus Reef Hotel, Hendala Point, Ceylon. He wrote them a letter which shows that he wanted everything of the highest standard ... .

• • •

He spoke on the telephone to Mrs. Bremner. She led him to believe that the hotel would come up to his expectations. She wrote on the booking form: "Remarks Twins Room with connecting door essential. Total charge, £1,432." He sent it in and booked the holiday.

In the middle of January it was discovered that the Pegasus Reef Hotel would not be ready in time. So Horizon Holidays recommended a substitute. This was Brown's Beach Hotel. It was described in the advertisement as being, "superbly situated right on the beach, with all facilities for an enjoyable holiday including mini-golf, excellent restaurant, cocktail lounge, swimming pool, beauty salon, hairdressers and gift shop ... . The bedrooms are well furnished and equipped in modern style. All rooms have private bath, shower, w.c., sea view and air-conditioning."

Mr. Jackson had some hesitation about this other hotel. But Horizon Holidays assured him that it would be up to his expectation. So Mr. Jackson accepted it. But Horizon Holidays reduced the charge. Instead of the price being the total sum of £1,432, now, because of the change of hotel, it would be £1,200. That included air travel to Ceylon and back and a holiday for four weeks. So they went there. The courier, Miss Redgrave, met them and took them to Brown's Beach Hotel. But they were greatly disappointed. Their room had not got a connecting door with the room for the children at all. The room for the children was mildewed—black with mildew, at the bottom. There was fungus growing on the walls. The toilet was stained. The shower was dirty. There was no bath. They could not let the children sleep in it. So for the first three days they had all the family in one room. The two children were put into one of the single beds and the two adults in the other single bed. After the first three days they were moved into what was said to be one of the best suites in the hotel. Even then, they had to put the children in to sleep in the sittingroom and the parents in the bedroom. There was dirty linen on the bed. There was no private bath but only a shower; no mini-golf course; no swimming pool, no beauty salon, no hairdressers' salon. Worst of all was the cooking. There was no choice of dishes. On some occasions, however, curry was served as an alternative to the main dish. They found the food very distasteful. It appeared to be cooked in coconut oil. There was a pervasive taste because of its manner of cooking. They were so uncomfortable at Brown's Hotel, that after a fortnight they moved to the Pegasus Reef Hotel. It appears that by that time it was nearing completion. But a lot of building work was still going on. At any rate, for the fortnight they were in the Pegasus Reef Hotel, where things were somewhat better than at Brown's Beach. They stayed out the four weeks and came home.

Soon after their return, Mr. Jackson wrote a letter setting out all his complaints from the beginning to the end. Then Mr. Jackson brought an action for damages in respect of the loss of his holiday for himself, his wife and the two small children. Horizon Holidays admitted liability. The contest was only on the amount of damages.

In *Jarvis v. Swans Tours Ltd.* [1973] Q.B. 233 it was held by this court that damages for the loss of a holiday may include not only the difference in value between what was promised and what was obtained, but also damages for mental distress, inconvenience, upset, disappointment and frustration caused by the loss of the holiday. The judge directed himself in accordance with the judgments in that case. He eventually awarded a sum of £1,100. Horizon Holidays Ltd. appeal. They say it was far too much. The judge did not divide up the £1,100. Counsel has made suggestions about it. Counsel for Horizon Holidays suggests that the judge gave £100 for diminution in value and £1,000 for the mental distress. But counsel for Mr. Jackson suggested that the judge gave £600 for the diminution in value and £500 for the mental distress. If I were inclined myself to speculate, I think the suggestion of counsel for Mr. Jackson may well be right. The judge took the cost of the holidays at £1,200. The family only had about half the value of it. Divide it by two and you get £600. Then add £500 for the mental distress.

On this question a point of law arises. The judge said that he could only consider the mental distress to Mr. Jackson himself, and that he could not consider the distress to his wife and children. He said: "... the damages are the Plaintiff's; that I can consider the effect upon his mind of his wife's discomfort, vexation and the like, although I cannot award a sum which represents her vexation."

Counsel for Mr. Jackson disputes that proposition. He submits that damages can be given not only for the leader of the party, in this case, Mr. Jackson's own distress, discomfort and vexation, but also for that of the rest of the party.

We have had an interesting discussion as to the legal position when one person makes a contract for the benefit of a party. In this case it was a husband making a contract for the benefit of himself, his wife and children. Other cases readily come to mind. A host makes a contract with a restaurant for a dinner for himself and his friends. The vicar makes a contract for a coach trip for the choir. In all these cases there is only one person who makes the contract. It is the husband, the host or the vicar, as the case may be. Sometimes he pays the whole price himself. Occasionally he may get a contribution from the others. But in any case it is he who makes the contract. It would be a fiction to say that the contract was made by all the family, or all the guests, or all the choir, and that he was only an agent for them. Take this very case. It would be absurd to say that the twins of three years old were parties to the contract or that the father was making the contract on their behalf as if they were principals. It would equally be a mistake to say that in any of these instances there was a trust. The transaction bears no resemblance to a trust. There was no trust fund and no trust property. No, the real truth is that in each instance, the father, the host or the vicar, was making a contract himself for the benefit of the whole party. In short, a contract by one for the benefit of third persons.

What is the position when such a contract is broken? At present the law says that the only one who can sue is the one who made the contract. None of the rest of the party can sue, even though the contract was made for their benefit. But when that one does sue, what damages can he recover? Is he limited to his own loss? Or can he recover for the others? Suppose the holiday firm puts the family into a hotel which is only half built and the visitors have to sleep on the floor? Or suppose the restaurant is fully booked and the guests have to go away, hungry and angry, having spent so much on fares to get there? Or suppose the coach leaves the choir stranded half-way and they have to hire cars to get home? None of them individually can sue. Only the father, the host or the vicar can sue. He can, of course, recover his own damages. But can he not recover for the others? I think he can. The case comes within the principle stated by Lush L.J. in *Lloyd's v. Harper* (1880) 16 Ch.D. 290, at 291: "... I consider it to be an established rule of law that where a contract is made with A for the benefit of B, A can sue on the contract for the benefit of B, and recover all that B could have recovered if the contract had been made with B himself."

It has been suggested that Lush L.J. was thinking of a contract in which A was trustee for B. But I do not think so. He was a common lawyer speaking of the common law. His words were quoted with considerable approval by Lord Pearce in *Beswick v. Beswick*. I have myself often quoted them. I think they should be accepted as correct, at any rate so long as the law forbids the third persons themselves to sue for damages. It is the only way in which a just result can be achieved. Take the instance I have put. The guests ought to recover from the restaurant their wasted fares. The choir ought to recover the cost of hiring the taxis home. There is no one to recover for them except the one who made the contract for their benefit. He should be able to recover the expense to which they have been put, and pay it over to them. Once recovered, it will be money had and received to their use. (They might even, if desired, be joined as plaintiffs.) If he can recover for the expense, he should also be able to recover for the discomfort, vexation and upset which the whole party have suffered by reason of the breach of contract, recompensing them accordingly out of what he recovers.

Applying the principles to this case, I think that the figure of £1,100 was about right. It would, I think, have been excessive if it had been awarded only for the damage suffered by Mr. Jackson himself. But when extended to his wife and children, I do not think it is excessive. People look forward to a holiday. They expect the promises to be fulfilled. When it fails, they are greatly disappointed and upset. It is difficult to assess in terms of money; but it is the task of the judges to do the best they can. I see no reason to interfere with the total award of £1,100.

I would therefore dismiss this appeal.

ORR LJ: I agree.

JAMES LJ: In this case, Mr. Jackson, as found by the judge on the evidence, was in need of a holiday at the end of 1970. He was able to afford a holiday for himself and his family. According to the form which he completed, which was the form of Horizon Holidays Ltd., he booked what was a family holiday. The wording of that form might in certain circumstances give rise to a contract in which the person signing the form is acting as his own principal and as agent for others. In the circumstances of this case, as indicated by Lord Denning M.R. it would be wholly unrealistic to regard this contract as other than one made by Mr. Jackson for a family holiday. The judge found that he did not get a family holiday. The costs were some £1,200. When he came back he felt no benefit. His evidence was to the effect that, without any exaggeration, he felt terrible. He said: "The only thing, I was pleased to be back, very pleased, but I had nothing at all from that holiday." For my part, on the issue of damages in this matter, I am quite content to say that £1,100 awarded was the right and proper figure in those circumstances. I would dismiss the appeal.

Appeal dismissed. Leave to appeal to the House of Lords refused.

NOTE

Jackson was disapproved by Lord Wilberforce in *Woodar Investment Development Ltd v Wimpey Construction UK Ltd*, [1980] 1 WLR 277 (HL), but, in the same case, Lord Keith (at 297) explained *Jackson* as a case where the promisee's own loss was augmented by the losses of his family, and Lord Scarman (at 300) said, "If the opportunity arises I hope the House will reconsider *Tweddle v. Atkinson* ... and the other cases which stand guard over this unjust rule."

Midland Silicones Ltd v Scruttons Ltd. [1962] AC 446 (HL). Scruttons Ltd. were stevedores hired to handle a drum of silicone diffusion pump fluid from the ship to a lorry provided by the consignee, Midland Silicones Ltd. The stevedores were just lowering the drum on to the lorry when by their negligence it was dropped and some of the contents were lost. The loss was assessed at £593 12s. By virtue of the bill of lading between the shipper and the carrier, the carrier who moved the drum from New York to London was not to be liable for more than $500 (£179 1s.) in the event of damage. By virtue of the stevedoring contract between the carrier and Scruttons Ltd., Scruttons Ltd. agreed to be liable for damage while they were handling the drum, but they were entitled to "such protection as is afforded by the terms, conditions and exceptions of the bills of lading." By virtue of the sale of goods contract between the shipper and Midland, the title in the drum passed from the shipper, or seller, to Midland while it was on board the ship, and thereafter Midland became subject to the same rights in respect of the drum as if the contract in the bill of lading had been made directly with Midland. There was no express contract between Midland and Scruttons Ltd. Diplock J. directed judgment for Midland for £593 12s. 2d. plus interest. The Court of Appeal dismissed an appeal. The House of Lords affirmed the Court of Appeal. On the question whether Scruttons Ltd., who had no contract with Midland, could take advantage of the clause in the bill of lading limiting the carrier's liability to $500, the House, with the exception of Lord Denning, who dissented, denied the protection on the ground that a third party cannot take advantage of a clause in a contract to which he is not a party. VISCOUNT SIMONDS: But, my Lords, all these contentions were but a prelude to one which, had your Lordships accepted it, would have been the foundation of a dramatic decision of this House. It was argued, if I understood the argument, that if A contracts with B to do something for the benefit of C, then C, though not a party to the contract, can sue A to enforce it. This is independent of whether C is A's undisclosed principal or a beneficiary under a trust of which A is trustee. It is sufficient that C is an "interested person." My Lords, if this is the law of England, then, subject always to the question of consideration, no doubt, if the carrier purports to contract for the benefit of the stevedore, the latter can enforce the contract. Whether that premiss is satisfied in this case is another matter, but, since the argument is advanced, it is right that I should deal with it. Learned counsel for the respondents met it, as they had successfully done in the courts below, by asserting a principle which is, I suppose, as well established as any in our law, a "fundamental" principle, as Lord Haldane called it in *Dunlop Pneumatic Tyre Co. Ltd. v. Selfridge & Co. Ltd.*, [1915] A.C. 847, an "elementary" principle, as it has been called times without number, that only a person who is a party to a contract can sue upon it. "Our law," said Lord Haldane, "knows nothing of a *jus quaesitum tertio* arising by way of contract." Learned counsel for the respondents claimed that this was the orthodox view and asked your Lordships to reject any proposition that impinged upon it. To that invitation I readily respond. For to me heterodoxy, or, as some might say, heresy, is not the more attractive because it is dignified by the name of reform. Nor will I easily be led by an undiscerning zeal for some abstract kind of justice to ignore our first duty, which is to administer justice according to law, the law which is established for us by Act of Parliament or the binding authority of precedent. The law is developed by the application of old principles to new circumstances. Therein lies its genius. Its reform by the abrogation of those principles is the task not of the courts of law but of Parliament. Therefore I reject the argument for the appellants under this head and invite your Lordships to say that certain statements which appear to support it in recent cases such as *Smith & Snipes Hall Farm v. River Douglas Catchment Board*, [1949] 2 K.B. 500, and *White v. John Warwick & Co. Ltd.*, [1953] 1 W.L.R. 1285, must be rejected. If the principle of *jus quaesitum tertio* is to be introduced into our law, it must be done by Parliament after a due consideration of its merits and demerits. I should not be prepared to give it my support without a greater knowledge than I at present possess of its operation in other systems of law.

LORD DENNING (dissenting): [T]he question is: Did the owners of the goods impliedly authorize the carrier to employ stevedores on the terms that their liability should be limited to $500? I think they did. ... The carrier simply passed on the self-same limitation as he himself had, and this must have been within his implied authority. It seems to me that when the owner of goods allows the person in possession of them to make a contract in regard to them, then he cannot go back on the terms of the contract, if they are such as he expressly or impliedly authorized to be made, even though he was no party to the contract and could not sue or be sued upon it. It is just the same as if he stood by and watched it being made. And his successor in title is in no better position.

[Lord Reid pointed out that the House had been informed that questions of this kind frequently arise and that this action had been brought as a test case. How will the result affect the revision of the standard forms of the three contracts involved here?]

NEW ZEALAND SHIPPING CO LTD V AM SATTERTHWAITE & CO LTD (THE EURYMEDON)
[1975] AC 154 (PC)

LORD WILBERFORCE: The facts of this case are not in dispute. An expensive drilling machine was received on board the ship *Eurymedon* at Liverpool for transhipment to Wellington pursuant to the terms of a bill of lading no. 1262 dated June 5, 1964. The shipper was the maker of the drill, Ajax Machine Tool Co. Ltd. ("the consignor"). The bill of lading was issued by agents for the Federal Steam Navigation Co. Ltd. ("the carrier"). The consignee was A.M. Satterthwaite & Co. Ltd. of Christchurch, New Zealand ("the consignee"). For several years before 1964 the New Zealand Shipping Co. Ltd. ("the stevedore") had carried out all stevedoring work in Wellington in respect of the ships owned by the carrier, which was a wholly owned subsidiary of the stevedore. In addition to this stevedoring work the stevedore generally acted as agent for the carrier in New Zealand; and in such capacity as general agent (not in the course of their stevedoring functions) the stevedore received the bill of lading at Wellington on July 31, 1964. Clause 1 of the bill of lading, on the construction of which this case turns, was in the same terms as bills of lading usually issued by the stevedore and its associated companies in respect of ordinary cargo carried by their ships from the United Kingdom to New Zealand. The consignee became the holder of the bill of lading and owner of the drill prior to August 14, 1964. On that date the drill was damaged as a result of the stevedore's negligence during unloading.

At the foot of the first page of the bill of lading the following words were printed in small capitals: "In accepting this bill of lading the shipper, consignee and the owners of the goods, and the holders of this bill of lading agree to be bound by all of its conditions, exceptions and provisions whether written, printed or stamped on the front or back hereof." On the back of the bill of lading a number of clauses were printed in small type. It is only necessary to set out the following. The first and third paragraph of clause 1 provided:

This bill of lading shall have effect (a) subject to the provisions of any legislation giving effect to the International Convention for the unification of certain rules relating to bills of lading dated Brussels, August 25, 1924, or to similar effect which is compulsorily applicable to the contract of carriage evidenced hereby and (b) where no such legislation is applicable as if the Carriage of Goods by Sea Act 1924, of Great Britain and the rules scheduled thereto applied hereto and were incorporated herein. Nothing herein contained shall be deemed to be a surrender by the carrier of any of his rights or immunities or an increase of any of his responsibilities or liabilities under the provisions of the said legislation or Act and rules (as the case may be) and the said provisions shall not (unless and to the extent that they are by law compulsorily applicable) apply to that portion of the contract evidenced by this bill of lading which relates to forwarding under clause 4 hereof. If anything herein contained be inconsistent with or repugnant to the said provisions, it shall to the extent of such inconsistency or repugnance and no further be null and void. ...

It is hereby expressly agreed that no servant or agent of the carrier (including every independent contractor from time to time employed by the carrier) shall in any circumstances whatsoever be under any liability whatsoever to the shipper, consignee or owner of the goods or to any holder of this bill of lading for any loss or damage or delay of whatsoever kind arising or resulting directly or indirectly from any act neglect or default on his part while acting in the course of or in connection with his employment and, without prejudice to the generality of the foregoing provisions in this clause, every exemption, limitation, condition and liberty herein contained and every right, exemption from liability, defence and immunity of whatsoever nature applicable to the carrier or to which the carrier is entitled hereunder shall also be available and shall extend to protect every such servant or agent of the carrier acting as aforesaid and for the purpose of all the foregoing provisions of this clause the carrier is or shall be deemed to be acting as agent or trustee on behalf of and for the benefit of all persons who are or might be his servants or agents from time to time (including independent contractors as aforesaid) and all such persons shall to this extent be or be deemed to be parties to the contract in or evidenced by this bill of lading.

Clause 11 provided:

The carrier will not be accountable for goods of any description beyond £100 in respect of any one package or unit unless the value thereof shall have been stated in writing both on the broker's order which must be obtained before shipment and on the shipping note presented on shipment and extra freight agreed upon and paid and bills of lading signed with a declaration of the nature and value of the goods appearing thereon. When the value is declared and extra freight agreed as aforesaid the carrier's liability shall not exceed such value or pro rata on that basis in the event of partial loss or damage.

No declaration as to the nature and value of the goods having appeared in the bill of lading, and no extra freight having been agreed upon or paid, it was acknowledged by the consignee that the liability of the carrier was accordingly limited to £100 by the application of clause 11 of the bill of lading. Moreover, the incorporation in the bill of lading of the rules scheduled to the *Carriage of Goods by Sea Act 1924* meant that the carrier and the ship were discharged from all liability in respect of damage to the drill unless suit was brought against them within one year after delivery. No action was commenced until April 1967, when the consignee sued the stevedore in negligence, claiming £880 the cost of repairing the damaged drill.

The question in the appeal is whether the stevedore can take the benefit of the time limitation provision. The starting point, in discussion of this question, is provided by the House of Lords decision in *Midland Silicones Ltd. v. Scruttons Ltd.* [1962] A.C. 446. There is no need to question or even to qualify that case in so far as it affirms the general proposition that a contract between two parties cannot be sued on by a third person even though the contract is expressed to be for his benefit. Nor is it necessary to disagree with anything which was said to the same effect in the Australian case of *Wilson v. Darling Island Stevedoring and Lighterage Co. Ltd.* (1956) 95 C.L.R. 43. Each of these cases was dealing with a simple case of a contract the benefit of which was sought to be taken by a third person not a party to it, and the emphatic pronouncements in the speeches and judgments were directed to this situation. But *Midland Silicones* left open the case where one of the parties contracts as agent for the third person: in particular Lord Reid's speech spelt out, in four propositions, the prerequisites for the validity of such an agency contract. There is of course nothing unique to this case in the conception of agency contracts: well known and common instances exist in the field of hire purchase, of bankers' commercial credits and other transactions. Lord Reid said, at p. 474:

> I can see a possibility of success of the agency argument if (first) the bill of lading makes it clear that the stevedore is intended to be protected by the provisions in it which limit liability, (secondly) the bill of lading makes it clear that the carrier, in addition to contracting for these provisions on his own behalf, is also contracting as agent for the stevedore that these provisions should apply to the stevedore, (thirdly) the carrier has authority from the stevedore to do that, or perhaps later ratification by the stevedore would suffice, and (fourthly) that any difficulties about consideration moving from the stevedore were overcome. And then to affect the consignee it would be necessary to show that the provisions of the Bills of Lading Act 1855 apply.

The question in this appeal is whether the contract satisfies these propositions.

Clause 1 of the bill of lading, whatever the defects in its drafting, is clear in its relevant terms. The carrier, on his own account, stipulates for certain exemptions and immunities: among these is that conferred by article III, rule 6, of the Hague Rules which discharges the carrier from all liability for loss or damage unless suit is brought within one year after delivery. In addition to these stipulations on his own account, the carrier as agent for, inter alios, independent contractors stipulates for the same exemptions.

Much was made of the fact that the carrier also contracts as agent for numerous other persons; the relevance of this argument is not apparent. It cannot be disputed that among such independent contractors, for whom, as agent, the carrier contracted, is the appellant company which habitually acts as stevedore in New Zealand by arrangement with the carrier and which is, moreover, the parent company of the carrier. The carrier was, indisputably, authorised by the appellant to contract as its agent for the purposes of clause 1. All of this is quite straightforward and was accepted by all the judges in New Zealand. The only question was, and is, the fourth question presented by Lord Reid, namely that of consideration.

It was on this point that the Court of Appeal differed from Beattie J., holding that it had not been shown that any consideration for the shipper's promise as to exemption moved from the promisee, i.e., the appellant company.

If the choice, and the antithesis, is between a gratuitous promise, and a promise for consideration, as it must be in the absence of a tertium quid, there can be little doubt which, in commercial reality, this is. The whole contract is of a commercial character, involving service on one side, rates of payment on the other, and qualifying stipulations as to both. The relations of all parties to each other are commercial relations entered into for business reasons of ultimate profit. To describe one set of promises, in this context, as gratuitous, or nudum pactum, seems paradoxical and is prima facie implausible. It is only the precise analysis of this complex of relations into the classical offer and acceptance, with identifiable consideration, that seems to present difficulty, but this same difficulty exists in many situations of daily life, e.g., sales at auction; supermarket purchases; boarding an omnibus; purchasing a train ticket; tenders for the supply of goods; offers of rewards; acceptance by post; warranties of authority by agents; manufacturers' guarantees; gratuitous bailments; bankers' commercial credits. These are all examples which show that English law, having committed itself to a rather technical and schematic doctrine of contract, in application takes a practical approach, often at the cost of forcing the facts to fit uneasily into the marked slots of offer, acceptance and consideration.

In their Lordship's opinion the present contract presents much less difficulty than many of those above referred to. It is one of carriage from Liverpool to Wellington. The carrier assumes an obligation to transport the goods and to discharge at the port of arrival. The goods are to be carried and discharged, so the transaction is inherently contractual. It is contemplated that a part of this contract, viz. discharge, may be performed by independent contractors—viz. the appellant. By clause 1 of the bill of lading the shipper agrees to exempt from liability the carrier, his servants and independent contractors in respect of the performance of this contract of carriage. Thus, if the carriage, including the discharge, is wholly carried out by the carrier, he is exempt. If part is carried out by him, and part by his servants, he and they are exempt. If part is carried out by him and part by an independent contractor, he and the independent contractor are exempt. The exemption is designed to cover the whole carriage from loading to discharge, by whomsoever it is performed: the performance attracts the exemption or immunity in favour of whoever the performer turns out to be. There is possibly more than one way of analysing this business transaction into the necessary components; that which their Lordships would accept is to say that the bill of lading brought into existence a bargain initially unilateral but capable of becoming mutual, between the shipper and the appellant, made through the carrier as agent. This became a full contract when the appellant performed services by discharging the goods. The performance of these services for the benefit of the shipper was the consideration for the agreement by the shipper that the appellant should have the benefit of the exemptions and limitations contained in the bill of lading. The conception of a "unilateral" contract of this kind was recognised in *Great Northern Railway Co. v. Witham* (1873) L.R. 9 C.P. 16 and is well established. This way of regarding the matter is very close to if not identical to that accepted by Beattie J.

in the Supreme Court: he analysed the transaction as one of an offer open to accept-ance by action such as was found in *Carlill v. Carbolic Smoke Ball Co.* [1893] 1 Q.B. 256. But whether one describes the shipper's promise to exempt as an offer to be accepted by performance or as a promise in exchange for an act seems in the present context to be a matter of semantics. The words of Bowen L.J. in *Carlill v. Carbolic Smoke Ball Co.* [1893] 1 Q.B. 256, 268: "why should not an offer be made to all the world which is to ripen into a contract with anybody who comes forward and per-forms the condition?" seem to bridge both conceptions: he certainly seems to draw no distinction between an offer which matures into a contract when accepted and a promise which matures into a contract after performance, and, though in some special contexts (such as in connection with the right to withdraw) some further refinement may be needed, either analysis may be equally valid. On the main point in the appeal, their Lordships are in substantial agreement with Beattie J.

The following points require mention:

1. In their Lordships' opinion, consideration may quite well be provided by the appellant, as suggested, even though (or if) it was already under an obligation to discharge to the carrier. (There is no direct evidence of the existence or nature of this obligation, but their Lordships are prepared to assume it.) An agreement to do an act which the promisor is under an existing obligation to a third party to do, may quite well amount to valid consideration and does so in the present case: the promisee obtains the benefit of a direct obligation which he can enforce. This proposition is illustrated and supported by *Scotson v. Pegg* (1861) 6 H. & N. 295 which their Lordships consider to be good law.

2. The consignee is entitled to the benefit of, and is bound by, the stipulations in the bill of lading by his acceptance of it and request for delivery of the goods thereunder. This is shown by *Brandt v. Liverpool, Brazil and River Plate Steam Navigation Co. Ltd.* [1924] 1 K.B. 575 and a line of earlier cases. The Bills of Lading Act 1855, section 1 (in New Zealand the Mercantile Law Act 1908, sec-tion 13) gives partial statutory recognition to this rule, but, where the statute does not apply, as it may well not do in this case, the previously established law remains effective.

3. The appellant submitted, in the alternative, an argument that, quite apart from contract, exemptions from, or limitation of, liability in tort may be conferred by mere consent on the part of the party who may be injured. As their Lordships consider that the appellant ought to succeed in contract, they prefer to express no opinion upon this argument: to evaluate it requires elaborate discussion.

4. A clause very similar to the present was given effect by a United States District Court in *Carle & Montanari Inc. v. American Export Isbrandtsen Lines Inc.* [1968] 1 Lloyd's Rep. 260. The carrier in that case contracted, in an exemption clause, as agent, for, inter alios, all stevedores and other independent con-tractors, and although it is no doubt true that the law in the United States is more liberal than ours as regards third party contracts, their Lordships see no reason why the law of the Commonwealth should be more restrictive and technical as regards agency contracts. Commercial considerations should have the same force on both sides of the Pacific.

In the opinion of their Lordships, to give the appellant the benefit of the exemp-tions and limitations contained in the bill of lading is to give effect to the clear intentions of a commercial document, and can be given within existing principles. They see no reason to strain the law or the facts in order to defeat these intentions. It should not be overlooked that the effect of denying validity to the clause would be to encourage actions against servants, agents and independent contractors in order to get round exemptions (which are almost invariable and often compulsory) accepted by shippers against carriers, the existence, and presumed efficacy, of which is reflected in the rates of freight. They see no attraction in this consequence.

Their Lordships will humbly advise Her Majesty that the appeal be allowed and the judgment of Beattie J. restored. The respondent must pay the costs of the appeal and in the Court of Appeal.

[Viscount Dilhorne dissented.]

NOTES

1. In *ITO v Miida Electronics Ltd*, [1986] 1 SCR 752, the Supreme Court of Canada followed the *New Zealand Shipping* case.

2. In *Greenwood Shopping Plaza Ltd v Beattie*, [1980] 2 SCR 228, the lessor of business premises covenanted with its tenant to insure against fire. A loss by fire occurred, allegedly caused by the negligence of two of the lessee's employees. The Supreme Court of Canada held that the employees were not entitled to rely on the lease to limit their liability.

LONDON DRUGS LTD V KUEHNE & NAGEL INTERNATIONAL LTD
[1992] 3 SCR 299

IACOBUCCI J (L'Heureux-Dubé, Sopinka, and Cory JJ concurring): This appeal and cross-appeal raise two principal issues: (1) the duty of care owed by employees to their employer's customers, and (2) the extent to which employees can claim the benefit of their employer's contractual limitation of liability clause.

I. FACTS

The facts are not complicated. On August 31, 1981, London Drugs Limited (hereinafter "appellant"), delivered a transformer weighing some 7,500 pounds to Kuehne and Nagel International Ltd. (hereinafter "Kuehne & Nagel") for storage pursuant to the terms and conditions of a standard form contract of storage. The transformer had been purchased from its manufacturer, Federal Pioneer Limited, and was to be installed in the new warehouse facility being built by the appellant. The contract of storage included the following limitation of liability clause:

> LIABILITY—Sec. 11(a) The responsibility of a warehouseman in the absence of written provisions is the reasonable care and diligence required by the law.
>
> (b) The warehouseman's liability on any one package is limited to $40 unless the holder has declared in writing a valuation in excess of $40 and paid the additional charge specified to cover warehouse liability.

With full knowledge and understanding of this clause, the appellant chose not to obtain additional insurance from Kuehne & Nagel and instead arranged for its own all-risk coverage. At the time of entering into the contract, the appellant knew, or can be assumed to have known, that Kuehne & Nagel's employees would be responsible for moving and upkeeping the transformer.

On September 22, 1981, Dennis Gerrard Brassart and Hank Vanwinkel (hereinafter "respondents"), both employees of Kuehne & Nagel, received orders to load the transformer onto a truck which would deliver it to the appellant's new warehouse. The respondents attempted to move the transformer by lifting it with two forklift vehicles when safe practice required it to be lifted from above using brackets which were attached to the transformer and which were clearly marked for that purpose. While being lifted, the transformer toppled over and fell causing damages in the amount of $33,955.41.

Alleging breach of contract and negligence, the appellant brought an action for damages against Kuehne & Nagel, Federal Pioneer Limited, and the respondents. In a judgment rendered on April 14, 1986, Trainor J. of the Supreme Court of British Columbia held that the respondents were personally liable for the full amount of damages, limiting Kuehne & Nagel's liability to $40 and dismissing the claim against Federal Pioneer Limited. On March 30, 1990, the majority of the Court of Appeal allowed the respondents' appeal and reduced their liability to $40. The appellant was granted leave to appeal to this Court on December 7, 1990. The respondents have cross appealed in order to argue that they should be completely free of liability. A written intervention was made by the General Truck Drivers & Helpers Local Union No. 31, the union authorized to negotiate the collective agreement with Kuehne & Nagel which, at all material times, governed the respondents' employment relationship.

• • •

III. ISSUES

The cross-appeal raises the following question:

(1) Did the respondents, acting in the course of their employment and performing the very essence of their employer's contractual obligations with the appellant, owe a duty of care to the appellant?

If so, it is not disputed before this Court that the respondents were negligent in their handling of the appellant's transformer. In other words, the finding of the trial judge that the respondents breached their duty of care is not contested. Moreover, it is not disputed that it is the respondents' negligence which was the cause of the damages to the transformer and that these damages amount to $33,955.41. The next question which is raised by the appeal would thus become one of the appropriate liability for this breach, namely:

(2) Can the respondents obtain the benefit of the limitation of liability clause contained in the contract of storage between their employer and the appellant so as to limit their liability to $40?

For reasons that follow, I am of the opinion that both questions should be answered in the affirmative. By so concluding, both the cross-appeal and the appeal should therefore be dismissed. ...

(A) SHOULD THE DOCTRINE OF PRIVITY BE RELAXED?

Without doubt, major reforms to the rule denying third parties the right to enforce contractual provisions made for their benefit must come from the legislature. Although I have strong reservations about the rigid retention of a doctrine that has undergone systematic and substantial attack, privity of contract is an established principle in the law of contracts and should not be discarded lightly. Simply to abolish the doctrine of privity or to ignore it, without more, would represent a major change to the common law involving complex and uncertain ramifications. This Court has in the past indicated an unwillingness to sanction judge-made changes of this magnitude. ...

This Court has also recognized, however, that in appropriate circumstances courts have not only the power but the duty to make incremental changes to the common law to see that it reflects the emerging needs and values of our society. ... It is my view that the present appeal is an appropriate situation for making such an incremental change to the doctrine of privity of contract in order to allow the respondents to benefit from the limitation of liability clause.

As we have seen earlier, the doctrine of privity has come under serious attack for its refusal to recognize the right of a third party beneficiary to enforce contractual provisions made for his or her benefit. Law reformers, commentators and judges have pointed out the gaps that sometimes exist between contract theory on the one hand, and commercial reality and justice on the other. We have also seen that many jurisdictions around the world, including Quebec and the United States, have chosen from an early point (as early as the doctrine became "settled" in the English common law) to recognize third party beneficiary rights in certain circumstances. As noted by the appellant, the common law recognizes certain exceptions to the doctrine, such as agency and trust, which enable courts, in appropriate circumstances, to arrive at results which conform with the true intentions of the contracting parties and commercial reality. However, as many have observed, the availability of these exceptions does not always correspond with their need. Accordingly, this Court should not be precluded from developing the common law so as to recognize a further exception to privity of contract merely on the ground that some exceptions already exist.

While these comments may not, in themselves, justify doing away with the doctrine of privity, they nonetheless give a certain context to the principles that this Court is now dealing with. This context clearly supports in my view some type of reform or relaxation to the law relating to third party beneficiaries. Again, I reiterate that any substantial amendment to the doctrine of privity is a matter properly left with the legislature. But this does not mean that courts should shut their eyes to criticisms when faced with an opportunity, as in the case at bar, to make a very specific incremental change to the common law.

At this point, it is useful to recall briefly the salient facts with which this Court is seized. The appellant entered into a contract with Kuehne & Nagel for certain services, namely, the storing of its transformer. When the contract was signed, the appellant knew that it contained a clause limiting the liability of the "warehouseman" to $40. It also knew, or can be assumed to have known, that Kuehne & Nagel employed many individuals and that these employees would be directly involved in the storing of the transformer. The appellant chose not to obtain additional insurance from Kuehne & Nagel and instead arranged for its own all-risk coverage. When the damages to the transformer occurred, the respondents, two of Kuehne & Nagel's employees, were acting in the course of their employment and were performing services directly related to the contract of storage. The appellant is now seeking to recover the full amount of damages from these employees since it can only obtain $40 from the employer. As a defence to such a claim, the respondents are attempting to obtain the benefit of the limitation of liability clause.

There are few principled reasons for upholding the doctrine of privity in the circumstances of this case. Maintaining the alleged status quo by itself is an unhelpful consideration since I am considering whether or not a relaxation, or change, to the law should be made. Similarly, most of the traditional reasons or justifications behind the doctrine are of little application in cases such as this one, when a third party beneficiary is relying on a contractual provision as a defence in an action brought by one of the contracting parties. There are no concerns about double recovery or floodgates of litigation brought by third party beneficiaries. The fact that a contract is a very personal affair, affecting only the parties to it, is simply a restatement of the doctrine of privity rather than a reason for its maintenance. Nor is there any concern about "reciprocity," that is, there is no concern that it would be unjust to allow a party to sue on a contract when he or she cannot be sued on it.

Moreover, recognizing a right for a third party beneficiary to rely on a limitation of liability clause should have relatively little impact on the rights of contracting parties to rescind or vary their contracts, in comparison with the recognition of a third party right to sue on a contract. In the end, the most that can be said against the extension of exceptions to the doctrine of privity in this case is that the respondent employees are mere donees and have provided no consideration for the contractual limitation of liability.

The doctrine of privity fails to appreciate the special considerations which arise from the relationships of employer-employee and employer-customer. There is clearly an identity of interest between the employer and his or her employees as far as the performance of the employer's contractual obligations is concerned. When a person contracts with an employer for certain services, there can be little doubt in most cases that employees will have the prime responsibilities related to the performance of the obligations which arise under the contract. This was the case in the present appeal, clearly to the knowledge of the appellant. While such a similarity or closeness might not be present when an employer performs his or her obligations through someone who is not an employee, it is virtually always present when employees are involved. Of course, I am in no way suggesting that employees are a party to their employer's contracts in the traditional sense so that they can bring an action on the contract or be sued for breach of contract. However, when an employer and a customer enter into a contract for services and include a clause limiting the liability of the employer for damages arising from what will normally be conduct contemplated by the contracting parties to be performed by the employer's employees, and in fact so performed, there is simply no valid reason for denying the benefit of the clause to employees who perform the contractual obligations. The nature and scope of the limitation of liability clause in such a case coincides essentially with the nature and scope of the contractual obligations performed by the third party beneficiaries (employees).

Upholding a strict application of the doctrine of privity in the circumstances of this case would also have the effect of allowing the appellant to circumvent or escape the limitation of liability clause to which it had expressly consented. ...

In a similar fashion, it would be absurd in the circumstances of this case to let the appellant go around the limitation of liability clause by suing the respondent employees in tort. The appellant consented to limit the "warehouseman's" liability to $40 for anything that would happen during the performance of the contract. When the loss occurred, the respondents were acting in the course of their employment and performing the very services, albeit negligently, for which the appellant had contracted with Kuehne & Nagel. The appellant cannot obtain more than $40 from Kuehne & Nagel, whether the action is based in contract or in tort, because of the limitation of liability clause. However, resorting to exactly the same actions, it is trying to obtain the full amount from the individuals ("warehousemen") who were directly responsible for the storing of its goods in accordance with the contract. As stated earlier, there is an identity of interest between the respondents and Kuehne & Nagel as far as performance of the latter's contractual obligations is concerned. When these facts are taken into account, and it is recalled that the appellant knew the role to be played by employees pursuant to the contract, it is clear to me that this Court is witnessing an attempt in effect to "circumvent or escape a contractual exclusion or limitation of liability for the act or omission that would constitute the tort." In my view, we should not sanction such an endeavour in the name of privity of contract.

Finally, there are sound policy reasons why the doctrine of privity should be relaxed in the circumstances of this case. A clause such as one in a contract of storage limiting the liability of a "warehouseman" to $40 in the absence of a declaration by the owner of the goods of their value and the payment of an additional insurance fee makes perfect commercial sense. It enables the contracting parties to allocate the risk of damage to the goods and to procure insurance accordingly. If the owner declares the value of the goods, which he or she alone knows, and pays the additional premium, the bargain will have placed the entire risk on the shoulders of the "warehouseman." On the other hand, if the owner refuses the offer of additional coverage, the bargain will have placed only a limited risk on the "warehouseman" and the owner will be left with the burden of procuring private insurance if he or she decides to diminish its own risk. In either scenario, the parties to the contract agree to a certain allocation and then proceed, based on this agreement, to make additional insurance arrangements if required. It stretches commercial credulity to suggest that a customer, acting prudently, will not obtain insurance because he or she is looking to the employees for recovery when generally little or nothing is known about the financial capacity and professional skills of the employees involved. That does not make sense in the modern world.

In addition, employees such as the respondents do not reasonably expect to be subject to unlimited liability for damages that occur in the performance of the contract when said contract specifically limits the liability of the "warehouseman" to a fixed amount. According to modern commercial practice, an employer such as Kuehne & Nagel performs its contractual obligations with a party such as the appellant through its employees. As far as the contractual obligations are concerned, there is an identity of interest between the employer and the employees. It simply does not make commercial sense to hold that the term "warehouseman" was not intended to cover the respondent employees and as a result to deny them the benefit of the limitation of liability clause for a loss which occurred during the performance of the very services contracted for. Holding the employees liable in these circumstances could lead to serious injustice especially when one considers that the financial position of the affected employees could vary considerably such that, for example, more well off employees would be sued and left to look for contribution from their less well off colleagues. Such a result also creates uncertainty and requires excessive expenditures on insurance in that it defeats the allocations of risk specifically made by the contracting parties and the reasonable expectations of everyone involved, including the employees. When parties enter into commercial agreements and decide that one of them and its employees will benefit from limited liability, or when these parties choose language such as "warehouseman" which implies that employees will also benefit from a protection, the doctrine of privity should not stand in the way of commercial reality and justice.

For all the above reasons, I conclude that it is entirely appropriate in the circumstances of this case to call for a relaxation of the doctrine of privity.

(B) HOW SHOULD THE DOCTRINE OF PRIVITY BE RELAXED?

Regardless of the desirability of making a particular change to the law, I have already noted that complex changes with uncertain ramifications should be left to the legislature. Our power and duty as a court to adapt and develop the common law must only be exercised generally in an incremental fashion. This is particularly important when, as here, changes to substantive law are concerned, as opposed to changes to procedural law. The respondents submit that this Court should relax the doctrine of privity so as to permit non-contracting employees to take the benefit of any immunities or limitations of liability granted to their employer. They offer three requirements for the application of this new exception, namely: (1) there is a contractual limitation of liability between an employer and another party; (2) the loss occurs during the employer's performance of its contractual obligations to that party; and (3) the employees are acting in the course of their employment when the loss occurs.

In my opinion, not only does the respondents' submission go beyond what is required to dispose of the present appeal, but it also does not represent an incremental change to the law. The main problem I have is with their first requirement. As we have seen earlier, the criticisms and statutory inroads into the doctrine of privity of contract have mostly, if not exclusively, occurred with respect to third party beneficiaries. That is, with respect to third parties to whom contracting parties have extended, either expressly or impliedly, some form of benefit arising under the contract. However, this is not the thrust of the respondents' submission. In essence, what they are requesting is the recognition of a third party right, or ius tertii, for complete strangers to their employer's contracts, without any regard whatsoever to the intention of the contracting parties. While this may be an appropriate step for the legislature, it is not the type of incremental change that this Court should endorse.

In my opinion, a threshold requirement for employees to obtain the benefit of their employer's contractual limitation of liability clause is the express or implied stipulation by the contracting parties that the benefit of the clause will also be shared by said employees. Without such a stipulation, it is my view that the employees are in a no better situation than this Court held those employees involved in *Greenwood Shopping Plaza*, supra, to be in, and should not therefore be able to rely on the clause as a means of defence. This Court found that the employees were strangers to the contract, as I discussed above. As for the other requirements proposed by the respondents, I agree with their substance although I would express them in a different manner.

In the end, the narrow question before this Court is: in what circumstances should employees be entitled to benefit from a limitation of liability clause found in a contract between their employer and the plaintiff (customer)? Keeping in mind the comments made earlier and the circumstances of this appeal, I am of the view that employees may obtain such a benefit if the following requirements are satisfied:

(1) The limitation of liability clause must, either expressly or impliedly, extend its benefit to the employees (or employee) seeking to rely on it; and

(2) the employees (or employee) seeking the benefit of the limitation of liability clause must have been acting in the course of their employment and must have been performing the very services provided for in the contract between their employer and the plaintiff (customer) when the loss occurred.

Although these requirements, if satisfied, permit a departure from the strict application of the doctrine of privity of contract, they represent an incremental change to the common law. I say "incremental change" for a number of reasons.

First and foremost, this new exception to privity is dependent on the intention of the contracting parties. An employer and his or her customer may choose the appropriate language when drafting their contacts so as to extend, expressly or impliedly, the benefit of any limitation of liability to employees. It is their intention as stipulated in the contract which will determine whether the first requirement is met. In this connection, I agree with the view that the intention to extend the benefit of a limitation of liability clause to employees may be express or implied in all the circumstances: see e.g. *Mayfair Fabrics v. Henley*, 244 A.2d 344 (N.J. 1968); *Employers Casualty Co. v. Wainwright*, 473 P. 2d 181 (Colo. Ct. App. 1970) (cert. denied).

Second, taken as a whole, this new exception involves very similar benchmarks to the recognized agency exception, applied in *The Eurymedon* and by this Court in *ITO-International Terminal Operators* [[1986] 1 SCR 752]. As discussed in the latter decision, the four requirements for the agency exception were inspired from the following passage of Lord Reid's judgment in *Midland Silicones*, supra (at p. 474):

> I can see a possibility of success of the agency argument if (first) the bill of lading makes it clear that the stevedore is intended to be protected by the provisions in it which limit liability, (secondly) the bill of lading makes it clear that the carrier, in addition to contracting for these provisions on his own behalf, is also contracting as agent for the stevedore that these provisions should apply to the stevedore, (thirdly) the carrier has authority from the stevedore to do that, or perhaps later ratification by the stevedore would suffice, and (fourthly) that any difficulties about consideration moving from the stevedore were overcome.

The first requirement of both exceptions is virtually identical. The second and third requirements of the agency exception are supplied by the identity of interest between an employer and his or her employees as far as the performance of contractual obligations are concerned; this is implicit in the recognition of this new exception. As for the fourth requirement of agency, while this new exception makes no specific mention of consideration moving from the employees to the customer, the second requirement of the new exception embraces the same elements which were adopted by courts to recognize consideration moving from stevedores in cases involving "Himalaya clauses."

Third, it must be remembered that I am proposing a very specific and limited exception to privity in the case at bar; viz. permitting employees who qualify as third party beneficiaries to use their employer's limitation of liability clauses as "shields" in actions brought against them, when the damage they have caused was done in the course of their employment and while they were carrying out the very services for which the plaintiff (customer) had contracted with their employer. In sum, I am recognizing a limited jus tertii.

In closing on this point, I wish to add the obvious comment that nothing in the above reasons should be taken as affecting in any way recognized exceptions to privity of contract such as trust and agency. In other words, even if the above requirements are not satisfied, an employee may still establish the existence of a trust or agency so as to obtain a benefit which the contracting parties intended him or her to have, notwithstanding lack of privity.

(C) APPLICATION OF THE NEW EXCEPTION

The only question in the case at bar is whether the respondents are third party beneficiaries with respect to the limitation of liability clause so as to come within the first requirement of the test I set forth above. Based on uncontested findings of fact, the respondents were acting in the course of their employment when they caused the transformer to topple over. Moreover, at that time they were performing the very services provided for in the contract between Kuehne & Nagel and the appellant, namely, the storage and upkeep of the transformer.

For convenience, I reproduce again the limitation of liability clause. ... Does the language chosen indicate that the benefit of the clause is specifically restricted to Kuehne & Nagel? I think not. On the contrary, when all of the relevant circumstances are considered, it is my view that the parties must be taken as having intended that the benefit of this clause would also extend to Kuehne & Nagel's employees.

It is clear that the parties did not choose express language in order to extend the benefit of the clause to employees. For example, there is no mention of words such as "servants" or "employees" in s. 11(b) of the contract. As such, it cannot be said that the respondents are express third party beneficiaries with respect to the limitation of liability clause. However, this does not preclude a finding that they are implied third party beneficiaries. In view of the identity of interest between an employer and his or her employees with respect to the performance of the former's contractual obligations and the policy considerations discussed above, it is surely open to a court, in appropriate circumstances, to conclude that a limitation of liability clause in a commercial contract between an employer and his or her customer impliedly extends its benefit to employees.

In the case at bar, the parties have not chosen language which inevitably leads to the conclusion that the respondents were not to benefit from s. 11(b) of the contract of storage. The term "warehouseman" as used in s. 11(b) is not defined in the contract and the definition provided in the Warehouse Receipt Act, s. 1, is of no use in determining whether it includes employees for the purpose of the contractual limitation of liability. While it is true that s. 10(e) of the contract uses the term "warehouse employee," this by itself does not preclude an interpretation of "warehouseman" in s. 11(b) of the same contract as implicitly including employees for the purposes of the limitation of liability clause. Such a conclusion does not offend the words chosen by the parties.

When all the circumstances of this case are taken into account, including the nature of the relationship between employees and their employer, the identity of interest with respect to contractual obligations, the fact that the appellant knew that employees would be involved in performing the contractual obligations, and the absence of a clear indication in the contract to the contrary, the term "warehouseman" in s. 11(b) of the contract must be interpreted as meaning "warehousemen." As such, the respondents are not complete strangers to the limitation of liability clause. Rather, they are unexpressed or implicit third party beneficiaries with respect to this clause. Accordingly, the first requirement of this new exception to the doctrine of privity is also met.

IV. CONCLUSION

The respondents owed a duty of care to the appellant in their handling of its transformer. According to the uncontested findings of the trial judge, they breached this duty causing damages in the amount of $33,955.41. While neither trust nor agency is applicable, the respondents are entitled to benefit directly from the limitation of liability clause in the contract between their employer and the appellant. This is so because they are third party beneficiaries with respect to that clause and because they were acting in the course of their employment and performing the very services contracted for by the appellant when the damages occurred. I acknowledge that this, in effect, relaxes the doctrine of privity and creates a limited jus tertii. However, when viewed in its proper context, it merely represents an incremental change to the law, necessary to see that the common law develops in a manner that is consistent with modern notions of commercial reality and justice.

V. DISPOSITION

For the foregoing reasons, I would dismiss the appeal and cross-appeal, both with costs.

NOTE

The two judges who did not join in the judgment of the majority agreed that the employees were not liable. McLachlin J held that the limitation clause could not be interpreted to include the employees, but she held that the plaintiff had voluntarily assumed the risk of damage exceeding the sum of $40. La Forest J held that the employees owed no duty of care to the plaintiff at all, and he would have allowed the cross-appeal by the employees to remove their liability entirely. Stevenson J took no part in the judgment.

FRASER RIVER PILE & DREDGE LTD V CAN-DIVE SERVICES LTD
[1999] 3 SCR 108

[A marine insurer waived its subrogation rights against, among others, "any charterer." The insured vessel was sunk by a charterer's negligence, and the insurer then sought to bring a subrogated action in the owner's name. The court held that the insurer was bound by the waiver and could not, even by express agreement with the owner, exercise any subrogation rights after the occurrence of the loss.]

IACOBUCCI J: ...

[30] As a preliminary matter, I note that it was not our intention in *London Drugs* ... to limit application of the principled approach to situations involving only an employer–employee relationship. That the discussion focused on the nature of this relationship simply reflects the prudent jurisprudential principle that a case should not be decided beyond the scope of its immediate facts.

[31] In terms of extending the principled approach to establishing a new exception to the doctrine of privity of contract relevant to the circumstances of the appeal, regard must be had to the emphasis in *London Drugs* that a new exception first and foremost must be dependent upon the intention of the contracting parties. Accordingly, extrapolating from the specific requirements as set out in *London Drugs*, the determination in general terms is made on the basis of two critical and cumulative factors: (a) did the parties to the contract intend to extend the benefit in question to the third party seeking to rely on the contractual provision; and (b) are the activities performed by the third party seeking to rely on the contractual provision the very activities contemplated as coming within the scope of the contract in general, or the provision in particular, again as determined by reference to the intentions of the parties?

(A)   INTENTIONS OF THE PARTIES

[32] As to the first inquiry, Can-Dive has a very compelling case in favour of relaxing the doctrine of privity in these circumstances, given the express reference in the waiver of subrogation clause to "charterer(s)," a class of intended third-party beneficiaries that, on a plain reading of the contract, includes Can-Dive within the scope of the term. Indeed, there is no dispute between the parties as to the meaning of the term within the waiver of subrogation clause; disagreement exists only as to whether the clause has legal effect. Accordingly, there can be no question that the parties intended to extend the benefit in question to a class of third-party beneficiaries whose membership includes Can-Dive. Given the lack of ambiguity on the face of the provision, there is no need to resort to extrinsic evidence for the purposes of determining otherwise. If the parties did not intend the waiver of subrogation clause

to be extended to third-party beneficiaries, they need not have included such language in their agreement.

[33] In essence, Fraser River's argument in terms of the intention of the parties is not that the scope of the waiver of subrogation clause does not extend to third parties such as Can-Dive, but that the provision can only be enforced by Fraser River on Can-Dive's behalf, and not by Can-Dive acting independently. A plain reading of the provision, however, does not support this conclusion. There is no language in the clause indicating that the waiver of subrogation is intended to be conditional upon Fraser River's initiative in favour of any particular third-party beneficiary. It appears to me that Fraser River has conflated arguments concerning the intentions of the parties in drafting the provision and the legal effect to be given to the provision. In no uncertain terms, the waiver of subrogation clause indicates that the insurers are precluded from proceeding with an action against third-party beneficiaries coming within the class of "charterer(s)," and the relevant inquiry is whether to give effect to these intentions by enforcing the contractual term, notwithstanding the doctrine of privity of contract.

[34] In my opinion, the case in favour of relaxing the doctrine of privity is even stronger in the circumstances of this appeal than was the case in *London Drugs*, *supra*, wherein the parties did not expressly extend the benefit of a limitation of liability clause covering a "warehouseman" to employees. Instead, it was necessary to support an implicit extension of the benefit on the basis of the relationship between the employers and its employees, that is to say, the identity of interest between the employer and its employees in terms of performing the contractual obligations. In contrast, given the express reference to "charterer(s)" in the waiver of subrogation clause in the policy, there is no need to look for any additional factors to justify characterizing Can-Dive as a third party beneficiary rather than a mere stranger to the contract.

[35] Having concluded that the parties intended to extend the benefit of the waiver of subrogation clause to third parties such as Can-Dive, it is necessary to address Fraser River's argument that its agreement with the insurers to pursue legal action against Can-Dive nonetheless effectively deleted the third-party benefit from the contract. A significant concern with relaxing the doctrine of privity is the potential restrictions on freedom of contract which could result if the interests of a third-party beneficiary must be taken into account by the parties to the initial agreement before any adjustment to the contract could occur. It is important to note, however, that the agreement in question was concluded subsequent to the point at which what might be termed Can-Dive's inchoate right under the contract crystallized into an actual benefit in the form of a defence against an action in negligence by Fraser River's insurers. Having contracted in favour of Can-Dive as within the class of potential third-party beneficiaries, Fraser River and the insurers cannot revoke unilaterally Can-Dive's rights once they have developed into an actual benefit. At the point at which Can-Dive's rights crystallized, it became for all intents and purposes a party to the initial contract for the limited purposes of relying on the waiver of subrogation clause. Any subsequent alteration of the waiver provision is subject to further negotiation and agreement among all of the parties involved, including Can-Dive.

[36] I am mindful, however, that the principle of freedom of contract must not be dismissed lightly. Accordingly, nothing in these reasons concerning the ability of the initial parties to amend contractual provisions subsequently should be taken as applying other than to the limited situation of a third party's seeking to rely on a benefit conferred by the contract to defend against an action initiated by one of the parties, and only then in circumstances where the inchoate contractual right has

crystallized prior to any purported amendment. Within this narrow exception, however, the doctrine of privity presents no obstacle to contractual rights conferred on third-party beneficiaries.

(B) THIRD-PARTY BENEFICIARY IS PERFORMING THE ACTIVITIES CONTEMPLATED IN THE CONTRACT

[37] As to the second requirement that the intended third-party beneficiary must rely on a contractual provision in connection with the very activities contemplated by the contract in general, or by the relevant clause in particular, Fraser River has argued that a significant distinction exists between the situation in *London Drugs*, ... and the circumstances of the present appeal. In *London Drugs*, the relationship between the contracting parties and the third-party beneficiary involved a single contract for the provision of services, whereas in the present circumstances, such a "contractual nexus," to use Fraser River's phrase, does not exist. In other words, the waiver of subrogation clause upon which Can-Dive seeks to rely is contained in an unrelated contract that does not pertain to the charter contract in effect between Fraser River and Can-Dive.

[38] With respect, I do not find this argument compelling, given that a similar contractual relationship could be said to exist in *London Drugs*, in terms of the service contract between the parties and a contract of employment which presumably existed between the employer and employees. At issue is whether the purported third-party beneficiary is involved in the very activity contemplated by the contract containing the provision upon which he or she seeks to rely. In this case, the relevant activities arose in the context of the relationship of Can-Dive to Fraser River as a charterer, the very activity anticipated in the policy pursuant to the waiver of subrogation clause. Accordingly, I conclude that the second requirement for relaxing the doctrine of privity has been met.

(C) POLICY REASONS IN FAVOUR OF AN EXCEPTION IN THESE CIRCUMSTANCES

[39] Having found that Can-Dive has satisfied both of the cumulative threshold requirements for the purposes of introducing a new, principled exception to the doctrine of privity of contract as it applies to third party beneficiaries, I nonetheless wish to add that there are also sound policy reasons for relaxing the doctrine in these circumstances. In this respect, it is time to put to rest the unreasonable application of the doctrine of privity to contracts of insurance established by the Privy Council in *Vandepitte* [v *Preferred Accident Insurance Corp of New York*, [1933] AC 70 (PC)], a decision characterized since its inception by both legislatures and the judiciary as out of touch with commercial reality. As Esson J.A. noted, the decision in *Vandepitte* received little attention outside the field of automobile insurance, where it had been promptly overruled by legislative amendment in British Columbia and other provinces. In addition, Esson J.A. was correct in holding that *Vandepitte* has been impliedly overruled in the course of decisions by the Court, given that in cases where the rule of privity might have been applied, the decision was ignored .... Of particular interest is the Court's decision in *Commonwealth Construction Co.* [v *Imperial Oil Ltd*, [1978] 1 SCR 317] .... The case concerned a general contractor's "builder's risk" policy that purported to extend coverage to subcontractors who were not parties to the original contract. In holding that subrogation was not available against the subcontractors, de Grandpre J., writing for the Court, made the following comments regarding the "Additional Insureds" and "Trustee" clauses, at p. 324:

While these conditions may have been inserted to avoid the pitfalls that were the lot of the unnamed insured in *Vandepitte v. Preferred Accident Ins. Co.* [citations omitted], a precaution that in my view was not needed, they without doubt cover additional ground.

[40] When considered in light of the Court's discussion of the necessary interdependence of various contractors involved in a common construction enterprise, the comment reflects the Court's acknowledgment that the rule of privity set out in *Vandepitte*, *supra*, was inconsistent with commercial reality. In a similar fashion, Fraser River in the course of this appeal has been unable to provide any commercial reason for failing to enforce a bargain entered into by sophisticated commercial actors. In the absence of any indication to the contrary, I must conclude that relaxing the doctrine of privity in these circumstances establishes a default rule that most closely corresponds to commercial reality as is evidenced by the inclusion of the waiver of subrogation clause within the contract itself.

[41] A plain reading of the waiver of subrogation clause indicates that the benefit accruing in favour of third parties is not subject to any qualifying language or limiting conditions. When sophisticated commercial parties enter into a contract of insurance which expressly extends the benefit of a waiver of subrogation clause to an ascertainable class of third party beneficiary, any conditions purporting to limit the extent of the benefit or the terms under which the benefit is to be available must be clearly expressed. The rationale for this requirement is that the obligation to contract for exceptional terms most logically rests with those parties whose intentions do not accord with what I assume to be standard commercial practice. Otherwise, notwithstanding the doctrine of privity of contract, courts will enforce the bargain agreed to by the parties and will not undertake to rewrite the terms of the agreement.

[42] Fraser River has also argued that to relax the doctrine of privity of contract in the circumstances of this appeal would be to introduce a significant change to the law that is better left to the legislature. As was noted in *London Drugs*, *supra*, privity of contract is an established doctrine of contract law, and should not be lightly discarded through the process of judicial decree. Wholesale abolition of the doctrine would result in complex repercussions that exceed the ability of the courts to anticipate and address. It is by now a well-established principle that courts will not undertake judicial reform of this magnitude, recognizing instead that the legislature is better placed to appreciate and accommodate the economic and policy issues involved in introducing sweeping legal reforms.

[43] That being said, the corollary principle is equally compelling, which is that in appropriate circumstances, courts must not abdicate their judicial duty to decide on incremental changes to the common law necessary to address emerging needs and values in society ... . In this case, I do not accept Fraser River's submission that permitting third party beneficiaries to rely on a waiver of subrogation clause represents other than an incremental development. To the contrary, the factors present in *London Drugs*, *supra*, in support of the incremental nature of the exception are present as well in the circumstances of this appeal. As in *London Drugs*, a third-party beneficiary is seeking to rely on a contractual provision in order to defend against an action initiated by one of the contracting parties. Fraser River's concerns regarding the potential for double recovery are unfounded, as relaxing the doctrine to the extent contemplated by these reasons does not permit Can-Dive to rely on any provision in the policy to establish a separate claim. In addition, the exception is dependent upon the express intentions of the parties, evident in the language of the waiver of subrogation clause, to extend the benefit of the provision to certain named classes of third-party beneficiaries.

V. CONCLUSION AND DISPOSITION

[44] I conclude that the circumstances of this appeal nonetheless meet the requirements established in *London Drugs*, *supra*, for a third-party beneficiary to rely on the terms of a contract to defend against a claim initiated by one of the parties to the contract. As a third-party beneficiary to the policy, Can-Dive is entitled to rely on the waiver of subrogation clause whereby the insurers expressly waived any right of subrogation against Can-Dive as a "charterer" of a vessel included within the policy's coverage.

[See McCamus at 303-30; Waddams at paras 280-95; JW Neyers, "Explaining the Principled Exception to Privity of Contract" (2007) 52 McGill LJ 757.]

NOTES

1. In *District of Kitimat v Alcan Inc* (2006), 265 DLR (4th) 462 (BCCA), the District of Kitimat brought a petition seeking declaratory relief against a company for its sale of hydroelectric power to the United States, alleging that this was in contravention of various agreements between the provincial government and the company. The petition was dismissed. The BC Court of Appeal said (at paras 69-71): "In both *London Drugs* and *Fraser River*, the third party sought the benefit of the contract to protect itself from a claim advanced against them. The learned chambers judge distinguished these cases from this one, correctly in my view, on the basis that here Kitimat seeks to avail itself of the statutory and contractual relationship between Alcan and the Province so that it can advance a claim against Alcan. If, however, Kitimat had standing to advance its claim against Alcan for the latter's breach of its public obligations, it would have no need to resort to a third party beneficiary claim under the contract. In attempting to extend the third party beneficiary principle to permit it to advance, rather than to defend a claim, Kitimat is simply trying to circumvent the well settled principles governing private interest standing. In my respectful view, such a claim is well beyond anything contemplated by the decisions in *London Drugs* or *Fraser River*."

2. In *Brown v Belleville (City)*, 2013 ONCA 148, a covenant by a municipality to maintain and repair a drainage system on certain land was held to be enforceable by a successor in title to the land. The court said at para 110: "I recognize that *London Drugs* and *Fraser River* were cases where the third-party beneficiaries sought to rely, by way of defence, on the benefit of the contractual provisions at issue to resist claims brought against them—they were not seeking to enforce the affirmative benefit of the relevant contractual provisions. Nevertheless, it is my view that the Browns' status as successors of the original covenantee under the Agreement affords them the right to seek to enforce the original covenantor's contractual obligations as against the original covenantor."

RESTATEMENT OF THE LAW OF CONTRACTS (SECOND)
American Law Institute, 1981

302. Intended and Incidental Beneficiaries.
(1) Unless otherwise agreed between promisor and promisee, a beneficiary of a promise is an intended beneficiary if recognition of a right to performance in the beneficiary is appropriate to effectuate the intention of the parties and either
(a) the performance of the promise will satisfy an obligation of the promisee to pay money to the beneficiary; or
(b) the circumstances indicate that the promisee intends to give the beneficiary the benefit of the promised performance.
(2) An incidental beneficiary is a beneficiary who is not an intended beneficiary. ...

304. Creation of Duty to Beneficiary.

A promise in a contract creates a duty in the promisor to any intended beneficiary to perform the promise, and the intended beneficiary may enforce the duty.

305. Overlapping Duties to Beneficiary and Promisee.

(1) A promise in a contract creates a duty in the promisor to the promisee to perform the promise even though he also has a similar duty to an intended beneficiary.

(2) Whole or partial satisfaction of the promisor's duty to the beneficiary satisfies to that extent the promisor's duty to the promisee.

306. Disclaimer by a Beneficiary.

A beneficiary who has not previously assented to the promise for his benefit may in a reasonable time after learning of its existence and terms render any duty to himself inoperative from the beginning by disclaimer.

307. Remedy of Specific Performance.

Where specific performance is otherwise an appropriate remedy, either the promisee or the beneficiary may maintain a suit for specific enforcement of a duty owed to an intended beneficiary. ...

309. Defences against the Beneficiary.

(1) A promise creates no duty to a beneficiary unless a contract is formed between the promisor and the promisee; and if a contract is voidable or unenforceable at the time of its formation the right of any beneficiary is subject to the infirmity.

(2) If a contract ceases to be binding in whole or in part because of impracticability, public policy, non-occurrence of a condition, or present or prospective failure of performance, the right of any beneficiary is to that extent discharged or modified.

(3) Except as stated in Subsections (1) and (2) and in §311 or as provided by the contract, the right of any beneficiary against the promisor is not subject to the promisor's claims or defences against the promisee or to the promisee's claims or defences against the beneficiary.

(4) A beneficiary's right against the promisor is subject to any claim or defence arising from his own conduct or agreement.

310. Remedies of the Beneficiary of a Promise to pay the Promisee's Debt; Reimbursement of Promisee.

(1) Where an intended beneficiary has an enforceable claim against the promisee, he can obtain a judgment or judgments against either the promisee or the promisor or both based on their respective duties to him. Satisfaction in whole or in part of either of these duties, or of a judgment thereon, satisfies to that extent the other duty or judgment, subject to the promisee's right of subrogation.

(2) To the extent that the claim of an intended beneficiary is satisfied from assets of the promisee, the promisee has a right of reimbursement from the promisor, which may be enforced directly and also, if the beneficiary's claim is fully satisfied, by subrogation to the claim of the beneficiary against the promisor, and to any judgment thereon and to any security therefor.

311. Variation of a Duty to Beneficiary.

(1) Discharge or modification of a duty to an intended beneficiary by conduct of the promisee or by a subsequent agreement between promisor and promisee is ineffective if a term of the promise creating the duty so provides.

(2) In the absence of such a term, the promisor and promisee retain power to discharge or modify the duty by subsequent agreement.

(3) Such a power terminates when the beneficiary, before he receives notification of the discharge or modification, materially changes his position in justifiable reliance on the promise or brings suit on it or manifests assent to it at the request of the promisor or promisee.

(4) If the promisee receives consideration for an attempted discharge or modification of the promisor's duty which is ineffective against the beneficiary, the beneficiary can assert a right to the consideration so received. The promisor's duty is discharged to the extent of the amount received by the beneficiary.

312. Mistake as to Duty to Beneficiary.

The effect of an erroneous belief of the promisor or promisee as to the existence or extent of a duty owed to an intended beneficiary is determined by the rules making contracts voidable for mistake.

315. Effect of a Promise of Incidental Benefit.

An incidental beneficiary acquires by virtue of the promise no right against the promisor or the promisee.

CONTRACTS (RIGHTS OF THIRD PARTIES) ACT 1999
(UK), c 31

1(1) Subject to the provisions of this Act, a person who is not a party to a contract (a "third party") may in his own right enforce a term of the contract if—

(a) the contract expressly provides that he may, or

(b) subject to subsection (2), the term purports to confer a benefit on him.

(2) Subsection (1)(b) does not apply if on a proper construction of the contract it appears that the parties did not intend the term to be enforceable by the third party.

(3) The third party must be expressly identified in the contract by name, as a member of a class or as answering a particular description but need not be in existence when the contract is entered into.

(4) This section does not confer a right on a third party to enforce a term of a contract otherwise than subject to and in accordance with any other relevant terms of the contract.

(5) For the purpose of exercising his right to enforce a term of the contract, there shall be available to the third party any remedy that would have been available to him in an action for breach of contract if he had been a party to the contract (and the rules relating to damages, injunctions, specific performance and other relief shall apply accordingly).

(6) Where a term of a contract excludes or limits liability in relation to any matter, references in this Act to the third party enforcing the term shall be construed as references to his availing himself of the exclusion or limitation.

(7) In this Act, in relation to a term of a contract which is enforceable by a third party—

"the promisor" means the party to the contract against whom the term is enforceable by the third party, and

"the promisee" means the party to the contract by whom the term is enforceable against the promisor.

2(1) Subject to the provisions of this section, where a third party has a right under section 1 to enforce a term of the contract, the parties to the contract may not, by agreement, rescind the contract, or vary it in such a way as to extinguish or alter his entitlement under that right, without his consent if—

(a) the third party has communicated his assent to the term to the promisor,

(b) the promisor is aware that the third party has relied on the term, or

(c) the promisor can reasonably be expected to have foreseen that the third party would rely on the term and the third party has in fact relied on it.

(2) The assent referred to in subsection (1)(a)—

(a) may be by words or conduct, and

(b) if sent to the promisor by post or other means, shall not be regarded as communicated to the promisor until received by him.

(3) Subsection (1) is subject to any express term of the contract under which—

(a) the parties to the contract may by agreement rescind or vary the contract without the consent of the third party, or

(b) the consent of the third party is required in circumstances specified in the contract instead of those set out in subsections (1)(a) to (c).

(4) Where the consent of a third party is required under subsection (1) or (3), the court or arbitral tribunal may, on the application of the parties to the contract, dispense with his consent if satisfied—

(a) that his consent cannot be obtained because his whereabouts cannot reasonably be ascertained, or

(b) that he is mentally incapable of giving his consent.

(5) The court or arbitral tribunal may, on the application of the parties to a contract, dispense with any consent that may be required under subsection (1)(c) if satisfied that it cannot reasonably be ascertained whether or not the third party has in fact relied on the term.

(6) If the court or arbitral tribunal dispenses with a third party's consent, it may impose such conditions as it thinks fit, including a condition requiring the payment of compensation to the third party.

(7) The jurisdiction conferred on the court by subsections (4) to (6) is exercisable by both the High Court and a county court.

3(1) Subsections (2) to (5) apply where, in reliance on section 1, proceedings for the enforcement of a term of a contract are brought by a third party.

(2) The promisor shall have available to him by way of defence or set-off any matter that—

(a) arises from or in connection with the contract and is relevant to the term, and

(b) would have been available to him by way of defence or set-off if the proceedings had been brought by the promisee.

(3) The promisor shall also have available to him by way of defence or set-off any matter if—

(a) an express term of the contract provides for it to be available to him in proceedings brought by the third party, and

(b) it would have been available to him by way of defence or set-off if the proceedings had been brought by the promisee.

(4) The promisor shall also have available to him—

(a) by way of defence or set-off any matter, and

(b) by way of counterclaim any matter not arising from the contract,

that would have been available to him by way of defence or set-off or, as the case may be, by way of counterclaim against the third party if the third party had been a party to the contract.

(5) Subsections (2) and (4) are subject to any express term of the contract as to the matters that are not to be available to the promisor by way of defence, set-off or counterclaim.

(6) Where in any proceedings brought against him a third party seeks in reliance on section 1 to enforce a term of a contract (including, in particular, a term purporting to exclude or limit liability), he may not do so if he could not have done so (whether by reason of any particular circumstances relating to him or otherwise) had he been a party to the contract.

4. Section 1 does not affect any right of the promisee to enforce any term of the contract.

5. Where under section 1 a term of a contract is enforceable by a third party, and the promisee has recovered from the promisor a sum in respect of—

(a) the third party's loss in respect of the term, or

(b) the expense to the promisee of making good to the third party the default of the promisor,

then, in any proceedings brought in reliance on that section by the third party, the court or arbitral tribunal shall reduce any award to the third party to such extent as it thinks appropriate to take account of the sum recovered by the promisee. ...

[Section 6 contains a series of exceptions where the Act does not apply.]

7(1) Section 1 does not affect any right or remedy of a third party that exists or is available apart from this Act.

[For a critical analysis of this statute, see R Stevens, "Contracts (Rights of Third Parties) Act 1999" (2004) 120 Law Q Rev 292.]

QUÉBEC CIVIL CODE
LRQ, c C-1991

1444. A person may make a stipulation in a contract for the benefit of a third person. The stipulation gives the third person beneficiary the right to exact performance of the promised obligation directly from the promisor. ...

1446. The stipulation may be revoked as long as the third person beneficiary has not advised the stipulator or the promisor of his will to accept it.

1447. Only the stipulator may revoke a stipulation; neither his heirs nor his creditors may do so. If the promisor has an interest in maintaining the stipulation, however, the stipulator may not revoke it without his consent.

PROBLEM

Able takes tickets for a voyage by himself and his wife on a ship owned by Baker. Mr. and Mrs. Able are both injured when the gangway is carelessly removed by Charlie, one of the crew. On the face of the tickets is a clause that reads: "Neither Baker nor his servants shall be made liable for any injury whatsoever to the person of any passenger arising from the activities of Baker's servants, whether occasioned or caused by negligence or otherwise, and in this regard it is agreed that Baker contracts as agent for his servants." Advise Mr. and Mrs. Able. See *Adler v Dickson*, [1955] 1 QB 158; *Gore v Van Der Lann*, [1967] 2 QB 31; *Cockerton v Naviera Aznar SA*, [1960] 2 Ll LR 450 (SC); Odgers, "The Strange Case of Mrs. Gore" (1970) 86 Law Q Rev 69. See also MacDougall at Chapter 7; Waddams at paras 281-98.

II. ASSIGNMENT

Contractual rights have long been treated as a species of property, and like other kinds of property, they have been bought and sold. The common law courts before the *Judicature Act* refused to recognize assignments, but the Courts of Equity did recognize and enforce them. In the case of contractual rights enforceable at law (choses in action), the Court of Equity, because it could not directly affect the decisions of the courts of law, achieved its end indirectly by permitting the assignee to bring his action in the name of the assignor, if necessary, enjoining the assignor from objecting. In the case of rights enforceable in equity (choses in equity), the assignee's right was directly enforceable by the Court of Equity.

The *Judicature Act* included a provision, now s 53(1) of the Ontario *Conveyancing and Law of Property Act*, RSO 1990, c C.34, and in force in all the common law provinces, but with variations in Saskatchewan and Manitoba, permitting assignments subject to certain restrictions. It was held in *Brandt's Sons & Co v Dunlop Rubber Co Ltd*, [1905] AC 454 (HL) that the effect of the statute was not to impair the validity of the old equitable procedure. An assignment that fails to comply with the statute, therefore, may still be valid as an equitable assignment.

It is ironic that the establishment of free assignability coincided with the strengthening of the rule against third-party beneficiaries (*Tweddle v Atkinson*, above). If A makes a promise to B, B can, in the next instant of time, assign the benefit of it to C as a gift, if he wishes. It seems odd to prevent A and B from agreeing to do the same thing directly—that is, to confer a direct benefit on C.

It will be noted that assignment under the statute is "subject to equities"—that is, to defences that the debtor could have asserted against the assignor. The assignee of a debt, therefore, is generally in no better position than the assignor, even if he gives value for the debt in good faith without notice of the defences, and the debtor is generally no worse off by the assignment. This rule obviously limits the negotiability of debts; it is the assignee, and not the debtor, who takes the risk of the assignor's fraud or insolvency.

The commercial need for negotiability is met by the concept of the negotiable instrument defined by the *Bills of Exchange Act*, RSC 1985, c B-4 to mean a promissory note or a bill of exchange (including a cheque). The chief significance of a negotiable instrument is that the holder of one for value in good faith does *not* take "subject to equities," and so if a debt is embodied in a negotiable instrument and negotiated to a third party, it is generally the debtor, not the holder of the instrument, who takes the risk of the creditor's fraud or insolvency. This rule is subject to an important qualification in the case of consumer transactions.

CONVEYANCING AND LAW OF PROPERTY ACT
RSO 1990, c C.34

53(1) Any absolute assignment, made on or after the 31st day of December, 1897, by writing under the hand of the assignor, not purporting to be by way of charge only, of any debt or other legal chose in action of which express notice in writing has been given to the debtor, trustee or other person from whom the assignor would have been entitled to receive or claim such debt or chose in action is effectual in law, subject to all equities that would have been entitled to priority over the right of the assignee if this section had not been enacted, to pass and transfer the legal right to such debt or chose in action from the date of such notice, and all other remedies for the same and the power to give a good discharge for the same without the concurrence of the assignor.

[This provision is substantially the same as s 25(6) of the *English Judicature Act* of 1873, later s 136 of the *Law of Property Act*. See also Waddams at paras 269-80.]

III. AGENCY

If A authorizes B to act on her behalf, and B contracts on A's behalf with C, B is A's agent, and there is a contract between A and C. Such an arrangement creates three sets of relationships—those between A and B, B and C, and A and C.

The relationship between the principal and his agent is a contractual one, but no detailed attention is given to it here, though some of the cases elsewhere in the book arise out of agency relationships. The agent is generally held to owe his principal a special duty of trust that prevents him from profiting at his principal's expense.

The relationship between the agent and the third party is on the borderline of contract, tort, and restitution. If a contract is formed between A and C, the agent, B, is ordinarily not personally liable, but there are a number of important exceptions to this rule, as where the agent undertakes to guarantee payment by the principal or where justice for some other reason requires the imposition of personal liability on the agent. If an agent claims to have authority that he does not in fact have and the principal in consequence is not liable to the third party, the agent can be held liable for what is called "breach of warranty of authority." Whether the basis of the warranty is contractual or tortious, the effect is to hold the agent to a guarantee that she has the authority she claims to have.

The relationship between principal and third party is the most interesting and significant aspect of agency, and the extract below from Seavey's article on the subject is a useful account.

SEAVEY, "THE RATIONALE OF AGENCY"
(1920) 29 Yale LJ 859

[Reprinted by permission of the Yale Law Book Company and Fred B. Rothman & Company from the *Yale Law Journal*, vol. 29, pp. 860, 872-89, 880-86.]

Authority. This word is combined usually with the idea of representation and with delegation. It cannot be discarded since its long continued use has made it an essential part of our legal vocabulary. Unfortunately, however, it is used indiscriminately in two very different senses, e.g.: the power held by the agent, and the power coupled with the privilege of exercising it. Thus we have the qualifying and confusing words "real" and "apparent" added to it to explain that the principal may be bound by an act in excess of the agent's real authority if the act was within the scope of his apparent authority. This double use leads to inaccuracy and is unnecessary. Authority is from *auctoritas* meaning legal power, or power exercised in conformity to law. The confusion is due to using a word conveying a combination of elementary ideas, where one idea is to be expressed and where both are.

Using the single-idea word "power" to describe that which the agent holds, we escape confusion, and reserve "authority" for its proper and more limited use. "Power" has a definite meaning in law and its use is not limited to agency. It may be classified and analyzed. It is therefore both more exact and more helpful in connecting what are said to be the special rules of agency with the general body of the law. For present purposes, it may be said that a power is a legal ability by which a person may create, change, or extinguish legal relations.

"Authority" should be limited to its primitive meaning of a power which can be rightfully exercised, or a power which can be exercised without going beyond the privilege given to A by P. Thus the phrase given above would be paraphrased: a principal is bound where the agent acts in the exercise of his power, although without authority, i.e., although not privileged by his principal to exercise it. The existence and extent of the power is determined by public policy; authority is limited by the expression of the principal's will in accordance with the agreement with or direction to the agent. The agent always has both the power and an authority, the latter being sometimes identical with, sometimes smaller, but never larger, than the former. ...

The Power. In the following discussion will be included cases of agency and also cases which resemble it only in externals, i.e., those situations where the law, operating upon the voluntary act of P, creates in A a power to affect the legal relations of P, this being created in order to prevent injustice. It will not include tort cases, being limited to those powers the exercise of which results in some form of contractual liability. These may be divided into two classes:

(a) *Powers, the exercise of which results in true contracts.* In this class is included all cases where the parties to be held, i.e., both principal and third party, expressed an intention to create the specific agreement or an agreement of the sort made. Cases where the existence of the principal was unknown to the third party are excluded since the parties are as much a part of an agreement as the terms. Also excluded are certain cases where the agent exceeded his orders. For convenience, a further subdivision may be made:

(1) The powers originated by direct grant to the agent create what is usually called "real authority," so called, I presume, because the agent is privileged to exercise them in the performance of his fiduciary obligations. They are again subclassified into those created by "express authority" and those created by "implied authority," the latter referring to powers created by the conduct of the principal in connection with the usages and customs of the business of the locality.

That the existence of these powers is no departure from the operation of the ordinary principles relating to contracts is clear in most cases. If the principal has agreed to become a party to a particular contract and the agent obeys orders, there is an expressed consent, conveyed as intended to the other party. Where the agent is given discretion as to the creation or terms of such contracts, there is a variation from the usual offer and acceptance situation where there is not the intervention of an agent. It is not true that the contract is completed by the will of the principal alone, or that the agent is "a referee who settles the price," a mere "tetotum." The contract comes into existence through the independent will of the agent, for the latter is responsible for his acts and words so far as his status as an individual permits. But the contract does come into existence in accordance with the expressed will of the principal and there is no departure from the theory of contracts. Nor is there anything peculiar in "implied authority," which corresponds to contracts implied in fact. Actions have the same weight in expressing intentions as do words, and in neither agency nor contracts do we inquire what a party thinks; we interpret his words and acts. The power, therefore, includes all that the agent reasonably believes it contains and this is determined by custom, if there are no instructions to the contrary.

Where the existence, but not the name, of the principal is known, it might be thought that a true contract is not created. But in this case, T, the third person, by his agreement with A, the agent, shows his intention to contract with a person indicated by description and of course it is not necessary to know personally the other party to a contract. It is sufficient if he falls within the class intended to be dealt with. It may be objected that the agent is a party to the contract and that there is but one contract. It is true that in many cases the agent has been a successful plaintiff and an unsuccessful defendant. But those cases may be placed upon a number of different grounds—the form of the written agreement, a custom to hold the agent as guarantor, a right in the agent to sue created by his personal interest in the goods. In all of these cases there may be alternative or secondary agreements with the agent but these do not affect the existence of the intent to deal with the principal nor the reality of a consensual relationship with him. Of course if the third party chooses to deal exclusively with the agent, we have no question of agency, at least within the principles now discussed.

(2) The power created where the principal has led T to believe that a power existed in A. This refers, of course, to "ostensible authority" or the so-called "agency by estoppel." In this class of cases also, there is created a true contract. As has been pointed out we may discard the use of the word estoppel as unnecessary, although doubtless the basis for liability is much the same as in estoppel. If P represents to T that A has authority to contract, the legal result is exactly the same as if A had authority to contract. Here A has a power to create contractual relations between P and T identical to those which would have been created by the same words spoken to A. It is objected that if A is not an agent, a misrepresentation that he is one will not make him one and, since, by hypothesis, there is no true agent, the obligation must rest upon estoppel. This is not, however, an accurate statement of the representation. In the statement by P that A is his agent, the only part material to T is that A has a power to create certain ascertainable contractual relations between P and T. This representation may be made, of course, by any action which indicates to a normal person that A has the particular power in question. This is indicated by conduct leading T to believe that A is a certain kind of an agent and that he has power to deal with the class of persons to which T belongs.

The situation is not different from that where P makes an offer personally to T. P's actual consent is unnecessary. The offer is made by the speaking of the words or the doing of an act with communication through authorized channels. With P's mental processes we are not concerned. In the case of agency the courts have used the language of estoppel, very largely because of the double use of the word "authority," a use which has led to phrasing indicating that the power is real only where it can be rightly exercised. That the contract is real, however, has never been questioned and therefore the power to make it must be real. If in these cases, A purports to exercise the power, he has, as against P, the rights and duties of an agent only where P's representations are such that A reasonably believed that P intended him to act as agent in the matter. But the existence of agency is not essential to the reality of the powers or of the contracts made by their exercise.

Entirely irrespective of this excursus upon estoppel, however, there are in these cases all the essentials of contracts and there is no divergence from general principles. But two points call for further notice.

The representation that another is an agent of a particular kind or has authority to do certain classes of acts, sweeps into the power conferred all acts that the customs and usages of the trade or locality have made usual. But as Ewart points out, there would be no real contract created by such acts if T were not aware of the custom, since there would be no communication of P's holding out or offer, it being assumed that A is not authorized to make the representations as to the extent of his powers. Thus where there is a holding out to T that A is a particular kind of an agent and by the custom of the place such agents have authority to warrant, there is no holding out to T that A has this authority unless T knows the custom. In this, the situation differs from that where there is a direct grant of authority to A to warrant, for in this case A is authorized to state that he has such power.

The representation may be made in a great variety of ways, and so also the communication. T may receive his information individually or as one of a class. The communication may be by advertisements, by an office being kept open with signs indicating its character, or it may be through A himself. That "the authority of the agent cannot be proved by the agent's statement of it," is true; but there may be a power based upon statements which the principal has authorized the agent to make. If he so authorizes a statement, the fact that at the same time he instructs the agent not to exercise the power does not affect the rights of third persons who do not know of the instructions. This is the basis of the cases where an agent disobeys instructions and there are no elements of misrepresentation except in the agent's statements. Thus if P tells A to represent to buyers that he is P's horse selling agent and instructs him not to warrant, as is the custom, but also not to disclose this want of authority, A creates in himself a power to warrant by following the instructions. This is true whether A is a "general" or a "special" agent, since the power is created not by the agreement between P and A as to A's authority, but by the authorized statement of A that he is a horse selling agent. These "secret instructions" must be distinguished from the instructions considered later.

In much the same way where a principal intrusts goods to a selling agent, it is inferable as a fact that he causes the agent to represent that he has authority to sell the goods in the normal manner with the usual incidents of sale in the locality to which they are sent. Merely giving possession of goods to another is not a representation of ownership, even, perhaps, when they are sent to a place where such goods are commonly sold; but to intrust goods or the *indicia* of title to one for the purpose of sale or as security for a loan may be said to be equivalent to a representation that the agent has the usual power of sale. If this is such a representation, as most courts have considered it, the result is the same whether the goods were given to a "special" or to a "general" agent.

In all of these cases classified as containing powers resulting in true contracts, we find that either the act of the agent was rightful, i.e., he had authority, or there was a manifestation of assent given by the principal through some authorized channel to the third party. There can be no contract made by "holding out to the world" an agent as having a particular character or particular powers. In the absence of authority or representation, there is nothing to which the principal has expressed assent to the third person, and hence nothing to which the general rules of contract can be applied. This does not prevent, however, obligations arising the remedy for which lies in an action of assumpsit.

(b)   In the second class of cases I have placed *powers, the exercise of which does not result in a contract, but which does create obligations enforceable in an action of assumpsit.* For further consideration, they may be divided into two groups: (1) where the existence of the principal is unknown and the agent acts in conformity to orders, and (2) where the agent acts contrary to orders and there is no element of representation of his authority by the principal to the third person. These are distinctive agency powers, existing only where all the elements of agency exist and seemingly created by the relationship. That they do exist cannot be denied in view of the cases, and their existence prevents, if nothing else does, the conception that the agent is a sort of human machine conveying the assent of the principal to the third party. For in the case where the existence of the principal is undisclosed, the third person did not assent to the principal as a party to the contract, and in the second group of cases the principal never assented nor expressed assent to the contract as made. It is for this reason that it cannot be said that the resulting obligation is a true contract, there being no mutual assent, even by the use of the most violent presumptions.

In group (1) where the existence of the principal is unknown, the resulting obligations are accepted by the commentators as something like an excrescence. It may be that historically it can be explained only through the fiction of the identity of master and servant, or as the outcome of "a kind of common law equity, powerfully aided and extended by the fiction of the identity of principal and agent and the doctrine of reciprocity or mutuality of contractual obligations." Pollock says frankly that "the position of an undisclosed principal is an anomaly." Ames goes further. He charges the doctrine with the two sins of ignoring fundamental principles and of producing injustice. Of course if it ignores fundamental principles, we must expect that it will produce injustice, if we have faith in our principles. But I think that the doctrine is not as black or as peculiar as it is painted and that the case against it is somewhat overstated.

Of course it is a fiction, though not because of that an anomaly at common law, to designate as a contract that which is obviously not consensual. There is nothing necessarily inconsistent, however, in allowing an action of assumpsit either by or against the principal, based upon the agreement made by the agent. Accepting Lewis' theory as sound, that assumpsit lies against one who has caused the plaintiff to change his position for a stipulated reward, the technical objection against allowing suit by the third person fails. And the common law was accustomed to enforce promises made to another than the plaintiff. It created an obligation to pay when land was left upon a condition, and later created out of whole cloth, by the fiction of an implied promise, all those obligations now known as quasi-contractual. In the case of the undisclosed principal, the only fiction alleged is that of treating the principal as a party to the contract, and this fiction is not needed either to create rights in favor of or obligations against the principal. ... A principal receives profits and controls the manner of making them. It is for this reason that his duty to exonerate is both personal and unlimited. Liability follows control and it is not unjust, therefore, to allow the third person to recover against one who is both the receiver of the profits and the *dominus* of the one making the contract. ...

In group (2) where the agent acts contrary to instructions and there is no element of representation by the principal to the third person, the courts have created a power in the agent in certain cases:

1. Where the agent is intrusted with the management of a business or with a series of transactions, he has the powers usual to an agent of his class, and limitations sought to be placed upon it are ineffective unless brought to the attention of the third person dealing with the agent.

   (a) Where the existence of the principal is unknown. This result has been severely criticized, but has been accepted without hesitation by a great majority of the courts.

   (b) Where the existence of the principal is disclosed, the existence of this agency power has been denied, explicitly by many and implicitly by all who, admitting the soundness of the general rules of undisclosed principal, disagree with *Watteau v. Fenwick*. For if this case is correct, it must be because of a principal that an agent has a power, in certain cases, greater than his authority, although there has been no element of representation to the third person. That such a power does exist where the existence of the principal is disclosed as well as where it is not, is seen by an examination of the cases. As seen before, "a holding out to the world" is not a representation to the particular third person. Nor can there be a holding out to him that an agent has a power to contract in conformity to the customs of the trade or locality unless such third person knows of such customs. If, therefore, liability were placed upon grounds of representation, it should be a part of the case of a third person seeking to hold a principal where the agent had acted in accordance with the powers usually conferred upon such agents, but contrary to his individual orders, to show that he, the third person, knew of such holding out or knew of the customs. In fact the cases do not require this. It follows, therefore, that the power must be created by the relationship of principal and agent, and that the principal is not bound upon a theory that he assented or manifested any assent; he is bound because he is a principal.

This method of approach assists in solving the difficult question of what is meant by instructions. Where the power is based solely upon representation, the only instructions which do not affect third persons are those intended to be kept secret and those which are purely by way of advice. But, as pointed out by Mechem, there are many instructions not intended to be kept secret which affect the third person only if he is informed of them. For example, there is no reason to suppose that ordinarily a principal intends that an agent not authorized to warrant should keep this limitation secret. Yet in the case of a general agent, the principal would be held liable were a warranty such as is customary in the business to be given. In dealing with the situations coming within the class considered here, the principal's intent as to this concealment by the agent becomes immaterial; the third person is unaffected by any instructions not in conformity with the customs of the locality or business, unless he knew or should have known of the instructions.

2. Where the agent is intrusted with the management of a particular transaction, and is given neither the possession of goods, nor documents indicating a more extended authority, I have discovered no cases where the principal has been held liable for unauthorized acts. In making this distinction, I am aware that modern text writers and some courts are inclined either to cast aside or minimize the effect of the classification into general and special agents. But although the necessity for its application may be infrequent, the classification was made by the older judges and commentators, and it plays an important part in the development of the law. It cannot be said that it is difficult to contrast a general agent with a special agent. Justice Strong, in *Butler v. Mapes*, has summed up the judicial attitude: "The purpose of [a special agency] is a single transaction, or a transaction with designated persons. ... Authority to buy for a principal a single article of merchandise by one contract, or to buy several articles from a person named, is a special agency, but authority to make purchase from any persons with whom the agent may choose to deal, or to make an indefinite number of purchases, is a general agency."

There is considerable business sense in the classifications, which in effect creates powers in proportion to the authority created in another and adopts a convenient rule of thumb for easy measurement. It must be borne in mind, of course, that a special agent may be given the most complete authority in dealing with the particular matter intrusted to him. If it is said in some cases that a special agent has "general powers," the meaning is that the agent has been given such authority in dealing in the particular transaction as a general agent normally has. It must be remembered also that there may be a representation by the principal that the agent has greater authority than that given him and that the power will be commensurate with the representation. Furthermore the instructions given a special agent may be intended to be kept secret, or may be merely advice, intended not to limit the agent's powers but to guide his discretion. In these cases the instructions do not limit his powers. Furthermore, the fact that the agent acted in bad faith and in fraud of the principal is immaterial, unless known to the third person, since the motive with which the act is done does not affect the exercise of the power.

Reasons for the creation of agency powers. Unless it is true that an agent's power may be greater than his authority in cases where there has been no representation of authority, there would be no necessity to discuss the reasons for the liability of the principal. Assuming that such powers have been created by law, there must be some reasons of public policy which require their existence. It must be in the protection of some conceived interest of business that, except in the case of a special agent, one is prevented from creating powers limited to the express authority given. The employer's interests are fully protected only if he is allowed to create powers of any kind and limited in any manner so long as he does not affirmatively mislead others.

In the first place it is to be noted that the conception that interests can be protected only in certain defined ways is not limited to the law of agency or to powers. Only certain interests in land will be protected by the creation of easements; the desire of the parties to create an easement is not enough. So a statement of an intention to make an instrument negotiable will not make it such. A mortgagor cannot in advance cut off his equity of redemption. "The law will not permit the owner of an estate to grant it alternately to his heirs male and female." For one reason or another the law prevents the creation of extraordinary types of dealing, because conceived to be injurious to the individual or to the public. It is, therefore, not inconsistent with the custom of judicial decision to create powers in accordance with general customs, if there are affirmative reasons for so doing.

In all the cases where an agent exceeds his authority, one of two persons, both innocent, must suffer. Between these two classes of persons, we must select the class which, in the long run, should suffer. The reasons which have actuated the courts in placing the burden upon the employer may be grouped under three heads.

Trust reposed in the agent. It is said that there is no reason for preferring the third person for he has trusted the agent. True, he does trust, but not equally with, nor in the same way as does the principal. In the case where the principal is undisclosed, T trusts the solvency of the agent; where the principal is known, he trusts his truthfulness. In both cases A and T are adversary parties. On the other hand the principal trusts the truthfulness, the honesty, the loyalty and the discretion of the agent, for that is what A has agreed to give him. When the agency relationship has been established A and P are not adversary parties; the agent is a fiduciary and subject to the stringent rules created upon the hypothesis that the fiduciary exists only to benefit the *cestui*. There is a trusting with a power, as in the case of a trustee there is a trusting with a title. It is true that there is no general principal that a known trustee may bind the trust estate where he acts in excess of the authority given him but, in the absence of notice of the existence of a written authorization, he may create rights in favor of third persons by such act.

Control. Liability follows control and the principal has a power of control at all times. It is true that normally liability for unintended results comes only where there has been negligent conduct on the part of the one who is held. There are, however, extrahazardous uses where liability for injurious results is absolute. And one of the elements of such liability is that the use shall be both dangerous and novel. It is not introducing an incongruity to subject the principal to liability where he has attempted to create an unusual power which may be expected to cause injury to third persons dealing with reference to the usual business methods.

Business convenience. Agency is essentially commercial; generally there is neither time nor opportunity to examine the extent of the powers of the individual agent by tracing them to their source. They have to be classified and taken at a face value. The general agent must circulate more or less as does a negotiable instrument without hindering conditions. Because of this, an agent sent out habitually with powers limited in certain abnormal ways would be in a position to cause injury to third persons. In sending out an agent, the principal knows, or should know, that his vouchers will not be carefully looked to. And he knows that the agent will not be apt to mention a lack of authority, for this might often interfere with sales. He knows of the human qualities which, at times, will lead even a faithful agent to overstep his authority in the desire to make sales. It is said that the third party need not deal with the agent. But if business is to continue, agents must be dealt with and protection given as experience rather than logic dictates.

In reaching this result, the courts have had before them the more or less imperfect analogy of the liability of a master for the torts of his servant. In both cases, the courts cannot avoid the conclusion that it is good business sense to hold that where one employs and controls another in the performance of acts for the benefit of a business, that business ought to pay for the mistakes, negligence and errors of judgment of the one so employed. For this purpose, the general agent may be said to bear the same relation to the special agent that a servant bears to an independent contractor.

[See also Waddams at paras 255-68.]

IV. MERCANTILE AGENTS

An agent in possession of her principal's goods was thought to present something of a trap to third parties, who might be induced by the agent's possession to believe that she had the right to dispose of the goods. In this situation, the *Factors Act* provides that the third party is protected, even though the agent acts in defiance of the true owner's express instructions. To this extent the common law moves some way toward the maxim of French law, "possession *vaut titre*"—that is, toward protection of the third party, in contradistinction to the general common law maxim, "*nemo dat quod non habet*" (no one can give what he does not own), which tends to protect the true owner in such situations.

FACTORS ACT
RSO 1990, c F.1

1. (1) In this Act,
    (a) "document of title" includes any bill of lading and warehouse receipt, as defined by The Mercantile Law Amendment Act, any warrant or order for the delivery of goods, and any other document used in the ordinary course of business as proof of the possession or control of goods, or authorizing or purporting to authorize, either by endorsement or delivery, the possessor of the document to transfer or receive goods thereby represented;
    (b) "goods" includes wares and merchandise;

(c) "mercantile agent" means a mercantile agent having, in the customary course of his business as such agent, authority either to sell goods or to consign goods for the purpose of sale, or to buy goods, or to raise money on the security of goods;

(d) "pledge" includes any contract pledging or giving a lien or security on goods, whether in consideration of an original advance or of any further or continuing advance or of any pecuniary liability.

(2) A person shall be deemed to be in possession of goods or of the documents of title to goods where the goods or documents are in the person's actual custody or are held by another person subject to the person's control or for the person or on the person's behalf.

2. (1) Where a mercantile agent is, with the consent of the owner, in possession of goods or of the documents of title to goods, a sale, pledge or other disposition of the goods made by the agent, when acting in the ordinary course of business of a mercantile agent, is, subject to this Act, as valid as if the agent were expressly authorized by the owner of the goods to make the disposition, if the person taking under it acts in good faith and has not at the time thereof notice that the person making it has not authority to make it.

(2) Where a mercantile agent has, with the consent of the owner, been in possession of goods or of documents of title to goods, a sale, pledge or other disposition that would have been valid if the consent had continued, is valid despite the determination of the consent; if the person taking under the disposition acts in good faith and has not at the time thereof notice that the consent has been terminated.

(3) Where a mercantile agent has obtained possession of any documents of title to goods by reason of being or having been, with the consent of the owner, in possession of the goods represented thereby, or of any other documents of title of the goods, the agent's possession of the first mentioned documents shall, for the purposes of this Act, be deemed to be with the consent of the owner.

(4) For the purposes of this Act the consent of the owner shall be presumed in the absence of evidence to the contrary.

3. A pledge by a mercantile agent of the documents of title to goods shall be deemed to be a pledge of the goods.

• • •

10. The provisions of this Act shall be construed in amplification and not in derogation of the powers exercisable by an agent independently of this Act.

V. BUYERS AND SELLERS IN POSSESSION

Another instance of protecting one who relies on the apparent ownership of goods signified by possession is the case of the buyer or seller of goods left in possession of them with the true owner's consent.

SALE OF GOODS ACT
RSO 1990, c S.1

25(1) Where a person having sold goods continues or is in possession of the goods or of the documents of title to the goods, the delivery or transfer by that person, or by a mercantile agent acting for that person, of the goods or documents of title under a sale, pledge, or other disposition thereof, to any person receiving the same in good faith and without notice of the previous sale, has the same effect as if the person making the delivery or transfer were expressly authorized by the owner of the goods to make the delivery or transfer.

(2) Where a person having bought or agreed to buy goods obtains, with the consent of the seller, possession of the goods or the documents of title to the goods, the delivery or transfer by that person, or by a mercantile agent acting for that person, of the goods or documents of title, under a sale, pledge or other disposition thereof to any person receiving the same in good faith and without notice of any lien or other right of the original seller in respect of the goods, shall have the same effect as if the person making the delivery or transfer were a mercantile agent in possession of the goods or documents of title with the consent of the owner.

• • •

(4) In this section "mercantile agent" means a mercantile agent having, in the customary course of business as such agent, authority either to sell goods or to consign goods for the purpose of sale, or to buy goods, or to raise money on the security of goods.

[This section was originally in the English *Factors Act* of 1889 as ss 8-9.]

NOTES AND QUESTIONS

1. Where a transaction creates what is, in substance, a security interest in goods—for example, a conditional sale agreement or a chattel mortgage, where interest in goods is retained in order to secure payment of a debt—the *Personal Property Security Act*, RSO 1990, c P.10 applies. In general, this Act requires registration by the secured party of his interest and gives in return priority over subsequent purchasers from and creditors of the debtor.

2. A problem that the courts frequently confront in a variety of situations is which of two more-or-less innocent parties to favour when one or both of them must suffer for the fraud of a third party. The problem arises in the assignment cases: a creditor assigns a debt to a bona fide purchaser, who pays full value for it; it then turns out that the debtor has a defence against the creditor. Should the debtor be able to assert that defence against the assignee? Consider the problem of the mercantile agent who, contrary to the principal's instructions, disposes of goods to an innocent third party. Should the principal be able to assert against the third party the agent's lack of authority?

We now consider two further situations in which a similar problem arises. The first is the case of mistaken identity. The owner of goods sells them to a rogue, mistakenly believing that the rogue is a wealthy and respectable citizen; the rogue promises to pay to the owner the price of the goods, takes the goods, sells them to an innocent third party, and disappears. Should the original owner be able to recover the goods without compensation from the third party? The other case is that of documents mistakenly signed. Here the rogue obtains a signature to a document by misrepresenting its nature; an innocent third party, relying on the signature, then pays value to the rogue who, as usual, disappears or is insolvent. Should the signer be able to allege against the third party that the signature is void? These problems have not always been considered together, and it is hoped that the analogy drawn here will be useful in analyzing them.

VI. MISTAKE OF IDENTITY

BOULTON V JONES
(1857), 2 H & N 564, 157 ER 232, 27 LJ Ex 117

At the trial before the Assessor of the Court of Passage at Liverpool, it appeared that the plaintiff had been foreman and manager of one Brocklehurst, a pipe hose manufacturer, with whom the defendants had been in the habit of dealing, and with whom they had a running account. On the morning of the 13th of January, 1857, the plaintiff bought Brocklehurst's stock, fixtures and business, and paid for them. In the afternoon of the same day, the defendant's servant brought a written order, addressed to Brocklehurst, for some leather hose. The goods were supplied by the plaintiff. The plaintiff's bookkeeper struck out the name of Brocklehurst and inserted the name of the plaintiff in the order. An invoice was afterwards sent in by the plaintiff to the defendants, who said they knew nothing of him. Upon these facts, the jury, under direction of the Assessor, found a verdict for the plaintiff, and leave was reserved to the defendants to move to enter a verdict for them.

POLLOCK CB: The point raised is, whether the facts proved did not show an intention on the part of the defendants to deal with Brocklehurst. The plaintiff, who succeeded Brocklehurst in business, executed the order without any intimation of the change that had taken place, and brought this action to recover the price of the goods supplied. It is a rule of law, that if a person intends to contract with A, B cannot give himself any right under it. Here the order in writing was given to Brocklehurst. Possibly Brocklehurst might have adopted the act of the plaintiff in supplying the goods, and maintained an action for their price. But, since the plaintiff has chosen to sue, the only course the defendants could take was to plead that there was no contract with him.

MARTIN B: I am of the same opinion. This is not a case of principal and agent. If there was any contract at all, it was not with the plaintiff. If a man goes to a shop and makes a contract, intending it to be with one particular person, no other person can convert that into a contract with him.

BRAMWELL B: The admitted facts are, that the defendants sent to a shop an order for goods, supposing they were dealing with Brocklehurst. The plaintiff, who supplied the goods, did not undeceive them. If the plaintiff were now at liberty to sue the defendants, they would be deprived of their right of set-off as against Brocklehurst. When a contract is made in which the personality of the contracting party is or may be of importance, as a contract with a man to write a book, or the like, or where there might be a set-off, no other person can interpose and adopt the contract. As to the difficulty that the defendants need not pay anybody, I do not see why they should, unless they made a contract either express or implied. I decide the case on the ground that the defendants did not know that the plaintiff was the person who supplied the goods, and that allowing the plaintiff to treat the contract as made with him would be a prejudice to the defendants. ... The defendant has, it is true, had the goods; but it is also true that he has consumed them and cannot return them.

CHANNELL B: In order to entitle the plaintiff to recover he must show that there was a contract with himself. The order was given to the plaintiff's predecessor in business. The plaintiff executes it without notifying to the defendants who it was who executed the order. When the invoice was delivered in the name of the plaintiff, it may be that the defendants were not in a situation to return the goods. ... Here the defendant had no notice of the plaintiff's claim, until the invoice was sent to him, which was not until after he had consumed the goods, and when he could not, of course, have returned them. Without saying what might have been the effect of the receipt of the invoice before the consumption of the goods, it is sufficient to say that in this case the plaintiff clearly is not entitled to sue and deprive the defendant of his set-off.

Rule absolute.

[From the *Law Journal* report (27 LJ Ex 117), it appears that the defendant had a set-off against Brocklehurst, and that the case was argued on that basis.]

CUNDY V LINDSAY
(1878), 3 App Cas 459 (HL)

In 1873, one Alfred Blenkarn hired a room at a corner house in Wood Street, Cheapside; it had two side windows opening into Wood Street, but though the entrance was from Little Love Lane it was by him constantly described as 37, Wood Street, Cheapside. His agreement for this room was signed "Alfred Blenkarn." The now respondents, Messrs. Lindsay & Co., were linen manufacturers carrying on their business in Belfast. In the latter part of 1873, Blenkarn wrote to the plaintiffs on the subject of a purchase from them of goods of their manufacture—chiefly, cambric handkerchiefs. His letters were written as from "37, Wood Street, Cheapside," where he pretended to have a warehouse, but in fact occupied only a room on the top floor, and that room, though looking into Wood Street on one side, could only be reached from the entrance in 5, Little Love Lane. The name signed to these letters was always signed without any initial as representing a Christian name, and was, besides, so written as to appear "Blenkiron & Co." There was a highly respectable firm of W. Blenkiron & Son, carrying on business in Wood Street—but at number 123, Wood Street, and not at 37. Messrs. Lindsay, who knew the respectability of Blenkiron & Son, though not the number of the house where they carried on business, answered the letters, and sent the goods addressed to "Messrs. Blenkiron & Co., 37, Wood Street, Cheapside," where they were taken in at once. The invoices sent with the goods were always addressed in the same way. Blenkarn sold the goods, thus fraudulently obtained from Messrs. Lindsay, to different persons, and among the rest he sold 250 dozen of cambric handkerchiefs to the Messrs. Cundy, who were bona fide purchasers and who resold them in the ordinary way of their trade. Payment not being made, an action was commenced in the Mayor's Court of London by Messrs. Lindsay, the junior partner of which firm, Mr. Thompson, made the ordinary affidavit of debt, as against Alfred Blenkarn, and therein named Alfred Blenkarn as the debtor. Blenkarn's fraud was soon discovered, and he was prosecuted at the Central Criminal Court, and convicted and sentenced. Messrs. Lindsay then brought an action against Messrs. Cundy for unlawful conversion of the handkerchiefs. The cause was tried before Mr. Justice Blackburn, who left it to the jury to consider whether Alfred Blenkarn with a fraudulent intent to induce the plaintiffs to give him the credit belonging to the good character of Blenkiron & Son, wrote the letters and by fraud induced the plaintiffs to send the goods to 37, Wood Street—were they the same goods as those bought by the defendants, and did the plaintiffs by the affidavit of debt intend, as a matter of fact, to adopt Alfred Blenkarn as their debtor. The first and second questions were answered in the affirmative, and the third in the negative. A verdict was taken for the defendants, with leave reserved to move to enter the verdict for the plaintiffs. On motion accordingly, the court, after argument, ordered the rule for entering judgment for the plaintiffs to be discharged, and directed judgment to be entered for the defendants. On appeal, this decision was reversed and judgment ordered to be entered for the plaintiffs, Messrs. Lindsay. This appeal was then brought.

LORD CAIRNS LC: My Lords, you have in this case to discharge a duty which is always a disagreeable one for any court, namely to determine as between two parties, both of whom are perfectly innocent, upon which of the two consequences of a fraud practised upon both of them must fall. My Lords, in discharging that duty your Lordships can do no more than apply, rigorously, the settled and well-known rules of law. Now, with regard to the title to personal property, the settled and well-known rules of law may, I take it, be thus expressed: by the law of our country the purchaser of a chattel takes the chattel, as a general rule, subject to what may turn out to be certain infirmities in the title. If he purchases the chattel in market overt, he obtains a title which is good against all the world; but if he does not purchase the chattel in market overt, and if it turns out that the chattel has been found by the person who professed to sell it, the purchaser will not obtain a title good as against the real owner. If it turns out that the chattel has been stolen by the person who has professed to sell it, the purchaser will not obtain a title. If it turns out that the chattel has come into the hands of the person who professed to sell it, by a *de facto* contract, that is to say, a contract which has purported to pass the property to him from the owner of the property, there the purchaser will obtain a good title, even although afterwards it should appear that there were circumstances connected with that contract, which would enable the original owner of the goods to reduce it, and to set it aside because these circumstances so enabling the original owner of the goods, or of the chattel, to reduce the contract and to set it aside, will not be allowed to interfere with a title for valuable consideration obtained by some third party during the interval while the contract remained unreduced.

My Lords, the question, therefore, in the present case, as your Lordships will observe, really becomes the very short and simple one which I am about to state. Was there any contract which, with regards to the goods in question in this case, had passed the property in the goods from Messrs. Lindsay to Alfred Blenkarn? If there was any contract passing that property, even although, as I have said, that contract might afterwards be open to a process of reduction upon the ground of fraud, still, in the meantime, Blenkarn might have conveyed a good title for valuable consideration to the present appellants.

Now, my Lords, there are two observations bearing upon the solution of that question which I desire to make. In the first place, if the property in the goods in question passed, it could only pass by way of contract; there is nothing else which could have passed the property. The second observation is this, your Lordships are not here embarrassed by any conflict of evidence, or any evidence whatever as to conversations or as to acts done; the whole history of the whole transaction lies upon paper. The principal parties concerned, the respondents and Blenkarn, never came in contact personally—everything that was done was done by writing. What has to be judged of, and what the jury in the present case had to judge of, was merely the conclusion to be derived from that writing, as applied to the admitted facts of the case.

Now, my Lords, discharging that duty and answering that inquiry, what the jurors have found is in substance this: it is not necessary to spell out the words, because the substance of it is beyond all doubt. They have found that by the form of the signatures to the letters which were written by Blenkarn, by the mode in which his letters and his applications to the respondents were made out, and by the way in which he left uncorrected the mode and form in which, in turn, he was addressed by the respondent; that by all those means he led, and intended to lead, the respondents to believe, and they did believe that the person with whom they were communicating was not Blenkarn, the dishonest and irresponsible man, but was the well known and solvent house of Blenkiron & Co., doing business in the same street. My Lords, those things are found as matters of fact, and they are placed beyond the range of dispute and controversy in the case.

If that is so, what is the consequence? It is that Blenkarn—the dishonest man, as I call him—was acting here just in the same way as if he had forged the signature of Blenkiron & Co., the respectable firm, to the application for goods, and as if, when in return, the goods were forwarded and letters were sent, accompanying them, he had intercepted the goods and intercepted the letters and had taken possession of the goods, and of the letters which were addressed to, and intended for, not himself, but the firm of Blenkiron & Co. Now, my Lords, stating that matter shortly in that way, I ask the question, how is it possible to imagine that in the state of things any contract could have arisen between the respondents and Blenkarn, the dishonest man? Of him they knew nothing, and of him they never thought. With him they never intended to deal. Their minds never, even for an instant of time, rested upon him, and as between him and them there was no consensus of mind which could lead to any agreement or any contract whatever. As between him and them there was merely the one side to a contract, where, in order to produce a contract, two sides would be required. With the firm of Blenkiron & Co., of course there was no contract, for as to them the matter was entirely unknown, and therefore the pretence of a contract was a failure.

The result, therefore, my Lords, is this, that your Lordships have not here to deal with one of those cases in which there is *de facto* a contract made which may afterwards be impeached and set aside, on the ground of fraud; but you have to deal with a case which ranges itself under a completely different chapter of law, the case namely in which the contract never comes into existence. My Lords, that being so, it is idle to talk of the property passing. The property remained, as it originally had been, the property of the respondents, and the title which was intended to be given to the appellants was a title which could not be given to them.

My Lords, I therefore move your Lordships, that this appeal be dismissed with costs, and the judgment of the Court of Appeal affirmed.

[Lords Hatherly and Penzance also gave reasons for dismissing the appeal. Lord Gordon concurred.]

NOTE

In *Shogun Finance Ltd v Hudson*, [2004] 1 AC 919 (HL), the reasoning in *Cundy v Lindsay* was approved by a majority, over vigorous dissents by two of the law lords, and applied to a provision of the *Hire Purchase Act, 1964* (UK).

KING'S NORTON METAL CO LTD
V EDRIDGE, MERRETT & CO LTD
(1897), 14 TLR 98 (CA)

The action was brought to recover damages for the conversion of one ton of brass rivet wire. The plaintiffs were metal manufacturers at King's Norton, Worcestershire, and the defendants were metal merchants at Birmingham. It appeared that in 1896 the plaintiffs received a letter purporting to come from Hallam & Co., Soho Hackle Pin and Wire Works, Sheffield, at the head of which was a representation of a large factory with a number of chimneys, and in one corner was a printed statement that Hallam & Co. had depots and agencies at Belfast, Lille, and Ghent. The letter contained a request by Hallam & Co. for a quotation of prices for brass rivet wire. In reply, the plaintiffs quoted prices, and Hallam & Co. then by letter ordered some goods, which were sent off to them. These goods were never paid for. It turned out that a man named Wallis had adopted the name of Hallam & Co., and fraudulently obtained goods by the above means, and that Wallis sold the goods to the defendants, who bought them bona fide, and with no notice of any defect of title in Wallis. It appeared that the plaintiffs had been paid for some goods previously ordered by Hallam & Co., by a cheque drawn by "Hallam and Co." The plaintiffs brought this action to recover damages for the conversion of these goods. At the trial, the learned judge non-suited the plaintiffs upon the ground that the property in the goods had passed to Wallis, who sold them to the defendants before the plaintiffs had disaffirmed the contract.

A.L. SMITH LJ said the case was a plain one. The question was whether the plaintiffs, who had been cheated out of their goods by a rogue called Wallis, or the defendants were to bear the loss. The law seemed to him to be well settled. If a person induced by false pretences contracted with a rogue to sell goods to him and the goods were delivered the rogue could until the contract was disaffirmed give a good title to the goods to a bona fide purchaser for value. The facts here were that Wallis, for the purpose of cheating, set up in business as Hallam and Co., and got note-paper prepared for the purpose, and wrote to the plaintiffs representing that he was carrying on business as Hallam and Co. He got the goods in question and sold them to the defendants, who bought them bona fide for value. The question was, With whom, upon this evidence, which was all one way, did the plaintiffs contract to sell goods? Clearly with the writer of the letters. If it could have been shown that there was a separate entity called Hallam and Co. and another entity called Wallis then the case might have come within the decision in *Cundy v. Lindsay* (1878), 3 App. Cas. 459. In his opinion there was a contract by the plaintiffs with the person who wrote the letters, by which the property passed to him. There was only one entity, trading it might be under an *alias*, and there was a contract by which the property passed to him. Mr. Justice CAVE said that this was nothing more than a long firm fraud. Did any one ever hear of an attempt being made by a person who had delivered his goods to a long firm to get his goods back on the ground that he had made no contract with the long firm? The indictment against a long firm was always for obtaining the goods by false pretences, which presupposed the passing of the property. For these reasons there was no question to go to the jury, and the non-suit was right.

[Rigby and Collins LJJ delivered judgments to the same effect.]

Phillips v Brooks. [1910] 2 KB 243 (Eng HC). On April 15, 1918, a man entered the plaintiff's shop and asked to see some pearls and some rings. He selected pearls at the price of £2,550 and a ring at the price of £450. He produced a cheque book and wrote out a cheque for £3,000. In signing it, he said: "You see who I am, I am Sir George Bullough," and he gave an address in St. James's Square. The plaintiff knew there was such a person as Sir George Bullough, and finding on reference to a directory that Sir George lived at the address mentioned, he said, "Would you like to take the articles with you?" to which the man replied: "You had better have the cheque cleared first, but I should like to take the ring, as it is my wife's birthday tomorrow," whereupon the plaintiff let him have the ring. The cheque was dishonoured, the person who gave it being in fact a fraudulent person named North, who was subsequently convicted of obtaining the ring by false pretences. In the meantime—namely, on April 16, 1918—North, in the name of Firth, had pledged the ring with the defendants, pawnbrokers, who, bona fide and without notice advanced £350 on it. Held, for the defendants. HORRIDGE J: I think the seller intended to contract with the person present, and there was no error as to the person with whom he contracted, although the plaintiff would not have made the contract if there had not been a fraudulent misrepresentation.

INGRAM V LITTLE
[1961] 1 QB 31 (CA)

The Misses Ingram advertised their car for sale for £725. A stranger calling himself Hutchinson came to the house on August 3, 1957, and after an examination of the car offered Miss Elsie Ingram £700 for it. The offer was refused. After some discussion he offered £717, which was accepted. Hutchinson then took out his cheque book, but at this time Miss Elsie immediately told him that she was only willing to sell for cash, that she was not prepared to accept a cheque, and started to leave the room. Hutchinson then described himself as Mr. P.G.M. Hutchinson, with business interests at Guildford and as living at Stanstead House, Stanstead Road, Caterham. Miss Hilda Ingram, who was present, slipped out and checked in the area telephone directory at the local post office. Finding an entry for "Hutchinson, P.G.M., Stanstead House, Stanstead Road, Caterham 4665" Miss Hilda returned, reported this fact, and the Misses Ingram decided to take Hutchinson's cheque and the deal was concluded. Hutchinson disappeared with the car and has not been heard of since under that name. On August 6, 1957, a man calling himself Hardy sold the Ingram car to Reginald Little in Blackpool. Hardy, or Hutchinson, disappeared and has not been heard of since under either name. In December 1957, Little sold the car to another dealer. The plaintiffs sued Little for the return of the car or damages for its conversion. Slade J. held that Hutchinson and Hardy were the same person, and that Little had bought in good faith, but he held that the plaintiffs' mistake as to the identity of the person with whom they were dealing prevented the formation of a contract. He gave judgment for the plaintiffs for £720, the agreed value of the car. The defendant appealed.

SELLERS LJ: ... The decision in the present case turns solely on whether "Hutchinson" entered into a contract which gave him a title to the car which would subsist until it was avoided on the undoubted fraud being discovered. ...

It does not seem to me to matter whether the right view of the facts is, as the judge has held and as I would agree, that there was no concluded contract before the cheque was produced and before the vital fraudulent statements were made or that there was a concluded contract which "Hutchinson" at once repudiated by refusing to pay cash and that this repudiation was accepted by the plaintiffs and the transaction was then and there at an end. The property would not have passed until cash had been paid and it never was paid or intended to be paid.

Was there a contract of sale subsequently made which led to the plaintiffs taking "Hutchinson's" cheque and in exchange for it handing over the car and its log book?

The judgment held that there never was a concluded contract, applying, as I understand it, the elementary factors required by law to establish a contract.

The judge, treating the plaintiffs as the offerors and the rogue "Hutchinson" as the offeree, found that the plaintiffs in making their offer to sell the car not for cash but for a cheque (which in the circumstances of the Bank Holiday week-end could not be banked before the following Tuesday, August 6, 1957) were under the belief that they were dealing with, and therefore making their offer to, the honest P.G.M. Hutchinson of Caterham, whom they had reason to believe was a man of substance and standing.

"Hutchinson" the offeree, knew precisely what was in the minds of the two ladies for he had put it there and he knew that their offer was intended for P.G.M. Hutchinson of Caterham and that they were making no offer to and had no intention to contract with him, as he was. There was no offer which he "Hutchinson" could accept and, therefore, there was no contract.

The judge pointed out that the offer which the plaintiffs made was one which was capable of being accepted only by the honest P.G.M. Hutchinson of Caterham and was incapable of acceptance by "Hutchinson."

In all the circumstances of the present case I would accept the judge's findings. Indeed the conclusion so reached seems self-evident.

Is the conclusion to be held wrong in law? If it is, then, as I see it, it must on the sole ground that as "Hutchinson" was present, albeit making fraudulent statements to induce the plaintiffs to part with their car to him in exchange for his worthless cheque and was successful in so doing, then a bargain must have been struck with him personally, however much he deceived the plaintiffs into thinking they were dealing with someone else.

Where two parties are negotiating together and there is no question of one or the other purporting to act as agent for another, and an agreement is reached, the normal and obvious conclusion would no doubt be that they are the contracting parties. A contrary finding would not be justified unless very clear evidence demanded it. The unfortunate position of the defendant in this case illustrates how third parties who deal in good faith with the fraudulent person may be prejudiced.

The mere presence of an individual cannot, however, be conclusive that an apparent bargain he may make is made with him. If he were disguised in appearance and in dress to represent someone else and the other party, deceived by the disguise, dealt with him on the basis that he was that person and would not have contracted had he known the truth then, it seems clear, there would be no contract established. If words are substituted for outward disguise so as to depict a different person from the one physically present, in what circumstances would the result be different?

Whether the person portrayed, by disguise or words, is known to the other party or not is important in considering whether the identity of the person is of any moment or whether it is a matter of indifference. If a man said his name was Brown when it was in fact Smith, and both were unknown to the other party, it would be difficult to say that there was any evidence that the contract was not made and intended to be made with the person present. In *King's Norton Metal Co. Ltd. v. Edridge, Merrett & Co. Ltd.* (1897), 14 T.L.R. 98, one Wallis fraudulently described himself as Hallam & Co., making it appear a substantial firm with a large factory. The court held that the use of an assumed name by the buyer did not prevent a finding that the plaintiffs, the sellers of some brass rivet wire, had contracted with him.

But personal knowledge of the person fraudulently represented cannot, I think, be an essential feature. It might be a very strong factor but the qualities of a person not personally known might be no less strong. If a man misrepresented himself to be a Minister of the Crown or a stockbroker, confidence in the person so identified might arise although the individual so described was wholly unknown personally or by sight to the other party.

It would seem that there is an area of fact in cases of the type under consideration where a fraudulent person is present purporting to make a bargain with another and that the circumstances may justify a finding that, notwithstanding some fraud and deceit, the correct view may be that a bargain was struck with the person present, or on the other hand they may equally justify, as here, a finding the other way.

Some of the difficulties and perhaps confusion which have arisen in some of the cases do not, in my view, arise here.

If less had been said by the rogue, and if nothing had been done to confirm his statements by Miss Hilda Ingram, who communicated what she had learnt to Miss Elsie who was doing the main negotiation, the result might have been different, for the sellers' concern about the stability and standing of the buyer might not have been revealed and it might have been held that an offer in such circumstances was to the party present, whatever his true identity would be.

In *Phillips v. Brooks Ltd.*, [1919] 2 K.B. 243, the rogue had apparently been in the shop some time inspecting the goods which were brought and displayed for sale to him without any regard to his identity—he was a "customer" only. The judgment of Horridge J. is, as I read it, based on a finding of fact that Phillips intended to deal with North as a customer. Viscount Haldane, in *Lake v. Simmons*, [1927] A.C. 487, has taken the view that the case could be explained on the ground that the fraudulent misrepresentation was not made until after the parties had agreed upon a sale.

That opinion has been criticised, mainly, I think, by academic writers, but if, as must be conceded, it is a possible view, and as *Phillips v. Brooks Ltd.* has stood for so long and is, as I think, a decision within an area of fact, I would not feel justified in saying it was wrong.

It is not an authority to establish that where an offer or acceptance is addressed to a person (although under a mistake as to his identity) who is present in person, then it must in all circumstances be treated as if actually addressed to him. I would regard the issue as a question of fact in each case depending on what was said and done and applying the elementary principles of offer and acceptance in the manner in which Slade J. directed himself.

The judgment quotes extensively from the article by Dr. Goodhart, the editor of the *Law Quarterly Review*, called "Mistake as to Identity in the Law of Contract" (1941), 57 *L.Q.R.* 228, and I would join the judge in his expression of indebtedness to the author. Referring to *Phillips v. Brooks Ltd.*, Dr. Goodhart asked, "Did the shopkeeper believe that he was entering into a contract with Sir George Bullough and did North know this? If both answers are in the affirmative, then it is submitted that there was no contract."

I think there may be a doubt in that case whether both the answers should have been in the affirmative, but on the facts of the present case I feel no doubt and I would uphold the judge's views of no contract.

Dr. Goodhart might well be right when he said that "There is no branch of the law of contract which is more uncertain and difficult" than that involved in the present case, and I am conscious that our decision here will not have served to dispel the uncertainty. ...

I am in agreement with the judge when he quotes, accepts and applies the following passage from Dr. Goodhart's article—"It is the interpretation of the promise which is the essential thing. This is usually based on the interpretation which a reasonable man, in the promisee's position, would place on it, but in those cases where the promisor knows that the promisee has placed a peculiar interpretation on his words, then this is the binding one. The English law is not concerned with the motives of the parties nor with the reasons which influenced their actions. For practical reasons it has limited itself to the simple questions: what did the promisor promise, and how should this be interpreted?"

Phillips v. Brooks Ltd. is the closest authority on which the defendant relies. Once that is distinguished on its facts, without going so far as to say it is wrong, authority leans strongly in favour of the judgment appealed from. ...

DEVLIN LJ (dissenting): ... Before, therefore, I consider mistake, I shall inquire whether there is offer and acceptance in form. There is no doubt that H's offer was addressed to Miss Ingram and her acceptance apparently, addressed to him. But, it is argued, the acceptance was in reality addressed to P.G.M. Hutchinson, who was not the offeror, and, therefore, no contract was made. There can be no doubt upon the authorities that this argument must be settled by inquiring with whom Miss Ingram intended to contract: was it with the person to whom she was speaking or was it with the person whom he represented himself to be? ... All that Miss Ingram or any other witness in her position can say is that she did in fact accept the offer made to her; and that, if she had not been tricked or deceived, she would not have accepted it.

Courts of law are not inexperienced in dealing with this sort of situation. They do so by means of presumptions. ... Whether the court, when it acts in this way, is really ascertaining the intentions of the parties or whether it is simply providing a just solution of their difficulties is a theoretical question which I need not explore. ...

In my judgment, the court cannot arrive at a satisfactory solution in the present case except by formulating a presumption and taking it at least as a starting point. The presumption that a person is intending to contract with the person to whom he is actually addressing the words of contract seems to me to be a simple and sensible one and supported by some good authority. ...

I do not think it can be said that the presumption is conclusive, since there is at least one class of case in which it can be rebutted. If the person addressed is posing only as an agent it is plain that the party deceived has no thought of contracting with him but only with his supposed principal; if then there is no actual or ostensible authority, there can be no contract. *Hardman v. Booth* (1863), 1 H. & C. 803, is, I think, an example of this. Are there any other circumstances in which the presumption can be rebutted? It is not necessary to strain to find them, for we are here dealing only with offer and acceptance; contracts in which identity really matters may still be avoided on the ground of mistake. I am content to leave the question open, and do not propose to speculate on what other exceptions there may be to the general rule. What seems plain to me is that the presumption cannot in the present case be rebutted by piling up the evidence to show that Miss Ingram would never have contracted with H. unless she had thought him to be P.G.M. Hutchinson. That fact is conceded and, whether it is proved simpliciter or proved to the hilt, it does not go any further than to show that she was the victim of fraud. With great respect to the judge, the question that he propounded as the test is not calculated to show any more than that. He said: "Is it to be seriously suggested that they were willing to accept the cheque of the rogue other than in the belief, created by the rogue himself, that he, the rogue, was in fact the honest P.G.M. Hutchinson of the address in Caterham with the telephone number which they had verified?" In my judgment, there is everything to show that Miss Ingram would never had accepted H.'s offer if she had known the truth, but nothing to rebut the ordinary presumption that she was addressing her acceptance, in law as well as in fact, to the person to whom she was speaking. I think, therefore, that there was offer and acceptance in form.

On my view of the law, it, therefore, becomes necessary to consider next whether there has been a mistake that vitiates the contract. As both my brethren are of opinion that there has been no offer and acceptance, the result of this further inquiry cannot affect the decision in the present case or its ratio, and I shall, therefore, state my conclusion and my reasons for it as briefly as may be.

In my judgment there has been no such mistake. I shall assume without arguments what I take to be the widest view of mistake that is to be found in the authorities, and that is that a mistake avoids the contract if at the time it is made there exists some state of fact which, as assumed, is the basis of the contract and as it is in truth, frustrates its object. ...

The fact that Miss Ingram refused to contract with H. until his supposed name and address had been "verified" goes to show that she regarded his identity as fundamental. In this she was misguided. She should have concerned herself with creditworthiness rather than with identity. The fact that H. gave P.G.M. Hutchinson's address in the directory was no proof that he was P.G.M. Hutchinson; and if he had been, that fact alone was no proof that his cheque would be met. Identity, therefore, did not really matter. Nevertheless, it may truly be said that to Miss Ingram, as she looked at it, it did. In my judgment, Miss Ingram's state of mind is immaterial to this question. When the law avoids a contract ab initio, it does so irrespective of the intentions or opinions or wishes of the parties themselves. ... This rule applies in the case of mistake because the reason for the avoidance is the same, namely, that the consent is vitiated by non-agreement about essentials. It is for the court to determine what in the light of all the circumstances is to be deemed essential. In my judgment, in the present case H.'s identity was immaterial. His creditworthiness was not, but creditworthiness in relation to contract is not a basic fact; it is only a way of expressing the belief that each party normally holds that the other will honour his promise. ...

There can be no doubt, as all this difference of opinion shows, that the dividing line between voidness and voidability, between fundamental mistake and incidental deceit, is a very fine one. That a fine and difficult distinction has to be drawn is not necessarily any reproach to the law. But need the rights of the parties in a case like this depend on such a distinction? The great virtue of the common law is that it sets out to solve legal problems by the application to them of principles which the ordinary man is expected to recognise as sensible and just; their application in any particular case may produce what seems to him a hard result, but as principles they should be within his understanding and merit his approval. But here, contrary to its habit, the common law, instead of looking for a principle that is simple and just, rests on theoretical distinctions. Why should the question whether the defendant should or should not pay the plaintiff damages for conversion depend upon voidness or voidability, and upon inferences to be drawn from a conversation in which the defendant took no part? The true spirit of the common law is to override theoretical distinctions when they stand in the way of doing practical justice. For the doing of justice, the relevant question in this sort of case is not whether the contract was void or voidable, but which of two innocent parties shall suffer for the fraud of a third. The plain answer is that the loss should be divided between them in such proportion as is just in all the circumstances. If it be pure misfortune, the loss should be borne equally; if the fault or imprudence of either party has caused or contributed to the loss, it should be borne by that party in the whole or in the greater part. In saying this, I am suggesting nothing novel, for this sort of observation has often been made. But it is only in comparatively recent times that the idea of giving to a court power to apportion loss has found a place in our law. I have in mind particularly the Law Reform Acts of 1935, 1943 and 1945, that dealt respectively with joint tortfeasors, frustrated contracts and contributory negligence. These statutes, which I believe to have worked satisfactorily, show a modern inclination towards a decision based on a just apportionment rather than one given in black or white according to the logic of the law. I believe it would be useful if Parliament were now to consider whether or not it is practicable by means of a similar act of law reform to provide for the victims of a fraud a better way of adjusting their mutual loss than that which has grown out of the common law.

[The judgment of Pearce LJ is omitted. The appeal was dismissed but leave was granted to appeal to the House of Lords.]

LEWIS V AVERAY
[1972] 1 QB 198 (CA)

LORD DENNING MR: This is another case where one of two innocent persons has to suffer for the fraud of a third. It will no doubt interest students and find its place in the textbooks.

Mr. Lewis is a young man who is a post-graduate student of chemistry. He lives at Clifton near Bristol. He had an Austin Cooper "S" motor car. He decided to sell it. He put an advertisement in the newspaper offering it for £450. On May 8, 1969, in reply to the advertisement a man—I will simply call him the "rogue," for so he was—telephoned and asked if he could come and see the car. He did not give his name. He said he was speaking from Wales, in Glamorganshire. Mr. Lewis said he could come and see it. He came in the evening to Mr. Lewis's flat. Mr. Lewis showed him the car, which was parked outside. The rogue drove it and tested it. He said he liked it. They then went along to the flat of Mr. Lewis's fiancée, Miss Kershaw (they have since married). He told them he was Richard Green and talked much about the film world. He led both of them to believe that he was the well-known film actor, Richard Greene, who played Robin Hood in the "Robin Hood" series. They talked about the car. He asked to see the logbook. He was shown it and seemed satisfied. He said he would like to buy the car. They agreed a price of £450. The rogue wrote out a cheque for £450 on the Beckenham Branch of the Midland Bank. He signed it "R.A. Green." He wanted to take the car at once. But Mr. Lewis was not willing for him to have it until the cheque was cleared. To hold him off, Mr. Lewis said there were one or two small jobs he would like to do on the car before letting him have it, and that would give time for the cheque to be cleared. The rogue said, "Don't worry about those small jobs. I would like to take the car now." Mr. Lewis said: "Have you anything to prove that you are Mr. Richard Green?" The rogue thereupon brought out a special pass of admission to Pinewood Studios which had an official stamp on it. It bore the name of Richard A. Green and the address, and also a photograph which was plainly the photograph of this man, who was the rogue.

On seeing this pass, Mr. Lewis was satisfied. He thought this man was really Mr. Richard Greene, the film actor. By that time it was 11 o'clock at night. Mr. Lewis took the cheque and let the rogue have the car and the logbook and the Ministry of Transport test certificate. Each wrote and signed a receipt evidencing the transaction. Mr. Lewis wrote:

Received from
Richard A. Green, 59 Marsh Rd., Beckenham, Kent
the sum of £450 in return for Austin Cooper S Reg.
No. AHT 484B chassis No. CA257—549597
   Keith Lewis.

The rogue wrote:

> Received logbook No. 771835 and M.O.T. for Mini-Cooper S No. AHT 484B
>   R.A. Green.

Next day, May 9, 1969, Mr. Lewis put the cheque into the bank. A few days later the bank told him it was worthless. The rogue had stolen a cheque book and written this £450 on a stolen cheque.

Meanwhile, while the cheque was going through, the rogue sold the car to an innocent purchaser. He sold it to a young man called Mr. Averay. He was at the time under 21. He was a music student in London at the Royal College of Music. His parents live at Bromley. He was keen to buy a car. He put an advertisement in the "Exchange and Mart," seeking a car for £200. In answer he had a telephone call from the rogue. He said he was speaking from South Wales. He said that he was coming to London to sell a car. Mr. Averay arranged to meet him on May 11, 1969. The rogue came with the car. Young Mr. Averay liked it, but wanted to get approval of his parents. They drove it to Bromley. The parents did approve. Young Mr. Averay agreed to buy it for £200. The rogue gave his name as Mr. Lewis. He handed over the car and logbook to young Mr. Averay. The logbook showed the owner as Mr. Lewis. In return Mr. Averay, in entire good faith, gave the rogue a cheque for £200. The rogue signed this receipt:

> Sale of Cooper S to A.J. Averay.
> Received £200 for the Cooper S Registration No.
> AHT 484B, the said car being my property absolutely,
> there being no hire purchase charges outstanding or
> other impediment to selling the car:
>   Keith Lewis
>   May 13, 1969.

A fortnight later, on May 29, 1969, Mr. Averay wanted the workshop manual for the car. So his father on his behalf wrote to the name and address of the seller as given in the logbook—that is, Mr. Lewis. Then, of course, the whole story came to light. The rogue had cashed the cheque and disappeared. The police have tried to trace him, but without success.

Now Mr. Lewis, the original owner of the car, sues young Mr. Averay. Mr. Lewis claims that the car is still his. He claims damages for conversion. The judge found in favour of Mr. Lewis and awarded damages of £330 for conversion.

The real question in the case is whether on May 8, 1969, there was a contract of sale under which the property in the car passed from Mr. Lewis to the rogue. If there was such a contract, then, even though it was voidable for fraud, nevertheless Mr. Averay would get a good title to the car. But if there was no contract of sale by Mr. Lewis to the rogue—either because there was, on the face of it, no agreement between the parties, or because any apparent agreement was a nullity and void ab initio for mistake, then no property would pass from Mr. Lewis to the rogue. Mr. Averay would not get a good title because the rogue had no property to pass to him.

There is no doubt that Mr. Lewis was mistaken as to the identity of the person who handed him the cheque. He thought that he was Richard Greene, a film actor of standing and worth: whereas in fact he was a rogue whose identity is quite unknown. It was under the influence of that mistake that Mr. Lewis let the rogue have the car. He would not have dreamed of letting him have it otherwise.

What is the effect of this mistake? There are two cases in our books which cannot, to my mind, be reconciled the one with the other. One of them is *Phillips v. Brooks*

Ltd. [1919] 2 K.B. 23, where a jeweller had a ring for sale. The other is *Ingram v. Little* [1961] 1 Q.B. 31, where two ladies had a car for sale. In each case the story is very similar to the present. A plausible rogue comes along. The rogue says he likes the ring, or the car, as the case may be. He asks the price. The seller names it. The rogue says he is prepared to buy it at that price. He pulls out a cheque book. He writes, or prepares to write, a cheque for the price. The seller hesitates. He has never met this man before. He does not want to hand over the ring or the car not knowing whether the cheque will be met. The rogue notices the seller's hesitation. He is quick with his next move. He says to the jeweller, in *Phillips v. Brooks*: "I am Sir George Bullough of 11 St. James's Square"; or to the ladies in *Ingram v. Little* "I am P.G.M. Hutchinson of Stanstead House, Stanstead Road, Caterham"; or to the post-graduate student in the present case: "I am Richard Greene, the film actor of the Robin Hood series." Each seller checks up the information. The jeweller looks up the directory and finds there is a Sir George Bullough at 11 St. James's Square. The ladies check up too. They look at the telephone directory and find there is a "P.G.M. Hutchinson of Stanstead House, Stanstead Road, Caterham." The post-graduate student checks up too. He examines the official pass of the Pinewood Studios and finds that it is a pass for "Richard A. Green" to the Pinewood Studios with this man's photograph on it. In each case the seller feels that this is sufficient confirmation of the man's identity. So he accepts the cheque signed by the rogue and lets him have the ring, in the one case, and the car and logbook in the other two cases. The rogue goes off and sells the goods to a third person who buys them in entire good faith, and pays the price to the rogue. The rogue disappears. The original seller presents the cheque. It is dishonoured. Who is entitled to the goods? The original seller? Or the ultimate buyer? The courts have given different answers. In *Phillips v. Brooks*, the ultimate buyer was held to be entitled to the ring. In *Ingram v. Little* the original seller was held to be entitled to the car. In the present case the deputy county court judge has held the original seller entitled.

It seems to me that the material facts in each case are quite indistinguishable the one from the other. In each case there was, to all outward appearance, a contract; but there was a mistake by the seller as to the identity of the buyer. This mistake was fundamental. In each case it led to the handing over of the goods. Without it the seller would not have parted with them.

This case therefore raises the question: What is the effect of a mistake by one party as to the identity of the other? It has sometimes been said that if a party makes a mistake as to the identity of the person with whom he is contracting there is no contract, or, if there is a contract, it is a nullity and void, so that no property can pass under it. This has been supported by a reference to the French jurist Pothier; but I have said before, and I repeat now, his statement is no part of English law. I know that it was quoted by Lord Haldane in *Lake v. Simmons* [1927] A.C. 487, 501, and, as such, misled Tucker J. in *Sowler v. Potter* [1940] 1 K.B. 271, into holding that a lease was void whereas it was really voidable. But Pothier's statement [to the effect that the mistake destroys consent and annuls the agreement] has given rise to such refinements that it is time it was dead and buried altogether.

For instance, in *Ingram v. Little* [1961] 1 Q.B. 31 the majority of the court suggested that the difference between *Phillips v. Brooks* [1919] 2 K.B. 243 and *Ingram v. Little* was that in *Phillips v. Brooks* the contract of sale was concluded (so as to pass the property to the rogue) before the rogue made the fraudulent misrepresentation: see [1961] 1 Q.B. 31, 51, 60: whereas in *Ingram v. Little* the rogue made the fraudulent misrepresentation before the contract was concluded. My own view is that in each case the property in the goods did not pass until the seller let the rogue have the goods.

Again it has been suggested that a mistake as to the identity of a person is one thing: and a mistake as to his attributes is another. A mistake as to identity, it is said, avoids a contract: whereas a mistake as to attributes does not. But this is a distinction without a difference. A man's very name is one of his attributes. It is also a key to his identity. If then, he gives a false name, is it a mistake as to his identity? or a mistake as to his attributes? These fine distinctions do no good to the law.

As I listened to the argument in this case, I felt it wrong that an innocent purchaser (who knew nothing of what passed between the seller and the rogue) should have his title depend on such refinements. After all, he has acted with complete circumspection and in entire good faith: whereas it was the seller who let the rogue have the goods and thus enabled him to commit the fraud. I do not, therefore, accept the theory that a mistake as to identity renders a contract void. I think the true principle is that which underlies the decision of this court in *King's Norton Metal Co. Ltd. v. Edridge Merrett & Co. Ltd.* (1897) 14 T.L.R. 98 and of Horridge J. in *Phillips v. Brooks* [1919] 2 K.B. 243, which has stood for these last 50 years. It is this: When two parties have come to a contract—or rather what appears, on the face of it, to be a contract—the fact that one party is mistaken as to the identity of the other does not mean that there is no contract, or that the contract is a nullity and void from the beginning. It only means that the contract is voidable, that is, liable to be set aside at the instance of the mistaken person, so long as he does so before third parties have in good faith acquired rights under it.

Applied to the cases such as the present, this principle is in full accord with the presumption stated by Pearce L.J. and also Devlin L.J. in *Ingram v. Little* [1961] 1 Q.B. 31, 61, 66. When a dealing is had between a seller like Mr. Lewis and a person who is actually there present before him, then the presumption in law is that there is a contract, even though there is a fraudulent impersonation by the buyer representing himself as a different man than he is. There is a contract made with the very person there, who is present in person. It is liable no doubt to be avoided for fraud, but it is still a good contract under which title will pass unless and until it is avoided. In support of that presumption, Devlin L.J. quoted, at p. 66, not only the English case of *Phillips v. Brooks*, but other cases in the United States where "the courts hold that if A appeared in person before B, impersonating C, an innocent purchaser from A gets the property in the goods against B." That seems to me to be right in principle in this country also.

In this case Mr. Lewis made a contract of sale with the very man, the rogue, who came to the flat. I say that he "made a contract" because in this regard we do not look into his intentions, or into his mind to know what he was thinking or into the mind of the rogue. We look to the outward appearances. On the face of the dealing. Mr. Lewis made a contract under which he sold the car to the rogue, delivered the car and the logbook to him, and took a cheque in return. The contract is evidenced by the receipts which were signed. It was, of course, induced by fraud. The rogue made false representations as to his identity. But it was still a contract, though voidable for fraud. It was a contract under which this property passed to the rogue, and in due course passed from the rogue to Mr. Averay, before the contract was avoided.

Though I very much regret that either of these good and reliable gentlemen should suffer, in my judgment it is Mr. Lewis who should do so. I think the appeal should be allowed and judgment entered for the defendant.

[Phillimore and Megaw LJJ agreed. See also McCamus at 539-48; MacDougall at 238-40; Waddams at paras 299-306.]

VII. DOCUMENTS MISTAKENLY SIGNED

FOSTER V MACKINNON
(1869), LR 4 CP 704

This was an action by an indorsee against an indorser on a bill of exchange for £3000. One Callow, who was called as a witness for the plaintiff testified that the defendant, an elderly man, signed the note in his presence, he having taken the bill, as drawn and endorsed by one Cooper, to the defendant and asked him to sign it telling him it was a guarantee. The defendant had previously signed a guarantee for £3000 for Callow but no liability had resulted to him. Callow only showed the defendant the back of the paper; it was, however, in the ordinary shape of a bill of exchange, and bore a stamp, the impress of which was visible through the paper. The defendant wrote his signature right after Cooper's. Bovill C.J. at the trial told the jury that, if the endorsement was not the signature of the defendant, or if, being his signature, it was obtained upon a fraudulent representation that it was a guarantee, and the defendant signed it without knowing that it was a bill, and under the belief that it was a guarantee, and if the defendant was not guilty of any negligence in so signing the paper, he was entitled to the verdict. The jury found for the defendant. On a rule nisi for a new trial on grounds of misdirection and that the verdict was against the weight of evidence.

BYLES J (for the court): ... The case presented by the defendant is, that he never made the contract declared on; that he never saw the face of the bill; that the purport of the contract was fraudulently mis-described to him; that, when he signed one thing, he was told and believed that he was signing another and an entirely different thing; and that his mind never went with his act.

It seems plain, on principle and on authority, that, if a blind man, or man who cannot read, or who for some reason (not implying negligence) forgot to read, has a written contract falsely read over to him, the reader misreading to such a degree that the written contract is of a nature altogether different from the contract pretended to be read from the paper which the blind or illiterate man afterwards signs; then, at least if there is no negligence, the signature so obtained is of no force. And it is invalid not merely on the ground of fraud, where fraud exists, but on the ground that the mind of the signer did not accompany the signature; in other words that he never intended to sign, and therefore in contemplation of law never did sign, the contract to which his name is appended.

The authorities appear to us to support this view of the law. In *Thoroughgood's Case* (1582), 2 Co. Rep. 9a; 76 E.R. 408, it was held that, if an illiterate man have a deed falsely read over to him, and he then seals and delivers the parchment; that parchment is nevertheless not his deed. In a note to *Thoroughgood's Case*, in Fraser's edition of *Coke's Reports*, it is suggested that the doctrine is not confined to the condition of an illiterate grantor; and a case in Keilway's *Reports*, 70, pl. 6, is cited in support of this observation. On reference to that case it appears that one of the judges did there observe that it made no difference whether the grantor were lettered or unlettered. That, however, was a case where the grantee himself was the defrauding party. But the position that, if a grantor or covenantor be deceived or misled as to the *actual contents* of the deed, the deed does not bind him, is supported by many authorities. ... Accordingly, it has recently been decided in the Exchequer Chamber, that, if a deed be delivered, and a blank left therein be afterwards improperly filled up (at least if that be done without the grantor's negligence), it is not the deed of the grantor: *Swan v. North British Australasian Land Company* (1863), 2 H. & C. 175; 159 E.R. 73.

These cases apply to deeds; but the principle is equally applicable to other written contracts. Nevertheless, this principle, when applied to negotiable instruments, must be and is limited in its application. These instruments are not only assignable, but they form part of the currency of the country. A qualification of the general rule is necessary to protect innocent transferees for value. If, therefore, a man write his name across the back of a blank bill-stamp, and part with it, and the paper is afterwards improperly filled up, he is liable as indorser. If he write it across the face of the bill, he is liable as acceptor, when the instrument has once passed into the hands of an innocent indorsee for value before maturity, and liable to the extent of any sum which the stamp will cover.

In these cases, however, the party signing knows what he is doing; the indorser intended to indorse, and the acceptor intended to accept, a bill of exchange to be thereafter filled up, leaving the amount, the date, the maturity, and the other parties to the bill undetermined.

But, in the case now under consideration, the defendant, according to the evidence, if believed, and the finding of the jury, never intended to indorse a bill of exchange at all, but intended to sign a contract of an entirely different nature. It was not his design, and, if he were guilty of no negligence, it was not even his fault that the instrument he signed turned out to be a bill of exchange. It was as if he had written his name on a sheet of paper for the purpose of franking a letter, or in a lady's album, or on an order for admission to the Temple Church, or on the fly-leaf of a book, and there had already been, without his knowledge, a bill of exchange or a promissory note payable to order inscribed on the other side of the paper. To make the case clearer, suppose the bill or note on the other side of the paper in each of these cases to be written at a time subsequent to the signature, then the fraudulent misapplication of that genuine signature to a different purpose would have been a counterfeit alteration of a writing with intent to defraud, and would therefore have amounted to a forgery. In that case, the signer would not have been bound by his signature, for two reasons, first, that he never in fact signed the writing declared on, and, secondly, that he never intended to sign any such contract.

In the present case, the first reason does not apply, but the second reason does apply. The defendant never intended to sign that contract, or any such contract. He never intended to put his name to any instrument that then was or thereafter might become negotiable. He was deceived, not merely as to the legal effect, but as to the *actual contents* of the instrument.

We are not aware of any case in which the precise question now before us has arisen on bills of exchange or promissory notes, or been judicially discussed. ... But, in *Putnam v. Sullivan*, an American case, reported in 4 Mass. 45, and cited in *Parsons on Bills*, vol. i, p. 111 n., a distinction is taken by Chief Justice Parsons between a case where an endorser intended to indorse such a note as he actually indorsed, being induced by fraud to indorse it, and a case where he intended to indorse a different note and for a different purpose. And the Court intimated an opinion that, even in such a case as that, a distinction might prevail and protect the indorsee.

The distinction in the case now under consideration is a much plainer one; for, on this branch of the rule, we are to assume that the indorser never intended to indorse at all, but to sign a contract of an entirely different nature.

For these reasons, we think the direction of the Lord Chief Justice was right.

[A new trial was granted because "the case should undergo further investigation."]

HOWATSON V WEBB
[1907] 1 Ch 537

Webb was the managing clerk of one Hooper, a solicitor, who was engaged in building speculations near Edmonton, north of London, for the purposes of which Hooper had had various leases put in Webb's name as nominee for him. Some time after Webb had left Hooper's service, Hooper called him on the phone and asked him to come over and sign some deeds "transferring the Edmonton property." Webb went the same day and arrived about lunch time. Hooper seemed to be in a great hurry and asked Webb to sign and "Hurry up and come and join me at lunch." Webb asked "What are the deeds?" to which Hooper replied, "They are just deeds transferring that property," presumably meaning the Edmonton property. Hooper then went out and Webb signed a number of deeds left open for signature on a table. One was a mortgage dated that day, June 2, 1899, between Webb and one Whitaker as mortgagee and contained Webb's covenant to pay the mortgagee £1000. During the next seven years Hooper paid the interest and £200 on principal. Webb was not called upon to pay any interest, but on February 2, 1906, the plaintiff, Miss Howatson, asked for payment of the principal. Miss Howatson took a transfer of the mortgage from Whitaker in October 1902, and paid Whitaker, or possibly Hooper, as solicitor in the transaction, £800. Webb raised the defence of *non est factum*.

WARRINGTON J: The question in this case is which of two innocent parties is to suffer for the roguery of a third party. ...

[After a careful review of *Foster v Mackinnon* and some other cases, Warrington J continued:]

What does the evidence in the present case shew? I may go so far in the defendant's favour as to say that Webb, having regard to his knowledge of Hooper, when Hooper said that the deeds were "deeds for transferring the Edmonton property" was justified in believing that they were deeds such as a nominee could be called upon to execute either in favour of a new nominee or for the purpose of putting an end to his own position of nominee, and certainly not a deed creating a mortgage to another person. But in my opinion that is not enough. He was told that they were deeds relating to the property to which they did in fact relate. His mind was therefore applied to the question of dealing with that property. The deeds did deal with that property. The misrepresentation was as to the contents of the deed, and not as to the character and class of the deed. He knew he was dealing with the class of deed with which in fact he was dealing, but did not ascertain its contents. The deed contained a covenant to pay. Under those circumstances I cannot say that the deed is absolutely void. It purported to be a transfer of the property, and it was a transfer of the property. If the plea of *non est factum* is to succeed the deed must be wholly, and not partly, void. If that plea is an answer in this case, I must hold it to be an answer in every case of misrepresentation. In my opinion the law does not go as far as that. The defence therefore fails. There must therefore be judgment for the plaintiff on the claim with costs.

[The judgment of Warrington J, which has been drastically cut, was unanimously affirmed on appeal—[1908] 1 Ch 1.]

SAUNDERS V ANGLIA BUILDING SOCIETY (GALLIE V LEE)
[1971] AC 1004 (HL)

LORD PEARSON: My Lords, this appeal raises questions of law as to the limits of the plea of *non est factum*, in a case where the person who signed the deed of assignment of a long lease of a house alleges that she was deceived by the assignee as to the nature and character of the deed, so that it was not her deed, and she relies on the plea not only against the assignee who is alleged to have deceived her but also against an innocent third party, the defendant building society who afterwards in good faith and with no knowledge of any defect affecting her signature lent money to the assignee on the security of the house. There are also questions of fact on which two members at least of the Court of Appeal took different views from that of the learned trial judge.

In 1962 the plaintiff, Mrs. Gallie, was 78 years of age. She owned a long lease of a house, where she resided and earned her living by taking in lodgers. The ground rent was small, so that in broad effect she was the owner of the house. The only one of her relatives who frequently visited her was her nephew, Walter Parkin, aged about 40. He had a small garage at which he did motor repairing work. He had a friend and business associate, named William Robert Lee, whom she trusted, although in the event Lee proved to be untrustworthy.

The plaintiff told Parkin that she had made a will leaving her house to him. Later she handed over to him the deeds of her house thinking apparently that she was thereby transferring to him the ownership of the house or at any rate enabling him to raise money on the security of the house. She made it a condition that she would have the use of the house for the rest of her life. Parkin needed money for his business, and she wished to help him in this way. If a further step, such as the making of a deed of gift, was required, she would be willing to do this.

Parkin consulted with Lee. Parkin was in a difficulty. He had left his wife and three children, and for years had been living with another woman who had become known as "Mrs. Parkin." He was in arrear with maintenance payments to his wife, and he was afraid that if he became the owner of the house his wife might be able to force him to pay the maintenance. Lee needed money in order to purchase a house for himself and his family, as they were still living in his father's house. He saw the opportunity of raising money on the security of the plaintiff's house if he could become the owner of it. It was arranged, or at any rate proposed, between Parkin and Lee that the plaintiff should transfer the house to Parkin by deed of gift, and when she had done so Parkin should sell the house to Lee at a price of £2,000 or £2,500 (the evidence is not clear as to the amount of the proposed price) and Lee should raise money from a building society on the security of the house and should pay the price of £2,000 or £2,500 by making monthly payments to the woman known as "Mrs. Parkin." Lee consulted a firm of solicitors about the proposed transaction and was advised that a recent deed of gift on the title would be likely to deter a building society from lending money on the security of the house and that a direct sale by the plaintiff to Lee would be preferable. Accordingly, the solicitors drafted a deed of assignment of the house from the plaintiff to Lee at a stated price of £3,000. It may be that the conduct of the solicitors or their managing clerk fell below professional standards, but it is not necessary to investigate that aspect of the matter.

Lee and Parkin went to see the plaintiff. Lee had the deed, and he put it before the plaintiff for her to sign. The plaintiff had broken her spectacles and could not read effectively without them. She asked what the deed was, and Lee said, in the presence of Parkin and without any dissent from him, that the deed was "to do with the gift by deed to Wally for the house." The plaintiff, not having asked Parkin to read the deed to her or give his explanation of it, but assuming that Parkin and Lee knew what they were doing, and desiring to help Parkin in the way that he wished, signed the deed. Parkin witnessed the plaintiff's signature to the deed. The price of £3,000 was not paid or intended to be paid, so that in practical reality the assignment from the plaintiff to Lee was for no consideration. As between Lee and Parkin the intention was that £2,000 or £2,500 was to be made available in some way by Lee to Parkin: he might pay monthly instalments to the woman known as "Mrs. Parkin" or he might from time to time put money into the business of Parkin, in which Lee had some interest. It is not easy to gather from the evidence exactly what the arrangement was, and it probably was somewhat indefinite in its details, but I think that was the broad effect of it. If this arrangement or something on these lines, had been duly carried out, the plaintiff's signature to the deed would have enabled Parkin through Lee to raise money on the security of the house in the way that Parkin considered most beneficial to himself.

Lee made to the defendant building society an application containing some false statements and supported it with a testimonial, drafted by him and signed by Parkin, also containing some false statements. The defendant building society, in response to the application, and in reliance on the title deeds including the plaintiff's assign- ment to Lee, and having no notice of any defect in the assignment or of anything unusual affecting it and acting in complete good faith, lent £2,000 to Lee on the security of the house.

Then things went wrong. Lee failed to carry out his arrangement with Parkin. Lee was heavily indebted, and the sum which he had borrowed from the defendant building society was used up in paying his debts, and probably his other resources were insufficient to enable him to make any money available to Parkin. At any rate, he did not make the sum of £2,500 or £2,000 or any sum available to Parkin in any way. Thus, in the event, the plaintiff's execution of the deed of assignment did not bring any benefit to Parkin, although it would have done if his arrangement with Lee had been duly carried out by Lee.

The plaintiff commenced her action in July, 1964. By her amended statement of claim she claimed (1) against Lee a declaration that the assignment of the house to him was void, return of the title deeds or their value and damages for their detention, and damages for fraudulent misrepresentation, and (2) against the defendant build- ing society a declaration that the assignment of the house to Lee was void, and the delivery up of the title deeds or their value and damages for their detention.

The plaintiff's evidence was, owing to her age and infirmity, taken on commis- sion, so that the learned judge did not have the advantage of seeing and hearing her as she was giving her evidence. Evidence was given at the trial by Parkin, Lee and a witness named Hall who had been managing clerk of the solicitors concerned. The learned judge found that Lee and Hall had told lies in the witness box and he could not rely on their evidence. As to Parkin, he found that he had told some lies in the witness box and that his evidence showed a high degree of confusion and inaccu- racy, but nevertheless there were times in his evidence when he was saying simple things when the learned judge had the conviction that he was telling the truth. With regard to the plaintiff's evidence the learned judge said: "It is apparent from the transcript of that evidence first that she must have been a difficult witness, that her evidence is not very clear in a number of respects and in some respects it is contradictory."

He did, however, find as a fact that the plaintiff did not read the document, that Lee represented it to be a deed of gift to Parkin and that the plaintiff executed it in the belief that that was what it was. He also found as a fact that the plaintiff had no idea that the document took the form of an assignment on sale from her to Lee and that a sale or gift to him was something which she did not and would not for one moment have contemplated.

As at least two members of the Court of Appeal did not accept these findings of the learned judge, and I prefer their views to his (though undoubtedly these questions of fact are difficult), I will set out a few extracts from the plaintiff's evidence taken on commission, in order to show in outline what was the basis of their views:

> Q. Do you know that Mr. Parkin—that is Wally—gave the building society a testimonial about Mr. Lee so that he could get a mortgage on this house? Do you know that? A. I did not know what they were doing when they came to see me. I only said to my nephew—I didn't refer to Mr. Lee; I referred to my nephew, and I said to my nephew—"I don't mind, helping you at all. I have helped you in the past and I will still help you as long as I can; but mind you are doing the right thing." I have always trusted my nephew.
>
> Q. And if he told you a document was all right you believed him? A. I believe my nephew. I don't believe Mr. Lee.
>
> Q. And, of course, when your nephew and Mr. Lee came along with the document you thought it must be all right? A. I did.
>
> Q. And it was because your nephew was there that you were willing to sign it? A. Yes. ...
>
> Q. Did you know that Mr. Lee stated that he would buy the house from Mr. Parkin? A. No, I did not know he was buying the house. I just thought he was having a loan on my house.
>
> Q. Mr. Lee was? A. Yes. But if my nephew had have come to me and said, "Auntie, I am in difficulties," I would have got him the money instead of bothering Mr. Lee.
>
> Q. But the money was to be borrowed on your deeds through Mr. Lee. Is that right? A. Yes.
>
> Q. And you were quite satisfied about that? A. Yes. I done it to help my nephew with his business. ...
>
> Q. Have you brought this action to help your nephew? A. I have, sir. ...
>
> Q. Did it occur to you to ask Wally to read the document to you? A. I never thought of that, sir.
>
> Q. You thought it was all right. If Wally was there, it must be all right? A. I did.

The learned judge (1) made a declaration as against Lee that the alleged assignment of June 15, 1962 was void and of no effect, and directed an inquiry as to damages; (2) made a declaration in the same terms as against the defendant building society, and ordered them to deliver up the title deeds. There was no appeal by Lee. There was an appeal by the defendant building society, and it was allowed by the Court of Appeal.

The Master of the Rolls decided the case on a broad principle to which I will refer later.

Russell L.J. carefully examined the facts of the case and made two comments on the plaintiff's evidence, and these were in effect his grounds of decision. He said, [1969] 2 Ch. 17, 40–41:

> The first is ... it is inadequate to establish the minimum facts necessary to establish the plea of *non est factum*, assuming that it would be sufficient for that plea to show that the plaintiff was induced wholly by Lee's falsehood to think that she was signing a deed of gift to Parkin whereas she executed an assignment in terms for value to Lee. I think that the plaintiff's evidence in this regard was unsatisfactory, and was inadequate to

discharge the burden of proof that is laid by law on this plea, which requires strong and clear evidence for its discharge. ... At first sight, of course, it is easy to see the difference between a voluntary assignment of the leasehold property to A and an assignment for value of that property to B. But what upon the plaintiff's own evidence was the essential character of the document she was intending to execute? It was a document intended by her to divest herself of her leasehold property by transferring it to another, not as mere trustee for her, but so that transferee should be in a position to deal with the property and in particular by borrowing money on the security of the property. Her evidence in my view makes it plain that she understood that Lee and Parkin were jointly concerned in a project of raising money on security of the property and this was her intention. In those circumstances I do not consider that it is correct to say that, for the purposes of the plea of *non est factum*, a transfer by her to Lee is to be regarded as of a totally different character or nature from a transfer to Parkin. The judge relied on the identity of the transferee as constituting the essential nature or character of the instrument. In so doing I think that he paid insufficient regard to what I may call the object of the exercise. Suppose that Lee had carried through the arrangement that Parkin had understood was made—had in fact paid Parkin. This would have fulfilled the plaintiff's purpose in executing the document put before her.

I respectfully agree with the reasoning of Russell L.J. and in particular with the principle that importance should be attached to the "object of the exercise," when dissimilar legal documents may have similar practical effects. Another example of this will be found in *Mercantile Credit Co. Ltd. v. Hamblin*, [1965] 2 Q.B. 242, 267. In that case the defendant had signed hire-purchase documents, and there was some evidence that she intended to raise money by means of a mortgage of her car, and she had pleaded *non est factum*. It became plain, however, that the object of the proposed hire-purchase transaction was to produce the same practical effect as a mortgage of the car would have produced (if it had been lawful). She would sell the car through a dealer to a finance company, and take it back from the finance company on hire purchase, with the result that she would receive a lump sum down and would repay it with additions by instalments over a period, so that she would for practical purposes be in much the same position as if she had mortgaged the car. The plea of *non est factum* failed.

I think Salmon L.J.'s view of the facts in the present case was consistent with that of Russell L.J., but his main conclusion on the facts was this, [1969] 2 Ch. 17, 45:

> In the present case it seems plain from Mrs. Gallie's evidence, which was given before an examiner and which we are, therefore, in just as good a position to evaluate as was the judge, that Mrs. Gallie would have executed the conveyance even if its true character and class and the nature of the transaction had been properly explained to her and she had understood the explanation. Certainly she was not induced to sign by any false representation made to her by Lee.

In the later passage Salmon L.J. said, at p. 47: "... [I]f Parkin had taken the trouble to explain the true nature of the document to her and told her that the solicitors had advised that it should be in that form and asked her to sign it, there can in my view be no real doubt but that she would have done so."

I think that conclusion of Salmon L.J. is probably right but there may be an element of doubt as to what the plaintiff would have done if she had been given a full explanation of the document. I would dismiss the appeal for the reasons given by Russell L.J. because they seem to me free from doubt.

In the judgments of the Court of Appeal in this case there was an elaborate and, if I may respectfully say so, illuminating and valuable discussion of the law relating to the plea of *non est factum*. It is not practicable in this opinion to examine what they have said at length and in detail, dealing with every point. It seems to me that the right course here is to examine the law on this subject with the aid of the judgments in the Court of Appeal and to endeavour to arrive at clear general propositions for the future on the basis of the earlier law which I think has become distorted in some respects.

I must, however, deal specifically with the broad principle stated by the Master of the Rolls as his conclusion from his investigation of the law, at pp. 36-37:

> ... [W]henever a man of full age and understanding, who can read and write, signs a legal document which is put before him for signature—by which I mean a document which, it is apparent on the face of it, is intended to have legal consequences—then, if he does not take the trouble to read it, but signs it as it is, relying on the word of another as to its character or contents or effect, he cannot be heard to say that it is not his document. By his conduct in signing it he has represented, to all those into whose hands it may come, that it is his document; and once they act upon it as being his document, he cannot go back on it, and say it was nullity from the beginning.

In applying the principle to the present case, the Master of the Rolls said, at p. 37:

> ... Mrs. Gallie cannot in this case say that the deed of assignment was not her deed. She signed it without reading it, relying on the assurance of Lee that it was a deed of gift to Wally. It turned out to be a deed of assignment to Lee. But it was obviously a legal document. She signed it: and the building society advanced money on the faith of it being her document. She cannot now be allowed to disavow her signature.

There can be no doubt that this statement of principle by the Master of the Rolls is not only a clear and concise formulation but also a valuable guide to the right decision to be given by a court in any ordinary case. The danger of giving an undue extension to the plea of *non est factum* has been pointed out in a number of cases. For instance in *Muskham Finance Ltd. v. Howard*, [1963] 1 Q.B. 904, 912 Donovan L.J. delivering the judgment of the court said:

> The plea of *non est factum* is a plea which must necessarily be kept within narrow limits. Much confusion and uncertainty would result in the field of contract and elsewhere if a man were permitted to try to disown his signature simply by asserting that he did not understand that which he had signed.

In *Hunter v. Walters* (1871), L.R. 7 Ch. App. 75, 87, Mellish L.J. said: "Now, in my opinion, it is still a doubtful question at law, on which I do not wish to give any decisive opinion, whether, if there be a false representation respecting the contents of a deed, a person who is an educated person, and who might, by very simple means, have satisfied himself as to what the contents of the deed really were, may not, by executing it negligently be estopped as between himself and a person who innocently acts upon the faith of the deed being valid, and who accepts an estate under it."

This passage was referred to by Farwell L.J. in *Howatson v. Webb*, [1908] 1 Ch. 1, being 3-4, where he said:

> I think myself that the question suggested, but not decided, by Mellish L.J. in that case will some day have to be determined, viz., whether the old cases on misrepresentation as to the contents of a deed were not based upon the illiterate character of the person to whom the deed was read over, and on the fact that an illiterate man was treated as being in the same position as a blind man: see *Thoroughgood's Case* and *Sheppard's Touchstone* p. 56; and whether at the present time an educated person, who is not

blind, is not estopped from availing himself of the plea of *non est factum* against a person who innocently acts upon the faith of the deed being valid.

The principle stated by the Master of the Rolls can and should be applied so as to confine the scope of the plea of *non est factum* within narrow limits. It rightly prevents the plea from being successful in the normal case of a man who, however much he may have been misinformed about the nature of a deed or document, could easily have ascertained its true nature by reading it and has taken upon himself the risk of not reading it.

I think, however, that, unless the doctrine of *non est factum*, as it has been understood for at least a hundred years, is to be radically transformed, the statement of principle by the Master of the Rolls, taken just as it stands, is too absolute and rigid and needs some amplification and qualification. Doubts can be raised as to the meaning of the phrase "a man of full age and understanding, who can read and write." There are degrees of understanding and a person who is a great expert in some subjects may be like a child in relation to other subjects. Does the phrase refer to understanding of things in general, or does it refer to capacity for understanding (not necessarily in more than a general and elementary way) legal documents and property transactions and business transactions?

In my opinion, the plea of *non est factum* ought to be available in a proper case for the relief of a person who for permanent or temporary reasons (not limited to blindness or illiteracy) is not capable of both reading and sufficiently understanding the deed or other document to be signed. By "sufficiently understanding" I mean understanding at least to the point of detecting a fundamental difference between the actual document and the document as the signer had believed it to be. There must be a proper case for such relief. There would not be a proper case if (a) the signature of the document was brought about by negligence of the signer in failing to take precautions which he ought to have taken, or (b) the actual document was not fundamentally different from the document as the signer believed it to be. I will say something later about negligence and about fundamental difference.

In the present case the plaintiff was not at the material time a person who could read, because on the facts found she had broken her spectacles and could not effectively read without them. In any case her evidence (unless it was deliberately false, which has not been argued) shows that she had very little capacity for understanding legal documents and property transactions, and I do not think a reasonable jury would have found that she was negligent. In my opinion, it would not be right to dismiss the plaintiff's appeal on the ground that the principle stated by the Master of the Rolls is applicable to her case. I do not think it is.

The principle as stated is limited to a case in which it is apparent on the face of the document that it is intended to have legal consequences. That allows for possible success of the plea in a case such as *Lewis v. Clay* (1897), 67 L.J. Q.B. 224, where Clay had been induced to sign promissory notes by the cunning deception of a false friend, who caused him to believe that he was merely witnessing the friend's signature on several private and highly confidential documents, the material parts of which had been covered up.

I wish to reserve the question whether the plea of *non est factum* would ever be rightly successful in a case where (1) it is apparent on the face of the document that it is intended to have legal consequences; (2) the signer of the document is able to read and sufficiently understand the document; (3) the document is fundamentally different from what he supposes it to be; (4) he is induced to sign it without reading it. It seems unlikely that the plea ought ever to succeed in such a case, but it is inadvisable to rule out the wholly exceptional and unpredictable case.

I have said above that the statement of principle by the Master of Rolls needs to be amplified and qualified unless the doctrine of *non est factum*, as it has been understood for at least a hundred years, is to be radically transformed. What is the doctrine, and should it be radically transformed?

As to the early history, the authorities referred to in the judgment of Byles J. in *Foster v. Mackinnon* (1869), L.R. 4 C.P. 704, 711-12 (and also referred to in *Holdsworth's History of England Law*, Vol. 8, pp. 50-51) were cited in the argument of this appeal. Having considered them I think they show that the law relating to the plea of *non est factum* remained in an undeveloped state until the judgment in *Foster v. Mackinnon*, and the modern development began with that judgment. It was the judgment of the court (Bovill C.J., Byles, Keating and Montague Smith JJ.) delivered by Byles J. He said, at p. 711:

> It seems plain, on principle and on authority, that, if a blind man, or a man who cannot read, or who for some reason (not implying negligence) forbears to read, has a written contract falsely read over to him, the reader misreading to such a degree that the written contract is of a nature altogether different from the contract pretended to be read from the paper which the blind or illiterate man afterwards signs; then, at least if there be no negligence, the signature so obtained is of no force. And it is invalid not merely on the ground of fraud, where fraud exists, but on the ground that the mind of the signer did not accompany the signature; in other words, that he never intended to sign, and therefore in contemplation of law never did sign, the contract to which his name is appended.

In my opinion, the essential features of the doctrine are contained in that passage and the doctrine does not need any radical transformation. A minor comment is that the phrase "who for some reason (not implying negligence) forbears to read" is (to use a currently fashionable word) too "permissive" in its tone. If a person forbears to read the document, he nearly always should be reckoned as negligent or otherwise debarred from succeeding on the plea of *non est factum*.

The passage which I have set out from Byles J.'s judgment, though I think it contains the essential features, was only a brief summary in a leading judgment, and there are further developments which need to be considered.

Ascertainment of the intention. I think the doctrine of *non est factum* inevitably involves applying the subjective rather than the objective test to ascertain the intention. It takes the intention which a man has in his own mind rather than the intention which he manifests to others (the intention which as reasonable men they would infer from his words and conduct).

There are, however, some cases in which the subjective test of intention can be applied so as to produce the same result as would be produced by the objective test. Suppose a man signs a deed without knowing or inquiring or having any positive belief or formed opinion, as to its nature or effect: he signs it because his solicitor or other trusted adviser advises him to do so. Then his intention is to sign the deed that is placed before him, whatever it may be or do. That is the intention in his own mind as well as the intention which by signing he manifests to others. Examples of this will be found in *Hunter v. Walters* (1871), 7 Ch. App. 75; *National Provincial Bank of England v. Jackson* (1886), 33 Ch. D. 1; *King v. Smith*, [1900] 2 Ch. 425. In *King v. Smith*, Farwell J., at p. 430, cited and relied upon a passage in the judgment of Mellish L.J. in *Hunter v. Walters* (1817), L.R. 7 Ch. App. 75, 88, where he said:

> [W]hen a man knows that he is conveying or doing something with his estate, but does not ask what is the precise effect of the deed, because he is told it is a mere form, and

has such confidence in his solicitor as to execute the deed in ignorance, then, in my opinion, a deed so executed, although it may be voidable upon the ground of fraud, is not a void deed.

Farwell J. said, [1900] 2 Ch. 425, 430 that Mr. King "had absolute confidence in his solicitor, and executed any deed relating to his property that Eldred put before him."

I think this principle affords a solution to a problem that was raised in the course of the argument. Suppose that the very busy managing director of a large company has a pile of documents to be signed in a few minutes before his next meeting, and his secretary has arranged them for maximum speed with only the spaces for signature exposed, and he "signs them blind," as the saying is, not reading them or even looking at them. He may be exercising a wise economy of his time and energy. There is the possibility of some extraneous document, involving him in unexpected personal liability, having been fraudulently inserted in the pile, but this possibility is so improbable that a reasonable man would disregard it: *Bolton v. Stone*, [1951] A.C. 850, 858. Such conduct is not negligence in any ordinary sense of the word. But the person who signs documents in this way ought to be held bound by them, and ought not to be entitled to avoid liability so as to shift the burden of loss on to an innocent third party. The whole object of having documents signed by him is that he makes them his documents and takes responsibility for them. He takes the chance of a fraudulent substitution. I think the right view of such a case is that the person who signs intends to sign the documents placed before him, whatever they may be, and so there is no basis on which he could successfully plead *non est factum*.

Negligence. It is clear that by the law as it was laid down in *Foster v. Mackinnon* (1869), L.R. 4 C.P. 704 a person who had signed a document differing fundamentally from what he believed it to be would be disentitled from successfully pleading *non est factum* if his signing of the document was due to his own negligence. The word "negligence" in this connection had no special, technical meaning. It meant carelessness, and in each case it was a question of fact for the jury to decide whether the person relying on the plea had been negligent or not. In *Foster v. Mackinnon* the Lord Chief Justice had told the jury that, if the indorsement was not the defendant's signature, or if, being his signature, it was obtained upon a fraudulent representation that it was a guarantee, and the defendant signed it without knowing that it was a bill, and under the belief that it was a guarantee and if the defendant was not guilty of any negligence in so signing the paper, the defendant was entitled to the verdict. On appeal this direction was held to be correct. In *Vorley v. Cooke* (1857), 1 Giffard 230, 236-237, Stuart V.-C. said: "It cannot be said that Cooke's conduct was careless or rash. He was deceived, as anyone with the ordinary amount of intelligence and caution would have been deceived, and he is therefore entitled to be relieved." Whatever may be thought of the merits of the decision in that case, this passage illustrates the simple approach to the question whether the signer of the deed had been negligent or not. Similarly, in *Lewis v. Clay* (1898), 67 L.J.Q.B. 224, 225, Lord Russell of Killowen C.J. left to the jury the question: "Was the defendant, in signing his name as he did, recklessly careless, and did he thereby enable Lord William Nevill to perpetrate the fraud?"

Unfortunately this simple and satisfactory view as to the meaning and effect of negligence in relation to the plea of *non est factum* became distorted in the case of *Carlisle and Cumberland Banking Co. v. Bragg*, [1911] 1 K.B. 489. The defendant was induced to sign the document by fraud, and did not know that it was a guarantee, but thought that it was a mere proposal for insurance. The jury found that he had been negligent. Pickford J. considered that the finding of negligence was immaterial, and on appeal his view was upheld. Vaughan Williams L.J. said on p. 494:

I do not know whether the jury understood that there could be no material negligence unless there was a duty on the defendant towards the plaintiff. Even if they did understand that, in my opinion, in the case of this instrument, the signature to which was obtained by fraud, and which was not a negotiable instrument, Pickford J. was right in saying that the finding of negligence was immaterial. I wish to add for myself that in my judgment there is no evidence whatsoever to show that the proximate cause of the plaintiff's advancing money on this document was the mere signature of it by the defendant. In my opinion, the proximate cause of the plaintiffs' making the advance was that Rigg fraudulently took the document to the bank, having fraudulently altered it by adding the forged signature of an attesting witness, and but for Rigg having done these things the plaintiffs would never have advanced the money at all.

The reasoning of the Court of Appeal in *Carlisle and Cumberland Banking Co. v. Bragg* has been criticised, for example, by Sir William Anson in the year 1912 in 28 *Law Quarterly Review*, at p. 190, and by Professor Guest in the year 1963 in 79 *Law Quarterly Review*, at p. 346. Also doubts as to the correctness of the reasoning were expressed by Donovan L.J. delivering the judgment of the Court of Appeal in *Muskham Finance Ltd. v. Howard*, [1963] 1 Q.B. 9-4, 913 and by Gavan Duffy J. in *Carlton and United Breweries Ltd. v. Elliott*, [1960] V.R. 320. In my opinion *Carlisle and Cumberland Banking Co. v. Bragg*, [1911] 1 K.B. 489 was wrong in the reasoning and the decision.

I think it is not right to say that in relation to the plea of *non est factum*, negligence operates by way of estoppel. The phrase "estoppel by negligence" tends, in this connection at any rate, to be misleading in several ways:

(1) The phrase is inaccurate in itself, as has been pointed out in *Spencer Bower and Turner on Estoppel by Representation*, 2nd ed. (1966), p. 69 and in the judgments of the Court of Appeal in this case. Estoppel in the normal sense of the word does not arise from negligence: it arises from a representation made by words or conduct.

(2) The phrase tends to bring in the technicalities of estoppel, and the requirement that the representation must be intended to be acted upon may cause difficulties.

(3) The phrase tends to bring in the technicalities of negligence as they have been developed in the tort of negligence. This is what happened in *Carlisle and Cumberland Banking Co. v. Bragg*, as shown by the passage cited above. The innocent third party who has paid or lent money on the faith of a negligently signed document should not have to prove the signer owed a duty to him, nor that the signer's negligence was the proximate cause of the money paid or lent.

(4) An estoppel must be pleaded and proved by the party relying on it. In relation to the plea of *non est factum*, this could put the burden of proof on the wrong party. The person who has signed the document knows with what knowledge or lack of knowledge and with what intention he signed the document, and how he was induced or came to sign it. He should have the burden of proving that his signature was not brought about by negligence on his part.

Salmon L.J. has said in his judgment in this case [1969] 2 ch. 17, 48: "If, ... a person signs a document because he negligently failed to read it, I think he is precluded from relying on his own negligent act for the purpose of escaping from the ordinary consequences of his signature. In such circumstances he cannot succeed on a plea of *non est factum*. This is not in my view a true estoppel, but an illustration of the principle that no man may take advantage of his own wrong."

I agree.

The degree of difference required. The judgments in the older cases used a variety of expressions to signify the degree or kind of difference that, for the purpose of the plea of *non est factum*, must be shown to exist between the document as it was and the document as it was believed to be. More recently there has been a tendency to draw a firm distinction between (a) a difference in character or class, which is sufficient for the purposes of the plea, and (b) a difference only in contents, which is not sufficient. This distinction has been helpful in some cases, but, as the judgments of the Court of Appeal have shown, it would produce wrong results if it were applied as a rigid rule for all cases. In my opinion, one has to use a more general phrase, such as "fundamentally different" or "radically different" or "totally different."

I would dismiss the appeal.

LORD REID: My Lords, I am in general agreement with the speech of my noble and learned friend, Lord Pearson. In my opinion this appeal must fail however one states the law. The existing law seems to me to be in a state of some confusion. I do not think that it is possible to reconcile all the decisions, let alone all the reasons given for them. In view of some general observations made in the Court of Appeal I think that it is desirable to try to extract from the authorities the principles on which most of them are based. When we are trying to do that my experience has been that there are dangers in there being only one speech in this House. Then statements in it have often tended to be treated as definitions and it is not the function of a court or of this House to frame definitions; some latitude should be left for future developments. The true ratio of a decision generally appears more clearly from a comparison of two or more statements in different words which are intended to supplement each other.

The plea of *non est factum* obviously applies when the person sought to be held liable did not in fact sign the document. But at least since the sixteenth century it has also been held to apply in certain cases so as to enable a person who in fact signed a document to say that it is not his deed. Obviously any such extension must be kept within narrow limits if it is not to shake the confidence of those who habitually and rightly rely on signatures when there is no obvious reason to doubt their validity. Originally this extension appears to have been made in favour of those who were unable to read owing to blindness or illiteracy and who therefore had to trust someone to tell them what they were signing. I think that it must also apply in favour of those who are permanently or temporarily unable through no fault of their own to have without explanation any real understanding of the purport of a particular document, whether that be from defective education, illness or innate incapacity.

But that does not excuse them from taking such precautions as they reasonably can. The matter generally arises where an innocent third party has relied on a signed document in ignorance of the circumstances in which it was signed, and where he will suffer loss if the maker of the document is allowed to have it declared a nullity. So there must be a heavy burden of proof on the person who seeks to invoke this remedy. He must prove all the circumstances necessary to justify its being granted to him, and that necessarily involves his proving that he took all reasonable precautions in the circumstances. I do not say that the remedy can never be available to a man of full capacity. But that could only be in very exceptional circumstances; certainly not where his reason for not scrutinising the document before signing it was that he was too busy or too lazy. In general I do not think that he can be heard to say that he signed in reliance on someone he trusted. But, particularly when he was led to believe that the document which he signed was not one which affected his legal rights, there may be cases where this plea can properly be applied in favour of a man of full capacity.

The plea cannot be available to anyone who was content to sign without taking the trouble to try to find out at least the general effect of the document. Many people do frequently sign documents put before them for signature by their solicitor or other trusted advisers without making any enquiry as to their purpose or effect. But the essence of the plea *non est factum* is that the person signing believed that the document he signed had one character or one effect whereas in fact its character or effect was quite different. He could not have such a belief unless he had taken steps or been given information which gave him some grounds for his belief. The amount of information he must have and the sufficiency of the particularity of his belief must depend on the circumstances of each case. Further the plea cannot be available to a person whose mistake was really a mistake as to the legal effect of the document, whether that was his own mistake or that of his adviser. That has always been the law and in this branch of the law at least I see no reason for any change.

We find in many of the authorities statements that a man's deed is not his deed if his mind does not go with his pen. But that is far too wide. It would cover cases where the man had taken no precautions at all, and there was no ground for his belief that he was signing something different from that which in fact he signed. I think that it is the wrong approach to start from that wide statement and then whittle it down by excluding cases where the remedy will not be granted. It is for the person who seeks the remedy to show that he should have it.

Finally, there is the question to what extent or in what way must there be a difference between that which in fact he signed and that which he believed he was signing. In an endeavour to keep the plea within bounds there have been many attempts to lay down a dividing line. But any dividing line suggested has been difficult to apply in practice and has sometimes led to unreasonable results. In particular I do not think that the modern division between the character and the contents of a document is at all satisfactory. Some of the older authorities suggest a more flexible test so that one can take all factors into consideration. There was a period when here as elsewhere in the law hard and fast dividing lines were sought, but I think that experience has shown that often they do not produce certainty but do produce unreasonable results.

I think that in the older authorities difference in practical result was more important than difference in legal character. If a man thinks that he is signing a document which will cost him £10 and the actual document would cost him £1,000 it could not be right to deny him this remedy simply because the legal character of the two was the same. It is true that we must then deal with questions of degree but that is a familiar task for the courts and I would not expect it to give rise to a flood of litigation.

There must I think be a radical difference between what he signed and what he thought he was signing—or one could use the words "fundamental" or "serious" or "very substantial." But what amounts to a radical difference will depend on all the circumstances. If he thinks he is giving property to A whereas the document gives it to B the difference may often be of vital importance, but in the circumstances of the present case I do not think that it is. I think that it must be left to the courts to determine in each case in light of all the facts whether there was or was not a sufficiently great difference. The plea *non est factum* is in a sense illogical when applied to a case where the man in fact signed the deed. But it is none the worse for that if applied in a reasonable way.

I would dismiss this appeal.

[Lord Hodson, Lord Wilberforce, and Viscount Dilhorne delivered concurring speeches.]

MARVCO COLOUR RESEARCH LTD V HARRIS
[1982] 2 SCR 774, 141 DLR (3d) 577

ESTEY J: This is an action for foreclosure on a mortgage (or more accurately, a charge under the *Land Titles Act*, R.S.O. 1970, c. 234) securing the sum of $55,650.43 granted by the respondents to the appellant. The only defence raised in the action was that of *non est factum.* The respondents unquestionably executed the charge in favour of the appellant and it is clear that the appellant has not been guilty of fraud or improper conduct of any kind and in concurrent findings below has been found to be, but for *non est factum*, fully entitled to the relief requested. The respondents executed the charge at the request of a third party, Johnston, in connection with the acquisition by Johnston of an interest of an associate in a firm owned by Johnston and the associate. In connection with this acquisition the respondents had advanced $15,000 in cash raised by them through an earlier mortgage on the same property, granted by them to the Bank of Montreal. The husband, Dennis Harris, one of the respondents, had also executed a contract of guarantee in favour of the appellant of the same principal sum as secured by the mortgage which is the subject of this action. In this guarantee the appellant, in consideration of the covenants by the respondent husband and Johnston, released its claims against Suwald, the person whose interest in the firm was being purchased by Johnston. Prior to the release, Suwald had been liable to the appellant on a covenant in a chattel mortgage which had been given by Johnston and Suwald at the time of the purchase of the firm from the appellant. Apparently on the same day, but after this contract of guarantee was executed, the respondents signed the mortgage or charge in question, the last paragraph of which included the following passage typed in a blank space in the form of charge used by the parties:

> This mortgage is given as collateral security for the liability of Dennis Albert Harris under the terms of a Deed of Covenants bearing even data wherein the said Dennis Albert Harris and the Mortgagee are (inter alia) parties as co-covenantor and covenantee respectively. No financial liability on the part of the Mortgagors shall arise hereunder unless and until there shall be default on the part of the covenantors of the terms of the said Deed of Covenants and no rights shall accrue to the Mortgagee prior to any such default. The Mortgagee agrees with the Mortgagors that it will pursue all other remedies under the Deed of Covenants and Chattel Mortgage referred to therein before enforcing the security hereby constituted. Discharge of the liabilities arising under the Deed of Covenants and the said Chattel Mortgage shall rank pro tanto as a discharge (or partial discharge, as the case may be) of the principal secured hereby. All other terms and conditions of this Mortgage shall be read and construed accordingly.

The mortgage was in fact, therefore a collateral security grant by the respondents in favour of the appellant securing the performance by the covenantors, including the respondent husband, and it was relied upon by the appellant in releasing Suwald from his obligations under the chattel mortgage.

Johnston was at all material times living with the daughter of the respondents. The daughter also executed the aforementioned contract of guarantee as trustee because she had been the trustee under a bill of sale executed by the appellant in favour of a company owned or controlled by Suwald and Johnston at the time the appellant sold its business to those individuals or their corporate nominee. The daughter did not personally guarantee the indebtedness to the appellant. Other than the association of their daughter with Johnston, the purchaser of the Suwald interest in the firm in question, there appears to be no reason for the participation by the respondents in the financing of Johnston's purchase of Suwald's interest in the firm.

The mortgage in question was executed by the respondents individually at different times and places on the same date, apparently January 27, 1976. When the respondent wife signed the document her daughter was present, but the finding is that in executing the mortgage the respondent wife relied upon the representations made by Johnston, who was also present, as to the nature and content of the document, and did not do so in reliance upon anything said by the daughter. The respondent husband executed the mortgage later on the same day in the presence of Johnston upon whose representations he likewise apparently relied. The learned trial judge stated this about the execution of the mortgage by the respondents [107 DLR (3d) 632 at 634, 27 OR (2d) 686, aff'd 115 DLR (3d) 512nl, 30 OR (2d) 162n (CA)]:

> When she [the respondent wife] arrived Johnston said they were to wait for Clay [an employee in the lawyer's office] who was bringing a paper for her to sign. Clay arrived, said there was an error in the document, left and returned and presented the document to the wife. At some point Johnston, perhaps in the presence of Clay, said it was "just to correct the date" in the Bank of Montreal mortgage. In any event the defendant wife signed it without reading it. Later that day Johnston and Clay attended upon her husband at home and got him to sign as well. The husband testified they told him it related to discrepancies in the date of the Bank of Montreal mortgage. He signed without question and without reading. ...
>
> There is also no doubt that the defendants were careless in not reading the document before signing. The wife is well educated, the husband less so, but both are literate and English-speaking and both have a basic understanding of mortgages, having executed at least three others since the purchase of their home. It is the undisputed evidence, however, that they were told it was an unimportant amendment to the Bank of Montreal mortgage when in reality it was a second substantial mortgage to the plaintiff.

The mortgage in favour of the Bank of Montreal has been paid off and the only issue arising on this appeal, concerns the mortgage which is the subject of the action, and in that connection this issue was put by the appellant:

> Is the defence of *non est factum* available to a party who, knowing that a document has legal effect, carelessly fails to read the document thereby permitting a third party to perpetrate a fraud on another innocent party?

This issue turns on the decision of this Court in *Prudential Trust Co. Ltd. v. Cugnet et al.* (1956), 5 D.L.R. (2d) 1, [1956] S.C.R. 914, a four-to-one decision. The majority, applying the decision of the English Court of Appeal in *Carlisle & Cumberland Banking Co. v. Bragg*, [1911] 1 K.B. 489 found that where a document was executed as a result of a misrepresentation as to its nature and character and not merely its contents the defendant was entitled to raise the plea of *non est factum* on the basis that his mind at the time of the execution of the document did not follow his hand. In such a circumstance, the document was void *ab initio*. So went the judgment of Nolan J. with whom Justices Taschereau and Fauteux, as they then were, concurred. Locke J. reached the same result, but added the following comment on the effect of careless conduct on the ability of the defendant to raise the plea of *non est factum* (at p. 4 D.L.R., p. 929 S.C.R.):

> It is my opinion that the result of the authorities was correctly stated in the *Bragg*'s case. To say that a person may be estopped by careless conduct such as that in the present case, when the instrument is not negotiable, is to assert the existence of some duty on

the part of the person owing to the public at large, or to other persons unknown to him who might suffer damage by acting upon the instrument on the footing that it is valid in the hands of the holder. I do not consider that the authorities support the view that there is any such general duty, the breach of which imposes a liability in negligence.

Cartwright J., as he then was, dissented. His Lordship commenced with a recitation of the general proprieties (at p. 7 D.L.R., p. 932 S.C.R.):

... [G]enerally speaking, a person who executes a document without taking the trouble to read it is liable on it and cannot plead that he mistook its contents, at all events, as against a person who acting in good faith in the ordinary course of business has changed his position in reliance on such document

and then moved to the exception arising under the principle of *non est factum*. After making reference to *Carlisle v. Bragg, supra.* His Lordship said (at p. 9 D.L.R., p. 934 S.C.R.):

An anxious consideration of all the authorities referred to by counsel and the Courts below has brought me to the conclusion that, insofar as *Carlisle v. Bragg* decides that the rule that negligence excludes a plea of *non est factum* is limited to the case of negotiable instruments and does not extend to a deed such as the one before us, we should refuse to follow it.

He concluded, therefore, that any person who fails to exercise reasonable care in signing a document is precluded from relying on the plea of *non est factum* as against a person who relies upon that document in good faith and for value.

As the basis for the judgments of Justice Nolan, concurred in by two other members of the court, and of Justice Locke was the judgment of the Court of Appeal of England in *Carlisle v. Bragg, supra*, it should be pointed out at once that that case has been overruled by the House of Lords in *Saunders v. Anglia Building Society* (reported in the Court of Appeal as *Gallie v. Lee*, [1969] 2 Ch. 17, [1969] 1 All E.R. 1062, [1969] 2 W.L.R. 901, *sub nom. Gallie v. Lee*), [1971] A.C. 1004, *per* Lord Pearson at p. 1038, *per* Lord Wilberforce at p. 1027, *per* Viscount Dilhorne at p. 1023, and *per* Lord Hodson at p. 1019. Lord Reid stated (at p. 1015): "I am in general agreement with the speech of my noble and learned friend, Lord Pearson."

The doctrine of *non est factum* sprang into prominence with the judgment in *Foster v. Mackinnon* (1869), L.R. 4 C.P. 704. At trial in that case the jury was directed that if the defendant's signature on the document in question "was obtained upon a fraudulent representation that it was a guarantee and that the defendant signed it without knowing that it was a bill, and under the belief that it was a guarantee, and if the defendant was not guilty of any negligence in so signing the paper, he was entitled to the verdict." On appeal, the Court of Common Pleas endorsed the direction of the trial judge, and held that (at p. 712):

... [I]n the case now under consideration, the defendant, according to the evidence, if believed, and the finding of the jury, never intended to indorse a bill of exchange at all, but intended to sign a contract of an entirely different nature. It was not his design, and, if he were guilty of no negligence, it was not even his fault that the instrument he signed turned out to be a bill of exchange.

In *Foster v. Mackinnon* a distinction is drawn between negotiable instruments and other documents. A qualification of the general rule was felt to be necessary when applied to negotiable instruments in order to protect innocent transferees for value. As a result, the court concluded that where "the party signing knows what he is doing: the indorser intended to indorse, and the acceptor intended to accept, a bill of exchange," the party signing the document cannot deny its validity against a holder in due course whether or not he was negligent in affixing his signature. This rule was said to be a limitation on the general principle of *non est factum* established in earlier cases under which the signor, in order to deny successfully his signature, had to show that he had not been careless in executing the document. This general rule was applicable to deeds, and "equally applicable to other written contracts" (at p. 712).

Following the decision in *Foster v. Mackinnon*, and prior to the decision of the Court of Appeal in *Carlisle v. Bragg*, it is clear that the presence or absence of negligence on the part of the defendant was a critical factor in determining his ability to raise successfully the plea of *non est factum.* The rule as stated in two of the leading textbooks of the day was as follows:

> So a man may avoid a deed or other instrument, which he was induced to execute by a fraudulent misrepresentation of its contents, as was held in *Foster v. Mackinnon* ...
>
> And if the party who executes an instrument in such circumstances has not been guilty of negligence in so doing, he may avoid it, not only against him who made the fraudulent misrepresentation, but as against a third party who has acted innocently, on the faith of the instrument being genuine.

(*Chitty on Contracts*, 15th ed. (1909), at pp. 673-74)

> Mistake as to the nature of the transaction entered into ... must arise from some deceit which ordinary diligence could not penetrate, or some mischance which ordinary diligence could not avert. ...

(Anson, *Law of Contracts*, 12th ed. (1910), at pp. 151-52)

Only one exception to this rule was recognized: if the document signed was a bill of exchange and the signor intended to sign a bill of exchange, he could not successfully plead *non est factum*, even though he had not been negligent.

Almost a half a century after the decision in *Foster v. Mackinnon, supra*, the Court of Appeal in *Carlisle v. Bragg, supra*, substantially modified the law in the United Kingdom with reference to the plea of *non est factum*. In that case the court allowed the plea to be entered by a defendant who had executed a guarantee believing it to be a document of a different character, and went on to hold that the defendant was not estopped from raising the plea even though it was the negligence of the defendant which led to the loss in question. The jury indeed had found the defendant to be negligent in signing the document. The Court of Appeal concluded that any doctrine which limited the application of the plea where the defendant was negligent was confined to negotiable instruments.

The decision of the Court of Appeal in *Carlisle v. Bragg* may be summarized as follows:

(1) *Foster v. Mackinnon* applies only to bills of exchange.

(2) Negligence on the part of the signor is therefore relevant only to bills of exchange.

(3) Negligence is used in the tortious sense, and therefore, only when a duty of care exists in the signor and his act is the proximate cause of the loss by the third party, can it be a bar to a successful plea of *non est factum*.

(4) n all other cases negligence is irrelevant, and *non est factum* may be pleaded where the document signed is of a different nature from that which the signor intended to execute: *vide Chitty on Contracts*, 18th ed. (1930), at p. 803, and Anson, *Law of Contracts*, 14th ed. (1917), at p. 164.

Carlisle v. Bragg has attracted unfavourable comment in legal writings and the following is an example of the criticisms of the judgment written shortly after its issuance:

> A man who signs a document which he has not taken the trouble to read, who makes therein a promise on which other persons may act to their detriment, and who is found by a jury to have acted without reasonable care, is not liable for the consequences of his act to the party who has suffered by reliance on his promise, unless the document, the nature and contents of which he has neglected to ascertain, should chance to be a negotiable instrument; or unless the promisee, whose identity he has also neglected to ascertain, should chance to be a person to whom he owes a duty to take care. Such is the decision of the Court of Appeal in *Carlisle and Cumberland Banking Co. v. Bragg*, [1911] 1 K.B. 489, 80 L.J.K.B. 472.
>
> Shortly stated, the Court was asked to say which of two innocent parties should suffer for the fraud of a third, and the Lords Justices decided in favour of the man whose admitted negligence was the cause of the trouble.

(Anson, *Carlisle and Cumberland Banking Co. v. Bragg*, 28 L.Q.R. 190 (1912) at p. 190.)

Although the decision in *Carlisle v. Bragg* was the subject of much criticism, it was adopted by the majority of this court in *Prudential Trust Co. Ltd. v. Cugnet, supra*. ...

It was not until *Saunders v. Anglia Building Society, supra*, that the law was put back to the position which it was in after *Foster v. Mackinnon*. It is interesting to note that in doing so all the judges dealt with the meaning of the word negligence as employed by the court in *Foster v. Mackinnon* as meaning "carelessness" in the same way that Cartwright J. did in *Prudential, supra*. Thus the rule with reference to *non est factum* in the United Kingdom requires that the defendant be not guilty of carelessness in order to be entitled to raise the defence of *non est factum*.

It is not necessary for us to concern ourselves with the second leg of *Saunders v. Anglia*, namely, those circumstances in which a defendant who has not been guilty of negligence may raise the defence of *non est factum*. Here the respondents, by concurrent findings below, were found to be negligent or careless. I do note in passing, however, that it was the consensus of the several members of the House of Lords participating in the *Saunders* case that for the principle to operate, the document must be fundamentally different, either as to content, character or otherwise from the document that the signor intended to execute. Prior to this decision the plea of *non est factum* was available only if the mistake was as to the very nature or character of the transaction. It was not sufficient that there be a mistake as to the contents of the document: *Howatson v. Webb*, [1907] 1 Ch. 537, affirmed [1908] 1 Ch. 1; *Muskham Finance Ltd. v. Howard*, [1963] 1 Q.B. 904. This distinction was rejected by the House of Lords in favour of a more flexible test. In the words of Lord Pearson (at p. 1039): "In my opinion, one has to use a more general phrase, such as 'fundamentally different' or 'radically different' or 'totally different.'" Lord Wilberforce at pp. 1026-7 concluded that the principle would come into play on "rare occasions." ...

In my view, with all due respect to those who have expressed views to the contrary, the dissenting view of Cartwright J. (as he then was) in *Prudential, supra*, correctly enunciated the principles of the law of *non est factum*. In the result the defendants-respondents are barred by reasons of their carelessness from pleading that their minds did not follow their hands when executing the mortgage so as to be able to plead that the mortgage is not binding upon them. The rationale of the rule is simple and clear. As between an innocent party (the appellant) and the respondents, the law must take into account the fact that the appellant was completely innocent of any negligence, carelessness or wrongdoing, whereas the respondents by their careless conduct have made it possible for the wrongdoers to inflict a loss. As between the appellant and the respondents, simple justice requires that the party, who by the application of reasonable care was in a position to avoid a loss to any of the parties, should bear any loss that results when the only alternative available to the courts would be to place the loss upon the innocent appellant. In the final analysis, therefore, the question raised cannot be put more aptly than in the words of Cartwright J. in *Prudential, supra*, at p. 5 D.L.R., p. 929 S.C.R.: "... [W]hich of two innocent parties is to suffer for the fraud of a third." The two parties are innocent in the sense that they were not guilty of wrongdoing as against any other person, but as between the two innocent parties there remains a distinction significant in the law, namely that the respondents, by their carelessness, have exposed the innocent appellant to risk of loss, and even though no duty in law was owed by the respondents to the appellant to safeguard the appellant from such loss, nonetheless the law must take this discarded opportunity into account.

In my view, this is so for the compelling reason that in this case, and no doubt generally in similar cases, the respondents' carelessness is but another description of a state of mind into which the respondents have fallen because of their determination to assist themselves and/or a third party for whom the transaction has been entered into in the first place. Here the respondents apparently sought to attain some advantage indirectly for their daughter by assisting Johnston in his commercial venture. In the *Saunders* case, *supra*, the aunt set out to apply her property for the benefit of her nephew. In both cases the carelessness took the form of a failure to determine the nature of the document the respective defendants were executing. Whether the carelessness stemmed from an enthusiasm for their immediate purpose or from a confidence in the intended beneficiary to save them harmless matters not. This may explain the origin of the careless state of mind but is not a factor limiting the operation of the principle of *non est factum* and its application. The defendants, in executing the security without the simple precaution of ascertaining its nature in fact and in law, have nonetheless taken an intended and deliberate step in signing the document and have caused it to be legally binding upon themselves. In the words of *Foster v. Mackinnon* this negligence, even though it may have sprung from good intentions, precludes the defendants in this circumstance from disowning the document, that is to say, from pleading that their minds did not follow their respective hands when signing the document and hence that no document in law was executed by them.

This principle of law is based not only upon the principle of placing the loss on the person guilty of carelessness but also upon a recognition of the need for certainty and security in commerce. ... The appellant, as it was entitled to do, accepted the mortgage as valid, and adjusted its affairs accordingly. For example, the appellant released Suwald from the chattel mortgage held by the appellant.

I wish only to add that the application of the principle that carelessness will disentitle a party to the document of the right to disown the document in law must depend upon the circumstances of each case. This has been said throughout the judgments written on the principle of *non est factum* from the earliest times. The magnitude, and extent of the carelessness, the circumstances which may have contributed to such carelessness, and all other circumstances must be taken into account in each case before a court may determine whether estoppel shall arise in the defendant so as to prevent the raising of this defence. The policy considerations inherent in the plea of *non est factum* were well stated by Lord Wilberforce in his judgment in *Saunders, supra*, at pp. 1023-4:

> ... [T]he law ... has two conflicting objectives: relief to a signer whose consent is genuinely lacking ... [and] protection to innocent third parties who have acted upon an

apparently regular and properly executed document. Because each of these factors may involve questions of degree or shading any rule of law must represent a compromise and must allow to the court some flexibility in application.

The result in this case has depended upon the intervention by this court in the development of the principle of *non est factum* and its invocation in a way inconsistent with that applied many years ago in the *Prudential* case, *supra*. The respondents have pleaded their case in the courts below and in this court consistent with the result in the *Prudential* judgment. In these circumstances consideration can and should be given to the application·of the general principle that costs follow the event. The appellant, of course, was required to persevere to the level of this court in order to bring about a review of the reasoning which led to the determination in the *Prudential* case. The respondents, on the other hand, acted reasonably in founding their position upon that decision notwithstanding the revision of the law of England consequent upon the judgments in *Saunders*. In all these circumstances, therefore, I would award to the appellant costs only before the court of first instance with no costs being awarded either party in the Court of Appeal or in this court.

Appeal allowed.

[See also McCamus at 548-56; MacDougall at 240-42; Waddams at paras 307-14.]

CHAPTER FIVE

WRITTEN DOCUMENTS

I. UNSIGNED DOCUMENTS (THE TICKET CASES)

PARKER V THE SOUTH EASTERN RAILWAY COMPANY
(1877), 2 CPD 416 (CA)

The plaintiff deposited a bag in a cloak-room at the defendants' railway station, paid the clerk 2d., and received a paper ticket, on one side of which were written a number and a date, and were printed notices as to when the office would be opened and closed, and the words "See Back." On the other side were printed several clauses relating to articles left by passengers, the last of which was, "The company will not be responsible for any package exceeding the value of £10." The plaintiff on the same day presented his ticket and demanded his bag, and the bag could not be found, and has not been since found. Parker claimed £24 10s. as the value of his bag. The company pleaded that they had accepted the goods on the condition that they would not be responsible for the value if it exceeded £10; and at the trial they relied on the words printed on the back of the ticket, and also on the fact that a notice to the same effect was printed and hung up in the cloak-room. The plaintiff gave evidence and denied that he had seen the notice, or read what was printed on the ticket. He admitted that he had often received such tickets and knew there was printed matter on them, but said that he did not know what it was. He said that he imagined the ticket to be a receipt for the money paid by him. Another case with very similar facts was tried at the same time.

Parker's case was tried at Westminster on the 27th of February, 1876, before Pollock B. The questions left by the judge to the jury were: 1. Did the plaintiff read or was he aware of the special condition upon which the articles were deposited? 2. Was the plaintiff, under the circumstances, under any obligation, in the exercise of reasonable and proper caution, to read or make himself aware of the condition?

The jury answered both questions in the negative, and the judge thereupon directed judgment to be entered for the plaintiff for the amount claimed, reserving leave to the defendants to move to enter judgment for them.

The defendants moved to enter judgment, and also obtained from the Common Pleas Division an order *nisi* for a new trial, on the ground of misdirection. The order was discharged, and the motion was refused by the Common Pleas Division. The Defendants appealed.

MELLISH LJ: In this case we have to consider whether a person who deposits in the cloak-room of a railway company articles which are lost through the carelessness of the company's servants is prevented from recovering, by a condition on the back of the ticket, that the company would not be liable for the loss of goods exceeding the value of £10. It was argued on behalf of the railway company that the company's servants were only authorized to receive goods on behalf of the company upon the terms contained in the ticket. ... I am of opinion that this objection cannot prevail. It is clear that the company's servants did not exceed the authority given them by the company. They did the exact thing they were authorized to do. They were authorized to receive articles on deposit as bailees on behalf of the company, charging 2d. for each article, and delivering a ticket properly filled up to the person leaving the article. This is exactly what they did in the present cases, and whatever may be the legal effect of what was done, the company must, in my opinion, be bound by it. The directors may have thought, and no doubt did think, that delivering the ticket to the person depositing the article would be sufficient to make him bound by the conditions contained in the ticket, and if they were mistaken in that, the company must bear the consequences.

The question then is, whether the plaintiff was bound by the conditions contained in the ticket. In an ordinary case, where an action is brought on a written agreement which is signed by the defendant, the agreement is proved by proving his signature, and, in the absence of fraud, it is wholly immaterial that he has not read the agreement and does not know its contents. The parties may, however, reduce their agreement into writing, so that the writing constitutes the sole evidence of the agreement, without signing it; but in that case there must be evidence independently of the agreement itself to prove that the defendant has assented to it. In that case, also, if it is proved that the defendant has assented to the writing constituting the agreement between the parties, it is, in the absence of fraud, immaterial that the defendant had not read the agreement and did not know its contents. Now if in the course of making a contract one party delivers to another a paper containing writing, and the party receiving the paper knows that the paper contains conditions which the party delivering it intends to constitute the contract, I have no doubt that the party receiving the paper does, by receiving and keeping it, assent to the conditions contained in it, although he does not read them, and does not know what they are. I hold therefore that the case of *Harris v. Great Western Ry. Co.* (1876), 1 Q.B.D. 515, was rightly decided, because in that case the plaintiff admitted, on cross-examination, that he believed there were some conditions on the ticket. On the other hand, the case of *Henderson v. Stevenson* (1875), L.R. 2 Sc. & Div. 470, is a conclusive authority that if the person receiving the ticket does not know that there is any writing upon the back of the ticket, he is not bound by a condition printed on the back. The facts in the cases before us differ from those in both *Henderson v. Stevenson*, and *Harris v. Great Western Ry. Co.* because in both the cases which have been argued before us, though the plaintiffs admitted that they knew there was writing on the back of the ticket, they swore not only that they did not read it, but that they did not know or believe that the writing contained conditions, and we are to consider whether, under those circumstances, we can lay down as a matter of law either that the plaintiff is bound or that he is not bound by the conditions contained in the ticket, or whether his being bound depends on some question of fact to be determined by the jury, and if so, whether, in the present case, the right question was left to the jury.

Now, I am of opinion that we cannot lay down, as a matter of law, either that the plaintiff was bound or that he was not bound by the conditions printed on the ticket, from the mere fact that he knew there was writing on the ticket, but did not know that the writing contained conditions. I think there may be cases in which a paper containing writing is delivered by one party to another in the course of a business transaction, where it would be quite reasonable that the party receiving it should assume that the writing contained in it no condition, and should put it in his pocket unread. For instance, if a person driving through a turnpike gate received a ticket upon paying the toll, he might reasonably assume that the object of the ticket was that by producing it he might be free from paying toll at some other turnpike gate, and might put it in his pocket unread. On the other hand, if a person who ships goods to be carried on a voyage by sea receives a bill of lading signed by the master, he would plainly be bound by it, although afterwards in an action against the shipowner for the loss of the goods, he might swear that he had never read the bill of lading, and that he did not know that it contained the terms of the contract of carriage, and that the shipowner was protected by the exceptions contained in it. Now the reason why the person receiving the bill of lading would be bound seems to me to be that in the great majority of cases persons shipping goods do know that the bill of lading contains the terms of the contract of carriage; and the shipowner, or the master delivering the bill of lading, is entitled to assume that the person shipping goods has that knowledge. It is, however, quite possible to suppose that a person who is neither a man of business nor a lawyer might on some particular occasion ship goods without the least knowledge of what a bill of lading was, but in my opinion such person must bear the consequences of his own exceptional ignorance, it being plainly impossible that business could be carried on if every person who delivers a bill of lading had to stop to explain what a bill of lading was.

Now the question we have to consider is whether the railway company were entitled to assume that a person depositing luggage, and receiving a ticket in such a way that he could see that some writing was printed on it, would understand that the writing contained the conditions of contract, and this seems to me to depend upon whether people in general would in fact and naturally, draw that inference. The railway company, as it seems to me, must be entitled to make some assumptions respecting the person who deposits luggage with them: I think they are entitled to assume that he can read, and that he understands the English language, and that he pays such attention to what he is about as may be reasonably expected from a person in such a transaction as that of depositing luggage in a cloak-room. The railway company must, however, take mankind as they find them, and if what they do is sufficient to inform people in general that the ticket contains conditions, I think that a particular plaintiff ought not to be in a better position than other persons on account of his exceptional ignorance or stupidity or carelessness. But if what the railway company do is not sufficient to convey to the minds of people in general that the ticket contains conditions, then they have received goods on deposit without obtaining the consent of the persons depositing them to the conditions limiting their liability. I am of opinion, therefore, that the proper direction to leave to the jury in these cases is, that if the person receiving the ticket did not see or know that there was any writing on the ticket he is not bound by the conditions; that if he knew there was writing, and knew or believed that the writing contained conditions, then he is bound by the conditions; that if he knew there was writing on the ticket, but did not know or believe that the writing contained conditions, nevertheless he would be bound, if

445

the delivering of the ticket to him in such a manner that he could see there was writing upon it, was, in the opinion of the jury, reasonable notice that the writing contained conditions.

I have lastly to consider whether the direction of the learned judge was correct, namely, "Was the plaintiff under the circumstances, under any obligation, in the exercise of reasonable and proper caution, to read and to make himself aware of the condition?" I think that this direction was not strictly accurate, and was calculated to mislead the jury. The plaintiff was certainly under no obligation to read the ticket, but was entitled to leave it unread if he pleased, and the question does not appear to me to direct the attention of the jury to the real question, namely, whether the railway company did what was reasonably sufficient to give the plaintiff notice of the condition.

On the whole, I am of opinion that there ought to be a new trial.

BRAMWELL LJ: ... Has not the giver of the paper a right to suppose that the receiver is content to deal on the terms in the paper? What more can be done? Must he say, "Read that?" As I have said, he does so in effect when he puts it into the other's hands. The truth is, people are content to take these things on trust. They know that there is a form which is always used—they are satisfied it is not unreasonable, because people do not usually put unreasonable terms into their contracts. If they did, then dealing would soon be stopped. Besides, unreasonable practices would be known. The very fact of not looking at the paper shews that this confidence exists. It is asked: What if there was some unreasonable condition, as for instance to forfeit £1000 if the goods were not removed in forty-eight hours? Would the depositors be bound? I might continue myself by asking: Would he be, if he were told, "our conditions are on this ticket," and he did not read them. In my judgment, he would not be bound in either case. I think there is an implied understanding that there is no condition unreasonable to the knowledge of the party tendering the document and not insisting on its being read—no condition not relevant to the matter in hand. I am of opinion, therefore, that the plaintiffs, having notice of the printing, were in the same situation as though the porter had said, "Read that, it concerns the matter in hand": that if the plaintiffs did not read it, they were as much bound as if they had read it and had not objected.

The difficulty I feel as to what I have written is that it is too demonstrative. But, put in practical language, it is this: The defendants put into the hands of the plaintiff a paper with printed matter on it, which in all good sense and reason must be supposed to relate to the matter in hand. This printed matter the plaintiff sees, and must either read it, and object if he does not agree to it, or if he does read it and not object, or does not read it, he must be held to consent to its terms; therefore, on the facts, the judges should have directed verdicts for the defendants.

[The opinion of Bramwell LJ has been severely cut and the opinion of Baggallay LJ omitted altogether. The court ordered a new trial.]

Lamont v Canadian Transfer Co Ltd. (1909), 19 OLR 291 (CA). The plaintiff, having arrived in Toronto by steamer, handed his baggage checks to his father-in-law in order that his trunks might be sent to his residence. The father-in-law gave the checks to a friend of his, one Horn, a customs officer, and asked him to have the trunks delivered. Horn took the checks and handed them, together with 25¢, to Dunn, an agent of the Canadian Transfer Co., with instructions to send along the trunks. Dunn offered to do it without charge, but Horn refused, saying that he had been given the 25¢. The agent then removed the steamer checks and replaced them by checks of the Can. Transfer Co. Fifteen minutes later Horn came back to Dunn and asked him for a receipt, which, without being read, was later passed on to the plaintiff, and not read by the latter until some ten days afterwards. On the face of the receipt, there was legibly printed a notice that the company should "not be liable for any loss or damage of any trunk for over $50." The trunk was either lost or stolen and the plaintiff sued the company for the value of his trunk, refusing to accept the $50 tendered by the defendants. Held, for the plaintiff. GARROW JA: [T]he real question is, ought knowledge to be imputed to him under the circumstances? This is a pure question of fact, and, in my opinion, the reasonable inference is the other way. He had already made an unconditional contract after having been offered free cartage. He came back, not to get a new or different contract, but a mere receipt. That was what he asked for, and he might under the circumstances fairly and without negligence assume without reading it that he was merely getting what he had asked for and nothing more. If he had not come back no question could have been raised as to the defendants' liability, and the burden is of course upon them to shew that the new contract was substituted, with the plaintiff's consent, for the old, and in this they, in my opinion, fail.

Chapelton v Barry Urban District Council. [1940] 1 KB 532 (CA). The plaintiff was injured when using a deck chair supplied for public use by the defendant Council. When he took the chair from the attendant he was handed a ticket. He glanced at it and slipped it into his pocket. He claimed to have no idea that there were conditions on it. In fact, the ticket contained these words: "Available for 3 hours. Time expires where indicated by cut-off and should be retained and shown on request. The Council will not be made liable for any accident or damage arising from hire of chair." Near the pile of chairs was a notice: "Barry Urban District Council. Cold Knap. hire of chairs 2d. per session of 3 hours. The public are respectfully requested to obtain tickets properly issued from the automatic punch in their presence from the Chair Attendants." The county court judge found the damages to be £50 in addition to special damages, but held the plaintiff bound by the notice on the ticket. The Court of Appeal reversed him. SLESSER LJ: The very language of that "respectful request" shows clearly, to my mind, that for the convenience of the local authority the public were asked to obtain from the chair attendants tickets, which were mere vouchers or receipts showing how long a person hiring a chair is entitled to use that chair. It is wrong, I think, to look at the circumstance that the plaintiff obtained his receipt at the same time as he took his chair as being in any way a modification of the contract which I have indicated. This was a general offer to the general public, and I think that it is right to say that one must take into account here that there was no reason why anybody taking one of these chairs should necessarily obtain a receipt at the moment he took his chair—and, indeed, the notice is inconsistent with that, because it "respectfully requests" the public to obtain receipts for their money. It may be that somebody might sit in one of these chairs for one hour, or two hours, or, if the holiday resort was a very popular one, for a longer time, before the attendant came round for his money, or it may be that the attendant would not come to him at all for payment for the chair, in which case I take it that there would be an obligation upon the person who used the chair to search out the attendant, like a debtor searching for his creditor, in order to pay him the sum of 2d. for the use of the chair and to obtain a receipt for the 2d. paid.

I think the learned county court judge has misunderstood the nature of this agreement. I do not think that the notice excluding liability was a term of the contract at all. ... I think the object of the giving and the taking of this ticket was that the person taking it might have evidence at hand by which he could show that the obligation he was under to pay 2d. for the use of the chair for three hours had been duly discharged, and I think it is altogether inconsistent, in the absence of any qualification of liability in the notice put up near the pile of chairs, to attempt to read into it the qualification contended for. In my opinion, this ticket is no more than a receipt, and is quite different from a railway ticket which contains upon it the terms upon which a railway company agrees to carry the passenger.

Olley v Marlborough Court Ltd. [1949] 1 KB 532 (CA). A man and his wife checked into a hotel, and paid a week's board and lodging in advance. They then went up to their room, where a notice was displayed as follows: "The proprietors will not hold themselves responsible for articles lost or stolen, unless handed to the manageress for safe custody in a sealed package and a receipt obtained." The wife's furs were stolen from her room because of the negligence of the hotel's servants, who gave the key to an unauthorized person. It was held by the majority of the court that the notice was seen by the plaintiffs too late for it to be a part of their contract with the hotel. DENNING LJ: The first question is whether that notice formed part of the contract. Now people who rely on a contract to exempt themselves from their common law liability must prove that contract strictly. Not only must the terms of the contract be clearly proved, but also the intention to create legal relations—the intention to be legally bound—must also be clearly proved. The best way of proving it is by a written document signed by the party to be bound. Another way is by handing him before or at the time of the contract a written notice specifying its terms and making it clear to him that the contract is on those terms. A prominent public notice which is plain for him to see when he makes the contract or an express oral stipulation would, no doubt, have the same effect. But nothing short of one of these three ways will suffice. It has been held that mere notices put on receipts for money do not make a contract (see *Chapelton v. Barry Urban District Council*). So, also, in my opinion, notices put up in bedrooms do not of themselves make a contract. As a rule, the guest does not see them until after he has been accepted as a guest. The hotel company no doubt hope that the guest will be held bound by them, but the hope is vain unless they clearly show that he agreed to be bound by them, which is rarely the case.

J Spurling Ltd v Bradshaw. [1956] 2 All ER 121. The plaintiffs were warehousemen, and the defendant, who had had previous dealings with the plaintiffs, delivered to them for storage eight barrels of orange juice. A few days later the plaintiffs sent to the defendant a document, called a landing account, acknowledging receipt of the goods, and referring to conditions on the back of the document. On the back, in small print, was included the following clause: "We will not in any circumstances ... be liable for any loss, damage or detention howsoever, whensoever or wheresoever occasioned in respect of any goods entrusted to ... us in the course of our business, even when such loss, damage or detention may have been occasioned by the negligence, wrongful act or default of ourselves or our servants or agents." When the defendant came to collect the barrels, they were found to be empty, and the defendant refused to pay the storage charges on the ground that the plaintiff had been negligent in storing the goods. The plaintiff brought an action, relying on the printed exemption clause. The court held that the plaintiff could rely on the clause. DENNING LJ: This brings me to the question whether this clause was part of the contract. Counsel for the defendant urged us to hold that the plaintiffs did not do what was reasonably sufficient to give notice of the conditions within *Parker v. South Eastern Ry. Co.* I agree that the more unreasonable a clause is, the greater the notice which must be given of it. Some clauses which I have seen would need to be printed in red ink on the face of the document with a red hand pointing to it before the notice could be held to be sufficient. The clause in this case, however, in my judgment, does not call for such exceptional treatment, especially when it is construed, as it should be, subject to the proviso that it only applies when the warehouseman is carrying out his contract and not when he is deviating from it or breaking it in a radical respect. So construed, the judge was, I think, entitled to find that sufficient notice was given. It is to be noticed that the landing account on its face told the defendant that the goods would be insured if he gave instructions; otherwise they were not insured. The invoice, on its face, told him they were warehoused "at owner's risk." The printed conditions, when read subject to the proviso which I have mentioned, added little or nothing to those explicit statements taken together. Next it was said that the landing account and invoice were issued after the goods had been received and could not therefore be part of the contract of bailment: but the defendant admitted that he had received many landing accounts before. True he had not troubled to read them. On receiving this account, he took no objection to it, left the goods there, and went on paying the warehouse rent for months afterwards. It seems to me that by the course of business and conduct of the parties, these conditions were part of the contract.

QUESTION

Is it relevant to ask who, as between plaintiff and defendant, could more efficiently insure against the loss of the goods?

MCCUTCHEON V DAVID MACBRAYNE LTD
[1964] 1 All ER 430 (HL)

LORD DEVLIN: My Lords, when a person in the Isle of Islay wishes to send goods to the mainland he goes into the office of MacBrayne (the respondents) in Port Askaig which is conveniently combined with the local Post Office. There he is presented with a document headed "Conditions" containing three or four thousand words of small print divided into twenty-seven paragraphs. Beneath them there is a space for the sender's signature which he puts below his statement in quite legible print that he thereby agrees to ship on the conditions stated above. The appellant, Mr. McCutcheon, described the negotiations which preceded the making of this formidable contract in the following terms:

> Q.—Tell us about that document; how did you come to sign it? A.—You just walk in the office and the document is filled up ready and all you have to do is to sign your name and go out. Q.—Did you ever read the conditions? A.—No. Q.—Did you know what was in them? A.—No.

There are many other passages in which the appellant and his brother-in-law, Mr. McSporran, endeavour more or less successfully to appease the forensic astonishment aroused by this statement. People shipping calves, the appellant said (he was dealing with an occasion when he had shipped thirty-six calves), had not much time to give to the reading. Asked to deal with another occasion when he was unhampered by livestock, he said that people generally just tried to be in time for the boat's sailing; it would, he thought, take half a day to read and understand the conditions and then he would miss the boat. In another part of his evidence he went so far as to say that if everybody took time to read the document, "MacBrayne's office would be packed out the door." Mr. McSporran evidently thought the whole matter rather academic because, as he pointed out, there was no other way to send a car.

There came a day, Oct. 8, 1960, when one of the respondents' vessels was negligently sailed into a rock and sank. She had on board a car belonging to the appellant, which he had got Mr. McSporran to ship for him, and the car was a total loss. It would be a strangely generous set of conditions in which the persistent reader, after wading through the verbiage, could not find something to protect the carrier against "any loss ... wheresoever or whensoever occurring"; and condition 19 by itself is enough to absolve the respondents several times over for all their negligence. It is conceded that if the form had been signed as usual, the appellant would have had no case. But by a stroke of ill luck for the respondents it was on this day of all days that they omitted to get Mr. McSporran to sign the conditions. What difference does that make? If it were possible for your lordships to escape from the world of make-believe, which the law has created, into the real world in which transactions of this sort are actually done, the answer would be short and simple. It should make no difference whatever. This sort of document is not meant to be read, still less to be understood. Its signature is in truth about as significant as a handshake that marks the formal conclusion of a bargain.

Your Lordships were referred to the dictum of Blackburn J., in *Harris v. Great Western Ry. Co.* (1876) 1 Q.B.D. 515. The passage is as follows: "And it is clear law that where there is a writing, into which the terms of any agreement are reduced, the terms are to be regulated by that writing. And though one of the parties may not have read the writing, yet, in general, he is bound to the other by those terms; and that, I apprehend, is on the ground that, by assenting to the contract thus reduced to writing, he represents to the other side that he has made himself acquainted with the contents of that writing and assents to them, and so induces the other side to act upon that representation by entering into the contract with him, and is consequently precluded from denying that he did make himself acquainted with those terms. But then the preclusion only exists when the case is brought within the rule so carefully and accurately laid down by Parke B., in delivering the judgment of the Exchequer in *Freeman v. Cooke* (1848) 2 Exch. 654, that is, if he 'means his representation to be acted upon, and it is acted upon accordingly: or if, whatever a man's real intentions may be, he so conduct himself that a reasonable man would take the representation to be true, and believe that it was meant that he should act upon it, and did act upon it as true.'" If the ordinary law of estoppel was applicable to this case, it might well be argued that the circumstances leave no room for any representation by the sender on which the carrier acted. I believe that any other member of the public in the appellant's place—and this goes for lawyers as well as for laymen—would have found himself compelled to give the same sort of answers as the appellant gave; and I doubt if any carrier who serves out documents of this type could honestly say that he acted in the belief that the recipient had "made himself acquainted with the contents." But Blackburn J. was dealing with an unsigned document, a cloakroom ticket. Unless your Lordships are to disapprove the decision of the Court of Appeal in *L'Estrange v. F. Graucob, Ltd.* [1934] 2 K.B. 394—and there has been no suggestion in this case that you should—the law is clear, without any recourse to the doctrine of estoppel, that a signature to a contract is conclusive.

This is a matter that is relevant to the way in which the respondents put their case. They say that the previous dealings between themselves and the appellant, being always on the terms of their "risk note," as they call their written conditions, the contract between themselves and the appellant must be deemed to import the same conditions. In my opinion, the bare fact that there have been previous dealings between the parties does not assist the respondents at all. The fact that a man has made a contract in the same form ninety-nine times (let alone three or four times which are here alleged) will not of itself affect the hundredth contract, in which the form is not used. Previous dealings are relevant only if they prove knowledge of the terms, actual and not constructive, and assent to them. If a term is not expressed in a contract, there is only one other way in which it can come into it and that is by implication. No implication can be made against a party of a term which was unknown to him. If previous dealings show that a man knew of and agreed to a term on ninety-nine occasions, there is a basis for saying that it can be imported into the hundredth contract without an express statement. It may or may not be sufficient to justify the importation—that depends on the circumstances; but at least by proving knowledge the essential beginning is made. Without knowledge there is nothing.

It is for the purpose of proving knowledge that the respondents rely on the dictum of Blackburn J. which I have cited. My lords, in spite of the great authority of Blackburn J., I think that this is a dictum which some day your lordships may have to examine more closely. It seems to me that when a party assents to a document forming the whole or a part of his contract, he is bound by the terms of the document, read or unread, signed or unsigned, simply because they are in the contract; and it is unnecessary, and possibly misleading, to say that he is bound by them because he represents to the other party that he has made himself acquainted with them. But if there be an estoppel of this sort, its effect is in my opinion limited to the contract in relation to which the representation is made; and it cannot (unless of course there be something else on which the estoppel is founded besides the mere receipt of the document) assist the other party in relation to other transactions. The respondents in the present case have quite failed to prove that the appellant made himself acquainted with the conditions that they had introduced into previous dealings. He is not estopped from saying that for good reasons or bad he signed the previous contracts without the slightest idea of what was in them. If that is so, previous dealings are no evidence of knowledge and so are of little or no use to the respondents in this case. I say "of little or no use" because the appellant did admit that he knew that there were some conditions, though he did not know what they were. He certainly did not know that they were conditions which exempted the respondents from liability for their own negligence, though, I suppose, if he had thought about them at all, he would have known that they probably exempted the respondents from the strict liability of a carrier. Most people know that carriers exact some conditions and it does not matter in this case whether the appellant's knowledge was general knowledge of this sort or was derived from previous dealings. Your lordships can therefore leave previous dealings out of it and ask yourselves simply what is the position of a man who, with that amount of general knowledge, apparently makes a contract into which no conditions are expressly inserted? The answer must surely be that either he does not make a contract at all because the parties are not ad idem or he makes the contract without the conditions. You cannot have a contract subject to uncommunicated conditions the terms of which are known only to one side.

It is at this point, I think, that their lordships in the Second Division fell into error. The Lord Justice-Clerk said: "It is, I think, well settled that, if A contracts with B for the carriage by B of A's goods, in the knowledge, gained through previous experience of similar transactions, that B carries goods subject to conditions, A is bound by these conditions under this later contract, if it is of a similar nature to those which have gone before, in the absence of agreement or information to the contrary. This applies even if A, knowing that there are conditions, does not take the trouble to ascertain precisely what these conditions are."

Similarly LORD MACKINTOSH said: "In these circumstances, I am of the opinion, following what I understand to be the law as laid down in *Parker v. South Eastern Ry. Co.* and particularly by Baggallay, L.J., that the [appellant], being aware by reason of his own previous experience, and of that of the agent who happened to be acting for him in the present transaction, that goods were carried on the [respondents'] vessels subject to certain conditions, and having been given no reason to think that these conditions were not still operative on Oct. 8, 1960, was bound by the conditions, although, as was proved to have been the case, he had never at any time acquainted himself with their purport."

My lords, I think, with great respect, that this is to introduce a new and fundamentally erroneous principle into the law of contract. There can be no conditions in any contract unless they are brought into it by expression, incorporation or implication. They are not brought into it simply because one party has inserted them into similar transactions in the past and has not given the other party any reason to think that he will not want to insert them again. The error is based, I think, on a misunderstanding of what are commonly called the ticket cases; I say this because the single authority cited for the proposition is one of the leading ticket cases, *Parker v. South Eastern Ry. Co.* The question in these cases is whether or not the passenger has accepted the ticket as a contractual document. If he knows that it contains conditions of some sort, he must know that it is meant to be contractual. If he accepts it as a contractual document, then prima facie (I am not dealing with questions of reasonable notice) he is bound by the conditions that are printed on it or incorporated in it by sufficient reference to some other document, whether he has inquired about them or not. That is all that Baggallay, L.J., is saying in *Parker v. South Eastern Ry. Co.* In the present case there is no contractual document at all. There is not so much as a peg on which to hang any terms that are not expressed in the contract nor a phrase which is capable of expansion. It is as if the appellant had been accepted as a passenger without being given a ticket at all. There is then no special contract and the contract is the ordinary one which the law imposes on carriers. As Baggallay, L.J., said, "This clearly would be the nature of the contract if no ticket were delivered, as occasionally happens."

If a man is given a blank ticket without conditions or any reference to them, even if he knows in detail what the conditions usually exacted are, he is not, in the absence of any allegation of fraud or of that sort of mistake for which the law gives relief, bound by such conditions. It may seem a narrow and artificial line that divides a ticket that is blank on the back from one that says "For conditions see time-tables," or something of that sort, that has been held to be enough notice. I agree that it is an artificial line and one that has little relevance to every day conditions. It may be beyond your lordships' power to make the artificial line more natural: but at least you can see that it is drawn fairly for both sides, and that there is not one law for individuals and another for organizations that can issue printed documents. If the respondents had remembered to issue a risk note in this case, they would have invited your lordships to give a curt answer to any complaint by the appellant. He might say that the terms were unfair and unreasonable, that he had never voluntarily agreed to them, that it was impossible to read or understand them and that anyway, if he had tried to negotiate any change, the respondents would not have listened to him. The respondents would expect him to be told that he had made his contract and must abide by it. Now the boot is on the other foot. It is just as legitimate, but also just as vain, for the respondents to say that it was only a slip on their part, that it is unfair and unreasonable of the appellant to take advantage of it and that he knew perfectly well that they never carried goods except on conditions. The law must give the same answer: they must abide by the contract which they made. What is sauce for the goose is sauce for the gander. It will remain unpalatable sauce for both animals until the legislature, if the courts cannot do it, intervenes to secure that when contracts are made in circumstances in which there is no scope for free negotiation of the terms, they are made on terms that are clear, fair and reasonable and settled independently as such. That is what Parliament has done in the case of carriage of goods by rail and on the high seas.

I have now given my opinion on the main point in the case and the one on which the respondents succeeded below. On the other points on which the respondents failed below and which they put forward again as grounds for dismissing the claim, I have nothing to add to what your lordships have already said. In my opinion the appeal should be allowed.

THORNTON V SHOE LANE PARKING LTD
[1971] 2 QB 163 (CA)

LORD DENNING MR: In 1964 Mr. Thornton, the plaintiff, who was a free-lance trumpeter of the highest quality, had an engagement with the BBC at Farringdon Hall. He drove to the City in his motor car and went to park it at a multi-storey automatic car park. It had only been open a few months. He had never gone there before. There was a notice on the outside headed "Shoe Lane Parking." It gave the parking charges, 5s for two hours, 7s 6d for three hours, and so forth; and at the bottom: "All Cars Parked At Owners Risk." The plaintiff drove up to the entrance. There was not a man in attendance. There was a traffic light which showed red. As he drove in and got to the appropriate place, the traffic light turned green and a ticket was pushed out from the machine. The plaintiff took it. He drove on into the garage. The motor car was taken up by mechanical means to a floor above. The plaintiff left it there and went off to keep his appointment with the BBC. Three hours later he came back. He went to the office and paid the charge for the time that the car was there. His car was brought down from the upper floor. He went to put his belongings into the boot of the car; but unfortunately there was an accident. The plaintiff was severely injured. The judge has found it was half his own fault, but half the fault of Shoe Lane Parking Ltd., the defendants. The judge awarded him £3,637 6s 11d.

On this appeal the defendants do not contest the judge's findings about the accident. They acknowledge that they were at fault, but they claim that they are protected by some exempting conditions. They rely on the ticket which was issued to the plaintiff by the machine. They say that it was a contractual document and that it incorporated a condition which exempts them from liability to him. The ticket was headed "Shoe Lane Parking." Just below there was a "box" in which was automatically recorded the time when the car went into the garage. There was a notice alongside: "Please present this ticket to cashier to claim your car." Just below the time, there was some small print in the left hand corner which said: "This ticket is issued subject to the conditions of issue as displayed on the premises." That is all.

The plaintiff says that he looked at the ticket to see the time on it, and put it in his pocket. He could see there was printing on the ticket, but he did not read it. He only read the time. He did not read the words which said that the ticket was issued subject to the conditions as displayed on the premises. If the plaintiff had read those words on the ticket and had looked round the premises to see where the conditions were displayed, he would have had to have driven his car on into the garage and walked round. Then he would have found, on a pillar opposite the ticket machine, a set of printed conditions in a panel. He would also have found, in the paying office (to be visited when coming back for the car) two more panels containing the printed conditions. If he had the time to read the conditions—it would take him a very considerable time—he would read this:

CONDITIONS

The following are the conditions upon which alone motor vehicles are accepted for parking:

1. The Customer agrees to pay the charges of [the defendants]. ...
2. The Customer is deemed to be fully insured at all times against all risks (including, without prejudice to the generality of the foregoing, fire, damage and theft, whether due to the negligence of others or not) and [the defendants] shall not be responsible or liable for any loss or misdelivery of or damage of whatever kind to the Customer's motor vehicle, or any articles carried therein or thereon or of or to any accessories carried thereon or therein *or injury to the Customer* or any other person *occurring when the Customer's motor vehicle is in the Parking Building howsoever that loss, misdelivery, damage or injury shall be caused*; and it is agreed and understood that the Customer's motor vehicle is parked and permitted by [the defendants] to be parked in the Parking Building in accordance with this Licence entirely at the Customer's risk.

There is a lot more. I have only read about one-tenth of the conditions. The important thing to notice is that the defendants seek by this condition to exempt themselves from liability, not only for damage to the car, but also for injury to the customer howsoever caused. The condition talks about insurance. It is well known that the customer is usually insured against damage to the car; but he is not insured against damage to himself. If the condition is incorporated into the contract of parking, it means that the plaintiff will be unable to recover any damages for his personal injuries which were caused by the negligence of the company.

We have been referred to the ticket cases of former times from *Parker v. South Eastern Ry. Co.* to *McCutcheon v. David MacBrayne Ltd.* They were concerned with railways, steamships and cloakrooms where booking clerks issued tickets to customers who took them away without reading them. In those cases the issue of the ticket was regarded as an *offer* by the company. If the customer took it and retained it without objection, his act was regarded as an *acceptance* of the offer: see *Watkins v. Rymill* and *Thompson v. London, Midland and Scottish Ry. Co.* These cases were based on the theory that the customer, on being handed the ticket, could refuse it and decline to enter into a contract on those terms. He could ask for his money back. That theory was, of course, a fiction. No customer in a thousand ever read the conditions. If he had stopped to do so, he would have missed the train or the boat.

None of those cases has any application to a ticket which is issued by an automatic machine. The customer pays his money and gets a ticket. He cannot refuse it. He cannot get his money back. He may protest to the machine, even swear at it; but it will remain unmoved. He is committed beyond recall. He was committed at the very moment when he put his money into the machine. The contract was concluded at that time. It can be translated into offer and acceptance in this way. The offer is made when the proprietor of the machine holds it out as being ready to receive the money. The acceptance takes place when the customer puts his money into the slot. The terms of the offer are contained in the notice placed on or near the machine stating what is offered for the money. The customer is bound by those terms as long as they are sufficiently brought to his notice beforehand, but not otherwise. He is not bound by the terms printed on the ticket if they differ from the notice, because the ticket comes too late. The contract has already been made: see *Olley v. Marlborough Court Ltd.* The ticket is no more than a voucher or receipt for the money that has been paid (as in the deckchair case, *Chapelton v. Barry Urban District Council*) on terms which have been offered and accepted before the ticket is issued. In the present case the offer was contained in the notice at the entrance giving the charges for garaging and saying "at owners risk," i.e. at the risk of the owner so far as damage to the car was concerned. The offer was accepted when the plaintiff drove up to the entrance and, by the movement of his car, turned the light from red to green, and the ticket was thrust at him. The contract was then concluded, and it could not be altered by any words printed on the ticket itself. In particular, it could not be altered so as to exempt the company from liability for personal injury due to their negligence.

Assuming, however, that an automatic machine is a booking clerk in disguise, so that the old fashioned ticket cases still apply to it, we then have to go back to the three questions put by Mellish L.J. in *Parker v. South Eastern Ry. Co.*, subject to this qualification: Mellish L.J. used the word "conditions" in the plural, whereas it would be more apt to use the word "condition" in the singular, as indeed Mellish L.J. himself did at the end of his judgment. After all, the only condition that matters for this purpose is the exempting condition. It is no use telling the customer that the ticket is issued subject to some "conditions" or other, without more; for he may reasonably regard "conditions" in general as merely regulatory, and not as taking away his rights, unless the exempting condition is drawn specifically to his attention. (Alternatively, if the plural "conditions" is used, it would be better prefaced with the word "exempting," because the exempting conditions are the only conditions that matter for this purpose.) Telescoping the three questions, they come to this: the customer is bound by the exempting condition if he knows that the ticket is issued subject to it: or, if the company did what was reasonably sufficient to give him notice of it. Counsel for the defendants admitted here that the defendants did not do what was reasonably sufficient to give the plaintiff notice of the exempting condition. That admission was properly made. I do not pause to enquire whether the exempting condition is void for unreasonableness. All I say is that it is so wide and so destructive of rights that the court should not hold any man bound by it unless it is drawn to his attention in the most explicit way. It is an instance of what I had in mind in *J. Spurling Ltd. v. Bradshaw*. In order to give sufficient notice, it would need to be printed in red ink with a red hand pointing to it, or something equally startling.

However, although reasonable notice of it was not given, counsel for the defendants said that this case came within the second question propounded by Mellish L.J., namely that the plaintiff "knew or believed that the writing contained conditions." There was no finding to that effect. The burden was on the defendants to prove it, and they did not do so. Certainly there was no evidence that the plaintiff knew of this exempting condition. He is not, therefore, bound by it. Counsel for the defendants relied on a case in this court last year, *Mendelssohn v. Normand Ltd.* Mr. Mendelssohn parked his car in the Cumberland Garage at Marble Arch and was given a ticket which contained an exempting condition. There was no discussion as to whether the condition formed part of the contract. It was conceded that it did. That is shown by the report. Yet the garage company were not entitled to rely on the exempting condition for the reasons there given. That case does not touch the present, where the whole question is whether the exempting condition formed part of the contract.

I do not think it did. The plaintiff did not know of the condition, and the defendants did not do what was reasonably sufficient to give him notice of it.

I do not think the defendants can escape liability by reason of the exempting condition. I would, therefore, dismiss the appeal.

[Megaw LJ and Sir Gordon Wilmer delivered concurring judgments.]

QUESTIONS

1. A runs a photographic transparency lending library. B ordered 50 transparencies by telephone, which were delivered with a printed "delivery note" stipulating that unless transparencies were returned within 14 days of delivery a "holding fee" of $20 per transparency per day would be payable. B had not previously used the library and did not read the note. She returned the transparencies 24 days after delivery. Is she liable to pay $10,000? See *Interfoto Picture Library Ltd v Stiletto Visual Programmes Ltd*, [1989] QB 433 (CA).

2. When are terms incorporated in a contract made by computer? Is it necessary for the recipient to click on an "agree" box? See *Century 21 Canada Limited Partnership v Rogers Communications Inc*, 2011 BCSC 1196, 338 DLR (4th) 32.

BRITISH CRANE HIRE CORP LTD V IPSWICH PLANT HIRE LTD
[1975] QB 303 (CA)

LORD DENNING MR: In June, 1970, a big earth-moving machine got stuck in the mud. It sank so far as to be out of sight. It cost much money to get it out. Who is to pay the cost?

The defendants, Ipswich Plant Hire Ltd., were doing drainage and other engineering works in the marshy land next the River Stour, near Cattawade Bridge in Essex. They are themselves in the hiring business, letting out cranes and so forth. But on this occasion they were doing the work themselves. They needed a dragline crane urgently. They got in touch with the plaintiffs, the British Crane Hire Corporation Ltd., and asked if they could hire a dragline crane. The plaintiffs responded quickly. They delivered it on Sunday, June 28, 1970. They let it on hire to the defendants, together with the driver, Mr. Humphrey. No doubt the driver remained the servant of the plaintiffs when he was driving the crane. The plaintiffs took it as far as they could by road. Then it was unloaded.

On the next day, Monday, June 29, 1970, the defendants' site agent, a Mr. Meadows, directed the driver the way to go across the marsh. When they got to a particularly bad patch, Mr. Meadows warned the driver that he ought to have "navimats," that is, sets of timber baulks which could be laid on the marsh and form a kind of roadway for the machine. The defendants ought to have supplied the "navimats," but they had not yet arrived. Mr. Meadows told the driver to wait for the "navimats." But the driver did not wait. He took his chance. He went on without "navimats." He got over that patch safely. Further on, there was another bad patch of marsh. The driver took his chance again. This time he fared worse. The dragline crane sank into the marsh. That was the "first mishap." They got it out after a good deal of work. There was no doubt that it was the fault of the driver, Mr. Humphrey, in not waiting for the "navimats." His negligence was the cause of that first mishap. His employers, the plaintiffs, must bear the cost of it.

On the next day, Tuesday, June 30, 1970, the "navimats" arrived. But there was a second mishap. On that day the dragline crane had to cross another bad patch. The driver, Mr. Humphrey, was this time using the "navimats." He had to make a turning movement or "spragging." He had just completed it when, in spite of the "navimats," this machine sank into the marsh. It went out of sight. Great efforts were needed to get it out. Heavy equipment was brought in. Eventually, at great expense, the machine was got out.

The question arises on the second mishap. Who is to bear the expense of recovering the machine from the marsh? The judge found that the sinking into the marsh was not the fault of the driver, Mr. Humphrey, but the fault of Mr. Meadows, the site agent of the defendants. The judge thought that Mr. Meadows ought to have directed the crane by a safer route across the marshy ground. On that account he held the defendants liable for the expense. That finding was challenged before us by Mr. McCowan for the defendants. He pointed out that the driver and the site agent had gone together over the ground and decided on this route. I was impressed by Mr. McCowan's submissions on this point. I doubt whether it would be right to hold the site agent guilty of negligence. It seems to me that this second mishap may have been a piece of bad luck which occurred without the fault of anyone. It was a hazard due to the nature of the marsh itself at that point.

But it does not follow that the plaintiffs fail on their claim. Even though the defendants were not negligent, nevertheless the plaintiffs say that the defendants are liable in contract for the costs of recovering the machine from the marsh. The plaintiffs say that the contract incorporated the conditions on a printed form under which the defendants are liable for the costs.

The judge found that the printed conditions were not incorporated into the contract. The plaintiffs appeal from that finding. The facts are these: the arrangements for the hire of the crane were all on the telephone. The plaintiffs agreed to let the defendants this crane. It was to be delivered on the Sunday. The hiring charges and transport charges were agreed. Nothing was said about conditions. There was nothing in writing. But soon after the crane was delivered, the plaintiffs, in accordance with their practice, sent forward a printed form to be signed by the hirer. It set out the order, the work to be done, and the hiring fee, and that it was subject to the conditions set out on the back on the form. The defendants would ordinarily have sent the form back signed: but this time they did not do so. The accident happened before they signed it. So they never did so. But the plaintiffs say that nevertheless, from the previous course of dealing, the conditions on the form govern the relationship between the parties. They rely on no. 6:

> Site conditions: The hirer shall take all reasonable precautions to ensure that the crane can safely be taken onto and kept upon or at the site and in particular to ensure that the ground is in a satisfactory condition to take the weight of the crane and/or its load. The hirer shall where necessary supply and lay timber or other suitable material for the crane to travel over and work upon and shall be responsible for the recovery of the crane from soft ground.

Also on no. 8: "The hirer shall be responsible for and indemnify the owner against ... all expenses in connection with or arising out of the use of the plant." In support of the course of dealing, the plaintiffs relied on two previous transactions in which the defendants had hired cranes from the plaintiffs. One was February 20, 1969; and the other October 6, 1969. Each was on a printed form which set out the hiring of a crane, the price, the site, and so forth; and also setting out the conditions the same as those here. There were thus only two transactions many months before and they were not known to the defendants' manager who ordered this crane. In the circumstances I doubt whether those two would be sufficient to show a course of dealing.

In *Hollier v. Rambler Motors (A.M.C.) Ltd.* [1972] 2 Q.B. 71, 76, Salmon L.J. said he knew of no case "in which it has been decided or even argued that a term could be implied into an oral contract on the strength of a course of dealing (if it can be so called) which consisted at the most of three or four transactions over a period of five years." That was a case of a private individual who had had his car repaired by the defendants and had signed forms with conditions on three or four occasions. The plaintiff there was not of equal bargaining power with the garage company which repaired the car. The conditions were not incorporated.

But here the parties were both in the trade and were of equal bargaining power. Each was a firm of plant hirers who hired out plant. The defendants themselves knew that firms in the plant-hiring trade always imposed conditions in regard to the hiring of plant; and that their conditions were on much the same lines. The defendants' manager, Mr. Turner (who knew the crane), was asked about it. He agreed that he had seen these conditions or similar ones in regard to the hiring of plant. He said that most of them were, to one extent or another, variations of a form which he called "the Contractors' Plant Association form." The defendants themselves (when they let out cranes) used the conditions of that form. The conditions on the plaintiffs' form were in rather different words, but nevertheless to much the same effect. He was asked one or two further questions which I would like to read:

> (Q) If it was a matter of urgency, you would hire that machine out, and the conditions of hire would no doubt follow? (A) They would.   (Q) Is it right that, by the very nature of your business, this is not something that happens just once a year, nor does it happen every day either, but it happens fairly regularly? (A) It does.   (Q) You are well aware of the condition that it is the hirer's responsibility to make sure that soft ground is suitable for a vehicle or machine? (A) It is: it is also the owner's responsibility to see that the machine is operated competently.

Then the judge asked: "But it is the hirer's job to see what in relation to the ground? (A) That suitable timber was supplied for the machine to operate on in relation to soft ground." Then counsel asked: "And in fact it is the hirer's job to recover the crane from the soft ground, if it should go into it? (A) If the crane sank overnight of its own accord, I dare say it would be."

From that evidence it is clear that both parties knew quite well that conditions were habitually imposed by the supplier of these machines: and both parties knew the substance of those conditions. In particular that if the crane sank in soft ground it was the hirer's job to recover it: and that there was an indemnity clause. In these circumstances, I think the conditions on the form should be regarded as incorporated into the contract. I would not put it so much on the course of dealing, but rather on the common understanding which is to be derived from the conduct of the parties, namely, that the hiring was to be on the terms of the plaintiffs' usual conditions.

As Lord Reid said in *McCutcheon v. David MacBrayne Ltd.* [1964] 1 W.L.R. 125, 128 quoting from the Scottish textbook, *Gloag on Contract*, 2nd ed. (1929), p. 7: "The judicial task is not to discover the actual intentions of each party; it is to decide what each was reasonably entitled to conclude from the attitude of the other." It seems to me that, in view of the relationship of the parties, when the defendants requested his crane urgently and it was supplied at once—before the usual form was received—the plaintiffs were entitled to conclude that the defendants were accepting it on the terms of the plaintiffs' own printed conditions—which would follow in a day or two. It is just as if the plaintiffs had said: "We will supply it on our usual conditions," and the defendants said "Of course, that is quite understood."

458

Applying the conditions, it is quite clear that nos. 6 and 8 cover the second mishap. The defendants are liable for the cost of recovering the crane from the soft ground.

But, so far as the first mishap is concerned, neither condition 6 nor condition 8 (the indemnity clause) is wide enough to cover it: because that mishap was due to the negligence of their own driver. It requires very clear words to exempt a person from responsibility for his own negligence: see *Gillespie Bros. & Co. Ltd. v. Roy Bowles Transport Ltd.* [1973] Q.B. 400, 415. There are no such words here.

Even though the judge did not find that the conditions were incorporated, he held that there was an implied term that the hirer should return the chattel to the owner at the end of the hiring. Mr. McCowan pointed out that that implied term was not distinctly pleaded or relied upon. But, nevertheless, there is much to be said for it. When a machine is let out on hire for us on marshy land, and both parties know that it may sink into a marsh, then it seems to me that, if it sinks into the marsh, it is the hirer's job to recover it, so as to restore it to the owner at the end of the hiring. Take a motor car which is let out on hire, and by reason of a gale, or an icy road, it goes off the road into a ditch. It is the hirer's job to get it back on the road and restore it at the end of the hiring. Just as when he takes it on a long journey and falls ill a long distance away. It still is his duty to get it back and restore it to the owner at the end of the hiring. Of course, if it is lost or damaged and he can prove that it was not due to any fault on his part, he would not be liable. A bailee is not liable for loss or damage which he can prove occurred without any default on his part: but the return of the vehicle is different. It is the duty of the hirer to return the vehicle at the end of the hiring to the owner, and to pay the cost of doing so. Although he is not liable for loss or damage occurring without his fault, nevertheless he is liable to do what is reasonable to restore the property to the owner.

So, apart from the express conditions, it may well be, if it had been pleaded, that the plaintiffs could have recovered for the second mishap on an implied term. But, as it was not distinctly pleaded, I prefer to decide the case on the ground that conditions 6 and 8 formed part of the contract of hiring: and under them the plaintiffs are entitled to succeed in regard to mishap no. 2. I would affirm the decision of the judge, but on a different ground.

[Megaw LJ agreed and Sir Eric Sachs delivered separate concurring reasons.]

Appeal and cross-appeal dismissed.

[See also McCamus at 184-97; Waddams at paras 61-67; MacDougall at 159-65.]

II. PAROL EVIDENCE RULE

It is often said that the general rule is that a party who signs a contractual document is bound by its contents, even though he or she has not read the document, and even though the contents of the document may differ from the signer's understanding of the agreement. A statement often quoted is that of Scrutton LJ in *L'Estrange v Graucob*, [1934] 2 KB 394 at 403: "In cases in which the contract is contained in a railway ticket or other unsigned document, it is necessary to prove that an alleged party was aware, or ought to have been aware of its terms and conditions. These cases have no application when the document has been signed. When a document containing contractual terms is signed, then, in the absence of fraud, or, I will add, misrepresentation, the party signing it is bound, and it is wholly immaterial whether he has read the document or not." The following cases include a variety of techniques by which courts have managed to give relief to a party in spite of his signature to a contractual document.

Running through the cases are frequent references to the so-called parol evidence rule, of which it has been said that it is not concerned especially with parol statements, that it is not a rule of evidence, and that it is not even a rule at all. Nevertheless, references to it are so frequent that it cannot be ignored. A typical statement of the rule, per Denman CJ in *Goss v Lord Nugent* (1833), 5 B & Ad 58, follows: "By the general rules of the common law, if there be a contract which has been reduced into writing, verbal evidence is not allowed to be given of what passed between the parties, either before the written instrument was made, or during the time that it was in a state of preparation, so as to add to, or subtract from, or in any manner to vary or qualify the written contract."

The parties to a contract can seek to ensure the parol evidence rule applies by agreeing on it in their contract. Such a term in a contract is called an "entire agreement" or "entire contract" or "entire obligations" clause.

FEDERAL COMMERCE & NAVIGATION CO LTD V TRADAX EXPORT SA
[1978] AC 1 (HL)

[Under a charterparty the owners of a ship chartered her to carry grain to the port of Brake. No berths were available at Brake, and the ship anchored at a lightship some miles away. The charterer was bound to pay a fee for delay (demurrage) after the ship had "arrived." The shipowners claimed demurrage based on the ship having become an arrived ship when she reached the lightship. The House of Lords, reversing the Court of Appeal, held that the ship had not "arrived" until it had reached a port where it could effectively be unloaded.]

LORD DIPLOCK: My Lords, the freight market for chartered vessels still remains a classic example of a free market. It is world-wide in coverage, highly competitive and sensitive to fluctuations in supply and demand. It is a market in which the individual charterers and shipowners are matched in bargaining power and are at liberty to enter into charterparties in whatever contractual terms they please.

In practice the contracts negotiated in this market by the parties or their brokers are based upon one or other of a number of printed forms of charterparties appropriate to the various kinds of use to which vessels are put. These forms incorporate numerous standard clauses to which additions, often in the form of other well-known standard clauses, and deletions are agreed in the course of the bargaining process in which agreement is also reached upon such basic terms as rates of freight, demurrage and dispatch money.

No market such as a freight, insurance or commodity market, in which dealings involve the parties entering into legal relations of some complexity with one another, can operate efficiently without the use of standard forms of contract and standard clauses to be used in them. Apart from enabling negotiations to be conducted quickly, standard clauses serve two purposes. First, they enable those making use of the market to compare one offer with another to see which is the better; and this, as I have pointed out, involves considering not only the figures for freight, demurrage and dispatch money, but those clauses of the charterparty that deal with the allocation of misfortune risks between charterer and shipowner, particularly those risks which may result in delay. The second purpose served by standard clauses is that they become the subject of exegesis by the courts so that the way in which they will apply to the adventure contemplated by the charterparty will be understood in the same sense by both the parties when they are negotiating its terms and carrying them out.

It is no part of the function of a court of justice to dictate to charterers and ship-owners the terms of the contracts into which they ought to enter on the freight market; but it is an important function of a court, and particularly of your Lordships' House, to provide them with legal certainty at the negotiation stage as to what it is that they are agreeing to. And if there is that certainty, then when occasion arises for a court to enforce the contract or to award damages for its breach, the fact that the members of the court themselves may think that one of the parties was unwise in agreeing to assume a particular misfortune risk or unlucky in its proving more expensive to him than he expected, has nothing to do with the merits of the case or with enabling justice to be done. The only merits of the case are that parties who have bargained on equal terms in a free market should stick to their agreements. Justice is done by seeing that they do so or compensating the party who has kept his promise for any loss he has sustained by the failure of the other party to keep his.

PRENN V SIMMONDS
[1971] 3 All ER 237 (HL)

LORD WILBERFORCE: My Lords, Dr. Simmonds's claim in this action is that under the terms of an agreement under seal dated 6th July 1960, he is entitled to acquire from Mr. Prenn, for a consideration of £6,000, a 4 per cent interest in the ordinary capital of a company controlled by Mr. Prenn called now Controls & Communications Ltd., but at the relevant date Radio & Television Trust Ltd. ("RTT"). This interest was worth at the date of the trial about £200,000. Mr. Prenn disputes the claim on the ground that a necessary condition set by the agreement has not been satisfied because less than £300,000 profits available for dividend on the ordinary stock of RTT over the relevant period has been earned. Dr. Simmonds maintains that the condition has been fulfilled. The dispute relates not to the figures, which are agreed, but to the definition of profits of RTT available for dividend on its ordinary stock. If this means the separate profits of RTT alone, the amount over the period fell just short of the target, by less than £10,000. If it means the consolidated profits of the group consist-ing of RTT and subsidiaries, the amount was largely exceeded. The small margin of deficiency, although capable of arousing sympathy for Dr. Simmonds, is not an argument for one or other side. A similar situation might arise on either interpreta-tion and is inherent in the nature of "target" agreements.

The question is thus simply one of construction of the agreement and it should be capable of resolution shortly and cheaply. But Dr. Simmonds has claimed in the alternative that, if the agreement did not bear the meaning he contended for, it should be rectified so as to do so. This let in a mass of evidence, oral and documen-tary, as to the parties' intentions, which would not be admissible on construction, although (as I shall explain) counsel for Dr. Simmonds tried to bring some of it in on that issue. It also involved some issues of law. This part of the case overshadowed the rest, so that by far the greater part of the time spent both at first instance and in the Court of Appeal was concerned with it. In this House argument was heard first exclusively on the question of construction and, as your Lordships reached on it a conclusion in favour of Dr. Simmonds, no argument on rectification was heard. I now deal with this construction issue.

In order for the agreement of 6th July 1960 to be understood, it must be placed in its context. The time has long passed when arguments, even those under seal, were isolated from the matrix of facts in which they were set and interpreted purely on internal linguistic considerations. There is no need to appeal here to any modern, anti-literal, tendencies, for Lord Blackburn's well-known judgment in *River Wear Comrs. v. Adamson* (1877) 2 App. Cas. 743 at 763 provides ample warrant for a liberal approach. We must, as he said, enquire beyond the language and see what the circumstances were with reference to which the words were used, and the object, appearing from those circumstances, which the person using them had in view. Moreover, at any rate since 1859 (*Macdonald v. Longbottom* (1860) 1 E. & E. 977) it has been clear enough that evidence of mutually known facts may be admitted to identify the meaning of a descriptive term.

Counsel for Dr. Simmonds, however, contended for even greater extension of the court's interpretative power. They argued that later authorities have gone further and allow prior negotiations to be looked at in aid of the construction of a written document. In my opinion, they did not make good their contention. A modern authority in this House, which counsel for Dr. Simmonds invoked, is *Hvalfangersels-kapet Polaris Aktieselskap v. Unilever Ltd.* (1933) 39 Com. Cas. 1 where it was necessary to interpret the words "entire production." There, as here, there was a claim for rectification in the alternative so that a great deal of evidence of matters prior to the contract was called. But the speeches give no support for a contention that negotiations leading up to the contract can be taken into account; at most they support the admission of evidence to establish a trade or technical meeting (not in question here) and, of course, they recognise the admissibility of evidence of surrounding circumstances. But they contain little to encourage, and much to discourage, evidence of negotiation or of the parties' subjective intentions.

I may refer to one other case to dispel the idea that English law is left behind in some island of literal interpretation. In *Utica City National Bank v. Gunn* (1918) 118 N.E. 607 the New York Court of Appeals followed precisely the English line. Cardozo J. in his judgment refers to "the genesis and aim of the transaction" citing Stephen's *Digest of the Law of Evidence*, and *Wigmore on Evidence*. Surrounding circumstances may, he says, "stamp upon a contract a popular or looser meaning" than the strict legal meaning, certainly when to follow the latter would make the transaction futile. "It is easier to give a new shade of meaning to a word than to give no meaning to a whole transaction." The whole judgment, as one may expect, combines classicism with intelligent realism.

So I think that Dr. Simmonds gains little support from authority. On principle, the matter is worth pursuing a little, because the present case illustrates very well the disadvantages and danger of departing from established doctrine and the virtue of the latter. There were prolonged negotiations between solicitors, with exchanges of draft clauses, ultimately emerging in cl. 2 of the agreement. The reason for not admitting evidence of these exchanges is not a technical one or even mainly one of convenience (although the attempt to admit it did greatly prolong the case and add to its expense). It is simply that such evidence is unhelpful. By the nature of things, where negotiations are difficult, the parties' positions, with each passing letter, are changing and until the final agreement, although converging, still divergent. It is only the final document which records a consensus. If the previous documents use different expressions, how does construction of those expressions, itself a doubtful process, help on the construction of the contractual words? If the same expressions are used, nothing is gained by looking back; indeed, something may be lost since the relevant surrounding circumstances may be different. And at this stage there is no consensus of the parties to appeal to. It may be said that previous documents may be looked at to explain the aims of the parties. In a limited sense this is true; the commercial, or business object, of the transaction, objectively ascertained, may be a surrounding fact. Cardozo J. thought so in the *Utica Bank* case. And if it can be shown that one interpretation completely frustrates that object, to the extent of rendering the contract futile, that may be a strong argument for an alternative interpretation, if that can reasonably be found. But beyond that it may be difficult to go; it may be a matter of degree, or of judgment, how far one interpretation, or another, gives effect to a common intention; the parties, indeed, may be pursuing that intention with differing emphasis, and hoping to achieve it to an extent which may differ, and in different ways. The words used may, and often do, represent a formula which means different things to each side, yet may be accepted because that is the only way to get "agreement" and in the hope that disputes will not arise. The only course then can be to try to ascertain the "natural" meaning. Far more, and indeed totally, dangerous is it to admit evidence of one party's objective—even if this is known to the other party. However strongly pursued this may be, the other party may only be willing to give it partial recognition, and in a world of give and take, men often have to be satisfied with less than they want. So, again, it would be a matter of speculation how far the common intention was that the particular objective should be realised. In the present case, Lord Denning M.R. seems to have taken into account Dr. Simmonds's anxiety (as testified by a witness) to protect himself against unilateral decisions by Mr. Prenn; and an argument pressed on us was that, if Mr. Prenn's interpretation (i.e. that only the holding company's profits were relevant) was correct, Dr. Simmonds would, in this matter on which he felt so anxious, in some respect at least, be completely in Mr. Prenn's hands, for Mr. Prenn could decide just how much, or how little, of the subsidiaries' profits were to be passed to the holding company. I cannot see how any of this can be admissible because, I repeat, I cannot see how it is helpful. Given the fact of Dr. Simmonds's anxiety, the whole question is how far does the agreement meet it; how can we know, except by interpreting the agreement, how far Mr. Prenn was willing to meet him or how far Dr. Simmonds decided to take what he could get? Even the argument that Mr. Prenn's interpretation would put Dr. Simmonds's position—a professional man—entering into relations with the source of finance and benefits to come, might decide, in his own interest, that if he could not get all the protection he wanted, the risk of partial protection was one to accept; that Mr. Prenn had to be trusted to act fairly. To say that the clause had this result is not to say that it was futile or frustratory: it is to say that a better clause could, with hindsight, in Dr. Simmonds's interest have been drawn. But the court cannot construct such a clause out of the material given.

In my opinion, then, evidence of negotiations, or of the parties' intentions, and a fortiori of Dr. Simmonds's intention, ought not to be received, and evidence should be restricted to evidence of the factual background known to the parties at or before the date of the contract, including evidence of the "genesis" and objectively the "aim" of the transaction.

As to the circumstances, and the object of the parties, there is no controversy in the present case. The agreement itself, on its face, almost supplies enough, without the necessity to supplement it by outside evidence. But some expansion, from undisputed facts, makes for clearer understanding and I include a reference to these in what follows.

In the year (1959) before the making of the contract, RTT was controlled by Crompton Parkinson Ltd., a large public electrical engineering company. RTT itself did not trade, but had a wholly-owned trading subsidiary, Airmec Ltd., which employed

Dr. Simmonds as managing director and as its leading technician. The structure of RTT was such that Crompton Parkinson held 94 per cent of its ordinary capital, and the whole of an issue of redeemable preference stock; the amount required to redeem it being £294,716 (there were also some capital certificates but I need not refer to this complication). Mr. Prenn desired to secure the services of Dr. Simmonds in his group of companies and decided to do so by purchasing, from Crompton Parkinson, RTT together, of course, with its subsidiary, Airmec, which in turn would bring with it Dr. Simmonds's services. So in July-August, 1959, an agreement was reached by which Mr. Prenn agreed to buy the 94 per cent of the ordinary capital and the preference stock. For this he paid £160,000 in cash. The balance, £294,716, was to be paid by four equal instalments on 19th August 1960, 1961, 1962 and 1963. The agreement provided that any money applied by RTT in redeeming preference stock was to go in reduction of the balance of the purchase price; and it was no doubt in Mr. Prenn's prima facie interest that the preference stock should be redeemed out of profits of RTT so as to avoid his having to find cash from his own resources.

The critical sale agreement between Mr. Prenn and Dr. Simmonds was dated 6th July 1960, after a period of negotiation. Its connection with the Crompton Parkinson agreement is manifest, both from the recital of the latter in it, and from the coincidence of the critical date in cl. 2 with the date—19th August 1963—stated in the Crompton Parkinson agreement as the terminal date for payment. A reading of the agreement shows that it was intended to secure for Dr. Simmonds the provision of an interest in the equity of RTT and that this was to be conditional on Dr. Simmonds remaining with RTT long enough to ensure that the Crompton Parkinson debt was paid off out of profits of RTT and on RTT in fact earning enough to enable the debts to be paid. Thus cl. 3 of the agreement provided for the sale to go off if Dr. Simmonds left RTT before the terminal date either voluntarily or through dismissal for gross misconduct. In order to make good this description of the agreement, I must set out a number of its provisions. After stating the parties there are recitals and definitions:

WHEREAS:

A. In this agreement the following words and expressions shall have the meanings set opposite them:

R.T.T.: Radio and Television Trust Limited ...
Ordinary Stock Units: The Ordinary stock units of 6d. each in the capital of R.T.T. ...
The Contract: The contract created by exchange of letters dated 21st July 1959 from Mr. Prenn to K.R. Cork as agent for C.P. and 29th July 1959 from C.P. to Mr. Prenn as varied by a Memorandum in writing dated 19th August 1959 being a contract for the purchase by Mr. Prenn of the interest of C.P. in R.T.T. and which includes 356,944 Preference Stock Units remaining in the hands of C.P. Under the terms of this contract as varied there is an obligation on the part of Mr. Prenn to pay the sum of £294,716, being the balance of the purchase money by your equal instalments on 19th August in 1960, 1961, 1962 and 1963 respectively.

B. Under the Contract any money received by C.P. from R.T.T. for any of the said 356,944 Preference Stock Units redeemed after 19th August 1959 is to be applied by C.P. in or towards payment of the balance of the said purchase money ...

Then the operative part:

1(a) [Provided for a payment by Mr. Prenn to Dr. Simmonds of £6,600.]
    (b) [Provided for the sale to Dr. Simmonds of shares in RTT.]
    (c) [Provided for sale of further shares to Dr. Simmonds.]

2. The provisions of Clause 1 hereof shall not take effect unless and until any one of the following conditions has been satisfied:

(a) The said sum of £294,716 has been paid or satisfied in full on or before the due dates for payment thereof under the Contract out of monies provided by R.T.T. redeeming its Preference Stock Units out of its profits which would otherwise be available for dividend or

(b) The aggregate profits of R.T.T. earned during the four years ending 19th August 1963 and available for dividend on the Ordinary Stock. Units for the time being issued whether declared or not shall have amounted to £300,000 after payment or provision for income tax and profits tax *provided always* that the conditions of this sub-paragraph (b) shall only apply if the Preference Stock Units or any of them are redeemed otherwise than out of the profits of R.T.T. which would otherwise be available for dividend or the terms of payment of the said balance of the purchase price under the Contract or any part thereof shall be re-arranged or all or any part of the said sum of £294,716 shall be satisfied from any other source.

3. The provisions of clause 1 shall not take effect if at any time before 20th August 1963 Dr. Simmonds ceases to be employed by R.T.T. either directly or through any of its subsidiaries by reason of his own act or is dismissed for gross misconduct and at the time of such termination neither of the conditions in clause 2 shall have been fulfilled.

Clauses 4 and 5 contained other consequential provisions.

What, then with this background, is the meaning of cl. 2? Its purpose is plain. Paragraph (a) provides that Dr. Simmonds is not to get his shares unless the outstanding debt to Crompton Parkinson has been repaid by means of redemption of preference stock out of profits of RTT. But this might not be fair to Dr. Simmonds, for Mr. Prenn, under his agreement with Crompton Parkinson, was not obliged to redeem the preference stock, or, if he did, might not use RTT's profits to do so. So para (b) is evidently designed to protect Dr. Simmonds against these possibilities. There are three alternative events which might bring it into operation, stated under the proviso. If any of these happened, Dr. Simmonds was to get his shares if the aggregate profits of RTT earned over the four years ending 19th August 1963 and available for dividend on the ordinary stock units whether declared or not should have amounted to £300,000 after payment or provision for income tax and profits tax. All of this was in the nature of an inducement to Dr. Simmonds, to procure whose expert services was a main object of the Crompton Parkinson purchase, and who was the mainspring of the profit earning activities of RTT through Airmec, to ensure that enough profits were earned to match the £294,716 which, on this hypothesis, was to be paid by Mr. Prenn, otherwise than out of RTT's profits, to Crompton Parkinson.

What profits, then, are contemplated by this clause? The profits of the RTT group, including Airmec, or only such separate profits as reach RTT as holding company? This is the whole question in the case.

As a final preliminary matter, before answering this question, it is necessary to state a few more matters of fact which must have been present to the minds of both parties. First, it must have been known to those businessmen, at least in general terms, that under the Companies Act 1948 there had to be placed before the shareholders of RTT in general meeting a consolidated profit and loss account giving a true and fair view of the profits of RTT and its subsidiaries combined just as if it was an account of a single company. No doubt there would also be separate profit and loss accounts of each individual company, including RTT itself, but I have no hesitation in asserting that both under the scheme of the Act and in accepted business practice, the significant document is the consolidated account which alone would show whether the enterprise represented by the group was making profit or not.

Secondly, as one would expect, accounts in this form had been prepared by RTT. There are among the documents consolidated profit and loss accounts of RTT and subsidiaries for the year ended 31st March 1958, the fifteen months ended 30th June 1959, the nine months ended 31st March 1960, the three relevant periods immediately before the agreement. Each of these shows the consolidated profit on trading (i.e. of the group), the dividend paid (i.e. on the preference and ordinary capital of RTT) and the balance on profit and loss account (of RTT and the subsidiaries). Thirdly, there are minutes showing how the decisions as to dividends (on RTT capital) out of the profits (of the group) were made. Minutes of 11th August 1959 and 10th June 1960 show, as one would expect, that these were made by the board of the holding company, which then instructed the subsidiaries to declare the appropriate amount by way of dividend, in favour of the holding company.

In the light of this, the meaning of cl. 2 of the agreement seems to me clear. The references to "profits" in para (a) and in para (b) can only, in my opinion, be to the consolidated profits of the group consisting of RTT and its subsidiaries. It is only these profits which could provide an incentive to Dr. Simmonds to remain and work with the group and which could be a measure of his success. On the other hand, no purpose can be discerned why the reference should be to the separate profits of RTT, which in fact means such part of the group profits as the board of that company, effectively Mr. Prenn, decided to pass up to the parent company.

Linguistically, the arguments point decidedly the same way. The reference to profits "earned," and that to income and profits tax, point strongly to consolidated profits. The use of the words "R.T.T." even coupled with the definition appears to me perfectly neutral, since other usages of "R.T.T." in the agreement (definition of "the Contract" and cl. 3) dispel any idea that the draftsman had in mind any segregation of RTT (qua parent) from the rest of its group. The reference (in para (b)) to profits "available for dividend on the Ordinary Stock Units," so far from pointing towards the limited construction, points, for me, the other way. For both commercially and on the established accounting practice, all profits of the group are available for these dividends. It is true that a large part of the profits was ploughed back into the business of the subsidiaries, and that both parties must have contemplated that this would be done, but this is not to the point. To say so is to confuse the earning of profits with their appropriation; all profits earned are available for dividend; what is done with them is a matter of choice which rests with those who control the company. Even if they decided to "plough them back" they still remain "available for dividend," so long as they remain in the balance sheet as "balance on profit and loss account."

One other argument I must mention. It is based on para (a). The reference there to profits otherwise available for dividend must, it is said, be to profits of the holding company, because it is only out of them that preference stock can be redeemed. This is said to be borne out by s. 58 of the Companies Act 1948, which requires that redeemable preference shares can only be redeemed out of "profits available for dividend" (or by a new issue). The use of these same words in para (a) is argued to show that only separate profits of RTT can be meant. In my opinion, this argument is fallacious. Paragraph (a) can just as well be referring to group profits; in a real sense (since RTT does not trade) its preference stock can only be redeemed by profits earned by the group. Admittedly, before redemption can occur, they have to be passed up to RTT (holding) by way of dividend on the subsidiaries; but they are still group profits. The only difference between para (a) and para (b) is that in the one case a "passing up" operation is presupposed, in the other not. But the "profits" are the same—group profits. The use of the words "available for dividend" in s. 58 proves nothing, since that section is not concerned with any particular type of company or with any distinction between parent and subsidiary. It is simply, in effect, saying that redeemable preference shares must be redeemed out of profits, not out of capital. What those profits are, in the case of a group, must be decided on arguments outside the section.

To sum up, Mr. Prenn's construction does not fit in any way the aim of the agreement, or correspond with commercial good sense, nor is it, even linguistically, acceptable. The converse of each of these propositions applies to Dr. Simmonds's interpretation. I would accept it. It follows, in consequence, that the alternative claim for rectification does not arise.

NOTES

1. In *Investors Compensation Scheme, Ltd v West Bromwich Building Society*, [1998] 1 WLR 896 (HL), Lord Hoffmann said, referring to *Prenn v Simmonds*:

> The background was famously referred to by Lord Wilberforce as the "matrix of fact," but this phrase is, if anything, an understated description of what the background may include. Subject to the requirement that it should have been reasonably available to the parties and to the [exclusion of the parties' previous negotiations and their declarations of subjective intent], it includes absolutely anything which would have affected the way in which the language of the document would have been understood by a reasonable man.

2. In *Eli Lilly & Co v Novopharm Ltd*, [1998] 2 SCR 129, evidence of the subjective intentions of the parties to an agreement for the supply of pharmaceuticals was excluded. Iacobucci J said at para 54: "The contractual intent of the parties is to be determined by reference to the words they used in drafting the document, possibly read in the light of the surrounding circumstances which were prevalent at the time."

3. In *Sattva Capital Corp v Creston Moly Corp*, 2014 SCC 53, Rothstein J acknowledged that the parol evidence rule is justified on the basis of certainty but has been subject to numerous critiques. He left for another day the issue of the role of the rule in general, but did say at para 60 that:

> The parol evidence rule does not apply to preclude evidence of the surrounding circumstances. Such evidence is consistent with the objectives of finality and certainty because it is used as an interpretive aid for determining the meaning of the written words chosen by the parties, not to change or overrule the meaning of those words. The surrounding circumstances are facts known or facts that reasonably ought to have been known to both parties at or before the date of contracting; therefore, the concern of unreliability does not arise.

FARAH V BARKI
[1955] SCR 107, 2 DLR 657

[On March 8, 1951, Barki wrote out and signed a document stating: "I hereby declare having sold today to Mr. Bryan Farah 650 shares of Joy Heat and Equipment Company for the price of $6500 payable by Mr. Farah on the 15th of December 1951." Farah read over and signed the document, but, in an action by Barki on the alleged contract, Farah testified that although he had read the document he did not appreciate that he was personally becoming the purchaser of the shares. He thought, as Barki had previously proposed to him, that the shares were to be transferred to him and that he should act for Barki in controlling the company and carry out a sale of the shares to one Joy, if that should prove possible. Farah had introduced Barki to Joy, who carried on the furnace business and he and Barki incorporated the company. Joy was given 350 shares at a par value of $10 and continued to manage the business. Barki invested $6,500, for which he got 650 shares. The company did very poorly. Arrangements were proposed, but which fell through, for the sale of Barki's shares to Joy. It was at this stage that Barki made the proposal to Farah on which he relied. The trial judge accepted Farah's evidence and dismissed the action and remarked that the contract looked to him very much like a "smart trick" by which Barki endeavoured to recompense himself for a bad investment. The Ontario Court of Appeal allowed an appeal and concluded that the trial judge had made no finding of fraud. Farah appealed to the Supreme Court.]

KELLOCK J [after discussing the facts and evidence]: ... In these circumstances, I think the finding of the learned trial Judge is to be interpreted as a finding of fraudulent misrepresentation on the part of the respondent as to the nature of the document which he asked the appellant to sign, and which he trusted he would sign, as he did, under the influence of the previous discussion without appreciating the real nature of the document, understanding that it was to be followed by a more formal document. The question therefore arises as to whether or not in such circumstances the appellant can successfully resist an action upon the document.

Winfield in his 13th edition of *Pollock on Contracts* at p. 384, quotes the language of Lord Chelmsford in *Wythes v. Labouchere* (1858), 3 De G. & J. 593 at p. 601, 44 E.R. 1397, namely: "It may be said generally that a man of business who executes 'an instrument of a short and intelligible description cannot be permitted to allege that he executed it in blind ignorance of its real character.'"

Winfield goes on to state that: "Strictly this may be an *inference of fact* rather than a rule of law; but under such conditions the inference is irresistible."

This puts the point too rigidly. As stated by Farwell J. in *May v. Platt*, [1900] 1 Ch. 616 at p. 623, fraud "unravels everything." The cases, however, such as that presently before the Court, in which a man may escape from a short and clear document, which he admits reading before signing, must be few. But that is not impossible. ...

In *Blay v. Pollard*, [1930] 1 K.B. 628, where fraud was not pleaded, Scrutton L.J., in the course of his judgment, said at p. 633: "As a general rule mistake as to the legal effect of what you are signing, when you have read the document, does not avail. ... It would be very dangerous to allow a man over the age of legal infancy to escape from the legal effect of a document he has, after reading it, signed, in the absence of an express misrepresentation by the other party of that legal effect."

The learned Lord Justice continued, however, quoting from *Fry on Specific Performance* as follows: "'It equally follows that the mistake of one party to a contract can never be a ground for compulsory rectification, so as to impose on the second party the erroneous conception of the first. The error of the plaintiff alone may, however, where (but, it is conceived, only where) there has been fraud or conduct equivalent to fraud on the part of the defendant, be a ground for putting the defendant to elect between having the transaction annulled altogether or submitting to the rectification of the deed in accordance with the plaintiff's intention.' ... This rests on unilateral mistake in one party, fraud or conduct equivalent to fraud in the other party."

[The opinions of Kerwin CJC and Rand J also allowing the appeal are omitted. Cartwright and Fauteux JJ concurred with Kellock J.]

Curtis v Chemical Cleaning and Dyeing Co, Ltd. [1951] 1 All ER 631 (CA). The defendants are cleaners and dyers. The plaintiff took a white satin wedding dress to them for cleaning. When the dress was returned it had a stain on it which had not been there when it was left for cleaning. The trial judge found that the stain was caused by the defendant's negligence. The defendants relied on a receipt that the plaintiff signed. The receipt set out her name and address and a description of the dress and in the bottom right hand corner under the amount to be charged, was printed: "This or these articles is accepted on condition that the company is not liable for any damage howsoever arising, or delay." The plaintiff was told she had to sign the document because she had to accept responsibility for damage to the beads and sequins on the dress. The trial judge awarded damages at £32 10s. The defendants appealed. The Court of Appeal dismissed the appeal. DENNING LJ: If the party affected signs a written document, knowing it to be a contract which governs the relations between him and the other party, his signature is irrefragable evidence of his assent to the whole contract, including the exempting clauses, unless the signature is shown to be obtained by fraud or misrepresentation. ... What is a sufficient misrepresentation for this purpose? ... In my opinion, any behaviour by words or conduct is sufficient to be a misrepresentation if it is such as to mislead the other party about the existence or extent of the exemption. If it conveys a false impression, that is enough. If the false impression is created knowingly, it is a fraudulent misrepresentation; if it is created unwittingly, it is an innocent misrepresentation. But either is sufficient to disentitle the creator of it to the benefit of the exemption. ... In those circumstances, by failing to draw attention to the width of the exemption clause, the assistant created the false impression that the exemption related to the beads and sequins only, and that it did not extend to the material of which the dress was made. it was done perfectly innocently, but, nevertheless, a false impression was created. It was probably not sufficiently precise and unambiguous to create an estoppel ... but, nevertheless, it was a sufficient misrepresentation to disentitle the cleaners from relying on the exemption, except in regard to the beads and sequins. ...

The second point made by counsel for the defendant was that, even if there was an innocent misrepresentation, the plaintiff cannot, in point of law, avoid the terms of the contract. He said that an innocent misrepresentation gives no right to damages but only to rescission, that rescission was not possible because the contract was executed, and that in any case rescission was of no use to the plaintiff, because, once rescission has taken place, there would be no contract to sue upon. That is an attractive argument, but I do not think it is right. One answer to it is that an executed contract can in a proper case be rescinded for innocent misrepresentation; and if the present contract was rescinded, the plaintiff could sue in tort for negligence, because any task undertaken must be done carefully.

QUESTION

If the "receipt" signed in the *Curtis* case had carried the words, "None of our agents or employees has any authority to alter, vary, or qualify in any way these terms and conditions," would the case have been decided differently?

Canadian Indemnity Co v Okanagan Mainline Real Estate Board. [1971] SCR 493. JUDSON JA: A party who misrepresents, albeit innocently, the contents or effect of a clause inserted by him into a contract cannot rely on the clause in the face of his misrepresentation: *Mendelssohn v Normand Ltd*, [1969] 3 WLR 139; *Curtis v Chemical Cleaning & Dying Co*, [1951] 1 KB 805; *Jaques v Lloyd D George & Partners Ltd*, [1968] 2 All ER 187.

HAWRISH V BANK OF MONTREAL
[1969] SCR 515

JUDSON JA (for the court): This action was brought by the Bank of Montreal against Andrew Hawrish, a solicitor in Saskatoon, on a guarantee which the solicitor had signed for the indebtedness and liability of a newly formed company, Crescent Dairies Limited. This company had been formed for the purpose of buying the assets of Waldheim Dairies Limited, a cheese factory in which Hawrish had an interest.

By January 1959, the line of credit granted by the bank to the new company was almost exhausted. The bank then asked Hawrish for a guarantee, which he signed on January 30, 1959. The guarantee was on the bank's usual form and stated that it was to be a continuing guarantee and to cover existing as well as future indebtedness of the company up to the amount of $6,000.

The defence was that when he signed the guarantee, Hawrish had an oral assurance from the assistant manager of the branch that the guarantee was to cover only existing indebtedness and that he would be released from his guarantee when the bank obtained a joint guarantee from the directors of the company. The bank did obtain a joint guarantee from the directors on July 22, 1959, for the sum of $10,000. Another joint guarantee for the same amount was signed by the directors on March 22, 1960. Between the dates of these two last-mentioned guarantees there had been some changes in the directorate.

Hawrish was never a director or officer of the new company but at the time when the action was commenced, he was a shareholder and he was interested in the vendor company. At all times the new company was indebted to the vendor company in an amount between $10,000 and $15,000. Hawrish says that he did not read the guarantee before signing. On February 20, 1961, Crescent Dairies Ltd., whose overdraft was at that time $8,000, became insolvent. The bank then brought its action against Hawrish for the full amount of his guarantee—$6,000.

The trial Judge dismissed the bank's action. He accepted the guarantor's evidence of what was said before the guarantee was signed and held that parol evidence was admissible on the ground that it was a condition of signing the guarantee that the appellant would be released as soon as a joint guarantee was obtained from the directors. He relied upon *Standard Bank v. McCrossan*, 55 D.L.R. 238. ... The Court of Appeal ... reversed this decision and gave judgment for the bank. In their view the parol evidence was not admissible and the problem was not the same as that in *Standard Bank v. McCrossan*. Hall J.A. correctly stated the *ratio* of the *Standard Bank* case in the following paragraph of his reasons [at 373]: "In my opinion the learned trial judge erred in holding that the respondent was able to establish such condition by parol evidence. The condition found, if indeed it is one, was not similar to that which existed in *Standard Bank v. McCrossan*, *supra*, in that it did not operate merely as a suspension or delay of the written agreement. It may be permissible to prove by extraneous evidence an oral agreement which operates as a suspension only."

The relevant provisions of this guarantee may be summarized as follows:

(a) It guarantees the present and future debts and liabilities of the customer (Crescent Dairies Ltd.) up to the sum of $6,000.

(b) It is a continuing guarantee and secures the ultimate balance owing by the customer.

(c) The guarantor may determine at any time his further liability under the guarantee by notice in writing to the bank. The liability of the guarantor continues until determined by such notice.

(d) The guarantor acknowledges that no representations have been made to him on behalf of the bank; that the liability of the guarantor is embraced in the guarantee; that the guarantee has nothing to do with any other guarantee; and that the guarantor intends the guarantee to be binding whether any other guarantee or security is given to the bank or not.

The argument before us was confined to two submissions of error contained in the reasons of the Court of Appeal:

(a) that the contemporaneous oral agreement found by the trial Judge neither varied nor contradicted the terms of the written guarantee but simply provided by an independent agreement a manner in which the liability of the appellant would be terminated; and

(b) that oral evidence proving the making of such agreement, the consideration for which was the signing of the guarantee, was admissible.

I cannot accept these submissions. In my opinion, there was no error in the reasons of the Court of Appeal. This guarantee was to be immediately effective. According to the oral evidence it was to terminate as to all liability, present or future, when the new guarantees were obtained from the directors. But the document itself states that it was to be a continuing guarantee for all present and future liabilities and could only be terminated by notice in writing, and then only as to future liabilities incurred by the customer after the giving of the notice. The oral evidence is also in plain contradiction of the terms of para. (d) of my summary above made. There is nothing in this case to permit the introduction of the principle in *Pym v. Campbell* (1856), 6 El. & Bl. 370, 119 E.R. 903, which holds that the parol evidence rule does not prevent a defendant from showing that a document formally complete and signed as a contract, was in fact only an escrow.

The appellant further submitted that the parol evidence was admissible on the ground that it established an oral agreement which was independent of and collateral to the main contract.

In the last half of the 19th century a group of English decisions, of which *Lindley v. Lacey* (1864), 17 C.B. (N.S.) 578, 144 E.R. 232; *Morgan v. Griffith* (1871), L.R. 6 Ex. 70; and *Erksine v. Adeane* (1873), L.R. 8 Ch. 764, are representative, established that where there was parol evidence of a distinct collateral agreement which did not contradict nor was inconsistent with the written instrument, it was admissible. These were cases between landlord and tenant in which parol evidence of stipulations as to repairs and other incidental matters and as to keeping down game and dealing with game was held to be admissible although the written leases were silent on these points. These were held to be independent agreements which were not required to be in writing and which were not in any way inconsistent with or contradictory of the written agreement.

The principle formulated in these cases was applied in *Byers v. McMillan* (1887), 15 S.C.R. 194. In this case Byers, a woodcutter, agreed in writing with one Andrew to cut and deliver 500 cords of wood from certain lands. The agreement contained no provision for security in the event that Byers was not paid upon making delivery. However, before he signed, it was orally agreed that Byers was to have a lien on the wood for the amount to which he would be entitled for his work and labour. Byers was not paid and eventually sold the wood. The respondents, the McMillans, in whom the contract was vested as a result of various assignments, brought an action of replevin. It was held by a majority of this Court that they could not succeed on the ground that the parol evidence of the oral agreement in respect of the lien was admissible. Strong J., with whom the other members of the majority agreed, said at pp. 202-3:

> *Erskine v. Adeane*, 8 Ch. App. 764; *Morgan v. Griffith*, L.R. 6 Ex. 70; *Lindley v. Lacey*, 17 C.B. (N.S.) 578, afford illustrations of the rule in question by the terms of which any agreement collateral or supplementary to the written agreement may be established by parol evidence, provided it is one which as an independent agreement could be made without writing, and that it is not in any way inconsistent with or contradictory of the written agreement. ...
>
> These cases (particularly *Erskine v. Adeane* which was a judgment of the Court of Appeal) appear to be all stronger decisions than that which the appellant calls upon us to make in the present case, for it is difficult to see how an agreement, that one who in writing had undertaken by his labor to produce a chattel which is to become the property of another shall have a lien on such product for the money to be paid as the reward of his labor, in any way derogates from the contemporaneous or prior writing. By such a stipulation no term or provision of the writing is varied or in the slightest degree infringed upon; both agreements can well stand together; the writing provides for the performance of the contract, and the consideration to be paid for it, and the parol agreement merely adds something respecting security for the payment of the price to these terms.

In *Heilbut, Symons & Co. v. Buckleton*, [1913] A.C. 30 at p. 47, a case having to do with the existence of a warranty in a contract for the sale of shares, there is comment on the existence of the doctrine and a note of caution as to its application:

> It is evident, both on principle and on authority, that there may be a contract the consideration for which is the making of some other contract. "If you will make such and such a contract, I will give you one hundred pounds," is in every sense of the word a complete legal contract. It is collateral to the main contract, but each has an independent existence, and they do not differ in respect of their possessing to the full the character and status of a contract. But such collateral contracts must from their very nature be rare. The effect of a collateral contract such as that which I have instanced would be to increase the consideration of the main contract by 100l., and the more natural and usual way of carrying this out would be by so modifying the main contract and not by executing a concurrent and collateral contract. Such collateral contracts, the sole effect of which is to vary or add to the terms of the principal contract, are therefore viewed with suspicion, by the law. They must be proved strictly. Not only the terms of such contracts but the existence of an animus contrahendi on the part of all the parties to them must be clearly shewn. Any laxity on these points would enable parties to escape from the full performance of the obligations of contracts unquestionably entered into by them and more especially would have the effect of lessening the authority of written contracts by making it possible to vary them by suggesting the existence of verbal collateral agreements relating to the same subject-matter.

Bearing in mind these remarks to the effect that there must be a clear intention to create a binding agreement, I am not convinced that the evidence in this case indicates clearly the existence of such intention. Indeed, I am disposed to agree with what the Court of Appeal said on this point. However, this is not in issue in this appeal. My opinion is that the appellant's argument fails on the ground that the collateral agreement allowing for the discharge of the appellant cannot stand as it clearly contradicts the terms of the guarantee bond which state that it is a continuing guarantee.

The appellant has relied upon *Byers v. McMillan*. But upon my interpretation that the terms of the two contracts conflict, this case is really against him as it is there stated by Strong J., that a collateral agreement cannot be established where it is inconsistent with or contradicts the written agreement. To the same effect is the unanimous judgment of the High Court of Australia in *Hoyt's Proprietary Ltd. v. Spencer* (1919), 27 C.L.R. 133, which rejected the argument that a collateral contract which contradicted the written agreement could stand with it. Knox C.J., said at p. 139: "A distinct collateral agreement, whether oral or in writing, and whether prior to or contemporaneous with the main agreement, is valid and enforceable even though the main agreement be in writing, provided the two may consistently stand together so that the provisions of the main agreement remain in full force and effect notwithstanding the collateral agreement. This proposition is illustrated by the decisions in *Lindley v. Lacey* (17 C.B. (N.S.), 578), *Erskine v. Adeane* (L.R. 8 Ch. 756), *De Lassalle v. Guildford* ([1901] 2 K.B. 215) and other cases."

I would dismiss the appeal with costs.

Appeal dismissed.

NOTE

Hawrish was approved in *Bauer v The Bank of Montreal*, [1980] 2 SCR 102 and *Carman Construction Ltd v Canadian Pacific Railway Co*, [1982] 1 SCR 958. The misrepresentation cases, however, have been held to survive: *Bank of Nova Scotia v Zackheim* (1983), 3 DLR (4th) 760 (Ont CA). How the parol evidence rule operates on misrepresentations depends on whether the written evidence of the contract excludes both oral terms and representations that are not specifically set out within the writing: *Tender Choice Foods Inc v Planet Energy (Ontario) Corp*, 2016 ONCA 192.

MORGAN V GRIFFITH
(1871), LR 6 Ex 70

The plaintiff became tenant of the defendant on Michaelmas Day, 1867, on oral terms that included the signing of a lease. The plaintiff found the land was overrun with rabbits and when the lease was presented for signature he refused to sign unless the rabbits were destroyed. The defendant later promised to destroy them when the plaintiff threatened to quit. At Michaelmas, 1868, the lease was again tendered. The plaintiff refused to sign it, but the defendant repeated his promise. The plaintiff then asked to have the promise incorporated in the lease, which the defendant refused, although he repeated his promise. The plaintiff signed. The lease contained the plaintiff's promise that he would not hunt or destroy game, but preserve it and allow the defendant and his friends to hunt. The rabbits were not destroyed and the plaintiff quit at Michaelmas, 1870. He then brought this action. The defendant pleaded the parol evidence rule, but the trial judge admitted the oral evidence of his promise, and the plaintiff got a verdict. The defendant appealed this ruling of the judge.

KELLY CB: All that is possible has been said on behalf of the defendant, but it has failed to convince me. I think the verbal agreement was entirely collateral to the lease, and was founded on a good consideration. The plaintiff, unless the promise to destroy the rabbits had been given, would not have signed the lease, and a court of equity would not have compelled him to do so, or only on the terms of the defendant performing his undertaking. The decision of the county court judge must therefore be affirmed.

[Pigott B, who was of the same opinion, observed that the "verbal agreement" did not appear to contain any terms that conflicted with the written document.]

PYM V CAMPBELL
(1856), 6 E & B 370, 119 ER 903

[Campbell proposed to purchase Pym's invention and arranged a meeting at which Pym, Campbell, and two engineers, Fergusson and Abernethie, were to attend and the engineers were to inspect and approve the invention. Pym arrived late, after the engineers had left. It was agreed that, because the parties were together, if the engineers could be found the sale might be arranged. Fergusson was found and approved, but Abernethie could not be found; however, Campbell drew up a paper that both he and Pym signed and it was agreed that if later Abernethie approved the invention the paper should be an agreement and if he did not it should not be one. Abernethie did not approve.

The Lord Chief Justice told the jury that if they were satisfied that, before the paper was signed, it was agreed among them all that it should not operate as an agreement until Abernethie approved of the invention, they should find for the defendant on the pleas denying the agreement. Verdict for the defendant.

Thomas Serjt., in the ensuing term, obtained a rule nisi for a new trial on the ground of misdirection.]

ERLE J: I think that this rule ought to be discharged. The point made is that this is a written agreement, absolute on the face of it, and that evidence was admitted to shew it was conditional: and if that had been so it would have been wrong. But I am of opinion that the evidence shewed that in fact there was never any agreement at all. The production of a paper purporting to be an agreement by a party, with his signature attached, affords a strong presumption that it is his written agreement; and, if in fact he did sign the paper *animo contrahendi*, the terms contained in it are conclusive, and cannot be varied by parol evidence: but in the present case the defence begins one step earlier: the parties met and expressly stated to each other that, though for convenience they would then sign the memorandum of the terms, yet they were not to sign it as an agreement until Abernethie was consulted. I grant the risk that such a defence may be set up without ground; and I agree that a jury should therefore always look on such a defence with suspicion: but, if it be proved that in fact the paper was signed with the express intention that it should not be an agreement, the other party cannot fix it as an agreement upon those so signing. The distinction in point of law is that evidence to vary the terms of an agreement in writing is not admissible, but evidence to shew that there is not an agreement at all is admissible.

[The opinions of Lord Campbell CJ and Crompton J to the like effect are omitted.]

Long v Smith. (1911), 23 OLR 121. Smith bought a piano from Long for a price expressed in their written agreement to be $575. The printed form provided it was the whole agreement. The parties had, however, what Smith called a "wordable understanding" that, if he afterward found that he had been overcharged or that the piano was unsatisfactory, Smith could return it and get back his $10 deposit or exchange the piano for another. When Smith wanted his oral agreement added to the printed form of the contract of sale, Long said he could not alter it but that his word could be relied on. After Smith paid a $10 deposit and had the piano for 2-3 weeks, an expert valued it at $400. Smith wanted to return it and be relieved from any obligation beyond the $10 deposit. BOYD J, for the court, said: ... it is argued that it is contrary to the rule of evidence and the decisions of the Courts to allow oral testimony to be given which is inconsistent with or repugnant to the terms of the written instrument. No little difficulty and confusion has arisen in the application of this rule to the varying transactions of business life, which is not lessened by the discordant opinions of the Judges. But, without trying to reconcile differences, there is a well-marked line of cases establishing this doctrine, that evidence may be given of a prior or a contemporaneous oral agreement which constitutes a condition upon which the performance of the written agreement is to depend. The oral evidence may be such as to affect the performance of the written agreement by shewing that it is not to be operative till the condition is complied with. The enforcement of the contract may be suspended or arrested till the stipulation orally agreed on has been satisfied. Here there was to be in substance and in essence no bargain if the piano was not worth the price stated in the writing. At the outset, and before the signing of the contract, the defendant was practically prevented from getting correct information as to the value from a competent person, but it was left for him to satisfy himself on that point forthwith thereafter. Ten dollars he had paid, but there was no intention of paying any more till he was satisfied as to the truth of the representation as to value.

City and Westminster Properties (1934) Ltd v Mudd. [1959] 1 Ch 129. To the knowledge of his landlord, a tenant had for years used the back part of his shop for living and sleeping, despite a prohibition of such use in his lease. A new lease was drawn up containing a covenant by the tenant to use the premises for "showrooms, workrooms and offices only," but the landlord orally assured the tenant that he could continue to live on the premises, and on the strength of that assurance the tenant signed the lease. Now the landlord brings an action for forfeiture of the lease on the ground that the tenant is living on the premises in breach of his covenant. HARMAN J, holding that the oral promise prevailed over the writing, said: If the defendant's evidence is to be accepted, as I hold it is, it is a case of a promise made to him before the execution of the lease that, if he would execute it in the form put before him, the landlord would not seek to enforce against him personally the covenant about using the property as a shop only. The defendant says that it was in reliance on this promise that he executed the lease and entered on the onerous obligations contained in it. He says, moreover, that but for the promise made he would not have executed the lease, but would have moved to other premises available to him at the time. If these be the facts, there was a clear contract acted upon by the defendant to his detriment and from which the plaintiffs cannot be allowed to resile. ...

The plea that this was a mere licence retractable at the plaintiffs' will does not bear examination. The promise was that so long as the defendant personally was tenant, so long would the landlords forbear to exercise the rights which they would have if he signed the lease. He did sign the lease on this promise and is therefore entitled to rely on it so long as he is personally in occupation of the shop.

NOTE

It is interesting to consider this case in connection with *Central London Property Trust Ltd v High Trees House Ltd* in Chapter 3. What would have been the tenant's remedy in the *Mudd* case if the landlord's assurance had been given after the lease had been executed?

TILDEN RENT-A-CAR CO V CLENDENNING
(1978), 83 DLR (3d) 400 (Ont CA)

DUBIN JA: Upon his arrival at Vancouver airport, Mr. Clendenning, a resident of Woodstock, Ontario, attended upon the office of Tilden Rent-A-Car Company for the purpose of renting a car while he was in Vancouver. He was an experienced traveller and had used Tilden Rent-A-Car Company on many prior occasions. He provided the clerk employed at the airport office of Tilden Rent-A-Car Company with the minimum information which was asked of him, and produced his American Express credit card. He was asked by the clerk whether he desired additional coverage, and, as was his practice, he said "yes." A contract was submitted to him for his signature, which he signed in the presence of the clerk, and he returned the contract to her. She placed his copy of it in an envelope and gave him the keys to the car. He then placed the contract in the glove compartment of the vehicle. He did not read the terms of the contract before signing it, as was readily apparent to the clerk, and in fact he did not read the contract until this litigation was commenced, nor had he read a copy of a similar contract on any prior occasion.

The issue on the appeal is whether the defendant is liable for the damage caused to the automobile while being driven by him by reason of the exclusionary provisions which appear in the contract.

On the front of the contract are two relevant clauses set forth in box form. They are as follows:

> 15. Collision Damage Waiver By Customers Initials "J.C."
> *In consideration of the payment of $2.00 per day customers liability for damage to rented vehicle including windshield is limited to nil.* But notwithstanding payment of said fee, customer shall be fully liable for all collision damage if vehicle is used, operated or driven in violation of any of the provisions of this rental agreement or off highways serviced by federal, provincial, or municipal governments, and for all damages to vehicle by striking overhead objects.
>
> 16. I, the undersigned have read and received a copy of above and reverse side of this contract.
> Signature of customer or employee of customer "John T. Clendenning"

(Emphasis added.)

On the back of the contract in particularly small type and so faint in the customer's copy as to be hardly legible, there are a series of conditions, the relevant ones being as follows:

> 6. The customer agrees not to use the vehicle in violation of any law, ordinance, rule or regulation of any public authority.
> 7. The customer agrees that the vehicle will not be operated:
> (a) By any person who has drunk or consumed any intoxicating liquor, whatever be the quantity, or who is under the influence of drugs or narcotics.

The rented vehicle was damaged while being driven by Mr. Clendenning in Vancouver. His evidence at trial, which was accepted by the trial Judge, was to the effect that in endeavouring to avoid a collision with another vehicle and acting out of a sudden emergency, he drove the car into a pole. He stated that although he had pleaded guilty to a charge of driving while impaired in Vancouver, he did so on the advice of counsel, and at the time of the impact he was capable of the proper control of the motor vehicle. This evidence was also accepted by the trial Judge.

Mr. Clendenning testified that on earlier occasions when he had inquired as to what added coverage he would receive for the payment of $2 per day, he had been advised that "such payment provided full non-deductible coverage." It is to be observed that the portion of the contract reproduced above does provide that "In consideration of the payment of $2.00 per day customers liability for damage to rented vehicle including windshield is limited to nil."

A witness called on behalf of the plaintiff gave evidence as to the instructions given to its employees as to what was to be said by them to their customers about the conditions in the contract. He stated that unless inquiries were made, nothing was to be said by its clerks to the customer with respect to the exclusionary conditions. He went on to state that if inquiries were made, the clerks were instructed to advise the customer that by the payment of the $2 additional fee the customer had complete coverage "unless he were intoxicated, or unless he committed an offence under the *Criminal Code* such as intoxication."

Mr. Clendenning acknowledged that he had assumed, either by what had been told to him in the past or otherwise, that he would not be responsible for any damage to the vehicle on payment of the extra premium unless such damage was caused by reason of his being so intoxicated as to be incapable of the proper control of the vehicle, a provision with which he was familiar as being a statutory provision in his own insurance contract.

The provisions fastening liability for damage to the vehicle on the hirer, as contained in the clauses hereinbefore referred to, are completely inconsistent with the express terms which purport to provide complete coverage for damage to the vehicle in exchange for the additional premium. It is to be noted, for example, that if the driver of the vehicle exceeded the speed-limit even by one mile per hour, or parked the vehicle in a no-parking area, or even had one glass of wine or one bottle of beer, the contract purports to make the hirer completely responsible for all damage to the vehicle. Indeed, if the vehicle at the time of any damage to it was being driven off a federal, provincial or municipal highway, such as a shopping plaza for instance, the hirer purportedly would be responsible for all damage to the vehicle.

Mr. Clendenning stated that if he had known of the full terms of the written instrument, he would not have entered into such a contract. Having regard to the findings made by the trial Judge, it is apparent that Mr. Clendenning had not in fact acquiesced to such terms.

It was urged that the rights of the parties were governed by what has come to be known as "the rule in *L'Estrange v. F. Graucob, Ltd.*," [1934] 2 K.B. 394, and in particular the following portion from the judgment of Scrutton, L.J., at p. 403:

> In cases in which the contract is contained in a railway ticket or other unsigned document, it is necessary to prove that an alleged party was aware, or ought to have been aware, of its terms and conditions. These cases have no application when the document has been signed. *When a document containing contractual terms is signed, then, in the absence of fraud, or, I will add, misrepresentation, the party signing it is bound, and it is wholly immaterial whether he has read the document or not.*

(Emphasis added.)

In the same case Maugham, L.J., added at p. 406:

There can be no dispute as to the soundness in law of the statement of Mellish L.J. in *Parker v. South Eastern Ry. Co.*, 2 C.P.D. 416, 421, which has been read by my learned brother, to the effect that where a party has signed a written agreement it is immaterial to the question of his liability under it that he has not read it and does not know its contents. That is true in any case in which the agreement is held to be an agreement in writing.

There are, however, two possibilities to be kept in view. The first is that it might be proved that the document, though signed by the plaintiff, was signed in circumstances which made it not her act. That is known as the case of Non est factum.

And at p. 407:

Another possibility is that the plaintiff might have been induced to sign the document by misrepresentation.

Consensus ad idem is as much a part of the law of written contracts as it is of oral contracts. The signature to a contract is only one way of manifesting assent to contractual terms. However, in the case of *L'Estrange v. F. Graucob, Ltd.*, there was in fact no *consensus ad idem*. Miss L'Estrange was a proprietor of a cafe. Two salesmen of the defendant company persuaded her to order a cigarette machine to be sold to her by their employer. They produced an order form which Miss L'Estrange signed without reading all of its terms. Amongst the many clauses in the document signed by her, there was included a paragraph, with respect to which she was completely unaware, which stated "any express or implied condition, statement, or warranty, statutory or otherwise not stated herein is hereby excluded." In her action against the company she alleged that the article sold to her was unfit for the purposes for which it was sold and contrary to the *Sale of Goods Act*. The company successfully defended on the basis of that exemption clause.

Although the subject of critical analysis by learned authors (see, for example, J.R. Spencer, "Signature, Consent, and the Rule in *L'Estrange v. Graucob*," [1973] *C.L.J.* 104), the case has survived, and it is now said that it applies to all contracts irrespective of the circumstances under which they are entered into, if they are signed by the party who seeks to escape their provisions.

Thus, it was submitted that the ticket cases, which in the circumstances of this case would afford a ready defence for the hirer of the automobile, are not applicable.

As is pointed out in Waddams, *The Law of Contracts*, at p. 191:

From the 19th century until recent times an extraordinary status has been accorded to the signed document that will be seen in retrospect, it is suggested, to have been excessive.

The justification for the rule in *L'Estrange v. F. Graucob Ltd.*, appears to have been founded upon the objective theory of contracts, by which means parties are bound to a contract in writing by measuring their conduct by outward appearance rather than what the parties inwardly meant to decide. This, in turn, stems from the classic statement of Blackburn J., in *Smith v. Hughes* (1871), L.R. 6 Q.B. 597 at p. 607:

I apprehend that if one of the parties intends to make a contract on one set of terms, and the other intends to make a contract on another set of terms, or, as it is sometimes expressed, if the parties are not ad idem, there is no contract, unless the circumstances are such as to preclude one of the parties from denying that he has agreed to the terms of the other. The rule of law is that stated in *Freeman v. Cooke* (1848), 2 Ex. 654, 154

E.R. 652. *If, whatever a man's real intention may be, he so conducts himself that a reasonable man would believe that he was assenting to the terms proposed by the other party, and that other party upon that belief enters into the contract with him, the man thus conducting himself would be equally bound as if he had intended to agree to the other party's terms.*

(Emphasis added.)

Even accepting the objective theory to determine whether Mr. Clendenning had entered into a contract which included all the terms of the written instrument, it is to be observed that an essential part of that test is whether the other party entered into the contract in the belief that Mr. Clendenning was assenting to all such terms. In the instant case, it was apparent to the employee of Tilden Rent-A-Car that Mr. Clendenning had not in fact read the document in its entirety before he signed it. It follows under such circumstances that Tilden Rent-A-Car cannot rely on provisions of the contract which it had no reason to believe were being assented to by the other contracting party.

As stated in Waddams, *The Law of Contracts*, p. 191:

One who signs a written document cannot complain if the other party reasonably relies on the signature as a manifestation of assent to the contents, or ascribes to words he uses their reasonable meaning. But the other side of the same coin is that only a reasonable expectation will be protected. If the party seeking to enforce the document knew or had reason to know of the other's mistake the document should not be enforced.

In ordinary commercial practice where there is frequently a sense of formality in the transaction, and where there is a full opportunity for the parties to consider the terms of the proposed contract submitted for signature, it might well be safe to assume that the party who attaches his signature to the contract intends by so doing to acknowledge his acquiescence to its terms, and that the other party entered into the contract upon that belief. This can hardly be said, however, where the contract is entered into in circumstances such as were present in this case.

A transaction, such as this one, is invariably carried out in a hurried, informal manner. The speed with which the transaction is completed is said to be one of the attractive features of the services provided.

The clauses relied on in this case, as I have already stated, are inconsistent with the over-all purpose for which the contract is entered into by the hirer. Under such circumstances, something more should be done by the party submitting the contract for signature than merely handing it over to be signed.

In an analogous situation Lord Devlin in the case of *McCutcheon v. David Mac-Brayne Ltd.*, [1964] 1 W.L.R. 125, commented as follows, at pp. 132-4:

It would be a strangely generous set of conditions in which the persistent reader, after wading through the verbiage, could not find something to protect the carrier against "any loss ... wheresoever or whensoever occurring"; and condition 19 by itself is enough to absolve the respondents several times over for all their negligence. *It is conceded that if the form had been signed as usual, the appellant would have had no case.* But, by a stroke of ill luck for the respondents, it was upon this day of all days that they omitted to get Mr. McSporran to sign the conditions. What difference does that make?

If it were possible for your Lordships to escape from the world of make-believe which the law has created into the real world in which transactions of this sort are actually done, the answer would be short and simple. It should make no difference whatever. This sort of document is not meant to be read, still less to be understood.

Its signature is in truth about as significant as a handshake that marks the formal conclusion of a bargain.

Your Lordships were referred to the dictum of Blackburn J. in *Harris v. Great Western Railway Co.* (1876) 1 Q.B.D. 515, 530. The passage is as follows:

> And it is clear law that where there is a writing, into which the terms of any agreement are reduced, the terms are to be regulated by that writing. And though one of the parties may not have read the writing, yet, in general, he is bound to the other by those terms; and that, I apprehend, is on the ground that, by assenting to the contract thus reduced to writing, he represents to the other side that he has made himself acquainted with the contents of that writing and assents to them, and so induces the other side to act upon that representation by entering into the contract with him, and is consequently precluded from denying that he did make himself acquainted with those terms. But then the preclusion only exists when the case is brought within the rule so carefully and accurately laid down by Parke B., in delivering the judgment of the Exchequer in *Freeman v. Cooke* (1848), 2 Ex. 654, that is, if he "means his representation to be acted upon, and it is acted upon accordingly: or if, whatever a man's real intentions may be, he so conduct himself that a reasonable man would take the representation to be true, and believe that it was meant that he should act upon it, and did act upon it as true."

If the ordinary law of estoppel was applicable to this case, it might well be argued that the circumstances leave no room for any representation by the sender on which the carrier acted. I believe that any other member of the public in Mr. McCutcheon's place—and this goes for lawyers as well as for laymen—would have found himself compelled to give the same sort of answers as Mr. McCutcheon gave; and I doubt if any carrier who serves out documents of this type could honestly say that he acted in the belief that the recipient had "made himself acquainted with the contents." But Blackburn J. was dealing with an unsigned document, a cloakroom ticket. Unless your Lordships are to disapprove the decision of the Court of Appeal in *L'Estrange v. F. Graucob Ltd.*, [1934] 2 K.B. 394, C.A.—and there has been no suggestion in this case that you should— the law is clear, without any recourse to the doctrine of estoppel, that a signature to a contract is conclusive.

(Emphasis added.)

An analysis of the Canadian cases, however, indicates that the approach in this country has not been so rigid. In the case of *Colonial Investment Co. of Winnipeg, Man. v. Borland*, [1911] 1 W.W.R. 171 at p. 189, 19 W.L.R. 588, 5 Alta. L.R. at p. 72 [aff'd 6 DLR 21, 2 WWR 960, 22 WLR 145, 5 Alta LR 71], Beck, J., set forth the following propositions:

> *Consensus ad idem* is essential to the creation of a contract, whether oral, in writing or under seal, subject to this, that as between the immediate parties (and merely voluntary assigns) apparent—as distinguished from real—consent will on the ground of estoppel effect a binding obligation unless the party denying the obligation proves:
>
> (1) That the other party knew at the time of the making of the alleged contract that the mind of the denying party did not accompany the expression of his consent; or
> (2) Such facts and circumstances as show that it was not reasonable and natural for the other party to suppose that the denying party was giving his real consent and he did not in fact give it;

In commenting on the *Colonial Investment Co. of Winnipeg v. Borland* case, Spencer, in the article above cited, observes at p. 121:

> It is instructive to compare a Canadian approach to the problem of confusing documents which are signed but not fully understood.

And at p. 122 the author concludes his article with the following analysis:

> Policy considerations, but of different kinds, no doubt lay behind both the Canadian and the English approaches to this problem. The Canadian court was impressed by the abuses which would result—and, in England, *have* resulted—from enabling companies to hold ignorant signatories to the letter of sweeping exemption clauses contained in contracts in standard form. The English courts, however, were much more impressed with the danger of furnishing an easy line of defence by which liars could evade contractual liabilities freely assumed. It would be very dangerous to allow a man over the age of legal infancy to escape from the legal effect of a document he has, after reading it, signed, in the absence of any express misrepresentation by the other party of that legal effect. Forty years later, most lawyers would admit that the English courts made a bad choice between two evils.

The significance of the circumstances under which a contract is entered into is noted by Taschereau, J., in *Provident Savings Life Ass'ce Society of New York v. Mowat et al.* (1902), 32 S.C.R. 147, as follows at p. 162:

> As remarked by Mr. Justice Maclennan [27 O.A.R. 675]:
>
> > The case of a formal instrument like the present, prepared and executed, after a long negotiation, and correspondence delivered and accepted, and acted upon for years, is wholly different from the cases relating to railways and steamship and cloak-room tickets, in which it has been held that conditions qualifying the principal contract of carriage or bailment, not sufficiently brought to the attention of the passenger or bailor are not binding upon him. Such contracts are usually made in moments of more or less haste and confusion and stand by themselves.

I see no real distinction in contracts such as these, where the signature by itself does not truly represent an acquiescence of unusual and onerous terms which are inconsistent with the true object of the contract, and the ticket cases. This point was made by Beck, J.A., in *Can. Bk. Commerce v. Foreman*, [1927] 2 D.L.R. 530 at p. 537, [1927] 1 W.W.R. 783, 22 Alta. L.R. 443, where he stated:

> Personally I have a very strong opinion, which is not to the full extent shared by other members of the Court and expressed in *Gray-Campbell Ltd. v. Flynn*, [1923] 1 D.L.R. 51, 18 Alta. L.R. 547, and for which I see some support in some circumstances in *Ball v. Gutschenritter*, [1925] 1 D.L.R. 901, at p. 908 (and see also *Jadis v. Porte* (1915), 23 D.L.R. 713, 8 Alta. L.R. 489)—*the opinion that when a contract of a common type contains special onerous and unusual provisions it is the duty of the party in whose interests such provisions are inserted to see that they are effectively called to the attention of the other party under the penalty of their being held not binding upon the latter party* but I think that would not ordinarily affect the residue of the contract and consequently the question does not arise in the present case. The only special provision which the bank needs to invoke, and which is of that special character that it alters the rights of the parties, is that permitting the giving of time to the debtor etc.; but this I would not place under the category of special provisions of an onerous or special character but would consider to be such a provision as the ordinary layman would suppose to express the law independently of special provision.

(Emphasis added.)

The same point of view was expressed by Lord Denning in the case of *Jaques v. Lloyd D. George & Partners Ltd.*, [1968] 1 W.L.R. 625 at p. 630:

> The principles which in my opinion are applicable are these: When an estate agent is employed to find a purchaser for a business or a house, the ordinary understanding of

mankind is that the commission is payable out of the purchase price when the matter is concluded. If the agent seeks to depart from that ordinary and well-understood term, then he must make it perfectly plain to his client. He must bring it home to him such as to make sure he agrees to it. When his representative produces a printed form and puts it before the client to sign, he should explain its effect to him, making it clear that it goes beyond the usual understanding in these matters. In the absence of such explanation, a client is entitled to assume that the form contains nothing unreasonable or oppressive. If he does not read it and the form is found afterwards to contain a term which is wholly unreasonable and totally uncertain, as this is, then the estate agent cannot enforce it against the innocent vendor.

In commenting on *Jaques v. Lloyd D. George & Partners Ltd.*, and on the case of *O'Connor Real Estate Ltd. v. Flynn* (1969), 3 D.L.R. (3d) 345; affirmed 11 D.L.R. (3d) 559, 1 N.S.R. (2d) 949, in 49 *Can. Bar Rev.*, Professor Waddams makes the following observations, at pp. 590-1:

> These cases suggest that there is a special onus on the supplier to point out any terms in a printed form which differ from what the consumer might reasonably expect. If he fails to do so, he will be guilty of a "misrepresentation by omission," and the court will strike down clauses which "differ from the ordinary understanding of mankind" or (and sometimes this is the same thing) clauses which are "unreasonable or oppressive." If this principle is accepted, the rule about written documents might be restated as follows: the signer is bound by the terms of the document if, and only if, the other party believes on reasonable grounds that those terms truly express the signer's intention. This principle retains the role of signed documents as a means of protecting reasonable expectations; what it does not allow is that a party should rely on a printed document to contradict what he knows, or ought to know, is the understanding of the other party. Again this principle seems to be particularly applicable in situations involving the distribution of goods and services to consumers, though it is by no means confined to such situations.

In modern commercial practice, many standard form printed documents are signed without being read or understood. In many cases the parties seeking to rely on the terms of the contract know or ought to know that the signature of a party to the contract does not represent the true intention of the signer, and that the party signing is unaware of the stringent and onerous provisions which the standard form contains. Under such circumstances, I am of the opinion that the party seeking to rely on such terms should not be able to do so in the absence of first having taken reasonable measures to draw such terms to the attention of the other party, and, in the absence of such reasonable measures, it is not necessary for the party denying knowledge of such terms to prove either fraud, misrepresentation or *non est factum*.

In the case at bar, Tilden Rent-A-Car took no steps to alert Mr. Clendenning to the onerous provisions in the standard form of contract presented by it. The clerk could not help but have known that Mr. Clendenning had not in fact read the contract before signing it. Indeed the form of the contract itself with the important provisions on the reverse side and in very small type would discourage even the most cautious customer from endeavouring to read and understand it. Mr. Clendenning was in fact unaware of the exempting provisions. Under such circumstances, it was not open to Tilden Rent-A-Car to rely on those clauses, and it was not incumbent on Mr. Clendenning to establish fraud, misrepresentation or *non est factum*. Having paid the premium, he was not liable for any damage to the vehicle while being driven by him.

As Lord Denning stated in *Neuchatel Asphalte Co. Ltd. v. Barnett*, [1957] 1 W.L.R. 356 at p. 360: "We do not allow printed forms to be made a trap for the unwary."

In this case the trial Judge held that "the rule in *L'Estrange v. Graucob*" governed. He dismissed the action, however, on the ground that Tilden Rent-A-Car had by their prior oral representations misrepresented the terms of the contract. He imputed into the contract the assumption of Mr. Clendenning that by the payment of the premium he was "provided full non-deductible coverage unless at the time of the damage he was operating the automobile while under the influence of intoxicating liquor to such an extent as to be for the time incapable of the proper control of the automobile." Having found that Mr. Clendenning had not breached such a provision, the action was dismissed.

For the reasons already expressed, I do not think that in the circumstances of this case "the rule in *L'Estrange v. Graucob*" governed, and it was not incumbent upon Mr. Clendenning to prove misrepresentation.

In any event, if "the rule in *L'Estrange v. Graucob*" were applicable, it was in error, in my respectful opinion, to impute into the contract a provision which Tilden Rent-A-Car had not in fact represented as being a term of the contract.

As was stated in *Canadian Indemnity Co. v. Okanagan Mainline Real Estate Board et al.*, [1971] S.C.R. 493 at p. 500, 16 D.L.R. (3d) 715 at p. 720, [1971] 1 W.W.R. 289:

> A party who misrepresents, albeit innocently, the contents or effect of a clause inserted by him into a contract cannot rely on the clause in the face of his misrepresentation.

Under such circumstances, absent the exclusionary provisions of the contract, the defendant was entitled to the benefit of the contract in the manner provided without the exclusionary provisions, and the action, therefore, had to fail.

In the result, therefore, I would dismiss the appeal with costs.

[Zuber JA concurred. Lacourcière JA dissented.]

GALLEN V ALLSTATE GRAIN CO LTD
(1984), 9 DLR (4th) 496 (BCCA)

LAMBERT JA:

I. THE ISSUES

[25] An oral representation was made by Mr. Nunweiler, the president of Allstate Grain Company Ltd., to the plaintiffs. Later, the plaintiffs reached an agreement with Allstate, and signed Allstate's standard form contract. The representation turned out to be wrong, and the plaintiffs suffered a loss. The plaintiffs sued and won. This appeal by Allstate is now limited to questions about the parol evidence rule. These are the questions:

(a) Is evidence of the oral representation admissible?
(b) Is the oral representation a warranty?
(c) Can the oral representation add to, subtract from, vary or contradict the signed document?
(d) Is there a contradiction between the oral representation and the signed document?

The answer to each of these questions depends, to some extent, on the answers to the others. So I suppose to discuss them separately, but to answer them all at the end.

II. THE FACTS

[26] Allstate Grain Company Ltd. is a Saskatchewan company. It is in the business of selling seed to farmers and buying farm crops. It had sold buckwheat seed to farmers in Saskatchewan and bought their buckwheat crops. It had developed a standard form contract covering that type of transaction.

[27] Allstate discovered that there was a very good market for early buckwheat in Japan. But buckwheat for that market had to be planted at the beginning of May and harvested before the end of July. That could not be done in Saskatchewan. So Allstate decided to embark on a new venture in contracting with farmers in the Lower Fraser Valley to grow first crop buckwheat for the Japanese market. Allstate started off by advertising for farmers who might be interested in such a project.

[28] The plaintiffs were experienced farmers in Ladner. But first crop buckwheat was not a crop which had ever been grown in the Fraser Valley, though buckwheat had been grown as a second crop.

[29] The plaintiffs answered Allstate's advertisement and a meeting took place between the plaintiffs and Mr. Nunweiler in March, 1980. They discussed planting procedures, yield, returns, and details of growth. The plaintiffs asked about weeds. They were assured by Mr. Nunweiler that there would be no problem with weeds; the buckwheat would grow up and cover the field like an umbrella, and the weeds would all be smothered. On May 1, 1980, the plaintiffs signed Allstate's standard Buckwheat Marketing Agreement, 1980, by which they agreed to buy buckwheat seed from Allstate and to sell back the buckwheat crop. The contract contained this clause:

> 23. Allstate gives no warranty as to the productiveness or any other matter pertaining to the seed sold to the producer and will not in any way be responsible for the crop.

The plaintiffs had prepared a substantial acreage for this project. They took delivery of Allstate's buckwheat seed and planted it. The buckwheat grew, but the weeds grew faster; they could not be controlled, and they destroyed the growing buckwheat.

[30] The plaintiffs brought this action for breach of warranty, breach of collateral contract and negligent misrepresentation. Paris J. found that the plaintiffs relied on Mr. Nunweiler's statement when, two months or so after the statement was made, they entered the buckwheat contract; and he found that Mr. Nunweiler was perfectly aware of the plaintiffs' concerns about weeds when he gave the assurances that he did. On that basis, Paris J. decided that the assurances constituted a warranty, and that the defendant company was liable to the plaintiffs for breach of warranty. Paris J. said it was clear on the law that an exclusionary clause in the standard form contract would not avail the defendants if a collateral warranty was made out. Seaton J.A. has set out the relevant passages from the reasons of Paris J. and I will not repeat them.

[31] Paris J. also considered the claim for negligent misrepresentation. He did not decide whether a duty of care existed, because, assuming that it did exist, Mr. Nunweiler had complied with a reasonable standard of care. Mr. Nunweiler had relied on his experience in Saskatchewan, and he had relied on an expert in buckwheat, and he had relied on government publications. They all turned out to be wrong. But Mr. Nunweiler was not negligent when he relied on them and assured the plaintiffs that the buckwheat would smother the weeds.

[32] Paris J. decided that the other personal defendant, Ronald Butterley, was not involved in the misrepresentation. So he dismissed the claims against the two individual defendants. He awarded $18,000 damages, calculated from the profit lost in not growing barley, plus prejudgment interest and costs, against Allstate. This appeal is brought by Allstate from that judgment. There is no cross-appeal.

III. IS EVIDENCE OF THE ORAL REPRESENTATION ADMISSIBLE?

[33] The parol evidence rule is not only a rule about the admissibility of evidence. It reaches into questions of substantive law. But it is a rule of evidence, as well as a body of principles of substantive law, and if the evidence of the oral representation in this case was improperly admitted, the appeal should be allowed.

[34] The rule of evidence may be stated in this way: Subject to certain exceptions, when the parties to an agreement have apparently set down all its terms in a document, extrinsic evidence is not admissible to add to, subtract from, vary or contradict those terms.

[35] So the rule does not extend to cases where the document may not embody all the terms of the agreement. And even in cases where the document seems to embody all the terms of the agreement, there is a myriad of exceptions to the rule. I will set out some of them. Evidence of an oral statement is relevant and may be admitted, even where its effect may be to add to, subtract from, vary or contradict the document:

(a) to show that the contract was invalid because of fraud, misrepresentation, mistake, incapacity, lack of consideration, or lack of contracting intention;

(b) to dispel ambiguities, to establish a term implied by custom, or to demonstrate the factual matrix of the agreement;

(c) in support of a claim for rectification;

(d) to establish a condition precedent to the agreement;

(e) to establish a collateral agreement;

(f) in support of an allegation that the document itself was not intended by the parties to constitute the whole agreement;

(g) in support of a claim for an equitable remedy, such as specific performance or rescission, on any ground that supports such a claim in equity, including misrepresentation of any kind, innocent, negligent or fraudulent; and

(h) in support of a claim in tort that the oral statement was in breach of a duty of care.

I do not consider that I am setting out an exhaustive list. I am only showing that appropriate allegations in the pleadings will require that the evidence be admitted.

[36] So, if it is said that an oral representation, that was made before the contract document was signed, contains a warranty giving rise to a claim for damages, evidence can be given of the representation, even if the representation adds to, subtracts from, varies or contradicts the document, if the pleadings are appropriate, and if the party on whose behalf the evidence is tendered asserts that from the factual matrix it can be shown that the document does not contain the whole agreement. The oral representation may be part of a single agreement, other parts of which appear in the document (the one-contract theory). Alternatively, the document may record a complete agreement, but there may be a separate collateral agreement with different terms, one of which is the oral representation (the two-contract theory).

[37] On the basis of the pleadings in this case, I do not doubt that the evidence was properly admitted on the question of whether the document constituted a record of the whole agreement.

[38] I should add that I can see very little residual practicality in the parol evidence rule, as a rule of evidence, in cases tried by a judge alone.

IV. IS THE ORAL REPRESENTATION A WARRANTY?

[39] A warranty is one of the terms that may form a part of a contractual relationship and affect the scope of the relationship. It may be either a representation as to

the existence of a present fact ("This car has travelled only 10,000 kms."); or it may be a promise to bear the risk of the loss that will flow from a failure of a fact to occur in the future ("This car is guaranteed rust-proof.").

[40] It is not necessary to distinguish, in this case, between conditions, warranties, and other contractual terms that may give rise to claims in damages. But what must be done in this case is to distinguish between a warranty, where the breach gives rise to a claim for damages, and a bare and innocent misrepresentation, which may give rise to a claim in equity for rescission, but does not give rise to a claim for damages.

[41] The distinction does not turn on whether the recipient of the representation acted on it. The distinction turns on whether the representation became a part of the contractual relationship between the maker and the recipient. That, in turn, depends on the intention of the parties, as derived from objective evidence, including but not limited to, evidence that tends to show whether the representation was intended to be acted upon and was in fact acted upon.

[42] Seaton J.A., whose reasons I have seen in draft form, has set out six factors listed in Halsbury as aids in determining whether a statement is a warranty or a bare representation. The six factors are only straws in the wind, but, to the extent that they are helpful, I think that the second factor, namely, that the recipient makes it clear that he regards the matter as so important that he would not contract without the assurance, and the third factor, namely, that the maker is stating a matter that should be within his knowledge and of which the recipient is known to be ignorant, both apply on the facts of this case, and both tend to show a warranty rather than a bare representation.

[43] More helpful than Halsbury, in my opinion, are the reasons of Robertson J.A. in *Yorke v. Duval*, [1953] 3 D.L.R. 820, 9 W.W.R. (N.S.) 523, a decision of this court. They contain two guides for determining whether a pre-contractual representation is a warranty. First, at p. 821 D.L.R., p. 545-5 W.W.R., Robertson J.A. said that the way to decide is to look at the contract in the light of all the surrounding circumstances, and that one of the first things to look to is to what extent the accuracy of the statement—the truth of what is promised—would be likely to affect the substance and foundation of the adventure which the contract is intended to carry out. Then, second, at p. 822 D.L.R., p. 525 W.W.R., Robertson J.A. said that the essence of a warranty is that it becomes plain by the words and actions of the parties that it is intended that, in the purchase, the responsibility of the soundness will rest upon the vendor.

[44] That seems to me to put the question squarely. What the trier of fact is trying to find out is this: who was to bear the risk that the statement might be wrong, the person who made it, or the person who acted on it? If it must be taken to have been intended, and understood, when said, to form a part of the contractual relations between the parties, then it is a warranty.

[45] As was said by Robertson J.A. in *Yorke v. Duval*, in the end it is a question of fact as to whether what was said was a warranty or just a statement. I will return to that question of fact in this case in Part VII of these reasons.

V. CAN THE ORAL REPRESENTATION ADD TO, SUBTRACT FROM, VARY, OR CONTRADICT THE SIGNED DOCUMENT?

[46] Once the oral evidence has been properly admitted under the application of the parol evidence rule, the body of principles of substantive law that are also customarily treated as being encompassed by the rule must be considered.

[47] In Part III of these reasons, I concluded that evidence of the oral representation was admissible in this case either on the basis that the document did not contain the whole agreement (the "one-contract" theory), or on the basis that the document contained one complete agreement, but that the oral representation formed the basic term of another complete agreement (the "two-contract" theory).

[48] But I wish to emphasize that these theories are legal analysis only. They are not real life. So the substantive law ought to be the same, whichever theory is adopted. It makes no sense to say that if the warranty is cast as part of a single contract ("I am selling you a rust-proof car."), the consequence in law is different than if the warranty is cast as part of a separate collateral contract ("If you buy this car from me, I will guarantee that it is rust-proof.").

[49] The crucial parol evidence principle of substantive law, for the purposes of this case, is the principle that forms one of the reasons for decision in *Hawrish v. Bank of Montreal* (1969), 2 D.L.R. (3d) 600, [1969] S.C.R. 515, 66 W.W.R. 673; *Bauer v. Bank of Montreal* (1980), 110 D.L.R. (3d) 424, [1980] 2 S.C.R. 102, 33 C.B.R. (N.S.) 291, and *Carman Construction Ltd. v. C.P.R. Co.* (1982), 136 D.L.R. (3d) 193, [1982] 1 S.C.R. 958, 18 B.L.R. 65, all decisions of the Supreme Court of Canada, and also in *First National Mortgage Co. Ltd. v. Grouse Nest Resorts Ltd.* (1977), 2 B.C.L.R. 300, a decision of this court. That principle was stated in this way by Martland J., for the Supreme Court of Canada, in the *Carman Construction* case, at p. 201 D.L.R., p. 969 S.C.R.: "[A] collateral agreement cannot be established where it is inconsistent with or contradicts the written agreement."

[50] I propose to make eight comments about that principle.

[51] The first is that the principle has its root in the parol evidence rule as a rule of evidence, and in the "two-contract" or "collateral contract" exception to that rule of evidence. There is no objection to the introduction of evidence to establish an oral agreement separate from the written agreement and made at the same time: see *Heilbut, Symons & Co. v. Buckleton*, [1913] A.C. 30. But it is unreasonable to contemplate that, at the same time, and between the same parties, two contracts will be made dealing with the same subject-matter, one of which contradicts the other. So, since the written one was clearly and demonstrably made, reason requires one to conclude that the oral one, contradicting it, was never made. This point was set out clearly by Isaacs J. in the High Court of Australia, in *Hoyt's Proprietary Ltd. v. Spencer* (1919), 27 C.L.R. 133 at pp. 145-6, and it is consistent with the reasons of Strong J., in the Supreme Court of Canada, in *Byers v. McMillan* (1887), 15 S.C.R. 194. Those are the two roots which Judson J. relied on in *Hawrish v. Bank of Montreal* when he framed the modern restatement of the principle.

[52] The second is that the principle cannot be an absolute one. Let us suppose that a bank manager, acting within his authority, agrees that, if his customer will agree to sign and be bound by the bank's standard form of guarantee, then the guarantee will only be in effect for one year. The customer agrees on the basis of that assurance and he signs the standard form of guarantee which contains no mention of the one-year period. Two years pass by. The bank manager is replaced. The principal debtor goes bankrupt and the bank sues the guarantor, who pleads the collateral agreement as a defence. At trial, evidence is given by the former bank manager. He says that he agreed on behalf of the bank that the guarantee would only be in effect for a year. The second bank manager says that he knows about the agreement made by the first bank manager, but he also knows about the *Hawrish* case, which he thinks says that the agreement made by the first bank manager on behalf of the bank does not bind the bank, and that, if that is so, then he thinks that his duty to the bank's shareholders is to sue on the written guarantee. I do not consider that

the bank would succeed in that case. The principle in *Hawrish* is not a tool for the unscrupulous to dupe the unwary.

[53] The third comment is that *Hawrish*, *Bauer* and *Construction* illustrate, by the attention given to the evidence, that the principle is not an absolute one. In *Hawrish*, at p. 605 D.L.R., p. 520 S.C.R., Judson J. said:

> Bearing in mind these remarks to the effect that there must be a clear intention to create a binding agreement, I am not convinced that the evidence in this case indicates clearly the existence of such intention. Indeed, I am disposed to agree with what the Court of Appeal said on this point.

In *Bauer*, at p. 431 D.L.R., p. 111 S.C.R., McIntyre J. said:

> For reasons which will appear later in that part of this judgment dealing with the collateral contract argument, I am of the view that there is no evidence which would support any such finding against the bank.

In *Carman Construction*, at p. 199 D.L.R., p. 967 S.C.R., Martland J. said:

> In any opinion there is no evidence in the present case to establish an intention to warrant the accuracy of the statement made by the C.P.R. employee to Fielding, *i.e.*, no promise to make it good.

If the principle were an absolute one, there would have been no need in those cases to mention the evidence, because the statement alleged in each case, if established by the evidence, clearly contradicted the document. So the cases could have been disposed of by the application of the absolute principle, no matter how convincing the evidence, even if both parties agreed that the oral warranty was given, and was intended to be binding, and was intended to override or modify the document.

[54] The fourth point is that *Bauer v. Bank of Montreal* explicitly recognizes a particular exception to the principle, where, at p. 430 D.L.R., p. 111 S.C.R., McIntyre J., for the Supreme Court of Canada, said:

> Various authorities were cited for the proposition that a contract induced by misrepresentation or by an oral representation, inconsistent with the form of the written contract, would not stand and could not bind the party to whom the representation had been made. These authorities included *Canadian Indemnity Co. v. Okanagan Mainline Real Estate Board et al.* (1970), 16 D.L.R. (3d) 715 at p. 720, [1971] S.C.R. 493 at p. 500, *per* Judson, J.; *Jaques v. Lloyd D. George & Partners Ltd.*, [1968] 1 W.L.R. 625 (C.A.), *per* Lord Denning at pp. 630-1; *Firestone Tyre & Rubber Co. Ltd. v. Vokins & Co. Ltd.*, [1951] 1 Lloyd's Rep. 32 (K.B.), see Devlin, J., at p. 39, and *Mendelssohn v. Normand Ltd.*, [1970] 1 Q.B. 177 (C.A.).
>
> No quarrel can be made with the general provision advanced on this point by the appellant. To succeed, however, this argument must rest upon a finding of some misrepresentation by the bank, innocent or not, or on some oral representation inconsistent with the written document which caused a misimpression in the guarantor's mind, or upon some omission on the part of the bank manager to explain the contents of the document which induced the guarantor to enter into the guarantee upon a misunderstanding as to its nature.

So, if the contract is induced by an oral misrepresentation that is inconsistent with the written contract, the written contract cannot stand.

[55] The fifth point is that the *rationale* of the principle, as discussed in the first point, above, does not apply with equal force where the oral representation adds to, subtracts from, or varies the agreement recorded in the document, as it does where

the oral representation contradicts the document. As far as "adding to" is concerned, there is nothing inherently unreasonable about two agreements which add to each other. "Subtracting from" and "varying" represent a half-way stage between "adding to," on the one hand, which is wholly reasonable, and "contradicting," on the other hand, which is wholly unreasonable.

[56] The sixth point is that, if *Hawrish*, *Bauer* and *Carman Construction* are properly considered on their facts, the law in Canada is no different from that stated by K.W. Wedderburn in his article "Collateral Contracts," [1959] *Camb. L.J.* 58 at p. 62, where he says:

> What the parol evidence rule has bequeathed to the modern law is a presumption—namely that a document which looks like a contract is to be treated as the whole contract. This presumption is "very strong" but "it is a presumption only, and it is open to either of the parties to allege that there was, in addition to what appears in the written agreement, an antecedent express stipulation not intended by the parties to be excluded, but intended to continue in force with the express written agreement."

The presumption is always strong. But it is strongest when the oral representation is alleged to be contrary to the document, and somewhat less strong when the oral representation only adds to the document.

[57] The seventh point is that, if it is correct to view the principle only as a strong presumption, which I think is the correct view of *Hawrish*, *Bauer* and *Carman*, then that presumption would be more rigorous in a case where the parties had produced an individually negotiated document than it would be where a printed form was used, though it would be a strong presumption in both cases.

[58] The eighth and final point is that, if it is correct to consider the principle only as a strong presumption, then the presumption would be less strong where the contradiction was between a specific oral representation, on the one hand, and a general exemption or exclusion clause that excludes liability for any oral representation, whatsoever, on the other hand, than it would be in a case where the specific oral representation was contradictory to an equally specific clause in the document. This point is made by Anderson J.A., whose reasons I have read in draft, and I agree with him that the point is established by the cases to which he refers.

[59] I will return to this principle, on the facts of this case, in Part VII of these reasons.

VI. IS THERE A CONTRADICTION BETWEEN THE ORAL REPRESENTATION AND THE SIGNED DOCUMENT?

[60] I propose to set out the oral representation and cl. 23. If the oral representation is to have effect at all, it can be stated in this way:

> Allstate warrants that weeds will not be a cause of loss; the buckwheat will grow up and smother the weeds.

[61] Clause 23 reads:

> 23. Allstate gives no warranty as to the productiveness or any other matter pertaining to the seed sold to the producer and will not in any way be responsible for the crop.

In my opinion, the oral warranty and the printed document do not contradict each other. Taking cl. 23 without regard to the oral warranty, and having regard to the fact that the clause does not exclude all warranties, I think that the proper interpretation of cl. 23, in its context, is that all warranties pertaining to the seed are excluded, and that Allstate is not responsible for the yield. In the context, I think that the word "crop" means "yield."

[62] But even if I am wrong, and cl. 23, if it stood alone, would bear the meaning that Allstate was not to be liable for anything that prevented the production and harvesting of a buckwheat crop grown from the seed, I think it is proper to interpret cl. 23 in its relationship with the oral representation that was made in this case, because it is in the light of that representation that the parties would have interpreted cl. 23 when they read it over before signing the document. If that approach to inter-pretation is the correct one, then the oral representation and cl. 23 must be interpreted harmoniously, if that can be done without depriving cl. 23 of a natural and sensible meaning. Under that interpretation, Allstate would not be responsible for matters relating to the seed, for the yield, or for matters that might affect the production of the buckwheat arising from soil conditions or from farming methods and practices, but Allstate would assume any risk that the crop would be destroyed by weeds. There is no reason why the usual rule that an harmonious construction should be preferred to a contradictory construction should not apply.

[63] But, of course, the *rationale* of the harmonious construction rule is that the parties cannot have intended to agree to inconsistent obligations. So the rule only applies where both obligations have contractual force. And that depends on whether the oral representation was a warranty. But the question of whether it was a warranty or a bare representation is a question of fact, determined by the objective evidence of whether it was intended to have contractual force. So the interpretation of the representation and the document, on the one hand, and the question of whether the representation is a warranty, on the other hand, are bound together and should be answered together.

VII. CONCLUSION

[64] The trial judge said:

> It is clear on the law that the exclusionary clause in the contract will not avail the defend-ant, Allstate, if such a warranty is made out on the evidence. Is it so made out?

For the reasons I have set out in Parts V and VI, I think that it is a considerable over-simplification of the law to say that an exclusionary clause will not avail the defendant if a collateral warranty is made out on the evidence. Sometimes it will, sometimes it would not; the court must strive to reach the true contractual intention of the parties, guided, in the case of contradiction, by the strong presumption in favour of the document.

[65] But even if the trial judge oversimplified the law, he considered the right ques-tion on the evidence, namely: Is a warranty made out as a matter of fact? I do not think that he misdirected himself on the principles to be applied in answering that question of fact. It involved a nice question of judgment and an assessment of the testimony and demeanour of the witnesses. Paris J. concluded that Mr. Nunweiler's statement regarding weed control constituted a warranty. There is ample evidence to support that conclusion, much of it referred to by Paris J. in his reasons. I do not think that it is open to me to consider that matter afresh, or, if I were to reach a different conclu-sion on the facts than Paris J., to substitute my view of the facts for his.

[66] Once it has been decided that the oral representation was a warranty, then, in my opinion,

(a) evidence accepted on the basis that there would be a subsequent ruling on admissibility, becomes admissible;

(b) the oral warranty and the document must be interpreted together, and, if possible, harmoniously, to attach the correct contractual effect to each;

(c) if no contradiction becomes apparent in following that process, then the principle in *Hawrish*, *Bauer* and *Carman* has no application; and

(d) if there is a contradiction, then the principle in *Hawrish*, *Bauer* and *Carman* is that there is a strong presumption in favour of the written document, but the rule is not absolute, and if on the evidence it is clear that the oral warranty was intended to prevail, it will prevail.

[67] Since, in my opinion, there is no contradiction in this case between the specific oral warranty and the signed standard form Buckwheat Marketing Agreement, 1980, I have concluded that the warranty has contractual effect and that the defendant, Allstate Grain Co. Ltd., is liable to the plaintiffs for breach of that warranty.

[68] But if it were correct, in this case, to conclude that the oral representation and the Buckwheat Marketing Agreement, 1980 contradicted each other, then, on the basis of the facts found by the trial judge and his conclusion that the oral representation was intended to affect the contractual relationship of the parties, as a warranty, I would have concluded that, in spite of the strong presumption in favour of the document, the oral warranty should prevail.

[69] I would dismiss the appeal.

[Anderson JA agreed. Seaton JA dissented.]

NOTES

1. In consumer transactions within the scope of the Ontario *Consumer Protection Act*, oral evidence is admissible to prove an "unfair practice." See Chapter 6. In British Columbia, s 187 of the *Consumer Protection and Business Practices Act*, SBC 2004, c 2, has the effect of abolishing the "parole" evidence rule for proceedings in respect of a consumer transaction. In Saskatchewan, s 17 of the *Consumer Protection and Business Practices Act*, SS 2013, c C-30.2, allows parol evidence to establish the existence of an express warranty in any action between a consumer and a retail seller or manufacturer. In England, a Law Commission Working Paper (no 70, 1976) recommended total abolition of the rule, as did the Ontario Law Reform Commission in its *Report on Sale of Goods* (1979). The English Law Commission reversed its view in its report in 1988. See also McCamus at 193-207; Waddams at paras 315-35, 344-51; MacDougall, ch 5.

2. In *Bhasin v Hrynew*, 2014 SCC 71, the Supreme Court of Canada said that the "duty of honest performance," discussed in Chapter 8, cannot be excluded, even through the use of an entire obligations clause.

III. RECTIFICATION

USA V MOTOR TRUCKS, LIMITED
[1924] AC 196 (Ont PC)

By contract dated May 18, 1918, the respondent company contracted to machine high-explosive shells for the appellant Government; the contract provided for cancellation by notice in the event of anticipated termination of the war, and for payments to be made to the respondents thereupon. The payments were to include reimbursement for the cost of buildings, plant, etc., which the respondents had to add to their facilities for the purpose of carrying out the contract. Notice to terminate the contract was given in November 1918, and the parties thereupon negotiated as to the sum to be paid to the respondents. Ultimately a sum of $1,653,115 was agreed, which included $376,496, being the full amount which the respondents claimed in respect of land and buildings. After deducting from the above total a large sum which had been advanced by the appellant Government to the respondents, together with interest thereon, it was agreed that $637,812 was due to the respondents.

The parties accordingly entered into a formal contract dated October 7, 1919, but not actually signed until November 8. The contract provided that it should supersede the original contract of May 18, 1918, which was thereby terminated, and that the appellant Government should pay to the respondents the sum of $637,812 in full settlement for work and goods delivered and expenses incurred under the original contract; it further provided as follows: "(4) Title to all property specified in Schedule A, hereto annexed and made a part hereof, shall vest in the United States immediately upon execution of this agreement."

The land and buildings were not included in the schedule.

The agreed sum was paid on November 10, 1919, but the respondents subsequently denied the right of the appellant Government to possession of the land and buildings.

The appellant Government brought an action against the respondents in the Supreme Court of Ontario, claiming rectification of the schedule by the inclusion of the land and buildings, and specific performance of the contract as so rectified; alternatively they claimed repayment of the sum paid in respect of the land and buildings.

The trial judge (Kelly J.) found that the intention was that the land and buildings should become the property of the appellant Government. He ordered and declared that the respondents were trustees of the land and buildings for such person as the appellant Government might direct, with rectification of the schedule, the respondents to convey the land accordingly.

On appeal to the Appellate Division the judgment of Kelly J. was reversed and the action dismissed, Meredith C.J. dissenting. The judgments of the majority of the Court were based mainly upon the conclusions of fact.

THE EARL OF BIRKENHEAD: ... The question which requires the decision of the Board is whether or not it was the intention of the parties that the land and buildings, which had been paid for as claimed without deduction, should be inserted in schedule A and whether, if so, they were omitted therefrom by mutual mistake, so that rectification of an incomplete schedule should be ordered, or whether on the true interpretation of the intentions of the parties the respondents were entitled to receive all that they had expended upon acquiring the land and erecting the building, and, being so compensated, to retain both as their own.

The answer to these questions can only be found by reference to some legal considerations which their Lordships will hereinafter examine. If the parties intended that the lands and buildings should be included in schedule A, so that the omission in the instrument was accidental, rectification ought undoubtedly to be decreed. The Board, therefore, finds it necessary to examine the actions and the words of the parties at the relevant periods.

Their Lordships have reached the conclusion that both the appellants and the respondents intended that the land and buildings should be included in schedule A. That the appellants so intended has not been seriously disputed; and upon this point the Board entertains no doubt. Their Lordships, after giving careful attention to the matter, are no less confident that the respondents clearly understood that the award contemplated the transfer as owners to the United States of the land and buildings for which under its terms that Government had paid the respondents complete and generous compensation. ...

It was further suggested that the present action involved an attempt to enforce a parol contract inconsistently with the principle of the Statute of Frauds. It is however, well settled by a series of familiar authorities that the Statute of Frauds is not allowed by any Court administering the doctrines of equity to become an instrument for enabling sharp practice to be committed. And indeed the power of the Court to rectify mutual mistake implies that this power may be exercised notwithstanding that the true agreement of the parties has not been expressed in writing. Nor does the rule make any inroad upon another principle, that the plaintiff must show first that there was an actually concluded agreement antecedent to the instrument which is sought to be rectified; and secondly, that such agreement has been inaccurately represented in the instrument. When this is proved either party may claim, in spite of the Statute of Frauds, that the instrument on which the other insists does not represent the real agreement. The statute, in fact, only provides that no agreement not in writing and not duly signed shall be sued on; but when the written instrument is rectified there is a writing which satisfies the statute, the jurisdiction of the Court to rectify being outside the prohibition of the statute.

The respondents, however, advance still a further point of law. They contend that a plaintiff was not allowed to sue in the old Court of Chancery for the specific performance of a contract with a parol variation. There seems no reason on principle why a Court of Equity should not at one and the same time reform and enforce a contract; the matter, however, has been much discussed in the Court, and the balance of distinguished authority not unequally maintained. But the difficulty, which was almost entirely technical, has been, in the view of the Board, removed by the provisions of the Judicature Act, 1873, s. 24, which are reproduced in s. 16 of the Judicature Act of the Province of Ontario, ch. 56 of the Revised Statutes of 1914. This section provides that the Court, which is to administer equity as well as law, is to grant, either absolutely or on such reasonable terms and conditions as it shall deem best, all such remedies as any of the parties may appear to be entitled to in respect of any and every legal and equitable claim properly brought forward by them in such cause or matter, so that, as far as possible, all matters so in controversy between the parties may be completely and finally determined, and all multiplicity of legal proceedings discouraged.

The analogous provisions of the English Judicature Act are stated by Sir Edward Fry in his book on *Specific Performance*, 5th ed. para. 816. The learned author holds (and the Board agrees with him) that the controversy between the Chancery judges has now become obsolete, inasmuch as since the Judicature Act the Court can entertain an action in which combined relief will be given simultaneously for the reformation of a contract, and for the specific performance of the reformed contract.

Despite some differences in subsequent decisions, in which the principles of s. 24 of the Judicature Act have not been sufficiently considered, it has been held by P. O. Lawrence J., and by the Court of Appeal in the very recent case of *Craddock Brothers v. Hunt*, [1922] 2 Ch. 809, that the principle that as laid down by Sir Edward Fry must now prevail.

Their Lordships are of the same opinion, and conclude that under this head no difficulty confronts the appellants in the present case.

The board has thought it proper to consider the matters raised in this appeal with some particularity, partly because of the importance of the case, and partly out of respect for the learned judges who took a different view in the Appellate Division. But on analysis the issue has proved to be extremely simple. Both parties intended the lands and buildings to be included in the schedule. These were inadvertently omitted. Rectification must follow unless some exceptional ground for excluding this remedy is advanced. The respondents have attempted only to show that they agreed to the schedule in its intended form by reason of an error as to their existing legal rights. This contention has been rightly negatived on the facts, and would, in any event, be irrelevant in law.

Their Lordships will, therefore, humbly advise His Majesty that this appeal should be allowed, the judgment of the Appellate Division of the Supreme Court set aside with costs, and the judgment of Kelly J. restored. The respondents will pay the costs of the appeal.

Bercovici v Palmer. (1966), 59 DLR (2d) 513 (Sask CA). [In connection with a written agreement for the sale of land, both parties claimed relief, but in different ways. The question arose as to whether their conduct after the agreement was reached could be used to establish how, if at all, the written agreement should be rectified.] CULLITON CJS (for the court) said: Learned counsel contended that in an action for rectification the only evidence that can be considered is the evidence of what took place prior to the execution of the written document and that in the instant case the learned trial Judge erred in law in considering the conduct of the parties subsequent to that time. In support of this argument learned counsel relied upon the judgments in *Lovell and Christmas, Ltd. v. Wall* (1911), 104 L.T. 85; *Earl of Bradford v. Earl of Romney* (1862), 30 Beav. 431, 54 E.R. 956, and *Brown v. Hillar*, [1951] 4 D.L.R. 383, [1951] O.R. 634. With all deference I must say that I do not think the judgments in these cases advance the appellant's argument. In each case there is reiterated the established principle that subsequent declarations of the parties are not admissible for the purpose of construing a written contract. In this case the learned trial Judge was not faced with the question of construction but with the question of rectification.

In *The M.F. Whalen v. Pointe Anne Quarries Ltd.*, [(1921), 63 D.L.R. 545], Duff J. (as he then was), at p. 568: "Where one of the parties denies the alleged variation the parol evidence of the other party is not sufficient to entitle the Court to act. Such parol evidence must be adequately supported by documentary evidence *and by considerations arising from the conduct of the parties* satisfying the Court beyond reasonable doubt that the party resisting rectification did in truth enter into the agreement alleged. It is not sufficient that there should be a mere preponderance of probability, the case must be proved to a demonstration in the only sense in which in a Court of law an issue of fact can be established to a demonstration, that is to say, the evidence must be so satisfactory as to leave no room for such doubt. *Hart v. Boutilier* (1916), 56 D.L.R. 620, at p. 630; *Fowler v. Fowler* (1859), 4 De G. and J. 250 at p. 264, 45 E.R. 97; *Clarke v. Joselin* (1888), 16 O.R. 68 at p. 78." [The italics are mine.]

In *Hart v. Boutilier, supra*, it is obvious that Duff J. gave effect to considerations arising from the conduct of the parties for at p. 636 he said: "The respondent's subsequent conduct is not less difficult to understand." In the same case Idington J., makes it clear that in an action for rectification reliance may be placed upon considerations arising from the conduct of the parties. At p. 630 he stated: "The conduct of the parties and the outstanding features and nature of the transaction must in such cases often be relied upon as a better guide than what either may merely swear to."

PERFORMANCE INDUSTRIES LTD V SYLVAN
LAKE GOLF & TENNIS CLUB LTD
2002 SCC 19, [2002] 1 SCR 678

[As part of a joint venture the parties agreed orally on development of a strip of land 110 yards wide, but when the agreement was reduced to writing the measurement was stated as 110 *feet*. The president of the plaintiff corporation (Frederick Bell) signed the document without reading it. The trial judge granted rectification, and was upheld on this point by the Alberta Court of Appeal. A further appeal to the Supreme Court of Canada was dismissed.]

BINNIE J: ...

[31] Rectification is an equitable remedy whose purpose is to prevent a written document from being used as an engine of fraud or misconduct "equivalent to fraud." The traditional rule was to permit rectification only for mutual mistake, but rectification is now available for unilateral mistake (as here), provided certain demanding preconditions are met. Insofar as they are relevant to this appeal, these preconditions can be summarized as follows. Rectification is predicated on the existence of a prior oral contract whose terms are definite and ascertainable. The plaintiff must establish that the terms agreed to orally were not written down properly. The error may be fraudulent, or it may be innocent. What is essential is that at the time of execution of the written document the defendant knew or ought to have known of the error and the plaintiff did not. Moreover, the attempt of the defendant to rely on the erroneous written document must amount to "fraud or the equivalent of fraud." The court's task in a rectification case is corrective, not speculative. It is to restore the parties to their original bargain, not to rectify a belatedly recognized error of judgment by one party or the other: *Hart v. Boutilier* (1916), 56 D.L.R. 620 (S.C.C.), at p. 630; *Ship M.F. Whalen v. Pointe Anne Quarries Ltd.* (1921), 63 S.C.R. 109, at pp. 126-27, 63 D.L.R. 545, at p. 557; *Downtown King West Development Corp. v. Massey Ferguson Industries Ltd.* (1996), 133 D.L.R. (4th) 550 (Ont. C.A.), at p. 558; G.H.L. Fridman, *The Law of Contract in Canada* (4th ed. 1999), at p. 867; S.M. Waddams, *The Law of Contracts* (4th ed. 1999), para. 336. In *Hart*, supra, at p. 630, Duff J. (as he then was) stressed that "[t]he power of rectification must be used with great caution." Apart from everything else, a relaxed approach to rectification as a substitute for due diligence at the time a document is signed would undermine the confidence of the commercial world in written contracts.

• • •

[35] As stated, high hurdles are placed in the way of a business person who relies on his or her own unilateral mistake to resile from the written terms of a document which he or she has signed and which, on its face, seems perfectly clear. The law is determined not to open the proverbial floodgates to dissatisfied contract makers who want to extricate themselves from a poor bargain.

[36] I referred earlier to the four conditions precedent, or "hurdles" that a plaintiff must overcome. To these the appellants wish to add a fifth. Rectification, they say, should not be available to a plaintiff who is negligent in reviewing the documentation of a commercial agreement. To the extent the appellants' argument is that in such circumstances the Court may exercise its discretion to refuse the equitable remedy to such a plaintiff, I agree with them. To the extent they say the want of due diligence (or negligence) on the plaintiff's part is an absolute bar, I think their proposition is inconsistent with principle and authority and should be rejected.

[37] The first of the traditional hurdles is that Sylvan (Bell) must show the existence and content of the inconsistent prior oral agreement. Rectification is "[t]he most

venerable breach in the parol evidence rule" (Waddams, supra, at para. 336). The requirement of a prior oral agreement closes the "floodgate" to unhappy contract makers who simply failed to read the contractual documents, or who now have misgivings about the merits of what they have signed.

[38] The second hurdle is that not only must Sylvan (Bell) show that the written document does not correspond with the prior oral agreement, but that O'Connor either knew or ought to have known of the mistake in reducing the oral terms to writing. It is only where permitting O'Connor to take advantage of the error would amount to "fraud or the equivalent of fraud" that rectification is available. This requirement closes the "floodgate" to unhappy contract makers who simply made a mistake. Equity acts on the conscience of a defendant who seeks to take advantage of an error which he or she either knew or ought reasonably to have known about at the time the document was signed. Mere unilateral mistake alone is not sufficient to support rectification, but, if permitting the non-mistaken party to take advantage of the document would be fraud or equivalent to fraud, rectification may be available: *Hart*, supra, at p. 630; *Ship M.F. Whalen*, supra, at pp. 126-27.

[39] What amounts to "fraud or the equivalent of fraud" is, of course, a crucial question. In *First City Capital Ltd. v. British Columbia Building Corp.* (1989), 43 B.L.R. 29 (B.C. S.C.), McLachlin C.J.S.C. (as she then was) observed that "in this context 'fraud or the equivalent of fraud' refers not to the tort of deceit or strict fraud in the legal sense, but rather to the broader category of equitable fraud or constructive fraud ... . Fraud in this wider sense refers to transactions falling short of deceit but where the Court is of the opinion that it is unconscientious for a person to avail himself of the advantage obtained" (p. 37). Fraud in the "wider sense" of a ground for equitable relief "is so infinite in its varieties that the Courts have not attempted to define it," but "all kinds of unfair dealing and unconscionable conduct in matters of contract come within its ken": *McMaster University v. Wilchar Construction Ltd.* (1971), 22 D.L.R. (3d) 9 (Ont. H.C.), at p. 19. See also *Montreal Trust Co. v. Maley* (1992), 99 D.L.R. (4th) 257 (Sask. C.A.), per Wakeling J.A.; *Alampi v. Swartz* (1964), 43 D.L.R. (2d) 11 (Ont. C.A.); *Stepps Investments Ltd. v. Security Capital Corp.* (1976), 73 D.L.R. (3d) 351 (Ont. H.C.), per Grange J. (as he then was), at pp. 362-63; and Waddams, supra, at para. 342.

[40] The third hurdle is that Sylvan (Bell) must show "the precise form" in which the written instrument can be made to express the prior intention (*Hart*, supra, per Duff J., at p. 630). This requirement closes the "floodgates" to those who would invite the court to speculate about the parties' unexpressed intentions, or impose what in hindsight seems to be a sensible arrangement that the parties might have made but did not. The court's equitable jurisdiction is limited to putting into words that—and only that—which the parties had already orally agreed to.

[41] The fourth hurdle is that all of the foregoing must be established by proof which this Court has variously described as "beyond reasonable doubt" (*Ship M.F. Whalen*, supra, at p. 127), or "evidence which leaves no 'fair and reasonable doubt'" (*Hart*, supra, at p. 630), or "convincing proof" or "more than sufficient evidence" (*Augdome Corp. v. Gray*, [1975] 2 S.C.R. 354, at pp. 371-72, 49 D.L.R. (3d) 372). The modern approach, I think, is captured by the expression "convincing proof," i.e., proof that may fall well short of the criminal standard, but which goes beyond the sort of proof that only reluctantly and with hesitation scrapes over the low end of the civil "more probable than not" standard.

[42] Some critics argue that anything more demanding than the ordinary civil standard of proof is unnecessary (e.g., Waddams, supra, at para. 343), but, again, the objective is to promote the utility of written agreements by closing the "floodgate" against marginal cases that dilute what are rightly seen to be demanding preconditions to rectification.

[43] It was formerly held that it was not sufficient if the evidence merely comes from the party seeking rectification. In *Ship M.F. Whalen*, supra, Duff J. (as he then was) said, at p. 127, "[s]uch parol evidence must be adequately supported by documentary evidence and by considerations arising from the conduct of the parties." Modern practice has moved away from insistence on documentary corroboration (Waddams, supra, at para. 337; Fridman, supra, at p. 879). In some situations, documentary corroboration is simply not available, but if the parol evidence is corroborated by the conduct of the parties or other proof, rectification may, in the discretion of the Court, be available.

[44] It is convenient at this point to deal with the trial judge's findings in relation to these traditional requirements. I will then turn to the appellants' proposed fifth precondition—due diligence on the part of the plaintiff. ...

[45] The appellants' principal argument against rectification is that the alleged prior oral agreement is void for uncertainty. Reliance is placed on *I.C.R.V. Holdings Ltd. v. Tri-Par Holdings Ltd.* (1994), 53 B.C.A.C. 72, where rectification of an agreement to purchase a recreational vehicle park was refused because, per Finch J.A. (now C.J.B.C.), at para. 7, the parties never agreed on "the precise location of the eastern boundary," and *Gordeyko v. Edmonton* (1986), 45 Alta. L.R. (2d) 201 (Q.B.), where Stratton J. (as he then was) found the evidence uncertain about a notice period envisaged by the prior oral agreement. See also *Kerr v. Cunard* (1914), 16 D.L.R. 662 (N.B. S.C.). Appellants' counsel quotes Lord Denning's "pithy" observation that "[a] mistake made by one party to the knowledge of the other is a ground for avoiding a contract, but not for making one" (*Byrnlea Property Investments Ltd. v. Ramsay*, [1969] 2 Q.B. 253 (C.A.), at p. 265).

[46] I agree with the appellants that on this point the trial judge's reasons are somewhat unsatisfactory, but this appears to be because the "uncertainty" argument now made against rectification was not before him. The issue of uncertainty of subject matter was raised neither in the pleadings nor at trial. The trial judge directed his reasons to the points that he believed were in controversy. As to the appellants' new arguments, one may echo the words of James V.C. in *Rumble v. Heygate* (1870), 18 W.R. 749 (Ch.), who said, at p. 750, that the objections to the agreement in that case on the basis of uncertainty of quantity of land and of its site "are mere shadows which vanish when examined by the light of common sense."

[47] The Court should attempt to uphold the parties' bargain where the terms can be ascertained with a reasonable level of comfort, i.e., convincing proof. Here the trial judge predicated his award of compensatory damages on the finding that the optioned land could accommodate 58 single family houses located along the 480-yard length of the 18th fairway. There is no argument about the 480 yards. O'Connor himself plucked the 480 figure from the length of play listed on the Sylvan Lake Golf Club score card. O'Connor's number for the width of the development (110) may also be accepted. The issue is whether the number was intended to express yards or feet. The trial judge appears to have concluded that the dispute about the depth of the residential development (which is all that divided the parties) came down to a simple choice between Bell's version (Plan A) and O'Connor's version (Plan B). Both plans were predicated on the length of the 18th fairway, namely 480 yards. Plan B, which O'Connor had described in the document, contemplated a single row of houses on a development plan 110 feet deep. Bell's Plan A was based on two rows of housing separated by a road allowance, in a configuration similar to that shown in the aerial photo of the Bayview development discussed by Bell and O'Connor at their December 16-17 meeting. Plan A called for a depth of about 110 yards. If Plan B's 110-foot depth is tripled to 110 yards, the acreage under option would be roughly tripled from about 3.6 acres (Plan B) to about 10.8 acres (Plan A), which accommodates the 58 lots

plus the standard municipal road allowance. The problem in *I.C.R.V. Holdings Ltd.*, *supra*, was that the parties never agreed on the boundary. Here the trial judge concluded that there was agreement even though the parties did not express themselves to each other in lawyerly language. ...

[48] The trial judge thus found that the parties had made a verbal agreement with reference to a residential development along the 18th hole. It was more than an agreement to agree. He concluded that there was a definite project in a definite location to which O'Connor and Bell had given their definite assent.

[49] Although the parties did not discuss a metes and bounds description, they were working on a defined development proposal. O'Connor cannot complain if the numbers he inserted in clause 18 (110 [times] 480) are accepted and confirmed. The issue, then, is the error created by his apparently duplicitous substitution of feet for yards in one dimension. We know the 480 must be yards because it measures the 18th fairway. If the 110 is converted from feet to yards, symmetry is achieved, certainty is preserved and Bell's position is vindicated. ...

[50] The notion of "equivalent to fraud" as distinguished from fraud itself, is often utilized where "the court is unwilling to go so far as to find actual knowledge on the side of the party seeking enforcement" (Waddams, supra, at para. 342). The trial judge had no such hesitation in this case. He characterized O'Connor's actions as "fraudulent, dishonest and deceitful" (para. 114).

[51] The trial judge was persuaded not only of the terms of the prior oral agreement and of Bell's mistake but "beyond any reasonable doubt" of O'Connor's knowledge of that mistake. He states (at para. 79):

> This court is satisfied beyond any reasonable doubt that O'Connor knew of Bell's mistake and he chose to permit Bell to sign it in the mistaken belief that it represented the verbal agreement. He did so with the full intention that he would in the future rely on the terms of the Agreement to thwart or reduce any plan by Bell to develop an increased area of the golf course for residential development.

[52] O'Connor thus fraudulently misrepresented the written document as accurately reflecting the terms of the prior oral contract. He knew that Bell would not sign an agreement without the option for sufficient land to create the "Bayview" layout development with two rows of housing as specified in the prior oral contract. O'Connor therefore knew when Bell signed the document that he had not detected the substitution of 110 feet for 110 yards. O'Connor knowingly snapped at Bell's mistake "to thwart or reduce any plan by Bell to develop an increased area of the golf course for residential development." Bell's loss would be O'Connor's gain, as O'Connor (Performance) would come into sole ownership of the optioned land as of December 31, 1994.

[53] Although on occasion the trial judge describes O'Connor's conduct as "equivalent to fraud," and elsewhere he describes it as actual fraud, his reasons taken as a whole can only be characterized as a finding of actual fraud. ...

[54] It follows from the foregoing that "the precise form" in which the written document can be made to conform to the oral agreement would be simply to change the word "feet" in the phrase "one hundred and ten (110) feet in width" to "yards." ...

[55] The trial judge made his key findings in respect of the prior oral agreement, Bell's unilateral mistake and O'Connor's knowledge of that mistake to a standard of "beyond any reasonable doubt."

[56] He also found that Bell's version of the verbal agreement was sufficiently corroborated on significant points by other witnesses (including his wife, his former partner, his lawyer and, subsequently, the development consultants), and documents

(including his lawyer's notes and the plan of the Bayview Golf Course development discussed in mid-December 1989). ...

[57] The appellants seek, in effect, to add a fifth hurdle (or condition precedent) to the availability of rectification. A plaintiff, they say, should be denied such a remedy unless the error in the written document could not have been discovered with due diligence.

[58] O'Connor says that Bell's failure to read clause 18 and note the mixture of yards and feet should be fatal to his claim because the Court ought not to assist business persons who are negligent in protecting their own interests. Alternatively, the effective cause of Bell's loss is not the fraudulent document but Bell's failure to detect the fraud when he had an opportunity to do so.

[59] I agree that Bell, an experienced businessman, ought to have examined the text of clause 18 before signing the document. The terms of clause 18 were clear on their face (even though many readers might have misread a description of land that mixed units of measurement as clause 18 did here). He had time to review the document with his lawyer. He did so. Changes were requested. He did not catch the substitution of 110 feet for 110 yards; indeed, he says he did not read clause 18 at all.

[60] The trial judge, at para. 76, accepted the evidence of Bell's lawyer who admitted that he had not directed his mind to the limitations of the size of the development parcel found in clause 18, nor had he made any note of bringing those to Bell's attention which would have been his normal practice. He could offer no explanation for why he had not done so other than the fact that his focus on receipt of the Agreement signed by Bell was to ensure the completion and registration of documentation to facilitate the closing of [the purchase] on or before December 31, 1989. This court accepts the evidence offered by Mr. Hancock and that of Bell that they at no time discussed the description of property contained in clause 18.

[61] It is undoubtedly true that courts ought to hold commercial entities to a reasonable level of due diligence in documenting their transactions. Otherwise, written agreements will lose their utility and commercial life will suffer. Rectification should not become a belated substitute for due diligence.

[62] On the other hand, most cases of unilateral mistake involve a degree of carelessness on the part of the plaintiff. A diligent reading of the written document would generally have disclosed the error that the plaintiff, after the fact, seeks to have corrected. The mistaken party will often have failed to read the document entirely, or may have read it too hastily or without parsing each word. ...

[63] One reason why the defence of contributory negligence or want of due diligence is not persuasive in a rectification case is because the plaintiff seeks no more than enforcement of the prior oral agreement to which the defendant has already bound itself.

• • •

[66] I conclude, therefore that due diligence on the part of the plaintiff is not a condition precedent to rectification. However, it should be added at once that rectification is an equitable remedy and its award is in the discretion of the court. The conduct of the plaintiff is relevant to the exercise of that discretion. In a case where the court concludes that it would be unjust to impose on a defendant a liability that ought more properly to be attributed to the plaintiff's negligence, rectification may be denied. That was not the case here.

NOTE

The Ontario Court of Appeal, in *Royal Bank of Canada v El-Bris Ltd* (2008), 92 OR (3d) 779 (CA), rejected the four-part test in *Performance Industries* for cases of common mistake, preferring the two-part test in *Bank of Montreal v Vancouver Professional Soccer Ltd* (1987), 15 BCLR (2d) 34 (CA) at 36-37 where McLachlin JA, as she then was, said a petitioner for rectification of any document must establish:

1. that the written instrument does not reflect the true agreement of the parties; and
2. that the parties shared a common continuing intention up to the time of signature that the provision in question stand as agreed rather than as reflected in the instrument.

CANADA (ATTORNEY GENERAL) V FAIRMONT HOTELS INC
2016 SCC 56, [2016] 2 SCR 720

[In the case of *Juliar v Canada (Attorney General)* (2000), 50 OR (3d) 728 (CA), it was held that an agreement could be rectified where it did not achieve the *effect* the parties had intended, which was to avoid the payment of certain taxes. *Fairmont Hotels* was another tax case. The facts were fairly straightforward. Fairmont Hotels, through its subsidiaries, helped finance Legacy Hotels' purchase of two hotels. This financing arrangement was meant to operate on a tax-neutral basis. Because of ownership changes at Fairmont Hotels, a new plan was put in place that covered Fairmont Hotels but not its subsidiaries. Still further changes in the arrangement caused Fairmont Hotels to redeem its shares in its subsidiaries, by resolutions of the directors. This step resulted, however, in unanticipated tax liability for the subsidiaries, revealed through a tax audit. Fairmont Hotels sought to avoid that liability by rectifying the directors' resolutions.]

BROWN J: ...

[12] If by mistake a legal instrument does not accord with the true agreement it was intended to record—because a term has been omitted, an unwanted term included, or a term incorrectly expresses the parties' agreement—a court may exercise its equitable jurisdiction to rectify the instrument so as to make it accord with the parties' true agreement. Alternatively put, rectification allows a court to achieve correspondence between the parties' agreement and the substance of a legal instrument intended to record that agreement, when there is a discrepancy between the two. Its purpose is to give effect to the parties' true intentions, rather than to an erroneous transcription of those true intentions (Swan and Adamski, [*Canadian Contract Law* (3rd ed 2012)] at s.8.229).

[13] Because rectification allows courts to rewrite what the parties had originally intended to be the final expression of their agreement, it is "a potent remedy" (*Snell's Equity* (33rd ed. 2015), by J. McGhee, at pp. 417-18). It must, as this Court has repeatedly stated (*Shafron v KRG Insurance Brokers (Western) Inc.*, 2009 SCC 6, [2009] 1 SCR 157, at para. 56, citing *Performance Industries Ltd.* ... , at para. 31), be used "with great caution," since a "relaxed approach to rectification as a substitute for due diligence at the time a document is signed would undermine the confidence of the commercial world in written contracts": *Performance Industries*, at para. 31. It bears reiterating that rectification is limited solely to cases where a written instrument has incorrectly recorded the parties' antecedent agreement (Swan and Adamski, at s.8.229). It is not concerned with mistakes merely in the making of that antecedent agreement: E. Peel, *The Law of Contract* (14th ed. 2015), at para. 8-059; *Mackenzie v Coulson* (1869),

LR 8 Eq 368, at p. 375 ("Courts of Equity do not rectify contracts; they may and do rectify instruments"). In short, rectification is unavailable where the basis for seeking it is that one or both of the parties wish to amend not the instrument recording their agreement, but the agreement itself. More to the point of this appeal, and as this Court said in *Performance Industries* (at para. 31), "[t]he court's task in a rectification case is ... to restore the parties to their original bargain, not to rectify a belatedly recognized error of judgment by one party or the other."

[14] Beyond these general guides, the nature of the mistake must be accounted for: Swan and Adamski, at s.8.233. Two types of error may support a grant of rectification. The first arises when both parties subscribe to an instrument under a *common* mistake that it accurately records the terms of their antecedent agreement. In such a case, an order for rectification is predicated upon the applicant showing that the parties had reached a prior agreement whose terms are definite and ascertainable; that the agreement was still effective when the instrument was executed; that the instrument fails to record accurately that prior agreement; and that, if rectified as proposed, the instrument would carry out the agreement: ...

[15] In *Performance Industries* (at para. 31) and again in *Shafron* (at para. 53), this Court affirmed that rectification is also available where the claimed mistake is unilateral—either because the instrument formalizes a unilateral act (such as the creation of a trust), or where (as in *Performance Industries* and *Shafron*) the instrument was intended to record an agreement between parties, but one party says that the instrument does not accurately do so, while the other party says it does. In *Performance Industries* (at para. 31), "certain demanding preconditions" were added to rectify a putative unilateral mistake: specifically, that the party resisting rectification knew or ought to have known about the mistake; and that permitting that party to take advantage of the mistake would amount to "fraud or the equivalent of fraud" (para. 38).

• • •

[19] ... [R]ectification is available not to cure a party's error in judgment in entering into a particular agreement, but an error in the recording of that agreement in a legal instrument. Alternatively put, rectification aligns the instrument with what the parties agreed to do, and not what, with the benefit of hindsight, they should have agreed to do. The parties' mistake in *Juliar*, however, was not in the recording of their intended agreement to transfer shares for a promissory note, but in selecting that mechanism instead of a shares-for-shares transfer. By granting the sought-after change of mechanism, the Court of Appeal in *Juliar* purported to "rectify" not merely the instrument recording the parties' antecedent agreement, but that agreement itself where it failed to achieve the desired result or produced an unanticipated adverse consequence—that is, where it was the product of an error in judgment.

• • •

C. TWO FURTHER CONCERNS

[25] Before applying the test for rectification—which test, I emphasize, is to be applied in a tax context just as it is in a non-tax context—to the facts of this appeal, I turn to two matters in need of clarification, the first of which was raised by the respondents.

(1) "COMMON CONTINUING INTENTION" TO AVOID TAX LIABILITY

[26] The respondents argue that, in the case of a common mistake, it is unnecessary for the party seeking rectification to prove a prior agreement concerning the

term or terms for which rectification is sought. Rather, they say that evidence of a "common continuing intention"—in this case, their common continuing intention that the value of the shares in FHIW and FHIS should be transferred in a way that would avoid immediate tax liability—should suffice to ground a grant of rectification.

• • •

[29] ... *Joscelyne* [*Joscelyne v Nissen*, [1970] 2 QB 86 (CA)] should not be taken as authorizing any departure from this Court's direction that a party seeking to correct an erroneously drafted written instrument on the basis of a common mistake must first demonstrate its inconsistency with an antecedent agreement with respect to that term. In *Shafron*, this Court unambiguously rejected the sufficiency of showing mere intentions to ground a grant of rectification, insisting instead on erroneously recorded terms. As Denning LJ said in *Frederick E Rose (London) Ld v William H Pim Jnr & Co*, [1953] 2 QB 450 (CA), at p 461 (quoted in *Shafron*, at para. 52):

> Rectification is concerned with contracts and documents, not with intentions. In order to get rectification it is necessary to show that the parties were in complete agreement on the terms of their contract, but by an error wrote them down wrongly; and in this regard, in order to ascertain the terms of their contract, you do not look into the inner minds of the parties—into their intentions—any more than you do in the formation of any other contract.

[30] This Court's statement in *Performance Industries* (at para. 31) that "[r]ectification is predicated on the existence of a prior oral contract whose terms are definite and ascertainable" is to the same effect. The point, again, is that rectification corrects the recording in an instrument of an agreement (here, to redeem shares). Rectification does not operate simply because an agreement failed to achieve an intended effect (here, tax neutrality)—irrespective of whether the intention to achieve that effect was "common" and "continuing."

• • •

[32] It therefore falls to a party seeking rectification to show not only the putative error in the instrument, but also the way in which the instrument should be rectified in order to correctly record what the parties intended to do. "The court's task in a rectification case is corrective, not speculative": *Performance Industries*, at para. 31. Where, therefore, an instrument recording an agreed-upon course of action is sought to be rectified, the party seeking rectification must identify terms which were omitted or recorded incorrectly and which, correctly recorded, are sufficiently precise to constitute the terms of an enforceable agreement. The inclusion of imprecise terms in an instrument is, on its own, not enough to obtain rectification; absent evidence of what the parties had specifically agreed to do, rectification is not available. While imprecision may justify setting aside an instrument, it cannot invite courts to find an agreement where none is present. It was for this reason that the Court in *Shafron* declined to enforce the restrictive covenant covering the "Metropolitan City of Vancouver." The term was imprecise, but there was "no indication that the parties agreed on something and then mistakenly included something else in the written contract": *Shafron*, at para. 57.

• • •

(2) STANDARD OF PROOF

[34] The second point requiring clarification is the standard of proof. In *Performance Industries*, at para. 41, this Court held that a party seeking rectification will have

to meet all elements of the test by "convincing proof," which it described as "proof that may fall well short of the criminal standard, but which goes beyond the sort of proof that only reluctantly and with hesitation scrapes over the low end of the civil 'more probable than not' standard." This, as was observed in *Performance Industries*, was a relaxation of the standard from the Court's earlier jurisprudence, in which the criminal standard of proof was applied: ...

[35] In light, however, of this Court's more recent statement in *F H v McDougall*, 2008 SCC 53, [2008] 3 SCR 41, at para. 40, that there is "only one civil standard of proof at common law and that is proof on a balance of probabilities," the question obviously arises of whether the Court's description in *Performance Industries* of the standard to which the elements of the test for obtaining rectification must be proven is still applicable.

[36] In my view, the applicable standard of proof to be applied to evidence adduced in support of a grant of rectification is that which *McDougall* identifies as the standard generally applicable to all civil cases: the balance of probabilities. But this merely addresses the standard, and not the quality of evidence by which that standard is to be discharged. As the Court also said in *McDougall* (at para. 46), "evidence must always be sufficiently clear, convincing and cogent." A party seeking rectification faces a difficult task in meeting this standard, because the evidence must satisfy a court that the true substance of its unilateral intention or agreement with another party was not accurately recorded in the instrument to which it nonetheless subscribed. A court will typically require evidence exhibiting a high degree of clarity, persuasiveness and cogency before substituting the terms of a written instrument with those said to form the party's true, if only orally expressed, intended course of action. This idea was helpfully encapsulated, in the context of an application for rectification of a common mistake, by Brightman LJ in *Thomas Bates and Son Ltd v Wyndham's (Lingerie) Ltd.*, [1981] 1 WLR 505 (CA), at p. 521:

> The standard of proof required in an action of rectification to establish the common intention of the parties is, in my view, the civil standard of balance of probability. But as the alleged common intention ex hypothesi contradicts the written instrument, convincing proof is required in order to counteract the cogent evidence of the parties' intention displayed by the instrument itself. It is not, I think, the standard of proof which is high, so differing from the normal civil standard, but the evidential requirement needed to counteract the inherent probability that the written instrument truly represents the parties' intention because it is a document signed by the parties.

[37] In brief, while the standard of proof is the balance of probabilities, the essential concern of *Performance Industries* remains applicable, being (at para. 42) "to promote the utility of written agreements by closing the 'floodgate' against marginal cases that dilute what are rightly seen to be demanding preconditions to rectification."

D. APPLICATION TO THE PRESENT APPEAL

[38] To summarize, rectification is an equitable remedy designed to correct errors in the recording of terms in written legal instruments. Where the error is said to result from a mistake common to both or all parties to the agreement, rectification is available upon the court being satisfied that, on a balance of probabilities, there was a prior agreement whose terms are definite and ascertainable; that the agreement was still in effect at the time the instrument was executed; that the instrument fails to accurately record the agreement; and that the instrument, if rectified, would carry out the parties' prior agreement. In the case of a unilateral mistake, the party seeking

rectification must also show that the other party knew or ought to have known about the mistake and that permitting the defendant to take advantage of the erroneously drafted agreement would amount to fraud or the equivalent of fraud.

[39] A straightforward application of these principles to the present appeal leads unavoidably to the conclusion that the respondents' application for rectification should have been dismissed, since they could not show having reached a prior agreement with definite and ascertainable terms. I have already noted (1) the chambers judge's finding that, in 2006, Fairmont intended to address the "unhedged position of [FHIW and FHIS] in a way that would be tax and accounting neutral although [it] had no specific plan as to how [it] would do that" (para. 33); and (2) the Court of Appeal's description of Fairmont's intention as being "to unwind [the Legacy transactions] on a tax free basis" (para. 7). It is therefore clear that Fairmont intended to limit, if not avoid altogether, its tax liability in unwinding the Legacy transactions. And, by redeeming the shares in 2007, this intention was frustrated. Without more, however, these facts do not support a grant of rectification. The error in the courts below is of a piece with the principal flaw I have identified in the Court of Appeal's earlier reasoning in *Juliar*. Rectification is not equity's version of a mulligan. Courts rectify instruments which do not correctly record agreements. Courts do not "rectify" agreements where their faithful recording in an instrument has led to an undesirable or otherwise unexpected outcome.

[40] Relatedly, the respondents do not show how Fairmont's intention, held in common and on a continuing basis with FHIW and FHIS, was to be achieved in definite and ascertainable terms while unwinding the Legacy transactions. The respondents' factum refers to "the original 2006 plan," but that plan was not only imprecise: it really was not a plan at all, being at best an inchoate wish to protect, by unspecified means, FHIW and FHIS from foreign exchange tax liability.

[41] The respondents' application for rectification therefore fails at the first hurdle. They show no prior agreement whose terms were definite and ascertainable.

• • •

[43]   ABELLA J (dissenting)

• • •

[63] Whether a mistake is unilateral or mutual, rectification is, ultimately, an equitable remedy that seeks to give effect to the true intention of the parties, and prevent errors from causing windfalls. The doctrine is also "based on simple notions of relief against unjust enrichment," namely, that it would be unfair to rigidly enforce an error that enriches one party at the expense of another: Waddams, at p. 240. As Professor Waddams notes, "[t]he doctrine is a far-reaching and flexible tool of justice" (p. 243).

• • •

[66] While I acknowledge that rectification seems most often to have been granted in the context of agreed upon terms having been transcribed incorrectly, since unjust enrichment can also result from a mistake in carrying out the intention of the parties, the remedy is also available to correct errors in implementation. Courts have, as a result, granted rectification where a corporate transaction was conducted in the wrong sequence (*GT Group Telecom Inc., Re* (2004), 5 CBR (5th) 230 (Ont Sup Ct J)), where an underlying calculation in a contract was incorrect (*Oriole Oil & Gas Ltd v American Eagle Petroleums Ltd* (1981), 27 AR 411 (CA)), and where the requisite steps of an amalgamation were not correctly carried out (*Prospera Credit Union, Re* (2002), 32 BLR (3d) 145 (BCSC)).

[67] Whether the errors are in transcription or in implementation, courts may refuse to exercise their discretion where allowing rectification would prejudice the

rights of third parties (*Wise v Axford*, [1954] OWN 822 (CA)). But the mere existence of a third party will not bar rectification. In *Augdome Corp v Gray*, [1975] 2 SCR 354, this Court concluded that the presence of a third party is only a bar to rectification where the third party has actually relied on the flawed agreement. This principle was subsequently explained by Gray J. in *Consortium Capital Projects Inc v Blind River Veneer Ltd* (1988), 63 OR (2d) 761 (H Ct J), at p. 766, aff'd (1990), 72 OR (2d) 703 (CA): "... the proper test is whether the third party relied on the document as executed and took action based on that document." ...

[68] This is consistent with one of the underlying purposes of rectification, namely to prevent unjust enrichment: Waddams, at p. 240; ... Just as rectification can prevent one party from enforcing an error and being unjustly enriched by the other's mistake, rectification can also prevent a third party who has not relied on the agreement from enforcing a mistake and receiving a windfall. This theory was on display in *Love v Love*, [2013] 5 WWR 662 (Sask CA). The Saskatchewan Court of Appeal allowed the rectification of a life insurance contract, in which a husband had designated his wife as the beneficiary of his life insurance policy. When the couple divorced, the husband completed a new form to designate his son as the policy's beneficiary instead of his former wife. He filled the paperwork out incorrectly. After he died, the former wife and the son both attempted to claim the proceeds of the insurance policy. The court rectified the contract to reflect what it saw as the husband's true intention, namely to designate his son as the beneficiary.

[69] This brings us to the tax context.

• • •

[83] ... Civil law and common law rectification in the tax context are clearly based on analogous principles, namely, that the true intention of the parties has primacy over errors in the transcription or implementation of that agreement, subject to a need for precision and the rights of third parties who detrimentally rely on the agreement.

[84] That means that there is no principled basis in either the common or civil law for a stricter standard in the tax context simply because it is the government which is positioned to benefit from a mistake. The tax department is not entitled to play "Gotcha" any more than any other third party who did not rely to its detriment on the mistake.

• • •

[90] Fairmont was found by Newbould J to have always had a clear, continuing intention to unwind the reciprocal loan structure on a tax-neutral basis and never to redeem the preferred shares. But, by mistake, the preferred share redemption terms were included in the directors' resolutions. This is exactly the kind of mistake rectification exists to remedy. Once Newbould J was satisfied of the true intention of the parties, he was entitled to give effect to it by allowing the replacement loan arrangement terms to be inserted into the directors' resolutions.

[91] To require an exhaustive account of how the transaction was supposed to have proceeded would amount to imposing a uniquely high threshold for rectification in the tax context. As Newbould J explained, denying the application to rectify the agreement in these circumstances would "give [the Canada Revenue Agency] an unintended gain because of the mistake": para. 44. There is no basis for permitting a windfall to the Canada Revenue Agency that no other third party would have been entitled to.

[Appeal allowed. McLachlin CJ, and Cromwell, Moldaver, Karakatsanis, Wagner and Gascon JJ agreed with Brown J. Côté J agreed with Abella J's dissent.]

PAGET V MARSHALL
(1884), 28 ChD 255

BACON VC: The case before me is in a very narrow compass. The Plaintiff had taken the lease of a site from the *Goldsmiths' Company* upon a contract to build upon it a very valuable and commodious structure. He did so, and his plans are in evidence; it is quite clear what his intention was. He built two separate ground-floor tenements, Nos. 49 and 50, to be let to two separate tenants. He kept a third, No. 48, including ground and first floors, intending to occupy it himself, and the fourth part, that coloured blue on the model, he had to let when the negotiation commenced with the Defendant. So that the subject in dispute is beyond all question. The two shops, Nos. 49 and 50, were separate and distinct things—as separate as if they had been in some other street—and the third, No. 48, was equally separate and distinct—built by the Plaintiff for his own occupation, and for carrying on his own business, and constructed so that those objects might be conveniently performed by him. To that end he built on the ground floor of No. 48 a staircase communicating with the first floor of No. 48, and he partitioned off the first floor of No. 48, so that in its turn it became just as distinct a building—just as distinct a tenement—as Nos. 49 and 50, and the purpose was distinct. Then, the part coloured blue (which included the whole first floor of the block except that of No. 48, and all the upper floors without any exception) being still available, and the Plaintiff willing to let it, he constructed a staircase which led from the street past the first floor of No. 48, and landed upon the blue part, I will call it, that is sufficient description,—no communication whatever either in fact being made, or according to the evidence ever intended to be made, between the ground or first floor of No. 48 and the part coloured blue. That was the state of things when these parties met to negotiate. The partition which effectually severed the first floor of No. 48 from the part coloured blue, had been completely settled and arranged. The Defendant on his first visit looked over all that was then to let, ascertained what the Plaintiff meant to let, saw the first floor over No. 48, said that it would make a very handsome warehouse, but knew at the same time that it was not to be let, because, to use his own expression in his own evidence, the Plaintiff told him "we mean to use that for ourselves." That is the evidence which the Defendant has given on this occasion. He says that he was satisfied to some extent with what he looked at, and desired to acquire it, but he must have a packing-room. He could not mean the first floor, that which he said was a magnificent warehouse could not be a packing-room, it could not in the nature of things; and he does not say that that was in his mind, still he insists more than once on the necessity of having a packing-room. I am mentioning these facts in order to ascertain, as it is my duty to do, what I must take to be proved to have been the intention of the parties when they entered into the negotiation. He asks for a packing-room. The brother goes with him down into a cellar—a cellar under No. 48, in the basement of No. 48—they look about there, and the brother comes in and says, "You cannot have it." No wonder, because there can be no access to it but from the floor of No. 48, and that went off.

Now, it would be impossible for me to connect, and there was a very faint attempt made to connect, the necessity which was present in the Defendant's mind to have a packing-room, with the magnificent first floor, which he now says he had in his mind when he was present. The statement about putting up the inscription by no means encourages any such notion. The Defendant desired to advertise to the public by means of a large inscription on the front of that which was to be his the trade which he was carrying on. He wished also to have a similar inscription over No. 48. That was resisted. It was the subject of discussion between them; the reason it was resisted was explained to him: "If we granted you that, it would look as if you were carrying on your business in our warehouse"; but they said, that, in order to accommodate him they would be willing to insert a tablet, containing his name and business, provided it did not interfere with the architectural decorations of No. 48. These facts are beyond all question. Both parties are agreed. Then the Plaintiff writes a letter in which he offers to let, among other things, the first floor of No. 48. This is answered very readily by the Defendant, who accepts the offer. Instructions are sent to the solicitors, instructions consisting only of this letter. Mr. Marten made a point that the Plaintiff, in his pleadings, said they had no other instructions. They must have had some other instructions. I should read the word "other" used by him in the pleadings as meaning no different instructions, no variation in form or otherwise from the words that appear in the letter. Then the lease is prepared and executed in accordance with the letter, including the first floor of No. 48.

Under these circumstances, the facts being as I have stated, am I, because the lease has been executed under seal, demising to the Defendant that which the Plaintiff never meant to let him have, that which the Defendant says he knew at one time the Plaintiff intended to keep for himself, that which he has never claimed at any period prior to the letter—am I to say that the agreement is to be held to be irrevocable? It would be against every principle that regulates the law relating to mistakes, and it would be directly at variance with the proved facts in this case. On the evidence, it looks like a common mistake. The Defendant, it is true, says in his defence, that he took it on the faith that the first floor of No. 48 was intentionally included in the letter of the 13th of November, 1883. Certainly he never said so until it is said in the defence, which I am looking at now; but he has not said so in his evidence. He has never said that he intended to take that. The argument addressed to me has been this:—"The separation of No. 48 and the blue, is effected solely by means of a brick-on-end partition; and that is easily removed." People building brick-on-end partitions do not mean them to be easily removed, unless there is some purpose to remove them, and here, using the Defendant's own evidence on this occasion, at that time the partition was effectually finished, and the Defendant knew that the Plaintiff intended to reserve it for his own use in his own business. The law being such as I have said, it is not necessary to say anything about how easily you can make holes in a partition, and how you can knock down a partition; you can pull down the front of a house with equal ease if you have proper appliances and proper workmen to do it. The way it is forced on my attention is the reason why the partition was first made, why it was found to be in existence when the Defendant first inspected it, why he knew from that time as well as he knows now that it was never the intention of the Plaintiff that he should have that "magnificent" room which formed one of two rooms which constituted the business place intended by the Plaintiff for his own use, and to which the access was made by one staircase communicating with nothing but the upper room.

But without being certain, as I cannot be certain on the facts before me, whether the mistake was what is called a common mistake—that is, such a common mistake as would induce the Court to strike out of a marriage settlement a provision or limitation—that there was to some extent a common mistake I must in charity and justice to the Defendant believe, because I cannot impute to him the intention of taking advantage of any incorrect expression in this letter. He may have persuaded himself that the letter was right; but if there was not a common mistake it is plain and palpable that the Plaintiff was mistaken, and that he had no intention of letting his own shop, which he had built and carefully constructed for his own purposes.

Upon that ground, therefore, I must say that the contract ought to be annulled. I think it would be right and just and perfectly consistent with other decisions that the Defendant should have an opportunity of choosing whether he will submit, as the Plaintiff asks that he should submit, to have the lease rectified by excluding from it the first floor of No. 48, whether he will choose to take his lease with that rectification, or whether he will choose to throw up the thing entirely, because the object of the Court is, as far as it can, to put the parties into the position in which they would have been if the mistake had not happened. Therefore I give the Defendant an opportunity of saying whether he will or will not submit to rectification. If he does not, then I shall declare that the agreement is annulled. Then we shall have to settle the terms on which it should be annulled. The Plaintiff does not object, if the agreement is annulled, to pay the Defendant any reasonable expenses to which he may have been put by reason of the Plaintiff's mistake; but it must be limited to that. I should like, if it be convenient for counsel or for the parties, to have an answer to the proposition I have made, in order that that may be fully before the persons whom it interests. I may say that I can find no reason for a reduction of the rent. I listened attentively to what Sir John Ellis said, and to what Mr. Farmer said, and I cannot but think that the rent of £500, if the lease is rectified, ought not, with any show of justice, to suffer any reduction.

Marten for the Defendant, agreed to strike out the first floor of No. 48 from the lease; the lease in other respects standing as it was executed.

BACON VC: Then the decree will be, the Defendant electing to have rectification instead of cancellation of the lease, let the lease be rectified by omitting from it all mention of the first floor of No. 48. Then as to the costs of the action, the Plaintiff is not entitled to costs, because he has made a mistake, and the Defendant ought not to have any costs, because his opposition to the Plaintiff's demand has been unreasonable, unjust, and unlawful.

NOTES AND PROBLEMS

1. Compare the approach of the court to a somewhat similar problem in *Alampi v Swartz* (1964), 43 DLR (2d) 11 (Ont CA). *Paget v Marshall* was followed in *Devald v Zigeuner* (1958), 16 DLR (2d) 285 (Ont H Ct J); *Stepps Investments Ltd v Security Capital Corp* (1976), 73 DLR (3d) 351 (Ont H Ct J); and *Murphy's Ltd v Fabricville Co Inc* (1980), 117 DLR (3d) 668 (NSSC (TD)). See, however, *Riverlate Properties Ltd v Paul*, [1975] Ch 133, and "Comment" (1975) 53 Can Bar Rev 340.

2. You are assisting in the drafting of a new Contracts Code. It is to take the form of statutory text, with each section followed by an official comment explaining the purpose and effect of the text. Draft the section or sections (with official comment) on the effect of written documents on contractual relationships.

3. See also McCamus at 587-97; Waddams at paras 336-43; MacDougall at 243-47.

CHAPTER SIX

PROTECTION OF WEAKER PARTIES

I. INTRODUCTION

The materials in this chapter address various categories of situations and correlative legal doctrines that raise questions about the extent to which the legal system should protect weaker parties in the contracting process. Section II addresses the doctrine of contractual incapacity, which renders contracts entered into by minors unenforceable in a wide range of circumstances. Section III deals with the enforceability of forfeiture and penalty clauses in contracts. Section IV deals with the problem of the enforceability of disclaimer, exclusion, or limitation of liability clauses in contracts—often standard form contracts—thus raising similar issues to those addressed in the "ticket" and related cases in Chapter 5, where these terms may not have been read or fully understood by the party against whom they are sought to be enforced. Sections V and VI address a wide variety of residual cases that may fall within the scope of legal doctrines like unconscionability and undue influence, duress, or inequality of bargaining power. In these cases, legal grounds for relief from contractual obligations may be granted if the circumstances provided for exploitation of constrained choices, special relationships, or cognitive incapacities between the contracting parties. These circumstances create asymmetries in the relative abilities of the contracting parties to evaluate information on the potential impact of a contractual transaction on their respective interests. More general philosophical concepts of coercion, information asymmetries, and paternalism are raised in many of these cases (see Trebilcock, ch 4, 5, and 7). Section VII sets out some relevant consumer protection legislation and Section VIII deals with restitution.

II. MINORS

REX V RASH
(1923), 53 OLR 245 (CA)

ROSE J: The question as put in the stated case is whether the magistrate was right as a matter of law in holding that a person under the age of 21 years can be convicted of the offence of removing, concealing, or disposing of any of his property, with intent to defraud his creditors (the *Criminal Code*, sec. 417(1)). To that question, put in that broad way, the answer is: "Yes: an infant, in some circumstances, can incur debts of certain kinds, and can have creditors; and if he disposes of his property with intent to defraud those creditors he can be convicted." But upon the whole case it is apparent that the question intended to be submitted for the opinion of the Court is a much narrower question than the one formally put. It is, in effect: "Are persons who have supplied goods to an infant trader for the purposes of his trade, and who have not been paid, 'creditors' within the meaning of sec. 417?" That is the question which was argued and which must be answered. ...

At common law, certain contracts made by infants are void, in the strict sense, and incapable of ratification: see *Beam v. Beatty* (1902), 3 O.L.R. 345; 4 O.L.R. 554; *Phillips v. Greater Ottawa Development Co.* (1916), 38 O.L.R. 315.

Others are usually described as valid. Such are contracts for necessaries, although, considering the fact that the person who supplied necessaries recovers, not the agreed price, but the value, probably confusion would have been avoided if it had been recognised that, as pointed out by Fletcher Moulton L.J., in *Nash v. Inman*, [1908] 2 K.B. 1, an infant, like a lunatic, is incapable of making a contract of purchase in the strict sense of the words; that, if a man satisfies the needs of an infant or lunatic by supplying to him necessaries, the law will imply an obligation to repay him for the services so rendered, and will enforce that obligation against the estate of the infant or lunatic; that consequently the basis of the action is hardly contract—the obligation arises *re* and not *consensu*.

Contracts of a third (and this the largest) class may be avoided or enforced at the option of the infant: *Bruce v. Warwick* (1815), 6 Taunt. 118; 128 E.R. 978, "The law so far protects him, as to give him an opportunity to consider it when he comes of age; and it is good or voidable at his election": *Holt v. Ward Clarencieux* (1732), 2 Str. 937; 93 E.R. 954. These contracts are usually described as voidable. Contracts, such as are here in question, by which the infant undertakes to pay for goods supplied to him for use in trade are of this class, and what has to be determined is the precise meaning of the word "voidable" as applied to them—is it correct to say quite generally, as in Halsbury's *Laws of England*, vol. 17, p. 64, note (1), that "voidable means valid until repudiated, not invalid until confirmed"; or ought it to be said, as in *Anson on Contracts*, 15th ed., p. 186, that an infant's "voidable" contracts must be divided under two heads, (a) those which are valid and binding on the infant until disaffirmed, and (b) those which are not binding until ratified after majority? If such a division as is suggested by Anson is justified, there is no doubt that contracts such as we have to deal with in this case, will fall into the author's class (b); and that it is justified, will, I think, appear when there are considered, first, some of the cases which have arisen out of contracts by an infant for the purchase of goods (other than necessaries) or out of other contracts which would clearly be in class (b), if there is such a class, and secondly, some of the cases that are usually cited in support of the broad general proposition that voidable means valid until repudiated. ...

[A long discussion of cases is omitted.]

My conclusion accords with that reached, in a civil case, by the Supreme Court of Mississippi in *Edmunds v. Mister* (1881), 58 Miss. 765 (cited in 27 Corpus. Juris., p. 476). There, soon after attaining his majority, a man who, while an infant, had contracted debts (I use the expression in the popular sense) conveyed his property to his daughter for life with reversion to himself, the conveyance being without consideration, and with the avowed intention of defeating "creditors"—although, as the grantor said, he was unwilling to plead infancy and intended to pay his debts. The Court held that the conveyance was valid, because the holders of the demands for goods furnished during the grantor's minority were not creditors. ... For these reasons, my answer to the question submitted is in the negative.

[The concurring opinions of Mulock CJ Ex and Kelly, Masten, and Orde JJ are omitted. See MASTEN J at 253: "If an adult contracts with an infant, the infant can enforce the contract though the adult cannot. This was decided by the Court of King's Bench in 1813 ... and has ever since been accepted as the law. Such a right of action by the infant predicates and necessitates as its foundation, an existing valid contract."]

NOTES

1. Compare the following statements in *Re Sovereign Bank* (1915), 35 OLR 448 (SC (AD)): Middleton J at 453—"No doubt in ordinary cases, an infant is called upon to repudiate within a reasonable time after attaining majority"—and Garrow JA at 456—"An infant may by contract become the holder of shares in a bank. The legal effect of such a contract is the same as that of other voidable contracts of an infant, namely, that it is valid until repudiated. See *Edwards v. Carter*, [1893] A.C. 360 ... . And, the repudiation must, to be effective, take place within a reasonable time after full age is reached." Notice, however, that the court is here dealing with a situation of the kind described by Anson as one "when an infant acquired an interest in permanent property to which obligations attach, etc."

2. In some jurisdictions, the enforceability of infants' contracts is regulated by statute. See e.g. the *Infants Act*, RSBC 1996, c 223.

SALE OF GOODS ACT
RSO 1990, c S.1

3(1) Capacity to buy and sell is regulated by the general law concerning capacity to contract and to transfer and acquire property, but where necessaries are sold and delivered to a minor or to a person who by reason of mental incapacity or drunkenness is incompetent to contract, he or she shall pay a reasonable price therefor.

(2) In this section, "necessaries" means goods suitable to the conditions in life of the minor or other person and to his or her actual requirements at the time of the sale and delivery.

NASH V INMAN
[1908] 2 KB 1 (CA)

The action was brought by specially indorsed writ by a tailor carrying on business in Saville Row, London, for £145 10s. 3d. for clothes supplied to the defendant while an undergraduate at Cambridge University between October 29, 1902, and June 16, 1903. The defendant was an infant at the time of the sale and delivery of the goods. He had been at school at Uppingham, and in October 1902, he went up as a freshman to Trinity College, Cambridge. He was the son of an architect of good position, who had a town house at Hampstead, and a country establishment called Wade Court, near Havant. The clothes supplied to the defendant included, among other things, eleven fancy waistcoats at two guineas each, or £1 15s. for cash. Upon an application for judgment under Order xiv., the defendant set up the plea of infancy, and the action was adjourned into Court and was tried before Ridley J. and in a special jury. At the trial the plaintiff claimed only £122 19s. 6d., the cash price of the goods, in lieu of £145 10s. 3d., the credit price. The only witness called on behalf of the plaintiff was a travel-ler in his employ, who stated that he went to Cambridge and other places to solicit orders for the plaintiff, and that, hearing that the defendant was spending money freely and was likely to be a good customer, he called upon him personally at his lodgings in Cambridge and obtained the first order for clothes; and he gave evidence as to the goods supplied, and stated that they were charged for at the usual prices.

Counsel for the defendant thereupon submitted that, subject to his formally prov-ing infancy, which was not admitted, there was no evidence to go to the jury, and he called the defendant's father, who proved the date of the defendant's birth, and then went on to state that he was satisfied that his son on going to the university was amply supplied with proper clothes according to his position; and he gave particulars of his outfit. The learned judge then held that there was no evidence to go to the jury that the goods were necessaries, and directed judgment to be entered for the defendant.

The plaintiff applied for judgment or a new trial, on the ground that the judge himself had decided the issues of fact instead of leaving them to the jury.

COZENS-HARDY MR: This case is undoubtedly one of difficulty and also, I think, one of importance. It is an action by a tailor against Mr. Inman, who was at the date of the transactions in question an infant. There were no pleadings in the action. There was merely a hint and an application under Order xiv., and the action was adjourned into Court, and came on for trial before Ridley J. and a special jury. In substance the position is this: The plaintiff sues the defendant for goods sold and delivered. The defendant pleads infancy at the date of the sale, and his plea is proved. What is the consequence of that? The consequence of that is that the *Infants' Relief Act, 1874*, becomes applicable. Under that Act all contracts for goods supplied are absolutely void, the only exception being contracts for necessaries. Then s. 2 of the *Sale of Goods Act, 1893*, provides as follows: "Capacity to buy and sell is regulated by the general law concerning capacity to contract, and to transfer and acquire property." That, of course, includes the Act of 1874. Then follows this proviso: "Provided that where necessaries are sold and delivered to an infant, or minor, or to a person who by reason of mental incapacity or drunkenness is incompetent to contract, he must pay a reasonable price therefor." The section then defines necessaries as follows: "Necessaries in this section mean goods suitable to the condition in life of such infant or minor or other person, and to his actual requirements at the time of the sale and delivery." What is the effect of that? The plaintiff sues for goods sold and delivered. The defendant pleads infancy. The plaintiff must then reply, "The goods sold were necessaries within the meaning of the definition in s. 2 of the *Sale of Goods Act, 1893*." It is not sufficient, in my view, for him to say, "I have discharged the onus which rests upon me if I simply shew that the goods supplied were suitable to the condition in life of the infant at the time."

There is another branch of the definition which cannot be disregarded. Having shewn that the goods were suitable to the condition in life of the infant, he must then go on to shew that they were suitable to his actual requirement at the time of the sale and delivery. Unless he establishes that fact, either by evidence adduced by himself or by cross-examination of the defendant's witnesses, as the case may be, in my opinion he has not discharged the burden which the law imposes upon him. Our attention has been called by Mr. McCardie, in his very able and learned argument, to a number of authorities going back for a very long period, which he said established that the burden on a plaintiff who supplied goods to an infant was simply to shew that the goods were of a class which might be necessaries, having regard to the position in life of the defendant and his family, and that, unless the judge withdrew the case from the jury on the ground that the articles in question could not be necessaries, it was for the jury to find as a matter of fact, Aye or No, were these articles necessaries. It had never, he said, been the law that the plaintiff was required to go into the question, which might present great difficulties, of whether or not the goods were actually required by the defendant at the date of the sale, or, in other words, to say what was the state of the defendant's wardrobe at the time when the goods were ordered.

I think there is very great force up to a certain point in that argument. But it must be remembered that the law on this subject has been developed and altered in the course of the last century. It was until quite recently doubted whether it was even admissible to prove that the infant was supplied with goods of the class—being goods which might properly be necessary—at the date when the contract was made, so that he really did not want any more. It was not until the decision of the Divisional Court in *Barnes v. Toye*, 13 Q.B.D. 410, in 1884, overruling the direction given by A.L. Smith J., that it could be said to be at all established that that was even admissible evidence unless you went further and proved that the plaintiff knew he was sufficiently supplied. The point arose again in *Johnstone v. Marks* (1887), 19 Q.B.D. 509, before what was no doubt a Divisional Court, but it was composed of three members of the Court of Appeal, Lord Esher M.R., Lindley L.J., and Lopes L.J. In that case the county court judge had rejected evidence to prove that the defendant was sufficiently supplied with clothes at the time of the sale. Lord Esher said: "I am of opinion that the evidence was improperly rejected. It lies upon the plaintiff to prove, not that the goods supplied belong to the class of necessaries as distinguished from that of luxuries, but that the goods supplied when supplied were necessaries to the infant. The circumstance that the infant was sufficiently supplied at the time of the additional supply is obviously material to this issue, as well as fatal to the contention of the plaintiff with respect to it." Lindley L.J. said: "If an infant can be made liable for articles which may be necessaries without proof that they are necessaries, there is an end to the protection which the law gives him. If he has enough of such articles, more cannot possibly be necessary to him." Although it may be true that the language which I have just read from the judgments of Lord Esher and Lindley L.J. goes further than was absolutely necessary for the decision of the case, that language is perfectly clear and unambiguous, and seems to me to be logically involved in the definition of necessaries. ...

The learned judge ruled as a matter of law that there was no evidence fit to be submitted to the jury that these articles, or any of them, were necessaries within the meaning of the statutory definition, and, thinking, as I do that there was no evidence in support of that which was a necessary issue, I cannot say that the learned judge was wrong in the view which he took. We have scarcely heard any suggestion that there was even a scintilla of evidence to support that which is an affirmative issue, that the goods were suitable to the requirements of the infant. Nay more, I think, if the matter had been left to the jury, and the jury had found that they were suitable to the require-ments of the infant at that time, and application had been made for a new trial, it would have been the duty of this Court to grant a new trial on the ground that there was no evidence to support the verdict, and that it was perverse. Under these cir-cumstances it seems to me that this appeal fails, and that there is no ground for interfering with the judgment which was entered for the defendant.

FLETCHER MOULTON LJ: I am of the same opinion. I think that the difficulty and at the same time the suggestion of hardship to the plaintiff in such a case as this disap-pear when one considers what is the true basis of an action against an infant for necessaries. It is usually spoken of as a case of enforcing a contract against the infant, but I agree with the view expressed by the Court in *Rhodes v. Rhodes* (1890), 44 Ch. D. 94, in the parallel case of a claim for necessaries against a lunatic, that this lan-guage is somewhat unfortunate. An infant, like a lunatic, is incapable of making a contract of purchase in the strict sense of the words; but if a man satisfied the needs of the infant or lunatic by supplying to him necessaries, the law will imply an obliga-tion to repay him for the services rendered, and will enforce that obligation against the estate of the infant or lunatic. The consequence is that the basis of the action is hardly contract. Its real foundation is an obligation which the law imposes on the infant to make a fair payment in respect of needs satisfied. In other words the obliga-tion arises *re* and not *consensu*. I do not mean that this nicety of legal phraseology has been adhered to. The common and convenient phrase is that an infant is liable for goods sold and delivered provided that they are necessaries, and there is no objection to that phraseology so long as its true meaning is understood. But the treatment of such actions by the Courts of Common Law has been in accordance with that principle I have referred to. That the articles were necessaries had to be alleged and proved by the plaintiff as part of his case, and the sum he recovered was based on a *quantum meruit*. If he claimed anything beyond this he failed, and it did not help him that he could prove that the prices were agreed prices. All this is very ancient law, and is confirmed by the provisions of s. 2 of the *Sale of Goods Act, 1893*—an Act which was intended to codify the existing law. That section expressly provides that the consequence of necessaries sold and delivered to an infant is that he must pay a reasonable price therefor.

    The *Sale of Goods Act, 1893*, gives a statutory definition of what are necessaries in a legal sense, which entirely removes any doubt, if any doubt previously existed, as to what that word in legal phraseology means. ... Hence, if an action is brought by one who claims to enforce against an infant such an obligation, it is obvious that the plaintiff in order to prove his case must shew that the goods supplied come within this definition. That a plaintiff has to make out his case is, I should have thought, the first lesson that any one studying English law would learn; and the elaborate argument of Mr. McCardie that if you look at the authorities in the past, going back nearly a hundred years, you will find cases in which particular defendants might have taken a higher standpoint and insisted upon a right which they did not insist on does not appear to me to touch the plain and obvious conclusion that in order to succeed in the action the plaintiff must shew that he has supplied neces-saries. That is to say, the plaintiff has to shew, first, that the goods were suitable to the condition in life of the infant; and secondly, that they were suitable to his actual requirements at the time—or, in other words, that the infant had not at the time an adequate supply from other sources. ...

The issue is not only whether the articles in question were suitable to the defendant's condition in life, but whether they were suitable to his actual requirements at the time of the sale and delivery; and how does the evidence stand? The evidence for the plaintiff shewed that one of his travellers, hearing that a freshman at Trinity College was spending money pretty liberally, called on him to get an order for clothes, and sold him within nine months goods which at cash price came to over £120, including an extravagant number of waistcoats and other articles of clothing, and that is all that the plaintiff proved. The defendant's father proved the infancy, and then proved that the defendant had an adequate supply of clothes, and stated what they were. That evidence was uncontradicted. Not only was it not contradicted by any other evidence, but there was no cross-examination tending to shake the credit of the witness, against whose character and means of knowledge nothing could be said. On that uncontradicted evidence the judge came to the conclusion that there was no evidence on which the jury might properly find that these goods were necessary to the actual requirements of the infant at the time of sale and delivery, and therefore, in accordance with the duty of the judge in all cases of trial by jury, he withdrew the case from the jury and directed judgment to be entered for the defendant. In my opinion he was justified by the practice of the Court in so doing, and this appeal must be dismissed.

[The concurring opinion of Buckley LJ is omitted. See also Waddams, ch 18 and 19; MacDougall at 185-88.]

NOTES

1. With the expanding availability of online contracts, courts have had to deal with the enforceability of these transactions when the signatory who clicks through them is a minor. In Canada, the law is that contracts with infants are voidable unless they are for "necessaries." With regard to online contracts and whether they are treated differently, there does not appear to be any reported decisions in Canada. In the United States, the law is different when dealing with minors and online agreements. In *AV v iParadigms LLC*, No 08-1424 (4th Cir 2009), a group of high school students brought a copyright infringement claim based on the use of an "online technology system" in its plagiarism detection service. The high school subscribed to the service, which required students to submit their essays through a web-based system and which would digitally store the work submitted by students. In order to submit an assignment, "a student must create a user profile on the web site, a process that requires the student to click on 'I Agree' under the 'terms of agreement' or 'Clickwrap Agreement.'" Part of the agreement contained a limitation of liability clause, maintaining that the services offered were "conditioned on [the user's] acceptance without modification of the terms, conditions, and notices contained herein," and that "[i]n no event shall iParadigms ... be liable for any ... damages arising out of or in any way connected with the use of this web site." The district court had refused to void the contract based on the doctrine of infancy, concluding that the plaintiffs could not use the doctrine as a "sword" to void the contract but retain its benefits ("high school credit and standing to bring this action"). The findings on the copyright infringement claim were upheld on appeal.

2. Similarly, the court would not allow the infancy defence in *EKD v Facebook, Inc*, 885 F Supp 2d 894, 2012 WL 324392, 4 (SDIII). There, Facebook invoked a forum selection clause found in its terms of service when minors brought a claim against it. With regard to whether the terms of service were void or voidable on the basis that the plaintiffs were minors, the court maintained that "[t]he infancy defense may not be used inequitably to retain the benefits

of a contract while reneging on the obligations attached to that benefit" and upheld the forum selection clause. However, see *IB ex rel Fife v Facebook, Inc*, F Supp 2d 989 (NDCal 2012), where the court distinguished *EKD* on the basis that it was limited to enforcing a forum selection clause, and not the entire agreement.

III. FORFEITURES AND PENALTY CLAUSES

SHATILLA V FEINSTEIN
[1923] 3 DLR 1035 (Sask CA)

[Feinstein carried on business as a wholesale drygoods merchant in Saskatoon, and on April 16, 1920, sold his business to Shatilla on the express understanding that Feinstein and his brother, who were most active in the business, would not compete within the corporate limits of Saskatoon for five years. They agreed to pay $10,000 on breach of the covenant recoverable on each and every such breach as liquidated damages and not as a penalty. In 1921 Feinstein became a shareholder and director of Harley Henry Ltd., which engaged in the wholesale drygoods business. Shatilla sued to recover on the covenant. The trial judge held the covenant to be a penalty and unenforceable, but he also held that there had been a breach and directed a reference to ascertain actual damages. The plaintiff appealed on the ground, among others not here material, that the covenant was valid as a genuine pre-estimate of liquidated damages.]

MARTIN JA (for the court): ...

[9] The main question to be determined is whether or not the sum fixed by the covenant is a penalty, or whether it is recoverable by way of liquidated damages. When the damages which may arise out of the breach of a contract are in their nature uncertain, the law permits the parties to agree beforehand as to the amount to be paid in case of breach. Whether such an agreement has been made by the parties or not, or whether the sum agreed upon is a penalty, must depend upon the circumstances of each case. If the sum fixed is in excess of any actual damage which can possibly arise from the breach of the contract, the sum fixed as damage is not considered to be a *bona fide* pre-estimate of the damage. The same principle is applied when the payment of a larger sum is stipulated in the event of the breach of a covenant to pay a smaller sum. In the case of a contract containing a single stipulation which, if broken at all, can be broken once only—such as a covenant not to reveal a trade secret—when the parties have agreed to the amount which shall be paid in case of breach and referred to such sum as liquidated damages, there would appear to be no reason, on the authorities, why the Court should not treat such sum as liquidated damages. If, however, the covenant is one which is capable of being broken more than once, such as an agreement not to solicit the customers of a firm, or an agreement not to sell certain specified articles below a certain price, the question is a more difficult one. In such a case, however, the damage in the case of each breach is of the same kind, and the fact that such damage may vary in amount for each breach has not been held by the Courts to raise a presumption that the sum agreed upon is a penalty, particularly where the parties have agreed to the sum as liquidated damages. This, I think, is a fair deduction from the decision in the House of Lords in *Dunlop Pneumatic Tyre Co. Ltd. v. New Garage and Motor Co.*, [1915] A.C. 79.

[10] In cases, however, where it is agreed to pay a fixed sum on the breach of a number of stipulations of various degrees of importance, a presumption is said to

be raised against the sum so fixed being treated as liquidated damages, even though the parties have referred to it as such; that is, there is a presumption against the parties having pre-estimated the damages. The damage likely to accrue from breaches of various kinds in such a case is different in kind and amount, and a separate estimate in the case of each breach would be necessary. Such a presumption may, however, be rebutted if it is shown on the face of the agreement, or on the evidence, that the parties have taken into consideration the different amounts of damages that might occur, and had actually arrived at an amount which was considered proper under all the circumstances. Even then, however, the amount fixed must not be extravagant or unreasonable.

• • •

[24] The covenant in the present case covers a number of matters which would constitute breach of it. It provides that the defendant shall not

> carry on or be engaged in or take part in or be in any way interested in the business of wholesale drygoods, etc.

[25] This, the main portion of the covenant, is further described by words preceding it:

> directly or indirectly, either as principal or agent or as director or manager of a company, or as a servant in any capacity.

[26] There could be many breaches of this covenant, some of which would be very important, others of a less important and even trivial character. For instance, if the defendant had engaged as a clerk with some one carrying on a similar business, or if he purchased a small amount of stock in a similar business, it could scarcely be said that such action would cause serious damage to the plaintiffs, nor that it would constitute an important breach of the agreement; certainly it would seem "extravagant and unconscionable" that for either one of such breaches he should pay damages amounting to $10,000. On the other hand, if he actually went into business in partnership with some one or carried on a competing business on his own account, or became manager of a company carrying on a similar business, or purchased a large interest in a similar concern carrying on business as a company and became a director of such company, such breaches would be of an important character and might conceivably cause serious damage to the plaintiffs. The covenant provides for the payment of a lump sum upon the occurrence of any one of a number of things differing in importance, and some of them trivial in character, and where a sum is stipulated to be paid as liquidated damages, and is payable not on the happening of a single event but of one or more of a number of events, some of which might result in inconsiderable damage, the Court may decline to construe the words "liquidated damages" according to their ordinary meaning and may treat such a sum as a penalty. Lord Dunedin, in the *Dunlop* case, [1915] A.C. at p. 89, considers that if there are various breaches to which an indiscriminate sum is applied, "then the strength of the chain must be taken to be its weakest link," and if it can be seen clearly that the loss in one particular breach could never amount to the sum stated then the conclusion that the sum is a penalty may be reached. I think this statement of the law is peculiarly applicable to the facts of the present case.

PROBLEM

Draft a clause for Shatilla that would have achieved his object.

HF CLARKE LIMITED V THERMIDAIRE CORP LTD
[1976] 1 SCR 319, 54 DLR (3d) 385

[Clarke agreed to distribute (as sole distributor) a product manufactured by Thermidaire and not to sell competing products. He further agreed that "in the event of breach by Clarke of this covenant pertaining to competitive products, Clarke shall pay to Thermidaire by way of liquidated damages an amount equal to the gross trading profit realized through the sale of such competitive products." In breach of contract (found by the trial judge to be "unscrupulous, brazen and flagrant"), Clarke did sell competing products. The trial judge and the Ontario Court of Appeal held the liquidated damages clause to be enforceable, the latter court stressing that there were elements of Thermidaire's loss that were difficult to calculate, such as loss of product identification. The Supreme Court of Canada, however, reversed.]

LASKIN CJC: The primary concern in breach of contract cases ... is compensation, and judicial interference with the enforcement of what the courts regard as penalty clauses is simply a manifestation of a concern for fairness and reasonableness, rising above contractual stipulation, whenever the parties seek to remove from the courts their ordinary authority to determine not only whether there has been a breach but what damages may be recovered as a result thereof. ...

I regard the exaction of gross trading profits as a penalty in this case because it is, in my opinion, a grossly excessive and punitive response to the problem to which it was addressed; and the fact that the appellant subscribed to it, and may have been foolish to do so, does not mean that it should be left to rue its unwisdom. ...

... The fact that the highest amount put forward by the respondent as its actual loss was $92,017 [this figure was based on estimated loss of profits] is plainly indicative of the disproportion that resides in the exaction of gross trading profits of $239,449.05.

STOCKLOSER V JOHNSON
[1954] 1 QB 476 (CA)

The plaintiff agreed to buy certain plant and machinery from the defendant. The price was payable in instalments, and the agreement provided that in case of default by the purchaser, the vendor was entitled (after giving notice) to retake possession of the machinery and to retain all payments made by the purchaser. The purchaser did default, and now claims the return of the instalments paid.

DENNING LJ: There was acute contest as to the proper legal principles to apply in this case. On the one hand [counsel for the plaintiff] urged us to hold that the buyer was entitled to recover the instalments at law. He said that the forfeiture clause should be ignored as it was of a penal character; and once it was ignored it meant that the buyer was left with a simple right to repayment of his money ... subject only to a cross-claim for damages. In asking us to ignore the forfeiture clause, [counsel for the plaintiff] relied on the familiar tests which are used to distinguish between penalties and liquidated damages. ... There is, I think, a plain distinction between penalty cases, strictly so called, and cases like the present.

It is this: when one party seeks to exact a penalty from the other, he is seeking to exact payment of an extravagant sum either by action at law or by appropriating to himself moneys belonging to [the other party]. The claimant invariably relies, like

Shylock, on the letter of the contract to support his demand, but the courts decline to give him their aid because they will not assist him in an act of oppression. ...

In the present case, however, the seller is not seeking to exact a penalty. He only wants to keep money which already belongs to him. The money was handed to him in part payment of the purchase price, and, as soon as it was paid, it belonged to him absolutely. He did not obtain it by extortion or oppression or anything of that sort, and there is an express clause—a forfeiture clause, if you please—permitting him to keep it. It is not the case of a seller seeking to enforce a penalty, but a buyer seeking restitution of money paid. If the buyer is to recover it, he must, I think, have recourse to somewhat different principles from those applicable to penalties, strictly so called.

On the other hand, [counsel for the defendant] urged us to hold that the buyer could only recover the money if he was able and willing to perform the contract, and for this purpose he ought to pay or offer to pay the instalments which were in arrears and be willing to pay the future instalments as they became due; ... I think that this contention goes too far in the opposite direction. If the buyer was seeking to re-establish the contract, he would of course have to pay up the arrears and to show himself willing to perform the contract in the future, just as a lessee, who has suffered a forfeiture, has to do when he seeks to re-establish the lease. So also if the buyer were seeking specific performance he would have to show himself able and willing to perform his part. But the buyer's object here is not to re-establish the contract. It is to get his money back, and to do this I do not think that it is necessary to go so far as to show that he is ready and willing to perform the contract.

I reject, therefore, the arguments of counsel at each extreme. It seems to me that the cases show the law to be this: (1) *When there is no forfeiture clause.* If money is handed over in part payment of the purchase price, and then the buyer makes default as to the balance, then so long as the seller keeps the contract open and available for perform-ance, the buyer cannot recover the money; but once the seller rescinds the contract or treats it as at an end owing to the buyer's default, then the buyer is entitled to recover his money by action at law subject to a cross-claim by the seller for damages: ... (2) *But when there is a forfeiture clause or the money is expressly paid as a deposit (which is equivalent to a forfeiture clause)*, then the buyer who is in default cannot recover the money at law at all. He may, however, have a remedy in equity, for, despite the express stipulation in the contract, equity can relieve the buyer from forfeiture of the money and order the seller to repay it on such terms as the court thinks fit. ...

The difficulty is to know what are the circumstances which give rise to this equity. ... Two things are necessary: first, the forfeiture clause must be of a penal nature, in this sense, that the sum forfeited must be out of all proportion to the dam-age, and, secondly, it must be unconscionable for the seller to retain the money. ...

In the course of the argument before us Somervell L.J. put an illustration which shows the necessity for this equity even though the buyer is not ready and willing to perform the contract. Suppose a buyer has agreed to buy a necklace by instal-ments, and the contract provides that, on default in payment of any one instalment, the seller is entitled to rescind the contract and forfeit the instalments already paid. The buyer pays 90 per cent of the price but fails to pay the last instalment. He is not able to perform the contract because he simply cannot find the money. The seller thereupon rescinds the contract and retakes the necklace and resells it at a higher price. Surely equity will relieve the buyer against forfeiture of the money on such terms as may be just.

Again, suppose that a vendor of property, in lieu of the usual 10 per cent deposit, stipulates for an initial payment of 50 per cent of the price as a deposit and part payment; and later, when the purchaser fails to complete, the vendor resells the property at a profit and in addition claims to forfeit the 50 per cent deposit. Surely the court will relieve against the forfeiture. The vendor cannot forestall this equity by describing an extravagant sum as a deposit, any more than he can recover a penalty by calling it liquidated damages. ...

[Denning LJ concluded that in this particular case it was not unconscionable for the vendor to retain the money. Somervell and Romer LJJ agreed in the result, but Romer LJ expressly dissented from Denning LJ's view of the power of the court to relieve against forfeiture. He thought that the powers of the court ought to be considerably narrower. See also Waddams at para 468.]

NOTES

1. The common law principles dealing with penalties have been generally based on the House of Lords' judgment in *Dunlop Pneumatic Tyre Co, Ltd v New Garage and Motor Co, Ltd*, [1915] AC 79, which was based on a clause, where the pre-estimate of damages was a fixed sum: "We agree to pay to the Dunlop company the sum of 5 pounds for each and every tyre, cover, or tube sold or offered in breach of this agreement, as and by way of liquidated damages and not as a penalty." The principles on the distinction between penalty clauses and liquidated damages were provided in the judgment of Lord Dunedin:

1. Though the parties to a contract who use the words "penalty" or "liquidated damages" may prima facie be supposed to mean what they say, yet the expression used is not conclusive. The Court must find out whether the payment stipulated is in truth a penalty or liquidated damages ...
2. The essence of a penalty is a payment of money stipulated as in terrorem of the offending party; the essence of liquidated damages is a genuine covenanted pre-estimate of damage ...
3. The question whether a sum stipulated is penalty or liquidated damages is a question of construction to be decided upon the terms and inherent circumstances of each particular contract, judged as at the time of the making of the contract, not as at the time of the breach ...
4. To assist this task of construction various tests have been suggested ... . Such are:
   (a) It will be held to be penalty if the sum stipulated for is extravagant and unconscionable in amount in comparison with the greatest loss that could conceivably be proved to have followed from the breach ...
   (b) It will be held to be a penalty if the breach consists only in not paying a sum of money, and the sum stipulated is a sum greater than the sum which ought to have been paid ...
   (c) There is a presumption (but no more) that it is penalty when "a single lump sum is made payable by way of compensation, on the occurrence of one or more or all of several events, some of which may occasion serious and others but trifling damage." ...

   On the other hand:
   (d) It is no obstacle to the sum stipulated being a genuine pre-estimate of damage, that the consequences of the breach are such as to make precise pre-estimation almost an impossibility. On the contrary, that is just the situation when it is probable that pre-estimated damage was the true bargain between the parties.

2. In *Elsley Estate v JG Collins Ins Agencies*, [1978] 2 SCR 916, the Supreme Court determined that when the actual loss is greater than the penalty clause, the amount in the penalty

clause would be the upper limit on the damage awarded. Speaking for a unanimous court, Dickson J held:

> It is now evident that the power to strike down a penalty clause is a blatant interference with freedom of contract and is designed for the sole purpose of providing relief against oppression for the party having to pay the stipulated sum. It has no place where there is no oppression. If the actual loss turns out to exceed the penalty, the normal rules of enforcement of contract apply to allow recovery of only the agreed sum. The party imposing penalty should not be able to obtain the benefit of whatever intimidating force the penalty clause may have in inducing performance, and then ignore the clause when it turns out to be to his advantage to do so. A penalty clause should function as a limitation on the damages recoverable while still being ineffective to increase damages above the actual loss sustained when such loss is less than the stipulated amount. ... Of course, if an agreed sum is a valid liquidated damages clause, the plaintiff is entitled at law to recover this sum regardless of the actual loss sustained.
>
> In the context of the present discussion of the measure of damages, the result is that an agreed sum payable on breach represents the maximum amount recoverable whether the sum is a penalty or a valid liquidated damages clause. [at 937]

3. In *McKeen v The Mortgage Makers Inc and Libby*, 2009 NBCA 61, the court attempted to resolve the three cases (*Dunlop*, *Thermidaire*, and *Elsley Estate*) by providing the following summary (at para 38): "One way of resolving this apparent conflict is to reformulate the applicable rules as follows: A clause providing a fixed sum representing a genuine pre-estimate of damages will be deemed enforceable unless at the time of the breach the amount fixed is deemed extravagant or unconscionable."

4. Using the doctrine of unconscionability to analyze the enforceability of penalty clauses in a contract is not new. In 1976, in "Unconscionability in Contracts" (1976) Mod L Rev 369 at 373-75, Stephen Waddams advocated that "clarity, justice and, in the long run, certainty, would be served by an open recognition of a principle of unconscionability." Cases since then have also used the doctrine of unconscionability. In *Birch v Union of Taxation Employees, Local 70030*, 2008 ONCA 809, 93 OR (3d) 1, leave to appeal denied, the issue was whether a union is entitled to enforce a fine against strike-breaking members pursuant to the provisions in the union constitution. Instead of approaching the issue from the common law rule against penalty clauses, the Ontario Court of Appeal opted to look at whether the clause was unconscionable, thereby adopting an approach suggested in *obiter* by Sharpe JA in *869163 Ontario Ltd v Torrey Springs II Associates Ltd Partnership (2005)* (*sub nom Peachtree II Associates-Dallas LP v 857486 Ontario Ltd*) (2005), 76 OR (3d) 362, 200 OAC 159, leave to appeal refused, [2005] SCCA No 420. See also Kevin E Davis, "Penalty Clauses Through the Lens of Unconscionability Doctrine: Birch v Union of Taxation Employees, Local 70030" (2010) 55 McGill LJ 151. For other commentary on the issue, see *Yarra Capital Group Pty Ltd v Sklash Pty Ltd*, [2006] VSCA 109, which suggests that "unconscionability" is an additional basis on which to have a penalty struck down; *Hav-A-Kar Leasing Ltd v Vekselshtein*, 2012 ONCA 826, [2012] OJ No 5592 (QL), which upheld the trial judge's findings that "the accelerated amount provided for in the challenged provision of the Lease ... 'is not excessive or unconscionable' and that it 'merely puts [Hav-A-Kar] in the position it would have been in if [ZV] had performed his obligations under the contract'" (para 49); John Carter and Elisabeth Peden, "A Good Faith Perspective on Liquidated Damages" (2007) 23 Journal of Contract Law 157; MacDougall at 368-78; and S Waddams, "Abusive or Unconscionable Clauses from a Common Law Perspective" (2010) 49 Can Bus LJ 378.

5. While the majority of penalty clause cases fall within the commercial law context, the analysis is also applicable in the family law context. See *Dundas v Schafer*, 2014 MBCA 92.

6. *Andrews v Australia and New Zealand Banking Group Ltd*, [2012] HCA 30 involved a class action lawsuit where customers sued ANZ Bank with regard to "service fees" being charged by the bank for their account transactions. In a controversial decision, a unanimous High Court

of Australia determined that the penalty doctrine can be applied to bank fees that were levied on customers for incidences that were not breaches of contract. The UK Supreme Court declined to follow *Andrews* in *Cavendish Square Holding BV v Talal El Makdessi; ParkingEye Limited v Beavis*, [2015] UKSC 67. Similarly, in *Paciocco v Australia and New Zealand Banking Group Limited*, [2016] HCA 28, the High Court of Australia dealt with the issue of whether late payment fees applied to credit cards could be classified as penalties and should be unenforceable. A majority of the court held they were not void as penalties, and maintained that costs outside the "direct costs" of contractual breach can be considered when determining whether an amount can be classified as a penalty.

7. For further reading, see Prince Saprai, "The Penalties Rule and the Promise Theory of Contract" (2013) 26 Can JL & Jur 443 and Katy Barnett, "Paciocco v Australia and New Zealand Banking Group Ltd: Are Late Payment Fees on Credit Cards Enforceable?" (2015) 37 Sydney L Rev 595.

IV. CLAUSES EXCLUDING LIABILITY

MARGARET J RADIN, *Boilerplate, the Fine Print,*
Vanishing Rights, and the Rule of Law
(Princeton, NJ: Princeton University Press, 2013)
at 138-40 (footnotes omitted)

It is not unusual for boilerplate to eliminate tort remedies, such as all damages for personal injury, by means of what are called "exculpatory clauses." For example, many contracts that you might sign at a fitness studio or at a summer camp to which you take your children provide that the establishment will not be liable for any injury it may cause to you or your children, no matter what the cause .... The question arises whether such a waiver can be valid.

Courts have tended to look at exculpatory clauses in contracts differently depending on the level of fault (in tort) of the injurer. Probably no court would enforce the aspect of a blanket exculpatory clause that would immunize the injurer from harm inflicted intentionally on a person, because that would allow a boilerplate contract to excuse a crime—the crime of assault. Nor would most courts enforce the aspect of a blanket exculpatory clause that would immunize the injurer from paying damages for harm caused by its own recklessness or gross negligence. Such contractual clauses would be declared violative of public policy.

In view of these judicial limits on enforcement, why do firms nonetheless use blanket exculpatory clauses that purport to immunize them against all injuries including death, and no matter how caused? ... Perhaps the firm hopes (or even knows) that the clause will deter some people from even thinking about suing them. Most people, supposing that they read the clause, probably would be unaware that an over-reaching aspect of the clause would be held invalid in their jurisdiction. Some who consult an attorney may know that the question whether the clause would be held invalid as applied to their particular case is in doubt and would be expensive to adjudicate, because the validity of the clause would have to be litigated in addition to the particular events that caused the injury.

Although courts would most likely uniformly invalidate as against public policy exculpatory clauses that immunize intentional harm or reckless or grossly negligent behavior causing harm (and thus many of the clauses in use today are unenforceable to the extent that they cover harm *however caused*), some courts now do enforce exculpatory clauses insofar as they apply to merely negligent behavior. One often finds such clauses in boilerplate deployed by gyms, training facilities, summer camps, resorts, and tour companies ... . Anecdotal evidence suggests that firms are using these clauses because their insurance companies make it a condition of their coverage. ...

Exculpatory clauses for merely negligent harm-causing behavior are upheld against public policy challenge in many states, but not uniformly. Some courts now hold that they are generally enforceable; others that they are enforceable unless they relate to essential services, or unless the parties have unequal bargaining power. A few courts still adhere to the older view that such clauses are generally unenforceable if they fall into the categories delineated in a California case from the early 1960s.

It seems that the argument in favor of exculpation for harm caused by negligence (which would otherwise subject the firm to tort liability) is that it is efficient to force clients and customers to bear the risk of harm because it will incentivize them to bear the cost of insuring against it. Many would see this as a weak rationale for validating these clauses. For one thing, this practice seems to entail some risk of moral hazard. ("Moral hazard" refers to the risk that firms may not take the proper level of precaution against accidents causing harm to customers if no liability ensues for their negligence.) Also, to the extent that insurance companies require their insureds to impose these clauses on their clients or customers, insurance companies seem to be insuring firms against liability they will not have to cover, since as a condition of coverage the insurance company is requiring the firm to disclaim liability and shunt it to the client or customer.

If the real argument in support of allowing firms to exculpate themselves from tort liability for their own negligence is not this weak efficiency argument, but is simply an argument based on "freedom of contract," one would expect to find courts making a distinction between how they evaluate such a clause in a commercial contract between parties who have apparently engaged in cognizant risk allocation versus how they evaluate it in a boilerplate rights deletion scheme. Some courts will make this distinction, and some will not.

GEORGE MITCHELL LTD V FINNEY LOCK SEEDS LTD
[1983] QB 284 (CA), aff'd [1983] 2 AC 803 (HL)

LORD DENNING MR:

THE HEYDAY OF FREEDOM OF CONTRACT

None of you nowadays will remember the trouble we had—when I was called to the Bar—with exemption clauses. They were printed in small print on the back of tickets and order forms and invoices. They were contained in catalogues or timetables. They were held to be binding on any person who took them without objection. No one ever did object. He never read them or knew what was in them. No matter how unreasonable they were, he was bound. All this was done in the name of "freedom of contract." But the freedom was all on the side of the big concern which had the use of the printing press. No freedom for the little man who took the ticket or order form or invoice. The big concern said, "Take it or leave it." The little man had no option but to take it. The big concern could and did exempt itself from liability in its own interest without regard to the little man. It got away with it time after time. When the courts said to the big concern, "You must put it in clear words," the big concern had no hesitation in doing so. It knew well that the little man would never read the exemption clauses or understand them.

It was a bleak winter for our law of contract. It is illustrated by two cases, *Thompson v. London, Midland and Scottish Railway Co.* [1930] 1 K.B. 41 (in which there was exemption from liability, not on the ticket, but only in small print at the back of the timetable, and the company were held not liable) and *L'Estrange v. F. Graucob Ltd.* [1934] 2 K.B. 394 (in which there was complete exemption in small print at the bottom of the order form, and the company were held not liable).

THE SECRET WEAPON

Faced with this abuse of power—by the strong against the weak—by the use of the small print of the conditions—the judges did what they could to put a curb upon it. They still had before them the idol, "freedom of contract." They still knelt down and worshipped it, but they concealed under their cloaks a secret weapon. They used it to stab the idol in the back. This weapon was called "the true construction of the contract." They used it with great skill and ingenuity. They used it so as to depart from the natural meaning of the words of the exemption clause and to put upon them a strained and unnatural construction. In case after case, they said that the words were not strong enough to give the big concern exemption from liability; or that in the circumstances the big concern was not entitled to rely on the exemption clause. If a ship deviated from the contractual voyage, the owner could not rely on the exemption clause. If a warehouseman stored the goods in the wrong warehouse, he could not pray in aid the limitation clause. If the seller supplied goods different in kind from those contracted for, he could not rely on any exemption from liability. If a shipowner delivered goods to a person without production of the bill of lading, he could not escape responsibility by reference to an exemption clause. In short, whenever the wide words—in their natural meaning—would give rise to an unreasonable result, the judges either rejected them as repugnant to the main purpose of the contract, or else cut them down to size in order to produce a reasonable result. ...

But when the clause was itself reasonable and gave rise to a reasonable result, the judges upheld it; at any rate, when the clause did not exclude liability entirely but only limited it to a reasonable amount. So where goods were deposited in a cloakroom or sent to a laundry for cleaning, it was quite reasonable for the company to limit their liability to a reasonable amount, having regard to the small charge made for the service. ...

FUNDAMENTAL BREACH

No doubt has ever been cast thus far by anyone. But doubts arose when in this court—in *Karsales (Harrow) Ltd. v. Wallis* [1956] 1 W.L.R. 936—we ventured to suggest that if the big concern was guilty of a breach which went to the "very root" of the contract—sometimes called a "fundamental breach"—or at other times a "total failure" of its obligations—then it could not rely on the printed clause to exempt itself from liability. ...

But we did make a mistake—in the eyes of some—in elevating it—by inference—into a "rule of law." That was too rude an interference with the idol of "freedom of contract." We ought to have used the secret weapon. We ought to have said that in each case, on the "true construction of the contract" in that case, the exemption clause did not avail the party where he was guilty of a fundamental breach or a breach going to the root. That is the lesson to be learnt from the "indigestible" speeches in

Suisse Atlantique Société d'Armement Maritime S.A. v. N.V. Rotterdamsche Kolen Centrale
[1967] 1 A.C. 361. They were all obiter dicta. The House were dealing with an agreed
damages clause and not an exemption clause and the point had never been argued
in the courts below at all. It is noteworthy that the House did not overrule a single
decision of the Court of Appeal. Lord Wilberforce, at p. 433, appears to have approved
them. At any rate, he cast no doubt upon the actual decision in any case.

THE CHANGE IN CLIMATE

In 1969 there was a change in climate. Out of winter into spring. It came with the
Law Commission's Exemption Clauses in Contracts. First Report: Amendments to
the Sale of Goods Act 1893 (Law Com. No. 24, H.C. 403) which was implemented in
the Supply of Goods (Implied Terms) Act 1973. In 1975 there was a further change.
Out of spring into summer. It came with the Law Commission's Exemption Clauses,
Second Report (Law Com. No. 69, H.C. 605) which was implemented by the Unfair
Contract Terms Act 1977. No longer was the big concern able to impose whatever
terms and conditions it liked in a printed form—no matter how unreasonable they
might be. These reports showed most convincingly that the courts could and should
only enforce them if they were fair and reasonable in themselves and it was fair and
reasonable to allow the big concern to rely on them. So the idol of "freedom of contract" was shattered. In cases of personal injury or death, it was not permissible to
exclude or restrict liability at all. In consumer contracts any exemption clause was
subject to the test of reasonableness.

These reports and statutes have influenced much the thinking of the judges. At
any rate, they influenced me as you will see if you read *Gillespie Bros. & Co. Ltd. v.
Roy Bowles Transport Ltd.* [1973] Q.B. 400, 416 and *Photo Production Ltd. v. Securicor
Transport Ltd.* [1978] 1 W.L.R. 856, 865:

> Thus we reach, after long years, the principle which lies behind all our striving: the court
> will not allow a party to rely on an exemption or limitation clause in circumstances in which
> it would not be fair or reasonable to allow reliance on it: and, in considering whether it
> is fair and reasonable, the court will consider whether it was in a standard form, whether
> there was equality of bargaining power, the nature of the breach, and so forth.

THE EFFECT OF THE CHANGES

What is the result of all this? To my mind it heralds a revolution in our approach to
exemption clauses; not only where they exclude liability altogether [but] also where
they limit liability; not only in the specific categories in the Unfair Contract Terms
Act 1977, but in other contracts too. Just as in other fields of law we have done away
with the multitude of cases on "common employment," "last opportunity," "invitees"
and "licensees" and so forth, so also in this field we should do away with the multitude
of cases on exemption clauses. We should no longer have to go through all kinds of
gymnastic contortions to get round them. We should no longer have to harass our
students with the study of them. We should set about meeting a new challenge. It is
presented by the test of reasonableness.

THE TWO SECURICOR CASES

The revolution is exemplified by the recent two *Securicor* cases ([1980] A.C. 827 and
1982 S.L.T. 377) in the House of Lords. In each of them the Securicor company provided a patrolman to keep watch on premises so as to see that they were safe from
intruders. They charged very little for the service. In the first case it was a factory

with a lot of paper in it. The patrolman set light to it and burnt down the factory. In the second case it was a quay at Aberdeen where ships were berthed. The patrolman went off for the celebrations on New Year's Eve. He left the ships unattended. The tide rose. A ship rose with it. Its bow got "snubbed" under the deck of the quay. It sank. In each case the owners were covered by insurance. The factory owners had their fire insurance. The shipowners had their hull insurance. In each case the Securicor company relied on a limitation clause. Under it they were protected from liability beyond a limit which was quite reasonable and their insurance cover was limited accordingly. The issue in practical terms was: which of the insurers should bear the loss? The question in legal terms in each case was whether Securicor could avail themselves of the limitation clause. In each case the House held that they could.

In the first case ([1980] A.C. 827) the House made it clear that the doctrine of "fundamental breach" was no longer applicable. They replaced it by the test of reasonableness. That was the test applied by the trial judge, MacKenna J., which I myself quoted with approval: See *Photo Production Ltd. v. Securicor Transport Ltd.* [1978] 1 W.L.R. 856, 865. He said:

> Condition 1, as I construe it, is, I think, a reasonable provision ... Either the owner of the premises, or the person providing the service, must bear the risk. Why should the parties not agree to its being borne by the owners of the premises? He is certain to be insured against fire and theft, and is better able to judge the cover needed than the party providing the service ... That is only another way of shifting the risk from the party who provides the service to the party who receives it. There is, as I have said, nothing unreasonable, nothing impolitic, in such a contract.

His judgment was approved by the House of Lords who themselves held that the limitation clause was valid because it was a reasonable way of apportioning the risks—as between the insurers on either side. I would set out two passages to prove it. Lord Wilberforce said in *Photo Production Ltd. v. Securicor Transport Ltd.* [1980] A.C. 827, 846:

> Securicor undertook to provide a service of periodical visits for a very modest charge which works out at 26p. per visit. It did not agree to provide equipment. It would have no knowledge of the value of the plaintiffs' factory: that, and the efficacy of their fire precautions, would be known to the respondents. In these circumstances nobody could consider it unreasonable, that as between these two equal parties the risk assumed by Securicor should be a modest one, and that the respondents should carry the substantial risk of damage or destruction.

And Lord Diplock said, at p. 851:

> For the reasons given by Lord Wilberforce it seems to me that this apportionment of the risk of the factory being damaged or destroyed by the injurious act of an employee of Securicor while carrying out a visit to the factory is one which reasonable businessmen in the position of Securicor and the factory owners might well think was the most economical. An analogous apportionment of risk is provided for by the Hague Rules in the case of goods carried by sea under bills of lading.

I do hope, however, that we shall not often have to consider the newfound analysis of contractual obligations into "primary obligations," "secondary obligations," "general secondary obligations" and "anticipatory secondary obligations." No doubt it is logical enough but it is too esoteric altogether. It is fit only for the rarified atmosphere of the House of Lords. Not at all for the chambers of the practitioner. Let alone for the student at the university.

In the second case (1982 S.L.T. 377) the House made a distinction between clauses which excluded liability altogether, and those which only limited liability to a certain sum. Exclusion clauses were to be construed strictly contra proferentem, whereas limitation clauses were to be construed naturally. This must be because a limitation clause is more likely to be reasonable then an exclusive clause. If you go by the plain natural meaning of the words (as you should do) there is nothing to choose between them.

As Lord Sumner said 50 years ago in *Atlantic Shipping and Trading Co. v. Louis Dreyfus and Co.* [1922] 2 A.C. 250, 260:

> There is no difference in principle between words which save them from having to pay at all [and] words which save them from paying as much as they would otherwise have had to pay.

If you read the speeches in the second *Securicor* case, 1982 S.L.T. 377, it does look as if they were relying on the reasonableness of the limitation clause. They held it was applicable even though the failure of the Securicor company was a "total failure" to provide the service contracted for. They also said, obiter, that they would construe an exclusion clause much more strictly—just as was done in the old cases decided in the winter time. But I would suggest that the better reason is because it would not be fair or reasonable to allow the propounder of them to rely on them in the circumstances of the case.

NOTES

1. In England, legislative and judicial changes brought to an end the doctrine of fundamental breach. There, the *Unfair Contract Terms Act 1977* (UK), c 50 was enacted, to apply to clauses excluding liability in consumer and standard form contracts. In cases where the legislation was not applicable, such as in *Photo Production Ltd v Securicor Transport Ltd*, [1980] AC 827 (HL), the courts started utilizing the construction approach in place of the doctrine of fundamental breach, which entails analyzing the exclusion clause as follows: "These words [in the exclusion clause] have to be approached with the aid of the cardinal rules of construction that they must be read *contra proferentem* and that in order to escape from the consequences of one's own wrongdoing, or that of one's servant, clear words are necessary" (Lord Wilberforce in *Photo Production*).

2. On the Canadian side, prior to *Tercon Contractors Ltd v British Columbia (Transportation and Highways)*, 2010 SCC 4, in which the Supreme Court of Canada laid the doctrine of fundamental breach to rest, the application of the doctrine to exclusionary clauses had been difficult to predict. The Supreme Court of Canada had an opportunity, before *Tercon*, to clarify its position on the application of the doctrine, in *Hunter Engineering Co v Syncrude Canada Ltd*, [1989] 1 SCR 426. However, although the court was unanimous in dismissing the plaintiff's claims, the court rendered two decisions, by Dickson CJC and Wilson J, neither of which had the majority support of the court. This left lower courts to grapple with which test to apply to exclusionary clauses, and the application of the doctrine remained unclear until *Tercon*. In *Tercon*, a unanimous Supreme Court discarded the doctrine of fundamental breach and, instead, laid out a three-step framework to determine the enforceability of exclusion clauses. However, the *Tercon* court split on the analysis of the framework and its application to the facts before it.

HUNTER ENGINEERING CO V SYNCRUDE CANADA LTD
[1989] 1 SCR 426

[Syncrude contracted for 32 gearboxes from Hunter US for its tar sands oil processing plant in Alberta. Syncrude also contracted with Allis-Chalmers for 4 more gearboxes. These contracts included a warranty limiting the liability of the suppliers to 24 months from the date of shipment or to 12 months from the date of start-up, whichever period lapsed first. The warranty by Allis-Chalmers provided that "no other warranty or conditions, statutory or otherwise shall be implied." A third contract was concluded between Syncrude and Aco for 11 more gearboxes. The gearboxes turned out to be poorly designed for their intended purpose and developed cracks necessitating costly repairs after the expiry of the warranties. Syncrude sued for damages on the basis that the gearboxes were inherently defective, unsafe, and unfit for their intended purpose and were not of merchantable quality. The BC Court of Appeal awarded $1 million against Hunter US for the cost of repairs and interest on the basis of breach of a statutory warranty of fitness in the Ontario *Sale of Goods Act*, RSO 1990, c S.1, because the contractual warranty had expired, and found Allis-Chalmers liable for fundamental breach of contract, because the statutory warranty was excluded by the terms of the contract. The parties appealed to the Supreme Court. The following excerpts are from the opinions of Dickson CJ and Wilson J, on the issue of fundamental breach.]

DICKSON CJ (La Forest J concurring): ... I have had the advantage of reading the reasons for judgment prepared by my colleague, Justice Wilson, in this appeal and I agree with her disposition of the liability of Allis-Chalmers. In my view, the warranty clauses in the Allis-Chalmers contract effectively excluded liability for defective gearboxes after the warranty period expired. With respect, I disagree, however, with Wilson J.'s approach to the doctrine of fundamental breach. I am inclined to adopt the course charted by the House of Lords in *Photo Production Ltd. v. Securicor Transport Ltd.*, [1980] A.C. 827, and to treat fundamental breach as a matter of contract construction. I do not favour, as suggested by Wilson J., requiring the court to assess the reasonableness of enforcing the contract terms after the court has already determined the meaning of the contract based on ordinary principles of contract interpretation. In my view, the courts should not disturb the bargain the parties have struck, and I am inclined to replace the doctrine of fundamental breach with a rule that holds the parties to the terms of their agreement, provided the agreement is not unconscionable. ...

In light of the unnecessary complexities the doctrine of fundamental breach has created, the resulting uncertainty in the law, and the unrefined nature of the doctrine as a tool for averting unfairness, I am much inclined to lay the doctrine of fundamental breach to rest, and where necessary and appropriate, to deal explicitly with unconscionability. In my view, there is much to be gained by addressing directly the protection of the weak from over-reaching by the strong, rather than relying on the artificial legal doctrine of "fundamental breach." There is little value in cloaking the inquiry behind a construct that takes on its own idiosyncratic traits, sometimes at odds with concerns of fairness. This is precisely what has happened with the doctrine of fundamental breach. It is preferable to interpret the terms of the contract, in an attempt to determine exactly what the parties agreed. If on its true construction the contract excludes liability for the kind of breach that occurred, the party in breach will generally be saved from liability. Only where the contract is unconscionable, as might arise from situations of unequal bargaining power between the parties, should the courts interfere with agreements the parties have freely concluded. The courts do not blindly enforce harsh or unconscionable bargains and, as Professor Waddams has argued, the doctrine of "fundamental breach" may best be understood as but one manifestation of a general underlying principle which explains judicial intervention in a variety of contractual settings. Explicitly addressing concerns of unconscionability and inequality of bargaining power allows the courts to focus expressly on the real grounds for refusing to give force to a contractual term said to have been agreed to by the parties. ...

WILSON J (L'Heureux-Dubé J concurring) (dissenting in cross-appeal): ... I would reject the concept that an exclusion clause in order to be enforceable must be *per se* a fair and reasonable provision at the time it was negotiated. The exclusion clause cannot be considered in isolation from the other provisions of the contract and the circumstances in which it was entered into. The purchaser may have been prepared to assume some risk if he could get the article at a modest price or if he was very anxious to get it. Conversely, if he was having to pay a high price for the article and had to be talked into the purchase, he may have been concerned to impose the broadest possible liability on his vendor. A contractual provision that seems unfair to a third party may have been the product of hard bargaining between the parties and, in my view, deserves to be enforced by the courts in accordance with its terms.

It is, however, in my view an entirely different matter for the courts to determine after a particular breach has occurred whether an exclusion clause should be enforced or not. This, I believe, was the issue addressed by this Court in *Beaufort Realties*. In *Beaufort Realties* this Court accepted the proposition enunciated in *Photo Production* that no rule of law invalidated or extinguished exclusion clauses in the event of fundamental breach but rather that they should be given their natural and true construction so that the parties' agreement would be given effect. Nevertheless the Court, in approving the approach taken by the Ontario Court of Appeal in *Beaufort Realties*, recognized at the same time the need for courts to determine whether in the context of the particular breach which had occurred it was fair and reasonable to enforce the clause in favour of the party who had committed that breach even if the exclusion clause was clear and unambiguous. The relevant question for the Court in *Beaufort Realties* was: is it fair and reasonable in the context of this fundamental breach that the exclusion clause continue to operate for the benefit of the party responsible for the fundamental breach? In other words, should a party be able to commit a fundamental breach secure in the knowledge that no liability can attend it? Or should there be room for the courts to say: this party is now trying to have his cake and eat it too. He is seeking to escape almost entirely the burdens of the transaction but enlist the support of the courts to enforce its benefits.

It seems to me that the House of Lords was able to come to a decision in *Photo Production* untrammelled by the need to reconcile the competing values sought to be advanced in a system of contract law such as ours. We do not have in this country legislation comparable to the United Kingdom's *Unfair Contract Terms Act 1977*. I believe that in the absence of such legislation Canadian courts must continue to develop through the common law a balance between the obvious desirability of allowing the parties to make their own bargains and have them enforced through the courts and the obvious undesirability of having the courts used to enforce bargains in favour of parties who are totally repudiating such bargains themselves. I fully agree with the commentators that the balance which the courts reach will be made much clearer if we do not clothe our reasoning "in the guise of interpretation." Exclusion clauses do not automatically lose their validity in the event of a fundamental breach by virtue of some hard and fast rule of law. They should be given their natural and true construction so that the meaning and effect of the exclusion clause the parties agreed to at the time the contract was entered into is fully understood and appreciated. But, in my view, the court must still decide, having ascertained the parties' intention at the time the contract was made, whether or not to give effect to it in the context of subsequent events such as a fundamental breach committed by the party seeking its enforcement through the courts. Whether the courts address this narrowly in terms of fairness as between the parties (and I believe this has been a source of confusion, the parties being, in the absence of inequality of bargaining power, the best judges of what is fair as between themselves) or on the broader policy basis of the need for the courts (apart from the interests of the parties) to balance conflicting values inherent in our contract law (the approach which I prefer), I believe the result will be the same since the question essentially is: in the circumstances that have happened should the court lend its aid to A to hold B to this clause? ...

As I have noted, this is not the place for an exposition of the doctrine of unconscionability as it relates to inequality of bargaining power and I do not necessarily endorse the approaches taken in the cases to which I have just referred. I use them merely to illustrate the broader point that in situations involving contractual terms which result from inequality of bargaining power the judicial armory has weapons apart from strained and artificial constructions of exclusion clauses. Where, however, there is no such inequality of bargaining power (as in the present case) the courts should, as a general rule, give effect to the bargain freely negotiated by the parties. The question is whether this is an absolute rule or whether as a policy matter the courts should have the power to refuse to enforce a clear and unambiguous exclusion clause freely negotiated by parties of equal bargaining power and, if so, in what circumstances? In the present state of the law in Canada the doctrine of fundamental breach provides one answer.

To dispense with the doctrine of fundamental breach and rely solely on the principle of unconscionability, as has been suggested by some commentators, would, in my view, require an extension of the principle of unconscionability beyond its traditional bounds of inequality of bargaining power. The court, in effect, would be in the position of saying that terms freely negotiated by parties of equal bargaining power were unconscionable. Yet it was the inequality of bargaining power which traditionally was the source of the unconscionability. What was unconscionable was to permit the strong to take advantage of the weak in making of the contract. Remove the inequality and we must ask, wherein lies the unconscionability? It seems to me that it must have its roots in subsequent events, given that the parties themselves are the best judges of what is fair at the time they make their bargain. The policy of the common law is, I believe, that having regard to the conduct (pursuant to the contract) of the party seeking the indulgence of the court to enforce the clause, the court refuses. This conduct is described for convenience as "fundamental breach." It marks off the boundaries of tolerable conduct. But the boundaries are admittedly uncertain. Will replacing it with a general concept of unconscionability reduce the uncertainty?

When and in what circumstances will an exclusion clause in a contract freely negotiated by parties of equal bargaining power be unconscionable? If both fundamental breach and unconscionability are properly viewed as legal tools designed to relieve parties in light of subsequent events from the harsh consequences of an automatic enforcement of an exclusion clause in accordance with its terms, is there anything to choose between them as far as certainty in the law is concerned? Arguably, unconscionability is even less certain than fundamental breach. Indeed, it may be described as "the length of the Chancellor's foot." Lord Wilberforce may be right that parties of equal bargaining power should be left to live with their bargains regardless of subsequent events. I believe, however, that there is some virtue in a residual power residing in the court to withhold its assistance on policy grounds in appropriate circumstances.

Turning to the case at bar, it seems to me that, even if the breach of contract was a fundamental one, there would be nothing unfair or unreasonable (and even less so unconscionable, if this is a stricter test) in giving effect to the exclusion clause. The contract was made between two companies in the commercial market place who are of roughly equal bargaining power. Both are familiar and experienced with this type of contract. As the trial judge noted:

> Warranty cl. 8 was put forward by Syncrude. Presumably it provided the protection Syncrude wanted. Indeed, the first sentence thereof is sufficiently all-embracing that it is difficult to conceive of a defect which would not be caught by it. Syncrude freely accepted the time limitations; there is no evidence that they were under any disadvantage or disability in the negotiating of them. There is no reason why they should not be held to their bargain, including that part which effectively excludes the implied condition of s. 15(1) of the Ontario *Sale of Goods Act* [*Syncrude Can Ltd v Hunter Enrg Co* (1985), 27 BLR 59 (BCSC) at 77].

There is no evidence to suggest that Allis-Chalmers who seeks to rely on the exclusion clause was guilty of any sharp or unfair dealing. It supplied what was bargained for (even although it had defects) and its contractual relationship with Syncrude, which included not only the gears but the entire conveyer system, continued on after the supply of the gears. It cannot be said, in Lord Diplock's words, that Syncrude was "deprived of substantially the whole benefit" of the contract. This is not a case in which the vendor or supplier was seeking to repudiate almost entirely the burdens of the transaction and invoking the assistance of the courts to enforce its benefits. There is no abuse of freedom of contract here.

NOTE

If a limitation of liability clause is imposed by statute, should that affect the analysis in the case? In *Beaulieu v Day & Ross Inc*, 250 DLR (4th) 533, [2005] NBJ No 77 (QL) (CA), the limitation of liability clause in a bill of lading, restricting the carrier's liability to $2 per pound unless a higher value were declared, was upheld after the carrier lost the goods. In finding, *inter alia*, that to hold the clause to be unenforceable would be unfair to the consignor, and that the limitation term in the bill of lading is prescribed under provincial regulation, Robertson JA held (at para 21):

> In light of the statutory framework applicable in both Ontario and New Brunswick, I cannot subscribe to the view that the limitation clause found in the bill of lading in question is unfair, unconscionable or unreasonable. Even if one were to hold a contrary view, the fact that the legislatures have imposed a statutory solution to a problem is a sufficient basis on which to oust the application of the fundamental breach doctrine to the extent that it continues to be viewed as a rule of law.

See also Anthony Duggan, "Stolen Goods, Disaster, and a Right of Way Gone Wrong: Three Unconscionable Contracts Cases from a Law and Economics Perspective" (2004) 40 Can Bus LJ 3.

DAVIDSON V THREE SPRUCES REALTY LTD
(1977), 79 DLR (3d) 481 (BCSC)

ANDERSON J: The plaintiffs' claims are for damages for breach of contract of bailment or, alternatively, for negligence.

The three actions were consolidated for the purposes of trial, and it was agreed by counsel that the evidence of all witnesses and the discovery read in by counsel for Mr. and Mrs. Farr could be considered by me in reaching my decision in each of the cases.

The defendant "The Three Spruces Realty Ltd." (hereinafter called the "bailee") carried on the business and operation of "safety deposit" vaults at 402 West Pender St., Vancouver, British Columbia. These vaults provided bulk storage space for the safekeeping of the property of customers. The property of the customers was stored in the vaults in containers supplied by the customers. The bailee also rented "safety deposit" boxes to its customers. This aspect of the bailee's business is not in issue here except perhaps to demonstrate the higher risk involved in placing valuables in bulk storage as opposed to placing such valuables in a safety deposit box.

Each of the plaintiffs entered into an agreement with the bailee whereby the bailee agreed to keep their valuables in safekeeping. Each of the plaintiffs paid an annual fee for this service.

In the *Farr* and *Elsdon* cases a written agreement was executed by the plaintiffs, which agreement contained a "limitation of liability" clause. In the *Davidson* case the agreement was simply an oral contract whereby the bailee, for a fee, agreed to keep the Davidsons' valuables in safekeeping. ...

The bailee relies on cl. 9 appearing on the back page of the contract, which clause reads as follows:

> 9. Neither the lessor nor its officers, agents and servants, shall be in any way liable directly or indirectly for any theft, robbery, embezzlement, loss or destruction of, or any injury or damage whatsoever to any papers or property which may at any time be deposited or stored in the box or held by the lessor under clause 11 below, or for any act, neglect, or omission whatsoever of the lessor or its officers, agents and servants, or of the tenant or any deputy or any stranger.

The following matters may be relevant in determining whether the limitation clause is applicable in the circumstances:

- (a) The contract is a standard form prepared by the bailee.
- (b) The contract refers to the rental of a safety deposit box and not to bulk storage.
- (c) A copy of the contract was not given to any of the plaintiffs.
- (d) The contract was executed by each of the plaintiffs after representations of almost absolute safety had been made by the bailee.
- (e) The contract was not read by any of the plaintiffs and their attention was not drawn to the limitation clause.
- (f) The rules and regulations made it clear that, in so far as safety deposit boxes are concerned, access to the box is limited to the holder of the box or his agent, and that the contents of the box are to be examined outside the vault in rooms specially provided for that purpose (see rules 2 and 4).
- (g) The contract contains a release form whereby the customer may waive the liability of the bailee.

(h) Almost immediately after the contract was signed the plaintiffs were assured that it was not necessary to insure their valuables against loss by theft or otherwise. ...

Counsel for the bailee submits that the Courts should not interfere with freedom of contract. He submits that if the parties to contracts are not held to the terms of their bargain, however harsh or one-sided, the element of certainty so important in the commercial world will be eliminated. He submits that the plaintiffs agreed in writing, in clear terms, that the bailee would not be responsible for any negligence on its part. He submits that negligence cannot in itself constitute a fundamental breach or, in any event, the limitation clause protected the bailee in respect of all acts of negligence.

I agree that as a general rule, apart from fraud, it would be a dangerous thing to hold that contracts freely entered into should not be fully enforced. It is not correct, however, to suppose that there are no limitations on freedom of contract. The point has been reached in the development of the common law where, in my opinion, the Courts may say, in certain circumstances, that the terms of a contract, although perfectly clear, will not be enforced because they are entirely unreasonable. I quote from the judgment of Lord Denning, M.R., in *Gillespie Brothers & Co. Ltd. v. Roy Bowles Transport Ltd.*, [1973] Q.B. 400 at pp. 415-6, as follows:

> The time may come when this process of "construing" the contract can be pursued no further. The words are too clear to permit of it. Are the courts then powerless? Are they to permit the party to enforce his unreasonable clause, even when it is so unreasonable, or applied so unreasonably, as to be unconscionable? When it gets to this point, I would say, as I said many years ago: "there is the vigilance of the common law which, while allowing freedom of contract, watches to see that it is not abused": *John Lee & Son (Grantham) Ltd. v. Railway Executive* [1949] 2 All E.R. 581, 584. It will not allow a party to exempt himself from his liability at common law when it would be quite unconscionable for him to do so.

I take the view that the Courts are not bound to accept all contracts at face value and enforce those contracts without some regard to the surrounding circumstances. I do not think that standard form contracts should be construed in a vacuum. I do not think that mere formal consensus is enough. I am of the opinion that the terms of a contract may be declared to be void as being unreasonable where it can be said that in all the circumstances it is unreasonable and unconscionable to bind the parties to their formal bargain.

In ascertaining whether "freedom of contract has been abused" so as to make it unconscionable for the bailee to exempt itself from liability, I think regard may be had to the following:

(1) Was the contract a standard form contract drawn up by the bailee?
(2) Were there any negotiations as to the terms of the contract or was it a commercial form which may be described as a "sign here" contract?
(3) Was the attention of the plaintiffs drawn to the limitation clause?
(4) Was the exemption clause unusual in character?
(5) Were representations made which would lead an ordinary person to believe that the limitation clause did not apply?
(6) Was the language of the contract when read in conjunction with the limitation clause such as to render the implied covenant made by the bailee to use reasonable care to protect the plaintiffs' property meaningless?

(7) Having regard to all the facts including the representations made by the bailee and the circumstances leading up to the execution of the contract, would not the enforcement of the limitation clause be a tacit approval by the Courts of unacceptable commercial practices?

In the case at bar, the plaintiffs were not asked to read the contract. They were not advised of the contents of the contract. They were asked to "sign here" and pay the annual rental fee. Prior to signing the contract they were assured that proper precautions would be taken to secure their valuables. When the plaintiffs asked whether they should obtain insurance coverage they were advised that it was not necessary to obtain such coverage. The plaintiffs were not given a copy of the contract. The fact a theft had taken place was not made known to them.

Even if the language of the limitation clause extends to all acts or omissions on the part of the bailee, including such negligence as would amount to a fundamental breach of contract, I hold, in the circumstances here, that the limitation clause is so unreasonable that it cannot be enforced. It amounts to a clear "abuse of freedom of contract." ...

[Anderson J also held for the plaintiffs on the basis of strict construction, fundamental breach, and misrepresentation.]

DELANEY V CASCADE RIVER HOLIDAYS LTD
(1983), 44 BCLR 24, 24 CCLT 6 (CA)

NEMETZ CJBC (dissenting): Dr. Fergus Delaney, an Ontario veterinarian, visited British Columbia on business on the weekend of May 5, 1979. While in Vancouver he met a school friend, Dr. Stein Hoff. Dr. Hoff told Dr. Delaney that he (Hoff) was taking part in a "white water adventure" down the Fraser River and invited Delaney to join him. Delaney was enthusiastic about the idea. Inquiries were made and, because the raft was not full for that trip, Delaney's name was added to the passenger list. The trip ended in tragedy with the drowning of Dr. Delaney and two other passengers. The plaintiff (widow), executrix of the estate of Fergus Michael Delaney, brought this action under the provision of the Family Compensation Act, R.S.B.C. 1979, c. 120, for the benefit of herself and for three infant children of Dr. Delaney. Her action was dismissed [reported (1981), 34 BCLR 62, 19 CCLT 78, 16 BLR 114 (SC)]. She now appeals to this Court.

The history of the disastrous trip is as follows: The passenger group travelled to Yale on Friday night. On Saturday morning, May 5, 1979, they assembled in a parking lot and met with representatives of Cascade River Holidays Ltd. (Cascade) including the reservations manager, Louella Morrison, and the defendant, Philip Reambeault, the raftsman. Sometime prior to this meeting Delaney paid $100 to Mr. Sims, president of Cascade, for the trip. The other passengers had made earlier bookings and paid in advance.

It was an overcast, rainy day. As Cascade's van was being loaded with gear and passengers, and T-shirts were being distributed, Louella Morrison obtained the signature of the eight paying passengers on a form entitled "Standard Liability Release." I will discuss the effect of Delaney's signing of this release later. All passengers, save Delaney, had received brochures from Cascade which contained the following statement:

LIABILITY

Cascade River Holidays Ltd. does not guarantee safe passage and assumes no responsibility for patron's safety or property. Patrons must sign our liability release before
departure. Cascade River Holidays has operated since 1973 without major loss and uses
all the standard safety devices. We recommend the patron purchase personal insurance
to protect himself.

Dr. Hoff had received one of these brochures, but there is no evidence that Dr. Delaney saw it. Hoff, who had been on such an expedition before, described the trip to
Delaney as being "not necessarily a terribly adventuresome trip" and said that some
elderly people had been on it the previous occasion. Hoff gave Delaney the impression that it was a safe thing to do. ...

[The defendant provided life jackets that he knew were inadequate for the Fraser
River. When the raft overturned, Delaney drowned. At trial, the defendant was found
negligent for not using more buoyant life jackets. The majority of the Court of Appeal
held that the plaintiff had failed to prove that Delaney would have lived if he had
been provided with a better life jacket. Nemetz CJBC in his dissent held that the
plaintiff had shown causation of loss and decided that the liability release did not
preclude the action for two reasons:]

(I) PAST CONSIDERATION

It is contended for the plaintiff that notice of the terms of the liability release were not
contemporaneous with the entry into the contract; in other words, the terms of the
liability release are not a part of the contract, and since there was no "new" consideration for them, the release is unenforceable. This raises the question whether the
maxim "past consideration is no consideration" is applicable to the facts of this case.
The trial Judge found that Dr. Delaney paid his $100 at or about the time the release
was signed. Since the issue of past consideration was not canvassed by the trial Judge,
it was not essential for him to analyze the timing of the payment. There is evidence
before the Court from Mr. Sims that Dr. Delaney paid his fare to take the trip on the
morning of May 5, 1979 before the release was presented for signature. Mr. Sims
testified that he received the payment personally and that he was not present later
when the release was signed. Therefore, we know that some time elapsed between
the two events.

The crucial factor is that notice of the terms, or indeed of the existence of a liability
release was not contemporaneous with the entry into the contract evidenced by the
payment of the fare to Sims earlier that morning. At the moment of payment, Cascade
was obligated to take Dr. Delaney on the expedition on the terms existing at that
moment. The subsequent requirement of signing the release was an attempt by
Cascade to impose additional and onerous terms to a contract which had already
been finalized. Although the company policy was that no one could go on the trip
without signing the release, they had no more right to require him to agree to the
additional contractual terms of the release than they would have had to try to exact
a higher fare from him to secure their performance of the contract (*Gilbert Steel Ltd.
v. University Const. Ltd.* [see Chapter 3]). Simply stated, there was no consideration
for Dr. Delaney's signature on the release form because Cascade was bound to take
him whether or not he signed.

(II) THE INSUFFICIENCY OF THE NOTICE

I reproduce the principal portion of the liability release:

CASCADE RIVER HOLIDAYS

P.O. Box 65, Yale, B.C., Canada
V0K 2S0
Phone (604) 863-2332

Standard Liability Release

TRIP NAME 2 day Fraser TRIP NO. C10 TRIP DATE May 5-6 1979

DISCLAIMER CLAUSE: Cascade River Holidays Ltd. is not responsible for any loss or damage suffered by any person either in travelling to the location of the trip, before, during or after the trip, for any reason whatsoever including negligence on the part of the company, its agents or servants.

AGREEMENT: I agree to assume all risks involved in taking the trip including travelling before and after, and agree to pay the cost of any emergency evacuation of my person and belongings that may become necessary. I agree to Cascade River Holidays Ltd. its agents and servants relieving themselves of all liability for losses and damages of all and every descriptions. I acknowledge having read this Liability release and that I am of full age and my acceptance of the above disclaimer clause by my signature and seal. (Parents or Guardians please sign for minors.)

(Signatures follow)

This document must be read together with the relevant portions of the brochure. ...

[See above. Nemetz CJBC held that there was no evidence that Delaney had read the brochure.]

On the morning of May 5, Miss Morrison met with the members of the group in the hotel parking lot at Yale and either singly or in groups presented them with the release. She asked each to read it and sign it and said that those who would not sign would not be allowed to embark on the journey on the river. All passengers signed. It is evident that the releases were signed in a hurried manner. Miss Morrison's evidence is clear and frank. She pointed out that "it always seemed we were always in a hurry trying to get everybody out." She approached the passengers for signature when they were busy with other matters, i.e., "getting things out of their car and they are getting fishing things and things like that. ..." This testimony is amply supported by a number of the passengers. Dr. Hoff, when asked in cross-examination, "If you wished to read the release it would not have taken you very long, at all, would it?" He replied, "It would under the circumstances have taken an inappropriate time." The reason was, of course, that he was anxious to get onto the van for the embarkation place. Mr. Lundie, a chartered accountant, was also a passenger. He described the signing operation:

> As I understood it one of the procedures that we had to do was sign that standard form of liability and it was done in a rather perfunctory manner by somebody just standing by the van or sitting at the opening of the side door of the van and thus they could ask people to come over and they did. I think as we stowed our gear in the van, we signed the liability document and got a T-shirt.

He did not read the document. He was told it was a standard liability form but there was no discussion as to implications. Mr. Steeves, another passenger, confirms that the signing was done "very quickly." He said, "I think I can compare it to signing a rent-a-car form." Miss Morrison was not sure whether Delaney read the release.

[Nemetz CJBC referred to the *Tilden Rent-A-Car* case, compared the signing of the release to the signing of a car rental contract, and held that the release was misleading in the following two respects.]

(1) The use of the adjective "standard" would tend to induce a sense of security in the passenger asked to sign the release. This is borne out in the testimony of Lundie, who, having read the word "standard," refrained from reading further.

(2) The clause speaks generally of "loss or damage" but does not mention the risk of personal injury or death. Cascade's president, Sims, conceded that if he mentioned the possibility of a fatal accident, his business would suffer. ...

The release contained provisions so onerous and unusual that it was the duty of Cascade to see that the provisions were "effectively called to the attention of the other party under the penalty of their being held non-binding on the latter party." ... It was not sufficient that a clerk, minutes before passengers were to depart on this unusual voyage, when the passengers' minds were directed to the voyage and packing their gear, should place before them this document containing the onerous terms it did. A reasonably intelligent person was entitled to assume that a form titled "standard" did not contain the unusual provisions contained in this one. This was indeed what Professor Waddams has termed "misrepresentation by omission" (see *Tilden* [18 OR (2d) 609]). In the case of Delaney, Cascade had not sent him a brochure. They could not assume that he had a clear idea of the risk of which they had forewarned the others in the brochure under the heading "Liability" which speaks of Cascade not guaranteeing safe passage and not assuming responsibility for the patron's safety. And, a fortiori, the brochure recommended that "the patron purchase personal insurance to protect himself." Had Delaney been so warned, would he have assumed the risk to absolve Cascade from negligence of not providing him with the best life-saving jackets available? I do not think so. ...

McFARLANE JA (Taggart JA concurring): The trial judge held that the corporate defendant was negligent in failing to provide personal flotation devices of greater buoyancy. While I find it difficult to agree that finding is correct I think I am bound by decisions of the Supreme Court of Canada to accept it for the purposes of this appeal.

I am, however, clearly of the opinion that the appellant has failed to show that the failure to provide a life-jacket of greater buoyancy caused, or contributed to, the death of the deceased. Stated in another way, I think the plaintiff has failed to show on balance that the deceased would have survived if he had worn a 30 or 32-pound jacket. ...

I think the argument of "past consideration" must fail. It seems clear that the deceased was informed that unless he signed the release form he would not be taken on the trip. The immediate consideration which he received was, therefore, that he was permitted to enter the van and carry on with the venture.

While it is possible to criticize the language of the "Standard Liability Release," I think it must be interpreted and understood, having regard to the whole purpose of the relationship between the deceased and the corporate respondent. That purpose, so far as the deceased was concerned, was to engage in what must have been intended to be an exciting and thrilling challenge of the power of the Fraser River in the Canyon. Construed in that way, there is, in my opinion, no doubt of the intent involved in the language of the release. I think also the trial Judge was correct in applying the principles stated in *L'Estrange v. F. Graucob Ltd.* [1934] 2 K.B. 394. Having regard to the nature of the venture involved I think that there is no sufficient ground for making an exception to the general principles enunciated in that case.

[The appeal was dismissed. Leave to appeal to the Supreme Court of Canada was granted, but the appeal was discontinued on September 24, 1984.]

TERCON CONTRACTORS LTD V BRITISH COLUMBIA (TRANSPORTATION AND HIGHWAYS)
2010 SCC 4, [2010] 1 SCR 69

[The court was unanimous in laying the doctrine of fundamental breach to rest and on the approach to be taken in analyzing exclusion clauses. It was, however, divided on the interpretation of the clause in issue.]

CROMWELL J (LeBel, Deschamps, Fish, and Charron JJ concurring):

I. INTRODUCTION

[1] The Province accepted a bid from a bidder who was not eligible to participate in the tender and then took steps to ensure that this fact was not disclosed. The main question on appeal, as I see it, is whether the Province succeeded in excluding its liability for damages flowing from this conduct through an exclusion clause it inserted into the contract. I share the view of the trial judge that it did not.

• • •

[5] On Tercon's appeal to this Court, the questions for us are whether the successful bidder was eligible to participate in the RFP and, if not, whether Tercon's claim for damages is barred by the exclusion clause.

• • •

III. ISSUES

[13] The issues for decision are whether the trial judge erred in finding that:

1. the Province breached the tendering contract by entertaining a bid from an ineligible bidder.
2. the exclusion clause does not bar the appellant's claim for damages for the breaches of the tendering contract found by the trial judge.

IV. ANALYSIS

[The discussion on tendering has been omitted. The court found that the province had breached the tendering contract by entertaining a bid from an ineligible bidder.]

• • •

B. THE EXCLUSION CLAUSE:

1. Introduction

[60] As noted, the RFP includes an exclusion clause which reads as follows:

2.10 ... Except as expressly and specifically permitted in these Instructions to Proponents, *no Proponent shall have any claim for compensation of any kind whatsoever, as a result of participating in this RFP*, and by submitting a Proposal each Proponent shall be deemed to have agreed that it has no claim. [Emphasis added.]

[61] The trial judge held that as a matter of construction, the clause did not bar recovery for the breaches she had found. The clause, in her view, was ambiguous and, applying the *contra proferentem* principle, she resolved the ambiguity in Tercon's favour. She also found that the Province's breach was fundamental and that it was not fair or reasonable to enforce the exclusion clause in light of the nature of the Province's breach. The Province contends that the judge erred both with respect to the construction of the clause and her application of the doctrine of fundamental breach.

[62] On the issue of fundamental breach in relation to exclusion clauses, my view is that the time has come to lay this doctrine to rest, as Dickson C.J. was inclined to do more than 20 years ago: *Hunter Engineering Co. v. Syncrude Canada Ltd.*, [1989] 1 S.C.R. 426, at p. 462. I agree with the analytical approach that should be followed when tackling an issue relating to the applicability of an exclusion clause set out by my colleague Binnie J. However, I respectfully do not agree with him on the question of the proper interpretation of the clause in issue here. In my view, the clause does not exclude Tercon's claim for damages, and even if I am wrong about that, the clause is at best ambiguous and should be construed *contra proferentem* as the trial judge held. As a result of my conclusion on the interpretation issue, I do not have to go on to apply the rest of the analytical framework set out by Binnie J.

[63] In my view, the exclusion clause does not cover the Province's breaches in this case. The RFP process put in place by the Province was premised on a closed list of bidders; a contest with an ineligible bidder was not part of the RFP process and was in fact expressly precluded by its terms. A "Contract A" could not arise as a result of submission of a bid from any other party. However, as a result of how the Province proceeded, the very premise of its own RFP process was missing, and the work was awarded to a party who could not be a participant in the RFP process. That is what Tercon is complaining about. Tercon's claim is not barred by the exclusion clause because the clause only applies to claims arising "as a result of participating in [the] RFP," not to claims resulting from the participation of other, ineligible parties. Moreover, the words of this exclusion clause, in my view, are not effective to limit liability for breach of the Province's implied duty of fairness to bidders. I will explain my conclusion by turning first to a brief account of the key legal principles and then to the facts of the case.

2. Legal Principles

[64] The key principle of contractual interpretation here is that the words of one provision must not be read in isolation but should be considered in harmony with the rest of the contract and in light of its purposes and commercial context. The approach adopted by the Court in *M.J.B.* is instructive. The Court had to interpret a privilege clause, which is somewhat analogous to the exclusion clause in issue here. The privilege clause provided that the lowest or any tender would not necessarily be accepted, and the issue was whether this barred a claim based on breach of an implied term that the owner would accept only compliant bids. In interpreting the privilege clause, the Court looked at its text in light of the contract as a whole, its purposes and commercial context ... .

[65] In a similar way, it is necessary in the present case to consider the exclusion clause in the RFP in light of its purposes and commercial context as well as of its overall terms. The question is whether the exclusion of compensation for claims

resulting from "participating in this RFP," properly interpreted, excludes liability for the Province having unfairly considered a bid from a bidder who was not supposed to have been participating in the RFP process at all.

3. Application to This Case

[66] Having regard to both the text of the clause in its broader context and to the purposes and commercial context of the RFP, my view is that this claim does not fall within the terms of the exclusion clause.

• • •

[70] The closed list of bidders was the foundation of this RFP and there were important competitive advantages to a bidder who could side-step that limitation. Thus, it seems to me that both the integrity and the business efficacy of the tendering process support an interpretation that would allow the exclusion clause to operate compatibly with the eligibility limitations that were at the very root of the RFP.

• • •

[74] I turn to the text of the clause which the Province inserted in its RFP. It addresses claims that result from "participating in this RFP." As noted, the limitation on who could participate in this RFP was one of its premises. These words must, therefore, be read in light of the limit on who was eligible to participate in this RFP. As noted earlier, both the ministerial approval and the text of the RFP itself were unequivocal: only the six proponents qualified through the earlier RFEI process were eligible and *proposals received from any other party would not be considered*. Thus, central to "participating in this RFP" was participating in a contest among those eligible to participate. A process involving other bidders, as the trial judge found the process followed by the Province to be, is not the process called for by "this RFP" and being part of that other process is not in any meaningful sense "participating in this RFP."

[75] The Province would have us interpret the phrase excluding compensation "as a result of participating in this RFP" to mean that compensation is excluded that results from "submitting a Proposal." However, that interpretation is not consistent with the wording of the clause as a whole. The clause concludes with the phrase that "by submitting a Proposal each Proponent shall be deemed to have agreed that it has no claim." If the phrases "participating in this RFP" and "submitting a Proposal" were intended to mean the same thing, it is hard to understand why different words were used in the same short clause to express the same idea. The fact that the Minister had approved a closed list of participants strengthens the usual inference that the use of different words was deliberate so as not to exclude compensation for a departure from that basic eligibility requirement.

[76] ... In short, limiting eligibility of bidders to those who had responded to the RFEI was the foundation of the whole RFP. As the judge found, acceptance of a bid from an ineligible bidder "attacks the underlying premise of the process" established by the RFP: para. 146. Liability for such an attack is not excluded by a clause limiting compensation resulting from participation in this RFP.

[77] This interpretation is also supported by another provision of the RFP. Under s. 2.9, as mentioned earlier, the Province reserved to itself the right to unilaterally cancel the RFP and the right to propose a new RFP allowing additional bidders. If the exclusion clause were broad enough to exclude compensation for allowing ineligible bidders to participate, there seems to be little purpose in this reservation of the ability to cancel the RFP and issue a new one to a wider circle of bidders. It is also significant that the Province did not reserve to itself the right to accept a bid from an ineligible bidder or to unilaterally change the rules of eligibility. The RFP

expressly did exactly the opposite. None of this, in my opinion, supports the view that the exclusion clause should be read as applying to the Province's conduct in this case.

[78] To hold otherwise seems to me to be inconsistent with the text of the clause read in the context of the RFP as a whole and in light of its purposes and commercial context. In short, I cannot accept the contention that, by agreeing to exclude compensation for participating in this RFP process, the parties could have intended to exclude a damages claim resulting from the Province unfairly permitting a bidder to participate who was not eligible to do so. I cannot conclude that the provision was intended to gut the RFP's eligibility requirements as to who may participate in it, or to render meaningless the Minister's statutorily required approval of the alternative process where this was a key element. The provision, as well, was not intended to allow the Province to escape a damages claim for applying different eligibility criteria, to the competitive disadvantage of other bidders and for taking steps designed to disguise the true state of affairs. I cannot conclude that the parties, through the words found in this exclusion clause, intended to waive compensation for conduct like that of the Province in this case that strikes at the heart of the integrity and business efficacy of the tendering process which it undertook.

[79] If I am wrong about my interpretation of the clause, I would hold, as did the trial judge, that its language is at least ambiguous. If, as the Province contends, the phrase "participating in this RFP" could reasonably mean "submitting a Proposal," that phrase could also reasonably mean "competing against the other eligible participants." Any ambiguity in the context of this contract requires that the clause be interpreted against the Province and in favour of Tercon under the principle *contra proferentem* ... . Following this approach, the clause would not apply to bar Tercon's damages claim.

V. DISPOSITION

[80] ... I would therefore allow the appeal, set aside the order of the Court of Appeal and restore the judgment of the trial judge ... .

BINNIE J (McLachlin CJ and Abella and Rothstein JJ concurring):

[81] The important legal issue raised by this appeal is whether, and in what circumstances, a court will deny a defendant contract breaker the benefit of an exclusion of liability clause to which the innocent party, not being under any sort of disability, has agreed. Traditionally, this has involved consideration of what is known as the doctrine of fundamental breach, a doctrine which Dickson C.J. in *Hunter Engineering Co. v. Syncrude Canada Ltd.*, [1989 1 S.C.R. 426, suggested should be laid to rest 21 years ago (p. 462).

[82] On this occasion we should again attempt to shut the coffin on the jargon associated with "fundamental breach." Categorizing a contract breach as "fundamental" or "immense" or "colossal" is not particularly helpful. Rather, the principle is that a court has no discretion to refuse to enforce a valid and applicable contractual exclusion clause unless the plaintiff (here the appellant Tercon) can point to some paramount consideration of public policy sufficient to override the public interest in freedom of contract and defeat what would otherwise be the contractual rights of the parties. Tercon points to the public interest in the transparency and integrity of the government tendering process (in this case, for a highway construction contract) but in my view such a concern, while important, did not render unenforceable the terms of the contract Tercon agreed to. There is nothing inherently unreasonable about exclusion clauses. Tercon is a large and sophisticated corporation. Unlike my

colleague Justice Cromwell, I would hold that the respondent Ministry's conduct, while in breach of its contractual obligations, fell within the terms of the exclusion clause. In turn, there is no reason why the clause should not be enforced. I would dismiss the appeal.

I. OVERVIEW

• • •

[86] I accept, as did the courts below, that the respondent Ministry breached the terms of its own RFP when it contracted with Brentwood... However, I also agree with the B.C. Court of Appeal that the exclusion of compensation clause is clear and unambiguous and that no legal ground or rule of law permits us to override the freedom of the parties to contract (or to decline to contract) with respect to this particular term, or to relieve Tercon against its operation in this case.

II. THE TENDERING PROCESS

• • •

[95] Tercon is a large and experienced contractor. As noted by Donald J.A. in the B.C. Court of Appeal, it had earlier "successfully recovered damages from the [Ministry] on a bidding default on a previous case" ... . Thus Tercon would have been more sensitive than most contractors to the risks posed by an exclusion of compensation clause. It nevertheless chose to bid on the project on the terms proposed by the Ministry.

III. TERCON'S CLAIM FOR RELIEF FROM THE EXCLUSIONARY CLAUSE IT AGREED TO

[96] In these circumstances, the first question is whether there is either a statutory legal obstacle to, or a principled legal argument against, the freedom of these parties to contract out of the obligation that would otherwise exist for the Ministry to pay compensation for a breach of Contract A. If not, the second question is whether there is any other barrier to the court's enforcement of the exclusionary clause in the circumstances that occurred. On the first branch, Tercon relies on the *Ministry of Transportation and Highways Act* ... . On the second branch, Tercon relies on the doctrine of fundamental breach.

• • •

[The discussion of the Act has been omitted.]

B. THE DOCTRINE OF THE FUNDAMENTAL BREACH

[104] The trial judge considered the applicability of the doctrine of fundamental breach. Tercon argued that the Ministry, by reason of its fundamental breach, had forfeited the protection of the exclusion of compensation clause.

[105] The leading case is *Hunter* which also dealt with an exclusion of liability clause. The appellants Hunter Engineering and Allis-Chalmers Canada Ltd. supplied gearboxes used to drive conveyor belts at Syncrude's tar sands operations in Northern Alberta. The gearboxes proved to be defective. At issue was a broad exclusion of warranty clause that limited time for suit and the level of recovery available against Allis-Chalmers (i.e. no recovery beyond the unit price of the defective products). Dickson C.J. observed: "In the face of the contractual provisions, Allis-Chalmers can only be found liable under the doctrine of fundamental breach" (p. 451).

[106] This doctrine was largely the creation of Lord Denning in the 1950s (see, e.g., *Karsales (Harrow) Ltd. v. Wallis*, [1956] 1 W.L.R. 936 (C.A.)). It was said to be a rule of law that operated independently of the intention of the parties in circumstances where the defendant had so egregiously breached the contract as to deny the plaintiff substantially the whole of its benefit. In such a case, according to the doctrine, the innocent party was excused from further performance but the defendant could still be held liable for the consequences of its "fundamental" breach even if the parties had excluded liability by clear and express language. ...

[107] The five-judge *Hunter* Court was unanimous in the result and gave effect to the exclusion clause at issue. Dickson C.J. and Wilson J. both emphasized that there is nothing inherently unreasonable about exclusion clauses and that they should be applied unless there is a compelling reason not to give effect to the words selected by the parties. At that point, there was some divergence of opinion.

[108] Dickson C.J. (La Forest J. concurring) observed that the doctrine of fundamental breach had "spawned a host of difficulties" (p. 460), the most obvious being the difficulty in determining whether a particular breach is fundamental. The doctrine obliged the parties to engage in "games of characterization" (p. 460) which distracted from the real question of what agreement the parties themselves intended. Accordingly, in his view, the doctrine should be "laid to rest." The situations in which the doctrine is invoked could be addressed more directly and effectively through the doctrine of "unconscionability," as assessed at the time the contract was made: ... Dickson C.J. explained that "[t]he courts do not blindly enforce harsh or unconscionable bargains" (p. 462), but "there is much to be gained by addressing directly the protection of the weak from over-reaching by the strong, rather than relying on the artificial legal doctrine of 'fundamental breach'" (p. 462). To enforce an exclusion clause in such circumstances could tarnish the institutional integrity of the court. In that respect, it would be contrary to public policy. However, a *valid* exclusion clause would be enforced according to its terms.

[109] Wilson J. (L'Heureux-Dubé J. concurring) disagreed. In her view, the courts retain some residual discretion to refuse to enforce exclusion clauses in cases of fundamental breach where the doctrine of *pre*-breach unconscionability (favoured by Dickson C.J.) did not apply. Importantly, she rejected the imposition of a general standard of reasonableness in the judicial scrutiny of exclusion clauses, affirming that "the courts ... are quite unsuited to assess the fairness or reasonableness of contractual provisions as the parties negotiated them" (p. 508). Wilson J. considered it more desirable to develop through the common law a *post*-breach analysis seeking a "balance between the obvious desirability of allowing the parties to make their own bargains ... and the obvious undesirability of having the courts used to enforce bargains in favour of parties who are totally repudiating such bargains themselves" (p. 510).

[110] Wilson J. contemplated a two-stage test, in which the threshold step is the identification of a fundamental breach where "the foundation of the contract has been undermined, where the very thing bargained for has not been provided" (p. 500). Having found a fundamental breach to exist, the exclusion clause would *not* automatically be set aside, but the court should go on to assess whether, having regard to the circumstances of the breach, the party in fundamental breach should escape liability: ...

[111] Wilson J. reiterated that "as a general rule" courts should give effect to exclusion clauses *even in the case of fundamental breach* (p. 515). Nevertheless, a residual discretion to withhold enforcement [on policy grounds] exists:

• • •

[113] The law was left in this seemingly bifurcated state until *Guarantee Co. of North America v. Gordon Capital Corp.*, [1999] 3 S.C.R. 423. In that case, the Court breathed some life into the dying doctrine of fundamental breach while nevertheless affirming (once again) that whether or not a "fundamental breach prevents the breaching party from continuing to rely on an exclusion clause is a matter of construction rather than a rule of law" (at para. 52). In other words, the question was whether the parties *intended* at the time of contract formation that the exclusion or limitation clause would apply "in circumstances of contractual breach, whether fundamental or otherwise" (para. 63). The Court thus emphasized that what was important was not the label ("fundamental or otherwise") but the intent of the contracting parties when they made their bargain. "The *only limitation* placed upon enforcing the contract as written in the event of a fundamental breach," the Court in *Guarantee Trust* continued,

> would be to refuse to enforce an exclusion, of liability in circumstances where to do so would be unconscionable, according to Dickson C.J., *or* [note the disjunctive "or"] unfair, unreasonable or otherwise contrary to public policy, according to Wilson J. [Emphasis added; para. 52.]

What has given rise to some concern is not the reference to "public policy," whose role in the enforcement of contracts has never been doubted, but to the more general ideas of "unfair" and "unreasonable," which seemingly confer on courts a very broad after-the-fact discretion.

[114] The Court's subsequent observations in *ABB Inc. v. Domtar Inc.*, 2007 SCC 50, [2007] 3 S.C.R. 461, should be seen in that light. *Domtar* was a products liability case arising under the civil law of Quebec, but the Court observed with respect to the common law:

> Once the existence of a fundamental breach has been established, the court must still analyse the limitation of liability clause in light of the general rules of contract interpretation. If the words can reasonably be interpreted in only one way, it will not be open to the court, *even on grounds of equity or reasonableness*, to declare the clause to be unenforceable since this would amount to rewriting the contract negotiated by the parties. [Emphasis added; para. 84.]

While the *Domtar* Court continued to refer to "fundamental breach," it notably repudiated any judicial discretion to depart from the terms of a valid contract upon vague notions of "equity or reasonableness." It did not, however, express any doubt about the residual category mentioned in *Guarantee Trust*, namely a refusal to enforce an exclusion clause on the grounds of public policy.

• • •

[116] While memorably described as an unruly horse, public policy is nevertheless fundamental to contract law, both to contractual formation and enforcement and (occasionally) to the court's relief *against* enforcement...

[117] As Duff C.J. recognized, freedom of contract will often, but not always, trump other societal values. The residual power of a court to decline enforcement exists but, in the interest of certainty and stability of contractual relations, it will rarely be exercised. Duff C.J. adopted the view that public policy "should be invoked only in clear cases in which the harm to the public is substantially incontestable, and does not depend upon the idiosyncratic inferences of a few judicial minds" (p. 7). While he was referring to public policy considerations pertaining to the nature of the *entire contract*, I accept that there may be well-accepted public policy considerations that

relate directly to the nature of the *breach*, and thus trigger the court's narrow jurisdiction to give relief against an exclusion clause.

[118] There are cases where the exercise of what Professor Waddams calls the "ultimate power" to refuse to enforce a contract may be justified, even in the commercial context. Freedom of contract, like any freedom, may be abused. Take the case of the milk supplier who adulterates its baby formula with a toxic compound to increase its profitability at the cost of sick or dead babies ... .

[119] A less extreme example in the commercial context is *Plas-Tex Canada Ltd. v. Dow Chemical of Canada Ltd.* [see reference to *Plas-Tex* in Note 9 below]. ... What was demonstrated in *Plas-Tex* was that the defendant Dow was so contemptuous of its contractual obligation and reckless as to the consequences of the breach as to forfeit the assistance of the court. The public policy that favours freedom of contract was outweighed by the public policy that seeks to curb its abuse.

[120] Conduct approaching serious criminality or egregious fraud are but examples of well-accepted and "substantially incontestable" considerations of public policy that may override the countervailing public policy that favours freedom of contract ... . Such misconduct may disable the defendant from hiding behind the exclusion clause. But a plaintiff who seeks to avoid the effect of an exclusion clause must identify the overriding public policy that it says outweighs the public interest in the enforcement of the contract ... .

[121] The present state of the law, in summary, requires a series of enquiries to be addressed when a plaintiff seeks to escape the effect of an exclusion clause or other contractual terms to which it had previously agreed.

[122] The first issue, of course, is whether as a matter of interpretation the exclusion clause even *applies* to the circumstances established in evidence. This will depend on the Court's assessment of the intention of the parties as expressed in the contract. If the exclusion clause does not apply, there is obviously no need to proceed further with this analysis. If the exclusion clause applies, the second issue is whether the exclusion clause was unconscionable at the time the contract was made, "as might arise from situations of unequal bargaining power between the parties" (*Hunter*, at p. 462). This second issue has to do with contract formation, not breach.

[123] If the exclusion clause is held to be valid and applicable, the Court may undertake a third enquiry, namely whether the Court should nevertheless refuse to enforce the valid exclusion clause because of the existence of an overriding public policy, proof of which lies on the party seeking to avoid enforcement of the clause, that outweighs the very strong public interest in the enforcement of contracts.

IV. APPLICATION TO THE FACTS OF THIS CASE

[124] I proceed to deal with the issues in the sequence mentioned above.

[The court proceeded with the analysis on the basis that Contract A was breached by the Ministry.]

• • •

B. WHAT IS THE PROPER INTERPRETATION OF THE EXCLUSION OF COMPENSATION CLAUSE AND DID THE MINISTRY'S CONDUCT FALL WITHIN ITS TERMS?

[127] It is at this stage that I part company with my colleague Cromwell J. The exclusion clause is contained in the RFP and provides as follows:

> 2.10 ... Except as expressly and specifically permitted in these Instructions to Proponents, no Proponent shall have any claim for compensation of any kind whatsoever, as a result of participating in this RFP, and by submitting a Proposal each Proponent shall be deemed to have agree that it has no claim.

In my view, "participating in this RFP" began with "submitting a Proposal" for consideration. The RFP process consisted of more than the final selection of the winning bid and Tercon participated in it. Tercon's bid *was* considered ... .

[128] I accept the trial judge's view that the Ministry was at fault in its performance of the RFP, but the conclusion that the process thereby ceased to be the RFP process appears to me, with due respect to colleagues of a different view, to be a "strained and artificial interpretatio[n] in order, indirectly and obliquely, to avoid the impact of what seems to them *ex post facto* to have been an unfair and unreasonable clause." ... Accordingly, I conclude that on the face of it, the exclusion clause applies to the facts described in the evidence before us.

• • •

C. WAS THE CLAIM EXCLUDING COMPENSATION UNCONSCIONABLE AT THE TIME CONTRACT A WAS MADE?

[130] At this point, the focus turns to contract formation. Tercon advances two arguments: firstly, that it suffered from an inequality of bargaining power and secondly, (as mentioned) that the exclusion clause violates public policy as reflected in the *Transportation Act*.

(1) Unequal Bargaining Power

[131] In *Hunter*, Dickson C.J. stated, at p. 462: "Only where the contract is unconscionable, as might arise from situations of unequal bargaining power between the parties, should the courts interfere with agreements the parties have freely concluded." Applying that test to the case before him, he concluded:

> I have no doubt that unconscionability is not an issue in this case. Both Allis-Chalmers and Syncrude are large and commercially sophisticated companies. Both parties knew or should have known what they were doing and what they had bargained for when they entered into the contract. [p. 464]

While Tercon is not on the same level of power and authority as the Ministry, Tercon is a major contractor and is well able to look after itself in a commercial context. It need not bid if it doesn't like what is proposed. There was no relevant imbalance in bargaining power.

(2) Policy of the *Transportation Act*

• • •

[134] The Court should not be quick to declare such a clause, negotiated between savvy participants in the construction business, to be "contrary to the Act."

D. ASSUMING THE VALIDITY OF THE EXCLUSION CLAUSE AT THE TIME THE CONTRACT WAS MADE, IS THERE ANY OVERRIDING PUBLIC POLICY THAT WOULD JUSTIFY THE COURT'S REFUSAL TO ENFORCE IT?

[135] If the exclusion clause is not invalid from the outset, I do not believe the Ministry's performance can be characterized as so aberrant as to forfeit the protection

of the contractual exclusion clause on the basis of some overriding public policy. While there is a public interest in a fair and transparent tendering process, it cannot be ratcheted up to defeat the enforcement of Contract A in this case. There *was* an RFP process and Tercon participated in it.

• • •

[137] While the Ministry's conduct was in breach of Contract A, that conduct was not so extreme as to engage some overriding and paramount public interest in curbing contractual abuse as in the *Plas-Tex* case. Brentwood was not an outsider to the RFP process. It was a legitimate competitor. All bidders knew that the road contract (i.e. Contract B) would not be performed by the proponent alone. The work required a large "team" of different trades and personnel to perform. The issue was whether EAC would be on the job as a major sub-contractor (to which Tercon could not have objected) or identified with Brentwood as a joint venture "proponent" with EAC. All bidders were made aware of a certain flexibility with respect to the composition of any proponent's "team." Section 2.8(b) of the RFP provided that if "a material change has occurred to the Proponent since its qualification under the RFEI, including if the composition of the Proponent's team members has changed, ... the Ministry may request [further information and] ... reserves the right to disqualify that Proponent, and reject its Proposal." Equally, "[i]f a qualified Proponent is concerned that it has undergone a material change, the Proponent can, at its election, make a preliminary submission to the Ministry, in advance of the Closing Date, and before submitting a Proposal. ... The Ministry will, within three working days of receipt of the preliminary submission give a written decision as to whether the Proponent is still qualified to submit a Proposal."

• • •

[139] The Ministry did obtain legal advice and did not proceed in defiance of it. On March 29, 2001, the Ministry noted in an internal e-mail that a Ministry lawyer (identified in the e-mail) had come to the conclusion that the joint venture was not an eligible proponent but advised that Contract B could lawfully be structured in a way so as to satisfy both Brentwood/EAC's concerns and avoid litigation from disappointed proponents.

[140] I do not wish to understate the difference between EAC as a sub-contractor and EAC as a joint-venturer. Nor do I discount the trial judge's condemnation of the Ministry's lack of fairness and transparency in making a contract B which on its face was at odds with what the trial judge found to be the true state of affairs. Tercon has legitimate reason to complain about the Ministry's conduct. I say only that based on the jurisprudence, the Ministry's misconduct did not rise to the level where public policy would justify the court in depriving the Ministry of the protection of the exclusion of compensation clause freely agreed to by Tercon in the contract.

[141] The construction industry in British Columbia is run by knowledgeable and sophisticated people who bid upon and enter government contracts with eyes wide open. No statute in British Columbia and no principle of the common law override their ability in this case to agree on a tendering process including a limitation or exclusion of remedies for breach of its rules. A contractor who does not think it is in its business interest to bid on the terms offered is free to decline to participate. As Donald J.A. pointed out, if enough contractors refuse to participate, the Ministry would be forced to change its approach. So long as contractors are willing to bid on such terms, I do not think it is the court's job to rescue them from the consequences of their decision to do so. Tercon's loss of anticipated profit is a paper loss. In my view, its claim is barred by the terms of the contract it agreed to.

NOTES

1. *Tercon* has now clarified this area by supporting Dickson CJ's analysis from *Hunter Engineering*. In *Tercon*, the doctrine of fundamental breach was laid to rest and the court determined that freedom of contract would prevail unless the exclusion clause was unconscionable at the time the contract was made or there is some overriding public policy concern to defeat what would otherwise be the contractual right of parties to draft their own agreements. For the effect of *Tercon* on exclusion clauses in the tendering process, see Jassmine Girgis, "*Tercon Contractors*: The Effect of Exclusion Clauses on the Tendering Process" (2010) 49 Can Bus LJ 187. For an analysis of the *Tercon* decision, see Shannon O'Byrne, "Assessing Exclusion Clauses: The Supreme Court of Canada's Three Issue Framework in *Tercon Contractors Ltd v British Columbia (Transportation and Highways)*" (2012) 35 Dal LJ 215.

2. The first prong of the *Tercon* framework involves analyzing the clause to determine its applicability to the situation, using the principles of contract interpretation. Courts must do this in any decision involving limitation of liability clauses, whether or not they explicitly apply *Tercon*. See e.g. *Niedermeyer v Charlton*, 2014 BCCA 165, where the plaintiff was injured when the bus on which she was riding on her return from a zip-lining tour was overturned. The plaintiff argued that "the intention of the words 'travel to and from the tour area' were not intended to exclude liability for negligence in the operation of motor vehicles on highways" (para 65). At trial, the judge dismissed the action, finding that the waiver was a complete defence to the appellant's claim, and that the accident happened in the circumstances envisioned by the exclusion clause. The judgment was overturned on appeal for public policy reasons. See note 4 below. In *Chamberlin v Canadian Physiotherapy Assn*, 2015 BCSC 1260, the plaintiff was injured when she partook in a continuing education course set up by the defendant. The judge agreed with the plaintiff's argument, in that she had understood the waiver to refer to pain and soreness, and not to the legal risks of the course, which excluded liability for negligence. The judge applied the principle of *contra proferentem* to the ambiguity, resolving it against the drafters of the clause.

3. The test for the traditional doctrine of unconscionability has involved both an inequality of bargaining power and a grossly improvident transaction. On the second prong of the *Tercon* framework, whether there was unconscionability at the time the agreement was made, the question that arose after *Tercon* was whether the Supreme Court was referring only to procedural unconscionability, which would focus on the state of the parties at the time the agreement was made, or whether it also encompassed a substantive element, to enable courts to analyze the contractual terms for unfairness. Courts have tended to focus on the procedural aspect, but they do conduct a substantive analysis as well, and it has been noted that Binnie J was not departing from the traditional test in *Tercon* (see *Roy v 1216393 Ontario Inc*, 2011 BCCA 500 at para 30). In *1539304 Ontario Inc v ICICI Bank Canada*, 2013 ONSC 2737, [2013] OJ No 2132 (QL), the court focused on procedural aspects and looked at whether parties were represented by counsel at the time the agreements were signed and whether the documents were subject to negotiation. In *Loychuk v Cougar Mountain Adventures Ltd*, 2012 BCCA 122, [2012] BCJ No 504 (QL), the court considered both procedural and substantive factors, and determined that there is no power imbalance where a person engages in a potentially risky recreational activity that is controlled by another and that it is not inherently unfair for the operator to require that a customer sign a release that bars claims for negligence against the operator or its employees as a condition of participating in the activity. In *Hans v Volvo Trucks North America Inc*, 2011 BCSC 1574, the court applied the four-part test set out in *Cain v Clarica Life Insurance Company*, 2005 ABCA 437, and again in *Titus v William F Cooke Enterprises Inc*, 2007 ONCA 573, which contains both procedural and substantive elements:

1. a grossly unfair and improvident transaction; and
2. victim's lack of independent legal advice or other suitable advice; and

3. overwhelming imbalance in bargaining power caused by victim's ignorance of business, illiteracy, ignorance of the language of the bargain, blindness, deafness, illness, senility, or similar disability; and
4. other party's knowingly taking advantage of this vulnerability.

In *Hans*, above, the court maintained that the words "grossly" and "imprudent" denote a transaction that is more than simply unfair, and that it must be "egregiously unfair" (para 86). In *Raabe v 4042492 Manitoba Ltd*, [2011] MJ No 320 (QL) (QB), to determine whether there was unconscionability, the court relied on criteria such as age, education, employment of the claimant, and the defendant's knowledge of the problem with the product sold to the claimant. However, as the court noted in *Hans*, unconscionability does not have a low bar; all four elements of the test must be met, and each element must be considered in context. For example, the absence of legal advice does not mean the transaction is unconscionable. Similarly, an imbalance of bargaining power, which will typically exist when consumers deal with corporations, does not necessarily give rise to unconscionability, nor will the failure to read the agreement prior to signing it, if there was an opportunity to read it that was simply not utilized.

4. On the third prong of the *Tercon* framework, the courts have had to weigh the balance of enforcing the exclusion clause with overriding public policy concerns, or determine whether public policy concerns are even triggered. To invalidate an exclusion clause on the basis of public policy concerns, the behaviour must be so deplorable that it would be contrary to the public interest to allow a party to avoid liability by relying on the exclusion clause, or the matter must be of such public importance that it should not be left to be adjudicated by an exclusion clause. In *Skypower CL 1 LP v Ontario (Minister of Energy)*, [2012] OJ No 4458 (QL) (Sup Ct J (Div Ct)), the court decided that the objectives of a renewable energy program by government were matters of public policy, not strict commercial dealings. In *Niedermeyer* (above, note 2), a majority of the court of appeal determined it was "contrary to public policy to permit the owner and/or operator of a motor vehicle to contract out of liability for damages for personal injuries suffered in a motor vehicle accident in British Columbia" (para. 72). The legislature intended to enact a statutory insurance scheme that provided mandatory and compulsory coverage when motor vehicles are involved. This means that motor vehicle accidents will trigger public policy interests that can override freedom of contract. Finally, in *Roy v 1216393 Ontario Inc.*, 2011 BCCA 500, the court refused to allow the vendor to escape liability for fraudulently breaching the contract by relying on the exclusion clause. However, in *Felty v Ernst & Young LLP*, 2015 BCCA 445, the court found that avoiding liability for giving erroneous tax advice pursuant to a limitation of liability clause did not trigger public policy concerns. It went on to note that if holding accountants to that standard was important, the legislature could enact provisions similar to those prohibiting lawyers and law firms from relying on limitation of liability clauses. In *Loychuk*, the court maintained that there were no public policy concerns where a release for negligence was signed in a contract for a dangerous activity, even where the safety of the activity was not within the control of the participant.

5. In *Douez v Facebook, Inc*, 2017 SCC 33 (see longer note in Chapter 7), Abella J, in a concurring judgment, found in favour of not enforcing a forum selection clause on the basis of unconscionability and public policy (though unconscionability was not argued before the court). She maintained that it would "be contrary to public policy to enforce a forum selection clause in a consumer contract that has the effect of depriving a party of access to a statutorily mandated court" (para 108). She also found that the doctrine of unconscionability could be applied to render the clause unenforceable, procedurally and possibly substantively. There was inequality of bargaining power between the parties as well as unfairness, given that Facebook had "the unilateral ability to require that any legal grievances Ms. Douez had, could not be vindicated in British Columbia where the contract was made, but only in California where Facebook has its head office" (para 116).

6. A broadly worded exclusion clause can be found to cover negligence, even if negligence is not explicitly mentioned. In *ITO-Int'l Terminal Operators v Miida Electronics*, [1986] 1 SCR 752, the Supreme Court of Canada laid out a test for determining when an exclusion clause that does not expressly exclude negligence can nevertheless extend to negligent action. When an exclusion clause is worded broadly enough to exclude negligence by implication, the court must look to the parties' intentions. If negligence can reasonably be construed as being within the contemplation of the parties in formulating their agreement, then the clause will extend to liability for negligence. *ITO* was applied in *MacKay v Scott Packing and Warehousing Co (Canada) Ltd*, [1996] 2 FC 36 (CA), in which the defendant invoked an exclusion clause in an action for losses due to the defendant's non-delivery of goods. The Federal Court of Appeal held that the exclusion clause extended to negligence. However, in *Chamberlin v Canadian Physiotherapy Assn*, above, the judge found that a waiver of liability for a physiotherapy training course did not include negligence, noting that "a reasonable participant at the Course would not have understood or expected that he or she was agreeing to such onerous legal risks, particularly given the general language of the Waiver and its lack of specificity with respect to negligence" (para 88).

7. In *Canadian Pacific Forest Products Ltd-Tahsis Pacific Region v Beltimber (The)*, [1999] 4 FC 320, 175 DLR (4th) 449, the Federal Court of Appeal ruled that if an exclusion clause can reasonably contemplate any head of liability other than negligence, it is generally construed as *not* extending to negligence. *MacKay* was distinguished from *Belships* because the defendant in *Belships* was a "carrier of goods at sea." At common law, such a carrier is liable for safe carriage and delivery and seaworthiness; as such, the exclusion clause could reasonably contemplate heads of liability other than negligence and did not, therefore, extend to negligence.

8. In *Meditek Laboratory Services v Purolator Courier Ltd* (1995), 125 DLR (4th) 738 (Man CA), a customer's package was delivered by a Purolator employee to the wrong address. Mis-delivery was concealed by the employee's falsification of documents. When the customer sued for breach of contract, Purolator relied on its bill of lading, which included a clause explicitly limiting liability due to negligence. The Manitoba Court of Appeal held that once a breach of contract has been established, the onus is on a defendant to prove that the breach resulted from actions falling within the four corners of the limitation clause. Wilful misconduct is separate and distinct from negligence, and did not fall within the scope of Purolator's clause. As a result, Purolator was liable for damages for breach of contract.

9. In *Plas-Tex Canada Ltd v Dow Chemical of Canada Limited*, 2004 ABCA 309, the defendant Dow, a large petrochemical company, knowingly sold defective polyethylene resin to the respondents without advising them. When the pipe cracked because of defective resin, and the escaping natural gas caused an explosion, the respondents sought assistance from Dow for the repair, but Dow refused. Picard JA, writing for the court, found that Dow knew of the defects before it signed the contract, but, rather than disclosing its knowledge, it protected itself from liability by inserting clauses limiting liability for loss or damage resulting from the use of resin in the contract. The conduct was found to be unconscionable because of the potential danger to people and property and Dow was prevented from relying on the limitation of liability clauses.

10. Do you think it is a socially desirable policy decision to allow companies that run potentially dangerous recreational activities to utilize limitation of liability clauses? See Philip H Osborne, "The Battle of Contractual Waivers of Liability for Personal Injury in Sporting and Recreational Activities: An Annotation to *Loychuk v Cougar Mountain Adventures Ltd*" (2011) 81 CCLT (3d) 100.

11. Most provinces have enacted legislation that provides in all contracts for the sale of goods implied conditions as to the fitness for purpose and merchantability of the goods involved (e.g. see the Ontario *Sale of Goods Act*, RSO 1990, c S.1, s 15). In Ontario, any attempt to contract out of any implied condition or warranty under the *Sale of Goods Act* in a consumer

agreement is void (see the Ontario *Consumer Protection Act, 2002*, SO 2002, c 30, sch A, s 9). See generally on disclaimer clauses Waddams at paras 471-90; McCamus at 796-834.

V. UNCONSCIONABILITY AND UNDUE INFLUENCE

MICHAEL J TREBILCOCK, *The Limits of Freedom of Contract*
(Cambridge, MA: Harvard University Press, 1993) at 115-20

INEQUALITY OF BARGAINING POWER

A provocative approach to this problem has been proposed by Gordley [James Gordley, "Equality in Exchange" (1981) 69 Cal L Rev 1583]. In contrast to the Paretian principle, which merely requires in order for an exchange to be Pareto superior that both parties gain *something* from the exchange, even if the gains from exchange are unequal, Gordley's proposal holds that both parties should gain equally, in effect postulating a principle of commutative or corrective justice as originally articulated by Aristotle and designed to maintain the pre-existing distribution of wealth. Gordley argues for an ethical principle of equality in exchange such that inequalities in the value of the performances exchanged should be grounds for contractual invalidation or judicial reconstruction of the contract, without examination of the causes of the disparity. He argues that most legal systems from classical Greek and Roman times forward, including the medieval theory of the just price, have recognized some such principle but that in the nineteenth century, courts under the influence of will theories of contract and theories about the subjectivity of value became much less self-conscious in applying the principle, despite similar patterns of judicial outcomes disguised under other principles. Gordley reformulates classical theories of commutative justice and medieval theories of the just price in a modern economic context as requiring contractual relief where parties have contracted for substantially more or substantially less than the market price. For example, A buys from a door-to-door salesman for $1,000 a freezer that commonly sells for $500 at normal retail outlets (holding constant characteristics of consumers in terms of default risk, and so on), or, alternatively, A sells his farm to B for $50,000, when its market value is $100,000. In both cases, it is assumed that A is ignorant of the prevailing market price, and on Gordley's theory we should not be concerned to inquire whether B did or did not deliberately take advantage of his ignorance. In cases where the contract subject matter does not have a readily ascertainable market price, Gordley's theory would apparently be more respectful of the parties' valuation unless there is compelling evidence that the price reflects much more or much less than the seller's costs. The ethical intuition that lies behind Gordley's reformulation of the theory of the just price appears to be that a party to an arm's-length exchange does not intend to make a gift to the other party, which is implied by selling for less than the market price or buying for more than the market price.

Although provocative, Gordley's theory raises a number of questions. From an individual autonomy perspective, to take a case outside the fungible goods context, suppose that I am extremely attached to my house for family, sentimental, historical, or locational reasons and would not contemplate selling it for less than a large premium over the going market price for otherwise similar houses. A buyer, perhaps motivated by similar factors to those which weigh with me, agrees to pay me this price. Is this price unjust? From a communitarian perspective of the kind adopted by McPherson, one might imagine a challenge to Gordley's theory along the lines of asking why we should sanctify or even exalt market prices as the dominant indicia of fairness. In terms of the practical implications of Gordley's theory, we need to ask whether a recognition of a reconstituted theory of the just price would yield substantially different results in particular cases from a Paretian test with the conventional conditions attached. In order to violate Gordley's doctrine of equality in exchange, he envisages that the disproportionality between contract and market price must be substantial. Thus, some range of inequalities in values exchanged is still envisaged, and to that extent, Gordley's theory moves closer to a Paretian theory of mutually beneficial exchanges but does not completely elide with it, since, provided that both parties derive *any* gains from the exchange, however they are shared, the Paretian test would be met. Moreover, where the disproportionalities are as large as Gordley apparently envisages in order for the doctrine to be invoked, one would need to ask whether this would be compelling evidence in many settings of a violation of the Paretian conditions, including coercion or fraud or misrepresentation. However, his theory does offer the advantage that one need not investigate the precise source of procedural irregularities or deficiencies in the contract formation process—it is a theory of substantive, not procedural, fairness—and may provide more precision than either Kronman's modified Paretian test or Fried's established conventions test in dealing with cases where, because of asymmetric information, as the facts are subsequently revealed, there is a major disparity between the contract price and the market price for the contract subject matter in the fully revealed state of the facts. It needs to be added, though, that this certainty comes at a price: Gordley is largely insensitive to the dynamic incentive considerations which emphasize the welfare gains from the acquisition and utilization of information that moves assets from less productive to more productive uses. It needs also to be added that whatever virtues Gordley's theory of equality in exchange might have, the obligations it implies are certainly not consensually based and entail an appeal to external ethical norms, which he presumably believes the community widely endorses. ...

INFORMATION PROCESSING DISABILITIES: COGNITIVE DEFICIENCIES

Under this category, I include cases where there has been no misrepresentation of information by one contracting party to the other and no non-disclosure of some material fact, but rather where the two parties, while sharing equal access to the relevant body of information about the contract subject matter, have sharply differential capacities to evaluate the implications of that information for their respective welfare. Eisenberg [Melvin Eisenberg, "The Bargain Principle and Its Limits" (1982) 95 Harv L Rev 741] cites two sub-classes of case, both of which he argues should be addressed by a modern doctrine of unconscionability. The first sub-class he characterizes as "transactional incapacity." The paradigm case he envisages is one where A knows or has reason to know of B's inability to deal with a given complex transaction, because of lack of aptitude, experience, or judgemental ability to make a deliberative and well-informed decision concerning the desirability of entering into the transaction, and exploits that incapacity by inducing B to make a bargain that a person who had the capacity to deal with the transaction probably would not make. He cites as an example a very complex real estate proposal put by a commercial developer to an aging testamentary beneficiary of a commercial building. He also cites the well-known decision of Lord Denning of the English Court of Appeal in *Lloyds Bank v. Bundy*, where an elderly farmer was induced by his son's bank to sign a guarantee of his son's indebtedness to the bank in circumstances where it was highly unlikely that the farmer was able to evaluate prudentially all the implications of the transaction. The other sub-class of case which Eisenberg identifies is what he calls "unfair persuasion." By this he means the use of bargaining methods that seriously impair the free and competent exercise of judgement and produce a state of acquiescence that the promisee knows or should know is likely to be highly transitory. Examples of such situations which he cites are a creditor's obtaining a promise from a bereaved and distraught widow to pay debts of her husband's business shortly after his death, or a door-to-door salesman's employing importuning and intrusive sales tactics.

I believe that both of Eisenberg's sub-classes of cognitive deficiencies fall within the concerns that in order for contractual promises to be binding, they should in general arise out of the autonomous consent of the parties and reflect base-line conditions of voluntariness and information. Thus, they seem entirely appropriate candidates for a doctrine of unconscionability.

STANDARD FORM CONTRACTS

Standard form contracts have suffered a bad press from both judicial and academic members of the legal fraternity over many years. At least in a consumer setting, the hostility to standard form contracts is based on two principal propositions. First, it is said that the use of standard form contracts is a manifestation of monopoly. Second, it is pointed out that the use of standard form contracts is typically characterized by imperfect information on the part of some of the parties to them. In both cases, the legal implications are much the same: courts should be extremely cautious about enforcing such contracts. These two arguments require evaluation.

The monopoly argument essentially rests on the "take it or leave it" character of most standard form contractual offerings. However, as I have argued elsewhere, the principal justification for standard form contracts is the dramatic reduction in transaction costs that they permit in many contexts. That they may be offered on a take it or leave it basis is as consistent with the benign transaction cost conservation rationale for them as it is with a monopoly or collusion rationale. Simply observing the fact of standard form contracts yields no meaningful implications as to the underlying structure of the market. Indeed, we observe them being used in many settings where manifestly the market is highly competitive, for example, in dry-cleaning stores, hotel registration forms, insurance contracts, and so on. Indeed, even in the absence of standard form contracts, we see many goods being offered on a take it or leave it basis in some of the most competitive retail markets in the economy. For example, corner variety stores (mom and pop stores) typically offer their goods on a take it or leave it basis, presumably to avoid the transaction costs entailed in haggling over price or product offerings.

The imperfect information argument against standard form contracts is clearly more substantial. Almost necessarily implicit in the transaction cost justification for standard form contracts is the assumption that parties will often not read them or, if they do, will not wish to spend significant amounts of time attempting to renegotiate the terms. Thus, to hold parties bound to standard form contracts which they had entered into but which they had not read or understood does not rest comfortably with a theory of contractual obligation premised on individual autonomy and consent. Clearly, in many, perhaps most cases, meaningful consent is absent. Thus, to justify contractual enforcement of these kinds of standard form contracts requires us, once again, to move outside the purely internal, non-instrumental basis for contractual obligation as deriving from the will of the parties and appeal instead to external benchmarks of fairness. In this respect, I have argued first that problems of unfairness resulting from imperfect information are not so severe as they might seem at first sight. To the extent that there is a margin of informed, sophisticated, and aggressive consumers in any given market, who understand the terms of the standard form contracts on offer and who either negotiate over those terms or switch their business readily to competing suppliers offering more favourable terms, they may in effect discipline the entire market, so that inframarginal (less well informed, sophisticated, or mobile) consumers can effectively free-ride on the discipline brought to the market by the marginal consumers, although there is the potential for a collective action problem if every consumer attempts to free-ride on the efforts of others in effective monitoring of contract terms. In addition, where suppliers are able either to term or to performance discriminate between marginal and inframarginal consumers, this generalized discipline will be undermined, and there is a clear risk that the inframarginal consumers will be exploited because of their imperfect knowledge of the contract terms. Here, I have proposed that courts, in evaluating the fairness of standard form contracts in particular cases, should investigate whether a particular consumer seeking relief from the contract or some particular provision in it has received a deal that is significantly inferior, in relation to either the explicit terms of the contract or the performance provided under it, to that realized by marginal consumers in the same market, with the economic as opposed to personal characteristics of consumers in these two classes held constant. In other words, where a supplier has deliberately exploited a consumer's ignorance of terms generally available, in the market for like goods or services, to consumers in an economically similar situation in order to exact terms substantially inferior to these generally prevailing terms, the supplier's actions should be viewed as unconscionable, perhaps again invoking the equal concern and respect basis for protection of individual autonomy. In markets which are so badly disrupted by imperfect information that there is no identifiable margin of informed consumers from which appropriate benchmarks can be derived, then judicial sniping in case-by-case litigation seems less appropriate than legislative or regulatory intervention of the kind that has occurred in many jurisdictions, for example, with respect to various classes of door-to-door sales.

NOTE

For a critical analysis of Trebilcock's article, see Marc Ramsay, "The Buyer/Seller Asymmetry: Corrective Justice and Material Non-Disclosure" (2006) 56 UTLJ 115.

ARTHUR A LEFF, "UNCONSCIONABILITY AND THE CODE: THE EMPEROR'S NEW CLAUSE"
(1967) 115 U Pa L Rev 485

Let us begin the story the way so many good stories begin, with ritual incantation: to make a contract one needs (i) parties with capacity, (ii) manifested assent, and (iii) consideration. This is all very simple. If these criteria are met, a party to the resulting nexus who has made promises is obligated to carry them out, unless he can maintain successfully one of the standard contract-law defenses, such as fraud, duress, mistake, impossibility or illegality. These "defenses" might be classified in diverse ways to serve various analytical purposes. For our particular needs, however, there is a simple way of grouping them which is signally illuminating: some of these defenses have to do with the *process of contracting* and others have to do with the resulting *contract*. When fraud and duress are involved, for instance, the focus of attention is on what took place between the parties at the making of the contract. With illegality, on the other hand, the material question is instead the content of the contract once "made." The law may legitimately be interested both in the way agreements come about and in what they provide. A "contract" gotten at gunpoint may be avoided; a classic dicker over Dobbin may come to naught if horse owning is illegal. Hereafter, to distinguish the two interests, I shall often refer to bargaining naughtiness as "procedural unconscionability," and to evils in the resulting contract as "substantive unconscionability."

Getting down to cases, section 2-302 of the Uniform Commercial Code provides in its entirety as follows:

Section 2-302. Unconscionable Contract or Clause.

(1) If the court as a matter of law finds the contract or any clause of the contract to have been unconscionable at the time it was made the court may refuse to enforce the contract, or it may enforce the remainder of the contract without the unconscionable clause, or it may so limit the application of any unconscionable clause as to avoid any unconscionable result.

(2) When it is claimed or appears to the court that the contract or any clause thereof may be unconscionable the parties shall be afforded a reasonable opportunity to present evidence as to its commercial setting, purpose, and effect to aid the court in making the determination.

If reading this section makes anything clear it is that reading this section alone makes nothing clear about the meaning of "unconscionable" except perhaps that it is pejorative. More particularly, one cannot tell from the statute whether the key concept is something to be predicated on the bargaining process or on the bargain or on some combination of the two, that is, to use our terminology, whether it is procedural or substantive. Nonetheless, determining whether the section's target is a species of quasi-fraud or quasi-duress, or whether it is a species of quasi-illegality, is obviously the key to the bite and scope of the provision. ...

Strictly speaking, only one reported case relies upon section 2-302 of the Code even as an alternative ground of holding. In *American Home Improvement, Inc. v. MacIver*, the plaintiff was in the business of selling and installing home improvements. It agreed with the defendant to "furnish and install 14 combination windows and one door" and "flintcoat the side walls" on defendant's home, all for $1,759.00. Since the defendant was apparently unwilling or unable to pay cash, the plaintiff undertook to arrange long-term financing, and furnished defendant with an application to a finance company (apparently in some way allied or affiliated with the plaintiff). This application was shortly "accepted," and defendant was notified in writing that his payments for the improvements would be $42.81 per month for sixty months (a grand total of $2,568.60) which included "principal, interest and life and disability insurance." Plaintiff commenced work, but after it had completed only a negligible portion of the job it was asked by defendant to stop and it complied, thereafter suing defendant for damages for breach of contract.

On these facts, the New Hampshire court need never have reached any unconscionability question. There was in effect in the jurisdiction a "truth-in-lending" statute which applied to the transaction. The court could have relied upon that statute to strike the contract, and indeed did so as an alternative ground of decision. But the court most specifically made it a point not to rest its decision solely upon the disclosure statute. It said:

There is another and independent reason why the recovery should be barred in the present case because the transaction was unconscionable. "The courts have often avoided the enforcement of unconscionable provisions in long printed standardized contracts, in part by the process of 'interpretation' against the parties using them, and in part by the method used by Lord Nelson at Copenhagen." 1 Corbin, Contracts, s. 128 (1963). Without using either of these methods reliance can be placed upon the Uniform Commercial Code (U.C.C. 2-302(1)).

Inasmuch as the defendants have received little or nothing of value and under the transaction they entered into they were paying $1,609 for goods and services valued at far less, the contract should not be enforced because of its unconscionable features. This is not a new thought or a new rule in this jurisdiction. See *Morrill v. Bank*, 90 N.H. 358, 365, 9 A.2d 519, 525: "It has long been the law in this state that contracts may be declared void because unconscionable and oppressive. ..."

All right, then. As of the time of writing, the only case which has relied upon section 2-302 as a basis of decision has decided that "unconscionable" means "too expensive." And certainly there is no immutable principle displayed in fixed stars that would make that particular meaning of unconscionable inconceivable. I have earlier suggested that in fact that was the primary meaning of unconscionability in some of the early drafts of the Code, and that it was its *only* meaning as used by courts of equity. Certainly the idea that a strikingly disproportionate exchange should be voidable has not destroyed the commerce of the many jurisdictions which utilize a *laesio enormis* doctrine in one form or another. On the other hand one may certainly speculate on whether the legislatures which have flocked to embrace the Code would have been willing to adopt a provision which frankly and openly declared that overcharges of some large but unspecified degree could be invalidated by courts on an *ad hoc* basis, at least as part of a *commercial* code.

Let us assume, however, that a system of jurisprudence ought to have some way to deal with transactions in which one party is giving up vastly more than he is getting, and that this purpose is at least one of those that section 2-302 is designed to serve. Even given that assumption, one has still to ask whether the best way to inject that supervisory power into the law is to subsume it under a high-level abstraction like "unconscionability." After all, a *laesio enormis* type of statute is not very hard to draft, as either a flat-percentage or a "grossly-too-much" provision. ...

As noted earlier, the *MacIver* case is the only one reported which has relied upon 2-302 as a basis of decision. One very recent case, however, which has attracted substantial attention from the commentators, clearly would have been decided on the basis of 2-302 had the statute been in effect at the time of the relevant transaction, and in fact was decided as if the section were the law of the jurisdiction. In that case, *Williams v. Walker-Thomas Furniture Co.*, the appellant, a Mrs. Williams, "a person of limited education separated from her husband," had, during the period 1957-1962, purchased "a number of household items" from appellee furniture company on printed-form installment sale contracts (in the transparent guise of leases). One sentence in this printed contract, part of "a long paragraph in extremely fine print" had the net effect of keeping

a balance due on every item purchased until the balance due on all items, whenever purchased, was liquidated. As a result, the debt incurred at the time of purchase of each item was secured by the right to repossess all the items previously purchased by the same purchaser. ...

When Mrs. Williams' outstanding balance was only $164, she bought a $515 stereo phonograph set. At the time of this purchase, the furniture company was perfectly aware (since the information was endorsed on the back of the installment contract) that Mrs. Williams' sole income was a government payment (apparently some species of relief) of $218 per month. The Circuit Court opinion also indicated that the store knew that Mrs. Williams was supposed to support herself and her seven children on that amount (though that seems not to have been endorsed on the back of the contract). At any rate, the stereo set was apparently just too great a burden for the $218 per month to bear. Mrs. Williams defaulted, the store replevied every item it could lay its hands on and won in the trial court and the intermediate appeals court. On appeal to the United States Court of Appeals for the District of Columbia Circuit, the case was remanded to make findings on the issue of unconscionability.

For those of us who have an instinctive and infallible sense of justice (and which of us does not), any other result in this case is unimaginable. But there are grounds for quibbling about the court's (and the Code's) methodology. Judge Wright found unconscionability easy to describe:

> Unconscionability has generally been recognized to include an absence of meaningful choice on the part of one of the parties together with contract terms which are unreasonably favorable to the other party. ... [In the footnote which supports this statement, citation is to *Henningsen v. Bloomfield Motors, Inc.*, 32 N.J. 358, 161 A.2d 69 (1960) and *Campbell Soup Co. v. Wentz*, 172 F.2d 80 (3d Cir. 1948) only.] In many cases the meaningfulness of the choice is negated by a gross inequality of bargaining power.

That is, there is immediate recognition that unconscionability has to have two foci, the negotiation which led to the contract and that contract's terms. As for the procedural aspect, while there is no finding that this was the only credit furniture store open to Mrs. Williams, or that even if it were not, they all had substantially the same contract (which was the situation in the Henningsen case so heavily relied upon by the court), one may assume that the form Mrs. Williams signed was essentially the only kind of form open to her. A person's "relevant market" may fairly be the one he can reasonably be expected to know about or dare to use. In other words, the local stores may be a local person's relevant market because of his ignorance, and if they are all as one on something, as to him they are a monopoly. And besides, in this case the court made an almost-finding of contracting procedures which went beyond the mere use of a form or even of a contract of adhesion, which reached, in fact, at least some level of quasi-fraud. Judge Wright asks:

> Did each party to the contract, considering his obvious education or lack of it, have a reasonable opportunity to understand the terms of the contract, or were the important terms hidden in a maze of fine print and minimized by deceptive sales practices?

There was apparently no problem with the answer, for after giving lip service to the "usual rule" that one who signs an agreement is bound to all of its terms, he said:

> But when a party of little bargaining power, and hence little real choice, signs a commercially unreasonable contract with little or no knowledge of its terms ... the usual rule ... should be abandoned. ...

It is hard to fault the court's argument on the procedural unconscionability aspects of this case. While it might sometimes be difficult to decide whether a species or level of bargaining ought to protect a contract from section 2-302, it is not difficult here. If the unconscionability section is to be applicable to any contract, it must be to one "bargained" as this one was.

But there is no need to labor this point. Finding that the bargaining procedure involved will not insulate the contract from judicial scrutiny under section 2-302 is only the first and less difficult step in the process of using that section. Once one decides that the contract is vulnerable to judicial meddling, there still remains to be decided whether the provision or contract is "unconscionable." For that determination Judge Wright also articulated a test:

> In determining reasonableness or fairness, the primary concern must be with the terms of the contract considered in light of the circumstances existing when the contract was made. The test is not simple, nor can it be mechanically applied. The terms are to be considered "in the light of the general commercial background and the commercial needs of the particular trade or case" [citing "Comment, Uniform Commercial Code sec. 2-307," but obviously meaning 2-302]. Corbin suggests the test as being whether the terms are "so extreme as to appear unconscionable according to the mores and business practices of the time and place." ... We think this formulation correctly states the test to be applied in those cases where no meaningful choice was exercised upon entering the contract.

How does that test apply to the *Williams* facts? What is it about Mrs. Williams' contract which is "unconscionable"? Surprisingly, the answer is not clear, even about *what* in the contract is bad. It seems, however, that there are two possibilities. First, it may be that the provision by which each item purchased became security for all items purchased was the objectionable feature of the contract. Or it might be that the furniture company sold this expensive stereo set to this particular party which forms the unconscionability of the contract. If the vice is the add-on clause, then one encounters the now-familiar problem: such a clause is hardly such a moral outrage as by itself meets Judge Wright's standard of being "so extreme as to appear unconscionable according to the mores and business practices of the time and place." The lower court in the *Williams* case called attention, for instance, to a Maryland statute regulating retail installment sales under which Mrs. Williams might have been relieved, noting with regret that the statute was not in effect in the District. What was not pointed out by the lower court (and *certainly* not by the upper court) was that the Statute of Maryland had found nothing illegal per se about add-on provisions, in fact specifically permitting them and setting out to regulate them in some detail. Of the thirty-seven jurisdictions which have statutes regulating retail installment sales, only one has a provision making add-on clauses impermissible. In such circumstances it does seem a bit much to find "so extreme as to appear unconscionable according to the mores and business practices of the time and place" an add-on clause in the District of Columbia which is used and statutorily permitted almost everyplace else, including contiguous Maryland. One's gorge can hardly be expected to rise with such nice geographic selectivity.

If one is not convinced that the unconscionability inheres in the add-on provision, it may be argued that it inheres in the contract as a whole, in the act of having sold this expensive item to a poor person knowing of her poverty. This is quite clearly the primary significance of the case to some of the commentators. That is the kind of action which the Maryland statute does not deal with, nor do any of the statutes like it: the unconscionability of aiding or encouraging a person to live beyond his means (without much hope of eventual success). Well, why not make that "unconscionable" for purposes of section 2-302? After all, in this case Walker-Thomas did know for a fact that Mrs. Williams was on relief; they knew her income and needs with great particularity: $218 per month and seven children. This case does not present any of the sticky close questions of how much of what a seller would have to know (or inquire about) before being deemed to know that the buyer shouldn't buy. Moreover, what Mrs. Williams bought this time was a stereo record player. No one could argue that such an article is a "necessity" to a relief client, and thus the dissenting judge's suggestion that "what is a luxury to some may seem an outright necessity to others" hardly applies in this case. Who can doubt but that this purchase was a frill? So in this case all we would have is a holding that one cannot enforce a contract pursuant to which one has sold luxuries to a poor person (or at least one on relief) with knowledge or reason to know that he will not be able to pay for them. This is just another class distinction, and distinctions among persons on the basis of the "class" to which they belong, that is, on the basis of some common supra-personal characteristics, are exceedingly common in the law (not to mention life). Such a process immensely simplifies decision by limiting the required inquiry to the person's membership in the class. Once that determination is made, a certain legal result will flow. The classic instance is the majority–minority dichotomy. Persons under twenty-one cannot, as a general rule, make self-binding contracts. This may be considered a shorthand form of a syllogism which would go something like (a) persons lacking sufficient probity ought not to be allowed to bind themselves; (b) all persons under twenty-one lack sufficient probity; (c) persons under twenty-one cannot bind themselves. This illustrates some of the strengths and weaknesses of the class system. The rule is easy to administer because a party's age is much easier to determine than his probity. The difficulty is that the easier the classification the less likely it is to be accurate, because classes are, in fact, hardly ever wholly homogeneous. In our case, for instance, the "minor premise," is false; not all persons under twenty-one lack sufficient probity to bind themselves.

When faced with the difficulties inherent in deciding the bargaining fairness of any given transaction, the equity courts, in working out *their* unconscionability doctrine, similarly leaned heavily on relatively gross classifications. In effect, they seem continually to have taken a kind of *sub rosa* judicial notice of the amount of power of certain classes of people to take care of themselves, often without too much inquiry into the actual individual bargaining situation. And it is arguable that some-times they were wrong; not all old ladies or farmers are without defenses. Put briefly, the typical has a tendency to become stereotypical, with what may be unpleasant results even for the beneficiaries of the judicial benevolence. One can see it enshrined in the old English equity courts' jolly treatment of English seamen as members of a happy, fun-loving race (with, one supposes, a fine sense of rhythm), but certainly not to be trusted to take care of themselves. What effect, if any, this had upon the sailors is hidden behind the judicial chuckles as they protected their loyal sailor boys, but one cannot help wondering how many sailors managed to get credit at any reasonable price. In other words, the benevolent have a tendency to colonize, whether geographically or legally.

Far more economically significant and widespread as an example of the Chancel-lors' temptation toward stereotypical jurisprudence is found in the expectant-heir cases. The most important thing about expectant-heir cases is that there are expectant-heir cases, classifiable separately as such in treatises. The Chancellors did not find unfairness in the price and refuse to enforce because they had no conception of how an expectancy had to be discounted for risk; that kind of sophistication came early. They just set out to protect heirs from the full effect of their tendency to live beyond their governors' life expectancies. This was easy to do; it was rare that a judge had to enter into too long a discussion of the actual facts, or to face the real basis of his easy decision in the battle between his (there but for the grace of God) grandson and the most-likely Jewish moneylender. After all, he had the rubric "unconscion-able" with which to explain (to himself and to the public) that decision.

Thus, when one asks why a court (like the District of Columbia Court in the *Williams* case) ought not be allowed to subsume its social decisions under a high-level abstraction like "unconscionability," one may point to the equity cases so many other commentators have pointed to, but for a different reason. One may suggest that first (and less important) it tends to make the true bases of decisions more hidden to those trying to use them as the basis of future planning. But more important, it tends to permit a court to be nondisclosive about the basis of its decision even to itself; the class determination is so easy and so tempting (and often so heart-warming). More particularly with respect to the *Williams* case concept that the poor should be discouraged from frill-buying, no legislature in America could be persuaded openly to pass such a statute, nor should any be permitted to do so sneakily. If the selling of frills to the poor is to be discouraged, if the traditional middle-class virtues of thrift and child care are to be fostered in the deserving poor by a commercial statute, if one wants to protect a class, improvident by definition, from the depredations of another class, it is at least arguable that one should just up and do so—but clearly. This is not to suggest, for a moment, anything as stupid as that some "freedom-of-contract" concept ought to prevent, for instance, the statutory interdiction of an eleven-hour day. It is only to say that when you forbid a contractual practice, you ought to have the political nerve to do so with some understanding (and some disclosure) of what you are doing.

I have attempted to describe in some detail the pathology, developmental, morphological and functional, of section 2-302 of the Code and its official and unofficial commentaries. The gist of the tale is simple: it is hard to give up an emotionally satisfying incantation, and the way to keep the glow without the trouble of the meaning is continually to increase the abstraction level of the drafting and explaining language. If for one reason or another (in this case the desire to forward the passage of the whole Code) the academic community is generally friendly to the drafting effort, a single provision in a massive Code may get by even if it has, really, no reality referent, and all of its explanatory material ranges between the irrelevant and the misleading. That this happened with respect to 2-302 the few cases using it are beginning to show more and more clearly. The world is not going to come to an end. The courts will most likely adjust, encrusting the irritating aspects of the section with a smoothing nacre of more or less reasonable applications, or the legislatures may act if things get out of hand. Commerce in any event is not going to grind to a halt because of the weaknesses in 2-302. But the lesson of its drafting ought nevertheless to be learned: it is easy to say nothing with words. Even if those words make one feel all warm inside, the result of sedulously preventing thought about them is likely to lead to more trouble than the draftsmen's cozy glow is worth, as a matter not only of statutory elegance but of effect in the world being regulated. Subsuming problems is not as good as solving them, and may in fact retard solutions instead. Or, once more to quote Karl Llewellyn (to whom, after all, the last word justly belongs), "Covert tools are never reliable tools."

NOTES

1. For commentary on the effects of Leff's "frontal assault on the unconscionability norm," see Jeffrey W Stempel, "Arbitration, Unconscionability, and Equilibrium: The Return of Unconscionability Analysis as a Counterweight to Arbitration Formalism" (2004) 19 Ohio St J Disp Resol 757.

2. For a critical analysis of Canada's unconscionability doctrine, see Rick Bigwood, "Antipodean Reflections on the Canadian Unconscionability Doctrine" (2005) 84 Can Bar Rev 171.

RICK BIGWOOD, *Exploitative Contracts*
(Oxford: Oxford University Press, 2003) at 505-10, 514-15
(footnotes omitted)

[T]he area of present inquiry ... is to determine whether, for corrective justice purposes, some lesser form of agency-responsible conduct than "exploitation"—in particular, "legal negligence"—should function as the justificatory paradigm for state interference with contracts entered into under conditions where exploitation was at least an eventuality, if not an event. If, as I have argued in this book, the fundamental reason for regulation in the precontractual bargaining setting is sufficiently analogous with our ordinary motivations for and style of private law regulation and responsibility, as exemplified in particular by tort law, then we can only profit by transferring, *mutatis mutandis*, relevant principles and insights from the tort context to the present one. ...

[I]t makes sense to return to what I argued ... lay as a possible basis for objection to exploitative contracts, namely, that such contracts involved a certain violation of a "legal neighbourhood" norm that, properly understood, defines and constrains the precontractual interactions of bargaining parties operating under whatever conditions trigger such a norm. ...

To summarize ... "legal neighbourhood" depicts the situation where "serious" vulnerability or dependency exists on the one side of an interpersonal relationship or dealing, and where that vulnerability or dependency is sufficiently known to the party on the other side of the relationship, who enjoys an atypical degree of interpersonal power as a result. The known possession of such power generates special responsibilities on the part of the power-holder not to "abuse" his peculiarly advantaged position. I enlisted this particular conception of legal neighbourhood in order to give content to "corrective justice" in this area. That is to say, I argued that legal neighbourhood generates norms of decent treatment toward parties who are known to be especially vulnerable to or dependent upon the other, more powerful party's choices and actions within a contract bargaining relationship, and that the violation of those norms is sufficient to justify state interference with any resulting transactions. As in both morals and tort law, the point of recognizing the neighbourhood norm is to prevent vulnerable parties from coming to "harm," which can be understood in terms of a vulnerable party's welfare interests, autonomy interests, or both. Most important, at least in the contract bargaining context, legal neighbourhood generates two separate (negative) responsibilities—each of which is best viewed ... in terms of a Hohfeldian "disability" or a Nozickian "side-constraint," rather than a full-blown legal duty or independent goal of action or condition vis-à-vis P ["exploited" contracting party].

The first responsibility, which for convenience I shall call "responsibility 1," comprises a responsibility not to create serious vulnerability to harm in bargaining. The second responsibility, which for convenience I shall call "responsibility 2," is a responsibility not unfairly to derive benefit in virtue of another's known serious bargaining disadvantage relative to you, even though such disadvantage was not of your making.

Violation of either responsibility ought to suffice ... to justify state-assisted rescission of a bargain transaction so resulting. ...

Whether negligence should be seen as too rigorous a burden in this area will depend on what we consider is a just balance between the parties' interests as "agents in freedom of action" and potential victims in contract formation settings, given all that we understand and accept about the liberal conception of contract in modern legal systems. ... [W]e ought to consider in this balance the consequences of lowering the threshold of agency responsibility in this area, not just for the immediate parties involved (D ["exploiting" contracting party] and P), but also for society generally, which has a wider interest in the continuance of valuable social activities such as private contract. Certainly, one reason for requiring *exploitation* and not merely neglect on the part of D in this context, and hence for preferring D's contractual freedom over P's personal and proprietary security, is that such a requirement at least pays lip-service to "sanctity of contract." ...

But no longer do we operate under a "primitive" conception of contract (if we ever really did), under which every moral tie is thought to be submerged in "the icy waters of egotistical calculation." Ours is reportedly an era in which commerce and commercial law place their "imprimatur on the accepted moral standards and condemn conduct which fails to match 'the reflection of moral uprightness, of fundamental honesty, fair play and right dealing in the general business life of members of society.'" Still, even under such an "enlightened" vision of commerce and commercial law, sanctity of contract is unlikely to be cast aside lightly, for the stability of our economic system is ultimately at stake.

Yet for all that, who is really going to believe that a paradigm shift from exploitation to negligence in this area of the law will endanger the general security of contractual relations? Surely no one reflecting thoughtfully on the matter; for ... such a paradigm shift would make no difference at all to the doctrinal formulations, qualifying thresholds, and decisions historically rendered in the name of (especially passive) "exploitation." Only the nomenclature at the conceptual justificatory level ought to change. Thus, it should not be thought that the substitution of "negligence" for "exploitation" as the justificatory paradigm for official interference with certain species of defeasible bargain transaction would result in more contracts becoming vulnerable to rescission than is possible under current formulations of law, or would require radical surgery to existing doctrine. Moreover, the *end result* of both exploitation and negligence upon their respective victims in this area is the same, as is the wrongdoer's *essential conduct*. Under both complaints the wrongdoer fails to be influenced by relevant disabilities that attend the parties' bargaining relationship circumscribed by legal neighbourhood, resulting in his victim being used merely instrumentally for the advancement of the wrongdoer's own interests. In both events the wrongdoer fails to meet the legal standard of caring for the relevant interests of his victim. Only the *quality of the will* that accompanies such failure, and hence the consequent receipt of the impugned benefit, varies as between the "exploitative" merely instrumental user and the "neglectful" merely instrumental user.

POST V JONES
60 US 150 (1857)

GRIER J (for the court): ... As many of the circumstances attending this case are peculiar and novel, it may not be improper to give a brief statement of them. The Richmond, after a ramble of three years on the Pacific, in pursuit of whales, had passed through the sea of Anadin, and was near Behring's Straits, in the Arctic ocean, on the 2d of August, 1849. She had nearly completed her cargo, and was about to return; but, during a thick fog, she was run upon rocks, within half a mile of the shore, and in a situation from which it was impossible to extricate her. The master and crew escaped in their boats to the shore, holding communication with the vessel, without much difficulty or danger. They could probably have transported the cargo to the beach, but this would have been unprofitable labor, as its condition would not have been improved. Though saved from the ocean, it would not have been safe. The coast was barren; the few inhabitants, savages and thieves. This ocean is navigable for only about two months in the year; during the remainder of the year it is sealed up with ice. The winter was expected to commence within fifteen or twenty days, at farthest. The nearest port of safety and general commercial intercourse was at the Sandwich Islands, five thousand miles distant. Their only hope of escape from this inhospitable region was by means of other whaling vessels, which were known to be cruising at no great distance, and who had been in company with the Richmond, and had pursued the same course.

On the 5th of August the fog cleared off, and the ship Elizabeth Frith was seen at a short distance. The officers of the Richmond immediately went on board, and the master informed the master of the Frith of the disaster which had befallen the Richmond. He requested him to take his crew on board, and said, "You need not whale any more; there is plenty of oil there, which you may take, and get away as soon as possible." On the following day they took on board the Frith about 300 barrels oil from the Richmond. On the 6th, the Panama and the Junior came near; they had not quite completed their cargoes; as there was more oil in the Richmond than they could all take, it was proposed that they also should complete their cargoes in the same way. Captain Tinkham, of the Junior, proposed to take part of the crew of the Richmond, and said he would take part of the oil, "provided it was put up and sold at auction." In pursuance of this suggestion, advertisements were posted on each of the three vessels, signed *by* or *for* the master of the Richmond. On the following day the forms of an auction sale were enacted; the master of the Frith bidding one dollar per barrel for as much as he needed, and the others seventy-five cents. The ship and tackle were sold for five dollars; no money was paid, and no account kept or bill of sale made out. Each vessel took enough to complete her cargo of oil and bone. The transfer was effected in a couple of days, with some trouble and labor, but little or no risk or danger, and the vessels immediately proceeded on their voyage, stopping as usual at the Sandwich Islands.

Now, it is evident, from this statement of the facts, that, although the Richmond was stranded near the shore upon which her crew and even her cargo might have been saved from the dangers of the sea, they were really in no better situation as to ultimate safety than if foundered or disabled in the midst of the Pacific ocean. The crew were glad to escape with their lives. The ship and cargo, though not actually derelict, must necessarily have been abandoned. The contrivance of an auction sale, under such circumstances, where the master of the Richmond was hopeless, helpless, and passive—where there was no market, no money, no competition—where one party had absolute power, and the other no choice but submission—where the vendor must take what is offered or get nothing—is a transaction which has no characteristic of a valid contract. It has been contended by the claimants that it would be a great hardship to treat this sale as a nullity, and thus compel them to assume the character of salvors, because they were not bound to save this property, especially at so great a distance from any port of safety, and in a place where they could have completed their cargo in a short time from their own catchings, and where salvage would be no compensation for the loss of this opportunity. The force of these arguments is fully appreciated, but we think they are not fully sustained by the facts of the case. Whales may have been plenty around their vessels on the 6th and 7th of August, but, judging of the future from the past, the anticipation of filling up their cargo in the few days of the season in which it would be safe to remain, was very uncertain, and barely probable. The whales were retreating towards the north pole, where they could not be pursued, and, though seen in numbers on one day, they would disappear on the next; and, even when seen in greatest numbers, their capture was uncertain. By this transaction, the vessels were enabled to proceed at once on their home voyage; and the certainty of a liberal salvage allowance for the property rescued will be ample compensation for the possible chance of greater profits, by refusing their assistance in saving their neighbor's property.

It has been contended, also, that the sale was justifiable and valid, because it was better for the interests of all concerned to accept what was offered, than suffer a total loss. But this argument proves too much, as it would justify every sale to a salvor. Courts of admiralty will enforce contracts made for salvage service and salvage compensation, where the salvor has not taken advantage of his power to make an unreasonable bargain; but they will not tolerate the doctrine that a salvor can take the advantage of his situation, and avail himself of the calamities of others to drive a bargain; nor will they permit the performance of a public duty to be turned into a traffic of profit. (See 1 Sumner, 210.) The general interests of commerce will be much better promoted by requiring the salvor to trust for compensation to the liberal recompense usually awarded by courts for such services. We are of opinion, therefore, that the claimants have not obtained a valid title to the property in dispute, but must be treated as salvors.

NOTE

See Trebilcock, ch 4, "Coercion." See also Rick Bigwood, *Exploitative Contracts* (Oxford: Oxford University Press, 2003) ch 7, "Contracting Under Duress."

MARSHALL V CANADA PERMANENT TRUST CO
(1968), 69 DLR (2d) 260 (Alta SC)

KIRBY J: This is an action for specific performance of an agreement for sale of land.

On January 30, 1967, the plaintiff offered to purchase the S.E. ¼ of section 27, and the N.W. ¼ of section 26, both in township 38, range 14, west of the 4th meridian, from the defendant for the sum of $7,000 cash, payable immediately upon execution of a transfer by the vendor. The offer was accepted by the owner of these lands, John A. Walsh, on the same date. Both the offer and acceptance are in writing. Cash in the sum of $100 was paid by the purchaser to the vendor. At the time the document was executed, Walsh was a patient at Bow View Rest Home, Calgary.

The plaintiff, in relating the circumstances under which the transaction was made, testified that having tried without success to purchase farm lands from Walsh's brother in the same general area, and on hearing that John Walsh might sell his half-section of land, he went to see him at the rest home and asked him if he wanted to sell his farm near Castor. He stated that Walsh said that he did wish to sell for cash, and felt that he should get between $7,000 and $8,000; that Walsh pointed out that the land was under a lease; that he offered $7,000 cash and would take over the lease. He stated that through an employee of the rest home he was put in touch with Canada Permanent Mortgage Company, who in turn referred him to a solicitor who drew up the offer to purchase and acceptance. The solicitor, he said, showed him a copy of the lease. He related that he returned to the home on Monday, January 30th, with the offer to purchase, which was signed by him and Walsh in the presence of a witness—a member of the staff, and gave him a cheque for $100, which Walsh signed and instructed him to give to his solicitor for deposit in the main branch of the Bank of Montreal, which he did. On February 22nd, he received a letter from a firm of solicitors, informing him that they were acting in this matter, did not intend to deliver a transfer, and were in the process of applying for appointment of a committee for Walsh.

On February 24th, agents for the solicitor for the plaintiff sent a prepared transfer of the lands from Walsh to the plaintiff, together with a certified cheque for $7,000, to the solicitors for Walsh. On March 11th, the cheque was returned with a letter declining to deliver a transfer to the lands in question.

On March 30th, Canada Permanent Trust Company was appointed a committee for the estate of John A. Walsh, pursuant to the provisions of the *Mentally Incapacitated Persons Act*, 1955 (Alta.), c. 3.

The defendant seeks a declaration of rescission of the memorandum of agreement on the grounds that the consideration which the plaintiff proposed to pay to Walsh for the lands in question, was grossly inadequate, that the agreement entered into between the plaintiff and Walsh was not fair and reasonable, and that the plaintiff took advantage of Walsh by reason of the inequality of their positions. In the alternatives to specific performance the plaintiff claims damages.

Simply stated, the ground on which the defendant seeks to have the agreement rescinded is that the transaction was unconscionable. In *Knupp v. Bell* (1966), 58 D.L.R. (2d) 466 [aff'd 67 DLR (2d) 256 (Sask CA)], in considering the equitable jurisdiction of the Court to set aside unconscionable transactions, MacPherson, J. (Saskatchewan Court of Queen's Bench), refers to an article by Bradley E. Crawford in the *Canadian Bar Review*, vol. 44, No. 1 (March 1966), p. 142, entitled "Restitution—Unconscionable Transaction—Undue Advantage Taken of Inequality Between Parties," which he accepts as a fair statement of the law in this matter. The author says at p. 143:

> The jurisdiction of equity to set aside bargains contracted by persons under [undue] influence is well known. But what is referred to here is something distinct from that. It is also technically distinct from the simple refusal of the courts to grant specific performance where the contract has been obtained by sharp practice. In the cases now under discussion the courts intervene to rescind the contract whenever it appears that one of the parties was incapable of adequately protecting his interests and the other has made some immoderate gain at his expense. If the bargain is fair the fact that the parties were not equally vigilant of their interest is immaterial. Likewise if one was not preyed upon by the other, an improvident or even grossly inadequate consideration is no ground upon which to set aside a contract freely entered into. It is the combination of inequality and improvidence which alone may invoke this jurisdiction. Then the onus is placed upon the party seeking to uphold the contract to show that his conduct throughout was scrupulously considerate of the other's interests.

Applying this law, the learned Justice held that where a senile woman of no business experience and who was very easily led was induced to sell her lands to a neighbour at the grossly inadequate price of $35 per acre without taking independent advice from competent members of her family, no binding obligation was created. Hence, no action for specific performance would lie to enforce the contract.

In the *Bar Review* article, reference is made to the judgment in *Waters v. Donnelly* (1884), 9 O.R. 391, in which Boyd, C., said at p. 401:

> There is an important decision in 1876, by Sir Edward Sullivan then M.R., and now Lord Chancellor of Ireland, which was affirmed by the Court of Appeal and in which he thus defines the law applicable to this case: "I take the law of the Court to be, that if two persons, no matter whether a confidential relationship exists between them or not, stand in such a relation to each other that one can take an undue advantage of the

other, whether by reason of distress, or recklessness, or wildness, or want of care, and when the facts shew that one party has taken undue advantage of the other by reason of the circumstances I have mentioned, a transaction resting upon such unconscionable dealing will not be allowed to stand; and there are several cases which shew, even where no confidential relationship exists, that where parties were not on equal terms, the party who gets a benefit cannot hold it without proving that everything has been right and fair and reasonable on his part:" *Slator v. Nolan*, Ir. R. 11 Eq. 386.

The method of investigation is to determine first whether the parties were on equal terms, if not, and the transaction is one of purchase, and any matters requiring explanation arise, then it lies on the purchaser to shew affirmatively that the price given was the value.

The Chancellor referred to *Baker v. Monk* (1864), 4 De G.J. & S. 386, 46 E.R. 968, in which Turner, L.J., referred to *Evans v. Llewellin* (1787), 1 Cox 333, 29 E.R. 1191, in laying down the principle on which the Court acts in cases of purchase, that though there was no actual fraud, it is something like fraud for an undue advantage was taken of the vendor's situation, and then proceeded to eliminate moral fraud on the part of the purchaser, but said that it is enough if the parties are not on equal terms, that an improvident contract has been entered into, in order to invoke the protection of the Court. The Chancellor then alluded to the doctrine elucidated by Lord Selborne, L.C., in *Earl of Aylesford v. Morris* (1873), L.R. 8 Ch. 484, that if the parties met under such circumstances as in the particular transaction to give the stronger party dominion over the weaker, then the principle is applied of requiring the one who gets the benefit to prove that the transaction was fair, just and reasonable.

Applying these principles, the Court affirmed a decision rescinding an agreement for the exchange of land and chattels which had been held to be improvident, the plaintiff having been found to be ignorant, wanting skill in business, and comparatively an imbecile of intellect, and the transaction, one into which he would not have entered had he been properly advised and protected.

On the basis of these principles, in this case, the plaintiff's claim for specific performance must fail, and the defendant is entitled to rescission, if it is established:

(1) That Walsh was incapable of protecting his interests;
(2) That it was an improvident transaction for Walsh.

With respect to (1), it is not material whether Marshall was aware of Walsh's incapacity; with respect to (2), the onus rests with the plaintiff to show that the price given for the land corresponded to its fair value.

Was Walsh incapable of protecting his interests?

Marshall, 52 years of age, described himself as a farmer, merchant, auctioneer. It was quite evident that he was an alert, intelligent businessman.

The rest home records indicate Walsh to have been 68 years of age at the time of his admission to the home on June 14, 1966. Dr. Mortis, the house physician for the rest home, referring to the medical records of the home with respect to Walsh, testified that the symptoms reflected in these records were typical of brain damage due to hardening of the arteries: that Walsh had been from the time of his admission, given different forms of medication, some, sedative in nature; that Walsh had a minor stroke on December 14, 1966, and that following such a stroke, ability to think, to rationalize, to speak, gets progressively worse. He expressed the opinion that after the stroke Walsh was definitely not capable of transacting business, and that while it was not surprising that he could read a document, he could not relate to the past or future.

On the basis of this medical evidence, I am satisfied, and find, that Walsh was incapable of protecting his interests at the time the memorandum of agreement was entered into.

Was it an improvident transaction for Walsh? ...

The evidence of Hunt as to the values of comparable land in the same general area in 1967 must be taken as more realistic than that of comparable land in the same general area sold in 1958 and 1959. The offer made by Dunkle to Walsh in 1967 for this half-section is in line with Hunt's valuation of this land at $50 per acre. On the basis of this evidence I am satisfied, and find, that the price agreed upon by Walsh was considerably less than the actual value of this land, and it therefore was an improvident transaction for him.

By virtue of the authorities cited above, the defendant is entitled to rescission of the agreement, and it is ordered accordingly. The caveat and certificate of *lis pendens* will forthwith be withdrawn. The plaintiff has not established that he has suffered, or is entitled to any damage by reason of the non-performance of the agreement.

There was nothing in the conduct of Walsh on the two occasions when Marshall visited him in the rest home, and consummated this transaction, as related by him in his evidence, to suggest that Walsh was suffering from mental incapacity. This is supported by the evidence of the receptionist at the home, who witnessed the signatures to the offer and acceptance. The house physician testified that Walsh, by the nature of his disability, could give the impression of reasonable understanding, even though he was not capable of transacting business. An officer of Canada Permanent Trust Company accepted instructions from Walsh for his last will and testament, and pursuant to these instructions a will was prepared by the trust company and executed by Walsh in the presence of a trust officer of the company, on January 12, 1967. Dr. Mortis gave as his opinion, that he doubted whether Walsh could have understood the will at the time of its execution. He testified that he was not consulted by the trust company as to Walsh's competence to make a will, and was not consulted as to his mental capacity until March, 1967.

Since Walsh's mental capacity was not evident to the trust officer in the early part of January, one who could be expected to be observant and cautious in matters of this kind, and was not evident to the receptionist, who witnessed his signature, it is reasonable to conclude that it was not evident to Marshall when the transaction was effected. For this reason there will be no costs.

Action dismissed.

NOTE

See *Van De Geer Estate v Penner*, [2006] 7 WWR 575 (Sask CA), rev'g in part (2004), 252 Sask R 213 (QB), and *Hittinger v Turgeon*, 2005 ABQB 257, 30 RPR (4th) 123, where, in each case, the court held that the seller was not under the power of the purchaser and, in any event, the agreement of sale was not unreasonable or unfair such as to "shock the conscience of the court."

MUNDINGER V MUNDINGER
(1968), 3 DLR (3d) 338 (Ont CA)

SCHROEDER JA (for the court): This is an appeal from a judgment pronounced by Hartt, J., on September 5, 1967, whereby he dismissed the plaintiff's action against her husband for alimony; for an order declaring that a certain separation agreement entered into between the parties on June 9, 1965, was null and void and should be set aside on the ground that the plaintiff was induced to execute it through the husband's fraud and threats and by reason of duress and undue influence, at a time when, to his knowledge, she was suffering from a serious nervous breakdown and was not in a mentally competent condition to appreciate the nature and quality of her act; and further dismissing the plaintiff's claim for an order declaring null and void a certain conveyance by the wife to the husband of property known and described for municipal purposes as 23 Oriole Gardens in the City of Toronto, and a conveyance by the wife to the husband of her interest in a 50-acre parcel of land in the Township of Uxbridge in the County of Ontario both of which properties had been registered in the names of the spouses as joint tenants.

The parties were married on April 5, 1939, and resided throughout their married life in the City of Toronto. There were three children of the marriage who are now of age and married. The wife complained of many acts of cruelty on the part of the husband during their married life and more particularly of his conduct to her towards the end of the period of cohabitation. Her principal complaint was as to an intimate and adulterous relationship between the husband and one Doris Johnson, which he stubbornly continued notwithstanding his wife's emphatic objections. She alleged that her husband's maltreatment had caused her to have a nervous breakdown. She became so depressed in this unhappy state of affairs that while under the care of her family physician who was administering tranquilizers to her she took an overdose of those drugs and became so dangerously ill that she was confined to the hospital on April 26, 1965, where she remained until May 14, 1968.

During her confinement in the hospital the husband demanded a separation. This ill-timed and inconsiderate request was a severe shock to the appellant which aggravated the condition of tension and anxiety under which she was then labouring. Shortly after her return from the hospital the husband presented and asked her to sign a separation agreement which had been prepared by his solicitor, which provided, *inter alia*, that in consideration of $5,000 she was to relinquish all rights to support and maintenance, was to convey to her husband her undivided one-half interest in the Oriole Gardens property the equity value of which was said to be $20,000, and to convey her one-half interest in the farm property near Uxbridge, which was said to have a value of approximately $40,000. Although she was advised by the respondent that she did not require a solicitor she heeded the advice of a friend and consulted Mr. Bowden McLean, a solicitor, who wrote a letter dated June 1, 1965, to Messrs. Rowland and Givertz, the respondent's solicitors, expressing his client's dissatisfaction with the agreement and stating the terms which would be acceptable to her.

When the husband was apprised of the terms so proposed he flew into a violent rage and a quarrel ensued, in the course of which he addressed his wife in an abominable manner and adopted a very threatening attitude towards her. He stated that he had a solicitor who could look after their affairs and it was not necessary that she be separately advised. On or about June 9, 1965, the defendant redrafted the agreement as previously prepared by his solicitors in the same terms but substituting for the sum of $5,000 to be paid to the wife, the sum of $10,000. In the result the appellant was induced to telephone Mr. McLean, to advise him that she had settled her affairs with her husband and that he should submit his account for services rendered.

The defendant is the president of the Mundinger Company Limited and related enterprises which engages in the merchandising of musical instruments and provides musical instruction. For many years following the marriage the wife took an active part in the business as an officer and employee of the company and more especially in the teaching activity. In 1952 or 1953 the said Doris Johnson entered the service of the company and almost immediately thereafter replaced the wife not only in the conduct of the company's affairs but apparently, also, in the husband's affections. The learned Judge found that the continued association between the defendant and Mrs. Johnson on a personal basis "was such that the defendant well knew that it was injurious to the health of the plaintiff." "On this ground alone," he stated, "I would have found that the plaintiff, Mrs. Mundinger, was entitled to alimony." He held, however, that the separation agreement signed by the wife was a bar to her cause of action. He stated: "I have given to the evidence prolonged and anxious consideration, and I have come to the conclusion that on the evidence before me, and having in mind the onus of proof that a case had not been made out." He found on the evidence of one Jack Souter and Dr. Caroline Hobbs, a resident intern at St. Michael's Hospital, that the wife was mentally capable of entering into these transactions, disregarding almost entirely the evidence of her family physician who had treated her for many years and of Dr. Fischer, an eminent psychiatrist under whose care she had been for several years prior to the dates with which we are concerned. Both of these medical witnesses, who were familiar with the unhappy situation in which this unfortunate plaintiff was involved, testified that, in their opinion, she was not in a mental condition to exercise proper judgment in matters affecting her property rights and temporal welfare. The evidence of the witnesses Souter and Givertz, the solicitor, was based on their observation of the appellant during the short period when she executed the separation agreement and deeds respectively. The young resident intern formed no settled opinion as to the mental capacity of the appellant to transact business of such a nature and, in any event, her testimony upon this point was quite inconclusive. There was no proper ground for preferring it to the evidence of her general physician and Dr. Fischer.

With deference to the learned Judge's view we are all of the opinion that he arrived at his decision in this case under the belief that despite the circumstances disclosed in evidence the onus of proof lay throughout on the plaintiff. The transactions in question are unconscionable and improvident on their very face as the learned Judge suggested. The plaintiff, now 52 years of age, has devoted the most important years of her life to her husband and their three children. She was influenced by her husband when suffering from the effects of a serious nervous breakdown, while under the influence of tranquillizers and other forms of sedation prescribed for her condition and doubtless also while affected by brandy which was liberally provided by the husband for reasons best known to himself, to surrender all rights to future support and maintenance and to part with a valuable interest in two pieces of real estate for the paltry consideration of $10,000. Her condition was such that it can clearly be asserted that her husband was in a position of dominance and control over her of which he took full advantage by exercising undue influence upon her to carry off this improvident and nefarious transaction.

The governing principle applicable here was laid down by this Court in the oft-cited case of *Vanzant v. Coates* (1917), 40 O.L.R. 556, 39 D.L.R. 485. It was there held that the equitable rule is that if the donor is in a situation in which he is not a free agent and is not equal to protecting himself, a Court of Equity will protect him, not against his own folly or carelessness, but against his being taken advantage of by those in a position to do so because of their position. In that case the circumstances were the advanced age of the donor, her infirmity, her dependence on the donee; the position of influence occupied by the donee, her acts in procuring the drawing and execution of the deed; and the consequent complete change of a well-understood and defined purpose in reference to the disposition of the donor's property. It was held that in those circumstances the onus was on the plaintiff to prove by satisfactory evidence that the gift was a voluntary and deliberate act by a person mentally competent to know, and who did know, the nature and effect of the deed, and that it was not the result of undue influence. That onus had not been discharged; and it was therefore held to be unnecessary for the defendant to prove affirmatively that the influence possessed by the plaintiff had been unduly exercised.

The principle enunciated in *Vanzant v. Coates, supra*, has been consistently followed and applied by the Courts of this Province and the other common law Provinces of Canada. The effect of the relevant decisions was neatly stated by Professor Bradley E. Crawford in a commentary written by him and appearing in 44 *Canadian Bar Review* 142 (1966) at p. 143, from which I quote the following extract:

> If the bargain is fair the fact that the parties were not equally vigilant of their interest is immaterial. Likewise if one was not preyed upon by the other, an improvident or even grossly inadequate consideration is no ground upon which to set aside a contract freely entered into. It is the combination of inequality and improvidence which alone may invoke this jurisdiction. Then the onus is placed upon the party seeking to uphold the contract to show that his conduct throughout was scrupulously considerate of the other's interests.

This correctly sets forth the effect of the decisions bearing upon this and like problems and I adopt it as an accurate statement of the law. On the evidence in the present case there was that combination of inequality and improvidence which justifies the Court in saying that the defendant has failed to discharge the onus which, in the circumstances, was cast upon him.

The appeal is allowed with costs. The separation agreement shall be declared null and void and set aside. The deed of the farm property shall likewise be declared null and void and be set aside. There shall be a declaration that the wife is entitled to alimony for a sum to be determined on a reference to the Master for that purpose which shall be payable from the date of the commencement of the action. There shall also be a reference to the Master with respect to the residential property at Oriole Gardens which has been sold by the defendant and to fix the proportion of the proceeds thereof payable to the appellant. Counsel stated that since the conveyance of the farm property to the husband he has expended certain monies in the making of improvements thereto. On the reference to the Master there shall also be an inquiry as to the extent of these improvements and their value, the wife to be allowed occupation rent for the period during which she was excluded from enjoyment of the property. The sum of $10,000 paid by the husband to the wife will, of course, be taken into account by the Master in determining what is due to the appellant. The appellant shall have the costs of the trial, the costs of the appeal and the costs of the reference on a solicitor-and-client basis.

Appeal allowed.

HARRY V KREUTZIGER
(1978), 95 DLR (3d) 231 (BCCA)

[The appellant sold his fishing boat, the *Glenda Marion*, to the respondent for approximately $4,000, but the boat, which came with a salmon fishing license, was worth approximately $16,000. The claim at the Court of Appeal was on the ground of an unconscionable bargain. The Court of Appeal noted that the appellant "suffers from a congenital hearing defect, but is by no means totally deaf. He has [a] grade 5 education, and ... is a mild, inarticulate, retiring person, and it would appear from the evidence that he is not widely experienced in business matters."]

McINTYRE JA (29 December 1978): ...

[11] For this recital it is at once clear that the appellant made an improvident bargain. ... The question for decision is: Did he enter into this bargain under such circumstances that the court will exercise its equitable jurisdiction to rescind the contract and return the parties to their original positions? The trial judge held that he had not. ...

[12] The principles upon which a court will interfere with a concluded transaction and nullify it upon the ground that it is unconscionable have found frequent expression. An early Canadian case is *Waters v. Donnelly* (1884), 9 O.R. 391. The leading pronouncement on the subject in British Columbia is to be found in *Morrison v. Coast Finance Ltd.* (1965), 54 W.W.R. 257, 55 D.L.R. (2d) 710 (C.A.), where Davey J.A., speaking for himself and Bull J.A., said at p. 259:

> The equitable principles relating to undue influence and relief against unconscionable bargains are closely related, but the doctrines are separate and distinct. The finding here against undue influence does not conclude the question whether the appellant is entitled to relief against an unconscionable transaction. A plea of undue influence attacks the sufficiency of consent; a plea that a bargain is unconscionable invokes relief against an unfair advantage gained by an unconscientious use of power by a stronger party against a weaker. On such a claim the material ingredients are proof of inequality in the position of the parties arising out of the ignorance, need or distress of the weaker, which left him in the power of the stronger, and proof of substantial unfairness of the bargain obtained by the stronger. On proof of those circumstances, it creates a presumption of fraud which the stronger must repel by proving that the bargain was fair, just and reasonable.

• • •

[14] From these authorities, this rule emerges. Where a claim is made that a bargain is unconscionable, it must be shown for success that there was inequality in the position of the parties due to the ignorance, need or distress of the weaker, which would leave him in the power of the stronger, coupled with proof of substantial unfairness in the bargain. When this has been shown a presumption of fraud is raised, and the stronger must show, in order to preserve his bargain, that it was fair and reasonable.

[15] ... The appellant, by education, physical infirmity and economic circumstances, was clearly not the equal of the respondent. The evidence supports the conclusion that the appellant wanted to continue fishing and wanted to retain his licence or tonnage. It shows as well that the respondent proceeded aggressively with full knowledge of the value of the licence. He expressed regret at one stage that he had not acquired three or four more licences, they were so valuable. The appellant did not wish to sell, and resisted for a time by returning the cheque and delaying a decision. ... The respondent also knew that the preservation of his licence was a vital consideration to the appellant. The respondent sought out the appellant and in his dealings would not take no for an answer. He persuaded the appellant to enter a bargain after, by his own admission, making assurances which were untrue regarding the chance of the appellant to get a licence. He thereby procured an asset worth $16,000 for $4,500, which he later chose to reduce by $570. The position taken by the appellant's counsel was that the appellant's ignorance, coupled with pressures exerted upon him by the respondent, caused the inequality of the bargaining position. In my view, the improvidence of the bargain is shown. On the whole of the evidence, it is also my view that the appellant was so dominated and overborne by the respondent

that he was, in the sense of that term used by Davey J.A. in the *Morrison* case, supra, within the power of the respondent in these dealings.

• • •

[18] ... It is true, as [the trial judge] has pointed out, that the appellant could have sought advice; he could have torn up the cheque; he could have refused to have any dealings with the respondent; but this will be true of almost any case where an unconscionable bargain is claimed. If the appellant had done these things, no problem would have arisen. The fact remains, however, he did not, and in my view of the evidence it was because he was overborne by the respondent because of the inequality in their positions, and the principles of the cases cited apply.

[19] I would allow the appeal and direct that the contract be rescinded; that the respondent deliver the "Glenda Marion" to the appellant upon payment by the appellant to the respondent of the sum of $3,930.

[20] CRAIG JA (19 January 1979): I agree that this appeal should be allowed for the reasons given by McIntyre J.A. and also for the reasons given by Lambert J.A. ...

[21] LAMBERT JA (19 January 1979): I have had the advantage of reading the opinion of my erstwhile brother McIntyre. ... I would allow the appeal and make the order proposed by McIntyre J.A.

• • •

[26] In my opinion, questions as to whether use of power was unconscionable, an advantage was unfair or very unfair, a consideration was grossly inadequate, or bargaining power was grievously impaired, to select words from both statements of principle, the *Morrison* case and the *Bundy* case [*Lloyds Bank Ltd v Bundy,* [1974] 3 WLR 501, [1974] 3 All ER 757 (CA)], are really aspects of one single question. That single question is whether the transaction, seen as a whole, is sufficiently divergent from community standards of commercial morality that it should be rescinded. To my mind, the framing of the question in that way prevents the real issue from being obscured by an isolated consideration of a number of separate questions; as, for example, a consideration of whether the consideration was grossly inadequate, rather than merely inadequate, separate from the consideration of whether bargaining power was grievously impaired, or merely badly impaired. Such separate consideration of separate questions produced by the application of a synthetic rule tends to obscure rather than aid the process of decision.

[27] The single question of whether the transaction, seen as a whole, is sufficiently divergent from community standards of commercial morality that it should be rescinded must be answered by an examination of the decided cases and a consideration, from those cases, of the fact patterns that require that the bargain be rescinded and those that do not. In that examination, Canadian cases are more relevant than those from other lands, where different standards of commercial morality may apply, and recent cases are more germane than those from earlier times when standards were in some respects rougher and in other respects more fastidious. In my opinion, it is also appropriate to seek guidance as to community standards of commercial morality from legislation that embodies those standards in law. ...

[28] I have applied the standards derived from those authorities to the facts in this case, which are that the respondent purchased for $4,500 a boat that he knew to be worth $16,000 from the appellant, whom he knew to be partially deaf, easily intimidated and ill-advised, by a process of harassment. In my opinion, the whole circumstances of the bargain reveal such a marked departure from community standards of commercial morality that the contract of purchase and sale should be rescinded.

NOTES

1. In *Williams v Downey-Waterbury* (1995), 120 DLR (4th) 737 (Man CA), a separation agreement provided for the equal division between husband and wife of all assets, including $350,000 worth of shares held by the husband in a family corporation. The husband challenged the agreement as unconscionable and brought about by the undue influence of the wife. It was found as fact that the wife had been extraordinarily dominant during the marriage. Nevertheless, the Manitoba Court of Appeal rejected the husband's claim, holding that it was necessary to focus on the circumstances surrounding the execution of the separation agreement rather than the circumstances of the marriage. When the husband signed the agreement he was no longer within the wife's "orbit of influence." There was no longer a dominant–subservient relationship or an atmosphere of tension. The husband signed because he felt it was the right thing to do. In *Virc v Blair*, 2016 ONSC 49, the court maintained that signing the agreement in stressful circumstances where there has been financial misrepresentation should be distinguished from situations in which there is "a power imbalance that impacts a party's ability to understand and freely assent to a legally binding agreement" (para 102).

2. The contract negotiation principles governing commercial relationships are different from those governing separation agreement negotiations between spouses. In *Rick v Brandsema*, 2009 SCC 10, the validity of a separation agreement was in issue when the wife sought to set it aside one year after the divorce on the grounds of unconscionability and misrepresentation. Relying on *Miglin v Miglin*, 2003 SCC 24, [2003] 1 SCR 303 for guidance, the court found that the uniqueness of the negotiating environment (the breakdown of the relationship) meant that the principles governing commercial contracts negotiated between parties of equal strength were inapplicable. Rather, to protect the integrity of the negotiating environment between spouses, there is a duty to make full and honest disclosure of all relevant financial information, a duty that "anchors the ability of separating spouses to genuinely decide for themselves what constitutes an acceptable bargain." And because "[a]n agreement based on full and honest disclosure is an agreement that, *prima facie*, is based on the informed consent of both parties," the court would be less likely to set it aside. The court allowed the appeal and restored the trial judge's decision, which had determined the agreement to be unconscionable. At trial, it was found that the husband had failed to provide full disclosure of his finances and had deliberately exploited his wife's mental fragility, a vulnerability ineffectively compensated for by the lawyer who was present. The remedy for unconscionability here was equitable compensation, requiring the husband to pay the wife an amount representing the difference between the negotiated "equalization payment" and the wife's entitlement under the *Family Relations Act* [repealed by the *Family Law Act*, SBC 2011, c 25].

3. Knowledge of financial affairs is a significant component of the analysis involving the enforceability of separation agreements, but it is not the only one. In *C (SL) v C (CJR)*, 2014 BCSC 1814, the court found that the wife handled the financial affairs of the parties, but that she had been afraid of her husband at the time she entered into the separation agreement. "She feared that he would hurt her, at least emotionally, such as through the children, if she did not sign the Separation Agreement on the terms dictated by the Husband. The Wife knew the Separation Agreement was unfair to her. She signed it only because of her fear. The Husband exploited the Wife's vulnerability by insisting that she enter into a profoundly unfair agreement" (para 427).

4. The environment surrounding the signing of a prenuptial agreement is different from the "emotional environment that follows the disintegration of a marriage," identified in *Rick v Brandsema* (*Dyck v Bashold*, 2009 CanLII 65813, [2009] OJ No 4999 (QL) (Sup Ct J), In *Melnyk v Melnyk*, 2010 MBQB 121, [2010] MJ No 176 (QL), the wife sought to have the pre-nuptial agreement set aside when the marriage fell apart. The court held that the circumstances in which she signed the agreement—namely, one month before the wedding date and the request was sudden—did not amount to duress. Other cases have also found that the embarrassment of

cancelling a wedding (*Toscano v Toscano*, 2015 ONSC 487) or of having a child out of wed-lock (*Verkaik v Verkaik* (2009), 68 RFL (6th) 293 (Ont Sup Ct J)) is not a valid basis for duress. In *Melnyk*, the wife had known of her husband's assets at the time she signed the agreement, chose to sign rather than pose questions to a lawyer, and was both young and healthy at the time and not dependent on her husband-to-be. The court found that the fact that the hus-band told the wife that the wedding would not proceed if she did not sign the agreement did not amount to unconscionability. The court determined that the standard for considering the validity of a pre-nuptial agreement was the usual common law threshold for unconscionability. It distinguished its decision from *Rick v Brandsema* because of the different statutory regimes between Manitoba, where the legislation prescribes an equal division of property, and British Columbia, which allows the courts to ignore unfair agreements and reapportion marital assets in a way the court deems fair. The point of a pre-nuptial agreement is to avoid the statutory regime for the marital division of property, which, the court determined, meant that the legis-lature did not intend that pre-nuptial agreements be measured against a standard of fairness.

5. Legislation enables courts to alter agreements between spouses in circumstances that could encompass unconscionability. For example, in Ontario, the court has express jurisdiction to set aside a domestic contract (1) if a party failed to disclose to the other significant assets, or significant debts or other liabilities, existing when the domestic contract was made; (2) if a party did not understand the nature or consequences of the domestic contract; or (3) other-wise in accordance with the law of contract: see *Family Law Act*, RSO 1990, c F.3, s 56(4). In British Columbia, a judge can reapportion property between spouses under their marriage agreement on the basis of fairness: see *Family Law Act*, SBC 2011, c 25, s 95.

6. Although misrepresentation was claimed in *Rick v Brandsema*, the court did not deal with the claim. Would the results have been different if the case had been treated as one involving fraudulent misrepresentation?

LLOYDS BANK LIMITED V BUNDY
[1975] 1 QB 326

LORD DENNING MR: Broadchalke is one of the most pleasing villages in England. Old Herbert Bundy, the defendant, was a farmer there. His home was at Yew Tree Farm. It went back for 300 years. His family had been there for generations. It was his only asset. But he did a very foolish thing. He mortgaged it to the bank. Up to the very hilt. Not to borrow money for himself, but for the sake of his son. Now the bank have come down on him. They have foreclosed. They want to get him out of Yew Tree Farm and to sell it. They have brought this action against him for possession. Going out means ruin for him. He was granted legal aid. His lawyers put in a defence. They said that, when he executed the charge to the bank he did not know what he was doing; or at any rate that the circumstances were such that he ought not to be bound by it. At the trial his plight was plain. The judge was sorry for him. He said he was a "poor old gentleman." He was so obviously incapacitated that the judge admitted his proof in evidence. He had a heart attack in the witness-box. Yet the judge felt he could do nothing for him. There is nothing, he said, "which takes this out of the vast range of commercial transactions." He ordered Herbert Bundy to give up possession of Yew Tree Farm to the bank. Now there is an appeal to this court. The ground is that the circumstances were so exceptional that Herbert Bundy should not be held bound.

Herbert Bundy had only one son, Michael Bundy. He had great faith in him. They were both customers of Lloyd's Bank Ltd., the plaintiff, at the Salisbury branch. They had been customers for many years. The son formed a company called M.J.B. Plant

Hire Ltd. It hired out earth-moving machinery and so forth. The company banked at Lloyds too at the same branch.

In 1961 the son's company was in difficulties. The father on September 19, 1966, guaranteed the company's overdraft for £1,500 and charged Yew Tree Farm to the bank to secure the £1,500. Afterwards the son's company got further into difficulties. The overdraft ran into thousands. In May 1969 the assistant bank manager, Mr. Bennett, told the son the bank must have further security. The son said his father would give it. So Mr. Bennett and the son went together to see the father. Mr. Bennett produced the papers. He suggested that the father should sign a further guarantee for £5,000 and to execute a further charge for £6,000. The father said that he would help his son as far as he possibly could. Mr. Bennett did not ask the father to sign the papers there and then. He left them with the father so that he could consider them overnight and take advice on them. The father showed them to his solicitor, Mr. Trethowan, who lived in the same village. The solicitor told the father that £5,000 was the utmost that he could sink in his son's affairs. The house was worth about £10,000 and this was half his assets. On that advice the father on May 27, 1969, did execute the further guarantee and the charge, and Mr. Bennett witnessed it. So at the end of May, 1969 the father had charged the house to secure £7,500.

During the next six months the affairs of the son and his company went from bad to worse. The bank had granted the son's company an overdraft up to a limit of £10,000, but this was not enough to meet the outgoings. The son's company drew cheques which the bank returned unpaid. The bank were anxious. By this time Mr. Bennett had left to go to another branch. He was succeeded by a new assistant manager, Mr. Head. In November 1969 Mr. Head saw the son and told him that the account was unsatisfactory and that he considered that the company might have to cease operations. The son suggested that the difficulty was only temporary and that his father would be prepared to provide further money if necessary.

On December 17, 1969, there came the occasion which, in the judge's words, was "important and disastrous" for the father. The son took Mr. Head to see his father. Mr. Head had never met the father before. This was his first visit. He went prepared. He took with him a form of guarantee and a form of charge filled in with the father's name ready for signature. There was a family gathering. The father and mother were there. The son and the son's wife. Mr. Head said that the bank had given serious thought as to whether they could continue to support the son's company. But that the bank were prepared to do so in this way: (i) the bank would continue to allow the company to draw money on overdraft up to the existing level of £10,000, but the bank would require the company to pay 10 per cent of its incomings into a separate account. So that 10 per cent would not go to reduce the overdraft. Mr. Head said that this would have the effect "of reducing the level of borrowing." In other words, the bank was cutting down the overdraft. (ii) The bank would require the father to give a guarantee of the company's account in a sum of £11,000 and to give the bank a further charge on the house of £3,500, so as to bring the total charge to £11,000. The house was only worth about £10,000, so this charge for £11,000 would sweep up all that the father had.

On hearing the proposal, the father said that Michael was his only son and that he was 100 per cent behind him. Mr. Head produced the forms that had already been filled in. The father signed them and Mr. Head witnessed them there and then. On this occasion, Mr. Head, unlike Mr. Bennett did not leave the forms with the father: nor did the father have any independent advice.

It is important to notice the state of mind of Mr. Head and of the father. Mr. Head said in evidence:

Defendant asked me what in my opinion the company was doing wrong and company's position. I told him. I did not explain the company's affairs very fully as I had only just taken over the account. ... Michael said that company had a number of bad debts. I was not entirely satisfied with this. I thought the trouble was more deep seated. ... It did not occur to me that there was any conflict of interest. I thought there was no conflict of interest. I would think the defendant relied on me implicitly to advise him about the transaction as bank manager. ... I knew he had no other assets except Yew Tree Cottage.

The father said in evidence: "I always thought Head was genuine. I have always trusted him. ... No discussion how business was doing that I can remember. I simply sat back and did what they said." The solicitor, Mr. Trethowan, said of the father: "He is straightforward. Agrees with anyone. ... I doubt if he understood all that Head explained to him."

So the father signed the papers. Mr. Head witnessed them and took them away. The father had charged the whole of his remaining asset, leaving himself with nothing. The son and his company gained a respite. But only for a short time. Five months later, in May 1970, a receiving order was made against the son. Thereupon the bank stopped all overdraft facilities for the company. It ceased to trade. The father's solicitor, Mr. Trethowan, at once went to see Mr. Head. He said he was concerned that the father had signed the guarantee.

In due course the bank insisted on the sale of the house. In December 1971 they agreed to sell it for £9,500 with vacant possession. The family were very disappointed with this figure. It was, they said, worth much more. Estate agents were called to say so. But the judge held it was a valid sale and that the bank could take all the proceeds. The sale has not been completed because Herbert Bundy is still in possession. The bank have brought these proceedings to evict Herbert Bundy.

Now let me say at once that in the vast majority of cases a customer who signs a bank guarantee or a charge cannot get out of it. No bargain will be upset which is the result of the ordinary interplay of forces. There are many hard cases which are caught by this rule. Take the case of a poor man who is homeless. He agrees to pay a high rent to a landlord just to get a roof over his head. The common law will not interfere. It is left to Parliament. Next take the case of a borrower in urgent need of money. He borrows it from the bank at high interest and it is guaranteed by a friend. The guarantor gives his bond and gets nothing in return. The common law will not interfere. Parliament has intervened to prevent moneylenders charging excessive interest. But it has never interfered with banks.

Yet there are exceptions to this general rule. There are cases in our books in which the courts will set aside a contract, or a transfer of property, when the parties have not met on equal terms—when the one is so strong in bargaining power and the other so weak—that, as a matter of common fairness, it is not right that the strong should be allowed to push the weak to the wall. Hitherto those exceptional cases have been treated each as a separate category in itself. But I think the time has come when we should seek to find a principle to unite them. I put on one side contracts or transactions which are voidable for fraud or misrepresentation or mistake. All those are governed by settled principles. I go only to those where there has been inequality of bargaining power, such as to merit the intervention of the court.

The first category is that of "duress of goods." A typical case is when a man is in a strong bargaining position by being in possession of the goods of another by virtue of a legal right, such as by way of pawn or pledge or taken in distress. The owner is in a weak position because he is in urgent need of the goods. The stronger demands of the weaker more than is justly due: and he pays it in order to get the goods. Such a transaction is voidable. He can recover the excess: see *Astley v. Reynolds* (1731) 2 Stra. 915 and *Green v. Duckett* (1883) 11 Q.B.D. 275. To which may be added the cases of "colore officii," where a man is in a strong bargaining position by virtue of his official position or public profession. He relies upon it so as to gain from the weaker—who is urgently in need—more than is justly due: see *Pigott's* case cited by Lord Kenyon C.J. in *Cartwright v. Rowley* (1799) 2 Esp. 723, 723-724; *Parker v. Bristol and Exeter Railway Co.* (1851) 6 Exch. 702 and *Steele v. Williams* (1853) 8 Exch. 625. In such cases the stronger may make his claim in good faith honestly believing that he is entitled to make his demand. He may not be guilty of any fraud or misrepresentation. The inequality of bargaining power—the strength of the one versus the urgent need of the other—renders the transaction voidable and the money paid to be recovered back: see *Maskell v. Horner* [1915] 3 K.B. 106.

The second category is that of the "unconscionable transaction." A man is so placed as to be in need of special care and protection and yet his weakness is exploited by another far stronger than himself so as to get his property at a gross undervalue. The typical case is that of the "expectant heir." But it applies to all cases where a man comes into property, or is expected to come into it—and then being in urgent need—another gives him ready cash for it, greatly below its true worth, and so gets the property transferred to him: see *Evans v. Llewellin* (1787) 1 Cox 333. Even though there be no evidence of fraud or misrepresentation, nevertheless the transaction will be set aside. ... This second category is said to extend to all cases where an unfair advantage has been gained by an unconscientious use of power by a stronger party against a weaker. ...

The third category is that of "undue influence" usually so called. These are divided into two classes as stated by Cotton L.J. in *Allcard v. Skinner* (1887) 36 Ch. D. 145, 171. The first are those where the stronger has been guilty of some fraud or wrongful act—expressly so as to gain some gift or advantage from the weaker. The second are those where the stronger has not been guilty of any wrongful act, but has, through the relationship which existed between him and the weaker, gained some gift or advantage for himself. Sometimes the relationship is such as to raise a presumption of undue influence, such as parent over child, solicitor over client, doctor over patient, spiritual adviser over follower. At other times a relationship of confidence must be proved to exist. But to all of them the general principle obtains which was stated by Lord Chelmsford L.C. in *Tate v. Williamson* (1866) 2 Ch. App. 55, 61:

> Wherever two persons stand in such a relation that, while it continues, confidence is necessarily reposed by one, and the influence which naturally grows out of that confidence is possessed by the other, and this confidence is abused, or the influence is exerted to obtain an advantage at the expense of the confiding party, the person so availing himself of his position will not be permitted to retain the advantage, although the transaction could not have been impeached if no such confidential relation had existed.

The fourth category is that of "undue pressure." The most apposite of that is *Williams v. Bayley* (1866) L.R. 1 H.L. 200, where a son forged his father's name to a promissory note and, by means of it, raised money from the bank of which they were both customers. The bank said to the father, in effect: "Take your choice—give us security for your son's debt. If you do take that on yourself, then it will all go smoothly: if you do not, we shall be bound to exercise pressure." Thereupon the father charged his property to the bank with payment of the note. The House of Lords held that the charge was invalid because of undue pressure exerted by the bank. Lord Westbury said, at pp. 218-219:

A contract to give security for the debt of another, which is a contract without consideration, is above all things, a contract that should be based upon the free and voluntary agency of the individual who enters into it.

Other instances of undue pressure are where one party stipulates for an unfair advantage to which the other has no option but to submit. As where an employer—the stronger party—has employed a builder—the weaker party—to do work for him. When the builder asked for payment of sums properly due (so as to pay his workmen) the employer refused to pay unless he was given some added advantage. Stuart V.-C. said: "Where an agreement, hard and inequitable in itself, has been exacted under circumstances of pressure on the part of the person who exacts it, this court will set it aside": see *Ormes v. Beadel* (1860) 2 Giff. 166, 174 (reversed on another ground, 2 De G.F. & J. 333) and *D. & C. Builders Ltd. v. Rees* [1966] 2 Q.B. 617, 625.

The fifth category is that of salvage agreements. When a vessel is in danger of sinking and seeks help, the rescuer is in a strong bargaining position. The vessel in distress is in urgent need. The parties cannot be truly said to be on equal terms. ...

Gathering all together, I would suggest that through all these instances there runs a single thread. They rest on "inequality of bargaining power." By virtue of it, the English law gives relief to one who, without independent advice, enters into a contract upon terms which are very unfair or transfers property for a consideration which is grossly inadequate, when his bargaining power is grievously impaired by reason of his own needs or desires, or by his own ignorance or infirmity, coupled with undue influences or pressures brought to bear on him by or for the benefit of the other. When I use the word "undue" I do not mean to suggest that the principle depends on proof of any wrongdoing. The one who stipulates for an unfair advantage may be moved solely by his own self-interest, unconscious of the distress he is bringing to the other. I have also avoided any reference to the will of the one being "dominated" or "overcome" by the other. One who is in extreme need may knowingly consent to a most improvident bargain, solely to relieve the straits in which he finds himself. Again, I do not mean to suggest that every transaction is saved by independent advice. But the absence of it may be fatal. With these explanations, I hope this principle will be found to reconcile the cases. Applying it to the present case, I would notice these points:

(1) The consideration moving from the bank was grossly inadequate. The son's company was in serious difficulty. The overdraft was at its limit of £10,000. The bank considered that its existing security was insufficient. In order to get further security, it asked the father to charge the house—his sole asset—to the uttermost. It was worth £10,000. The charge was for £11,000. That was for the benefit of the bank. But not at all for the benefit of the father, or indeed for the company. The bank did not promise to continue the overdraft or to increase it. On the contrary, it required the overdraft to be reduced. All that the company gained was a short respite from impending doom.

(2) The relationship between the bank and the father was one of trust and confidence. The bank knew that the father relied on it implicitly to advise him about the transaction. The father trusted the bank. This gave the bank much influence on the father. Yet the bank failed in that trust. It allowed the father to charge the house to his ruin.

(3) The relationship between the father and the son was one where the father's natural affection had much influence on him. He would naturally desire to accede to his son's request. He trusted his son.

(4) There was a conflict of interest between the bank and the father. Yet the bank did not realise it. Nor did it suggest that the father should get independent advice. If the father had gone to his solicitor—or to any man of business—there is no doubt that any one of them would say: "You must not enter into this transaction. You are giving up your house, your sole remaining asset, for no benefit to you. The company is in such a parlous state that you must not do it."

These considerations seem to me to bring this case within the principles I have stated. But, in case that principle is wrong, I would also say that the case falls within the category of undue influence of the second class stated by Cotton L.J. in *Allcard v. Skinner*, 36 Ch. D. 145, 171. I have no doubt that the assistant bank manager acted in the utmost good faith and was straightforward and genuine. Indeed the father said so. But beyond doubt he was acting in the interests of the bank—to get further security for a bad debt. There was such a relationship of trust and confidence between them that the bank ought not to have swept up his sole remaining asset into its hands—for nothing—without his having independent advice. I would therefore allow this appeal.

[Cairns LJ and Sir Eric Sachs agreed in the result, but on the narrower ground mentioned in Lord Denning's last paragraph. The document executed on December 17 was set aside.]

CREDIT LYONNAIS BANK NEDERLAND NV V BURCH
[1997] 1 All ER 144 (CA)

[The defendant worked for a company whose primary shareholder was Mr. Pelosi. The company maintained an overdraft facility with the plaintiff bank. Pelosi requested that the defendant provide the bank with an unlimited guarantee, supported by a second mortgage on the defendant's home, so that the company's overdraft could be extended by £20,000. When the company went into liquidation, the bank sued the defendant for the amount outstanding on the overdraft. The defendant argued that her guarantee had been procured by the undue influence of her employer, Mr. Pelosi.]

MILLETT LJ: This transaction cannot possibly stand. ... It is an extreme case. The transaction was not merely to the manifest disadvantage of Miss Burch; it was one which, in the traditional phrase, "shocks the conscience of the court." Miss Burch committed herself to a personal liability far beyond her slender means, risking the loss of her home and personal bankruptcy, and obtained nothing in return beyond a relatively small and possibly temporary increase in the overdraft facility available to her employer, a company in which she had no financial interest. The transaction gives rise to grave suspicion. It cries aloud for an explanation. ...

In the present case, the excessively onerous nature of the transaction into which she was persuaded to enter, coupled with the fact that she did so at the request of, and after discussion with Mr. Pelosi, is, in my judgment, quite enough to justify the inference, which is really irresistible, that the relationship of employer and employee had ripened into something more and that there had come into existence between them a relationship of trust and confidence which he improperly exploited for his own benefit. ...

I repeat that the mere fact that a transaction is improvident or manifestly disadvantageous to one party is not sufficient by itself to give rise to a presumption that it has been obtained by the exercise of undue influence; but where it is obtained by a party between whom and the complainant there is a relationship like that of employer and junior employee which is easily capable of developing into a relationship of trust and confidence, the nature of the transaction may be sufficient to justify the inference that such a development has taken place; and where the transaction is so extravagantly improvident that it is virtually inexplicable on any other basis, the inference will be readily drawn. ...

The bank had actual notice of the facts from which the existence of a relationship of trust and confidence between Mr. Pelosi and Miss Burch could be inferred. It knew that they were respectively employer and junior employee working in a small business, and should have "appreciated that the possibility of influence exist[ed]." ...

The bank submitted that it had discharged its duty to Miss Burch by urging her to obtain independent legal advice. This does not accurately reflect the legal position. The bank owed no duty to Miss Burch. If it urged Miss Burch to take independent legal advice, this was for its own protection. If it had not had cause to suspect that Miss Burch's agreement to enter into the transaction might have been improperly obtained, it would have had no need to encourage her to take legal advice. Since it did have cause to suspect it, it could not avoid the consequences unless two conditions were satisfied: (i) it must have taken reasonable steps to allay any such suspicion; and (ii) the result of the steps which it took must be such as would reasonably allay any such suspicion.

The bank urged Miss Burch to obtain independent legal advice. In a letter obviously written at the instance of Mr. Pelosi and after consultation with him, she declined to do so. The bank had taken all reasonable steps open to it to allay any suspicion it might have had that Miss Burch's agreement to the transaction had been procured by the exercise of undue influence on the part of Mr. Pelosi. But what followed could not reasonably have allayed any such suspicion; on the contrary, it should have confirmed it.

That is sufficient to dispose of this appeal, but I should not be taken to accept that it would necessarily have made any difference even if Miss Burch had entered into the transaction after taking independent legal advice. Such advice is neither always necessary nor always sufficient. It is not a panacea. The result does not depend mechanically on the presence or absence of legal advice. ...

It is first necessary to consider the position as between the complainant and the alleged wrongdoer. The alleged wrongdoer may seek to rebut the presumption that the transaction was obtained by undue influence by showing that the complainant had the benefit of independent legal advice before entering into it. It is well established that in such a case the court will examine the advice which was actually given. It is not sufficient that the solicitor has satisfied himself that the complainant understands the legal effect of the transaction and intends to enter into it. That may be a protection against mistake or misrepresentation; it is no protection against undue influence. As Lord Eldon L.C. said in *Huguenin v. Baseley* (1807) 14 Ves 273 at 300, [1803-13] All E.R. Rep. 1 at 13: "The question is, not, whether she knew what she was doing, had done, or proposed to do, but how the intention was produced ... ."

Accordingly, the presumption cannot be rebutted by evidence that the complainant understood what she was doing and intended to do it. The alleged wrongdoer can rebut the presumption only by showing that the complainant was either free from any undue influence on his part or had been placed, by the receipt of independent advice, in an equivalent position. That involves showing that she was advised as to the propriety of the transaction by an adviser fully informed of all the material facts. ...

Some of those cases were concerned with the equity to set aside a harsh and unconscionable bargain rather than one obtained by the exercise of undue influence, but the role of the independent adviser, while not identical, is not dissimilar. The solicitor may not be concerned to protect the complainant against herself, but he is concerned to protect her from the influence of the wrongdoer. The cases show that it is not sufficient that she should have received independent advice unless she has acted on that advice. If this were not so, the same influence that produced her desire to enter into the transaction would cause her to disregard any advice not to do so. They also show that the solicitor must not be content to satisfy himself that his client understands the transaction and wishes to carry it out. His duty is to satisfy himself that the transaction is one which his client could sensibly enter into if free from improper influence; and if he is not so satisfied to advise her not to enter into it, and to refuse to act further for her if she persists. He must advise his client that she is under no obligation to enter into the transaction at all and, if she still wishes to do so, that she is not necessarily bound to accept the terms of any document which has been put before her but (where this is appropriate) that he should ascertain on her behalf whether less onerous terms might be obtained.

It is next necessary to consider the position of the third party who has been put on enquiry of the possible existence of some impropriety and who wishes to avoid being fixed with constructive notice. One means of doing so is to ensure that the complainant obtains competent and independent legal advice before entering into the transaction. If she does so, and enters into the transaction nonetheless, the third party will usually escape the consequences of notice. This is because he is normally entitled to assume that the solicitor has discharged his duty and that the complainant has followed his advice. But he cannot make any such assumption if he knows or ought to know that it is false.

In the present case, the bank did not have actual notice of the exercise of undue influence, or even of the existence of a relationship of trust and confidence between Miss Burch and Mr. Pelosi. It did not know for a fact that Miss Burch had no incentive to enter into the transaction. For all the bank knew, for example, the parties might be intending to set up home together and live off the profits of the company's business. It did not, therefore, know (as was the case) that no competent solicitor could possibly advise Miss Burch to guarantee the company's overdraft.

But it must have known that no competent solicitor could advise her to enter into a guarantee in the terms she did. He would be bound to inquire, of the bank if necessary, of the reason why it required additional security. Having discovered that it was to enable the limit of the company's overdraft to be increased from £250,000 to £270,000, he would be bound to advise Miss Burch that an unlimited guarantee was unnecessary and inappropriate for this purpose, and that, if she felt that she must accommodate Mr. Pelosi's wishes, she should offer a limited guarantee with a limit of £20,000 or (better still) a guarantee of the company's liability in excess of £250,000 with a maximum of £270,000. The terms of Miss Burch's letters indicate that if she had been given appropriate advice of the alternatives which were legally available, she would have chosen one which was less onerous to her while still meeting the bank's ostensible requirements.

I do not, therefore, accept that a bank, in circumstances where it ought to appreciate the possibility that undue influence has been exercised, can escape the consequences by putting forward an unnecessarily onerous form of guarantee and relying on the failure of the guarantor's solicitor to advise her of the possibility of offering a guarantee on less onerous terms and more appropriate to the situation.

In the present case, the bank accepted an unlimited guarantee of her employer's indebtedness obtained by the employer from a junior employee with no incentive to give it; and who had, at the instance of her employer, declined to obtain legal advice, was known to be concerned at the unlimited nature of the obligation which she was undertaking, and was almost certainly unaware of the alternatives open to her. In my opinion, the transaction must be set aside and the appeal must be dismissed.

[The judgments of Nourse and Swinton-Thomas LJJ have been omitted.]

ROYAL BANK OF SCOTLAND PLC V ETRIDGE (NO 2) AND OTHER APPEALS
[2002] 2 AC 773, [2001] 4 All ER 449 (HL)

PANEL

Lord Bingham of Cornhill, Lord Nicholls of Birkenhead, Lord Clyde, Lord Hobhouse of Woodborough, Lord Scott of Foscote

LORD NICHOLLS OF BIRKENHEAD: ...

[5] My Lords, before your Lordships' House are appeals in eight cases. Each case arises out of a transaction in which a wife charged her interest in her home in favour of a bank as security for her husband's indebtedness or the indebtedness of a company through which he carried on business. The wife later asserted she signed the charge under the undue influence of her husband. In *Barclays Bank plc v. O'Brien* [1993] 4 All E.R. 417, [1994] 1 A.C. 180 your Lordships enunciated the principles applicable in this type of case. Since then, many cases have come before the courts, testing the implications of the *O'Brien* decision in a variety of different factual situations. Seven of the present appeals are of this character. In each case the bank sought to enforce the charge signed by the wife. The bank claimed an order for possession of the matrimonial home. The wife raised a defence that the bank was on notice that her concurrence in the transaction had been procured by her husband's undue influence. The eighth appeal concerns a claim by a wife for damages from a solicitor who advised her before she entered into a guarantee obligation of this character.

UNDUE INFLUENCE

[6] The issues raised by these appeals make it necessary to go back to first principles. Undue influence is one of the grounds of relief developed by the courts of equity as a court of conscience. The objective is to ensure that the influence of one person over another is not abused. In everyday life people constantly seek to influence the decisions of others. They seek to persuade those with whom they are dealing to enter into transactions, whether great or small. The law has set limits to the means properly employable for this purpose. To this end the common law developed a principle of duress. Originally this was narrow in its scope, restricted to the more blatant forms of physical coercion, such as personal violence.

[7] Here, as elsewhere in the law, equity supplemented the common law. Equity extended the reach of the law to other unacceptable forms of persuasion. The law will investigate the manner in which the intention to enter into the transaction was secured: "how the intention was produced," in the oft repeated words of Lord Eldon L.C., from as long ago as 1807 (*Huguenin v. Basely* (1807) 14 Ves. Jun. 273 at 300, [1803-13] All E.R. Rep. 1 at 13). If the intention was produced by an unacceptable means, the law will not permit the transaction to stand. The means used is regarded as an

exercise of improper or "undue" influence, and hence unacceptable, whenever the consent thus procured ought not fairly to be treated as the expression of a person's free will. It is impossible to be more precise or definitive. The circumstances in which one person acquires influence over another, and the manner in which influence may be exercised, vary too widely to permit of any more specific criterion.

[8] Equity identified broadly two forms of unacceptable conduct. The first comprises overt acts of improper pressure or coercion such as unlawful threats. Today there is much overlap with the principle of duress as this principle has subsequently developed. The second form arises out of a relationship between two persons where one has acquired over another a measure of influence, or ascendancy, of which the ascendant person then takes unfair advantage. ...

[9] In cases of this latter nature the influence one person has over another provides scope for misuse without any specific overt acts of persuasion. The relationship between two individuals may be such that, without more, one of them is disposed to agree a course of action proposed by the other. Typically this occurs when one person places trust in another to look after his affairs and interests, and the latter betrays this trust by preferring his own interests. He abuses the influence he has acquired. ...

[10] The law has long recognised the need to prevent abuse of influence in these "relationship" cases despite the absence of evidence of overt acts of persuasive conduct. The types of relationship, such as parent and child, in which this principle falls to be applied cannot be listed exhaustively. Relationships are infinitely various. Sir Guenter Treitel Q.C. has rightly noted that the question is whether one party has reposed sufficient trust and confidence in the other, rather than whether the relationship between the parties belongs to a particular type ... .

[11] Even this test is not comprehensive. The principle is not confined to cases of abuse of trust and confidence. It also includes, for instance, cases where a vulnerable person has been exploited. Indeed, there is no single touchstone for determining whether the principle is applicable. Several expressions have been used in an endeavour to encapsulate the essence: trust and confidence, reliance, dependence or vulnerability on the one hand and ascendancy, domination or control on the other. None of these descriptions is perfect. None is all embracing. Each has its proper place.

[12] In *CIBC Mortgages plc v. Pitt* [1993] 4 All E.R. 433, [1994] 1 A.C. 200 your Lordships' House decided that in cases of undue influence disadvantage is not a necessary ingredient of the cause of action. It is not essential that the transaction should be disadvantageous to the pressurised or influenced person, either in financial terms or in any other way. However, in the nature of things, questions of undue influence will not usually arise, and the exercise of undue influence is unlikely to occur, where the transaction is innocuous. The issue is likely to arise only when, in some respect, the transaction was disadvantageous either from the outset or as matters turned out.

BURDEN OF PROOF AND PRESUMPTIONS

[13] Whether a transaction was brought about by the exercise of undue influence is a question of fact. Here, as elsewhere, the general principle is that he who asserts a wrong has been committed must prove it. The burden of proving an allegation of undue influence rests upon the person who claims to have been wronged. This is the general rule. The evidence required to discharge the burden of proof depends on the nature of the alleged undue influence, the personality of the parties, their relationship, the extent to which the transaction cannot readily be accounted for by the ordinary motives of ordinary persons in that relationship, and all the circumstances of the case.

[14] Proof that the complainant placed trust and confidence in the other party in relation to the management of the complainant's financial affairs, coupled with a transaction which calls for explanation, will normally be sufficient, failing satisfactory evidence to the contrary, to discharge the burden of proof. On proof of these two matters the stage is set for the court to infer that, in the absence of a satisfactory explanation, the transaction can only have been procured by undue influence. In other words, proof of these two facts is prima facie evidence that the defendant abused the influence he acquired in the parties' relationship. He preferred his own interests. He did not behave fairly to the other. So the evidential burden then shifts to him. It is for him to produce evidence to counter the inference which otherwise should be drawn.

[15] *Bainbrigge v. Browne* (1881) 18 Ch. D. 188, already mentioned, provides a good illustration of this commonplace type of forensic exercise. Fry J. held (at 196) that there was no direct evidence upon which he could rely as proving undue pressure by the father. But there existed circumstances "from which the court will infer pressure and undue influence." None of the children were entirely emancipated from their father's control. None seemed conversant with business. These circumstances were such as to cast the burden of proof upon the father. He had made no attempt to discharge that burden. He did not appear in court at all. So the children's claim succeeded. Again, more recently, in *Morgan's* case [1985] 1 All E.R. 821 at 829, [1985] A.C. 686 at 707, Lord Scarman noted that a relationship of banker and customer may become one in which a banker acquires a dominating influence. If he does, and a manifestly disadvantageous transaction is proved, "there would then be room" for a court to presume that it resulted from the exercise of undue influence. ...

[17] The availability of this forensic tool in cases founded on abuse of influence arising from the parties' relationship has led to this type of case sometimes being labelled "presumed undue influence." This is by way of contrast with cases involving actual pressure or the like, which are labelled "actual undue influence" ... . This usage can be a little confusing. In many cases where a plaintiff has claimed that the defendant abused the influence he acquired in a relationship of trust and confidence the plaintiff has succeeded by recourse to the rebuttable evidential presumption. But this need not be so. Such a plaintiff may succeed even where this presumption is not available to him; for instance, where the impugned transaction was not one which called for an explanation.

[18] The evidential presumption discussed above is to be distinguished sharply from a different form of presumption which arises in some cases. The law has adopted a sternly protective attitude towards certain types of relationship in which one party acquires influence over another who is vulnerable and dependent and where, moreover, substantial gifts by the influenced or vulnerable person are not normally to be expected. Examples of relationships within this special class are parent and child, guardian and ward, trustee and beneficiary, solicitor and client, and medical advisor and patient. In these cases the law presumes, irrebuttably, that one party had influence over the other. The complainant need not prove he actually reposed trust and confidence in the other party. It is sufficient for him to prove the existence of the type of relationship.

[19] It is now well established that husband and wife is not one of the relationships to which this latter principle applies. ... Although there is no presumption, the court will nevertheless note, as a matter of fact, the opportunities for abuse which flow from a wife's confidence in her husband. The court will take this into account with all the other evidence in the case. ...

INDEPENDENT ADVICE

[20] Proof that the complainant received advice from a third party before entering into the impugned transaction is one of the matters a court takes into account when weighing all the evidence. The weight, or importance, to be attached to such advice depends on all the circumstances. In the normal course, advice from a solicitor or other outside advisor can be expected to bring home to a complainant a proper understanding of what he or she is about to do. But a person may understand fully the implications of a proposed transaction, for instance, a substantial gift, and yet still be acting under the undue influence of another. Proof of outside advice does not, of itself, necessarily show that the subsequent completion of the transaction was free from the exercise of undue influence. Whether it will be proper to infer that outside advice had an emancipating effect, so that the transaction was not brought about by the exercise of undue influence, is a question of fact to be decided having regard to all the evidence in the case.

MANIFEST DISADVANTAGE

[21] As already noted, there are two prerequisites to the evidential shift in the burden of proof from the complainant to the other party. First, that the complainant reposed trust and confidence in the other party, or the other party acquired ascendancy over the complainant. Second, that the transaction is not readily explicable by the relationship of the parties.

[22] Lindley L.J. summarised this second prerequisite in the leading authority of *Allcard v. Skinner* (1887) 36 Ch. D. 145, [1886-90] All E.R. Rep. 90, where the donor parted with almost all her property. Lindley L.J. pointed out that where a gift of a small amount is made to a person standing in a confidential relationship to the donor, some proof of the exercise of the influence of the donee must be given. The mere existence of the influence is not enough. He continued:

> But if the gift is so large as not to be reasonably accounted for on the ground of friendship, relationship, charity, or other ordinary motives on which ordinary men act, the burden is upon the donee to support the gift.

(See (1887) 36 Ch. D. 145 at 185, [1886-90] All E.R. Rep. 90 at 100-101.)

• • •

[24] The second prerequisite, as expressed by Lindley L.J., is good sense. It is a necessary limitation upon the width of the first prerequisite. It would be absurd for the law to presume that every gift by a child to a parent, or every transaction between a client and his solicitor or between a patient and his doctor, was brought about by undue influence unless the contrary is affirmatively proved. Such a presumption would be too far-reaching. ... So something more is needed before the law reverses the burden of proof, something which calls for an explanation. When that something more is present, the greater the disadvantage to the vulnerable person, the more cogent must be the explanation before the presumption will be regarded as rebutted.

[25] This was the approach adopted by Lord Scarman in *Morgan's* case ... . He noted that whatever the legal character of the transaction, it must constitute a disadvantage sufficiently serious to require evidence to rebut the presumption that in the circumstances of the parties' relationship, it was procured by the exercise of undue influence. ...

[26] Lord Scarman attached the label "manifest disadvantage" to this second ingredient necessary to raise the presumption. This label has been causing difficulty. ...

[27] The problem has arisen in the context of wives guaranteeing payment of their husband's business debts. In recent years judge after judge has grappled with the baffling question whether a wife's guarantee of her husband's bank overdraft, together with a charge on her share of the matrimonial home, was a transaction manifestly to her disadvantage.

[28] In a narrow sense, such a transaction plainly ("manifestly") is disadvantageous to the wife. She undertakes a serious financial obligation, and in return she personally receives nothing. But that would be to take an unrealistically blinkered view of such a transaction. Unlike the relationship of solicitor and client or medical advisor and patient, in the case of husband and wife there are inherent reasons why such a transaction may well be for her benefit. Ordinarily, the fortunes of husband and wife are bound up together. ...

[29] Which, then, is the correct approach to adopt in deciding whether a transaction is disadvantageous to the wife: the narrow approach, or the wider approach? The answer is neither. The answer lies in discarding a label which gives rise to this sort of ambiguity. The better approach is to adhere more directly to the test outlined by Lindley L.J. in *Allcard v. Skinner*, and adopted by Lord Scarman in *Morgan's* case, in the passages I have cited.

[30] I return to husband and wife cases. I do not think that, in the ordinary course, a guarantee of the character I have mentioned is to be regarded as a transaction which, failing proof to the contrary, is explicable only on the basis that it has been procured by the exercise of undue influence by the husband. ...

[31] I have emphasised the phrase "in the ordinary course." There will be cases where a wife's signature of a guarantee or a charge of her share in the matrimonial home does call for explanation. Nothing I have said above is directed at such a case.

A CAUTIONARY NOTE

[32] I add a cautionary note, prompted by some of the first instance judgments in the cases currently being considered by the House. It concerns the general approach to be adopted by a court when considering whether a wife's guarantee of her husband's bank overdraft was procured by her husband's undue influence. ... [W]hen a husband is forecasting the future of his business, and expressing his hopes or fears, a degree of hyperbole may be only natural. Courts should not too readily treat such exaggerations as misstatements.

[33] Inaccurate explanations of a proposed transaction are a different matter. So are cases where a husband, in whom a wife has reposed trust and confidence for the management of their financial affairs, prefers his interests to hers and makes a choice for both of them on that footing. Such a husband abuses the influence he has. He fails to discharge the obligation of candour and fairness he owes a wife who is looking to him to make the major financial decisions.

THE COMPLAINANT AND THIRD PARTIES: SURETYSHIP TRANSACTIONS

• • •

[35] If the freedom of home-owners to make economic use of their homes is not to be frustrated, a bank must be able to have confidence that a wife's signature of the necessary guarantee and charge will be as binding upon her as is the signature of anyone else on documents which he or she may sign. Otherwise banks will not be willing to lend money on the security of a jointly owned house or flat.

[36] At the same time, the high degree of trust and confidence and emotional interdependence which normally characterises a marriage relationship provides scope for abuse. ...

[37] In *O'Brien's* case this House decided where the balance should be held between these competing interests. On the one side, there is the need to protect a wife against a husband's undue influence. On the other side, there is the need for the bank to be able to have reasonable confidence in the strength of its security. Otherwise it would not provide the required money. The problem lies in finding the course best designed to protect wives in a minority of cases without unreasonably hampering the giving and taking of security. The House produced a practical solution. The House decided what are the steps a bank should take to ensure it is not affected by any claim the wife may have that her signature of the documents was procured by the undue influence or other wrong of her husband. Like every compromise, the outcome falls short of achieving in full the objectives of either of the two competing interests. In particular, the steps required of banks will not guarantee that, in future, wives will not be subjected to undue influence or misled when standing as sureties. Short of prohibiting this type of suretyship transaction altogether, there is no way of achieving that result, desirable although it is. What passes between a husband and wife in this regard in the privacy of their own home is not capable of regulation or investigation as a prelude to the wife entering into a suretyship transaction.

[38] The jurisprudential route by which the House reached its conclusion in *O'Brien's* case has attracted criticism from some commentators. It has been said to involve artificiality and thereby create uncertainty in the law. I must first consider this criticism. In the ordinary course a bank which takes a guarantee security from the wife of its customer will be altogether ignorant of any undue influence the customer may have exercised in order to secure the wife's concurrence. In *O'Brien's* case Lord Browne-Wilkinson prayed in aid the doctrine of constructive notice. In circumstances he identified, a creditor is put on inquiry. When that is so, the creditor "will have constructive notice of the wife's rights" unless the creditor takes reasonable steps to satisfy himself that the wife's agreement to stand surety has been properly obtained (see [1993] 4 All E.R. 417 at 429, [1994] 1 A.C. 180 at 196).

• • •

[40] The traditional view of equity in this tripartite situation seems to be that a person in the position of the wife will only be relieved of her bargain if the other party to the transaction (the bank, in the present instance) was privy to the conduct which led to the wife's entry into the transaction. Knowledge is required ... . The law imposes no obligation on one party to a transaction to check whether the other party's concurrence was obtained by undue influence. But *O'Brien's* case has introduced into the law the concept that, in certain circumstances, a party to a contract may lose the benefit of his contract, entered into in good faith, if he ought to have known that the other's concurrence had been procured by the misconduct of a third party.

[41] There is a further respect in which *O'Brien's* case departed from conventional concepts. Traditionally, a person is deemed to have notice (that is, he has "constructive" notice) of a prior right when he does not actually know of it but would have learned of it had he made the requisite inquiries. A purchaser will be treated as having constructive notice of all that a reasonably prudent purchaser would have discovered. In the present type of case, the steps a bank is required to take, lest it have constructive notice that the wife's concurrence was procured improperly by her husband, do not consist of making inquiries. Rather, *O'Brien's* case envisages that the steps taken by the bank will reduce, or even eliminate, the risk of the wife entering into the transaction under any misapprehension or as a result of undue influence by her husband. The steps are not concerned to discover whether the wife has been wronged by her husband in this way. The steps are concerned to minimise the risk that such a wrong may be committed.

• • •

[43] The route selected in *O'Brien*'s case ought not to have an unsettling effect on established principles of contract. *O'Brien*'s case concerned suretyship transactions. These are tripartite transactions. They involve the debtor as well as the creditor and the guarantor. The guarantor enters into the transaction at the request of the debtor. The guarantor assumes obligations. On the face of the transaction the guarantor usually receives no benefit in return, unless the guarantee is being given on a commercial basis. Leaving aside cases where the relationship between the surety and the debtor is commercial, a guarantee transaction is one-sided so far as the guarantor is concerned. The creditor knows this. Thus the decision in *O'Brien*'s case is directed at a class of contracts which has special features of its own. ...

THE THRESHOLD: WHEN THE BANK IS PUT ON INQUIRY

[44] In *O'Brien*'s case the House considered the circumstances in which a bank, or other creditor, is "put on inquiry." Strictly this is a misnomer. As already noted, a bank is not required to make inquiries. But it will be convenient to use the terminology which has now become accepted in this context. The House set a low level for the threshold which must be crossed before a bank is put on inquiry. For practical reasons the level is set much lower than is required to satisfy a court that, failing contrary evidence, the court may infer that the transaction was procured by undue influence. Lord Browne-Wilkinson said:

> Therefore, in my judgment a creditor is put on inquiry when a wife offers to stand surety for her husband's debts by the combination of two factors: (a) the transaction is on its face not to the financial advantage of the wife; and (b) there is a substantial risk in transactions of that kind that, in procuring the wife to act as surety, the husband has committed a legal or equitable wrong that entitles the wife to set aside the transaction.

(See [1993] 4 All E.R. 417 at 429, [1994] 1 A.C. 180 at 196.)
In my view, this passage, read in context, is to be taken to mean, quite simply, that a bank is put on inquiry whenever a wife offers to stand surety for her husband's debts.

• • •

[47] The position is likewise if the husband stands surety for his wife's debts. Similarly, in the case of unmarried couples, whether heterosexual or homosexual, where the bank is aware of the relationship ... . Cohabitation is not essential. The Court of Appeal rightly so decided in *Massey v. Midland Bank plc* [1995] 1 All E.R. 929 at 933, per Steyn L.J.

[48] As to the type of transactions where a bank is put on inquiry, the case where a wife becomes surety for her husband's debts is, in this context, a straightforward case. The bank is put on inquiry. On the other side of the line is the case where money is being advanced, or has been advanced, to husband and wife jointly. In such a case the bank is not put on inquiry, unless the bank is aware the loan is being made for the husband's purposes, as distinct from their joint purposes. That was decided in *CIBC Mortgages plc v. Pitt* [1993] 4 All E.R. 433, [1994] 1 A.C. 200.

[49] Less clear cut is the case where the wife becomes surety for the debts of a company whose shares are held by her and her husband. Her shareholding may be nominal, or she may have a minority shareholding or an equal shareholding with her husband. In my view the bank is put on inquiry in such cases, even when the wife is a director or secretary of the company. ...

THE STEPS A BANK SHOULD TAKE

[50] The principal area of controversy on these appeals concerns the steps a bank should take when it has been put on inquiry. In *O'Brien*'s case Lord Browne-Wilkinson

([1993] 4 All E.R. 417 at 429-430, [1994] 1 A.C. 180 at 196-197) said that a bank can reasonably be expected to take steps to bring home to the wife the risk she is running by standing as surety and to advise her to take independent advice. That test is applicable to past transactions. All the cases now before your Lordships' House fall into this category. For the future a bank satisfies these requirements if it insists that the wife attend a private meeting with a representative of the bank at which she is told of the extent of her liability as surety, warned of the risk she is running and urged to take independent legal advice. In exceptional cases the bank, to be safe, has to insist that the wife is separately advised.

• • •

[53] My Lords, it is plainly neither desirable nor practicable that banks should be required to attempt to discover for themselves whether a wife's consent is being procured by the exercise of undue influence of her husband. This is not a step the banks should be expected to take. Nor, further, is it desirable or practicable that banks should be expected to insist on confirmation from a solicitor that the solicitor has satisfied himself that the wife's consent has not been procured by undue influence. As already noted, the circumstances in which banks are put on inquiry are extremely wide. They embrace every case where a wife is entering into a suretyship transaction in respect of her husband's debts. Many, if not most, wives would be understandably outraged by having to respond to the sort of questioning which would be appropriate before a responsible solicitor could give such a confirmation. In any event, solicitors are not equipped to carry out such an exercise in any really worthwhile way, and they will usually lack the necessary materials.

• • •

[54] The furthest a bank can be expected to go is to take reasonable steps to satisfy itself that the wife has had brought home to her, in a meaningful way, the practical implications of the proposed transaction. This does not wholly eliminate the risk of undue influence or misrepresentation. But it does mean that a wife enters into a transaction with her eyes open so far as the basic elements of the transaction are concerned.

• • •

[56] I shall return later to the steps a bank should take ... . Suffice to say, these steps, together with advice from a solicitor acting for the wife, ought to provide the substance of the protection which *O'Brien*'s case intended a wife should have. Ordinarily it will be reasonable that a bank should be able to rely upon confirmation from a solicitor, acting for the wife, that he has advised the wife appropriately.

[57] The position will be otherwise if the bank knows that the solicitor has not duly advised the wife or, I would add, if the bank knows facts from which it ought to have realised that the wife has not received the appropriate advice. In such circumstances the bank will proceed at its own risk.

THE CONTENT OF THE LEGAL ADVICE

[58] In *Royal Bank of Scotland plc v. Etridge (No. 2)* [1998] 4 All E.R. 705 at 715 (para. 19), the Court of Appeal set out its views of the duties of a solicitor in this context:

A solicitor who is instructed to advise a person who may be subject to the undue influence of another must bear in mind that [it] is not sufficient that she understands the nature and effect of the transaction if she is so affected by the influence of the other that she cannot make an independent decision of her own. ... His duty is to satisfy himself that his client is free from improper influence, and the first step must be to ascertain whether it is one into which she could sensibly be advised to enter if free from such influence. If he is not so satisfied it is his duty to advise her not to enter into it, and to refuse to act further for her in the implementation of the transaction if she persists ... .

[59] I am unable to accept this as an accurate formulation of a solicitor's duties in cases such as those now under consideration. In some respects it goes much too far.

• • •

[61] Thus, in the present type of case it is not for the solicitor to veto the transaction by declining to confirm to the bank that he has explained the documents to the wife and the risks she is taking upon herself. If the solicitor considers the transaction is not in the wife's best interests, he will give reasoned advice to the wife to that effect. But at the end of the day the decision on whether to proceed is the decision of the client, not the solicitor. A wife is not to be precluded from entering into a financially unwise transaction if, for her own reasons, she wishes to do so.

[62] That is the general rule. There may, of course, be exceptional circumstances where it is glaringly obvious that the wife is being grievously wronged. In such a case the solicitor should decline to act further. ...

[63] In *Etridge's* case ([1998] 4 All E.R. 705 at 722 (para. 49)), the Court of Appeal said that if the transaction is "one into which no competent solicitor could properly advise the wife to enter," the availability of legal advice is insufficient to avoid the bank being fixed with constructive notice. It follows from the views expressed above that I am unable to agree with the Court of Appeal on this point.

[64] I turn to consider the scope of the responsibilities of a solicitor who is advising the wife. In identifying what are the solicitor's responsibilities the starting point must always be the solicitor's retainer. What has he been retained to do? As a general proposition, the scope of a solicitor's duties is dictated by the terms, whether express or implied, of his retainer. ...

[65] Typically, the advice a solicitor can be expected to give should cover the following matters as the core minimum. (1) He will need to explain the nature of the documents and the practical consequences these will have for the wife if she signs them. She could lose her home if her husband's business does not prosper. Her home may be her only substantial asset, as well as the family's home. She could be made bankrupt. (2) He will need to point out the seriousness of the risks involved. The wife should be told the purpose of the proposed new facility, the amount and principal terms of the new facility, and that the bank might increase the amount of the facility, or change its terms, or grant a new facility, without reference to her. She should be told the amount of her liability under her guarantee. The solicitor should discuss the wife's financial means, including her understanding of the value of the property being charged. The solicitor should discuss whether the wife or her husband has any other assets out of which repayment could be made if the husband's business should fail. These matters are relevant to the seriousness of the risks involved. (3) The solicitor will need to state clearly that the wife has a choice. The decision is hers and hers alone. Explanation of the choice facing the wife will call for some discussion of the present financial position, including the amount of the husband's present indebtedness, and the amount of his current overdraft facility. (4) The solicitor should check whether the wife wishes to proceed. She should be asked whether she is content that the solicitor should write to the bank confirming he has explained to her the nature of the documents and the practical implications they may have for her, or whether, for instance, she would prefer him to negotiate with the bank on the terms of the transaction. Matters for negotiation could include the sequence in which the various securities will be called upon or a specific or lower limit to her liabilities. The solicitor should not give any confirmation to the bank without the wife's authority.

[66] The solicitor's discussion with the wife should take place at a face-to-face meeting, in the absence of the husband. It goes without saying that the solicitor's

explanations should be couched in suitably non-technical language. It also goes without saying that the solicitor's task is an important one. It is not a formality.

[67] The solicitor should obtain from the bank any information he needs. If the bank fails for any reason to provide information requested by the solicitor, the solicitor should decline to provide the confirmation sought by the bank.

[68] As already noted, the advice which a solicitor can be expected to give must depend on the particular facts of the case. But I have set out this "core minimum" in some detail, because the quality of the legal advice is the most disturbing feature of some of the present appeals. The perfunctory nature of the advice may well be largely due to a failure by some solicitors to understand what is required in these cases.

INDEPENDENT ADVICE

[69] I turn next to the much-vexed question whether the solicitor advising the wife must act for the wife alone.

• • •

[The court concludes that the solicitor can act for both husband and wife, as long as the solicitor fully discharges his professional duty to look after the wife's interests. If there is any doubt of his ability to do this, or any conflict of interest, the lawyer should decline to act for both parties.]

AGENCY

[75] No system ever works perfectly. There will always be cases where things go wrong, sometimes seriously wrong. The next question concerns the position when a solicitor has accepted instructions to advise a wife but he fails to do so properly. He fails to give her the advice needed to bring home to her the practical implications of her standing as surety. What then? The wife has a remedy in damages against the negligent solicitor. But what is the position of the bank who proceeded in the belief that the wife had been given the necessary advice?

[76] Mr. Sher contended that, depending on the facts, the solicitor should be regarded as the agent of the bank. ...

[77] I cannot accept this analysis. ...

[78] In the ordinary case, therefore, deficiencies in the advice given are a matter between the wife and her solicitor. The bank is entitled to proceed on the assumption that a solicitor advising the wife has done his job properly. I have already mentioned what is the bank's position if it knows this is not so, or if it knows facts from which it ought to have realised this is not so.

OBTAINING THE SOLICITOR'S CONFIRMATION

[79] I now return to the steps a bank should take when it has been put on inquiry and for its protection is looking to the fact that the wife has been advised independently by a solicitor. (1) One of the unsatisfactory features in some of the cases is the late stage at which the wife first became involved in the transaction. In practice she had no opportunity to express a view on the identity of the solicitor who advised her. She did not even know that the purpose for which the solicitor was giving her advice was to enable him to send, on her behalf, the protective confirmation sought by the bank. Usually the solicitor acted for both husband and wife. Since the bank is looking for its protection to legal advice given to the wife by a solicitor who, in this respect, is acting solely for her, I consider the bank should take steps to check directly

with the wife the name of the solicitor she wishes to act for her. To this end, in future the bank should communicate directly with the wife, informing her that for its own protection it will require written confirmation from a solicitor, acting for her, to the effect that the solicitor has fully explained to her the nature of the documents and the practical implications they will have for her. She should be told that the purpose of this requirement is that thereafter she should not be able to dispute she is legally bound by the documents once she has signed them. She should be asked to nominate a solicitor whom she is willing to instruct to advise her, separately from her husband, and act for her in giving the necessary confirmation to the bank. She should be told that, if she wishes, the solicitor may be the same solicitor as is acting for her husband in the transaction. If a solicitor is already acting for the husband and the wife, she should be asked whether she would prefer that a different solicitor should act for her regarding the bank's requirement for confirmation from a solicitor. The bank should not proceed with the transaction until it has received an appropriate response directly from the wife. (2) Representatives of the bank are likely to have a much better picture of the husband's financial affairs than the solicitor. If the bank is not willing to undertake the task of explanation itself, the bank must provide the solicitor with the financial information he needs for this purpose. Accordingly it should become routine practice for banks, if relying on confirmation from a solicitor for their protection, to send to the solicitor the necessary financial information. What is required must depend on the facts of the case. Ordinarily this will include information on the purpose for which the proposed new facility has been requested, the current amount of the husband's indebtedness, the amount of his current overdraft facility, and the amount and terms of any new facility. If the bank's request for security arose from a written application by the husband for a facility, a copy of the application should be sent to the solicitor. The bank will, of course, need first to obtain the consent of its customer to this circulation of confidential information. If this consent is not forthcoming the transaction will not be able to proceed. (3) Exceptionally there may be a case where the bank believes or suspects that the wife has been misled by her husband or is not entering into the transaction of her own free will. If such a case occurs the bank must inform the wife's solicitors of the facts giving rise to its belief or suspicion. (4) The bank should in every case obtain from the wife's solicitor a written confirmation to the effect mentioned above.

[80] These steps will be applicable to future transactions. In respect of past transactions, the bank will ordinarily be regarded as having discharged its obligations if a solicitor who was acting for the wife in the transaction gave the bank confirmation to the effect that he had brought home to the wife the risks she was running by standing as surety.

THE CREDITOR'S DISCLOSURE OBLIGATION

[81] It is a well-established principle that, stated shortly, a creditor is obliged to disclose to a guarantor any unusual feature of the contract between the creditor and the debtor which makes it materially different in a potentially disadvantageous respect from what the guarantor might naturally expect. The precise ambit of this disclosure obligation remains unclear. ... It is sufficient for me to say that, contrary to submissions made, the need to provide protection for wives who are standing as sureties does not point to a need to revisit the scope of this disclosure principle. Wives require a different form of protection. They need a full and clear explanation of the risks involved. Typically, the risks will be risks any surety would expect. The protection needed by wives differs from, and goes beyond, the disclosure of information. The *O'Brien* principle is intended to provide this protection.

A WIDER PRINCIPLE

[82] ... The *O'Brien* decision cannot sensibly be regarded as confined to sexual relationships, although these are likely to be its main field of application at present. What is appropriate for sexual relationships ought, in principle, to be appropriate also for other relationships where trust and confidence are likely to exist.

• • •

[84] The crucially important question raised by this wider application of the *O'Brien* principle concerns the circumstances which will put a bank on inquiry. A bank is put on inquiry whenever a wife stands as surety for her husband's debts. It is sufficient that the bank knows of the husband/wife relationship. That bare fact is enough ... . What, then, of other relationships where there is an increased risk of undue influence, such as parent and child? Is it enough that the bank knows of the relationship? ... [A]s with wives, so with other relationships, the test of what puts a bank on inquiry should be simple, clear and easy to apply in widely varying circumstances. This suggests that, in the case of a father and daughter, knowledge by the bank of the relationship of father and daughter should suffice to put the bank on inquiry. ...

[86] But the law cannot stop at this point, with banks on inquiry only in cases where the debtor and guarantor have a sexual relationship or the relationship is one where the law presumes the existence of trust and confidence. That would be an arbitrary boundary, and the law has already moved beyond this, in the decision in the *Credit Lyonnais* case. As noted earlier, the reality of life is that relationships in which undue influence can be exercised are infinitely various. They cannot be exhaustively defined. Nor is it possible to produce a comprehensive list of relationships where there is a substantial risk of the exercise of undue influence, all others being excluded from the ambit of the *O'Brien* principle. Human affairs do not lend themselves to categorisations of this sort. The older generation of a family may exercise undue influence over a younger member, as in parent/child cases such as *Bainbrigge v. Browne* (1881) 18 Ch. D. 188 and *Powell v. Powell* [1900] 1 Ch. 243. Sometimes it is the other way round, as with a nephew and his elderly aunt in *Inche Noriah v. Shaik Allie Bin Omar* [1929] A.C. 127, [1928] All E.R. Rep. 189. An employer may take advantage of his employee, as in the *Credit Lyonnais* case. But it may be the other way round, with an employee taking advantage of her employer, as happened with the secretary/companion and her elderly employer in *Re Craig (decd.)* [1970] 2 All E.R. 390, [1971] Ch. 95. The list could go on.

[87] These considerations point forcibly to the conclusion that there is no rational cut-off point, with certain types of relationship being susceptible to the *O'Brien* principle and others not. Further, if a bank is not to be required to evaluate the extent to which its customer has influence over a proposed guarantor, the only practical way forward is to regard banks as "put on inquiry" in every case where the relationship between the surety and the debtor is non-commercial. ...

[88] Different considerations apply where the relationship between the debtor and guarantor is commercial, as where a guarantor is being paid a fee, or a company is guaranteeing the debts of another company in the same group. Those engaged in business can be regarded as capable of looking after themselves and understanding the risks involved in the giving of guarantees.

[89] By the decisions of this House in *O'Brien*'s case and the Court of Appeal in the *Credit Lyonnais* case, English law has taken its first strides in the development of some such general principle. It is a workable principle. It is also simple, coherent and eminently desirable. I venture to think this is the way the law is moving, and should continue to move. Equity, it is said, is not past the age of child-bearing. In the present context the equitable concept of being "put on inquiry" is the parent of

a principle of general application, a principle which imposes no more than a modest obligation on banks and other creditors. The existence of this obligation in all non-commercial cases does not go beyond the reasonable requirements of the present times. In future, banks and other creditors should regulate their affairs accordingly.

• • •

LORD SCOTT OF FOSCOTE: ...

SUMMARY

[191] My Lords I think, given the regrettable length of this opinion, I should try and summarise my views about the principles that apply and the practice that should be followed in surety wife cases. (1) The issue as between the surety wife and the lender bank is whether the bank may rely on the apparent consent of the wife to the surety-ship transaction. (2) If the bank knows that the surety wife's consent to the transaction has been procured by undue influence or misrepresentation, or if it has shut its eyes to the likelihood that that was so, it may not rely on her apparent consent. (3) If the wife's consent has in fact been procured by undue influence or misrepresentation, the bank may not rely on her apparent consent unless it has good reason to believe that she understands the nature and effect of the transaction. (4) Unless the case has some special feature, the bank's knowledge that a solicitor is acting for the wife and has advised her about the nature and effect of the transaction will provide a good reason for the purposes of (3) above. That will also be so if the bank has a reasonable belief that a solicitor is acting for her and has so advised her. Written confirmation by a solicitor acting for the wife that he has so advised her will entitle the bank to hold that reasonable belief. (5) So, too, a sufficient explanation of the nature and effect of the transaction given by a senior bank official would constitute good reason for the purposes of (3) above. (6) If there are any facts known to the bank which increase the inherent risk that the wife's consent to the transaction may have been procured by the husband's undue influence or misrepresentation, it may be necessary for the bank to be satisfied that the wife has received advice about the transaction from a solicitor independent of the husband before the bank can reasonably rely on the wife's apparent consent. (7) If the bank has not taken reasonable steps to satisfy itself that the wife understands the nature and effect of the transaction, the wife will, subject to such matters as delay, acquiescence, change of position etc., be able to set aside the transaction if her consent was in fact procured by undue influence or misrepresentation. (8) Subject to special instructions or special circumstances, the duty of a solicitor instructed to act for a wife proposing to stand as surety, or to give security, for her husband's debts is to try and make sure that she understands the nature and effect of the transaction. (9) In all surety wife cases the bank should disclose to the surety wife, or to the solicitor acting for her, the amount of the existing indebtedness of the principal debtor to the bank and the amount of the proposed new loan or drawing facility. (10) Subject to (9) above, a creditor has no greater duty of disclosure to a surety wife than to any other intending surety.

[192] I am in full agreement with the analysis of the applicable principles of law and with the conclusions expressed in the opinion of my noble and learned friend Lord Nicholls of Birkenhead. I believe the analysis I have sought to give in this opinion and my conclusions are consistent with them. ...

DISPOSITION

The Harris, Wallace, Moore, Bennett and Desmond Banks & Co. appeals allowed. The Etridge, Gill and Coleman appeals dismissed.

Decision of the Court of Appeal in *Royal Bank of Scotland plc v. Etridge (No 2)* [1998] 4 All E.R. 705 reversed in part.

Decision of the Court of Appeal in *Barclays Bank plc v. Coleman* [2000] 1 All E.R. 385 affirmed.

[The judgments of Lord Bingham of Cornhill, Lord Clyde, and Lord Hobhouse of Woodborough (concurring in substance with Lord Nicholls) have been omitted.]

NOTES

1. Lord Nicholls spent a significant amount of time discussing the exact nature of the presumptions to be applied in the spousal guarantor cases. This issue has also caused controversy in Canada. Compare *Bank of Montreal v Duguid* (2000), 47 OR (3d) 737 (CA) with *CIBC Mortgage Corp v Rowatt* (2002), 61 OR (3d) 737 (CA).

2. *Barclays Bank plc v O'Brien*, discussed above in *Etridge (No 2)*, was cited with approval by the Supreme Court of Canada in *Gold v Rosenberg*, [1997] 3 SCR 767 at para 60, 152 DLR (4th) 385 at 402. Speaking for the majority, Iacobucci J stated that in certain circumstances a creditor's duty to inquire will extend beyond spousal relationships to other relationships in which the surety reposes trust and confidence in the principal debtor, such as parent–child or employer–employee relationships.

3. Spousal relationships are frequently analyzed by the courts in guarantee cases, as courts commonly see people who guarantee loans for their spouses or partners, but then later seek to have the transaction put aside (perhaps because of a divorce) on the basis of unconscionability and undue influence. The courts consider many factors, and make assessments based on the circumstances of the case and the roles occupied by the parties throughout their relationship. For example, in *Bank of Montreal v Courtney* 2005 NSCA 153, 261 DLR (4th) 665, the court denied relief to the guarantor wife. The husband, who had attended to the couple's financial affairs, had persuaded his reluctant wife to sign the guarantee. However, the wife had had considerable work experience, a good educational background, and an appreciation of financial and business matters. The fact that she had not sought independent legal advice did not affect the outcome because she already knew and appreciated her rights and obligations regarding the loans and risks she was undertaking. Similarly, although this case did not involve a spousal relationship, in *DRL Coachlines Ltd v GE Canada Equipment Financing GP*, 2011 NSCA 23, [2011] NSJ No 93 (QL), the court upheld the trial judge's findings that the guarantor, "despite her limited education ... was a capable and experienced businessperson who understood just what she was signing." Because she had time to seek advice and ask questions before signing the personal guarantee, "her bargaining power was not 'grievously impaired by reason of ... ignorance or infirmity.'" See also *Van Der Ros v Van Der Ros* (2003), 182 BCCA 211.

See also *Susan Hilary Hurley v The Darjan Estate Company plc*, [2012] EWHC 189 (Ch), where the court had to determine whether a statutory demand for a debt should be set aside in order to decide whether a bankruptcy order was properly granted. Mr and Mrs Hurley were joint signatories to a lease for 21 years, but, after they failed to pay the rent, the landlord forfeited the lease, retook possession of the property, and served statutory demands on the couple. Mrs Hurley contested the debt, claiming that her signature on the lease was procured by Mr Hurley's undue influence to enter into the contract. The court questioned whether the principle of constructive notice from *Etridge (No 2)* would apply outside the context of a suretyship to one "where the complainant derives a direct benefit under the contract in the form of an interest in land." The court went on to consider whether there was "anything about this case to suggest to [the lessor] that Mrs Hurley was taking on a position akin to a surety and thus susceptible to pressure from her husband" (at paras 34-35). The court concluded that this was a standard lease of a licensed premises to spouses and did not require an explanation. Nonetheless, it went on to consider the principles relating to undue influence and concluded (at para 39) that Mrs Hurley "was not a lady who was accustomed to entrusting her financial affairs to her husband. She had her own job, and a measure of financial independence ... . Mrs Hurley must have been well aware that her husband's outburst was just a facet of the heightened emotion generally displayed in the course of a domestic argument ... . Indeed it was his manifest unhappiness that, above all, appears to have made her decide to sign the document then and there. None of this suggests that her independent judgment as to whether or not she should sign the Lease was being overborne." Compare to *Etridge (No 2)*, where Lord Nicholls cited *CIBC Mortgages plc v Pitt*, [1993] 4 All ER 433, [1994] 1 AC 200. There, the House of Lords determined (at para 12) that "[i]t is not essential that the transaction should be disadvantageous to the pressurised or influenced person, either in financial terms or in any other way. However, in the nature of things, questions of undue influence [are] unlikely to occur, where the transaction is innocuous. The issue is likely to arise only when, in some respect, the transaction was disadvantageous either from the outset or as matters turned out."

4. In *Garcia v National Australia Bank Ltd*, [1998] 155 ALR 614 (Austl HC), the court explained that the consideration of spousal relations in guarantee cases was not a result of antiquated notions of female dependency on male partners but, rather, because of the trust inherent in marital relations. Mr and Mrs Garcia executed a mortgage over their home in order to secure all moneys owing to the bank, including moneys owing under future guarantees. Mrs Garcia subsequently guaranteed several loans with the bank in order to secure her husband's business ventures. After the couple divorced, Mrs Garcia commenced proceedings to void the transactions and the bank cross-claimed for the moneys owing under the guarantees. The High Court of Australia ruled that it would be unconscionable for the bank to enforce the guarantees because Mrs Garcia did not understand the purport and effect of the transactions she had entered into. The bank should have understood that, as a wife, Mrs Garcia may have reposed trust in her husband in matters of business. The bank should have realized that Mr Garcia may not have fully and accurately explained the transactions to his wife. However, the bank took no steps to explain the nature of the transactions to Mrs Garcia, or to ascertain whether the effect of the transactions had been explained to her by a competent, independent, and disinterested party. The court addressed concerns that the case law governing the setting aside of a wife's guarantee of her husband's debt were founded on outdated notions of the subservience and inferior economic position of women. The court held that, instead, the case law recognized the ordinary trust and confidence between marriage partners. In many relationships, one spouse might handle the business affairs and might not provide the other spouse with a complete or accurate description of transactions. That this is the case is not always attributable to deception, to an imbalance of power within the relationship, or to exploitation due to emotional involvement. It is often simply a reflection of the trust and confidence that each spouse has for the other. See also *Padden v Bevan Ashford Solicitors*, [2012] 2 Costs LO 223, relying on *Etridge (No 2)*. There, the court maintained (at para 29) that "[w]here a wife provides her interest in the family home (and often other assets) to a bank as security for her husband's liabilities, there is an obvious risk that she may subsequently allege that the security should be set aside because it was obtained by her husband's undue influence, of which the bank had notice. In order to minimize the risk of such a claim being successfully advanced, a bank should ensure that the wife has proper legal advice."

5. Did the court in *Hewett v First Plus Financial Group Plc*, [2010] EWCA Civ 312 go too far in finding that the husband's concealment of his extramarital affair from his wife amounted to undue influence against her when she signed a charge against their matrimonial home as security for his personal debts? In *Hewett*, Briggs J found that "Mrs Hewett reposed a sufficient

degree of trust and confidence in her husband to give rise to what Lord Nicholls described as an obligation of candour and fairness owed to her." This finding was made because Mr Hewitt was in charge of the family finances and this particular transaction required her "to take on trust his promise to make the instalment payments." With regard to whether Mr Hewett's affair was something he was required to disclose as a result of his obligation of trust and candour, the court found that it was a material fact calling for disclosure, noting that "[t]he issue may be best addressed by asking whether a solicitor, consulted by Mrs Hewett for advice about the wisdom of the transaction, would have thought it relevant to know that her husband was, while asking for her unqualified trust, at the same time conducting a clandestine affair." The court concluded that "Mrs Hewett's decision to participate in the charge ... was ... vitiated by his abuse of her trust" and set the mortgage aside.

6. Banks are well advised to ensure guarantors have full knowledge of the documents they are signing and the potential consequences for them. One of the best ways to protect against a transaction being set aside at a later date is to require a guarantor to obtain independent legal advice prior to signing the documents. In *McKenzie v Bank of Montreal* (1975), 55 DLR (3d) 641 (Ont H Ct J), aff'd (1976), 12 OR (2d) 719 (CA), the plaintiff was a middle-aged widow whose intimate companion, Mr Lawrence, had accumulated substantial bad debts with the defendant bank. The plaintiff attended the bank with Mr Lawrence and signed several documents about which she was told nothing. One of the documents signed was a mortgage by the plaintiff to the bank, to be used as additional security for Lawrence's indebtedness. The Ontario Court of Appeal upheld the trial court's decision to set aside the mortgage. Given the bank's knowledge of Lawrence's precarious financial situation and of several dubious dealings in which he was involved, the bank was under an obligation to ensure that in mortgaging her land the plaintiff was doing what she wanted to do, with full knowledge of the probable consequences. To discharge this obligation, the bank should have required the plaintiff to obtain independent legal advice or, in the alternative, should have ensured that full disclosure was made to her of Lawrence's substantial indebtedness to the bank. Similarly, in *Canadian Kawasaki Motors Ltd v McKenzie* (1981), 126 DLR (3d) 253, the plaintiff, in granting a dealership to Colin McKenzie, induced McKenzie's wife and father to sign guarantees for the credit the company was extending to him. The Ontario County Court held that the plaintiff owed a duty to explain the effect of the guarantee, to disclose all relevant facts, and to advise the defendants to get independent advice. The court also held that because McKenzie had so little money and the timing was unfavourable for starting a business, the plaintiff should have explained to the guarantors that the chances of success were low, and held that failure to do so was a breach of a trust relationship. Therefore the guarantees were unenforceable.

7. Family settings, beyond spousal relations, frequently provide a context for guarantee cases. In these settings, where trust and familiarity form the basis for one party agreeing to guarantee a loan for another, the same principles will apply. In *Bomek v Bomek* (1983), 146 DLR (3d) 139 (Man CA), a credit union obtained a home mortgage from the plaintiffs, a husband and wife with grades 3 and 9 education respectively, in order to secure existing loans it had made to their son's company, on the representation that the loan was for investment by their son. The credit union applied the money to reduce the company's debt and did not advance any money to the son. The company went bankrupt a year later. The Manitoba Court of Appeal set aside the mortgage because the documents were misleading and the transaction was unconscionable. The court held that the credit union had a duty to ensure that the plaintiffs obtained independent legal advice. Similarly, in *Bertolo v Bank of Montreal* (1986), 33 DLR (4th) 610 (Ont CA), the defendant bank recognized the need for an elderly widow to obtain independent legal advice before securing her son's indebtedness. However, the legal advice on which the bank ultimately relied was provided by a member of the same firm representing the bank and the plaintiff's son. In setting aside the mortgage, the Ontario Court of Appeal ruled that the plaintiff had never been properly apprised of the nature of the transaction or the

extent of her potential liability. The transaction was manifestly disadvantageous to the plaintiff in that it subjected her to the prospect of losing her only asset—her home. As such, the plaintiff's interests conflicted with the interests of the other parties to the transaction, who simply wanted to complete the deal. Independent legal advice was therefore essential. The bank was, or ought to have been, aware that the plaintiff had not had the benefit of such advice. See also *Lewis v Central Credit Union Ltd,* 2012 PECA 9, where the court commented, "[i]n the present case, the applications judge found it was apparent that the mother would want to help her son in the circumstances. The relevant circumstances included her being 77 years of age, not personally involved in her son's business and having little knowledge of his financial affairs, having deep regard for her son and relying heavily on his advice and ability, having previously provided collateral security for his business loans with the creditor, and having received no financial benefit or remuneration for mortgaging her property interests for her son's benefit. It is plain to see that the relationship between the son and his mother was such that a potential existed for the son to exercise persuasive influence over his mother" (para 67).

8. As mentioned above, one significant factor that comes out of all these cases is the importance of legal advice. As a standing rule, legal advice is not required, but, as the Supreme Court said in *Gold v Rosenberg,* above, "[w]hether or not someone requires independent legal advice will depend on two principal concerns: whether they understand what is proposed to them and whether they are free to decide according to their own will. The first is a function of information and intellect, while the second will depend, among other things, on whether there is undue influence" (para 85). The extent of the solicitor's responsibility (and therefore the financial institution's) was specified in *Etridge (No 2)* (at para 54) as:

> [t]he furthest a bank can be expected to go is to take reasonable steps to satisfy itself that the wife has had brought home to her, in a meaningful way, the practical implications of the proposed transaction. This does not wholly eliminate the risk of undue influence or misrepresentation. But it does mean that a wife enters into a transaction with her eyes open so far as the basic elements of the transaction are concerned.

This principle is currently expressed in legislation. See e.g. the *Guarantees Acknowledgment Act,* RSA 2000, c G-11, s 4, which requires, if a guarantee is to have any effect, that the person signing it appear before a notary public, who must certify that the person is "aware of the contents of the guarantee and understands it." For a recent application of *Etridge (No 2),* see *Lewis v Central Credit Union Limited,* above.

9. In *Australian Competition and Consumer Commission v CG Berbatis Holdings Pty Ltd,* [2003] HCA 18, the Australian High Court tested the "small business" unconscionability provisions of the *Trade Practices Act 1974* for the first time. It held that it was not unconscionable for a commercial landlord to require its small business tenants to drop legal claims against him in exchange for the renewal of their lease. Although the landlord knew that his tenants wanted to sell their business (which they could not do without a lease), the High Court held that the landlord did not take special advantage of them. In rendering its decision, the court considered it important that the tenants had no legal entitlement to the renewal of the lease and had the benefit of legal advice and representation. For more, see Anthony Duggan, "The Trumping of Mateship: Unconscionability in the High Court of Australia" (2003) 39 Can Bus LJ 275. For a critical analysis of the case, see Rick Bigwood, "Curbing Unconscionability: Berbatis in the High Court of Australia" (2004) 28 Melbourne UL Rev 203.

10. In *Rogers v Lane Realty Corp,* 2005 SKQB 330, the court found that the failure to read an agreement before signing does not, of itself, make the agreement unconscionable.

11. For extended commentary on the issues surrounding financial transactions and family ties, see Michael Trebilcock & Steven Elliot, "The Scope and Limits of Legal Paternalism: Altruism and Coercion in Family Financial Arrangements" in Benson, and Belinda Fehlberg, *Sexually Transmitted Debt: Surety Experience and English Law* (Oxford: Clarendon Press, 1997).

MACAULAY V A SCHROEDER MUSIC PUBLISHING CO LTD
[1974] 1 WLR 1308 (HL)

[A song writer, aged 21 and unknown, entered into an agreement with music publishers in their "standard form" whereby the publishers engaged his exclusive services during the term of the agreement. By clause 1 the agreement was, subject as thereinafter provided, to remain in force for five years. By clause 3(a) the song writer assigned to the publishers the full copyright for the whole world in all his musical compositions during the term. Clauses 5 to 8 dealt with the song writer's remuneration, which was to be by royalties on works published. By clause 9(a) if the total royalties during the term exceeded £5,000 the agreement was automatically extended for a further five years. By clause 9(b) the publishers could terminate the agreement at any time by one month's written notice. No such right was given to the song writer. By clause 16(a) the publishers had the right to assign the agreement. By clause 16(b) the songwriter agreed not to assign his rights under the agreement without the publishers' prior written consent. The song writer brought an action claiming, *inter alia*, a declaration that the agreement was contrary to public policy and void. Plowman J. so held and made the declaration sought, and his judgment was affirmed by the Court of Appeal.

The publishers appealed to the House of Lords.]

LORD DIPLOCK: My Lords, the contract under consideration in this appeal is one whereby the respondent accepted restrictions upon the way in which he would exploit his earning power as a song writer for the next ten years. Because this can be classified as a contract in restraint of trade the restrictions that the respondent accepted fell within one of those limited categories of contractual promises in respect of which the courts still retain the power to relieve the promisor of his legal duty to fulfil them. In order to determine whether this case is one in which that power ought to be exercised, what your Lordships have in fact been doing has been to assess the relative bargaining power of the publisher and the song writer at the time the contract was made and to decide whether the publisher had used his superior bargaining power to exact from the song writer promises that were unfairly onerous to him. Your Lordships have not been concerned to inquire whether the public have in fact been deprived of the fruit of the song writer's talents by reason of the restrictions, nor to assess the likelihood that they would be so deprived in the future if the contract were permitted to run its full course.

It is, in my view, salutary to acknowledge that in refusing to enforce provisions of a contract whereby one party agrees for the benefit of the other party to exploit or to refrain from exploiting his own earning power, the public policy which the court is implementing is not some 19th-century economic theory about the benefit to the general public of freedom of trade, but the protection of those whose bargaining power is weak against being forced by those whose bargaining power is stronger to enter into bargains that are unconscionable. Under the influence of Bentham and of laissez-faire the courts in the 19th century abandoned the practice of applying the public policy against unconscionable bargains to contracts generally, as they had formerly done to any contract considered to be usurious; but the policy survived in its application to penalty clauses and to relief against forfeiture and also to the special category of contracts in restraints of trade. If one looks at the reasoning of 19th-century judges in cases about contracts in restraint of trade one finds lip service paid to current economic theories, but if one looks at what they said in the light of what they did, one finds that they struck down a bargain if they thought it was unconscionable as between the parties to it and upheld it if they thought that it was not.

So I would hold that the question to be answered as respects a contract in restraint of trade of the kind with which this appeal is concerned is: "Was the bargain fair?" The test of fairness is, no doubt, whether the restrictions are both reasonably necessary for the protection of the legitimate interests of the promisee and commensurate with the benefits secured to the promisor under the contract. For the purpose of this test all the provisions of the contract must be taken into consideration.

My Lords, the provisions of the contract have already been sufficiently stated by my noble and learned friend, Lord Reid. I agree with his analysis of them and with his conclusion that the contract is unenforceable. It does not satisfy the test of fairness as I have endeavoured to state it. I will accordingly content myself with adding some observations directed to the argument that because the contract was in a "standard form" in common use between music publishers and song writers the restraints that it imposes upon the song writer's liberty to exploit his talents must be presumed to be fair and reasonable.

Standard forms of contracts are of two kinds. The first, of very ancient origin, are those which set out the terms upon which mercantile transactions of common occurrence are to be carried out. Examples are bills of lading, charterparties, policies of insurance, contracts of sale in the commodity markets. The standard clauses in these contracts have been settled over the years by negotiation by representatives of the commercial interests involved and have been widely adopted because experience has shown that they facilitate the conduct of trade. Contracts of these kinds affect not only the actual parties to them but also others who may have a commercial interest in the transactions to which they relate, as buyers or sellers, charterers or shipowners, insurers or bankers. If fairness or reasonableness were relevant to their enforceability the fact that they are widely used by parties whose bargaining power is fairly matched would raise a strong presumption that their terms are fair and reasonable.

The same presumption, however, does not apply to the other kind of standard form of contract. This is of comparatively modern origin. It is the result of the concentration of particular kinds of business in relatively few hands. The ticket cases in the 19th century provide what are probably the first examples. The terms of this kind of standard form of contract have not been the subject of negotiation between the parties to it, or approved by any organisation representing the interests of the weaker party. They have been dictated by that party whose bargaining power, either exercised alone or in conjunction with others providing similar goods or services, enables him to say: "If you want these goods or services at all, these are the only terms on which they are obtainable. Take it or leave it."

To be in a position to adopt this attitude towards a party desirous of entering into a contract to obtain goods or services provides a classic instance of superior bargaining power. It is not without significance that on the evidence in the present case music publishers in negotiating with song writers whose success has been already established do not insist upon adhering to a contract in the standard form they offered to the respondent. The fact that the appellants' bargaining power vis-à-vis the respondent was strong enough to enable them to adopt this take-it-or-leave-it attitude raises no presumption that they used it to drive an unconscionable bargain with him, but in the field of restraint of trade it calls for vigilance on the part of the court to see that they did not.

NOTES AND QUESTIONS

1. In "The Doctrine of Inequality of Bargaining Power: Post-Benthamite Economics in the House of Lords" (1976) 26 UTLJ 359, Michael Trebilcock criticized the *Schroeder* decision for its attempt to regulate contractual terms and argued that the decision would not have the intended effect—namely, to make contracts between music producers and songwriters more balanced. See also Rick Bigwood, *Exploitative Contracts* (Oxford: Oxford University Press, 2003) ch 6, "Exploitation of Special Advantage: Unconscionable Dealing," and Stephen Waddams, "Unconscionable Contracts: Competing Perspectives" (1999) 62 Sask L Rev 1.

2. At least one commentator has suggested that the doctrines of inequality of bargaining power, undue influence, and unconscionability reflect the principle of equality in exchange. In this view, the "bad" behaviour of the parties per se is irrelevant: see e.g. Peter Benson, "The Unity of Contract Law" in Benson.

3. In *Techform Products Ltd v Wolda* (2001), 56 OR (3d) 1 (CA), an independent contractor signed an employee technology agreement (ETA) that transferred his rights to any inventions that he created while in the plaintiff's employ. It was the contractor's contention that he did not want to sign the agreement, but that he did so because he was afraid that his services would be terminated if he did not. The Ontario Court of Appeal drew a sharp distinction between an employee's lack of choice and the illegitimacy of the pressure applied by the employer, requiring that both be present for a finding of economic duress. In deciding that there was no economic duress in this case, the court made the following remarks:

> The trial judge gave extensive attention to whether the defendant was deprived of choice, but did not return to the question of whether pressure was illegitimate. In failing to do so, she erred in law. There were a number of characteristics of this case that required a finding that the pressure was not illegitimate. First, the defendant was an independent contractor. The plaintiff could have insisted on something like the ETA as a condition for renewing the consultancy agreement for the following year. Second, the plaintiff genuinely believed that it was entitled to ownership of inventions by its employees and consultants. The fact that the law appears to be that absent an express or implied agreement to the contrary, an employee or independent contractor owns inventions did not mean that the plaintiff's request or demand that the defendant execute such an agreement was illegitimate. The plaintiff was paying the defendant for his work on the various inventions, and, while the plaintiff did not expressly assign the concept of the 3D Hinge to the defendant, he was generally assigned to work on hinges. The plaintiff's bona fide belief that it was the owner of the inventions told strongly in favour of finding that the pressure was not illegitimate. Finally, it was important that the defendant was not forced to sign the ETA on the spot. He took it away with him and had ample opportunity to obtain independent advice. Thereafter, he had many years to reconsider, obtain the benefit of legal advice, seek a revised agreement or repudiate the agreement. He did not do so, and the lengthy passage of time told strongly against there being illegitimate pressure. The trial judge erred in finding that the ETA was unenforceable on the basis of economic duress.

What *should* be the determining factors in cases like these: the employer's sincerely held belief in the legitimacy of the contractual terms, the plaintiff's actual lack of choice, or the contractual terms themselves (note that the law appeared to allocate the right in question to the independent contractor)? Does this depend on how you view the purposes of the unconscionability/duress doctrine? See Leff, "Unconscionability and the Code: The Emperor's New Clause," excerpted above.

PRIDMORE V CALVERT
(1975), 54 DLR (3d) 133 (BCSC)

[The plaintiff was injured in a motor accident by the defendants' negligence. The defendants relied on a release signed by the plaintiff.]

TOY J: The final question for determination has given me the greatest concern. The plaintiff was attended by an insurance adjuster within 48 hours of the accident. After signing a statement disclosing the circumstances of the accident, the plaintiff then signed a release of all her claims in favour of the defendants and their insurers. The defendants' counsel has pleaded and relied on that release as a complete defence to the plaintiff's claims.

Although the plaintiff's version of the signing of the release—or releases—is in many respects uncertain and vague, and in some instances she professed not to remember, I ascribe her lack of recollection to her state of mind and general condition at that time. The insurance adjuster gave his evidence in an admirably frank fashion, and I am prepared to accept his evidence as accurate and truthful.

In coming to the conclusion that I have, I have relied on a recent judgment of my brother Anderson J., in *Towers v. Affleck*, [1974] 1 W.W.R. 714. Anderson J. at p. 717 said: "... the true question to be determined here is whether the parties were on such unequal footing in all the circumstances, that it would be inequitable to hold the plaintiff to her bargain." He said further, at pp. 719-20:

> I have reached the conclusion that on the whole of the evidence the plaintiff has proved by a preponderance of evidence that the parties were on such an unequal footing that it would be unfair and inequitable to hold her to the terms of the agreement which she signed. Having reached the conclusion that the defendants [were] in a dominant position, it becomes necessary to consider whether the settlement was fair and reasonable. I have asked myself the question whether any practising lawyer would have approved the settlement. The answer is in the negative.
>
> While the Court will not lightly set aside settlement agreements, the Court will set aside contracts and bargains of an improvident character made by poor and ignorant persons acting without independent advice unless the other party discharges the onus on him to show that the transaction is fair and reasonable: see *Whittet v. Bush* (1888), 40 Ch.D. 312. While there is no evidence of poverty or financial distress in this case, I think that one of the major factors in the *Whittet* case was that the purchaser's solicitors acted for all parties and that the vendors did not receive any independent advice. *An experienced insurance adjuster plays the same role as a practising solicitor.* (Italics my own.)

In my view, the plaintiff should not be bound by the release that she signed for the reasons which I will detail shortly, but which in my judgment are supported by facts of greater weight than those relied on by my brother Anderson, in *Towers v. Affleck, supra*:

1. The plaintiff is a woman of limited intelligence. I do not mean that in a disparaging sense, but she told me that she started her training as a practical nurse at age 15. There was no evidence of any later academic training.
2. The plaintiff had worked throughout her married life as a practical nurse and in 1971 her husband died. The plaintiff had no close personal friends to whom she turned for advice or counselling of a confidential nature.
3. At the material time she sought no legal advice nor any lay advice concerning the signing of the release.

4. There was no evidence to suggest that the plaintiff had any business acumen at all, much less any knowledge of "releases."
5. The defendants' adjuster courteously arranged for an interview with the plaintiff at her home where she was recuperating on the second day after the accident.
6. The plaintiff's poor physical condition was apparent to the defendants' adjuster, who observed that the plaintiff was taking pills, that she was suffering from headaches, that she was in pain, and when walking, she did so in a guarded fashion.
7. The defendants' adjuster, without having examined the scene of the accident, without having solicited the plaintiff's doctor's opinion, or even having interviewed the defendant driver, was prepared to assess the claim and settle it "on the spot" at his first meeting with the plaintiff. There was a second release executed by the plaintiff two days later which is the operative release, but I do not attach great significance to that fact, as for all realistic purposes, the plaintiff was in the same condition and position of reliance on the adjuster on the second day as she was on the first. ...
9. The stated consideration of $331.40 which the plaintiff received "on the spot" on September 1, 1972, was calculated by the adjuster on August 30th as follows:

    — For out-of-pocket expenses, such as torn clothing, damaged wig, etc. $131.40
    — Extra $200.00

The adjuster asked the plaintiff how much she wanted for her "injuries" and she apparently asked the adjuster's opinion. He volunteered the figure of $200. That amount, one could only conclude as being in satisfaction of the plaintiff's whole general damage claim, except her actual loss of earnings, providing they did not exceed 180 days.

10. The adjuster computed the plaintiff's monthly income and broke it down to a daily wage loss claim and arrived at the figure of $17.66 per day. That amount the plaintiff was to receive in addition to medical expenses not otherwise covered and the above-mentioned sum of $331.40.
11. The adjuster was a man experienced in his work, and, before me, acknowledged that he had three interests to serve: one, his employer, the insurer; two, the defendants, namely, the insured persons; and three, the plaintiff, because she was, in any event, entitled to receive no-fault benefits of $50 per week for as long as she was off work up to a maximum of 108 weeks. I pause here to note that of the $17.66 daily benefit to be paid, as calculated by the adjuster, the plaintiff was entitled as of right to receive $7.15 as a result of her entitlement to no-fault benefits. I find that at the times the plaintiff was solicited to sign the two releases, she was not advised of her right to claim no-fault benefits of $50 per week and postpone her claims for general damages and out-of-pocket expenses until she had effected a complete recovery.
12. I further find that with respect to the $200 extra paid to her as referred to in para. 9 above, that she advanced no such claim herself, but was induced by the adjuster to advance such a claim. It is accordingly my opinion that the figure selected by the adjuster of $200 was not one that could properly be construed as a fair and reasonable estimate for the plaintiff's pain and suffering or loss of amenities, but one deliberately designed by the defendants' insurers to foreclose the possibility of a future claim by the plaintiff from anything in excess of 180 days of loss of income and her no-fault benefits. The defendants'

adjuster and counsel on the defendants' behalf at trial sought to justify the adjuster's conduct by relating that the plaintiff had told the adjuster that her doctor had said she would probably be back to work in a couple or three weeks. If that estimate was entitled to be acted upon, the $200 figure for loss of amenities and pain and suffering might be construed as reasonable. But if the agreement and release form ran its full course of $2,000 or a 180 days off work, could a figure of $200 be justified to compensate a person for suffering, or continued suffering in the manner that the defendants' adjuster observed when he attended at the plaintiff's residence?

13. The defendants' adjuster further conceded, with admirable candor that he did not explain the harshness of the release to the plaintiff.

Would any lawyer purporting to advise the plaintiff as to her rights have advised her to accept such a settlement? Posing the question that Anderson J. did in *Towers v. Affleck* brings quickly to mind numerous reasons why a complete settlement and release under the conditions which existed on both August 30, and September 1, 1972, should not have been made, only a few of which I will mention:

(a) The attending doctor's concurrence to settle should have been considered.

(b) Lawyers, and adjusters, exposure to these matters militates against a quick "on the spot" settlement.

(c) Without a firm, if not written, medical opinion, no settlement should have been made.

(d) A doctor's first opinion, or prognosis, many times has been shown to be inaccurate and the majority of [doctors] are quick to concede the point.

(e) The pain, headaches and general demeanour of the plaintiff, witnessed by the defendants' adjuster on the second and fourth days after the accident, should have been sufficient for any person purporting to give her independent advice to counsel her against signing such a serious document.

Accordingly, the plaintiff has satisfied me, on the balance of probabilities, that she was on such an unequal footing with respect to the defendants and their representatives, that in all the circumstances, it would be inequitable to hold her to the bargain that was made. There will accordingly be judgment for the plaintiff for general damages, special damages and allowing deductions as previously detailed, for the net amount of $20,995.11.

Judgment for plaintiff.

HORRY V TATE
[1982] 2 Lloyd's Rep 416 (QB)

[The plaintiff was injured in an accident at his place of employment. The defendants' insurers, represented by Mr. Oram, the claims inspector of the Iron Trades Association, had negotiated a contract with the plaintiff, who lacked legal representation, in which Horry accepted £1,000 in full settlement of his claim. The court rejected the contract as a defence to Horry's action.]

PETER PAIN J: ... So far as this case goes, I find that the plaintiff did rely on the guidance or advice of the Iron Trades as to the settlement of his claim. I find that the insurers knew that he so relied, and I find—this is perhaps almost a glimpse of the obvious—

that they had an interest in the figure at which the claim was settled, and their interest conflicted with the plaintiff's interest.

Further, I find here that there was a quality of confidence between the plaintiff and the insurers, which extended beyond that inherent in the confidence that can well exist between trustworthy persons who in business affairs deal with each other at arm's length.

The relationship existed, of course, between the plaintiff and the Iron Trades, not between the plaintiff and Mr. Oram personally, although, of course, Mr. Oram was closely involved, because he was the agent through whom the Iron Trades acted.

On this basis, there was in my view a duty of fiduciary care lying upon the Iron Trades. They might have discharged that duty as late as Jan. 28, if Mr. Oram had said to the plaintiff "Look here, you really ought to get some independent advice about this before you settle." But, that not having been done, in my view it was incumbent on the Iron Trades to have offered a figure which was considerably higher and towards the upper part of the bracket appropriate to hernia claims, in view of the severity of the hernia in this case.

Secondly, it was their duty to specify what reduction they were making which was inherent in their offer in respect of contributory negligence; that is to say, they should have made it clear what they thought the claim was worth in toto and how much they were deducting in respect of the plaintiff's contributory negligence. That could have been done, of course, either by way of percentage or by way of figures.

I think that they should have supplied the plaintiff with a copy of the medical report which was provided by his doctor. It is all very well to read a report out to someone in an interview, but if he has got it to read it over and consider himself it makes a great deal more of an impression on the mind. Mr. Oram told me that it was company policy not to hand such a document over to a claimant in person, although it would have been disclosed had the plaintiff been legally represented. The company policy to my mind provides no answer here. There is nothing whatever in this report which the plaintiff should not have seen and there seems to me to have been no good grounds for not giving him an opportunity to see exactly what the doctor said before he settled. I dare say that there was a fairly substantial reading of the report, but that is not sufficient.

Fourthly, they should have made sure that the plaintiff understood that this settlement, if entered into, was the end of the road and that no further claim could be made in respect of this accident, and in view of the fact that the risk of recurrence at 15 per cent was by no means insubstantial, they should have made sure that he understood that and that nothing further could be taken up if the injury did recur. As to that, as I have already said, I think they left the plaintiff in a state of considerable confusion.

Finally, I take the view that they should have advised the plaintiff to think the matter over and to delay until he had had an opportunity of testing himself back at work and had had a proper opportunity of considering the offer. I hold that the defendants were in breach of their duty of fiduciary care, in that they did none of these things and that therefore, in my view, they are not entitled to rely upon the settlement, or the alleged settlement of the plaintiff's claim.

In saying this, I ought to make it plain that I do not regard Mr. Oram as someone who is morally to blame, as having overreached a simple man. He was a claims inspector settling a claim, but I think he failed to appreciate that if he encouraged a layman to act without independent advice, then he, Mr. Oram, put himself in a position quite different from the position he was in, in the ordinary way, when he is negotiating a claim with a man's trade union or solicitor.

605

I also want to say that I am not seeking to lay down any general principle with regard to insurance companies and claimants who act for themselves. The insurance company which encourages a layman with no legal knowledge to act for himself without advice clearly puts itself in a position of risk; but the decision I am giving is simply an exercise in applying the principles of *Lloyd's Bank Ltd. v. Bundy*, [1975] Q.B. 326 (C.A.), as set out in Sir Eric Sach's judgment, to the facts of the present case.

WOODS V HUBLEY
(1995), 130 DLR (4th) 119 (NSCA)

[The plaintiff was injured in an automobile accident caused by the defendant. Surgery was recommended. A few days before the surgery a representative of the defendant's insurer offered the plaintiff a small amount of money in settlement for her claim. The plaintiff accepted and signed a release. In a subsequent action for damages by the plaintiff, the trial court set aside the release as unconscionable. The defendants appealed. Chipman JA delivered the judgment of the court on the issue of the release.]

CHIPMAN JA (dissenting in part): ... In coming to these conclusions the trial judge was guided by the summary of principles enunciated by Hallet J. (as he then was) in *Stephenson v. Hilti (Canada) Ltd.* (1989), 63 D.L.R. (4th) 573 at pp. 578-9 ... :

> To summarize the principles set out in the foregoing cases, it seems to me that a transaction may be set aside as being unconscionable if the evidence shows the following:
>
> (1) That there is an inequality of bargaining position arising out of ignorance, need or distress of the weaker party;
> (2) The stronger party has unconscientiously used a position of power to achieve an advantage; and
> (3) The agreement reached is substantially unfair to the weaker party or, as expressed in the *Harry v. Kreutziger* case, it is sufficiently divergent from community standards of commercial morality that it should be set aside.

• • •

[The respondent] was ignorant of the legal system, not well educated and ... a person of limited accomplishments for her age (then 25). In my opinion she was no match for the adjuster who appears to have had considerable training and a degree of sophistication in bargaining with people over numbers. The inequality of their respective positions is clear.

Counsel for the appellants has strongly urged that the agreement reached was not substantially unfair. He emphasized that the time for testing the value of the claim was at the time of settlement and not at the time of the trial when it was obvious that the respondent's condition had deteriorated substantially, leaving her in a position of permanent disability. ...

While I agree with counsel for the appellants that the relevant time to evaluate the bargain is the time of settlement ... [t]o anybody with the slightest experience in dealing with claims, it would be clear that [at the time of settlement] the respondent was facing an uncertain prognosis. While an early and complete recovery was a possibility, chances of long-term problems were so high that the only sound advice to the respondent would be not to settle the claim at an early stage. Only when the true extent of the disability was finally measured by expert medical persons after the effect of the operation and the progress of convalescence became known could one seriously entertain the possibility of settlement. It is really for this reason that the bargain was improvident, substantially unfair and divergent from community standards of commercial morality. No informed person would countenance settlement at such an uncertain stage.

I am satisfied therefore that it has not been shown that the trial judge was wrong in finding that the first and third elements listed by Hallett J. were established. As to the second, I am of the opinion that the burden fell upon the defence to establish that the bargain was not brought about as a result of the unconscientious use of the power to achieve the advantage. It is apparent to me on reading the record and the trial judge's findings that the adjuster did not overtly pressure the respondent. However, he must have been well aware of the complete folly of anybody in settling so uncertain a claim at that early stage, let alone for such a modest amount as $3,500. He certainly used tactics designed to make her think that $3,500 was all that she would ever get. The implication was that she might as well take it now rather than later. While not overt, it was clearly pressure which meets the test.

• • •

There is no suggestion that the adjuster deliberately set up his records to deceive, or specifically that he ever did deceive the respondent or make any false statements to her. However, deceit is not a necessary ingredient in the establishment of an unconscionable transaction. The adjuster was obviously thoughtless or indifferent to the position of the respondent and the high risk that she was taking in settling her claim at the time she did.

VI. DURESS

NAV CANADA V GREATER FREDERICTON
AIRPORT AUTHORITY INC
2008 NBCA 28

[The facts of this case are set out in Chapter 3. The court determined that a variation to an existing contract (the Airport Authority's promise to pay for the distance-measuring equipment (DME)), although unsupported by fresh consideration, may nonetheless be enforceable provided it was not procured under economic duress. The court set out the following analysis for economic duress.]

JT ROBERTSON JA (for the court): In the reasons that follow, I conclude that the arbitrator erred in finding that the variation was supported by fresh consideration. As a matter of law, however, I am prepared to recognize and adopt an "incremental" change in the traditional rules by holding that a variation unsupported by consideration remains enforceable provided it was not procured under economic duress. This refined approach leads us to consider how the contractual variation in issue was procured. In my view, the Airport Authority had no "practical alternative" but to agree to pay money that it was not legally bound to pay. Nav Canada implicitly threatened to withhold performance of its own obligation until the Airport Authority capitulated to the demand that it pay the cost of the navigational aid. However, the absence of practical alternatives is merely evidence of economic duress, not conclusive proof of its existence. The true cornerstone of the doctrine is the lack of "consent." In that regard, the uncontroverted fact is that the Airport Authority never "consented to" nor "acquiesced in" the variation, as is evident from the letter agreeing to payment "under protest." But this is not the end of the matter. There is jurisprudence that holds that the exercise of "illegitimate pressure" is a condition precedent to a finding of economic duress. I respectfully decline the invitation to recognize such pressure as an essential component of the duress doctrine, at least in cases involving the enforceability of variations to an existing contract. It is not the legitimacy of the pressure that is important but rather its impact on the victim, unless, perhaps, one is attempting to establish that a finding of economic duress qualifies as an independent tort.

• • •

V. THE ISSUE OF ECONOMIC DURESS

[33] Accepting that, in law, a variation to an existing contract, unsupported by fresh consideration, may be enforceable provided that it was not procured under economic duress, it follows that Nav Canada's appeal falls to be decided on the basis of that doctrine. It should also follow that the party seeking to enforce the variation must establish either that it was not procured under economic duress or that the other party is precluded from raising the duress doctrine for having subsequently affirmed the variation. Hence, the onus is on Nav Canada to establish that the post-contractual modification was not procured under economic duress. ...

A. THE DEVELOPING DOCTRINE OF ECONOMIC DURESS & ILLEGITIMATE PRESSURE

• • •

[37] Given the paucity of Supreme Court decisions in this area of the law, Canadian courts have traditionally turned to the English jurisprudence. Under English law, and prior to 1975, duress as a ground for holding a contract unenforceable was limited to the categories of duress to the person (actual or threatened violence) and duress of goods. With respect to duress to the person, the "gun to the head" inducement to contract formation has never been acceptable according to the common law's consensual model of contract formation. As to duress of goods, the classic case is the one in which a pawn broker demands an excess payment before agreeing to release goods that are being held: *Astley v. Reynolds* (1731), 93 E.R. 939 (Eng. K.B.). However, in 1975, the English courts began to recognize economic duress as a form of coercion that would render "voidable" an otherwise enforceable agreement: *Occidental Worldwide Investment Corp. v. Skibs A/S Avanti*, [1976] 1 Lloyd's Rep. 293 (Eng. Q.B.).

[38] In 1979, the Privy Council extended the duress doctrine to include economic duress in the leading case of *Pao On v. Lau Yiu Long*, [1979] 3 All E.R. 65, [1980] A.C. 614 (Hong Kong P.C.). ...

[39] In *Pao On*, Lord Scarman defined duress as "a coercion of the will so as to vitiate consent" and went on to indicate that "in a contractual situation commercial pressure is not enough." Again, the compulsion had to be such that the party was "deprived of 'his freedom of exercising his will.'" In applying this test, Lord Scarman indicated, at page 79 (All E.R.), that the following evidence could be relevant: "American judges pay great attention to such evidential matters as the effectiveness of the alternative remedy available, the fact or absence of protest, the availability of independent advice, the benefit received, and the speed with which the victim has sought to avoid the contract." In order to meet the test for economic duress, then, it must be shown that the conduct coerced did not amount to a voluntary act. Applying

these criteria to the facts of *Pao On*, Lord Scarman held that the defendant had submitted to commercial pressure, but not to coercion in the requisite sense. The Privy Council accepted the trial judge's finding that the defendant had "considered the matter thoroughly, chose to avoid litigation, and formed the opinion that the risk in giving the guarantee was more apparent than real."

[40] While commentators agree that the "overborne will" threshold is either too difficult to meet or too vague, Lord Scarman soon had the opportunity to revisit his earlier formation of the doctrine, only this time sitting as a member of the House of Lords in *Universe Tankships Inc. of Monrovia v. International Transport Workers' Federation*, [1982] 2 All E.R. 67, [1983] 1 A.C. 366 (U.K. H.L.). The litigation in that case arose after the defendant trade union threatened to "black" the plaintiff's ships unless the latter complied with the union's demands by making certain monetary payments and entering into collective agreements governing the conditions of employment for the vessel's crew. The objective was to prevent the employment of cheap labour on ships flying flags of convenience. The effect of "blacking" is to prevent a ship from leaving port because of the corresponding refusal by tugboat owners to provide the necessary services. One of the trade union's demands was that the ship owners make a payment to the trade union's "welfare fund." The plaintiff complied with the demands but, after leaving port, sought recovery of the amounts paid on the basis that they were paid under economic duress. By the time the case reached the House of Lords, the trade union conceded that the payment to the welfare fund was made under economic duress but argued that the union was immunized from a restitutionary claim under the *Trade Union and Labour Relations Act*, 1974. The majority of their Lordships held that although the legislation conferred immunity against an action in tort in respect of interference with contractual relations (here, between the ship owners and the tugboat owners), the legislation did not confer immunity in respect of a restitutionary action and, therefore, the money was recoverable.

[41] In dissent, Lord Scarman took the opportunity to reform the tenets of the economic duress doctrine as stated in *Pao On*. He cited *Barton v. Armstrong* (1973), [1975] 2 All E.R. 465, [1976] A.C. 104 (New South Wales P.C.) and *Pao On* for the proposition that the test for economic duress now comprises two elements: "(1) pressure amounting to compulsion of the will of the victim; and (2) the illegitimacy of the pressure exerted." With respect to the first branch of the test, Lord Scarman observed that the requirement is variously stated in the authorities as "coercion or the vitiation of consent." In his view, however, "[t]he classic case of duress is ... not the lack of will to submit but the victim's intentional submission arising from the realisation that there is no other practical choice open to him." Lord Scarman then proceeded to consider the matters set out in *Pao On* as relevant to but not dispositive of this issue. Thus, even though the ship owners had not protested at the time of entering into the agreements with the trade union, it was nonetheless clear that they had no practical alternative but to submit to the arrangement. Having satisfied the first branch of the test, Lord Scarman held that it was necessary to determine whether the pressure exerted was "legitimate." With respect to this branch of the test, he held that two matters "may" have to be considered. The first is the "nature of the pressure," which in many cases will be decisive, though not in every case. The second consideration is stated in terms of the "nature of the demand." With respect to the first branch, the nature of the pressure, Lord Scarman held that the threat of unlawful action is invariably regarded by the law as "illegitimate." On the facts, however, the unlawful threatened action was immunized from suit by the legislation; accordingly, it was a legitimate exercise of pressure that did not constitute duress. Consequently, Lord Scarman next examined the "nature of the demand." In that regard, he held that it was necessary

to decide whether the demand for contributions to the welfare fund was lawful, which depended on "whether it was an act done in contemplation or furtherance of a trade dispute" and, specifically, on whether the contributions were connected with the terms and conditions of employment as set out in the legislation. Lord Scarman answered those questions in the positive. The nature of the demand being lawful, he held that the contributions were not recoverable. In short, *Universe Tankships* is a case in which the House of Lords was asked to decide whether contractual concessions procured through the exercise of otherwise unlawful acts were legitimatized by legislation.

[42] It is of significance to the law that the majority of the House of Lords did not take issue with Lord Scarman's contention that the economic duress doctrine includes the concept of illegitimate pressure. ...

[43] No one questions that tortious or criminal conduct amounts to unlawful pressure and that unlawful pressure qualifies as illegitimate pressure. However, it is equally clear that pressure does not have to be characterized as "unlawful" in order to be found "illegitimate." This leads one to ask when lawful pressure moves from the category of legitimate to illegitimate pressure? Regrettably, no one, judge or commentator alike, has been able to explain how one goes about answering that question. ...

[44] Although Canadian Courts are no longer bound to follow the English authorities, regrettably, the criterion of illegitimate pressure has been absorbed into the fabric of the Canadian jurisprudence without comment. The three most cited decisions on economic duress in Canada are *Stott v. Merit Investment Corp.* (1988), 63 O.R. (2d) 545, [1988] O.J. No. 134 (Ont. C.A.); *Gordon v. Roebuck* (1992), 9 O.R. (3d) 1, [1992] O.J. No. 1499 (Ont. C.A.) and *Techform Products Ltd. v. Wolda*. In each instance, the Court applied the tenets of the economic duress doctrine stated in the English authorities.

[45] No one has been as critical of the introduction of the additional test of illegitimate pressure as Professor Ogilvie in "Economic Duress in Contract: Departure, Detour or Dead-End?" (at pp. 219-220 and 224):

> This survey shows the English case law to date on economic duress is characterized by false starts, pregnant remarks and loose ends. ... Defining illegitimacy has proven difficult, especially after its extension to acts otherwise lawful, requiring yet another test to determine when legitimate conduct becomes illegitimate for the purposes of economic duress. Why legitimacy should be the sole criterion or even a criterion, as Lord Goff suggests in *The Evia Luck*, is unclear, especially once it is extended beyond criminal and tortious conduct.

• • •

[46] Like Professor Ogilvie, I am not convinced that the doctrine of economic duress should incorporate a criterion of illegitimate pressure when it comes to cases involving a variation to an existing contract. If we apply Lord Scarman's approach it should follow that most contractual variations will be classified as having been procured through the exercise of legitimate commercial pressure. Let me explain. According to Lord Scarman, two matters must be considered when determining what pressure is illegitimate: (1) the nature of the pressure; and (2) the nature of the demand. In cases involving the variation of an existing contract, inevitably the nature of the pressure is the threatened breach of the contract: the "coercer" threatens to withhold performance under the contract until such time as the "victim" capitulates to the coercer's demands. Of course, a threatened breach of contract is not only

lawful but in fact constitutes a right which can be exercised subject to the obligation to pay damages and possibly to an order for specific performance: *Hillspring Farms Ltd. v. Leland Walton & Sons Ltd.* (2007), 312 N.B.R. (2d) 109, [2007] N.B.J. No. 19, 2007 NBCA 7 (N.B. C.A.). This takes us to the second prong of Lord Scarman's framework: the nature of the demand. Once again, the typical variation case is one in which the coercer demands a variation to the contract. Invariably, the coercer demands that the victim pay or do more than is required under the existing contract. But once again there is nothing to support the argument that the nature of this typical demand should be classified as illegitimate. In brief, the application of the two-fold test articulated by Lord Scarman, when applied to cases involving a contractual modification, should lead to the conclusion that the pressure typically exerted falls within the "legitimate" category. In other words, courts would be forced to begin their analysis on the premise that the pressure exerted falls within the category of "legitimate commercial pressure."

[47] In my view, the criterion of illegitimate pressure adds unnecessary complexity to the law of economic duress, and presently lacks a compelling juridical justification, at least with respect to its application in the context of the enforcement of contractual variations. The law does not provide a workable template for distinguishing between legitimate and illegitimate pressure. Admittedly, we know that tortious or criminal conduct qualifies as illegitimate pressure and I would be prepared to go so far as to say that a party who acts in "bad faith" in demanding a variation to a contract is exerting illegitimate pressure. However, without a template for distinguishing between legitimate and illegitimate pressure in other contexts, litigants and courts are forced to find that some other aspect of the demand for the variation is unacceptable conduct that justifies a finding of illegitimate pressure. There is already evidence that this is what is happening under English law: *Vantage Navigation Corp. v. Suhail*, [1989] 1 Lloyd's Rep. 138 (Eng. Q.B.) and *Atlas Express Ltd. v. Kafco Ltd.*, [1989] 1 All E.R. 641 (Eng. Q.B.).

[48] My concern is that just as the courts developed legal fictions to enforce otherwise gratuitous promises, so too will they spend too much time trying to explain the difference between illegitimate and legitimate pressure. If we are going to permit the enforcement of gratuitous variations that are not the product of economic duress in order to avoid "fictional" attempts to justify the enforcement of such promises, it follows that we should not introduce a criterion that may well lead to the development of other legal fictions. Moreover, I am afraid that the distinction between legitimate and illegitimate pressure will soon lead to the understanding that a plea of economic duress can be defeated by a plea of "good faith" on the part of the coercer, a point I shall return to in these reasons.

[49] ... [F]or purposes of deciding this appeal, I need only hold that illegitimate pressure is not a condition precedent to a finding of economic duress where the remedy being sought is declaratory or restitutionary in nature. It is one thing to have a contractual variation declared unenforceable or to demand the return of property extracted under economic duress and quite another to seek damages for the exercise of illegitimate pressure.

[50] In conclusion, I am not prepared to hold that illegitimate pressure is a condition precedent to a finding of economic duress in cases involving post-contractual modifications to executory contracts. I am in complete agreement with Professor Ogilvie when she writes that the legitimacy of the pressure is not what is important but rather its impact on the "victim": "Forbearance and Economic Duress: Three Strikes and You're Still Out at the Ontario Court of Appeal," at para. 26.

B. ECONOMIC DURESS—THE ANALYTICAL FRAMEWORK

[51] Having rejected illegitimate pressure as a criterion to be applied when deciding whether a contractual variation was procured under economic duress, it is incumbent on this Court to identify the tenets of that doctrine. Once again, I must reiterate that my analysis applies to the plea of economic duress being raised with respect to the enforceability of variations to an existing contract and not in regard to the formation of the underlying contract. Is the distinction a valid one? I have already indicated as much when it comes to the issue whether the doctrine of economic duress also serves as an independent source of tortious liability. As well, the distinction avoids adding further and unnecessary complexity to the law. I do not feel that anything is to be gained by infusing into the economic duress doctrine concepts such as inequality of bargaining power, unconscionability and undue influence, all of which are key doctrines when it comes to the formation of a contract and its enforceability. By contrast, cases involving modification of variation of an existing contract are not decided on the basis of whether the victim is a sophisticated or unsophisticated party. The critical factor is whether the victim had any practical alternative but to capitulate to the demand for the contract change. ...

[52] While the jurisprudence continues to speak of the economic duress doctrine in terms of whether the will was overborne, the consent vitiated, or the contract varied voluntarily, the objective of the exercise is to determine whether the variation was the product of an agreement. I begin with the premise that the hallmark of every commercial agreement is a "consensual bargain" and this applies equally to variations to existing contracts. So far as the element of "bargain" is concerned, that component is measured according to the consideration doctrine, but as discussed earlier, a lack of consideration should not inevitably lead to the conclusion that a gratuitous promise is unenforceable. A gratuitous promise may still be enforceable, if it is the product of a consensual agreement. Leaving aside for the moment the issue of whether the contractual variation is supported by consideration and accepting that "consent" or "agreement" remains the hallmark of an enforceable agreement, I offer the following general framework for deciding whether a contractual variation was the product of "coercion" or "economic duress." I say general framework because some cases are easier to decide than others. For example, special consideration might be given to variations extracted in the employment context, some of which are regulated by the common law or statute or both. What I am dealing with is a commercial contract regulating the business affairs of two corporations that were formed for purposes of promotion and protecting the public interest.

[53] Subject to the above observations, a finding of economic duress is dependent *initially* on two conditions precedent. First, the promise (the contractual variation) must be extracted as a result of the exercise of "pressure," whether characterized as a "demand" or a "threat." Second, the exercise of that pressure must have been such that the coerced party had no practical alternative but to agree to the coercer's demand to vary the terms of the underlying contract. However, even if those two conditions precedent are satisfied, a finding of economic duress does not automatically follow. Once these two threshold requirements are met, the legal analysis must focus on the ultimate question: whether the coerced party "consented" to the variation. To make that determination three factors should be examined: (1) whether the promise was supported by consideration; (2) whether the coerced party made the promise "under protest" or "without prejudice"; and (3) if not, whether the coerced party took reasonable steps to disaffirm the promise as soon as practicable. Admittedly, the last two factors are more likely to have a bearing on the ultimate outcome

of a case than the first. As well, note that under this general framework, no reference is made to the supposed victim having "independent legal advice" or to the "good faith conduct" on the part of the supposed coercer. I shall also deal with these matters separately. For the moment, I am going to focus on the framework outlined above.

[54] While it might appear trite to hold that, to meet the first threshold requirement, the contractual variation must be the product of pressure exerted by the promisee (the coercer), there may be cases where this is not so. If the variation comes at the instance of the promisor (the so-called victim), as happened in *Williams v. Roffey Bros. & Nicholls (Contractors) Ltd.*, it cannot be credibly argued that variation was coerced. Admittedly, such a case may be rare. In most instances pressure for the contractual variation will come from the promisee in the form of an *express* or *implied* threat to breach the underlying contract, usually by withholding future performance. I have included implied threats in anticipation of the sophisticated promisee, aided by astute counsel, who attempts to camouflage the coercive nature of the variation demand by avoiding the use of combative language amounting to a threat to withhold promised goods or services until such time as the promisor capitulates to the demand. In the end, it may be a question of judgment whether the facts support the contention that the promisee exerted the requisite pressure, such as by threatening to breach the contract by withholding performance.

[55] Once we accept that pressure has been exerted, we turn to the second condition precedent: whether the promisor could have resisted the pressure and refused to agree to the modification. It is a central feature of the doctrine that a plea of economic duress will fail unless is it established that the promisor (victim) had no practical alternative but to capitulate to the demands of the promisee (coercer). Thus, for example, it is a question of judgment whether the victim could have resisted the coercer's demands and gone to a third party to obtain the performance promised in the underlying contract, while suing the coercer for damages for breach of contract. If the evidence establishes that other practical alternatives were available to the victim, the plea of economic duress must fail at the threshold stage. On the other hand, if the evidence establishes a lack of practical alternatives, the law requires the analysis to continue before a finding of economic duress is warranted. In short, the absence of practical alternatives is evidence of a lack of consent, but is not conclusive of the issue. The law is still concerned with the possibility that the contractual variation may have been consented to for reasons that the promisor alone deems sufficient. This leads us to ask how one goes about assessing the presence or absence of "consent."

[56] If the variation is not supported by consideration, in the classical sense, the court may be more sympathetic to the plea of economic duress. After all, why would anyone agree to pay more or do more in return for nothing? There is one ready answer to that question: the promisor had no practical alternative other than to submit to the coercer's demands. The variation is not the product of an agreement for which the promisor's "consent" or "agreement" is essential if the variation is to be deemed enforceable at law. But as we know, even if there is consideration for the contractual variation, it may still be unenforceable under the doctrine of economic duress. It is of little consolation to those who have been held to commercial ransom that their promise is enforceable under the doctrine of consideration because the variation was procured under "seal" or with the payment of a "peppercorn" in exchange. In summary, and as a basic proposition, we must accept that a contractual variation unsupported by consideration in the classical sense bolsters the argument that it was procured under economic duress. On the other hand, a variation supported by fresh consideration lends weight to the argument that it was the product of commercial pressure and not economic duress.

[57] There is no doubt that the easiest and most convincing way to establish that a contractual variation was procured under economic duress and, therefore unenforceable, is to show that it was made "under protest" or "without prejudice" to the promisor's right to insist on performance in accordance with the original contract. While some American courts have declared that "protest" is an essential component of the right to avoid a contract under duress (see A.L. Corbin, *Corbin on Contracts*, rev. ed., vol 2. (St. Paul, Minn.: West Pub. Co., 1993), at 7:21), this is not true according to English and Canadian law. In brief, a failure to "object" to the variation is not necessarily fatal to a plea of economic duress. However, the failure of the promisor to voice any objection at the time that contractual variation was extracted may ultimately prove fatal to the plea of economic duress. Let me explain.

[58] Assuming that the promisor fails to agree under protest or without prejudice to existing legal rights, his or her plea of economic duress is weakened as the court struggles with the promisee's contention that the variation was the product of agreement and not coercion. If the variation is supported by fresh consideration and there has been no protest, one has to seriously question the validity of the plea of economic duress. While the failure to agree under protest is not fatal to a successful plea of economic duress, the plea may become unavailable with the passage of time, whether or not the contractual variation was supported by consideration. In the absence of a promise made under protest, the law insists that the victim take reasonable steps to repudiate or disaffirm the promise as soon as practicable. Generally, this will occur after the pressure dissipates, which is usually once the threat of breaching the contract has lost its persuasive force. If money has been paid under the variation and the coercer has performed his or her part of the bargain as outlined in the underlying contract, then the victim should act responsibly in seeking its recovery. If the variation is a bald promise to pay and the coercer performs his or her part of the bargain, then the victim should continue to resist payment (as happened in this case).

[59] The law is clear that a promisor who, for example, sits back and waits several years before challenging the enforceability of the variation will be deemed guilty of acquiescence and though the plea of economic duress may have been made out, it will fail on this ground. This is what happened in *Stott v. Merit Investment Corp.* Although the Court of Appeal found the agreement was entered into under economic duress, the failure of the defendant promisor to disavow himself of the agreement until several years after it was signed was fatal to his defence. Once again, it is important to note that the law will reject a plea of economic duress where commercial parties make deliberate decisions that they later regret. In "Economic Duress in Contract: Departure, Detour or Dead-End?," Professor Ogilvie expresses this accurately at p. 204:

> The [cases] demonstrate that parties who voluntarily negotiate agreements that they believe to be advantageous cannot subsequently rely on economic duress to avoid those agreements. ... [E]conomic duress does not function to relieve parties from commercial bargains subsequently perceived or experienced to be burdensome.

[60] To this point, I have not addressed whether "independent legal advice" is a relevant consideration. According to the Privy Council's decision in *Pao On*, and relying on the American jurisprudence, it is a factor that must be examined. On the other hand, courts have questioned the relevance of this factor. In *Gordon v. Roebuck*, McKinlay J.A. adroitly observed that the independent advice is likely to focus on whether the victim has any practical alternative other than to capitulate to the demands of the coercer. Indeed, one cannot help but speculate that it would be rare for sophisticated commercial parties, such as those before us, not to consult legal counsel and have their solicitors draft correspondence to bolster their clients'

respective positions in anticipation of a possible plea of economic duress. The fact of the matter is that access to independent legal advice on the part of the victim is not sufficient to overcome the finding that he or she had no alternative but to submit to the contractual variation demanded by the coercer. As stated earlier, it seems to me that the notion of "independent legal advice" is more amenable to cases where a person has entered into an improvident bargain which is attacked on the grounds of unconscionability, undue influence and duress. Insurance settlements come quickly to mind: *Permaform Plastics Ltd. v. London & Midland General Insurance Co.* (1996), 110 Man. R. (2d) 260, [1996] M.J. No. 322 (Man. C.A.). These are the cases where the law favours the consumer and the courts are favourably disposed to scrutinize the fairness of the bargain. But in most cases where economic duress is pleaded, the parties are commercial entities with ready access to legal counsel. That said, there may be cases where independent legal advice becomes a relevant consideration in cases involving a contractual modification. For example, an unsophisticated promisor is dilatory in disaffirming the contractual variation. The fact that the promissor did not act as quickly as he or she should have might be forgiven because of a lack of independent legal advice. At the end of the day, however, I am hesitant to embrace the notion of independent legal advice as an integral component of the economic duress doctrine.

[61] Finally, both the literature and jurisprudence make reference to the motives or reasons underscoring the coercer's demands for a contractual variation, as though they are a relevant consideration. I label this the "good faith" argument or requirement. For example, if the coercer refuses to perform under an existing contract unless the other party agrees to pay more than the contract price and the reason for the demand is that the coercer's supplier has imposed a corresponding increase in price, it could be perceived that the coercer's demands reflect good faith on his or her part. More so, if the price increase is critical to the coercer's survival as a commercial enterprise. Implicit in all of this is the understanding that if the promissor is not acting "opportunistically" one should be less sympathetic to the plea of economic duress. The question remains whether that fact should have an impact on the finding of economic duress. In my view, it should not, subject to the following caveat.

[62] I have no doubt that, where the party exerting the pressure is acting in a commercially reasonable manner, in "good faith," a party faced with a demand for a contractual variation might consent for sound business reasons tied to the financial crisis that the demanding party faces. In short, the good faith of the supposed coercer may be a reason why the supposed victim consents to the variation. Thus, the reasons or motives of the promisee for demanding the contractual variation are relevant so far as they may impact on the decision of the promissor to consent to the demand. It is in that limited sense that I believe the reasons underscoring the decision to secure a contractual variation by threatened breach of the underlying contract become relevant. But I do not believe that a plea of good faith should be regarded as either a complete defence to a plea of economic duress or a central tenet of the economic duress doctrine. A person who puts a gun to my head and demands my wallet should be in no better a legal position because he or she is acting in response to a third person who placed a gun against his or her head. I am still entitled to be restored to the position I was in before the gun was put to my head. My wallet must be returned despite the good faith exercised by my coercer.

[63] In summary, the supposed good faith of the coercer should not impact on the victim's contractual right and expectation to receive performance in accordance with the original terms of the contract. This is why it is important to reiterate that it is not the legitimacy of the pressure that is important, but rather its impact on the

victim. The victim may also regret having agreed to the original terms of the contract. But neither party has the right to cry "hardship" and demand changes to the underlying contract in the absence of a contractual provision that provides such relief (e.g. a *force majeure* clause) or the application of the frustration doctrine.

C. APPLICATION TO THE FACTS OF THE PRESENT CASE

[64] This is not a difficult case when it comes to adjudicating on the validity of the plea of economic duress. Once again, the facts as found by the arbitrator are central to Nav Canada's argument that the promise to pay for the navigational aid (the DME) was not procured under economic duress. Nav Canada insists that it did not exert any pressure on the Airport Authority. According to Nav Canada's argument, the Airport Authority was given the option to relocate the old equipment (the NDB) or to go with the new DME, but that if it elected the latter it would have to pay for the DME. Nav Canada argues further that as the Airport Authority was given this option it could not claim that the promise was given because it had no practical alternative but to agree to pay the $223,000 acquisition cost. As discussed earlier, those are not the facts as found by the arbitrator. He held that Nav Canada had the contractual right to decide whether to relocate the existing equipment or purchase new equipment and that Nav Canada elected to go with the new. The evidence also established that Nav Canada had refused to purchase and install the navigational equipment until such time as the Airport Authority agreed to pay for the DME. Admittedly, Nav Canada did not word its letter to the Airport Authority in terms of withholding performance under the ASF Agreement. Nav Canada chose its words carefully when it said that it was not prepared to provide for the purchase of the equipment when preparing its fiscal budget for the upcoming year. But the practical effect of that letter was to force the Airport Authority to promise to pay the $223,000. Nav Canada's threat to breach the contract by withholding performance arose by implication, but as stated earlier that is sufficient for purposes of establishing the plea of economic duress.

[65] As to the question of whether there were practical alternatives available to the Airport Authority, it must be emphasized that Nav Canada exercises a monopoly when it comes to providing aviation services and equipment to public airports throughout Canada. In reality, the Airport Authority could not unilaterally withdraw from the ASF Agreement and turn to another service provider in the industry. The Airport Authority had already expended $6 million to extend one of its two runaways and Nav Canada was threatening to hold up the use of the extended runway for at least another year. In brief, the Airport Authority had no practical alternative but to submit Nav Canada's demand that it agree to pay the cost of the navigational aid.

[66] The two threshold conditions precedent to a successful plea of economic duress have been met in this case: Nav Canada exerted pressure to obtain what amounts to a contractual modification to the ASF Agreement, and the Airport Authority was left with no practical alternative but to capitulate to Nav Canada's demand. This does not end the legal analysis. It remains to be decided whether the Airport Authority consented to the variation notwithstanding the circumstances in which the promise was made. The fact that the promise was not supported by fresh consideration suggests that consent was lacking and, indeed, this inference is confirmed by the phrasing of the Airport Authority's letter of February 20, 2003: "Your arbitrary deadline has now forced us to make funds available under protest." Even if those words had not been used, there is nothing in the record to indicate that the Airport Authority acquiesced to Nav Canada's demand and pressure by virtue of the lapse of time. This is not a case where money was paid and the plaintiff did nothing in an effort to secure its repayment. This is a case in which the victim (the Airport Authority)

refused to pay from the very outset and has not deviated from that position now that the coercer (Nav Canada) has fulfilled its contractual obligations under the underlying contract (the ASF) in accordance with the analytical framework set out in these reasons for judgment.

[67] In concluding that the plea of economic duress was established and that the arbitrator erred in finding that the subsequent correspondence qualified as a separate and enforceable contract, I have not made reference to the matters of "independent legal advice" and "good faith." Nav Canada argues that the Airport Authority was in receipt of independent legal advice over the relevant period of time. I will not speculate on whether Nav Canada also retained legal counsel in the months leading up to the exchange of correspondence, other than to state that the correspondence reflects an awareness of the tenets of the doctrine of economic duress. In any event, this factor could have no bearing on the determination regarding economic duress. Finally, it may well be that Nav Canada truly believed that it had no contractual obligation to pay for the cost of the navigational aid and as such was acting in good faith. But it is equally plausible, as claimed by the Airport Authority, that Nav Canada was simply attempting to offload its responsibility to purchase navigational equipment onto an unwilling and unrelenting "victim." If that were its true intent then it failed to achieve that objective because of the economic duress doctrine. In any event, "good faith" is not a defence to a plea of economic duress when dealing with the enforceability of a contractual variation.

[Larlee and Turnbull JJA agreed in dismissing the appeal.]

Appeal dismissed.

NOTES

1. For a critique of the court's reasoning in *NAV Canada*, see Rick Bigwood, "Doctrinal Reform and Post-Contractual Modifications in New Brunswick: *NAV Canada v Greater Fredericton Airport Authority Inc*" (2010) 49 Can Bus LJ 256, where Bigwood argues that "the court's new framework for analyzing economic duress claims in Nav Canada [does not] represent the best comprehension and rationalization of economic duress in cases involving postcontractual modifications of executory contracts, even when the claim is merely declaratory or restitutionary in nature." Rather, he maintains that "Lord Scarman's dual test [in *Pao On v Lau Yiu Long*, [1980] AC 614 (PC)] for duress is superior to Robertson JA's new analytical framework precisely because it responds to both the quality of the conduct of the promisee and the quality of its effect on the promisor's contractual assent, acknowledging their respective roles in the reckoning."

2. In *Pao On*, Lord Scarman held:

Duress, whatever form it takes, is a coercion of the will so as to vitiate consent. ... [I]n a contractual situation commercial pressure is not enough. There must be present some factor "which could in law be regarded as a coercion of his will so as to vitiate his consent." ... In determining whether there was a coercion of will such that there was no true consent, it is material to inquire whether the person alleged to have been coerced did or did not protest; whether, at the time he was allegedly coerced into making the contract, he did or did not have an alternative course open to him such as an adequate legal remedy; whether he was independently advised; and whether after entering the contract he took steps to avoid it. All these matters are, as was recognised in *Maskell v Horner*, [1915] 3 KB 106, relevant in determining whether he acted voluntarily or not. ... In their Lordships' view, there is nothing contrary to principle in recognising economic duress as a factor which may render a contract voidable, provided always that the basis of such recognition is that it must amount to a coercion of will, which vitiates consent. It must be shown that the payment made or the contract entered into was not a voluntary act.

3. Later English cases have departed from the "overborne will" theory of duress to an approach that emphasizes the legitimacy of the threat and the availability of reasonable alternatives. For example, in *CTN Cash and Carry Ltd v Gallaher Ltd*, [1994] 4 All ER 714 (CA), the court considered whether a threat to perform a lawful act, when made together with a bona fide (but mistaken) demand for payment, amounted to economic duress. The court held, in the context of dealings between two commercial enterprises, that it did not. See also *The Evia Luck*, [1993] 2 AC 152 (HL).

4. In *Burin Peninsula Community Business Development Corporation v Grandy*, 2010 NLCA 69, the Court of Appeal had to consider whether personal guarantees executed by the Grandys in favour of the corporation were unenforceable for having been obtained under economic duress. The appellate court maintained (at para 30) that "[t]his appears to be a classic case where the lender's representative, mindful of the absence of a contractual provision requiring personal guarantees, coerced the principal shareholders of the borrower who were under pressure from an existing lender to agree to vary the terms of an existing loan commitment without the provision of further consideration." It upheld the trial judge's findings that the Grandys were in a "precarious financial position" and lacked alternatives because the corporation was the lender of last resort and they were being pressured for payment by their existing lender. In addition, although the Grandys were told they could take time to consider their position, they were advised by the corporation's executive officer that it was unlikely that the corporation would be advancing additional funds to the Grandys without the additional security. Finally, the corporation's counsel (who was found by the trial judge to be, in the minds of the Grandys, their counsel as well) advised the Grandys to sign the guarantees without advising them to seek another opinion. There was a finding of economic duress, meaning that the corporation was not entitled to enforce its guarantee against Mr. Grandy.

5. For more discussion of economic duress, see H Stewart, "Economic Duress in Canadian Law: Towards a Principled Approach" (2003) 82 Can Bar Rev 359; Waddams at paras 509-13; McCamus at 248-56, 379-402. For a discussion on the doctrines of duress, undue influence, and unconscionable dealing in New Zealand, see Rick Bigwood, "Ill-Gotten Contracts in New Zealand: Parting Thoughts on Duress, Undue Influence and Unconscionable Dealing: Kiwi Style?" (2011) 42 VUWLR 83.

VII. CONSUMER PROTECTION

CONSUMER PROTECTION ACT, 2002
SO 2002, c 30, Schedule A

1. In this Act, ...

"consumer" means an individual acting for personal, family or household purposes and does not include a person who is acting for business purposes; ...

"representation" means a representation, claim, statement, offer, request or proposal that is or purports to be,

(a) made respecting or with a view to the supplying of goods or services to consumers, or

(b) made for the purpose of receiving payment for goods or services supplied or purporting to be supplied to consumers;

"services" means anything other than goods, including any service, right, entitlement or benefit; ...

14(1) It is an unfair practice for a person to make a false, misleading or deceptive representation.

(2) Without limiting the generality of what constitutes a false, misleading or deceptive representation, the following are included as false, misleading or deceptive representations:

1. A representation that the goods or services have sponsorship, approval, performance characteristics, accessories, uses, ingredients, benefits or qualities they do not have.

2. A representation that the person who is to supply the goods or services has sponsorship, approval, status, affiliation or connection the person does not have.

3. A representation that the goods or services are of a particular standard, quality, grade, style or model, if they are not.

4. A representation that the goods are new, or unused, if they are not or are reconditioned or reclaimed, but the reasonable use of goods to enable the person to service, prepare, test and deliver the goods does not result in the goods being deemed to be used for the purposes of this paragraph.

5. A representation that the goods have been used to an extent that is materially different from the fact.

6. A representation that the goods or services are available for a reason that does not exist.

7. A representation that the goods or services have been supplied in accordance with a previous representation, if they have not.

8. A representation that the goods or services or any part of them are available or can be delivered or performed when the person making the representation knows or ought to know they are not available or cannot be delivered or performed.

9. A representation that the goods or services or any part of them will be available or can be delivered or performed by a specified time when the person making the representation knows or ought to know they will not be available or cannot be delivered or performed by the specified time.

10. A representation that a service, part, replacement or repair is needed or advisable, if it is not.

11. A representation that a specific price advantage exists, if it does not.

12. A representation that misrepresents the authority of a salesperson, representative, employee or agent to negotiate the final terms of the agreement.

13. A representation that the transaction involves or does not involve rights, remedies or obligations if the representation is false, misleading or deceptive.

14. A representation using exaggeration, innuendo or ambiguity as to a material fact or failing to state a material fact if such use or failure deceives or tends to deceive.

15. A representation that misrepresents the purpose or intent of any solicitation of or any communication with a consumer.

16. A representation that misrepresents the purpose of any charge or proposed charge.

17. A representation that misrepresents or exaggerates the benefits that are likely to flow to a consumer if the consumer helps a person obtain new or potential customers.

15(1) It is an unfair practice to make an unconscionable representation.

(2) Without limiting the generality of what may be taken into account in determining whether a representation is unconscionable, there may be taken into account

that the person making the representation or the person's employer or principal knows or ought to know,

(a) that the consumer is not reasonably able to protect his or her interests because of disability, ignorance, illiteracy, inability to understand the language of an agreement or similar factors;

(b) that the price grossly exceeds the price at which similar goods or services are readily available to like consumers;

(c) that the consumer is unable to receive a substantial benefit from the subject-matter of the representation;

(d) that there is no reasonable probability of payment of the obligation in full by the consumer;

(e) that the consumer transaction is excessively one-sided in favour of some-one other than the consumer;

(f) that the terms of the consumer transaction are so adverse to the consumer as to be inequitable;

(g) that a statement of opinion is misleading and the consumer is likely to rely on it to his or her detriment; or

(h) that the consumer is being subjected to undue pressure to enter into a consumer transaction. ...

18(1) Any agreement, whether written, oral or implied, entered into by a consumer after or while a person has engaged in an unfair practice may be rescinded by the consumer and the consumer is entitled to any remedy that is available in law, including damages.

(2) A consumer is entitled to recover the amount by which the consumer's payment under the agreement exceeds the value that the goods or services have to the consumer or to recover damages, or both, if rescission of the agreement under subsection (1) is not possible,

(a) because the return or restitution of the goods or services is no longer possible; or

(b) because rescission would deprive a third party of a right in the subject-matter of the agreement that the third party has acquired in good faith and for value.

(3) A consumer must give notice within one year after entering into the agreement if,

(a) the consumer seeks to rescind an agreement under subsection (1); or

(b) the consumer seeks recovery under subsection (2), if rescission is not possible.

(4) The consumer may express notice in any way as long as it indicates the intention of the consumer to rescind the agreement or to seek recovery where rescission is not possible and the reasons for so doing and the notice meets any requirements that may be prescribed.

• • •

(10) In the trial of an issue under this section, oral evidence respecting an unfair practice is admissible despite the existence of a written agreement and despite the fact that the evidence pertains to a representation in respect of a term, condition or undertaking that is or is not provided for in the agreement.

(11) A court may award exemplary or punitive damages in addition to any other remedy in an action commenced under this section.

(12) Each person who engaged in an unfair practice is liable jointly and severally with the person who entered into the agreement with the consumer for any amount to which the consumer is entitled under this section.

UNCONSCIONABLE TRANSACTIONS RELIEF ACT
RSO 1990, c U.2

1. In this Act,

"cost of the loan" means the whole cost to the debtor of money lent and includes interest, discount, subscription, premium, dues, bonus, commission, brokerage fees and charges, but not actual lawful and necessary disbursements made to a land registrar, a local registrar of the Superior Court of Justice, a sheriff or a treasurer of a municipality; ...

"creditor" includes the person advancing money lent and the assignee of any claim arising or security given in respect of money lent;

"debtor" means a person to whom or on whose account money lent is advanced and includes every surety and endorser or other person liable for the repayment of money lent or upon any agreement or collateral or other security given in respect thereof;

"money lent" includes money advanced on account of any person in any transaction that, whatever its form may be, is substantially one of money-lending or securing the repayment of money so advanced and includes and has always included a mortgage within the meaning of the *Mortgages Act*.

2. Where, in respect of money lent, the court finds that, having regard to the risk and to all the circumstances, the cost of the loan is excessive and that the transaction is harsh and unconscionable, the court may,

(a) reopen the transaction and take an account between the creditor and the debtor;

(b) despite any statement or settlement of account or any agreement purporting to close previous dealings and create a new obligation, reopen any account already taken and relieve the debtor from payment of any sum in excess of the sum adjudged by the court to be fairly due in respect of the principal and the cost of the loan;

(c) order the creditor to repay any such excess if the same has been paid or allowed on account by the debtor;

(d) set aside either wholly or in part or revise or alter any security given or agreement made in respect of the money lent, and, if the creditor has parted with the security, order the creditor to indemnify the debtor.

3. The powers conferred by section 2 may be exercised,

(a) in an action or proceeding by a creditor for the recovery of money lent;

(b) in an action or proceeding by the debtor despite any provision or agreement to the contrary, and despite the fact that the time for repayment of the loan or any installment thereof has not arrived;

(c) in an action or proceeding in which the amount due or to become due in respect of money lent is in question.

4(1) In addition to any right that a debtor may have under this or any other Act or otherwise in respect of money lent, the debtor may apply for relief under this Act to the Superior Court of Justice which may exercise any of the powers of the court under section 2.

• • •

5. Nothing in this Act affects the rights of an assignee or holder for value without notice, or derogates from the existing powers or jurisdiction of any court.

VIII. RESTITUTION

In many of the categories of situations considered in this chapter, opportunities for the assertion of restitutionary claims for the value of benefits conferred by one party on the other may
arise. In the main, the doctrines examined in this chapter, if applicable, have the effect of
rendering unenforceable an agreement entered into by parties manifesting an inequality of
bargaining power. As in all cases of ineffective transactions, the possibility exists that prior to
an awareness of the unenforceability of the agreement, one party will confer a valuable benefit
on the other. In such circumstances, the party conferring the benefit has no claim to enforce
the contract and, as an alternative, may wish to pursue a claim for restitutionary relief in order
to prevent the unjust enrichment of the other party.

In these contexts, however, there exists some tension between the general policy favouring
recovery of benefits conferred under ineffective transactions in order to prevent unjust enrichment and the policies underlying the rules that have rendered the agreement unenforceable
on the ground of inequality of bargaining power. Nowhere is this tension more evident than in
the context of restitution for benefits conferred under agreements entered into by minors. If,
for example, restitutionary claims against minors were generally available, the policy of affording protection to minors that underlies the unenforceability rule might be severely undermined. Although, as we have seen in *Nash v Inman*, above, the common law clearly permits
restitutionary recovery of the value of necessaries supplied to a minor, and courts have been
generally unreceptive to restitutionary claims against minors. At the same time, an absolute bar
against such relief would provide minors with an opportunity to engage in strategic or, indeed,
fraudulent behaviour in order to exploit their status of contractual incapacity. Thus, claims
against minors have been permitted in circumstances where the minor has acted fraudulently.
See e.g. *Stocks v Wilson*, [1913] 2 KB 235. Although the doctrine on these issues does not yield
to a concise summary, courts have tended to protect minors from restitutionary claims where
the minor has lost or dissipated the benefit or where the adult party has engaged in oppressive
conduct. In some cases, courts have restricted the adult party to recovery of benefits that can
be returned *in specie*.

Turning to the restitutionary rights of the minor, however, an understandably straightforward pattern emerges. It would be consistent with the underlying policy of protection of
minors to grant restitutionary relief to a minor who has conferred value on an adult party.
Canadian courts appear to have embraced the proposition that restitutionary relief should
generally be available to minors, at least in cases where the minor can make restitution to the
other party. See e.g. *LaFayette v WW Distributors & Co Ltd* (1965), 51 WWR 685 (Sask Dist Ct).
Presumably, however, the minor would be relieved of the obligation to make counterrestitution in any case where its application would severely prejudice the minor. This, at least, is the
majority rule in American jurisdictions. See e.g. *Quality Motors, Inc v Hays*, 225 SW 2d 326 (Ark
SC 1949). For more detailed accounts, see generally Waddams, ch 18, and JD McCamus,
"Restitution of Benefits Conferred Under Minors' Contracts" (1979) 28 UNBLJ 98.

In the context of transactions rendered unenforceable on grounds of unconscionability and
undue influence, a different balance is struck between the impulse to afford protection to the
weaker party and the impulse to prevent unjust enrichment by affording restitutionary relief. If
either of these doctrines is applicable to a particular transaction, the only traditional means of
relief available to the weaker party is to seek an equitable decree of rescission. Although the
obtaining of such a decree will be coupled with restitutionary relief for the weaker party, equitable rescission takes an even-handed approach to restitutionary matters. Thus, in order to obtain
a decree of rescission, the weaker party must meet a number of conditions for the granting of
such relief, the most important of which for present purposes is that the weaker party must be
able to make counterrestitution to the other party. In other words, in order to grant a declaration
that the agreement is unenforceable on grounds of either undue influence or unconscionability,
the court must be satisfied that it is possible to achieve a mutual restitution. As it is sometimes

said, "there must be a giving back and a taking back on both sides." Thus, if the weaker party has acquired an asset that can no longer be restored to the other party, perhaps because it has been consumed, the decree of rescission is not available to the weaker party. Similarly, rescission will be unavailable if, prior to the attempt to rescind, third-party rights have intervened. If, for example, the subject matter of a purchase from the weaker party has been sold by the stronger party to a bona fide third-party purchaser who is unaware of the undue influence or unconscionability, rescission will not be decreed.

It is not self-evident, however, that this limitation on relief meets the needs of justice in the context of inequality of bargaining power. If, for example, in *Marshall v Canada Permanent Trust Co*, excerpted above, Walsh had transferred title to his property to Marshall and Marshall, in turn, had sold the property to an innocent third-party purchaser, a decree of rescission would not be available and the agreement would remain enforceable. Walsh would have no ability to recover the value obtained by Marshall through unconscionable conduct. The traditional explanation for this outcome is that equity normally did not award monetary relief, damages being the special preserve of the common law. Little more than history commends such a result, however, and it is of interest, therefore, that in recent years both English and Canadian courts in such circumstances appear to be moving in the direction of allowing monetary relief that achieves a form of restitutionary relief for the innocent party.

In *Mahoney v Purnell*, [1996] 3 All ER 61 (QB), the plaintiff, who jointly owned and operated a hotel business with his son-in-law, Purnell, acting under the undue influence of Purnell, sold his interest in the business to his son-in-law at a severely undervalued price. Purnell then sold the business in a rising market, at great profit, to a bona fide purchaser. Under traditional doctrine, rescissionary relief would be unavailable in such circumstances. Nonetheless, the trial judge awarded equitable compensation in an amount representing the difference between the value of the interest Mahoney transferred to Purnell and the purchase price received from Purnell in return. In effect, then, Mahoney was allowed to recover the amount by which Purnell had unjustly enriched himself through the exercise of undue influence. Similar results have been achieved in Canadian cases of undue influence and unconscionability. See e.g. *Paris v Machnick* (1972), 32 DLR (3d) 723 (NSSC (TD)); *Junkin v Junkin* (1978), 86 DLR (3d) 751 (Ont H Ct J); *Treadwell v Martin* (1976), 67 DLR (3d) 493 (NBCA). This approach has recently been confirmed in the unconscionability context by the Supreme Court of Canada in *Rick v Brandsema*, 2009 SCC 10, [2009] 1 SCR 295, the facts and holding of which have been described above. In explaining that monetary compensation could be awarded in lieu of rescission, Abella J (for the court) observed:

> Historically, rescission was the remedy when a contract was found to be unenforceable because of unconscionability. Increasingly, however, when rescission is not available because restitution, as a practical matter, cannot be made, damages in the form of equitable compensation are imposed to provide relief to the wronged party. This is because [quoting from the British Columbia Court of Appeal in *Dusik v Newton*(1985), 62 BCLR 1 at 47 (CA)] "where rescission is impossible or inappropriate, it would be inequitable for the defendant to retain the benefits of an unconscionable bargain."

In a case where rescission is unavailable, then, monetary restitution for the value of benefits wrongfully obtained by the defendant may be awarded as an alternative.

In addition to the requirements that there must be mutual restitution, or, as is said, a *restitutio in integrum*, and that third-party rights must not have intervened, there are additional defences or "bars" generally applicable to equitable rescission. Thus, relief will be denied where the impugned transaction has been affirmed by the weaker party or where undue delay or "laches" has occurred. One would expect that in the context of inequality of bargaining power, courts would apply these defences in a manner that is sensitive to the policies underlying the rules rendering the transaction unenforceable. Thus, for example, it is well established in the context of rescission for undue influence that an affirmation of the weaker party will not be effective unless made after the undue influence has ceased to operate.

In the context of forfeiture clauses, under the rule in *Stockloser v Johnson*, excerpted above, the striking down of the particular forfeiture clause, rather than the agreement itself, provides a basis for the restitutionary recovery of the moneys that would otherwise have been forfeited. When placed in context, the restitutionary claim recognized by Denning LJ in *Stockloser* appears boldly innovative. The plaintiff in *Stockloser*, of course, was in breach of a contractual obligation to continue making installment payments. It may be asked, then, whether a party in breach of contract may be entitled to recover moneys paid under the agreement with respect to which no value has been received in return. The general rule is that moneys paid as a deposit by the party in breach are irrecoverable. It is established that use of the term "deposit" indicates that the payment is made as an earnest to bind performance. If the payer refuses to proceed with the agreement, the deposit will be forfeited. See *Howe v Smith* (1884), 27 Ch D 89 (CA). Where, on the other hand, the money has been paid by the party in default as a partial payment of the contract price, the traditional rule is that the money is recoverable in a restitutionary claim. See *Dies v British & International Mining Financing Corp Ltd*, [1939] 1 KB 724.

Under traditional doctrine, then, an agreement on the part of the party in default to forfeit moneys paid would normally preclude restitutionary relief. The decision in *Stockloser* thus creates a potentially powerful exception to this traditional approach by allowing recovery of moneys subject to a forfeiture clause in circumstances where the clause is considered by the courts to be oppressive in its effect. As we shall see in Chapter 8, a similar issue arises in the context of partial performance by a party in default who has agreed to supply goods and services. In Chapter 8 we examine the traditional authority, *Sumpter v Hedges*, [1898] 1 QB 673 (CA), which holds that where a builder withdraws from an agreement after partial completion of the contracted work under a contract that provides for payment on completion of the work, the value of the partial performance is, in effect, forfeited and no restitutionary claim will lie. When considering the possible reform of *Sumpter v Hedges*, it will be useful to reflect back on the approach adopted by Denning LJ in the *Stockloser* case. See generally Maddaugh & McCamus, ch 5 at 500 (rescission) and ch 19 at 300 (restitution for the party in breach of contract).

CHAPTER SEVEN

PUBLIC POLICY

I. INTRODUCTION

The freedom to contract, to voluntarily enter into agreements enforceable at law, is fundamental to the law of contracts. That freedom, however, can be overridden in the name of public policy when it is determined that other social policies are more important, or when it would not be in the public interest to enforce a contract. This chapter is about contracts that are, on their face, valid, but that are not enforced for public policy reasons. As Professor Waddams writes in *Dimensions of Private Law: Categories and Concepts in Anglo-American Legal Reasoning* (New York: Cambridge University Press, 2003) at 19: "From one point of view, there is an identity of meaning [between private law and public policy], because protection of property, enforcement of contracts, redress of wrongs, and avoidance of unjust enrichment are public policies but 'policy' is often used to denote the residual or overriding sense of justice between the parties and 'public policy' often indicates enlargement or restriction of liability because of anticipated salutary effects on the future behaviour of others."

Constricting agreements that have been freely entered into through the vague reference to the "paramount public policy" has elicited concern, but the concern has fallen on both sides of the argument. Courts have emphasized both the freedom to contract and to have those contracts enforced, as well as public interest considerations that protect society—considerations that should not be disregarded in favour of private interests. Buttough J famously cautioned against reliance on public policy in *Richardson v Mellish* (1824), 2 Bing 229 at 252 (CP), saying, "Public policy ... is a very unruly horse, and when once you get astride it you never know where it will carry you." Similarly, Jessel MR urged caution when interfering with freedom of contract in *Printing & Numerical Registering Co v Sampson* (1875), LR 19 Eq 462 at 465, maintaining, "[I]f there is one thing which more than another public policy requires it is that men of full age and competent understanding shall have the utmost liberty of contracting and that their contracts when entered into freely and voluntarily shall be held sacred and shall be enforced by Courts of justice."

On the other side, courts have acknowledged that the freedom to contract is not infinite, and have recognized that constraints are necessary to protect the public. Lord Denning, in *Enderby Town Football Club Ltd v The Football Association Ltd*, [1971] Ch 591 at 606, directly countered Buttough J's concerns: "I disagree. With a good man in the saddle, the unruly horse can be kept in control. It can jump over obstacles. It can leap the fences put up by fictions and come down on the side of justice." The Canadian Supreme Court in *Miller Estate, Re*, ([1938] SCR 1 at paras 5 and 15) also recognized that while contracts must be given effect, there is nonetheless the "paramount consideration of public policy which over-rides the interest [of giving effect to contracts and testamentary dispositions] and what otherwise would be the rights and powers of individuals." However, the court went on to urge caution when courts utilize public interest considerations, and articulated, "two conditions which must be fulfilled to justify a refusal by the courts on grounds of public policy to give effect to the rule of law according to its proper application." First, "... such prohibition is imposed in the interest of the safety of the state, or the economic or social well-being of the state and its people as a whole ... [and second], the doctrine should be invoked only in clear cases, in which harm to the public is substantially uncontestable, and does not depend upon the idiosyncratic inferences of a few judicial minds."

More recently, in *Tercon Contractors Ltd v British Columbia (Transportation and Highways)*, 2010 SCC 4, excerpted in Chapter 6, the Supreme Court emphasized the power of public policy and urged restraint in its application, saying, "[t]he residual power of a court to decline enforcement exists but, in the interests of certainty and stability of contractual relations, it will rarely be exercised" (at paras 117-18). But the court went on to say, "[t]here are cases where the exercise of what Professor Waddams calls the 'ultimate power' to refuse to enforce a contract may be justified, even in the commercial context. Freedom of contract, like any freedom, may be abused." It is against this background that the following cases should be studied.

II. THE EFFECTS OF ILLEGALITY

When a court declares a contract illegal as contrary to public policy, it must then determine how to treat the parties to that agreement. Usually, one of those parties to the contract is before the court, seeking to enforce the agreement or to recover some benefit paid under the now-inoperative contract.

HOLMAN V JOHNSON
(1775), 1 Cowp 341, 98 ER 1120 (KB)

Assumpsit for goods sold and delivered: Plea *non assumpsit*, and verdict for the plaintiff. Upon a rule to show cause why a new trial should not be granted, Lord Mansfield reported the case, which was shortly this: The plaintiff, who was resident at and inhabitant of Dunkirk, together with his partner, a native of that place, sold and delivered a quantity of tea, for the price of which the action was brought, to the order of the defendant, knowing it was intended to be smuggled by him into England; they had, however, no concern in the smuggling scheme itself, but merely sold this tea to him, as they would have done to any other person in the common and ordinary course of their trade.

LORD MANSFIELD: There can be no doubt that every action tried here must be tried by the law of England; but the law of England says that in a variety of circumstances, with regard to contracts legally made abroad, the laws of the country where the cause of action arose shall govern. There are a great many cases which every country says shall be determined by the laws of foreign countries where they arise. But I do not see how the principles on which that doctrine obtains are applicable to the present case. For no country ever takes notice of the revenue laws of another.

The objection that a contract is immoral or illegal as between plaintiff and defendant, sounds at all times very ill in the mouth of the defendant. It is not for his sake, however, that the objection is ever allowed; but it is founded in general principles of policy, which the defendant has the advantage of, contrary to the real justice as between him and the plaintiff, by accident, if I may so say. The principle of public policy is this: *Ex dolo malo non oritur actio.* No court will lend its aid to a man who founds his cause upon an immoral or illegal act. If from the plaintiff's own stating or otherwise, the cause of action appears to arise *ex turpi causa*, or the transgression of a positive law in this country, there the court says he has no right to be assisted. It is upon that ground the court goes; not for the sake of the defendant, but because they will not lend their aid to such a plaintiff. So if the plaintiff and defendant were to change sides, and the defendant was to bring his action against the plaintiff, the latter would then have the advantage of it; for where both are *equally* in fault, *potior est conditio defendantis.*

The question therefore is, whether in this case the plaintiff's demand is founded upon the ground of any immoral act or contract, or upon the ground of his being guilty of anything which is prohibited by a positive law of this country. An immoral contract it certainly is not; for the revenue laws themselves, as well as the offences against them, are all *positivi juris*. What, then, is the contract of the plaintiff? It is this: being a resident and inhabitant of Dunkirk, together with his partner, who was born there, he sells a quantity of tea to the defendant, and delivers it at Dunkirk to the defendant's order, to be paid for in ready money there, or by bills drawn personally upon him in England. This is an action brought merely for the goods sold and delivered at Dunkirk. Where, then, or in what respect is the plaintiff guilty of any crime? Is there any law of England transgressed by a person making a complete sale of a parcel of goods at Dunkirk, and giving credit for them? The contract is complete, and nothing is left to be done. The seller, indeed, knows what the buyer is going to do with the goods, but he has no concern in the transaction itself. It is not a bargain to be paid in case the vendee should succeed in landing the goods; but the interest of the vendor is totally at an end, and his contract complete by the delivery of the goods at Dunkirk.

To what a dangerous extent would this go if it were to be held a crime. If contraband clothes are bought in France, and brought home hither, or if glass bought abroad, which ought to pay a great duty, is run into England, shall the French tailor or the glass manufacturer stand to the risk or loss attending their being run into England? Clearly not. Debt follows the person, and may be recovered in England, let the contract of debt be made where it will; and the law allows a fiction for the sake of expediting the remedy. Therefore, I am clearly of the opinion that the vendors of these goods are not guilty of any offence, nor have they transgressed against the provisions of any act of Parliament ...

... Therefore, let the rule for a new trial be discharged.

[The three other judges concurred.]

NOTES

1. The principle in *Holman v Johnson* is that "no court will lend its aid to a man who founds his cause upon an immoral or illegal act." This principle has been applied and mitigated in Canadian decisions. Particularly important has been the development of the law of restitution. See the material below in Section V.B, "Restitution," and, for example, the decision of the Ontario Court of Appeal in *Koliniotis v Tri Level Claims Consultants Ltd* (2005), 201 OAC 282, in which the court allowed a paralegal recovery on the basis of *quantum meruit* despite a finding that the contract, which provided for services on a contingency-fee basis, was illegal. The court found that having a rule absolutely barring *quantum meruit* would create an injustice that cannot stand, given the public policy underlying the statutory prohibition against champertous agreements.

2. For a general discussion of public policy in contract law, see Brandon Kain & Douglas T Yoshida, "The Doctrine of Public Policy in Canadian Contract Law" in Todd L Archibald & Randall Echlin JJ, eds, *Annual Review of Civil Litigation, 2007* (Toronto: Carswell, 2007) 1.

III. CONTRACTS CONTRARY TO PUBLIC POLICY EXPRESSED IN THE COMMON LAW

The following cases provide examples of some kinds of agreements that the courts have refused to enforce on the ground of public policy, including contracts in restraint of trade, contracts under which a criminal would receive a benefit from his or her crime, and contracts to defraud a third party. Courts have also refused to enforce sexually immoral contracts, contracts to commit a crime or a tort, contracts prejudicial to public safety, contracts prejudicial to the administration of justice or designed to oust the jurisdiction of the court, contracts to promote corruption in public life, and contracts prejudicial to the status of marriage. One question is whether the "heads of public policy" are closed or may be expanded. Consider the following excerpts and notes.

> **Egerton v Brownlow.** (1853), 4 HLC 1, 10 ER 359. PARKE B (ER at 409): Public policy is a vague and unsatisfactory term ... it is capable of being understood in different senses ... and in that sense there may be every variety of opinion, according to education, habits, talents, and dispositions of each person, who is to decide whether an act is against public policy or not. To allow this to be a ground of judicial decision, would lead to the greatest uncertainty and confusion.... It is the province of the judge to expound the law only; the written from the statutes, the unwritten or common law from the decisions of our predecessors and of our existing Courts, from text writers of acknowledged authority, and upon the principles to be clearly deduced from them by sound reason and just inference; not to speculate upon what is best, in his opinion, for the advantage of the community. Some of these decisions may have no doubt been founded upon the prevailing and just opinions of the public good; for instance, the illegality of covenants in restraint of marriage or trade. They have become part of the recognized law, and we are therefore bound by them, but we think we are not thereby authorised to establish as law everything which we may think for the public good, and prohibit everything which we think otherwise.
>
> POLLOCK LCB (ER at 419): My Lords, it may be that Judges are no better able to discern what is for the public good than other experienced and enlightened members of the community; but that is no reason for their refusing to entertain the question, and declining to decide upon it.

NOTES

1. Lord Wright, in *Fender v St John-Mildmay*, [1938] AC 1 at 42, said: "[It] is, I think, clear that this dictum of Pollock C.B. and certain observations in *Egerton v Brownlow* to a similar effect cannot be regarded as fixing the modern law, which in my opinion is as stated by Parke B." Why is it that two centuries ago judges could develop ideas of "public policy," but today the subject is closed? Compare Samuel Williston, *The Law of Contracts*, vol 3 (1920), s 1629 at 2864; Williston "respectfully doubts," as inconsistent with the history of our law, the dictum of Lord Halsbury in *Janson v Driefontein Consolidated Mines, Ltd*, [1902] AC 484 at 491: "I deny that any court can 'invent a new public policy.'"

In *Bursey v Bursey*, 1999 CanLII 19021 (NLCA), the court urged caution in applying the doctrine of public policy, "lest it become a catch-all for invalidating too wide a variety of con-tractual objectives, and unduly impinge on the basic right to enforce engagements freely and voluntarily made." The court went on to state that "... such restraint [could be observed] by relating the scope of judicial intervention to precedent, while at the same time not absolutely foreclosing the doctrine evolving to meet changing conditions" (at para 24).

2. A US view was expressed in *Henningsen v Bloomfield Motors*, 32 NJ 358, 121 A2d 69 (SC 1960). The court was dealing with a contract for the sale of an automobile, certain clauses of which severely limited the right of the buyer to recover for damage caused by any defects in the automobile. The court said: "Public policy is a term not easily defined. Its significance varies as the habits and needs of a people may vary. It is not static and the field of application is an ever increasing one. A contract or a particular provision therein, valid in one era, may be totally opposed to the public policy of another."

3. In *Douez v Facebook, Inc*, 2017 SCC 33, a majority of the Supreme Court of Canada used public policy principles to decide that a forum selection clause was unenforceable. The Kara-katsanis judgment (for three of the judges) determined the clause to be unenforceable on public policy grounds. Abella J, concurring, also determined the clause could not be enforced, on public policy and unconscionability grounds. The dissent would have enforced the clause.

In British Columbia, a class action was brought against Facebook, Inc, on behalf of 8.1 mil-lion people. They alleged Facebook used the names and pictures of certain members for advertising without their consent, contrary to the *Privacy Act*, RSBC 1996, c 373. Facebook sought to stay the proceedings on the basis of a forum selection clause contained in the terms of use, terms to which all Facebook members must agree before they access the site.

To determine the enforceability of the forum selection clause, the Karakatsanis judgment applied the two-step common law test, established by the Supreme Court in *ZI Pompey Industrie v ECU-Line NV*, 2003 SCC 27 (the *Pompey* test). Under the first step, the party seek-ing to stay the proceeding must establish that the clause is "valid, clear and enforceable and that it applies to the cause of action before the court" (*Douez v Facebook*, at para 28). Basic principles of contract law apply to the first step of the test, to determine the enforceability and applicability of the clause, and a plaintiff may use doctrines such as mistake, unconscionability, undue influence, etc. to argue that the clause is unenforceable, as with any contract claim. Once the first part is met, the onus shifts to the plaintiff under the second part, to show reasons the court should nonetheless not enforce the clause. This part of the test is referred to as the "strong cause" part. Under the strong cause test, the court exercises its discretion to consider "'all the circumstances,' including the 'convenience of the parties, fairness between the parties and the interests of justice'" (at para 29). The Karakatsanis judgment found the clause enforce-able under the first step, but not under the second. The judges determined that, because the strong cause test has been utilized in commercial contexts, the test should be expanded to include public policy to account for the consumer context before them.

There were two aspects to the public policy considerations. First, there is an inequality of bargaining power between the parties, as determined by Facebook's profits, and by consum-ers' inability to reject Facebook's terms of use. Facebook's argument that customers could

629

simply remain offline if they chose, was rejected, as the court found that "there are few comparable alternatives to Facebook, a social networking platform with extensive reach" (at para 56). Second, it is important to adjudicate these matters in Canadian courts. "There is an inherent public good in Canadian courts deciding these types of claims. Through adjudication, courts establish norms and interpret the rights enjoyed by all Canadians" (at para 58). Given that privacy legislation is quasi-constitutional, "only a local court's interpretation of privacy rights under the Privacy Act will provide clarity and certainty about the scope of the rights to others in the province" (at para 59). In sum, the public policy concerns provided a strong cause to not enforce the clause. The Karakatsanis decision maintained (at para 52):

> There are generally strong public policy reasons to hold parties to their bargain and it is clear that forum selection clauses are not inherently contrary to public policy. But freedom of contract is not unfettered. A court has discretion under the strong cause test to deny the enforcement of a contract for reasons of public policy in appropriate circumstances. Generally, such limitations fall into two broad categories: those intended to protect a weaker party or those intended to protect "the social, economic, or political policies of the enacting state in the collective interest".... In this case, both of these categories are implicated. It raises both the reality of unequal bargaining power in consumer contracts of adhesion and the local court's interest in adjudicating claims involving constitutional or quasi-constitutional rights.

In the light of these comments, consider the following US case.

IN THE MATTER OF BABY "M"
537 A 2d 1227 (NJSC 1988)

[Mr. and Mrs. Stern were advised against having children for fear that pregnancy would exacerbate Mrs. Stern's mild form of multiple sclerosis. They were considered unlikely candidates for adoption due to their age (30s) and differing religious commitments. As well, Mr. Stern's parents were Holocaust survivors and it was important to him to have a child biologically connected to him. The couple pursued an ad from the Infertility Center in New York and was matched with Mrs. Whitehead, who agreed to serve as a surrogate mother.

The contract provided that Mrs. Whitehead would be artificially inseminated with Mr. Stern's sperm and assume the risks of childbirth; submit to a psychiatric examination at Mr. Stern's expense and to amniocentesis; and, upon the birth of the child, surrender all parental rights. Mr. Stern agreed to assume the risk of the child being born with any defects and to pay $10,000 plus all expenses.

After the child was born, Mrs. Whitehead refused to surrender custody. The Sterns sued for specific performance of the contract. At trial, Judge Sorkow concluded that the contract was enforceable. There was no law against it and he found no evidence of fraud or unconscionability. Because specific performance is a discretionary remedy, he refused to order it unless convinced that giving custody to the Sterns would be in the best interests of the child. After reviewing the evidence, he concluded that that was the case. Mrs. Whitehead appealed.

The appeal court decided that the surrogacy contract was void, both because it was contrary to laws of the state prohibiting money being used in adoptions and because it was contrary to public policy of the state. However, the court also awarded custody to the Sterns, finding that it was in the best interests of the child. On the public policy question, the court stated:]

WILENTZ CJ: The point is made that Mrs. Whitehead agreed to the surrogacy arrangement, supposedly fully understanding the consequences. Putting aside the issue of how compelling her need for money may have been, and how significant her understanding of the consequences, we suggest that her consent is irrelevant. There are, in a civilized society, some things that money cannot buy. In America, we decided long ago that merely because conduct purchased by money was "voluntary" did not mean that it was good or beyond regulation and prohibition. ... There are, in short, values that society deems more important than granting to wealth whatever it can buy, be it labor, love, or life. Whether this principle recommends prohibition of surrogacy which presumably sometimes results in great satisfaction to all of the parties, is not for us to say. We note here only that, under existing law, the fact that Mrs. Whitehead "agreed" to the arrangement is not dispositive.

The long-term effects of surrogacy contracts are not known, but feared—the impact on the child who learns her life was bought, that she is the offspring of someone who gave birth to her only to obtain money; the impact on the natural mother as the full weight of her isolation is felt along with the full reality of the sale of her body and her child; the impact on the natural father and adoptive mother once they realize the consequences of their conduct. Literature in related areas suggests these are substantial considerations, although, given the newness of surrogacy, there is little information. ...

The surrogacy contract creates, it is based upon, principles that are directly contrary to the objectives of our laws. It guarantees the separation of a child from its mother; it looks to adoption regardless of suitability; it totally ignores the child; it takes the child from the mother regardless of her wishes and her maternal fitness; and it does all of this, it accomplishes all of its goals, through the use of money.

Beyond that is the potential degradation of some women that may result from this arrangement. In many cases, of course, surrogacy may bring satisfaction, not only to the infertile couple, but to the surrogate mother herself. The fact, however, that many women may not perceive surrogacy negatively but rather see it as an opportunity does not diminish its potential for devastation to other women.

In sum, the harmful consequences of this surrogacy arrangement appear to us all too palpable. In New Jersey the surrogate mother's agreement to sell her child is void. Its irrevocability infects the entire contract, as does the money that purports to buy it.

NOTES AND QUESTIONS

1. Why would the infertility centre try to use contract law to formalize the arrangement between surrogate mothers and infertile couples?

2. In both courts, Mrs Whitehead lost custody of Baby M. What if the $10,000 fee had not been paid to Mrs Whitehead before the appeal? Consider yourself in the role of Mrs Whitehead's lawyer, explaining to her that, at trial, she lost custody of the baby but would have received her fee; after her appeal, despite winning on the ground that the surrogacy contract was void, she now can neither keep the baby nor claim the fee.

3. What if the $10,000 fee had been paid prior to the appeal? The question of what happens to payments made pursuant to illegal contracts is treated below.

4. The question of surrogacy contracts has also been debated in Canada. See Felicia Daunt, "Exploitation or Empowerment? Debating Surrogate Motherhood" (1991) 55 Sask L Rev 415; Angela Campbell, "Law's Suppositions About Surrogacy Against the Backdrop of Social Science" (2011-12) 43 Ottawa L Rev 29. The *Assisted Human Reproduction Act*, SC 2004, c 2, s 6 prohibits paying any consideration to a surrogate mother or to anyone arranging a surrogacy contract. Sections of the Act relating to surrogacy have been upheld as constitutional under the federal powers over criminal law, although various other sections of the original act were declared

beyond the federal powers. See *Reference Re Assisted Human Reproduction Act*, 2010 SCC 61, [2010] 3 SCR 457.

5. The Supreme Court of Canada in *Bruker v Marcovitz*, 2007 SCC 54, [2007] 3 SCR 607 held (at para 64) that a contract to give a *get* or religious divorce as part of a divorce settlement was an enforceable contract and not "contrary to public order" because it "harmonizes with Canada's approach to religious freedom, to equality rights, to divorce and remarriage generally." The case arose in Quebec where the *Québec Civil Code*, LRQ, c C-1991 provides in art 1413: "A contract whose object is prohibited by law or contrary to public order is null."

6. See also *Canadian Taxpayers Federation v Ontario (Minister of Finance)* (2004), 73 OR (3d) 621 (Sup Ct J), excerpted in Chapter 3.

A. CONTRACTS IN RESTRAINT OF TRADE

Historically, common law courts have been opposed to agreements that reduced competition and created monopolies in the market, and such agreements were promptly overturned. Now, agreements creating monopolies and anticompetitive practices are governed by legislation. What continues to be an issue at common law, however, are contracts in which the restraint is voluntarily expressed, in clauses called "covenants in restraint of trade." These clauses limit a party's right to carry on business in the future, and are most notably found in employment contracts and contracts for the sale of businesses, in the form of non-competition and non-solicitation clauses. At common law, these covenants are unenforceable on public policy grounds, but courts are now more permissive with their interpretation depending on the type of agreement before them. As the cases below will show, courts are stricter in interpreting these covenants in employment contracts than they are in commercial contracts. See also Waddams at paras 564-66 and MacDougall at 278-81.

SHAFRON V KRG INSURANCE BROKERS (WESTERN) INC
2009 SCC 6, [2009] 1 SCR 157

[In 1988, Mr. Shafron sold the shares in his insurance brokerage business to KRG Insurance Brokers ("KRG"). He continued to be employed in the business and as part of his employment contract signed a contract that contained a non-competition clause providing that if he left the employment of KRG he would not carry on a similar business for three years within the "Metropolitan City of Vancouver." A few years later, the shares were sold to another purchaser, but Mr. Shafron's employment continued under a contract containing a similar clause. In 2000, Mr. Shafron left KRG and began working as an insurance salesman in Richmond for another company. KRG sued Mr. Shafron for breach of his contract. At trial, the judge held that there was no clear definition for the "Metropolitan City of Vancouver" and the clause was unenforceable. The Court of Appeal reversed and Mr. Shafron appealed to the Supreme Court.]

ROTHSTEIN J (after reviewing the facts and the issues): A restrictive covenant in a contract is what the common law refers to as a restraint of trade. Restrictive covenants are frequently found in agreements for the purchase and sale of a business and in employment contracts. A restrictive covenant precludes the vendor in the sale of a business from competing with the purchaser and, in an employment contract, the restrictive covenant precludes the employee, upon leaving employment, from competing with the former employer.

Restrictive covenants give rise to a tension in the common law between the concept of freedom to contract and public policy considerations against restraint of trade. In the seminal decision of the House of Lords in *Nordenfelt v. Maxim Nordenfelt Guns and Ammunition Co.*, [1894] A.C. 535, this tension was explained. At common law, restraints of trade are contrary to public policy because they interfere with individual liberty of action and because the exercise of trade should be encouraged and should be free. Lord Macnaghten stated, at p. 565:

> The public have an interest in every person's carrying on his trade freely: so has the individual. All interference with individual liberty of action in trading, and all restraints of trade of themselves, if there is nothing more, are contrary to public policy, and therefore void. That is the general rule.

However, recognition of the freedom of the parties to contract requires that there be exceptions to the general rule against restraints of trade. The exception is where the restraint of trade is found to be reasonable. At p. 565, Lord Macnaghten continued:

> But there are exceptions: *restraints of trade and interference with individual liberty of action may be justified by the special circumstances of a particular case. It is a sufficient justification, and indeed it is the only justification, if the restriction is reasonable*—reasonable, that is, in reference to the interests of the parties concerned and reasonable in reference to the interests of the public, so framed and so guarded as to afford adequate protection to the party in whose favour it is imposed, while at the same time it is in no way injurious to the public. That, I think, is the fair result of all the authorities. [Emphasis added.]

Therefore, despite the presumption that restrictive covenants are *prima facie* unenforceable, a reasonable restrictive covenant will be upheld.

It is important at this juncture to differentiate between a contract for the sale of a business and an employment contract.

In *Nordenfelt*, Lord Macnaghten pointed out that there is greater freedom to contract between buyer and seller than between employer and employee. At p. 566, he wrote:

> To a certain extent, *different considerations must apply in cases of apprenticeship and cases of that sort, on the one hand, and cases of the sale of a business or dissolution of partnership on the other.* A man is bound as an apprentice because he wishes to learn a trade and to practise it. A man may sell because he is getting too old for the strain and worry of business, or because he wishes for some other reason to retire from business altogether. *Then there is obviously more freedom of contract between buyer and seller than between master and servant or between an employer and a person seeking employment.* [Emphasis added.]

Although the comments of Lord Macnaghten focus on apprenticeship, the same concept has been extended and applied to contracts between employers and employees.

In the House of Lords' decision of *Herbert Morris, Ltd. v. Saxelby*, [1916] 1 A.C. 688, Lord Atkinson made some observations on the difference between contracts of employment and those for sale of a business. He cited with approval *Leather Cloth Co. v. Lorsont* (1869), L.R. 9 Eq. 345, at p. 354, quoting James V.-C. in that case:

> The principle is this: Public policy requires that every man shall be at liberty to work for himself, and shall not be at liberty to deprive himself or the State of his labour, skill, or talent, by any contract that he enters into. On the other hand, public policy requires that when a man has by skill or by any other means obtained something which he wants to sell, he should be at liberty to sell it in the most advantageous way in the market; and in order to enable him to sell it advantageously in the market it is necessary that he should be able to preclude himself from entering into competition with the purchaser.

Lord Atkinson then stated that "[t]hese considerations in themselves differentiate, in my opinion, the case of the sale of goodwill from the case of master and servant or employer and employee" (p. 701).

The sale of a business often involves a payment to the vendor for goodwill. In consideration of the goodwill payment, the custom of the business being sold is intended to remain and reside with the purchaser. As Lord Ashbourne observed at p. 555 of *Nordenfelt*:

> I think it is quite clear that the covenant must be taken as entered into in connection with the sale of the goodwill of the appellant's business, and that it was entered into with the plain and bona fide object of protecting that business.

And as stated by Dickson J. (as he then was) in *Elsley v. J.G. Collins Insurance Agencies Ltd.*, [1978] 2 S.C.R. 916, at p. 924:

> A person seeking to sell his business might find himself with an unsaleable commodity if denied the right to assure the purchaser that he, the vendor, would not later enter into competition.

See also *Burgess v. Industrial Frictions & Supply Co.* (1987), 12 B.C.L.R. (2d) 85 (C.A.), *per* McLachlin J.A. (as she then was), at p. 95.

The same considerations will not apply in the employer/employee context. No doubt an employee may build up a relationship with customers of the employer, but there is normally no payment for goodwill upon the employee leaving the employment of the employer. It is also accepted that there is generally an imbalance in power between employee and employer. For example, an employee may be at an economic disadvantage when litigating the reasonableness of a restrictive covenant because the employer may have access to greater resources (see, for example, *Elsley*, at p. 924, and *Mason v. Provident Clothing and Supply Co.*, [1913] A.C. 724 (H.L.), *per* Lord Moulton, at p. 745 ... .

The absence of payment for goodwill as well as the generally accepted imbalance in power between employee and employer justifies more rigorous scrutiny of restrictive covenants in employment contracts compared to those in contracts for the sale of a business. ...

Normally, the reasonableness of a restrictive covenant is determined by considering the extent of the activity sought to be prohibited and the extent of the temporal and spatial scope of the prohibition. This case is different because of the added issue of ambiguity. As indicated, a restrictive covenant is *prima facie* unenforceable unless it is shown to be reasonable. However, if the covenant is ambiguous, in the sense that what is prohibited is not clear as to activity, time, or geography, it is not possible to demonstrate that it is reasonable. Thus, an ambiguous restrictive covenant is, by definition, *prima facie* unreasonable and unenforceable. Only if the ambiguity can be resolved is it then possible to determine whether the unambiguous restrictive covenant is reasonable.

The trial judge found that there was no legal or judicial definition of the term "Metropolitan City of Vancouver." In finding that the spatial area covered by the restrictive covenant was not clear and certain, the trial judge referred to the evidence of the principal of KRG Western. ... On the basis of this and other evidence, the trial judge found that the language of the restrictive covenant was neither clear nor certain and for this and other reasons dismissed the claim of KRG Western against Shafron.

[The court held that the ambiguity could not be resolved and that the clause was therefore unenforceable.]

NOTES

1. See also MJ Trebilcock, *The Common Law Doctrine of Restraint of Trade* (Scarborough, ON: Carswell, 1988).

2. For a discussion of the use of severance in the context of statutory illegality, see below, Section V.C, "Severance of Illegal Provisions."

3. A covenant prohibiting employees from soliciting customers of the employer, "... in any manner whosoever, in any business or activity for any client of [the employer] with which he/she had dealings on behalf of [the employer] at any time within the twelve (12) months preceding" the date of the employee's departure was found too ambiguous to be reasonable. See *Globex Foreign Exchange Corporation v Kelcher*, 2011 ABCA 240. Similarly, a covenant prohibiting a former employee from providing or soliciting services or products to or from "any business entity which was a customer of the Company" during the period in which he was employed with the company, which was 17 years, for a period of one year following termination, was found to be unreasonable due to being "overly broad and unworkable in practice." See *Mason v Chem-Trend Ltd Partnership*, 2011 ONCA 344.

4. Courts interpret restrictive covenants in contracts for the sale of assets in a commercial context less strictly than restrictive covenants in contracts for employment: *Guay inc c Payette*, 2013 SCC 45. In a commercial context, Wagner J explained that the test for reasonableness depends on the limitations of the clause, "... as to its term and to the territory and activities to which it applies, to whatever is necessary for the protection of the legitimate interests of the party in whose favour it was granted" (para 61). See *MEDIchair LP v DME Medequip Inc*, 2016 ONCA 168, for a discussion about reasonableness and geographical limitations contained in the restrictive covenant when the business has yet to expand to the area covered.

5. It is not always easy to distinguish between the types of contracts in which restrictive covenants are contained. The *Payette* Court quoted Dickson J's distinction in *JG Collins Insurance Agencies v Elsley*, [1978] 2 SCR 916 at p 924:

> The distinction made in the cases between a restrictive covenant contained in an agreement for the sale of a business and one contained in a contract of employment is well-conceived and responsive to practical considerations. A person seeking to sell his business might find himself with an unsaleable commodity if denied the right to assure the purchaser that he, the vendor, would not later enter into competition. Difficulty lies in definition of the time during which, and the area within which, the non-competitive covenant is to operate, but if these are reasonable, the courts will normally give effect to the covenant.
>
> A different situation, at least in theory, obtains in the negotiation of a contract of employment where an imbalance of bargaining power may lead to oppression and a denial of the right of the employee to exploit, following termination of employment, in the public interest and in his own interest, knowledge and skills obtained during employment.

The *Payette* Court went on to say, "determin[ing] whether a restrictive covenant is linked to a contract for the sale of assets or to a contract of employment, it is ... important to clearly identify the reason why the covenant was entered into. ... The goal of the analysis is to identify the nature of the principal obligations under the master agreement and to determine why and for what purpose the accessory obligations of non-competition and non-solicitation were assumed" (para 45).

B. CONTRACTS RELATED TO GAMING

BOARDWALK REGENCY CORP V MAALOUF
(1992), 6 OR (3d) 737 (CA)

CARTHY JA: The respondent, a resident of Ontario, borrowed money and built up a gambling debt at the appellant's casino in Atlantic City, New Jersey, failed to honour a cheque representing the ultimate debt of $43,000, permitted a default judgment to be entered in New Jersey, and now resists an action on that judgment in Ontario. The trial judge, in a judgment reported at (1988), 68 O.R. (2d) 753, found that the Ontario *Gaming Act*, R.S.O. 1980, c. 183 (now R.S.O. 1990, c. G.2) and particularly ss. 1, 4 and 5 represent a public policy in Ontario discouraging gambling, and accordingly that the action based upon the New Jersey judgment should be dismissed. The appellant says that the loan agreement was not a wagering agreement within s. 4 of the *Gaming Act*, that the proper law of the contract is that of New Jersey and s. 1 on the Act therefore has no application, and, finally, that it is not contrary to public policy in Ontario to enforce the New Jersey judgment. The respondent takes the contrary position on each of these three issues.

[Having found that the proper law of the contract was New Jersey law, the court concluded that the Ontario *Gaming Act* had no application. Carthy JA continued:]

The Saskatchewan Court of Appeal accurately summarized the public policy concerns which may stand in the way of enforcement of foreign contracts or judgments. In *Canadian Acceptance Corp. v. Matte* (1957), 9 D.L.R. (2d) 304, Martin C.J.S. states:

> In Dicey's Conflict of Laws, 6th ed., pp. 19-20, the learned author states: "English courts refuse to give legal effect to transactions, even when governed by foreign law, which our tribunals hold to be immoral. Thus a promise made in consideration of future illicit cohabitation, or an agreement which, though innocent in itself, is intended by the parties to promote an immoral purpose, or a promise obtained through what our courts consider duress or coercion, champertous contracts and contracts in restraint of trade are according to English law based on an immoral consideration. Such a promise or agreement, therefore, even were it valid under the law of the country which governs the contract, will not be enforced by English judges."

... The common ground of all expressed reasons for imposing the doctrine of public policy is essential morality. This must be more than the morality of some persons and must run through the fabric of society to the extent that it is not consonant with our system of justice and general moral outlook to countenance the conduct, no matter how legal it may have been where it occurred. If that be so, the *Gaming Act* must be viewed in the context of the community's sense of morality. An important element of that sense of morality is what the community has consensually determined is not to be tolerated, as found in the *Criminal Code*. The *Gaming Act* may reflect that general morality or may, upon analysis, appear to have a very narrow focus related to recovery of debts with no present relevance as a moral statement.

If this case concerned enforcement of a judgment based upon a contract relating to the corruption of children, our instinctive moral repugnance would find confirmation in s. 172 of the *Criminal Code*, declaring such corruption a criminal offence. It is not so easy with gaming laws because of the history of their development and the unique form they take in the *Criminal Code*. In an article entitled "Recent Amendments to Canadian Lottery and Gaming Laws: The Transfer of Power Between Federal and

Provincial Governments" (1988), 26 *Osgoode Hall Law Journal* 19, Judith A. Osborne and Colin S. Campbell describe the background to our present legislation. It is founded in English statute law rather than the common law, and one of the earliest of these is a statute of 1388 prohibiting all games except archery [*Gaming Act*, 1388 (12 Ric 2, Eng), c 6]. It is said that this prohibition was occasioned by the fear of Richard II that his skilled archers were losing their talents by spending time playing games of dice. This general prohibition, in revised form, was incorporated in the *Criminal Code* of 1892.

In 1956, a joint committee of both Canadian Houses of Parliament recommended new gaming laws emphasizing supervision and control by workable laws in order to avoid abuses such as had been experienced under alcohol prohibition laws. In other words, the prohibitions against gambling were seen as not being consonant with the public perception of morality. In 1969, the *Criminal Code* was amended to permit the federal or the provincial government to conduct lottery schemes (encompassing gaming enterprises generally). ... Then, in what the authors characterize as a political contract, the federal government divested itself of the power in 1985, leaving the provinces as the sole licensors. ...

Returning to the example of corrupting children, it is unimaginable to consider an amendment to make this an offence only if not licensed by a provincial body or conducted at an annual fair, but that very fact makes the point that the morality of gambling as a part of our social fibre is very different from other offences in the Criminal Code. In 1991, $10 bets were made at blackjack tables at the Canadian National Exhibition. Those participating cannot be generally viewed as engaged in an immoral venture, although some persons may so view it. If money is loaned by a friend to enable another to play the games, which is inevitable in any gaming situation, is that to be considered immoral? The provincial legislature may bar recovery of the loan, but the statute doing so can hardly be interpreted as establishing a moral policy when the same government licenses the opportunity.

In my view, activities occurring in an enterprise licensed by the State of New Jersey cannot carry a different colour of morality. The federal parliament would be inconsistent in decreeing that what is licensed by Ontario or under the auspices of an annual exhibition has moral integrity, while what is licensed and regulated by New Jersey does not.

It is, therefore, my conclusion that an Ontario court cannot say that a judgment founded upon a contract related to gambling is tainted by immorality and should be refused enforcement.

NOTES

1. This case raises two issues that arise with public policy. One is the enforcement of foreign judgments; the other is the application of foreign laws that may be contrary to public policy in Canada. The dissenting judgment of Arbour JA is omitted, but it raises both issues. Arbour JA determined that she did not have to decide the morality issue. For her, it was sufficient that, had the contract been made in Ontario, it would have been unenforceable. However, that position is questionable, for the reasons articulated in *Atlantic City Showboat Inc v Smith*, [1993] OJ No 1561 (QL) (Gen Div), which also involved a gambling debt from New Jersey, where the plaintiff commenced an action in Ontario, but did not have an existing judgment in New Jersey. The court, citing *Maalouf*, maintained, at para 6:

The defence argument, taken to its logical conclusion, is not without its irony because, presumably, implicit in the *Gaming Act* argument is the principle that the courts will not enforce a contract the moral foundation of which is dubious. The irony lies in the fact that an Ontario citizen could incur foreign debt, legally enforceable in that foreign jurisdiction, without the slightest intention of honouring that debt; rank dishonesty by any standard. Such an Ontario resident could then return to Ontario and, under the umbrella of the *Gaming Act*, crave the indulgence of the court in circumstances where the would-be beneficiary of the Act so much more richly deserves the court's contempt. Should such a refuge be found in the courts, a right-thinking citizen may well conclude that the *Gaming Act* had served to spawn an evil more heinous than the one, ostensibly, it was intended to guard against.

2. In *Di Manno Estate v Valenzisi*, 2007 CanLII 57463 (Ont Sup Ct J), the court refused to aid a plaintiff in various complaints against the defendant because the complaints related to a café business run by the parties in conjunction with an illegal gambling club that provided about 50 percent of the income from the business. However, the plaintiff was awarded damages for property unrelated to the gaming establishment that had been unlawfully removed by the defendant from the premises.

C. CONTRACTS IN FURTHERANCE OF ILLEGAL PURPOSES

ZIMMERMANN V LETKEMAN
[1978] 1 SCR 1097 (footnotes omitted)

[The parties entered into an agreement under which Mr. Letkeman was to purchase Mr. Zimmermann's property for a price of $135,000. By a document signed contemporaneously with this agreement, the parties also agreed that the purchase price of the first agreement was a nullity and the actual price to be paid was $117,500. The purpose of the two agreements was so that the purchaser could represent to the mortgage company that the purchase price was higher than it actually was, thus enabling him to obtain a larger mortgage than he would otherwise have been able to secure. The representative of the mortgage company testified at trial that he was aware of the true purchase price. Before the conveyance was completed, the vendor, Mr. Zimmermann, withdrew from the deal, having received legal advice that the two documents could constitute a fraud on the mortgage company. The purchaser then sued for specific performance. At trial, the court held that the transaction was illegal and denied the claim. The Court of Appeal reversed the trial judgment. After reviewing the facts, Martland J continued:]

MARTLAND J: ...
    The majority of the Court of Appeal held that the appeal of the respondent should be allowed on two grounds. The first ground was that the case was within the principles enunciated by Anglin J., as he then was, in *Elford v. Elford*.
    In that case a husband had put land into his wife's name, with her knowledge, for the purpose of defeating his creditors. He held a general power of attorney from her. A quarrel having occurred between them, the husband registered the power of attorney and proceeded to transfer title to the land into his own name. The wife sued to have the title re-transferred into her name.
    It was held that the wife was entitled to have the transfer set aside. The wide general authority conferred by the power of attorney did not embrace the power to execute a conveyance in favour of the agent himself. *Prima facie*, the wife was entitled to have the husband declared a trustee for her. The husband could not display that right by alleging that her title was acquired in pursuance of his unlawful design to defeat his creditors.
    The passage from the judgment of Anglin J., relied upon by the majority of the Court of Appeal, appears at p. 129, as follows:

In order to succeed the plaintiff merely requires to establish that in executing the transfer to himself of the property in question, which stood registered in her name, her husband committed a fraud on the power of attorney from her under which he professed to act. She does not have to disclose the alleged intent to defraud her husband's creditors in which her own title to the land is said to have originated, or to invoke any of the transactions tainted by that fraud. *Simpson v. Bloss* (1816) 7 Taunt, 246; *Taylor v. Chester* (1869) L.R. 4 Q.B. 309, at p. 314; *Clark v. Hagar* (1893) 22 Can. S.C.R. 510, at p. 525; 20 Ont. App. R. 198, at pp. 221-2. It is the defendant who brings that aspect of the matter before the court in his effort to retain the fruits of his abuse of his position as his wife's attorney; and to him the maxim applies *memo allegans turpitudinem suam est audiendus.* *Montefiori v. Montefiori* (1762) 1 W. Bl. 363.

After citing this passage, the Court of Appeal went on to say:

In order to succeed here the plaintiff was merely required to establish that the documents executed by the parties constituted the contract between the parties. In order to do so he needed only to produce such documents and prove the execution thereof by himself and the defendant. In the present case this presented no difficulty as the defendant admitted in his statement of defence the execution of the documents and did not suggest that they did not constitute the contract between the parties. It is apparent that the defendant alone invoked the suggestion of illegality in order to avoid his obligation under the contract.

With respect, this statement fails to take account of the fact that in the present case it is the respondent purchaser who is seeking to enforce the contract which is tainted with illegality. His position is akin to the position, not of the wife, but of the husband in the *Elford* case.

The fact that the documents on their face did not disclose the respondent's unlawful purpose, which was disclosed by the evidence, does not improve his position. He is still in the position of seeking to enforce an illegal contract. This point is well made by Gwynne J. in the case of *Clark v. Hagar, supra,* mentioned by Anglin J. At p. 525 Gwynne J. said this:

What is meant in this case, and in all cases as to the application of the test is, that in every case, whether in *indebitatus assumpsit* or in an action upon a bond, note or other instrument, it appears either by admission on the pleadings, or in the evidence given upon the issues joined upon the pleadings in the case, that the action is connected with an illegal transaction to which the plaintiff was a party, the question arises whether he can or cannot succeed in his action without relying upon the illegal transaction. If he cannot, the action fails; if he can, it prevails. But it never has been held, nor so far as I have been able to find hitherto contended, that in an action upon a note or other instrument in security for money requiring *prima facie* no evidence of consideration the plaintiff is entitled to recover upon the mere production of the instrument, notwithstanding that the defence is that the instrument sued upon was executed for an illegal consideration in respect of a transaction to which the defendant was himself a party. Such a proposition could not be maintained without reversing a legion of cases from *Guichard v. Roberts*, 1 Wm. Black, 445, down to *Windhill Board of Health v. Vint*, 45 Ch. D. 351, which establish that illegality in the consideration of an instrument, whether under seal or not, to enforce which an action is brought, not only may be pleaded, but if it does not appear upon the plaintiff's own pleading must be pleaded.

In the present case, in order to succeed in his suit for specific performance, the respondent had to rely upon the illegal contract. The wife, in the *Elford* case, had acquired title to the land. She was seeking to set aside a conveyance of her land by her husband founded on an improper purported exercise of his power of attorney. She did not have to rely upon an illegal contract.

The second ground stated by the majority of the Court of Appeal was that as the respondent had abandoned his intention of relying upon the first document in order to obtain a larger loan, the law would allow him a *locus poenitentiae*. Reliance was placed on the statement of Mellish L.J., in *Taylor v. Bowers* [(1876), 1 QBD 291], at p. 300:

> ... If money is paid or goods delivered for an illegal purpose, the person who had so paid the money or delivered goods may recover them back before the illegal purpose is carried out; but if he waits till the illegal purpose is carried out, or if he seeks to enforce the illegal transaction, in neither case can he maintain an action; the law will not allow that to be done.

As this passage indicates, the rule as to *locus poenitentiae* is applicable to enable a party to an illegal contract, which is still executory, to recover what he has paid or transferred to his co-contractor, pursuant to the contract, provided he repents in time before the illegal purpose has been substantially performed. The only payment made by the respondent to the appellant was the deposit of $1,000, which the appellant returned to the respondent. The respondent in these proceedings is not seeking from the appellant the return of anything. He is seeking to enforce a contract of sale and purchase, tainted with illegality, on the basis that the intended deception of Credit Foncier was not carried through. In my opinion the doctrine of *locus poenitentiae* has no application in favour of the respondent in the circumstances of this case. In fact it was the appellant who repented of the transaction, returned the respondent's deposit and refused to proceed with the transaction.

In my opinion the grounds relied upon by the majority of the Court of Appeal were insufficient to justify their allowing the appeal from the judgment at trial. I agree with the dissenting reasons of Bayda J.A., that the trial judge correctly applied the principle stated in *Alexander v. Rayson* in the circumstances of this case.

I would allow the appeal, set aside the judgment of the Court of Appeal, and restore the judgment at trial.

NOTE

In *Alexander v Rayson*, [1936] 1 KB 169 (CA) (relied on in *Zimmermann*, above), the Court of Appeal refused to enforce a lease where the parties signed two documents, one stating a much lower rent than the other, with the intent to deceive the Westminster City Council as to the true rateable value of the premises. Similarly, in *Stevens Pools Ltd v Carlsen*, 2015 BCPC 23, a $50,000 pool purchase was documented in two contracts, one for a contract price of $35,000 and the other in an addendum, for $15,000 to be payable in cash. The court found that the only purpose to arrange their dealings as such was to ensure taxes would not be payable on the $15,000 "under the table" payment. Finding it to be an "immoral" and illegal contract, and therefore presumptively unenforceable, the court went on to examine whether the presumption against enforceability could yield under one of the exceptions, namely if the contract had not yet been executed and one party "repented," or where the parties were not equally culpable for the wrong. Finding neither exception to apply, nor any way to sever the unenforceable bargain from the rest of the contract, the court determined the agreement to be unenforceable.

D. CONTRACTS CONFERRING BENEFITS OBTAINED AS A RESULT OF CRIME

BRISSETTE ESTATE V WESTBURY LIFE INSURANCE CO; BRISSETTE ESTATE V CROWN LIFE INSURANCE CO
[1992] 3 SCR 87

[A married couple took out a life insurance policy in which both were named as "the insured." The terms of the policy provided that, upon the death of one, the insurance proceeds would be paid to the survivor. The husband murdered his wife. The husband brought a claim, seeking to be paid the proceeds of his wife's life insurance policy, and alleged that if he was not personally entitled to the proceeds, then the estate of his deceased wife was entitled to them. Once he had been convicted of her murder, the husband surrendered any rights he had had under the policy. However, the estate of the deceased wife claimed entitlement to the proceeds of insurance and prior to her death, the wife had appointed her husband as the primary beneficiary of her estate.]

SOPINKA J: ... The contract in this case is not reasonably capable of the interpretation contended for by the appellant. It cannot be construed to require payment to the estate of Mary Brissette.

• • •

Moreover, there is nothing ambiguous about the wording of the contract. The money is to be paid to the survivor. The problem is that something has occurred that the parties neither contemplated nor provided for. The survivor acceded to this status by killing the other party. Public policy prevents the money from being paid in accordance with the explicit terms of the contract. These terms cannot simply be rewritten under the guise of interpretation. The resort to a constructive trust to achieve the result contended for by the appellant is an acknowledgement that this is so. A constructive trust is ordinarily resorted to when the application for other accepted legal principles would produce a result that is unjust and that would not be countenanced by a court applying the principles of equity. The question, therefore, is not one of interpretation but whether the result of the application of the rules of interpretation are unjust so as to require the court to employ a constructive trust and whether it can do so in accordance with the applicable principles of equity. ...

In order to determine whether, as a matter of public policy, the Court should resort to the device of a constructive trust, it is appropriate to consider whether the application of public policy which denies payment to the felonious beneficiary would work an injustice if recovery is denied to the appellants. After all, it is this policy that prevents the contract from taking effect in accordance with its terms. If denial of recovery by the estate is not inconsistent with this policy, then there is no misuse of public policy which would warrant a conclusion that its application is unjust.

The results reached in *Demeter v. Dominion Life Assurance Co.* (1982), 35 O.R. (2d) 560 and *Cleaver v. Mutual Reserve Fund Life Association*, [1892] 1 Q.B. 147 define the parameters of the application of this public policy. In *Demeter* the assured took out an insurance policy on his wife's life naming himself as beneficiary. He then arranged for her murder. Although the claim for the proceeds of insurance was made by the daughter of the deceased wife, the court made it clear that it would have been equally consistent with public policy to deny recover to the wife's estate. MacKinnon A.C.J.O. concluded as follows (at p. 562):

We are in agreement with the Motions Court judge that the life insured had no interest in the policy, legal or equitable, which vested in her estate. In our view it could be stretching equitable principles beyond recognizable limits to grant either the infant plaintiff or her mother's estate an equitable interest in the policies and the proceeds of those policies.

The rationale of the policy which denies recovery to the felonious beneficiary is that a person should not profit from his or her own criminal act. It is consistent with this policy that a person should not be allowed to insure against his or her own criminal act irrespective of the ultimate payee of the proceeds. Denial of recovery in *Demeter* to either the daughter or the wife's estate would have been consistent with public policy. There was nothing unjust about such a result calling for the special assistance of equitable principles.

On the other hand, in *Cleaver* the insured took out an insurance policy on his own life with his wife as beneficiary. The wife-beneficiary who murdered the insured-husband was not a party to the contract of insurance. By virtue of the *Married Women's Property Act, 1882* (U.K.), the moneys were payable to the estate of the insured to be held in trust for the beneficiary. Public policy stepped in to deny payment to the wife-beneficiary leaving the insurance moneys in the estate. Public policy was not allowed to abrogate a right that the estate had by virtue of the statute. The principles of equity were not resorted to in order to remedy a perceived injustice.

The contract of insurance in this case is not identical to the contract in either *Demeter* or *Cleaver*. It is necessary, therefore, to examine the whole of the contract in order to determine whether in its essential features it more closely resembles one or the other of the contracts in those cases so as to attract the policy underlying that decision. After review of the contract of insurance in this case, I am of the opinion that it cannot be viewed as two separate contracts with each of Gerald and Mary insuring their own lives with the other as beneficiary so as to resemble the policy in *Cleaver*. The contract lists the two of them together as the "insured" and provides for payment to "the beneficiary" who is defined as "the survivor." ...

On this basis, the result reached in *Demeter* is appropriate in this case. There is nothing unjust in refusing to pay the proceeds of insurance to a beneficiary not designated by the insurance contract when to do so would allow the insured to insure against his own criminal act. Moreover, even if the contract of insurance can be characterized as two separate contracts, as submitted by the appellants, so as to resemble the contract in *Cleaver*, the result in *Cleaver* cannot be achieved in the absence of a provision, statutory or in the contract, providing for payment to the estate of the wife. Such a result can only be attained by invoking the equitable principle of a constructive trust. Those principles should only be invoked to cure an unjust application of public policy. There is nothing unjust about the application of that public policy in this case.

But, even if I had concluded that the denial of recovery to the estate was inconsistent with public policy, in my opinion it would be contrary to established principles of equity to employ a constructive trust in this case. A constructive trust will ordinarily be imposed on property in the hands of a wrongdoer to prevent him or her from being unjustly enriched by profiting from his or her own wrongful conduct.

• • •

In this case, no claim of unjust enrichment has been made out. It cannot be said that but for Gerald's act, Mary's estate would have recovered the money. The wrongdoer does not benefit from his own wrong, nor is the insurer in breach of its duty to Mary. It is simply complying with the express terms of the contract. Moreover, there is no property in the hands of the wrongdoer upon which a trust can be fastened.

642

By virtue of public policy the provision for payment in the insurance policy is unenforceable and no money is payable to the wrongdoer. The effect of a constructive trust would be to first require payment to the wrongdoer and then impress the money with a trust in favour of the estate. A constructive trust cannot be used to bring property into existence by determining the liability of the insurer to pay. The situation would be different, if, as in *Cleaver*, the insurance money were payable to the estate to be held in trust for the beneficiary. Public policy would step in to prevent the execution of the trust leaving the proceeds in the hands of the estate. But where, as here, there is no provision for payment to the estate, a constructive trust cannot be used to rewrite the contract which clearly and explicitly provides that the insured "agrees to pay the Sum Insured at its Head Office to the beneficiary."

NOTES AND QUESTIONS

1. Cory and Gonthier JJ dissented. First, they pointed out that the contract of insurance did not have an exempting clause for this type of death for one of the insureds, but did have one for suicide. An ambiguity of this type would be construed against the insurance company, since it drafts the standard form contract. Second, they maintained that principles of public policy applied to prevent the husband from benefiting from his crime. However, they went on to note that those same principles of public policy should not operate to benefit the insurance company, which would happen if the insurance company were permitted to avoid paying its contractual obligations. Third, in order for the insurer to not benefit by virtue of the application of the doctrine of public policy, Cory and Gonthier JJ maintained that the survivor must hold those funds in trust for the administrator of the wife's estate. Doing so "ensures the performance of the contract in compliance with the real intent of the parties" (para 69). Since the wife was the co-owner of the insurance policy, she had both a legal and beneficial interest to the insurance proceeds, an interest upon which her estate could assert its right to the policy.

2. Would an insured likely think that there was a major difference between a contract of insurance with proceeds paid to the deceased's estate in trust for the heirs of the deceased and a contract explicitly naming the person likely to be the insured's chief heir?

3. The majority view was that payment to the estate of the deceased would allow the murderer to insure against his own conduct. Is there any policy objection to requiring the payment to be made to the husband, but requiring him to hold it in trust for the deceased's estate? Who is the beneficiary of the majority decision?

4. A later decision of the Supreme Court of Canada, *Oldfield v Transamerica Life Insurance Co of Canada*, 2002 SCC 22, [2002] 1 SCR 742, recognized the arbitrary nature of this decision. However, the court considered that reform ought to be left to the legislature. Compare *Brissette* with the decision excerpted below.

OLDFIELD V TRANSAMERICA LIFE INSURANCE CO OF CANADA
2002 SCC 22, [2002] 1 SCR 742

[Maria Oldfield was claiming the proceeds of a life insurance policy under which she was the named beneficiary. The policy was taken out by her husband as part of their separation agreement, which required him to maintain insurance with her as the named beneficiary until their two children became 18 years old. The insured, Paul Oldfield, died in Bolivia from a heart attack when one of 30 condoms in his stomach containing cocaine burst. It was not contested that Paul Oldfield's actions were contrary to both Bolivian and Canadian law. The insurer refused to pay on public policy grounds.

The Ontario Court of Appeal upheld Maria Oldfield's entitlement to payment. After stating the facts, Major J continued:]

MAJOR J (McLachlin CJ and Gonthier, Iacobucci, Bastarache, Binnie, Arbour, and LeBel JJ concurring): ...

The public policy rule at issue is that a criminal should not be permitted to profit from crime. Unless modified by statute, public policy operates independently of the rules of contract. For example, courts will not permit a husband who kills his spouse to obtain her life insurance proceeds, regardless of the manner in which the life insurance contract was worded. As Ferguson J. held in the court below, public policy "applies regardless of the policy wording—it is imposed because of the courts' view of social values" (p. 119).

Generally, though, an insurer seeks the shelter of public policy rules because they have failed to specifically provide for the contingency that gives rise to the dispute. In the present appeal, the insurance policy did not provide for the result that would occur if the insured died while committing a criminal act. If the policy specifically excluded coverage, there would be no need to resort to public policy.

The public policy rule that prevents criminals from profiting from crime has existed for many years.

[The court reviewed authority from England and Canada to this effect and continued:]

In *Brissette Estate v. Westbury Life Insurance Co.*, [1992] 3 S.C.R. 87, Sopinka J. held that "a person should not be allowed to insure against his or her own criminal act irrespective of the ultimate payee of the proceeds" (p. 94).

The rule extends to those who claim through the criminal's estate. In *Cleaver*, Fry L.J. held that "the rule of public policy should be applied so as to exclude from benefit the criminal *and all claiming under her*" (p. 159 (emphasis added)). Technically, the reason why no distinction is drawn between the criminal and his or her estate is that the estate's claim is equivalent to a claim brought by the criminal. ...

However, innocent beneficiaries are neither criminals nor claim through the criminal's estate. Because of that, the public policy rule is inapplicable. Section 195 of Ontario's *Insurance Act*, R.S.O. 1990, c. I.8, states that "[a] beneficiary may enforce for the beneficiary's own benefit ... the payment of insurance money made payable to him, her or it in the contract ... ." In *Kerslake v. Gray*, [1957] S.C.R. 516, the Court held that insurance money paid to an ordinary beneficiary does not form part of the insured's estate. In Borins J.A.'s words, Maria Oldfield "has not asserted her right to the insurance proceeds as a successor of the insured, but as an ordinary beneficiary, with the result that her claim is not tainted by any illegality on the part of her husband" (p. 748). ...

In total, Sopinka J.'s decision in *Brissette* demonstrated that he did not intend to displace the principle that innocent beneficiaries who do not take through the criminal's estate should not be affected by public policy. In *Brissette*, Sopinka J. held that "[t]here is nothing unjust in refusing to pay the proceeds of insurance to a beneficiary *not designated by the insurance contract* when to do so would allow the insured to insure against his own criminal act" (p. 95 (emphasis added)). ...

A universal rule that "a person should not be allowed to insure against his or her own criminal act irrespective of the ultimate payee of the proceeds" would have serious repercussions for bona fide creditors who provide value to obtain an interest in life insurance. Creditors in numerous instances such as a mortgage and other debt instruments will insist on obtaining an assignment of an insurance policy or being the named beneficiary sufficient to discharge the debt to protect their interest in the event of the debtor dying insolvent. ...

In *Brissette*, Sopinka J. did not intend to eliminate long-established exceptions to the public policy rule. *Brissette* does not bar a claim by an innocent beneficiary where the insured does not intend the insured loss. ...

(6) RATIONALE FOR THE PUBLIC POLICY RULE

Two reasons have been advanced to support the public policy rule. One is that to enforce certain illegal contracts would "take away one of those restraints operating on the minds of men against the commission of crimes, namely, the interest we have in the welfare and prosperity of our connections" (*Amicable Society v. Bolland*, [1824-34] All E.R. Rep. 570 (1830) (H.L.) ("*Fauntleroy's Case*"), at p. 572). ...

Over time, courts have criticized the idea that a less than strict application of public policy would encourage crime. In *Hardy* ... [*v Motor Insurers' Bureau*, [1964] 2 QB 745], Diplock L.J. held (at p. 770):

> It seems to me to be slightly unrealistic to suggest that a person who is not deterred by the risk of a possible sentence of life imprisonment from using a vehicle with intent to commit grievous bodily harm would be deterred by the fear that his civil liability to his victim would not be discharged by his insurers. I do not myself feel that by dismissing this appeal we shall add significantly to the statistics of crime.

... The second reason for the public policy rule simply recognizes that a court will not permit injustice. ...

It is consistent with justice that innocent beneficiaries not be disentitled to insurance proceeds merely because an insured accidentally dies while committing a criminal act. Many decisions have recognized the long-standing principle (see e.g. *Cleaver*, at pp. 159-60). To deny recovery would penalize the victim for the insured's anti-social behaviour (C. Brown, *Insurance Law in Canada* (loose-leaf ed.), vol. 1, at pp. 8-28 to 8-29). ...

(8) IS THERE A NEED TO REFORM THE PUBLIC POLICY RULE?

For the purposes of the present appeal, it is sufficient to conclude that an innocent beneficiary named in an insurance policy should not be disentitled to insurance proceeds where the insured dies while committing a criminal act and does not intend the loss. Public policy does not bar Maria Oldfield's claim.

Nevertheless, the distinction between an innocent beneficiary and those who claim through the criminal's estate should be considered. Public policy has consistently refused to permit the criminal or those who claim through the criminal to obtain insurance proceeds. Those who claim through the criminal are denied, while innocent beneficiaries named in the policy are not. Ferguson J. noted and I agree that the distinction seems arbitrary. As he held, "it is difficult to explain why a criminal can benefit his family by naming them as beneficiaries in an insurance policy but not by naming them in his will" (p. 128). That there is an arbitrary distinction suggests the need to loosen the public policy rule rather than restrict it. ...

It might be appropriate to modify the public policy rule so as to permit an innocent person who claims through the criminal's estate to take insurance proceeds. Indeed, in *Hardy*, Diplock L.J. thought that the public policy rule could be modified to permit the criminal to take insurance proceeds, depending on "the nature of the anti-social act" and "the nature of the right asserted" (p. 768). Under England's *Forfeiture Act 1982*, courts can modify the effect of the forfeiture rule even where a person who has unlawfully killed another seeks to acquire a benefit in consequence of the killing. I leave the question to be decided either by the legislature or in another case where the issue arises.

III. CONCLUSION

In conclusion, public policy does not apply to bar a claim by an innocent beneficiary named in an insurance policy merely because the insured dies while committing a crime. Maria Oldfield's claim is not barred by public policy or by any rule of contractual interpretation.

[The separate, but concurring, opinion of L'Heureux-Dubé J is omitted.]

NOTES AND QUESTIONS

1.   The common law principle has been expanded by statute in some provinces to include a situation where the criminal seeks to make a profit from his or her criminal activity after the crime has been committed—for example, by publishing a book about his or her experiences. See *The Profits of Criminal Notoriety Act*, CCSM c P141 and SS 2009, c P-28.1. How far should this principle extend?

2.   The public policy rule that a criminal should not be allowed to profit from crime does not extend to situations in which a person is found not criminally responsible as a result of having a mental disorder at the time of the crime. See *Nordstrom v Baumann*, [1962] SCR 147 and *Re Dreger* (1976), 12 OR (2d) 371 (H Ct J).

IV. CONTRACTS CONTRARY TO PUBLIC POLICY EXPRESSED IN STATUTE

In *Boardwalk Regency Corp v Maalouf*, the court gave a statute, although not directly applicable in the circumstances, considerable weight in determining whether a contract should be considered unenforceable as contrary to public policy. See also *In the Matter of Baby "M,"* above. In many modern cases, the problem stems from a contract that is made in contravention of a statute. The wide range of statutory prohibition and regulation in modern society raises a variety of difficult questions. The first issue is whether the contract is illegal. But, given a finding of illegality, even more complex is the issue of what the result should be. The next cases deal with contracts that are illegal because they are contrary to public policy expressed in statute. In Section V, "Mitigating the Consequences of Illegality," we turn to the complex issues surrounding the results of that illegality.

A. WHEN A CONTRACT IS RENDERED VOID BY STATUTE

KINGSHOT V BRUNSKILL
[1953] OWN 133 (CA)

ROACH JA (for the court): The facts of this case are simple but it raises an important question under *The Farm Products Grades and Sales Act*, R.S.O. 1950, c. 130, and the regulations passed thereunder.

The plaintiff operates a fruit and market garden on 34 acres of land in the county of Peel. On that land he has a small apple orchard. He is not a large producer of apples and his main income is derived from the operation of greenhouses. In the fall of

1950 he had harvested his apple crop and the apples were stored on his premises. Among these apples were 846 bushels of Spy and Delicious apples. They were in bushel baskets. No effort had been made by him to grade or sort them, although there was no mixture of the two varieties in any basket. In harvesting the apples the plaintiff had taken the empty baskets and marked some of them "Fancy Delicious" and the others of them "Fancy Grade Spies." It was stated in evidence that the usual practice is to mark the baskets or hampers with the name and quality of the variety which the producer intends, after grading, that those hampers shall contain. The hampers were then sent out to the orchard and the apples were picked from the tree and placed in the appropriate hampers. The plaintiff had no intention of offering those apples for sale to the public until they were first graded in compliance with the regulations passed under the Act.

The defendant resides on land about one mile from the plaintiff's premises. His main business is the growing and marketing of apples and purchasing apples from other apple growers, grading them and marketing them.

On 14th December the defendant came to the plaintiff's premises and inquired whether or not the plaintiff would sell his Spy apples. The plaintiff replied that he would not sell the Delicious and Spies separately and that if he sold them he wanted to sell the whole lot. It was apparent to the defendant that the apples had not been graded. After some preliminary discussion, the defendant entered into a contract with the plaintiff to purchase the apples at $1.10 per bushel and paid the plaintiff a deposit of $25. As the learned trial judge said in his reasons there was no warranty, express or implied. The defendant inspected the apples and simply bought what he saw in the premises where they were stored. Under the terms of the contract it was the defendant's obligation to remove the apples. From time to time he removed quantities of them to his own premises, graded them and sold them. By April, 1951 there were still some hampers of apples which the defendant had not yet removed. The plaintiff requested the defendant to remove them because he needed the space, and when the defendant delayed removing them the plaintiff sent them over to the defendant's premises. During the course of the removal by the defendant he paid the plaintiff on account the further sum of $200. When the last of the apples had been delivered by the plaintiff to the defendant, the defendant called an inspector appointed under the regulations and the inspector marked the last consignment of delivery with a detention order, as he was permitted to do under the regulations. Notice of that detention order was given to the plaintiff. The defendant, alleging that of the total quantity of apples received by him there were certain defective apples, computed the balance that he owed to the plaintiff and sent him a cheque for $619.80, being the amount which the defendant considered represented the balance owing by him. This cheque was marked "in full payment for apples." This cheque was not accepted by the plaintiff but was returned to the defendant. The plaintiff thereupon sued the defendant for the sum of $719.60, which sum was made up of $705.60, being the balance owing for the apples, plus $14.00 being the value of hampers which the defendant had not returned to the plaintiff.

The defendant pleaded that the apples had not been graded, packed or marked in accordance with *The Farm Products Grades and Sales Act* and the regulations passed thereunder and in particular, regulation 3(a), (c), (d), (f) and (g), and that the sale of the apples was thereby prohibited by statute and illegal. The learned trial judge gave effect to that plea and it is with some regret that I feel myself constrained to agree with that decision.

Section 2(1) of the statute authorizes the Minister of Agriculture, subject to the approval of the Lieutenant-Governor in Council, to make certain regulations respecting farm products as defined in the statute. Farm products as there defined include fruit. The regulations that the Minister may make as aforesaid include regulations

(a) establishing grades and classes for any farm product;

(b) providing for the inspection, grading, packages and packing, marketing, handling, shipping, transporting, advertising, purchasing and selling of farm products within Ontario.

Pursuant to the authority contained in the statute, regulations were made and they are known as Regulations 87 (1 C.R.O. 1950, p. 431). Regulation 3 thereof provides in part as follows:

No person shall pack, transport, ship, advertise, sell, offer for sale or have in possession for sale any produce

(a) unless the produce has been graded, packed and marked in accordance with the provisions of the Act and these regulations;

(b) which is below the minimum grade for the produce but this provision shall not apply to produce for an establishment [establishment is defined in Regulation 1 as including any plant, factory or premises where produce is canned, preserved or otherwise processed];

(c) where the faced or shown surface falsely represents the contents;

(d) in a package unless the package is properly filled and packed; ...

(f) in a package which has been previously marked unless the marks are completely removed;

(g) which is so immature or so diseased or otherwise affected as to be unfit for human consumption.

By s. 8 of the statute every person who contravenes any of the provisions of the Act or the regulations is guilty of an offence and liable on summary conviction to the penalties therein set out.

It must be concluded that the main object of the statute and the regulations passed thereunder is the protection of the public. The penalty authorized by the statute is imposed wholly for the protection of the public. Therefore, if the sale here in question was forbidden by the regulations, then it was illegal and notwithstanding that the defendant resold the apples after having graded them and made a profit thereby, the plaintiff cannot recover in an action for the price of those apples. Reference may be made to *Anderson, Limited v. Daniel*, [1924] 1 K.B. 183, and *Little v. Poole* (1829), 9 B. & C. 192.

I have looked in vain for any provision in the regulations that would exempt the plaintiff in the circumstances of this case from their application. It is not difficult to conceive a case in which a farmer who has a small orchard on his farm may have neither the manpower nor the equipment necessary to grade and pack the product of his orchard, in accordance with the regulations. His neighbour, with a much larger orchard and specializing in the growing of fruit, has the necessary help and equipment for the grading and packing of the produce not only of his own orchard but of others in the neighbourhood. It would seem not unreasonable that the first of those two farmers should be permitted to sell his whole crop of fruit to the second of those two farmers, who, having the necessary help and equipment, could grade it and pack it in accordance with the regulations before offering it for sale to the public. The regulations, however, do not appear to provide for such a case. There is no provision in the regulations that would exempt the first of those two farmers in that hypothetical case from compliance with the regulations. The Court cannot read into the regulations exemptions which might appear to the Court to be justifiable in a given set of circumstances.

For these reasons the appeal must be dismissed with costs.

QUESTION ON LEGAL METHOD

The court's interpretation of the Act and regulations is obviously possible; however, is it a necessary one? Consider *Still v MNR* (below) and the following case.

DOHERTY V SOUTHGATE (TOWNSHIP)
(2006), 214 OAC 30, 271 DLR (4th) 59 (CA)

[The appellant, the Corporation of the Township of Southgate ("Southgate"), entered into a contract with a developer (Doherty) for sale of a piece of property it had decided was surplus. Section 268(3) of the *Municipal Act of Ontario*, SO 2001, c 25 provided that a municipality had to meet certain conditions prior to selling land. It had to have a bylaw setting out procedures for the sale, and the bylaw also had to provide notice to the public. Southgate passed such a bylaw, but did not give the required public notice prior to entering into the contract with Doherty. The contract stipulated that Southgate would rezone the land prior to the sale closing. Southgate failed to fulfill this condition and the sale did not close. Doherty sued Southgate for breach of contract. Southgate moved for summary judgment, arguing that the contract was void because public notice as required by the town bylaw and the *Municipal Act* had not been given. The motions judge allowed Doherty to proceed with an action for damages and Southgate appealed. After finding that the Act required public notice to be given prior to entering into the contract of sale, the court proceeded as follows:]

O'CONNOR ACJO: That then brings me to the second question: Did Southgate's failure to give that notice render the agreement of purchase and sale void and unenforceable?

In my view, the answer to that question is in the negative. Not every statutory breach results in a contract being void or unenforceable. The decision of this court in *Beer v. Townsgate I* (1997), 36 O.R. (3d) 136, is instructive.

In *Beer*, a developer of residential condominiums entered into a number of agreements of purchase and sale when it was not registered under the Ontario New Home Warranty Program in contravention of s. 6 of the *Ontario New Home Warranties Plan Act*. The developer had applied for registration and was subsequently granted registration. The purchasers were at all times protected under the Act. This court rejected an argument that the agreements of purchase and sale were void and unenforceable because of the breach of the statute at the time they were executed. At page 144, Brooke J.A., for the court, said:

> I think it is significant that while the Act provides for a financial penalty for a breach of s. 6 it does not expressly provide that the contract so made is unenforceable. If a statute does not expressly deprive a party of his or her rights under the contract, the question is whether, having regard to the purpose of the Act, and the circumstances under which the contract was made, and to be performed, it would be contrary to public policy to enforce it because of illegality: see the judgment of Devlin L.J. in *St. John Shipping Corp. v. Joseph Rank Ltd.*, [1956] 3 All E.R. 683 at p. 690, [1957] 1 Q.B. 267 (Q.B.).

On the same page, Brooke J.A. continued:

> As Waddams notes in *The Law of Contracts*, 3rd ed. (1993), at p. 381:
>
> > If every statutory illegality, however trivial, in the course of performance of a contract, invalidated the agreement, the result would be an unjust and haphazard allocation of loss without regard to any rational principles.
>
> I think public policy favours that contracts should not be rendered unenforceable merely because of technical deficiencies.

There are three reasons why I consider that it would not be contrary to public policy to conclude that the agreement of purchase and sale in this case was not rendered void or unenforceable as a result of the non-compliance with s. 268(3)(c) of the *Municipal Act*.

First, as was the case in *Beer*, there is nothing in the statute under consideration, here the *Municipal Act*, expressly providing that a contract made in contravention of s. 268(3), is unenforceable.

Second, there is nothing in the record to suggest that giving notice to the public of the proposed sale of the property to Doherty would have resulted in any different outcome. No one, including Southgate, has suggested that the property was not surplus to the needs of the municipality. On the contrary, Southgate has passed a resolution declaring it to be surplus. Nor is there any suggestion that the sale price in the agreement of purchase and sale was in any way improvident. Significantly, by the time Doherty agreed to buy the property, it had been on the market for close to a year. The sale price was 72 percent of the value estimated by Southgate's realtor and Southgate does not now take the position that it could have obtained any higher price. On two occasions, Southgate's council approved the sale and no ratepayers have challenged the sale. Thus, it appears that even if Southgate had given notice to the public of the proposed sale, it would have ended up selling the property to Doherty on exactly the same terms as are in the agreement of purchase and sale.

Third, Southgate's position in this litigation with respect to the public notice is a disingenuous attempt to take advantage of its own failure. Significantly, Southgate's decision not to complete the sale on March 5, 2004 was based on its unwillingness to proceed with the zoning amendment called for in the agreement of purchase and sale and not on the fact that it had not given the public notice required by s. 268(3)(c). Indeed, had Southgate taken that position prior to closing, it is fair to conclude that Doherty would have agreed to an extension of the closing date, if necessary, to permit such notice to be given. While s. 268(3)(c) requires notice to the public before the municipality enters into an agreement to sell land, giving notice after the agreement was executed would still have provided an opportunity for the public to register any objections. As I have said, I do not think that in this case it would have made any difference. Be that as it may, Southgate did not raise the notice issue as a reason for not closing and first raised it in its statement of defence in an attempt to extricate itself from an action for breach of contract.

While it may be said that Doherty should have been aware of Southgate's obligation to give notice and its failure to do so, there is no evidence to suggest that he did not act in good faith throughout. Doherty, through his lawyer, took steps necessary to prepare for a closing of the sale and Southgate's actions would have led him to believe that Southgate had fulfilled all of the statutory requirements necessary to complete the transaction.

In summary, I am satisfied that it would not be against public policy to hold that the agreement of purchase and sale in this case was not rendered void and unenforceable by the breach of the statute by Southgate. Accordingly, I am satisfied that the motion judge did not err in making a declaration to that effect.

B. A COMMON INTENT TO PERFORM A CONTRACT ILLEGALLY

ASHMORE, BENSON, PEASE & CO LTD V AV DAWSON LTD
[1973] 1 WLR 828 (CA)

LORD DENNING MR: In February, 1967 a big piece of engineering equipment called a tube bank was being carried from Stockton-on-Tees to Hull where it was to be shipped to Poland. It was very heavy. It weighed 25 tons. It was loaded on an articulated lorry. Halfway to Hull that lorry with its load tipped over. Damage was done to the load. It cost £2,225 to repair. The manufacturers claim damages from the hauliers. In answer the hauliers plead that the load was too heavy for the vehicle: and that the contract of carriage, or the performance of it, was illegal.

The relevant regulations are the Motor Vehicles (Construction and Use) Regulations 1966 (S.I. 1966 No. 1288). They were made by virtue of the Road Traffic Act 1960, section 64. Subsection (2) of section 64 says: "... [I]t shall not be lawful to use on a road a motor vehicle or trailer which does not comply with any such regulations as aforesaid. ..."

In the present case the vehicle was an articulated vehicle with a tractor and trailer. Under regulation 73(2) the maximum weight laden was specified as 30 tons. Now the unladen weight of the vehicle was 10 tons. This load (consisting of the tube bank) was 25 tons. So the total weight laden was 35 tons. So it was five tons over the regulation weight. Furthermore, the tube bank was top heavy. It had fittings on the top which made its centre of gravity high. Not only was it in breach of the regulations, but it was a dangerous and unsafe load to be carried on this vehicle along the roads of England. The evidence showed clearly that the only vehicle suitable for this load was a "low loader," which is underslung so that it can take heavier weights and bigger loads. So the expedition was certainly illegal.

I turn now to consider the contract of carriage. The makers of the tube bank were Ashmore, Benson, Pease & Co. Ltd. of Stockton-on-Tees. Their transport manager was a Mr. Bulmer. His assistant was Mr. Jones. Two of these tube banks were to be sent from the works at Stockton-on-Tees to the port of Hull. Mr. Bulmer told Mr. Jones to arrange for the carriage of the two tube banks and to give the work to A.V. Dawson Ltd. That was a small firm in which the principals were Mr. Arthur Vernon Dawson, the father, and Mr. Maurice Dawson, the son. This firm had 10 articulated vehicles. The biggest of them was only a 30 tonner. They had no low loaders. They had worked for Ashmores for several years. Mr. Jones knew the whole of their fleet well; and Mr. Bulmer had known it for some six months. On getting the instructions, Mr. Jones telephoned Dawsons and spoke to Mr. Maurice Dawson, the son. He suggested that Maurice Dawson should come up and see the nature of the load. Maurice Dawson did so. The weight of it was shown plainly on the plate and on each tube bank and on the case. It was "25 tons." It was arranged that Dawson should take the loads. The price was arranged: it was £55 for the trip for each of the two articulated vehicles. If it had been on low loaders (which Dawsons had not got), the price would have been £85 or more for each: but here it was £55. Later that day Dawsons sent two of their drivers with the articulated vehicles to get the two loads. The tube banks were loaded on to the trailers. Mr. Bulmer was there for a short time. He saw them loaded, and so did Mr. Jones. The tube banks were firmly secured in by chains. Early next morning the two drivers came and set off on the journey for Hull. When they were about half-way there, the leading vehicle toppled over. It was driven by Mr. Harvey, the best and most experienced driver that Dawsons had. Mr. Harvey was asked the cause: "What do you say caused your lorry to topple over?" He answered: "The camber in the road to the left plus the weight of the load, plus the height of the load." The judge found that Mr. Harvey made an error of judgment. But that was not the real cause of the toppling over. The real cause was the overweight. The articulated lorry was a most unsuitable vehicle on which to carry it. The whole transaction was illegal, being in breach of the regulations.

Assuming, however, that Mr. Harvey was negligent, the question is whether the illegality prevents Ashmores from suing for that negligence. This depends on whether the contract itself was unlawful, or its performance was unlawful.

The first question is whether the contract of carriage, when made, was lawful or not. ...

Although I have these misgivings, I am prepared to accept the judge's finding that the contract was lawful when it was made. But then the question arises: was it lawful in its performance? The judge's attention does not seem to have been drawn to this point. Yet there are authorities which show that illegality in the performance of a contract may disable a person from suing on it, if he participated in the illegality. This was pointed out by Atkin L.J. in *Anderson Ltd. v. Daniel* [1924] 1 K.B. 138, 149 in a passage which was quoted by Devlin J. in *St. John Shipping Corporation v. Joseph Rank Ltd.* [1957] 1 Q.B. 267, 282:

> The question of illegality in a contract generally arises in connection with its formation, but it may also arise, as it does here, in connection with its performance. In the former case, where the parties have agreed to do something which is prohibited by Act of Parliament, it is indisputable that the contract is unenforceable by either party. And I think that it is equally unenforceable by the offending party where the illegality arises from the fact that the mode of performance adopted by the party performing it is in violation of some statute, even though the contract as agreed upon between the parties was capable of being performed in a perfectly legal manner.

That passage was further approved by Jenkins L.J. in *B. and B. Viennese Fashions v. Losane* [1952] 1 All E.R. 909, 913, where he said: "that illegality in the performance of a contract may avoid it although the contract was not illegal ab initio."

In this case the parties entered into the performance of the contract when Dawson's driver took the articulated vehicle (the 30-tonner) up to Ashmore's works to pick up this load. Mr. Bulmer, the transport manager, came along and saw it. Mr. Jones, his assistant, was there. Both saw this 25-ton tube bank being loaded on to the articulated lorry. Mr. Bulmer must have known that this was illegal: and Mr. Bulmer's knowledge would affect Ashmores. Mr. Jones was asked: "Mr. Bulmer would know the specific loads for articulated lorries, would he not? (A.) Like the back of his hand, yes." Then as to these particular lorries, Mr. Jones was asked: "Mr. Bulmer would have had all the knowledge in the world and would have known what weight these lorries were permitted to carry but you didn't know?" "Well," said Mr. Jones, "I would say he would have a good idea what they would carry, yes."

Now Mr. Bulmer was not called to give evidence. The reason was because he left the employment of Ashmores some years ago and had gone to Zambia. But he had given a statement in which he had said: "Identical loads to the one in question have been carried on similar vehicles belonging to G. Stiller (Haulage) Ltd., Middleton St. George, Darlington, completely without incident."

On that evidence I think that Mr. Bulmer must have known that those articulated lorries of Dawsons were only permitted to carry 20 tons. Nevertheless, realising that 25 tons was too heavy—much too heavy—for them, he was content to let them carry the loads because it had happened before without trouble. He was getting the transport done cheaper too by £30 saved on each trip by each load. Not only did Mr. Bulmer know of the illegality. He participated in it by sanctioning the loading of the vehicle with a load in debars Ashmores from suing Dawsons on it or suing Dawsons for negligence. I know that Dawsons were parties to the illegality. They knew, as well as Mr. Bulmer, that the load was overweight in breach of the regulations. But in such a situation as this, the defendants are in a better position. In pari delicto, potior est conditio defendantis. I would therefore allow the appeal and enter judgment for the defendants.

V. MITIGATING THE CONSEQUENCES OF ILLEGALITY

The variety of situations in which a contract may be illegal has impelled the development of a number of exceptions that permit the court to intervene to assist a party to an action. These exceptions have been frequently criticized as overly technical and lacking in logic and consistency. For an example, see the Law Reform Commission of British Columbia, *Report on Illegal Contracts*. The cases below illustrate several of the exceptions. In addition, a number of these technical exceptions may have developed to protect interests that, today, would be seen as a part of the law relating to restitution.

A. WHEN THE CLAIM IS FOUNDED ON AN INDEPENDENT RIGHT

MISTRY AMAR SINGH V SERWANO WOFUNIRA KULUBYA
[1964] AC 142 (JCPC, on appeal from the
Court of Appeal for Eastern Africa)

[The respondent, an African, who was the registered proprietor of certain "mailo" lands, purported by three agreements to lease the lands to the appellant, an Indian, but the consents of the governor and the Lukiko to the transactions were not obtained as required by s 2(d) of the *Buganda Possession of Land Law*, c 25 of 1957 Revision, and s 2 of the *Uganda Land Transfer Ordinance*, s 114 of the 1951 Revisions, the result of the omission being that under the above statutes both the respondent and the appellant had contravened the law and committed punishable offences. On a claim by the respondent, based on his registered ownership of the lands—his claim for rent and mesne profits having been abandoned—to possession and eviction of the appellant, the latter pleaded that the agreements by which the lands were leased were illegal in the absence of the necessary consents and that the respondent could not file an action on them. The respondent acknowledged that the transactions were illegal.
    Lord Morris of Borth-y-Gest stated the facts set out above and continued:]

LORD MORRIS OF BORTH-Y-GEST (for the court):
    In the judgments of the Court of Appeal it was pointed out (rightly as their Lordships think) that a rejection of the plaintiff's claim would have the result that the defendant, a non-African, would be entitled to remain permanently in possession of African land, to the exclusion of the registered African owner, and without payment of any nature whatsoever.
    Although, as has been seen, the plaintiff set out in his plaint that he had entered into agreements to lease the plots of land to the defendant, his right to claim possession did not depend upon those agreements. His claim was in the end based independently of those agreements. Though the plaintiff did in his plaint claim mesne profits and damages, he later abandoned those claims and at the trial he made

no claim for rent or for mesne profits. He was able to rest his claim upon his registered ownership of the property. The defendant did not have and could not show any right to the property. In view of the terms of the legislative provisions he could not assert that he had acquired any leasehold interest. For the same reason the defendant could not assert that he had any right to occupy. As a non-African he had no right without the consent in writing of the Governor to occupy or enter into possession of the land or to make any contract to take the land on lease. Quite irrespective of the circumstance that the plaintiff by giving certain notices to quit had purported to withdraw any permission to occupy, the defendant was not and never had been in lawful occupation.

The defendant, for his part, could not point to or rely upon the illegal agreements as justifying any right or claim to remain in possession, and without doing so he could not defeat the plaintiff's claim to possession.

Appeal dismissed.

NOTES AND QUESTIONS

1. In *International Paper Industries Ltd v Top Line Industries Inc*, 1996 CanLII 3340, 135 DLR (4th) 423 (BCCA), a landlord and tenant had entered into a lease agreement for a term of five years with a right to renew. Unknown to both, the lease was contrary to s 73 of the *Land Title Act*, RSBC 1979, c 219, which stated that no lease for a term of three years for an unsubdivided parcel of land could be registered. When the tenant claimed the right to renew, the landlord argued that the lease was illegal. At trial, the judge found that the lease, although it was illegal and could not be registered, created personal rights between the landlord and tenant. The Court of Appeal overruled this decision. In later proceedings, the BC Supreme Court awarded use and occupation rent to the landlord because the tenant had remained in possession pending the appeal. This too was reversed by the Court of Appeal, which held that the consent to occupy on which the landlord relied to claim use and occupation rent was given only by virtue of the illegal lease (see 2000 BCCA 23).

2. The *Land Title Act* (now RSBC 1996, c 250) was subsequently amended to provide that a lease in violation of s 73 was not, by that reason alone, unenforceable between the parties. This may suggest that the Court of Appeal's approach did not reflect the legislative intent of the statute.

3. There are many similarities between the *Singh* case, excerpted above, and *Top Line*, discussed in note 1. Are the results similarly satisfactory? Are there differences between the two cases that could have led to differing results? Consider the policies that underlay the statutes in the two cases. Consider also that in *Top Line* the only penalty provided by the statute was that the agreement could not be registered. Registration under the *Land Title Act* would have only one benefit—to protect the registered tenant from parties to whom the landlord might transfer other interests in the land.

4. Even if the conveyance (by way of the lease) in *Top Line* was illegal, why could the contract not provide an independent right under which the landlord could claim rent, especially after the tenant was in possession of the premises by virtue of the holding (reversed on appeal) by the BC Supreme Court? Was this result possible in *Singh*?

B. RESTITUTION

As a matter of general principle, where benefits have been conferred by one party on the other to an agreement that is unenforceable by reason of a doctrine of common law or equity, restitutionary relief will be available to the conferring party to enable recovery of the value of the benefit conferred. In the context of an illegal transaction, however, application of this general approach is complicated by the principle articulated in *Holman v Johnson*, above. The common law has generally assumed that Lord Mansfield's statement to the effect that "[n]o court will lend its aid to a man who founds his cause upon an immoral or illegal act" not only precludes an action to enforce an illegal agreement but also precludes the bringing of a restitutionary claim for the value of benefits conferred. Although the right to recover benefits conferred under an illegal contract is recognized to some extent, it is recognized only by way of exception to the general *Holman v Johnson* principle. Where such rights are recognized, it must be emphasized, they do not render the agreement enforceable. Rather, they allow the party who has conferred benefits under the agreement to seek recovery of their value.

The traditional exceptions to the principle in *Holman v Johnson* permitting restitutionary relief are applicable in circumstances, broadly speaking, where the party seeking restitution is in some sense less at fault than the other party. The consequence of this approach is that a party who has, for example, acted in contravention of a statutory provision is normally unable to pursue restitutionary relief. Thus, the plaintiff farmer in *Kingshot v Brunskill*, above, is not only unable to enforce the contract to sell ungraded apples, he is unable to bring a restitutionary claim for the value of the apples transferred to the defendant. After briefly considering the traditional restitutionary exceptions to *Holman v Johnson*, we will return to this point with a view to considering whether this traditional approach is a satisfactory one.

An obvious case for restitutionary relief is made out in circumstances where the party conferring the benefit was unaware of the facts that render the transaction illegal. An exception to *Holman v Johnson* on this ground is well established, if rarely applied. In *Oom v Bruce* (1810), 12 East 225 (KB), the plaintiff was allowed to recover moneys paid for insurance of goods on board a Russian vessel. The plaintiff was unaware that war had broken out with Russia, thus rendering the contract unenforceable.

A second exception pertains to circumstances where the defendant has induced the plaintiff to enter the agreement by oppressive conduct such as fraud or undue influence. *Mohamed v Alaga & Co (a firm)*, [1999] 3 All ER 699 (CA) suggests that it is not necessary to establish that the defendant's conduct meets the technical requirements of fraud, duress, or undue influence. In *Mohamed v Alaga*, the plaintiff, a Somali speaker, entered into a fee-splitting arrangement with a law firm under which he was to introduce potential clients to the firm and provide translation services in return for half the legal-aid fees earned by the firm in providing services to the clients. Pursuant to this arrangement, the plaintiff introduced several clients to the firm and provided translation services. Fee-splitting arrangements of this kind are prohibited by the rules of professional practice of the legal profession on the theory that paying for such referrals is contrary to the public interest. Accordingly, the fee-splitting agreement was held unenforceable as contrary to public policy. The plaintiff was nonetheless entitled to recover for the value of the translation services he had provided on the basis that his conduct was less culpable than that of the defendant firm. Two further exceptions to the general principle denying restitution are considered in the following two cases.

KIRIRI COTTON CO LTD V RACHHODDAS KESHAVJI DEWANI
[1960] AC 192 (JCPC, on appeal from the
Court of Appeal for Eastern Africa)

The facts were simple. The plaintiff came to Kampala in March 1953, and looked for somewhere to live. At the end of May 1953, he took a flat in Salisbury Road, but he had to pay 10,000 shillings premium. He now said that the premium was illegal because it was in contravention of the Rent Restriction Ordinance, and he claimed the return of it.

The oral evidence was so short that it could be set out in full. Only the plaintiff gave evidence. He said:

> I came to Kampala, Uganda, in 1953—March. I lived with a brother for 1½ months. I took a flat but I had to pay key money. I was searching for some time.
>
> I got a flat at Kololo but after 2-3 days I had to leave as I had trouble with a co-tenant. Then I got in touch with C.B. Patel, after having difficulty. I borrowed 10,000 shillings from the company as my brother was a director.

Cross-examination: "I paid the money by borrowing the money."

It was apparent from that evidence, as the trial judge said, that during the negotiations for the flat the plaintiff was at a disadvantage. He was having difficulty in obtaining accommodation—and he only got the flat by paying a premium of 10,000 shillings, which he borrowed for the purpose. He took it under a sublease dated September 17, 1953. This was prepared by lawyers. It contained provisions whereby the defendant company, in consideration of the sum of 10,000 shillings paid by the plaintiff by way of premium, subleased to him Flat No. 1 on the first floor for residence only, having three rooms, one kitchen, one bathroom and one lavatory. The term was seven years and one day from May 31, 1953. The rent was 300 shillings a month payable monthly in advance. And there were several covenants on either side.

The Rent Restriction Ordinance, 1949, of Uganda, provided by section 3(2): "Any person whether the owner of the property or not who in consideration of the letting or subletting of a dwelling-house ... to a person asks for, solicits or receives any sum of money other than rent ... shall be guilty of an offence and liable to a fine not exceeding Shs. 10,000 or imprisonment for a period not exceeding six months or to both such fine and imprisonment. ..."

The judgment of their Lordships was delivered by LORD DENNING, who stated the facts set out above, and continued: Their Lordships desire to point out at once that neither party thought they were doing anything illegal. The lease was for more than seven years and it was thought that, on a lease for that length of time, there was nothing wrong in asking for a premium or receiving it.

This was an easy mistake to make, as will be seen if one reads section 3(1) and (2) of the Rent Restriction Ordinance:

> 3(1) No owner or lessee of a dwelling-house or premises shall let or sublet such dwelling-house or premises at a rent which exceeds the standard rent.
>
> (2) Any person whether the owner of the property or not who in consideration of the letting or subletting of a dwelling-house or premises to a person asks for, solicits or receives any sum of money other than rent or any thing of value whether such asking, soliciting or receiving is made before or after the grant of a tenancy shall be guilty of an offence and liable to a fine not exceeding Shs. 10,000 or imprisonment for a period not exceeding six months or to both such fine and imprisonment:
>
> Provided that a person acting bona fide as an agent for either party to the intended tenancy agreement shall be entitled to a reasonable commission for his services:
>
> And provided further that nothing in this section shall be deemed to make unlawful the charging of a purchase price or premium on the sale, grant, assignment or renewal of a long lease of premises where the term or unexpired term is seven years or more.

Anyone reading the last proviso to that section—without more—might well think that a premium could be charged on the lease of this flat for seven years and one day. He would readily assume that the word "premises" included a flat. But he would be wrong. For if he took pains to look back to the definition section 2, he would find that in this Ordinance, the word "premises" refers only to business premises and not to residential flats at all. And so this proviso does not apply to this flat—because by the very terms of the sublease it was let "for residence only." Their Lordships ought perhaps to set out the material words of the definition clause which produces this result—it says that "dwelling-house" means any building let for human habitation as a separate dwelling and "premises" means any building or part of a building let for business, trade or professional purpose or for the public service.

It was owing to the failure of the lawyers to refer to those definitions—or at any rate to appreciate the importance of them—that the mistake arose.

Their Lordships also think it right to point out that there was no evidence to show whether the premium of 10,000 shillings was extortionate or not. Their Lordships were told that no standard rent had been fixed for this flat because it was a new flat. It is obvious that if the standard rent were to be fixed at, say 450 shillings a month for seven years, there would be nothing extortionate in a premium of 10,000 shillings down and a rent of 300 shillings a month thereafter: for it would come in the long run to much about the same.

Nevertheless, no matter whether the mistake was excusable or inexcusable, or the premium fair or extortionate, the fact remains that the landlord received a premium contrary to the provisions of the Ordinance: and the question is whether the tenant can recover it back—remembering always that there is nothing in the Uganda Ordinance, comparable to the English Acts, enabling a premium to be recovered back.

This omission in the Ordinance was considered to be decisive by the Court of Appeal for Eastern Africa in a case a few years ago. ... The court was then differently constituted from what it is now. The judges argued in this wise: "We do not know the reason, but the Uganda legislature in its wisdom has included in the Ordinance no provision comparable to section 8(2) of the Rent Restriction Act of 1920. ... Without this statutory right of recovery, the giver of the illegal premium is left in the position of one who, although he himself has committed no substantive offence, has aided and abetted the commission of an offence by another. In these circumstances he could not go to a civil court with clean hands, and the principle stated by Lord Ellenborough in *Langton v. Hughes*, (1813) 1 M. & S. 593, would have application: 'What is done in contravention of an Act of Parliament, cannot be made the subject-matter of an action.'"

In considering the validity of this reasoning, their Lordships would point out that the observation of Lord Ellenborough was made in a case where a party was seeking the aid of the court in order positively to enforce an illegal contract. It should be confined to cases of that description. His observation has no application to cases such as the present, where a party is seeking to recover money paid or property transferred under an illegal transaction. In such cases the general principle was stated by Littledale J. in *Hastelow v. Jackson*, (1828), 8 B. & C. 221, "If two parties enter into an illegal contract, and money is paid upon it by one to the other, that may be recovered back from the execution of the contract, but not afterwards." In accordance with this principle, so long as the illegal transaction has not been fully executed and carried out, the courts have in many cases shown themselves ready to entertain a suit for recovery of the money paid or property transferred. These were cases in which it appeared to the court that, even though the transaction was illegal, nevertheless it was better to allow the plaintiff to resile from it before it was completed, and to award restitution to him rather than to allow the defendant to remain in possession of his illegal gains. ... But so soon as the illegal transaction has been fully executed and carried out the courts will not entertain a suit for recovery ... unless it appears that the parties were not in pari delicto. ...

It is clear that in the present case the illegal transaction was fully executed and carried out. The money was paid. The lease was granted. It was and still is vested in the plaintiff. In order to recover the premium, therefore, the plaintiff must show that he was not in pari delicto with the defendant. That was, indeed, the way he put his claim in the pleadings. After setting out the lease, the payment of the premium and the entry into occupation, the statement of claim proceeded simply to say: "By virtue of the provisions of subsection (2) of section 3 of the Rent Restriction Ordinance, the receipt of the said sum of Shs. 10,000 by the defendant from the plaintiff ... was illegal but the plaintiff is entitled to recover the same since he (the plaintiff) was not in pari delicto with the defendant.

The plaintiff claims the sum of Shs. 10,000 as money received by the defendant for the use of the plaintiff."

The issue thus becomes: Was the plaintiff in pari delicto with the defendant? Mr. Elwyn Jones, for the appellant, said they were both in pari delicto. The payment was, he said, made voluntarily, under no mistake of fact, and without any extortion, oppression or imposition, and could not be recovered back. True, it was paid under a mistake of law, but that was a mistake common to them both. They were both equally supposed to know the law. They both equally mistook it and were thus in pari delicto. ...

Their Lordships cannot accept this argument. It is not correct to say that everyone is presumed to know the law. The true proposition is that no man can excuse himself from doing his duty by saying that he did not know the law on the matter. Ignorantia juris neminem excusat. Nor is it correct to say that money paid under a mistake of law can never be recovered back. The true proposition is that money paid under a mistake of law, by itself and without more, cannot be recovered back. ... If there is something more in addition to a mistake of law—if there is something in the defendant's conduct which shows that, of the two of them, he is the one primarily responsible for the mistake—then it may be recovered back. Thus, if as between the two of them the duty of observing the law is placed on the shoulders of the one rather than the other—it being imposed on him specially for the protection of the other—then they are not in pari delicto and the money can be recovered back; ... Likewise, if the responsibility for the mistake lies more on the one than the other—because he has misled the other when he ought to know better—then again they are not in pari delicto and the money can be recovered back. ... These propositions are in full accord with the principles laid down by Lord Mansfield relating to the action for money had and received. Their Lordships have in mind particularly ... his celebrated judgment ... on May 19, 1760, in *Moses v. Macferlan*, 2 Burr. 1005, when he sat in banco. Their Lordships were referred to some cases 30 or 40 years ago where disparaging remarks were made about the action for money had and received: but their Lordships venture to suggest that these were made under a misunderstanding of its origin. It is not an action on contract or imputed contract. If it were none such could be imputed here, as their Lordships readily agree. It is simply an action for restitution of money which the defendant has received but which the law says he ought to return to the plaintiff. This was explained by Lord Wright in *Fibrosa Spolka Akcyjna v. Fairbairn Lawson Combe Barbour Ltd.*, [1943] A.C. 32. All the particular heads of money had and received, such as money paid under a mistake of fact, paid under a consideration that has wholly failed, money paid by one who is not in pari delicto with the defendant, are only instances where the law says the money ought to be returned.

In applying these principles to the present case, the most important thing to observe is that the Rent Restriction Ordinance was intended to protect tenants from being exploited by landlords in days of housing shortage. One of the obvious ways in which a landlord can exploit the housing shortage is by demanding from the tenant "key-money." Section 3(2) of the Rent Restriction Ordinance was enacted so as to protect tenants from exploitation of that kind. This is apparent from the fact that the penalty is imposed only on the landlord or his agent and not upon the tenant. It is imposed on the person who "asks for, solicits or receives any sum of money," but not on the person who submits to the demand and pays the money. It may be that the tenant who pays money is an accomplice or an aider and abettor ... but he can hardly be said to be in pari delicto with the landlord. The duty of observing the law if firmly placed by the Ordinance on the shoulders of the landlord for the protection of the tenant: and if the law is broken, the landlord must take the primary responsibility. Whether it be a rich tenant who pays a premium as a bribe in order to "jump the queue," or a poor tenant who is at his wits' end to find accommodation, neither is so much to blame as the landlord who is using his property rights so as to exploit those in need of a roof over their heads.

Seeing then that the parties are not in pari delicto, the tenant is entitled to recover the premium by the common law: and it is not necessary to find a remedy given by the Ordinance, either expressly or by implication. The omission of a statutory remedy does not, in cases of this kind, exclude the remedy by money had and received. That is amply shown by the numerous cases to which their Lordships were referred, such as those arising under the statutes against usury, lotteries and gaming, in which there was no remedy given by the statute but nevertheless it was held that an action lay for money had and received. ...

Their Lordships find themselves in full agreement with the judgment of the High Court of Uganda and of the Court of Appeal for Eastern Africa, and will humbly advise Her Majesty that this appeal should be dismissed. The appellant must pay the costs.

OUTSON V ZUROWSKI
(1985), 63 BCLR 89 (CA)

[The plaintiffs had been induced by the defendants to enter into a pyramid scheme that was illegal under s 189(1)(e) of the *Criminal Code*. The scheme called for each participant to contribute $2,200 to an "Investment Board" and then to recruit eight others to do the same. If the board was completed, the return for the original investors would be $17,600.

The defendants had successfully participated in the scheme twice before. They promised the plaintiffs that if the board stopped, the defendants would indemnify the plaintiffs against the loss of their $2,200. This promise was found by the trial judge to be contractual. The trial judge also found that the plaintiffs were not aware that the scheme was illegal, but that the defendants knew that to be the case.

Before the plaintiffs had made any serious efforts to recruit their participants to the scheme, publicity regarding such schemes and investigations by the police caused the defendants to decide to abandon the plan. The plaintiffs sued on the basis of the defendants' promise of indemnity to recover the money they had paid.]

TAGGART JA (Anderson JA concurring): ... I regard the contract as one contract with the parties having disparate obligations. I think the contract is illegal. That gives rise to the defendants' argument that because the plaintiffs seek to enforce an illegal contract their action must fail. I do not accept that argument.

Two issues must be resolved. First, I think it is necessary to decide if the parties are in pari delicto. If they are not and the plaintiffs are blameless, as on the findings of the judge they are, no further inquiry is necessary and they may recover on the contract of indemnity. If, however, the parties are in pari delicto, then it is necessary to consider whether, notwithstanding that, the plaintiffs may recover.

As I read his reasons for judgment, that is the process of reasoning followed by Laycraft J.A., now C.J.A., in *McDonald v. Fellows*, [1979] 6 W.W.R. 544. I refer particularly to this passage from his judgment at pp. 554-55:

> Where the plaintiff must rely on the illegal transaction, the learned author of Cheshire and Fifoot's Law of Contract recognizes two true exceptions to the rule of law that there can be no *recovery* of money paid under an illegal contract. In the 8th edition at pp. 342-43 it is said:
>
>> There are two exceptions to the general rule that a party cannot recover what he has given to the other party under an illegal contract. These are (a) where the parties are not in pari delicto and (b) where the plaintiff repents before the contract has been performed.
>>
>> If the parties to an illegal contract are not in pari delicto, the court in certain circumstances will allow the less blameworthy to recover what he may have transferred to the other. This relief is granted to the plaintiff upon proof that he has been the victim of fraud, duress or oppression at the hands of the defendant, or that the latter stood in a fiduciary position towards him and abused it. ...
>>
>> The second exception to the ban on restitution recognizes the virtue of repentance in the case of a contract which is still executory. A party to such a contract, despite its illegality, is allowed a locus poenitentiae, and he may recover what he has transferred to his co-contractor, provided that he takes proceedings before the illegal purpose has been substantially performed. If he repents in time, he will be assisted by the court, but in the present state of the authorities it is not clear at what point his repentance is to be regarded as overdue.
>
> It is therefore necessary to consider whether in this case the vendors and purchasers were in pari delicto and, if they were, whether the plaintiffs may nevertheless recover the deposit because the agreement has not been substantially performed.

... I turn now to consider whether the plaintiffs here were in pari delicto. Certainly they were unaware the contract they had made committed them to participation in an illegal scheme. But I think that makes no difference. In *J.M. Allan (Merchandising) Ltd. v. Cloke*, [1963] 2 Q.B. 340 (C.A.), the plaintiffs hired to the defendants, who were interested in the management of a proprietary club, a roulette table, a roulette wheel and a croupier's rake at a weekly rent payable quarterly in advance. A booklet was provided which contained the rules of the game and which stated the game was designed to be conducted in accordance with the provisions of the Betting and Gaming Act, 1960. The defendants did not pay the second instalment of the rent on the ground that the agreement was illegal, though at the date the agreement was entered into neither party knew the game was unlawful.

Lord Denning M.R. decided the game was unlawful. He went on to say at pp. 260-61:

> ... As I read *Waugh v. Morris* [(1873), L.R. 8 Q.B. 202], there was there no participation in any unlawful purpose and the plaintiff could recover. In this case, however, there was participation. The common design was that a game should be played which was in fact unlawful. I hold that such a contract is unlawful; and it is no answer for those concerned to say that they did not know the law. It would be an easy way round the law if we were to permit a person to excuse himself by saying that he did not know the law. Here the judge was, I think, quite right in holding that there was an express purpose of both that this roulette-table and appurtenances should be used for this unlawful game. The contract was, in my judgment, illegal in its inception, and no action lies to recover the rent.

Danckwerts L.J. did not refer to that aspect of the matter, but Davies L.J. concurred with Lord Denning.

I think the reasoning of Lord Denning has application on the first issue. I think it is not open to the plaintiffs to say they are not in pari delicto because they did not know the law and believed the scheme to be legal.

Then can the plaintiffs bring themselves within the second exception referred to by the authors of *Cheshire and Fifoot's Law of Contract*? In my opinion, they can. I think this contract was clearly executory. The plaintiffs had each paid $2,200 into the scheme. But while that enabled the defendants to take their "winnings," the plaintiffs each had still to find eight persons to join the scheme. The defendants had succeeded for the second time in obtaining $17,600 for an investment of $2,200 on their part. But their obligation to indemnify the plaintiffs was a continuing obligation.

There has been much discussion concerning the scope of the exception. All judges and commentators are agreed that the illegal contract must remain executory if parties in the position of the plaintiffs are to succeed in recovering their money. But differing answers have been given to the question of the stage at which they may "repent" by withdrawing from the illegal contract. ...

As Laycraft J.A. pointed out at p. 557 of *McDonald v. Fellows*, Fry L.J. in *Kearley v. Thomson* (1890), 24 Q.B.R. 742 at 747 (C.A.), said:

> I hold, therefore, that where there has been a partial carrying into effect of an illegal purpose in a substantial manner, it is impossible, though there remains something not performed, that the money paid under that illegal contract can be recovered back.

That would appear to limit considerably the circumstances in which there is a right to recovery. ...

Whatever may be the limits of the exception, I think even on the basis adopted by Fry L.J. in *Kearley v. Thomson* the plaintiffs here are entitled to succeed. They had taken only the initial step of paying money into the scheme and two of them had made desultory efforts to persuade others to enter the scheme. The defendants, on the other hand, had received benefits as a result of the participation of the plaintiffs in the scheme.

On this aspect of the matter I think it is appropriate to consider the relative degrees of turpitude of the parties. The plaintiffs had barely begun their participation in the scheme and did not know it was unlawful. The defendants, on the other hand, at the very least, had doubts about the legality of the scheme but, notwithstanding those doubts, induced the plaintiffs to participate by assuring them it was lawful.

I am therefore of the view the plaintiffs fall within the second exception and are entitled to recover from the defendants the amounts which they claim.

NOTES AND QUESTIONS

1. In the typical *locus poenitentiae* case, or repentance case, as the excerpt from *McDonald v Fellows* quoted by Taggart JA illustrates, the relief made available to the party who repents in time is a restitutionary claim for the value of benefits conferred prior to the repentance. Is that the type of relief made available in *Outson*? Should it have been?

2. The separate judgment of Esson JA is omitted. He concurred in the result. He also found that the plaintiffs had "repented" and noted that the word in this context "is used without any moral connotation. What is important is that they abandoned their participation in the scheme before the illegal purpose was carried out in any substantial way, that they entered into it without knowledge of its illegality and were induced to do so by the defendants who had such

knowledge." In *Bigos v Boustead*, [1951] 1 All ER 92 (KB), the plaintiff had entered into an unlawful agreement with the defendant foreign national for the purpose of evading English currency controls. The plaintiff had advanced securities to the defendant but the defendant refused to carry out his side of the bargain. The plaintiff's restitutionary claim was denied on the basis that his "repentance" was not genuine. The real reason for the claim was that the defendant's non-performance had frustrated the scheme. Was the repentance in *Outson* genuine in this sense? In *Tribe v Tribe*, [1995] 4 All ER 236 (CA), the English Court of Appeal suggested that a plaintiff who transferred assets to a defendant under an unlawful scheme to hide assets from a potential creditor could recover the assets even though the plaintiff sought relief only after the claim failed to materialize and the need for deception had passed. Millett LJ observed (at 260) that "restitution should not be confined to the penitent." Which approach do you prefer?

3. For further discussion of the repentance doctrine, see R Merkin, "Restitution by Withdrawal from Executory Illegal Contracts" (1981) 97 Law Q Rev 420; J Beatson, "Repudiation of a Legal Purpose as a Ground for Restitution" (1975) 91 Law Q Rev 420.

4. Would any of the restitutionary exceptions to *Holman v Johnson* considered above provide a basis for granting relief to the plaintiff farmer in *Kingshot v Brunskill*, above? If not, is it possible to devise a rule that would provide a basis for recovery in such a case? In *Berne Development Ltd v Haviland* (1983), 40 OR (2d) 238 (H Ct J), the plaintiff developer sold a condominium unit to the defendant, accepting a second mortgage on the unit as part of the purchase price. The developer refrained from disclosing the existence of the second mortgage, as it was required to do, to the first mortgagee and a government agency, the CMHC, because the existence of the second mortgage would have precluded the requisite CMHC approval of the first mortgage. Although the scheme was initiated and implemented by the plaintiff, the defendant was also aware of the deception. When the plaintiff sought to enforce the second mortgage, the defendant raised a defence of illegality. Saunders J noted that the traditional exceptions to the *Holman v Johnson* principle would not be available to the plaintiff in these circumstances and went on to observe (at 250) as follows:

> In recent years, there has been a recognition of the desirability [of] balancing the need to preserve public policy by not enforcing illegal agreements and the need to avoid unjust enrichment ... . [T]he striking of the balance may depend in each case on the extent of the illegality and the unjust enrichment.

Applying this framework, Saunders J then reasoned that the conduct of the plaintiff developer, though reprehensible, should not attract the severe consequence of inability to recover the balance of the purchase price. At the same time, however, the plaintiff was not entitled to recover further interest or enforce its security or other remedies under the mortgage because of the illegal nature of the transaction.

Similarly in *Koliniotis v Tri Level Claims Consultant Ltd* (2005), 201 OAC 282, 257 DLR (4th) 297 (CA), the Ontario Court of Appeal applied the balancing test articulated by Saunders J in *Berne* and allowed *quantum meruit* relief for services rendered by a paralegal under a service agreement rendered illegal by virtue of a provincial statutory prohibition against champertous agreements. The unlawful contingency fee stipulated for in the agreement was not recoverable but recovery for the reasonable value of the services rendered was awarded. Sharpe JA, for the Court of Appeal, observed that "an absolute bar on *quantum meruit* recovery creates an injustice that is unacceptable when considered in the light of the public policy informing the statutory prohibition against champertous agreements." Sharpe JA noted that the plaintiff was not aware that the agreement was illegal and had not engaged in sharp or dishonest practice with the defendant client. The underlying purpose of the legislation—protecting the administration of justice from abuse—had not been sufficiently undermined by the conduct of the plaintiff to warrant a complete denial of relief.

Can you fashion an argument for overturning the result in *Kingshot v Brunskill* on the basis of these authorities? See, further, the similar analysis provided by Robertson JA at the Federal Court of Appeal in *Still v MNR*, below. Should we consider this a fifth restitutionary exception to the rule in *Holman v Johnson*? See generally Maddaugh & McCamus, ch 15.

5.   The approach adopted in *Berne Development Ltd v Haviland* and *Kolionotis v Tri-Level Claims Consultant Ltd* requires, in essence, that one simply ask whether the granting of restitutionary relief in the particular circumstances would undermine or frustrate the policies underlying the rule or prohibition rendering the transaction unlawful to such a degree that restitution should be denied. If granting such relief does not offend this principle, restitution will be allowed. In such cases the burden would be on the plaintiff to establish that the restitution claim should not be denied on this basis. Once such an approach is clearly adopted, the traditional exceptions to *Holman v Johnson* permitting restitutionary recovery—such as the protected class and repentance exceptions—may be seen as applications of that new approach or rule. That is, in a protected class or repentance case, restitution could be said to be granted because the plaintiff has successfully established that doing so will not undermine the rule that renders the transaction invalid. If this approach is accepted, the rule in *Holman v Johnson* and its exceptions could simply be replaced by or absorbed by the new principle.

6.   A similar approach to reform of the rule in *Holman v Johnson* has recently been adopted by the United Kingdom Supreme Court in *Patel v Mirza*, [2016] UKSC 42 (SC). The facts of the *Patel* case are not complicated. The plaintiff, Patel, had been persuaded to transfer a substantial sum to the defendant, Mirza, who undertook to engage, on the plaintiff's behalf, in an illicit insider trading scheme with these funds. In due course, the insider information did not become available to Mirza and accordingly, it became impossible to proceed with the scheme. Mirza, however, refused to return the funds to Patel. On traditional grounds, Patel's restitutionary claim would be precluded by his willing participation in the illicit scheme. None of the traditional exemptions to *Holman v Johnson* would be available to him. Nonetheless, as between Patel and Mirza, Patel's claim for restitution appears just.

The English Court of Appeal was able to ground relief for Patel on the basis of what many would consider an extended application of the *locus poenitentiae* exception. In the court's view, the exception could apply where, as here, the impossibility of carrying out the scheme had the consequence that the scheme was not implemented. This holding may be thought to be inconsistent with the underlying repentance rationale underlying the *locus poenitentiae* doctrine. Mr Patel did not experience a "change of heart" at a time when the illicit scheme could still be implemented. On the other hand, the holding is consistent with the suggestion in *Tribe*, above, that "restitution should not be confined to the penitent."

On appeal to the United Kingdom Supreme Court, however, a majority of the Court upheld the result on a more radical ground. The majority favoured a reinterpretation of the law granting restitution of benefits conferred under illegal transactions to the effect that, presumptively, relief should be granted unless the granting of such relief would stultify the purpose underlying the prohibition or some other ground of public policy or, alternatively, the withholding of relief would constitute a disproportionately punitive response to the plaintiff's conduct. In the leading majority opinion of Lord Toulson, it was suggested that in undertaking this analysis, a number of factors should be taken into account such as "the seriousness of the conduct, its centrality to the contract, whether it was intentional and whether there was a marked disparity in the parties' respective culpability" (*Patel*, at para 107). Applying this approach to the present facts, it was the majority's view that there was no consideration of public policy that would require Mr Patel to forfeit moneys which were never used for the illicit purpose for which they were paid. A concurring minority of the court would have granted relief essentially on the grounds that had been adopted by the Court of Appeal.

Although the majority reasoning in *Patel* appears consistent with the reasoning in the Canadian *Koliniotis* line of authority and current American law, there is an important, if subtle, distinction between the new English rule and developments in North America. In order to understand the new English rule, it is important to draw a distinction between "reasons for restitution," proof of the existence of which lies upon the plaintiff, and "defences" to restitution, proof of which lies upon the defendant. Some English scholars have taken the view that the "illegality" of a transaction should not be considered to be a reason for restitution but, rather, should be considered to be a "defence" to a restitution claim. Indeed, a number of them have taken the view that where the plaintiff is a member of a protected class or is entitled to rely on the *locus poenitentiae* exception, these constitute "reasons for restitution" that must be established by the plaintiff in order to ground relief. Where the plaintiff is a perpetrator of the illegality, however, no such "reasons for restitution" are available and, under traditional doctrine, relief would be denied. These scholars also suggest, however, that the traditional rule in *Holman v Johnson* should simply be ignored in such cases and that the perpetrator should be presumptively entitled to relief, unless the defendant can raise the "defence" of illegality. That defence should not be available, it is argued, where relief does not result in the stultification of the rationale underlying the prohibition offended by the transaction or where other considerations of public policy are not offended and, further, where denying recovery would amount to a disproportionate response to the plaintiff's conduct. In this rather indirect way, then, the traditional rule of *Holman v Johnson* is overruled and restitutionary relief is made available to the perpetrator by adopting a new rule presumptively granting such relief, subject to a "defence" of illegality that will not invariably be available to the defendant. The odd effect of this manner of structuring the reform of *Holman v Johnson,* however, is that in cases where the plaintiff is a perpetrator or willing participant in the illicit scheme, the burden is on the defendant to establish a "defence" of illegality on the various public policy grounds making the defence available to the defendant. The better view, arguably, is that the burden should be on the plaintiff perpetrator to establish that the various policy factors weigh in favour of relief. That is the approach taken in the Canadian *Koliniotis* line of authority and in American law. One difficulty with the majority reasoning in *Patel*, then, is that it is not entirely clear whether the reformed illegality doctrine constitutes, in the court's view, a "reason for restitution" or a "defence." Although the doctrine appears to be at least assumed to operate as a "defence," the implications of this characterization for the burden of proof are not explored in the majority opinion. See further, Maddaugh & McCamus, s 15 800.40.

7. For examples of recent English scholarship suggesting that illegality operates (at least sometimes) as a defence, see, G Virgo, "The Defence of Illegality in Unjust Enrichment," in A Dyson et al, *Defences in Unjust Enrichment* (Oxford: Hart Publishing, 2016) ch 8; AS Burrows, *A Restatement of the English Law of Unjust Enrichment* (Oxford: Oxford University Press, 2012) at 107-10, 136-41. For a review of the latter volume, see, JD McCamus, (2016), 58 Can Bus LJ 208.

C. SEVERANCE OF ILLEGAL PROVISIONS

One means that the courts have developed to prevent unjust enrichment of one party to an illegal contract is to sever an illegal part of the contract and enforce the remainder. The questions of how severance is to be applied and when it will be applied were, at least before the 1980s, little explored. However, in one area, the courts have developed these doctrines. Pursuant to s 347 of the *Criminal Code*, it is an offence to charge or receive a rate of interest in excess of 60 percent per annum. Prosecution requires the consent of the attorney general.

The section has been most frequently used in commercial cases in which one party is trying to recover a loan from another. The defendant pleads the illegality of the transaction. Particularly when both parties are sophisticated with access to legal advice, courts have been reluctant to allow the defendant to retain the principal money of the loan. The following two cases illustrate the development of the doctrine of severance in these cases. See also MA Waldron, "White Collar Usury: Another Look at the Conventional Wisdom" (1994) 72 Can Bar Rev 1.

WILLIAM E THOMSON ASSOCIATES INC V CARPENTER
(1989), 61 DLR (4th) 1 (Ont CA)

[The court found that a "facility fee" fell within the definition of interest under the *Criminal Code*, making the rate of return on a loan illegal. The loan was made to Jamestown Resources Inc. The appellants, Carpenter and Martin, were directors of Jamestown and gave, in connection with the loan, personal guarantees for a limited amount. When the company failed to repay the loan, the lender called on the guarantees of Carpenter and Martin. They resisted payment on the ground that the guarantees were void because the effective rate on the loan exceeded the criminal rate. Only the court's discussion of severance is quoted.]

BLAIR JA: ... I now turn to the question whether the loan agreement can be severed so that the agreement to repay the principal of the loan can be enforced even though the agreement to pay a criminal rate of interest is void. Two questions arise. The first is whether severance is possible, which presents no difficulties in this case. The three clauses providing for payment of interest referred to above can be excised from the agreement without affecting the substance of the obligation to repay the principal of the loan and without making a new agreement for the parties.

The important question is whether public policy prevents the severance of the agreement because it is tainted by illegality. In deciding whether the agreements in this case are capable of severance and partial enforcement, a number of principles from the decided cases must be taken into account. They include the object and policy of s. 347; whether that object and policy would be subverted by a partial performance of the agreements; whether one or both parties intended to break the law; whether the parties were in an equal bargaining position and were professionally advised; and whether one party would be unjustly enriched if the contract were not enforced. ...

The first consideration is whether the purpose and policy of s. 347 would be subverted by severance. The section was enacted to curb the reprehensible practice of loan sharking. In this case, it does not seem to me that its purpose would be subverted by severing the loan agreements to permit recovery of the principal amount of the guarantees. The deterrent effect of the punishment it provides is not undermined by severance for proper reasons. The enforcement of the valid part of the loan agreement does not absolve the respondent company from criminal responsibility under s. 347.

The second consideration is whether the parties entered into the agreement for an illegal purpose or with an evil intention ... . This is not a case where it can be said that the agreement was made for an illegal purpose. ...

The third consideration is the relative bargaining position of the parties and their conduct in reaching the agreement. This is not a case of a desperate borrower who was forced to submit to terms dictated by a sophisticated usurious lender. The parties to this agreement were all businessmen who bargained from a position of equality and who, in additions, acted on the advice of their own solicitors. In *La Foncière Compagnie d'Assurance de France v. Perras*, [1943] 2 D.L.R. 129, the Supreme Court of Canada warned that the maxim ex turpi causa should be applied carefully to persons who seek to use the rule to avoid performance of contracts for which they have received full consideration. Davis J. at p. 139, quoted with approval the dictum of Lord Esher in *Cleaver v. Mutual Reserve Fund Life Ass'n*, [1892] 1 Q.B. 147 at p. 151:

> No doubt there is a rule that, if a contract be made contrary to public policy, or if the performance of a contract would be contrary to public policy, performance cannot be

enforced either at law or in equity; but when people vouch that rule to excuse themselves from the performance of a contract, in respect of which they have received the full consideration, and when all that remains to be done under the contract is for them to pay the money, the application of the rule ought to be narrowly watched, and ought not to be carried a step further than the protection of the public requires.

There can be no doubt that in this case the appellants are attempting on technical grounds to avoid performance of an important business obligation. Their conduct does not entitle them to any favourable exercise of the court's discretion.

The fourth consideration is related to the third in this case. It is whether the appellants can be considered to have been unjustly enriched at the expense of the company. The principle is expressed by Professor Waddams [*The Law of Contracts*, 2nd ed] at p. 420:

> [I]t seems inadequate to say of an illegal contract simply that it is "void" without taking account of the effect that such a holding will have on the particular case and whether the seriousness of the contravention of public policy justifies the particular consequences, including often the enrichment of one party at the other's expense.

Because of the collapse of Jamestown, the enrichment might not be regarded as continuing but it remains a consideration which should be taken into account. The words of Krever J. in *Menard v. Genereux* (1982), 39 O.R. (2d) 55, in a case where a deposit had been paid under an illegal transaction, are apt and militate against the avoidance of the agreement to repay the principal and the guarantors' obligation in this case. He said at p. 72:

> As between the plaintiffs and the defendants, there is at work a conflict between two policies of the law, the first, that unjust enrichment should, where possible, be prevented and the second, that the law will not come to the assistance of persons who behave illegally. It is apparent that in these circumstances, to prefer the second policy of the law would result in the unacceptable situation I have described and, therefore, it seems to me that the only reasonable recourse is to adopt a position that would return the deposit to the plaintiffs and thus prevent the unjust enrichment of the defendants.

Whether or not a contract tainted by illegality is completely unenforceable depends upon all the circumstances surrounding the contract and the balancing of the considerations discussed above and, in appropriate cases, other considerations. This careful case by case approach was anticipated more than half a century ago by Masten J.A. in *Steinberg v. Cohen*, [1930] 64 O.L.R. 545 (H.C.J.), where he said at p. 558:

> It is possible that each case should depend upon its own facts, and upon a balancing by the Court of the public interest on the one hand and of the private injustice on the other.

In the present case, J. Holland J. properly exercised his discretion, in my opinion, in permitting the severance of the loan agreement and the enforcement of the guarantees of the principal given by both appellants. The exercise of his discretion accords with the principles governing the intervention of public policy to strike down a contract. In the result, I agree that the agreements should be severed and that the appellants should be liable for the principal amounts of their guarantees.

TRANSPORT NORTH AMERICAN EXPRESS INC V
NEW SOLUTIONS FINANCIAL CORP
2004 SCC 7, [2004] 1 SCR 249

[The appellant, New Solutions, had entered into a credit agreement with Transport North American Express. Under the terms of the agreement, interest was charged at 4 percent per month, calculated daily; there were also a "monitoring fee," "royalty payments," and various other fees and charges, all of which fell within the statutory definition of interest. The monthly interest rate alone, converted to an annualized rate, produced a rate of 60.1 percent per annum; the various other payments amounted to 30.8 percent per annum. The application judge, Cullity J, determined that to reduce the interest rate using the traditional method of severance—that is, by striking out entire provisions of the agreement with the "blue pencil"—his only option was to strike the provision for monthly interest, leaving the lender with only 30.8 percent per annum in interest charges. Instead, while criticizing the blue-pencil test as overly formalistic and outdated, Cullity J applied a "notional severance" test and permitted interest to be paid up to the legal rate of 60 percent per annum without identifying a particular provision of the contract to be struck out. The Ontario Court of Appeal reversed the judgment and reaffirmed the blue-pencil test as the only acceptable method of severance. The lender appealed to the Supreme Court of Canada.]

ARBOUR J (Iacobucci, Major, and LeBel JJ concurring):

I. OVERVIEW

[1] In March 2000, the appellant, New Solutions Financial Corp. ("New Solutions"), and the respondent, Transport North American Express Inc. ("TNAE"), entered into a credit agreement pursuant to which New Solutions advanced TNAE the sum of $500,000. In addition to various other fees and charges, the agreement provided for interest to be paid at the rate of four percent per month, calculated daily and payable monthly in arrears. By all accounts, the various payments called for by the agreement constituted a "criminal rate" of interest as defined in s. 347 of the *Criminal Code*, R.S.C. 1985, c. C-46 (the "Code"). The payments soon became too onerous for TNAE to meet, and the company applied to the Ontario Superior Court of Justice for a declaration that the agreement contained an illegally high rate of interest and should not be enforced.

[2] The application judge, Cullity J., ruled that he was not confined to the so-called "blue-pencil" approach to severance in dealing with the statutory illegality of the contract, whereby only discrete illegal promises could be excised. Using "notional severance," he read down the offending interest rate so the contract provided for the maximum legal rate of interest: (2001), 54 O.R. (3d) 144.

[3] Upon appeal to the Court of Appeal for Ontario, Rosenberg J.A., for the majority, concluded that the doctrine of severance only permits the striking of distinct promises from a contract: (2002), 60 O.R. (3d) 97. He reversed the application judge's finding that notional severance was an available remedial instrument. Rosenberg J.A. found that it was appropriate to strike out or blue-pencil the provision calling for interest at four percent per month, calculated daily and payable monthly in arrears, leaving the balance of the agreement to be enforced in accordance with its terms. Sharpe J.A., agreeing with the reasons of Cullity J., dissented.

[4] There is broad consensus that the traditional rule that contracts in violation of statutory enactments are void ab initio is not the approach courts should necessarily take in cases of statutory illegality involving s. 347 of the Code. Instead, judicial

discretion should be employed in cases in which s. 347 has been violated in order to provide remedies that are tailored to the contractual context involved. The primary issue in this appeal by New Solutions is whether notional severance, as formulated and applied by Cullity J., is valid in Canadian law and applicable here.

[5] Given the desirability of remedial flexibility in cases of statutory illegality arising in connection with s. 347 of the Code, the evolving nature of the law regarding statutory illegality generally and the sound policy basis in which the concept is rooted, I find that notional severance is available as a matter of law as a remedy in cases arising under s. 347.

[6] A spectrum of remedies is available to judges in dealing with contracts that violate s. 347 of the Code. The remedial discretion this spectrum affords is necessary to cope with the various contexts in which s. 347 illegality can arise. At one end of the spectrum are contracts so objectionable that their illegality will taint the entire contract. For example, exploitive loan-sharking arrangements and contracts that have a criminal object should be declared void ab initio. At the other end of the spectrum are contracts that, although they do contravene a statutory enactment, are otherwise unobjectionable. Contracts of this nature will often attract the application of the doctrine of severance. The agreement in this case is an example of such a contract. In each case, the determination of where along the spectrum a given case lies, and the remedial consequences flowing therefrom, will hinge on a careful consideration of the specific contractual context and the illegality involved.

[7] The application judge in this case found that (i) the agreement between New Solutions and TNAE only inadvertently violated s. 347; (ii) the parties were experienced in commercial matters and negotiated at arm's length; (iii) there was no evidence that they did not have equal bargaining power; and (iv) they each had the benefit of independent legal advice in the course of the negotiations leading to the agreement. Consequently, the application of notional severance to the agreement between New Solutions and TNAE in this case by Cullity J. was appropriate. I would allow the appeal.

• • •

[On the question of the blue-pencil test, the court stated:]

[27] The blue-pencil approach is understood both as a test of the availability of severance to remedy contractual illegality and also as a technique for effecting severance. The blue-pencil approach as a test of the appropriateness of severance requires a consideration of whether an illegal contract can be rendered legal by striking out (i.e., by drawing a line through) the illegal promises in the agreement. The resulting set of legal terms should retain the core of the agreement. If the nature or core of the agreement is disturbed, then on this test the illegal clause in the contract is not a candidate for severance and the entire contract is void. The blue-pencil approach as a technique of effecting severance involves the actual excision of the provisions leading to the illegality, leaving those promises untainted by the illegality to be enforced.

[28] The use of the blue-pencil approach to sever one or more provisions from a contract alters the terms of the agreement between the parties. The only agreement that one can say with certainty the parties would have agreed to is the one that they actually entered into. The insistence in the case law that the blue-pencil test derives its validity from refusing to change or add words or provisions to the contract is unconvincing. It is doubtful, for example, that the lenders in cases such as *Thomson*, supra, or *Mira Design* ... would have entered into the agreements at issue had they been aware ex ante that they would only be entitled to the return of the principal advanced. The change effected by the blue-pencil technique will often fundamentally alter the consideration associated with the bargain and do violence to the

intention of the parties. Indeed, in many cases, the application of the blue-pencil approach will provide for an interest-free loan where the parties demonstrated in the agreement a clear intention to charge and pay considerable interest.

[29] The blue-pencil test was developed in cases where the courts were considering instruments under seal, where the form of the deed governed and where the intention of the parties was irrelevant. It was therefore important that what remained after severance would be a valid deed:

> In the deed form was everything; the actual intention of the parties was immaterial. It was, therefore, natural that in considering the possibility of severance of promises in a deed, the court should be concerned to see that what was left remained a valid deed; there could be no question of implying a promise to take effect if part of the original bargain was illegal. This is the historical origin of what was later called the "blue-pencil test."

(N.S. Marsh, "The Severance of Illegality in Contract" (1948), 64 *L.Q.R.* 230 and 347, at pp. 351-52.)

Historically, courts were not concerned with the intention of the parties. The artificiality of the blue-pencil test arises from the common law constraints imposed on courts unaided by principles of equity.

[The detailed reasons and the dissenting judgment of Bastarache J are omitted.]

NOTE

In *Shafron v KRG Insurance Brokers*, excerpted above, the Supreme Court of Canada clarified the circumstances in which notional severance can be applied. The BC Court of Appeal in *Shafron* (2007), 64 BCLR (4th) 125 had used notional severance to construe the meaningless phrase "Metropolitan City of Vancouver" to mean the City of Vancouver, UBC Endowment Lands, Richmond, and Burnaby. The Supreme Court held that notional severance was not applicable in this case because there was no "bright line" test for illegality in cases such as this and to rewrite the clause would encourage employers to include unreasonable clauses regarding future competition in their contracts in the knowledge that the court would substitute what it considered reasonable.

VI. AN ALTERNATIVE APPROACH?

The technical exceptions to the courts' refusal to intervene to mitigate the consequences of the invalidity of a contract found void as illegal have been widely criticized. In the cases we have seen excerpted above, we can observe numerous inconsistencies. Reviewing the use of illegality as a defence in contracts, the UK Law Commission recommended that "the courts should consider in each case whether the application of the illegality defence can be justified on the basis of the policies that underlie that defence" (*The Illegality Defence: A Consultative Report* (2009), part 8 at para 8.3). The Commission called for a balancing approach, weighing the application of the various policies involved. Consider whether such an approach was used in *Still v MNR*, below. The development of the law of restitution, the influence of which can be seen in the judgment excerpted here, as well as in those included above, is likely to have an increasingly significant role to play in the modern development of the law of illegal contracts.

STILL V MNR
[1998] 1 FC 549 (FCA)

ROBERTSON JA (Strayer and Linden JJA concurring): ...

2. FACTS

The facts are not in dispute. The applicant married a Canadian citizen and immigrated to Canada to be with her husband. She applied for permanent resident status and on September 22, 1991 was provided with the following document by immigration officials:

> This will verify that, for the person(s) named hereunder, a recommendation has been sent to the Governor-in-Council for Canada for an exemption pursuant to subsection 114(2) of the *Immigration Act*.

> KATHLEEN STILL

> Pending Governor-in-Council approval and provided all other requirements are met, the above-named will be granted permanent resident status in Canada. The above-named is/are hereby eligible to apply for employment and/or student authorizations, as applicable.

The applicant took the above document to mean that she was entitled, at that point and without further action on her part, to work in Canada. From May 9, 1993 to October 1, 1993, she was employed as a housekeeper at Camp Hiawatha in Manitoulin Island, Ontario. On September 23, 1993 she was granted status as a permanent resident, which status embraced the right to work in Canada without a work permit. The applicant was laid off from work on October 1, 1993 and her application for unemployment benefits was denied on the ground that her contract of service was illegal and invalid for the period May 9 to September 23, 1993. The period during which she did work under a valid contract of service, September 23 to October 1, 1993, was not long enough to qualify her for benefits. Ultimately, the applicant appealed to the Tax Court of Canada [*Still v Canada (Minister of National Revenue)*, [1996] TCJ No 1228 (QL)].

The Tax Court Judge found that the applicant believed in good faith that she was lawfully entitled to work in Canada. ...

Specifically, the Tax Court Judge held that the applicant was not engaged in insurable employment because of a violation of subsection 18(1) of the *Immigration Regulations*, 1978 [SOR/78-172 (as am by SOR/89-80, s 1)] which states:

> 18(1) Subject to subsection 19(1) to (2.2), no person, other than a Canadian citizen or permanent resident, shall engage or continue in employment in Canada without a valid and subsisting employment authorization [a work permit].

There is no express penalty for a breach of this particular provision. ...

It is common ground that the applicant paid the insurance premiums and complied with all other requirements of the *Unemployment Insurance Act*. However, because she was not in possession of a work permit, the Tax Court Judge found that the contract of service with her employer was void for illegality. ...

[After a thorough review of the common law doctrine of illegality, the court determined that the contract here was expressly prohibited by statute and continued:]

First, I am of the view that the classical model has long since lost its persuasive force and is no longer being applied consistently. The doctrine is honoured more in its breach than in its observance through the proliferation of so-called judicial "exceptions" to the rule. I am not the first to recognize that these exceptions are truly a movement away from the doctrine itself ... and *Love's Realty & Fin. Services Ltd. v. Coronet Trust*, [1989] 3 W.W.R. 623 (Alta. C.A.), per Kerans J.A., at page 629). ...

In conclusion, the extent to which the precepts of the common law doctrine of illegality are ill-suited to resolving the issue at hand provides the impetus for this Court to chart a course of analysis which is reflective of both the modern approach and its public law milieu. In my opinion, the doctrine of statutory illegality in the federal context is better served by the following principle (not rule): where a contract is expressly or impliedly prohibited by statute, a court may refuse to grant relief to a party when, in all of the circumstances of the case, including regard to the objects and purposes of the statutory prohibition, it would be contrary to public policy, reflected in the relief claimed, to do so.

As the doctrine of illegality rests on the understanding that it would be contrary to public policy to allow a person to maintain an action on a contract prohibited by statute, then it is only appropriate to identify those policy considerations which outweigh the applicant's prima facie right to unemployment insurance benefits. ...

[The court considered the policy of the statutes and concluded:]

Moral disapprobation is likely to arise in those cases where a person gains entry to this country through stealth or deception, obtains employment and then seeks unemployment benefits after losing his or her job. Public policy, of course, cannot be equated with public opinion. But there are occasions when community values are rationally supported and not reflective of a "knee-jerk" reaction to a multi-layered problem. While moral disapprobation of employment obtained in flagrant disregard of Canadian laws is not an unreasonable policy consideration, this sentiment should not be permitted to degenerate into the belief that everyone who gains employment in Canada without a work permit should be so judged.

In my view, this is a case in which the bona fides of the party seeking relief is of critical significance. Ms. Still is not an illegal immigrant. In concluding that she acted in good faith, the Tax Court Judge took into consideration the government document provided to her. The significant portion [at paragraph 1] reads as follows: "The [applicant] is ... hereby eligible to apply for employment and/or student authorizations." That document can be said to serve one of two purposes. First, it reinforces the Tax Court Judge's conclusion that the applicant had acted in good faith (in ignorance of the law). Alternatively, it can be said that the document either induced or misled the applicant into believing that she could obtain employment without a work permit. As this argument was not raised before us, I refrain from commenting further.

There is one other factor I believe to be of significance. It is open to ask whether the denial of unemployment benefits is a de facto penalty which is disproportionate to the statutory breach. I note that here is no express penalty for the breach in question and that a conviction under the general penal provision could not be obtained because of the requirement that a person knowingly contravene the *Immigration Act*. In effect, the applicant is not subject to any penalty under that legislation because of the statutory breach. If the *Immigration Act* is only concerned with those who knowingly fail to obtain a work permit, why should this Court impose a penalty amounting to thousands of dollars in benefits? The Tax Court Judge expressed concerns about the possible depletion of the unemployment insurance fund by "illegal" workers;

however it should be noted in this case that both the claimant and the employer contributed to the fund during the period of "illegal" employment, [and] thus the solvency of the fund was not affected. The Tax Court Judge also concluded that the "social utility" in denying the applicant unemployment benefits lay in the understanding that it would discourage the employment of "non-citizens and non-residents." I take the Tax Court Judge's reasons to mean that the purpose of the requirement to obtain a work permit is to discourage illegal immigrants from undermining the laws of Canada. In response, I simply note that the applicant, Ms. Still, is not an illegal immigrant and that the *Immigration Act* does not seek to discourage her from working in Canada. Rather it encourages her to seek employment for which there are not enough qualified Canadians or employment which Canadians are unwilling to accept. The fabric of many a nation has been woven from the cloth of those who have fallen into the latter category.

Having regard to objects of the *Unemployment Insurance Act*, the fact that the applicant is a legal immigrant to this country and that she acted in good faith, I am not prepared to conclude that she is disentitled to unemployment insurance benefits on the ground of illegality.

CHAPTER EIGHT

PERFORMANCE AND BREACH

Non-performance of a contractual obligation may not only give rise to an action for damages, or specific enforcement, but also have the effect of excusing the party not in breach from that party's obligations. The first part of this chapter deals with this effect. We then turn to consider whether the party in breach might be considered to have waived the ability to seize on the other party's breach as an excuse for non-performance. As we shall see, there appear to be limits on the ability of a party not in breach to waive the other party's breach and enforce the agreement. In the third section, we consider the recently recognized duty to perform one's contractual obligations in good faith. In the final section, we consider the possible remedies of the party in breach of contract.

I. REPUDIATORY BREACH

KINGSTON V PRESTON
(1773), 2 Douglas 689, 99 ER 437 (in argument in *Jones v Barkley*)

This was an action of debt for non-performance of covenants contained in certain articles of agreement between the plaintiff and the defendant. The declaration stated: That, by articles made the 24th of March, 1770, the plaintiff, for the considerations thereinafter mentioned, covenanted with the defendant to serve him for one year and a quarter next ensuing, as a covenant servant, in his trade of a silk-mercer, at £200 a year, and, in consideration of the premises the defendant covenanted that, at the end of the year and a quarter, he would give up his business of a mercer to the plaintiff, and a nephew of the defendant or some other person to be nominated by the defendant, and give up to them his stock in trade, at a fair valuation; and that, between the young traders, deeds of partnership should be executed for fourteen years, and from and immediately after the execution of the said deeds the defendant would permit the said young traders to carry on the said business in the defendant's house.

Then the declaration stated a covenant by the plaintiff, that he would accept the business and stock-in-trade, at a fair valuation, with the defendant's nephew, or such other person, & c., and execute such deeds of partnership, and, further, that the plaintiff should and would, at and before the sealing and delivery of the deeds, cause and procure good and sufficient security to be given to the defendant, to be approved of by the defendant, for the payment of £250 monthly to the defendant, in lieu of a moiety of the monthly produce of the stock in trade, until the value of the stock should be reduced to £4000. Then the plaintiff averred that he had performed and been ready to perform and assigned for breach on the part of the defendant, that he had refused to surrender and give up his business at the end of the said year and a quarter.

The defendant pleaded: 1. That the plaintiff did not offer sufficient security; and, 2. that he did not give sufficient security for payment of the £250, & c.

And the plaintiff demurred generally to both pleas.

LORD MANSFIELD (for the court): There are three kinds of covenants: 1. Such as are called mutual and independent, where either party may recover damages from the other for the injury he may have received by a breach of the covenants in his favor, and where it is no excuse for the defendant to allege a breach of the covenants on the part of the plaintiff. 2. There are covenants which are conditions and dependent, in which the performance of one depends on the prior performance of another, and therefore, till this prior condition is performed, the other party is not liable to an action on his covenant. 3. There is also a third sort of covenants, which are mutual conditions to be performed at the same time; and in these, if one party was ready and offered to perform his part, and the other neglected or refused to perform his, he who was ready and offered has fulfilled his engagement, and may maintain an action for the default of the other though it is not certain that either is obliged to do the first act. His Lordship then proceeded to say, that the dependence or independence of covenants was to be collected from the evident sense and meaning of the parties, and that, however transposed they might be in the deed, their precedency must depend on the order of time in which the intent of the transaction requires their performance. That, in the case before the Court, it would be the greatest injustice if the plaintiff should prevail. The essence of the agreement was, that the defendant should not trust to the personal security of the plaintiff, but, before he delivered up his stock and business, should have good security for the payment of the money. The giving such security, therefore, must necessarily be a condition precedent. Judgment was accordingly given for the defendant, because the part to be performed by the plaintiff was clearly a condition precedent.

RULES OF CIVIL PROCEDURE
Ontario Superior Court of Justice, 1990, as am

25.06(3) Allegations of the performance or occurrence of all conditions precedent to the assertion of a claim or defence of a party are implied in the party's pleading and need not be set out, and an opposite party who intends to contest the performance or occurrence of a condition precedent shall specify in the opposite party's pleading the condition and its non-performance or non-occurrence.

McDonald v Murray. (1885), 11 OAR 101 (CA). PATTERSON JA: ... When people bargain together, whether it is to barter one piece of property for another, or to exchange property for money, each party ordinarily expects to receive what he bargains for when he parts with what he is to give. If the intention is that either of them is to part with his property, and take his chance of the other afterwards performing his part, or paying damages for his default, it is not the ordinary transaction of sale or exchange, and when it is intended we may reasonably expect to find some express declaration of that intention.

BETTINI V GYE
(1876), 1 QBD 183

The defendant was the director of the Royal Italian Opera in Covent Garden, London and the plaintiff was a professional singer who agreed with the defendant as follows (in an English translation from the French):

1. Mr. Bettini undertakes to fill the part of prime tenor assoluto in the theatres, halls, and drawing-rooms, both public and private, in Great Britain and in Ireland, during the period of his engagement with Mr. Gye.
2. This engagement shall begin on the 30th of March, 1875, and shall terminate on the 13th of July, 1875.
3. The salary of Mr. Bettini shall be £150 per month, to be paid monthly.
4. Mr. Bettini shall sing in concerts as well as in operas, but he shall not sing anywhere out of the theatre in the United Kingdom of Great Britain and Ireland, from the 1st of January to the 31st of December, 1875, without the written permission of Mr. Gye, except at a distance of more than fifty miles from London, and out of the season of the theatre.
5. Mr. Gye shall furnish the costumes to Mr. Bettini for his characters, according to the ordinary usage of theatres.
6. Mr. Bettini will conform to the ordinary rules of the theatre in case of sickness, fire, rehearsals, & c.
7. Mr. Bettini agrees to be in London without fail at least six days before the commencement of his engagement, for the purpose of rehearsals.
8. In case Mr. Gye shall require the services of Mr. Bettini at a distance of more than ten miles from London, he shall pay his travelling expenses.
9. Mr. Bettini shall not be obliged to sing more than four times a week in opera. Mr. Bettini, in order to assist the direction of Mr. Gye, will sing, upon the request of Mr. Gye, in the same characters in which he has already sung, and in other characters of equal position. In case of the sickness of other artists, Mr. Bettini agrees to replace them in their characters of first tenor assoluto.
10. Mr. Gye shall have the right to prolong the period limited above upon the same conditions, provided that the period does not go beyond the end of the month of August.

The plaintiff was prevented by temporary illness from being in London before March 28, although the agreement required him to be there "without fail" by March 24. The defendant terminated the agreement on the ground that the plaintiff was late in arrival and had given no notice of his inability to be in London for the purpose of rehearsals. The case was argued on a demurrer to the plea of the plaintiff's late arrival.

BLACKBURN J (for the court): In this case the parties have entered into an agreement in writing, which is set out on the record.

The Court must ascertain the intention of the parties, as is said by Parke B., in delivering the judgment of the Court in *Graves v. Legg* (1854), 156 E.R. 304, "To be collected from the instrument and the circumstances legally admissible in evidence with reference to which it is to be construed." He adds: "One particular rule well acknowledged is, that where a covenant or agreement goes to part of the consideration on both sides, and may be compensated in damages, it is an independent covenant or contract." There was no averment of any special circumstances existing in this case, with reference to which the agreement was made, but the Court must look at the general nature of such an agreement. By the 7th paragraph of the agreement, "Mr. Bettini agrees to be in London, without fail at least six days before the commencement of his engagement for the purpose of rehearsals." The engagement was to begin on the 30th of March, 1875. It is admitted on the record that the plaintiff did not arrive in London till the 28th of March, which is less than six days before the 30th, and therefore it is clear that he has not fulfilled his part of the contract.

The question raised by the demurrer is, not whether the plaintiff has any excuse for failing to fulfil this part of his contract, which may prevent his being liable in damages for not doing so, but whether his failure to do so justified the defendant in refusing to proceed with the engagement, and fulfil his, the defendant's part. And the answer to that question depends on whether this part of the contract is a condition precedent to the defendant's liability or only an independent agreement, a breach of which will not justify a repudiation of the contract, but will only be a cause of action for a compensation in damages. ...

We think the answer to this question depends on the true construction of the contract taken as a whole.

Parties may think some matter, apparently of very little importance, essential; and if they sufficiently express an intention to make the literal fulfilment of such a thing a condition precedent, it will be one; or they may think that the performance of some matter, apparently of essential importance and prima facie a condition precedent, is not really vital, and may be compensated for in damages, and if they sufficiently expressed such an intention, it will not be a condition precedent.

In this case, if to the 7th paragraph of the agreement there had been added words to this effect: "And if Mr. Bettini is not there at the stipulated time, Mr. Gye may refuse to proceed further with the agreement"; or if, on the other hand, it had been said, "And if not there, Mr. Gye may postpone the commencement of Mr. Bettini's engagement for as many days as Mr. Bettini makes default, and he shall forfeit twice his salary for that time," there could have been no question raised in the case. But there is no such declaration of the intention of the parties either way. And in the absence of such an express declaration, we think that we are to look to the whole contract, and applying the rule stated by Parke B. to be acknowledged, see whether the particular stipulation goes to the root of the matter, so that a failure to perform it would render the performance of the rest of the contract by the plaintiff a thing different in substance from what the defendant has stipulated for; or whether it merely partially affects it and may be compensated for in damages. Accordingly as it is one or the other, we think it must be taken to be or not to be intended to be a condition precedent.

If the plaintiff's engagement had been only to sing in operas at the theatre, it might very well be that previous attendance at rehearsals with the actors in company with whom he was to perform was essential. And if the engagement had been only for a few performances, or for a short time, it would afford a strong argument that attendance for the purpose of rehearsals during the six days immediately before the commencement of the engagement was a vital part of the agreement. But we find, on looking to the agreement, that the plaintiff was to sing in theatres, halls, and drawing rooms, both public and private, from the 30th of March to the 13th of July, 1875, and that he was to sing in concerts as well as in operas, and was not to sing anywhere out of the theatre in Great Britain or Ireland from the 1st of January to the 31st of December, 1875, without the written permission of the defendant, except at a distance of more than fifty miles from London.

The plaintiff, therefore, has, in consequence of this agreement, been deprived of the power of earning anything in London from the 1st of January to the 30th of March; and though the defendant has, perhaps, not received any benefit from this, so as to preclude him from any longer treating as a condition precedent what had originally been one, we think this at least affords a strong argument for saying that subsequent stipulations are not intended to be conditions precedent, unless the nature of the thing strongly shows they must be so.

And, as far as we can see, the failure to attend at rehearsals during the six days immediately before the 30th of March could only affect the theatrical performances and, perhaps, the singing in duets or concerted pieces during the first week or fortnight of this engagement, which is to sing in theatres, halls, and drawing-rooms, and concerts, for fifteen weeks.

We think, therefore, that it does not go to the root of the matter so as to require us to consider it a condition precedent.

The defendant must, therefore, we think, seek redress by a cross-claim for damages.

Judgment must be given for the plaintiff.

QUESTIONS

Is this decision consistent with *Kingston v Preston*, above? What is the test, according to Blackburn J, for determining whether a breach is of such a nature that it enables the other party to terminate the contract? If the defendant cross-claimed for damages, as suggested, would the plaintiff have any defence in the fact that his absence was caused by illness? See *Poussard v Spiers and Pond*, below. If the plaintiff's absence had been caused by some capricious delay on his part, would it have affected the decision in the case?

POUSSARD V SPIERS AND POND
(1876), 1 QBD 410

BLACKBURN J: This was an action for the dismissal of the plaintiff's wife from a theatrical engagement. On the trial before my brother Field it appeared that the defendants, Messrs. Spiers & Pond, had taken the Criterion Theatre, and were about to bring out a French opera, which was to be produced simultaneously in London and Paris. Their manager, Mr. Hingston, by their authority, made a contract with the plaintiff's wife, which was reduced to writing in the following letter:

Criterion Theatre, Oct. 16th, 1874.

To Madame Poussard,

On behalf of Messrs. Spiers & Pond I engage you to sing and play at the Criterion Theatre on the following terms:

You to play the part of Friquette in Lecocq's opera Les Pres Saint Gervais, commencing on or about the 14th of November next, at a weekly salary of eleven pounds (£11) and to continue on at that sum for a period of three months, providing the opera shall run for that period. Then, at the expiration of the said three months, I shall be at liberty to re-engage you at my option, on terms then to be arranged, and not to exceed fourteen pounds per week for another period of three months. Dresses and

677

tights requisite for the part to be provided by the management, and the engagement to be subject to the ordinary rules and regulations of the theatre.

E.P. Hingston, Manager

Ratified:
Spiers & Pond
Madame Poussard, 46 Gunter Grove, Chelsea.

The first performance of the piece was announced for Saturday, the 28th of November. No objection was raised on either side as to this delay, and Madame Poussard attended rehearsals, and such attendance, though not expressed in the written engagement, was an implied part of it. Owing to delays on the part of the composer, the music of the latter part of the piece was not in the hands of the defendants till a few days before that announced for the production of the piece, and the latter and final rehearsals did not take place till the week on the Saturday of which the performance was announced. Madame Poussard was unfortunately taken ill, and though she struggled to attend the rehearsals, she was obliged on Monday, the 23rd of November, to leave the rehearsal, go home and go to bed, and call in medical attendance. In the course of the next day or two an interview took place between the plaintiff and Mr. Leonard (Madame Poussard's medical attendant) and Mrs. Liston, who was the defendant's stage manager, in reference to Madame Poussard's ability to attend and undertake her part, and there was a conflict of testimony as to what took place. According to the defendant's version, Mrs. Liston requested to know as soon as possible what was the prospect of Madame Poussard's recovery, as it would be very difficult on such short notice to obtain a substitute; and that in the result the plaintiff wrote stating that his wife's health was such that she could not play on the Saturday night, and that Mrs. Liston had better, therefore engage a young lady to play the part; and this, if believed to be accurate, amounted to a rescission of the contract. According to the evidence of the plaintiff and the doctor, Mrs. Liston told them that Madame Poussard was to take care of herself and not come out till quite well, as she, Mrs. Liston, had procured, or would procure, a temporary substitute; and Madame Poussard could resume her place as soon as she was well. This, it was contended by the plaintiff, amounted to a waiver by the defendants of a breach of the condition precedent, if there was one.

The jury found that the plaintiff did not rescind the contract, and that Mrs. Liston, if she did waive the condition precedent (as to which they were not agreed), had no authority from the defendants to do so.

These findings, if they stand, dispose of those two questions.

There was no substantial conflict as to what was in fact done by Mrs. Liston. Upon learning, on the Wednesday (the 25th of November), the possibility that Madame Poussard might be prevented by illness from fulfilling her engagement, she sent to a theatrical agent to inquire what artistes of position were disengaged, and learning that Miss Lewis had no engagement till the 25th of December, she made a provisional arrangement with her, by which Miss Lewis undertook to study the part and be ready on Saturday to take the part, in case Madame Poussard was not then recovered so far as to be ready to perform. If it should turn out that this labour was thrown away, Miss Lewis was to have a douceur for her trouble. If Miss Lewis was called on to perform, she was to be engaged at £15 a week up to the 25th of December, if the piece ran so long. Madame Poussard continued in bed and ill, and unable to attend either the subsequent rehearsals or the first night of the performance on the Saturday, and Miss Lewis's engagement became absolute, and she performed the part on Saturday, Monday, Tuesday, Wednesday, and up to the close of her engagement, the

25th of December. The piece proved a success, and in fact ran for more than three months.

On Thursday, the 4th of December, Madame Poussard, having recovered, offered to take her place, but was refused, and for this refusal the action was brought.

On the 21st of January Madame Poussard left England.

My brother Field, at the trial, expressed his opinion that the failure of Madame Poussard to be ready to perform, under the circumstances, went so much to the root of the consideration as to discharge the defendants, and that he should therefore enter judgment for the defendants; but he asked the jury five questions.

The first three related to the supposed rescission and waiver. The other questions were in writing and were: 4. Whether the non-attendance on the night of the opening was of such material consequence to the defendants as to entitle them to rescind the contract? To which the jury said, "No." And, 5. Was it of such consequence as to render reasonable for the defendants to employ another artiste, and whether the engagement of Miss Lewis, as made, was reasonable? to which the jury said, "Yes." Lastly, he left the question of damages, which the jury assessed at £83.

On these answers he reserved leave to the plaintiff to move to enter judgment for £83.

A cross rule was obtained on the ground that the verdict was against evidence and that the damages were excessive.

We think that, from the nature of the engagement to take a leading, and, indeed, the principal, female part (for the prima donna sang her part in male costume as the Prince de Conti) in a new opera which (as appears from the terms of the engagement) it was known might run for a longer or shorter time, and so be a profitable or losing concern to the defendants, we can, without the aid of the jury, see that it must have been of great importance to the defendants that the piece should start well, and consequently that the failure of the plaintiff's wife to be able to perform on the opening and early performances was a very serious detriment to them.

This inability having been occasioned by sickness was not any breach of contract by the plaintiff, and no action can lie against him for the failure thus occasioned. But the damage to the defendants and the consequent failure of consideration is just as great as if it had been occasioned by the plaintiff's fault, instead of by the wife's misfortune. The analogy is complete between this case and that of a charter-party in the ordinary terms, where the ship is to proceed in ballast (the act of God, & c., excepted) to a port, and there load a cargo. If the delay is occasioned by excepted perils, the ship owner is excused. But if it is so great as to go to the root of the matter, it frees the charterer from his obligation to furnish a cargo; see per Bramwell B., delivering the judgment of the majority of the Court of Exchequer Chamber in *Jackson v. Union Marine Insurance Co.* (1874), L.R. 10 C.P. 125 at p. 141.

And we think that the question, whether the failure of a skilled and capable artiste to perform in a new piece through serious illness is so important as to go to the root of the consideration, must to some extent depend on the evidence; and is a mixed question of law and fact. Theoretically, the facts should be left to and found separately by the jury, it being for the judge or the Court to say whether they, being so found, show a breach of condition precedent or not. But this course is often (if not generally) impracticable; and if we can see that the proper facts have been found, we should act on these without regard to the form of the questions.

Now, in the present case, we must consider what were the courses open to the defendants under the circumstances. They might, it was said on the argument before us (though not on the trial), have postponed the bringing out of the piece till the recovery of Madame Poussard, and if her illness had been a temporary hoarseness incapacitating her from singing on the Saturday, but sure to be removed by the Monday, that might have been a proper course to pursue. But the illness here was a serious one, of uncertain duration, and if the plaintiff had at the trial suggested that this was the proper course, it would, no doubt, have been shown that it would have been a ruinous course; and that it would have been much better to have abandoned the piece altogether than to have postponed it from day to day for an uncertain time, during which the theatre would have been a heavy loss.

The remaining alternatives were to employ a temporary substitute until such time as the plaintiff's wife should recover; and if a temporary substitute capable of performing the part adequately could have been obtained upon such a precarious engagement on any reasonable terms, that would have been a right course to pursue; but if no substitute capable of performing the part adequately could be obtained, except on the terms that she should be permanently engaged at higher pay than the plaintiff's wife, in our opinion it follows, as a matter of law, that the failure on the plaintiff's part went to the root of the matter and discharged the defendants.

We think, therefore, that the fifth question put to the jury, and answered by them in favour of the defendants, does find all the facts necessary to enable us to decide as a matter of law that the defendants are discharged.

The fourth question is, no doubt, found by the jury for the plaintiff; but we think in finding it they must have made a mistake in law as to what was a sufficient failure of consideration to set the defendants at liberty, which was not a question for them.

This view taken by us renders it unnecessary to decide anything on the cross-rule for a new trial.

The motion must be refused with costs.

QUESTIONS

Was illness a material factor in this case? Why can no action lie against M Poussard for the failure occasioned by Madame Poussard's illness? Is there not a breach of the promise to sing? What terms must the court imply in this contract in order that Madame Poussard be excused? What reason in policy is there for such implied terms?

CEHAVE NV V BREMER HANDELGESELLESCHAFT GMBH
[1976] QB 44 (CA)

LORD DENNING MR: In 1970, the sellers, a German company, agreed to sell to the buyers, a Dutch company, 12,000 metric tons of U.S. citrus pulp pellets. Those pellets are a by-product of oranges. The juice is extracted and tinned. The orange rinds are dried and made into pellets. The pellets are used as an ingredient in making cattle food.

In September 1970, there were two contracts of sale, each for 6,000 metric tons, delivery in bulk to be made by six instalments of 1,000 tons each over the first six months of 1971. Under the first contract of September 24, the price was $73.50 per metric ton. Under the second contract of September 28, the price was $73.75. In each case c.i.f. Rotterdam. Each contract incorporated the terms issued by the Cattle Food Trade Association, form 100, for shipment of feeding stuffs in bulk "Talequale c.i.f. terms." That form contained two sentences material to this dispute in clause no. 7: "Shipment to be made in good condition. ... [E]ach shipment shall be considered a separate contract."

The first three or four shipments were quite satisfactory. This case is concerned with a shipment made early in May 1971. It was by the German vessel the *Hansa Nord*.

She took on about 3,400 metric tons of citrus pulp pellets at Port Manatee in Florida. Four bills of lading were issued. They were appropriated by the sellers as follows: two were for 1,000 tons each on the second contract. One for 1,000 tons and one for 419.856 tons on the first contract. But there was no physical appropriation of the cargo as between the two contracts.

On May 14 the buyers paid the price and got the shipping documents. The *Hansa Nord* arrived in Rotterdam on Friday, May 21, and started unloading on Saturday, May 22. It was finished by May 25. The cargo was discharged into lighters. The out-turn weights were:

Ex-hold no. 1 .... 1,260 metric tons.
Ex-hold no. 2 .... 2,053 metric tons.

It is to be noticed that by this time the market price had fallen greatly. The contract price for these 3,400 tons was (when converted into sterling) about £100,000. But the market price on May 24 in Rotterdam was, for sound goods, only £86,000. This may give an explanation of subsequent happenings.

The cargo ex no. 2 hold (2,053 tons) was in good condition. But some of the cargo ex no. 1 hold (1,260 tons) was found to be damaged. On May 24 the buyers rejected the whole cargo (both no. 2 and no. 1 holds) on the ground that it was not shipped in good condition and they claimed repayment of the purchase price of £100,000. On the next day the sellers refused, saying that the goods were shipped in good condition: and that the damage must have occurred at sea and that the buyers ought to lodge their claim with the insurers.

So there it was. The goods were in the lighters with both sellers and buyers disclaiming ownership. Now comes an astonishing sequence of events. There was a Mr. Baas in Rotterdam who was an importer of feeding products (including citrus pulp pellets). On May 29, 1971, if not before, he inspected the cargo in the lighters. On June 1, 1971, the lighter owners applied ex parte to the Rotterdam County Court, the Commercial court I expect, asking it to authorise a sale of the goods. They applied by their lawyer, a Mr. Driessen. The sellers were not told of this application. But the buyers were. They were represented by the same lawyer as the lighter owners, Mr. Driessen. On the same day this court granted the application and authorised the sale. It appointed agents to make the sale. The agents approached Mr. Baas. They did not approach any other possible bidders. They sold the whole cargo to Mr. Baas (out of both no. 2 and no. 1 holds) for a sum equivalent to £33,720. The expenses of sale were deducted, leaving the net proceeds at £29,903. These were paid into a Dutch bank "to the order of whom it may concern." On the self-same day, Mr. Baas sold the whole cargo to the buyers (i.e. the original buyers under the two contracts) at the same price and upon the same terms as he had himself bought them from the agents of the court. The board of appeal found: "as a fair inference from the evidence ... that the buyers and Mr. Baas intended that he (Baas) should acquire the cargo for their (the buyers') benefit, or on their behalf ... ."

Having bought the whole cargo from Mr. Baas, the buyers transported it in the same way as they would have done if it had never suffered any damage. They took the lighters by canal to their plant at Veghel, a journey of some 60 miles. The buyers then used the entire cargo to manufacture cattle food at their processing plant at Veghel. They used it in the self-same way as they would sound goods except that they used "smaller percentages in their compound feeds than would be normal with sound goods." This difference in manufacture did not cause them any loss. At any rate, there is no finding that it did. And it was surely for them to prove it.

The upshot of it all was, therefore, that the buyers took the whole cargo and used all of it for their business just as if they had never rejected it save for the smaller percentages. So the ubiquitous Mr. Baas had helped them greatly. They paid only £33,720 for it instead of the contract price of £100,000. The board of appeal of the trade association felt it necessary to make this comment:

> We wish to record that we are not satisfied that we have been presented with a full account of how the goods were disposed of in Rotterdam after rejection by the buyers. The witnesses produced by the buyers gave contradictory evidence on this question, as well as on other less vital issues.

That is a devastating comment. The buyers must have known the truth. But they did not tell it to the board of appeal. At any rate, not the whole truth.

Nevertheless, despite that devastating comment, the board of appeal made their award in favour of the buyers. They ordered the sellers to repay the buyers the £100,000 with interest, and directed the proceeds of sale (£29,903) to be repaid to the sellers. So the buyers have got the entire cargo and used it for their cattle food, but instead of paying £100,000 for it, they have only paid £30,000. The judge has upheld this award [1974] 2 Lloyd's Rep. 216,227. The sellers appeal to this court. They recognise that they may have to pay something by way of damages for the damaged goods, but they deny that the buyers had any right to reject the whole cargo.

The board of appeal found a breach of the express clause "Shipped in good condition." They said: " ... on the balance of probability, not all the goods in hold no. 1 were shipped in good condition as required by the contract, nor on balance of probability were they reasonably fit to be carried on the contemplated voyage."

The board of appeal also found a breach of the implied conditions as to merchantability contained in section 14(2) of the Sale of Goods Act 1893. They said:

> The goods in hold 1 were "merchantable" on arrival in Rotterdam in a commercial sense, though at a lower price than would be paid for sound goods: we find and hold, however, that they were not "of merchantable quality" within the meaning of the phrase when used in the Sale of Goods Act 1893.

The board of appeal did not find a breach of the implied condition of fitness contained in section 14(1) of the Act. They found all the elements about reliance and so forth, but they did not find that the goods were unfit. They could hardly have found them unfit, seeing that they were in fact used for that purpose.

"SHIPPED IN GOOD CONDITION"

The judge held that, in contracts for the sale of goods, a stipulation must either be a "condition" or a "warranty" and that there could be no tertium quid. Accepting that distinction, he held that this stipulation "shipped in good condition" was a "condition" and not a "warranty" [1974] 2 Lloyd's Rep. 216, 225; so that, for any breach of it by the seller, the buyer was entitled to treat the contract as repudiated.

Those decisions by the judge are so important that they deserve careful consideration.

THE GENERAL LAW APART FROM THE SALE OF GOODS

For the last 300 or 400 years the courts have had to grapple with this problem: in what circumstances can a party, who is in breach himself of a stipulation of the contract, call upon the other side to perform his part or sue him for non-performance? At one time the solution was thought to depend on the nature of the stipulation itself, and not on the extent of the breach or its consequences. Under the old forms of pleading, a plaintiff had to aver and prove that he had performed all conditions precedent or that he was ready and willing to perform them. The question, therefore, was whether the stipulation (which he had broken) was a condition precedent or not: or, in the terminology of the 18th century, whether it was an *independent* covenant (the breach of which did not debar him from suing the other side), or a *dependent* covenant (the breach of which did debar the plaintiff because the performance by the other was *dependent* on the plaintiff performing his). This distinction was well stated by Serjeant Williams in his notes to *Pordage v. Cole* (1669) 1 Wms. Saund. 319, 320b:

> ... [W]here there are several covenants, promises or agreements, which are *independent* of each other, one party may bring an action against the other for a breach of his covenants, etc. without averring a performance of the covenants, etc. on his, the plaintiff's part; and it is no excuse for the defendant to allege in his plea a breach of the covenants, etc. on the part of the plaintiff ... . But where the covenants, etc. are *dependent*, it is necessary for the plaintiff to aver and prove a performance of the covenants, etc. on his part, to entitle himself to an action for the breach of the covenants on the part of the defendant. ...

Although that division was treated as exhaustive, nevertheless, when the courts came to apply it, they had regard to the extent of the breach. ...

In short, if the breach went to the root of the matter, the stipulation was to be considered a condition precedent: but if the breach did not go to the root, the stipulation was considered to be an independent covenant which could be compensated for in damages: see *Davidson v. Gwynne* (1810) 12 East 381, 389, per Lord Ellenborough C.J.; *Ellen v. Topp* (1851) 6 Exch. 424, 441; and *Graves v. Legg* (1854) 9 Exch. 709, 716.

Apart from those cases of "breach going to the root," the courts at the same time were developing the doctrine of "anticipatory breach." When one party, before the day when he is obliged to perform his part, declares in advance that he will not perform it when the day comes, or by his conduct evinces an intention not to perform it, the other may elect to treat his declaration or conduct as a breach going to the root of the matter and to treat himself as discharged from further performance: see *Hochster v. De la Tour* (1853) 2 E. & B. 678. By his prior declaration or conduct, the guilty party is said to repudiate the contract. The word "repudiation" should be confined to those cases of an *anticipatory* breach, but it is also used in connection with cases of an *actual* breach going to the root of the contract: see *Heyman v. Darwins Ltd.* [1942] A.C. 356, 378-379 by Lord Wright. All of them were gathered together by Lord Blackburn in his famous speech in *Mersey Steel and Iron Co. Ltd. v. Naylor, Benzon & Co.* (1884) 9 App. Cas. 434, 443-444:

> The rule of law, as I always understand it, is that where there is a contract in which there are two parties, each side having to do something (it is so laid down in the notes to *Pordage v. Cole*, 1 Wms. Saund. 319, 320) if you see that the failure to perform one part of it goes to the root of the contract, goes to the foundation of the whole, it is a good defence to say, "I am not going on to perform any part of it when that which is the root of the whole and the substantial consideration for my performance is defeated by your misconduct." ... I repeatedly asked Mr. Cohen whether or not he could find any authority which justified him in saying that every breach of a contract ... must be considered to go to the root of the contract, and he produced no such authority. There are many cases in which the breach may do so; it depends upon the construction of the contract.

Those last words are clearly a reference to a "condition" strictly so called, in which any breach entitled the other to be discharged from further performance. But the earlier words are quite general. They refer to all terms other than conditions strictly so called.

THE SALE OF GOODS ACT

Such was the state of the law when the Sale of Goods Act 1893 was passed on February 20, 1894. I have studied the then current edition of Benjamin, *Sale of Personal Property*, 4th ed. (1888), and the little books which Judge Chalmers wrote before (1890) and after the Act (*Chalmers' Sale of Goods Act*, 1893, 1st ed. (1894)), and the proceedings in Parliament. These show that until the year 1893 there was much confusion in the use of the words "condition" and "warranty." But that confusion was removed by the Act itself and by the judgment of Bowen L.J. in *Bentsen v. Taylor, Sons & Co.* [1893] 2 Q.B. 274, 280. Thenceforward those words were used by lawyers as terms of art. The difference between them was that if the promisor broke a *condition* in any respect, however slight, it gave the other party a right to be quit of his obligations and to sue for damages: unless he by his conduct waived the condition, in which case he was bound to perform his future obligations but could sue for the damage he had suffered. If the promisor broke a *warranty* in any respect, however serious, the other party was not quit of his future obligations. He had to perform them. His only remedy was to sue for damages: see *The Mihalis Angelos* [1971] 1 Q.B. 164, 193 and *Wickman Machine Tool Sales Ltd. v. L. Schuler A.G.* [1972] 1 W.L.R. 840, 851.

Now that division was not exhaustive. It left out of account the vast majority of stipulations which were neither "conditions" nor "warranties" strictly so called: but were intermediate stipulations, the effect of which depended on the breach. The cases about these stipulations were legion. They stretched continuously from *Boone v. Eyre (Note)*, 1 Hy. Bl. 273, in 1777 to *Mersey Steel and Iron Co. Ltd. v. Naylor, Benzon & Co.* (1884) 9 App. Cas. 434. I cannot believe that Parliament in 1893 intended to give the go-by to all these cases: or to say that they did not apply to the sale of goods. Those cases expressed the rules of the common law. They were preserved by section 61(2) of the Act of 1893, which said: "The rules of the common law, including the law merchant, save in so far as they are inconsistent with the express provisions of this Act ... shall continue to apply to contracts for the sale of goods." There was nothing in the Act inconsistent with those cases. So they continued to apply.

In 1962 in the *Hongkong Fir Shipping Co. Ltd. v. Kawasaki Kisen Kaisha Ltd.* [1962] 2 Q.B. 26, the Court of Appeal drew attention to this vast body of case law. They showed that besides conditions and warranties, strictly so called, there are many stipulations of which the effect depends on this: if the breach goes to the root of the contract, the other party is entitled to treat himself as discharged: but if it does not go to the root, he is not. In my opinion, the principle embodied in these cases applies to contracts for the sale of goods just as to all other contracts.

The task of the court can be stated simply in the way in which Upjohn L.J. stated it at p. 64. First, see whether the stipulation, on its true construction, is a condition strictly so called, that is, a stipulation such that, for any breach of it, the other party is entitled to treat himself as discharged. Second, if it is not such a condition, then look to the extent of the actual breach which has taken place. If it is such as to go to the root of the contract, the other party is entitled to treat himself as discharged: but, otherwise, not. To this may be added an anticipatory breach. If the one party, before the day on which he is due to perform his part, shows by his words or conduct that he will not perform it in a vital respect when the day comes, the other party is entitled to treat himself as discharged.

"SHIPPED IN GOOD CONDITION"

This brings me back to the particular stipulation in this case: "Shipped in good condition." Was this a condition strictly so called, so that *any* breach of it entitled the buyer to reject the goods? Or was it an intermediate stipulation, so that the buyer cannot reject unless the breach is so serious as to go to the root of the contract?

If there was any previous authority holding it to be a *condition* strictly so called, we should abide by it, just as we did with the clause "expected ready to load": see *Finnish Government (Ministry of Food) v. H. Ford & Co. Ltd.* (1921) 6 Ll.L.Rep. 188; *The Mihalis Angelos* [1971] 1 Q.B. 164. But, there is no such authority with the clause "shipped in good condition." I regard this clause as comparable to a clause as to quality, such as "fair average quality." If a small portion of the goods sold was a little below that standard, it would be met by commercial men by an allowance off the price. The buyer would have no right to reject the whole lot unless the divergence was serious and substantial: see *Biggin & Co. Ltd. v. Permanite Ltd.* [1951] 1 K.B. 422, 439, *per* Devlin J. and *Christopher Hill Ltd. v. Ashington Piggeries Ltd.* [1972] A.C. 441, 511, *per* Lord Diplock. That is shown in this very case by clause 5 in form no. 100 which contains percentages of contamination, below which there is a price allowance, and above which there is a right in the buyer to reject. Likewise with the clause "shipped in good condition." If a small portion of the whole cargo was not in good condition and arrived a little unsound, it should be met by a price allowance. The buyers should not have a right to reject the whole cargo unless it was serious and substantial. This is borne out by the difficulty which often arises (as in this case) on a c.i.f. contract as to whether the damage was done before shipment or took place after shipment: for in the latter case the buyer would have no claim against the seller but would be left to his claim against the insurers. So, as a matter of good sense, the buyer should be bound to accept the goods and not reject them unless there is a serious and substantial breach, fairly attributable to the seller.

In my opinion, therefore, the term "shipped in good condition" was not a condition strictly so called: nor was it a warranty strictly so called. It was one of those intermediate stipulations which gives no right to reject unless the breach goes to the root of the contract.

On the facts stated by the board of appeal, I do not think the buyer was entitled to reject these instalments of the contract. The board only said that "not all the goods in hold no. 1 were shipped in good condition." That does not say how many were bad. In any case, their condition cannot have been very bad, seeing that all of them were in fact used for the intended purpose. The breach did not go to the root of the contract. The buyer is entitled to damages, but not to rejection.

"MERCHANTABLE"

The board of appeal made this finding: "The goods in hold 1 were 'merchantable' on arrival at Rotterdam in a commercial sense, though at a lower price than would be paid for sound goods; we find and hold, however, that they were not 'of merchantable quality' within the meaning of the phrase when used in the Sale of Goods Act 1893."

The board of appeal were not lawyers: but they had a legal adviser. And I am afraid that in reaching that finding they were not advised correctly. The statute uses the words "merchantable quality" in a commercial sense. The board should, therefore, have applied it in the commercial sense. They should not have been persuaded to give it some other "statutory sense."

Now we were taken through many of the definitions which have been given by judges of "merchantable quality," particularly that of Dixon J. in *Australian Knitting Mills Ltd. v. Grant* (1933) 50 C.L.R. 387, 418; of Lord Wright in *Cammell Laird & Co. Ltd. v. Manganese Bronze and Brass Co. Ltd.* [1934] A.C. 402, 430, as amended by Lord Reid in *Hardwick Game Farm v. Suffolk Agricultural Poultry Producers Association* [1969] 2 A.C. 31, 77 and by Lord Guest in *B.S. Brown & Son Ltd. v. Craiks Ltd.* [1970] 1 W.L.R. 752,

758. But, as Lord Reid pointed out in that case, at p. 754: " ... [J]udicial observations can never be regarded as complete definitions: they must be read in light of the facts and issues raised in the particular case. I do not think it is possible to frame, except in the vaguest terms, a definition of 'merchantable quality' which can apply to every kind of case."

For myself, I think the definition in the latest statute is the best that has yet been devised. It is contained in section 7(2) of the Supply of Goods (Implied Terms) Act 1973. The statute itself only applies to contracts made after May 18, 1973. But the definition seems to me appropriate for contracts made before it. It runs as follows:

> Goods of any kind are of merchantable quality within the meaning of this Act if they are as fit for the purpose or purposes for which goods of that kind are commonly bought as it is reasonable to expect having regard to any description applied to them, the price (if relevant) and all other relevant circumstances; and any reference in this Act to unmerchantable goods shall be construed accordingly.

In applying that definition, it is as well to remember that, by the statute, we are dealing with an implied *condition*, strictly so called, and not a warranty. For any breach of it, therefore, the buyer is entitled to *reject* the goods: or, alternatively, if he chooses to accept them or has accepted them, he has a remedy in damages. In these circumstances, I should have thought a fair way of testing merchantability would be to ask a commercial man: was the breach such that the buyer should be able to reject the goods? In answering that question the commercial man would have regard to the various matters mentioned in the new statutory definition. He would, of course, have regard to the purpose for which goods of that kind are commonly bought. If a buyer buys "waste silk" and it is of no use for the purpose of "waste silk," he can reject it: see *Gardiner v. Gray* (1815) 4 Camp. 144. If he buys dates for food and they are of no use for food, he can reject them: see *Asfar & Co. v. Blundell* [1896] 1 Q.B. 123, 127. But if he buys groundnuts for cattlefood, and they can reasonably be used for cattlefood, he may not be able to reject them, even though they are not suitable for poultry; see *Hardwick Game Farm v. Suffolk Agricultural Poultry Producers Association* [1969] 2 A.C. 31. The commercial man would also, of course, have regard to the description applied to them. If motor horns are sold, expressly or impliedly, as "new" and then the buyer finds that they are dented and scratched, he ought to be able to reject them: see *Jackson v. Rotax Motor and Cycle Co.* [1910] 2 K.B. 937. If they are sold as "second hand" or "shop soiled," then he must take them as they are: see *Bartlett v. Sidney Marcus Ltd.* [1965] 1 W.L.R. 1013; unless there is something radically wrong with them. He would also have regard to the price. If they are sold at the market price, the buyer would expect them to be of good quality and condition; and, if they were not, he would be able to reject them: see *Jones v. Just* and *B.S. Brown & Son Ltd. v. Craiks Ltd.* [1970] 1 W.L.R. 752, 754-755, per Lord Reid: but, if they are sold at a "cut" price or "bargain" price, or a lower price, he would have to put up with something less. He would not be entitled to reject them simply because they were not perfect. The commercial man would also have regard to any other relevant circumstances. If there was a clause, express or implied, which would give the buyer an allowance off the price for the particular shortcomings, such that a commercial man would say: "The buyer is entitled to a price allowance but not to reject them"—again the goods would be of merchantable quality. The buyer would be entitled to an allowance or damages in lieu, but not entitled to reject the lot.

Our present case comes within that last illustration. These citrus pulp pellets were bought for cattle food. That was the purpose for which such pellets are commonly bought. They were as fit for that purpose as it was reasonable to expect. That is shown by the fact that they were actually used for that purpose. Some of them arrived damaged, but not to such an extent that the buyer was entitled to reject the cargo in both holds, or either of them. That damage was such as to entitle the buyer to an allowance off the price for breach of the clause "shipped in good condition": but not such as to entitle him to reject the lot on the ground that it was not of "merchantable quality." That is, I think, what the board of appeal meant when they found that the goods were "merchantable" on arrival at Rotterdam in a commercial sense, though at a lower price than would be paid for sound goods. In short, the buyers are entitled to an allowance or damages for the damaged goods, but not entitled to reject the lot. This makes commercial good sense. It often happens that the market price falls between the making of the contract and the time for delivery. In such a situation, it is not fair that a buyer should be allowed to reject a whole consignment of goods just because a small quantity are not up to the contract quality or condition. The proper remedy is a price allowance and not complete rejection. I feel sure that is what the board of appeal thought in this case. They only found otherwise because they thought the law constrained them to do so. Their instinct was right. Having found that in a commercial sense the goods were merchantable, there was no breach of section 14(2).

DAMAGES

In my opinion, therefore, the buyers were not entitled to reject the goods. They are, however, entitled to damages for the difference in value between the damaged goods and sound goods on arrival at Rotterdam. The case must be remitted to the board for this to be determined.

I would allow the appeal, accordingly.

ORMROD LJ: ... We have all been brought up since our student days to ask the question in the form: "Is this stipulation a condition or a warranty?" But before the Sale of Goods Act 1893 was passed the question was whether the buyer was bound to accept the goods. The answer depended, to use modern language, on whether the stipulation "went to the root of the contract," although it was differently phrased, e.g., "the buyer was entitled to get what he bargained for" or "the seller had failed to perform an essential term of the contract." The words "condition" and "warranty" were used in various senses in different cases but the distinction depended largely on the old rules of pleading. Section 11(1)(b) of the Act was clearly intended to remove this confusion of terminology but the essential dichotomy was not affected; it was and is, between the right to reject or the right to damages. The modern form of the question tends to put the cart before the horse and to obscure the issue.

If one asks oneself the question in the form, "Did the parties intend that the buyer should be entitled to reject the goods if they were not shipped in good condition?" the answer must be that it depends on the nature and effects of the breach. This is directly in line with Diplock L.J.'s approach in the *Hongkong Fir Shipping Co.* case [1962] 2 Q.B. 26, 69-70, not surprisingly, since there can be very little difference in principle between whether the ship is seaworthy and whether goods are in good condition. There is obviously a strong case for applying the general principle of the *Hongkong Fir Shipping Co.* case to contracts for the sale of goods. The question remains, however, and it is the kernel of Mr. Hallgarten's submission, whether it is open to the court to do so. The parties themselves, of course, can do it by express agreement as, indeed, they have done in the present case in relation to quality. Clause 5 provides that breach of the terms as to quality shall entitle the buyer to an allowance but that if the goods contain over 5 per cent of sand or in excess of .005 per cent of castor seed husk, the buyer may reject the parcel. If it can be done expressly, it can be done by implication, unless it is in some way prohibited. Mr. Hallgarten argues that section 11(1)(b) compels the court to choose between condition and warranty. I do not think that the subsection was intended to have any prohibitory effect. It is essentially a definition, defining "condition" and "warranty" in terms of remedies. Nor is the classification absolutely rigid, for it provides that a buyer may treat a condition as a warranty if he wishes, by accepting the goods. It does not, however, envisage the possibility that a breach of warranty might go to the root of the contract, and so, in certain circumstances, entitle the buyer to treat the contract as repudiated. But the law has developed since the Act was passed. It is now accepted as a general principle since the *Hongkong Fir Shipping Co.* case [1962] 2 Q.B. 26 that it is the events resulting from the breach, rather than the breach itself, which may destroy the consideration for the buyer's promise and so enable him to treat the contract as repudiated.

[See also Waddams at paras 584-95.]

SALE OF GOODS ACT
RSO 1990, c S.1

30(2) Where there is a contract for the sale of goods to be delivered by stated instalments that are to be separately paid for and the seller makes defective deliveries in respect of one or more instalments or fails to deliver one or more instalments or the buyer neglects or refuses to take delivery of or pay for one or more instalments, it is a question in each case depending on the terms of the contract and the circumstances of the case whether the breach of contract is a repudiation of the whole contract or whether it is a severable breach giving rise to a claim for compensation but not to a right to treat the whole contract as repudiated.

MAPLE FLOCK COMPANY, LTD V UNIVERSAL FURNITURE PRODUCTS (WEMBLEY), LTD
[1934] 1 KB 148 (CA)

LORD HEWART CJ: The judgment which I am about to read is the judgment of the whole Court.

The appellant company are manufacturers of rag flock, and the respondents are manufacturers of furniture and bedding for which they use such flock. The action was brought by the appellants for breach by the respondents of a contract in writing, dated March 14, 1932, for the sale by the appellants to the respondents of 100 tons of black lindsey flock at £15 2s. 6d. per ton, to be delivered in three loads per week as required. It was further stipulated that there should be a written guarantee that all flock supplied under the contract should conform to the Government standard. The load was 1½ tons of 60 bags. The Government standard was that required under the *Rag Flock Act, 1911,* which had been fixed by regulation under the Act at not more than 30 parts of chlorine in 100,000 parts of flock. The Act made it a penal offence punishable by fine for any person (inter alia) to sell or have in his possession for sale or use or to use flock not conforming to that standard. A person charged under the Act might, however, if he could prove that he bought it from some one resident in the United Kingdom under a warranty that it complied with the Government standard, and that he had taken reasonable steps to ascertain and did in fact believe in the accuracy of the warranty, bring the seller before the Court by information and transfer the burden of the offence to him.

The appellant company duly gave a written guarantee as required by the contract and deliveries were at once commenced and continued of 1½ tons each. The sixteenth of these deliveries was made on April 28, 1932, and, according to the respondent's evidence, was duly accepted and the stuff put into use; a further delivery was made on April 29, 1932, and another on May 2, 1932. On that latter date the respondents notified the appellants that a sample drawn from the delivery of April 28, 1932 had been analysed and showed a contamination of 250 parts of chlorine, instead of the maximum allowed by law of 30 parts. The respondents thereupon claimed to rescind the contract; the appellants protested, and some negotiations took place, during which two more deliveries were tendered and taken, each of 1½ tons. Eventually the respondents adhered to their claim that they were entitled to rescind, and the writ was issued by the appellants claiming damages on the ground that the refusal of the respondents to take further deliveries was wrongful.

No complaint is made in respect of the 15 deliveries made before April 28, 1932, or in respect of the four deliveries made after that date. The respondents made no claim for damages in respect of the delivery said to be defective, because it had all been used before the report was received on the sample. The learned Judge finds that the sample was taken in the usual way—namely, one handful drawn from one bag of the 60 bags which constituted the delivery, and he held that the respondents were entitled, applying the ordinary rules of probability, to say that such must be the condition of the whole or substantially the whole of that delivery of 1½ tons. On the other hand the appellants produced analyses of the flock they had in store from time to time, including an analysis dated April 29, 1932, all of which showed percentages of chlorine well below the Government maximum, though they could not identify any sample as drawn from the flock actually delivered to the respondents. In their evidence they described the process of manufacture by washing which they used. The learned Judge finds that it would be quite wrong to make any general criticism at all of the way in which the appellants conducted their business; he was very favourably impressed, he said, by the evidence of Mr. Jebb, who gave evidence for them; he seemed to the Judge a careful, scrupulous and honourable man. Mr. Jebb could give no explanation of so gross a degree of contamination and was disposed to think some mistake had been made as to the sample. The learned Judge, however, finding that the sample must be taken as a fair test of the delivery, held that the defendants, as prudent traders, could properly say to themselves, in regard to the defective delivery, "it might happen again." He nowhere finds that it was a reasonable inference that it would happen again. His conclusion appears to us to be that there was a mere possibility, not a reasonable probability, that it would happen again. On the contrary, he finds that the occurrence was a very extraordinary thing. We think that on the evidence, and the findings of the learned judge, the true inference of fact is that there was no reasonable probability of any such improper delivery being repeated under the contract.

The decision of this case depends on the true construction and application of s. 31, sub-s. 2, of the *Sale of Goods Acts, 1893*, which is in [substantially the language of the Ontario Act reproduced above]. That subsection was based on decisions before the Act, and has been the subject of decisions since the Act. A contract for the sale of goods by instalments is a single contract, not a complex of as many contracts as there are instalments under it. The law might have been determined in the sense that any breach of condition in respect of any one or more instalments would entitle the party aggrieved to claim that the contract has been repudiated as a whole; or on the other hand the law as established might have been that any breach, however serious, in respect of one or more instalments should not have consequences extending beyond the particular instalment or instalments or affecting the contract as a whole. The sub-section, however which deals equally with breaches either by the buyer or the seller, requires the Court to decide on the merits of the particular case what effect, if any, the breach or breaches should have on the contract as a whole.

The language of the Act is substantially based on the language used by Lord Selborne L.C. in *Mersey Steel and Iron Co. v. Naylor, Benzon & Co.* (1884), 9 App. Cas. 434, where he said: "I am content to take the rule as stated by Lord Coleridge in *French v. Burr* (1874), L.R. 9 C.P. 208, which is in substance, as I understand it, that you must look at the actual circumstances of the case in order to see whether the one party to the contract is relieved from its future performance by the conduct of the other; you must examine what the conduct is, so as to see whether it amounts to a renunciation, to an absolute refusal to perform the contract, such as would amount to a rescission if he had the power to rescind, and whether the other party may accept it as a reason for not performing his part." In *Freeth v. Burr*, Lord Coleridge C. stated the true question to be: "Whether the acts and conduct of the party evince an intention no longer to be bound by the contract." These were both cases of breach by the buyer in not making punctual payment, and in each case it was clear that the buyer had some justification for the course he took. The case of breach by the seller in making defective deliveries may raise different questions. Lord Selborne in the passage above quoted did not refer to any question of intention, but said that what is to be examined is the conduct of the party. Lord Coleridge in *Freeth v. Burr*, citing *Hoare v. Rennie* (1859), 5 H. & N. 19; 157 E.R. 1083, on the question of a seller's breach, states thus one aspect of the rule: "Where by the non-delivery of part of the thing contracted for the whole object of the contract is frustrated, the party making default renounces on his part all the obligations of the contract." In other words, the true test will generally be, not the subjective mental state of the defaulting party, but the objective test of the relation in fact of the default to the whole purpose of the contract.

Since the Act, the sub-section has been discussed by a Divisional Court in *Millars' Karri and Jarrah Company (1902) v. Weddel, Turner & Co.* (1909), 14 Com. Cas. 25, where the contract being for 1100 pieces of timber, the first instalment of 750 pieces was rejected by the buyers; an arbitrator awarded "that the said shipment was, and is, so far from complying with the requirements of the said contract as to entitle the buyers to repudiate and to rescind the whole contract and to refuse to accept the said shipment and all further shipments under the said contract." The Court upheld the award. Bigham J. thus stated what in his opinion was the true test, "Thus, if the breach is of such a kind, or takes place in such circumstances as reasonably to lead to the inference that similar breaches will be committed in relation to subsequent deliveries, the whole contract may there and then be regarded as repudiated and may be rescinded. If, for instance, a buyer fails to pay for one delivery in such circumstances as to lead to the inference that he will not be able to pay for subsequent deliveries; or if a seller delivers goods differing from the requirements of the contract, and does so in such circumstances as to lead to the inference that he cannot, or will not, deliver any other kind of goods in the future, the other contracting party will be under no obligation to wait to see what may happen; he can at once cancel and rid himself of the difficulty." Watson J. concurred.

This ruling was more recently applied in *Robert A. Munroe & Co. v. Meyer*, [1930] 2 K.B. 312, where under a contract for the sale of 1500 tons of bone meal, 611 tons were delivered which were seriously adulterated. The sellers were middlemen, who relied on their suppliers, the manufacturers, for correct delivery: when the buyers discovered that the deliveries did not conform to the contract they claimed that they were entitled to treat the whole contract as repudiated by the sellers. It was held that they were right in so claiming, on the ground that "in such a case as this, where there is a persistent breach, deliberate so far as the manufacturers are concerned, continuing for nearly one-half of the total contract quantity, the buyer, if he ascertains in time what the position is, ought to be entitled to say that he will not take the risk of having put upon him further deliveries of this character." [1930] 2 K.B. 331, per Wright J. On the other hand in *Taylor v. Oakes Roncoroni & Co.*, [1922] 27 Com. Cas. 261, Greer J., as he then was, and the Court of Appeal, declined to hold that the buyers were entitled to refuse to go on with the contract, but held that the breach was a severable breach, as it was a case "where the instalment delivered failed in a slight but appreciable degree to come up to the standard required by the contract description."

With the help of these authorities we deduce that the main tests to be considered in applying the sub-section to the present case are, first, the ratio quantitatively which the breach bears to the contract as a whole, and secondly the degree of probability or improbability that such a breach will be repeated. On the first point, the delivery complained of amounts to no more than 1½ tons out of a contract for 100 tons. On the second point, our conclusion is that the chance of the breach being repeated is practically negligible. We assume that the sample found defective fairly represents the bulk; but bearing in mind the judge's finding that the breach was extraordinary and that the appellant's business was carefully conducted, bearing in mind also that the appellants were warned, and bearing in mind that the delivery complained of was an isolated instance out of 20 satisfactory deliveries actually made both before and after the instalment objected to, we hold that it cannot reasonably be inferred that similar breaches would occur in regard to subsequent deliveries. Indeed, we do not understand that the learned judge came to any different conclusion. He seems, however, to have decided against the appellants on a third and separate ground, that is, that a delivery not satisfying the Government requirements would or might lead to the respondents being prosecuted under this Act. Though we think he exaggerates the likelihood of the respondents in such a case being held responsible, we do not wish to under-rate the gravity to the respondents of their being even prosecuted. But we cannot follow the judge's reasoning that the bare possibility, however remote, of this happening would justify the respondents in rescinding in this case. There may indeed be such cases, as also cases where the consequences of a single breach of contract may be so serious as to involve a frustration of the contract and justify rescission, or furthermore, the contract might contain an express condition that a breach would justify rescission, in which case effect would be given to such a condition by the Court. But none of these circumstances can be predicated of this case. We think the deciding factor here is the extreme improbability of the breach being repeated, and on that ground, and on the isolated and limited character of the breach complained of, there was, in our judgment, no sufficient justification to entitle the respondents to refuse further deliveries as they did.

The appeal must accordingly be allowed and judgment entered for the appellants, with costs here and below, for damages for their breach of contract in refusing further deliveries.

RESTATEMENT OF THE LAW OF CONTRACTS (SECOND)
American Law Institute, 1981

241. In determining whether a failure to render or to offer performance is material, the following circumstances are significant.

(a) The extent to which the injured party will be deprived of the benefit which he reasonably expected;

(b) The extent to which the injured party can be adequately compensated for that part of the benefit of which he will be deprived;

(c) The extent to which the party failing to perform ... will suffer forfeiture;

(d) The likelihood that the party failing to perform ... will cure his failure, taking account of all the circumstances including any reasonable assurances;

(e) The extent to which the behavior of the party failing to perform ... comports with standards of good faith and fair dealing.

QUESTIONS

Why did the Institute not simply state rules? Why "significant" or persuasive "circumstances" rather than binding rules?

II. WAIVER AND THE TRUE CONDITION PRECEDENT

PANOUTSOS V RAYMOND HADLEY
CORPORATION OF NEW YORK
[1917] 2 KB 473 (CA)

By a contract in writing made in London and dated September 27, 1915, which was made on the printed form of the "London Flour Trade Association, American Flour Contract," the Raymond Hadley Corporation of New York (herein called the sellers), who had also a place of business in London, sold to Panoutsos (herein called the buyer) 4,000 tons of flour to be despatched from the Atlantic seaboard by steamer or steamers to Greece as per bills of lading dated not later than November 7, 1915; "each shipment shall be deemed a separate contract"; and there was this clause written into the contract: "Cash against documents in New York. Payment by confirmed bankers' credit." Any dispute arising out of the contract was to be referred to arbitration according to the printed rules indorsed thereon.

On October 16 the National Bank of Commerce of New York wrote to the sellers in New York stating that they had been requested to open a credit in favour of the sellers for about $270,000 in respect of the shipment of 4,000 tons of flour shipped up to November 7, 1915, and adding: "In advising you that this credit has been opened we are acting merely as agent for our foreign correspondents and cannot assume any responsibility for its continuance." This letter showed that the credit was not irrevocable and therefore was not a "confirmed bankers' credit." The sellers, however, on October 21 and again on October 27, 28, 29 and 30 made shipments of flour in part fulfilment of the contract, for which they were duly paid by the New York bank in pursuance of the credit exchange for shipping documents. Meanwhile on October 27, the sellers took exception to the credit as not being irrevocable. On November 15 they requested the buyer to extend the time for the shipment of the balance of the flour from November 7 to November 30, and to this the buyer agreed. On November 25 the sellers notified the buyer that the balance of their contract was cancelled on the ground (so far as material) that the buyer had failed to perform the condition as to "payment by confirmed bankers' credit." The buyer refused to accept the cancellation, and the dispute was referred to arbitration. The arbitrators found that the credit was not a confirmed bankers' credit within the meaning of the contract, but that the sellers took no exception to it at the time it was opened.

Before the arbitrators the sellers contended that the buyer had failed to comply with the conditions of the contract, as he had failed to open a credit at New York, which would be irrevocable until November 30; and that the fact that they had made shipments without insisting on this condition did not release the buyer in respect of subsequent shipments, especially having regard to the term of the contract that "each shipment shall be deemed a separate contract." The buyer contended that the sellers had accepted as satisfactory the credit which has been opened, and, having made a shipment under it, had waived any possible objection to it and could not repudiate their obligation to ship the balance of the flour, or could not do so without giving due notice to him so as to enable him to remove any valid objection and furnish such a credit as would satisfy them.

The arbitrators awarded that the sellers were in default in not shipping the balance of the flour in accordance with the contract, and that they should pay a certain sum as damages.

The question for the opinion of the Court was whether or not upon the above facts there was any evidence upon which the arbitrators could properly find that the sellers had waived the term in the contract that payment should be by confirmed bankers' credit.

If the Court should be of opinion that the question should be answered in the affirmative, then the award was to stand; if in the negative, then the award was to be in favour of the sellers.

Bailhache J. held that when the sellers knew that the credit was not in order, and yet proceeded to act upon it as if it was in order, they must be taken to have waived the informality so long as they chose to act upon that credit, but that they were not bound to act upon it to the end merely because they acted upon it at first and waived the informality up to a point. In his opinion the sellers could at any time insist upon the credit being put in order, but if they desired to cancel the contract because the credit upon which they had acted was not in order they must give reasonable notice to the buyer of their intention to do so; which they had not done. He therefore confirmed the award. The sellers appealed.

VISCOUNT READING CJ: ... The question put to the Court is "whether or not upon the above findings of fact"—to which must now be added "coupled with our findings of fact"—"there was any evidence upon which the arbitrators could properly find that the sellers had waived the term in the contract that payment should be by confirmed bankers' credit." It was therefore admitted that there was no confirmed bankers' credit, but the buyer contended that there had been a waiver of that condition of the contract. In answer to that the sellers said that there had been no such waiver, and if there had been a waiver that they were entitled at any time to insist upon the condition being performed. The buyer replied that no doubt the sellers were entitled to insist upon the performance of the condition, but that, having waived its performance hitherto, they must give reasonable notice to the buyer of their intention to insist upon its performance in the future so as to give him an opportunity of putting the credit right. Bailhache J. held that the sellers must be taken to have waived the performance of the condition, that the buyer was entitled to reasonable notice, and that such notice had not in fact been given. He therefore answered the question in favour of the buyer.

In my opinion the learned judge was right. It is open to a party to a contract to waive a condition which is inserted for his benefit. If the sellers chose to ship without the safeguard of a confirmed bankers' credit, they were entitled to do so, and the buyer performed his part of the contract by paying for the goods shipped, though there was no confirmed bankers' credit, inasmuch as that condition had been waived.

If at a later stage the sellers wished to avail themselves of the condition precedent, in my opinion there was nothing in the facts to prevent them from demanding the performance of the condition if they had given reasonable notice to the buyer that they would not ship unless there was a confirmed bankers' credit. If they had done that and the buyer had failed to comply with the condition, the buyer would have been in default, and the sellers would have been entitled to cancel the contract without being subject to any claim by the buyer for damages.

In *Bentsen v. Taylor, Sons & Co.*, [1893] 2 Q.B., Bowen L.J. stated the law as to waiver thus: "Did the defendants by their acts or conduct lead the plaintiff reasonably to suppose that they did not intend to treat the contract for the future as at an end, on account of the failure to perform the condition precedent?" Reading sellers for defendants and buyer for plaintiff in that passage, it applies exactly to the present case. The sellers did lead the buyer to think so, and when they intended to change that position it was incumbent on them to give reasonable notice of that intention to the buyer so as to enable him to comply with the condition which up to that time had been waived.

The case of *In re Tyrer & Co. and Hessler & Co.*, 6 Com. Cas. 143; 7 Com. Cas. 166 was cited as an authority for the proposition that the moment the sellers chose to avail themselves of the failure to perform the condition precedent they could put an end to the contract without giving the buyer an opportunity of remedying the default which had hitherto been waived. That case is not an authority for that proposition. It shows that, where there was stipulated times in a charterparty for payment of the hire of a ship and a power to withdraw the ship if the payment is not made at the stipulated time, the mere fact that there has been default in payment at one or more stipulated times, of which advantage has not been taken, does not entitle the party in default at a subsequent time to a notice so as to enable him to comply with the condition before the right to withdraw arises. That is a totally different case from the present. I cannot find any authority to support the proposition that, when one party has led another to believe that he may continue in a certain course of conduct without any risk of the contract being cancelled, the first-mentioned party can cancel the contract without giving any notice to the other so as to enable the latter to comply with the requirement of the contract. It seems to me to follow from the observations of Bowen L.J. in *Bentsen v. Taylor, Sons & Co.* that there must be reasonable notice given to the buyer before the sellers can take advantage of the failure to provide a confirmed bankers' credit. That is the decision of Bailhache J.

The only question which remains is whether reasonable notice has been given. We have more material before us than Bailhache J. had when he came to the conclusion that no reasonable notice had been given. I am not prepared to draw the inference of fact that reasonable notice had been given before the sellers cancelled the contract. If notice had been given on October 27, and on November 25 the sellers had cancelled the contract, I should have thought that that would have been ample notice to enable the buyer to provide the confirmed credit in New York. But I cannot find any such notice on the part of the sellers of their intention to insist upon the performance of the condition. ...

The result is that the decision of Bailhache J. is right, and the appeal must be dismissed.

[Lord Cozens-Hardy MR and Scrutton LJ agreed.]

NOTE

In *Sail Labrador Ltd v Challenge One (The)*, [1999] 1 SCR 265, 169 DLR (4th) 1, the charterer of a ship had an option to purchase the ship, conditional on "full performance of all its obligations" under the charter party. Payment was required in cash or by certified cheque in 35 installments, but the charterer submitted uncertified postdated cheques without objection from the owner. By bank error, payment of one of these cheques was slightly late, and the owner asserted that the option was void. The Supreme Court of Canada was unanimous in holding in the charterer's favour, but there was a division in its reasons. Bastarache J, for the majority, said that time was not of the essence, that the effect of accepting the cheques had been to vary the contract, and that substantial performance was sufficient. Binnie J held that the parties had contracted for full performance, and that "substantial" performance was not sufficient. But he concurred in the result on the basis that full performance had in fact been rendered, except as to the banking arrangements where the owner was estopped by its conduct from saying otherwise.

TURNEY V ZHILKA
[1959] SCR 578, 18 DLR (2d) 497

[A contract for the sale of "all and singular the land and not buildings situate on the East side of the 5th Line west in the township of Toronto and known as 60 acres or more having frontage of about 2046 feet on 5th Line more or less, by a depth of about ... feet, more or less (lot boundaries about as fenced), being part of west ½ lot 5 Con 5 west" contained the condition: "Providing the property can be annexed to the Village of Streetsville and a plan is approved by the Village Council for subdivision." The vendor owned only 62.37 acres, but he thought he had 65 acres and that he could retain 5 acres around his buildings. The purchaser claimed 60.87 acres, leaving the vendor 1.5 acres. The Village of Streetsville did not annex the property. An action for specific performance by the purchaser was dismissed. As to the defence of non-compliance with the *Statute of Frauds*, the court held that not only was there lack of sufficient certainty of description, "but the evidence makes it quite clear that the parties never reached any agreement, oral or written, on the quantity or description of the land to be retained or the land to be conveyed." The purchaser was willing to waive the annexation condition.]

JUDSON J (on this point): The date for the completion of the sale if fixed with reference to the performance of this condition—"60 days after plans are approved." Neither party to the contract undertakes to fulfil this condition, and neither party reserves a power of waiver. The purchaser made some enquiries of the village council but the evidence indicates that he made little or no progress and received little encouragement and that the prospects of annexation were very remote. After the trouble arose over the quantity and description of the land, the purchaser purported to waive this condition on the ground that it was solely for his benefit and was severable, and sued immediately for specific performance without reference to the condition and the time for performance fixed by the condition. The learned trial Judge found that the condition was one introduced for the sole benefit of the purchaser and that he could waive it. ...

But here there is no right to be waived. The obligations under the contract, on both sides, depend upon a future uncertain event, the happening of which depends entirely on the will of a third party—the village council. This is a true condition precedent—an external condition upon which the existence of the obligation depends. Until the event occurs there is no right to performance on either side. The parties

695

have not promised that it will occur. In the absence of such a promise there can be no breach of contract until the event does occur. The purchaser now seeks to make the vendor liable on his promise to convey in spite of the non-performance of the condition and this to suit his own convenience only. This is not a case of renunciation or relinquishment of a right but rather an attempt by one party, without the consent of the other, to write a new contract. Waiver has often been referred to as a troublesome and uncertain term in the law but it does at least presuppose the existence of a right to be relinquished.

QUESTIONS

1. What explanations are offered by Judson J for the conclusion that the condition precedent in this agreement cannot be waived? Would the doctrine of true condition precedent apply to every situation in which neither party to the contract undertakes to fulfill a particular condition? Would it apply to every case in which the fulfillment of the condition depends on the will of a third party?

2. Would the doctrine of true condition precedent apply to a financing condition in a real estate transaction pursuant to which the closing of the transaction is enforceable only if the purchaser is able to acquire "satisfactory financing"? In *Beauchamp v Beauchamp*, [1973] 2 OR 43 (CA), the Ontario Court of Appeal held that a condition in a real estate transaction to the effect that the purchaser be able to obtain a first mortgage in the amount of $10,000 at current rates and a second for $2,500 was not a true condition precedent. Do you agree?

3. In *O'Reilly v Marketers Diversified Inc* (1968), 1 DLR (3d) 387 (BCCA), the BC Court of Appeal held that a real estate transaction subject to a condition that the purchaser be able to purchase an adjacent lot was not a true condition precedent. Do you agree? This decision was overruled by the Supreme Court of Canada. See [1969] SCR 741.

BARNETT V HARRISON
[1976] 2 SCR 531, 57 DLR (3d) 225

DICKSON J: The rule in *Turney and Turney v. Zhilka* has been in effect since 1959, and has been applied many times. In the interests of certainty and predictability in the law, the rule should endure unless compelling reason for change be shown. If in any case the parties agree that the rule should not apply, that can be readily written into the agreement.

Laskin C.J.C. and Spence J. dissented on the ground that a party should be entitled to waive a condition inserted for his own benefit.

[See also Waddams at paras 607-10.]

III. THE DUTY TO PERFORM CONTRACTUAL OBLIGATIONS IN GOOD FAITH

In previous sections of this chapter, we have assumed that the content or nature of the performance obligations imposed by an agreement are clear and are understood by the parties. The questions we have considered in Section I relate to the impact of one party's failure to perform an obligation upon the other party's obligation to perform. In Section II we have considered whether the victim of a party in breach might be considered to have waived the right to rely on the default of that party as an excuse for non-performance of their own contractual obligations. Here we turn to consider the contents of the agreement which may be said to define or delineate the nature of each party's performance obligations. More particularly, we will consider whether every contract must be considered to contain an obligation imposed on each party, whether explicitly expressed by the parties or not, to perform their obligations in good faith.

The determination of the nature of the performance obligations imposed by an agreement may prove to be a complex or subtle issue in many circumstances. Where the parties have engaged in both written and oral communications concerning the nature of their agreement, the decision as to whether any or all of the oral communications may be taken into account in determining the contents of the agreement may prove to be a difficult matter. As we saw in Chapter 5, making such determinations will normally involve application of the "parol evidence rule." Once the contents of the agreement, in this sense, have been determined, subtle questions may arise with respect to the proper interpretation of particular terms of the agreement. Particular provisions may be drafted by the parties or their lawyers in language that is unclear or ambiguous or for other reasons difficult to apply to the circumstances of the agreement as they have unfolded. The drafting of the agreement in question may have failed to anticipate future circumstances in which the agreement may be required to operate, thus leaving what now appear to be "gaps" in the agreement. There may be an apparent conflict between the obligations imposed by two separate terms. Problems of this kind are addressed by the law of contractual interpretation, a subject that is not explored at length, however, in the present volume.

One of many devices made available by the law of contractual interpretation to assist in the interpretation of agreements is the judicial implication of terms in the agreement. The doctrine of implied terms is itself extensive, but, for present purposes, may be briefly summarized. Generally speaking, three different kinds of implication (or sources of implied terms) are permitted by the law of contractual interpretation. First, courts may imply terms in agreements when they reach the conclusion that such additional understandings fairly represent what must have been the implicit or tacit understandings of the parties to the agreement with respect to the matter in question. Such implied terms are commonly referred to as terms "implied in fact." The two tests for implying such terms are, first, that the implication of such a term is necessary to give "business efficacy" to the agreement or, second, that the need for such a term is otherwise so obvious that an "officious bystander" or the parties themselves, if asked, would agree that such an understanding must have been assumed by the parties. A second category of implied terms—terms "implied in law"—do not rest on the presumed intentions of the parties. Rather, they are terms implied by courts to ensure the fair functioning of standard types of contracts, such as those related to employment, leases of land, and insurance. In the context of employment contracts, for example, it is well established that in a contract of employment of indefinite duration, it is an implied term that the contract can be terminated by the employer only upon reasonable notice to the employee. Employment agreements are also considered to include implied terms imposing obligations on employees to provide service at a reasonable level of skill and care and to not disclose to third parties confidential information acquired in the course of their employment. A third type or source of implied terms—commonly referred to as terms "implied from custom or usage"—arise from well-established expectations within a particular trade or commercial context as to the terms on which business is normally conducted. Evidence of such customs or usage may provide a basis for adding terms to the agreement to give effect to these shared expectations.

In recent decades, Canadian courts have struggled with the question as to whether, in addition to all of the express or implied terms of contractual agreements, every agreement should be considered to contain an overarching and presumably implied duty on each party to perform their contractual obligations in good faith. The recognition of such a duty has been recommended by some law reform commissions and legal scholars. Those who favoured such recognition typically noted that such duties had been recognized in American law and in the law of Quebec. Other observers, however, were of the view that recognition of such a duty would introduce an unattractive level of uncertainty into contractual doctrine. What, after all, is the content of the notion of "good faith contractual performance"? How would one advise parties to conform with such a vague and uncertain obligation? Would such a concept not interfere with the concept of "freedom of contract" and the ability of parties to freely negotiate and understand the nature of their contractual obligations?

A similar division of opinion was manifest in Canadian judicial decisions touching upon the subject. Some Canadian judges embraced the good faith concept with some enthusiasm. Thus, in *Gateway Realty Ltd v Arton Holdings Ltd and LaHave* (No 3) (1991), 106 NSR (2d) 180 (SC (TD)), aff'd (1992) 112 NSR (2d) 180 (CA), for example, Kelly J held that all contracts should be considered to include a term requiring good faith performance or, what amounted in his view to the same thing, a term precluding bad faith performance. The concept of bad faith performance was articulated by Kelly J (at p 197) in the following terms:

> In most cases, bad faith can be said to occur when one party, without reasonable justification, acts in relation to the contract in a manner where the result would be to substantially nullify the bargained objective or benefit contracted for by the other, or to cause significant harm to the other, contrary to the original purpose and expectation of the parties.

Other courts expressed skepticism with respect to the desirability of recognizing such a doctrine. (See *e.g. Martselos Services Ltd v Arctic College,* [1994] NWTJ No 4, 111 DLR (4th) 65 (QL) (CA)).

It was not until the 2014 decision in *Bhasin v Hrynew,* 2014 SCC 71, however, that the Supreme Court of Canada resolved this debate in favour of recognition of a general underlying principle of contract law that requires all parties to agreements to perform their obligations in good faith.

BHASIN V HRYNEW
2014 SCC 71

[The controversy in *Bhasin v Hrynew* concerning the existence of an obligation to perform contracts in good faith arose in the following circumstances. The plaintiff appellant, Mr. Bhasin, was a retail dealer or so-called "enrolment director" for the defendant respondent, Canadian American Financial Corp (Can-Am). Can-Am was the supplier of education savings plans (ESPs) to investors through its network of enrolment directors. Under the agreements between Can-Am and its enrolment directors, the directors received compensation and bonuses for selling ESPs. Enrolment directors were obliged to sell Can-Am products exclusively and owed Can-Am fiduciary obligations. The agreements stipulated that Can-Am owned directors' client lists. The agreement with Mr. Bhasin had a three-year term and stipulated that the contract would automatically renew at the end of the three-year term unless one of the parties gave six months' written notice to terminate. Mr. Bhasin commenced his relationship with Can-Am in 1989 and built up a successful business in the ensuing years, winning numerous recognition awards from Can-Am as one of its top enrolment directors in Canada.

The defendant Hrynew was another Can-Am enrolment director. He was a competitor of Mr. Bhasin and there was considerable animosity between them. The principal source of the acrimony was that Mr. Hrynew wished to, in effect, merge Mr. Bhasin's business with his own. He planned that Mr. Bhasin would become an employee of the newly merged business to be owned by Hrynew. Mr. Hrynew was in a position to pressure Can-Am into supporting his efforts to absorb Mr. Bhasin's business. Hrynew was a very successful enrolment director. When he moved his business from one of Can-Am's competitors to Can-Am, he was promised that he would be given consideration for possible mergers with existing directors and, indeed, a number of mergers had taken place. Hrynew was Can-Am's largest dealer in Alberta. Moreover, he was said to have a "good working relationship" (2014 SCC 71 at para 8) with the Alberta Securities Commission, the regulator of Can-Am's business.

Mr. Bhasin steadfastly resisted Mr. Hrynew's frequent proposals to merge their two businesses. Nonetheless, Mr. Hrynew enjoyed success in pressuring Cam-Am to assist in achieving this objective and was said to have made "veiled threats" (2014 SCC 71 at para 9) that he would leave Can-Am if the merger could not be achieved. Matters came to a head in 1999 and 2000 when Can-Am developed a concern that the Securities Commission might revoke its licence. In discussions with the commission, Can-Am indicated that it was planning to restructure its agencies in Alberta in a manner that would involve Mr. Bhasin. Mr. Bhasin was not informed of these plans. In 1999, the commission required Can-Am to appoint a provincial trading officer (PTO) to audit its enrolment directors with respect to compliance with applicable securities laws. Can-Am appointed Mr. Hrynew to this position with the result that Mr. Hrynew was assigned the task of auditing Mr. Bhasin's business. Mr. Bhasin resisted the idea of allowing a competitor to have access to his confidential business records, even though Can-Am assured Bhasin that Hrynew would be subject to a duty of confidentiality.

When Mr. Bhasin continued to refuse to allow Mr. Hrynew access to his business records, Can-Am threatened to terminate their agreement and finally, in May of 2001, gave notice of non-renewal. At the expiry of the term, the majority of Mr. Bhasin's sales agents were successfully recruited by Mr. Hrynew and Mr. Bhasin lost the value of his business.

During the period leading up to termination, Mr. Bhasin was misled by Can-Am in a number of respects. Can-Am did not respond in a forthright manner when Mr. Bhasin asked in August 2000 whether or not the proposed merger was a "done deal" (2014 SCC 71 at para 12). The trial judge had held that Can-Am "equivocated" on this point (2011 ABQB 637 at para 247). Can-Am also advised Bhasin that the Securities Commission would not permit it to appoint an outsider as the PTO. This was not true. Further, Mr. Hrynew's contract of employment as PTO did not contain a requirement of confidentiality, as Bhasin had been assured by Can-Am.

Upon termination, Mr. Bhasin brought an action against Can-Am and Hrynew alleging that Can-Am was in breach of an implied term to perform its contractual obligations in good faith. He also claimed that Hrynew had committed the tort of inducing breach of contract and that the two defendant parties had conducted a civil conspiracy.

At trial, Moen J held in favour of the plaintiff on all counts (2011 ABQB 637). The defendant Can-Am had breached its implied duty of good faith performance by exercising the right to terminate for the improper purpose of forcing a merger and by appointing Hrynew to audit Bhasin's business records. As well, the defendants had engaged in a civil conspiracy, and Hrynew had committed the tort of inducing breach of contract. Importantly, the trial judge held that if Can-Am had been straightforward with Bhasin he would have been able to preserve the value of his business. The trial judge also made a finding that, notwithstanding any difficulties that might be encountered by Mr. Bhasin in transferring his business to a new owner, the value of the business at the date of termination could be assessed as $87,000.

The decision at trial was reversed, however, by the Alberta Court of Appeal. Canadian law did not, in its view, impose a general duty to perform contracts in good faith and, in any event, the trial judge had erred, in the court's view, by implying a term requiring good faith in the context of an unambiguous agreement containing an entire agreement clause. Accordingly, the plaintiff's claims were dismissed.

Against this background and on behalf of a unanimous Supreme Court, Cromwell J observed as follows:]

[33]   CROMWELL J: In my view, it is time to take two incremental steps in order to make the common law less unsettled and piecemeal, more coherent and more just. The first step is to acknowledge that good faith contractual performance is a general organizing principle of the common law of contract which underpins and informs the various rules in which the common law, in various situations and types of relationships, recognizes obligations of good faith contractual performance. The second is to recognize, as a further manifestation of this organizing principle of good faith, that there is a common law duty which applies to all contracts to act honestly in the performance of contractual obligations.

• • •

[In support of the view that the existing law was "unsettled and piecemeal," Cromwell J provided an account of the notion of good faith as it had appeared over time in English and Canadian common law. He noted the division of judicial opinion as to the existence or desirability of the doctrine. He noted, as well, that the notion of good faith underlies or is present in existing contractual doctrines, such as the doctrine of unconscionability and the law of implied terms in which the attempt to give effect to the intentions of the parties is informed by the concept of good faith. Cromwell J also indicated that there are numerous contexts in which the doctrine appears in more explicit form. These situations he described as follows:]

[47]   There have been many attempts to bring a measure of coherence to this piecemeal accretion of appeals to good faith: see, among many others, McCamus, at pp. 835-68; S. K. O'Byrne, "The Implied Term of Good Faith and Fair Dealing: Recent Developments" (2007), 86 *Can. Bar Rev.* 193, at pp. 196-204; Waddams, *The Law of Contracts*, at paras. 494-508; R. S. Summers, "'Good Faith' in General Contract Law and the Sales Provisions of the Uniform Commercial Code" (1968), 54 *Va. L. Rev.* 195; S. J. Burton, "Breach of Contract and the Common Law Duty to Perform in Good Faith" (1981), 94 *Harv. L. Rev.* 369. By way of example, Professor McCamus has identified three broad types of situations in which a duty of good faith performance of some kind has been found to exist: (1) where the parties must cooperate in order to achieve the objects of the contract; (2) where one party exercises a discretionary power under the contract; and (3) where one party seeks to evade contractual duties (pp. 840-56; *CivicLife.com Inc. v. Canada (Attorney General)* (2006), 215 O.A.C. 43, at paras. 49-50).

[48]   While these types of cases overlap to some extent, they provide a useful analytical tool to appreciate the current state of the law on the duty of good faith. They also reveal some of the lack of coherence in the current approach. It is often unclear whether a good faith obligation is being imposed as a matter of law, as a matter of implication or as a matter of interpretation. Professor McCamus notes:

Although the line between the two types of implication is difficult to draw, it may be realistic to assume that implied duties of good faith are likely, on occasion at least, to slide into the category of legal incidents rather than mere presumed intentions. Certainly, it would be difficult to defend the implication of terms on each of the cases considered here on the basis of the traditional business efficiency or officious bystander test. In the control of contractual discretion cases, for example, it may be more realistic to suggest that the implied limitation on the exercise of the discretion is intended to give effect to the "reasonable expectations of the parties." [pp. 865-66]

[49] The first type of situation (contracts requiring the cooperation of the parties to achieve the objects of the contract) is reflected in the jurisprudence of this Court. In *Dynamic Transport Ltd. v. O.K. Detailing Ltd.*, [1978] 2 S.C.R. 1072, the parties to a real estate transaction failed to specify in the purchase-sale agreement which party was to be responsible for obtaining planning permission for a subdivision of the property. By law, the vendor was the only party capable of obtaining such permission. The Court held that the vendor was under an obligation to use reasonable efforts to secure the permission, or as Dickson J. (as he then was) put it, "[t]he vendor is under a duty to act in good faith and to take all reasonable steps to complete the sale": p. 1084. It is not completely clear whether this duty was imposed as a matter of law or was implied based on the parties' intentions: see p. 1083; see also *Gateway Realty* and *CivicLife.com*.

[50] *Mitsui & Co. (Canada) Ltd. v. Royal Bank of Canada*, [1995] 2 S.C.R. 187, is an example of the second type of situation (exercise of contractual discretion). The lease of a helicopter included an option to buy at the "reasonable fair market value of the helicopter as established by Lessor": para. 2. This Court held, at para. 34, that, "[c]learly, the lessor is not in a position, by virtue of clause 32, to make any offer that it may feel is appropriate. It is contractually bound to act in good faith to determine the reasonable fair market value of the helicopters, which is the price that the parties had initially agreed would be the exercise price of the option." The Court did not discuss the basis for implying the term, but suggested that in the absence of a reasonableness requirement, the option would be a mere agreement to agree and thus would be unenforceable, which means that the implication of the term was necessary to give business efficacy to the agreement.

[51] This Court's decision in *Mason v. Freedman*, [1958] S.C.R. 483, falls in the third type of situation in which a duty of good faith arises (where a contractual power is used to evade a contractual duty). In that case, the vendor in a real estate transaction regretted the bargain he had made. He then sought to repudiate the contract by failing to convey title in fee simple because he claimed his wife would not provide a bar of dower. The issue was whether he could take advantage of a clause permitting him to repudiate the transaction in the event that he was "unable or unwilling" to remove this defect in title even though he had made no efforts to do so by trying to obtain the bar of dower. Judson J. held that the clause did not "enable a person to repudiate a contract for a cause which he himself has brought about" or permit "a capricious or arbitrary repudiation": p. 486. On the contrary, "[a] vendor who seeks to take advantage of the clause must exercise his right reasonably and in good faith and not in a capricious or arbitrary manner": p. 487.

[52] The jurisprudence is not always very clear about the source of the good faith obligations found in these cases. The categories of terms implied as a matter of law, terms implied as a matter of intention and terms arising as a matter of interpretation sometimes are blurred or even ignored, resulting in uncertainty and a lack of coherence at the level of principle.

• • •

[Cromwell J further observed that in addition to these types of *situations* in which particular good faith duties arise, there are *classes of relationships* "that call for a duty of good faith to be implied by law" (para 53). Illustrations provided by Cromwell J included the employer's obligation to behave in a good faith manner when exercising its right to terminate the employment relationship (*Honda Canada Inc v Keays*, 2008 SCC 39), the obligation on an insured to disclose material facts at the time of formation of an insurance contract and the insurer's duty to deal with its insured's claim fairly (*Fidler v Sun Life Assurance Co of Canada*, 2006 SCC 30) and the duty of fair dealing imposed on parties who conduct tendering processes (*MJB Enterprises Ltd v Defence Construction (1951) Ltd* [1991] 1 S.C.R. 619). Cromwell J also provided a survey of developments in other jurisdictions.

Cromwell J, having concluded that this survey supports the view that the current Canadian law is "piecemeal, unsettled and unclear" (para 59), proposed that recognition of a duty of good faith performance would be consistent with the reasonable expectations of the parties. As he explained:]

[60] Commercial parties reasonably expect a basic level of honesty and good faith in contractual dealings. While they remain at arm's length and are not subject to the duties of a fiduciary, a basic level of honest conduct is necessary to the proper functioning of commerce. The growth of longer term, relational contracts that depend on an element of trust and cooperation clearly call for a basic element of honesty in performance, but, even in transactional exchanges, misleading or deceitful conduct will fly in the face of the expectations of the parties: see Swan and Adamski, at §1.24.

· · ·

[Cromwell J then returned to the proposed two incremental steps to be taken in clarifying the existing law. The first step he described as follows:]

[63] The first step is to recognize that there is an organizing principle of good faith that underlies and manifests itself in various more specific doctrines governing contractual performance. That organizing principle is simply that parties generally must perform their contractual duties honestly and reasonably and not capriciously or arbitrarily.

[64] As the Court has recognized, an organizing principle states in general terms a requirement of justice from which more specific legal doctrines may be derived. An organizing principle therefore is not a free-standing rule, but rather a standard that underpins and is manifested in more specific legal doctrines and may be given different weight in different situations: see, e.g., *R. v. Jones*, [1994] 2 S.C.R. 229, at p. 249; *R. v. Hart*, 2014 SCC 52, [2014] 2 S.C.R. 544, at para. 124; R. M. Dworkin, "Is Law a System of Rules," in R. M. Dworkin, ed., *The Philosophy of Law* (1977), 38, at p. 47. It is a standard that helps to understand and develop the law in a coherent and principled way.

[65] The organizing principle of good faith exemplifies the notion that, in carrying out his or her own performance of the contract, a contracting party should have appropriate regard to the legitimate contractual interests of the contracting partner. While "appropriate regard" for the other party's interests will vary depending on the context of the contractual relationship, it does not require acting to serve those interests in all cases. It merely requires that a party not seek to undermine those interests in bad faith. This general principle has strong conceptual differences from the much higher obligations of a fiduciary. Unlike fiduciary duties, good faith performance does not engage duties of loyalty to the other contracting party or a duty to put the interests of the other contracting party first.

[66] This organizing principle of good faith manifests itself through the existing doctrines about the types of situations and relationships in which the law requires, in certain respects, honest, candid, forthright or reasonable contractual performance. Generally, claims of good faith will not succeed if they do not fall within these existing doctrines. But we should also recognize that this list is not closed. The application of the organizing principle of good faith to particular situations should be developed where the existing law is found to be wanting and where the development may occur incrementally in a way that is consistent with the structure of the common law of

contract and gives due weight to the importance of private ordering and certainty in commercial affairs.

• • •

[The second step—recognizing a new particularized duty or rule—was made necessary by the fact that the present fact situation did not come within any of the existing situations or relationships in which good faith duties have been found to exist. The need for a new duty of honesty to capture the facts of the present case was described as follows:]

[72] In my view, the objection to Can-Am's conduct in this case does not fit within any of the existing situations or relationships in which duties of good faith have been found to exist. The relationship between Can-Am and Mr. Bhasin was not an employment or franchise relationship. Classifying the decision not to renew the contract as a contractual discretion would constitute a significant expansion of the decided cases under that type of situation. After all, a party almost always has some amount of discretion in how to perform a contract. It would also be difficult to say that a duty of good faith should be implied in this case on the basis of the intentions of the parties given the clear terms of an entire agreement clause in the Agreement. The key question before the Court, therefore, is whether we ought to create a new common law duty under the broad umbrella of the organizing principle of good faith performance of contracts.

[73] In my view, we should. I would hold that there is a general duty of honesty in contractual performance. This means simply that parties must not lie or otherwise knowingly mislead each other about matters directly linked to the performance of the contract. This does not impose a duty of loyalty or of disclosure or require a party to forgo advantages flowing from the contract; it is a simple requirement not to lie or mislead the other party about one's contractual performance. Recognizing a duty of honest performance flowing directly from the common law organizing principle of good faith is a modest, incremental step. The requirement to act honestly is one of the most widely recognized aspects of the organizing principle of good faith: see Swan and Adamski, at § 8.135; O'Byrne, "Good Faith in Contractual Performance: Recent Developments," at p. 78; Belobaba; *Greenberg v. Meffert* (1985), 50 O.R. (2d) 755 (C.A.), at p. 764; *Gateway Realty*, at para. 38, *per* Kelly J.; *Shelanu Inc. v. Print Three Franchising Corp.* (2003), 64 O.R. (3d) 533 (C.A.), at para. 69. For example, the duty of honesty was a key component of the good faith requirements which have been recognized in relation to termination of employment contracts: *Wallace*, at para. 98; *Honda Canada*, at para. 58.

[Cromwell J went on to consider the view expressed by the Alberta Court of Appeal, below, to the effect that any implied duty of good faith would be excluded by the "entire agreement clause" set out in the dealership agreement:]

[74] There is a longstanding debate about whether the duty of good faith arises as a term implied as a matter of fact or a term implied by law: see *Mesa Operating*, at paras. 15-19. I do not have to resolve this debate fully, which, as I reviewed earlier, casts a shadow of uncertainty over a good deal of the jurisprudence. I am at this point concerned only with a new duty of honest performance and, as I see it, this should not be thought of as an implied term, but a general doctrine of contract law that imposes as a contractual duty a minimum standard of honest contractual performance. It operates irrespective of the intentions of the parties, and is to this extent analogous to equitable doctrines which impose limits on the freedom of contract, such as the doctrine of unconscionability.

[75] Viewed in this way, the entire agreement clause in cl. 11.2 of the Agreement is not an impediment to the duty arising in this case. Because the duty of honesty in contractual performance is a general doctrine of contract law that applies to all

contracts, like unconscionability, the parties are not free to exclude it: see *CivicLife.com*, at para. 52.

[76] It is true that the Anglo-Canadian common law of contract has been reluctant to impose mandatory rules not based on the agreement of the parties, because they are thought to interfere with freedom of contract: see *Gateway Realty, per* Kelly J.; O'Byrne, "Good Faith in Contractual Performance: Recent Developments," at p. 95; Farnsworth, at pp. 677-78. As discussed above, however, the duty of honest performance interferes very little with freedom of contract, since parties will rarely expect that their contracts permit dishonest performance of their obligations.

[77] That said, I would not rule out any role for the agreement of the parties in influencing the scope of honest performance in a particular context. The precise content of honest performance will vary with context and the parties should be free in some contexts to relax the requirements of the doctrine so long as they respect its minimum core requirements. The approach I outline here is similar in principle to that in § 1-302(b) of the U.C.C. (2012):

> The obligations of good faith, diligence, reasonableness, and care ... may not be disclaimed by agreement. The parties, by agreement, may determine the standards by which the performance of those obligations is to be measured if those standards are not manifestly unreasonable.

[78] Certainly, any modification of the duty of honest performance would need to be in express terms. A generically worded entire agreement clause such as cl. 11.2 of the Agreement does not indicate any intention of the parties to depart from the basic tenets of honest performance: see *GEC Marconi Systems Pty Ltd. v. BHP Information Technology Pty Ltd.*, [2003] FCA 50 (AustLII), at para. 922, *per* Finn J.; see also O'Byrne, "Good Faith in Contractual Performance: Recent Developments," at p. 96.

[With respect to the two standard objections made by the recognition of a duty of good faith contractual performance, Cromwell J responded in the following terms:]

[79] Two arguments are typically raised against an increased role for a duty of good faith in the law of contract: see Bridge; Clark; and Peden, "When Common Law Trumps Equity: the Rise of Good Faith and Reasonableness and the Demise of Unconscionability." The first is that "good faith" is an inherently unclear concept that will permit *ad hoc* judicial moralism to undermine the certainty of commercial transactions. The second is that imposing a duty of good faith is inconsistent with the basic principle of freedom of contract. I do not have to decide here whether or not these points are valid in relation to a broad, generalized duty of good faith. However, they carry no weight in relation to adopting a rule of honest performance.

[80] Recognizing a duty of honesty in contract performance poses no risk to commercial certainty in the law of contract. A reasonable commercial person would expect, at least, that the other party to a contract would not be dishonest about his or her performance. The duty is also clear and easy to apply. ...

[81] Any interference by the duty of honest performance with freedom of contract is more theoretical than real. It will surely be rare that parties would wish to agree that they may be dishonest with each other in performing their contractual obligations.

[82] Those who fear that this modest step would create uncertainty or impede freedom of contract may take comfort from experience of the civil law of Quebec and the common and statute law of many jurisdictions in the United States.

• • •

[For Cromwell J, the new duty of honest performance was not to be confused with a duty of disclosure or the existing doctrines of breach of fiduciary duty, fraud or estoppel:]

[86] The duty of honest performance that I propose should not be confused with a duty of disclosure or of fiduciary loyalty. A party to a contract has no general duty to subordinate his or her interest to that of the other party. However, contracting parties must be able to rely on a minimum standard of honesty from their contracting partner in relation to performing the contract as a reassurance that if the contract does not work out, they will have a fair opportunity to protect their interests. That said, a dealership agreement is not a contract of utmost good faith (*uberrimae fidei*) such as an insurance contract, which among other things obliges the parties to disclose material facts: *Whiten*. But a clear distinction can be drawn between a failure to disclose a material fact, even a firm intention to end the contractual arrangement, and active dishonesty.

[87] This distinction explains the result reached by the court in *United Roasters, Inc. v. Colgate-Palmolive Co.*, 649 F.2d 985 (4th Cir. 1981). The terminating party had decided in advance of the required notice period that it was going to terminate the contract. The court held that no disclosure of this intention was required other than what was stipulated in the notice requirement. The court stated:

> ... there is very little to be said in favor of a rule of law that good faith requires one possessing a right of termination to inform the other party promptly of any decision to exercise the right. A tenant under a month-to-month lease may decide in January to vacate the premises at the end of September. It is hardly to be suggested that good faith requires the tenant to inform the landlord of his decision soon after January. Though the landlord may have found earlier notice convenient, formal exercise of the right of termination in August will do. [pp. 989-90]

United Roasters makes it clear that there is no unilateral duty to disclose information relevant to termination. But the situation is quite different, as I see it, when it comes to actively misleading or deceiving the other contracting party in relation to performance of the contract.

[88] The duty of honest performance has similarities with the existing law in relation to civil fraud and estoppel, but it is not subsumed by them. Unlike promissory estoppel and estoppel by representation, the contractual duty of honest performance does not require that the defendant intend that his or her representation be relied on and it is not subject to the uncertainty around whether estoppel can be used to found an independent cause of action: *Ryan v. Moore*, 2005 SCC 38, [2005] 2 S.C.R. 53, at para. 5; *Maracle v. Travellers Indemnity Co. of Canada*, [1991] 2 S.C.R. 50; Waddams, *The Law of Contracts*, at paras. 195-203; B. MacDougall, *Estoppel* (2012), at pp. 142-44. As for the tort of civil fraud, breach of the duty of honest contractual performance does not require the defendant to intend that the false statement be relied on, and breach of it supports a claim for damages according to the contractual rather than the tortious measure: see, e.g., *Parna v. G. & S. Properties Ltd.*, [1971] S.C.R. 306, cited with approval in *Bruno Appliance and Furniture, Inc. v. Hryniak*, 2014 SCC 8, [2014] 1 S.C.R. 126, at para. 19.

[Finally, Cromwell J rejected the appellant's argument for the recognition of a more expansive duty of good faith in the following terms:]

[89] Mr. Bhasin, supported by many judicial and academic authorities, has argued for wholesale adoption of a more expansive duty of good faith in contrast to the modest, incremental change that I propose: A.F., at para. 51; Summers, at p. 206; Belobaba; *Gateway Realty*. In many of its manifestations, good faith requires more than honesty on the part of a contracting party. For example, in *Dynamic Transport*, this Court held that good faith in the context of that contract required a party to take reasonable steps to obtain the planning permission that was a condition precedent

to a sale of property. In other cases, the courts have required that discretionary powers not be exercised in a manner that is "capricious" or "arbitrary": *Mason*, at p. 487; *LeMesurier v. Andrus* (1986), 54 O.R. (2d) 1 (C.A.), at p. 7. In other contexts, this Court has been reluctant to extend the requirements of good faith beyond honesty for fear of causing undue judicial interference in contracts: *Wallace*, at para. 76.

[90] It is not necessary in this case to define in general terms the limits of the implications of the organizing principle of good faith. This is because it is unclear to me how any broader duty would assist Mr. Bhasin here. After all, the contract was subject to non-renewal. It is a considerable stretch, as I see it, to turn even a broadly conceived duty of good faith exercise of the non-renewal provision into what is, in effect, a contract of indefinite duration. This in my view is the principal difficulty in the trial judge's reasoning because, in the result, her decision turned a three year contract that was subject to an express provision relating to non-renewal into a contract of roughly nine years' duration. As the Court of Appeal pointed out, in my view correctly, "[t]he parties did not intend or presume a perpetual contract, as they contracted that either party could unilaterally cause it to expire on any third anniversary": para. 32. Even if there were a breach of a broader duty of good faith by forcing the merger, Can-Am's contractual liability would still have to be measured by reference to the least onerous means of performance, which in this case would have meant simply not renewing the contract. Since no damages flow from this breach, it is unnecessary to decide whether reliance on a discretionary power to achieve a purpose extraneous to the contract and which undermined one of its key objectives might call for further development under the organizing principle of good faith contractual performance.

[Applying the new duty of honesty to the present facts, Cromwell J held that the duty had been breached in several respects by Cam-Am including misrepresenting its intentions to Mr. Bhasin, misdescribing the role of the PTO and "equivocating" when asked directly by Mr. Bhasin concerning its intentions with respect to a merger. The court further held that if Mr. Bhasin had been dealt with honestly, he could have taken steps to preserve, to some extent at least, the value of his business. Damages were therefore calculated on the basis of the loss in value of the business directly attributable to Can-Am's dishonesty, an amount assessed by the trial judge to be $87,000.00.]

NOTES AND QUESTIONS

1. Is the new duty of honesty in contractual performance an implied term? Of fact? Of law? Are the other three existing duties implied terms? Of fact? Of law?

2. For Supreme Court of Canada authority confirming the existence of three different types of implied terms—of fact, of law, or of custom and usage—see *Canadian Pacific Hotels Ltd v Bank of Montreal*, [1987] 1 SCR 711; *Machtinger v HOJ Industries Ltd*, [1992] 1 SCR 986. For discussion of the law of implied contractual terms, see McCamus, ch 19; G Hall, *Canadian Contractual Interpretation Law*, 2d ed (Toronto: LexisNexis, 2016), ch 4.

3. In applying the rules supported by the underlying principle of good faith performance, is one restricted to relying upon the three pre-existing rules requiring good faith and the new fourth rule requiring honesty in performance?

4. Is it now a rule of contract law that a party must "have appropriate regard for the legitimate interests of the contracting partner"?

5. In *Bhasin*, Cromwell J suggests that the doctrine of unconscionability can be explained on the basis of the underlying principle requiring good faith contractual performance. Do you agree?

6. Do you agree that the two "steps" taken by the Supreme Court in *Bhasin* represent an "incremental change in the law"?

7. Is the underlying principle of good faith performance equivalent to or the same thing as the "policy" underlying the various good faith duties or rules? Are the terms "rules," "duties," "principles," and "policies" easily distinguishable? For discussion of possible meanings of the terms "principle" and "policy" in this context, see SM Waddams, *Principle and Policy in Contract Law: Competing or Complementary Concepts?* (Cambridge: Cambridge University Press, 2011), ch 1 and 2.

8. Cromwell J indicated that he "would not rule out any role for the agreement of the parties in influencing the scope of honest performance in a particular context." What kinds of provisions might enjoy success in exerting such influence?

IV. THE POSITION OF THE PARTY IN BREACH

JACOB & YOUNGS, INC V KENT
230 NY 239, 129 NE 889 (CA 1921)

CARDOZO J: The plaintiff built a country residence for the defendant at a cost of upwards of $77,000, and now sues to recover a balance of $3,483.46, remaining unpaid. The work of construction ceased in June 1914, and the defendant then began to occupy the dwelling. There was no complaint of defective performance until March 1915. One of the specifications for the plumbing works provides that "all wrought-iron pipe must be well galvanized, lap welded pipe of the grade known as 'standard pipe' of Reading manufacture."

The defendant learned in March 1915, that some of the pipe, instead of being made in Reading, was the product of other factories. The plaintiff was accordingly directed by the architect to do the work anew. The plumbing was then encased within the walls except in a few places where it had to be exposed. Obedience to the order meant more than the substitution of other pipe. It meant the demolition at great expense of substantial parts of the completed structure. The plaintiff left the work untouched, and asked for a certificate that the final payment was due. Refusal of the certificate was followed by this suit.

The evidence sustains a finding that the omission of the prescribed brand of pipe was neither fraudulent nor wilful. It was the result of the oversight and inattention of the plaintiff's subcontractor. Reading pipe is distinguished from Cohoes pipe and other brands only by the name of the manufacturer stamped upon it at intervals of between six and seven feet. Even the defendant's architect, though he inspected the pipe upon arrival, failed to notice the discrepancy. The plaintiff tried to show that the brands installed, though made by other manufacturers, were the same in quality, in appearance, in market value and in cost as the brand stated in the contract—that they were indeed the same thing, though manufactured in another place. The evidence was excluded, and a verdict directed for the defendant. The Appellate Division reversed, and granted a new trial.

We think the evidence, if admitted, would have supplied some basis for the inference that the defect was insignificant in its relation to the project. The courts never say that one who makes a contract fills the measure of his duty by less than full performance. They do say, however, that an omission, both trivial and innocent, will sometimes be atoned for by allowance of the resulting damage, and will not always be the breach of a condition to be followed by a forfeiture. ... The distinction is akin to that between dependent and independent promises, or between promises and conditions. ... Some promises are so plainly independent that they can never by fair construction be conditions of one another. ... Others are so plainly dependent that they must always be conditions. Others, though dependent and thus conditions when there is departure in point of substance, will be viewed as independent and collateral when the departure is insignificant. ... Considerations partly of justice and partly of presumable intention are to tell us whether this or that promise shall be placed in one class or in another. The simple and the uniform will call for different remedies from the multifarious and the intricate. The margin of departure within the range of normal expectation upon a sale of common chattels will vary from the margin to be expected upon a contract for the construction of a mansion or a "sky-scraper." There will be harshness sometimes and oppression in the implication of a condition when the thing upon which labor has been expended is incapable of surrender because united to the land, and equity and reason in the implication of a like condition when the subject-matter, if defective, is in shape to be returned. From the conclusion that promises may not be treated as dependent to the extent of their uttermost minutiae without a sacrifice of justice, the progress is a short one to the conclusion that they may not be so treated without a perversion of intention. Intention not otherwise revealed may be presumed to hold in contemplation the reasonable and probable. If something else is in view, it must not be left to implication. There will be no assumption of a purpose to visit venial faults with oppressive retribution.

Those who think more of symmetry and logic in the development of legal rules than of practical adaptation to the attainment of a just result will be troubled by a classification where the lines are so wavering and blurred. Something, doubtless, may be said on the score of consistency and certainty in favor of a stricter standard. The courts have balanced such considerations against those of equity and fairness, and found the latter to be the weightier. The decisions in this state commit us to the liberal view, which is making its way, nowadays, in jurisdictions slow to welcome it. *Dakin & Co. v. Lee*, [1916] 1 K.B. 566. Where the line is to be drawn between the import-ant and the trivial cannot be settled by a formula. "In the nature of the case precise boundaries are impossible." 2 *Williston on Contracts*, p. 841. The same omission may take on one aspect or another according to its setting. Substitution of equivalents may not have the same significance in fields of art on the one side and in those of mere utility on the other. Nowhere will change be tolerated, however, if it is so dom-inant or pervasive as in any real or substantial measure to frustrate the purpose of the contract. ... There is no general license to install whatever, in the builder's judg-ment, may be regarded as "just as good." ... The question is one of degree, to be answered, if there is doubt, by the triers of the facts, ... and, if the inferences are certain, by the judges of the law. ...

We must weigh the purpose to be served, the desire to be gratified, the excuse for deviation from the letter, the cruelty of enforced adherence. Then only can we tell whether literal fulfillment is to be implied by law as a condition. This is not to say that the parties are not free by apt and certain words to effectuate a purpose that performance of every term shall be a condition of recovery. That question is not here. This is merely to say that the law will be slow to impute the purpose, in the silence of the parties, where the significance of the default is grievously out of proportion to the oppression of the forfeiture. The wilful transgressor must accept the penalty of his transgression. ... For him there is no occasion to mitigate the rigor of implied conditions. The transgressor whose default is unintentional and trivial may hope for mercy if he will offer atonement for his wrong.

In the circumstances of this case, we think the measure of the allowance is not the cost of replacement, which would be great, but the difference in value, which would be either nominal or nothing. Some of the exposed sections might perhaps have been replaced at moderate expense. The defendant did not limit his demand to them, but treated the plumbing as a unit to be corrected from cellar to roof. In point of fact, the plaintiff never reached the stage at which evidence of the extent of the allowance became necessary. The trial court had excluded evidence that the defect was unsubstantial, and in view of that ruling there was no occasion for the plaintiff to go farther with an offer of proof. We think, however, that the offer, if it had been made, would not of necessity have been defective because directed to difference in value. It is true that in most cases the cost of replacement is the measure. The owner is entitled to the money which will permit him to complete, unless the cost of completion is grossly and unfairly out of proportion to the good to be attained. When that is true, the measure is the difference in value. Specifications call, let us say, for a foundation built of granite quarried in Vermont. On the completion of the building, the owner learns that through the blunder of a subcontractor part of the foundation has been built of the same quality quarried in New Hampshire. The measure of allowance is not the cost of reconstruction. "There may be omissions of that which could not afterwards be supplied exactly as called for by the contract without taking down the building to its foundations, and at the same time the omission may not affect the value of the building for use or otherwise, except so slightly as to be hardly appreciable." ... The rule that gives remedy in cases of substantial performance with compensation for defects of trivial or inappreciable importance, has been developed by the courts as an instrument of justice. The measure of the allowance must be shaped to the same end.

The order should be affirmed, and judgment absolute directed in favour of the plaintiff upon the stipulation, with costs in all courts.

McLAUGHLIN J: I dissent. The plaintiff did not perform its contract. Its failure to do so was either intentional or due to gross neglect which, under the uncontradicted facts, amounted to the same thing, nor did it make any proof of the cost of compliance, where compliance was possible. ...

No explanation was given why pipe called for by the contract was not used, nor was any effort made to show what it would cost to remove the pipe of other manufacturers and install that of the Reading Manufacturing Company. The defendant had a right to contract for what he wanted. He had a right before making payment to get what the contract called for. It is no answer to say that the pipe put in was just as good as that made by the Reading Manufacturing Company, or that the difference in value between such pipe and the pipe made by the Reading Manufacturing Company would be either "nominal or nothing." Defendant contracted for pipe made by the Reading Manufacturing Company. What his reason was for requiring this kind of pipe is of no importance. He wanted that and was entitled to it. It may have been a mere whim on his part, but even so, he had a right to the kind of pipe, regardless of whether some other kind, according to the opinion of the contractor or experts, would have been "just as good, better, or done just as well." He agreed to pay only upon condition that the pipe installed were made by that company and he ought not to be compelled to pay unless that condition be performed. ... The rule, therefore, of substantial performance, with damages for unsubstantial omissions, has no application.

QUESTIONS

1. What remedy was available to the party in breach in this case? What remedy was available to the party not in default?

2. Was the plaintiff's failure to install the correct pipe a breach of a "condition" of the agreement? If the contract plainly stipulated that payment of the final balance was conditional on completion of the work in strict compliance with the specifications, would a different result be warranted?

HOENIG V ISAACS
[1952] All ER 176 (CA)

The plaintiff, an interior designer, was employed by the defendant to decorate and furnish the defendant's apartment for a flat fee. The terms of payment were "net cash, as the work proceeds, and balance on completion." The defendant paid some installments but refused to pay the balance on the ground that some of the work done and some of the articles furnished were defective. The defendant resisted payment on the ground that the complete performance of the agreement was a condition precedent to the obligation to pay the balance.

SOMERVELL LJ: ... In a contract to erect buildings on the defendant's land for a lump sum, the builder can recover nothing on the contract if he stops before the work is completed in the ordinary sense—in other words, abandons the contract. He is also usually in a difficulty in recovering on a quantum meruit because no new contract can be inferred from the mere fact that the defendant remains in possession of his land; *Sumpter v. Hedges*. ...

The question here is whether in a contract for work and labour for a lump sum payable on completion the defendant can repudiate liability under the contract on the ground that the work though "finished" or "done" is in some respects not in accordance with the contract. ...

The learned official referee regarded *H. Dakin & Co., Ltd. v. Lee* as laying down that the price must be paid subject to set-off or counterclaim if there was a substantial compliance with the contract. I think on the facts of this case where the work was finished in the ordinary sense, though in part defective, this is right. ...

DENNING LJ: ... In determining this issue the first question is whether, on the true construction of the contract, entire performance was a condition precedent to payment. It was a lump sum contract, but that does not mean that entire performance was a condition precedent to payment. When a contract provides for a specific sum to be paid on completion of specified work, the courts lean against a construction of the contract which would deprive the contractor of any payment at all simply because there are some defects or omissions. The promise to complete the work is, therefore, construed as a term of the contract, but not as a condition. ...

I would point out that in these cases the question of quantum meruit only arises when there is a breach or failure of performance which goes to the very root of the matter. On any lump sum contract, if the work is not substantially performed and there has been a failure of performance which goes to the root of it, as, for instance, when the work has only been half done, or is entirely different in kind from that contracted for, then no action will lie for the lump sum. The contractor can then only succeed in getting paid for what he has done if it was the employer's fault that the work was incomplete, or there is something to justify the conclusion that the parties have entered into a fresh contract. ...

ROMER LJ: ... In certain cases it is right that the rigid rule for which the defendant contends should be applied, for example, if a man tells a contractor to build a ten foot wall for him in his garden and agrees to pay £X for it, it would not be right that he should be held liable for any part of the contract price if the contractor builds the wall to two feet and then renounces further performance of the contract, or builds the wall of a totally different material from that which was ordered, or builds it at the wrong end of the garden. The work contracted for has not been done and the corresponding obligation to pay consequently never arises. But when a man fully performs his contract in the sense that he supplies all that he agreed to supply but what he supplies is subject to defects of so minor a character that he can be said to have substantially performed his promise, it is, in my judgment, far more equitable to apply the *H. Dakin & Co., Ltd. v. Lee* principle than to deprive him wholly of his contractual rights and relegate him to such remedy (if any) as he may have on a quantum meruit.

QUESTIONS

1. Is there a difference between the reasoning of Denning and Romer LJJ? Does Romer LJ take the view that the plaintiff's promise has been performed? Does Denning LJ share this view? Which approach would be more satisfactory in a case where the contract plainly stipulates that payment is not to be made until completion of the work?

2. A agrees to supply and install a machine for the manufacture of soap chips on B's premises, payment to be made on completion of the work. When only a few remaining steps were to be made by A to make the machine functional, A declined to finish the work unless he first received payment from B. Is A entitled to rely on the doctrine of substantial performance? See *Fairbanks Soap Co Ltd v Sheppard*, [1953] 1 SCR 314 (declining to apply the doctrine on the ground that the work was incomplete rather than complete with defects).

CUTTER V POWELL
(1795), 6 TR 320, 101 ER 573 (KB)

To assumpsit for work and labour done by the intestate Cutter, the defendant pleaded the general issue. And at the trial at Lancaster the jury found a verdict for the plaintiff for £31 10s. subject to the opinion of this court on the following case.

The defendant being at Jamaica subscribed and delivered to T. Cutter the intestate a note, whereof the following is a copy: "Ten days after the ship Governor Parry, myself master, arrives at Liverpool, I promise to pay Mr. T. Cutter the sum of thirty guineas, provided he proceeds, continues and does his duty as second mate in the said ship from hence to the port of Liverpool, Kingston, July 31st, 1793." The ship Governor Parry sailed from Kingston on the 2nd of August, 1793, and arrived in the port of Liverpool on the 9th of October following. T. Cutter went on board the ship on the 31st of July, 1793, and sailed in her on the 2nd day of August, and proceeded, continued and did his duty as second mate in her from Kingston until his death, which happened on the 20th of September following, and before the ship's arrival in the port of Liverpool. The usual wages of a second mate of a ship on such a voyage, when shipped by the month out and home is four pounds per month; but when seamen are shipped by the run from Jamaica to England, a gross sum is usually given. The usual length of a voyage from Jamaica to Liverpool is about eight weeks.

ASHURST J: We cannot collect that there is any custom prevailing among merchants on these contracts; and therefore we have nothing to guide us but the terms of the contract itself. This is a written contract, and it speaks for itself. And as it is entire, and as the defendant's promise depends on a condition precedent to be performed by the other party, the condition must be performed before the other party is entitled to receive anything under it. It has been argued however that the plaintiff may now recover on a quantum meruit: but she has no right to desert the agreement; for wherever there is an express contract the parties must be guided by it; and one party cannot relinquish or abide by it as it may suit his advantage. Here the intestate was by the terms of his contract to perform a given duty before he could call upon the defendant to pay him anything; it was a condition precedent, without performing which the defendant is not liable. And that seems to me to conclude the question: the intestate did not perform the contract on his part; he was not indeed to blame for not doing it; but still as this was a condition precedent, and as he did not perform it, his representative is not entitled to recover.

Postea to the defendant: Unless some other information relative to the usage in cases of this kind should be laid before the Court before the end of this term; but the case was not mentioned again.

[The opinions of Lord Kenyon CJ and Gross and Lawrence JJ are omitted.]

NOTE

The rights of sailors in circumstances like those in *Cutter v Powell* are now governed by the *Canada Shipping Act*, RSC 1985, c S-9; see especially ss 195-204.

Stubbs v Holywell Railway Company. (1867), LR 2 Ex 311. Stubbs was appointed consulting engineer to the defendants, to complete the construction of certain works. The work was to be completed in fifteen months from Dec. 5th, and Stubbs was to be paid £500 as his salary, in five equal quarterly installments. Stubbs worked one quarter and was paid £100 in March. He worked for two more quarters, and part of the fourth quarter when he died. His administrator sued for £200.

MARTIN B: Suppose a man enters into a contract to do a certain piece of work for a certain sum, then if he die before he completes it, he can recover nothing, not even if before his death he had done nine-tenths of it. For the contract was for the whole work, and not for nine-tenths of it. But suppose that the contract is for performance of a certain piece of work for a certain sum, to be paid at the rate, say of £50 a month, then the person employed earns £50 at the end of each successive month. It is true that if, after doing a portion of the work, he refused to do the rest, he might not be able to recover, because he could not prove that he was ready and willing to perform his part of the contract. But such a case as the present has no analogy with that of a refusal by the person employed to continue performance. The contract, no doubt, is ended by the death of Stubbs, but only in this sense, that the act of God has made further performance impossible. ... No vested right of action is taken away by death. The contract is at an end, but it is not rescinded, for rescission is the act of two parties, not of one.

APPORTIONMENT ACT
RSO 1990, c A.23

3. All rents, annuities, dividends, and other periodical payments in the nature of income, whether reserved or made payable under an instrument in writing or otherwise, shall, like interest on money lent, be considered as accruing from day to day, and are apportionable in respect of time accordingly.

[See also Waddams at paras 604-6.]

SUMPTER V HEDGES
[1898] 1 QB 673 (CA)

The action was for work done and materials provided. The plaintiff, a builder, had contracted with the defendant to build upon the defendant's land two houses and stables for the sum of £565. The plaintiff did part of the work, amounting in value to about £333, and had received payment of part of the price. He then informed the defendant that he had no money, and could not go on with the work. The learned judge found that he had abandoned the contract. The defendant thereupon finished the buildings on his own account, using for that purpose certain building materials which the plaintiff had left on the ground. The judge gave judgment for the plaintiff for the value of the materials so used, but allowed him nothing in respect of the work which he had done upon the buildings.

AL SMITH LJ: ... In this case the plaintiff, a builder, entered into a contract to build two houses and stables on the defendant's land for a lump sum. When the buildings were still in an unfinished state the plaintiff informed the defendant that he had no money, and was not going on with the work any more. The learned judge has found as a fact that he abandoned the contract. Under such circumstances, what is a building owner to do? He cannot keep the buildings on his land in an unfinished state for ever. The law is that, where there is a contract to do work for a lump sum, until the work is completed the price of it cannot be recovered. Therefore the plaintiff could not recover on the original contract. It is suggested however that the plaintiff was entitled to recover for the work he did on a quantum meruit. But, in order that that may be so, there must be evidence of a fresh contract to pay for the work already done. With regard to that, the case of *Munro v. Butt* (1858), 8 E. & B. 738; 120 E.R. 274 appears to be exactly in point. That case decides that, unless the building owner does something from which a new contract can be inferred to pay for the work already done, the plaintiff in such a case as this cannot recover on a quantum meruit. In the case of *Lysaght v. Pearson* (not reported except in Times Newspaper of March 3, 1879), to which we have been referred, the case of *Munro v. Butt* does not appear to have been referred to. There the plaintiff had contracted to erect on the defendant's land two corrugated iron roofs. When he had completed one of them, he does not seem to have said that he abandoned the contract, but merely that he would not go on unless the defendant paid him for what he had already done. The defendant thereupon proceeded to erect for himself the second roof. The Court of Appeal held that there was in that case something from which a new contract might be inferred to pay for the work done by the plaintiff. That is not this case. In the case of *Whitaker v. Dunn* (1887), 3 Times L.R. 602, there was a contract to erect a laundry on defendant's land, and the laundry erected was not in accordance with the contract, but the official referee held that the plaintiff could recover on a quantum meruit. The case came before a Divisional Court, consisting of Lord Coleridge C.J. and myself, and we said that the decision in *Munroe v. Butt* applied, and there being no circumstances to justify an inference of a fresh contract the plaintiff must fail. My brother Collins thinks that that case went to the Court of Appeal, and that he argued it there, and that the Court affirmed the decision of the Queen's Bench Division. I think the appeal must be dismissed.

COLLINS LJ: ... I agree. I think the case is really concluded by the finding of the learned judge to the effect that the plaintiff had abandoned the contract. If the plaintiff had merely broken his contract in some way so as not to give the defendant the right to treat him as having abandoned the contract, and the defendant had then proceeded to finish the work himself, the plaintiff might perhaps have been entitled to sue on a quantum meruit on the ground that the defendant had taken the benefit of the work done. But that is not the present case. There are cases in which, though the plaintiff has abandoned the performance of a contract, it is possible for him to raise the inference of a new contract to pay for the work done on a quantum meruit from the defendant's having taken the benefit of that work, but, in order that that may be done, the circumstances must be such as to give an option to the defendant to take or not to take the benefit of the work done. It is only where the circumstances are such as to give that option that there is any evidence on which to ground the inference of a new contract. Where, as in the case of work done on land, the circumstances are such as to give the defendant no option whether he will take the benefit of the work or not, then one must look to other facts than the mere taking the benefit of the work in order to ground the inference of a new contract. In this case I see no other facts on which such an inference can be founded. The mere fact that a defendant is in possession of what he cannot help keeping, or even has done work upon it, affords no ground for such an inference. He is not bound to keep unfinished a building which in an incomplete state would be a nuisance on his land. I am therefore of opinion that the plaintiff was not entitled to recover for the work which he had done. I feel clear that the case of *Whitaker v. Dunn* to which reference has been made, was the case which as counsel I argued in the Court of Appeal, and in which the Court dismissed the appeal on the ground that the case was concluded by *Munro v. Butt*.

[The appeal was dismissed. The opinion of Chitty LJ to the same effect is omitted.]

QUESTIONS

1. The claim in *quantum meruit* is evidently restitutionary in nature. In Chapter 2, Section IX, we briefly examined the development of the law of restitution and the shift from the implied contract theory of liability to the explanation offered by the unjust enrichment principle. Is the reasoning in *Sumpter v Hedges* inconsistent with the reasoning in *Deglman v Guaranty Trust*, examined in Chapter 2?

2. Even if a claim on unjust enrichment grounds might be theoretically available on the facts of *Sumpter v Hedges*, are there reasons of public policy that weigh against granting this form of relief?

3. Is a lump-sum or entire contract either explicitly or implicitly an agreement under which the contractor has agreed to forfeit the value of any work done upon failure to complete the entire work? In Chapter 6, we considered the enforceability of forfeiture clauses and noted that, though they are generally enforceable, the decision in *Stockloser v Johnson*, excerpted in Chapter 6, developed an exception to the rule. In that case, the English Court of Appeal held that where moneys have been paid subject to a clause forfeiting the moneys paid if the payer is unable to complete performance of the agreement, the clause would not be enforceable in circumstances where the value conferred on the payee is out of all proportion to the loss sustained by the payee as a result of the breach of contract. Should a similar rule apply to a case like *Sumpter v Hedges*? Is there a difference between the receipt of money and the receipt of a partially constructed building that might warrant different results in these two different settings? From this perspective, is it relevant that the defendant in *Sumpter v Hedges* had contracted to acquire the work in question? See also Waddams at paras 604-5 and Maddaugh & McCamus, ch 19 at 300.

CHAPTER NINE

MISTAKE

I. INTRODUCTION

Even committed proponents of freedom of contract recognize that certain information pre-conditions must be met for a given exchange to justify enforcement. For example, Milton Friedman states: "The possibility of co-ordination through voluntary co-operation rests on the elementary—yet frequently denied—proposition that both parties to an economic transaction benefit from it, *provided the transaction is bilaterally voluntary and informed*" (*Capitalism and Freedom* (Chicago: University of Chicago Press, 1962) at 13). Economic justifications for private exchange assume that both parties to an exchange are rendered better off by it—in terms of the subjectively perceived impact of the exchange on their respective utility functions—or they would not have entered into it. But if at least one party inaccurately perceives or evaluates the impact of the exchange on her utility, we can no longer be confident that the exchange will in fact render both parties better off. However, almost no exchange is entered into with absolutely perfect information by both parties. Thus, if we were to insist on a blanket requirement of perfect information, very few contracts would be enforceable. Autonomy justifications for freedom of contract raise comparable challenges—it is difficult to conceive of a choice as autonomous without basic information about its implications, but, because information is often costly, it may be rational to choose to forgo the acquisition of further information where its expected benefits are less than its expected costs.

It is useful to think of information imperfections affecting the contracting process as falling into two broad categories: (1) asymmetric information imperfections, where one party to a contract is substantially less well informed about some aspect of the contract subject matter than the other party, and (2) symmetric information imperfections, where both parties are mistaken about either material facts at the time of contracting or the possible occurrence of future events that may affect the value of the contract. There is also a hybrid category where both parties have information imperfections but with respect to different aspects of the contract. Where one party has an information imperfection, there is said to be a *unilateral* mistake. Where both parties have information imperfections of the same type, there is a *common* mistake. This situation is sometimes referred to as a *mutual* mistake but that term is confusing because it is also the term used to describe the hybrid category of information imperfection.

The mistake might arise because of a misstatement by another person to the mistaken party. That other person could be—and often is—the other contracting party. The misstatement can be a negative rather than a positive in the sense of involving a material *non-disclosure* rather than an erroneous statement. The misstatement might also involve contexts of incomplete or partially false statements or true statements that later become false (or vice versa). In all such situations, the law on "misrepresentation" deals with the consequences of the resulting mistake. The maker of the misstatement (i.e. of the "misrepresentation") might have deliberately made it with intent to deceive the recipient (the "representee") in which case it is called a *fraudulent misrepresentation*. A fraudulent misrepresentation, by its very nature, will result in a unilateral mistake. If such knowledge and intent on the part of the maker of the statement are lacking, then there is what is called an *innocent misrepresentation*. An innocent misrepresentation may well be a context of common mistake, the maker's being mistaken and conveying that mistake to the representee. The maker of an innocent misrepresentation ought in many cases not to have been mistaken, in which case the innocent misrepresentation is better characterized as a *negligent misrepresentation*.

Misrepresentation cases typically deal with misstatements made before or at the time a contract is entered into, though there is no reason why a misrepresentation made after the contract is created cannot affect the contract. (See e.g. *Mafo v Adams*, [1970] 1 QB 548 (CA).) Despite Cromwell J's statement to the contrary, the new "duty of honest performance" recognized in *Bhasin v Hrynew*, 2014 SCC 71—a duty of contract parties not to "lie or otherwise knowingly mislead each other about matters directly linked to the performance of the contract"—can be seen as a new variant of the law on misstatements. (See B MacDougall, *Misrepresentation* (Toronto: LexisNexis, 2016) at pp 60-70.) The duty of honest performance and the *Bhasin* case are dealt with in Chapter 8.

Where the mistake of a contracting party is not caused by the misstatement of the other contracting party, the law on "mistake" proper, rather than that of "misrepresentation," is applicable. Such mistakes can be about various matters to do with the contract:

a. a mistake about the meaning or existence of a term in a contract;
b. a mistake about the nature of the contract ("*non est factum*");
c. a mistake about assumptions as to significant facts in existence (or not in existence) when the contract is entered into;
d. a mistake about the identity of the other contracting party (in fact often a subset of item (c));
e. a mistake about the future course of events and how they might affect the contract; and
f. a mistake in the written record of an agreement.

This chapter deals with all contexts of misrepresentation, except the duty of honest performance (which, as already noted, is discussed in Chapter 8), and also with certain types of mistake from the above list of six items. The items from that list dealt with in this chapter are items (a) and (c). Item (b), *non est factum*, is dealt with in Chapter 5. Item (d), mistaken identity, is dealt with in Chapter 4. Item (e) is dealt with in Chapter 10. Item (f) is dealt with in Chapter 5, Section III.

II. MISREPRESENTATIONS

GROTIUS, "WHETHER A PROMISE GIVEN UNDER A MISAPPREHENSION IS BY THE LAW OF NATURE BINDING, AND TO WHAT EXTENT" (1625)

in Hugo Grotius, *The Law of War and Peace*, Book II, ch 11, "On Promises," section VI, Francis W. Kelsey, trans (Indianapolis, Ind: Bobbs-Merrill, 1925)

[1] The treatment of agreements based on a misapprehension is perplexing enough. It is, in fact, customary to distinguish between errors which affect the substance of the matter and those which do not; to consider whether a contract was based on fraud or not, whether the person with whom the contract was made was a party to the fraud, and whether the act was one of strict justice or only of good faith. For in view of the diversity of these cases the writers declare some acts void and others binding, but in such a way that they may be annulled or changed at the choice of the one injured.

The majority of these distinctions come from the Roman law, not only the old civil law, but also the edicts and decisions of the praetors; and some of them are not entirely true or accurate.

[2] Now a method of ascertaining the truth according to nature is furnished to us by the fact that as regards the force and effect of laws nearly every one agrees that, if [the application of] a law rests upon the presumption of a certain fact which does not actually obtain, then that law does not apply; for the whole foundation for the [application of the] law is overthrown when the truth of the [alleged] fact fails. The decision when a law has been based on such a presumption must be inferred from the substance, words, and circumstances of the law.

In like manner, then, we shall say that, if a promise has been based on a certain presumption of fact which does not so obtain, by the law of nature it has no force. For the promisor did not consent to the promise except under a certain condition which, in fact, did not exist. To this principle should be referred the question in the first book of Cicero's *On the Orator*, concerning the man who, falsely believing that his son was dead, had named another as heir.

[3] If, however, the promisor was careless in investigating the matter, or in expressing his thought, and another has suffered loss therefrom, the promisor will be bound to make this loss good, not from the force of the promise, but by reason of the loss suffered through his fault, a subject which we shall treat below.

On the other hand, if there was an error present indeed, but the promise was not based thereon, the action will be valid, since true consent was not lacking. But in this case also, if the person to whom the promise is made has by fraud caused the error, according to that other principle of obligation he will have to make good whatever loss the promisor has suffered in consequence of the error. If the promise only in part was based on error, it will be valid as to the remainder.

HEILBUT, SYMONS & CO V BUCKLETON
[1913] AC 30 (HL)

VISCOUNT HALDANE LC: My Lords, the appellants, who were rubber merchants in London, in the spring of 1910 underwrote a large number of shares in a company called the Filisola Rubber and Produce Estates, Limited, a company which was promoted and registered by other persons about that time. They instructed a Mr. Johnston, who was the manager of their Liverpool business, to obtain applications for shares in Liverpool. Johnston, who had seen a draft prospectus in London but had at the time no copy of the prospectus, mentioned the company to several people in Liverpool, including a Mr. Wright, who sometimes acted as broker for the respondent.

On April 14 the respondent telephoned to Johnston from Wright's office. As to what passed there is no dispute. The respondent said "I understand you are bringing out a rubber company." The reply was "We are." The respondent then asked whether Johnston had any prospectuses, and his reply was in the negative. The respondent then asked "if it was all right," and Johnston replied "We are bringing it out," to which the respondent rejoined "That is good enough for me." He went on to ask how many shares he could have, and to say that he would take almost any number. He explained in his evidence in chief that his reason for being willing to do this was that the position the appellants occupied in the rubber trade was of such high standing that "any company they should see fit to bring out was a sufficient warranty" to him "that it was all right in every respect." Afterwards, as the result of the conversation, a large number of shares were allotted to the respondent.

About this time the rubber boom of 1910 was at its height and the shares of the Filisola Company were, and for a short time remained, at a premium. Later on it was discovered that there was a large deficiency in the rubber trees which were said in the prospectus to exist on the Filisola Estate, and the shares fell in value. The respondent brought an action against the appellants for fraudulent misrepresentation, and alternatively for damages for breach of warranty that the company was a rubber company whose main object was to produce rubber.

The action was tried at Liverpool Assizes before Lush J. and a special jury. The jury found that there was no fraudulent representation by the appellants or Johnston, but they found that the company could not be properly described as a rubber company, and that the appellants or Johnston, or both, had warranted that the company was a rubber company ... .

[The trial judge allowed damages at £406 5s. and the Court of Appeal affirmed the judgment.]

LORD MOULTON: There is no controversy between the parties as to certain points of fact and of law. It is not contested that the only company referred to was the Filisola Rubber and Produce Estates Limited, or that the reply of Mr. Johnston to the plaintiff's question over the telephone was a representation by the defendants that the company was a "rubber company," whatever may be the meaning of that phrase; nor is there any controversy as to the legal nature of that which the plaintiff must establish. He must shew a warranty, i.e., a contract collateral to the main contract to take the shares, whereby the defendants in consideration of the plaintiff taking the shares promised that the company itself was a rubber company. The question in issue is whether there was any evidence that such a contract was made between the parties.

It is evident, both on principle and on authority, that there may be a contract the consideration for which is the making of some other contract. "If you will make such and such a contract I will give you one hundred pounds," is in every sense of the word a complete legal contract. It is collateral to the main contract, but each has an independent existence, and they do not differ in respect of their possessing to the full the character and status of a contract. But such collateral contracts must from their very nature be rare. The effect of a collateral contract such as that which I have instanced would be to increase the consideration of the main contract by £100, and the more natural and usual way of carrying this out would be by so modifying the main contract and not by executing a concurrent and collateral contract. Such collateral contracts, the sole effect of which is to vary or add to the terms of the principal contract, are therefore viewed with suspicion by the law. They must be proved strictly. Not only the terms of such contracts but the existence of an *animus contrahendi* on the part of all the parties to escape from the full performance of the obligations of contracts unquestionably entered into by them, and more especially would have the effect of lessening the authority of written contracts by making it possible to vary them by suggesting the existence of verbal agreements relating to the same subject-matter.

There is in the present case an entire absence of any evidence to support the existence of such a collateral contract. The statement of Mr. Johnston in answer to plaintiff's question was beyond controversy a mere statement of fact, for it was in reply to a question for information and nothing more. No doubt it was a representation as to fact, and indeed it was the actual representation upon which the main case of the plaintiff rested. It was this representation which he alleged to have been false and fraudulent and which he alleged induced him to enter into the contracts and take the shares. There is no suggestion throughout the whole of his evidence that he regarded it as anything but a representation. Neither the plaintiff nor the defendants were asked any question or gave any evidence tending to shew the existence of any *animus contrahendi* other than as regards the main contracts. The whole case for the existence of a collateral contract therefore rests on the mere fact that the statement was made as to the character of the company, and if this is to be treated as evidence sufficient to establish the existence of a collateral contract of the kind alleged the same result must follow with regard to any other statement relating to the subject-matter of a contract made by a contracting party prior to its execution. This would negative entirely the firmly established rule that an innocent representation gives no right to damages. It would amount to saying that the making of any representation prior to a contract relating to its subject-matter is sufficient to establish the existence of a collateral contract that the statement is true and therefore to give a right to damages if such should not be the case.

In the history of English law we find many attempts to make persons responsible in damages by reason of innocent misrepresentation, and at times it has seemed as though the attempts would succeed. On the Chancery side of the Court the decisions favouring this view usually took the form of extending the scope of the action for deceit. There was a tendency to recognize the existence of what was sometimes called "legal fraud," i.e., that the making of an incorrect statement of fact without reasonable grounds, or of one which was inconsistent with information which the person had received or had the means of obtaining, entailed the same legal consequences as making it fraudulently. Such a doctrine would make a man liable for forgetfulness or mistake or even for honestly interpreting the facts known to him or drawing conclusions from them in a way which the Court did not think to be legally warranted. The high water mark of these decisions is to be found in the judgment by the Court of Appeal in the case of *Peek v. Derry* (1887), 37 Ch. D. 541, when they laid down that where a defendant has made a mis-statement of fact and the Court is of opinion that he had no reasonable grounds for believing that it was true he may be made liable in an action of deceit if it has materially tended to induce the plaintiff to do an act by which he has incurred damage. But on appeal to your Lordships' House, this decision was unanimously reversed, and it was definitely laid down that, in order to establish a cause of action sounding in damages for misrepresentation, the statement must be fraudulent or, what is equivalent thereto, must be made recklessly, not caring whether it be true or not. The opinions pronounced in your Lordships' House in that case shew that both in substance and in form the decision was, and was intended to be, a reaffirmation of the old common law doctrine that actual fraud was essential to an action for deceit, and it finally settled the law that an innocent misrepresentation gives no right of action sounding in damages.

On the Common Law side of the Court the attempts to make a person liable for an innocent misrepresentation have usually taken the form of attempts to extend the doctrine of warranty beyond its just limits and to find that a warranty existed in cases where there was nothing more than an innocent misrepresentation. The present case is, in my opinion, an instance of this. But in respect of the question of the existence of a warranty the Courts have had the advantage of an admirable enunciation of the true principle of law which was made in very early days by Holt C.J. with respect to the contract of sale. He says [c 1690]: "An affirmation at the time of the sale is a warranty, provided it appear on evidence to be so intended." So far as decisions are concerned, this has, on the whole, been consistently followed in the Courts of Common Law. But from time to time there have been dicta inconsistent with it which have, unfortunately found their way into textbooks and have given rise to confusion and uncertainty in this branch of the law. For example, one often sees quoted the dictum of Bayley J. in *Cave v. Coleman* 3 Man. & Ry. 2, where, in respect of a representation made verbally during the sale of a horse, he says that "being made in the course of dealing, and before the bargain was complete, it amounted to a warranty"— a proposition that is far too sweeping and cannot be supported. A still more serious deviation from the correct principle is to be found in a passage in the judgment of the Court of Appeal in *De Lassalle v. Guildford*, [1901] 2 K.B. 215, at p. 221, which was cited to us in the argument in the present case. In discussing the question whether a representation amounts to a warranty or not the judgment says: "In determining whether it was so intended, a decisive test is whether the vendor assumed to assert a fact of which the buyer is ignorant, or merely states an opinion or judgment upon a matter of which the vendor has no special knowledge, and on which the buyer may be expected also to have an opinion and to exercise his judgment."

With all deference to the authority of the Court that decided that case, the proposition which it thus formulates cannot be supported. It is clear that the Court did not intend to depart from the law laid down by Holt C.J. and cited above, for in the same judgment that dictum is referred to and accepted as a correct statement of the law. It is, therefore, evident that the use of the phrase "decisive test" cannot be defended. Otherwise it would be the duty of a judge to direct a jury that if a vendor states a fact of which the buyer is ignorant, they must, as a matter of law, find the existence of a warranty, whether or not the totality of the evidence shows that the parties intended the affirmation to form part of the contract; and this would be inconsistent with the law as laid down by Holt C.J. It may well be that the features thus referred to in the judgment of the Court of Appeal in that case may be criteria of value in guiding a jury in coming to a decision whether or not a warranty was intended; but they cannot be said to furnish decisive tests, because it cannot be said as a matter of law that the presence or absence of those features is conclusive of the intention of the parties. The intention of the parties can only be deduced from the totality of the evidence, and no secondary principle of such a kind can be universally true.

It is, my Lords, of the greatest importance, in my opinion, that this House should maintain in its full integrity the principle that a person is not liable in damages for an innocent misrepresentation, no matter in what way or under what form the attack is made. In the present case the statement was made in answer to an inquiry for information. There is nothing which can by any possibility be taken as evidence of an intention on the part of either or both of the parties that there should be a contractual liability in respect of the statement. It is a representation as to a specific thing and nothing more. The judge, therefore, ought not to have left the question of warranty to the jury, and if, as a matter of prudence, he did so in order to obtain their opinion in case of appeal, he ought then to have entered judgment for the defendants notwithstanding the verdict.

It will, of course, be evident that I have been dealing only with warranty or representation relation to a specific thing. This is wholly distinct from the question which arises when goods are sold by description and their answering to that description becomes a condition of the contract. It is, in my opinion, a failure to recognize that in the present case the parties were referring (as is evident by the written contract) to one specific thing only that led Farwell L.J. to come to a different conclusion from that to which your Lordships ought, in my opinion, to come in this appeal.

[Order of the Court of Appeal reversed and judgment entered for the appellants. Viscount Haldane LC and Lord Atkinson also gave reasons for allowing the appeal.]

NOTES AND QUESTIONS

1. If the defendant had sold his own shares to the plaintiff under the circumstances set out in *Heilbut*, could the plaintiff have claimed "rescission" of the contract? If the representation had been held to be a "term" of the contract, would the answer be different?

2. *Heilbut* was severely criticized by the US scholar Williston in "Representation and Warranty in Sales" (1914) 27 Harv L Rev 1. Williston's view was that a misrepresentation inducing a sale ought always to give the deceived buyer a remedy, even though the representation was innocent and no intention to contract could be inferred. Williston was the draftsman of the *Uniform Sales Act* (1913), and so it is not surprising to find that the definition of warranty in that Act includes "[a]ny affirmation of fact or any promise by the seller relating to the goods ... if the natural tendency of such affirmation or promise is to induce the buyer to purchase the goods, and if the buyer purchases the goods relying thereon." The *Uniform Sales Act* is now superseded by the *Uniform Commercial Code*. Section 2-313 of the Code provides:

(1) In this section, "immediate buyer" means a buyer that enters into a contract with the seller.

(2) Express warranties by the seller to the immediate buyer are created as follows:

(a) Any affirmation of fact or promise made by the seller to the buyer which relates to the goods and becomes part of the basis of the bargain creates an express warranty that the goods shall conform to the affirmation or promise. ...

(3) It is not necessary to the creation of an express warranty that the seller use formal words such as "warrant" or "guarantee" or that the seller have a specific intention to make a warranty, but an affirmation merely of the value of the goods or a statement purporting to be merely the seller's opinion or commendation of the goods does not create a warranty.

(4) Any remedial promise made by the seller to the immediate buyer creates an obligation that the promise will be performed upon the happening of the specified event.

3. In 2003, s 2-313 of the Code was amended to explicitly deal with remote purchasers of new goods, in conformity with pre-existing practice and case law. Section 2-313A of the Code now deals with the "record packaged with or accompanying goods," creating warranties by affirmative statements in documentation that is packaged with new goods. Section 2-313B deals with warranties created by "communications to the public," such as advertisements. Sections 2-313A and 2-313B both use the term "obligation," rather than "express warranty," to avoid the implication that the obligation must arise as part of an actual bargaining process.

4. In *Rick v Brandsema*, 2009 SCC 10, [2009] 1 SCR 295 (summary provided in Chapter 6), damages in the form of equitable compensation were provided as relief to the party wronged in an unconscionable bargain. The court, quoting *Dusik v Newton* (1985), 62 BCLR 1 (CA) at 47, said: "Where rescission is impossible or inappropriate, it would be inequitable for the defendant to retain the benefits of the unconscionable bargain."

BENTLEY (DICK) PRODUCTIONS LTD V
SMITH (HAROLD) (MOTORS) LTD
[1965] 1 WLR 623, [1965] 2 All ER 65 (CA)

LORD DENNING MR: The accused plaintiff, Mr. Charles Walter Bentley, sometimes known as Dick Bentley, brings an action against Harold Smith (Motors). Ltd., for damages for breach of warranty on the sale of a car. Mr. Bentley had been dealing with Mr. Smith (to whom I shall refer in the stead of the defendant company) for a couple of years and told Mr. Smith he was on the look-out for a well vetted Bentley car. In January 1960, Mr. Smith found one and bought it for £1,500 from a firm in Leicester. He wrote to Mr. Bentley and said: "I have just purchased a Park Ward power operated hood convertible. It is one of the nicest cars we have had in for quite a long time." Mr. Smith had told Mr. Bentley earlier that he was in a position to find out the history of cars. It appears that with a car of this quality the makers do keep a complete biography of it.

Mr. Bentley went to see the car. Mr. Smith told him that a German baron had had this car. He said that it had been fitted at one time with a replacement engine and gearbox, and had done twenty thousand miles only since it had been so fitted. The speedometer on the car showed only twenty thousand miles. Mr. Smith said the price was £1,850, and he would guarantee the car for twelve months, including parts and labour. That was on the morning of Jan. 23, 1960. In the afternoon Mr. Bentley took his wife over to see the car. Mr. Bentley repeated to his wife in Mr. Smith's presence what Mr. Smith had told him in the morning. In particular that Mr. Smith said it had done only twenty thousand miles since it had been refitted with a replacement engine and gearbox. Mr. Bentley took it for a short run. He bought the car for £1,850, gave his cheque and the sale was concluded. The car was a considerable disappointment to him. He took it back to Mr. Smith from time to time. ...

[His Lordship referred briefly to some work done on the car and continued:]

Eventually he brought this action for breach of warranty. The county court judge found that there was a warranty, that it was broken, and that the damages were more than £400, but as the claim was limited to £400, he gave judgment for the plaintiffs for that amount.

The first point is whether this representation, namely that the car had done twenty thousand miles only since it had been fitted with a replacement engine and gearbox, was an innocent misrepresentation (which does not give rise to damages), or whether it was a warranty. It was said ... in *Heilbut, Symons & Co. v. Buckleton* [above]:

> An affirmation at the time of the sale is a warranty, provided it appear on evidence to be so intended.

But that word "intended" has given rise to difficulties. I endeavoured to explain in *Oscar Chess Ltd. v. Williams* [[1957] 1 All ER 325 (CA)] that the question whether a warranty was intended depends on the conduct of the parties, on their words and behaviour, rather than on their thoughts. If an intelligent bystander would reasonably infer that a warranty was intended, that will suffice. What conduct, then? What words and behaviour, lead to the inference of a warranty?

Looking at the cases once more, as we have done so often, it seems to me that if a representation is made in the course of dealings for a contract for the very purpose of inducing the other party to act on it, and it actually induces him to act on it by entering into the contract, that is prima facie ground for inferring that the representation was intended as a warranty. It is not necessary to speak of it as being collateral.

Suffice it that the representation was intended to be acted on and was in fact acted on. But the maker of the representation can rebut this inference if he can show that it really was an innocent misrepresentation, in that he was in fact innocent of fault in making it, and that it would not be reasonable in the circumstances for him to be bound by it. In the *Oscar Chess* case the inference was rebutted. There a man had bought a second-hand car and received with it a log-book, which stated the year of the car, 1948. He afterwards resold the car. When he resold it he simply repeated what was in the log-book and passed it on to the buyer. He honestly believed on reasonable grounds that it was true. He was completely innocent of any fault. There was no warranty by him but only an innocent misrepresentation. Whereas in the present case it is very different. The inference is not rebutted. Here we have a dealer, Mr. Smith, who was in a position to know, or at least to find out, the history of the car. He could get it by writing to the makers. He did not do so. Indeed it was done later. When the history of this car was examined, his statement turned out to be quite wrong. He ought to have known better. There was no reasonable foundation for it. ...

The county court judge found that the representations were not dishonest. Mr. Smith was not guilty of fraud. But he made the statement as to twenty thousand miles without any foundation. And the judge was well justified in finding that there was a warranty. He said:

> I have no hesitation that as a matter of law the statement was a warranty. Mr. Smith stated a fact that should be within his own knowledge. He had jumped to a conclusion and stated it as a fact. A fact that a buyer would act on.

This is ample foundation for the inference of a warranty.

SALMON LJ: I agree. I have no doubt at all that the learned county court judge reached a correct conclusion when he decided that Mr. Smith gave a warranty to the second plaintiff, Mr. Bentley, and that that warranty was broken. Was what Mr. Smith said intended and understood as a legally binding promise? If so, it was a warranty and as such may be part of the contract of sale or collateral to it. In effect, Mr. Smith said:

> If you will enter into a contract to buy this motor car from me for £1,850, I undertake that you will be getting a motor car which has done no more than twenty thousand miles since it was fitted with a new engine and a new gearbox.

I have no doubt at all that what was said by Mr. Smith was so understood and was intended to be so understood by Mr. Bentley.

[Danckwerts LJ concurred with Lord Denning MR.]

Appeal dismissed.

REDGRAVE V HURD
(1881), 20 ChD 1 (CA)

[The plaintiff, a solicitor, advertised for "a partner, an efficient lawyer and advocate about forty, who would not object to purchase advertiser's suburban residence." After entering into an agreement for the purchase of the house, the defendant discovered that the law practice was "utterly worthless." He gave up possession and refused to complete the purchase.

The plaintiff brought this action for specific performance. The defendant denied liability because he had been induced into making the agreements by the plaintiff's false representations about the law practice made for that purpose. He counter-claimed for "rescission." At trial, Fry J held for the plaintiff and dismissed the counterclaim.]

JESSEL MR: ... It only remains to consider ... so much of the counterclaim of the defendant as asks to have the contract rescinded. ...

As regards the rescission of a contract, there was no doubt a difference between the rules of Courts of Equity and the rules of Courts of Common Law—a difference which of course has now disappeared by the operation of the Judicature Act, which makes the rules of equity prevail. According to the decisions of the Courts of Equity it was not necessary, in order to set aside a contract obtained by material false representation, to prove that the party who obtained it knew at the time when the representation was made that it was false. It was put in two ways, either of which was sufficient. One way of putting the case was, "A man is not to be allowed to get a benefit from a statement which he now admits to be false. He is not to be allowed to say, for the purpose of civil jurisdiction, that when he made it he did not know it to be false; he ought to have found that out before he made it." The other way of putting it was this: "Even assuming that moral fraud must be shewn in order to set aside a contract, you have it where a man, having obtained a beneficial contract by a statement which he now knows to be false, insists upon keeping that contract. To do so is a moral delinquency: no man ought to seek to take advantage of his own false statements." The rule in equity was settled, and it does not matter on which of the two grounds it was rested. As regards the rule of Common Law there is no doubt it was not quite so wide. There were, indeed, cases in which, even at Common Law, a contract could be rescinded for misrepresentation, although it could not be shewn that the person making it knew the representation to be false. They are variously stated, but I think, according to the later decisions, the statement must have been made recklessly and without care, whether it was true or false, and not with the belief that it was true. ...

There is another proposition of law of very great importance. ... If a man is induced to enter into a contract by a false representation it is not a sufficient answer to him to say, "If you had used due diligence you would have found out that the statement was untrue. You had the means afforded you of discovering its falsity, and did not choose to avail yourself of them." ...

... [F]or when a person makes a material representation to another to induce him to enter into a contract, and the other enters into that contract, it is not sufficient to say that the party to whom the representation is made does not prove that he entered into the contract, relying upon the representation. If it is a material representation calculated to induce him to enter into the contract, it is an inference of law that he was induced by the representation to enter into it, and in order to take away his title to be relieved from the contract on the ground that the representation was untrue, it must be shewn either that he had knowledge of the facts contrary to the representation, or that he stated in terms, or shewed clearly by his conduct, that he did not rely on the representation. If you tell a man, "You may enter into partnership with me, my business is bringing in between £300 and £400 a year," the man who makes that representation must know that it is a material inducement to the other to enter into the partnership, and you cannot investigate as to whether it was more or less probable that the inducement would operate on the mind of the party to whom the representation was made. Where you have neither evidence that he knew the facts to shew that the statement was untrue, or that he said or did anything to shew that he did not actually rely upon the statement, the inference remains that he did so rely, and the statement being a material statement, its being untrue is a sufficient ground for rescinding the contract.

[The opinions of Baggallay and Lush LJJ, who concurred in allowing the appeal, are omitted.]

NEWBIGGING V ADAM
(1886), 34 ChD 582 (CA)

[The plaintiff was induced by the misrepresentation of the defendants as to the adequacy of some machinery to contribute £10,024 2s. 7d. to a partnership to which he was admitted. The business proved unsuccessful and this action was brought to dissolve the partnership and for, among other claims, an order that the defendants repay the plaintiff £9,279 6s. 1d. and indemnify him against all liabilities to which he had or might become liable in the partnership name. It was so ordered and the defendants appealed on the ground that this order amounted to damages for innocent misrepresentation.]

BOWEN LJ: ... If we turn to the question of misrepresentation, damages cannot be obtained at law for misrepresentation which is not fraudulent, and you cannot, as it seems to me, give in equity any indemnity which corresponds with damages. If the mass of authority there is upon the subject were gone through I think it would be found that there is not so much difference as is generally supposed between the view taken at common law and the view taken in equity as to misrepresentation. At common law it has always been considered that misrepresentations which strike at the root of the contract are sufficient to avoid the contract on the ground explained in *Kennedy v. Panana, New Zealand, and Australian Royal Mail Company* (1867), L.R. 2 Q.B. 580; but when you come to misrepresentation it seems to me to be this, and nothing more, that he is entitled to have the contract rescinded, and is entitled accordingly to all the incidents and consequences of such rescission. It is said that the injured party is entitled to be replaced in *statu quo*. It seems to me that when you are dealing with innocent misrepresentation you must understand that proposition that he is to be placed *in statu quo* with this limitation—that he is not to be replaced in exactly the same position in all respects, otherwise he would be entitled to recover damages, but is to be replaced in his position so far as regards the rights and obligations which have been created by the contract into which he has been induced to enter. That seems to me to be the true doctrine, and I think it is put in the neatest way in *Redgrave v. Hurd* (1881) 20 Ch. D. 14. ...

Now those ... [rights and obligations] may be of two kinds. He may get an advantage in the shape of an actual benefit, as when he receives money; he may also get an advantage if the party with whom he contracts assumes some burthen in consideration of the contract. In such a case it seems to me that complete rescission would not be effected unless the misrepresenting party not only hands back the benefits which he has himself received—but also re-assumes the burthen which under the contract the injured person has taken upon himself. Speaking only for myself I should not like to lay down the proposition that a person is to be restored to the position which he held before the misrepresentation was made, nor that the person injured must be indemnified against loss which arises out of the contract, unless you place upon the words "out of the contract" the limited and special meaning which I have endeavoured to shadow forth. Loss arising out of the contract is a term which would be too wide. It would embrace damages at common law, because damages at common law are only given upon the supposition that they are damages which would naturally and reasonably follow from the injury done. I think *Redgrave v. Hurd* shews that it would be too wide, because in that case the Court excluded from the relief which was given the damages which had been sustained by the plaintiff in removing his business, and other similar items. There ought, as it appears to me, to be a giving back and a taking back on both sides, including the giving back and taking back of the obligations which the contract has created, as well as the giving back and taking back of the advantages.

[The decisions of Cotton and Fry LJJ concurring in dismissing the appeal are omitted.]

KUPCHAK V DAYSON HOLDINGS LTD
(1965), 53 WWR 65, 53 DLR (2d) 482 (BCCA)

DAVEY JA: The learned trial Judge found that the Kupchaks had been induced by fraud of the respondents to exchange their Haro Street and North Vancouver properties for shares of the Palms Motel Ltd., and to give mortgages over land and chattels of the motel in the sum of $64,500 to Dayson Holdings Ltd. to secure the difference in the value of the two sets of property. However, he held that the appellants were not entitled to rescission, because, while they were able to restore to the respondents the shares in the motel, the respondents could not restore the Haro St. property, as they had conveyed an undivided one-half interest in it to Marks Estates Ltd. on October 19, 1960, and as the buildings had been torn down, and a modern apartment house had been erected. ...

The appellants appeal against the learned trial Judge's refusal to grant rescission, and the respondents cross-appeal against the finding of fraud and the amount of damages.

Having read all the evidence of the principal actors in this litigation, I think there is ample evidence to support the finding of fraud inducing the contract, and there remains for consideration only the question of the relief to be granted appellants. ...

Under the authorities the respondents' dealing with the Haro St. property, which they acquired by fraud, ought not to bar rescission of the transaction unless it be impractical, or so unjust to the respondents that it ought not to be imposed upon a guilty party.

Equity as an incident of its peculiar remedy of rescission, or under its power to award compensation, may adjust the rights of the parties by ordering either one to pay compensation to the other to make good some deficiency in perfect restitution.

It being impractical and unjust to require the respondents upon rescission to restore the Haro St. property they had acquired from the appellants by fraud, the respondents ought to compensate the appellants for the property respondents are allowed to keep, the more so as their dealing with the property was after September 16, 1960, when they had notice of appellants' claim of fraud. ...

The respondents should also indemnify the appellants against the increase in the amount of the principal due on the mortgage on the North Vancouver property and the increase in the rate of interest on the whole principal from $4\frac{1}{2}$% to $7\frac{1}{2}$%: they will also have to account for the profits realized from the North Vancouver property from March 31, 1960. On the other hand, the appellants will have to account for any dividends received on the shares of Palms Motel Ltd. and monies, if any, received on the alleged indebtedness of Palms Motel Ltd. to its shareholders. ...

That leads to the question whether the appellants by conduct, word, or silence have elected to affirm the exchange, and whether their right to rescission is barred by laches. If a guilty party intends to allege that his victim has affirmed the contract or has been guilty of laches, he must plead and prove those defences to rescission. But in neither action did the respondents plead these bars to rescission. Nevertheless these defences were argued before us without objection by the appellants, who did object, however, that the respondents had not pleaded in bar of rescission that they could not restore the Haro St. property. Any objection that these defences to rescission had not been pleaded would fail if the evidence thereon had been fully canvassed at the trial. But the difficulty is that neither appellants nor respondents directed their attention at the trial to evidence of election or laches. ...

[Davey JA's discussion of election and laches has been omitted. The fact that the Kupchaks retained the shares and continued to manage the hotel did not amount to an affirmation of the contract, in part because they could not transfer the shares without the cooperation of the Daysons.]

SHEPPARD JA (dissenting): ... In the case at bar the Kupchaks have retained the shares and have remained on the register which in itself is evidence of affirmation, and the positive acts of continuing in management of the motel can only be evidence of asserting rights in respect to the shares and therefore of affirming the transaction. In *Barron v. Kelly* (1918), 56 S.C.R. 455, the Court held that there had been an election to affirm by reason of the purchaser, after learning of the fraudulent misrepresentations, having made subsequent payments and having made an offer to exchange whereby he had thereby elected not to rescind. That must be said of the Kupchaks.

[Norris JA concurred with Davey JA.]

NOTES

1. In *Samson v Lockwood* (1998), 40 OR (3d) 161 (CA), the Ontario Court of Appeal held that in cases of negligent misrepresentation, a party's lack of awareness of the legal right to rescind does not necessarily prevent that party from affirming a contract. When the party affirms the contract after becoming aware of the nature of the misrepresentation, he or she is bound by the affirmation if the opportunity to seek legal advice was available but was recklessly disregarded.

2. However, in *Halleran v O'Neill Brothers Auto Ltd* (1971), 1 Nfld & PEIR 455 (CA), the vendors of the car rolled back the odometer to erase 21,000 km before selling it. When the plaintiff purchaser discovered the fraud, he attempted to sell the vehicle but, when unsuccessful, he had it fixed to put it in reasonable running order. The court determined that the plaintiff's conduct did not amount to affirmation of the contract and was only an attempt to minimize the damages.

3. In *Harrity and Northeast Yachts 1998 Ltd v Kennedy*, 2009 NBCA 60, the vendor's agent represented a boat to be equipped with a "new" engine when, in fact, the engine had been reconditioned and installed a year earlier to replace the original engine. The agent testified that when he spoke of "new," he meant "new to the boat." The court reached three findings. First, the independent survey obtained by the plaintiff (which had not identified any engine problems) had not been intended to verify the accuracy of the agent's representations and the purchaser's reliance on the survey did not displace her reliance on the agent's representations. Accordingly, the agent was liable at common law for negligent misrepresentation. Second, on the issue of privity (because the agent had not been a party to the contract), the court determined that the agent would be able to rely on the disclaimer clause, so long as it was found to

be enforceable. This latter point led to the third point, which arose because the disclaimer clause had not been part of the original contract and was only entered into on the closing of the transaction. Because no consideration had been provided to the purchaser for its insertion (and the consequent extinguishment of the purchaser's legal recourse with respect to actionable misrepresentations), the clause was accordingly declared to be unenforceable.

4. An allegation of fraud is serious and must meet a high burden. In *Anderson v British Columbia Securities Commission*, 2004 BCCA 7 at para 29, Mackenzie JA described the standard of proof for fraud in a civil case:

> Fraud is a very serious allegation which carries a stigma and requires a high standard of proof. While proof in a civil or regulatory case does not have to meet the criminal law standard of proof beyond a reasonable doubt, it does require evidence that is clear and convincing proof of the elements of fraud, including the mental element.

The standard, however, is nonetheless the standard in a civil case, which is on a balance of probabilities. The Supreme Court of Canada also commented on this standard in *FH v McDougall*, 2008 SCC 53, [2008] 3 SCR 41 at para 45, where Rothstein J said:

> To suggest that depending upon the seriousness, the evidence in the civil case must be scrutinized with greater care implies that in less serious cases the evidence need not be scrutinized with such care. I think it is inappropriate to say that there are legally recognized different levels of scrutiny of the evidence depending upon the seriousness of the case. There is only one legal rule and that is that in all cases, evidence must be scrutinized with care by the trial judge.

Rothstein J went on to say (at para 49):

> In the result, I would reaffirm that in civil cases there is only one standard of proof and that is proof on a balance of probabilities. In all civil cases, the trial judge must scrutinize the relevant evidence with care to determine whether it is more likely than not that an alleged event occurred.

(See also *Canada (Attorney General) v Fairmont Hotels Inc*, 2016 SCC 56, [2016] 2 SCR 720.)

REDICAN V NESBITT
[1924] SCR 135

[The defendants entered into a contract to purchase a leasehold property from the plaintiff, represented by Wing, the plaintiff's agent. In due course, an assignment of lease executed by the plaintiff and assented to by the landlord (the city of Toronto) was delivered to the defendants' solicitor with the keys to the property; the cheque of one of the defendants for the purchase money was simultaneously handed to the plaintiff's solicitor. The defendants also took an assignment of insurance and paid some arrears of taxes. On inspecting the property two days later, which is said to have been their first opportunity to do so, they discovered, as they allege, that it had been misrepresented to them by Wing in several particulars, which they claim are of such importance that, had they known the truth in regard to them, they would not have purchased. On learning of these matters they stopped payment of the cheque given for the purchase money, having first notified the vendor's husband that that would be done. An action by the vendor was at once begun for the sum of $2,969.84, being the balance of account owing under an offer to purchase by the defendants from the plaintiff and accepted by her.

The defendants by way of counterclaim asked for rescission.]

ANGLIN J: ... In the present case the defendants plead misrepresentation as a ground both of defence and of counter-claim. They assert that it was fraudulent and, alternatively, that if innocent it was so material as to afford ground for rescission.

The jury negatived fraud and on this branch of the case, if they are not entitled to have the action dismissed on the other, the defendants ask for a new trial on the ground of misdirection and refusal by the learned trial judge to submit an essential element of it to the jury. I defer dealing with that aspect of the appeal.

The jury found that innocent misrepresentations inducing the contract had been made by the plaintiff's agent, and upon them the defendants maintain they are entitled to rescission. The trial judge rejected this claim on the ground that the contract for sale had been fully executed by the delivery of the deed and the acceptance of the cheque in payment, and that rescission of a contract after execution cannot be had for mere innocent misrepresentation unless it be such as renders the subject of sale different in substance from what was contracted for. ... The suggestion that the property differed so completely in substance from what the defendants intended to acquire that there was a failure of consideration is not borne out by the facts. Neither is there any foundation for a suggestion of mutual mistake as a basis for rescission. *Debenham v. Sawbridge* [1901] 2 Ch. 98, 109. The trial judge regarded the handing over of the cheque as absolute payment and as a completion of the contract by the defendants just as the delivery of the conveyance and possession constituted completion on the part of the plaintiff.

... [The proposition that] "where the conveyance has been executed ... a Court of Equity will set aside the conveyance only on the ground of fraud," ... is too well established to admit of controversy, assuming that his Lordship meant where the contract had been fully carried out. ...

But on the question when a contract will, for the purpose of this rule, be deemed to have ceased to be "executory" and to have become "executed" the authorities are not so clear. I have not found any reported case in which it has been determined whether or not after delivery and acceptance of the conveyance and taking of possession a contract of sale remains "executory" until actual payment of the purchase money then due; nor indeed have I found any authority in which the contrary has been categorically determined. In many of the cases it is broadly stated, as it was by Lord Campbell, that after conveyance rescission will not be granted for innocent misrepresentation. ...

[Anglin J then quoted from a number of text writers and concluded:]

The foundation of the rule that an executed contract will not be rescinded for innocent misrepresentation appears to be somewhat obscure. In *Angel v. Jay*, [1911] 1 K.B. 666, 671, Darling J. states, apparently without disapproval, the contention of counsel that "the foundation of the doctrine" is that "when property has passed the persons concerned cannot be placed in the same position as they were in before the estate became vested." In numerous cases the vesting of the property has been referred to as a serious obstacle to rescission. In other cases the supersession of the contract for sale by the executed conveyance accepted by the purchaser and the resultant restriction of his rights to those assured by the latter instrument appears to be the ground upon which rescission of the contract after acceptance of conveyance is refused. So far does the court go in maintaining this doctrine that, where under a court sale the purchase money was still in court, the purchaser who had accepted the title and taken his conveyance was refused relief in respect of subsequently discovered incumbrances.

729

In the case now before us it is probably unnecessary to determine the effect on the right of a purchaser to rescission of his acceptance of a conveyance and taking of possession without making payment. What might have been a formidable obstacle to the granting of rescission to the defendants was suggested by the trial judge, namely, the inability of the court to compel the landlord's assent to a re-assignment of the leasehold to the plaintiff. The effect of the acceptance of the conveyance assented to by the lessor and of the taking of possession of the property by the defendants may have been to give to the lessor rights against them as tenants the relinquishment of which the court could not exact.

Although the execution of the contract does not afford an answer to a claim for rescission in cases of fraudulent misrepresentation, inability to effect *restitutio in integrum*, unless that has become impossible owing to action of the wrong-doer, will ordinarily preclude rescission. *Kerr on Fraud* (5th ed.) 387-90. *A fortiori* is this the case where innocent misrepresentation only is relied upon. ...

But I strongly incline to the view that while the acceptance of the cheque as payment was in this sense conditional that, if it should be dishonoured, the right to sue for the money due under the contract would revive, the transaction was, nevertheless, intended to be closed and the contract completely executed so far as the purchasers were concerned by their taking of the deed and the keys and handing over the cheque. They had obtained the full consideration for which they contracted and, if the vendor saw fit to accept the cheque they tendered in payment in lieu of cash, they should not be heard to say that the contract had not been fully executed. I cannot think that the vendor's right to have the contract treated as executed and completed can be defeated by the fact that she took a cheque as the equivalent of a cash payment, and still less by the accident that the cheque was not presented for payment during the two days which intervened between the closing of the sale and the stopping of payment. ...

Without, therefore, necessarily affirming the position taken in the judgment of the majority of the learned judges of the Appellate Divisional Court, I am of the opinion that, under all the circumstances of this case, the contract for sale was executed and that, according to a well-settled rule in equity, rescission for innocent misrepresentation is not an available remedy for the defendants.

I am clearly of the opinion, however, that a new trial must be directed because the issue of fraud was not properly presented to the jury. In substance the learned trial judge charged that, in order to establish fraud, the defendants must show that Wing actually knew his representations were false. He did not tell the jury that the representations would be fraudulent if they were false and were made without belief in their truth, or recklessly, careless whether they were true or false.

[Appeal allowed with costs and a new trial granted; Davies CJ concurred with Anglin J. The opinions of Idington, Duff, and Mignault JJ are omitted. Although Idington J agreed in the result he also went beyond the grounds taken by the rest of the court in that he appeared willing to grant rescission even though the contract was executed on the apparent ground that the misrepresentation led to an "error *in substantialibus*." "I think a difference of a few acres, as therein, is no more important than the four rooms instead of five as misrepresented and electric light in this case to the appellants."]

NOTE

The remedy for agreements that have been induced by innocent misrepresentation is equitable rescission, so long as the contract has not been fully executed (although Canadian courts have been lenient with this requirement) and the promisee has moved relatively quickly to effect a remedy. The *Law Reform Act*, RSNB 2011, c 184, s 6(1), allows a court to take execution of a contract into account when determining whether to rescind the contract, but such execution is not itself to be a bar to rescission. The rule with regard to monetary remedies—namely, that the victim of an innocent misrepresentation is not able to claim common law damages in tort—has been problematic at common law. One potential resolution is found in the *Principles, Definitions and Model Rules of European Private Law: Draft Common Frame of Reference*, Outline Edition (Munich: Sellier, 2009) II at 7:201 and 7:212, which provides that "a party may avoid a contract for mistake of fact or law existing when the contract was concluded if ... the other party caused the mistake," and adds that "the question whether either party has a right to the return of whatever has been transferred or supplied under a contract which has been avoided under this section, or a monetary equivalent, is regulated by the rules on unjustified enrichment."

LEAF V INTERNATIONAL GALLERIES
[1950] 2 KB 86, [1950] 1 All ER 693 (CA)

DENNING LJ: In March 1944, the buyer bought from the sellers an oil painting of Salisbury Cathedral. On the back of the picture there was a label indicating that it had been exhibited as a Constable, and during the negotiations for the purchase the sellers represented that it was a painting by Constable. That representation, the judge has found, was incorporated as one of the terms of the contract. The receipt for the price, £85, was given in these terms: "Mar. 6, 1944. One original oil painting Salisbury Cathedral by J. Constable, £85." Nearly five years later the buyer was minded to sell the picture. He took it to Christie's to be put into an auction, and he was then advised that it was not a Constable. So he took it back to the sellers and told them he wanted to return it and get his money back. They did take the picture back temporarily for investigation, and they still adhered to the view that it was a Constable. Eventually the buyer brought a claim in the county court claiming rescission of the contract. In his particulars of claim he pleaded that the picture had been represented to be a Constable, and that he had paid £85 in reliance on that representation. The sellers resisted the claim. After hearing expert evidence the judge found as a fact, and this must be accepted, that the painting was not by Constable and was worth little.

The question is whether the buyer is entitled to rescind the contract on that account. I emphasize that this is a claim to rescind only. There is no claim in this action for damages for breach of condition or breach of warranty. The claim is simply one for rescission. At a very late stage before the county court judge counsel for the buyer did ask for leave to amend by claiming damages for breach of warranty, but it was not allowed. So no claim for damages is before us. The only question is whether the buyer is entitled to rescind. The way in which the case is put by counsel for the buyer is this. He says this was an innocent misrepresentation and that in equity he is entitled to claim rescission even of an executed contract of sale on that account. He points out that the judge has found that it is quite possible to restore the parties to the same position that they were in originally, by the buyer simply handing back the picture to the sellers in return for the repayment of the purchase price.

In my opinion, this case is to be decided according to the well-known principles applicable to the sale of goods. This was a contract for the sale of goods. There was a mistake about the quality of the subject-matter, because both parties believed the picture to be a Constable, and that mistake was in one sense essential or fundamental. Such a mistake, however, does not avoid the contract. There was no mistake about the subject-matter of the sale. It was a specific picture of "Salisbury Cathedral."

The parties were agreed in the same terms on the same subject-matter, and that is sufficient to make a contract. ... There was a term in the contract as to the quality of the subject-matter, namely, as to the person by whom the picture was painted—that it was by Constable. That term of the contract was either a condition or a warranty. If it was a condition, the buyer could reject the picture for breach of the condition at any time before he accepted it or was to be deemed to have accepted it, whereas, if it was only a warranty, he could not reject it but was confined to a claim for damages.

I think it right to assume in the buyer's favour that this term was a condition, and that, if he had come in proper time, he could have rejected the picture, but the right to reject for breach of condition has always been limited by the rule that once the buyer has accepted, or is deemed to have accepted, the goods in performance of the contract, he cannot thereafter reject, but is relegated to his claim for damages: see s. 11(1)(c) of the Sale of Goods Act, 1893. ... The circumstances in which a buyer is deemed to have accepted goods in performance of the contract are set out in s. 35 of the Act which provides that the buyer is deemed to have accepted the goods, among other things,

> ... when after the lapse of a reasonable time, he retains the goods without intimating to the seller that he has rejected them.

In this case this buyer took the picture into his house, and five years passed before he intimated any rejection. That, I need hardly say, is much more than a reasonable time. It is far too late for him at the end of five years to reject this picture for breach of any condition. His remedy after that length of time is for damages only, a claim which he has not brought before the court.

Is it to be said that the buyer is in any better position by relying on the representation, not as a condition, but as an innocent material misrepresentation? I agree that on a contract for the sale of goods an innocent material misrepresentation may in a proper case be a ground for rescission even after the contract has been executed. The observations of Joyce J., in *Seddon v. North Eastern Salt Co. Ltd.*, [1905] 1 Ch. 326, are, in my opinion, too widely stated. Many judges have treated it as plain that an executed contract of sale may, in a proper case, be rescinded for innocent misrepresentation. ... It is unnecessary, however, to pronounce finally on these matters because, although rescission may in some cases be a proper remedy, nevertheless it is to be remembered that an innocent misrepresentation is much less potent than a breach of condition. A condition is a term of the contract of a most material character, and, if a claim to reject for breach of condition is barred, it seems to me *a fortiori* that a claim to rescission on the ground of innocent misrepresentation is also barred. So, assuming that a contract for the sale of goods may be rescinded in a proper case for innocent misrepresentation, nevertheless, once the buyer has accepted, or is deemed to have accepted, the goods, the claim is barred. In this case the buyer must clearly be deemed to have accepted the picture. He had ample opportunity to examine it in the first few days after he bought it. Then was the time to see if the condition or representation was fulfilled, yet he has kept it all this time and five years have elapsed without any notice of rejection. In my judgment, he cannot now claim to rescind, and the appeal should be dismissed.

O'FLAHERTY V MCKINLEY
[1953] 2 DLR 514 (Nfld CA)

DUNFIELD J: The plaintiff in this case, a young lady who had not owned a car before, bought a second-hand Hillman sedan in April 1950, from the defendant, who is an automobile dealer and garageman. She says she wanted and asked for a 1950 model. He and his staff told her it was a 1950 Hillman, which had gone 4,000 odd miles; that is admitted. She was charged $1,325, so far as the defendant was concerned.

The defendant says that the previous owner, who traded the car to him against a Standard "Vanguard" car, for which defendant is agent, told him and his staff it was a 1950 Hillman, and they accepted that statement. It appears that in 1949 Hillman redesigned their car. As often happens in a new design, it had some shortcomings, and these were made good in the 1950 model, but the changes were mostly internal, and the 1949 and 1950 cars were externally very much alike, and would not be readily distinguishable except by their own agents. The previous owner, who was in the witness-box denies that he represented the car to be a 1950 model; but the plaintiff's counsel accepts the defence position that there was innocent misrepresentation only. The plaintiff asks for rescission of the contract of sale and the return of her money including certain collateral expenditures. ...

[T]he plaintiff claims a total payment of $1,580.14 with rescission of the contract of sale. The difference, $255.14, between $1,325 and $1,580.14 is made up of [registration, insurance, repairs, taxes, and carrying charges].

The defendant counterclaims for $158.53, an unpaid bill for repairs and maintenance done for the plaintiff.

The plaintiff, who was a novice driver, and her two brothers, also novices, drove the car about 7,000 miles during the summer of 1950. In early September 1950 the plaintiff happened to call at Adelaide Motors Ltd., who are agents for the Hillman, and happened to remark that the car was a 1950 model, and was then told that it was a 1949 model. She forthwith saw her solicitors and instructed them to write repudiating the contract of sale. The car was not run after that. It was, however, kept out of doors in the plaintiff's yard, she not having a garage, during the past winter. Defendant says he offered to house the car in his garage for the winter without prejudice to the rights of either party, but that this offer was refused. Fortunately it was not a hard winter; but nevertheless a winter in the open is not desirable.

Mr. Furlong K.C., for the defendant, takes the position that rescission cannot be granted unless the parties can be restored substantially to their original positions, which is not possible, because the car has done 7,000 miles and been subjected to a winter's exposure. But as to this, a dealer in the witness-box remarked that mileage on a second-hand car was not very serious until it began to get up to 15,000 miles. This car has now done about 11,700 miles. Again, it is a known fact that a good many people keep cars in the open during the winter, and most people keep them in unheated garages. There is evidence that plaintiff's brother started the engine now and then to keep the battery alive. I hear nothing about the battery freezing. ...

A well-made car ought to be able to go, with proper maintenance, 50,000 to 100,000 miles; therefore it seems to me that the mere increase of the mileage from 4,700 to 11,700 does not substantially alter the character of the vehicle. It is still a young car.

But I consider also that the representation as to the year-model of a car is very material. A car is not just a car. One make may be better than another, and a car of one year of a certain maker very different in its satisfaction-giving qualities from a car of the same maker of another year. Evidence in this case indicates that the 1950

Hillman is a much better car than the 1949 Hillman in respect of its internal structure, regardless of the similarity in appearance; and it may command a better price on resale. A contract to supply a 1950 model cannot be considered to be satisfied by the supply of a 1949 model. I think there is what is called an *error in substantialibus*. ...

I think the contract must be avoided, and that the plaintiff must have her money, namely, $1,325, back forthwith, without interest, following the Ontario Court of Appeal in the *Addison* case; and that the car must be immediately returned to the defendant. But as to the subsidiary claims of the plaintiff, for registration, insurance, repairs, tax, and the additional sums paid by her to the finance company, these are not directly connected with the misrepresentation; she would have had to pay such charges as these if it had been a 1950 car and not a 1949 car. And on looking over the bill for repairs and maintenance, after excluding the cost of repairing small damages which she or her brothers did to the car, I cannot see that there is any excessive cost; to my mind she paid or is charged no more than anyone might expect to pay for the maintenance of a second-hand car in good condition running 7,000 miles. Nor has any effort been made to prove the allegation that the defendant's repair or maintenance charges are excessive. The defendant must therefore have judgment for the full amount of his counter-claim on the repair and maintenance bill.

Let judgment be entered accordingly, with costs to plaintiff on the claim and to defendant on the counter-claim, the payment into Court not covering the counter-claim in full.

WINTER J (dissenting): ... The action was based upon innocent misrepresentation, the statement of the defendant that the car was a 1950 model. But it is clear that the statement was made in the course of a transaction which resulted in a very simple contract, a contract of sale, and that it was embodied in the contract as a term thereof. ...

Once the buyer has definitely accepted the goods, he is taken to have elected to rely upon any claim he may have for damages if any condition is afterwards proved to have been broken. (I am assuming what cannot be doubted in both cases, that the representation was a condition and not a mere warranty.) It is too late for him to claim to repudiate the contract and return the goods. At a certain critical time, before he finally accepts the goods or notifies the seller to that effect, he is given an election, a choice between two courses of action. He is supposed to envisage the possibility of the seller failing to carry out all his promises and any loss he may himself suffer as a result. He can, if he wish, rely entirely upon his right in that case to recover the loss. And so he may accept the goods there and then and leave it at that. In a pecuniary sense, in theory at least, he will not suffer. Or he may think it preferable to reject the goods altogether if they are not what they should be under the contract. For this purpose he is allowed a reasonable time in which to satisfy himself on that point, and that is usually done by an examination of the goods. What is a reasonable time depends upon the facts and the contract; in the case of unascertained goods it is usually appreciably longer than where the goods are specific. It follows that if the reasonable time passes and he does nothing, he is taken to have accepted the goods. He has made his election. He cannot have it both ways.

Applying all this to the present case and to *Leaf v. International Galleries*, [1950] 1 All E.R. 693, which I purposely include because I can see no essential difference between them, it is abundantly clear that in both instances the buyer kept the goods for a much longer time than could be considered reasonable before seeking any redress. In actual fact, neither buyer made any examination at all. Both clearly elected to follow the former of the two courses of action I have mentioned. Both chose to rely entirely upon what the seller had said and both afterwards complained, it seems to me, almost illogically, that the seller was unreliable and that they should be granted the election over again. ...

I think a distinction must be made between two very different things, though I have never seen it made in any reported case. It is one thing for a buyer to make a genuine inspection of goods, or inquiries about them, with a view to satisfying himself that they are what he wants, and quite another to make up his mind whether he will choose rejection or damages as a remedy if he should need one. It is the latter, as I see it, that the Act contemplates when it speaks of a reasonable time, not the former; or at least, the latter must always be there. The striking feature that I see in both this case and *Leaf v. International Galleries* is that they are cases of the latter. Both buyers made up their minds not to examine at all, and both learned the truth quite accidentally. In my view both made the election as to the remedy within a very short time after delivery, if not at that very moment. ...

I have to add one other observation. It might be argued that, if my view of the case is correct, the plaintiff is without remedy altogether; that, again as in *Leaf v. International Galleries*, she chose to limit her claim to rescission. I think that that view would be most unfair and in any case is not the true one. The original statement of claim was confused and it was doubtful whether it claimed rescission or damages. It was later amended to make it clear that rescission was in fact claimed. I think that, if there is any doubt whether damages are claimed in the alternative, the Court has power even now to amend the pleadings to make that clear also. There can be no doubt whatever, on the facts, that the plaintiff is entitled to damages.

MURRAY V SPERRY RAND CORPORATION
(1979), 96 DLR (3d) 113 (Ont H Ct J)

REID J: This action concerns the purchase by the plaintiff of a forage harvester. At the relevant times:

(a) Plaintiff was a farmer.
(b) Sperry Rand Corporation was the American manufacturer of the forage harvester.
(c) Sperry Rand Canada Limited was the Canadian distributor of the machine.
(d) Farm Supplies and Services was a business carried on by the late Charles Church in Barrie, Ontario. It was the New Holland dealer. For convenience I refer to this company, and the late Charles Church, as "Church."
(e) The forage harvester was the New Holland SP818. "SP" stood for "self-propelled."

A forage harvester simultaneously cuts and chops hay and grass crops. Plaintiff had been thinking for some time about purchasing a new forage harvester. He owned one and had used it for some time. It was not a self-propelled type. That is, it had to be pulled by a tractor. He was particularly interested in a self-propelled type because he had a back problem. He hoped to avoid having to twist in his seat on the tractor, a necessary part of pulling a harvester.

He had seen the SP818 in action at a ploughing match and, on a later occasion, displayed at a stand operated by Church at the 1967 Barrie Fall Fair. He discussed the machine with Church's salesman Hogarth, who was at the stand. Hogarth gave him a sales brochure describing the machine. Plaintiff took the brochure home and read it for several nights. It described the machine's features and performance. He was particularly interested in the "fineness of the cut," that is to say, the size to which the machine would chop the crops it harvested. The quality of silage rose as the fineness increased. He was also interested in the productive capacity of the machine for he was planning to expand his operations. On these points the brochure said:

> You'll fine-chop forage to $\frac{3}{16}$ of an inch ... season after season!
>
> You'll harvest over 45 tons per hour with ease. ...
>
> Under test conditions, the big New Holland harvesters have harvested well over 60 tons per hour.
>
> And Micro-Shear cutting action gives you a choice of crop fineness—from $\frac{3}{16}$ of an inch to $2\frac{1}{4}$.

In consequence of his interest, Church and Hogarth visited plaintiff's farm. So did William Hutchinson, a representative of Sperry Rand Canada. In the course of the conversations that occurred on these visits, plaintiff explained his type of farming and the operation for which he intended the machine. He received assurances that the harvester would perform as described in the brochure; that it was ideally suited to plaintiff's type of farming, and that it would do a better job than his existing machine.

In the result, plaintiff placed an order for the harvester. It was dated September 26, 1967, addressed to Farm Supplies and Services and signed by plaintiff as purchaser. It was accepted by Hogarth on behalf of Church as vendor. The order was written out on the date it bears by Hutchinson at plaintiff's farm. This was on the occasion of a meeting between plaintiff and Hutchinson at plaintiff's farm when the SP818 was discussed at length. The price was $12,600.

The harvester was delivered to plaintiff. He began to use it. This litigation arose out of his repeated but unsuccessful attempts to operate the harvester at anything like the promise of the brochure. ...

On the evidence I make the following findings:

(1) Plaintiff was induced to purchase the harvester through oral representations made by the personnel of Church and Sperry Rand Canada and through the sales brochure prepared and published by Sperry Rand Corporation.

(2) The performance of the machine fell seriously short of that represented in the sales brochure.

In relation to liability, the real questions in this litigation are not questions of fact. There is no doubt about the failure of the machine. It was confirmed very clearly by the evidence of both defendants. Defendants' attempts, particularly those of Sperry Rand Corporation, to blame the failure of the machine upon plaintiff were unsuccessful. There is no question in my mind that the machine failed because of an inherent defect or because the machine was not suitable for plaintiff's farming conditions, or both. Defendant manufacturer denied that the machine suffered from an inherent defect. Yet it was not able to explain why in the hands of its own people the machine would not perform properly.

(3) I find also that the consequence of the machine's failure was damage suffered by plaintiff.

THE LIABILITY OF CHURCH

Church was a signatory to the purchase-order contract. Plaintiff was induced to sign that contract by representations made by or on behalf of Church.

Church and his salesman, Hogarth, were familiar with plaintiff's needs. Plaintiff was given assurances by or on behalf of Church, (1) that the machine was ideal for his farm and his plans for it, and (2) that it would perform in accordance with the sales brochure.

There is no doubt in my mind that these representations were fundamental to his decision to purchase.

There is equally no doubt on the evidence that Church or Hogarth, or both, were aware of the significance of these assurances. It cannot be suggested that they were not aware of the conditions in which plaintiff proposed to operate the machine for they visited the farm and could see for themselves.

I am satisfied that these representations were made with the single purpose of inducing plaintiff to buy the machine.

THE REPRESENTATIONS AS COLLATERAL WARRANTIES

It has long been the law that an affirmation made with the intention of inducing contractual relations is a warranty: *Heilbut, Symons & Co. v. Buckleton*, [1913] A.C. 30; *Dick Bentley Productions Ltd. et al. v. Harold Smith (Motors) Ltd.*, [1965] 2 All E.R. 65; *Oscar Chess, Ltd. v. Williams*, [1957] 1 All E.R. 325, the breach of which creates liability in damages; *Esso Petroleum Co. Ltd. v. Mardon*, [1976] 2 All E.R. 5.

The representations made to plaintiff were, in my opinion, collateral warranties.

The failure of the machine was a clear breach of those warranties. On that ground Church is liable to plaintiff. ...

THE LIABILITY OF THE MANUFACTURER

Sperry Rand Corporation was not a party to the written contract between plaintiff and Church. It had manufactured the harvester. It had also published the sales brochure.

I refer to it as a sales brochure notwithstanding evidence from an official of Sperry Rand Corporation that it was not intended to persuade people to buy the machines it describes. That view is, in my opinion, contradicted by the brochure itself. Its tone is strongly promotional. It goes far beyond any simple intention to furnish specifications. It was, in my opinion, a sales tool. It was intended to be one and was used in this case as one.

The representations contained in it, so far as they related to this litigation, have already been set out. In the circumstances of this case those representations amounted to collateral warranties given by the manufacturer.

It is, in my opinion, the law that a person may be liable for breach of a warranty notwithstanding that he has no contractual relationship with the person to whom the warranty is given: *Shanklin Pier Ltd. v. Detel Products Ltd.*, [1951] 2 K.B. 854; *Traders Finance Corp. Ltd. v. Haley; Haley v. Ford Motor Co. of Canada Ltd.* (1966), 57 D.L.R. (2d) 15 at p. 18; affirmed [1967] S.C.R. 437, 62 D.L.R. (2d) 329, 60 W.W.R. 497; *Andrews v. Hopkinson*, [1957] 1 Q.B. 229. See also K.W. Wedderburn, "Collateral Contracts," [1959] C.L.J. 48 at p. 68, and Cheshire and Fifoot, *The Law of Contract*, 7th ed. (1969), at pp. 54-6.

It has been stressed that the intention behind the affirmations govern. I can see no difference whether the affirmations are made orally or in writing.

I have given my opinion that the brochure was put out to entice sales. I can see no other purpose for it. It contained a number of warranties that were proven to be inaccurate. The breach of these creates liability upon the dealer. I can see no legal basis for differentiating between dealer and manufacturer in relation to collateral warranties. The manufacturer initiated the affirmations; it was the manufacturer who apparently prepared and certainly published the brochure. The dealer would perforce have to rely on the manufacturer.

The dealer induced a sale through the use of the brochure and thus acquired liability. Should the manufacturer who published the brochure in an obvious attempt to induce sales be shielded from liability because it had no direct contact with plaintiff?

In *Shanklin*, McNair J. was dealing with a case in which a paint manufacturer made representations concerning the qualities of its paint to pier owners. Owners caused the paint to be specified in a contract for painting the pier. The painting contractors therefore purchased the paint and applied it to the pier. The paint failed. The owners sued the manufacturers; a mirror image of this case.

McNair J. held that the representations were warranties given by manufacturers to owners. The defence submitted [at 856] that "in law a warranty could give rise to no enforceable cause of action except between the same parties as the parties to the main contract in relation to which the warranty was given."

McNair J. said [at 856]:

> In principle his submission seems to me to be unsound. If, as is elementary, the consideration for the warranty in the usual case is the entering into of the main contract in relation to which the warranty is given, I see no reason why there may not be an enforceable warranty between A and B supported by the consideration that B should cause C to enter into a contract with A or that B should do some other act for the benefit of A.

In other words, manufacturers would have been liable if they had supplied the paint directly to the owners and were equally liable in supplying the paint indirectly.

I see no significant difference between the oral warranties given by the paint manufacturer in that case and the written warranties given by the harvester manufacturer in this. The intention was the same in both cases, *viz.*, to induce the recipient of such representations to purchase the product described. I see no real difference either in the way in which the representations were placed before the prospective purchasers. Dissemination of a sale brochure through dealers is a well-known and normal method of distribution for manufacturers whose products are not sold directly to the public. Through the brochure, the manufacturer presents his case to the potential customer just as directly as he would if they were sitting down together to discuss the matter.

Plaintiff's purchase from the dealer in this case seems clearly to be "some other act for the benefit of the manufacturer" contemplated by McNair J.

NOTES

1. In the United Kingdom, the Law Reform Commission sought to clarify and simplify the law of misrepresentation legislatively: see the *Misrepresentation Act 1967* (UK), c 7. The Act is not in force in any Canadian jurisdiction. For a detailed criticism of its provisions, see Atiyah & Treitel, "Misrepresentation Act, 1967" (1967) 30 Mod L Rev 369.

2. In *With v O'Flanagan*, [1936] Ch 575 (CA), the vendor physician stated a correct income for his practice. But, the income became significantly reduced before the contract was concluded because of the vendor's illness. The earlier statement as to income, if made later, would have been untrue, and Romer LJ thought the vendor had a duty to correct the ignorance of the recipient of the representation. This result seemed to Romer LJ "so obviously consistent with the plainest principles of equity." In *Xerex Exploration Ltd v Petro-Canada*, 2005 ABCA 224, the court said:

> Ordinarily in contractual negotiations between sophisticated parties, operating at arm's length, there is no general duty of disclosure. When a representation is made during the course of negotiations, however, the party making it must ensure that it is accurate so that it does not amount to a misrepresentation. This gives rise to a·further duty to speak when

silence effectively renders a representation, already made, inaccurate. Having brought a particular subject up in negotiations, a party assumes a duty to ensure that the other party is aware of all the material facts relevant to that assertion.

COMPETITION ACT
RSC 1985, c C-34

36(1) Any person who has suffered loss or damage as a result of (a) conduct that is contrary to any provision of Part VI [s 52 is in part VI] ... may, in any court of competent jurisdiction, sue for and recover from the person who engaged in the conduct ... an amount equal to the loss or damage proved to have been suffered by him. ...

52(1) No person shall, for the purpose of promoting, directly or indirectly, the supply or use of a product or for the purpose of promoting, directly or indirectly, any business interest, by any means whatever, knowingly or recklessly make a representation to the public that is false or misleading in a material respect.

(1.1) For greater certainty, in establishing that subsection (1) was contravened, it is not necessary to prove that (a) any person was deceived or misled. ...

(5) Any person who contravenes subsection (1) is guilty of an offence and liable (a) on conviction on indictment, to a fine in the discretion of the court or to imprisonment for a term not exceeding 14 years, or to both; or (b) on summary conviction, to a fine not exceeding $200,000 or to imprisonment for a term not exceeding one year, or to both.

NOTES

1. See also the *Consumer Protection Act, 2002*, SO 2002, c 30, s18, excerpted in Chapter 6, which may allow damages for innocent misrepresentation. Consumer protection legislation exists in several provinces—for example, see Alberta's *Fair Trading Act*, RSA 2000, c F-2 and BC's *Business Practices and Consumer Protection Act*, SBC 2004, c 2.

2. See generally on the law of misrepresentation Waddams, ch 13; McCamus, ch 18; MacDougall, ch 15; and see B MacDougall, *Misrepresentation* (Toronto: LexisNexis, 2016).

III. THE RELATIONSHIP BETWEEN CONTRACT AND TORT

HEDLEY BYRNE & CO LTD V HELLER & PARTNERS LTD
[1964] AC 465 (HL)

[The plaintiff, before advancing credit to a third party, asked the defendant banker for a credit report. The defendant replied, "[F]or your private use and without responsibility on the part of this bank or its officials ... Re [third party]. Respectably constituted company, considered good for its ordinary business engagements. Your figures are larger than we are accustomed to see." In reliance on this report the plaintiff advanced credit and lost a large sum of money when the third party failed to honour its obligations. The House of Lords held that an action would lie for negligent misrepresentation causing financial loss, but in this particular case the defendant was protected by the opening sentence of its report.]

LORD DEVLIN: The respondents [defendants] in this case cannot deny that they were performing a service. Their sheet anchor is that they were performing it gratuitously and therefore no liability for its performance can arise. My Lords, in my opinion this is not the law. A promise given without consideration to perform a service cannot be enforced as a contract by the promisee; but if the service is in fact performed and done negligently, the promisee can recover in an action in tort. This is the foundation of the liability of a gratuitous bailee. In the famous case of *Coggs v. Bernard* (1703), 2 Ld. Raym. 909 where the defendant had charge of brandy belonging to the plaintiff and had spilt a quantity of it, there was a motion in arrest of judgment "for that it was not alleged in the declaration that the defendant was a common porter, nor averred that he had anything for his pains." The declaration was held to be good notwithstanding that there was not any consideration laid. Gould J. said: "The reason of the action is, the particular trust reposed in the defendant, to which he has concurred by his assumption, and in the executing which he has miscarried by his neglect." This proposition is not limited to the law of bailment. In *Skelton v. London & North Western Railway Co.* (1867), L.R. 2 C.P. 631, 636 Willes J. applied it generally to the law of negligence. He said: "Actionable negligence must consist in the breach of some duty ... if a person undertakes to perform a voluntary act, he is liable if he performs it improperly, but not if he neglects to perform it. Such is the result of the decision in the case of *Coggs v. Bernard.*" Likewise in *Banbury v. Bank of Montreal*, [1918] A.C. 626, 654 where the bank had advised a customer on his investments, Lord Finlay L.C. said: "He is under no obligation to advise, but if he takes upon himself to do so, he will incur liability if he does so negligently."

The principle has been applied to cases where as a result of the negligence no damage was done to person or to property and the consequential loss was purely financial. In *Wilkinson v. Coverdale* 1 Esp. 75 the defendant undertook gratuitously to get a fire policy renewed for the plaintiff, but, in doing so, neglected formalities, the omission of which rendered the policy inoperative. It was held that an action would lie. In two similar cases the defendants succeeded on the ground that negligence was not proved in fact. Both cases were thus decided on the basis that in law an action would lie. In the first of them, *Shiells v. Blackburne*, 1 H. Bl. 158 the defendant had, acting voluntarily and without compensation, made an entry of the plaintiff's leather as wrought leather instead of dressed leather, with the result that the leather was seized. In *Dartnall v. Howard & Gibbs* (1825), 4 B. & C. 345 the defendants purchased an annuity for the plaintiff but on the personal security of two insolvent persons. The court, after verdict, arrested the judgment upon the ground that the defendants appeared to be gratuitous agents and that it was not averred that they had acted either with negligence or dishonesty. ...

I agree with Sir Frederick Pollock's note on the case of *De La Bere v. Pearson Ltd.* where he said in *Contracts*, 13th ed., p. 140, that "the cause of action is better regarded as arising from default in the performance of a voluntary undertaking independent of contract."

My Lords, it is true that this principle of law has not yet been clearly applied to a case where the service which the defendant undertakes to perform is or includes the obtaining and imparting of information. But I cannot see why it should not be: and if it had not been thought erroneously that *Derry v. Peek* 14 App. Cas. 337 negatived any liability for negligent statements, I think that by now it probably would have been. It cannot matter whether the information consists of fact or of opinion or is a mixture of both, nor whether it was obtained as a result of special inquiries or comes direct from facts already in the defendant's possession or from his general store of professional knowledge. One cannot, as I have already endeavoured to show, distinguish in this respect between a duty to inquire and a duty to state.

I think, therefore, that there is ample authority to justify your Lordships in saying now that the categories of special relationships which may give rise to a duty to take care in word as well as in deed are not limited to contractual relationships or to relationships of fiduciary duty, but include also relationships which in the words of Lord Shaw in *Nocton v. Lord Ashburton* [1914] A.C. 932, 972 are "equivalent to contract," that is, where there is an assumption of responsibility in circumstances in which, but for the absence of consideration, there would be a contract. Where there is an express undertaking, an express warranty as distinct from mere representation, there can be little difficulty. The difficulty arises in discerning those cases in which the undertaking is to be implied. In this respect the absence of consideration is not irrelevant. Payment for information or advice is very good evidence that it is being relied upon and that the informer or adviser knows that it is. Where there is no consideration, it will be necessary to exercise greater care in distinguishing between social and professional relationships and between those which are of a contractual character and those which are not. It may often be material to consider whether the adviser is acting purely out of good nature or whether he is getting his reward in some indirect form. The service that a bank performs in giving a reference is not done simply out of a desire to assist commerce. It would discourage the customers of the bank if their deals fell through because the bank had refused to testify to their credit when it was good.

I have had the advantage of reading all the opinions prepared by your Lordships and of studying the terms which your Lordships have framed by way of definition of the sort of relationship which gives rise to a responsibility towards those who act upon information or advice and so creates a duty of care towards them. I do not understand any of your Lordships to hold that it is a responsibility imposed by law upon certain types of persons or in certain sorts of situations. It is a responsibility that is voluntarily accepted or undertaken, either generally where a general relationship, such as that of solicitor and client or banker and customer, is created, or specifically in relation to a particular transaction. In the present case the appellants were not, as in *Woods v. Martins Bank Ltd.* [1959] 1 Q.B. 55 the customers or potential customers of the bank. Responsibility can attach only to the single act, that is, the giving of the reference, and only if the doing of that act implied a voluntary undertaking to assume responsibility. This is a point of great importance because it is, as I understand it, the foundation for the ground on which in the end the House dismisses the appeal. I do not think it possible to formulate with exactitude all the conditions under which the law will in a specific case imply a voluntary undertaking any more than it is possible to formulate those in which the law will imply a contract. But in so far as your Lordships describe the circumstances in which an implication will ordinarily be drawn, I am prepared to adopt any one of your Lordships' statements as showing the general rule; and I pay the same respect to the statement by Denning L.J. in his dissenting judgment in *Candler v. Crane, Christmas & Co.* [1951] 2 K.B. 164 about the circumstances in which he says a duty to use care in making a statement exists.

I do not go further than this for two reasons. The first is that I have found in the speech of Lord Shaw in *Nocton v. Lord Ashburton* and in the idea of a relationship that is equivalent to contract all that is necessary to cover the situation that arises in this case. Mr. Gardiner does not claim to succeed unless he can establish that the reference was intended by the respondents to be communicated by the National Provincial Bank to some unnamed customer of theirs, whose identity was immaterial to the respondents, for that customer's use. All that was lacking was formal consideration. The case is well within the authorities I have already cited and of which *Wilkinson v. Coverdale* is the most apposite example.

I shall therefore content myself with the proposition that wherever there is a relationship equivalent to contract, there is a duty of care. Such a relationship may be either general or particular. Examples of a general relationship are those of solicitor and client and of banker and customer. For the former *Nocton v. Lord Ashburton* has long stood as the authority and for the latter there is the decision of Salmon J. in *Woods v. Martins Bank Ltd.* which I respectfully approve. There may well be others yet to be established. Where there is a general relationship of this sort, it is unnecessary to do more than prove its existence and the duty follows. Where, as in the present case, what is relied on is a particular relationship created ad hoc, it will be necessary to examine the particular facts to see whether there is an express or implied undertaking of responsibility.

I regard this proposition as an application of the general conception of proximity. Cases may arise in the future in which a new and wider proposition, quite independent of any notion of contract, will be needed. There may, for example, be cases in which a statement is not supplied for the use of any particular person, any more than in *Donoghue v. Stevenson* [1932] A.C. 562 the ginger beer was supplied for consumption by any particular person; and it will then be necessary to return to the general conception of proximity and to see whether there can be evolved from it, as was done in *Donoghue v. Stevenson*, a specific proposition to fit the case. When that has to be done, the speeches of your Lordships today as well as the judgment of Denning L.J. to which I have referred—and also, I may add, the proposition in the *American Restatement of the Law of Torts*, Vol. III, p. 122, para. 552, and the cases which exemplify it—will afford good guidance as to what ought to be said. I prefer to see what shape such cases take before committing myself to any formulation, for I bear in mind Lord Atkin's warning, which I have quoted, against placing unnecessary restrictions on the adaptability of English law. I have, I hope, made it clear that I take quite literally the dictum of Lord Macmillan, so often quoted from the same case, that "the categories of negligence are never closed." English law is wide enough to embrace any new category or proposition that exemplifies the principle of proximity.

I have another reason for caution. Since the essence of the matter in the present case and in others of the same type is the acceptance of responsibility, I should like to guard against the imposition of restrictive terms notwithstanding that the essential condition is fulfilled. If a defendant says to a plaintiff: "Let me do this for you; do not waste your money in employing a professional, I will do it for nothing and you can rely on me." I do not think he could escape liability simply because he belonged to no profession or calling, had no qualifications or special skill and did not hold himself out as having any. The relevance of these factors is to show the unlikelihood of a defendant in such circumstances assuming a legal responsibility, and as such they may often be decisive. But they are not theoretically conclusive and so cannot be the subject of definition. It would be unfortunate if they were. For it would mean that plaintiffs would seek to avoid the rigidity of the definition by bringing the action in contract as in *De La Bere v. Pearson Ltd.* and setting up something that would do for consideration. That, to my mind, would be an undesirable development in the law; and the best way of avoiding it is to settle the law so that the presence or absence of consideration makes no difference.

ESSO PETROLEUM CO LTD V MARDON

[1976] QB 801 (CA)

LORD DENNING MR: "This is," said the judge, "a tragic story of wasted endeavour and financial disaster." It is a long story starting as long ago as 1961, and finishing in 1967. Since then eight years have been spent in litigation.

In 1961 Esso Petroleum wanted an outlet for their petrol in Southport. They found a vacant site which was very suitable. It was on Eastbank Street, one of the business streets of the town. It had already got outline planning permission for a filling station. Esso thought of putting in a bid for the site. But before doing so, they made calculations to see if it would be a paying proposition. They made a careful forecast of the "estimated annual consumption" of petrol. This was the yardstick by which they measured the worth of a filling station. They called it the "e.a.c." In this case they estimated that the throughput of petrol would reach 200,000 gallons a year by the second year after development. This would accrue to their benefit by sales of petrol. In addition, they would get a substantial rental from a tenant. On May 25, 1961, the Esso local representatives recommended the go ahead. They gave the figures, and said: "We feel most strongly that this does genuinely represent a first-class opportunity of gaining representation in the centre of Southport." On that recommendation Esso bought the site and proceeded to erect a service station.

But then something happened which falsified all their calculations. Esso had thought that they could have the forecourt and pumps fronting on to the busy main street. But the Southport Corporation, who were the planning authority, refused to allow this. They insisted that the station should be built "back to front." So that only the showroom fronted on to the main street. The forecourt and pumps were at the back of the site and only accessible by side streets. They could not be seen from the main street. Esso had no choice but to comply with these planning requirements. They built the station "back to front." It was finished early in 1963.

Now at this point Esso made an error which the judge described as a "fatal error." They did not revise their original estimate which they had made in 1961. They still assessed the e.a.c. (estimated annual consumption) of petrol at 200,000 gallons. Whereas they should have made a reappraisal in the light of the building being now "back to front." This adversely affected the site's potential: because passing traffic could not see the station. It would reduce the throughput greatly. The judge found that this "fatal error" was due to want of care on the part of Esso. There can be no doubt about it.

It was under the influence of this "fatal error" that Esso sought to find a tenant for the service station. They found an excellent man, Mr. Philip Lionel Mardon. He was seen by Esso's local manager, Mr. Leitch. Now Mr. Leitch had had 40 years' experience in the petrol trade. It was on his calculations and recommendations that Esso had bought this site and developed it. At the decisive interview Mr. Leitch was accompanied by the new area manager, Mr. Allen. I will give what took place in the words of the judge:

> Mr. Mardon was told that Esso estimated that the throughput of the Eastbank Street site, in its third year of operation, would amount to 200,000 gallons a year. I also find that Mr. Mardon then indicated that he thought 100,000 to 150,000 gallons would be a more realistic estimate, but he was convinced by the far greater expertise of, particularly, Mr. Leitch. Mr. Allen is a far younger man and, although on his appointment as manager for the area I am satisfied he made his own observations as to the potentiality of the Eastbank Street site, in the result he accepted Mr. Leitch's estimate. Mr. Mardon, having indicated that he thought that a lower figure would be a more realistic estimate, had

his doubts quelled by the experience and the estimate furnished by Mr. Leitch, and it was for that reason, I am satisfied, because of what he was told about the estimated throughput in the third year, that he then proceeded to negotiate for and obtain the grant of a three-year tenancy at a rent of £2,500 a year for the first two years, rising to £3,000 yearly in the last year.

To the judge's summary, I would only add a few questions and answers by Mr. Allen in evidence:

Q. Now we know that the person who originally put forward this estimated 200,000 gallons forecast was Mr. Leitch?   A. Yes.

Q. Would somebody have checked Mr. Leitch's figures before they reached you?   A. Oh, very much so. ...

Q. You have told my Lord that you accept that, at that interview ... you might have said that Eastbank was capable of achieving a throughput of 200,000 gallons after the second complete year?   A. Yes.

Q. Would that have been your honest opinion at the time?   A. Most certainly.

All the dealings were based on that estimate of a throughput of 200,000 gallons. It was on that estimate that Esso developed the site at a cost of £40,000: and that the tenant agreed to pay a rent of £2,500, rising to £3,000. A few answers by Mr. Allen will show this:

Q. Would you agree that the potential throughput of a station is an important factor in assessing what rent to charge a tenant?   A. Yes. ...

Q. The rent would be substantially higher if your estimate was one of 200,000 gallons than if your estimate was one of 100,000 gallons?   A. Generally speaking, that is right. ...

Q. You would be able to command a higher rent if the throughput was 200,000 than if it was 100,000?   A. Had it been an estimated throughput of 100,000 gallons, they [Esso] would not have bought it in the first place.

Having induced Mr. Mardon to accept, Mr. Leitch and Mr. Allen sent this telegram to their head office: "We have interviewed a Mr. Philip Lionel Mardon for tenancy and find him excellent in all respects. We recommend strongly that he be granted tenancy." So a tenancy was granted to Mr. Mardon. It was dated April 10, 1963, and was for three years at a rent of £2,500 for the first two years, and £3,000 for the third year. It required him to keep open all day every day of the week, including Sunday. It forbade him to assign or underlet.

On the next day Mr. Mardon went into occupation of the service station and did everything that could be desired of him. He was an extremely good tenant and he tried every method to increase the sales and profitability of the service station. Esso freely acknowledge this.

But the throughput was most disappointing. It never got anywhere near the 200,000 gallons. Mr. Mardon put all his available capital into it. It was over £6,000. He raised an overdraft with the bank and used it in the business. He put all his work and endeavour into it. No one could have done more to make it a success. Yet when the accounts were taken for the first 15 months, the throughput was only 78,000 gallons. After paying all outgoings, such as rent, wages and so forth, there was a net loss of £5,800. The position was so serious that Mr. Mardon felt he could not continue. On July 17, 1964, he wrote to Mr. Allen: "I reluctantly give notice to quit forthwith. This is an endeavour to salvage as much as I can in lieu of inevitable bankruptcy." Mr. Allen did not reply in writing, but saw Mr. Mardon. As a result he put in a written report to his superiors recommending that Mr. Mardon's rent should be reduced to

£1,000 a year, plus a surcharge according to the amount of petrol sold. Mr. Allen telexed to his superiors on several occasions pressing for a decision. It culminated in a telex he sent on August 28, 1964: "Unless we hear soon the tenant is likely to resign and we will have difficulty in replacing this man with a tenant of the same high standard." This brought results. On September 1, 1964, a new tenancy agreement was made in writing. It granted Mr. Mardon a tenancy for one year certain and thereafter determinable on three months' notice. The rent was reduced to £1,000 a year, and a surcharge of 1d. to 2d. a gallon, according to the amount sold.

Again Mr. Mardon tried hard to make a success of the service station: but again he failed. It was not his fault. The site was simply not good enough to have a through-put of more than 60,000 or 70,000 gallons. He lost more and more money over it. In order to help him, Esso tried to get another site for him—a "cream" site—so that he could run the two sites in conjunction to offset his losses. But they never found him one. Eventually on January 1, 1966, he wrote to Esso appealing to them to find a solution. He consulted solicitors who wrote on his behalf. But Esso did nothing to help. Quite the contrary. They insisted on the petrol being paid for every day on delivery. On August 28, 1966 (by some mistake or misunderstanding while Mr. Mardon was away), they came and drained his tanks of petrol and cut off his supplies. That put him out of business as a petrol station. He carried on as best he could with odd jobs for customers, like washing cars. Esso had no pity for him. On December 1, 1966, they issued a writ against him claiming possession and £1,333 13s. 9d. for petrol supplied. This defeated him. On March 7, 1967, he gave up the site. He had tried for four years to make a success of it. It was all wasted endeavour. He had lost all his capital and had incurred a large overdraft. It was a financial disaster.

Such being the facts, I turn to consider the law. It is founded on the representation that the estimated throughput of the service station was 200,000 gallons. No claim can be brought under the Misrepresentation Act 1967, because that Act did not come into force until April 22, 1967: whereas the representation was made in April 1963. So the claim is put in two ways. First, that the representation was a collateral warranty. Second, that it was a negligent misrepresentation. I will take them in order.

COLLATERAL WARRANTY

Ever since *Heilbut, Symons & Co. v. Buckleton* [1913] A.C. 30, we have had to contend with the law as laid down by the House of Lords that an innocent misrepresentation gives no right to damages. In order to escape from that rule, the pleader used to allege—I often did it myself—that the misrepresentation was fraudulent, or alternatively a collateral warranty. At the trial we nearly always succeeded on collateral warranty. We had to reckon, of course, with the dictum of Lord Moulton, at p. 47, that "such collateral contracts must from their very nature be rare." But more often than not the court elevated the innocent misrepresentation into a collateral warranty: and thereby did justice—in advance of the Misrepresentation Act 1967. I remember scores of cases of that kind, especially on the sale of a business. A representation as to the profits that had been made in the past was invariably held to be a warranty. Besides that experience, there have been many cases since I have sat in this court where we have readily held a representation—which induces a person to enter into a contract—to be a warranty sounding in damages. I summarised them in *Dick Bentley Productions Ltd. v. Harold Smith (Motors) Ltd.* [1965] 1 W.L.R. 623, 627, where I said:

> Looking at the cases once more, as we have done so often, it seems to me that if a representation is made in the course of dealings for a contract for the very purpose of inducing the other party to act upon it, and actually inducing him to act upon it, by

entering into the contract, that is prima facie ground for inferring that it was intended as a warranty. It is not necessary to speak of it as being collateral. Suffice it that it was intended to be acted upon and was in fact acted on.

Mr. Ross-Munro, retaliated, however, by citing *Bisset v. Wilkinson* [1927] A.C. 177, where the Privy Council said that a statement by a New Zealand farmer that an area of land "would carry 2,000 sheep" was only an expression of opinion. He submitted that the forecast here of 200,000 gallons was an expression of opinion and not a statement of fact: and that it could not be interpreted as a warranty or promise.

Now I would quite agree with Mr. Ross-Munro that it was not a warranty—in this sense—that it did not *guarantee* that the throughput *would be* 200,000 gallons. But, nevertheless, it was a forecast made by a party—Esso—who had special knowledge and skill. It was the yardstick (the e.a.c.) by which they measured the worth of a filling station. They knew the facts. They knew the traffic in the town. They knew the throughput of comparable stations. They had much experience and expertise at their disposal. They were in a much better position than Mr. Mardon to make a forecast. It seems to me that if such a person makes a forecast, intending that the other should act upon it—and he does act upon it, it can well be interpreted as a warranty that the forecast is sound and reliable in the sense that they made it with reasonable care and skill. It is just as if Esso said to Mr. Mardon: "Our forecast of throughput is 200,000 gallons. You can rely upon it as being a sound forecast of what the service station should do. The rent is calculated on that footing." If the forecast turned out to be an unsound forecast such as no person of skill or experience should have made, there is a breach of warranty. Just as there is a breach of warranty when a forecast is made—"expected to load" by a certain date—if the maker has no reasonable grounds for it: see *Samuel Sanday and Co. v. Keighley, Maxted and Co.* (1922) 27 Com. Cas. 296; or bunkers "expected 600/700 tons": see *Efploia Shipping Corporation Ltd. v. Canadian Transport Co. Ltd. (The Pantanassa)* [1958] 2 Lloyd's Rep. 449, 455-457 by Diplock J. It is very different from the New Zealand case where the land had never been used as a sheep farm and both parties were equally able to form an opinion as to its carrying capacity: see particularly *Bisset v. Wilkinson* [1927] A.C. 177, 183-184.

In the present case it seems to me that there was a warranty that the forecast was sound, that is, Esso made it with reasonable care and skill. That warranty was broken. Most negligently Esso made a "fatal error" in the forecast they stated to Mr. Mardon, and on which he took the tenancy. For this they are liable in damages. The judge, however, declined to find a warranty. So I must go further.

NEGLIGENT MISREPRESENTATION

Assuming that there was no warranty, the question arises whether Esso are liable for negligent misstatement under the doctrine of *Hedley Byrne & Co. Ltd. v. Heller & Partners Ltd.* [1964] A.C. 465. It has been suggested that *Hedley Byrne* cannot be used so as to impose liability for negligent pre-contractual statements: and that, in a pre-contract situation, the remedy (at any rate before the Act of 1967) was only in warranty or nothing. Thus in *Hedley Byrne* itself Lord Reid said, at p. 483: "Where there is a contract there is no difficulty as regards the contracting parties: the question is whether there is a warranty." And in *Oleificio Zucchi S.P.A. v. Northern Sales Ltd.* [1965] 2 Lloyd's Rep. 496, 519, McNair J. said: " ... [A]s at present advised, I consider the submission advanced by the buyers, that the ruling in ... [*Hedley Byrne*, [1964] A.C. 465] applies as between contracting parties, is without foundation."

As against these, I took a different view in *McInerny v. Lloyds Bank Ltd.* [1974] 1 Lloyd's Rep. 246, 253 when I said: " ... [I]f one person, by a negligent misstatement, induces another to enter into a contract—with himself or with a third person—he may be liable in damages."

In arguing this point, Mr. Ross-Munro took his stand in this way. He submitted that when the negotiations between two parties resulted in a contract between them, their rights and duties were governed by the law of contract and not by the law of tort. There was, therefore, no place in their relationship for *Hedley Byrne* [1964] A.C. 465, which was solely on liability in tort. He relied particularly on *Clark v. Kirby-Smith* [1964] Ch. 506 where Plowman J. held that the liability of a solicitor for negligence was a liability in contract and not in tort, following the observations of Sir Wilfrid Greene M.R. in *Groom v. Crocker* [1939] 1 K.B. 194, 206. Mr. Ross-Munro might also have cited *Bagot v. Stevens Scanlan & Co. Ltd.* [1966] 1 Q.B. 197, about an architect; and other cases too. But I venture to suggest that those cases are in conflict with other decisions of high authority which were not cited in them. These decisions show that, in the case of a professional man, the duty to use reasonable care arises not only in contract, but is also imposed by the law apart from contract, and is therefore actionable in tort. It is comparable to the duty of reasonable care which is owed by a master to his servant, or vice versa. It can be put either in contract or in tort: see *Lister v. Romford Ice and Cold Storage Co. Ltd.* [1957] A.C. 555, 587 by Lord Radcliffe and *Matthews v. Kuwait Bechtel Corporation* [1959] 2 Q.B. 57. The position was stated by Tindal C.J., delivering the judgment of the Court of Exchequer Chamber in *Boorman v. Brown* (1842) 3 Q.B. 511, 525-526:

> That there is a large class of cases in which the foundation of the action springs out of privity of contract between the parties, but in which, nevertheless, the remedy for the breach, or non-performance, is indifferently either assumpsit or case upon tort, is not disputed. Such are actions against attorneys, surgeons, and other professional men, for want of competent skill or proper care in the service they undertake to render: ... The principle in all these cases would seem to be that the contract creates a duty, and the neglect to perform that duty, or the nonfeasance, is a ground of action upon a tort.

That decision was affirmed in the House of Lords in (1844) 11 Cl. & Fin. 1, when Lord Campbell, giving the one speech, said, at p. 44: " ... [W]herever there is a contract, and something to be done in the course of the employment which is the subject of that contract, if there is a breach of a duty in the course of that employment, the plaintiff may either recover in tort or in contract."

To this there is to be added the high authority of Viscount Haldane L.C., in *Nocton v. Lord Ashburton* [1914] A.C. 932, 956: " ... [T]he solicitor contracts with his client to be skilful and careful. For failure to perform his obligation he may be made liable at law in contract or even in tort, for negligence in breach of a duty imposed on him."

That seems to me right. A professional man may give advice under a contract for reward; or without a contract, in pursuance of a voluntary assumption of responsibility, gratuitously without reward. In either case he is under one and the same duty to use reasonable care: see *Cassidy v. Ministry of Health* [1951] 2 K.B. 343, 359-360. In the one case it is by reason of a term implied by law. In the other, it is by reason of a duty imposed by law. For a breach of that duty he is liable in damages: and those damages should be, and are, the same, whether he is sued in contract or in tort.

It follows that I cannot accept Mr. Ross-Munro's proposition. It seems to me that *Hedley Byrne & Co. Ltd. v. Heller & Partners Ltd.* [1964] A.C. 465, properly understood, covers this particular proposition: if a man, who has or professes to have special knowledge or skill, makes a representation by virtue thereof to another—be it advice, information or opinion—with the intention of inducing him to enter into a contract with him, he is under a duty to use reasonable care to see that the representation is correct, and that the advice, information or opinion is reliable. If he negligently gives unsound advice or misleading information or expresses an erroneous opinion, and thereby induces the other side to enter into a contract with him, he is liable in damages. This proposition is in line with what I said in *Candler v. Crane, Christmas & Co.* [1951] 2 K.B. 164, 179-80, which was approved by the majority of the Privy Council in *Mutual Life and Citizens' Assurance Co. Ltd. v. Evatt* [1971] A.C. 793. And the judges of the Commonwealth have shown themselves quite ready to apply *Hedley Byrne* [1964] A.C. 465, between contracting parties; see ... *Sealand of the Pacific Ltd. v. Ocean Cement Ltd.* (1973) 33 D.L.R. (3d) 625; and ... *Capital Motors Ltd. v. Beecham* [1975] 1 N.Z.L.R. 576.

Applying this principle, it is plain that Esso professed to have—and did in fact have—special knowledge or skill in estimating the throughput of a filling station. They made the representation—they forecast a throughput of 200,000 gallons—intending to induce Mr. Mardon to enter into a tenancy on the faith of it. They made it negligently. It was a "fatal error." And thereby induced Mr. Mardon to enter into a contract of tenancy that was disastrous to him. For this misrepresentation they are liable in damages.

THE MEASURE OF DAMAGES

Mr. Mardon is not to be compensated for "loss of a bargain." He was given no bargain that the throughput *would* amount to 200,000 gallons a year. He is only to be compensated for having been induced to enter into a contract which turned out to be disastrous for him. Whether it be called breach of warranty or negligent misrepresentation, its effect was *not* to warrant the throughput, but only to induce him to enter the contract. So the damages in either case are to be measured by the loss he suffered. Just as in *Doyle v. Olby (Ironmongers) Ltd.* [1969] 2 Q.B. 158, 167 he can say: " ... I would not have entered into this contract at all but for your representation. Owing to it, I have lost all the capital I put into it. I also incurred a large overdraft. I have spent four years of my life in wasted endeavour without reward: and it will take me some time to re-establish myself."

For all such loss he is entitled to recover damages. It is to be measured in a similar way as the loss due to a personal injury. You should look into the future so as to forecast what would have been likely to happen if he had never entered into this contract: and contrast it with his position as it is now as a result of entering into it. The future is necessarily problematical and can only be a rough-and-ready estimate. But it must be done in assessing the loss.

[Ormrod and Shaw LJJ agreed.]

NOTES AND QUESTIONS

1. The "special relationships which may give rise to a duty to take care," as articulated in *Hedley Byrne*, are not limited to professional advisers, but only in exceptional cases, such as in *Esso Petroleum v Mardon*, do they apply "between counterparties in a commercial context," because "as between commercial counterparties, a representor is in general less likely to know that the Claimant is relying upon its representation, and it is less likely to be reasonable for the Claimant to rely upon the Defendant." See *ParOS plc v Worldlink Group plc*, [2012] EWHC 394 (Comm) at paras 103, 107. Special relationships can arise in a number of different contexts. In *Krawchuk v Scherbak*, 2011 ONCA 352, 106 OR (3d) 598, the court found a special relationship giving rise to a duty of care between vendors of a home who had made particular comments on the Seller Property Information Sheet with respect to the property. And in *Albionex (Overseas)*

Ltd v Conagra Ltd, 2011 MBCA 95, [2011] MJ No 412 (QL), the court found that the Canadian Wheat Board had a special relationship with potential purchasers for whom it prepared an information letter and type samples "for the express purpose of informing potential purchasers around the world of the availability and quality of [Wheat-Ex. Special Bin]."

2. In *Esso Petroleum v Mardon*, [1976] QB 801 (CA), excerpted above, the court held that Esso was liable on the basis of negligent misrepresentation. It also held that the same facts could support a claim either in contract or in tort. The view of the majority of the Supreme Court of Canada in *J Nunes Diamonds Ltd v Dominion Electric Protection Company*, [1972] SCR 769, 26 DLR (3d) 699, that a tort action is inapplicable in any case where the relationship between the parties is governed by contract unless the negligence relied on can properly be considered as an independent tort unconnected with the performance of the contract, appears largely to have been rejected in later cases: see *Central Trust Co v Rafuse*, [1986] 2 SCR 147, 31 DLR (4th) 481; *BG Checo International Ltd v British Columbia Hydro and Power Authority*, [1993] 1 SCR 12, 99 DLR (4th) 577; and *Queen v Cognos Inc*, [1993] 1 SCR 87, 99 DLR (4th) 626. However, it is still the case that a tort claim cannot be used to circumvent a contractual limitation of liability. In *Central Trust Co*, the court determined that "[a] concurrent or alternative liability in tort will not be admitted if its effect would be to permit the plaintiff to circumvent or escape a contractual exclusion or limitation of liability for the act or omission that would constitute the tort. Subject to this qualification, where concurrent liability in tort and contract exists the plaintiff has the right to assert the cause of action that appears to be most advantageous to him in respect of any particular legal consequence." For what reasons might a party prefer to bring a suit on the basis of tort rather than contract? See also Waddams at paras 412-14; McCamus at 358-64; MacDougall at 201-9.

3. See *Sealand of the Pacific Ltd v Robert C McHaffie Ltd* (*sub nom Sealand of the Pacific Ltd v Ocean Cement Ltd*) (1974), 51 DLR (3d) 702 (BCCA), where the court found that "[a]n employee's act or omission that constitutes his employer's breach of contract may also impose a liability on the employee in tort. However, this will only be so if there is breach of a duty owed (independently of the contract) by the employee to the other party. ... The duty in negligence and the duty in contract may stand side by side but the duty in contract is not imposed upon the employee as a duty in tort."

IV. MISTAKE ABOUT CONTRACTUAL TERMS

HOBBS V ESQUIMALT AND NANAIMO RAILWAY CO
(1899), 29 SCR 450

[Hobbs paid the railway company $120 on account of the purchase of a quarter section of land at $3 an acre, payment to be made over three years. The receipt described the land without reservation and was signed by John Trutch, Land Commissioner for the Railway. The company claimed that Mr. Trutch had no authority to convey the minerals and three years later offered a conveyance with minerals reserved. Hobbs asked for specific performance. The trial judge refused it but declared that Hobbs was entitled to a conveyance with the reservation or to repayment of the purchase money with interest and compensation for improvements. The Court of Appeal denied him the option of repayment.]

TASCHEREAU J (dissenting): I would dismiss this appeal. The reasons given in the courts below against the appellant's right to specific performance are, in my opinion, unanswerable. There has been no contract between this company and Hobbs. The company thought they were selling the land without the minerals. Hobbs thought he was buying the land with the minerals. So that the company did not sell what Hobbs thought he was buying, and Hobbs did not buy what the company thought they were selling. Therefore, there was no contract between them. Hobbs would not have bought it if he had known that the company were selling only surface rights, and the company would not have sold if they had thought that Hobbs intended to buy the land with the minerals. The ratification by the company stands upon no better ground. It was nothing but ratification of a sale without the minerals.

The rule that any one dealing with another has the right to believe that this other one means what he says, or says what he means, is one that cannot be gainsaid. But it has no application here. Assuming that the agent sold the land with the minerals, he did what he had not the power to do. However, he did not do it.

I would dismiss the appeal with costs.

KING J: The facts are stated in the judgment of the late Chief Justice Davie before whom the case was tried.

It is found by him that Mr. Trutch acted beyond the scope of his authority in agreeing to a sale of the land without reservation of the minerals, but that the contract so made was [ratified] by the company. He, however, was of opinion that, in so ratifying it, the company were under a mistake as to its legal effect, and upon this ground he declined to compel performance but left the plaintiff to his common law remedy for breach of contract.

A first question is as to whether there was, by reason of the alleged mistake, a contract at all. ...

Here the parties were *ad idem* as to the terms of the contract. It was expressed in perfectly unambiguous language in the offer of the plaintiff and in the acceptance of defendants; and the alleged difference is in a wholly esoteric meaning which one of them gives to the plain words.

Then the legal right existing (as held by the Court below) is it a case (as also held by it) where a court will leave the party aggrieved by a breach to his common law remedy? As already mentioned *Stewart v. Kennedy* (1895), 15 App. Cas. 75 is not a case relating to the effect of mistake upon the exercise of the equitable jurisdiction of English Courts of Equity, but English authorities having been referred to, the jurisprudence is thus summarized by Lord Macnaghton (p. 105):

> It cannot be disputed that the Court of Chancery had refused specific performance in cases of mistake when the mistake has been on one side only, and even when the mistake on the part of the defendant resisting specific performance has not been induced or contributed to by any act or omission on the part of the plaintiff. But I do not think it is going too far to say that in all those cases—certainly in all that have occurred in recent times—the court has thought rightly or wrongly that the circumstances of the particular case under consideration were such that (to use a well known phrase) it would be "highly unreasonable" to enforce the agreement specifically.

In *Tamplin v. James* (1880), 15 Ch. D. 215, James L.J. says:

> If a man will not take reasonable care to ascertain what he is buying he must take the consequences. It is not enough for a purchaser to swear: "I thought the farm sold contained twelve fields which I knew, and I find it does not include them all," or "I thought it contained 100 acres and it only contains 80." It would open the door to fraud if such a defence was to be allowed. Perhaps some of the cases on this subject go too far (i.e. in the direction of allowing such defence) but for the most part the cases where a defendant has escaped on the ground of a mistake not contributed to by the plaintiff have been cases where a hardship amounting to injustice would have been inflicted upon him by holding him to his bargain and it was unreasonable to hold him to it.

Hence it may be, as stated in *Fry on Specific Performance*, that the court considers with more favour as a defence the allegation of mistake in an agent than in a principal.

The alleged mistake is given in the evidence of Mr. Dunsmuir, the vice-president of the company. Speaking of the contract entered into by Mr. Trutch, he says:

> It only sold the surface. That is, we term it land in our office. We do not say surface right, we say land, land minus the minerals.

It is evident, then, that we may put Mr. Trutch aside, and treat the case on this point as if the company, upon an application by plaintiff for purchase of 160 acres of land, had entered into an agreement to sell the land in the identical words used by Mr. Trutch. In effect they say:

> We agreed to sell the land, but this means land reserving the minerals.

It may well be that in the administration of their varied business a loose but convenient form of speech may have been used in the office, but it is not stated that it was supposed to be a correct one, and it appears incredible that a company, a large part of whose business is that of a land company could reasonably suppose that in dealings with third persons for the sale of land, the word "land" means land with reservation of minerals. Mr. Trutch does not say that he misconceived the meaning of the word. His impression was that he had verbally notified the plaintiff that the minerals were to be reserved, and if he had done so the plaintiff would be precluded from obtaining the specific performance he seeks; but it has been found that notice was not given. The form of the company conveyances expressly reserving the minerals show that they were aware how to effect such object. The alleged mistake was therefore an unreasonable and careless one, and in view of the fact that the plaintiff went into possession under the contract, I do not think that it can be said to be unconscionable or highly unreasonable to enforce the specific performance of the contract.

[Appeal allowed with costs. Gwynne, Sedgwick, and Girouard JJ concurred, Gwynne J with written reasons. In the Appendix of Privy Council Appeals in 31 SCR a note indicates that the appeal was dismissed upon settlement between the parties.]

RAFFLES V WICHELHAUS
(1864), 2 H & C 906, 159 ER 375

It was agreed at Liverpool that the plaintiff should sell to the defendants 125 bales of Surat cotton, guaranteed middling fair merchant's Dhollerah, to arrive ex "Peerless" from Bombay; and that the cotton should be taken from the quay, and that the defendants would pay the plaintiff at the rate of 17¼ d. per pound after the arrival of the goods in England. The goods did arrive by the "Peerless" but the defendants refused to accept the goods or pay the plaintiff for them. It was pleaded that the ship mentioned in the agreement was meant by the defendants to be the ship called the "Peerless" that sailed from Bombay in October; and that the plaintiff was only ready and willing and offered to deliver to the defendants cotton which arrived by another and different ship, which was also called the "Peerless," and which sailed from Bombay in December. Demurrer and joinder therein.

Milward, in support of the demurrer: The contract was for the sale of a number of bales of cotton of a particular description, which the plaintiff was ready to deliver. It is immaterial by what ship the cotton was to arrive, so that it was a ship called the

"Peerless." The words "to arrive ex 'Peerless'" only meant that, if the vessel is lost on the voyage, the contract is to be at an end.

[POLLOCK CB: [I]t would be a question for the jury whether both parties meant the same ship called the "Peerless."]

That would be so if the contract was for the sale of a ship called the "Peerless," but it is for the sale of cotton on board a ship of that name.

[POLLOCK CB: The defendant only bought that cotton which was to arrive by a particular ship. It may as well be said that, if there is a contract for the purchase of certain goods in warehouse A, that is satisfied by the delivery of goods of the same description in warehouse B.]

In that case there would be goods in both warehouses; here it does not appear that the plaintiff had any goods on board the other "Peerless."

[MARTIN B: It is imposing on the defendant a contract different from that which he entered into.]

[POLLOCK CB: It is like a contract for the purchase of wine coming from a particular estate in France or Spain, where there are two estates of that name.]

The defendant has no right to contradict by parol evidence a written contract good upon the face of it. He does not impute misrepresentation or fraud, but only says that he fancied the ship was a different one. Intention is of no avail, unless stated at the time of the contract.

[POLLOCK CB: One vessel sailed in October and the other in December.]

The time of sailings is no part of the contract.

Mellish (Cohen with him), in support of the plea: There is nothing on the face of the contract to show that any particular ship called the "Peerless" was meant; but the moment it appears that two ships called the "Peerless" were about to sail from Bombay, there is a latent ambiguity, and parol evidence may be given for the purpose of showing that the defendant meant one "Peerless" and the plaintiff another. That being so, there was no *consensus ad idem*, and therefore no binding contract.

[He was then stopped by the court.]

PER CURIAM: There must be judgment for the defendants.

NOTES AND QUESTIONS

1. A offers to sell goods to B ex *Peerless* from Bombay. B accepts. There are two ships called *Peerless*. What is the situation if

   a. A knows or has reason to know this fact, but B does not know, or have reason to know;
   b. B knows or has reason to know of it, but A does not;
   c. both know or have reason to know of it;
   d. neither of them knows or has reason to know of it at the time of communication?

2. For illuminating discussions of *Raffles v Wichelhaus*, see Robert Birmingham, "Holmes on 'Peerless': *Raffles v Wichelhaus* and the Objective Theory of Contract" (1985) U Pitt L Rev 183 and AWB Simpson, "Contracts for Cotton to Arrive: The Case of the Two Ships Peerless" (1989) 11 Cardozo L Rev 287, reprinted in AWB Simpson, *Leading Cases in the Common Law* (Oxford: Oxford University Press, 1996).

STAIMAN STEEL LTD V COMMERCIAL & HOME BUILDINGS LTD
(1976), 71 DLR (3d) 17 (Ont H Ct J)

SOUTHEY J: This is an action for damages for breach of an alleged contract for the sale of goods from the defendant Commercial & Home Builders Limited ("Commercial") to the plaintiff. The contract was alleged to have been made by the defendant F. Caldarone Auctions Limited ("Caldarone Auctions") as agent for Commercial at an auction sale conducted by Caldarone Auctions on the premises of Commercial on June 15, 1972. ...

When the auctioneer started to offer the lots of used steel, one or two of the buyers suggested that the items of used steel be sold in bulk, instead of by individual lot. ...

Before the bidding commenced, there was specific agreement that a number of items in the yard would not be included in the bulk sale, because they were not structural steel. Most of the items thus excluded were mechanical items. ...

At one point, according to some of the witnesses, the auctioneer described the bulk lot in general terms as being all the steel in the yard except mechanical items. When this general description was given, Bernard Staiman, president of the plaintiff, picked up a piece of scrap steel from the ground and asked "Even this?" The auctioneer replied "Yes."

The plaintiff was the successful bidder for the bulk lot at a unit price of $32 per ton.

The action relates to a pile of steel beams, doors and other members, which were the component members of a prefabricated steel building with craneway. This steel had been sold by Commercial several weeks before the auction sale, but was still piled in the yard of Commercial on the day of the sale. The plaintiff contended that this pile of steel was included in the bulk lot, whereas the defendants asserted that it was never their intention to include this steel in the sale, because it did not belong to Commercial.

The difference between the parties became apparent soon after the bulk lot was knocked down to the plaintiff and the auction sale was disrupted for a substantial time by a heated dispute between Staiman and the auctioneer as to the contents of the bulk lot. Staiman asserted that the steel he had purchased included the steel for the prefabricated building (hereinafter called the "building steel"). Commercial and the auctioneer both took the position that the steel purchased by the plaintiff in bulk did not include the building steel.

After consulting its solicitor, the plaintiff agreed on the day of the sale to take the lot without the building steel, but gave notice that it might bring legal proceedings to establish that the building steel should have been included in the lot. The auctioneer, acting on instructions from Commercial, required the plaintiff to sign a waiver to the effect that the lot purchased by it did not include the building steel. When the plaintiff refused to sign such waiver, the defendants refused to deliver any of the bulk lot to the plaintiff. The defendants' position was that if the plaintiff intended to bid for the building steel as part of the bulk lot, when the defendant had not intended that the bulk lot include such sale, then there was no *consensus ad idem* as to the subject of the sale and, therefore, no contract of sale. The positions thus taken by the parties remained substantially unchanged at trial.

The first question to be decided is whether the building steel was included in the bulk lot offered for sale at the auction. There is some conflict in the evidence bearing on this question and I must first make findings as to the credibility of some of the witnesses. ...

I was not impressed by Staiman's reliance on the question he put to the auctioneer as to whether the bulk lot included a piece of scrap steel and the answer received thereto as being of critical significance. ... If Staiman had any question that he genuinely wanted answered as to whether the building steel was included in the bulk lot, he should have made specific inquiries, as did Frank Clark and Irving Greenspoon, who were present at the auction and also gave evidence at trial.

... Staiman's evidence was that Szillard approached him and said he would like to buy back the building steel, because it had already been sold. Staiman said he and Szillard left it that they would try and work out a deal after the entire sale had been completed. I do not believe Staiman's evidence as to this conversation and accept instead the evidence of Szillard that when he discovered that Staiman thought he had bought the building steel, he pointed out to Staiman that it was not part of the bulk lot, because it had already been sold. ...

Returning then to the first question, as to whether the building steel was part of the bulk lot, I have concluded that it was never the intention of Commercial or Caldarone Auctions to offer the building steel for sale at the auction. That steel had already been sold. Furthermore, in my view, the defendants at no time manifested an intention to offer the building steel for sale. When the auctioneer agreed to sell the remaining inventory of steel in bulk, he was agreeing, in my view, to include in one bulk lot the items that had previously been offered for sale in separate lots. Even if he said that the bulk lot included all the steel in the yard except mechanical items, as some witnesses said he did, I think it should have been apparent to Staiman and the others at the sale that the auctioneer was offering only the steel belonging to Commercial that had been included in the auction sale. It should have been obvious that the auctioneer was not including the building steel in the bulk lot because that steel was separately piled from the rest; was not tagged; and was not listed in the catalogue. It was new steel, painted grey, that had obviously been fabricated for a particular purpose, whereas the other steel in the yard was all used.

For the foregoing reasons, I find that the bulk lot for which the plaintiff was the successful bidder, did not include the building steel.

... Frank Caldarone, the auctioneer, acting on the instructions of Commercial, refused to recognize the plaintiff as the buyer of any of the steel in the bulk lot, unless Staiman would execute an acknowledgement that the building steel was not included in the bulk lot.

Counsel for Commercial sought to justify the position thus taken by Commercial on the ground that if the plaintiff intended to buy a bulk lot containing the building steel, whereas Commercial intended to sell a lot without that steel, then there was no *consensus ad idem* and, therefore, no contract for the sale of any steel.

Counsel for Commercial relied on *Raffles v. Wichelhaus et al.* (1864), 2 H. & C. 906, 159 E.R. 375, involving two ships named "Peerless" which sailed from Bombay, one in October and one in December, and *Scriven Brothers & Co. v. Hindley & Co.*, [1913] 3 K.B. 564, where the purchaser at an auction bid an extravagant price for the bales of tow in the mistaken belief that they were bales of hemp. In both cases the Courts held that there was no contract, apparently because there was no *consensus ad idem*.

Counsel for the plaintiff, on the other hand, relied on the basic rule of contract law that it is not a party's actual intention that determines contractual relationships, but rather the intention manifested by the words and actions of the parties. ...

Mr. Catzman submitted that if the Court found that the building steel was not a part of the bulk lot, then the result should not be a finding that there was no contract. He contended that there should then be a finding that there was a contract for the sale of the lot without the building steel, even though it was not the plaintiff's intention to bid for the lot without the building steel.

In my judgment the plaintiff must succeed on this secondary point. The basis of the successful defence by Commercial on the first point is that the circumstances were such that a reasonable man would infer that the auctioneer, despite his words, was manifesting an intention to offer for sale the bulk lot without the building steel. By making the highest bid, Staiman so conducted himself that a reasonable man would believe that he was assenting to the purchase of that lot. A contract for the sale of that lot to the plaintiff thereupon came into existence. That contract was never subsequently repudiated by Staiman. The plaintiff was at all times willing to take delivery of and to pay for the bulk lot without the building steel, which was what Commercial and Caldarone Auctions said was the subject of the contract of sale, although the plaintiff made it quite clear that it might still commence proceedings to establish that the bulk lot should have included the building steel.

Commercial had the right to insist that the plaintiff take delivery and pay for the bulk lot excluding the building steel, but Commercial had no right, in my judgment, to require the plaintiff to give up its claim that the contract included the building steel as well as the remainder of the bulk lot. By insisting on such waiver or acknowledgement, Commercial was attempting to introduce unilaterally a new term into the contract of sale.

If, as appears to have been the case, the plaintiff thought the bulk lot he was purchasing included the building steel and the defendants thought that the bulk lot they were selling did not include the building steel, then the case was one of mutual mistake, as that expression is used in Cheshire and Fifoot's *Law of Contract*, 8th ed. (1972), p. 221. In such a case, the court must decide what reasonable third parties would infer to be the contract from the words and conduct of the parties who entered into it. It is only in a case where the circumstances are so ambiguous that a reasonable bystander could not infer a common intention that the Court will hold that no contract was created. As pointed out in Cheshire and Fifoot at p. 212:

> If the evidence is so conflicting that there is nothing sufficiently solid from which to infer a contract in any final form without indulging in mere speculation, the court must of necessity declare that no contract whatsoever has been created.

In this case, in my judgment, a reasonable man would infer the existence of a contract to buy and sell the bulk lot without the building steel and therefore I have held that there was a contract to that effect binding on both parties, notwithstanding such mutual mistake.

The case is quite unlike *Raffles v. Wichelhaus* and *Scriven Brothers & Co. v. Hindley & Co.*, because, in those cases, it was impossible for the Court to impute any definite agreements to the parties.

In *Raffles v. Wichelhaus*, the Court had no more reason to find that both parties had manifested an intention to deal in cotton shipped on the "Peerless" sailing in October than to deal with cotton shipped in the "Peerless" sailing in December. In *Scriven Brothers & Co. v. Hindley & Co.*, there was no reason to find that both parties had manifested an intention to buy and sell tow. The purchaser had manifested an intention to buy hemp, whereas the auctioneer had put tow up for sale.

By refusing to deliver any steel from the bulk lot to the plaintiff, Commercial has clearly breached its contract for the sale of such bulk lot to the plaintiff. It remains to assess the damages suffered by the plaintiff because of such breach of contract. ...

There will be judgment for the plaintiff against Commercial for $16,436. The plaintiff is also entitled to recover its costs of the action from Commercial.

Caldarone Auctions acted throughout within the scope of its authority as agent for Commercial. The action against Caldarone Auctions will be dismissed with costs, but the costs recovered by Caldarone Auctions from the plaintiff will be added to the costs to be recovered by the plaintiff from Commercial.

The third party proceedings by Commercial against Caldarone Auctions and by Caldarone Auctions against Commercial will be dismissed without costs.

Judgment for plaintiff.

HENKEL V PAPE
(1870), LR 6 Ex 7

Declaration for goods bargained and sold, and for goods sold and delivered.

Pleas, first, except as to £7 never indebted; and, secondly, as to £7, payment into Court. The plaintiffs accepted the money paid into Court, and joined issue on the first plea.

The plaintiffs are gun manufacturers in London and Birmingham, and the defendant is a gun-maker at Newcastle-upon-Tyne. On the 4th of June, 1870, the plaintiffs received from the defendant the following letter: "Send sample, Snider, with sword-bayonet, forward immediately. I can fix an order for fifty, I think, and it may lead to many large orders. Can you do them at 34s. net cash on delivery, so as to secure the order? I shall have to cut very fine, and several will be in for it." In reply the plaintiffs wrote: "We have forwarded you this day sample Snider, with sword-bayonet. We cannot possibly do them for less than 35s. net cash." With this letter the sample was sent. On the 7th of June the plaintiffs received the following telegram purporting to come from the defendant: "Send by mail immediately *the* Snider rifles same as pattern. Must be here in the morning. Ship sails then." The plaintiffs on receipt of this communication sent fifty rifles to the defendant. On the 9th of June they received the following letter from him. "I am surprised that you sent fifty instead of three rifles. The telegram was to send three." In fact, the clerk who sent the telegraph message had by mistake telegraphed the word "the" instead of "three." The defendant had written "three," and not "the," on the message paper. Under these circumstances the plaintiffs insisted on the defendant accepting the fifty rifles sent, but the defendant declined to take more than three. This action was then brought. The defendant paid a sum into court sufficient to cover the price of three rifles and their carriage. He denied his liability as to the residue of the plaintiffs' claim, contending that he could not be made responsible for the mistake of the telegraph clerk.

The cause was tried before Blackburn J., at the Surrey Summer Assizes, 1870, when a verdict was directed for the defendant, with leave to move to enter a verdict for the plaintiffs for the invoice price of the remaining forty-seven rifles.

H. Thompson Chitty moved accordingly: The telegraph clerk was the defendant's agent to transmit the message, and the defendant is responsible for the mistake in the transmission. *Chitty on Contracts*, 6th ed., p. 197. There is no privity between the plaintiffs and the telegraph clerk, nor can they proceed against the Post-Office, his employers: *Playford v. United Kingdom Telegraph Company*, L.P. 4 Q.B. 706. Their right remedy is against the defendant. Suppose in a letter written by himself he had made the mistake, he would clearly have been liable; and in the transmission of each particular message the telegraph clerk is the agent of the sender. Upon the sender therefore must rest the responsibility of any error committed by the agent in the course of his employment.

KELLY CB: We are of opinion that in this case there should be no rule. The question is whether the defendant has entered into a contract to purchase fifty rifles, and there is no doubt he might have bound himself either by letter or a telegraphic message. But the Post-office authorities are only agents to transmit messages in the terms in which the senders deliver them. They have no authority to do more. Now in this case the evidence is that the defendant agreed to take three rifles, and three only, and he authorized the telegraph clerk to send a message to that and to no other effect. That being so, there was no contract between the plaintiffs and defendant for the purchase of fifty rifles. The defendant cannot be made responsible because the telegraph clerk made a mistake in the transmission of the message. There was no contract between the parties such as the plaintiffs rely on. The verdict therefore ought to stand.

[Bramwell, Piggott, and Cleasby BB concurred. Rule refused.]

QUESTIONS

Suppose A writes an offer to buy 60 rifles, which B accepts. A intended to write 6. Is there a contract? A dictates a letter to his secretary offering to buy 6 rifles. The secretary takes it down as 60. A signs the letter without reading it over. B accepts. Is there a contract? A, after dictating, tells his secretary to sign the letter and mail it, and B accepts. Is there a contract? In *Henkel v Pape* was there a contract for 3 rifles? Suppose the plaintiff were unwilling to sell 3 at the price quoted. Was any offer for 3 communicated to him?

SMITH V HUGHES
(1871), LR 6 QB 597

[The plaintiff, a farmer, took a sample of some oats to Hughes, the manager of the defendant, who was an owner and trainer of horses. The plaintiff claimed to have said "I have some good oats for sale" and when Hughes replied "I am always a buyer of good oats," offered 40 to 50 quarters at 35s. a quarter. Hughes took away a sample, and later wrote to say that he would take the oats at 34s. and the plaintiff sent him 16 quarters, which Hughes complained were *new* oats. The plaintiff admitted they were and denied that he had any old oats. Hughes claimed that he had replied to the plaintiff, "I am always a buyer of good *old* oats," and that the plaintiff had replied, "I have some good old oats for sale." Hughes insisted that the plaintiff take the oats back. At the trial the judge put two questions to the jury for their consideration: Was the word "old" used by the plaintiff or the defendant? If so, they must find for the defendant. If the word "old" was not used, were they of the opinion that the plaintiff believed that Hughes believed, or was under the impression, that he was contracting for the purchase of old oats? If so, they must find for the defendant; otherwise, for the plaintiff. The jury did not answer the question specifically, but found a verdict for the defendant. On appeal the question was whether the direction was correct.]

COCKBURN CJ: ... It is to be regretted that the jury were not required to give specific answers to the questions so left to them. For, it is quite possible that their verdict may have been given for the defendant on the first ground; in which case there could, I think, be no doubt as to the propriety of the judge's direction; whereas now, as it is possible that the verdict of the jury—or at all events of some of them—may have proceeded on the second ground, we are called upon to consider and decide whether the ruling of the learned judge with reference to the second question was right.

For this purpose we must assume that nothing was said on the subject of the defendant's manager desiring to buy old oats, nor of the oats having been said to be old; while on the other hand, we must assume that the defendant's manager believed the oats to be old oats, and that the plaintiff was conscious of the existence of such belief, but did nothing, directly or indirectly, to bring it about, simply offering his oats and exhibiting his sample, remaining perfectly passive as to what was passing in the mind of the other party. The question is whether, under such circumstances, the passive acquiescence of the seller in the self-deception of the buyer will entitle the latter to avoid the contract. I am of opinion that it will not. ...

I take the true rule to be, that where a specific article is offered for sale, without express warranty, or without circumstances from which the law will imply a warranty—as where, for instance, an article is ordered for a specific purpose—and the buyer has full opportunity of inspecting and forming his own judgment, if he chooses to act on his own judgment, the rule *caveat emptor* applies. If he gets the article he contracted to buy, and that article corresponds with what it was sold as, he gets all he.is entitled to, and is bound by the contract. Here the defendant agreed to buy a specific parcel of oats. The oats were what they were sold as, namely, good oats according to the sample. The buyer persuaded himself they were old oats, when they were not so; but the seller neither said nor did anything to contribute to his deception. He has himself to blame. The question is not what a man of scrupulous morality or nice honour would do under such circumstances. The case put of the purchase of an estate, in which there is a mine under the surface, but the fact is unknown to the seller, is one in which a man of tender conscience or high honour would be unwilling to take advantage of the ignorance of the seller; but there can be no doubt that the contract for the sale of the estate would be binding. ...

Now, in this case, there was plainly no legal obligation in the plaintiff in the first instance to state whether the oats were new or old. He offered them for sale according to the sample, as he had a perfect right to do, and gave the buyer the fullest opportunity of inspecting the sample, which, practically, was equivalent to an inspection of the oats themselves. What, then, was there to create any trust or confidence between the parties, so as to make it incumbent on the plaintiff to communicate the fact that the oats were not, as the defendant assumed them to be, old oats? If, indeed, the buyer, instead of acting on his own opinion, had asked the question whether the oats were old or new or had said anything which intimated his understanding that the seller was selling the oats as old oats, the case would have been wholly different; or even if he had said anything which shewed that he was not acting on his own inspection and judgment, but assumed as the foundation of the contract that the oats were old, the silence of the seller, as a means of misleading him, might have amounted to a fraudulent concealment, such as would have entitled the buyer to avoid the contract. Here, however, nothing of the sort occurs. The buyer in no way refers to the seller, but acts entirely on his own judgment. ...

In the case before us it must be taken that, as the defendant, on a portion of the oats being delivered, was able by inspection to ascertain that they were new oats, his manager might, by due inspection of the sample, have arrived at the same result. The case is, therefore, one of the sale and purchase of a specific article after inspection by the buyer. Under these circumstances the rule *caveat emptor* clearly applies; more especially as this cannot be put as a case of latent defect, but simply one in which the seller did not make known to the buyer a circumstance affecting the quality of the thing sold. The oats in question were in no sense defective, on the contrary they were good oats, and all that can be said is that they had not acquired the quality which greater age would have given them. There is not, so far as I am aware, any authority for the position that a vendor who submits the subject matter of sale to the inspection of the vendee, is bound to state circumstances which may tend to detract from the estimate which the buyer may injudiciously have formed of its value. Even the civil law, and the foreign law, founded upon it, which require that the seller shall answer for latent defects, have never gone the length of saying that, so long as the thing sold answers to the description under which it is sold, the seller is bound to disabuse the buyer as to any exaggerated estimate of its value.

It only remains to deal with an argument which was pressed upon us, that the defendant in the present case intended to buy old oats, and the plaintiff to sell new, so that the two minds were not *ad idem*; and that consequently there was no contract. This argument proceeds on the fallacy of confounding what was merely a motive operating on the buyer to induce him to buy with one of the essential conditions of the contract. Both parties were agreed as to the sale and purchase of this particular parcel of oats. The defendant believed the oats to be old, and was thus induced to agree to buy them, but he omitted to make their age a condition of the contract. All that can be said is, that the two minds were not *ad idem* as to the age of the oats; they certainly were *ad idem* as to the sale and purchase of them. Suppose a person to buy a horse without warranty, believing him to be sound, and the horse turns out unsound could it be contended that it would be open to him to say that, as he had intended to buy a sound horse, and the seller to sell him an unsound one, the contract was void, because the seller must have known from the price the buyer was willing to give, or from his general habits as a buyer of horses, that he thought the horse was sound? The cases are exactly parallel.

The result is that, in my opinion, the learned judge of the county court was wrong in leaving the second question to the jury, and that, consequently, the case must go down to a new trial.

BLACKBURN J: In this case I agree that on the sale of a specific article, unless there be a warranty making it part of the bargain that it possesses some particular quality, the purchaser must take the article he has bought though it does not possess that quality. And I agree that even if the vendor was aware that the purchaser thought that the article possessed that quality, and would not have entered into the contract unless he had so thought, still the purchaser is bound, unless the vendor was guilty of some fraud or deceit upon him, and that a mere abstinence from disabusing the purchaser of that impression is not fraud or deceit; for, whatever may be the case in a court of morals, there is no legal obligation on the vendor to inform the purchaser that he is under a mistake, not induced by the act of the vendor. And I also agree that where a specific lot of goods are sold by a sample, which the purchaser inspects instead of the bulk, the law is exactly the same, if the sample truly represents the bulk; though, as it is more probable that the purchaser in such a case would ask for some further warranty, slighter evidence would suffice to prove that, in fact, it was intended there should be such a warranty. On this part of the case I have nothing to add to what the Lord Chief Justice has stated.

But I have more difficulty about the second point raised in the case. I apprehend that if one of the parties intends to make a contract on one set of terms, and the other intends to make a contract on another set of terms, or, as it is sometimes expressed, if the parties are not ad idem, there is no contract, unless the circumstances are such as to preclude one of the parties from denying that he has agreed to the terms of the other. The rule of law is that stated in *Freeman v. Cooke* [(1848), 2 Ex. 654, 154 E.R. 652]. If, whatever a man's real intention may be, he so conducts himself that a reasonable man would believe that he was assenting to the terms proposed by the other party, and that other party upon that belief enters into the contract with him, the man thus conducting himself would be equally bound as if he had intended to agree to the other party's terms.

The jury were directed that, if they believed the word "old" was used, they should find for the defendant—and this was right; for if that was the case it is obvious that neither did the defendant intend to enter into a contract on the plaintiff's terms, that is, to buy his parcel of oats without any stipulation as to their quality; nor could the plaintiff have been led to believe he was intending to do so.

But the second direction raises the difficulty. I think that, if from that direction the jury would understand that they were first to consider whether they were satisfied that the defendant intended to buy this parcel of oats on the terms that it was part of his contract with the plaintiff that they were old oats, so as to have the warranty of the plaintiff to that effect, they were properly told that, if that was so, the defendant could not be bound to a contract without any warranty unless the plaintiff was misled. But I doubt whether the direction would bring to the minds of the jury the distinction between agreeing to take the oats under the belief that they were old, and agreeing to take the oats under the belief that the plaintiff contracted that they were old.

The difference is the same as that between buying a horse believed to be sound, and buying one believed to be warranted sound; but I doubt if it was made obvious to the jury, and I doubt this the more because I do not see much evidence to justify a finding for the defendant on this latter ground if the word "old" was not used. There may have been more evidence than is stated in the case; and the demeanour of the witness may have strengthened the impression produced by the evidence there was; but it does not seem a very satisfactory verdict if it proceeded on this latter ground. I agree, therefore, in the result that there should be a new trial.

HANNEN J: ... It is essential to the creation of a contract that both parties should agree to the same thing in the same sense. Thus, if two persons enter into an apparent contract concerning a particular person or ship, and it turns out that each of them, misled by a similarity of name, had a different person or ship in his mind, no contract would exist between them: *Raffles v. Wichelhaus*.

But one of the parties to an apparent contract may, by his own fault, be precluded from setting up that he had entered into it in a different sense to that in which it was understood by the other party. Thus in the case of a sale by sample where the vendor, by mistake, exhibited a wrong sample, it was held that the contract was not avoided by this error of the vendor: *Scott v. Littledale*.

But if in the last-mentioned case the purchaser, in the course of the negotiations preliminary to the contract, had discovered that the vendor was under a misapprehension as to the sample he was offering, the vendor would have been entitled to shew that he had not intended to enter into the contract by which the purchaser sought to bind him. The rule of law applicable to such a case is a corollary from the rule of morality which Mr. Pollock cited from Paley [*Paley's Moral and Political Philosophy*, book III, ch 5], that a promise is to be performed "in that sense in which the promiser apprehended at the time the promisee received it," and may be thus expressed: "The promiser is not bound to fulfil a promise in a sense in which the promisee knew at the time the promiser did not intend it." And in considering the question, in what sense a promisee is entitled to enforce a promise, it matters not in what way the knowledge of the meaning in which the promiser made it is brought to the mind of the promisee, whether by express words, or by conduct, or previous dealings, or other circumstances. If by any means he knows that there was no real agreement between him and the promiser, he is not entitled to insist that the promise shall be fulfilled in a sense to which the mind of the promiser did not assent.

If, therefore, in the present case, the plaintiff knew that the defendant, in dealing with him for oats, did so on the assumption that the plaintiff was contracting to sell him old oats, he was aware that the defendant apprehended the contract in a different sense to that in which he meant it, and he is thereby deprived of the right to insist that the defendant shall be bound by that which was only the apparent, and not the real bargain.

This was the question which the learned judge intended to leave to the jury; as I have already said, I do not think it was incorrect in its terms, but I think that it was likely to be misunderstood by the jury. The jury was asked "whether they were of opinion, on the whole of the evidence, that the plaintiff believed the defendant to believe, or to be under the impression that he was contracting for the purchase of old oats? If so, there would be a verdict for the defendant." The jury may have understood this to mean that, if the plaintiff believed the defendant to believe that he was buying old oats, the defendant would be entitled to the verdict, but a belief on the part of the plaintiff that the defendant was making a contract to buy the oats, of which he offered him a sample, under a mistaken belief that they were old, would not relieve the defendant from liability unless his mistaken belief were induced by some misrepresentation of the plaintiff, or concealment by him of the fact which it became his duty to communicate. In order to relieve the defendant it was necessary that the jury should find not merely that the plaintiff believed the defendant to believe that he was buying old oats, but that he believed the defendant to believe that he, the plaintiff, was contracting to sell old oats.

I am the more disposed to think the jury did not understand the question in this last sense because I can find very little, if any, evidence to support a finding upon it in favour of the defendant. It may be assumed that the defendant believed the oats were old, and it may be suspected that the plaintiff thought he so believed, but the only evidence from which it can be inferred that the plaintiff believed that the defendant thought that the plaintiff was making it a term of the contract that the oats were old is that the defendant was a trainer, and that trainers, as a rule, use old oats and that the price given was high for new oats, and more than a prudent man would have given.

Having regard to the admitted fact that the defendant bought the oats after two days' detention of the sample, I think that the evidence was not sufficient to justify the jury in answering the question put to them in the defendant's favour, if they rightly understood it; and I therefore think there should be a new trial.

NOTES AND PROBLEMS

1. In *Bell v Lever Brothers Ltd*, [1932] AC 161 (HL), Lord Atkin states:

The Court [in *Smith v Hughes*] ordered a new trial. It is not quite clear whether they considered that if the defendant's contention was correct, the parties were not *ad idem* or there was a contractual condition that the oats were old oats. In either case the defendant would succeed in defeating the claim.

In these cases I am inclined to think that the true analysis is that there is a contract, but that the one party is not able to supply the very thing whether goods or services that the other party contracted to take; and therefore the contract is unenforceable by the one if executory, while if executed the other can recover money paid on the ground of failure of consideration.

2. More recently, in *Statoil ASA v Louis Dreyfus Energy Services LP*, [2008] EWHC 2257 (Comm), Mr. Justice Aikens states:

However, if one party has made a mistake about a fact on which he bases his decision to enter into the contract, but that fact does not form a term of the contract itself, then, even if the other party knows that the first is mistaken as to this fact, the contract will be binding. That was the effect of the decision of the Court of Queen's Bench, on appeal from the County Court, in *Smith v Hughes* ... . The correctness of that decision and the analysis in it has never been doubted.

Mr. Justice Aikens went on to determine that there was no jurisdiction in equity to render a contract voidable for unilateral mistake, especially in light of *Great Peace Shipping Ltd v Tsavliris Salvage (International) Ltd*, [2002] 4 All ER 689 (CA), excerpted and commented on below.

3. Able has two racehorses for sale by auction: "Pegasus" worth $10,000, described in the auction catalogue as "lot 1," and "Glanders" worth $500 and described as "lot 2." By mistake the sale numbers attached to the horses' hips are interchanged and "Glanders" is led in as "lot 1" and knocked down to Baker for $8,000. "Pegasus" is led in as "lot 2" to Charlie for $500. Baker and Charlie pay the prices and take delivery respectively of "Glanders" and "Pegasus." The mistake comes to light the next day. What is the legal position of the three parties? See *Diamond v British Columbia Thoroughbred Breeders' Society* (1965), 52 DLR (2d) 146 (BCSC).

4. Able agreed to sell and Baker agreed to buy a house at "300 Spadina" for $50,000. Able's house was at 300 Spadina Avenue, but Baker mistakenly assumed that it was at 300 Spadina Road and had inspected the outside of that house. Able's house is worth $25,000; 300 Spadina Road is worth $75,000. Upon discovering his error, Baker refused to buy Able's house. Able brings an action for specific performance, and Baker counterclaims for damages.

The house was accurately described in the document as 300 Spadina Avenue, but Baker mistakenly thought it was the house at 300 Spadina Road. During the course of negotiations Baker had said that he was pleased that the new subway would be so close. The new subway is close to 300 Spadina Road but not to 300 Spadina Avenue. Able wondered at the time what Baker meant but then dismissed the matter from his mind. See generally on mistake as to contractual terms Waddams, ch 11; McCamus, ch 13; MacDougall at 223-28.

V. MISTAKE IN ASSUMPTIONS

ANTHONY DUGGAN, "SILENCE AS MISLEADING CONDUCT: AN ECONOMIC ANALYSIS"
in M Richardson & P Williams, *The Law and the Market*
(Sydney: Federation Press, 1995) at 207-21

ECONOMIC ANALYSIS

According to the economic approach, contractual nondisclosure is subject to two competing efficiency considerations, and it is the interplay between them that shapes the pattern of the case law. These considerations are:

1. the desirability of preventing mistakes in the contracting process; and
2. the need to preserve incentives for the discovery and exploitation of socially useful information. ...

THE ECONOMIC ISSUES

Preventing mistakes. In the normal case, a contract can be assumed to make both parties better off (otherwise at least one of them would not have transacted). For example, if A sells a painting to B for $15,000, the indications are that A values the money more highly than the painting, whereas B's preferences are the reverse. One result of contracting is therefore to satisfy each party's individual preferences. Another result is an improved resource allocation (the movement of scarce resources to more highly valued uses), and this is a social benefit. However, these outcomes depend on both parties being fully informed, at the time of the contract negotiations, about all material aspects of the transaction. If one party is mistaken, the result may be a net social loss (or misallocation of resources). Assume, for example, that A sells the painting to B for $15,000 because she mistakenly thinks it is a copy. If she had known that the painting was an original, she would not have been prepared to sell it for less than $150,000. B knows the truth, but he would have been prepared to pay no more than $50,000. The contract therefore results in a gain to B of $35,000 ($50,000 − $15,000), but a loss to A of $135,000 ($150,000 − $15,000). The net result is a loss of $100,000 ($135,000 − $35,000), and this can be counted as the social cost of A's mistake.

Accordingly, it might be thought that the appropriate thing for the courts to do is set aside contracts routinely whenever [a] mistake is established. However, while such a rule might be beneficial in correcting past mistakes, it would also have a perverse effect on the incentives confronting parties in the future. It would be likely to result in parties taking too little care in their own interests at the time of contracting, because they will be secure in the knowledge that if they make a mistake, a court will correct it for them later (given that the courts are publicly subsidised, this outcome would represent an externalisation of the costs of contracting). Conversely, it may also result in one party taking excessive precautions to ensure that the other is not mistaken (for fear that otherwise a court will set the contract aside). Depending on which of these influences predominates, the end result will be either too much litigation or too much disclosure.

Given the costs of litigation, a policy which focuses on the prevention of mistakes will nearly always be preferable to one that concentrates on their correction. (This ceases to be true only at the point where the cost of additional precautions begins to exceed the savings from any further reduction in the risk of a mistake occurring.) Precautions against the making of a mistake might be taken by the party who would otherwise end up being disadvantaged (for example, in the case of a pricing error, by taking more care to read the contract before signing it or, in the case of a valuation error, by the mistaken party having an appraisal made of the contract subject-matter before transacting). Alternatively, precautions might be taken by the party who would otherwise end up being advantaged (by disclosing what the other party needs to know). From an economic perspective, the choice between the two alternatives depends on which is the cheaper. This suggests that an appropriate rule would be one which confronts the lowest cost information gatherer with the appropriate incentive to take the necessary action. In cases where the mistaken party could have taken the precautions more cheaply, then the contract should be allowed to stand, despite the mistake. In other cases, there should be a rule making the non-mistaken party liable for non-disclosure. Where one party (B) knows that the other party (A) is mistaken then, other things being equal, it will usually be cheaper to require B to disclose than to leave A to discover the mistake for herself and then make the necessary correction.

Creating incentives to discovery. There is a social benefit in the generation of information concerning the attributes of assets. Such information is relevant to the uses to which an asset can be put. If the information is not available, there is a risk that the asset will be allocated to a use that is less socially valuable than it might be. For example, if there is an undiscovered oil deposit lying beneath a farm then, for as long as the information is unavailable, the land is likely to remain devoted to farming purposes rather than oil production.

The problem is that information is costly to produce, while the gains from its production are difficult to capture. This is because, typically, the exploitation of information will result in its disclosure, but once it is disclosed there is nothing to prevent others from using it as well. This "public goods" character of information acts as a natural disincentive to its production. Why would someone invest resources in search if there is no way of appropriating the gains from discovery? To return to the example of the oil-rich farmland, oil exploration is an expensive undertaking. A prospector is unlikely to incur the cost unless assured of the gains from discovery. However, once news of the oil deposit gets out, there can be no such assurance (assuming private ownership of minerals and the like). The farmer will be likely to insist on a higher sale price for the land (or, alternatively, will offer rights of entry to the highest bidder), with a view to securing as large a share as possible of the new-found wealth. The prospect of this occurring will act as a deterrent to exploration in the first place, so that the oil deposit may remain undiscovered. A solution is to allow the successful searcher to trade on the information without disclosing it to the other contracting party. If the law permits the prospector to purchase the farm without telling the farmer about the existence of the oil deposit, then the gains from exploration and production will be secure, to the encouragement of both activities.

Synthesis. Of course, with full information, the farmer would be likely to decide differently. She may not agree to sell at all or, alternatively, she might insist on a substantially higher price. A rule favouring non-disclosure does nothing to ensure that mistaken contracting decisions will be prevented in future, and in this respect it involves a misallocation of resources in the sense just mentioned. However, there would be a greater misallocation if disclosure was required because then it is likely that the information would not be produced at all. In that event, the individual farmer might not be any worse off (she would still have her farm), but society as a whole would be deprived of the oil that the land is capable of yielding, and constrained to take the farm produce instead (a second-best alternative). There is a "powerful tension" between the public interest in the free use of information once it is in existence; and the creation of new information for future use (Easterbrook, 1981, p. 313). As a general rule, longer-run considerations require that the tension be resolved in favour of the second because the alternative implies that, while information might be more readily available, there would be less produced (Easterbrook, p. 313).

On the other hand, not all information concerning asset attributes is socially valuable in the sense that its discovery is likely to be wealth-increasing. Information concerning the existence of an oil deposit lying beneath a farm is socially valuable for the reasons that have just been discussed. By contrast, information concerning the volume of oil contained in a deposit which has already been discovered is not socially valuable unless it affects total production or extraction costs. It merely creates a bargaining advantage that can be used to redistribute wealth in favour of the knowledgeable party (Shavell, 1991, pp. 1, 2; drawing on Hirshleifer, 1971). Information that the oil deposit exists is vital to whether it is extracted. By contrast, where both parties already know that the oil deposit exists, the only matter that will turn on information about its size is how much the farmer ends up receiving for the land (Cooter and Ulen, 1988, p. 259). Information of the first kind comprises "productive facts," whereas information of the second kind comprises "redistributive facts" (Cooter and Ulen, p. 259). Incentives are required for the discovery of productive facts, but not for the discovery of purely redistributive facts. On the contrary, to allow speculative trading on the basis of purely redistributive facts would induce wasteful expenditure in the search for them. It would also induce (wasteful) defensive expenditure by parties seeking to avoid the loss of their wealth to more knowledgeable people (Cooter and Ulen, p. 259). These considerations suggest that in a case involving purely redistributive facts, disclosure should be required. Mistake prevention considerations will usually point in the same direction. ...

BUYER AND SELLER NON-DISCLOSURE

Where a valuation error is made by the seller, the court will not intervene in the absence of special circumstances. By contrast, where a valuation error is made by the buyer, the court will often be at pains to discover a misrepresentation or misleading conduct as a basis for setting the contract aside. Why are buyer and seller non-disclosure treated differently?

The conventional response is to say that mere passive silence is not actionable, but since it is more difficult for a seller to behave passively than it is for a buyer the consequence is that, in practice, a seller is less likely to escape liability. However, this rationalisation breaks down in the face of the "reasonable expectations" test. This makes the defendant's liability turn on the court's view as to whether or not it was reasonable for the plaintiff to expect disclosure. The more liberal the court's view, the closer the "reasonable expectations" test comes to a general rule that seller non-disclosure is actionable. There is no corresponding tension in the area of buyer non-disclosure. This raises the possibility that the court's willingness in cases of seller non-disclosure to find that the plaintiff had a reasonable expectation of disclosure is not so much a cause as a consequence of the desired outcome (Birmingham, 1988, p. 268).

The economic explanation is sounder. It runs as follows. There is a critical difference between the dynamics of the buyer and seller non-disclosure cases. A buyer will have an incentive to withhold favourable information (good news) with a view to keeping the price down, whereas the seller will want to disclose favourable information but withhold unfavourable information (bad news), in order to keep the price up (Shavell, 1991, p. 29). In both cases, the effect of a disclosure requirement will be to reduce the likelihood of a trade occurring. This may be a socially undesirable outcome where it is the buyer who is the knowledgeable party and the undisclosed good news comprises productive facts. By contrast, where the knowledgeable party is the seller (and the information is bad news), there is a social benefit in the trade not going ahead. If the trade does proceed, there is a risk that the buyer will incur expenditure before discovering the true facts. Furthermore, upon discovering the truth, the buyer will probably want to dispose of the asset, and this will entail transactions costs. The likely end result is a reversion to at least an approximation of the status quo, with (wasted) costs being incurred along the way. Therefore, sellers should be required to disclose. A disclosure requirement is unlikely to inhibit the acquisition by sellers of productive facts relating to assets for sale. There are all sorts of reasons why it will be in their interest to have this information, apart from the desire (if any) to obtain an advantage over potential purchasers. So, for example, the private owner of a painting may decide to have it appraised for insurance purposes or out of curiosity, while an art dealer may do so in order to avoid the risk of underselling the item. ...

MISREPRESENTATION AND NON-DISCLOSURE

Introduction. The distinction between active and passive behaviour is central to the law governing liability for non-disclosure, and this has been true since ancient times ("*aliud est celare, aliud tacere*"). Accordingly, to tell a lie is nearly always actionable, while merely to withhold information usually is not. On the other hand, there is a difference between *suppressio veri* and *suggestio falsi*, and the courts will intervene in the latter case. Non-disclosure which implies a falsehood is treated on the same footing as express misrepresentation, though the willingness of the courts to make this kind of implication is greater in cases of seller than buyer non-disclosure.

The reasons for the asymmetry between cases of buyer and seller non-disclosure have already been discussed, but it remains to consider why the courts discriminate between wilful misrepresentation and wilful non-disclosure. Given that the consequences to the uninformed party are the same in either case, what makes activity so much worse than passivity in this context? As before, the economic analysis turns on two sets of considerations, namely: the desirability of preventing mistakes in the contracting process; and the need to preserve incentives for productive activity.

Preventing mistakes. As explained earlier, a mistaken contracting decision is likely to result in a misallocation of resources, on the basis that the loss to the mistaken party (A) exceeds the gain to the knowledgeable party (B) ... . However, it does not follow that courts should intervene routinely whenever mistake is established, because the effect of this would be to encourage contracting parties in future to take insufficient precautions against their own mistakes, and excessive precautions against the other party's mistakes. Intervention is only warranted where B is the lowest cost information gatherer. This condition is most likely to be met where B knows of A's mistake, because in these circumstances it would usually be cheaper for B to correct the mistake than for A to discover that she is mistaken, and then make her own correction. ...

Where A's mistake is deliberately induced by B (where B lies to A), the case for intervention is even stronger. In these circumstances, B will always be the party best placed to take precautions at lowest cost. All he has to do is to refrain from lying, and this is a socially costless option (Darby and Karni, 1973, p. 83). By contrast, if B's lie was not actionable, A would be induced to take precautions against mistake, and these will always entail some costs. ...

Creating incentives to discovery. Information is valuable because it serves to move resources to more productive uses. Accordingly, there is a social benefit in encouraging the discovery and exploitation of information and this must be taken into account when deciding whether the law should require disclosure. Is there any corresponding social value in misinformation? The conventional response to this question is, "no." Misinformation is likely to result in the allocation of assets to lower valued uses ... and it lessens the efficiency of the market as an allocative mechanism because it undermines the signalling function of price movements. ...

Levmore takes a contrary view. He argues that there are cases where lying is socially productive, and that there is room for a policy of "optimal dishonesty." ... The law does not reflect a policy of optimal dishonesty. ... If dishonesty was allowed contracting parties would be induced to invest in measures to protect themselves from being defrauded. The taking of these precautions would require tricksters to spend resources in devising more ingenious methods of deception, leading in turn to the adoption of more elaborate precautions. ... These precaution and deception costs are totally wasteful from a social viewpoint. Moreover, there would be spillover effects in the form of a lessening of confidence in the contract system overall. People would become more reluctant to transact, with adverse implications for the socially beneficial movement of resources. In short, the costs of a policy favouring dishonesty (even selectively) would be likely to exceed the benefits.

NOTE

For an economic analysis on the doctrines of mutual and unilateral mistake and information that was or was not communicated prior to contracting, see Anthony T Kronman, "Mistake, Disclosure, Information, and the Law of Contracts" (1978) 7 J Legal Stud 1. See, further, Anthony Duggan, Michael Bryan & Frances Hanks, *Contractual Non-Disclosure* (Melbourne:

Longman Professional, 1994); Melvin A Eisenberg, "Disclosure in Contract Law" (2003) 91 Cal L Rev 1645; "Mistake in Contract Law" (2003) 91 Cal L Rev 1573; and Richard Craswell, "Taking Information Seriously: Misrepresentation and Nondisclosure in Contract Law and Elsewhere" (2006) 92 Va L Rev 565. For a critical analysis of Eisenberg, see James Gordley, "Mistake in Contract Formation" (2004) 52 Am J Comp L 433.

LAIDLAW V ORGAN
15 US (2 Wheat) 178 (1817)

Organ sued Laidlaw & Co., New Orleans merchants, to recover possession of 111 hogsheads of tobacco, alleged to have been wrongfully taken from him by Laidlaw. Organ introduced in evidence a written memorandum dated February 18, 1815, stating that he had bought 111 hogsheads of tobacco from Laidlaw & Co. for $7,544.69. Laidlaw denied liability on the ground that the contract had been induced by fraud. Laidlaw claimed that Organ had learned of the Treaty of Ghent ending the War of 1812, and that the British blockade of New Orleans would be lifted, before Laidlaw knew. When Laidlaw had asked Organ if he knew of anything which would increase the value of the tobacco, Organ had remained silent. There was no evidence that Organ said anything to lead Laidlaw to believe that peace did not exist. The contract was completed, and Laidlaw delivered the tobacco after the news became public. The value of the tobacco then rose between 30 and 50 percent. Laidlaw retook possession of the tobacco. At trial the jury was instructed to find for Organ, the plaintiff (defendant in error), which it did.

C.J. INGERSOLL (for the plaintiffs in error): The first question is, whether the sale, under the circumstances of the case, was a valid sale; whether fraud, which vitiates every contract, must be proved, by the communication of positive misinformation, or by withholding information when asked. Suppression of material circumstances, within the knowledge of the vendee, and not accessible to the vendor, is equivalent to fraud, and vitiates the contract. Pothier, in discussing this subject, adopts the distinction of the forum of conscience, and the forum of law; but he admits that *fides est servanda*. The parties treated on an unequal footing, as the one party had received intelligence of the peace of Ghent, at the time of the contract, and the other had not. This news was unexpected, even at Washington, much more at New Orleans, the recent scene of the most sanguinary operations of the war. In answer to the question, whether there was any news calculated to enhance the price of the article, the vendee was silent. This reserve, when such a question was asked, was equivalent to a false answer, and as much calculated to deceive as the communication of the most fabulous intelligence. Though the plaintiffs in error, after they heard the news of peace, still went on, in ignorance of their legal rights, to complete the contract, equity will protect them. ...

KEY (contra): ... The only real question in the cause is, whether the sale was invalid, because the vendee did not communicate information which he received precisely as the vendor might have got it, had he been equally diligent or equally fortunate? And, surely, on this question, there can be no doubt. Even if the vendor had been entitled to the disclosure, he waived it, by not insisting on an answer to his question; and the silence of the vendee might as well have been interpreted into an affirmative as a negative answer. But, on principle, he was not bound to disclose. Even admitting that his conduct was unlawful, in foro conscientiae, does that prove that it was so, in the civil forum? Human laws are imperfect in this respect, and the sphere of morality is more extensive than the limits of civil jurisdiction. The maxim of caveat emptor could never have crept into the law, if the province of ethics had been co-extensive with it. There was, in the present case, no circumvention or manoeuvre practised by the vendee, unless rising earlier in the morning, and obtaining, by superior diligence and alertness, that intelligence by which the price of commodities was regulated, be such. It is a romantic equality that is contended for on the other side. Parties never can be precisely equal in knowledge, either of facts or of the inferences from such facts, and both must concur, in order to satisfy the rule contended for. The absence of all authority in England and the United States, both great commercial countries, speaks volumes against the reasonableness and practicability of such a rule.

C.J. INGERSOLL (in reply): Though the record may not show that anything tending to mislead, by positive assertion, was said by the vendee, in answer to the question proposed by [the seller's representative], yet it is a case of manoeuvre; of mental reservation; of circumvention. The information was monopolized by the messengers from the British fleet, and not imparted to the public at large, until it was too late for the vendor to save himself. The rule of law and of ethics is the same. It is not a romantic, but a practical and legal rule of equality and good faith, that is proposed to be applied. ...

MARSHALL CH J (for the court): The question in this case is, whether the intelligence of extrinsic circumstances, which might influence the price of the commodity, and which was exclusively within the knowledge of the vendee, ought to have been communicated by him to the vendor. The court is of opinion that he was not bound to communicate it. It would be difficult to circumscribe the contrary doctrine within proper limits; where the means of intelligence are equally accessible to both parties. But at the same time, each party must take care not to say or do anything tending to impose upon the other. The court thinks that the absolute instruction of the judge was erroneous, and that the question whether any imposition was practiced by the vendee upon the vendor ought to have been submitted to the jury. For these reasons the judgment must be reversed, and the cause remanded to the District Court of Louisiana, with directions to award a venire facias de novo.

Venire de novo awarded.

NOTES AND QUESTIONS

1. In *Bank of BC v Wren Development Ltd* (1973), 38 DLR (3d) 759 (BCSC), Monroe J held that the failure of the plaintiff to disclose material facts was a misrepresentation which induced the defendant Allan to sign the contract.

On June 21, 1971, he [Allan] went to see plaintiff's credit supervisor who told him that Smith had recently made satisfactory arrangements for payment of the company loan and had signed a new guarantee and asked Allan to do likewise, saying it was a routine procedure. Allan inquired of the credit supervisor as to the collateral security (shares) held by the bank and was told by the latter that he did not know particulars thereof but would make an investigation and report later to Allan. Thereupon Allan signed the new form of guarantee. When he did so, he did not know that any of the shares had been released or exchanged by the bank as aforesaid. On the contrary, since he had not been informed of any sale or exchange of shares and because his signature was required on banking transactions entered into by the company, and because neither he nor the company had ever authorized Smith to act as their agent, he felt reasonably certain that the collateral security pledged by the company was still held by the bank. In that mistaken belief he executed and delivered the new guarantee to the plaintiff. ...

Upon the evidence I find that the defendant Allan, when he signed the second guarantee, was misled by the words, acts and conduct of the plaintiff into believing that there had been no change in the collateral securities held by the plaintiff, and otherwise he would not have signed it. In short, there was a unilateral mistake on the part of the defendant Allan which was induced by the misrepresentation of the plaintiff in failing to disclose material facts to him. In those circumstances, the defendant Allan is not liable to the plaintiff upon the second personal guarantee.

Did the "words, acts and conduct of the plaintiff" really amount to a misrepresentation? How does the holding in this case compare with that of *Laidlaw*, where silence in response to a question was held not to be a misrepresentation?

2. American law recognizes an exception to the rule that parties negotiating agreements have no duty to disclose material facts to each other. The American Law Institute, *Restatement of Contracts* (St Paul, Minn: American Law Institute, 1981), s 161(b) recognizes a duty to disclose "where [the representor] knows that disclosure of the fact would correct a mistake of the other party as to a basic assumption on which that party is making the contract and if non-disclosure of the fact amounts to a failure to act in good faith and in accordance with reasonable standards of fair dealing." Canadian common law has not recognized a comparable doctrine, but in a recent decision the Ontario Court of Appeal in *obiter* articulated five factors that would determine when such a duty should be imposed:

(1) a past course of dealing between the parties in which reliance for advice, etc., has been an accepted feature;
(2) the explicit assumption by one party of advisory responsibilities;
(3) the relative positions of the parties, particularly in their access to information and in their understanding of the possible demands of the dealing;
(4) the manner in which the parties were brought together and the expectation that could create in the relying party; and
(5) whether trust and confidence has been knowingly reposed by one party in the other.

978011 Ontario Ltd v Cornell Engineering Co (2001), 198 DLR (4th) 615 (Ont CA), leave to appeal refused (2001), 158 OAC 195n (SCC), additional reasons at (2001), 148 OAC 250 (CA), drawing the factors from P Finn, "The Fiduciary Principle" in T Youdan, ed, *Equity, Fiduciaries and Trusts* (Toronto: Carswell, 1989) 1 at 10-24.

BELL V LEVER BROTHERS LTD
[1932] AC 161 (HL)

Lever Brothers, Ltd., holding practically all the stock of the Niger Company, Limited, entered into an agreement with Bell in 1926 by which the latter was to be employed by Lever Brothers for five years at £8,000 a year, and to act as chairman of the Niger Company. In 1929, in view of the amalgamation of the Niger Company with other companies, Lever Brothers entered into an agreement with Bell on March 19, to pay him £30,000 in satisfaction of all Bell's claims against them. The money was paid and the employment terminated.

Later in the year, Lever Brothers discovered that Bell had been, in 1927, dealing in, and making profits on his own account amounting to perhaps £1,000, in the same materials that the Niger Company dealt in, and had not disclosed these secret profits.

Lever Brothers thereupon brought action claiming the return of the £30,000 paid under the agreement of 1929, alleging fraudulent misrepresentation, and breach of the former employment contracts.

At the trial before Wright J. the jury denied that the agreement of 1929 was induced by fraud, but found that Bell had committed a breach of the employment contract by undertaking the private dealings, and that Lever Brothers were entitled to terminate the employment contract by reason of such breach, and would have terminated such contract had the facts been known. They further found that Lever Brothers did not know of the private dealings in 1929 and would not have entered into the agreement of March 19, 1929, had such facts been known to them.

On these findings Wright J. gave judgment for the plaintiffs, Lever Brothers, stating that the agreement was based on a mutual mistake, which in the language of *Kennedy v. Panama Royal Mail Co.* (1867), L.R. 2 Q.B. 580, went "to the substance ... or root of the matter." The mistake was the existence of the previous service agreement. Bell appealed.

In the Court of Appeal, Scrutton L.J. said, in part: " ... In my opinion, on the facts of the present case the defendants were under an obligation, before and at the time of their negotiation of the contracts to terminate their services to disclose their dealings in breach of their contracts, and the contracts to terminate can be avoided by this non-disclosure. Wright J.'s ground of decision, with which I agree, is sufficient to support his judgment, but I think it could also be supported on the ground of failure to disclose material facts.

"I only desire to add that, in my view, the case of *Kennedy v. Panama etc. Co.* so far as it decides that an innocent misrepresentation, though material, is not a ground for rescission unless it is also fundamental, is no longer law, in view of the fusion of common law and equity by the Judicature Acts, the rule of equity prevailing. Also I reserve liberty to consider the decision in *Seddon v. North Eastern Salt Co.*, [1905] 1 Ch. 326, so far as it decides that executed contracts cannot be rescinded for innocent and material misrepresentation. The appeal must be dismissed with costs." Lawrence and Greer L.JJ. agreed with Scrutton L.J. So Bell appealed again. In the House of Lords, Lords Atkin, Blanesburgh and Thankerton gave reasons for allowing the appeal. Viscount Hailsham and Lord Warrington of Clyffe dissented, taking the view that, in the words of Lord Warrington, "the erroneous assumption on the part of both parties to the agreement that the service contracts were undeterminable except by agreement was of such a fundamental character as to constitute an underlying assumption without which the parties would not have made the contract."

LORD ATKIN: ... Two points present themselves for decision. Was the agreement of March 19, 1929, void by reason of a mutual mistake of Mr. D'Arcy Cooper and Mr. Bell?

Could the agreement of March 19, 1929, be avoided by reason of the failure of Mr. Bell to disclose his misconduct in regard to the cocoa dealings?

My Lords, the rules of law dealing with the effect of mistake on contract appear to be established with reasonable clearness. If mistake operates at all it operates so as to negative or in some cases nullify consent. The parties may be mistaken in the identity of the contracting parties, or in the existence of the subject-matter of the contract. These mistakes may be by one party, or by both, and the legal effect may depend upon the class of mistake above mentioned. Thus a mistaken belief by A, that he is contracting with B, whereas in fact he is contracting with C, will negative consent where it is clear that the intention of A was to contract only with B. So the agreement of A and B to purchase a specific article is void if in fact the article had perished before the date of sale. In this case, though the parties in fact were agreed about the subject-matter, yet a consent to transfer or take delivery of something not existent is deemed useless, [and] the consent is nullified. As codified in the Sale of Goods Act the contract is expressed to be void if the seller was in ignorance of the destruction of the specific chattel. I apprehend that if the seller with knowledge that a chattel was destroyed purported to sell it to a purchaser, the latter might sue for damages for non-delivery though the former could not sue for non-acceptance, but I know of no case where a seller has so committed himself. This is a case where mutual mistake certainly and unilateral mistake by the seller of goods will prevent a contract from arising. Corresponding to mistake as to the existence of the subject-matter is mistake as to title in cases where, unknown to the parties, the buyer is already the owner of that which the seller purports to sell to him. The parties intended to effectuate a transfer of ownership: such a transfer is impossible: the stipulation is naturali ratione inutilis. This is the case of *Cooper v. Phibbs* (1867), L.R. 2 H.L. 149 where A. agreed to take a lease of a fishery from B., though contrary to the belief of both parties at the time. A. was tenant for life of the fishery and B. appears to have had no title at all. To such a case Lord Westbury applied the principle that if parties contract under a mutual mistake and misapprehension as to their relative and respective rights the result is that the agreement is liable to be set aside as having proceeded upon a common mistake. Applied to the context the statement is only subject to the criticism that the agreement would appear to be void rather than voidable. Applied to mistake as to rights generally it would appear to be too wide. Even where the vendor has not title, though both parties think he has, the correct view would appear to be that there is a contract: but that the vendor has either committed a breach of the stipulation as to title, or is not able to perform his contract. The contract is unenforceable by him but is not void.

Mistake as to quality of the thing contracted for raises more difficult questions. In such a case a mistake will not affect assent unless it is the mistake of both parties, and is as to the existence of some quality which makes the thing without the quality essentially different from the thing as it was believed to be. Of course it may appear that the parties contracted that the article should possess the quality which one or other or both mistakenly believed it to possess. But in such a case there is a contract and the inquiry is a different one, being whether the contract as to quality amounts to a condition or a warranty, a different branch of the law. The principles to be applied are to be found in two cases which as far as my knowledge goes, have always been treated as authoritative expositions of the law. The first is *Kennedy v. Panama Royal Mail Co.*

In that case the plaintiff had applied for shares in the defendant company on the faith of a prospectus which stated falsely but innocently that the company had a binding contract with the Government of New Zealand for the carriage of mails. On discovering the true facts the plaintiff brought an action for the recovery of the sums he had paid on calls. The defendant brought a cross action for further calls. ...

The Court came to the conclusion in that case that, though there was a misapprehension as to that which was a material part of the motive inducing the applicant to ask for the shares, it did not prevent the shares from being in substance those he applied for.

The next case is *Smith v. Hughes* (1871), L.R. 6 Q.B. 597, the well known case as to new and old oats. ...

In these cases I am inclined to think that the true analysis is that there is a contract, but that the one party is not able to supply the very thing whether goods or services that the other party contracted to take; and therefore the contract is unenforceable by the one if executory, while if executed the other can recover back money paid on the ground of failure of the consideration.

We are now in a position to apply to the facts of this case the law as to mistake as far as it has been stated. It is essential in this part of the discussion to keep in mind the finding of the jury acquitting the defendants of fraudulent misrepresentation or concealment in procuring the agreements in question. Grave injustice may be done to the defendants and confusion introduced into the legal conclusion, unless it is quite clear that in considering mistake in this case no suggestion of fraud is admissible and cannot strictly be regarded by the judge who has to determine the legal issues raised. The agreement which is said to be void is the agreement contained in the letter of March 19, 1929, that Bell would retire from the Board of the Niger Company and its subsidiaries, and that in consideration of his doing so Levers would pay him as compensation for the termination of his agreements and consequent loss of office the sum of £30,000 in full satisfaction and discharge of all claims and demands of any kind against Lever Brothers, the Niger Company or its subsidiaries. The agreement, which as part of the contract was terminated, had been broken so that it could be repudiated. Is an agreement to terminate a broken contract different in kind from an agreement to terminate an unbroken contract, assuming that the breach has given the one party the right to declare the contract at an end? I feel the weight of the plaintiffs' contention that a contract immediately determinable is a different thing from a contract for an unexpired term, and that the difference in kind can be illustrated by the immense price of release from the longer contract as compared with the shorter. And I agree that an agreement to take an assignment of a lease for five years is not the same thing as to take an assignment of a lease for three years, still less a term for a few months. But, on the whole, I have come to the conclusion that it would be wrong to decide that an agreement to terminate a definite specified contract is void if it turns out that the agreement had already been broken and could have been terminated otherwise. The contract released is the identical contract in both cases, and the party paying for release gets exactly what he bargains for. It seems immaterial that he could have got the same result in another way, or that if he had known the true facts he would not have entered into the bargain. A buys B's horse; he thinks the horse is sound and he pays the price of a sound horse; he would certainly not have bought the horse if he had known as the fact is that the horse is unsound. If B has made no representation as to soundness and has not contracted that the horse is sound, A is bound and cannot recover back the price. A buys a picture from B; both A and B believe it to be the work of an old master, and a high price is paid. It turns out to be a modern copy. A has no remedy in the absence of representation or warranty. A agrees to take on lease or to buy from B an unfurnished dwelling-house. The house is in fact uninhabitable. A would never have entered into the bargain if he had known the fact. A has no remedy, and the position is the same whether B knew the facts or not, so long as he made no representation or gave no warranty. A buys a roadside garage business from B abutting on a public thoroughfare; unknown to A, but known to B, it has already been decided to construct a bypass road which will divert substantially the whole of the traffic from passing A's garage. Again A has no remedy. All these cases involve hardship on A and benefit B, as most people would say, unjustly. They can be supported on the ground that it is of paramount importance that contracts should be observed, and that if parties honestly comply with the essentials of the formation of contracts—i.e., agree in the same terms on the same subject-matter—they are bound, and must rely on the stipulations of the contract for protection from the effect of facts unknown to them.

This brings the discussion to the alternative mode of expressing the result of a mutual mistake. It is said that in such a case as the present there is to be implied a stipulation in the contract that a condition of its efficacy is that the facts should be as understood by both parties—namely, that the contract could not be terminated till the end of the current term. The question of the existence of conditions, express or implied, is obviously one that affects not the formation of contract, but the investigation of the terms of the contract when made. A condition derives its efficacy from the consent of the parties express or implied. They have agreed, but on what terms. One term may be that unless the facts are or are not of a particular nature, or unless an event has or has not happened, the contract is not to take effect. With regard to future facts such a condition is obviously contractual. Till the event occurs the parties are bound. Thus the condition (the exact terms of which need not here be investigated) that is generally accepted as underlying the principle of the frustration cases is contractual, an implied condition. Sir John Simon formulated for the assistance of your Lordships a proposition which should be recorded: "Whenever it is to be inferred from the terms of a contract or its surrounding circumstances that the consensus has been reached upon the basis of a particular contractual assumption, and that assumption is not true, the contract is avoided: i.e., it is void ab initio if the assumption is of present fact and it ceases to bind if the assumption is of future fact."

I think few would demur to this statement but its value depends upon the meaning of "a contractual assumption," and also upon the true meaning to be attached to "basis," a metaphor which may mislead. When used expressly in contracts, for instance, in policies of insurance, which state that the truth of the statements in the proposal is to be the basis of the contract of insurance, the meaning is clear. The truth of the statements is made a condition of the contract, which failing, the contract is void unless the condition is waived. The proposition does not amount to more than this that, if the contract expressly or impliedly contains a term that a particular assumption is a condition of the contract, the contract is avoided if the assumption is not true. But we have not advanced far on the inquiry how to ascertain whether the contract does contain such a condition. Various words are to be found to define the state of things which make a condition. "In the contemplation of both parties fundamental to the continued validity of the contract," "a foundation essential to its existence," "a fundamental reason for making it," are phrases found in the important judgment of Scrutton L.J. in the present case. The first two phrases appear to me to be unexceptionable. They cover the case of a contract to serve in a particular place, the existence of which is fundamental to the service, or to procure the services of a professional vocalist, whose continued health is essential to performance. But "a fundamental reason for making a contract" may, with respect, be misleading. The reason of one party only is presumably not intended, but in the cases I have suggested above, of the sale of a horse or of a picture, it might be said that the fundamental reason for making the contract was the belief of both parties that the horse was sound or the picture an old master, yet in neither case would the condition as I think exist. Nothing is more dangerous than to allow oneself liberty to construct for the parties contracts which they have not in terms made by importing implications which would appear to make the contract more business-like or more just. The implications to be made are to be no more than are "necessary" for giving business efficacy to the transaction, and it appears to me that, both as to existing facts and future facts, a condition would not be implied unless the new state of facts makes the contract something different in kind from the contract in the original state of facts. Thus, in *Krell v. Henry*, [1903] 2 K.B. 740, Vaughan Williams L.J. finds that the subject of the contract was "rooms to view the procession": the postponement, therefore, made the rooms not rooms to view the procession. This also is the test finally chosen by Lord Sumner in *Bank Line v. Arthur Capel & Co.*, [1919] A.C. 435, agreeing with Lord Dunedin in *Metropolitan Water Board v. Dick Kerr*, [1918] A.C. 119, where, dealing with the criterion for determining the effect of interruption in "frustrating" a contract, he says: "An interruption may be so long as to destroy the identity of the work or service, when resumed, with the work or service when interrupted." We therefore get a common standard for mutual mistake and implied conditions whether as to existing or as to future facts. Does the state of the new facts destroy the identity of the subject-matter as it was in the original state of facts? To apply the principle to the infinite combinations of facts that arise in actual experience will continue to be difficult, but if this case results in establishing order into what has been a somewhat confused and difficult branch of the law it will have served a useful purpose.

I have already stated my reasons for deciding that in the present case the identity of the subject-matter was not destroyed by the mutual mistake, if any, and need not repeat them.

It now becomes necessary to deal with the second point of the plaintiffs—namely, that the contract of March 19, 1929, could be avoided by them in consequence of the non-disclosure by Bell of his misconduct as to the cocoa dealings. Fraudulent concealment has been negatived by the jury; this claim is based upon the contention that Bell owed a duty to Levers to disclose his misconduct, and that in default of disclosure the contract was voidable. Ordinarily the failure to disclose a material fact which might influence the mind of a prudent contractor does not give the right to avoid the contract. The principle of caveat emptor applies outside contracts of sale. There are certain contracts expressed by the law to be contracts of the utmost good faith, where material facts must be disclosed; if not, the contract is voidable. Apart from the special fiduciary relationships, contracts for partnership and contracts of insurance are the leading instances. In such cases the duty does not arise out of contract; the duty of a person proposing an insurance arises before a contract is made, so of an intending partner. Unless this contract can be brought within this limited category of contracts *uberrimae fidei* it appears to me that this ground of defence must fail. I see nothing to differentiate this agreement from the ordinary contract of service; and I am aware of no authority which places contracts of service within the limited category I have mentioned. It seems to me clear that master and men negotiating for an agreement of services are as unfettered as in any other negotiation. Nor can I find anything in the relation of master and servant, when established, that places agreements between them within the protected category.

It is said that there is a contractual duty of the servant to disclose his past faults. I agree that the duty in the servant to protect his master's property may involve the duty to report a fellow servant whom he knows to be wrongfully dealing with that property. The servant owes a duty not to steal, but, having stolen, is there superadded a duty to confess that he has stolen? I am satisfied that to imply such a duty would be a departure from the well established usage of mankind and would be to create obligations entirely outside the normal contemplation of the parties concerned. If a man agrees to raise his butler's wages, must the butler disclose that two years ago he received a secret commission from the wine merchant; and if the master discovers it, can he, without dismissal or after the servant has left, avoid the agreement for the increase in salary and recover back the extra wages paid? If he gives his cook a month's wages in lieu of notice can he, on discovering that the cook has been pilfering the tea and sugar, claim the return of the month's wages? I think not. He takes the risk; if he wishes to protect himself he can question his servant, and will then be protected by the truth or otherwise of the answers.

I agree with the view expressed by Avory J. in *Healy v. Société Anonyme Française Rubastic*, [1917] 1 K.B. 946, on this point. It will be noticed that Bell was not a director of Levers, and, with respect, I cannot accept the view of Greer L.J. that if he was in fiduciary relationship to the Niger Company he was in a similar fiduciary relationship to the shareholders, or to the particular shareholders (Levers) who held 99 per cent of the shares. Nor do I think that it is alleged or proved that in making the agreement of March 19, 1929, Levers were acting as agents for the Niger Company.

In the matter of the release of the service contract and the payment of £30,000 they were acting quite plainly for themselves as principals. It follows that on this ground also the claim fails.

The result is that in the present case servants unfaithful in some of their work retain large compensation which some will think they do not deserve. Nevertheless it is of greater importance that well established principles of contract should be maintained than that a particular hardship should be redressed; and I see no way of giving relief to the plaintiffs in the present circumstances except by confiding to the Courts loose powers of introducing terms into contracts which would only serve to introduce doubt and confusion where certainty is essential.

I think therefore that this appeal should be allowed; and I agree with the order to be proposed by my noble and learned friend, Lord Blanesburgh.

SOLLE V BUTCHER
[1950] 1 KB 671

The plaintiff rented from the defendant an apartment, and took a lease at £250 a year for seven years. Both parties believed that the apartment was not governed by rent control legislation, and that £250 was a legal rent. In fact the apartment was controlled by the Rent Acts, and the maximum rent chargeable was £140 a year. But £250 was a fair rent, and by complying with certain formalities before the execution of the lease, the landlord could have charged that amount. The plaintiff now claims to be entitled to the lease at £140.

DENNING LJ: ... In this plight the landlord seeks to set aside the lease. He says, with truth, that it is unfair that the tenant should have the benefit of the lease for the outstanding five years of the term at £140 a year, when the proper rent is £250 a year. If he cannot give a notice of increase now, can he not avoid the lease? The only ground on which he can avoid it is on the ground of mistake. It is quite plain that the parties were under a mistake. They thought that the flat was not tied down to a controlled rent, whereas in fact it was. In order to see whether the lease can be avoided for this mistake it is necessary to remember that mistake is of two kinds: first, mistake which renders the contract void, that is, a nullity from the beginning, which is the kind of mistake which was dealt with by the courts of common law; and, secondly, mistake which renders the contract not void, but voidable, that is, liable to be set aside on such terms as the court thinks fit, which is the kind of mistake which was dealt with by the courts of equity. Much of the difficulty which has attended this subject has arisen because, before the fusion of law and equity, the courts of common law, in order to do justice in the case in hand, extended this doctrine of mistake beyond its proper limits and held contracts to be void which were really only voidable, a process which was capable of being attended with much injustice to third persons who had bought goods or otherwise committed themselves on the faith that there was a contract. In the well-known case of *Cundy v. Lindsay*, Cundy suffered such an injustice. He bought the handkerchiefs from the rogue, Blenkarn, before the *Judicature Acts* came into operation. Since the fusion of law and equity, there is no reason to continue this process, and it will be found that only those contracts are now held void in which the mistake was such as to prevent the formation of any contract at all.

Let me first consider mistakes which render a contract a nullity. All previous decisions on this subject must now be read in the light of *Bell v. Lever Bros. Ltd.* The correct interpretation of that case, to my mind, is that, once a contract has been made, that is to say, once the parties, whatever their inmost states of mind, have to all outward appearances agreed with sufficient certainty in the same terms on the same subject matter, then the contract is good unless and until it is set aside for failure of some condition on which the existence of the contract depends, or for fraud, or on some equitable ground. Neither party can rely on his own mistake to say it was a nullity from the beginning, no matter that it was a mistake which to his mind was fundamental, and no matter that the other party knew that he was under a mistake. A fortiori, if the other party did not know of the mistake, but shared it. The cases where goods have perished at the time of sale, or belong to the buyer, are really contracts which are not void for mistake but are void by reason of an implied condition precedent, because the contract proceeded on the basic assumption that it was possible of performance. ...

Applying these principles, it is clear that here there was a contract. The parties agreed in the same terms on the same subject-matter. It is true that the landlord was under a mistake which was to him fundamental: he would not for one moment have considered letting the flat for seven years if it meant that he could only charge £140 a year for it. He made the fundamental mistake of believing that the rent he could charge was not tied down to a controlled rent; but, whether it was his own mistake or a mistake common to both him and the tenant, it is not a ground for saying that the lease was from the beginning a nullity. Any other view would lead to remarkable results, for it would mean that, in the many cases where the parties mistakenly think a house is outside the Rent Restriction Acts when it is really within them, the tenancy would be a nullity, and the tenant would have to go; with the result that the tenants would not dare seek to have their rents reduced to the permitted amounts lest they should be turned out.

Let me next consider mistakes which render a contract voidable, that is, liable to be set aside on some equitable ground. Whilst presupposing that a contract was good at law, or at any rate not void, the court of equity would often relieve a party from the consequences of his own mistake, so long as it could do so without injustice to third parties. The court, it was said had power to set aside the contract whenever it was of opinion that it was unconscientious for the other party to avail himself of the legal advantage which he had obtained. ...

The court had, of course, to define what it considered to be unconscientious, but in this respect equity has shown a progressive development. It is now clear that a contract will be set aside if the mistake of the one party has been induced by a material misrepresentation of the other, even though it was not fraudulent or fundamental; or if one party, knowing that the other is mistaken about the terms of an offer, or the identity of the person by whom it is made, lets him remain under his delusion and concludes a contract on the mistaken terms instead of pointing out the mistake. That is, I venture to think, the ground on which the defendant in *Smith v. Hughes* would be exempted nowadays, and on which, according to the view by Blackburn J. of the facts, the contract in *Lindsay v. Cundy*, was voidable and not void: ...

A contract is also liable in equity to be set aside if the parties were under a common misapprehension either as to facts or as to their relative and respective rights, provided that the misapprehension was fundamental and that the party seeking to set it aside was not himself at fault. ...

The principle so established by *Cooper v. Phibbs* has been repeatedly acted on ... . It is in no way impaired by *Bell v. Lever Bros. Ltd.*, which was treated in the House of Lords as a case at law depending on whether the contract was a nullity or not. If it had been considered on equitable grounds, the result might have been different. ...

Applying that principle to this case, the facts are that the plaintiff, the tenant, was a surveyor who was employed by the defendant, the landlord, not only to arrange finance for the purchase of the building and to negotiate with the rating authorities as to the new rateable values, but also to let the flats. He was the agent for letting, and he clearly formed the view that the building was not controlled. He told the valuation officer so. He advised the defendant what were the rents which could be charged. He read to the defendant an opinion of counsel relating to the matter, and told him that in his opinion he could charge £250 and that there was no previous control. He said that the flats came outside the Act and that the defendant was "clear." The defendant relied on what the plaintiff told him, and authorized the plaintiff to let at the rentals which he had suggested. The plaintiff not only let the four other flats to other people for a long period of years at the new rentals, but also took one himself for seven years at £250 a year. Now he turns round and says, quite unashamedly, that he wants to take advantage of the mistake to get the flat at £140 a year for seven years instead of the £250 a year, which is not only the rent he agreed to pay but also the fair and economic rent; and it is also the rent permitted by the Acts on compliance with the necessary formalities. If the rules of equity have become so rigid that they cannot remedy such an injustice, it is time we had a new equity, to make good the omissions of the old. But, in my view, the established rules are amply sufficient for this case.

[Judgment was given for the defendant on terms that the plaintiff must elect between rescission and paying the full rent.]

MAGEE V PENNINE INSURANCE CO
[1969] 2 QB 507 (CA)

LORD DENNING MR: In 1961 Mr. Thomas Magee senior, the plaintiff, aged 58, acquired an Austin car. He signed a proposal form for insurance. In it he said that the car belonged to him. He was asked to give details of his driving licence "and of all other persons who to your present knowledge will drive." These were the details he gave:

(1) "Thomas Magee"—that is himself—"provisional licence aged 58."
(2) "John Magee"—that is his elder son—"Police mobile driver, aged 35." He had an annual licence.
(3) "John J. Magee"—that is his younger son—"joiner, aged 18—provisional licence."

Mr. Magee signed this declaration: "I ... do hereby declare that the car described is and shall be kept in good condition and that the answers above given are in every respect true and correct and I ... hereby agree that this declaration shall be the basis of the contract of insurance between the company and myself. ..." Those details were not written in by Mr. Magee himself. They were written in by Mr. Atkinson at the garage where he got the car. The details unfortunately were completely wrong. Mr. Thomas Magee had never driven a car himself. He had never had a licence, not even a provisional one. He was getting the car really for his son of 18 to drive. And we all know that a young man of 18 has to pay a much higher insurance than a man of 25 or over. This company said they would not have insured a young man of 18.

The judge found that Mr. Thomas Magee, the father, had not been fraudulent. He did not himself fill in the details. They were filled in by Mr. Atkinson, the man at the garage. And then Mr. Thomas Magee signed them. It was Mr. Atkinson who made some mistake or other. But there it was. A misrepresentation was made and on the faith of it being true, the insurance company granted an insurance policy to Mr. Magee.

Thereafter the policy was renewed each year and the premiums were paid. In 1964 that car was replaced by another. The policy was renewed for the new car without anything further being said about the drivers or the ownership. The company assumed, no doubt, that the same details applied.

On April 25, 1965, there was an accident. The younger son, John Magee, was driving the new car at 4 o'clock in the morning. He ran into a shop window. The plate glass was smashed and the car was a complete wreck. The father, Mr. Thomas Magee, put in a claim form, in which he said that the car was £600 in value. That was clearly wrong because the price new was only £547 the year before. The insurers thereupon got their engineer to look at it. On May 12, 1965, the broker wrote to Mr. Thomas Magee a letter, in which he said: " ... We have today been advised by your insurers that their engineer considers your vehicle is damaged beyond repair. The engineer considers that the pre-accident market value of the vehicle was £410 and they are therefore prepared to offer you this amount, less the £25 accidental damage excess in settlement of your claim. We should be pleased to receive your confirmation that this is acceptable. ..." There was no written acceptance, but it was accepted by word of mouth. That seemed to be a concluded agreement whereby the company agreed to pay £385.

But within the next few days the insurance company made further inquiries. One of their representatives saw Mr. Magee and took a statement from him. Then the truth was discovered. Mr. Magee did not drive at all. He had never had a driving licence, not even a provisional one. He said that the car was never his property but was his son's car: and that it was his son, the younger son, who had driven the car and was the only person who had ever driven it. On discovering those facts, the insurance company said they were not liable on the insurance policy.

They had been induced to grant it, they said, by the misrepresentations in the original proposal form; and also by reason of non-disclosure of material facts, namely, that the son aged 18 was normally to be the driver.

Mr. Magee brought an action in the county court in which he claimed the £385. He said it was payable under the insurance policy, or, alternatively, on an agreement of compromise contained in the letter of May 12.

The judge rejected the claim on the policy itself, because the insurance was induced by misrepresentation. He found that the company were entitled to repudiate the policy because of the inaccuracy of Mr. Magee's answers. That finding was not challenged in this court. Mr. Taylor, on behalf of Mr. Magee, admitted that he could not claim on the policy.

But the judge upheld the claim on the letter of May 12. He said it was a binding contract of compromise. I am not so sure about this. It might be said to be a mere quantification of the account which should be paid in case the insurance company were liable: and that it did not preclude them from afterwards contesting liability. But, on the whole, I do not think we should regard it as a mere quantification. The letter contains the important words: "in settlement of your claim," which import that it is to be settled without further controversy. In short, it bears the stamp of an agreement of compromise. The consideration for it was the ascertainment of a sum which was previously unascertained.

But then comes the next point. Accepting that the agreement to pay £385 was an agreement of compromise. Is it vitiated by mistake? The insurance company were clearly under a mistake. They thought that the policy was good and binding. They did not know, at the time of that letter, that there had been misrepresentations in the proposal form. If Mr. Magee knew of their mistake—if he knew that the policy was bad—he certainly could not take advantage of the agreement to pay £385. He would be "snapping at an offer which he knew was made under a mistake": and no man is allowed to get away with that. But I prefer to assume that Mr. Magee was innocent. I think we should take it that both parties were under a common mistake. Both parties thought that the policy was good and binding. The letter of March 12, 1968 was written on the assumption that the policy was good whereas it was in truth voidable.

What is the effect in law of this common mistake? Mr. Taylor said that the agreement to pay £385 was good, despite this common mistake. He relied much on *Bell v. Lever Brothers, Ltd.*, [1932] A.C. 161 and its similarity to the present case. He submitted that, inasmuch as the mistake there did not vitiate that contract, the mistake here should not vitiate this one. I do not propose today to go through the speeches in that case. They have given enough trouble to commentators already. I would say simply this: A common mistake, even on a most fundamental matter, does not make a contract void at law: but it makes it voidable in equity. I analysed the cases in *Solle v. Butcher*, [1950] 1 K.B. 671, and I would repeat what I said there, at p. 693: "A contract is also liable in equity to be set aside if the parties were under a common misapprehension either as to facts or as to their relative and respective rights, provided that the misapprehension was fundamental and that the party seeking to set it aside was not himself at fault." Applying that principle here, it is clear that, when the insurance company and Mr. Magee made this agreement to pay £385, they were both under a common mistake which was fundamental to the whole agreement. Both thought that Mr. Magee was entitled to claim under the policy of insurance, whereas he was not so entitled. That common mistake does not make the agreement to pay £385 a nullity, but it makes it liable to be set aside in equity.

This brings me to a question which has caused me much difficulty. Is this a case in which we ought to set the agreement aside in equity? I have hesitated on this point, but I cannot shut my eyes to the fact that Mr. Magee had no valid claim on the insurance policy: and, if he had no claim on the policy, it is not equitable that he should have a good claim on the agreement to pay £385, seeing that it was made under a fundamental mistake. It is not fair to hold the insurance company to an agreement which they would not have dreamt of making if they had not been under a mistake. I would, therefore, uphold the appeal and give judgment for the insurance company.

[Fenton Atkinson LJ agreed. Winn LJ dissented.]

NOTE

In *Toronto-Dominion Bank v Fortin (No 2)* (1978), 88 DLR (3d) 232 (BCSC), a fundamental mistake was held to be grounds to set aside a compromise agreement. Fortin contracted to buy a group of companies from a receiver-manager, but subsequently changed his mind and repudiated the agreement, consenting to pay $10,000 to the receiver-manager in a compromise agreement in satisfaction of all claims arising from the original contract. Shortly thereafter, the BC Supreme Court ruled that the receiver did not have authority to offer the companies for sale, and thus the original contract had been void. Fortin argued for the return of the $10,000, because the compromise agreement had been entered into under a mistake of law. Although the basic rule is that a compromise agreement is valid despite a mistake of law as long as the claim compromised is bona fide even though invalid, in this case the parties had not sought legal advice on this point, and therefore were not bound. The court went on to say that a mistake can be so fundamental that a compromise agreement cannot stand, where the *consensus* was reached on the basis of a mistaken fundamental assumption. The original contract was void *ab initio*, and the compromise agreement could be set aside in equity.

GREAT PEACE SHIPPING LTD V TSAVLIRIS
SALVAGE (INTERNATIONAL) LTD
[2002] 4 All ER 689 (CA)

The defendants offered salvage services to a vessel which had suffered serious structural damage in the South Indian Ocean. The offer having been accepted, the defendants approached London brokers for a tug, but the tug found was five to six days sailing time away. Fearing for the safety of the crew, the defendants sought a merchant vessel in the vicinity to assist. The defendants were given the names of four vessels reported to be in the area, the nearest being the claimant's vessel, which was believed to be about 35 miles away from the damaged vessel. Negotiations between the defendants and the claimants resulted in a hire contract for a minimum of five days to escort and stand by the damaged vessel for the purpose of saving life. The agreement contained a cancellation clause giving a right to cancel on payment of five days' hire. When it was discovered that the vessels were in fact 410 miles apart, not 35 miles as previously understood, the defendants did not immediately cancel the contract but sought a nearer vessel to assist. A few hours later such assistance was obtained. The defendants then cancelled the contract with the claimants and refused to make any payment for the hire of their vessel. The claimants brought an action claiming US$82,500 as moneys payable under the contract or as damages for wrongful repudiation. The defendants disputed the claim on the ground that the purported contract had been concluded by reason of a fundamental mistake of fact in that both parties had proceeded on the fundamental assumption that the two vessels were in close proximity when they were not, and that therefore the contract was either void at law or voidable and the defendants were entitled to rescission in equity. The judge gave judgment for the claimants.

LORD PHILLIPS OF WORTH MATRAVERS MR (for the court):

INTRODUCTION

[1] In 1931 in *Bell v. Lever Bros. Ltd.* [1932] A.C. 161 Lord Atkin made a speech which he must have anticipated would be treated as the definitive exposition of the rules of law governing the effect of mistake on contract. In 1949 in *Solle v. Butcher* [1950] 1 K.B. 671 Denning L.J. identified an equitable jurisdiction which permits the court to intervene where the parties have concluded an agreement that was binding in law under a common misapprehension of a fundamental nature as to the material facts or their respective rights. Over the last 50 years judges and jurists have wrestled with the problem of reconciling these two decisions and identifying with precision the principles that they lay down.

[2] In the court below Toulson J. used this case as a vehicle to review this difficult area of jurisprudence. He reached the bold conclusion that the view of the jurisdiction of the court expressed by Denning L.J. in *Solle v. Butcher* was "over-broad," by which he meant wrong. Equity neither gave a party a right to rescind a contract on grounds of common mistake nor conferred on the court a discretion to set aside a contract on such grounds.

• • •

THE MISTAKE IN THIS CASE

[31] ... In the present case the parties were agreed as to the express terms of the contract. The defendants agreed that the Great Peace would deviate towards the Cape Providence and, on reaching her, escort her so as to be on hand to save the lives of

her crew, should she founder. The contractual services would terminate when the salvage tug came up with the casualty. The mistake relied upon by the defendants is as to an assumption that they claim underlay the terms expressly agreed. This was that the Great Peace was within a few hours sailing of the Cape Providence. They contend that this mistake was fundamental in that it would take the Great Peace about 39 hours to reach a position where she could render the services which were the object of the contractual adventure.

[32] Thus what we are here concerned with is an allegation of a common mistaken assumption of fact which renders the service that will be provided if the contract is performed in accordance with its terms something different from the performance that the parties contemplated. This is the type of mistake which fell to be considered in *Bell v. Lever Bros. Ltd.* [1932] A.C. 161. We shall describe it as "common mistake," although it is often alternatively described as "mutual mistake."

[33] Mr. Reeder for the defendants puts his case in two alternative ways. First he submits that performance of the contract in the circumstances as they turned out to be would have been fundamentally different from the performance contemplated by the parties, so much so that the effect of the mistake was to deprive the agreement of the consideration underlying it. Under common law, so he submits, the effect of such a mistake is to render the contract void. ... The foundation for this submission is *Bell v. Lever Bros. Ltd.*

[34] If the facts of this case do not meet that test, Mr. Reeder submits that they none the less give rise to a right of rescission in equity. He submits that such a right arises whenever the parties contract under a common mistake as to a matter that can properly be described as "fundamental" or "material" to the agreement in question. Here he draws an analogy with the test for rescission where one party, by innocent misrepresentation, induces the other to enter into a contract—indeed that is one situation where the parties contract under a common mistake. The foundation for this submission is *Solle v. Butcher* [1950] 1 K.B. 671.

• • •

BELL V. LEVER BROS. LTD.

[The court quotes extensively from the decision in *Bell v Lever Brothers Ltd.*]

[50] It is generally accepted that the principles of the law of common mistake expounded by Lord Atkin in *Bell v. Lever Bros. Ltd.* [1932] A.C. 161 were based on the common law. The issue raised [here] ... is whether there subsists a separate doctrine of common mistake founded in equity which enables the court to intervene in circumstances where the mistake does not render the contract void under the common law principles. The first step is to identify the nature of the common law doctrine of mistake that was identified, or established, by *Bell v. Lever Bros. Ltd.*

[51] ... Lord Atkin and Lord Thankerton were breaking no new ground in holding void a contract where, unknown to the parties, the subject matter of the contract no longer existed at the time that the contract was concluded.

• • •

[55] The position is very different where there is "a mistake as to the existence of some quality of the subject matter which makes the thing without the quality essentially different from the thing as it was believed to be." In such a situation it may be possible to perform the letter of the contract. In support of the proposition that a contract is void in such circumstances, Lord Atkin cited two authorities, in which he said that the principles to be applied were to be found. The first was *Lord Kennedy v. Panama, New Zealand and Australian Royal Mail Co. Ltd.* L.R. 2 Q.B. 580.

• • •

[60] The other case to which Lord Atkin referred was *Smith v. Hughes* (1871) L.R. 6 Q.B. 597. On no view did that difficult case deal with common mistake and we are not able to see how it supported the test formulated by Lord Atkin, as set out ... above. Indeed, Lord Atkin himself commented [1932] A.C. 161, 222:

> In these cases I am inclined to think that the true analysis is that there is a contract, but that the one party is not able to supply the very thing whether goods or services that the other party contracted to take; and therefore the contract is unenforceable by the one if executory, while if executed the other can recover back money paid on the ground of failure of the consideration.

[61] We conclude that the two authorities to which Lord Atkin referred provided an insubstantial basis for his formulation of the test of common mistake in relation to the quality of the subject matter of a contract. Lord Atkin advanced an alternative basis for his test: the implication of a term of the same nature as that which was applied under the doctrine of frustration, as it was then understood. In so doing he adopted the analysis of Scrutton L.J. in the Court of Appeal. It seems to us that this was a more solid jurisprudential basis for the test of common mistake that Lord Atkin was proposing. At the time of *Bell v. Lever Bros. Ltd.* [1932] A.C. 161 the law of frustration and common mistake had advanced hand in hand on the foundation of a common principle. Thereafter frustration proved a more fertile ground for the development of this principle than common mistake, and consideration of the development of the law of frustration assists with the analysis of the law of common mistake.

· · ·

[The court discusses the frustration cases.]

[73] ... What do these developments in the law of frustration have to tell us about the law of common mistake? First that the theory of the implied term is as unrealistic when considering common mistake as when considering frustration. Where a fundamental assumption upon which an agreement is founded proves to be mistaken, it is not realistic to ask whether the parties impliedly agreed that in those circumstances the contract would not be binding. The avoidance of a contract on the ground of common mistake results from a rule of law under which, if it transpires that one or both of the parties have agreed to do something which it is impossible to perform, no obligation arises out of that agreement.

[74] In considering whether performance of the contract is impossible, it is necessary to identify what it is that the parties agreed would be performed. This involves looking not only at the express terms, but at any implications that may arise out of the surrounding circumstances. In some cases it will be possible to identify details of the "contractual adventure" which go beyond the terms that are expressly spelt out, in others it will not.

[75] Just as the doctrine of frustration only applies if the contract contains no provision that covers the situation, the same should be true of common mistake. If, on true construction of the contract, a party warrants that the subject matter of the contract exists, or that it will be possible to perform the contract, there will be no scope to hold the contract void on the ground of common mistake.

[76] ... [T]he following elements must be present if common mistake is to avoid a contract: (i) there must be a common assumption as to the existence of a state of affairs; (ii) there must be no warranty by either party that that state of affairs exists; (iii) the non-existence of the state of affairs must not be attributable to the fault of either party; (iv) the non-existence of the state of affairs must render performance of the contract impossible; (v) the state of affairs may be the existence, or a vital

attribute, of the consideration to be provided or circumstances which must subsist if performance of the contractual adventure is to be possible.

• • •

[84] Once the court determines that unforeseen circumstances have, indeed, resulted in the contract being impossible of performance, it is next necessary to determine whether, on true construction of the contract, one or other party has undertaken responsibility for the subsistence of the assumed state of affairs. This is another way of asking whether one or other party has undertaken the risk that it may not prove possible to perform the contract, and the answer to this question may well be the same as the answer to the question of whether the impossibility of performance is attributable to the fault of one or other of the parties.

• • •

[94] [O]n the facts of the present case, the issue in relation to common mistake turns on the question of whether the mistake as to the distance apart of the two vessels had the effect that the services that the Great Peace was in a position to provide were something essentially different from that to which the parties had agreed. We shall defer answering that question until we have considered whether principles of equity provide a second string to the defendants' bow.

MISTAKE IN EQUITY

[95] In *Solle v. Butcher* [1950] 1 K.B. 671 Denning L.J. held that a court has an equitable power to set aside a contract that is binding in law on the ground of common mistake. …

[96] It is axiomatic that there is no room for rescission in equity of a contract which is void. Either Lord Denning M.R. was purporting to usurp the common law principle in *Bell v. Lever Bros. Ltd.* and replace it with a more flexible principle of equity, or the equitable remedy of rescission that he identified is one that operates in a situation where the mistake is not of such a nature as to avoid the contract. Decisions have, hitherto, proceeded on the basis that the latter is the true position. …

[97] Toulson J. has taken a different view. He has concluded that it is not possible to differentiate between the test of mistake identified in *Bell v. Lever Bros. Ltd.* and that advanced by Lord Denning M.R. as giving rise to the equitable jurisdiction to rescind. He has examined the foundations upon which Lord Denning M.R. founded his decision in *Solle v. Butcher* and found them defective. These are conclusions that we must review. If we agree with them the question will then arise of whether it was open to him, or is open to this court, to rule that the doctrine of common mistake leaves no room for the intervention of equity.

[98] The following issues fall to be considered in relation to the effect of common mistake in equity. (1) Prior to *Bell v. Lever Bros. Ltd.* was there established a doctrine under which equity permitted rescission of a contract on grounds of common mistake in circumstances where the contract was valid at common law? (2) Could such a doctrine stand with *Bell v. Lever Bros. Ltd.*? (3) Is this court none the less bound to find that such a doctrine exists having regard to *Solle v. Butcher* and subsequent decisions?

• • •

[The court answers all of these questions in the negative.]

SUMMARY

[153] A number of cases, albeit a small number, in the course of the last 50 years have purported to follow *Solle v. Butcher* [1950] 1 K.B. 671, yet none of them defines

the test of mistake that gives rise to the equitable jurisdiction to rescind in a manner that distinguishes this from the test of a mistake that renders a contract void in law, as identified in *Bell v. Lever Bros. Ltd.* [1932] A.C. 161. This is, perhaps, not surprising, for Denning L.J., the author of the test in *Solle v. Butcher*, set *Bell v. Lever Bros. Ltd.* at nought. It is possible to reconcile *Solle v. Butcher* and *Magee v. Pennine Insurance Co. Ltd.* [1969] 2 Q.B. 507 with *Bell v. Lever Bros. Ltd.* only by postulating that there are two categories of mistake, one that renders a contract void at law and one that renders it voidable in equity. Although later cases have proceeded on this basis, it is not possible to identify that proposition in the judgment of any of the three Lords Justices, Denning, Bucknill and Fenton Atkinson, who participated in the majority decisions in the former two cases. Nor, over 50 years, has it proved possible to define satisfactorily two different qualities of mistake, one operating in law and one in equity.

[154] In *Solle v. Butcher* Denning L.J. identified the requirement of a common misapprehension that was "fundamental," and that adjective has been used to describe the mistake in those cases which have followed *Solle v. Butcher*. We do not find it possible to distinguish, by a process of definition, a mistake which is "fundamental" from Lord Atkin's mistake as to quality which "makes the thing [contracted for] essentially different from the thing [that] it was believed to be": [1932] A.C. 161, 218.

[155] A common factor in *Solle v. Butcher* and the cases which have followed it can be identified. The effect of the mistake has been to make the contract a particularly bad bargain for one of the parties. Is there a principle of equity which justifies the court in rescinding a contract where a common mistake has produced this result? ...

[156] [T]he premise of equity's intrusion into the effects of the common law is that the common law rule in question is seen in the particular case to work injustice, and for some reason the common law cannot cure itself. But it is difficult to see how that can apply here. Cases of fraud and misrepresentation, and undue influence, are all catered for under other existing and uncontentious equitable rules. We are only concerned with the question whether relief might be given for common mistake in circumstances wider than those stipulated in *Bell v. Lever Bros. Ltd.* [1932] A.C. 161. But that, surely, is a question as to where the common law should draw the line; not whether, given the common law rule, it needs to be mitigated by application of some other doctrine. The common law has drawn the line in *Bell v. Lever Bros. Ltd.* The effect of *Solle v. Butcher* [1950] 1 K.B. 671 is not to supplement or mitigate the common law: it is to say that *Bell v. Lever Bros. Ltd.* was wrongly decided.

[157] Our conclusion is that it is impossible to reconcile *Solle v. Butcher* with *Bell v. Lever Bros. Ltd.*

• • •

THE RESULT IN THIS CASE

[162] We revert to the question that we [previously] left unanswered ... . It was unquestionably a common assumption of both parties when the contract was concluded that the two vessels were in sufficiently close proximity to enable the Great Peace to carry out the service that she was engaged to perform. Was the distance between the two vessels so great as to confound that assumption and to render the contractual adventure impossible of performance? If so, the defendants would have an arguable case that the contract was void under the principle in *Bell v. Lever Bros. Ltd.* [1932] A.C. 161.

[163] Toulson J. addressed this issue, at para. 56:

Was the Great Peace so far away from the Cape Providence at the time of the contract as to defeat the contractual purpose—or in other words to turn it into something essentially different from that for which the parties bargained? This is a question of fact and degree, but in my view the answer is No. ... A telling point is the reaction of the defendants on learning the true positions of the vessels. They did not want to cancel the agreement until they knew if they could find a nearer vessel to assist. Evidently the defendants did not regard the contract as devoid of purpose, or they would have cancelled at once.

• • •

[165] ... This reaction was a telling indication that the fact that the vessels were considerably further apart than the defendants had believed did not mean that the services that the Great Peace was in a position to provide were essentially different from those which the parties had envisaged when the contract was concluded. The Great Peace would arrive in time to provide several days of escort service. The defendants would have wished the contract to be performed but for the adventitious arrival on the scene of a vessel prepared to perform the same services. The fact that the vessels were further apart than both parties had appreciated did not mean that it was impossible to perform the contractual adventure.

[166] The parties entered into a binding contract for the hire of the Great Peace. That contract gave the defendants an express right to cancel the contract subject to the obligation to pay the "cancellation fee" of five days' hire. When they engaged the Nordfarer they cancelled the Great Peace. They became liable in consequence to pay the cancellation fee. There is no injustice in this result.

[167] For the reasons that we have given, we would dismiss this appeal.

NOTES AND QUESTIONS

1. *Great Peace* was affirmed and applied in the context of a *unilateral* mistake in *Statoil ASA v Louis Dreyfus Energy Services LP*, [2008] EWHC 2257 (Comm). The restriction on the operation of equity does not, however, apply to a voluntary disposition in England; see *Sieff v Fox*, [2005] EWHC 1312 (Ch) and *Pitt v Holt*, [2013] UKSC 26.

2. The decision in *Great Peace* has been roundly criticized by some commentators: see e.g. John D McCamus, "Mistaken Assumptions in Equity: Sound Doctrine or Chimera?" (2004) 40 Can Bus LJ 46 [McCamus, "Mistaken Assumptions in Equity"] at 75-76, 85 (footnotes omitted):

Although one must concede that there is some truth in the Court of Appeal's suggestion that in *Solle v. Butcher* Denning L.J. attempted to confine the doctrine of mistaken common law as articulated by Lord Atkin in *Bell v. Lever Brothers*, the decision in *The Great Peace* appears to be an unfortunate one for a variety of reasons. First, the test for operative mistake defined by the Court of Appeal in *The Great Peace* appears unduly restrictive and is likely, therefore, to lead to the manipulations characteristic of the earlier narrower versions of the test. Moreover, by failing to address the very problem identified by Denning L.J. in *Solle v. Butcher*—the impact of the common law void for mistake doctrine on the interests of third parties—the Court of Appeal has breathed renewed life into a doctrine that is quite unattractive from a policy perspective. Further, the attempted suppression of the equitable doctrine carries with it, at least for the purposes of English law, the suppression of the remedial flexibility afforded by that doctrine. The result is to leave mistaken assumptions doctrine in a very unsatisfactory state as, indeed, the Court of Appeal appears to concede in this case. Finally, the handling of matters of precedent and the impression the reader is given of the Court of Appeal's sense of the appropriate role of an appellate court in dealing with matters of this kind may appear troubling to some observers. ... [I]t would be most unfortunate indeed if Canadian courts were to embrace the reasoning of the Court of Appeal in *The Great Peace*.

And see James Edelman, "An Uncommon Mistake?" (2004) 15 KCLJ 127, who also argues that one of the problems arising from *Great Peace* is the failure to clarify when a contract will be void for common mistake. Edelman, however, lists some benefits to be taken from *Great Peace* (footnotes omitted):

> Lord Phillips was plainly correct to say that it solves the problem of differentiating between the common law "essentially different" test and the equitable "fundamental" test .... A further benefit of the *Great Peace* decision is that the test for common mistake is now identical to that for frustration. The only difference between common mistake and frustration is timing. With common mistake the event occurs before the contract automatically discharging all obligations immediately, with frustration it occurs once the contract is extant, automatically discharging all future obligations. The decision in the *Great Peace* case brings common mistake and frustration together and treats them alike.

See also Kelvin Low, "Coming to Terms with the Great Peace in Common Mistake" in Jason Neyers, Richard Bronaugh & Stephen Pitel, *Exploring Contract Law* (Portland, Or: Hart, 2009), who maintains that *Great Peace* has clarified the law in the area of common mistake and that "concerns over *Great Peace* are either unfounded or overstated."

3. Critics of the result in *Great Peace* often invoke equity's role in protecting the rights of innocent third parties. See e.g. McCamus, "Mistaken Assumptions in Equity," above. The paradigmatic "innocent third party" case can be found in *Cundy v Lindsay* (1878), 3 App Cas 459 (HL), in which title to property did not pass to an innocent good-faith purchaser because the initial contract for sale was void. But were there any innocent third parties in *Great Peace*? What is the practical effect of the result in the case? As McCamus notes, Lord Denning was very concerned with the rights of third parties when he founded the equitable jurisdiction to intervene in cases of mistake in *Solle v Butcher*. Who were the innocent third parties in *Solle*? In *Solle*, Denning LJ seemed concerned that the tenant sought to benefit from a "fortunate" mistake: "The plaintiff not only let the four other flats to other people for a long period of years at the new rentals, but also took one himself for seven years at £250 a year. Now he turns round and says, quite unashamedly, that he wants to take advantage of the mistake to get the flat at £140 a year for seven years instead of the £250 a year." Isn't such manipulation of the "innocent third parties" justification precisely what the court in *Great Peace* sought to avoid?

4. As McCamus rightly points out later in his article, the court in this case need not have undertaken an exhaustive review of the conflict between *Bell v Lever Brothers Ltd* and *Solle v Butcher*. According to the court's own decision, once the parties are shown to have allocated the risk of non-performance, the inquiry should be at an end. Recall that there was exactly such a provision in the contract in this case. However, if we accept the reasoning of commentators that *Solle v Butcher* was meant to protect the interests of innocent third parties, then on their reasoning *should* the contractual allocation of risk end the inquiry?

5. The effect of *Great Peace* decision in England is significant because the Court of Appeal was of the opinion that *Solle v Butcher* and *Bell v Lever Brothers Ltd* could not stand together and, therefore, that *Solle* should not be followed. In Canada, the effect of *Great Peace* is seen in the following excerpt.

MILLER PAVING LIMITED V B GOTTARDO CONSTRUCTION LTD
2007 ONCA 422

GOUDGE JA (for the court):

[1] The appellant Miller Paving Limited ("Miller") contracted to supply aggregate materials to the respondent B. Gottardo Construction Ltd. ("Gottardo"), which then used the materials for a highway extension it had contracted to build for the owner of the highway. On December 20, 2001, Miller and Gottardo signed an agreement in which Miller acknowledged that it had been paid in full for all the materials it had

supplied. Then, on January 31, 2002, it rendered a further invoice after discovering deliveries for which it had not billed Gottardo. Gottardo relied on the December 20 agreement to resist the claim, although Gottardo had itself been paid by the owner for most of these materials.

. . .

[The trial judge had concluded that the misapprehension as to facts did not justify setting the contract aside. Miller appealed, arguing that the trial judge erred in failing to properly apply the doctrine of common mistake to the December 20 agreement. On appeal, it was determined that it was a case of common mistake. After discussing the views put forward in *Solle* and *Bell*, the court went on to discuss Canada's response to *Great Peace*.]

[24] As is well documented by Professor McCamus at p. 68 of his article, I think it is now undeniable that not just the common law doctrine of common mistake, but also the equitable doctrine, have been woven into the fabric of Canadian contract law. Indeed, in this appeal, neither party takes issue with that proposition.

[25] In England, however, the decision of *Great Peace Shipping Ltd. v. Tsavliris Salvage (International) Ltd.*, [2003] Q.B. 679 (C.A.), may have changed things for that country. In that case, after a detailed analysis, the Court of Appeal was of the view that *Solle* could not stand with *Bell* and therefore should not be followed. In addition to apparently eliminating the equitable doctrine, the court also elaborated and restated the test for declaring a contract void at common law. ...

[26] *Great Peace* appears not yet to have been adopted in Canada and, in my view, there is good reason for not doing so. The loss of the flexibility needed to correct unjust results in widely diverse circumstances that would come from eliminating the ... doctrine of common mistake would ... be a step backward.

[In the end, however, the court did not find it necessary to decide on the question of eliminating the equitable doctrine of common mistake because the outcome would not be determined by its existence or lack thereof. Rather, it concluded that the contract itself governed.]

[27] ... [I]t must be noted that *Great Peace* does provide one useful reminder that is of significance here, whether or not its approach to common mistake is adopted in Canada. It is that in considering whether to apply the doctrine of common mistake either at common law or in equity, the court should look to the contract itself to see if the parties have provided for who bears the risk of the relevant mistake, because if they have, that will govern. ... When the contract language is read in the context of this factual matrix, I conclude that the contract clearly allocates to Miller the risk that payment in full has not been received. I would therefore find that the December 20 agreement itself requires Miller to bear the consequence when that risk transpires, rather than allowing it to invoke the doctrine of common mistake.

[The court concluded that even if the doctrine of mistake applied, Miller would not be successful in setting aside the contract.]

LEE V 1435375 ONTARIO LTD
2013 ONCA 516

[A purchaser of a dry-cleaning business attempted to have the sale contract declared void because the property was not zoned so as to allow a dry-cleaning business to be a "permitted use." The premises had been used for this type of business, but likely only as a "legal non-conforming use" which would permit the business to continue to operate as it had in the past. The court held that there was no common mistake because the vendor had had no assumptions and had made no assertions as to zoning and in any event if zoning as a "permitted use" was important to the purchaser, that party ought to have investigated the matter more fully. The matter was said to be at the risk of the purchaser. The lower court judge applied both common law and equitable mistake. The vendor argued that the motion judge had erred, not in her statement of common law mistake—she had simply cited *Bell v Lever Brothers*—but that her application of common law mistake to the facts effectively re-allocated the risk that had been contractually assumed by the purchaser. The Court of Appeal agreed with that argument and also with the argument that the onus of establishing a common mistake is on the party who wants rescission.]

STRATHY JA: ...

[77]   Related to the issue of onus is the question of risk. The motion judge found that the Purchaser did not expressly or impliedly assume "the risk that the commonly assumed facts [that the dry cleaning operation was a permitted use] were untrue."

[78]   This had the effect of putting the risk of the Purchaser's erroneous assumption on the Vendor. Instead of *caveat emptor*, it became *caveat venditor*.

[79]   The law of mistake cannot be used to place a risk on a party where the contract has allocated that risk to another party. ...

[80]   In this case, the Purchaser did not make the agreement conditional on zoning, notwithstanding the evidence of his solicitor that it was sometimes done. In fact, the only clause in the agreement of purchase and sale that spoke to the issue was an acknowledgement that the real estate broker had advised the parties to seek independent professional advice with respect to zoning changes. In apparently ignoring this advice, and signing the agreement without any condition as to zoning, the Purchaser implicitly assumed the risk that the zoning would not permit his contemplated use. Having found that there were no representations, warranties or implied terms concerning zoning, the trial judge should have found that the agreement precluded any "understanding" other than what the parties had expressed in their agreement and that the risk of any "misunderstanding" had been allocated to the Purchaser, not to the Vendor.

• • •

[The argument that there had been an equitable mistake also failed because it had not been established that both parties had been mistaken. In any event the purchaser had been at fault for making the mistake.]

STRATHY JA (continued):

[82]   [The Purchaser] was at fault, however. He failed to take reasonable measures to protect himself, either by investigating the zoning before he signed the agreement or by making the agreement conditional on zoning. He, not the Vendor, should be visited with the consequences. There is nothing inequitable in holding him to the contract, particularly in the absence of any evidence that the use of the premises for their intended purpose is impossible.

[There had been at best a unilateral mistake here and it was not unjust that the purchaser should bear the consequences of his mistake.]

Zavarella v Zavarella. 2013 ONCA 720. [The parties entered into settlement agreement on separation. They made mistakes relating to the wife's indebtedness for a car but the court held that the mistakes were not sufficiently serious to affect the agreement. The entire agreement had to be considered.] GILLESE JA said: ... the mistake about the car did not go to the root of the Agreement. While the Agreement does not form part of the record before this court, a review of the trial transcript shows that its terms govern a large number of disputed matters, including custody and access, as well as various matters related to the parties' NFP [net family property] statements and equalization. In the circumstances, the car—a single item with a relatively small dollar value attached to it—cannot be seen to be the "root" of the Agreement. That is, the mistaken assumption about the car did not change the subject matter of the Agreement so that it became something essentially different from what it was believed to be. The parties believed the Agreement to be the resolution of a host of matters relating to the demise of their familial relationship. The essential nature of the Agreement remained.

SCOTT V COULSON
[1903] 2 Ch 249

The plaintiff agreed to sell to the defendant an insurance policy on the life of a man called A.T. Death. Both parties then assumed that Death was living, and the price agreed to be paid by the defendant was £460, slightly more than the cash surrender value. Actually Death was dead, so that the policy was worth £777, its face value. The contract was executed by assignment of the policy, at which time the purchaser had some reason to suspect the truth. When the vendor later discovered the truth, he brought an action to set aside the sale.

VAUGHAN WILLIAMS LJ: On the facts of this case, if one takes those which were found by the learned judge in his judgment, I do not see what room there is for argument on any question of law. If we are to take it that it was common ground that, at the date of the contract for the sale of this policy, both the parties to the contract supposed the assured to be alive, it is true that both parties entered into this contract upon the basis of a common affirmative belief that the assured was alive; but as it turned out that this was a common mistake, the contract was one which cannot be enforced. This is so at law; and the plaintiffs do not require to have recourse to equity to rescind the contract, if the basis which both parties recognized as the basis is not true. Having regard to the evidence, it seems to be clear that the learned judge came to a right conclusion. If it had turned out that the vendors or their agent had requested Coulson to find out whether the assured was dead or alive, and Coulson had come back and said he could not find out, I should have said that, apart from argument, it would have been almost impossible to arrive at the conclusion that both parties had entered into the contract upon the basis that the assured was alive. But it turns out that no such inquiry was requested to be made. The only inquiry requested to be made was that contained in Coulson's letter of March 15, 1902, in which he requested inquiry to be made about the assured. Therefore the inference cannot arise which, if it had arisen, would have been fatal to the plaintiffs' contention that this contract was entered into upon the basis that the assured was still alive. If one gets rid of that, what is there left? We have before us the conditions of the proposed sale which were before both parties, in which it certainly seems to be assumed that the assured was still alive.

All I say with regard to the matter is that the material date all through is the date of the contract. If at that date a good contract was entered into, I cannot conceive that it could be rescinded. But it turns out that it was a contract entered into under a common mistake existing at the date of it, and therefore it follows that an assignment executed in pursuance of such a contract cannot be supported.

The learned judge has arrived at a right conclusion, and this appeal must therefore be dismissed, with costs.

ROMER LJ: I agree that this appeal must be dismissed. Upon the facts of the case it appears to me that the learned judge came to the right conclusion, namely, that the contract entered into between the parties to the sale and purchase of this policy rested upon the basis of the assured being still alive. It turns out that, before the matter was concluded by assignment to the defendants, the fact upon which the contract was based was not the fact. The defendant Coulson must be taken to have known that the basis upon which the contract had been entered into, and the common belief upon which both parties had acted, did not exist. That was a circumstance which went to the root of the matter, and rendered it improper to insist upon the completion of the contract. What did Coulson do when he received the information leading him to the knowledge or belief that the assured was dead? Did he do what he ought to have done—tell the plaintiffs? Not at all. He allowed the plaintiffs to go on under the old belief, and to execute the assignment on the footing that the old basis continued and that the defendants were entitled to an assignment. I need scarcely say that that was wholly unjustifiable from a legal point of view, and also from an equitable point of view, and none the less so because the defendants apparently thought they were justified in taking the assignment.

Such a transaction cannot be allowed to stand, and therefore this appeal must be dismissed.

COZENS-HARDY LJ: I agree. I think the case was argued by Mr. Clerke in the only possible way it could be put on behalf of the defendants. Having regard to the facts as found by the learned judge, it appears to me to be quite plain that at the date of the contract there was a common mistake, both parties being under the belief that the assured was alive.

It would be quite shocking to say that the defendants have rendered the contract absolute simply by having obtained from the vendors an assignment after one of the defendants, Coulson, had full notice that the basis on which the contract has been entered into had had no existence. Under such circumstances it is impossible that the defendants can be allowed to derive any benefit from the assignment.

The appeal must, therefore, be dismissed with costs.

SHERWOOD V WALKER
66 Mich 568, 33 NW 919 (Mich SC 1887)

MORSE J: Replevin for a cow. Suit commenced in justice's court. Judgment for plaintiff. Appealed to circuit court of Wayne County, and verdict and judgment for plaintiff in that court. The defendants bring error, and set out 25 assignments of the same.

The main controversy depends upon the construction of a contract for the sale of the cow. The plaintiff claims that the title passed, and bases his action upon such claim. The defendants contend that the contract was executory, and by its terms no title to the animal was acquired by plaintiff. ...

It appears from the record that both parties supposed this cow was barren and would not breed, and she was sold by the pound for an insignificant sum as compared with her real value if a breeder. She was evidently sold and purchased on the relation of her value for beef, unless the plaintiff had learned of her true condition, and concealed such knowledge from the defendants. Before the plaintiff secured possession of the animal, the defendants learned that she was with calf, and therefore of great value, and undertook to rescind the sale by refusing to deliver her. The question arises whether they had a right to do so.

The circuit judge ruled that this fact did not avoid the sale, and it made no difference whether she was barren or not. I am of the opinion that the court erred in this holding. I know that this is a close question, and the dividing line between the adjudicated cases is not easily discerned. But it must be considered as well settled that a party who has given an apparent consent to a contract of sale may refuse to execute it, or he may avoid it after it has been completed, if the assent was founded, or the contract made, upon the mistake of a material fact,—such as the subject-matter of the sale, the price, or some collateral fact materially inducing the agreement; and this can be done when the mistake is mutual. ...

If there is a difference or misapprehension as to the substance of the thing bargained for, if the thing actually delivered or received is different in substance from the thing bargained for and intended to be sold, then there is no contract; but if it be only a difference in some quality or accident, even though the mistake may have been the actuating motive to the purchaser or seller, or both of them, yet the contract remains binding. "The difficulty in every case is to determine whether the mistake or misapprehension is as to the substance of the whole contract, going, as it were, to the root of the matter, or only to some point, even though a material point, an error as to which does not affect the substance of the whole consideration." *Kennedy v. Panama, etc., Mail Co.*, L.R. 2 Q.B. 580, 588.

It has been held, in accordance with the principles above stated, that where a horse is bought under the belief that he is sound, and both vendor and vendee honestly believe him to be sound, the purchaser must stand by his bargain, and pay the full price, unless there was a warranty.

It seems to me, however, in the case made by this record, that the mistake or misapprehension of the parties went to the whole substance of the agreement. If the cow was a breeder, she was worth at least $750; if barren, she was worth not over $80. The parties would not have made the contract of sale except upon the understanding and belief that she was incapable of breeding, and of no use as a cow. It is true she is now the identical animal that they thought her to be when the contract was made; there is no mistake as to the identity of the creature. Yet the mistake was not of the mere quality of the animal, but went to the very nature of the thing. A barren cow is substantially a different creature than a breeding one. There is as much difference between them for all purposes of use as there is between an ox and a cow that is capable of breeding and giving milk. If the mutual mistake had simply related to the fact whether she was with calf or not for one season, then it might have been a good sale; but the mistake affected the character of the animal for all time, and for her present and ultimate use. She was not in fact the animal, or the kind of animal, the defendants intended to sell or the plaintiff to buy. She was not a barren cow, and, if this fact had been known, there would have been no contract. The mistake affected the substance of the whole consideration, and it must be considered that there was no contract to sell or sale of the cow as she actually was. The thing sold and bought had in fact no existence. She was sold as a beef creature would be sold; she is in fact a breeding cow, and a valuable one.

The court should have instructed the jury that if they found that the cow was sold, or contracted to be sold, upon the understanding of both parties that she was barren, and useless for the purpose of breeding, and that in fact she was not barren, but capable of breeding, then the defendants had a right to rescind, and to refuse to deliver, and the verdict should be in their favor.

The judgment of the court below must be reversed, and a new trial granted, with costs of this Court to defendants.

[Campbell CJ and Champlin J concurred.]

SHERWOOD J (dissenting): I do not concur in the opinion given by my brethren in this case. I think the judgments before the justice and at the circuit were right.

... I further agree with [my brother Morse] that the plaintiff was entitled to a delivery of the property to him when the suit was brought, unless there was a mistake made which would invalidate the contract; and I can find no such mistake.

There is no pretense that there was any fraud or concealment in the case, and an intimation or insinuation that such a thing might have existed on the part of either of the parties would undoubtedly be a greater surprise to them than anything else that has occurred in their dealings or in the case. ...

In the spring of 1886 the plaintiff, learning that the defendants had some "polled Angus cattle" for sale, was desirous of purchasing some of that breed, and, meeting the defendants, or some of them, at Walkerville, inquired about them, and was informed that they had none at Walkerville, "but had a few head left on their farm in Greenfield, and they asked the plaintiff to go and see them, stating that in all probability they were sterile and would not breed." In accordance with said request, the plaintiff, on the fifth day of May, went out and looked at the defendants' cattle at Greenfield, and found one called "Rose 2d," which he wished to purchase, and the terms were finally agreed upon at five and one-half cents per pound, live weight, 50 pounds to be deducted for shrinkage. The sale was in writing, and the defendants gave an order to the plaintiff directing the man in charge of the Greenfield farm to deliver the cow to plaintiff. This was done on the fifteenth of May. On the twenty-first of May plaintiff went to get his cow, and the defendants refused to let him have her; claiming at the time that the man in charge at the farm thought the cow was with calf, and, if such was the case they would not sell her for the price agreed upon.

The record further shows that the defendants, when they sold the cow, believed the cow was not with calf, and barren; that from what the plaintiff had been told by defendants (for it does not appear he had any other knowledge or facts from which he could form an opinion) he believed the cow was farrow, but still thought she could be made to breed.

The foregoing shows the entire interview and treaty between the parties as to the sterility and qualities of the cow sold to the plaintiff. The cow had a calf in the month of October.

There is no question but that the defendants sold the cow representing her of the breed and quality they believed the cow to be, and that the purchaser so understood it. And the buyer purchased her believing her to be of the breed represented by the sellers, and possessing all the qualities stated, and even more. He believed she would breed. There is no pretense that the plaintiff bought the cow for beef, and there is nothing in the record indicating that he would have bought her at all only that he thought she might be made to breed. Under the foregoing facts—and these are all that are contained in the record material to the contract—it is held that because it turned out that the plaintiff was more correct in his judgment as to one quality of the cow than the defendants, and a quality, too, which could not by any possibility be positively known at the time by either party to exist, the contract may be annulled by the defendants at their pleasure. I know of no law, and have not been referred to any, which will justify any such holding, and I think the circuit judge was right in his construction of the contract between the parties.

It is claimed that a mutual mistake of a material fact was made by the parties when the contract of sale was made. There was no warranty in the case of the quality of the animal. When a mistaken fact is relied upon as ground for rescinding, such fact must not only exist at the time the contract is made, but must have been known to one or both of the parties. Where there is no warranty, there can be no mistake of fact when no such fact exists, or, if in existence, neither party knew of it, or could know of it; and that is precisely this case. If the owner of a Hambletonian horse had speeded him, and was only able to make him go a mile in three minutes, and should sell him to another, believing that was his greatest speed, for $300, when the purchaser believed he could go much faster, and made the purchase for that sum, and a few days thereafter, under more favorable circumstances, the horse was driven a mile in 2 min. 16 sec., and was found to be worth $20,000, I hardly think it would be held, either at law or in equity, by any one, that the seller in such case could rescind the contract. The same legal principles apply in each case.

In this case neither party knew the actual quality and condition of this cow at the time of the sale. The defendants say, or rather said, to the plaintiff, "they had a few head left on their farm in Greenfield, and asked plaintiff to go and see them, stating to plaintiff that in all probability they were sterile and would not breed." Plaintiff did go as requested, and found there three cows, including the one purchased, with a bull. The cow had been exposed, but neither knew she was with calf or whether she would breed. The defendants thought she would not, but the plaintiff says that he thought she could be made to breed, but believed she was not with calf. The defendants sold the cow for what they believed her to be, and the plaintiff bought her as he believed she was, after the statements made by the defendants. No conditions whatever were attached to the terms of sale by either party. It was in fact as absolute as it could well be made, and I know of no precedent as authority by which this Court can alter the contract thus made by these parties in writing, and interpolate in it a condition by which, if the *defendants should be mistaken in their belief that the cow was barren*, she should be returned to them, and their contract should be annulled.

It is not the duty of courts to destroy contracts when called upon to enforce them, after they have been legally made. There was no mistake of any such material fact by either of the parties in the case as would license the vendors to rescind. There was no difference between the parties, nor misapprehension, as to the substance of the thing bargained for, which was a cow supposed to be barren by one party, and believed not to be by the other. As to the quality of the animal, subsequently developed, both parties were equally ignorant, and as to this each party took his chances. If this were not the law, there would be no safety in purchasing this kind of stock. ...

In this case, if either party had superior knowledge as to the qualities of this animal to the other, certainly the defendants had such advantage.

I understand the law to be well settled that "there is no breach of any implied confidence that one party will not profit by his superior knowledge as to facts and circumstances" equally within the knowledge of both, because neither party reposes in any such confidence unless it be specially tendered or required, and that a general sale does not imply warranty of any quality, or the absence of any; and if the seller represents to the purchaser what he himself believes as to the qualities of an animal, and the purchaser buys relying upon his own judgment as to such qualities, there is no warranty in the case, and neither has a cause of action against the other if he finds himself to have been mistaken in judgment.

MCRAE V COMMONWEALTH DISPOSALS COMM
(1951), 84 CLR 377 (Austl HC)

The Commonwealth Disposals Commission contracted to sell to McRae "one oil tanker including contents wrecked on Jourmand Reef approximately 100 miles north of Samarai. Price £285." The plaintiffs organized a salvage operation to recover the ship, but could not locate the tanker. In fact, there was no tanker at the location indicated in the contract, and there did not seem to be any place known as Jourmand Reef.

DIXON and FULLAGAR JJ: ... In the assumed background of the case lay the facts that during the war a considerable number of ships, including "oil tankers," became wrecked or stranded in the waters adjacent to New Guinea, that after the war the Commission had the function of disposing of these as it thought fit, and that a purchaser from the Commission of any of these wrecked or stranded vessels might, but not necessarily would, make a very large profit by salving and selling the vessel, or the materials of her hull and equipment, or her cargo. The realization of a profit in this way (and the evidence suggests that a purchaser would not contemplate a realization of profit by an immediate resale of what he had bought as such) could, of course, only be achieved after the expenditure of large sums of money. Such a purchaser would naturally regard himself as acquiring, at best, a chance of making a profit. But he would not regard himself as acquiring a certainty of making a loss. ...

Now, the simple fact is that there was not at any material time any oil tanker lying at or anywhere near the location specified in the letter of 18th April. There was, at a point about eleven miles east of the location specified, a wrecked vessel described as an "oil barge." ... The existence of the wrecked barge in question here is not, we think, a directly relevant factor in the case, though it may serve to explain to some extent how a rumour that there was a wrecked tanker somewhere began to circulate in the offices of the Commission.

We say advisedly that such a rumour began to circulate, because there was indeed no better foundation for any supposition on the part of the officers of the Commission that they had a tanker to sell. They had no more definite information than was derived from an offer by a man named Jarrett to buy for £50 the contents of a wrecked vessel, which he said was within a radius of 200 miles from Samarai, and from what can be quite fairly described as mere gossip. The reckless and irresponsible attitude of the Commission's officers is clearly indicated by the description in the advertisement of the locality of the tanker. In an even worse light appears an attempt which was made later, without any foundation whatever, to suggest that at the time of the making of the contract there had been a tanker in the place specified but that she had since been washed off the reef in a storm. Unfortunately the plaintiffs, for their part, took the matter seriously. They believed, and there is evidence that they had some reason for believing, that an oil tanker wrecked at the place indicated was likely to prove a profitable proposition, and accordingly they paid on 23rd April the balance of their purchase money, and then proceeded to fit up a small ship, which they owned, with diving and salvage equipment, and they engaged personnel, and proceeded from Melbourne to New Guinea. It is sufficient at this stage to say that they expended a large sum of money in discovering that they had bought a non-existent tanker.

The plaintiffs, as has been said, based their claim for damages on three alternative grounds. They claimed, in the first place, for damages for breach of a contract to sell a tanker lying at a particular place. Alternatively they claimed damages for a fraudulent representation that there was a tanker lying at the place specified. In the further alternative, they claimed damages for a negligent failure to disclose that there was no tanker at the place specified after that fact became known to the Commission. ...

The first question to be determined is whether a contract was made between the plaintiffs and the Commission. The argument that the contract was void, or, in other words, that there was no contract, was based, as has been observed, on *Couturier v. Hastie* [(1856), 10 ER 1065 (HL)]. It is true that *Couturier v. Hastie* has been commonly treated in the text-books as a case of a contract avoided by mutual mistake. ...

The case has not, however, been universally regarded as resting on mistake, and Sir Frederick Pollock, in his preface to vol. 101 of the Revised Reports, at p. vi, says: — "*Couturier v. Hastie* shows how a large proportion of the cases which swell the rubric of relief against mistake in the textbooks (with or without protest from the text-writer) are really cases of construction." And in *Solle v. Butcher* [above], Denning L.J. observed that the cases which it had been usual to classify under the head of "mistake" needed reconsideration since the decision of the House of Lords in *Bell v. Lever Bros. Ltd.*, [above]. No occasion seems to have arisen for a close examination of *Couturier v. Hastie*, but such an occasion does now arise.

The facts of the case were simple enough. ... A sold to B "1,180 quarters of Salonica Indian corn of fair average quality when shipped, at 27/- per quarter f.o.b., and including freight and insurance, to a safe port in the United Kingdom, payment at two months from date upon handing over shipping documents." At the date of the contract the vessel containing the corn had sailed from Salonica, but, having encountered very heavy weather, had put in at Tunis. Here the cargo had been found to have become so heated and fermented that it could not be safely carried further. It had accordingly been landed at Tunis and sold there. These facts were unknown to either party at the date of the contract. On discovering them, B repudiated the contract. After the expiration of the two months mentioned in the contract, A, being able and willing to hand over the shipping documents, sued B for the price. The case came on for trial before Martin B. and a jury. Martin B. directed the jury that "the contract imported that, at the time of the sale, the corn was in existence as such, and capable of delivery" [(1852), 155 ER 1250 at 1254]. The jury found a verdict for the defendant, and the plaintiff had leave to move. The Court of Exchequer made absolute a rule to enter a verdict for the plaintiff. This decision was reversed in the Court of Exchequer Chamber, and the House of Lords, after consulting the Judges affirmed the decisions of the Exchequer Chamber, so that the defendant ultimately had judgment.

In considering *Couturier v. Hastie* it is necessary to remember that it was, in substance, a case in which a vendor was suing for the price of goods which he was unable to deliver. If there had been nothing more in the case, it would probably never have been reported: indeed the action would probably never have been brought. But the vendor founded his claim on the provision for "payment upon handing over shipping documents." He was not called upon to prove a tender of the documents, because the defendant had "repudiated" the contract, but he was able and willing to hand them over, and his argument was, in effect, that by handing them over he would be doing all that the contract required of him. The question thus raised would seem to depend entirely on the construction of the contract, and it appears really to have been so treated throughout. In the Court of Exchequer, Pollock C.B., in the course of argument, said [(1852), 155 ER 1250 at 1254]: — "This question is purely one of construction. I certainly think that the plain and literal meaning of the language here used imports that the thing sold, namely, the cargo, was in existence and capable of being transferred." This was, in effect, what Martin B. had told the jury, and what it means is that the plaintiff had contracted that there was a cargo in existence and capable of delivery. ...

The judgment of the Exchequer Chamber was delivered by Coleridge J. The view that the contract was void is probably derived from certain expressions which were used in the course of this judgment. But it does seem clear that again the question of construction was regarded as the fundamental question in the case. In the light of these passages it seems impossible to regard the expressions [(1853), 156 ER 43 at 46] "[i]f the contract for the sale of the cargo was valid" and "the contract failed as to the principal subject-matter of it" as meaning that the contract was treated as being void. All that the passages in which those expressions occur seem in their context to mean is that the principal subject matter of the contract was a cargo of goods, that the purchaser did not buy shipping documents representing non-existent goods, that the consideration to the purchaser had failed, and that he could not therefore be liable to pay the contract price.

In the House of Lords again the Lord Chancellor, in giving judgment [(1856), 10 ER 1065 at 1068 and 1069], said: — "The whole question turns upon the meaning and construction of the contract." A little later he said: — "What the parties contemplated ... was that there was an existing something to be sold and bought, and, if sold and bought, then the benefit of insurance should go with it." In other words, there was not an absolute obligation to pay the price on delivery of the shipping documents (as the plaintiff contended), but an obligation to pay on delivery of those documents only if they represented at the time of the making of the contract goods in existence and capable of delivery. And this is all that the Lord Chancellor really had in mind, we think, when later he says: — "If the contract of the 15th May had been an operating contract, and there had been a valid contract at that time existing, I think the purchaser would have had the benefit of insurance in respect of all damage previously existing." ...

If the view so far indicated be correct, as we believe it to be, it seems clear that the case of *Couturier v. Hastie* does not compel one to say that the contract in the present case was void. But, even if the view that *Couturier v. Hastie* was a case of a void contract be correct, we would still think that it could not govern the present case. Denning L.J. indeed says in *Solle v. Butcher* [(1950), 1 KB 671 at 692 (CA)]: — "Neither party can rely on his own mistake to say it was a nullity from the beginning, no matter that it was a mistake which to his mind was fundamental, and no matter that the other party knew he was under a mistake. *A fortiori* if the other party did not know of the mistake, but shared it." But, even if this be not wholly and strictly correct, yet at least it must be true to say that a party cannot rely on mutual mistake where the mistake consists of a belief which is, on the one hand, entertained by him without any reasonable ground, and, on the other hand, deliberately induced by him in the mind of the other party ... even if they [officials of the Commission] be credited with a real belief in the existence of a tanker, they were guilty of the grossest negligence. It is impossible to say that they had any reasonable ground for such a belief. Having no reasonable grounds for such a belief, they asserted by their advertisement to the world at large, and by their later specification of locality to the plaintiffs, that they had a tanker to sell. They must have known that any tenderer would rely implicitly on their assertion of the existence of a tanker, and they must have known that the plaintiffs would rely implicitly on their later assertion of the existence of a tanker in the latitude and longitude given. They took no steps to verify what they were asserting, and any "mistake" that existed was induced by their own culpable conduct. In these circumstances it seems out of the question that they should be able to assert that no contract was concluded. It is not unfair or inaccurate to say that the only "mistake" the plaintiffs made was that they believed what the Commission told them.

The position so far, then, may be summed up as follows. It was not decided in *Couturier v. Hastie* that the contract in that case was void. The question whether it was void or not did not arise. If it had arisen, as in an action by the purchaser for damages, it would have turned on the ulterior question whether the contract was subject to an implied condition precedent. Whatever might then have been held on the facts of *Couturier v. Hastie*, it is impossible in this case to imply any such term. The terms of the contract and the surrounding circumstances clearly exclude any such implication. The buyers relied upon, and acted upon, the assertion of the seller that there was a tanker in existence. It is not a case in which the parties can be seen to have proceeded on the basis of a common assumption of fact so as to justify the conclusion that the correctness of the assumption was intended by both parties to be a condition precedent to the creation of contractual obligations. The officers of the Commission made an assumption, but the plaintiffs did not make an assumption in the same sense. They knew nothing except what the Commission had told them. If they had been asked, they would certainly not have said: "Of course, if there is no tanker, there is no contract." They would have said: "We shall have to go and take possession of the tanker. We simply accept the Commission's assurance that there is a tanker and the Commission's promise to give us that tanker." The only proper construction of the contract is that it included a promise by the Commission that there was a tanker in the position specified. The Commission contracted that there was a tanker there. ... If, on the other hand, the case of *Couturier v. Hastie* and this case ought to be treated as cases raising a question of "mistake," then the Commission cannot in this case rely on any mistake as avoiding the contract, because any mistake was induced by the serious fault of their own servants, who asserted the existence of a tanker recklessly and without any reasonable ground. There *was* a contract, and the Commission contracted that a tanker existed in the position specified. Since there was no such tanker, there has been a breach of contract, and the plaintiffs are entitled to damages for that breach. ...

The conclusion that there was an enforceable contract makes it unnecessary to consider the other two causes of action raised by the plaintiffs.

QUESTIONS

What damages should the plaintiffs recover? Would or should the decision have been different if an oil tanker had been on the reef but had been swept away in a storm before the contract was entered into? Consider why the case was not argued as one of misrepresentation.

WOOD V BOYNTON
64 Wis 265, 25 NW 42 (1885)

TAYLOR J: This action was brought in the circuit court for Milwaukee county to recover the possession of an uncut diamond of the alleged value of $1,000. The case was tried in the circuit court and, after hearing all the evidence in the case, the learned circuit judge directed the jury to find a verdict for the defendants. The plaintiff excepted to such instruction, and, after a verdict was rendered for the defendants, moved for a new trial upon the minutes of the judge. The motion was denied, and the plaintiff duly excepted, and, after judgment was entered in favor of the defendants, appealed to this court.

The defendants are partners in the jewelry business. On the trial it appeared that on and before the 28th of December, 1883, the plaintiff was the owner of and in the possession of a small stone, the nature and value of which she was ignorant; that on that day she sold it to one of the defendants for the sum of one dollar. Afterwards it was ascertained that the stone was a rough diamond, and of the value of about $700. After learning this fact the plaintiff tendered the defendants the one dollar, and ten cents as interest, and demanded a return of the stone to her. The defendants refused to deliver it, and therefore she commenced this action.

The plaintiff testified to the circumstances attending the sale of the stone to Mr. Samuel B. Boynton, as follows:

> The first time Boynton saw that stone he was talking about buying the topaz, or whatever it is, in September or October. I went into his store to get a little pin mended, and I had it in a small box,—the pin,—a small ear-ring; ... this stone, and a broken sleeve-button were in the box. Mr. Boynton turned to give me a check for my pin. I thought I would ask him what the stone was, and I took it out of the box and asked him to please tell me what that was. He took it in his hand and seemed some time looking at it. I told him I had been told it was a topaz and he said it might be. He says, "I would buy this; would you sell it?" I told him I did not know but what I would. What would it be worth? And he said he did not know; he would give me a dollar and keep it as a specimen, and I told him I would not sell it; and it was certainly pretty to look at. He asked me where I found it, and I told him in Eagle. He asked about how far out, and I said right in the village, and I went out. Afterwards, and about the 28th of December, I needed money pretty badly, and thought every dollar would help, and I took it back to Mr. Boynton and told him I had brought back the topaz, and he says, "Well, yes; what did I offer you for it?" and I says, "One dollar," and he stepped to the change drawer and gave me the dollar, and I went out.

In another part of her testimony she says:

> Before I sold the stone I had no knowledge whatever that it was a diamond. I told him that I had been advised that it was probably a topaz, and he said probably it was. The stone was about the size of a canary bird's egg, nearly the shape of an egg,—worn pointed at one end; it was nearly straw color,—a little darker.

She also testified that before this action was commenced she tendered the defendants $1.10, and demanded the return of the stone, which they refused. This is substantially all the evidence of what took place at and before the sale to the defendants, as testified to by the plaintiff herself. She produced no other witness on that point.

The evidence on the part of the defendant is not very different from the version given by the plaintiff, and certainly is not more favorable to the plaintiff. Mr. Samuel B. Boynton, the defendant to whom the stone was sold, testified that at the time he bought this stone, he had never seen an uncut diamond; had seen cut diamonds, but they are quite different from the uncut ones; "he had no idea this was a diamond, and it never entered his brain at the time." Considerable evidence was given as to what took place after the sale and purchase, but that evidence has very little if any bearing upon the main point in the case.

This evidence clearly shows that the plaintiff sold the stone in question to the defendants, and delivered it to them in December 1883, for a consideration of one dollar. The title to the stone passed by the sale and delivery to the defendants. How has that title been divested and again vested in the plaintiff? The contention of the learned counsel for the appellant is that the title became vested in the plaintiff by the tender to the Boyntons of the purchase money, with interest, and a demand of a return of the stone to her. Unless such tender and demand revested the title in the appellant, she cannot maintain her action.

The only question in the case is whether there was anything in the sale which entitled the vendor (the appellant) to rescind the sale and so revest the title in her. The only reasons we know of for rescinding a sale and revesting the title in the vendor so that he may maintain an action at law for the recovery of the possession against his vendee are (1) that the vendee was guilty of some fraud in procuring a sale to be made to him; (2) that there was a mistake made by the vendor in delivering an article which was not the article sold,—a mistake in fact as to the identity of the thing sold with the thing delivered upon the sale. This last is not in reality a rescission of the sale made, as the thing delivered was not the thing sold, and no title ever passed to the vendee by such delivery.

In this case, upon the plaintiff's own evidence, there can be no just ground for alleging that she was induced to make the sale she did by any fraud or unfair dealings on the part of Mr. Boynton. Both were entirely ignorant at the time of the character of the stone and of its intrinsic value. Mr. Boynton was not an expert in uncut diamonds, and had made no examination of the stone, except to take it in his hand and look at it before he made the offer of one dollar, which was refused at the time, and afterwards accepted without any comment or further examination made by Mr. Boynton. The appellant had the stone in her possession for a long time, and it appears from her own statement that she made some inquiry as to its nature and qualities. If she chose to sell it without further investigation as to its intrinsic value to a person who was guilty of no fraud or unfairness which induced her to sell it for a small sum, she cannot repudiate the sale because it is afterwards ascertained that she made a bad bargain. *Kennedy v. Panama, etc., Mail Co.*, L.R. 2 Q.B. 580.

There is no pretense of any mistake as to the identity of the thing sold. It was produced by the plaintiff and exhibited to the vendor before the sale was made, and the thing sold was delivered to the vendee when the purchase price was paid. *Kennedy v. Panama, etc., Mail Co.*, L.R. 2 Q.B. 587; *Street v. Blay*, 2 Barn. & Adol. 456; *Compertz v. Bartlett*, 2 El. & Bl. 849; *Gurney v. Womersly*, 4 El. & Bl. 133; *Ship's Case*, 2 De G., J. & S. 544. Suppose the appellant had produced the stone, and said she had been told that it was a diamond, and she believed it was, but had no knowledge herself as to its character or value, and Mr. Boynton had given her $500 for it, could he have rescinded the sale if it had turned out to be a topaz or any other stone of very small value? Could Mr. Boynton have rescinded the sale on the ground of mistake? Clearly not, nor could he rescind it on the ground that there had been a breach of warranty, because there was no warranty, nor could he rescind it on the ground of fraud, unless he could show that she falsely declared that she had been told it was a diamond, or, if she had been told, still she knew it was not a diamond. See *Street v. Blay, supra.*

It is urged, with a good deal of earnestness, on the part of the counsel for the appellant that, because it has turned out that the stone was immensely more valuable than the parties at the time of the sale supposed it was, such fact alone is a ground for the rescission of the sale, and that fact was evidence of fraud on the part of the vendee. Whether inadequacy of price is to be received as evidence of fraud, even in a suit in equity to avoid a sale, depends upon the facts known to the parties at the time the sale is made.

When this sale was made the value of the thing sold was open to the investigation of both parties, neither knew its intrinsic value, and, so far as the evidence in this case shows, both supposed that the price paid was adequate. How can fraud be predicated upon such a sale, even though after investigation showed that the intrinsic value of the thing sold was hundreds of times greater than the price paid? It certainly shows no such fraud as would authorize the vendor to rescind the contract and bring an action at law to recover the possession of the thing sold. Whether the fact would have any influence in an action in equity to avoid the sale we need not consider. See *Stettheimer v. Killip*, 75 N.Y. 287; *Etting v. Bank of U.S.*, 11 Wheat. 59.

We can find nothing in the evidence from which it could be justly inferred that Mr. Boynton, at the time he offered the plaintiff one dollar for the stone, had any knowledge of the real value of the stone, or that he entertained even a belief that the stone was a diamond. It cannot, therefore, be said that there was a suppression of knowledge on the part of the defendant as to the value of the stone which a court of equity might seize upon to avoid the sale. The following cases show that, in the absence of fraud or warranty, the value of the property sold, as compared with the price paid, is no ground for a rescission of the sale. *Wheat v. Cross*, 31 Md. 99; *Lambert v. Heath*, 15 Mees. & W. 487; *Bryant v. Pember*, 45 Vt. 487; *Kuelkamp v. Hidding*, 31 Wis. 503, 511.

However unfortunate the plaintiff may have been in selling this valuable stone for a mere nominal sum, she has failed entirely to make out a case either of fraud or mistake in the sale such as will entitle her to a rescission of such sale so as to recover the property sold in an action at law.

By the Court.—The judgment of the circuit court is affirmed.

R (ONT) V RON ENGINEERING
[1981] 1 SCR 111, 119 DLR (3d) 267

[A contractor submitted a bid of $2,748,000 to construct a project, along with a certified cheque for the deposit of $150,000, in compliance with para 13 of the Information for Tenderers:

> Except as otherwise herein provided the tenderer guarantees that if his tender is withdrawn before the Commission shall have considered the tenders or before or after he has been notified that his tender has been recommended to the Commission for acceptance or that if the Commission does not for any reason receive within the period of seven days as stipulated and as required herein, the Agreement executed by the tenderer, the Performance Bond and the Payment Bond executed by the tenderer and the surety company and the other documents required herein, the Commission may retain the tender deposit for the use of the Commission and may accept any tender, advertise for new tenders, negotiate a contract or not accept any tender as the Commission may deem advisable.

After the tenders were opened, the contractor discovered that its bid was $632,000 lower than the next lowest bid. The contractor informed the owner one hour after the tender opening that in its rush to put its bid together, it left out of the total $750,058 for its own workforce, which would have brought its bid to $3,498,058. The contractor attempted to withdraw the tender, but the owner offered it the contract. When the contractor declined to sign, the owner kept the deposit. Subsequently and throughout the proceedings, the contractor took the position that it had not withdrawn its tender, but the owner could not accept its tender after it had received notice of the error and, because the notice had come before acceptance of the tender, the owner must return the deposit. The contractor sued for the return of the deposit, losing at trial, but succeeding in the Ontario Court of Appeal. The owner appealed to the Supreme Court of Canada.]

ESTEY J (for the court): The Ontario Court of Appeal, reversing the trial Judge, directed the return to the respondent-contractor (hereinafter referred to as the "contractor") of $150,000 paid by the contractor to the appellant-owner (hereinafter referred to as the "owner") by way of a tender deposit at the time of filing a bid in response to a call for tenders by the owner. ...

The core of the submission by the contractor is simply that a mistake by a tenderer, be it patent or latent, renders the tender revocable or the deposit recoverable by the tenderer, notwithstanding the provisions of para. 13 quoted above, so long as notice is given to the owner of the mistake prior to the acceptance by the owner of the contractor's tender. There are subsidiary arguments advanced by the contractor to which I will later make reference.

We are not here concerned with a case where the mistake committed by the tendering contractor is apparent on the face of the tender. Rather the mistake here involved is one which requires an explanation outside of the tender documents themselves. The trial Judge has so found and there is evidence in support of that finding. Nor do we have here a case where a trial Court has found impropriety on the part of the contractor such as the attempted recall of an intended, legitimate bid once the contractor has become aware that it is the lowest bidder by a wide margin. ...

Relying on its decision in *Belle River Community Arena Inc. v. W.J.C. Kaufmann Co. Ltd. et al.* (1978), 87 D.L.R. (3d) 761, decided by the Court of Appeal after the trial judgment herein had been handed down, the Court of Appeal concluded "that an offeree cannot accept an offer which he knows has been made by mistake and which affects a fundamental term of the contract." The Court, speaking through Arnup J.A., continued [(1979), 98 D.L.R (3d) 548 at 550]:

> In our view, the principles enunciated in that case ought to be applied in this case. The error in question has been found to be, as it obviously was, material and.important. It was drawn to the attention of the Commission almost at once after the opening of tenders. Notwithstanding that, the Commission proceeded as if the error had not been made and on the footing that it was entitled to treat the tender for what it said on its face.

and concluded [at 550-51]:

> As I said in the course of the argument, a commission or other owner calling for tenders is entitled to be sceptical when a bidder who is the low tenderer by a very substantial amount attempts to say, after the opening of tenders, that a mistake has been made. However, when that mistake is proven by the production of reasonable evidence, the person to whom the tender is made is not in a position to accept the tender or to seek to forfeit the bid deposit.

In the *Belle River* case the contractor purported to withdraw the tender before any action to accept was taken by the owner. In the course of reaching the conclusion that the contractor was entitled to recover his bid bond, Arnup J.A. in that case found that the owner was unable to accept the offer once he became aware that it contained a mistake which affected a fundamental term of the contract. At p. 766 D.L.R., the learned Justice in Appeal put it this way:

> In substance, the purported offer, because of the mistake, is not the offer the offeror intended to make, and the offeree knows that.
> The principle applies even if there is a provision binding the offeror to keep the offer open for acceptance for a given period.

and continuing on p. 767 D.L.R.:

> In view of the conclusion I have reached as to the inability of the plaintiff to accept the tender, it does not matter, in my opinion, whether the purported tender could be withdrawn, or was in fact withdrawn, before the purported acceptance. ...
> If Kaufmann's tender could be withdrawn before acceptance (as occurred in *Hamilton Bd. Ed.* case ... [*Hamilton Bd. Ed. v. U.S.F. & G.*, [1960] O.R. 594]), then Kaufmann's tender was so withdrawn, and no contract came into existence. If it could not be withdrawn for 60 days, it nevertheless could not be accepted, for the reason already stated, and hence no contract came into existence.

This judgment is the basis for that given by the Court of Appeal in these proceedings. ...

The revocability of the offer must, in my view, be determined in accordance with the "General Conditions" and "Information for Tenderers" and the related documents upon which the tender was submitted. There is no question when one reviews the terms and conditions under which the tender was made that a contract arose upon the submission of a tender between the contractor and the owner whereby the tenderer could not withdraw the tender for a period of 60 days after the date of the opening of the tenders. Later in these reasons this initial contract is referred to as contract "A" to distinguish it from the construction contract itself which would arise on the acceptance of a tender, and which I refer to as contract "B." Other terms and conditions of this unilateral contract which arose by the filing of a tender in response to the call therefor under the aforementioned terms and conditions, included the right to recover the tender deposit 60 days after the opening of tenders if the tender was not accepted by the owner. This contract is brought into being automatically upon the submission of a tender. The terms and conditions specified in the tender documents and which become part of the terms of contract A between the owner and the contractor included the following provision:

> *6. Withdrawal or Qualifying of Tenders*
>
> A tenderer who has already submitted a tender may submit a further tender at any time up to the official closing time. The last tender received shall supersede and invalidate all tenders previously submitted by that tenderer for this contract.
>
> A tenderer may withdraw or qualify his tender at any time up to the official closing time by submitting a letter bearing his signature and seal as in his tender to the Commission Secretary or his authorized representative in his office who will mark thereon the time and date of receipt and will place the letter in the tender box. No telegrams or telephone calls will be considered.

Paragraph 13 ... provides for the return of the tender deposit on the execution of the construction contract and then goes on to provide ... :

> Except as otherwise herein provided the tenderer guarantees that if his tender is withdrawn ... or if the Commission does not for any reason receive within the period of seven days ... the Agreement executed by the tenderer ... the Commission may retain the tender deposit. ...

Paragraph 14 is also relevant:

> The tenderer agrees that, if requested so to do by the Commission or anyone acting on its behalf within 90 days after the date of opening tenders, he will execute a triplicate and return to the Commission the Agreement in the form found [*sic*] herein within seven days after being so requested.

Here the contractor expressly avoided employing any terminology indicating a withdrawal of the tender, and indeed affirmatively asserted the position throughout that the offer had not been revoked. The owner did proffer a construction agreement and this agreement was not executed by the tenderer within the seven-day period. ...

We are then left with the bare submission on behalf of the contractor that while the offer was not withdrawn it was not capable of acceptance and that by reason thereof the contractor is entitled to a return of the deposit.

I share the view expressed by the Court of Appeal that the integrity of the bidding system must be protected where under the law of contracts it is possible so to do. I further share the view expressed by that Court that there may be circumstances where a tender may not be accepted as for example where in law it does not constitute a tender, and hence the bid deposit might not be forfeited. That is so in my view, however, simply because contract A cannot come into being. It puts it another way to say that the purported tender does not in law amount to an acceptance of the call for tenders and hence the unilateral contract does not come into existence. Therefore, with the greatest of respect, I diverge from that Court where it is stated in the judgment below [at 551]:

> However, when that mistake is proven by the production of reasonable evidence, the person to whom the tender is made is not in a position to accept the tender or to seek to forfeit the deposit.

The test, in my respectful view, must be imposed at the time the tender is submitted and not at some later date after a demonstration by the tenderer of a calculation error. Contract A (being the contract arising forthwith upon the submission of the tender) comes into being forthwith and without further formality upon the submission of the tender. If the tenderer has committed an error in the calculation leading to the tender submitted with the tender deposit, and at least in those circumstances where at that moment the tender is capable of acceptance of law, the rights of the parties under contract A have thereupon crystallized. The tender deposit, designed to ensure the performance of the obligations of the tenderer under contract A, must therefore stand exposed to the risk of forfeiture upon the breach of those obligations by the tenderer. Where the conduct of the tenderer might indeed expose him to other claims in damages by the owner, the tender deposit might well be the lesser pain to be suffered by reason of the error in the preparation of the tender. This I will return to later.

Much argument was undertaken in this Court on the bearing of the law of mistake on the outcome of this appeal. In approaching the application of the principles of mistake it is imperative here to bear in mind that the only contract up to now in existence between the parties to this appeal is the contract arising on the submission of the tender whereunder the tender is irrevocable during the period of time stipulated in the contract. Contract B (the construction contract, the form of which is set out in the documents relating to the call for tenders) has not and did not come into existence. We are concerned therefore with the law of mistake, if at all, only in connection with contract A.

The tender submitted by the respondent brought contract A into life. This is sometimes described in law as a unilateral contract, that is to say a contract which results from an act made in response to an offer, as for example in the simplest terms, "I will pay you a dollar if you will cut my lawn." No obligation to cut the lawn exists in law and the obligation to pay the dollar comes into being upon the performance of the invited act. Here the call for tenders created no obligation in the respondent or in anyone else in or out of the construction world. When a member of the construction industry responds to the call for tenders, as the respondent has done here, that response takes the form of the submission of a tender, or a bid as it is sometimes called. The significance of the bid in law is that it at once becomes irrevocable if filed in conformity with the terms and conditions under which the call for tenders was made and if such terms so provide. There is no disagreement between the parties here about the form and procedure in which the tender was submitted by the respondent and that it complied with the terms and conditions of the call for tenders. Consequently, contract A came into being. The principal term of contract A is the irrevocability of the bid, and the corollary term is the obligation in both parties to enter into a contract (contract B) upon the acceptance of the tender. Other terms include the qualified obligations of the owner to accept the lowest tender, and the degree of this obligation is controlled by the terms and conditions established in the call for tenders.

The role of the deposit under contract A is clear and simple. The deposit was required in order to ensure the performance by the contractor-tenderer of its obligations under contract A. The deposit was recoverable by the contractor under certain conditions, none of which were met; and also was subject to forfeiture under another term of the contract, the provisions of which in my view have been met.

There is no question of a mistake on the part of either party up to the moment in time when contract A came into existence. The employee of the respondent intended to submit the very tender submitted, including the price therein stipulated. Indeed, the president, in instructing the respondent's employee, intended the tender to be as submitted. However, the contractor submits that as the tender was the product of a mistake in calculation, it cannot form the basis of a construction contract since it is not capable of acceptance and hence it cannot be subject to the terms and conditions of contract A so as to cause a forfeiture thereunder of the deposit. The fallacy in this argument is twofold. Firstly, there was no mistake in the sense that the contractor did not intend to submit the tender as in form and substance it was. Secondly, there is no principle in law under which the tender was rendered incapable of acceptance by the appellant. For a mutual contract such as contract B to arise, there must of course be a meeting of the minds, a shared *animus contrahendi*, but when the contract in question is the product of other contractual arrangements, different considerations apply. However, as already stated, we never reach that problem here as the rights of the parties fall to be decided according to the tender arrangements, contract A. At the point when the tender was submitted the owner had not been told about the mistake in calculation. Unlike the case of *McMaster University v. Wilchar Const. Ltd.* (1971), 22 D.L.R. (3d) 9 [aff'd 69 DLR (3d) 400n], there was nothing on the face of the tender to reveal an error. There was no inference to be drawn by the quantum of the tender ... that there had indeed been a miscalculation.

It was not seriously advanced that this was a case of patent error in the tender offer and I proceed on the basis that there was not a patent error present.

On the facts as found by the learned trial Judge, no mistake existed which impeded or affected the coming into being of contract A. The "mistake" occurred in the calculations leading to the figures that the contractor admittedly intended to submit in his tender. Therefore, the issue in my view concerns not the law of mistake but the application of the forfeiture provisions contained in the tender documents. The effect a mistake may have on the enforceability or interpretation of a contract subsequently arising is an entirely different question, and one not before us. Neither are we here concerned with a question as to whether a construction contract can arise between parties in the presence of a mutually known error in a tender be it, at least initially, either patent or latent.

It might be argued that by some abstract doctrine of law a tender which could not form the basis of a contract upon acceptance in the sense of contract B, could not operate as a tender to bring into being contract A. It is unnecessary to consider such a theory because it was not and could not be argued that the tender as actually submitted by the contractor herein was not in law capable of acceptance immediately upon its receipt by the owner, the appellant. There may well be, as I have indicated, a situation in the contemplation of the law where a form of tender was so lacking as not to amount in law to a tender in the case of the terms and conditions established in the call for tenders, and it may well be that such a form of tender could not be "snapped up" by the owner, as some cases have put it, and therefore it would not operate to trigger the birth of contract A. Such a situation might arise in the circumstances described in Fridman, *The Law of Contract in Canada* (1976), at p. 81: "An offer that is made in error, *e.g.*, as where the offeror intended to say $200 a ton but wrote $20 by mistake, may be an offer that cannot be validly accepted by the other party." The rule in *Foster v. Mackinnon* (1869), L.R. 4 C.P. 704 (*vide* Cheshire Fifoot, *The Law of Contract*, 9th ed. (1976), pp. 239-40, for a discussion of the *non est factum* rule), might also preclude the creation of a contract based upon such an offer. We do not have to decide that question here.

Nor are we concerned with the position of the parties where an action is brought upon a refusal to form contract B as was the case in *McMaster, supra*. It is true that the appellant-owner here has made a counterclaim for damages resulting from the refusal of the respondent to enter into the construction contract but such counterclaim was dismissed and the appeal herein is concerned only with the claim made by the respondent for the return of the tender deposit.

Left to itself, therefore, the law of contract would result in a confirmation of a dismissal by the learned trial Judge of the claim by the contractor for the return of the tender deposit. The terms of contract A, already set out, clearly indicate a contractual right in the owner to forfeit this money.

As the respondent has not raised the principle of the law of penalty as it applies to the retention of the deposit here by the appellant, it is not necessary to deal with that branch of the law. ...

For these reasons I would allow the appeal, set aside the order of the Court of Appeal, and restore the judgment of J. Holland J. at trial with costs, here and in all Courts below, to the appellant.

Appeal allowed.

NOTES AND PROBLEMS

1. The Supreme Court of Canada affirmed the decision in *Ron Engineering* in *MJB Enterprises Ltd v Defence Construction (1951) Ltd*, [1999] 1 SCR 619, 170 DLR (4th) 577. The court also rejected Estey J's characterization of "Contract A" in *Ron Engineering* as a unilateral contract. See *MJB Enterprises*, excerpted in Chapter 3.

2. In bidding situations, sometimes the party making a tender makes a mistake in calculating its offer. If the other party knows of the mistake, can it snap up the low offer by accepting the bid? In *Imperial Glass Ltd v Consolidated Supplies Ltd* (1960), 22 DLR (2d) 759 (BCCA), the court held that because the mistake was not in the offer, but merely in the information on which it was based, the offer had been intended and therefore there was a consensus. However, in *McMaster University v Wilchar Construction Ltd* (1971), 22 DLR (3d) 9 (Ont H Ct J), aff'd without reasons 69 DLR (3d) 400n (CA), the Ontario High Court held that if one party made an honest mistake as to a material term of the contract, a mistake of which the other party was aware, there is no consensus and therefore no valid contract. And in *Belle River Community Arena Inc v WJC Kaufmann Co Ltd* (1978), 20 OR (2d) 447, 87 DLR (3d) 761 (CA), the court harshly criticized *Imperial Glass* and held that if a contractor submits a tender containing a mistake as to a fundamental term and the other party knows of the mistake, the contractor is not bound: specifically (at para 13), "In my view, the authorities establish that an offeree cannot accept an offer which he knows has been made by mistake and which affects a fundamental term of the contract. Price is obviously one such term ... . In substance, the purported offer, because of the mistake, is not the offer the offeror intended to make, and the offeree knows that."

3. Is the *Ron Engineering* solution to mistaken bids satisfactory? It has been suggested that it tends to provide windfalls to issuers of invitations to bid. For a discussion of two Canadian appellate courts' articulation of a rule that excuses mistaken bids (*Calgary (City) v Northern Construction Co*, [1986] 2 WWR 426 (Alta CA) and *Toronto Transit Commission v Gottardo Construction Ltd* (2005), 257 DLR (4th) 539 (Ont CA)), see John McCamus, "Mistaken Bids and

Unilateral Mistaken Assumptions, A New Solution for an Old Problem?" (2008) 87 Can Bar Rev 1. McCamus says:

> In two recent decisions, Alberta and Ontario appellate judges have expressed the view that mistaken bidders should be excused from their obligations where the burden imposed by the error is so *grossly disproportionate* that enforcement of the mistaken bid would be *unconscionable*. What is being proposed, in effect, is the recognition of a rule permitting rescission of the bidder's contractual obligations on the basis of the bidder's *unilateral* mistaken *assumption*. The error is unilateral in the sense that the calculation error is the bidder's alone. It is not shared by the issuer. The error pertains to an *assumption* on the bidder's part that the calculation of the price was accurate.

There were no grounds for equitable intervention in either *Gottardo* or *Northern Construction*. In *Gottardo*, the Court of Appeal found that the bidder's mistake, a miscalculation of approximately 10 percent of the correct bid price, or a $557,000 error, did not preclude the formation of Contract A. Similarly, in *Northern Construction*, a calculation error of $181,274 in a bid priced at $9,342,000 was not found to be so grossly disproportionate to the contract price such that it would have been unconscionable to hold the mistaken bidder contractually liable.

4. See generally on mistake in assumptions Waddams, ch 12; McCamus at 556-87; Mac-Dougall at 228-37.

VI. RESTITUTION

In this chapter we have examined the principles on which apparent agreements may be held unenforceable on grounds of mistake—that is, where the mistake has been induced by a misrepresentation of one party; where the mistake has prevented the formation of a true *consensus ad idem*; and where a mistaken assumption concerning the context of the transaction rendered its enforcement unjust. In each of these contexts, the party who has transferred value to the other party on the assumption that a valid contract was in existence may choose to pursue restitutionary relief for the value of the benefit conferred. The precise means by which restitution will be achieved, however, rests, to some extent, on whether the doctrine providing a basis for the unenforceability of the apparent agreement is one developed by the courts of common law or the courts of equity.

In order to set aside an agreement on equitable grounds, it was necessary to obtain a decree of rescission. A decree of rescission could not be obtained unless the parties could make an effective restoration of benefits received from one to the other. That is, a decree of rescission required that there be achieved an effective *restitutio in integrum*. At common law, this particular form of decree was unavailable. Nonetheless, the courts of common law did grant recovery of benefits conferred under transactions considered ineffective at common law in what were once referred to as quasi-contractual claims. Such a claim was advanced, for example, in *Bell v Lever Brothers*, above, to recover the moneys paid to Bell. If the House of Lords had held, in this case, that the agreement was indeed void at common law by reason of a mistaken assumption that Bell was not dismissible, recovery of the moneys paid would have been granted. Similarly, if benefits were conferred under an agreement that failed for a lack of *consensus ad idem*, a claim to recover their value would lie at common law.

Further, in some contexts, the common law held that where property had been transferred under an agreement void for operative mistake, property would not pass to the other party, thus enabling the mistaken party to pursue proprietary relief that, if successful, would have the effect of restoring the benefit conferred to the party who had conferred it. The mistake of identity cases examined in Chapter 4, such as *Cundy v Lindsay*, provide a leading illustration of the phenomenon. If the transaction was merely vulnerable to rescission in equity, however, the contract, being valid at law, was effective to pass title to the asset in question until such time as the agreement was rescinded or avoided in equity. Upon rescission, title to the asset would be revested in the transferor.

Accordingly, an important difference between the effect of rules that render agreements void at common law and those that render them voidable in equity is their impact on third parties who may have purchased in good faith an asset initially transferred under an agreement that is void or voidable for mistake. If the agreement is void at common law, no property would pass to the third party. The third party would be vulnerable, therefore, to a proprietary claim brought by the owner of the asset. If the agreement was rendered merely voidable, however, and the third party purchased the asset prior to rescission of the agreement in equity, title would have passed at common law to the third party and the decree of rescission would be denied.

The precise interaction of common law and equitable doctrines, however, and their consequent impact on the means by which restitution is achieved is subtle and, in contexts such as misrepresentation and mistake, where both common law and equitable doctrines are in play, may vary from one context to another. In the context of misrepresentation, as we have seen, courts of common law recognized that agreements induced by fraudulent misrepresentation could not be enforced. Nonetheless, courts of common law did not necessarily conclude that in such circumstances common law title would not pass where an asset was transferred to the defrauded party. The differences in the remedial devices available to courts of common law and equity in the context of fraudulent misrepresentation were described by Lord Blackburn in *Erlanger v The New Sombrero Phosphate Company*, below.

Erlanger v The New Sombrero Phosphate Company. (1878), 3 App Cas 1218. Baron Erlanger, a Paris banker, headed a syndicate (or partnership) that on August 30, 1871 acquired for £55,000 a lease of an island in the West Indies believed to contain valuable phosphate mines. He proceeded to organize a corporation with directors of his own choosing and the corporation bought the mines for £110,000 on September 20, 1871. At the first ordinary general meeting of the company on February 2, 1872, a shareholder queried the sale, which the first directors had already confirmed, but no action was taken. At the first annual general meeting on June 19, 1872, a committee was appointed to investigate rumours about the sale. The committee reported on August 29, and on December 24 the company filed suit against Erlanger and others asking to have the contract set aside, the £110,000 repaid to the company, the company to deliver up the island and to account for profits (if any) made by working it. It was so ordered. Most of the judgments are taken up with the question of the duty of promoters in equity to make full disclosure, and with the question of the separate identities of the promoters, the company, and its handful of shareholders on September 20, 1871 and on June 19, 1872. On the question of restitution, LORD BLACKBURN said:

> It is, I think, clear on principles of general justice, that as a condition to a rescission there must be a *restitutio in integrum*. The parties must be put in *statu quo*. It is a doctrine which has often been acted upon both at law and in equity. But there is a considerable difference in the mode in which it is applied in Courts of Law and Equity, owing, as I think, to the difference of the machinery which the Courts have at command. I speak of these Courts as they were at the time when this suit commenced, without inquiring whether the Judicature Acts make any, or if any, what difference.
>
> It would be obviously unjust that a person who has been in possession of property under the contract which he seeks to repudiate should be allowed to throw that back on the other party's hands without accounting for any benefit he may have derived from the use of the property, or if the property, though not destroyed, has been in the interval

deteriorated, without making compensation for that deterioration. But as a Court of Law has no machinery at its command for taking an account of such matters, the defrauded party, if he sought his remedy at law, must in such cases keep the property and sue in an action for deceit, in which the jury, if properly directed, can do complete justice by giving as damages a full indemnity for all that the party has lost. ...

But a Court of Equity could not give damages, and, unless it can rescind the contract, can give no relief. And, on the other hand, it can take accounts of profits, and make allowance for deterioration. And I think the practice has always been for a Court of Equity to give this relief whenever, by the exercise of its powers, it can do what is practically just, though it cannot restore the parties precisely to the state they were in before the contract. And a Court of Equity requires that those who come to it to ask its active interposition to give them relief, should use due diligence, after there has been such notice or knowledge as to make it inequitable to lie by. And any change which occurs in the position of the parties or the state of the property after such notice or knowledge should tell much more against the party *in morâ*, than a similar change before he was *in morâ* should do.

Although, as explained by Lord Blackburn, the defrauded party who desired to revest property in the party committing the fraud might have no means available at common law to achieve that objective, we have also seen in *Redgrave v Hurd*, above, that courts of equity would grant a decree of rescission in such circumstances, provided that the usual conditions for granting such decrees were met. Thus, the defrauded party who wished to achieve a revesting of property in the fraudster could resort to equity, provided that a full *restitutio in integrum* could be achieved. As a practical matter, then, the rules of equity govern in cases of this kind where the defrauded party wishes to revest property in the fraudster in order to achieve a restoration of the *status quo ante*. In cases where the defrauded party does not need to revest property in the fraudster, as where the defrauded party had simply paid money and has not, as yet, received anything in return, a simple claim to recover the moneys paid would lie at common law. Some observers sum up the effect of this interplay of common law and equitable doctrines by suggesting that fraud renders agreements merely voidable both at common law and in equity.

As Lord Blackburn indicates, courts of equity coupled orders of rescission with an accounting of profits or allowances for deterioration in order to achieve a result that would be "practically just." The application of this principle is well-illustrated by the decision in *Kupchak v Dayson Holdings Ltd*, above. The *Kupchak* decision also illustrates the essentially restitutionary nature of rescission and the associated monetary awards. The award of monetary compensation in substitution for the Haro Street property has the effect of making restitution for the value of that property. As *Newbigging v Adam*, above, indicates, however, the giving back and taking back on both sides may include indemnification for burdens assumed by the misrepresentee. The restitutionary nature of such relief is neatly illustrated by *Whittington v Seale-Hayne* (1900), 82 LT 49. In this case, the plaintiff had leased the defendant's property for the purpose of breeding poultry on the faith of a false misrepresentation that the premises were sanitary. The plaintiff sought rescission coupled with a monetary award for expenditures made on municipal taxes; repairs to the premises ordered by the municipality; damages for loss of poultry, whose death was caused by the unsanitary conditions; and lost profits. The rescission decree ordered indemnification only for the first two items. These expenditures conferred value on the lessor. The latter two constituted claims for damages, a form of relief available only in a tort claim. As we have seen, such a tort claim may lie where the statement is either fraudulently or negligently false.

In addition, *Kupchak* illustrates the various bars or defences to rescission and, in particular, the requirement that there be a *restitutio in integrum*. Although, in *Kupchak*, precise restitution was not possible because of the modification of the Haro Street property and the change in its ownership, *Kupchak* also illustrates the traditional view that a complete inability to make restitution would simply preclude rescissionary relief and leave the misrepresentee to whatever remedies might be available in tort. Thus, in such circumstances, the victim of an innocent "non-careless" misrepresentation would be entitled to no relief whatsoever. Such an outcome is difficult to justify and it is therefore not surprising that Canadian courts have suggested that, even where a return of benefits received is completely impossible, a monetary award may be substituted for their value. See e.g. *Dusik v Newton* (1985), 62 BCLR 1 (CA); *Bank of Montreal v Murphy*, [1986] 6 WWR 610 (BCCA); *Fleischhaker v Fort Garry Agencies Limited* (1957), 11 DLR (2d) 599 (Man CA). In such cases, the courts are simply awarding restitutionary recovery for the value of benefits conferred by the misrepresentee.

When one turns to mistaken assumptions, however, the position of the common law is that a contract that is unenforceable for this reason is void, with the consequence that no property passes in assets transferred by virtue of the mistake. The transferor is therefore entitled to proprietary relief at common law, even against a bona fide purchaser of the property who has purchased the property from the transferee without any awareness of the vulnerability of the original transaction to rescission on the basis of mistake. As we have seen, it was this potential difficulty for third-party purchasers that appeared to motivate Lord Denning's attempt, in *Solle v Butcher*, above, to develop an equitable doctrine of mistake that would confine or, indeed, supplant to some extent the common law mistake doctrine with a view to providing protection to third-party purchasers through application of the equitable doctrine that the intervention of third-party rights would preclude rescission. As we have also seen, however, the validity of this approach has been questioned in the English Court of Appeal's decision in *Great Peace Shipping Ltd v Tsavliris Salvage (International) Ltd*, above.

A further innovation in *Solle v Butcher*, also questioned by the Court of Appeal in *Great Peace*, was Lord Denning's suggestion that equity possessed a discretion to impose terms on a rescissionary decree that might, for example, provide one party with an option to enter into a further agreement on the other party's terms. In *Solle*, Denning LJ conditioned rescission on a willingness of the landlord to offer the tenant a lease for the unexpired portion of the term on the terms that could have been secured by compliance with the rent control legislation. In *Great Peace*, however, Lord Phillips noted that the principal authority on which Lord Denning relied for the existence of such discretion, the decision in *Cooper v Phibbs*, described in *Bell v Lever Brothers*, above, was a case in which the terms imposed simply achieved a mutual restitution of the parties. Accordingly, Lord Phillips suggested that a discretion to impose terms for other purposes was simply not established by precedent. Nonetheless, there does appear to be some merit in Lord Denning's approach. Apart from the facts of *Solle v Butcher* itself, there are situations in which rescission subject to terms of this kind appears to achieve a just result. For example, illustration 3 to s 152 of the American Law Institute's *Restatement of Contracts*, 2nd reads as follows:

> A contracts to sell and B to buy a tract of land. B agrees to pay A $100,000 in cash and to assume a mortgage that C holds on the tract. Both A and B believe that the amount of the mortgage is $50,000, but in fact it is only $10,000. The contract is voidable by A, unless the Court supplies a term under which B is entitled to enforce the contract if he agrees to pay an additional appropriate sum, and B does so.

If the deciding court's remedial choice is restricted to rescission with restitution or no rescission, either the agreement will be rescinded, in which case B is deprived of an opportunity to purchase the property at the agreed-on price, or the agreement is not rescinded and B is unjustly enriched by being able to purchase the property at a bargain price. If the court can condition rescission on a requirement that A be willing to offer the property to B for an additional $40,000, a palpably fairer result will be achieved.

Should Canadian courts preserve the remedial discretion asserted by Lord Denning in *Solle v Butcher*? In *Miller Paving Limited v B Gottardo Construction Ltd*, above, Goudge JA, for the court, observed as follows:

> *Great Peace* appears not yet to have been adopted in Canada and, in my view, there is good reason for not doing so. The loss of the flexibility needed to correct unjust results in widely diverse circumstances that would come from eliminating the equitable doctrine of common mistake would, I think, be a step backward.

See generally Maddaugh & McCamus, ch 17 and 20.

FRUSTRATION

I. INTRODUCTION

The cases on mistake in assumptions set out in Chapter 9 were concerned with agreements entered into on the basis of a false assumption about past or existing circumstances. This chapter is concerned with false assumptions about future events. In many respects, the problems are similar. In both contexts, the court must ask: when is it appropriate to terminate a contract or revise its terms so as to prevent an unexpected loss from being borne by one party or an unexpected benefit being derived by another? The cases in this chapter are usually classified under the doctrinal label of "impossibility" or "frustration" or both. Because it is quite clear that a person may promise the impossible and a court may award damages on his or her inevitable breach of promise, impossibility is not always a defence. Moreover, what is legally "impossible" is sometimes capable of performance if the promisor goes to inordinate expense. This label is therefore somewhat misleading. Equally, "frustration" is far from an illuminating label.

The first difficult issue to arise in the present context is the identification of circumstances that trigger a case for the release from obligations under the initial contract owing to mistaken assumptions as to future courses of events. If it is accepted that a major function of contracts is to allocate various types of risk, then the materialization of an adverse risk cannot per se be a justification for contractual discharge or excuse. On this basis, all insurance policies would be invalid. Moreover, the mere fact that a given risk is a low probability risk does not mean that it has not been foreseen or assigned to one or the other party, reflecting an appropriately modest expected cost associated with it. Again, many insurance policies cover remote risks. Thus, courts face the elusive task of identifying risks that cannot reasonably be assumed to have been assigned to either party under the contract and impounded in the contract terms. However, assuming that there is some class of risks that contracting parties simply do not address their minds to at all in the contracting process, thus leaving what has sometimes been called "gaps" in the contract terms, the second difficult issue that arises is: how to fill in the gaps? The cases in Sections II and III of this chapter raise the first problem: when ought changed or unforeseen circumstances to provide a basis for release from contractual obligations? The cases in Section IV raise the question of compensation for partial benefits conferred and relief of partial losses sustained in the event that some relief from contractual obligations is found to be warranted.

II. THEORETICAL PERSPECTIVES ON THE DOCTRINE OF FRUSTRATION

GEORGE G TRIANTIS, "CONTRACTUAL ALLOCATIONS OF
UNKNOWN RISKS: A CRITIQUE OF THE DOCTRINE
OF COMMERCIAL IMPRACTICABILITY"
(1992) 42 UTLJ 450 at 464-68 and 483 (footnotes omitted)

Consider the following example. A shipping company contracts with a merchant to transport a large amount of valuable cargo from the merchant's warehouse in Colombia to consumer markets in California. The usual and cheapest route for the trip is through the Panama canal and up the west coast of Central America. In the course of the negotiations, the shipper estimates the cost of the trip, given circumstances existing at that time. However, changes in the environment occurring after the execution of the contract may cause the actual cost to exceed the estimated value.

In pricing any risk of cost increase, whether broadly or narrowly framed, the shipper must identify and assess state variables and decision variables. Suppose that the shipper uses the fault tree in the accompanying diagram to organize the state variables that threaten to increase the cost of performance. For simplicity, the diagram assumes that decision variables are fixed and that there are no interdependencies among state variables. The ultimate concern, the probability distribution of the cost of performance, is placed at the bottom of the tree (on the left side of the diagram). As one moves up any branch of the tree (from left to right), the event at each level may be caused by any of the factors listed in the immediately higher level. For instance, moving from level 1 to level 2 of the uppermost branch, an increase in the aggregate cost of fuel on the trip may be caused by increased fuel consumption or by a higher price per unit of fuel. In other words, each level on a given branch defines or frames risks more narrowly than the lower levels. The risk of an event that causes an increase in the cost of performance is defined more or less narrowly, depending on its level on the tree.

Fault trees are rarely complete. Some branches may have been identified but failed sensitivity tests due to their slight marginal impact on the broader risk assessments. Other branches are missing because they were not contemplated by the decision maker. However, an omitted risk, although unanticipated, is in a sense contemplated and managed at a broader level. For example, the risk of terrorism causing the closing of the canal is not foreseen (level 4), but the more broadly framed risk is contemplated—the closing of the canal and increased fuel consumption (level 3). Similarly, the risk of a nuclear accident in the Middle East that disables oil fields is not foreseen (level 4), but the possibility of increases in the price of oil is (level 3). Advocates of the doctrine of commercial impracticability are mistaken when they assert that the risks of unforeseen contingencies, like terrorism in Panama and nuclear accidents in the Middle East, are not allocated by contract because they are not contemplated by the parties. In fact, they are both contemplated and allocated: not specifically, in their narrow frame, but as part of the package of the broader risks of increases in fuel consumption and of increases in the price of oil.

Although the risk of unforeseen contingencies are indeed allocated by contract, the failure to anticipate a risk in its narrow frame may nevertheless raise the following two concerns. First, the allocation of a risk at a lower (broader frame) level rather than specifically may not be optimal. For instance, though one party is the superior bearer of the risk in its broader frame, the other party is the superior bearer of the risk in its narrow frame. However, this case is relatively rare. Unknown risks are typically remote and exogenous. As noted earlier, exogenous risks are often managed best on a broader level, packaged with other contributing risks. Therefore, the mere fact that they are not foreseen does not affect the efficiency of the level of risk management. Moreover, even if a sufficient portion of the risk is controllable and therefore more effectively managed on a specific basis, the expected benefit from addressing such a remote risk in its narrow rather than broader frame may be outweighed by the cost of identifying, assessing, and allocating the risk in its narrow frame. For these reasons the lower (broader) level of allocation of risks of unforeseen contingencies is not a significant concern.

The second concern is that, even though the unanticipated risk may be more efficiently managed at a broader level, the failure to foresee the specific contingency increases the uncertainty of the more broadly framed risk. If the shipping company does not foresee all the potential events that might lead to the closing of the canal, the assessment of the risk of the canal closing is less certain. In other words, the failure to foresee is the failure to identify one of the state variables associated with the more broadly framed risk. This is due to imperfect information and is therefore an instance of what Kahneman and Tversky call "internal uncertainty." However, removal of this uncertainty through the acquisition of additional information may not be cost-justified. In any event, the recent empirical and theoretical analyses of such social scientists as Gardenfors and Sahlin and Einhorn and Hogarth suggest that, as long as the decision maker is aware of the uncertainty caused by the presence of unforeseen contingencies, she can address such uncertainty rationally by making adjustments in the determination of broader risk assessments. To illustrate, the anchoring and adjustment model of Einhorn and Hogarth may be applied to the assessment of risk in the case where the decision maker is aware of the existence of unspecified state variables but not of their identity.

The intuitive idea behind the anchor and adjustment strategy in these circumstances is analogous to the manner in which a family might plan their vacation budget. To the sum of specific items, such as transportation and accommodation, the family adds an amount reserved for unforeseen contingencies. More formally, the decision maker determines an anchor probability on the basis of contemplated state variables or scenarios that are presented in the fault tree. Since the decision maker knows that there are unforeseen scenarios, she is aware of the internal uncertainty that results. Suppose she decides that the investment in additional information that may reveal the unforeseen contingencies is not cost-justified. Therefore, she must adjust the anchor probability for the uncertainty that remains unresolved. The adjustment may be positive or negative and is a function of (1) the level of the anchor, (2) the amount of uncertainty, and (3) the relative weighting of the contemplated probabilities that are higher and lower than the anchor, which reflects the decision maker's preference toward uncertainty.

Suppose that the risk is the closing of the canal and that the decision maker identifies two potential causes: a hostile regime and a severe earthquake. She is likely to assess a relatively low anchor probability on this basis. However, she must adjust for the possibility that other causes are not contemplated. Since the anchor probability is low and since the unforeseen contingencies are more likely to increase the probability of the canal closing than to decrease it, the adjustment is likely to be positive. Moreover, the magnitude of the adjustment will vary with the decision maker's aversion to uncertainty.

Fault Tree: Risk of Increase in Shipping Cost

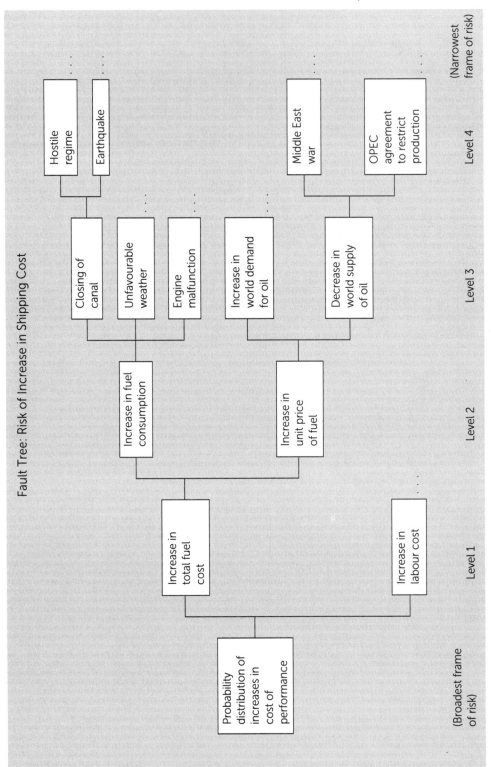

In sum, if information is costly, there is a point at which it becomes efficient for the decision maker to accept the existence of unknown risks rather than to invest in additional information. However, contrary to the widely held premise, risks of unforeseen contingencies are allocated by contract as part of more broadly framed risks to which they contribute as state variables. The decision maker accounts for the incompleteness in the specification of state variables in their narrow frame by adjusting the probability assessment of the more broadly framed risk. The broader risks are admittedly more uncertain because of the failure to specify all state variables. However, the discussion in this part suggests that these risks can nevertheless be priced, allocated and managed in a cost-effective and rational manner. ...

This article dispels the myth that an unknown risk cannot be managed or allocated in a rational manner. The question is not whether a risk is allocated in a contract, but at what level it is allocated. Since the prominent gap-filling rationales for the doctrine of commercial impracticability are premised on the myth that unforeseen risks are not allocated, this article proposes and evaluates alternative justifications for the doctrine. These justifications are concerned with how well, rather than whether, unforeseen risks are allocated in contracts. Given the empirical evidence on cognitive errors and judgmental biases in risk assessments, the intellectual capability of contracting parties to rationally allocate risks under uncertainty may be questioned. However, the ability of the courts to improve the efficiency of risk allocation or to redress inequities in compensation for risk bearing is severely limited. Thus, the intuition exhibited by most courts who decline to apply the doctrine of commercial impracticability is well-founded. The continued existence of the doctrine, even if substantially dormant, only serves to preserve the confusion and uncertainty as to its application and scope. The role of contract law should be limited to the interpretation and enforcement of the parties' risk allocations. It might be argued that, even without the modern doctrine of impracticability, the courts may effectively reallocate risks through the creative use of implied terms that was common in the development of the doctrine in the nineteenth century. However, that is a problem of policing judicial interpretative discretion that must be addressed on its own terms.

RICHARD A POSNER & ANDREW M ROSENFIELD, "IMPOSSIBILITY AND RELATED DOCTRINES IN CONTRACT LAW: AN ECONOMIC ANALYSIS"
(1977) 6 J Legal Stud 83

I. THE ECONOMICS OF IMPOSSIBILITY

The typical case in which impossibility or some related doctrine is invoked is one where, by reason of an unforeseen or at least unprovided-for event, performance by one of the parties of his obligations under the contract has become so much more costly than he foresaw at the time the contract was made as to be uneconomical (that is, the costs of performance would be greater than the benefits). The performance promised may have been delivery of a particular cargo by a specified delivery date—but the ship is trapped in the Suez Canal because of a war between Israel and Egypt. Or it may have been a piano recital by Gina Bachauer—and she dies between the signing of the contract and the date of the recital. The law could in each case treat the failure to perform as a breach of contract, thereby in effect assigning to the promisor the risk that war, or death, would prevent performance (or render it uneconomical).

Alternatively, invoking impossibility or some related notion, the law could treat the failure to perform as excusable and discharge the contract, thereby in effect assigning the risk to the promisee.

From the standpoint of economics—and disregarding, but only momentarily, administrative costs—discharge should be allowed where the promisee is the superior risk bearer; if the promisor is the superior risk bearer, nonperformance should be treated as a breach of contract. "Superior risk bearer" is to be understood here as the party that is the more efficient bearer of the particular risk in question, in the particular circumstances of the transaction. Of course, if the parties have expressly assigned the risk to one of them, there is no occasion to inquire which is the superior risk bearer. The inquiry is merely an aid to interpretation.

A party can be a superior risk bearer for one of two reasons. First, he may be in a better position to prevent the risk from materializing. This resembles the economic criterion for assigning liability in tort cases. It is an important criterion in many contract settings, too, but not in this one. Discharge would be inefficient in any case where the promisor could prevent the risk from materializing at a lower cost than the expected cost of the risky event. In such a case efficiency would require that the promisor bear the loss resulting from the occurrence of the event, and hence that occurrence should be treated as precipitating a breach of contract.

But the converse is not necessarily true. It does not necessarily follow from the fact that the promisor could not at any reasonable cost have prevented the risk from materializing that he should be discharged from his contractual obligations. Prevention is only one way of dealing with risk; the other is insurance. The promisor may be the superior insurer. If so, his inability to prevent the risk from materializing should not operate to discharge him from the contract, any more than an insurance company's inability to prevent a fire on the premises of the insured should excuse it from its liability to make good the damage caused by the fire.

The factors relevant to determining which party to the contract is the cheaper insurer are (1) risk-appraisal costs and (2) transaction costs. The former comprise the costs of determining (a) the probability that the risk will materialize and (b) the magnitude of the loss if it does materialize. The amount of risk is the product of the probability of loss and of the magnitude of the loss if it occurs. Both elements—probability and magnitude—must be known in order for the insurer to know how much to ask from the other party to the contract as compensation for bearing the risk in question.

The relevant transaction costs are the costs involved in eliminating or minimizing the risk through pooling it with other uncertain events, that is, diversifying away the risk. This can be done either through self-insurance or through the purchase of an insurance policy (market insurance). To illustrate, a corporation's shareholders might eliminate the risk associated with some contract the corporation had made by holding a portfolio of securities in which their shares in the corporation were combined with shares in many other corporations whose earnings would not be (adversely) affected if this particular corporation were to default on the contract. This would be an example of self-insurance. Alternatively, the corporation might purchase business-loss or some other form of insurance that would protect it (and, more important, its shareholders) from the consequences of a default on the contract; this would be an example of market insurance. Where good opportunities for diversification exist, self-insurance will often be cheaper than market insurance.

The foregoing discussion indicates the factors that courts and legislatures might consider in devising efficient rules for the discharge of contracts. An easy case for discharge would be one where (1) the promisor asking to be discharged could not reasonably have prevented the event rendering his performance uneconomical, and (2) the promisee could have insured against the occurrence of the event at lower cost than the promisor because the promisee (a) was in a better position to estimate both (i) the probability of the event's occurrence and (ii) the magnitude of the loss if it did occur, and (b) could have self-insured, whereas the promisor would have had to buy more costly market insurance.

NOTES

1. For a suggestion that frustration and mistake should be treated under a unified theoretical framework, see Andrew Kull, "Mistake, Frustration, and the Windfall Principle of Contract Remedies" (1991) 43 Hastings LJ 1. See also the discussion of the two doctrines in *The Great Peace*, excerpted in Chapter 9.

2. Gideon Parchomovsky, Peter Siegelman & Steve Thel, "Of Equal Wrongs and Half Rights" (2007) 82 NYUL Rev 738, suggested that fairness and efficiency dictate that parties should split the windfall loss when parties exchange a valuable interest that turns out to be worthless and neither party is in a better position to bear the risk of cancellation.

3. For a suggestion that the impossibility doctrine "has the potential to improve the efficiency and productivity of a wide range of long-term contractual agreements" and guidelines on how the doctrine should be applied to produce these results, see Donald J Smythe, "Bounded Rationality, the Doctrine of Impracticability, and the Governance of Relational Contracts" (2004) 13 S Cal Interdisciplinary LJ 227.

4. For a discussion on the doctrine of impossibility, see James Gordley, "Impossibility and Changed and Unforeseen Circumstances" (2004) 52 Am J Comp L 513; Shirley R Brener, "Outgrowing Impossibility: Examining the Impossibility Doctrine in the Wake of Hurricane Katrina" (2006) 56 Emory LJ 461. For a discussion of the principles that should govern the tension between unforeseen circumstances on one hand, and allocating risk and securing transactions on the other, see Melvin A Eisenberg, "Impossibility, Impracticability, and Frustration" 1 J Legal Analysis 207 (2009).

III. THE RULE OF ABSOLUTE PROMISES

PARADINE V JANE
(1647), Aleyn 26, 82 ER 897

[The defendant, Jane, failed to pay the rent under a lease, for which this action was brought against him. The defendant pleaded that Prince Rupert, an alien and an enemy of the King, had invaded the land with his army and expelled the defendant from the land, preventing the defendant from reaping profits from the land.]

... [W]here the law creates a duty or charge, and the party is disabled to perform it without any default in him, and hath no remedy over, then the law will excuse him ... but when the party by his own contract creates a duty or charge upon himself, he is bound to make it good, if he may, notwithstanding any accident by inevitable necessity, because he might have provided against it by his contract. And therefore if the lessee covenant to repair a house, though it be burnt by lightning, or thrown down by enemies, yet he ought to repair it. Dyer 33.3; 40E. Ill.6.h. Now the rent is a duty created by the parties upon the reservation, and had there been a covenant to pay it, there had been no question but the lessee must have made it good, notwithstanding the interruption by enemies, for the law would not protect him beyond his own agreement ... . Another reason was added, that as the lessee is to have the advantage of casual profits so he must run the hazard of casual losses, and not lay the whole burthen of them upon his lessor; ... that though the land be surrounded, or gained by the sea, or made barren by wildfire, yet the lessor shall have his whole rent: and judgment was given for the plaintiff.

NOTE

For a discussion of the historical origins of *Paradine v Jane*, see D Ibbetson, "Absolute Liability in Contract: The Antecedents of Paradine v Jayne" in FD Rose, ed, *Consensus ad Idem: Essays in the Law of Contract in Honour of Guenter Treitel* (London: Sweet & Maxwell, 1996). For views that *Paradine v Jane* has long been wrongly interpreted, see HWR Wade, "The Principle of Impossibility in Contract" (1940) 56 Law Q Rev 519 and John D Wladis, "Common Law and Uncommon Events: The Development of the Doctrine of Impossibility of Performance in English Contract Law" (1987) 75 Geo LJ 1575.

IV. RELAXATION OF THE RULE OF ABSOLUTE PROMISES

TAYLOR V CALDWELL
(1863), 3 B & S 826, 122 ER 309

BLACKBURN J (for the court): In this case the plaintiffs and the defendants had, on the 27th May, 1861, entered into a contract by which the defendants agreed to let the plaintiffs have the use of The Surrey Gardens and Music Hall on four days then to come viz., the 17th June, 15 July, 5th August, and 19th August, for the purpose of giving a series of four grand concerts, and day and night fetes at the Gardens and Hall on those days respectively; and the plaintiffs agreed to take the Gardens and Hall on those days, and pay £100 for each day. ...

After the making of the agreement, and before the first day on which a concert was to be given, the Hall was destroyed by fire. This destruction, we must take it on the evidence, was without the fault of either party, and was so complete that in consequence the concerts could not be given as intended. And the question we have to decide is whether, under these circumstances, the loss which the plaintiffs have sustained is to fall upon the defendants. The parties when framing their agreement evidently had not present to their minds the possibility of such a disaster, and have made no express stipulation with reference to it, so that the answer to the question must depend upon the general rules of law applicable to such a contract.

There seems no doubt that where there is a positive contract to do a thing, not in itself unlawful, the contractor must perform it or pay damages for not doing it, although in consequence of unforeseen accidents the performance of his contract has become unexpectedly burthensome or even impossible. The law is so laid down in 1 Roll. Abr. 450, Condition (G), and in the note (2) to *Walton* (1673), 2 Wms. Saund. 421 a. 6th ed.; 85 E.R. 1234, and is recognised as the general rule by all the judges in the much discussed case of *Hall v. Wright* (1859), 120 E.R. 695. But this rule is only applicable when the contract is positive and absolute, and not subject to any condition either express or implied; and there are authorities which, as we think, establish the principle that where, from the nature of the contract, it appears that the parties must from the beginning have known that it could not be fulfilled unless when the time for the fulfilment of the contract arrived some particular specified thing continued to exist, so that, when entering into the contract, they must have contemplated such continuing existence as the foundation of what was to be done; there, in the absence of any express or implied warranty that the thing shall exist, the contract is not to be construed as a positive contract, but as subject to an implied condition that the parties shall be excused in case, before breach, performance becomes impossible from the perishing of the thing without default of the contractor.

There seems little doubt that this implication tends to further the great object of making the legal construction such as to fulfil the intention of those who entered into the contract. For in the course of affairs men in making such contracts in general would, if it were brought to their minds, say that there should be such a condition.

Accordingly, in the Civil law, such an exception is implied [in some obligations]. ...

Although the Civil law is not of itself authority in an English Court, it affords great assistance in investigating the principles on which the law is grounded. And it seems to us that the common law authorities established that in such a contract the same condition of the continued existence of the thing is implied by English law.

There is a class of contracts in which a person binds himself to do something which requires to be performed by him in person; and such promises, e.g., promises to marry, or promises to serve for a certain time, are never in practice qualified by an express exception of the death of the party; and therefore in such cases the contract is in terms broken if the promisor dies before fulfilment. Yet it was very early determined that, if the performance is personal, the executors are not liable; *Hyde v. The Dean of Windsor* (1597), Cro. Eliz. 552; 78 E.R. 798. See 2 *Wms. Exors.* 1560, 5th ed. where a very apt illustration is given. "Thus," says the learned author, "if an author undertakes to compose a work, and dies before completing it, his executors are discharged from this contract: for the undertaking is merely personal in its nature, and, by the intervention of the contractor's death, has become impossible to be performed." For this he cites a dictum of Lord Lyndhurst in *Marshall v. Broadhurst* 1 Tyr. 348, 349, and a case mentioned by Patteson J. in *Wentworth v. Cock* (1839), 10 A. & E. 42; 113 E.R. 17 at p. 18. In *Hall v. Wright*, Crompton J., in his judgment, puts another case. "Where a contract depends upon personal skill, and the act of God renders it impossible, as, for instance, in the case of a painter employed to paint a picture who is struck blind, it may be that the performance might be excused."

It seems that in those cases the only ground on which the parties or their executors can be excused from the consequences of the breach of the contract is, that from the nature of the contract there is an implied condition of the continued existence of the life of the contractor, and perhaps, in the case of the painter of his eyesight. In the instances just given, the person, the continued existence of whose life is necessary to the fulfilment of the contract, is himself the contractor, but that does not seem in itself to be necessary to the application of the principle; as is illustrated by the following example. In the ordinary form of an apprentice deed the apprentice binds himself in unqualified terms to "serve until the full end and term of seven years to be fully complete and ended," during which term it is covenanted that the apprentice his master "faithfully shall serve," and the father of the apprentice in equally unqualified terms binds himself for the performance by the apprentice of all and every covenant on his part. (See the form, 2 Chitty on Pleading, 370, 7th ed. by Greening.) It is undeniable that if the apprentice dies within the seven years, the covenant of the father that he shall perform his covenant to serve for seven years is not fulfilled, yet surely it cannot be that an action would lie against the father? Yet the only reason why it would not is that he is excused because of the apprentice's death.

These are instances where the implied condition is of the life of a human being, but there are others in which the same implication is made as to the continued existence of a thing. For example, where a contract of sale is made amounting to a bargain and sale, transferring presently the property in specific chattels, without the fault of the vendor, perish in the interval, the purchaser must pay the price and the vendor is excused from performing his contract to deliver, which has thus become impossible. ...

It may, we think, be safely asserted to be now English law, that in all contracts of loan of chattels or bailments, if the performance of the promise of the borrower or bailee to return the things lent or bailed becomes impossible because it has perished, this impossibility (if not arising from the fault of the borrower or bailee from some risk which he has taken upon himself) excuses the borrower or bailee from the performance of his promise to redeliver the chattel. ...

In none of these cases is the promise in words other than positive, nor is there any express stipulation that the destruction of the person or thing shall excuse the performance; but that excuse is by law implied, because from the nature of the contract it is apparent that the parties contracted on the basis of the continued existence of the particular person or chattel. In the present case, looking at the whole contract, we find that the parties contracted on the basis of the continued existence of the Music Hall at the time when the concerts were to be given; that being essential to their performance.

We think, therefore, that the Music Hall having ceased to exist, without fault of either party, both parties are excused, the plaintiffs from taking the Gardens and paying the money, the defendants from performing their promise to give the use of the Hall and Gardens and other things. Consequently the rule must be absolute to enter the verdict for the defendants.

NOTES

1. In *Basic Contract Law* (St Paul, Minn: West, 1947) at 666-68, Professor Lon Fuller develops the notion of "tacit assumptions." He says:

> In *Taylor v. Caldwell* the court says that when framing their agreement the parties "had not present to their minds the possibility" of a disaster affecting the Music Hall, and concludes that the parties "must have contemplated" the "continuing existence" of the Hall "as the foundation of their agreement."

Is there a contradiction here? The court seems to say that the parties did not think of the possibility of the Hall's burning and therefore assumed it would not burn. But how can the parties assume that no fire will occur, when the possibility of a fire was never present to their minds? If this possibility was not present to their minds, would it not be more accurate to say that they assumed nothing about a fire, either that it would or would not occur? Fuller continues:

> The difficulty here does not lie in any dispute about psychological fact, but in the inappropriateness of the language ordinarily used to describe certain elementary psychological truths. Words like "intention," "assumption," "expectation" and "understanding" all seem to imply a *conscious* state involving an awareness of alternatives and a deliberate choice among them. It is, however, plain that there is a psychological state which can be described as "tacit assumption" that does not involve a consciousness of alternatives. The absent-minded professor stepping from his office into the hall as he reads a book "assumes" that the floor of the hall will be there to receive him. His conduct is conditioned and directed by this assumption, even though the possibility that the floor has been removed does not "occur" to him, that is, is not present in his conscious mental processes. ...

Underlying questions of this sort, and indeed, underlying much of contract law generally, are certain basic problems of psychology that have never been satisfactorily solved. We speak constantly of things that were "intended" or "assumed" without having a clear conception of the psychological processes involved in "intending" and "assuming." The lawyer or judge who turns to psychology for help in dealing with these problems is likely to be disappointed. ...

In spite of hopeful beginnings promising a more comprehensive psychological treatment of human behaviour, for the time being the only methods available for dealing with problems like that raised by *Taylor v. Caldwell* are essentially those resting on intuition and introspection. We "just know" that the burning of a music hall violates a tacit assumption of the parties who executed a contract for hiring it; we "just know" that a two per cent increase in the price of beans does not violate a tacit assumption underlying a contract to deliver a ton of beans for a fixed price.

2. In *Fishman v Wilderness Ridge at Stewart Creek Inc*, 2010 ABCA 345, the condominium that the appellants had contracted to purchase was destroyed by fire. Although the project was insured and being rebuilt, the appellants sought a declaration that the contract had been frustrated. The agreement contained a *force majeure* clause, which stated that the respondent company would not be in default for a delay caused by forces outside its reasonable control. While deciding whether the contract was frustrated, the Court of Appeal held that "[a] contract is only frustrated when it becomes incapable of performance, not just because performance might be more onerous, more costly, or different from what was anticipated." It determined that the late delivery of the condominium would be inconvenient for the appellants, but that the *force majeure* clause allocated that risk to them.

AMALGAMATED INVESTMENT AND PROPERTY CO LTD V JOHN WALKER & SONS LTD
[1977] 1 WLR 164 (CA)

The plaintiff agreed to buy, and the defendant to sell, a warehouse for £1,700,000. The plaintiff intended to redevelop the site. The day after the contract was made the defendant was informed that the building had been listed as of special architectural or historical interest, a designation that made redevelopment unlawful and reduced the value of the building to £200,000. The plaintiff sought rescission.

BUCKLEY LJ [after outlining the facts, continued]: ... Plowman V.-C. found as a fact that the value of the property with no redevelopment potential was probably 1½ million pounds less than the contract price. So the effect of the building being put into the list was this, that so long as it remained listed and "listed building consent" could not be obtained, the value of the property was depreciated from the £1,700,000 odd which was the sale price to something of the order of £200,000. Plowman V.-C. also found as a fact that the vendors knew at all material times that the purchasers were buying the property for redevelopment.

On December 12, 1973, the purchasers issued their writ against the vendors claiming rescission of the agreement on the ground of common mistake, a declaration that the agreement was void and of no effect, and a declaration that the agreement was voidable, and for an order rescinding the agreement. Those were, of course, alternative remedies. On December 14, 1973, the vendors issued a writ against the purchasers claiming specific performance of the contract and alternatively a declaration that the purchasers had wrongfully repudiated the contract, and forfeiture of the deposit and damages, with ancillary relief. Those two actions were consolidated on July 19, 1974, and the action came on with the purchasers as plaintiffs and the vendors as defendants. There was a counterclaim raised by the vendors for the relief sought in their action, specific performance and so forth. ... So Plowman V.-C. held that the contract stood and that the purchasers were liable for the full purchase price, and that the contract should be carried out.

It has been contended before us that there was here a common mistake of fact on a matter of fundamental importance, in consequence of which the contract ought to be set aside. Reliance has been placed upon the decision of the Court of Appeal in *Solle v. Butcher* [1950] 1 K.B. 671 and the decision of Goff J. in *Grist v. Bailey* [1967] Ch. 532.

Mr. Balcombe, appearing for the purchasers, says that the purchasers bought the property as property which was ripe for development and that the vendors sold upon the same basis, and that by reason of the decision to list the property, the property was not in fact ripe for development. Therefore he says there was a common mistake as to the nature of the property, and the purchaser is entitled to rescission. ... So the alleged common mistake was that the property was property suitable for and capable of being developed.

For the application of the doctrine of mutual mistake as a ground for setting the contract aside, it is of course necessary to show that the mistake existed at the date of the contract; and so Mr. Balcombe relies in that respect not upon the signing of the list by the officer who alone was authorised to sign it on behalf of the Secretary of State, but upon the decision of Miss Price to include the property in the list. That decision, although in fact it led to the signature of the list in the form in which it was eventually signed, was merely an administrative step in the carrying out of the operations of the branch of the ministry. It was a personal decision on the part of Miss Price that the list should contain the particular property with which we are concerned. But there was still the possibility that something else might arise before the list was signed. Some communication might have been received from some outside body which threw some light upon the qualifications of this building for listing, which might have resulted in its being excluded from the list as it was actually signed. Indeed, the head of the department might himself, had he known of the circumstances, have formed a different opinion from the opinion formed by Miss Price, or Miss Price might I suppose herself have changed her mind during the time between preparing the list, sending it to the typing pool, and eventually laying it before her superior for signature. Although she accepts the responsibility for the decision and says it was her decision, it was (as I say) no more than an administrative step leading to the ultimate signature of the list, just as the obtaining of the information that was eventually included in the report of the investigating officer was an administrative step, or the preparation of the report of the investigating officer. It seems to me that it is no more justifiable to point to that date as being the crucial date than it is to point to other earlier dates or later dates. The crucial date, in my judgment, is the date when the list was signed. It was then that the building became a listed building, and it was only then that the expectations of the parties (who no doubt both expected that this property would be capable of being developed, subject always of course to obtaining planning permission, without it being necessary to obtain listed building permission) were disappointed. For myself, I entirely agree with the conclusion which Plowman V.-C. reached on this part of the case. In my judgment, there was no mutual mistake as to the circumstances surrounding the contract at the time when the contract was entered into. The only mistake that there was, was one which related to the expectation of the parties. They expected that the building would be subject only to ordinary town planning consent procedures and that expectation has been disappointed. But at the date when the contract was entered into, I cannot see that there is any ground for saying that the parties were then subject to some mutual mistake of fact relating to the circumstances surrounding the contract. According, for my part, I think that the judge's decision on that part of the case is one which should be upheld. ...

I now turn to the alternative argument which has been presented to us in support of this appeal, which is upon frustration. Mr. Balcombe has relied upon what was said in the speeches in the House of Lords in *Davis Contractors Ltd. v. Fareham Urban District Council* [1956] A.C. 696, and it may perhaps be useful if I refer to what was said by Lord Radcliffe there, starting at p. 728:

> Perhaps it would be simpler to say at the outset that frustration occurs whenever the law recognises that without default of either party a contractual obligation has become incapable of being performed because the circumstances in which performance is called for would render it a thing radically different from that which was undertaken by the contract.

That is a passage which was referred to by Plowman V.-C. in the course of his judgment. Then, a little later on, after referring to *Denny, Mott & Dickson Ltd. v. James B. Fraser & Co. Ltd.* [1944] A.C. 265, 274-275, Lord Radcliffe says, at p. 729:

> It is for that reason that special importance is necessarily attached to the occurrence of any unexpected event that, as it were, changes the face of things. But, even so, it is not hardship or inconvenience or material loss itself which calls the principle of frustration into play. There must be as well such a change in the significance of the obligation that the thing undertaken would, if performed, be a different thing from that contracted for.

Now, the obligation undertaken to be performed in this case by the vendors was to sell this property for the contract price and, of course, to show a good title and so forth. The vendors did not warrant in any way that planning permission could be obtained for the development of the property. No doubt both parties considered that the property was property which could advantageously be developed and was property for which planning permission would probably be satisfactorily obtained. But there was no stipulation in the contract relating to anything of that kind; nor, as I say, was there any warranty on the part of the vendors. I am prepared to assume for the purposes of this judgment that the law relating to frustration of contracts is capable of being applied in the case of a contract for sale of land, though that is one of the matters which has been debated before us. But, making that assumption, I have reached the conclusion that there are not here the necessary factual bases for holding that this contract has been frustrated. It seems to me that the risk of property being listed as property of architectural or historical interest is a risk which inheres in all ownership of buildings. In many cases it may be an extremely remote risk. But it is a risk, I think, which attaches to all buildings and it is a risk that every owner and every purchaser of property must recognise that he is subject to. The purchasers in the present case bought knowing that they would have to obtain planning permission in order to develop the property. The effect of listing under the sections of the Act to which I have referred makes the obtaining of planning permission, it may be, more difficult, and it may also make it a longer and more complicated process. But still, in essence, the position is that the would-be developer has to obtain the appropriate planning permissions, one form of permission being the "listed building permission." The purchasers, when they entered into the contract, must obviously be taken to have known that they would need to get planning permission. They must also, in my judgment, be taken to have known that there was the risk, although they may not have regarded it as a substantial risk, that the building might at some time be listed, and that their chances of obtaining planning permission might possibly be adversely affected to some extent by that, or at any rate their chances of obtaining speedy planning permission. But, in my judgment, this is a risk of a kind which every purchaser should be regarded as knowing that he is subject to when he enters into his contract of purchase. It is a risk which I think the purchaser must carry, and any loss that may result from the maturing of that risk is a loss which must lie where it falls. Moreover, the purchasers have not yet established that they will be unable to obtain all the necessary planning permissions, including "listed building permission." So it has not yet, I think, been established that the listing of this building has had the drastic effect which the figures which I have mentioned suggest that it may have had. It may well turn out to be the case that "listed building permission" will be obtainable here and the purchasers will be able to carry out the development which they desire to carry into effect.

For these reasons, I reach the conclusion, as I say, that the necessary facts have not been established in this case to found a claim that the contract has been frustrated.

For these reasons, I would dismiss this appeal.

[Lawton LJ and Sir John Pennycuick agreed.]

CAPITAL QUALITY HOMES LTD V COLWYN CONSTRUCTION LTD
(1975), 9 OR (2d) 617 (CA)

EVANS JA: The defendant Colwyn Construction Limited appeals from the judgment of the Honourable Mr. Justice Keith granting the plaintiff recovery from the defendant of the sum of $13,980 being the return of a deposit paid by the plaintiff pursuant to an agreement for sale between the parties relative to certain undeveloped land in the City of Windsor.

The trial proceeded on an agreed statement of facts which was presented orally to the Court by counsel and which may be briefly summarized as follows: Under an agreement dated January 5, 1969, the plaintiff, purchaser, agreed to purchase from the defendant, vendor, 26 building lots each comprising parts of lots within a registered plan of subdivision. The date fixed for closing was July 30, 1970. Both parties were aware that the purchaser was buying building lots for the purpose of erecting a home on each lot with the intention of selling the several homes by way of separate conveyances. Under the terms of the agreement it was entitled to a conveyance of a building lot upon payment of $6,000 and, upon full payment, to 26 separate deeds of conveyance each representing one building lot. It is agreed that no demand for any conveyance was made prior to the date of closing.

When the sale agreement was executed the designated land was not within an area of subdivision control and not subject to any restriction limiting the right to convey. On June 27, 1970, certain amendments [1970, c 72, s 1] to the *Planning Act*, R.S.O. 1960, c. 296, came into effect whereby these lands came under the provisions of what is now s. 29 of the *Planning Act*, R.S.O. 1970, c. 349, which in certain circumstances restricts an owner's right to convey and makes necessary the obtaining of a consent from the relevant committee of adjustment designated in the amending legislation. In the absence of such consent no interest in part of a lot within a registered plan of subdivision can be conveyed.

The vendor was accordingly precluded from conveying the 26 building lots in 26 separate deeds without proper consents and while a conveyance to the purchaser of all lots in one deed may have been permissible, the purchaser in any event would be unable to reconvey individual building lots to prospective home buyers as it had intended without complying with the restrictive provisions of the new legislation.

This substantial change in the law, prohibiting and restricting conveyancing of the lands, 33 days prior to the anticipated closing date, resulted in some discussion between the parties relative to possible postponement of the closing date in order to devise some method of circumventing the restrictions to which the lands were now subject. No arrangement was made to extend closing. On the agreed date of closing the purchaser insisted that the vendor deliver conveyances for each individual building lot with the consents necessary to effectually transfer the lots. The vendor insisted that it was the responsibility of the purchaser to obtain the necessary consents. On the closing date the balance of the agreed purchase price was tendered by the solicitors for the purchaser but no conveyances were forthcoming in the mode contemplated by the agreement. It is common ground that the purchaser would not withdraw its demand for 26 individual conveyances with consents attached and that the vendor did not provide such conveyances. Following failure to close on the agreed date, the purchaser contended that the vendor was in default and on August 5, 1970, repudiated the agreement and made demand upon the vendor for the return of the balance of the deposit. ...

The issues for determination, as I apprehend them, are:

(1) Does the doctrine of impossibility of performance of a contract, *i.e.*, frustration, have any application when the contract is for the purchase and sale of land?

(2) Assuming that frustration is applicable to agreements for sale of land, does the factual situation in this case permit the doctrine to be invoked?

(3) Assuming that (1) and (2) are both answered in the affirmative what results flow therefrom?

In order to show the birth and development of the doctrine of frustration it is necessary to recall that the common law exacted strict performance of contractual obligations. A promise demanded performance and if performance became impossible, no matter what the reason, the defaulting party was liable in damages. *Paradine v. Jane* (1647), Aleyn 26; 82 E.R. 897 restated the principle and it is alleged that the justification for imposing such onerous obligations was that if contracting parties voluntarily entered into absolute and unconditional agreements they cannot complain if their lack of foresight in failing to provide against all contingencies created hardships to them.

English Courts, prior to *Taylor et al. v. Caldwell et al.* (1863), 3 B. & S. 826; 122 E.R. 309 followed the rule that impossibility of performance of a contract did not relieve the party unable to perform from liability in damages. Subsequently, that rigid rule was relaxed and contracts were held to be terminated and the parties discharged when the events which denied fulfilment of the contract were caused by some circumstances beyond the control of the contracting parties. In *Taylor et al. v. Caldwell*, the subject-matter of the contract was destroyed before the date upon which performance was required. Blackburn J. held that when a music-hall which was rented for the purpose of holding concerts was accidentally destroyed by fire prior to the concerts being held, the owner was discharged from his contract and not liable in damages. The common law doctrine of contract was uncompromising in its insistence on performance and if a party could not actually perform an act because some event made it physically impossible, then specific performance could not be ordered but the party failing would be liable in damages for non-performance. The breakthrough by Blackburn J. was accomplished by holding that a contract is not to be construed as absolute if the contracting parties from the beginning must have known that its fulfilment depended upon the continued existence of some peculiar thing and therefore must have realized that his continuing existence was the foundation of the bargain. He held that the contract is "subject to an implied condition that the parties shall be excused in case, before breach, performance becomes impossible from the perishing of the thing without default of the contract." He implied a term or condition into the contract. The doctrine of impossibility of performance or as it is now generally called, the doctrine of frustration, developed rapidly, particularly in commercial contracts and English Courts sought to do justice by holding that a contract was discharged when some catastrophic event occurred, the result of which was to destroy the very basis of the contract.

Krell v. Henry, [1903] 2 K.B. 740 (C.A.) dealt with a hire of premises to view a coronation subsequently cancelled and the Court held that the view of the coronation procession was the foundation of the contract and the non-happening of it prevented the performance of the contract. *Marshall v. Glanvill et al.*, [1917] 2 K.B. 87, was concerned with a contract of employment and the liability of the employee to compulsory military service was held to determine the contract.

In all these commercial contract cases in which the principle is referred to as "frustration of the adventure" the Court has implied into the contract a term or condition because the contract itself does not provide for the supervening act which produces the frustration. Lord Sumner in *Cheong Yne Steamship Co. Ltd. v. Hirji Mulji et al.*, [1926] 1 W.W.R. 917, [1926] A.C. 497, referred to the doctrine of frustration as "a device by which the rules as to absolute contracts can be reconciled with a special exception which justice demands." The legal effect of the frustration of a contract does not depend upon the intention of the parties, or their opinions or even knowledge as to the event that has brought about the frustration, but upon its occurrence in such circumstances as to show it to be inconsistent with the further prosecution of the adventure. On the contrary, it seems that when the event occurs, the meaning of the contract must be taken to be, not what the parties did intend (for they had neither thought nor intention regarding it) but that which the parties, as fair and reasonable men, would presumably have agreed upon if, having such possibility in view, they had made express provision as to their several rights and liabilities in the event of its occurrence: *Dahl v. Nelson et al.*, (1880), 6 App.Cas. 38.

The supervening event must be something beyond the control of the parties and must result in a significant change in the original obligation assumed by them. The theory of the implied term has been replaced by the more realistic view that the Court imposes upon the parties the just and reasonable solution that the new situation demands.

Lord Radcliffe in *Davis Contractors Ltd. v. Fareham Urban District Council*, [1956] A.C. 696 at pp. 728-9, stated:

> So perhaps it would be simpler to say at the outset that frustration occurs whenever the law recognizes that without default of either party a contractual obligation has become incapable of being performed because the circumstances in which performance is called for would render it a thing radically different from that which was undertaken by the contract. Non haec in foedera veni. It was not this that I promised to do.

The development of the doctrine briefly referred to above is traced with considerable detail in Cheshire & Fifoot, *Law of Contracts*, 7th ed. (1969), at p. 506, and following. The *Law Reform (Frustrated Contracts) Act*, 1943 (U.K.), c. 40, defined the position of the parties in England when a contract is discharged by frustration and set out those particular contracts to which the Act did not apply.

The controversial question that is still undecided by the House of Lords is whether the doctrine of frustration can be applied to a lease of land. Cases involving the destruction of a chattel, the subject of the contract, as in *Howell v. Coupland* (1876), 1 Q.B.D. 258, or the destruction of a music-hall, the existence of which was the foundation of the contract as in *Taylor et al. v. Caldwell et al., supra*, or those cases in which the performance of the contract has become illegal because of some supervening legislation are to be distinguished from land leases which are considered to be more than contracts, since they create estates in land which give rise to proprietary rights in addition to purely personal rights as found in all commercial contracts. In the development of the modern law of contracts an increasingly wider conception of the doctrine of frustration as a ground of discharge of commercial contracts came into operation but the English Courts have consistently held that the doctrine of frustration has no application when the contract creates an estate in land.

There can be no frustration if the supervening event results from the voluntary act of one of the parties or if the possibility of such event arising during the term of the agreement was contemplated by the parties and provided for in the agreement. In the instant case the planning legislation which supervened was not contemplated by the parties, not provided for in the agreement and not brought about through a voluntary act of either party. The factor remaining to be considered is whether the effect of the planning legislation is of such a nature that the law would consider the fundamental character of the agreement to have been so altered as to no longer reflect the original basis of the agreement. In my opinion the legislation destroyed the very foundation of the agreement. The purchaser was purchasing 26 separate building lots upon which it proposed to build houses for resale involving a reconveyance in each instance. This purpose was known to the vendor. The lack of ability to do so creates a situation not within the contemplation of the parties when they entered into the agreement. I believe that all the factors necessary to constitute impossibility of performance have been established and that the doctrine of frustration can be invoked to terminate the agreement.

The doctrine of frustration has been applied to commercial contracts since *Taylor et al. v. Caldwell et al., supra*. In *Cricklewood v. Leighton's* [[1945] AC 221], Viscount Simon L.C. and Lord Wright held against the accepted view that leases were outside the doctrine since a lease in addition to being a contract creates an estate in the land demised for the period of the agreed term. I adopt the reasoning of Viscount Simon L.C. and his conclusion that there is no binding authority precluding the application of the doctrine of frustration to contracts involving the lease of lands. I am also in accord with his observations that the doctrine is flexible and ought not to be restricted by any arbitrary formula. I see no reason why the doctrine cannot be logically extended to contracts involving the purchase and sale of land. If the supervening event makes the contract incapable of fulfilment as contemplated by the parties, then it appears to me illogical and unreasonable to contend that the fundamental object of the contract can be effected because the equitable interest in the land has passed to the purchaser.

I adopt the reasoning of Lord Simon in *Cricklewood v. Leighton's*, and accept his conclusion that there is no binding authority in England precluding the application of the doctrine of frustration to contracts involving a lease of land. I believe the situation to be the same in Ontario and I am unable to distinguish any difference between leases of land and agreements for the sale of land, so far as the application of the doctrine is concerned. Each is more than a simple contract. In the former an estate in land is created while in the latter an equitable estate arises. There does not appear to be any logical reason or binding legal authority which would prohibit the extension of the doctrine to contracts involving land.

If the factual situation is that there is a clear "frustration of the common venture" then the contract, whether it is a contract for the sale of land or otherwise, is at an end and the parties are discharged from further performance and the adjustment of the rights and liabilities of the parties are left to be determined under the *Frustrated Contracts Act*. In my opinion, on the facts of this case, the contract was frustrated; the doctrine was applicable and should be invoked with the result that both parties are discharged from performance of the contract and the purchaser is entitled to recover the full amount paid as it is not claimed that the vendor incurred any expenses in connection with the performance of the contract, prior to frustration, which would entitle it to retain a portion of the money paid as provided for in s. 3(2) of the *Frustrated Contracts Act*. Accordingly, the vendor must refund to the purchaser the balance of the deposit money, that is, $13,980.

The judgment below is affirmed and the appeal is dismissed with costs.

Appeal dismissed.

NOTES

1. In *National Carriers Ltd v Panalpina (Northern) Ltd*, [1981] AC 675, the House of Lords held that a lease could in some circumstances be frustrated, although rarely in the case of a long-term lease. There, the House of Lords found that a ten-year lease had not been frustrated, even though developments that were being done to the property temporarily interfered with the tenant's enjoyment of the land for a two-year period. For a comment on the decision, see Joseph Robertson, "Frustrated Leases: 'No to Never—But Rarely If Ever'" (1982) 60 Can Bar Rev 619. For a more recent application, see *Manufacturers Life Insurance Co v Huang & Danczkay Properties*, 2003 CarswellOnt 2990 (Ont Sup Ct J).

2. In *Petrogas Processing Ltd v Westcoast Transmission Co* (1988), 59 Alta LR (2d) 118 (QB), aff'd (1989), 66 Alta LR (2d) 254 (CA), O'Leary J discussed how changes in the law can lead to the frustration of existing contracts:

> Supervening illegality occurs when, after the making of a contract, a change in the law renders it illegal to perform the contract in accordance with its terms. The change in the law, to qualify as a frustrating event, must be one which was not foreseen by the parties and for which no express or implied provision is made in the contract. In addition, the illegality must not be temporary or trifling in nature when viewed in the context of the contract as a whole. If these conditions are met, the contract is automatically discharged by frustration the moment performance in accordance with its terms becomes illegal.

VICTORIA WOOD DEVELOPMENT CORP INC V ONDREY
(1977), 14 OR (2d) 723, 74 DLR (3d) 528 (HC)

[Victoria Wood and the Ondreys entered into a contract for the purchase and sale of approximately 90 acres of land in Oakville adjacent to the Queen Elizabeth Way. The contract was made on April 6, 1973, and the sale was to be completed on or before October 31, 1973. On June 22, the Ontario legislature passed the *Ontario Planning and Development Act, 1973*, c 51 and the *Parkway Belt Planning and Development Act, 1973*, each deemed to come into force on June 4, 1973. A regulation made under the Act (O Reg 481/73) on August 4, 1973 prohibited any use of land other than for agricultural purposes in Oakville.

Victoria Wood informed the Ondreys that because it entered into the contract with the intention to develop or subdivide the land, and this purpose was now prevented by the regulation, the agreement was frustrated. The plaintiff also demanded the return of the deposit of $50,000 paid on the signing of the contract.]

OSLER J (distinguishing *Capital Quality Homes Ltd*): ... In my view, in the present instance, "the very foundation of the agreement" has not been destroyed. Though it was as I have found well known to the vendor that the purchaser intended to make commercial use of its property by some form of subdivision, the agreement is in no sense made conditional upon the ability of the purchaser to carry out its intention. The "very foundation of the agreement" was that the vendor would sell and the purchaser would buy the property therein described upon the terms therein set out. The only obligations assumed by the vendor were to provide a deed and to join in or consent to any subsequent applications respecting the zoning and to give partial discharges of the mortgage it was taking back under certain circumstances. The only obligation of the purchaser was to complete the cash balance agreed to, execute and give back a mortgage and to pay such mortgage in accordance with its terms. Nothing in the supervening legislation affects, in the slightest degree, the abilities of the parties to carry out their respective obligations.

As it was put by counsel for the Ondreys, a developer in purchasing land is always conscious of the risk that zoning or similar changes may make the carrying out of his intention impossible, or may delay it. He may attempt to guard against such risk by the insertion of proper conditions in the contract and thereby persuade the vendor to assume some of the risk. In the present case he has not done so and, indeed, there is no evidence that he has attempted to do so. "The very foundation of the agreement" is not affected and there is no room for the application of the doctrine of frustration.

Counsel for the Ondreys advanced as a secondary argument the proposition that there is no absolute prohibition against development as now, some four years after the passage of the legislation, it has been shown to be possible to make application to a hearing board set up by the Minister for a recommendation to the Minister that any land affected by the legislation be exempted from such effect. Had I found that the ability to develop the land had formed part of the agreement between the parties, I would not have given effect to this second argument. Under the legislation, no development is permitted and the fact that it may, at some future time, become possible to persuade the Minister *ex gratia* to exempt the lands, would not, in my view, have affected the matter if I had found that development was at the heart of the agreement.

[The plaintiff's claim was dismissed and the Ondreys' claim for specific performance was successful; aff'd (1978), 22 OR (2d) 1, 92 DLR (3d) 229 (CA).]

NOTES AND QUESTIONS

1. In *KBK No 138 Ventures Ltd v Canada Safeway Limited*, 2000 BCCA 295, 185 DLR (4th) 650, the BC Court of Appeal ruled that a contract for the sale of land for commercial redevelopment was frustrated when the director of planning for the city (independently of the parties) rezoned the property in question, thereby preventing its use as a high-density commercial property. The court determined that the three-factor test set out in *Krell v Henry* (excerpted below) was satisfied, and the unilateral changes made by the city were not foreseeable by the parties. In distinguishing *Victoria Wood*, the court stated that because both parties knew of the intended commercial use of the land, there was "more than 'mere knowledge of the vendor that land was being bought for development or even for a particular kind of development.'" In *Troika Land Development Corp v West Jasper Properties Inc*, 2009 ABQB 590, two real estate developers entered into a purchase and sale agreement for a parcel of land. The purchaser later sought the return of its $250,000.00 deposit, claiming the agreement had been frustrated due to changes to a "neighbourhood structure plan" (NSP) required by the City of Edmonton. The purchaser, relying on *KBK*, above, argued the contract was frustrated and that *Victoria Wood* should be similarly distinguished on the basis that the vendor "had more than 'mere knowledge' of its intended

development." The court disagreed, finding that the changes to the NSP were reasonably foreseeable, were not radical, and that the agreement "continued to be capable of performance." Are these distinctions convincing? Does it seem these cases largely turn on the facts?

2. In *Ballenas Project Management Ltd v PSD Enterprises Ltd*, 2007 BCCA 166, 66 BCLR (4th) 122, the court ruled that a contract for the sale of land was not frustrated when the city rescinded third reading of a zoning bylaw that, if passed, would have allowed the appellant to transfer its liquor licence. The respondent had agreed to purchase the appellant's hotel for $2 million, but the appellant wanted to transfer its liquor licence to another location, which required rezoning of the other location by the city. In accordance with this objective, the purchase agreement between the parties contained a condition stating that the vendor's (appellant's) obligation to complete the transaction would be subject to the city giving third reading of a zoning amendment bylaw to allow a liquor store to be located at the new premises. In distinguishing *KBK*, the court maintained that the issue here was not at the core of the agreement. It also found that failure to obtain the zoning was foreseeable, even though it occurred by an unforeseen route.

3. In *Dinicola v Huang & Danczkay Properties* (1998), 40 OR (3d) 252 (CA), a condominium developer became embroiled in an unusually heated debate with city officials and neighbourhood groups about the redevelopment of harbourfront land in Toronto. The Ontario Court of Appeal rejected the argument that this "abnormal" municipal approval process for a condominium development frustrated the contract, because the parties contemplated what would happen in the event of a failed development application. See also *John E Dodge Holdings Ltd v 805062 Ontario Ltd* (2003), 63 OR (3d) 304 (CA), where the court found that the doctrine of frustration was inapplicable because the parties had made provision in the contract for the event that occurred, making it a foreseeable event.

HOWELL V COUPLAND
(1876), 1 QBD 258

The plaintiff is a potato merchant at Holbeach, Lincolnshire, and the defendant a farmer at Whaplode in the same county.

In 1872 the defendant, at the proper season, and in the due course of husbandry, appropriated between eighty and ninety acres of land for the growth of potatoes—sixty-eight acres at Whaplode, and about twenty at Holbeach.

In March of the same year the plaintiff and the defendant entered into the following contract: "A memorandum of agreement, made this ... day of ... 1872, between Robert Coupland, of Whaplode, and John Howell, of Holbeach, whereby Robert Coupland agrees to sell, and the said John Howell agrees to purchase, 200 tons of regent potatoes grown on land belonging to the said Robert Coupland in Whaplode, at and after the rate of £3 10s. 6d. per ton, to be riddled on 1⅝ in. riddle, and delivered at Holbeach railway station, good and marketable ware, during the months of September or October, as the said John Howell may direct, and, under his direction, the purchaser to find riddles. It is further agreed between the said Robert Coupland and the said John Howell that the said potatoes shall be paid for when and as they are taken away."

At the time of making the contract, out of the sixty-eight acres in Whaplode twenty-five were actually sown with potatoes, and the remaining forty-three acres were ready for sowing. The forty-three acres were afterwards sown in due course, and the whole sixty-eight acres together were amply sufficient, in an ordinary season and in the ordinary course of cultivation, to produce a much larger quantity than two hundred tons, the land producing, on an average, seven tons to the acre.

In July and August, without any fault on the part of the defendant, a disease, which no skill or care on the part of the defendant could have prevented attacked the crop and caused it to fail; and when the time for taking it up arrived, the whole marketable produce of the crop of the lands of the defendant, both in Whaplode and Holbeach together, amounted to no more than 79 tons 8 cwt., and this quantity the defendant delivered to the plaintiff. The rest of the crop had perished from the disease.

If the defendant had had other land to plant with potatoes at the time when the disease was discovered, which in fact he had not, it would have been too late to sow it.

The present action was brought to recover damages for the non-delivery of the residue of the two hundred tons. The verdict at the trial was entered for £432 5s., but a rule was obtained to enter the verdict for the defendant, on the ground that he was not liable to deliver the ungrown potatoes. It was made absolute by the Court of Queen's bench. The plaintiff appealed.

LORD COLERIDGE CJ: I am of opinion that the judgment ought to be affirmed.

[The Lord Chief Justice read the contract and facts.]

The Court of Queen's Bench held that, under these circumstances, the principle of *Taylor v. Caldwell* (1863), 122 E.R. 309 and *Appleby v. Myers* (1867), L.R. 2 C.P. 651 applied, and the defendant was excused from the performance of his contract. The true ground, as it seems to me, on which the contract should be interpreted, and which is the ground on which, I believe, the Court of Queen's Bench proceeded, is that by the simple and obvious construction of the agreement, both parties understood and agreed that there should be a condition implied that before the time for the performance of the contract the potatoes should be, or should have been in existence, and should still be existing when the time came for the performance. They had been in existence, and had been destroyed by causes over which the defendant, the contractor, had no control, and it became impossible for him to perform his contract; and, according to the condition which the parties had understood should be in the contract, he was excused from the performance. It was not an absolute contract of delivery under all circumstances, but a contract to deliver so many potatoes, of a particular kind, grown on a specific place, if deliverable from that place. On the facts the condition did arise and the performance was excused. I am, therefore, of opinion that the judgment of the Queen's Bench should be affirmed.

MELLISH LJ: I am of the same opinion. The words of the contract are clear: the defendant "agrees to sell two hundred tons of regent potatoes grown on land belonging to him in Whaplode." That is, potatoes which shall be grown in Whaplode. They are to be grown there, and delivered to the plaintiff provided they are grown there. Is not that a condition—so that, according to the case on which the Court of Queen's Bench acted, if the thing perishes before the time for performance, the vendor is excused from performance by the delivery of the thing contracted for? No doubt there is a distinction in the present case, that the potatoes, the things contracted for, were not in existence at the time the contract was entered into. But can that make any real difference in principle? Suppose the potatoes had been full grown at the time of the contract, and afterwards the disease had come and destroyed them; according to the authorities it is clear that the performance would have been excused; and I cannot think it makes any difference that the potatoes were not then in existence. This is not like the case of a contract to deliver so many goods of a particular kind, where no specific goods are to be sold. Here there was an agreement to sell and buy two hundred tons out of a crop to be grown on specific land, so that it is an agreement to sell what will be and may be called specific things; therefore neither party is liable if the performance becomes impossible. The language of this contract is much easier to imply a condition from than in most former cases where it has been held to be implied.

CANADIAN INDUSTRIAL ALCOHOL COMPANY
V DUNBAR MOLASSES COMPANY
258 NY 194 (1932)

CARDOZO CH J: A buyer sues a seller for breach of an executory contract of purchase and sale.

The subject-matter of the contract was "approximately 1,500,000 wine gallons Refined Blackstrap [molasses] of the usual run from the National Sugar Refinery, Yonkers, N.Y., to test around 60% sugars."

The order was given and accepted December 27, 1927, but shipments of the molasses were to begin after April 1, 1928, and were to be spread out during the warm weather.

After April 1, 1928, the defendant made delivery from time to time of 344,083 gallons. Upon its failure to deliver more, the plaintiff brought this action for the recovery of damages. The defendant takes the ground that, by an implied term of the contract, the duty to deliver was conditioned upon the production by the National Sugar Refinery at Yonkers of molasses sufficient in quantity to fill the plaintiff's order. The fact is that the output of the refinery, while the contract was in force, was 485,848 gallons, much less than its capacity, of which amount 344,083 gallons were allotted to the defendant and shipped to the defendant's customer. The argument for the defendant is that its own duty to deliver was proportionate to the refinery's willingness to supply, and that the duty was discharged when the output was reduced.

The contract, read in the light of the circumstances existing at its making, or more accurately in the light of any such circumstances apparent from this record, does not keep the defendant's duty within boundaries so narrow. We may assume, in the defendant's favor, that there would have been a discharge of its duty to deliver if the refinery had been destroyed ... . We may even assume that a like result would have followed if the plaintiff had bargained not merely for a quantity of molasses to be supplied from a particular refinery, but for molasses to be supplied in accordance with a particular contract between the defendant and the refiner, and if thereafter such contract had been broken without fault on the defendant's part ... . The inquiry is merely this, whether the continuance of a special group of circumstances appears from the terms of the contract, interpreted in the setting of the occasion, to have been a tacit or implied presupposition in the minds of the contracting parties, conditioning their belief in a continued obligation ... .

Accepting that test, we ask ourselves the question what special group of circumstances does the defendant lay before us as one of the presuppositions immanent in its bargain with the plaintiff? The defendant asks us to assume that a manufacturer, having made a contract with a middleman for a stock of molasses to be procured from a particular refinery would expect the contract to lapse whenever the refiner chose to diminish his production, and this in the face of the middleman's omission to do anything to charge the refiner with a duty to continue. Business could not be transacted with security or smoothness if a presumption so unreasonable were at the root of its engagements. There is nothing to show that the defendant would have been unable by a timely contract with the refinery to have assured itself of a supply sufficient for its needs. There is nothing to show that the plaintiff in giving the order for the molasses, was informed by the defendant that such a contract had not been made, or that performance would be contingent upon obtaining one thereafter. If the plaintiff had been so informed, it would very likely have preferred to deal with the refinery directly, instead of dealing with a middleman. The defendant does not even show that it tried to get a contract from the refinery during the months that intervened between the acceptance of the plaintiff's order and the time when shipments were begun. It has wholly failed to relieve itself of the imputation of contributory fault ... . So far as the record shows, it put its faith in the mere chance that the output of the refinery would be the same from year to year, and finding its faith vain, it tells us that its customer must have expected to take a chance as great. We see no reason for importing into the bargain this aleatory element. The defendant is in no better position than a factor who undertakes in his own name to sell for future delivery a special grade of merchandise to be manufactured by a special mill. The duty will be discharged if the mill is destroyed before delivery is due. The duty will subsist if the output is reduced because times turn out to be hard and labor charges high ... .

The defendant assigns as error the exclusion of correspondence that passed between itself and the plaintiff after April 10, 1928, when deliveries began. The letters, if received, would not have affected the result.

The judgment should be affirmed with costs.

Pound, Crane, Lehman, Kellogg, O'Brien and Hubbs, JJ. concur.

PARRISH & HEIMBECKER LTD V GOODING LUMBER LTD
[1968] 1 OR 716, 67 DLR (2d) 495 (CA), aff'd [1968] SCR viii

MacKAY JA (orally): This is an appeal by the defendant from a judgment awarding damages to the plaintiff for breach of contracts for the delivery of certain quantities of corn. The plaintiffs are dealers in grain. The defendant ordinarily is engaged in the trucking and lumber business and has a number of trucks. His place of operation or headquarters is Parkhill, Ontario. In that district one Sanderson, an employee of the plaintiff, had been buying corn from a farmer by the name of Willemse. Willemse suggested to Sanderson that he would prefer to deal through the defendant in the sale of his corn. Sanderson thereupon got in touch with the defendant Gooding and as a result of an oral agreement, certain written documents, which have been filed as ex. 1 in the action, were entered into by the parties. They are headed "Confirmation," addressed to Gooding Lumber Company Limited, Parkhill, and one of them is as follows:

Confirmation

Parrish & Heimbecker

43 Scott Street
Toronto 1, Ont.
Nov. 8th, 1965.

Gooding Lumber Ltd.,
Parkhill, Ontario

We confirm purchase from you as follows:
25 loads each about 23 tons #2CE Yellow K D Corn 47.93 per ton
Del'd Owen Sound

Shipping instructions: As available—Nov.–Dec.
1 load to C.W. Beattie
24 loads to Great Lakes Elevator Ltd.

There are a number of other similar orders, some providing for delivery to Hanover, some to one other location, but the orders are all in the same form.

It was the intention of Gooding to purchase the corn from three district farmers. It developed that because of weather conditions the farmers were unable to harvest all of their corn and only part of the orders for corn, which had been accepted by Gooding, were delivered. The plaintiff thereupon brought action for damages for failure to deliver. The confirmation orders to which I have referred contained at the bottom thereof the following clause: "If the above is not correct, please wire or phone us immediately; failure to do this is understood as acceptance to these terms. Subject to strikes, embargoes, etc. or other conditions beyond our control."

The learned trial Judge found as a fact that because of weather conditions there was no corn in the immediate vicinity of Parkhill available for the defendant to purchase to fill the balance of these contracts. The area referred to by the trial Judge was an area of within 10 to 20 miles of Parkhill. There was evidence that corn was available in other areas of the Province that the defendant could have purchased to fulfil the contracts.

I am in agreement with the conclusions of the learned trial Judge that these were contracts in writing and that they cannot be varied by any oral understanding. The submission of counsel for the defendant is that he says Sanderson learned at some time or knew who the farmers were from whom Gooding intended to purchase the corn and that by reason of this knowledge the provision in the orders in relation to strikes, embargoes or other conditions beyond their control applied and the corn not being available from these three farmers, there was frustration of the contract. Like the trial Judge, I am unable to accede to this proposition for the reasons I have briefly stated, that is that it was not part of the contract that the corn was to be purchased from any particular source. Sanderson, the agent of the plaintiff, said he did not know two of the farmers and that in making the contracts with the defendant he was not concerned as to from whom the defendant was to purchase the corn and that so far as he was concerned, the defendant could have obtained the corn from any source.

In our view, having regard to the wording of the contracts, it is immaterial that the plaintiff's agent Sanderson may have known of the defendant's intention to purchase the corn from particular sources. Therefore, for the reasons given by the learned trial Judge and accepting his findings, the appeal will be dismissed with costs.

[Kelly JA concurred with MacKay JA.]

LASKIN JA (orally) (dissenting): I cannot agree that these contracts should be viewed in the absolute terms in which the majority has treated them. I think it is clear that the original attitude of the common law that a contract duty is absolute has been considerably modified over the past one hundred years as we have come to recognize that mutual assumptions by parties that underlie their commercial relations cannot be ignored, and that, in the enforcement of a contract, allowance must be made if a failure of those assumptions supervenes, without fault of the contracting parties, after the contract has been made.

In this particular case, the contracts in question originated in oral discussions initiated by the representative of the plaintiff. They consist of written confirmations of the oral arrangements, these being sent by the plaintiff to the defendant and countersigned by the latter. I see nothing in the written documents, all of which are in common form, that in any way precludes the reliance by the defendant on what to me was a common understanding on which the contracts between them were made. The defendant is not in any professional or business sense a grainbroker. It is a lumber company engaged also in trucking, and this the plaintiff knew. When the plaintiff's representative approached the president of the defendant company, the conversation between them indicated that the corn, which was the subject-matter of their relations, would be coming from three farmers in particular or at the most from the Parkhill area and its environs which the trial Judge himself put at a 10 to 20 mile radius from Parkhill.

It is also material to the basis on which these contracts were concluded that the price to be paid by the defendant for the corn obtainable from the farmers was a price fixed by the plaintiff and the plaintiff also fixed the trucking charge that would be paid to the defendant for the transportation of the corn to the specified destinations set out in the written confirmations. It seems to me, therefore, that in the circumstances it would be changing the fundamental character of the contract to require the defendant who, for all practical purposes, was in a factoring position as between the plaintiff and the farmers in the area, to obtain the grain from some other area and at the same time insist that it accept payment on the basis of a price and trucking arrangement which contemplated that the grain would come from the area about which the representatives of the parties had reached an understanding.

I do not think that it is an answer to the defence proposed by the defendant that the plaintiff would have been prepared to receive grain from any source so long as it fulfilled the specifications of the contract. This, with great respect, does not meet the principle upon which I put my judgment. The question is whether the defendant is entitled to be excused from performance if grain is not available from the specified area for a reason not attributable to any fault on his part. It is undoubted that it was impossible to harvest the grain in order to meet the contract delivery dates. I do not say that the contracts themselves necessarily terminated when performance at the required time proved impossible, and I am prepared to assume that the plaintiff could have kept the contract alive and required the defendant to perform at a later time when it would be possible to harvest corn from the particular area. However, the plaintiff did not put his case on this basis but rather sued on the basis of the failure of the defendant to meet the contract delivery dates according to their specific terms. In my view, the foundation on which the arrangements between the parties proceeded collapsed. Accordingly, the defendant had a valid excuse for non-delivery.

I would, therefore, have allowed the appeal, set aside the judgment below and dismissed the plaintiff's action with costs, both at the trial and in this Court, to the defendant.

Appeal dismissed.

KRELL V HENRY
[1903] 2 KB 740 (CA)

The plaintiff, Paul Krell, sued the defendant, C.S. Henry, for £50, being the balance of a sum of £75 for which the defendant had agreed to hire a flat at 56A Pall Mall on the days of June 26 and 27, for the purpose of viewing the processions to be held in connection with the coronation of Edward VII. The defendant denied his liability, and counterclaimed for the return of the sum of £25, which had been paid as a deposit, on the ground that, the procession not having taken place owing to the serious illness of the King, there had been a total failure of consideration for the contract entered into by him.

Darling J. held that there was an implied condition in the contract that the procession should take place, and gave judgment for the defendant on the claim and counterclaim. The plaintiff appealed. The defendant on the appeal abandoned his counter-claim for £25.

VAUGHAN WILLIAMS LJ: The real question in this case is the extent of the application in English law of the principle of the Roman law which has been adopted and acted on in many English decisions, and notably in the case of *Taylor v. Caldwell* (1863), 122 E.R. 309. That case at least makes it clear that "where, from the nature of the contract, it appears that the parties must from the beginning have known that it could not be fulfilled unless, when the time for the fulfilment of the contract arrived, some particular specified thing continued to exist, so that when entering into the contract they must have contemplated such continued existence as the foundation of what was to be done; there, in the absence of any express or implied warranty that the thing shall exist, the contract is not to be considered a positive contract, but as subject to an implied condition that the parties shall be excused in case, before breach, performance becomes impossible from the perishing of the thing without default of the contractor."

Thus far it is clear that the principle of the Roman law has been introduced into the English law. The doubt in the present case arises as to how far this principle extends. The Roman law dealt with obligations *de certo corpore*. Whatever may have been the limits of the Roman law, the case of *Nickoll v. Ashton*, [1901] 2 K.B. 126 makes it plain that the English law applies the principle not only to cases where the performance of the contract becomes impossible by the cessation of existence of the thing which is the subject-matter of the contract, but also to cases where the event which renders the contract incapable of performance is the cessation or non-existence of an express condition or state of things, going to the root of the contract, and essential to its performance. It is said, on the one side, that the specified thing, state of things, or condition the continued existence of which is necessary for the fulfilment of the contract, so that the parties entering into the contract must have contemplated the continued existence of that thing, condition, or state of things as the foundation of what was to be done under the contract, is limited to things which are either the subject-matter of the contract or a condition or state of things, present or anticipated, which is expressly mentioned in the contract.

But, on the other side, it is said that the condition or state of things need not be expressly specified, but that it is sufficient if that condition or state of things clearly appears by extrinsic evidence to have been assumed by the parties to be the foundation or basis of the contract, and the event which causes the impossibility is of such a character that it cannot reasonably be supposed to have been in the contemplation of the contracting parties when the contract was made. In such a case the contracting parties will not be held bound by the general words which, though large enough to include, were not used with reference to a possibility of a particular event rendering performance of the contract impossible.

I do not think that the principle of the civil law as introduced into the English law is limited to cases in which the event causing the impossibility of performance is the destruction or non-existence of some thing which is the subject-matter of the contract or of some condition or state of things expressly specified as a condition of it. I think that you first have to ascertain, not necessarily from the terms of the contract, but, if required, from necessary inferences, drawn from surrounding circumstances recognised by both contracting parties, what is the substance of the contract, and then to ask the question whether that substantial contract needs for its foundation the assumption of the existence of a particular state of things. If it does, this will limit the operation of the general words, and in such case, if the contract becomes impossible of performance by reason of the non-existence of the state of things assumed by both contracting parties as the foundation of the contract, there will be no breach of the contract thus limited.

Now what are the facts of the present case? The contract is contained in two letters of June 20 which passed between the defendant and the plaintiff's agent, Mr. Cecil Bisgood. These letters do not mention the coronation, but speak merely of the taking of Mr. Krell's chambers, or, rather, of the use of them, in the daytime of June 26 and 27, for the sum of £75, £25 then paid, balance £50 to be paid on the 24th. But the affidavits, which by agreement between the parties are to be taken as stating the facts of the case, shew that the plaintiff exhibited on his premises, third floor, 56A Pall Mall, an announcement to the effect that windows to view the Royal coronation procession were to be let, and that the defendant was induced by that announcement to apply to the housekeeper on the premises, who said that the owner was willing to let the suite of rooms for the purpose of seeing the Royal procession for both days, but not nights, of June 26 and 27. In my judgment the use of the rooms was let and taken for the purpose of seeing the Royal procession. It was not a demise of the rooms, or even an agreement to let and take the rooms. It is a licence to use rooms for a particular purpose and none other. And in my judgment the taking place of these processions on the days proclaimed along the proclaimed route which passed 56A Pall Mall, was regarded by both contracting parties as the foundation of the contract; and I think that it cannot reasonably be supposed to have been in the contemplation of the contracting parties, when the contract was made, that the coronation would not be held on the proclaimed days, or the processions not take place on those days along the proclaimed route; and I think that the words imposing on the defendant the obligation to accept and pay for the use of the rooms for the named days, although general and unconditional, were not used with reference to the possibility of the particular contingency which afterwards occurred.

It was suggested in the course of the argument that if the occurrence, on the proclaimed days, of the coronation and the procession in this case were the foundation of the contract, and if the general words are thereby limited or qualified, so that in the event of the non-occurrence of the coronation and procession along the proclaimed route they would discharge both parties from further performance of the contract, it would follow that if a cabman was engaged to take some one to Epsom on Derby Day at a suitable enhanced price for such a journey, say £10, both parties to the contract would be discharged in the contingency of the race at Epsom for some reason becoming impossible; but I do not think this follows, for I do not think that in the cab case the happening of the race would be the foundation of the contract. No doubt the purpose of the engager would be to go to see the Derby, and the price would be proportionately high; but the cab had no special qualifications for the purpose which led to the selection of the cab for this particular occasion. Any other cab would have done as well. Moreover, I think that, under the cab contract, the hirer even if the race went off, could have said, "Drive me to Epsom; I will pay you the agreed sum; you have nothing to do with the purpose for which I hired the cab," and that if the cabman refused he would have been guilty of a breach of contract, there being nothing to qualify his promise to drive the hirer to Epsom on a particular day.

Whereas in the case of the coronation, there is not merely the purpose of the hirer to see the coronation procession, but it is the coronation procession and the relative position of the rooms which is the basis of the contract as much for the lessor as the hirer; and I think that if the King, before the coronation day and after the contract, had died, the hirer could not have insisted on having the rooms on the days named. It could not in the cab case be reasonably said that seeing the Derby race was the foundation of the contract, as it was of the licence in this case. Whereas in the present case, where the rooms were offered and taken, by reason of their peculiar suitability from the position of the rooms for a view of the coronation procession, surely the view of the coronation procession was the foundation of the contract, which is a very different thing from the purpose of the man who engaged the cab—namely, to see the race—being held to be the foundation of the contract.

Each must be judged by its own circumstances. In each case one must ask oneself, first, what, having regard to all the circumstances, was the foundation of the contract? Secondly, was the performance of the contract prevented? Thirdly, was the event which prevented the performance of the contract of such a character that it cannot reasonably be said to have been in the contemplation of the parties at the date of the contract? If all these questions are answered in the affirmative (as I think they should be in this case), I think both parties are discharged from further performance of the contract. I think that the coronation procession was the foundation of this contract, and that the non-happening of it prevented the performance of the contract; and, secondly, I think that the non-happening of the procession, to use the words of Sir James Hannen in *Baily v. De Crespigny* (1869), L.R. 4 Q.B. 180, was an event "of such a character that it cannot reasonably be supposed to have been in the contemplation of the contracting parties when the contract was made, and that they are not to be held bound by general words which, though large enough to include, were not used with reference to the possibility of the particular contingency which afterwards happened."

I myself am clearly of opinion that in this case, where we have to ask ourselves whether the object of the contract was frustrated by the non-happening of the coronation and its procession on the days proclaimed, parol evidence is admissible to shew that the subject of the contract was rooms to view the coronation procession, and was so to the knowledge of both parties. When once this is established, I see no difficulty whatever in the case. It is not essential to the application of the principle of *Taylor v. Caldwell* that the direct subject of the contract should perish or fail to be in existence at the date of the performance of the contract. It is sufficient if a state of things or condition expressed in the contract and essential to its performance perishes or fails to be in existence of that which was, in the contemplation of both parties, the foundation of the contract, is not expressly mentioned either as a condition of the contract or the purpose of it; but I think for the reasons which I have given that the principle of *Taylor v. Caldwell* ought to be applied.

... I think this appeal ought to be dismissed.

[The concurring opinions of Romer and Stirling LJJ are omitted.]

ALUMINUM CO OF AMERICA V ESSEX GROUP, INC
499 F Supp 53 (WD Pa 1980)

TEITELBAUM J: Plaintiff, Aluminum Company of America (ALCOA), brought the instant action against defendant, Essex Group, Inc. (Essex), in three counts. The first count requests the Court to reform or equitably adjust an agreement entitled the Molten Metal Agreement entered into between ALCOA and Essex.

COUNT ONE

ALCOA's first count seeks an equitable modification of the contract price for its services. The pleadings, arguments and briefs frame the issue in several forms. ALCOA seeks reformation or modification of the price on the basis of mutual mistake of fact, unilateral mistake of fact, unconscionability, frustration of purpose, and commercial impracticability.

A

The facts pertinent to count one are few and simple. In 1967 ALCOA and Essex entered into a written contract in which ALCOA promised to convert specified amounts of alumina supplied by Essex into aluminum for Essex. The service is to be performed at the ALCOA works at Warrick, Indiana. The contract is to run until the end of 1983. Essex has the option to extend it until the end of 1988. The price for each pound of aluminum converted is calculated by a complex formula which includes three variable components based on specific indices. ...

In the early years of the contract, the price formula yielded prices related, within the foreseeable range of deviation, to ALCOA's cost figures. Beginning in 1973, OPEC actions to increase oil prices and unanticipated pollution control costs greatly increased ALCOA's electricity costs. ... As a result, ALCOA's production costs rose greatly and unforeseeably beyond the indexed increase in the contract price. ...

ALCOA has sufficiently shown that without judicial relief or economic changes which are not presently foreseeable, it stands to lose in excess of $75,000,000 out of pocket, during the remaining term of the contract. ...

ALCOA initially argues that it is entitled to relief on the theory of mutual mistake. ...

[The discussion of mistake has been omitted.]

• • •

D

ALCOA argues that it is entitled to relief on the grounds of impracticability and frustration of purpose. The Court agrees.

In broad outline the doctrines of impracticability and of frustration of purpose resemble the doctrine of mistake. All three doctrines discharge an obligor from his duty to perform a contract where a failure of a basic assumption of the parties produces a grave failure of the equivalence of value of the exchange to the parties. And all three are qualified by the same notions of risk assumption and allocation. The doctrine of mistake of fact requires that the mistake relate to a basic assumption on which the contract was made. The doctrine of impracticability requires that the non-occurrence of the "event," Restatement 2d of Contracts § [261], or the non-existence of the "fact," *Id.* § [263], causing the impracticability be a basic assumption on which the contract is made. The doctrine of frustration of purpose similarly rests on the same "non-occurrence" or "non-existence," "basic assumption" equation. *Id.* §§ [265, 266].

The three doctrines further overlap in time. There may be some residual notion that the doctrine of frustration and impracticability relate to occurrences after the execution of the contract while the doctrine of mistake relates to facts as they stand at the time of execution. But that view has never won general acceptance. ...

Conversely the notion that the doctrines of frustration and impracticability apply only to events occurring after the execution of a contract appear to be drawn more from common experience with their application than from any inherent limitation of those doctrines. Nothing in the language of the first Restatement limits the doctrine to events occurring after the execution of the contract, though all three illustrations involve such supervening events. [Restatement of Contracts (1932), § 288.] The new Restatement recognizes that circumstances existing at the execution of a contract may render performance impracticable or they may frustrate the purpose of one of the parties so as to excuse his performance. § [266].

Thus there is a substantial area of similarity between the three doctrines. Within that area, the findings and holdings with respect to the claim of mistake also apply to the claims of impracticability and frustration. It requires no further discussion to establish that the non-occurrence of an extreme deviation of the WPI—IC and ALCOA's non-labor production costs was a basic assumption on which the contract was made. And it is clear that ALCOA neither assumed nor bore the risk of the deviation beyond the foreseeable limits of risk.

The court must still consider those aspects of doctrines of frustration and impracticability which differ from the doctrine of mistake. ...

The focus of the doctrines of impracticability and of frustration is distinctly on hardship. Section [261] [of the *Uniform Commercial Code*] declares a party is discharged from performing a contract where a supervening event renders his performance impracticable. Comment (d) discusses the meaning of "impracticability." The comment states the word is taken from Uniform Commercial Code §2-615(a). It declares that the word denotes an impediment to performance lying between "impossibility" and "impracticability."

> Performance may be impracticable because *extreme and unreasonable difficulty, expense, injury, or loss to one of the parties will be involved*. ...

A mere change in the degree of difficulty or expense due to such causes as increased wages, prices of raw materials, or costs of construction, unless well beyond the normal range, does not amount to impracticability since it is this sort of risk that a fixed-price contract is intended to cover. Restatement 2nd Contracts § [261] com. (d).

Similarly, § [265] declares a party is discharged from performing his contract where his principal purpose is *substantially* frustrated by the occurrence of a supervening event. The extent of the necessary frustration is further described in comment (a): "(T)he frustration must be substantial. It is not enough that the transaction has become less profitable for the affected party or even that he will sustain a loss. The frustration must be so severe that it is not fairly to be regarded as within the risks that he assumed under the contract." ...

This strict standard of severe disappointment is clearly met in the present case. ALCOA has sufficiently proved that it will lose well over $60 million out of pocket over the life of the contract due to the extreme deviation of the WPI—IC from ALCOA's actual costs. ...

Is this, then, a case of impracticability, of frustration, or both? The doctrine of impracticability and of frustration focus on different kinds of disappointment of a contracting party. Impracticability focuses on occurrences which greatly increase the costs, difficulty, or risk of the party's performance. Restatement 2d of Contracts § [261].

The doctrine of frustration, on the other hand, focuses on a party's severe disappointment which is caused by circumstances which frustrate his principal purpose for entering the contract. Restatement 2d of Contracts § [265]. The doctrine of frustration often applies to relieve a party of a contract which could be performed without impediment; relief is allowed because the performance would be of little value to the frustrated party. ...

In the present case ALCOA has satisfied the requirements of both doctrines. The impracticability of its performance is clear. The increase in its cost of performance is severe enough to warrant relief, and the other elements necessary for the granting of relief have been proven. Essex argues that the causes of ALCOA's losses are due to market price increases to which the doctrine of impracticability does not apply. The doctrine of impracticability of the new Restatement is one of recent evolution in the law. The first Restatement used the term as part of the definition of "impossibility." The interesting legal evolution from the strict standards of impossibility, evident at least by 0 in *Paradine v. Jane*, Aleyn, 26 (1647, K.B.), to modern standards of impracticability is traced in Professor Gilmore's *The Death of Contracts* 35-90 (1974). ...

[The court found actionable ALCOA's frustration of purpose claim. It then addressed the problem of fashioning an appropriate remedy.]

E

This leaves the question of framing a remedy for ALCOA. Essex argues that reformation is not available. It cites many Indiana cases declaring that reformation is only available to correct writings which, through mistake, do not reflect the agreement of the parties. The declarations to that effect are clear.

But the point is immaterial here. This case does not fall within reformation as a traditional head of equity jurisprudence. It does fall within the more general rules of equitable restitution. Courts have traditionally applied three remedial rules in cases of mistake, frustration and impracticability. In some cases courts declare that no contract ever arose because there was no true agreement between the parties, *Raffles v. Wichelhaus*, or because the parties were ignorant of existing facts which frustrated the purpose of one party or made performance impracticable. Restatement 2d of Contracts § [266]. In some other cases the courts hold that a contract is voidable on one of the three theories. In these cases the customary remedy is rescission. In both classes of cases where one or both parties have performed under the supposed contract, the courts award appropriate restitution in the light of the benefits the parties have conferred on each other. The aim is to prevent unjust enrichment. The courts in such cases often call this remedy "reformation" in the loose sense of "modification." See III Palmer, *Law of Restitution* §13.9 (1978). ... The same ends can be achieved under a long term executory contract by a similar remedy. To decree rescission in this case would be to grant ALCOA a windfall gain in the current aluminum market. It would at the same time deprive Essex of the assured long term aluminum supply which it obtained under the contract and of the gains it legitimately may enforce within the scope of the risk ALCOA bears under the contract. A remedy which merely shifts the windfall gains and losses is neither required nor permitted by Indiana law.

To frame an equitable remedy where frustration, impracticability or mistake prevent strict enforcement of a long term executory contract requires a careful examination of the circumstances of the contract, the purposes of the parties, and the circumstances which upset the contract. For some long term executory contracts rescission with or without restitution will be the only sensible remedy. Where developments make performance of the contract economically senseless or purposeless, to modify the contract and to enforce it as modified would be highly inappropriate. But in cases like the present one modification and enforcement may be the only proper remedy. See *Parev Products Co. v. I. Rokeach and Sons, Inc.*, 124 F.2d 147 (2nd Cir. 1941). In this case Essex sought an assured long term supply of aluminum at a price which would let it earn a profit on its finished products. ALCOA, facing ordinary market risks in 1967, sought a long term, limited risk use for its Warrick Works. A remedy modifying the price term of the contract in light of the circumstances which upset the price formula will better preserve the purposes and expectations of the parties than any other remedy. Such a remedy is essential to avoid injustice in this case.

NOTES

1. *Aluminum Co of America v Essex Group* [*ALCOA*] has been soundly criticized. See *Golsen v ONG Western, Inc*, 1988 OK 26, 756 P 2d 1209, 1221 (Okla 1988). See also *Wabash v Avnet Inc*, 516 F Supp 995, 999 n 5 (ND I11, 1981), where the court maintained that "under the logical consequences of [*ALCOA*], there would be no predictability or certainty for contracting parties who selected a future variable to measure their contract liability. Whichever way the variable fluctuated, the disappointed party would be free to assert frustrated expectations and seek relief via reformation."

2. For a discussion of the relation between the "frustration of purpose" doctrine and other forms of frustration, see Thomas Roberts, "Commercial Impossibility and Frustration of Purpose: A Critical Analysis" (2003) 16 Can JL & Jur 129.

3. Should the doctrine of frustration provide relief where there is a breakdown of relations between the contracting parties? In *Folia v Trelinski* (1997), 36 BLR (2d) 108 (BCSC), the plaintiff transferred her home to the defendants, her daughter and son-in-law, and, as part of the consideration for the transfer, the defendants promised they would take care of the plaintiff at their home for the rest of her life. When relations between them broke down, the defendants argued that the contract had been frustrated by the parties' inability to live together. In an oft-quoted excerpt, the court articulated the test for frustration (at para 18):

> In order to find that the contract at issue has been frustrated the following criteria would have to be satisfied. The event in question must have occurred after the formation of the contract and cannot be self-induced. The contract must, as a result, be totally different from what the parties had intended. This difference must take into account the distinction between complete fruitlessness and mere inconvenience. The disruption must be permanent, not temporary or transient. The change must totally affect the nature, meaning, purpose, effect and consequences of the contract so far as concerns either or both parties. Finally, the act or event that brought about such radical change must not have been foreseeable.

Applied to the case, the court found that the conflict between the parties did not "radically or totally [affect] the nature, meaning, purpose, effect and consequences of the contract ... . Although the parties no doubt expected to remain compatible, for the contract to be considered frustrated there must have been the occurrence of circumstances that could not be said to have been in the contemplation of the parties. Objectively viewed, the possibility of future incompatibility for any number of reasons must have been in the parties' contemplation when the agreement to care for [the plaintiff] was made." Death of a party, however, does frustrate a contract, when the contract is one for personal services. See *Rickards Estate v Diebold Election Systems Inc*, 2007 BCCA 246.

4. In *Exelon Generation Co, LLC v General Atomics Technologies Corp*, 559 F Supp 2d 892 (US Dist Ct, ND Illinois, Eastern Division, 2008), the court considered the doctrine of commercial impracticability, which has its roots in the common law doctrine of frustration or impossibility and which, under New York law, is "based on the notion that, where parties can reasonably anticipate events that may affect performance, [the] prudent course is to provide for such eventualities in their contract" (NY McKinney's *Uniform Commercial Code* § 2-615(a)). The court determined that the doctrine, "which is devised to '[shift] risk in accordance with the parties' presumed intentions,'" has no place when a contract explicitly assigns a particular risk to one of the parties. In this case, the risk of production costs was assigned to the defendant, who later argued that its obligations should be excused under the doctrine of commercial impracticability due to a confluence of unforeseeable contingencies.

EASTERN AIR LINES V GULF OIL CORP
415 F Supp 429 (SD Fla 1975)

KING J: Eastern Air Lines, Inc., hereafter Eastern, and Gulf Oil Corporation, hereafter Gulf, have enjoyed a mutually advantageous business relationship involving the sale and purchase of aviation fuel for several decades.

This controversy involves the threatened disruption of that historic relationship and the attempt, by Eastern, to enforce the most recent contract between the parties. On March 8, 1974 the correspondence and telex communications between the corporate entities culminated in a demand by Gulf that Eastern must meet its demand for a price increase or Gulf would shut off Eastern's supply of jet fuel within fifteen days.

Eastern responded by filing its complaint with this court, alleging that Gulf had breached its contract and requesting preliminary and permanent mandatory injunctions requiring Gulf to perform the contract in accordance with its terms. By agreement of the parties, a preliminary injunction preserving the status quo was entered on March 20, 1974, requiring Gulf to perform its contract and directing Eastern to pay in accordance with the contract terms, pending final disposition of the case.

Gulf answered Eastern's complaint, alleging that the contract was not a binding requirements contract, was void for want of mutuality, and, furthermore, was "commercially impracticable" within the meaning of Uniform Commercial Code §2-615; Fla. Stat. §§672.614 and 672.615.

The extraordinarily able advocacy by the experienced lawyers for both parties produced testimony at the trial from internationally respected experts who described in depth economic events that have, in recent months, profoundly affected the lives of every American. ...

In short, for U.C.C. §2-615 to apply there must be a failure of a pre-supposed condition, which was an underlying assumption of the contract, which failure was unforeseeable, and the risk of which was not specifically allocated to the complaining party. The burden of proving each element of claimed commercial impracticability is on the party claiming excuse. *Ocean Air Tradeways, Inc. v. Arkay Realty Corp.*, 480 F.2d 1112, 1117 (9th Cir. 1973).

The modern U.C.C. §2-615 doctrine of commercial impracticability has its roots in the common law doctrine of frustration or impossibility and finds its most recognized illustrations in the so-called "Suez Cases," arising out of the various closings of the Suez Canal and the consequent increases in shipping costs around the Cape of Good Hope. Those cases offered little encouragement to those who would wield the sword of commercial impracticability. As a leading British case arising out of the 1957 Suez closure declared, the unforeseen cost increase that would excuse performance "must be more than merely onerous or expensive. It must be positively unjust to hold the parties bound." *Ocean Tramp Tankers v. V/O Sovfracht (The Eugenia)*, 2 Q.B. 226, 239 (1964). ...

Other recent American cases similarly strictly construe the doctrine of commercial impracticability. For example, one case found no U.C.C. defense, even though costs had doubled over the contract price, the court stating, "It may have been unprofitable for defendant to have supplied the pickers, but the evidence does not establish that it was impossible. A mere showing of unprofitability, without more, will not excuse the performance of a contract." *Schafer v. Sunset Packing Co.*, 256 Or. 539 (1970).

Recently, the Seventh Circuit has stated: "The fact that performance has become economically burdensome or unattractive is not sufficient for performance to be excused. We will not allow a party to a contract to escape a bad bargain merely because it is burdensome." "(T)he buyer has a right to rely on the party to the contract to supply him with goods regardless of what happens to the market price. That is the purpose for which such contracts are made," *Neal-Cooper Grain Co. v. Texas Gulf Sulfur Co.*, 508 F.2d 283, 293, 294 (7th Cir. 1974). ...

Gulf's argument on commercial impracticability has two strings to its bow. First, Gulf contends that the escalator indicator does not work as intended by the parties by reason of the advent of so-called "two-tier" pricing under Phase IV government price controls. Second, Gulf alleges that crude oil prices have risen substantially without a concomitant rise in the escalation indicator, and, as a result, that performance of the contract has become commercially impracticable. ...

[The court held that Gulf's claim of hardship giving rise to "commercial impracticability" failed.]

But even if Gulf had established great hardship under U.C.C. §2-615, which it has not, Gulf would not prevail because the events associated with the so-called energy crises were reasonably foreseeable at the time the contract was executed. If a contingency is foreseeable, it and its consequences are taken outside the scope of U.C.C. §2-615, because the party disadvantaged by fruition of the contingency might have protected himself in his contract, *Ellwood v. Nutex Oil Co.*, 148 S.W.2d 862 (Tex. Civ. App. 1941).

The foreseeability point is illustrated by *Foster v. Atlantic Refining Co.*, 329 F.2d 485, 489 (5th Cir. 1964). There an oil company sought release from a gas royalty contract because the royalty provisions of the contract did not contain an escalation clause, with the result that the oil company came to receive a far smaller share of the royalties than it would then have been able to obtain on the market. Citing *Ellwood*, with approval, the Fifth Circuit answered the oil company's argument as follows:

> (O)ne who unconditionally obligates himself to do a thing possible of performance, must be held to perform it (citing cases); and though performance, subsequent to the contract, may become difficult or even impossible, (this) does not relieve the promisor, and particularly where he might have foreseen the difficulty and impossibility (citing cases).

The record is replete with evidence as to the volatility of the Middle East situation, the arbitrary power of host governments to control the foreign oil market, and repeated interruptions and interference with the normal commercial trade in crude oil. Even without the extensive evidence present in the record, the court would be justified in taking judicial notice of the fact that oil has been used as a political weapon with increasing success by the oil-producing nations for many years, and Gulf was well aware of and assumed the risk that the OPEC nations would do exactly what they have done.

With respect to Gulf's argument that "two-tier" was not "foreseeable," the record shows that domestic crude oil prices were controlled at all material times, that Gulf foresaw that they might be de-controlled, and that Gulf was constantly urging to the Federal Government that they should be de-controlled. Government price regulations were confused, constantly changing, and uncertain during the period of the negotiation and execution of the contract. During that time frame, high ranking Gulf executives, including some of its trial witnesses, were in constant repeated contact with officials and agencies of the Federal Government regarding petroleum policies and were well able to protect themselves from any contingencies.

Even those outside the oil industry were aware of the possibilities. Eastern's principal contract negotiator advised his superior in recommending this contract to him:

While Gulf is apparently counting on crude price increases, such increases are a fact of life for the future, except as the government may inhibit by price controls, therefore all suppliers have such anticipation.

1975 is the year during which the full effect of energy shortages will be felt in the United States according to most estimates.

Knowing all the factors, Gulf drafted the contract and tied the escalation to certain specified domestic postings in Platt's. The court is of the view that it is bound thereby. ...

Having found and concluded that the contract is a valid one, should be enforced, and that no defenses have been established against it, there remains for consideration the proper remedy.

The Uniform Commercial Code provides that in an appropriate case specific performance may be decreed. This case is a particularly appropriate one for specific performance. The parties have been operating for more than a year pursuant to a preliminary injunction requiring specific performance of the contract and Gulf has stipulated that it is able to perform. Gulf presently supplies Eastern with 100,000,000 gallons of fuel annually or 10 percent of Eastern's total requirements. If Gulf ceases to supply this fuel, the result will be chaos and irreparable damage.

Under the U.C.C. a more liberal test in determining entitlement to specific performance has been established than the test one must meet for classic equitable relief. U.C.C. §2-716(1); *Kaiser Trading Co. v. Associated Metals & Minerals Corp.*, 321 F. Supp 923, 932 (N.D. Cal. 1970), *appeal dismissed per curiam*, 443 F.2d 1364 (9th Cir. 1971).

It has previously been found and concluded that Eastern is entitled to Gulf's fuel at the prices agreed upon in the contract. In the circumstances, a decree of specific performance becomes the ordinary and natural relief rather than the extraordinary one. The parties are before the court, the issues are squarely framed, they have been clearly resolved in Eastern's favor, and it would be a vain, useless and potentially harmful exercise to declare that Eastern has a valid contract, but leave the parties to their own devices. Accordingly, the preliminary injunction heretofore entered is made a permanent injunction and the order of this court herein.

EDWINTON COMMERCIAL CORPORATION AND ANOTHER V TSAVLIRIS RUSS (WORLDWIDE SALVAGE AND TOWAGE) LTD (*"The Sea Angel"*)
[2007] 2 All ER (Comm) 634 (CA)

[Commercial salvagers, Tsavliris, engaged the *Sea Angel*, a vessel owned by Edwinton, to assist in the salvage operations of the oil tanker the *Tasman Spirit*. The *Tasman Spirit* had broken in two, causing a significant pollution incident in and around Karachi. The charter was to last up to 20 days. However, 3 days before Tsavliris was to redeliver the *Sea Angel*, the Karachi Port Trust (KPT) alleged negligence in the performance of Tsavliris' salvage duties and claimed compensation for the pollution cleanup from Tsavliris. During that time, as a result of the allegations, the *Sea Angel* was unable to depart due to the KPT's refusal to issue a "no demand certificate" (NDC), which was required as a prerequisite for port clearance. Tsavliris ceased paying hire for the *Sea Angel* 3 days after the contracted date for redelivery. By the time the court ordered the KPT to release the *Sea Angel*, the 20-day charter was exceeded by about 108 days. Edwinton claimed hire from Tsavliris for the time during which the vessel had been detained. Tsavliris took the position that the unlawful detention of the vessel had frustrated the charter party and that it owed no additional hire to Edwinton.]

RIX LJ: ... The general context is of course an allegation of frustration of a charter by reason of a foreseeable risk giving rise to delay, and the special context is that of a vessel chartered for a short period to assist in providing salvage services.

Two classic modern statements of the incidence of frustration are to be found in the dicta of Lord Radcliffe in *Davis Contractors Ltd v. Fareham Urban District Council* [1956] A.C. 696 at 729 and Lord Simon of Glaisdale in *National Carriers Ltd v. Panalpina (Northern) Ltd* [1981] A.C. 675 at 700. Lord Radcliffe said:

> ... frustration occurs whenever the law recognises that without default of either party a contractual obligation has become incapable of being performed because the circumstances in which performance is called for would render it a thing radically different from that which was undertaken by the contract. Non haec in foedera veni. It was not this that I promised to do.

Lord Simon said:

> Frustration of a contract takes place when there supervenes an event (without default of either party and for which the contract makes no sufficient provision) which so significantly changes the nature (not merely the expense or onerousness) of the outstanding contractual rights and/or obligations from what the parties could reasonably have contemplated at the time of its execution that it would be unjust to hold them to the literal sense of its stipulations in the new circumstances; in such case the law declares both parties to be discharged from further performance.

The reference by Lord Simon in that latter passage to the role that the concept of justice plays in the doctrine has a distinguished pedigree, which he elaborated at 701:

> In the first place, the doctrine has been developed by the law as an expedient to escape from injustice where such would result from enforcement of a contract in its literal terms after a significant change in circumstances. As Lord Sumner said, giving the opinion of a strong Privy Council in *Hirji Mulji v. Cheong Yue Steamship Co. Ltd.* [1926] A.C. 497, 510: "It is really a device, by which the rules as to absolute contracts are reconciled with a special exception which justice demands." ...
>
> Secondly, in the words of Lord Wright in the *Cricklehood Property* case [*Cricklewood Property and Investment Trust Ltd v Leighton's Investment Trust Ltd*, [1945] AC 221] at p. 241: " ... the doctrine of frustration is modern and flexible and is not subject to being constricted by an arbitrary formula." It is therefore on the face of it apt to vindicate justice wherever owing to relevant supervening circumstances the enforcement of any contractual arrangement in its literal terms would produce injustice.

Lord Wilberforce (at 696H) and Lord Roskill (at 712D/E) also referred to the doctrine of frustration as a means for finding just solutions or avoiding injustice.

In *The Super Servant Two* [1990] 1 Lloyd's Rep 1, at 8, Bingham L.J. on the same subject included the following as a proposition established by the highest authority and not open to question:

> The object of the doctrine was to give effect to the demands of justice, to achieve a just and reasonable result, to do what is reasonable and fair, as an expedient to escape from injustice where such would result from enforcement of a contract in its literal terms after a significant change in circumstances ...

The particular problem of delay as a cause of frustration has to be tested as at the time it had to be considered by the parties, but on an objective basis. For these purposes past and prospective delay has to be taken into account. The issue, if disputed, requires an informed judgment and the decision on such an issue by the tribunal of fact cannot easily be upset on appeal (subject of course to any error of law). As Lord Sumner famously said in *Bank Line, Limited v. Arthur Capel & Co* [1919] A.C. 435 at 454:

> The probabilities as to the length of the deprivation and not the certainty arrived at after the event are also material. The question must be considered at the trial as it had to be considered by the parties, when they came to know of the cause and the probabilities of the delay and had to decide what to do. On this the judgments in the above cases substantially agree. Rights ought not to be left in suspense or to hang on the chances of subsequent events. The contract binds or it does not bind, and the law ought to be that the parties can gather their fate then and there. What happens afterwards may assist in showing what the probabilities really were, if they had been reasonably forecasted, but when the causes of frustration have operated so long or under such circumstances as to raise a presumption of inordinate delay, the time has arrived at which the fact of the contract falls to be decided.

To which has to be added an equally well-known passage from the speech of Lord Roskill (with whom their other Lordships agreed) in *Pioneer Shipping Ltd v. BTP Tioxide Ltd (The "Nema")* [1982] A.C. 724 at 752:

> But in others, where the effect of that event is to cause delay in the performance of contractual obligations, it is often necessary to wait upon events in order to see whether the delay already suffered and the prospects of further delay from that cause, will make any ultimate performance of the relevant contractual obligations "radically different," to borrow Lord Radcliffe's phrase, from that which was undertaken under the contract. But, as has often been said, business men must not be required to await events too long. They are entitled to know where they stand. Whether or not the delay is such as to bring about frustration must be a question to be determined by an informed judgment based upon all the evidence of what has occurred and what is likely thereafter to occur. Often it will be a question of degree whether the effect of the delay suffered, and likely to be suffered, will be such as to bring about frustration of the particular adventure in question. ... That tribunal, properly informed as to the relevant law, must form its own view of the effect of that delay and answer the critical question accordingly. Your Lordships' House in *Tsakiroglou & Co. Ltd. v. Noblee Thorl G.m.b.H.* [1962] A.C. 93, decided that while in the ultimate analysis whether a contract was frustrated was a question of law, yet as Lord Radcliffe said at p. 124 in relation to that case "that conclusion is almost completely determined by what is ascertained as to mercantile usage and the understanding of mercantile men." ...

There were lengthy submissions before us from both parties as to the role in the doctrine of frustration of the fact that a risk might be foreseen or foreseeable ... .

The significance of foreseen or of unforeseen but foreseeable events is in my judgment well, if briefly, summarised in *Chitty on Contracts*, 29th ed, 2004 at paras 23-057/8. Para 23-057 which deals with foreseen events can be seen to make the point that there is no rule of exclusion, at best some prima facie indications. Thus:

> While an unforeseen event will not necessarily lead to the frustration of a contract, a foreseen event will generally exclude the operation of the doctrine. The inference that a foreseen event is not a frustrating event is only a prima facie one and so can be excluded by evidence of contrary intention.

However, there is no finding in terms that the detention by KPT which occurred in this case was actually foreseen (or unforeseen) even by Tsavliris, merely that unreasonable detention by port authorities is a "risk of the industry," and as such foreseeable. In such circumstances it is para 23-058 which is perhaps particularly pertinent, which reads:

> *Event foreseeable but not foreseen.* When the event was foreseeable but not foreseen by the parties, it is less likely that the doctrine of frustration will be held to be inapplicable. Much turns on the extent to which the event was foreseeable. The issue which the court must consider is whether or not one or other party has assumed the risk of the occurrence of the event. The degree of foreseeability required to exclude the doctrine of frustration is, however, a high one: "'foreseeability' will support the inference of risk-assumption only where the supervening event is one which any person of ordinary intelligence would regard as likely to occur, or ... the contingency must be 'one which the parties could reasonably be thought to have foreseen as a real possibility.'"

DISCUSSION

... In my judgment, the application of the doctrine of frustration requires a multi-factorial approach. Among the factors which have to be considered are the terms of the contract itself, its matrix or context, the parties' knowledge, expectations, assumptions and contemplations, in particular as to risk, as at the time of contract, at any rate so far as these can be ascribed mutually and objectively, and then the nature of the supervening event, and the parties' reasonable and objectively ascertainable calculations as to the possibilities of future performance in the new circumstances. Since the subject matter of the doctrine of frustration is contract, and contracts are about the allocation of risk, and since the allocation and assumption of risk is not simply a matter of express or implied provision but may also depend on less easily defined matters such as "the contemplation of the parties," the application of the doctrine can often be a difficult one. In such circumstances, the test of "radically different" is important: it tells us that the doctrine is not to be lightly invoked; that mere incidence of expense or delay or onerousness is not sufficient; and that there has to be as it were a break in identity between the contract as provided for and contemplated and its performance in the new circumstances.

What the "radically different" test, however, does not in itself tell us is that the doctrine is one of justice, as has been repeatedly affirmed on the highest authority. Ultimately the application of the test cannot safely be performed without the consequences of the decision, one way or the other, being measured against the demands of justice. Part of that calculation is the consideration that the frustration of a contract may well mean that the contractual allocation of risk is reversed. A time charter is a good example. Under such a charter, the risk of delay, subject to express provision for the cessation of hire under an off-hire clause, is absolutely on the charterer. If, however, a charter is frustrated by delay, then the risk of delay is wholly reversed: the delay now falls on the owner. If the provisions of a contract in their literal sense are to make way for the absolving effect of frustration, then that must, in my judgment, be in the interests of justice and not against those interests. Since the purpose of the doctrine is to do justice, then its application cannot be divorced from considerations of justice. Those considerations are among the most important of the factors which a tribunal has to bear in mind.

Mr Hamblen submitted that whereas the demands of justice play an underlying role, they should not be overstated. He referred the court to *Chitty* at para 23-008 ("But this appeal to the demands of justice should not be taken to suggest that the court has a broad absolving power whenever a change of circumstances causes hardship to one of the contracting parties. ... Such a test is too wide, and gives too much discretion to the court.") I respectfully agree. Mr Hamblen also referred to *Treitel* at para 16-009 ("The 'theory' does not, in other words, supersede the rules which determine the circumstances in which the doctrine of frustration operates.") I would again respectfully agree, as long as it is not sought to apply those rules as though they are expected to lead one automatically, and without an exercise of judgment, to a determined answer without consideration of the demands of justice. ...

I turn then to the facts of this case. I agree with Mr Hamblen that the critical question was whether, as of 13 October ..., the delay which had already occurred and prospective further delay would have led the parties at that time to have reasonably concluded that the charter was frustrated. ... For these purposes, since on the facts a delay of some 5 weeks had already occurred and the prospective delay involved in a revised strategy involving litigating in the Pakistani courts would involve a further 4 to 6 weeks at least, the first question to consider is whether Mr Hamblen is right in his submission that the Bailhache J. test of comparing the probable length of the delay with the unexpired duration of the charter is the critical or main and in any event overbearing test to apply ... .

In my judgment it is not. It may be an important consideration, but it is, on our facts, only the starting point. In the first place, the development of the law shows that such a single-factored approach is too blunt an instrument ... . Secondly, ... in our case, the consequences of the detention by the port authorities remained very much a matter for enquiry, negotiation, diplomacy, and, whatever the ordering of the tactics, legal pressure. Thirdly, where, as in our case, the supervening event comes at the very end of a charter, with redelivery as essentially the only remaining obligation, the effect of the detention on the performance of the charter is purely a question of the financial consequences of the delay, which will fall on one party or the other, depending on whether the charter binds or does not bind. It is not like the different situation where the supervening event either postpones or, which may be even worse, interrupts the heart of the adventure itself ... . In our case, the purpose for which the *Sea Angel* had been chartered, namely the lightening of the casualty, had been performed.

Fourthly, in general terms the contractual risk of such delay caused by detention by government authorities was firmly on the charterers, Tsavliris ... it follows from their obligation to pay hire, subject to the off-hire clause, until redelivery. And even the off-hire clause itself expressly provided for "detention by the authorities at home or abroad" but not in terms which were relied on as covering the particular event here. Fifthly, as was even common ground, the risk of detention by the littoral authorities arising out of a salvage situation where there was a concern about pollution was, at any rate in general terms, foreseeable. This remained the case even if, as Mr Hamblen submitted, the particular form in which that risk showed itself in this case was unforeseeable, or only weakly foreseeable, or was even unprecedented. Sixthly, that general risk was foreseeable by the salvage industry as a whole, and was provided for by the terms of that industry. ... Indeed, in my view the particular risk which occurred was within the provisions of SCOPIC [Special Compensation Protection and Indemnity Clause]. As such, those matters were part of the matrix itself of the charter under enquiry. In this connection, I bear in mind that [the other respondent] ... chartered the vessel to well-known international salvors, to perform salvage services directly to a casualty, at a high price which reflected the emergencies and risks of such services: and therefore the foreseeable risks of the salvage context, and the incidence of those risks subject to SCOPIC, are properly part of the matrix of the charter. In justice, they bear particularly on Tsavliris, the salvors, themselves.

Seventhly, it is now common ground, on the particular facts of this case, that, short as the charter was, a mere 20 days, and shorter still as the unexpired period of the charter was, a mere 3 days, there was no frustration until the strategy of commercial negotiation had initially failed (by 13 or 17 October), some five weeks after the detention began. So, in any event, this is not a case like *Anglo-Northern* and *Tatem v. Gamboa*, where the charters were frustrated then and there by the supervening event. Ours is one of those "wait and see" situations discussed in other authorities. In such situations, it is a matter for assessment, on all the circumstances of the case, whether by a particular date the tribunal of fact, putting itself in the position of the parties, and viewing the matter in the role of reasonable and well-informed men, concludes that those parties would or properly speaking should have formed the view that, in all fairness and consistently with the demands of justice, their contract, as something whose performance in the new circumstances, past and prospective, had become "radically different," had ceased to bind.

For these reasons, some of which have been sufficiently grounded above, and others of which I shall elaborate below, it seems to me that the primary point on which Tsavliris have founded their claim to frustration fails. I turn to discuss particular aspects of these reasons. ...

THE FORESEEABILITY OF THE RISK

... In a sense, most events are to a greater or lesser degree foreseeable. That does not mean that they cannot lead to frustration. Even events which are not merely foreseen but made the subject of express contractual provision may lead to frustration: as occurs when an event such as a strike, or a restraint of princes, lasts for so long as to go beyond the risk assumed under the contract and to render performance radically different from that contracted for. However, ... the less that an event, in its type and its impact, is foreseeable, the more likely it is to be a factor which, depending on other factors in the case, may lead on to frustration.

In the present case it was both highly relevant that the unreasonable detention of a vessel participating in salvage services, whether owned or contracted in by the salvors, could be foreseen and was actually provided for in SCOPIC, and also relevant, if it be the case, that the actual circumstances of the detention were comparatively unusual or even unprecedented and lasted for a long time. All such circumstances would need to be taken into account. ... Once a port authority acts unreasonably, the precise circumstances and consequences must essentially be variants on a theme. The foreseeability of this general risk, recognised within the industry, and provided for in its well-known terms of trade (SCOPIC), provides a special and highly relevant factor against which the issue of frustration needs to be assessed. ...

THE SPHERE OF RESPONSIBILITY

... The way I would therefore prefer to put the factor of the sphere of responsibility under the charter which the judge had in mind is to emphasise that, generally speaking, the risk of delay under the charter was upon Tsavliris as charterers. This is because of the essential structure of a time charter, under which, absent express provision, time runs continuously against the charterer until redelivery. Thus an off-hire clause is the place to find exceptions against the incidence of a continuous liability for hire, but such a clause did not avail Tsavliris in this case. ...

THE DICTATES OF JUSTICE

I have referred to this factor above. It is not an additional test, but it is a relevant factor which underlies all and provides the ultimate rationale of the doctrine. If one uses this factor as a reality check, its answer should conform with a proper assessment of the issue of frustration. If it does not appear to do so, it is probably a good indication of the need to think again. The question in this case is whether it would be just to relieve Tsavliris of the consequences of their bargain, or unjust to maintain the bargain, in a situation where they have assumed the general risk of delay, and have done so in a specific context where the risk of unreasonable detention is foreseeable and has at least in general been actually foreseen, as demonstrated by SCOPIC which, subject to the limits of frustration, protects the salvor from the financial consequences of the delay; where from the very beginning a solution was considered to be possible rather than impossible or hopeless, but only after a period of some three months, and where that solution, although not entirely or even mainly in Tsavliris's own control, was achievable with the co-operation of the owners of the casualty and their Club, known to be in principle available, and the assistance of legal action in the local courts; and where the outcome has confirmed the calculations of the objectively reasonable participants in the events.

In my judgment, the judge's conclusion, that the charter had not been frustrated by 13 or 17 October, shows the doctrine working justly, reasonably and fairly.

NOTES AND QUESTIONS

1. Two instances of a large corporation arguing that unforeseeable future events had rendered the performance of contractual obligations impractical are as follows. In the first case, *Re Westinghouse Elec Corp Uranium Contracts Litigation*, 517 F Supp 440, 31 UCC Rep Serv 930, Westinghouse Electric Corporation announced on September 8, 1975, that it would not fulfill contracts to provide about 70 million pounds of uranium to utilities at a fixed price. Westinghouse argued that under § 2-615 of the *Uniform Commercial Code* (UCC) it was legally excused from performance because of "commercial impracticability." It also argued that, due to the combined effects of the OPEC-induced oil-price shock and the formation of a cartel of uranium producers, uranium prices had unforeseeably risen to several times the price at which it had agreed to provide uranium to the utilities. It claimed that performance of its obligations would result in a loss of up to $2 billion. Twenty-seven utilities launched 14 lawsuits against Westinghouse for specific performance or damages. Which of the parties were better placed to insure against the risk of a price increase in the supply of uranium, Westinghouse or the utilities? The litigation was settled for about half the losses that Westinghouse claimed would have resulted from performance under the original contracts.

2. In the second case, *Florida Power and Light Co v Westinghouse Electric Corp*, 826 F 2d 239 (4th Cir 1987), Westinghouse had agreed to build a nuclear reactor for the utility and agreed to remove and dispose of spent reactor fuel. Westinghouse had planned to reprocess the fuel for a profit of $20 million, but changes in federal government policy discontinued reprocessing for commercial nuclear plants after the contract was signed. Westinghouse now stood to lose over $80 million to dispose of the waste. Florida Power sued for specific performance or damages. Westinghouse alleged in defence that its non-performance was excused by impossibility, commercial impracticability under UCC § 2-615, frustration, and mutual mistake. The court held for Westinghouse on the grounds of impossibility and commercial impracticability. Which party in this case could better bear the cost of waste disposal? See Alan Sykes, "The Doctrine of Commercial Impracticability in a Second-Best World" (1990) 19 J Legal Stud 43 and Trebilcock, ch 6.

TSAKIROGLOU & CO LTD V NOBLEE THORL GMBH
[1962] AC 93 (HL)

[On October 4, 1956, the respondents agreed to buy 300 tons of Sudanese groundnuts from the appellants for shipment from Port Sudan to Hamburg during November or December. On October 29 the British and French forces began military operations against Egypt to protect the Suez Canal. The Canal was blocked to navigation from November 2 until April 9, 1957. The usual route for such a shipment was via the Canal and the appellants refused to ship the nuts, although it was feasible to have shipped them via the Cape of Good Hope during November and December. The Cape route is 11,137 miles. The Canal route is 4,386 miles. Freight surcharges were imposed, first of 25 percent as from November 10, and then of 100 percent as from December 13. The rate was £7 10s. per ton. The market price of Sudanese nuts in Hamburg was about £68 15s. per ton between January 1 and 13, 1957.

The case was heard by an umpire arbitration proceeding, which awarded £5,625 as damages to the respondents. The board of appeal of the Incorporated Oil Seed Association upheld the award as did Diplock J on a stated case. Diplock J's decision was affirmed by the Court of Appeal. Clause 6 of the IOSA standard form contract provided that "in case of ... war ... and in all cases of force majeure preventing the shipment within the time fixed ... the period allowed ... shall be extended by not exceeding two months. After that, if the case of force majeure be still operating, the contract shall be cancelled." It was unanimously agreed that clause 6 did not relieve the defendants: there was no "war" and the "shipment" was not prevented via the Cape.]

VISCOUNT SIMONDS: ... I come then to the main issue and, as usual, I find two questions interlocked: (1) What does the contract mean? In other words, is there an implied term that the goods shall be carried by a particular route? (2) Is the contract frustrated?

It is convenient to examine the first question first, though the answer may be inconclusive. For it appears to me that it does not automatically follow that, because one term of a contract, for example, that the goods shall be carried by a particular route, becomes impossible of performance, the whole contract is thereby abrogated. Nor does it follow, because as a matter of construction a term cannot be implied, that the contract may not be frustrated by events. In the instant case, for example, the impossibility of the route via Suez, if that were assumed to be the implied contractual obligation, would not necessarily spell the frustration of the contract.

It is put in the forefront of the appellants' case that the contract was a contract for the shipment of goods via Suez. This contention can only prevail if a term is implied, for the contract does not say so. To say that that is nevertheless its meaning is to say in other words that the term must be implied. For this I see no ground. It has been rejected by the learned trial judge and each of the members of the Court of Appeal. ...

I turn now to what was the main argument for the appellants: that the contract was frustrated by the closure of the Canal from November 2, 1956 till April 1957. Were it not for the decision of McNair J. in *Green's* case, [1959] 1 Q.B. 131, I should not have thought this contention arguable and I must say with the greatest respect to that learned judge that I cannot think he has given full weight to the decisions old and new of this House upon the doctrine of frustration. He correctly held upon the authority of *Reardon Smith Line Ltd. v. Black Sea and Baltic General Insurance Co. Ltd.*, [1939] A.C. 562, that "where a contract, expressly or by necessary implication, provides that performance, or a particular part of the performance, is to be carried out in a customary manner, the performance must be carried out in a manner which is customary at the time when the performance is called for." But he concluded that the continued availability of the Suez route was a fundamental assumption at the time when the contract was made and that to impose upon the sellers the obligation to ship by an emergency route via the Cape would be to impose upon them a fundamentally different obligation which neither party could at the time when the contract was formed have dreamed that the sellers would be required to perform. Your Lordships will observe how similar this line of argument is to that which supports the implication of a term that the route should be via Suez and no other. I can see no justification for it. We are concerned with a c.i.f. contract for the sale of goods, not a contract of affreightment, though part of the sellers' obligation will be to procure a contract of affreightment. There is no evidence that the buyers attached any importance to the route. They were content that the nuts should be shipped at any date in November or December. There was no evidence, and I suppose could not be, that the nuts would deteriorate as the result of a longer voyage and a double crossing of the Equator, nor any evidence that the market was seasonable. In a word, there was no evidence that the buyers cared by what route or, within reasonable limits, when the nuts arrived. What, then, of the sellers? I recall the well-known passage in the speech of Lord Atkinson in *Johnson v. Taylor Bros. & Co. Ltd.*, [1920] A.C. 144, where he states the obligations of the vendor of goods under a c.i.f. contract, and ask which of these obligations is (to use McNair J.'s word) "fundamentally" altered by a change of route. Clearly the contract of affreightment will be different and so may be the terms of insurance. In both these respects the sellers may be put to greater cost: their profit may be reduced or even disappear. But it hardly needs reasserting that an increase of expense is not a ground of frustration: see *Larringa & Co. Ltd. v. Société Franco-Américaine de Phosphates de Medulla, Paris* (1922), 38 T.L.R. 739.

Nothing else remains to justify the view that the nature of the contract was "fundamentally" altered. That is the word used by Viscount Simon in *British Movietonews Ltd. v. London and District Cinemas Ltd.*, [1952] A.C. 166, at p. 185, and by my noble and learned friend Lord Reid in *Davis Contractors Ltd. v. Fareham Urban District Council*, [1956] A.C. 696, at p. 723. In the latter case my noble and learned friend Lord Radcliffe used the expression "radically different" and I think that the two expressions mean the same thing, as perhaps do other adverbs which have been used in this context. Whatever expression is used, I venture to say what I have said myself before and others more authoritatively have said before me: that the doctrine of frustration must be applied within very narrow limits. In my opinion this case falls far short of satisfying the necessary conditions. Reluctant as I am to differ from a judge so experienced in commercial law as McNair J., I am glad to find that my view is shared by Ashworth J. and all the members of the Court of Appeal. ...

In my opinion, the appeal should be dismissed with costs.

[The opinions of Lords Reid, Radcliffe, Hodson, and Guest dismissing the appeal are omitted.]

TRANSATLANTIC FINANCING CORP V UNITED STATES
363 F 2d 312 (DC Cir 1966)

WRIGHT J: This appeal involves a voyage charter between Transatlantic Financing Corporation, operator of the SS CHRISTOS, and the United States covering carriage of a full cargo of wheat from a United States Gulf port to a safe port in Iran. The District Court dismissed a libel filed by Transatlantic against the United States for costs attributable to the ship's diversion from the normal sea route caused by the closing of the Suez Canal. We affirm.

On July 26, 1956, the Government of Egypt nationalized the Suez Canal Company and took over operation of the Canal. On October 2, 1956, during the international crisis which resulted from the seizure, the voyage charter in suit was executed between representatives of Transatlantic and the United States. The charter indicated the termini of the voyage but not the route. On October 27, 1956, the SS CHRISTOS sailed from Galveston for Bandar Shapur, Iran, on a course which would have taken her through Gibraltar and the Suez Canal. On October 29, 1956, Israel invaded Egypt. On October 31, 1956, Great Britain and· France invaded the Suez Canal Zone. On November 2, 1956, the Egyptian Government obstructed the Suez Canal with sunken vessels and closed it to traffic.

On or about November 7, 1956, Beckmann, representing Transatlantic, contacted Potosky, an employee of the United States Department of Agriculture, who appellant concedes was unauthorized to bind the Government, requesting instructions concerning disposition of the cargo and seeking an agreement for payment of additional compensation for a voyage around the Cape of Good Hope. Potosky advised Beckmann that Transatlantic was expected to perform the charter according to its terms, that he did not believe Transatlantic was entitled to additional compensation for a voyage around the Cape, but that Transatlantic was free to file such a claim. Following this discussion, the CHRISTOS changed course for the Cape of Good Hope and eventually arrived in Bandar Shapur on December 30, 1956.

Transatlantic's claim is based on the following train of argument. The charter was a contract for a voyage from a Gulf port to Iran. Admiralty principles and practices, especially stemming from the doctrine of deviation, require us to imply into the contract the term that the voyage was to be performed by the "usual and customary" route. The usual and customary route from Texas to Iran was, at the time of contract, via Suez, so the contract was for a voyage from Texas to Iran via Suez. When Suez was closed this contract became impossible to perform. Consequently, appellant's argument continues, when Transatlantic delivered the cargo by going around the Cape of Good Hope, in compliance with the Government's demand under claim of right, it conferred a benefit upon the United States for which it should be paid in *quantum meruit*.

The doctrine of impossibility of performance has gradually been freed from the earlier fictional and unrealistic strictures of such tests as the "implied term" and the parties' "contemplation." Page, *The Development of the Doctrine of Impossibility of Performance*, 18 *Mich. L. Rev.* 589, 596 (1920). See generally 6 Corbin, *Contracts* 1320-1372 (rev. ed. 1962); 6 Williston, *Contracts* 1931-1979 (rev. ed. 1938). It is now recognized that "[a] thing is impossible in legal contemplation when it is not practicable; and a thing is impracticable when it can only be done at an excessive and unreasonable cost." *Mineral Park Land Co. v. Howard*, 172 Cal. 289, 293 (1916). The doctrine ultimately represents the ever-shifting line, drawn by courts hopefully responsive to commercial practices and mores, at which the community's interest in having contracts enforced according to their terms is outweighed by the commercial senselessness of requiring performance. When the issue is raised, the court is asked to construct a condition of performance based on the changed circumstances, a process which involves at least three reasonably definable steps. First, a contingency—something unexpected—must have occurred. Second, the risk of the unexpected occurrence must not have been allocated either by agreement or by custom. Finally, occurrence of the contingency must have rendered performance commercially impracticable. Unless the court finds these three requirements satisfied, the plea of impossibility must fail.

The first requirement was met here. It seems reasonable, where no route is mentioned in a contract, to assume the parties expected performance by the usual and customary route at the time of contract. Since the usual and customary route from Texas to Iran at the time of contract was through Suez, closure of the Canal made impossible the expected method of performance. But this unexpected development raises rather than resolves the impossibility issue, which turns additionally on whether the risk of the contingency's occurrence had been allocated and, if not, whether performance by alternative routes was rendered impracticable.

Proof that the risk of a contingency's occurrence has been allocated may be expressed in or implied from the agreement. Such proof may also be found in the surrounding circumstances, including custom and usages of the trade. The contract in this case does not expressly condition performance upon availability of the Suez route. Nor does it specify "via Suez" or, on the other hand, "via Suez or Cape of Good Hope." Nor are there provisions in the contract from which we may properly imply that the continued availability of Suez was a condition of performance. Nor is there anything in custom or trade usage, or in the surrounding circumstances generally, which would support our constructing a condition of performance. The numerous cases requiring performance around the Cape when Suez was closed, see e.g., *Ocean Tramp Tankers Corp. v. V/O Sovfracht (The Eugenia)* (1964), 2 Q.B. 226 and cases cited therein, indicate that the Cape route is generally regarded as an alternative means of performance. So the implied expectation that the route would be via Suez is hardly adequate proof of an allocation to the promisee of the risk of closure. In some cases, even an express expectation may not amount to a condition of performance. The doctrine of deviation supports our assumption that parties normally expect performance by the usual and customary route, but it adds nothing beyond this that is probative of an allocation of the risk.

If anything, the circumstances surrounding this contract indicate that the risk of the Canal's closure may be deemed to have been allocated to Transatlantic. We know or may safely assume that the parties were aware, as were most commercial men with interests affected by the Suez situation, see *The Eugenia*, that the Canal might become a dangerous area. No doubt the tension affected freight rates, and it is arguable that the risk of closure became part of the dickered terms. U.C.C. §2-615, comment 8. We do not deem the risk of closure so allocated, however. Foreseeability or even recognition of a risk does not necessarily prove its allocation. Compare U.C.C. §2-615, Comment 1; Restatement, Contracts 457 (1932). Parties to a contract are not always able to provide for all the possibilities of which they are aware, sometimes because they cannot agree, often simply because they are too busy. Moreover, that some abnormal risk was contemplated is probative but does not necessarily establish an allocation of the risk of the contingency which actually occurs. In this case, for example, nationalization by Egypt of the Canal Corporation and formation of the Suez Users Group did not necessarily indicate that the Canal would be blocked even if a confrontation resulted. The surrounding circumstances do indicate, however, a willingness by Transatlantic to assume abnormal risks, and this fact should legitimately cause us to judge the impracticability of performance by an alternative route in stricter terms than we would were the contingency unforeseen.

We turn then to the question whether occurrence of the contingency rendered performance commercially impracticable under the circumstances of this case. The goods shipped were not subject to harm from the longer, less temperate Southern route. The vessel and crew were fit to proceed around the Cape. Transatlantic was no less able than the United States to purchase insurance to cover the contingency's occurrence. If anything, it is more reasonable to expect owner-operators of vessels to insure against the hazards of war. They are in the best position to calculate the cost of performance by alternative routes (and therefore to estimate the amount of insurance required), and are undoubtedly sensitive to international troubles which uniquely affect the demand for and cost of their services. The only factor operating here in appellant's favor is the added expense, allegedly $43,972.00 above and beyond the contract price of $305,842.92, of extending a 10,000 mile voyage by approximately 3,000 miles. While it may be an overstatement to say that increased cost and difficulty of performance never constitute impracticability, to justify relief there must be more of a variation between expected cost and the cost of performing by an available alternative than is present in this case, where the promisor can legitimately be presumed to have accepted some degree of abnormal risk, and where impracticability is urged on the basis of added expense alone. ...

Affirmed.

DAVIS CONTRACTORS LTD V FAREHAM URBAN DISTRICT COUNCIL
[1956] AC 696 (HL)

[Davis tendered for the construction of 78 houses within a period of 8 months, at Gudgeheath Lane, Fareham, for £92,425. In a letter dated March 18, 1946 (ref. RL/JEM) accompanying the tender, Davis wrote: "Our tender is subject to adequate supplies of material and labour being available as and when required to carry out the work within the time specified." The agreement, which was later signed by Davis, contained only one reference to the letter. Appendix I to the agreement was headed "Materials and goods to be purchased directly by the contractor in respect of which variation of the contract sum is desired in accordance with clause 68B of the conditions of the contract." Under this heading Davis wrote: "As terms of letter attached dated March 18, 1946, reference RL/JEM." In later negotiations Davis actually supplied a detailed schedule of prices that was intended to constitute the appendix I schedule. The tender was made a part of the agreement. The contract took 22 months to complete, the delay being caused chiefly by the lack of skilled labour. With extras, the payments by Fareham amounted to £94,424. Davis claimed in this action that the contract price was inapplicable owing to the delay and asked to be paid a total of £115,233 on a *quantum meruit* basis. The arbitrator awarded damages amounting to £17,258, but the Court of Appeal held that the letter was not incorporated into the contract and the contract was not frustrated. Davis then appealed to the House of Lords. The appeal was dismissed. The following excerpt deals only with the question of frustration.]

LORD RADCLIFFE: ... But, in my opinion, full weight ought to be given to the requirement that the parties "must have made" their bargains on the particular footing. Frustration is not to be lightly invoked as the dissolvent of a contract.

Lord Loreburn ascribes the dissolution to an implied term of the contract that was actually made. This approach is in line with the tendency of English courts to refer all the consequences of a contract to the will of those who made it. But there is something of a logical difficulty in seeing how the parties could even impliedly have provided for something which ex hypothesi they neither expected nor foresaw; and the ascription of frustration to an implied term of the contract has been criticized as obscuring the true action of the court which consists in applying an objective rule of the law of contract to the contractual obligations that the parties have imposed upon themselves. So long as each theory produces the same result as the other, as normally it does, it matters little which theory is avowed (see *British Movietonews Ltd. v. London and District Cinemas Ltd.*, [1952] A.C. 166, at p. 184, *per* Viscount Simon). But it may still be of some importance to recall that, if the matter is to be approached by way of implied term, the solution of any particular case is not to be found by inquiring what the parties themselves would have agreed on had they been, as they were not, forewarned. It is not merely that no one can answer that hypothetical question: it is also that the decision must be given "irrespective of the individuals concerned, their temperaments and failings, their interest and circumstances" (*Hirji Mulji v. Cheong Yue Steamship Co. Ltd.*, [1962] A.C. 497, at p. 510). The legal effect of frustration "does not depend on their intention or their opinions, or even knowledge, as to the event." On the contrary, it seems that when the event occurs "the meaning of the contract must be taken to be, not what the parties did intend (for they had neither thought nor intention regarding it), but that which the parties, as fair and reasonable men, would presumably have agreed upon if, having such possibility in view, they had made express provision as to their several rights and liabilities in the event of its occurrence" (*Dahl v. Nelson* (1881), 6 App. Cas. 38, *per* Lord Watson).

By this time it might seem that the parties themselves have become so far disembodied spirits that their actual persons should be allowed to rest in peace. In their place there rises the figure of the fair and reasonable man. And the spokesman of the fair and reasonable man, who represents after all no more than the anthropomorphic conception of justice, is and must be the court itself. So perhaps it would be simpler to say at the outset that frustration occurs whenever the law recognizes that without default of either party a contractual obligation has become incapable of being performed because the circumstances in which performance is called for would render it a thing radically different from that which was undertaken by the contract. Non haec in foedera veni. It was not this that I promised to do.

There is, however, no uncertainty as to the materials upon which the court must proceed. "The data for decision are, on the one hand, the terms and construction of the contract, read in the light of the then existing circumstances, and on the other hand the events which have occurred" (*Denny, Mott & Dickson Ltd. v. James B. Fraser & Co. Ltd.*, [1944] A.C. 265, at p. 274, *per* Lord Wright). In the nature of things there is often no room for any elaborate inquiry. The court must act upon a general impression of what its rule requires. It is for that reason that special importance is necessarily attached to the occurrence of any unexpected event that, as it were, changes the face of things. But, even so, it is not hardship or inconvenience or material loss itself which calls the principle of frustration into play. There must be as well such a change in the significance of the obligation that the thing undertaken would, if performed, be a different thing from that contracted for.

I am bound to say that, if this is the law, the appellants' case seems to me a long way from a case of frustration. Here is a building contract entered into by a housing authority and a big firm of contractors in all the uncertainties of the post-war world. Work was begun shortly before the formal contract was executed and continued, with impediments and minor stoppages but without actual interruption, until the 78 houses contracted for had all been built. After the work had been in progress for a time the appellants raised the claim, which they repeated more than once, that they ought to be paid a larger sum for their work than the contract allowed; but the respondents refused to admit the claim and, so far as appears, no conclusive action was taken by either side which would make the conduct of one or the other a determining element in the case.

That is not in any obvious sense a frustrated contract. But the appellants' argument, which certainly found favour with the arbitrator, is that at some stage before completion the original contract was dissolved because it became incapable of being performed according to its true significance and its place was taken by a new arrangement under which they were entitled to be paid, not the contract sum, but a fair price on quantum meruit for the work that they carried out during the 22 months that elapsed between commencement and completion. The contract, it is said, was an eight months' contract, as indeed it was. Through no fault of the parties it turned out that it took 22 months to do the work contracted for. The main reason for this was that, whereas both parties had expected that adequate supplies of labour and material would be available to allow for completion in eight months, the supplies that were in fact available were much less than adequate for the purpose. Hence, it is said, the basis or the footing of the contract was removed before the work was completed; or, slightly altering the metaphor, the footing of the contract was so changed by the circumstances that the expected supplies were not available that the contract built upon that footing became void. These are the findings which the arbitrator has recorded in his supplemental award.

In my view, these are in substance conclusions of law, and I do not think that they are good law. All that anyone, arbitrator or court, can do is to study the contract in the light of the circumstances that prevailed at the time when it was made and, having done so, to relate it to the circumstances that are said to have brought about its frustration. It may be a finding of fact that at the time of making the contract both parties anticipated that adequate supplies of labour and material would be available to enable the contract to be completed in the stipulated time. I doubt whether it is, but even if it is, it is no more than to say that when one party stipulated for completion in eight months, and the other party undertook it, each assumed that what was promised could be satisfactorily performed. That is a statement of the obvious that could be made with regard to most contracts. I think that a good deal more than that is needed to form a "basis" for the principle of frustration.

The justice of the arbitrator's conclusion depends upon the weight to be given to the fact that this was a contract for specified work to be completed in a fixed time at a price determined by those conditions. I think that his view was that, if without default on either side the contract period was substantially extended, that circumstance itself rendered the fixed price so unfair to the contractor that he ought not to be held to his original price. I have much sympathy with the contractor, but, in my opinion, if that sort of consideration were to be sufficient to establish a case of frustration, there would be an untold range of contractual obligations rendered uncertain and, possibly, unenforceable.

Two things seem to me to prevent the application of the principle of frustration to this case. One is that the cause of the delay was not any new state of things which the parties could not reasonably be thought to have foreseen. On the contrary, the possibility of enough labour and materials not being available was before their eyes and could have been the subject of special contractual stipulation. It was not made so. The other thing is that, though timely completion was no doubt important to both sides, it is not right to treat the possibility of delay as having the same significance for each. The owner draws up his conditions in detail, specifies the time within which he requires completion, protects himself both by a penalty clause for time exceeded and by calling for the deposit of a guarantee bond and offers a certain measure of security to a contractor by his escalator clause with regard to wages and prices. In the light of these conditions the contractor makes his tender, and the tender must necessarily take into account the margin of profit that he hopes to obtain upon his adventure and in that any appropriate allowance for the obvious risks of delay. To my mind, it is useless to pretend that the contractor is not at risk if delay does occur, even serious delay. And I think it a misuse of legal terms to call in frustration to get him out of his unfortunate predicament.

[The judgments of Viscount Simonds and Lords Morton of Henryton, Reid, and Somervell of Harrow, dismissing the appeal, are omitted.]

NOTES

1. In *Wells v Newfoundland*, [1999] 3 SCR 199, 177 DLR (4th) 73, a senior civil servant claimed damages for breach of contract from the government of Newfoundland after his tenured position was eliminated pursuant to a newly enacted statute. The government argued that the statute had frustrated the claimant's employment contract. In rejecting this argument, the Supreme Court of Canada relied on the principle that self-induced frustration will not excuse non-performance. Because the government of Newfoundland was itself responsible for the impugned legislation, it could not rely on the doctrine of frustration.

2. In *Naylor Group Inc v Ellis-Don Construction Ltd*, 2001 SCC 58, [2001] 2 SCR 943, 204 DLR (4th) 513, the unfavourable results of a pending Labour Board decision did not frustrate the performance of a construction contract where the contractor knew that compliance with the pending decision was a condition of the bid.

3. In *Marshall v Harland & Wolff Ltd*, [1972] 2 All ER 715 (NIRC), Sir Donaldson provided a list of "inter-related and cumulative, but ... not necessarily exhaustive" factors to be taken into account when deciding whether an employment relationship has been frustrated due to the worker's incapacity caused by ill health, which later came to be known as the "*Marshall* Test." The test includes factors such as the nature of the employment, the expected length of future absence, and the period of past employment. It is now generally accepted that an employment contract will be frustrated when an employee's illness or disability is permanent in nature. In *Wilmot v Ulnooweg Development Group Inc* (2007), 283 DLR (4th) 237 (NSCA), the court, relying on the *Marshall* factors, determined that an employee's mental illness did not constitute a frustrating event, even though the employee had missed 138 days at the office and had been found to suffer from a "significant illness." In *Altman v Steve's Music*, 2011 ONSC 1480, the court applied the *Marshall* factors and found that an employee's illness did not render her unable to perform her job. The employee had worked at Steve's for more than 30 years when she developed lung cancer. She was terminated after she had been on medical leave for six months and reduced hours for the eight months prior. However, in *Trevitt v Blanche Equipment Rentals Ltd*, 2006 BCSC 94, when an employee, a licensed heavy equipment mechanic who was the shop foreman, was involved in a motor vehicle accident and suffered several injuries that rendered him unable to work, his employer hired someone else to perform his duties. The court found that the injured employee had been unable to return to work for more than one year and that while his injuries were not permanent, he was nonetheless unable to resume the same position he had held. As his disability was "clearly more than temporary," the court concluded his employment contract had been frustrated.

4. On the subject of how a disability affects an employment contract, the issue turns on the duration of the disability. In *Boucher v Black & McDonald Ltd*, 2016 ONSC 7220, the court noted that "[p]ermanent disability will frustrate a contract. However, employment is not frustrated by temporary sickness. The law permits temporary sickness and moreover, allows the disabled to recover" (at para 34). These issues do not operate in a vacuum, however, as they are affected by the application of human rights legislation, which may impose a duty on employers to accommodate disabilities. See *Jeffrey v Dofasco Inc* (2007), 161 ACWS (3d) 306 (Ont Div Ct).

5. In *Wightman Estate v 2774046 Canada Inc* (2007), 57 BCLR (4th) 79 (CA), a disabled employee was terminated without notice but, pursuant to the employment contract, continued to receive long-term disability benefits for the remainder of his working life. His estate argued

that the employment contract had not been frustrated because it had contemplated the disability by providing long-term disability insurance. The court determined that "foresee[ing] the possibility of a particular supervening event and [making] some provision for it in their contract does not necessarily preclude frustration of the contract upon the happening of the event." Rather, one must ask "whether the parties have provided that their contractual relationship will continue despite the radical change in circumstances brought about by the event." Here, although the parties contemplated the possibility of the disabling sickness and hedged their losses by purchasing long-term disability insurance, the contract did not provide that the employment relationship would continue indefinitely despite the change in circumstances.

6. The law is unsettled with respect to whether the employee's medical prognosis in a frustration context should be assessed as at the date of the dismissal, the date of the trial, or the date of the dismissal with the benefit of the hindsight available at the date of the trial.

V. RELIEF ON TERMS: RESTITUTION AND RELIANCE

APPLEBY V MYERS
(1867), LR 2 CP 651

This was an action brought to recover £419 for work done and materials provided by the plaintiffs, engineers, for the defendant, under the circumstances hereinafter mentioned. The following case was stated, by consent, without pleadings, for the opinion of the Court:

On the 30th of March 1865, the plaintiffs entered into an agreement with the defendant, which was headed, "Specification and estimate of engine, boiler, lifts, etc., for B. Meyers, Esq., Southward Street. Messrs. Tillott & Chamberland, architects, 30th March, 1865." This contract contained ten distinct parts or divisions, viz. 1. boiler; 2. Engine; 3. shafting; 4. lifts; 5. shafting; 6. drying-room; 7. copper pans; 8. tanks; 9. pump; 10. steamboxes; under each of which headings were particular descriptions of the work to be done in connection with each respectively, and the prices to be charged for the same; and the document concluded with these words:

> We offer to make and erect the whole of the machinery of the best materials and workmanship of their respective kinds, and to put it to work, for the sum above named respectively, and to keep the whole in order, under fair wear and tear, for two years from the date of completion. All brickwork, carpenters' and masons' work, and materials, are to be provided for us; but the drawings and general instructions required for them to work to will be provided by us, subject to the architects' approval.
>
> (signed) Appleby Brothers.

The total cost of the above works, if they had been completed under the contract, would have amounted to £459.

On the 4th of July, 1865, a fire accidentally broke out on the premises of the defendant in Southwark Street, which entirely destroyed the premises and the works which then had been erected by the plaintiffs in part performance of the contract. At the time of the fire the works contracted for had not been completed.

At the time of the fire, portions of the items Nos. 1 to 8 were erected and fixed, and some of the materials for the others were on the premises.

The defendant had not completed the carpenters' and masons' work. The tank had been erected by the plaintiffs, and was used by the defendant by taking water therefrom for the purpose of his business; but the other apparatus connected with it, as specified in No. 8 was not complete. The plaintiff's workmen were still engaged in continuing the erection and completion of the same at the time of the fire.

The premises were the property of the defendant, in his occupation, and under his entire control. The plaintiffs had access to them only for the purpose of performing their contract.

The question for the opinion of the Court was, whether, under the above circumstances, the plaintiffs were entitled to recover the whole or any portion of the contract price.

The Court of Common Pleas gave judgment for the plaintiffs for an amount equal to the value of the work and materials done and provided by them under the agreement. The defendants appealed to the Court of Exchequer Chamber.

BLACKBURN J (for the court): This case was partly argued before us at the last sittings; and the argument was resumed and completed at the present sittings.

Having had the advantage of hearing the very able argument of Mr. Holl and Mr. Hannen, and having during the interval had the opportunity of considering the judgment of the Court below, there is no reason that we should further delay expressing the opinion at which we have all arrived, which is, that the judgment of the Court below is wrong and ought to be reversed.

The whole question depends upon the true construction of the contract between the parties. We agree with the Court below in thinking that it sufficiently appears that the work which the plaintiffs agreed to perform could not be performed unless the defendant's premises continued in a fit state to enable the plaintiffs to perform the work on them; and we agree with them in thinking that, if by any default on the part of the defendant, his premises were rendered unfit to receive the work, the plaintiffs would have had the option to sue the defendant for this default, or to treat the contract as rescinded, and sue on a quantum meruit. But we do not agree with them in thinking that there was an absolute promise or warranty by the defendant that the premises should at all events continue so fit. We think that where, as in the present case the premises are destroyed without fault on either side, it is a misfortune equally affecting both parties, excusing both from further performance of the contract, but giving a cause of action to neither.

Then it was argued before us, that inasmuch as this was a contract of that nature which would in pleading be described as a contract for work, labour, and materials, and not as one of bargain and sale, the labour and materials necessarily became the property of the defendant as soon as they were at his risk. We think that, as to a great part at least of the work done in this case, the materials had not become the property of the defendant; for, we think that the plaintiffs, who were to complete the whole for a fixed sum, and keep it in repair two years, would have had a perfect right, if they thought that a portion of the engine which they had put up was too slight, to change it and substitute another in their opinion better calculated to keep in good repair during the two years, and without consulting or asking the leave of the defendant. But, even on the supposition that the materials had become unalterably fixed to the defendant's premises, we do not think that, under such a contract as this, the plaintiffs could recover anything unless the whole work was completed. It is quite true that materials worked by one into the property of another become part of that property. This is equally true, whether it be fixed or movable property. Bricks built into a wall become part of the house; thread stitched into a coat which is under repair, or planks and nails and pitch worked into a ship, under repair, become part of the coat or the ship; and therefore, generally, and in the absence of something to shew a contrary intention, the brick-layer or tailor, or shipwright, is to be paid for the work and materials he has done and provided, although the whole work is not complete.

It is not material whether in such a case the non-completion is because the ship-wright did not choose to go on with the work, as was the case in *Roberts v. Havelock* (1832), 3 B. & Ad. 404; 110 E.R. 145, or because in consequence of a fire he could not go on with it, as in *Menetone v. Athawes* (1764), 3 Burr. 1592; 97 E.R. 998. But, though this is the prima facie contract between those who enter into contracts for doing work and supplying materials, there is nothing to render it either illegal or absurd in the workman to agree to complete the whole, and be paid when the whole is complete, and not till then: and we think that the plaintiffs in the present case had entered into such a contract. Had the accidental fire left the defendant's premises untouched, and only injured a part of the work which the plaintiffs had already done, we apprehend that it is clear the plaintiffs under such a contract as the present must have done that part over again, in order to fulfil their contract to complete the whole and "put it to work for the sums above named respectively." As it is, they are, according to the principle laid down in *Taylor v. Caldwell* (1863), 122 E.R. 309 excused from completing the work; but they are not therefore entitled to any compensation for what they have done, but which has, without any fault of the defendant, perished. The case is in principle like that of a shipowner who has been excused from the performance of his contract to carry goods to their destination, because his ship has been disabled by one of the excepted perils, but who is not therefore entitled to any payment on account of the part-performance of the voyage, unless there is something to justify the conclusion that there has been a fresh contract to pay freight pro rata.

On the argument, much reference was made to the Civil Law. The opinions of the great lawyers collected in the Digest afford us very great assistance in tracing out any question of doubtful principle; but they do not bind us: and we think that, on the principles of English law laid down ... the plaintiffs, having contracted to do an entire work for a specific sum, can recover nothing unless the work be done, or it can be shewn that it was the defendant's fault that the work was incomplete, or that there is something to justify the conclusion that the parties have entered into a fresh contract.

FIBROSA SPOLKA AKCYNA V FAIRBAIRN LAWSON COMBE BARBOUR LTD
[1943] AC 32 (HL)

The respondents were a limited company carrying on at Leeds the business of manufacturing textile machinery, and by a contract in writing dated July 12, 1939, the respondents agreed to supply the appellants, a Polish company, of Vilna, with certain flax-hackling machines as therein specified and described, at a lump sum price of £4,800. The machines were of a special kind. The place of erection of the machinery was not mentioned in the contract, but it was agreed that it was the intention of the parties that it was to be erected at Vilna. By the terms of the contract, delivery was to be in three to four months from the settlement of final details. The machines were to be packed and delivered by the respondents c.i.f. Gdynia, the services of a skilled monteur to superintend erection were to be provided by the respondents and included in the price, and payment was to be made by cheque on London, one-third of the price (£1600) with the order and the balance (£3200) against shipping documents. By clause 7 of the conditions of sale attached to the contract: " ... Should dispatch be hindered or delayed by your instructions, or lack of instructions, or by any cause whatsoever beyond our reasonable control including strikes, lock-outs, war, fire, accidents ... a reasonable extension of time shall be granted ..." By clause 10 provisions were made for dispatch and possible storage pending dispatch.

On July 18, 1939, the appellants paid to the respondents £1000 on account of the initial payment of £1600 due under the contract. On September 1, 1939, Germany invaded Poland and on September 3, Great Britain declared war on Germany. On September 7, the appellants' agents in England wrote to the respondents: "Owing to the outbreak of hostilities, it is now quite evident that the delivery of the hackling machines on order for Poland cannot take place. Under the circumstances we shall be obliged if you will kindly arrange to return our initial payment of £1000 at your early convenience." To this request, the respondents replied on the next day refusing to return the sum and stating that "considerable work had been done upon these machines and we cannot consent to the return of this payment. After the war the matter can be reconsidered." There was further correspondence between the parties or their agents which failed to produce agreement, and on May 1, 1940, the appellants issued a writ and by their statement of claim alleged that the respondents had broken the contract by refusing to deliver the machines, while the appellants "are and have at all material times been ready and willing to take delivery of the said machinery and pay for the same." The prayer of the claim was (a) for damages for breach of contract, (b) for specific performance or, alternatively, return of the £1000 with interest, and (c) for further or other relief. The substantial defence of the respondents was that the contract had been frustrated by the German occupation of Gdynia in September 1939, and that in these circumstances the appellants had no right to the return of the £1000. Tucker J. dismissed the action on March 7, 1941, and the Court of Appeal affirmed his decision on May 15, 1941. The appellants appealed to the House of Lords.

VISCOUNT SIMON LC: My Lords, this is the appeal of a Polish company who were plaintiffs in the action against the decision of the Court of Appeal composed of MacKinnon and Luxmoore L.JJ. and Stable J., affirming the judgment of Tucker J. at the trial in favour of the respondents. After the Court of Appeal's judgment and before the appeal came to be argued at your Lordships' bar, the town of Vilna, where the appellants had carried on its business, and indeed the whole of Poland, under the laws of which state the appellants were incorporated, were occupied by our enemy, Germany. The question might, therefore, arise whether the appellants should now be debarred from prosecuting its appeal ... . To obviate any difficulty on this head, the appellants, at the suggestion of the House, applied to the Board of Trade, and the department gave to the appellants' solicitors a licence to proceed with the appeal, notwithstanding that their clients might be in the position of an alien enemy. The House was content to let the case proceed on this basis ... . If, as the result of the decision of the House, any payment becomes due to the appellants, and if they were in the position of alien enemies within the meaning of the *Trading with the Enemy Act, 1939*, the payment would be regulated by the Act.

Mr. Linton Thorp, in conducting the argument for the appellants before us, admitted that, if the point with which I have already dealt was decided against him, the only other issue to be determined was whether, when this contract became frustrated, the appellants could, in the circumstances of the present case, claim back from the respondents the £1000 which they had paid when placing the order. As to this, MacKinnon L.J., in delivering the judgment of the Court of Appeal said: "Tucker J. held that having regard to the principle laid down in *Chandler v. Webster* [1904] 1 K.B. 493, and other like cases, this claim must fail. We think he was right, and, further, that that principle must equally bind this court to reject the claim. Whether the principle can be overruled is a matter that can only concern the House of Lords."

This alleged principle is to the effect that where a contract has been frustrated by such a supervening event as releases from further performances, "the loss lies where it falls," with the result that sums paid or rights accrued before that event are not to be surrendered, but all obligations falling due for performance after that event are discharged. This proposition, whether right or wrong, first appears, not in *Chandler v. Webster* but in *Blakely v. Muller & Co.*, [1903] 2 K.B. 670n, decided in January 1903 by a Divisional Court, which was also a case arising out of the abandonment of the coronation procession owing to Kind Edward VII's sudden illness. In that case, Channell J. said: "If the money was payable on some day subsequent to the abandonment of the procession, I do not think it could have been sued for. If, however, it was payable prior to the abandonment of the procession, the position would be the same as if it had been actually paid and could not be recovered back, and could be sued for. ... It is impossible to import a condition into a contract which the parties could have imported and have not done so. All that can be said is that, when the procession was abandoned, the contract was off, not that anything done under the contract was void. The loss must remain where it was at the time of the abandonment. It is like the case of a charterparty where the freight is payable in advance, and the voyage is not completed, and the freight, therefore, not earned. Where the non-completion arose through impossibility of performance, the freight could not be recovered back."

If we are to approach this problem anew, it must be premised that the first matter to be considered is always the terms of the particular contract. If, for example, the contract is "divisible" in the sense that a sum is to be paid over in respect of completion of a defined portion of the work, it may well be that the sum is not returnable if completion of the whole work is frustrated. If the contract itself on its true construction stipulates for a particular result which is to follow in regard to money already paid, should frustration afterwards occur, this governs the matter. The ancient and firmly established rule that freight paid in advance is not returned if the completion of the voyage is frustrated ... should, I think, be regarded as a stipulation introduced into such contracts by custom, and not as the result of applying some abstract principle.

And so, a fortiori, if there is a stipulation that the prepayment is "out and out." To take an example, not from commerce, but from sport, the cricket spectator who pays for admission to see a match cannot recover the entrance money on the ground that rain has prevented play if, expressly or by proper implication, the bargain with him is that no money will be returned. Inasmuch as the effect of frustration may be explained as arising from an implied term: see *Joseph Constantine Steamship Line, Ltd. v. Imperial Smelting Corporation, Ltd.*, [1942] A.C. 154, it is tempting to speculate whether a further term could be implied as to what was to happen, in the event of frustration, to money already paid, but, if the parties were assumed to have discussed the point when entering into the contract, they could not be supposed to have agreed on a simple formula which would be fair in all circumstances, and all that could be said is that, in the absence of such agreement, the law must decide. The question now to be determined is whether, in the absence of a term in the contract dealing with the matter, the rule which is commonly called the rule in *Chandler v. Webster* should be affirmed. ...

The locus classicus for the view which has hitherto prevailed is to be found in the judgment of Collins M.R. in *Chandler v. Webster*. It was not a considered judgment, but it is hardly necessary to say that I approach this pronouncement of the then Master of the Rolls with all the respect due to so distinguished a common lawyer. When his judgment is studied, however, one cannot but be impressed by the circumstance that he regarded the proposition that money in such cases could not be recovered back as flowing from the decision in *Taylor v. Caldwell* (1863), 122 E.R. 309.

Taylor v. Caldwell, however, was not a case in which any question arises whether money could be recovered back, for there had been no payment in advance, and there is nothing in the judgment of Blackburn J., which, at any rate in terms, affirms the general proposition that "the loss lies where it falls." The application by Collins M.R. of *Taylor v. Caldwell* to the actual problem with which he had to deal in *Chandler v. Webster* deserves close examination. He said: "The plaintiff contends that he is entitled to recover the money which he has paid on the ground that there has been a total failure of consideration. He says that the condition on which he paid the money was that the procession should take place, and that, as it did not take place, there has been a total failure of consideration. That contention does no doubt raise a question of some difficulty, and one which has perplexed the courts to a consider-able extent in several cases. The principle on which it has been dealt with is that which was applied in *Taylor v. Caldwell*—namely, that where from causes outside the volition of the parties, something which was the basis of, or essential to the fulfilment of, the contract has become impossible, so that, from the time when the fact of that impossibility has been ascertained, the contract can no further be performed by either party, it remains a perfectly good contract up to that point, and everything previously done in pursuance of it must be treated as rightly done, but the parties are both discharged from further performance of it. If the effect were that the contract were wiped out altogether, no doubt the result would be that money paid under it would have to be repaid as on a failure of consideration. But that is not the effect of the doctrine; it only releases the parties from further performance of the contract. Therefore the doctrine of failure of consideration does not apply."

It appears to me that the reasoning in this crucial passage is open to two criticisms:

(a) The claim of a party, who has paid money under a contract, to get the money back, on the ground that the consideration for which he paid it has totally failed, is not based on any provision contained in the contract, but arises because, in the circumstances that have happened, the law gives a remedy in quasi-contract to the party who has not got that for which he bargained. It is a claim to recover money to which the defendant has no further right because in the circumstances that have developed the money must be regarded as received to the plaintiff's use. It is true that the effect of frustration is that, while the contract can no further be performed, "it remains a perfectly good contract up to that point, and everything previously done in pursuance of it must be treated as rightly done," but it by no means follows that the situation existing at the moment of frustration is one which leaves the party that has paid money and has not received the stipulated consideration without any remedy. To claim the return of money paid on the ground of total failure of consideration is not to vary the terms of the contract in any way. The claim arises not because the right to be repaid is one of the stipulated conditions of the contract, but because, in the circumstances that have happened, the law gives the remedy. It is the failure to distinguish between (1) the action of assumpsit for money had and received in a case where the consideration has wholly failed, and (2) an action on the contract itself, which explains the mistake which I think has been made in applying English law to this subject-matter. ...

(b) There is, no doubt, a distinction between cases in which a contract is "wiped out altogether," e.g., because it is void as being illegal from the start or as being due to fraud which the innocent party has elected to treat as avoiding the contract, and cases in which intervening impossibility "only releases the parties from further performance of the contract." But does the distinction between these two classes of case justify the deduction of Collins M.R. that "the doctrine of failure of consideration does not apply" where the contract remains a perfectly good contract up to the date of frustration? This conclusion seems to be derived from the view that, if the contract remains good and valid up to the moment of frustration, money which has already been paid under it cannot be regarded as having been paid for a consideration which has wholly failed. The party that has paid the money has had the advantage, whatever it may be worth, of the promise of the other party. That is true, but it is necessary to draw a distinction. In English law, an enforceable contract may be formed by an exchange of a promise for a promise, or by the exchange of a promise for an act—I am excluding contracts under seal—and thus, in the law relating to the formation of contract, the promise to do a thing may often be the consideration, but when one is considering the law of failure of consideration and of the quasi-contractual right to recover money on that ground, it is, generally speaking, not the promise which is referred to as the consideration, but the performance of the promise. The money was paid to secure performance and, if performance fails the inducement which brought about the payment is not fulfilled.

If this were not so, there could never be any recovery of money, for failure of consideration, by the payer of the money in return for a promise of future performance, yet there are endless examples which show that money can be recovered, as for a complete failure of consideration, in cases where the promise was given but could not be fulfilled. ... I can see no valid reason why the right to recover prepaid money should not equally arise on frustration arising from supervening circumstances as it arises on frustration from destruction of a particular subject-matter. The conclusion is that the rule in *Chandler v. Webster* is wrong, and that the appellants can recover their £1000.

While this result obviates the harshness with which the previous view in some instances treated the party who had made a prepayment, it cannot be regarded as dealing fairly between the parties in all cases, and must sometimes have the result of leaving the recipient who has to return the money at a grave disadvantage. He may have incurred expenses in connexion with the partial carrying out of the contract which are equivalent, or more than equivalent, to the money which he prudently stipulated should be prepaid, but which he now has to return for reasons which are no fault of his. He may have to repay the money, though he has executed almost the whole of the contractual work, which will be left on his hands. These results follow from the fact that the English common law does not undertake to apportion a prepaid sum in such circumstances—contrast the provision, now contained in s. 40 of the *Partnership Act, 1890*, for apportioning a premium if a partnership is prematurely dissolved. It must be for the legislature to decide whether provisions should be made for an equitable apportionment of prepaid moneys which have to be returned by the recipient in view of the frustration of the contract in respect of which they were paid. I move that the appeal be allowed, and that judgment be entered for the appellants.

[The opinions (allowing the appeal) of Lords Atkin, Russel of Killowen, Macmillan, Wright, Roche, and Porter are omitted.]

NOTE

The facts of *Chandler v Webster*, [1904] 1 KB 493 are stated briefly by Lord Atkin in *Fibrosa* as follows:

In that case the plaintiff had hired a room to view the coronation procession on Thursday, June 26, 1902. On June 10 he wrote to the defendant: "I beg to confirm my purchase of the first floor room of the Electric Lighting Board at 7 Pall Mall to view the procession on Thursday, June 26, for the sum of £141 15s., which amount is now due. I shall be obliged if you will take the room on sale, and I authorize you to sell separate seats in the room, for which I will erect a stand." It became the subject of controversy whether, in view of certain other terms arranged between the parties the whole sum became due before the procession became impossible, but the courts decided, as was clearly the case, that it did so become due. It may be noted that the defendant had nothing to do under the contract but allow the plaintiff the use of the room. On June 19 the plaintiff paid the defendant £100 on account of the price of the room, but had not paid the balance at the time the procession was abandoned. The plaintiff claimed the return of the £100 on a total failure of consideration, and the defendant counter-claimed for the balance of £41 15s. The plaintiff's claim failed, and the defendant's counter-claim succeeded.

For a defence of the view that the loss caused by the frustrating event should simply "lie where it falls," see A Kull, "Mistake, Frustration, and the Windfall Principle of Contract Remedies" (1991) 43 Hastings LJ 1.

FRUSTRATED CONTRACTS ACT
RSO 1990, c F.34

1. In this Act,
    (a) "contract" includes a contract to which the Crown is a party;
    (b) "court" means the court or arbitrator by or before whom a matter falls to be determined;
    (c) "discharged" means relieved from further performance of the contract.
    2(1) This Act applies to any contract that is governed by the law of Ontario, and that has become impossible of performance or been otherwise frustrated and to the parties which for that reason have been discharged.
    (2) This Act does not apply,
    (a) to a charterparty or a contract for the carriage of goods by sea, except a time charterparty or a charterparty by way of demise;
    (b) to a contract of insurance; or
    (c) to a contract for the sale of specific goods where the goods, without the knowledge of the seller, have perished at the time the contract was made, or where the goods, without any fault on the part of the seller or buyer, perished before the risk passed to the buyer.
    3(1) The sums paid or payable to a party in pursuance of a contract before the parties were discharged,
    (a) in the case of sums paid, are recoverable from the party as money received for the use of the party by whom the sums were paid; and
    (b) in the case of sums payable, cease to be payable.
    (2) If, before the parties were discharged, the party to whom the sums were paid or payable incurred expenses in connection with the performance of the contract, the court, if it considers it just to do so having regard to all the circumstances, may allow the party to retain or to recover, as the case may be, the whole or any part of

the sums paid or payable not exceeding the amount of the expenses, and, without restricting the generality of the foregoing, the court, in estimating the amount of the expenses, may include such sum as appears to be reasonable in respect of overhead expenses and in respect of any work or services performed personally by the party incurring the expenses.

(3) If, before the parties were discharged, any of them has, by reason of anything done by any other party in connection with the performance of the contract, obtained a valuable benefit other than a payment of money, the court, if it considers it just to do so having regard to all the circumstances, may allow the other party to recover from the party benefitted the whole or any part of the value of the benefit.

(4) Where a party has assumed an obligation under the contract in consideration of the conferring of a benefit by any other party to the contract upon any other person, whether a party to the contract or not, the court, if it considers it just to do so having regard to all the circumstances, may, for the purposes of subsection 3, treat any benefit so conferred as a benefit obtained by the party who has assumed the obligation.

(5) In considering whether any sum ought to be recovered or retained under this section by a party to the contract, the court shall not take into account any sum that, by reason of the circumstances giving rise to the frustration of the contract, has become payable to that party under any contract of insurance unless there was an obligation to insure imposed by an express term of the frustrated contract or by or under any enactment.

(6) Where the contract contains a provision that upon the true construction of the contract is intended to have effect in the event of circumstances that operate, or but for the provision would operate, to frustrate the contract, or is intended to have effect whether such circumstances arise or not, the court shall give effect to the provision and shall give effect to this section only to such extent, if any, as appears to the court to be consistent with the provision.

(7) Where it appears to the court that a part of the contract can be severed properly from the remainder of the contract, being a part wholly performed before the parties were discharged, or so performed except for the payment in respect of that part of the contract of sums that are or can be ascertained under the contract, the court shall treat that part of the contract as if it were a separate contract that had not been frustrated and shall treat this section as applicable only to the remainder of the contract.

NOTES AND QUESTIONS

1. Where a partially completed work product—for example, a building being constructed on the owner's land—is destroyed by the frustrating event, has a valuable benefit been conferred on the owner "before the parties were discharged"? If so, should a court exercise its discretion to allow recovery for that value under s 3(3) of the *Frustrated Contracts Act*? See *Parsons Bros Ltd v Shea* (1965), 53 DLR (2d) 86 (Nfld SC) (denying recovery) and *c.f. Laurwen Investments Inc v 814693 Northwest Territories Ltd* (1990), 48 BLR 100 (NWTSC) (assuming that such relief is available at common law).

2. In circumstances where expenses have been incurred by a supplier and either no valuable benefit has been produced or, perhaps, the frustrating event has destroyed the value of such a benefit, s 3(2) of the *Frustrated Contracts Act* appears to assume that one who agrees to make a prepayment is, in effect, agreeing to assume the risk of losses resulting from frustration. Is this a sound premise?

3. For a defence of the proposition that where a loss results from a frustrating event for which neither party is responsible the parties ought to share the loss, see C Fried, *Contract as Promise* (Cambridge, Mass: Harvard University Press, 1981) ch 5.

FRUSTRATED CONTRACT ACT
RSBC 1996, c 166

5(1) In this section, "benefit" means something done in the fulfillment of contractual obligations, whether or not the person for whose benefit it was done received the benefit.

(2) Subject to section 6, every party to a contract to which this Act applies is entitled to restitution from the other party or parties to the contract for benefits created by the party's performance or part performance of the contract.

(3) Every party to a contract to which this Act applies is relieved from fulfilling obligations under the contract that were required to be performed before the frustration or avoidance but were not performed, except in so far as some other party to the contract has become entitled to damages for consequential loss as a result of the failure to fulfil those obligations.

(4) If the circumstances giving rise to the frustration or avoidance cause a total or partial loss in value of a benefit to a party required to make restitution under subsection (2), that loss must be apportioned equally between the party required to make restitution and the party to whom the restitution is required to be made.

6(1) A person who has performed or partly performed a contractual obligation is not entitled to restitution under section 5 in respect of a loss in value, caused by the circumstances giving rise to the frustration or avoidance, of a benefit within the meaning of section 5 if there is

    (a) a course of dealing between the parties to the contract,

    (b) a custom or a common understanding in the trade, business or profession of the party so performing, or

    (c) an implied term of the contract,

to the effect that the party performing should bear the risk of the loss in value.

[See generally on the law of frustration Waddams at paras 362-82; Trebilcock, ch 6; MacDougall, ch 19; and Maddaugh & McCamus, ch 18.]